MICHEL NOSTRADAMUS

This portrait, painted by his son César from memory, hangs in the Bibliothèque Méjanes, Aix. (A copy hangs by Nostradamus' tomb in Salon.)

*War es ein Gott, der diese Zeichen schrieb?*
(Was it a god who penned these signs?)
—GOETHE. *Faust.* Sc. 1

# NOSTRADAMUS
## and His Prophecies

*INCLUDING*

*All the Prophecies in French and English,
With Complete Notes and Indexes*

*A Critical Biography of Nostradamus,
His Will and Personal Letters*

*Bibliography of Nostradamus and His Commentators*

*Historical, Geographical and Genealogical Background*

*A Review of Theories About Him, His Method
and Other Supplementary Material*

## Edgar Leoni

DOVER PUBLICATIONS, INC.
Mineola, New York

*Bibliographical Note*

This Dover edition, first published in 2000, is an unabridged republication of the work originally published in 1961 by the Exposition Press, New York under the title *Nostradamus: Life and Literature.*

*Library of Congress Cataloging-in-Publication Data*

Nostradamus, 1503–1566.
    [Prophéties. English & French]
    Nostradamus and his prophecies / by Edgar Leoni.
        p. cm.
    "Including all the Prophecies in French and English, with complete notes and indexes, a critical biography of Nostradamus, his will and personal letters, bibliography of Nostradamus and his commentators, historical, geographical, and genealogical background, a review of theories about him, his method and other supplementary material."
    Reprint. Originally published: Nostradamus: life and literature. New York: Exposition Press, 1961.
    Includes bibliographical references and index.
    ISBN 0-486-41468-X
    1. Prophecies (Occultism). I. Leoni, Edgar. II. Title.

BF1815.N8 A213 2000
133.3'092—dc21
[B]

                                    00-029513

Manufactured in the United States of America
Dover Publications, Inc., 31 East 2nd Street, Mineola, N.Y. 11501

To

MARY, ELLA *and* KITTY

# TO FRANCE AFTER THE DISASTER OF SAINT-QUENTIN

*Poem by Ronsard (1557)*

Tu te moques aussi des prophètes que Dieu
Choisit en tes enfants, et les fait au milieu
De ton sein apparaître, afin de te prédire
Ton malheur avenir; mais tu n'en fais que rire:
Ou soit que du grand Dieu l'immense éternité,
Aît de Nostradamus l'enthousiasme excité,
Ou soit que de démon bon ou mauvais l'agite,
Ou soit que de nature il aît l'âme subite,
Et outre les mortels s'élance jusqu'aux cieux,
Et de là nous redit des faits prodigieux;
Ou soit que son esprit sombre et mélancolique,
D'humeurs crasses repu, se rende fantastique;
Brief il est ce qu'il est, si est-ce toutesfois,
Que par les mots douteux de sa prophète voix
Comme un oracle antique, il a de mainte année,
Prédit la plus grande part de nôtre destinée.
Je ne l'eusse pas cru, si le ciel qui départ
Bien et mal aux humains, n'eût été de sa part.


## TRANSLATION

Thou mockest also the prophets that God chooses amongst thy children, and places in the midst of thy bosom, in order to predict to thee thy future misfortune.

But thou dost but laugh at them.

Perhaps it is the immense eternity of the great God that has aroused the fervor of Nostradamus.

Or perhaps a good or bad demon kindles it.

Or perhaps his spirit is moved by nature, and climbs to the heavens, beyond mortals, and from there repeats to us prodigious facts.

Or perhaps his somber and melancholy spirit is filled with crass humors, making him fanciful.

In brief, he is what he is; so it is that always with the doubtful words of his prophetic voice, like that of an ancient oracle, he has for many a year predicted the greater part of our destiny. I would not have believed him, had not Heaven, which assigns good and evil to mankind, been his inspiration.

# Contents

## LIST OF ILLUSTRATIONS

# Introduction

The purpose of this book is to provide *everything* by and about Nostradamus. As the title suggests, it deals primarily with both Nostradamus' life and the literature, mostly of a prophetic nature, produced *by* him. The literature *about* Nostradamus, so inextricably connected with his fame, is also the subject of considerable attention.

There is no particular design in this work for either the glorification or the debunking of Nostradamus. Indications of his seeming successes and his apparent failures in the prophetic field are dealt with, incidentally, in their place, as they arise.

After four hundred years, Nostradamus' name has remained so well known that it has become the very synonym for successful prognostication. There would seem to be three pre-eminent reasons why this is so:

1. He is the most pretentious of all prophets: he states blandly in his Preface that his prophecies run until 3797.
2. Many of his prophecies lend themselves to repeated interpretations, so that they never seem to be out of date. It is but human nature that when a man sees a fairly specific and detailed prophecy that applies impressively to events of his own day, he does not wonder how often similar events have occurred before.
3. Nostradamus has had a multitude of ardent propagandists, the like of which no other prophet has been blessed with. His memory has never been allowed to pass into oblivion. Down through the centuries, as the interest aroused by one enthusiastic book began to wane, another appeared.

The number of works on Nostradamus in the English language is second only to that in French, and they range in quality from the very impressive to the utterly ridiculous. And yet, surprisingly, in the four hundred years since the prophecies were first published, there has been no *truly complete* translation, with even the minimum of scholarly precision that the term implies. There exists only a very superficial and careless work, replete with every kind of error, dating from 1672, and a recent reprint of it, whose added errors and modifications have further compounded the inadequacies of the original.

It is the aim of this book to fill the void and to provide a complete and definitive work on Nostradamus, not only with respect to the needed translation, but also on all other aspects of Nostradamus.

The heart of this book consists of the prophecies of Nostradamus with the original French and the English translation on facing pages. Details as to

the source of the text, the new and original orthography and numbering
system, the use of italics, pointers and footnotes, etc., will be found in the
section entitled "Background and Rules of the Game in This Edition" (pp.
115-17). The reader will find there also the answer to many related questions
and would do well to be familiar with it.

To provide the greatest possible assistance in comprehending the subject
matter of the prophecies, this book includes also the following:

1. Commentary on each quatrain or paragraph of Nostradamus' prophecies,
   explaining, insofar as possible, what he seems to have had in mind. Where
   this cannot be determined, some clarification is provided, at least on the
   geographical references and the like. The Commentaries also include
   many interpretations of the past, noteworthy for any of several reasons—
   fame, ingenuity, general interest, or downright asininity.
2. The "Historical Background of the Prophecies," with a review of "The
   Historical Setting" and a "Chronology of Significant Dates." The events
   listed are significant as undoubtedly influencing the subject matter of
   Nostradamus' prophecies, with respect to the major part of the chronology.
   Events listed beyond the publication of the prophecies, and beyond Nostradamus' death, provide a framework for consideration of some of the
   best-known applications and interpretations of the prophecies.
3. Two "Genealogical Charts." The major one, "The House of France," is
   probably the most comprehensive and large-scale arrangement of the
   subjects concerned ever published on a single chart. Another, more
   limited in scope, deals with the House of Habsburg. As the reader will
   find, when he becomes familiar with Nostradamus, the personal rela-
   tionships of rival dynasties of the 16th century occupy a great deal of
   Nostradamus' attention.
4. A map of Nostradamus' Europe, giving the reader a graphic picture of the
   very different Europe in which the prophet lived.
5. A series of "Indexes to the Prophecies," the most complete ever published
   in any language, to assist the reader in promptly locating what is of most
   interest to him. In addition to the massive General Index, more special-
   ized indexes provide breakdowns of dated prophecies, of geographical
   setting, of cryptic words and proper names and various other categories.

Any study of Nostradamus must needs involve a consideration of bibliography—the history of the earliest editions of his prophecies as well as the
history of the works of his commentators, to whom he owes his lasting fame.
The two-part "Nostradamus Bibliography" provides the most complete treatment in any language of both the earliest editions of Nostradamus and virtually all the works of his commentators for four centuries.

The literature of Nostradamus, of necessity, occupies the greatest part
of this book. But the life of Nostradamus himself is of hardly less interest.
The "Biography of Nostradamus," with which this book begins, may perhaps
be the most complete in any language with respect to genuine biography,
although there are several heavily-padded books on only this aspect of
Nostradamus. It is of a considerably more critical nature than most biogra-

phies of the prophet presented by his propagandists, and includes a substantial amount of new material in this field. In addition to the biography proper, this book contains the complete original text and complete translation (on facing pages, like the prophecies) of three other biographical features now published for the first time:

1. Nostradamus' last will and testament, and its codicil
2. Nostradamus' letter to a M. Morel of Paris
3. Nostradamus' letter to the canons of the Cathedral of Orange, in which he plays clairvoyant detective over some stolen property

While this book is only incidentally concerned with the general topic of prophecy and, more particularly, with the source or basis of Nostradamus' prophecies, this subject is also dealt with in the section entitled "Background and Rules of the Game." All the various theories are presented, and some conclusions are advanced. This section also deals with the purely technical aspects of the prophecies, both on the part of Nostradamus in the 16th century, and on the part of the present author and translator.

A passing reference to one other section is in order. It is surely the least significant. In the "Miscellany" portion of the book, which contains also the will and the letters referred to above, are found prophecies falsely attributed to Nostradamus. Some have been accepted by many of the Nostradamian propagandists; others have fooled practically nobody.

Finally, occupying a traditional spot at the end, the reader will find yet another index. Entitled "Index of Historical and Eminent Persons," it is a rather curious index which requires for inclusion only that

*a*) the subject is to be found in a good encyclopedia or is a noted contemporary, and
*b*) he or she is mentioned somehow, somewhere in this book.°

Accordingly, the reader must not be too surprised to find such diverse names as Napoleon and Father Divine, or Charlemagne and Grace Kelly. They really are all mentioned!

---

°The number of the original prophecy in connection with which a name in this index is mentioned will be found on the page designated: each commentary is, of course, preceded by the number of the quatrain to which it refers.

# NOSTRADAMUS
## and His Prophecies

# Biography of Nostradamus

Michel de Nostredame, better known as Nostradamus, was born at noon on December 14,[1] 1503, at Saint-Rémy in Provence. His ancestors were Jews who appear to have lived in the Latin world ever since the Dispersion. Some of his biographers tell us that he was of the tribe of Issachar.[2] Many Jews had settled in Provence, which became the best of havens[3] under the rule of René the Good[4] (1434–80).

So tolerant was René that he had as his physician and adviser a Jewish doctor and astrologer (the combination was then quite ordinary) named Jean de Saint-Rémy. René's son Jean, Duke of Calabria and Lorraine, had taken as his physician one Pierre de Nostredame, who had had a flourishing practice in Arles until the pharmacists, annoyed at his making up his own prescriptions, had him driven out of town on charges of "falsifying his drugs." Both physicians traveled around Western Europe with their respective masters, whose dominions were far-flung, and in the course of their travels they learned much.

In 1470 Jean died, poisoned at Barcelona as he was about to add the County of Barcelona (in revolt against Aragon) to his other possessions. To his father he bequeathed his physician. René, greatly upset by the premature death of his son, abandoned Anjou and its brilliant court and settled down at Tarascon in Provence, which he had hitherto visited only rarely. The two physicians became fast friends, and after René's death, Jean persuaded his colleague to return with him to Saint-Rémy and to settle there. Accordingly, it was quite natural that Pierre's son Jacques, a prosperous notary, should marry Jean's daughter Renée.[5]

---

[1]December 23 by the Gregorian calendar. All dates are given in the calendar prevailing throughout Nostradamus' lifetime, the Julian.

[2]According to Smith and Fuller's *Dictionary of the Bible*, "they 'had understanding of the times to know what Israel ought to do . . . and all their brethren were at their commandment.' What this 'understanding of the times' was we have no clue. By the later Jewish interpreters it is explained as skill in ascertaining the periods of the sun and moon, the intercalation of months, and dates of solemn feasts, and the interpretation of the signs of the heavens. . . . Josephus gives it as 'knowing the things that were to happen.' . . ."

[3]By the Edict of 1454, they were authorized to practice medicine, commerce and the arts; they could be fiscal agents; and they could observe the rites of their religion with complete freedom.

[4]His full title was King of Naples, Sicily and Jerusalem, Duke of Anjou, Lorraine and Bar, Count of Provence and Piedmont.

[5]The original source of this lineage is Nostradamus himself, as reported by Chavigny, his first biographer. Similar details are found in the historical works of Nos-

With the death of René, followed six years later, in 1486, by that of his nephew and heir, Charles of Maine, the second House of Anjou expired in the male line, and Provence and Maine reverted to the French crown (Anjou having reverted upon René's death in 1480).[6] The kings of France did not propose to have Jews flourishing in their domain. In 1488 Charles VIII ordered the Jews of Provence to become baptized. However, the king was too busily engaged in Italy to have the order enforced. But when Louis XII came to the throne, he put teeth into the order, and by an Edict of September 26, 1501, all Jews were given three months to become baptized, or to leave Provence, under pain of severe penalties.

The young couple, as well as their respective fathers, decided on the wisdom of yielding, and were baptized.[7] The sons of Jacques de Nostredame were thus all born in the fold of the Church and duly baptized. The eldest son, Michel, became the most famous astrologer and prophet of his day, if not of modern times. Bertrand, the second son, passed into oblivion. Jean, the youngest, wrote a classic on the Provençal poets and was also Procureur of the Parliament of Provence.

At a very tender age Michel is said to have manifested signs of a very fine mind, so that his grandfather Jean asked to have Michel brought up at his home. Michel's parents were glad of this opportunity for their son, and willingly allowed the much-traveled old man to give Michel his earliest education. In addition to the rudiments of mathematics, Latin, Greek and Hebrew, he was given his first taste of the "celestial science" by his astrologically-minded grandsire.

---

tradamus' brother and his son, and are further amplified in Depping, *Histoire des Juifs*, pp. 334–35, where the suggestion is made that Pierre came from Italy and frenchified the name Nostra-done. More recently, in 1940, Reynaud-Plense, unable to find any name like that in the archives, identified Pierre with one Abraham Solomon, a baptized doctor who was ennobled by King René (*L'Encyclopédie du Département des Bouches-du-Rhône*, p. 357); this same suggestion had been made by Buget in 1862, who noted that Solomon was the only physician mentioned by Nostradamus' son in his historical account of René's court. Finally, years of laborious research in the scattered archives of Provence by a fanatical Nostradamus-hater of Saint-Rémy, Dr. Edgar Leroy, have led to a conclusion that this whole ancestry was sheer fabrication: Nostradamus' father Jaume (Jacques) was the son of Peyrot (Pierre) de Nostredame, of a long line of Avignon grain-dealers, recently converted and married to a gentile woman named Blanche. Jaume, himself in the grain business, gave it up when in 1495 he moved to Saint-Rémy to marry Reynière de Saint-Rémy, the granddaughter of Jean de Saint-Rémy, who had failed as a doctor and turned to more prosperous tax-collecting for the King. This family was also one of converted Jews. (*Mémoires de l'Institut historique de Provence*, Vol. 17, 1941; also reprinted in Busquet, 1950.)

[6]Lorraine, however, went to the son of René's daughter Yolande and the Count of Vaudemont. This House of Vaudemont, or Lorraine, of which René is the source, ultimately acceded to the Holy Roman and Austrian empires, and in the cadet branch (Guise) virtually ruled France for half a century. (See "Genealogy.")

[7]The archives of Aix list, for December 12, 1512, the names of Jean and Pierre, on the roll of taxes levied on the "new Christian community."

After Jean's death, Michel returned to his father's house in the rue de Barri. To a certain extent, his education was taken over by his other learned grandfather. When the old man had passed on all that he could teach Michel, the boy was sent off to Avignon to study the liberal arts of the time at this famous center of Renaissance learning, a century earlier the capital of Christendom. With or without justification, his biographers tell us that though apt enough in grammar, philosophy and rhetoric, he showed the greatest interest in the study of the stars. So marked was this early interest that as a result of his frequent discourses on the celestial movements, his classmates nicknamed him "the little astrologer."

On his return home, his father became worried about these "impractical" interests of Michel. On the advice of old Pierre, the doctor, this practical notary sent his son off to study medicine at the University of Montpellier, second only to that of Paris as a training place for doctors. So "modern" was Montpellier that in 1376 it had obtained from Louis I of Anjou the right to demand every year the body of one executed criminal for dissection.

It was 1522 and Nostradamus was nineteen. For three years he studied intensively, reading all the medical classics and listening to the lectures of the most celebrated physicians of Europe. The results was a *baccalauréat*, or bachelor's degree. The manner in which this was obtained has been recorded in detail. On the chosen day, from eight in the morning till noon, an oral examination was given, in which the candidate had to parry the questions of the professors, avoid their traps and give proof of a learning approaching their own. The successful candidates were then permitted to change their black student's robe for the red robe of the learned.

The next step for the aspiring doctor was to get a license to practice. To obtain this, the candidate had first to deliver five lectures on subjects chosen by the Dean over a period of three months. Next came the *per intentionem* exams, consisting of four different questions, presented one day in advance, each of which had to be discussed before a different professor. Each lasted one whole hour. Sometimes all were discussed in one day, at other times two each on two successive days. Eight days later, the candidate was given a question on a fifth malady by the Chancellor himself, and on this he had to do his best extemporaneously. Often the subject was one never treated before. Having finished, he was given an aphorism of Hippocrates on which to have a thesis finished by the following day. This final pair of hurdles to jump was called *les points rigoreux*. If the candidate was successful, and Michel was, he was given his license by the Bishop of Montpellier.

The year that Nostradamus obtained his license was 1525, and in this year a new outbreak of the ever-recurrent plague was devastating southern France. Abandoning for a time his education (there remained still a doctorate to obtain), Nostradamus left the university in order to make use of his knowledge. In the town of Montpellier itself he laid the foundations for a remarkable reputation. His phenomenal success seems to have been due to two factors. In the first place, he is said to have exhibited unusual self-confidence and unquenchable courage in the face of the plague. Second, he made great use of unorthodox prescriptions from his own formulas, which proved very successful, either medically or psychologically.

From Montpellier he extended his activity to the countryside and eventually came to Narbonne, where he attended the courses of the cele-brated Jewish[8] alchemists who flourished there. In that day, the distinction between alchemy and pharmacy was very hazy indeed. From Narbonne, Nostradamus moved on to Carcassonne, where he served the Bishop, Am-menien de Fays.[9] Some time later he was found living in Toulouse in the rue de la Triperie, and here he seems to have passed many months. In Bordeaux he found the plague in a particularly virulent form, and after offering his services for some time, he made his way eastward again. In Avignon, where he had had his first formal education, he is said to have spent many hours in the library, and it may be here that he first came across works on magic and the occult, works which were to influence him greatly.[10] Throughout his career, Nostradamus' pharmaceutical penchant led him to experiment not only with medical preparations but also with items whose sole purpose was to delight the stomach. Accordingly, we find that while in Avignon he presented "a quince jelly, of sovereign beauty, goodness, taste and excellence," to Cardinal Clermont, the Legate,[11] and to the Grand Master of the Knights of St. John.[12]

Four years had now passed since he had left Montpellier. The plague had abated and he had gained experience. It was but natural to return to Montpellier for his doctorate. The records of the university revealed his name inscribed anew on October 23, 1529. The new series of examinations was known as *les triduanes*. The candidate presented a list of twelve sub-jects on which he was prepared to be questioned. Of these, six were chosen, three by the Dean and three by lot. The candidate had then to argue the points involved with the professors. His biographers tell us that in Nostra-damus' case, he had to defend the unorthodox remedies which he had re-cently used. After making a successful showing, Dr. Nostradamus was

---

[8]Nominally Christian, of course.

[9]For him he prescribed an "elixir of life" in the form of a pomade, for which he later gave the formula in his *Opuscule, etc.* However, though Nostradamus himself is the authority for this, something doesn't check. The Bishop of Carcassonne from 1521 to 1545 was Martin de Saint-André. Either he had the name wrong, or it was someone less than a bishop. One Amanien de Foix was indeed Bishop of Mâcon between 1557 and 1579.

[10]Especially Marsilio Ficino's translation *De mysteriis Ægyptiorum . . .* , Nostrada-mus' how-to-do-it manual for prophecy.

[11]The Legate was the Pope's "viceroy" in Avignon, holding sovereign power there.

[12]Since 1522 known as the Knights of Malta.

given the distinctive cap, a gold ring and the book of Hippocrates. He was now on the same level as the great physicians of Christendom.

Dr. Nostradamus was offered a job on the faculty, and accepted. A splendid future lay before him there. But after a year, his independent spirit began chafing under the restrictions imposed upon him. Obliged to accept all the teachings of prescribed texts, he could not stress his own unorthodox conclusions.[13] Furthermore, the wanderlust was clearly in his blood.

And so one day in 1532[14] he saddled his mule, collected his books and instruments and set forth again. For two years he traveled over the scenes of what his biographers lyrically refer to as "his former triumphs."[15] His travels took him to Bordeaux again, to La Rochelle and to Toulouse. While in Toulouse he received a letter from Jules-César Scaliger, considered second only to Erasmus as the most learned man in Europe. Scaliger, whose attainments included medicine, poetry, philosophy, botany and mathematics, expressed a desire to meet this man of whom he had heard so much, and to see if his reputation was well founded. Nostradamus replied with a letter that was "at once ingenious, learned and spirited."[16] Scaliger forthwith invited him to Agen.

Nostradamus was highly pleased with both the personality of Scaliger and the clime of Agen, and decided to settle down near his new friend. Mothers with marriageable daughters looked with favor upon the eminent young doctor as a prospective son-in-law. Finally, he chose one whose name has not been preserved,[17] and of whom we know only that she was "of high estate, very beautiful and very amiable."[18] Within the usual space of time, his wife bore him a son and a daughter.

For three years Nostradamus led an idyllic life. He had a fine family, a lucrative practice and the intellectual stimulus of the near-by Scaliger and his learned visitors from all Christendom. Then disaster struck. One after another his wife and children were carried off by an outbreak of pestilence. We do not know whether or not it was the Black Death, but in any case, after saving so many he was unable to save those he loved most.

The loss of his family was a sufficiently heavy blow. But others followed in short order. Some of his patients decided they would just as soon not have a doctor who couldn't save his own family. He had a violent quarrel with Scaliger, the cause of which is unknown; they ceased to be friends and

---

[13]One seems to have been opposition to the often-fatal habit of bleeding patients for almost any ailment.

[14]Rabelais got his degree from Montpellier in 1530, but there is no record of any contact between the two famous men.

[15]Bareste goes well off the deep end here. ". . . no king, prince or count was ever received by the peasants of the Midi as . . . Nostradamus."

[16]In the biography of 1594 by Chavigny, his friend and eulogist.

[17]Some of the biographers call her "Adriète de Loubéjac," apparently confusing her with Scaliger's young wife, Andiette de Roques-Lobéjac.

[18]Chavigny.

Scaliger is said to have made abusive references to him later.[19] Finally, his wife's family started a lawsuit to recover her dowry.

But what appears to have prompted him to break all his ties in haste was a rather trivial matter. In 1534, seeing a workman cast a bronze model of the Virgin, Nostradamus remarked that he was only making devils. The workman, shocked, reported this to the authorities. Nostradamus' apologists maintain that he referred only to the inartistic Gothic form, but the similarity of his words to the iconoclasm of the Protestants was unmistakable. (Calvin was then in the same area, completing his theological masterwork.) It was rumored that the ecclesiastical authorities would soon send for Nostradamus. In 1538 came an official order to appear before the Inquisitor at Toulouse.

Once again he set out on his wanderings, which were to last about six years, 1538–44. Little is known of the route he followed. The only information comes from references to places, and occasionally dates, in his later works. He seems to have got as far north as Lorraine, as far east as Venice and as far south as Sicily.

Throughout his travels he seems to have sought contact with all who could in any way add to his medical and pharmaceutical knowledge. There is much reason to believe his round of calls included visits to alchemists, astrologers, cabalists, magicians and the like as well. But in those times, as we have seen, the distinction was only blurry.

This six-year odyssey is the setting for several of the Nostradamian legends, for none of which is there much in the line of proof. While in Italy, we are told, he saw coming towards him a young Franciscan from Ancona named Felice Peretti. As the ex-swineherd passed, the budding prophet put a knee to the ground devoutly. Asked the reason for his strange behavior, Nostradamus replied, "I must submit myself and bend a knee before His Holiness." It is almost superfluous to add that in 1585 Cardinal Peretti became Pope Sixtus V.

The source for the next legend is very distinct, so we shall see it as it first appeared.[20]

In the same place, visiting Monsieur and Madame de Florinville, I learned from them that Michel Nostradamus had lodged there and had treated there Madame de Florinville, grandmother of the said Lord of Florinville, who is still alive,[21] to whom happened this story which, to be entertaining, he tells in diverse places: Monsieur de Florinville, taking a walk in the courtyard of

---

[19]Nostradamus, however, did not retaliate. In 1552, in his *Traicté des fardemens*, he refers to Scaliger as one "who seems to have inherited Cicero's soul in the matter of eloquence, Virgil's in poetry and Galen's twice over in medicine. I owe to him more than to any other person in the world."

[20]Etienne Jaubert, *Eclaircissement* . . . (1656), pp. 40–41.

[21]If he was but twenty at the time, if Jaubert saw him twenty years before he wrote, he'd still be more than one hundred at that time.

his chateau, in the company of Nostradamus, saw two little suckling pigs, one white, the other black. At the sight of them he asked Nostradamus for sport what would happen to these two animals. To which the latter replied at once: "We will eat the black one and the wolf will eat the white one." Monsieur de Florinville, wishing to make a liar of the prophet, secretly commanded his cook to kill the white one and present it at supper. He killed the white one, dressed it and put it on the spit ready for roasting at the appropriate hour. However, while he was on an errand outside the kitchen, a little wolf's cub that was being nourished to tame it entered and ate the rumps of the little white pig ready to be roasted. When the cook returned, fearing to be scolded by his master, he took the black one, killed it, prepared it and served it for supper. Thereupon Monsieur de Florinville, believing he had won the day, knowing nothing of the accident which had occurred, said to Nostradamus: "Well, sir, we are now eating the white pig, and the wolf will not touch it here." "I do not believe it," said Nostradamus; "it is the black one which is on the table." As soon as the cook was made to come in he confessed the accident which provided the company with another more agreeable dish.[22]

We are also told of an extended stay at the Cistercian Abbey of Orval.[23] Two rather poorly faked prose prophecies, "predicting" the advent of Napoleon Bonaparte, were "discovered" in the early 19th century. The "Prophecy of Philip Olivarius, printed in 1542," seems to have actually been printed for the first time in 1820.[24] The "Prophecy of Orval, printed in 1544," seems to have appeared for the first time in 1839.[25] Bareste, the great Nostradamian enthusiast, took both of them to his heart and proclaimed Nostradamus their author, a claim taken up again shortly after by another great commentator of the 19th century, Torné-Chavigny.[26] Although it is highly improbable that Nostradamus or anyone else in the 16th century wrote the "prophecies," he may have passed some time at Orval amongst his other stops.

In 1544 Nostradamus was found in Marseilles, where, it seems, he thought of settling down. Together with Louis Serres, he fought a new outburst of

---

[22]Jaubert goes on to say, "All France recounts diverse events predicted by the Author, but not wishing to write anything without being assured about it, I omit them. . . ."

[23]Partially destroyed by the troops of Chatillon in 1637 and rebuilt in the 18th century, it was razed in 1793 by the armies of revolutionary France. The ruins stand in the Belgian commune of Villiers-devant-Orval in Belgian Luxembourg.

[24]As a footnote in *Historical and Secret Memoirs of the Empress Josephine*, by Mlle LeNormand, the Empress's friend and soothsayer. Napoleon was supposed to have carried a copy always on his person. For the text of it, see section on fake prophecies in the rear of this book.

[25]As part of "The Oracle for 1840" by Henri Dujardin. He pretends that five copies of it were made by *émigrés* who, taking refuge at Orval on the eve of its destruction, were shown the original by a monk who, familiar with it, was quite unsurprised by the catastrophic events of the day. See fake prophecies in rear for text.

[26]Bareste wrote in 1840. Torné made references to it in many writings, which extend from 1862 to 1878.

the plague here. In November of 1544, Provence suffered one of the worst floods of its history. The rivers becoming polluted by the corpses of men and animals, the death toll exacted by the plague reached new heights.

In 1546 the ever-worsening plague struck its mightiest blow at Aix, the capital of Provence. César Nostradamus later wrote a lurid description of conditions in Aix at the time, as reported to him by his father.[27]

> Persons stricken by the furor of this malady completely abandon all hope of recovery, wrap themselves in two white winding sheets, and give forth even while they live (unheard-of thing) their sad and lamentable obsequies. The houses are abandoned and empty, men disfigured, women in tears, children bewildered, old folk astonished, the bravest vanquished and animals pursued. The palace is shut and locked, justice silent and deserted, Themis absent and mute, the stretcher-bearers and street porters work on credit. The shops shut, arts halted, temples solitary and the priests all confused. In brief, all the streets villous, wild and full of weeds because of the lugubrious absence of man and beast for the 270 days that the evil lasted. . . .

In his later writings,[28] Nostradamus tells us that the plague began here on May 1, and that he was called in soon after. He gives many details of his work here, most interesting of which is the formula for his rose pills.[29] All who made use of them, he tells us, were saved, while those who didn't died. Anyhow, he himself had enough confidence in their effect to remain shut up with hundreds of patients over a period of many months. Whether or not his rose pills were supremely efficacious, he at least refrained from bleeding and physicking his patients to death, as many of his colleagues did.[30]

The next place to require his services was the little town of Salon. The dryness of the climate and its ideal location, between Marseilles, Aix, Arles and Avignon, made Salon more pleasing to him than any town he had seen

---

[27]*Histoire de Provence* (Lyons, 1614), p. 772.

[28]In his *Opuscule* (Lyons, 1555), parts of which were first printed in 1552. Chapter VIII is devoted entirely to his work in Aix.

[29]First a powder was made of the following ingredients:

> Sawdust from the greenest cyprus available, 1 oz.
> Iris of Florence, 6 oz.
> Cloves, 3 oz.
> Odorated calamus, 3 drams
> Lign-aloes, 6 drams

Three hundred to four hundred red roses, plucked before dawn, were pulverized and mixed with the above powder, carefully kept from exposure to air. The resulting mixture was made into pills or lozenges which the patient had to keep in his mouth at all times. The magnificent odor, he claimed, killed bad breath and bad smells and cleaned decayed teeth. Since Nostradamus felt that the pestilence was transmitted in the foul air, the purified air preserved the patient.

[30]Bareste makes up other details: He was voted a lifetime pension by the Parliament; he passed on the gifts given him by the wealthier of his patients to the widows and orphans of those he had been unable to save, etc.

since Agen. Once again he settled down, this time to stay. Salon remained his home for the rest of his life.

Soon after he settled in Salon, he was called away again, this time to Lyons. Nostradamus himself tells us only that he brought the pestilence raging there under control through mass prescriptions which were ably filled for him by one René Hepiliervard. But one of his most enthusiastic biographers, Bareste, added many more details of dubious authenticity, which have since become part of the stock Nostradamian biography.[31]

Returning to Salon loaded with honors and gifts, as we are told, Nostradamus married for a second time. The lady, whose name was Anne Ponsarde[32] Gemelle, was that always-useful person, a rich widow. Their marriage contract, still in the archives of Salon, was signed on November 11, 1547, before Master Étienne Hozier, Salon notary. Their house, in an impasse off the Place de la Poissonnerie, in the Farreiroux quarter (the street is now called after the prophet), can likewise still be seen, in its restored condition.

At best Salon, with its dry and healthy climate, did not offer a particularly turbulent practice. In his professional capacity, it appears that his chief job soon consisted mainly of making special cosmetic preparations for the wealthy gentry, by whom he was soon accepted. Whether his imminent mystical reputation was the cause of the hostility the lower classes had for him, or whether that hostility led him to his "secret studies," is still a matter of conjecture and conflict of opinion. Although we cannot be certain which of the two factors was the cause of the other, we know that by 1550 he was launched into his prophetic career, and that from the very beginning of his stay in Salon he was the subject of abuse as a minion of Satan, as a Jew (though converted, a fact that did not impress the mob) and as a suspected Huguenot sympathizer. For in these days of religious conflict, religion became the cloak for economic as well as political passions. When many of the Provençal gentry turned Huguenot, the peasantry periodically rose up and combined religious fervor with profit by looting the houses of the rich. These *Cabans*, as they were called, were guided more often by the wealth of their prospective victim than by evidence of their heresy.

---

[31]Bareste adds that at Lyons he came into conflict with Antoine Sarrazin (based on a misinterpretation of a remark of Sarrazin, who did not even get a license till many years later), a jealous colleague who would not heed his advice. When a delegation was sent to Nostradamus, begging him not to desert Aix in anger, he told them that because of the basic disagreement, they would have to choose between him and the rival doctor. To which they (or at least Bareste) replied enthusiastically, "We choose Dr. Nostradamus, liberator of the town of Aix." Bareste gives as authority for this touching recital "Astruc . . . Bouche . . . the historians of Lyons and the Provençal chronicles." Not only do neither Astruc nor Bouche mention it, but Parker, looking through the archives of Lyons in 1919, could not even find any trace of his being there at the time. However, the *Revue du Lyonnais pour 1835* mentions an epidemic of whooping cough which Nostradamus fought in 1547.

[32]The name appears also as *Pons, Ponce, Ponsart* and *Pousart.*

Retiring more and more from service amongst these "barbarians,"[33] Nostradamus converted the uppermost floor of his house into a study and observatory, and after consuming all the books on astrology and magic[34] on which he could lay his hands, he was ready to begin a career that was to make his one of the best known names in France.

In 1550[35] he published his first almanac.[36] The success which it enjoyed led him to publish one for almost every year until his death. Although many contained predictions that were never borne out, the prophet seems to have had many well-wishers ready to reply that if an almanac contained false predictions, it was only a forgery.[37] The profit[38] and the renown that he obtained from the fast-selling almanacs soon led him to conceive the most pretentious plan for a book of prophecies ever held by any man.

However, at no time in his career did prophecy absorb all his attention. Works on cosmetics, prescriptions, recipes for preserves and translations of classical literary pieces flowed from his pen at different times. In 1552 appeared the *Traicté des fardemens*, the first of his "professional" works.[39]

Another subject for concern during this period appeared when Nostradamus became a patron of Adam de Craponne, a young man with a dream. His dream was to make the arid desert of Crau around Salon into a fertile plain through a canal connecting the Rhône and the Durance. The prophet gave advice, encouragement and large sums of money on several occasions. Work was begun on August 17, 1554, and completed on April 20, 1559, when Craponne's dream was fully realized. Today eighteen communities owe their prosperity to him and his canal.

It may also have been in 1554 that another young man appeared on the horizon. Jean-Aymes[40] de Chavigny of Beaune, at the age of thirty in 1554, had a doctor's degree in both theology and law. In 1548 he had been mayor of Beaune. With this brilliant future ahead of him, he had suddenly decided

---

[33]In 1552, in the *Traicté*, he wrote, "Here where I reside I carry on my work among brute beasts, barbarous people, mortal enemies of learning and letters."

[34]In his Preface, he tells César of having destroyed books on magic he inherited. One theory is that some Hebrew lore was taken from the Temple by one of his ancestors at the time of the Dispersal. But most of his magical material clearly comes from Ficino's translation *De mysteriis Ægyptiorum* . . . printed at Venice in 1497 and reprinted at Lyons in 1547.

[35]On Chavigny's authority. This may mean the first one was printed in 1549 for 1550, or in 1550 for 1551.

[36]Sometimes titled "Prognostications," *et al.* See "Nostradamus Bibliography."

[37]LaCroix du Maine, in his *Bibliothèque* of 1594, without any Nostradamian bias, wrote, "He wrote an infinite number of Almanacs and Prognostications, which were very well received and sold so well that several imitations of them were made . . . under his name (which were composed by ignorant people and were consequently full of lies . . .)."

[38]The archives of Salon include a notarized receipt to two Lyons printers for twenty crowns for the sale of almanacs and prognostications for 1562.

[39]See "Nostradamus Bibliography" for this group of his works.

[40]Also written *Aimé*.

that judicial astrology and prophecy were the most interesting thing in the world for him. On the advice of his friend, Jean Dorat, court poet and professor of Greek at the College of France and a great admirer of Nostradamus, he had made his way to Salon. From his later works on Nostradamus, biographers have been led to believe that he lived with the prophet as friend, secretary and disciple until Nostradamus' death in 1566, but there are many reasons to doubt that their relationship was that close or of such long and uninterrupted duration.[41]

On various grounds, Nostradamus was convinced that a crucial period in history was on the horizon, a view which in fact most historians came to hold. Omens to right and left served to make him more sure of his convictions. One such omen is mentioned by César:[42]

The year 1554 . . . I don't know what sad and unhappy events begin and follow creatures hideously deformed and prodigious. Scarcely had January expired when one saw born at Senas a monstrous child, having two heads, which the eye could not look at without some sort of horror: he had been predicted some time previously by those who had knowledge of the course of future events. . . . He was carried to my father and seen by several persons.

This, and the birth of a two-headed horse near Salon forty-five days later, caused Nostradamus to declare profoundly that a deep cleavage in France was ahead.

While the almanacs contained prophecies for only one year in advance, the Centuries were to contain prophecies for more than two thousand years, or, specifically, until 3797. The literary form was to be a "Milliade" of ten Centuries, each Century containing one hundred quatrains, or four-line verses. There was no relationship whatever between the Century as a collection of one hundred quatrains and a calendar century. However, this ideal pattern was not to be realized. For reasons unknown, the 7th Century was never completed, and various quatrains which seem indeed the work of Nostradamus duplicate numbers of other predictions in some cases, or bear numbers for an additional 11th and 12th Centuries in other cases.[43]

In his brief biography of the prophet in 1594, Chavigny gave the following interesting background for the Centuries:

Foreseeing the signal mutations and changes which were to occur universally throughout Europe, and also the bloody civil wars, and the pernicious troubles fatally approaching the Gallic Realm, full of enthusiasm, and as if maddened by a furor entirely new, he set himself to write his Centuries, and other presages, which he kept a long time without wishing to publish them, feeling that the novelty of the matter could not fail to cause infinite detractions, calumnies and backbitings more than venomous, as indeed happened.

[41]See section on Chavigny in "Nostradamus Bibliography," below.
[42]*Histoire de Provence*, p. 775.
[43]For further details, see "Nostradamus Bibliography."

Finally, overcome by the desire that he had to be of service to the public, he brought them to light, with the result that their fame and renown ran quite incontinently through the mouths of Frenchmen and of foreigners with the greatest of admiration.

It is rather difficult to see how these predictions, admittedly obscured so as to be as incomprehensible as possible, could be "of service to the public." Whatever it was that impelled Nostradamus to cast aside his fears and publish the Centuries, this was certainly not the reason.

Although the first unit of the Centuries appears to have been seven Centuries, the first edition, printed in Lyons in 1555, contained only the Preface to the infant César,[44] Centuries I–III complete, and Century IV with but fifty-three quatrains. The rest of Century IV, as well as Centuries V–VII, may have been printed later that year. In any case, all seven were in print by 1557.[45]

The reaction to the Centuries was, as could be expected, mixed. The leisure classes who had enjoyed the almanacs gave these new predictions an even more enthusiastic reception.[46] To them the obscurity was intriguing and could definitely be clarified through their superior learning. The less-learned masses of the people could think only that the verses contained gibberish straight from hell, and that Nostradamus was, as they always suspected, a tool of the devil, to be feared and hated.

Although the quatrains were all the rage at court, there were also many educated people who joined the masses in villifying Nostradamus. Doctors and astrologers accused him of disgracing their respective professions; philosophers objected to his premises; poets reasonably enough objected to the miserable quality of his verses. Amongst the critics of the intelligentsia, a clever Latin distich at Nostradamus' expense sped across France:

> *Nostra damus cum falsa*[47] *damus, nam fallere nostrum est;*
> *Et cum falsa damus, nil nisi nostra damus.*[48]

This translates punlessly into English as "We give that which is our own when we give false things: for it is in our nature to deceive; And when we give false things, we give but our own things." Actually, many years had first to go by before he could be vilified for the most just reason—that very few of the things he intended to predict occurred as he foresaw.

Of all the great personages of France who formed Nostradamus' public, the greatest was undoubtedly the superstitious and astrology-conscious

---

[44]The Preface was actually intended for his spiritual sons, his interpreters, according to many commentators, including some critics.

[45]For further details, see "Nostradamus Bibliography."

[46]Says Parker: "The success of the Centuries was immediate and overwhelming. Although he had apparently aimed at the mediocre in intelligence and position, he had underestimated the range of his weapon or overestimated the intelligence of his public."

[47]A variant version has *verba* for *falsa*, but this is less effective.

[48]The author is either Calvin's right arm, Théodore de Bèze, or the court poet Jodelle.

Queen, Catherine de' Medici. At her request, Henry II sent a royal command to Claude de Savoy, Comte de Tende, Governor and Grand Seneschal of Provence, to send that Nostradamus fellow to Paris.

On July 14, 1556, Nostradamus set out upon the hazardous journey. Because he was traveling under royal orders, he was able to make use of the royal post from Pont-Saint-Esprit on, and thus the journey took *only* one month. Reaching Paris on August 15, he spotted the Inn of Saint-Michel near Notre Dame and, considering this a good augury, took lodgings here. Word of his arrival reached the Queen promptly, and next day there came to the inn no less a person that Anne de Montmorency, Grand Constable of France.

The Constable conducted him to the Court at Saint-Germain-en-Laye, outside Paris. As he waited to be admitted to Catherine's presence, he was surrounded on all sides by the curious courtiers, bombarding him with questions, serious or facetious, or just anxious to take a look at the Oracle of France.

For several hours he was closeted with the Queen. The range of probable subjects included astrology, Italy, cosmetics and the future of France. Henry II had less time for him. Some commentators have no doubt that Henry asked him about Quatrain 35 of Century I, since, if applied to himself, it tallied closely with the ominous warning by the famous Italian astrologer, Luc Gauric.[49] On this score, however, a great deal of skepticism is in order.

On his return to Paris, he was lodged at the palace of the Cardinal Bourbon-Vendôme, Archbishop of Sens. The king sent him a velvet purse with one hundred crowns, and Catherine added thirty. As the journey had cost him one hundred crowns, he had had to borrow money from a trusting stranger, Jean Morel, on his arrival.[50] He was furious about this niggardly reward for all his pains.

While thus comfortably lodged, he suffered an attack of gout and was confined for ten days. This is the setting for another Nostradamian legend. Many people had come by day, seeking his favor with presents, anxious to get a peek into the future. Grateful for the nocturnal peace in which he could occupy himself with his "secret studies," he was highly incensed when a

---

[49]We are told that the prophecy of Gauric was recalled when Catherine saw Nostradamus' quatrain. Upon her request, Gauric sent a letter which the King received on February 5, 1556, warning him "to avoid all single combat in an enclosed place, especially near his forty-first year, for in that period of his life he was menaced by a wound in the head which might rapidly result in blindness or even in death." Claude de l'Aubespine, who translated the letter into French (from Latin) for the King, mentions it in his *Histoire particulière de la Cour de Henry II* (Archives Curieuses de la France, S. I, Vol. III, 1835, pp. 295-96; see text in General Bibliography). Brantôme also mentions it. Half-inclined to believe it, Henry is reported to have said to Montmorency, "I care not if my death be in that manner more than in any other. I would even prefer it, to die by the hand of whoever he might be, so long as he was brave and valiant and that I kept my honor."

[50]This and other interesting details are found in a letter of Nostradamus to Jean Morel (ms. 8589 in the Bibliothèque Nationale). In this one authenticated letter of his,

persistent knocking sounded on the door. It was a page of the illustrious family of Beauveau, who had lost a fine dog entrusted to him. Before he could announce the cause of his impudence, Nostradamus called out, "What's the matter, king's page? You are making a lot of noise over a lost dog. Go and look on the road to Orléans. You will find it there, led on a leash." When the page followed directions, he found a servant leading the dog back. When he spread the story around court, we are told, the prophet's fame increased mightily.

The real purpose of his invitation to Paris was made known to him. He was to go to the royal chateau at Blois to cast the horoscopes of the Valois children. The Queen was impatient. As soon as he could walk again, he was off to Blois. Nostradamian commentators have no doubt that he saw the tragic fates that awaited most of them:

> . . . for, in the cloudy language of the Centuries, were not their fates already written? That boy of thirteen who shall one day be Francis II, who shall be married while still a child to that other unhappy child Mary Stuart, and who shall die miserably after one year of reign; that girl of eleven, destined also to die young, the child-wife of gloomy old Philip of Spain; that girl of nine who will die in her twenties as Duchess of Lorraine; that melancholy little boy of six in whose staring eyes shall one day be reflected the fires of St. Bartholomew; that boy of five who shall be twice a king, but in both kingdoms unhappy, and whose body will be pierced by the assassin's dagger; and that other boy of two, François, Duc d'Alençon, the perpetual *Malcontent*, titular sovereign of the Netherlands, suitor of Queen Elizabeth, laughing stock of Europe—what a nursery to prophesy for! The only child with any soundness and sweetness in the whole brood was the tempestuous Marguerite, then a girl of four, who was to be married to the enemy, Henry of

---

he acknowledges having received on November 29, 1561, a letter sent by Morel from Paris on October 12. It seems that when he was in dire financial straights in 1556 in Paris, Morel befriended him and lent him two rose nobles and twelve crowns. He mentioned this to Catherine, taking it for granted that she would repay Morel. She did not. Sometime later (maybe even several years) Morel, less worried about his money than he was anxious to claim intimacy with one of the most famous men in France, sent Nostradamus a letter by way of a captain from Aix. The letter was never received (or so Nostradamus writes). After waiting many months for an answer, Morel decided he was snubbing his former benefactor, and in anger sent him a very indignant and abusive letter, to which this is the reply.

The prophet is the epitome of tact. He praises Morel's generosity, protests that this is the first time he has heard from him, that only one unexpected event after another kept him from visiting Morel before he left Paris. He mentions enclosing two notes to friends at court, a Mlle de Saint-Rémy and M. de Fizes, from whom Morel can collect. He further states his willingness to be of any service possible to Morel or any friend of his. He will not fail to see Morel when he visits Paris again, as he expects to soon, to see about César's education, if the religious situation ever quiets down enough to make travel safe. The letter is first signed by its writer, Nostradamus' secretary (Chavigny?), but a postscript is followed by Nostradamus' own signature, the only known autograph. (See the complete text and translation in the Miscellany, at the back of the book.)

Navarre, to be repudiated by him for her adulteries, to outlive them all and to go down to history as the raffish, ragtaggle but not unlovable *Reine Margot*.[51]

Of course, Nostradamus could not inform Catherine of these tragic destinies. Accordingly, we are told, he simply told her that all her sons would be kings. This was not quite correct. François never quite made it. Maybe he said that in her sons she beheld four kings-to-be. Since Henry ruled Poland as well as France, this would do it. But whatever it was that he actually told Catherine, she never complained that he had been in the least inaccurate, and retained her confidence in him throughout.

Soon after his return to Paris, he left the city again hurriedly. A "very honest woman" who had the air of a lady of quality warned him that "these gentlemen from the Justice of Paris" intended to pay him a visit to inquire into the nature of the science that he practiced with so much success. Although in the end Catherine's protection would have pulled him out of any scrape, he took this as a good sign to leave the big city.[52]

The great man now returned to Salon in triumph. His house was constantly besieged by visitors. Craponne was nearing final success with his canal. He wrote more brief works of various sorts and probably worked on the new edition of the Centuries, with VIII–X, which would complete the Milliade. In 1557 his second son, André, was born.

It was probably at this time that the Bishop of Orange sent the famous prophet a plea for help. Some scoundrel had stolen a silver chalice. Could the prophet determine the culprit? The letter sent in reply by Nostradamus[53] is still in the archives of Arles. Nostradamus began his reply with an ominous-looking horoscope, unexplained. He wrote that if the chalice was not returned promptly, Orange would suffer the worst pestilence in its history, and the thief would die the most horrible death imaginable. He advised the Bishop to post the letter in a public place. Unfortunately, there is no further report of what happened thereafter.

This period is also the setting for another Nostradamian anecdote. One evening, as he was sitting in front of his house, the daughter of a neighbor passed him on her way to the woods to gather some firewood. She greeted him politely.

"*Bonjour, Monsieur de Nostredame.*"

"*Bonjour, fillette.*"

An hour later she returned and greeted him again.

"*Bonjour, Monsieur de Nostredame.*"

"*Bonjour, petite femme.*" True or not, a charming story.

---

[51]Laver, *Nostradamus; or, The Future Foretold* (London, 1942), pp. 49–50.

[52]In the letter to Jean Morel; see above.

[53]A copy of this letter was received and translated as this book was going to press (see the complete text and translation in the Miscellany). If not as authentic as the Morel letter, it sounds quite Nostradamian. The date is February 14, 1562, a few years later than we had previously supposed it.

The new edition of the Centuries was to be dedicated to the prophet's recent benefactor, the King of France. This Dedication, or Epistle, actually amounted to a prose outline of his view of things to come. Although it is dated June 27, 1558, and contains mention of March 14, 1557, as a starting point for the prophetic outline, this Epistle and the last three Centuries were not printed till 1568, two years after his death. However, it is likely that manuscript copies were circulated during his lifetime, for, as we shall see, at least one of the quatrains contained in this edition was known at court around 1560.[54] Why he refrained from publishing it during his lifetime is a matter for conjecture.

In the summer of 1559 the House of France celebrated two marriages. The King's daughter Elizabeth was married by proxy to Philip II of Spain on June 22. On June 28 the marriage contract of the King's sister Marguerite and the Duke of Savoy was signed. On June 28 there began three days of festivities, highlighted by tournaments in the rue Saint-Antoine. The King engaged in these and distinguished himself on the first two days. Towards sunset of the third day, July 1, Henry rode against Gabriel de Lorges, Comte de Montgomery, Captain of the Scottish Guard. Failing to unseat him, he insisted on another bout. Henry was perhaps conscious of riding headlong towards his fate. The lances met and splintered, Montgomery dropped his shaft a second too late, the jagged point pierced the King's visor and entered behind his eye. He reeled, clutched the pommel of his saddle desperately and fell into the arms of his grooms. After ten days of agony, he died on July 10.

"Cursed be the divine who predicted it, so evilly and so well," exclaimed Montmorency dramatically. Although he probably had Gauric in mind, there were many at court who thought of Quatrain 135 in the Centuries of Nostradamus. We are told by César that in the suburbs of Paris the populace burned Nostradamus in effigy and called on the Church to do the same to the prophet himself.

Henry was succeeded by his eldest son as Francis II. On November 17, 1560, the sickly young king had a shivering fit and swooned. On November 20, 1560, the Venetian ambassador, Michele Suriano, wrote to the Doge from Orléans, "Each courtier recalls now the 39th quatrain of Century X of Nostradamus and comments on it under his breath."[55] On December 3, Niccolo Tornabuoni, the Tuscan ambassador, wrote to Duke Cosimo of Florence, "The health of the King is very uncertain, and Nostradamus, in his predictions for this month, says that the royal house will lose two young members[56] from unforeseen malady."[57] Francis died December 5.

On January 12, 1561, Chantonnay, the Spanish ambassador, wrote to

---

[54]Parker writes that this was the custom in that day. It is the only way by which Henry II could have read the Epistle before he was killed in 1559.

[55]This is found in the Bibliothèque Nationale under Manuscript du fonds italien #1721-4-193. The latter, unfortunately, is a copy made in the 18th century (which does not, of course, imply fabrication).

Philip II, "It has been remarked that in one month the first and last members of the royal house have died. These catastrophes have struck the court with stupor, together with the warning of Nostradamus, whom it would be better to chastize than to allow to sell thus his prophecies, which lead to vain and superstitious beliefs."[58] In May, 1561, Suriano wrote another report to the Doge. "There is another prediction very widely spread in France, emanating from this famous divine astrologer named Nostradamus, and which threatens the three brothers, saying that the queen mother will see them all kings."[59]

Meanwhile, in Salon, Nostradamus could not know of his renown in the chancelleries of Europe. In October, 1559, the Duke of Savoy stopped at Salon on his way home to Nice. When he learned that a plague was raging in his domains, he decided to stay there awhile. In December he was joined here by Marguerite. The whole town turned out to honor her, and Nostradamus was called upon to compose a suitable inscription for the arches. He resolved on—

> SANGUINE TROIANNO, TROIANA STIRPE CREATA
> ET REGINA CYPRI.[60]

This was held to be in very fine taste. As for Marguerite, "a gentleman who was present at all these events assured me that this Princess entertained him a long time and did him much honor."[61]

Nostradamus continued to pass his time turning out yearly and periodical prophecies and defending himself from the attacks of the Cabans, which reached their height in 1560. In December of 1561 the prophet was called to Nice by his Savoy patrons to cast the horoscope of the unborn Charles-Emmanuel. Nostradamus predicted that he would be the greatest captain of his age; which turned out to be a bit of an exaggeration.[62]

---

[56]The other prince who died in December, 1560, was the young heir of the most-junior Capetian branch, that of Roche-sur-Yon, whose father was Governor of the future Charles IX. Presumably Ambassador Tornabuoni's reference to "predictions for this month" should point to Presage 57, but this Presage (see full text in French and English under "Presages") contains no such prediction.

[57]*Négociations diplomatiques de la France avec la Toscane* (Paris, 1865), Vol. III, p. 428.

[58]*Archives Nationales*, K 1494, #27.

[59]*Rélations des Ambassadeurs Vénitiens* . . . (Paris, 1838), Vol. I, p. 425.

[60]In English, "Of Trojan blood, created out of Trojan stock and queen of Cyprus." The first part refers to the claim of the ancient French kings to be descended from the Trojans, which was accepted by Nostradamus, who refers to "Trojan blood" in several quatrains. The second part refers to the fact that after the death of the last Lusignan king in 1475, one of the two female pretenders married the Duke of Savoy and of course bequeathed her rights to her son. Venice, supporting her rival, won out. Though politically empty, the title was justified poetically.

[61]*Histoire de Provence*, p. 783.

[62]He was indeed called Charles-Emmanuel the Great and was a dogged foe of Henry IV. His principal claim to fame is as the ruler of Savoy during the glorious career of St. Francis of Sales.

Early in 1564 Catherine conceived the idea of a Royal Progress through-out France, with the vain goal of pacifying the strife-torn land. The Progress was to terminate at the Spanish border in a conference with her daughter and Spanish leaders. If the Huguenots had not become reasonable by then, she could arrange for joint action with the Spanish. With a "reduced" court of eight hundred, including the entire royal family, she set out for a tour that was to last for two years.

The Progress of course had to include Provence, and Catherine would hardly pass through Provence without paying a visit to Nostradamus at Salon. César Nostradamus collected much information on this high-water mark of his father's career, so we shall see his own words:

Very soon afterwards there came to Provence the young King, who was making a tour of his kingdom, and arrived at this town of Salon on Tuesday, October 17th, at 3 P.M. The plague had already been declared in this little place, where it had been very suddenly caught by four or five persons: such that the town being empty and deserted by people who did not care to struggle against such a pitiless enemy, the structures looked very sad, and the houses were in a pitiful state to receive a royal train. This moved His Majesty to command through criers sent from there that all the absent were to return, along with their belongings, under pain of prompt and heavy penalties: upon which each returned to his hearth as much to obey the royal command as to see His Majesty and more princes than Salon had seen in its entire history. For the entry of this monarch, according to the custom of the times, several simple arches had been prepared, covered with branches of box, from the gate of Avignon by which he made his entry to the gates of the chateau, a magnificent and pontifical mansion. The streets were covered with sand and strewn with rosemary branches, which gave a very agreeable and scentful odor. He was seated on an African horse, with gray housing and a harness of black velvet with large trimmings and fringes of gold. His person was cloaked in a mantle of Tyrian crimson, vulgarly called purple, enriched with silver ribbons; his hat and plumage accorded with his clothing. Antoine de Cordova, an honorable and generous gentleman, who shortly afterwards was made a Knight of Saint-Michel, and Jacques Paul, one of the richest men of his time, who likewise was ennobled several years later, being Consuls, they received him at the gate by which he made his entry, under a curtain of violet and white damask. These two Magistrates, honorably accompanied by more nobles and bourgeois of the town, at once begged Michel de Nostredame, whose name was quite sufficient to account for their desire to have him along, to speak to Her Majesty at the reception, guessing quite correctly that she would especially desire to see him: but he excused himself as graciously as he could to Antoine de Cordova, his very intimate friend, and his companions, informing them that he wanted to move about independently and greet Her Majesty away from the vulgar mob, and from this crowd of men, being quite well warned that he would be asked for and sought when she arrived.

Thus, very decently covered, he awaited the moment to render this homage to his King; the Consuls pointed him out to His Majesty, to whom

Nostradamus and young Henry of Navarre (October 18, 1564). From a painting by L. Denis Valverane which hangs in the Museum of Old Salon.

he made a very humble and suitable reverence with a free and philosophical liberty, pronouncing this verse of the poet: *Vir magnus bello, nulli pietate secundus.*[63] Thereafter, as if completely beside himself with an extraordinary ease that he felt at this instant of seeing himself so humanely acclaimed by such a great Monarch, of whom he was born a subject, and as if indignant against his own land, he proclaimed these words: *O ingrata patria, veluti Abdera Democrito;*[64] as if he had wished to say: "O ungrateful land, to whom I have given such a name, see how much my King still deigns to make of me!" Which he doubtlessly said openly enough in these few words, against the rude and uncivilized treatment that certain seditious rogues, gallows-birds, bloody butchers and villainous Cabans had given to him, who gave such glory to his native land. Then my father, for it is of him I speak, accompanied him, always at his side, with his velvet hat in one hand, and a very large and beautiful Malacca cane, with a silver handle, in the other, to support him on the road (because he was often tormented by that troublesome pain in the feet vulgarly called gout) up to the gates of the chateau, and again in his own chamber, where he entertained this young

[63]"Man great in war, second to none in piety."

[64]"O native land, ungrateful as Democritus' Abdera." Abdera was a classical Greek town, proverbial for the stupidity of its citizens, who considered insane and persecuted its most brilliant son, the 5th century B.C. philosopher Democritus, who first conceived the atomic theory.

King for a very long time, as well as the Queen-Regent, his mother, who had a very benevolent curiosity to see all his little family, even to a little baby girl in arms. I remember this very well, for I was of the party.

His Majesty left the next morning[65] for Aix . . . and took again the road to Arles, where he stayed fifteen days. . . . While there, he desired to see more of my father, so he expressly sent to ask for him, and after several discourses, knowing very well that the late King, Henry II, his father, of very heroic memory, had made much of him, and had honored him greatly during his trip to France, he dispatched[66] to him a present of 200 gold crowns, to which the Queen added half as much, and gave him his patents as Counselor and Physician-in-Ordinary, with all the customary wages, prerogatives and honors. Sweet and agreeable things if they had had more durable import for him and his family, which could hardly have failed to raise itself by them to the best fortune if he did not abandon them. These royal favors which lasted only a moment seemed to be the signs and certain advance-couriers that a King greater than the one of France would very soon send for him to ask him to reply to His tribunal, as we shall see shortly.[67]

Chantonnay, that Spanish ambassador whose contempt for Nostradamus we have already noted, had been succeeded by a no less hostile Don Francisco de Alava. Some of his despatches to Philip II give us more interesting details on the royal visit. One provides a very interesting prophecy not borne out by history:[68] "Tomorrow there leaves secretly a gentleman sent to the Queen of England. I know that the Ambassador is jealous. The first day

---

[65]César omits one of the most interesting phases of the visit which is attested to by writers without any special bias for Nostradamus. Catherine had made Nostradamus cast a horoscope of her favorite, Edward of Anjou, who was to terminate the Valois line as Henry III. He satisfied her with the statement that Edward would be king. But Pierre L'Estoile, the French Samuel Pepys of the day, tells us (*Mémoires pour servir à l'histoire de France;* Cologne, 1718, Vol. II, p. 2) that he was far more interested in another prince.

. . . he begged his Governor to see this young prince. The next morning, the Prince being nude at his levee, Nostradamus was introduced into the chamber as he was being given his shirt, and after looking at him for a long time, he said that he would have the entire heritage ". . . and if God gives you grace to live till then," he added, "you will have as master a King of France and Navarre."

That which seemed incredible then has occurred in our own days: which prophetic story the King has since recounted often, even to the Queen, adding jestfully that because they delayed in giving him his shirt, so that Nostradamus could contemplate him at ease, he feared that they intended to whip him.

According to the Coudoulet manuscript (1789), this took place in the house of Pierre Tronc de Coudoulet. The date for this event is October 18, 1564, and is the subject of a painting. (See reproduction, p. 33.)

[66]There is a certain amount of confusion as to whether the added contact was by messenger or personal. Apparently he visited the King personally at Arles, but was sent the money and titles by messenger.

[67]*Histoire de Provence*, pp. 801–2.

[68]In *Archives Nationales*, K 1503, #37. Cited by De France, p. 252.

that the King and Queen saw Nostradamus he declared to them that the King would marry the aforesaid Queen."[69]

Another despatch, sent from Toulouse months later, verifies the high esteem in which Catherine held Nostradamus.[70]

In order that Your Majesty may see how light-minded people are here, I will say that the Queen, when she passed through the place where Nostradamus lives, summoned him and presented him with two hundred crowns.[71] She ordered him to draw up the horoscope of the King and that of the Queen.[72] As he is the most diplomatic man in the world and never says anything to displease anyone, he resolved in the two horoscopes to flatter the King and the Queen, so that they ordered him to follow their court, treating him royally until they separated and left him at Arles. The Queen said to me today, when I told her that I hoped, with the aid of God, that a great good would result from the future interview:[73] "Do you know," said she, "that Nostradamus had affirmed to me that in 1566 a general peace would reign over the world, that France would be peaceful and that the situation would become stronger?" And saying that, she had as confident an air as if she had quoted St. John or St. Luke.[74]

As a result of the visit, it was now clear to his opponents beyond all doubt that the House of France held the prophet in very high esteem. But his triumph was to be of short duration. Ever-worsening attacks of gout and arthritis weakened him to such a degree that he became confined to his home, surrounded only by his family and intimate friends. On June 17, 1566, Joseph Roche, notary, was called in to take down his will.[75]

In great detail Nostradamus enumerated the various species of coins he possessed, the sum and value of which was 3,444 crowns.[76] The largest

[69]Elizabeth made a witty reply to the proposal, which was actually made: "Charles IX is too great and too small to become my husband."

[70]*Archives Nationales*, K 1503, #30. Cited by De France, pp. 251–52.

[71]100, according to César. The reports of gifts Nostradamus received often seem to vary. According to César, Charles gave 200.

[72]Charles was affianced to Elizabeth of Austria in 1561 but did not marry her till 1570, so the Queen here must be Catherine herself.

[73]With her daughter, Elizabeth of Spain, at Bayonne near the frontier. At the meeting common measures against the Huguenots were to be concerted. (See above.)

[74]She had the same confidence in recording another "error" of our prophet. In a letter sent Montmorency from Salon, she quoted Nostradamus saying that he "promises a fine future to the King my son, and that he will live as long as you, whom he says will see ninety years before dying." The Constable died in 1567 at seventy-four, Charles IX in 1574 at twenty-four.

[75]Copied for Parker by the librarian of Arles from the Municipal Archives (*Testaments Curieux*, #298) in 1918. (See text and translation in Miscellany, at the back of the book.)

[76]Parker in 1920 estimated this sum to have the purchasing power of 500,000 francs. Allen in 1940 (*Window in Provence*) placed it at $11,000. The best idea can be got from Nostradamus' statement that his thirty-day trip to Paris cost one hundred crowns, or from the fact a room in a good house could be rented for four crowns a year.

*(Top)* The corner of the Church of St. Lawrence in Salon (Chapel of the Virgin) in which Nostradamus' tomb is located. *(Bottom)* Close-up of Nostradamus' tomb.

legacy went to his daughter Madeleine. While she got 600 crowns, her sisters Anne and Diana got only 500 each. Mme Nostradamus received 400 and most of the household furnishings. Each son was to get 100 crowns when he reached twenty-five. Minor bequests went to a girl named Madeleine Besaudine (ten crowns), Franciscan Friars (two), Friars of Saint-Pierre-de-Canon (one), the Chapel of Our Lady of the White Penitents (one) and thirteen beggars (six sous). The prophet, who could be very exact when he wanted to, provided for every possible event, ranging from the birth of posthumous twins to his wife to the death of a daughter before marriage. Instructions regarding his burial were also included. His body was to be laid in the church of the Franciscan monastery between the great door and the altar of St. Martha. For this, the friars got *one* crown. The executors were to be Pallamèdes Marc, Lord of Châteauneuf, and Jacques Suffren, bourgeois.

Notwithstanding his weakened condition, César and Madeleine, his eldest and apparently favorite son and daughter, respectively, must have plagued him about the inheritance of certain possessions of his which they most coveted. On June 30 Roche was called in again to draw up a codicil by which César got his astrolabe and a certain large gold ring immediately after his father's death, and Madeleine was to get two walnut coffers, with all the jewels, clothes and ornaments they contained, without having to wait for her marriage.

According to Chavigny, on about June 25 dropsy followed in the wake of Nostradamus' arthritis. Father Vidal, Superior of the Franciscan monastery, was sent for on July 1, heard his confession and administered the last rites. That evening, as Chavigny took his leave of him, politely saying, "Until tomorrow," Nostradamus replied, prophet to the last, "You will not find me alive at sunrise."[77] Early the next morning, after eight days of suffering, he expired.

He was buried in the chapel as specified. Although it was not specified in the will, he had also requested that he be buried upright, supposedly so that the boors of Salon could not tread upon him.[78] On a marble slab eight feet long an elaborate epitaph was erected in imitation of Livy's.[79]

D.O.M.

CLARISSIMI OSSA

MICHAELIS NOSTRADAMI

UNIUS OMNIUM MORTALIUM JUDICIO DIGNI,

CUIUS PENE DIVINO CALAMO TOTIUS ORBIS,

EX ASTRORUM INFLUXI, FUTURI EVENTUS

CONSCRIBERENTUR.

VIXIT ANNOS LXII. MENSES VI. DIES XVII.

OBIIT SALONE AN. MDLXVI.

QUIETUM POSTERI NE INVIDETE. ANNA PONTIA GEMELLA

CONIUGI OPT. V. FELICIT.

---

[77]However, Presage 141 indicates that he originally prophesied that he would die in November, 1567, or seventeen months after his actual death. It also indicates that the Almanacs were written about two years "in advance."

[78]Coudoulet, writing in the early 18th century, claimed Nostradamus had once scattered some mocking peasants in saying, "Be gone, scoundrels; you will never put your dirty feet on my throat, either during my life or after I'm dead."

[79]The composition has been ludicrously attributed to his wife. More likely Chavigny, who likened him to Livy elsewhere, is the author.

In English: "Here rest the bones of the illustrious Michael Nostradamus, alone of all mortals judged worthy to record with his almost divine pen, under the influence of the stars, the future events of the entire world. He lived 62 years, 6 months and 17 days. He died at Salon in the year 1566. Let not posterity disturb his rest. Anne Pons Gemelle wishes her husband true happiness."

As to Nostradamus' person and character, Chavigny's description is both thorough and unique, so we shall give his exact words.

He was a little under medium height, of robust body, nimble and vigorous. He had a large and open forehead, a straight and even nose, gray eyes which were generally pleasant but which blazed when he was angry and a visage both severe and smiling, such that along with his severity a great humanity could be seen; his cheeks were ruddy, even in his old age, his beard was long and thick,[80] his health good and hearty (except in his old age) and all his senses acute and complete. His mind was good and lively, understanding easily what he wanted to; his judgment was subtle, his memory quite remarkable. By nature he was taciturn, thinking much and saying little, though speaking very well in the proper time and place: for the rest, vigilant, prompt and impetuous, prone to anger, patient in labor. He slept only four to five hours. He praised and loved freedom of speech and showed himself joyous and facetious, as well as biting, in his joking. He approved of the ceremonies of the Roman Church and held to the Catholic faith and religion, outside of which, he was convinced, there was no salvation; he reproved grievously those who, withdrawn from its bosom, abandoned themselves to eating and drinking of the sweetness and liberties of the foreign and damned doctrines, affirming that they would come to a bad and pernicious end. I do not want to forget to say that he engaged willingly in fasts, prayers, alms and patience; he abhorred vice and chastised it severely; I can remember his giving to the poor, towards whom he was very liberal and charitable, often making use of these words, drawn from the Holy Scriptures: "Make friends of the riches of iniquity."[81]

Nostradamus left behind six children, three boys and three girls. César, who lived until 1631, has been described by a local historian[82] as a "good poet, excellent painter and able historian." He was Consul of Salon in 1598 and 1614. André, sent to Paris soon after his father's death, was arrested for killing an adversary in a duel. Vowing to become a Capuchin if freed, he

---

[80]There are three principal portraits of Nostradamus. The most famous one, done by César on copper, is in the Bibliothèque Méjanes in Aix; a copy hangs by the prophet's tomb in Salon. The second is in the Library of Grasse. The third is in the Museon Arlaten at Arles. (See Frontispiece for his son's portrait of him.)

[81]Some elements of this eulogy do not tally with other facts known about him, amongst them his great humanity, his love of freedom of speech, his sincere Catholic faith and his liberality towards the poor.

[82]Pitton, *Histoire de la ville d'Aix* (Aix, 1666), p. 604.

made good his vow and took orders after his release.[83] Charles followed in the footsteps of his uncle Jean as a Provençal poet. César alone was married[84] but he had no offspring.

In addition to these three sons, mention must be made of a fictitious son, referred to usually as Michel the younger.[85] He is said to have made an unsuccessful effort to follow in his father's footsteps, and to him are attributed various odds and ends of occult literature between about 1568 and 1615.[86] Frequent references are also found to the colorful close of his career at the siege of Poussin in 1574.[87] The story first appeared between 1616 and 1620 in print.[88]

The abandoned town was exposed to pillage and even to fire by a very novel means. They had in the army a young Nostradamus, son of Michel. Saint-Luc having asked him what would happen to Poussin, the prognosticator, after having thought it over profoundly, replied that it would perish by fire; this fellow was found, during the pillage of the town, starting fires everywhere. "Now then, our master, is any accident to happen to you today?" The divine had no sooner replied no than the other one drove his lance through his stomach, whereupon the horse upon which he sat kicked him, payment for his mischief.

Of the three daughters, Madeleine married Paul de Chonquin, a gentleman of Barbentane, according to César (p. 375). But the Coudoulet manuscript (1789) claims it was Anne who married him. Either Diana or Anne married the Lord of Isnard. The third one married into the family of de Seve and her son became mixed up with additional works attributed falsely to his grandfather.[89] There may be living descendants of Nostradamus from one or more of these marriages of his daughters.

---

[83]The Coudoulet manuscript (1789) has it that he was merely "converted" by one Basil of Bordeaux, took orders on December 4, 1587, and was buried in the monastery of Brignoles, near Toulon. A more prosaic version.

[84]To Claire de Grignon, granddaughter of Adam de Craponne.

[85]Jaubert, the first biographer after Chavigny (1656), wrote that Michel was the eldest son, César the second and André the third. This version omits Charles. A work of 1571, interpreting a recent earthquake, is by "Anthoine Crespin Nostradamus." Some have seen this person also as a son. Whether they are to be viewed as one and the same (some of the works in question have as author's name simply *Nostradamus le jeune;* while Michel has been presumed here, "Crespin" might be involved as well), neither is actually a son of his.

[86]In 1594 La Croix Du Maine wrote, "Michel de Notre-Dame, or Nostradamus the younger, son of the above, composed an Almanac or Prophecy in the year 1568, printed at Paris and in other places." His name also appears with a collection of non-Nostradamian prophecies, first printed in 1571, reprinted in 1611 and bound with the Pierre Chevillot edition of "his father's" Centuries.

[87]Sometimes dated 1629, when another siege took place there. But as the story was in print by 1620, the 1574 one is the only one possible.

[88]In *L'Histoire universelle* (Maillé, 1616–20) by Théodore-Agrippa d'Aubigné, grandfather of Madame de Maintenon (wife of Louis XIV).

[89]See "Nostradamus Bibliography."

The tomb of Nostradamus was visited on November 1, 1622, by Louis XIII. On January 16, 1660, another state visit was made, this time by Louis XIV, his mother Anne of Austria and Cardinal Mazarin.

The soldiers of Revolutionary France seemed to have an insatiable craving for the violation of churches and tombs, and Nostradamus' tomb was no exception. In 1791 some Gardes Nationales from Marseilles broke into his tomb, quite heedless of the solemn warning. One of them is said to have drunk some wine out of the prophet's skull. The bones were scattered during this drunken orgy and the Salonians were only too glad of this opportunity to gather new relics. The Mayor, M. David, gathered together all the bones he could still find, gaining the co-operation of the soldiery by ingeniously informing them that Nostradamus had predicted the Revolution. The remaining bones were placed in a wall of the Chapel of the Virgin in the Church of Saint-Laurent, Salon's other church, which escaped damage. There they remain. In the interests of poetic justice, we are told that the "sacreligious" soldier was killed the next morning in an ambush near Lançon.[90] The enterprising mayor had a new tombstone erected, the beginning of which must have caused the prophet to roll over in his nearby tomb.

In this Year 3 of Liberty[91] the tomb of Nostradamus, who honored Salon, his native land, and whose memory will always be dear to French patriots because of his predictions of the reign of Liberty, was opened. The citizens, anxious to save his precious remains, divided them amongst each other; with great pains the municipality has been able to recover part of them, which this tomb contains; it makes a gift of them to posterity, as well as of the portrait of this celebrated man and that of his son, the historian, painted by himself.

By 1813 ranting about Liberty was a bit out of date. The old epitaph was re-engraved on marble, and stands there today, with Nostradamus and Nostradamia the backbone of Salon's flourishing tourist trade.

In conclusion, it may be well to mention the last of the Nostradamian legends. It seems that after his death many of the yokels of Salon who had made his life so miserable were convinced that he was not really dead. They were sure he had shut himself up alive in a cave with a good supply of paper, pens and ink, and was continuing to turn out prophecies year after year.[92]

---

[90]This is the version of Reynaud-Plense (*Les vraies Centuries,* Salon, 1940, p. 26). Another version has it that he was caught with some stolen silverware and hanged.

[91]This is an interesting chance foreshadowing of the Republican calendar, which was only adopted at the end of 1793. In this case they seem to be counting from 1789 (not from 1792).

[92]Coudoulet manuscript (1789), p. 90.

# Nostradamus Bibliography:
# A Review of the Literature

In considering the works of any so-called prophet, it is extremely important to know which of the works attributed to him are actually his. It is equally important to know the dates by which the various elements of his prophecies were actually in print.

In even the largest and best of the world's libraries, which contain some of the oldest editions, the cataloguing of early editions of Nostradamus' prophecies is in a state of great chaos, with much confusion between dates when parts were written and dated by Nostradamus and dates when particular editions were printed. This condition is due principally to two factors. In the first place, several of the oldest editions are undated. In the second place, there exist several counterfeit editions, bearing false dates of more than a century before they were actually printed. Furthermore, a few of the earliest editions have vanished, leaving behind only vague traces.

To bring order out of chaos is a quality on which the Germans pride themselves, and so it was inevitably a German, Graf Karl von Klinckowström, who spent several years visiting the larger libraries of Western Europe, examining old editions and putting together the pieces of the jigsaw puzzle. His work[1] is the backbone of any bibliographical study, but it is by no means perfect. The Graf was not conscious of the falsity of some editions and accepted as accurate or approximate all dates he found on the titlepages. With due acknowledgment to the Graf and to others[2] whose painstaking research has been invaluable, we aim to present here a more complete and accurate coverage of the works of Nostradamus, and of his commentators and critics, than has ever been made.

Below we shall identify each edition briefly, and in English. Following will be found a list with titles arranged chronologically and given in their original tongue. The list of editions of the Centuries goes as far as 1643.[3] The list of works of which Nostradamus was the principal subject includes favorable and unfavorable ones alike and is also chronological, carried through to the present.[4] Works referred to of which Nostradamus is *not*

---

[1]In *Zeitschrift für Bücherfreunde*, 1912–13, pp. 361–72.

[2]Especially Eugene F. Parker, whose doctoral thesis on Nostradamus can be seen in the Harvard Archives Room.

[3]The latest possible date for the printing of any prophecies of which Nostradamus could seriously be considered the author.

[4]Probably over 90 per cent of the total of such works.

the principal subject will be found listed in the General Bibliography (A) at the end of the book.

## A. *Works of Nostradamus*

### 1. HIS PROPHETIC WORKS

#### *a) The Centuries*

The first edition of the Centuries bore in the back the date on which it was printed. On May 4, 1555, Macé Bonhomme of Lyons brought out the Preface to César Nostradamus and four Centuries, with the fourth containing only fifty-three quatrains. No reason is known for the odd number.

A copy of this edition was borrowed from Abbé James by Eugene Bareste, an ardent Nostradamian enthusiast and commentator, in the second quarter of the 19th century. In his book,[5] Bareste gives enough information about the book to convince the investigator that it really existed. There is now no record of a copy of this edition being in any public kind of library, though there may be copies in some private ones in Western Europe.[6]

The existence of the next few editions is somewhat hypothetical. The Antwerp edition of 1590 states that the quatrains in it have been reprinted from an edition of 1555 by Pierre Roux of Avignon.[7] As this 1590 edition contained seven Centuries, the implication is that seven Centuries were already in print in 1555.

Both the Rouen edition of 1649 and the Leyden edition of 1650 profess to be taken from "the first editions printed at Avignon in 1556 and at Lyons in 1558." The existence of an Avignon edition of 1556 is also confirmed by J. J. Held.[8] Klinckowström suggests that its printer was probably Barthélemy Bonhomme.[9]

Yet another edition of 1556 is mentioned by La Croix Du Maine in his article on Nostradamus.[10] He gives an edition by one Sixte Denyse of Lyons.[11]

---

[5]*Nostradamus* (Paris, 1840), pp. 253–55. For his text, Bareste uses the Bonhomme edition as far as it goes, which makes it very valuable.

[6]Parker was told in 1920 by a bookdealer of Lyons that he had sold a copy to an American in 1909, but he may have been confused about which edition it was.

[7]As such, this is impossible. From 1552 until his death in 1557, Barthélemy Bonhomme, running the Avignon branch of his brother Macé's, was the only printer in Avignon. Any Avignon edition, of 1555 or 1556, would have to be a Bonhomme edition. Pierre Roux and Jan Tramblay bought the Bonhomme business after Barthélemy's death in 1557; which may be the source of the confusion. Only from 1559 on did Roux own the whole business. (See P. Pansier, *L'Imprimerie à Avignon*, Vol. II, Avignon, 1922.)

[8]*Historischer Bericht* (Leipzig, 1711).

[9]It would have to be. See footnote 7, above.

[10]In *Bibliothèque françoise* (Paris, 1584), the first bibliography of French books.

[11]Who is not listed in any of the studies of Lyons printers.

In each of these cases, it must be remembered, there is a possibility of error through carelessness, misinformation or willful distortion. None of these editions since Bonhomme's has been seen and properly described by a trustworthy authority.

The next edition is that of 1557 by Antoine du Rosne of Lyons. There is no doubt about the existence of this edition; the reader will find Klinckowström's picture of its title-page in the following section. This edition contains the Preface and first seven[12] Centuries, and is thus the earliest authenticated edition containing this first block of the Centuries intact.

The next block of the Centuries, completing the Milliade, contains the Epistle to Henry II and Centuries VIII–X. We have already seen, in connection with the dubious 1556 Avignon edition, reference to a Lyons edition of 1558. This is certainly the earliest date at which this block could appear, for the Epistle is dated by Nostradamus June 27, 1558. A 1558 edition is also mentioned by Held,[13] and later by J. C. Adelung.[14] However, each of these references may simply have been based on the lightly-made assumption that the printing took place the same year that the Epistle was dated.

Brunet, the great 19th-century bibliographer, mentions the sale of an edition of 1560 by Barbe Regnault of Paris.[15] He says only that it contained seven Centuries—which brings us no further than the edition of 1557.

We now come to the first of the Rigaud editions, the most widely known of the earlier editions, the nearest thing to an *editio princeps* and the inspiration for both acknowledged reprints and counterfeit editions. It is also the first authenticated edition to have the Epistle and Centuries VIII–X.

The 1568 edition of Benoist Rigaud is divided into two sections. The first section contains the Preface and first seven Centuries, with two more quatrains in the Seventh than that of 1557 had. The second section contains the Epistle and last three Centuries. This second section has its own title-page, which gives the appearance of two separate works bound together. This is characteristic of all editions by the Rigaud family, and of many of their imitators.

Of the two counterfeits of this rare edition, the first appeared in 1649 in Paris or Troyes. This was the time of the Fronde, when Cardinal Mazarin, Richelieu's less-able successor, was confronted with widespread civil disturbances. The purpose of the counterfeit was to include two false quatrains at the expense of Mazarin.[16] They are very poorly done and do not resemble Nostradamus' style at all. Furthermore, the editors, who had actually copied

---

[12]The 7th containing only forty quatrains. It has never been completed.
[13]See footnote 8, above.
[14]*Geschichte der menschlichen Narrheit* (Leipzig, 1789).
[15]*Manuel du Libraire . . . Supplément* (Paris, 1880), Vol. II.
[16]As Quatrains 42 and 43 of Century VII. The old quatrain 42 became 44. See "Prophecies Falsely Attributed to Nostradamus," page 801.

the edition of 1605, even to the same vignette,[17] were so maladroit as to include a supplementary section with a dedication dated 1605.

The falsity of the second counterfeit is made glaring by the use of modern orthography on its title-page. Although most of the orthographical changes involved came into use in the last quarter of the 17th century,[18] some of them were still frowned upon in official documents as late as the first half of the 18th century. It was not until the 1740 edition of their *Dictionary* that the French Academy accepted all these changes. This edition must therefore be placed somewhere between 1675 and 1750.[19]

The next four editions can be considered together, for they all include the same material and the same text. Two of them are by Pierre Ménier of Paris, differing only in that one is undated (but probably of 1588), while the other is dated 1589, and in variations of the title-page. The third one, also of 1589, is by Charles Roger of Paris, who copied Ménier to the last detail. The fourth, dated 1588 but probably printed in 1589, by "The Widow Rossett," follows the same pattern again.

There are several reasons why this Ménier-Roger series is very interesting. They authenticate the Bonhomme edition with a note after Quatrain 53 of Century IV about a new edition. Century VI, for reasons unknown, stops with 71 in one and 74 in the other. Century VII has only twelve quatrains, numbered 72–83, which are not in the Rosne or Rigaud editions.[20] It does not have the Epistle. It does have a Century VIII, consisting of a mere six quatrains, numbered 1–6, all of which are again different from any in Century VIII of Rigaud. While none of these new quatrains is found in any known earlier edition, they are unmistakably in Nostradamus' style and, what is perhaps a more convincing proof of their being genuine, predict nothing on the political horizon of that day. But where they come from is still a mystery.[21] Otherwise, these Paris editions are poor ones, with all of

---

[17]Which suggests the edition came from the same printing house.

[18]However, not one of the changes involved was not amongst those advocated by several 16th-century printers and grammarians, and endorsed by Ronsard, the poet laureate. But experiments with them were abandoned for a long time. (See Beaulieux, *Les Accents,* 1927.)

[19]Le Pelletier, who in 1867 published the most able and extensive commentary on Nostradamus till then, professed to use as his text "Pierre Rigaud's edition of 1558–1566 with the variants from Benoist Rigaud's edition of 1568." The 1566 date is copied from Bareste, whose only authority is his own imagination and a date on a counterfeit edition (the Vallier), which we shall see later. Benoist's is indeed of 1568, but Pierre, his son, was not in business for several decades more. However, because Le Pelletier use the counterfeit Benoist Rigaud, the order is actually correct, but instead of being 1566 and 1568, it is *ca.* 1600 and *ca.* 1700.

[20]Only 73, 80, 82 and 83 are new; 72 is 631, 74–79 are Presages 59–64 (for 1561); 81 is Presage 65. There is doubtless a connection between Ménier's Century VI ending with 71, and Century VII beginning with 72.

[21]Possibly from the Regnault of 1560. Brunet does not explain whether its Century VII contained the traditional quatrains or these twelve. He mentions nothing of Century VIII, so the six would still be unexplained.

the "proper" quatrains of Centuries VII and VIII absent and the Epistle and Centuries IX and X completely ignored.

The next edition is the one of 1590, already referred to, by François de Sainct Jaure of Antwerp. As we have mentioned, it professes to be taken from a Pierre Roux edition of 1555. It contains the Preface and seven Centuries, with thirty-five quatrains in the seventh.[22] What is most interesting in this edition is that the Preface to César is dated June 22, 1555, instead of March 1 as in all other editions. This suggests that Nostradamus may in truth have released seven Centuries later that same year 1555.

The next edition, of no particular import, is one that neither Klinckowström nor Parker seems to have been aware of. It is another one by Benoist Rigaud, of which the first part bears the date 1594 and the second part the date 1596.[23]

Benoist having died in 1597, his sons, under the leadership of Pierre, set themselves up for four years as the "heirs of Benoist Rigaud." Somewhere in this period 1597–1601 they turned out an undated edition. This material contains the same layout as their father's but with certain variations in the text. On the whole, as with most variations of text, they are comparatively minor and insignificant.

In 1603 appeared an edition by Sylveste Moreau of Paris with a very pretentious and misleading title, containing nothing but the Epistle (with the "Henry II" removed, so as to make it appear to the ignorant addressed to Henry IV) and Centuries VIII–X. This edition is of no worth in any connection.

We now come to a period of conjectured dates, i.e., undated editions. This "oversight" on the part of the printers, which probably has some very good reason, has led to much confusion. It cannot be ascertained whether those of Jean Didier and of Jean Poyet preceded that of Pierre Rigaud, but because those of Didier and those of Poyet have not been counterfeited, while that of Rigaud was followed by two false ones, we shall look at the Poyet first. (Details of the Didier edition, of which the only known copy is in the U.S.S.R., are not available, but Didier took over his father's business in 1593.)

The edition by Jean Poyet of Lyons contains the same material and layout as the Rigaud editions; i.e., it is divided into two parts with the Preface and 642 quatrains in the first part, and the Epistle and 300 quatrains in the second. There is nothing particularly noteworthy about it. Poyet was a printer in Lyons from 1590 to 1614, a master printer after 1602. Within this period, the date is pure speculation.[24]

In 1601 the heirs of Benoist Rigaud split up and went into business for themselves. Pierre turned out another edition, which followed the traditional

---

[22]The missing ones are 3, 4, 8, 20 and 22, but the numbers are consecutive.
[23]Cited by Baudrier, *Bibliographie Lyonnaise,* Vol. III, pp. 434 and 443.
[24]Parker estimates after Pierre Rigaud but before 1605.

family pattern. The text varies in places from that of Benoist, or that of the heirs, or from both. Since it did not contain material included in the 1605 edition, Klinckowström and Parker have concluded that it was published before that date, as with the Poyet. However, many later editors preferred to ignore anything beyond the Milliade[25] mentioned by Nostradamus. Furthermore, although Pierre was not legally in business for himself until 1601, yet there appear editions bearing his name as early as 1580. The period for this edition is, therefore, anywhere between 1580 and 1625, but probably 1601–5.

A copy of this edition was "liberated" by the French Revolution from the Benedictine Abbey of Saint-Maur, and was found by both Le Pelletier and Bareste in the Bibliothèque Nationale, or, as it was called in Bareste's time, the Royal Library and, in Le Pelletier's time, the Imperial Library. Bareste wrote that "they pretend it's from 1558" but with careful precaution conceded "it was probably printed the same year that the author died, that is, 1566,"[26] at which time Pierre could not have been very far beyond the diaper stage.

There is one definitely false Pierre Rigaud counterfeit and another that is either counterfeit or a later edition of Pierre's.

This latter one, the dubious edition, has on its title-page the proper orthography of the period. However, the vignette and layout are different on the title-page, and the usual printer's address *ruë Mercière, au coing de ruë Ferrandière,* is followed by *à l'enseigne de la Fortune.* The most important difference, however, and that which has caused even the usually credulous Klinckowström to place it at "Soon after 1650"[27] is that it includes not only the supplementary material of 1605 but also Quatrains 43 and 44 of Century VII, whose first dated appearance is in the edition of 1643.

We tend to consider it authentic for three reasons. In the first place, the "sign of the Fortune" really was Pierre's sign. In the second place, there is no more reason to believe that the printer of this edition copied Garcin or Leffen than vice versa. In the third place, although the two title vignettes are not those of any of the previous Rigauds, in the back of the book there is a third vignette which is identical with the vignette of the second title-page of the 1568 edition. If this Fortune edition, as we shall henceforth refer to it, was actually from the press of Pierre Rigaud, it must be placed between 1605 and 1625. The text is generally an improvement over that in the other Rigauds.

The definitely false Pierre Rigaud edition has an orthography on its title-

---

[25]Consisting of ten Centuries with a nominal one hundred quatrains in each. But the incomplete Century VII has kept it at a maximum of 944.

[26]Bareste, p. 225. Le Pelletier accepted this also, and most writers on Nostradamus since then have accepted this baseless theory.

[27]Based on the theory that the first edition in which VII-43 and VII-44 appeared was the one of 1650 by Pierre Leffen of Leyden. Both Klinckowström and Parker seem unaware of the 1643 by Garcin of Marseilles.

page of the same modern vintage as the Benoist Rigaud counterfeit discussed above, and must likewise be placed at *ca.* 1700. Curiously, in this edition there is added to the usual title-page formula "Printed through the efforts of Friar Jean Vallier of the Franciscan Convent of Salon." Whether this was simply the inspiration of a printer brainy enough to think of this impressive formula to cloak its falsity[28] but not brainy enough to see that the right orthography was used, or whether it had some sort of historical foundation, is a matter for conjecture. It is of course possible that a Friar living *ca.* 1700 instead of *ca.* 1566 worked on the text, which happens to be particularly good by all accounts. This edition has the standard Rigaud material and layout.[29]

This completes the number of very rare early editions, none of which is known to be in the United States[30] (excluding the counterfeits, of which at least one is). We come now to the less-rare editions, most of which can be found in one or another of the larger libraries of the United States.

The edition of 1605 ranks in importance with the Benoist Rigaud of 1568 because it contains much new material and, for but two quatrains, completes the appearance of Nostradamus' Centuries. The title-page contains the name of neither the printer nor the town in which it was printed, but because of its striking resemblance to a later edition by Pierre Duruau of Troyes (this time without a date), it is assumed that Duruau is the printer and Troyes the place of origin of this edition of 1605.

On the title-page the printer acknowledges copying from Benoist Rigaud's edition. He includes the same material up to the end of Century VI. But there, instead of the usual Quatrain 100, the Latin "Incantation Against Inept Critics," there appears a quatrain which is identified as telling the future of the city of Orange. The ousted quatrain is then placed after, without numerical designation.

In Century VII, Quatrain 42 is followed by four more, numbered 73, 80, 82 and 83, preceded by a note that they have been "drawn from twelve under the seventh Century: of which eight have been rejected, having been found in the preceding Centuries." This of course refers to the Ménier edition of 1589, which has twelve quatrains, numbered 72–83.

Century VIII contains the usual one hundred quatrains, which are followed by six additional ones, with the heading "Previously printed under the eighth Century." Once again, Ménier is the source.

Centuries IX and X each contain the usual one hundred, but Quatrain 100 of Century X is followed by an additional quatrain, with the baffling heading "Added since the printing of 1568." This quatrain is singularly im-

---

[28]It was probably intended to pass for an *editio princeps.*

[29]Bareste (p. 262) mentions an undated variant of this edition, but Klinckowström does not seem to have come across it.

[30]That is, the Union Catalog Division of the Library of Congress has no record thereof. One or more of them may be in a private collection.

portant because it marks one of the few cases in which a dated prediction came pretty close to being realized at approximately that date, which in this case is 1660.

Next come the fragmentary Centuries XI and XII, whose existence seems in contradiction to Nostradamus' mention of Milliade.[31] Century XI has but two, 91 and 97. Century XII has eleven, numbered 4, 24, 36, 52, 55, 56, 59, 42 (misprint for 62), 65, 69 and 71.

Thus we see that of these twenty-five quatrains which were not in the 1568 edition, ten are taken from the eighteen of Ménier, while those assigned to Centuries VI, X, XI and XII appear for the first time[32] in this edition. The same comment made with regard to the authenticity of Ménier's holds here. Although their source is unknown, they are in Nostradamus' style and, what is more important, do not refer to any events of the period in which they were printed.

The next division of new material in this edition is that of the 141 four-lined verses entitled "Presages drawn from those made by M. Nostradamus, for the year 1555 and subsequent ones up to 1567." They are indeed the work of Nostradamus, but belong with his other prophecies rather than with the Centuries. Although technically quatrains, they are somewhat different in style from the quatrains of the Centuries, being yet more loose and grammatically disconnected.

They are actually drawn from the yearly almanacs published from 1550 till his death. In 1555 he began putting one of these verses as a heading for the almanac for each month. As a collected group, these 141 were first published in 1594 by Nostradamus' disciple and first great eulogist, Chavigny, in his *Janus Gallicus*. Chavigny faithfully transcribed the month and/or year for which each Presage was intended—which has not prevented interpreters from using them for any period that suits their fancies.

The perfect set for a year has thirteen, one for the whole year and one for each month. But whether through Nostradamus' own whimsies or through Chavigny's editing, the 141 are quite irregular.

At the beginning, we have not thirteen but fourteen, for the Presage for 1555 is followed by one labeled "From the luminary Epistle on the said year," whatever that means. For each of the months thereafter in 1555 there is one Presage. The year 1556 is skipped entirely, and it may indeed be that Nostradamus published none for that year. Presage 15 is for January, 1557. February, March and April are skipped, and 16 is for May, with one for each month thereafter. The year 1558 skips February and September.

---

[31]In *Bulletin du Bibliophile* (1862), p. 784, Buget states that they are to be found in Chavigny's *Janus Gallicus* of 1594.

[32]At least in an edition of the Centuries as such. If the *Janus* is the source for the thirteen of XI and XII it may be the source for the one of VI and the one of X. This would mean that all 25 or 27 had appeared previously, at latest in 1589 or 1594.

Neither 1557 nor 1558 has one for the whole year. The year 1559 is complete with thirteen. The year 1560 has none for the whole year and skips June. The year 1561 has one for the year but skips January, February, September, November and December. Years 1562, 1563, 1564 and 1565 are each complete with thirteen. Years 1566 and 1567 each have twelve, having one for the year but none for December. The last one, 141, said to be a prediction of his own death, is for November, 1567, a miss of seventeen months.

The most likely explanation for the lapses is that Presages that proved too ridiculous were removed by the faithful Chavigny. Even so, we know of no case where an interpretation given for one of the Presages has been for the year or month for which it was intended. Chavigny himself began the outrageous practice of applying them to other periods.

The final section of this edition contains the fifty-eight "Admirable Predictions for the years running in this century" with a note that they were presented to Henry IV on March 19, 1605, at the Château de Chantilly, residence of Montmorency, Constable of France. We shall have a look at the interesting dedication:

SIRE,

Having received (several years ago) certain Prophecies or Prognostications made by the late Michel Nostradamus, from the hands of one named Henry Nostradamus, nephew of the said Michel, before his death, I have held them in secret up to now. But since they concern the affairs of your State, and particularly of your person, and of your successors, and since the truth of several sixains has already been borne out exactly, as you can see, Sire, if Your Majesty will deign to glance at them, finding there some things worthy of admiration, I have taken the liberty (unworthy as I am) to present them to you, transcribed in this little Book, no less worthy and admirable than the other two books that he wrote, of which the last one expired in the year 1597, treating of that which will happen in this century, not as obscurely as he had done in the first ones; but by enigmas, and the things so specified and clear that one can safely judge when something has happened. Desiring that Your Majesty have cognizance of them before any other, acquitting myself by this means of my duty as one of your very obedient and faithful subjects . . . Your humble, very obedient and faithful servant and subject. From your town of Beaucaire in Languedoc.

SEVE.

There are several points of interest in this letter. There is no mention of any Henry Nostradamus elsewhere, neither in the will of Michel nor in the works of César or Chavigny. Nevertheless, the prophet did have two brothers and one of them may perfectly well have had a son named Henry. The "other two books" are presumably the Centuries and the Presages, which apparently he knew of only as published by Chavigny *en masse*. The date 1597 is either a misprint for 1567 or the result of misinformation, possibly

one of Chavigny's farfetched theories. Seve himself was a grandson of
Nostradamus.[33]

The style of the Sixains does not resemble too closely that of Nostradamus, and there is little evidence to support the belief that they really were
written by him. Furthermore, one of the Sixains deals far too explicitly with
an event which had shaken France a few years earlier.[34] Notwithstanding
Seve's clear and unequivocal statement that they are for the 17th century,
interpreters have applied them to events as late as those of World War II.

It seems rather unlikely that Seve made up the Sixains himself and had
the gall to present them to the King with such pomposity, knowing them to
be false. Although César was still to live another quarter of a century, he
was much less interested in the prophecies of his father than he was in the
social position his father's reputation gave him. If they enhanced his reputation, he was not interested in whether they were genuine or not. Chavigny
had died the year before (1604), so there was none to point the finger of
guilt.[35]

Garcin, who put out the 1643 edition, refers vaguely, as we shall see, to
the impositions of a dim-witted son. None of Nostradamus' three sons falls
in this category; possibly the apocryphal Michel Junior is alluded to once
again. As it is not the Sixains which Garcin rejects, his reference is rather
worthless anyhow. So the authorship still remains a mystery. There is a
remote possibility that their author was actually inspired by notes of Nostradamus, but this remains a very remote possibility.

This, then, is the framework of the 1605 edition. Subsequent editions
have made use of the material therein, but rearranged. A frequent change
has been to list the sixains as Century XI together with the two quatrains.
In a few editions the Sixains become Century XI, XI becomes XII and XII
becomes XIII. Several different series of numbers have been assigned to the
quatrains of XII. The extra quatrain of X is sometimes listed as 101 (10101).
Some editors have accepted parts of the supplementary material and omitted
other parts. Two of the most enthusiastic commentators, Jaubert and
Bareste, completely rejected the Sixains.

It has also been a frequent misconception to refer to all the material not
in the 1568 edition, extra quatrains, Presages and Sixains alike, as "The Supplement of Vincent Seve." This is completely inaccurate. It is only the
Sixains, or predictions, which Seve introduced.

Between this edition and the one of 1643, completing the material of the
Centuries with the appearance of VII-43 and VII-44, there are no editions of

---

[33]*Les Correspondants de Peiresc* (Marseilles, 1880) contains a letter from César to
Vincent Seve in which he refers to Seve as his nephew. In practice, César was practically
a father to him. His mother must have been either Anne or Diana Nostradamus.

[34]Sixain 6 gives a detailed account of the conspiracy of the Duc de Biron in 1602.

[35]Although it provides little clue to their authorship, Jaubert (1656) claims to have
seen an original manuscript of 132 (not 58) in the library of M. Barbotteal, Canon of
Amiens.

any particular importance. Two undated ones were put out by Pierre Chevillot of Troyes. One of these two is bound with a group of prophecies collected by "Michel Junior" and first printed in 1575. This latter work is dated 1611, and as its features are identical with those of the Centuries, it can be assumed that the Centuries were printed then also. The other Chevillot, whether printed before or after, shows its printer no longer content with the much overworked formula of "three Centuries never before printed";[36] he mentions using material "Found in a Library left by the Author."[37]

We have already mentioned the undated edition of Pierre Duruau, which is so similar to the one of 1605 as to suggest Duruau was its printer also.[38] We have also seen that both the Poyet and Pierre Rigaud editions may have come out after 1605, their respective editors choosing to ignore the supplementary material of 1605.

As far as we know, the next edition was that of 1643. But whether his word is to be relied on or not, we must note a contradictory opinion by Garencières, author of the first English translation of the Centuries.[39]

This was the first book after my primer wherein I did learn to read, it being the custom in France, about the year 1618, to initiate children by that book; first because of the crabbedness of the words; secondly, that they might be acquainted with the old and obsolete French, such as is now used in the English law; and thirdly, for the delightfulness and variety of the matter, so that this book was printed every year like an almanac or primer for children.

The 1643 edition by Claude Garcin of Marseilles is preceded by a very interesting note, entitled "The Printer to the Reader":

Do not be at all astonished (Friend Reader) if you do not find in these Prophecies of Nostradamus that I give you those which have been placed in the impressions which were made after those of the year 1568 on which I have based mine; this omission proceeds from neither malice nor negligence, and I have not withdrawn them without cause. The advantage which I had in having printed them in a place where I have been able to familiarize myself perfectly with all the author wrote,[40] prevents me from committing the fault of those who have printed more than I am giving you in this book. For

---

[36]This formula, generally understood for Centuries VIII–X (first printed in 1568) was actually first used for the first edition to contain Centuries V, VI and VII (whether the dubious Roux or the du Rosne) in contrast to the Bonhomme edition, with only three and a half Centuries.

[37]This assertion might warrant study in the light of the provision in the prophet's will whereby his papers were to remain locked up in a room until whichever son should most benefit by them would be of age.

[38]However, the only dated books of Duruau are between 1626 and 1629. Possibly he bought his shop from the printer of the 1605 edition.

[39]*The true prophecies* (London, 1672).

[40]What city he could be referring to is a mystery. It could not be Marseilles. Possibly he had close connections with the printers of Lyons and is acting as their spokesman in denouncing the parvenus of Troyes, who were breaking Lyons' monopoly of Nostradamus.

they had the text of several Prophecies which he never wrote imposed upon them by the son of this Great Astronomer. . . . Although it is undeniable that he was a very clever man, versed in many sciences, he had very little knowledge of the future, and his knowledge has been so weak that we have seen in him that which was anciently noted amongst the Hebrews, that all the children of Prophets prophesied nothing.

We have already mentioned the obscurity of Garcin's reference to the would-be prophet son of Nostradamus. Having read the story about Michel Junior, he may have merely assumed that he was the author of this false material.

What then is this false material that Garcin frowns upon? The Sixains? Not at all. He accepts them as Century XI, omitting for no apparent reasons Sixains 12, 16, 19, 24, 25, 54 and 55. He then makes Century XI into XII and XII into XIII, of which he omits 56, replacing it with the quatrain which appeared for Century X in 1605, all of which makes no particular sense. What he does omit are the perfectly acceptable Ménier additions for Centuries VII and VIII and the additional quatrain for Century VI of 1605. As he makes no mention of the Presages, we must assume he frowned on these too. Indeed, they are not part of the Centuries, but they certainly are the work of Nostradamus, as we have seen.

Thus, after a very promising introduction, this turns out to be a singularly poor edition. And although it is the first dated edition[41] to contain the elusive VII-43 and VII-44, he makes no mention of them. It is only the inclusion of these two quatrains, completing the first appearances of all the quatrains, that makes this edition worth any notice at all.

Logic would seem to dictate that since Nostradamus obviously intended to have ten Centuries whose very name required one hundred quatrains in each, all of the extra quatrains which appear to be his should be placed in the half-empty Century VII, adding 27 to 42, to make a total of 69, which is at least a little closer to 100. But this has never been done, and any attempt to do so would probably meet with the sharpest criticism from Nostradamian enthusiasts and critical scholars alike.

This completes the history of the Centuries and parts thereof attributed to Nostradamus with any degree of plausibility. In summary form, they are—
In print by 1568 and definitely genuine:

> Preface to his son (1555)
> Epistle to Henry II (1568)
> 10 Centuries with 942 quatrains
> 11-453[42] (1555)
> 11-740 (1555? or 1557)

---

[41]As we have seen, its only possibly rival is the dubious Fortune edition. If it really was Pierre Rigaud's, it is the first to contain these two quatrains, for Pierre died in 1625.

[42]According to the numbering system used in this edition (for details see p. 117), "11" is the first quatrain, i.e., [Century] One [Quatrain] One.

11-742 (1568)
11-10100 (1568)

In print by 1589 and probably genuine:

10 additional quatrains, i.e.,
VII-73, VII-80, VII-82, VII-83 (8 others are included
for Century VII which are either duplicates or Presages)
VIII-1 to VIII-6

In print by 1605 and probably genuine:

15 more quatrains
VI-100
X-100
XI-91 and XI-97
XII (11 odd quatrains)

In print by 1605 and not Nostradamus': 58 Sixains.

In print by 1643 and probably genuine: VII-43 and VII-44.

It should be noted that we have pointed out all the editions which have obviously false dates, or are subject to suspicion. In addition, there is always a possibility that genuine-seeming editions with early dates, such as the 1555 Bonhomme or the 1557 du Rosne, are the work of really clever counterfeiters, in contrast to the more clumsy ones whose maladroit handiwork we have noted. But as none of these early editions sold for particularly fabulous prices, were particularly sought after or contained any striking deviations in text, this is not at all likely.

It is estimated that since these early editions of the Centuries there have been at least one hundred more to date.

### b) The Almanacs, Prognostications et Al.

Until quite recently, even some of the best commentators, while aware of the fact that Nostradamus had published Almanacs, held to the view that all traces of these Almanacs had been lost. These same commentators were all familiar with the Presages which were, as we have mentioned, an integral part of the Almanacs. Some commentators chose to ignore the Presages while others considered them as more material to be interpreted for their own day.

In his brief biography of the prophet, Chavigny pays the Almanacs a quite unjustified tribute:

We have from him other presages in prose,[1] extending from 1550 to 1567, most of which I have collected and made up into twelve books as worthy of being handed down to posterity. They cover our history for about a hundred years, and all our troubles, wars and affairs from one end to the other.

[1]This refers not to the four-line verses called Presages but to the prose outline that also went with each month. See below.

This utter misconception of what the Presages were for, which is the inspiration for their loose handling by later commentators, is one of the many reasons which cause the careful observer to question the story that Chavigny himself gave out, that he was a virtual adopted son of Nostradamus, living with him as his disciple for many years. We discuss this further when we come to the commentators.

While we may take Chavigny's word for it that the first Almanac was for 1550, we know that it was only in 1555 that the Almanacs began to include the four-line prophecies for each month called Presages and the long prose prophecies called Prognostications, or "presage in prose." From the first, that of 1555, to the last, for 1567, there were twelve of these super-almanacs, since there was none for 1556. Chavigny collected these, making one year equal one book, choosing to disregard their chronological limitations. Because twelve was also the ultimate number of Centuries (as of 1605), many commentators have understood that these twelve prose books were a clear prose outline of world history, and have damned Chavigny for having ultimately refrained from publishing them as a unit.

Not only have the Presages come down to us, but there is also extant at least one of the original Almanacs and two English translations of the Almanacs.[2]

The original Almanac is the one for 1563, and it is fortunately a particularly rich one. The Almanac begins with the quatrain for the whole year which, as it should, coincides with Presage 79. Page 2 lists the eclipses, feastdays and various astrological data for the year. Pages 4–22 contain a calendar arranged by months. Each month has its own Presage. For each day we get something like this (for November 1):

> 1 *d* Toussaincts   [Gemini symbol]   3   Par force pacifique.

This means that on November 1, with the dominical letter *d*, the sun will be in Gemini, at noon the moon will be in position 3 of the ecliptic and that some event will occur to justify "Through force pacific."[3]

By page 22 all the months have been covered in this fashion. We now come to the dedication to some illustrious person. In 1562 it was no less a person that Pope Pius IV. In this case it is Fabritio de Serbelloni, the papal generalissimo in France,[4] who had recently distinguished himself by slaughtering several hundred Huguenots in Orange. A witty Epigram, full of puns

---

[2]Both are in the United States. Both omit the dedications and the prose Prognostications, but the correct Presages in the right place prove their inspiration to be genuine, though the translations are often poor. "An Almanacke for . . . 1559" is in the Huntington Library. "An Almanach For . . . M.D.LXII," located in the Folger Shakespeare Library, is actually the Almanac for 1555, not 1562.

[3]According to Buget, who covers it in detail in *Bulletin du Bibliophile* (1861), pp. 661–76.

[4]Until the Revolution, the Venaissin enclave around Avignon was ruled by the Papacy under a legate with complete sovereign powers.

on *Fabrice* or *Fabritio*, is followed by a long Epistle glorifying both Fabritio and astrology. For the remainder of the book there follows the Prognostication for each month, which is immense for January, decreases gradually and concludes with but a few lines for December. These are what Chavigny collected and extolled. As with all Nostradamus' prophecies, the Prognostications are filled with dire forebodings of bloody calamities, few of which, if any, occurred the following year in the month designated, or in any other, for that matter. Here is a sample, starting at the end of November:

> The wars of religion will still last very long, and there will be no peace until the year 1566[5] has gone by, when the Princes, Kings and monarchs, together with our Holy Father the Pope and all his holy college, will assemble for good deeds: and by ordinance of the council, from where the light of the world will be, there will be celebrated a feast of sovereign solemnity to commemorate a great accomplishment, and a victory won divinely. But at this point the death of several will cause trouble.
>
> DECEMBER. The easterners will levy a great army, which menaces us; but this will not be the new enemy, the *novus hostis*, which is to assail us, and the new pestilential enemy not to be understood at all. Then by these two quadrants of Saturn to Mars, and of Mars to Jupiter, a strange secret enterprise is signified. . . .

In addition to these Almanacs there are several works of a similar species still extant or bibliographically recorded. These include a "New Prognostication and portentous Prediction for the year 1555," a "Great New Prognostication, with a portentous prediction for the year 1557," "The Great New Prognostication with the ample declaration of 1559," "The Significance of the eclipse which will take place on September 16, 1559, which will cast its malign influence as far as 1560," and three Italian translations.

What were these New Prognostications? The monthly prose prophecies without the other parts of the almanac? Just another name for the almanac on certain years? Either of these may be possible. None of the New Prognostications has been described in detail, so we cannot say for certain. Whatever their framework, we know that they must have read like the Prognostication part of the Almanacs.

The opinion that unprincipled rascals used his name in almanacs of their own, containing predictions so absurd as to discredit Nostradamus, is a kindly one advanced by those who could not reconcile his eminent reputation with the nonsense they found in almanacs bearing his name. This kindly view was taken not only by Nostradamian enthusiasts but even by a disinterested scholar.[6] Although there is proof that unreliable printers made many changes, there is no evidence that any almanac that appeared under his name in France before his death was not actually from his pen. The

---

[5]The Council of Trent actually concluded its work in 1563.
[6]La Croix Du Maine. See footnote 37 in the preceding "Biography of Nostradamus."

Almanac of 1563 is both unquestionably in Nostradamus' style and lingo, and full of the absurdities which gave rise to the "imitations" theory.

## 2. HIS PROFESSIONAL WORKS

The bulk of this group of works, second only to the Centuries in popularity, is contained in a book first printed in 1555, the same year that saw the first edition of the Centuries, and the first edition of the super-almanacs. The lengthy title begins *Excellent and very useful Treatise necessary for all those who desire to have knowledge of several exquisite Recipes, divided into two parts.* The book contains a very interesting series of formulas for concocting such diverse items as beauty creams, love potients, preserves and a Black Death preventive. It contains also memoirs of his travels between 1536 and 1544, abuse of doctors of whom he disapproved and laurels for doctors and druggists who met with his approval. Some poems are included in the Preface, which, in the words of Buget, "resembles a little the language of a drunkard." He mentions that the work was undertaken at the request of a very great princess, by whom he is believed to mean Jeanne d'Albret, Queen of Navarre and mother of Henry IV.

This odd collection went through several reprints, notably in 1556 and 1572. The first of the two parts consisted of two works both of which had been published already in 1552 under separate titles. Other parts were published later under different titles. There was even an English translation of a part, and a German translation of the whole work.

## 3. HIS LITERARY WORKS

The first of these, which is undated, must have been written before 1555, because it is dedicated to the above-mentioned Princess of Navarre, who became Queen in 1555. The title is thoroughly misleading, informing the reader that he had in his hands *The Book of Orus Apollo, son of Osiris, king of Egypt . . . work of incredible and admirable erudition and antiquity.* Either the printer used his imagination in composing the title-page, or Nostradamus was incredibly misinformed.

"Orus Apollo" has actually no connection with the gods of Egypt at all. The name is a variant form of the name of Horapollon of Phaenebytis, a 4th-century writer under whose name there was extant in the Renaissance a pair of books entitled *Hieroglyphica,* supposed to be a translation from original Egyptian hieroglyphics into Greek by a mysterious Philippus, of whom nothing is known. Subject to much suspicion, the works have been placed as late as the 14th century A.D. The work contains nothing more mystical than a collection of treatises on ethical and philosophical problems. Several Latin translations had been made of them in Nostradamus' own day. His version turned it into two books of 182 Epigrams with a total of about two thousand lines. It is said to be totally lacking in literary merit. The second work, a translation of *Galen's Paraphrase of the exhortation of Menodotus for the studies of the fine Arts, especially Medicine,* is of such incredibly low calibre that it has led even the most level-headed to far-fetched conclusions. Buget came forth with the dramatic discovery that this was the key to Nostradamus: that the "offenses to grammar and common sense and the omissions breaking the chain of thought, of which the apparent aim is to repel the reader and make the author seem a madman," were designed to so disgust the "vulgar" that they would keep away from his works, leaving them only for the really learned, who could somehow or other see what he really meant. The dedication, to the Baron de la Garde, another of his heroes (he commanded the French fleet in the Mediterranean) is dated February 17, 1557.

## B. *Works of Commentators and Critics*

The first half-dozen printed reactions to the prophetic efforts of Nostradamus were extremely negative. Buget has made quite a study of these abusive pamphlets and has come to another of his dramatic, though by no means unreasonable, conclusions: some were the work of various of the Bolsheviks of the day, the Calvinists, operating from their Moscow, Geneva, and directed against Nostradamus as one of the pillars of the orthodox Catholic order of society. Indeed, Nostradamus missed no opportunity to abuse the Huguenots and never failed to predict what a bad end they would come to.

The first of these was printed in 1557, as the *First Invective of Seigneur Hercule le François against Nostradamus, translated from Latin (per l.u.c.m.)*[1] The initials, Buget discovered, stood for Latin *per lucem,* which suggested *phare* (French for lighthouse), which in turn suggested "Farel." Not only was Guillaume Farel the name of one of Calvin's henchmen but Farel was also the name of a Moor who made things rather hot for Charlemagne in Spain, the implication of which would not be lost, he hoped, on either Henry II or Nostradamus. Which may be true enough. The title suggested more *Invectives* to follow, but this seems to have been the only one.

The second one was called *The Monster of Abuse* and the full title contains such a long series of nonexistent and cryptographically pregnant proper names that we cannot blame Buget for letting his imagination roam. From it all he concluded that the author was the celebrated Calvinist scholar, wit, teacher and writer, Théodore de Bèze. The most interesting of the accusations is "You resemble that madman who, being unable to make

---

[1]Although all titles are given here in English, the works are all French unless otherwise specified. The titles in their original tongue can be found in the "List of Original Titles" following this section.

himself immortal by virtuous and praiseworthy acts, wanted to perpetuate his name by a deed of infamy—burning the temple of Ephesus." It was printed in 1558.

In 1558 there was also printed a vitriolic work that does not seem to have Calvinist inspiration. This vicious work, the *Declaration of the abuse, ignorance and sedition of Michel Nostradamus*, was written by one Laurens Videl, who in the course of his life was secretary to several notables, amongst them the Duc de Lesdiguières and the Maréchal de l'Hospital. Amongst things of which Videl accuses our prophet are impiety, magic, ignorance of astrology (which suggests a rival astrologer), promiscuous consumption of intoxicating beverages and having advised a sick patient to "sleep with a little black woman." The suspicious Buget questions the actual existence of Videl and guesses that the author is Pierre Viret, "Minister to Lausanne." Parker quotes some typical passages of this rather unscientific criticism.

> Where do you get that stuff? You intolerable pest, leading people astray with your false teachings full of abomination. . . . Believe me, Michel, study up a bit and don't be interested in those who tell you that Saturn is burning out, being so far away from the sun, contrary to the true rules . . . as you believe, you poor fool. . . . One thing which you have not stated in your almanacs is that I tell the world you are a lunatic brainless fool. . . . O poor fool . . . See here, Michel, I pray, whether you are not more stupid and a bigger ass than I can say . . . for you say, you big beast. . . .

Another non-Calvinist attack, dated 1560, contained *The Contradictions of the Seigneur du Pavillon . . . to the false and abusive Prophecies of Nostradamus and other astrologers*. In this one the venom also outweighs the wit. Buget feels that the author was merely trying to attract attention to himself by attacking the famous man.

In 1560 also, across the Channel in England, W. Fulke, incensed by his reading of various English translations of the almanacs, published in Latin an attack on the "useless astrological predictions" of Nostradamus and various long-forgotten confrères.

The last one, dated 1562, was admittedly printed in Geneva and contains satirical verses at Nostradamus' expense. The sole mention of this book, *The virtues of our master Nostradamus*, by Conrad Badius, is by Du Verdier,[2] who has preserved a section of the verses.[3]

Having passed these attacks, we come now to the first great propagandist, whose prolific works on Nostradamus were to be equaled only by Abbé Torné in the second half of the 19th century. Editions of his voluminous works have become almost as rare as the first editions of the Centuries. His commentaries have set the pattern for all commentators since then, including all the faults: lack of perspective, changing of text, glossing

---

[2] *Bibliothèque* (1584). Same year and same design as Du Maine's.
[3] See "List of Original Titles" for the text of these verses.

over lines that don't offer suitable explanations, vague or arbitrary notes and the like. For these two reasons, their importance and the fact that so little is known of them, we will discuss them in great detail.

According to the information we have about him, Jean-Aimé de Chavigny came from a noble family of Beaune, was well educated, achieving a doctorate in both law and theology, and in 1548 became mayor of Beaune. For reasons that can only be guessed at, Chavigny suddenly abandoned his career to study astrology under Nostradamus soon after 1550.

Along with César Nostradamus, Chavigny offers the only firsthand biographical information on Nostradamus. Inasmuch as his brief Biography gives an account of the last days of the prophet, the assumption is that Chavigny lived with him without interruption, as his friend, secretary and disciple. And yet in the will of Nostradamus, containing specific bequests of all sorts for various members of his family and for friends, and couched in detailed, non-Nostradamian language, there is no mention of Chavigny. Nor is there any reference to him in the writings of César Nostradamus. Furthermore, in his commentary on various Nostradamian hybrid words or veiled proper names, he displays not one iota of "inside knowledge." If anything, his explanations are far less satisfactory than those of much-later commentators.

The only conclusion that one can reach is that he merely paid occasional visits to Nostradamus and was informed about astrological and prophetic matters in a very impersonal sort of way. If this theory is correct, then we may assume that his presence during the prophet's last days was due merely to his having hurried to Salon when he heard of his approaching death. Chavigny himself seems to have been quite willing to have people believe him Nostradamus' confidant.

However close or remote his personal relationship with Nostradamus was, Chavigny did spend more than a score of years collecting his works and mulling over them. His known works include three published books, two manuscripts never published and one book which, though unauthorized by Chavigny and merely lifted from one of his books, has come to be regarded as a separate work.

The first known work of Chavigny on Nostradamus has never been seen by a Nostradamian researcher, but its complete title has survived[4] and gives a good idea of its contents. The heading of the title is *Collection of prose presages of M. Nostradamus.* The rest of the title resembles the claims quoted in the discussion of the Almanacs. In short, this book constituted Chavigny's collection of the Prognostications for each month, whose time limitations he chose to ignore. He can only have felt that the stipulated dates were some sort of code for a later period. Buget concluded that though this manuscript was dated 1589, Chavigny intended to hold it back until his theory was confirmed by history, as of course it never was. But

---

[4]In Papillon's work, *Bibliothèque des auteurs de Bourgogne* (1742), p. 141.

although he never published this complete collection of Prognostications, his other works include so many scattered excerpts from them as to make almost a complete mosaic.

Chavigny's next known work was the one for which he is best known, *The First Face of the French Janus,* which was published in 1594. Janus being the two-faced Roman god, this book was to cover history, according to Nostradamus and Chavigny, up to 1589, with Henry of Navarre, to whose star Chavigny had wisely hitched his wagon, as the pivotal figure. The second face of this bilingual work (French and Latin), he assured the nominal but still uncrowned King, would cover all the victories and conquests that would fall to Henry, provided, of course, he didn't drop back into his Huguenot heresy. The censors having demanded that Chavigny remove the word "prophet" with reference to Nostradamus, as a sort of sacrilege, the not-so-dumb scholar informed the reader of this removal in an extremely conspicuous spot at the beginning of his book.

Of the six sections of the book, it is the second that contains the famous Biography which has been reprinted in so many editions of the Centuries. It is this Biography that contains the promise to publish the "twelve books of prose Presages," which reference has excited so many poorly informed readers.[5]

In the third section, Nostradamus the historian is eulogized and the reader is promised that the second face will cover 1589–1607.

The fourth section consists of an imaginary dialogue between Chavigny and Jean Dorat, discussing such varied topics as Nostradamus' prophetic powers, the reasons for the barbarity and obscurity of his style and Chavigny's own woes.

The fifth section is the main part of the book. It contains the 141 verse Presages, the same ones that appeared in the 1605 edition of the Centuries, and which are merely the quatrains given with the almanac for each month. In addition, there are 126 quatrains from the Centuries, arranged according to Chavigny's interpretation of them, an arrangement inevitably copied by all succeeding commentators and interpreters. As we have mentioned, the interpretations are incomplete, vague, arbitrary and totally lacking in the "inside knowledge" one would expect of the prophet's "disciple." One of the most noteworthy items is that one or two interpretations are for events that occurred before the publication of the quatrain concerned. This theory of "retroactive" prophecy is one which some of Nostradamus' sharpest critics have enjoyed toying with.

The last section is devoted entirely to the coming of Henry IV to the crown of France, and his ensuing prosperity. Paris will fall to him in May or June, but not until practically every inhabitant is dead and the Duc de Mayenne, Henry's archfoe, is in exile. After that Henry will conquer Italy, overthrow the Ottoman Empire and of course wind up as Emperor of the

---

[5]See the section "The Almanacs, Prognostications, *et Al.*," above.

world. As it happened, Paris was quietly surrendered to Henry before *Janus* even came off the presses, and Mayenne was loaded with honors.

Nothing daunted by these failures, Chavigny prepared another book for Henry's perusal, dated December, 1594. It was never published.[6] In it, Nostradamus is co-ordinated with the prophecy of St. Cataldus about a forty-year-old king who would chase the tyrants from his own kingdom, conquer England, Spain and Italy, subjugate all the rulers of Christendom and, after conquering the Greeks, Turks and Barbarians, rule the world. Furthermore, on the basis of a coming celestial configuration, an epic battle in Italy was predicted for August 3, 1596, in which Mayenne would be utterly crushed. Finally, Henry was given the prophecy of the "Tiburtine sibyl," once unsuccessfully presented to Charles VIII, to have a crack at. The hero of this one comes from Bohemia, has a name that begins with E and ends up King of the French, the Greeks and the Romans, bringing the earth peace and universal Christianity. The fact that Chavigny, with only Nostradamus behind him, could make Henry of Navarre into E— from Bohemia shows just how talented he was.

In 1596 there appeared under Chavigny's name *Commentaries . . . on the centuries and prognostications of the late M. Michel de Nostradamus . . .* According to Buget, this work consisted merely of the French version of parts two and six of the bilingual *Janus* and was not authorized by Chavigny.

In 1603 appeared *The Pleiades*. This word can refer to seven heavenly stars or to a group of seven terrestrial luminaries. In this case, Chavigny compromised by selecting seven ancient prophecies and assigning to the section devoted to each of them the name of one of the stars. Once again Nostradamus is dragged in for confirmation, and insofar as the first and second of the seven are those of St. Cataldus and the Tiburtine sibyl, this book constitutes an enlargement of the unpublished work of 1594. The other five are "An anonymous prediction of 1580," one by Laurent Miniati (*ca.* 1460), one by Antonio Torquato of Ferrara (*ca.* 1480), a "Vulgar vaticination of the Turks"[7] and that of Saint-Hippolyte, which takes up half the book. In each case, isolated lines or pairs of lines are drawn from any work of Nostradamus for confirmation, quatrains, Presages and Prognostications being treated alike. The theme is always the same: the great, new Charlemagne, who will overthrow and convert the Turks and other infidels and establish universal peace and Christianity. One or two involve the Antichrist and the Second Coming.

Although Chavigny died in 1604, a second edition of *The Pleiades* appeared in 1606. It contained a supplementary "Parenetic discourse on

[6]The manuscript was seen by Buget (*ca.* 1860) in the library of Aix in Provence. Buget is the authority on all these works of Chavigny except *The Pleiades* which we have seen in the Harvard Library.

[7]The prophecy is given in the original Renaissance Turkish first, which may be of interest to some scholars.

Turkish matters" and a discussion of the import of a new star seen on October 17, 1604. Chavigny seems to have passed away without being too much upset by Henry's not having conquered the world. It is certainly a tribute to the character of Henry IV that his head was not turned by all the extravagances of Chavigny.

Chavigny's works are important not only as those of a supposed disciple of Nostradamus, and as those of the first of the commentators. In quoting Nostradamian passages in connection with other prophecies or predictions of his own, Chavigny, well-trained scholar that he was, gives the associated dates and thus provides the only information on the substance and language of the lost almanacs. Buget compared his version with the actual text in the one surviving one, that of 1563, and found that the deviations were usually very insignificant and that Chavigny had faithfully transcribed their substance. Furthermore, it should be noted that the comparison of Nostradamus' predictions with those of previous prophets is not necessarily an arbitrary idea of Chavigny. Nostradamus may indeed have been influenced by them.

In 1656 there appeared the *Explanation of the true quatrains of . . . Nostradamus.* Although the book was anonymous, those interested seemed to know that its author was Étienne Jaubert, a doctor of Amiens, who had had his work printed, for reasons unknown, in Amsterdam. Jaubert reveals that he had discovered 1,800 accomplished predictions of Nostradamus, the proofs of which he set out to put in fourteen volumes, of which seven would deal with France and seven with the rest of the world. In addition, he intended to write two on Christianity *vs.* Islam and the Antichrist, etc., two with a "corrected" text and paraphrase of the Preface and the Epistle, and one on other prophecies. Of these nineteen, he got as far as the first, containing the inevitable preliminary material and commentaries covering the period 1555–60.

Although in readability his book marks quite an improvement over the works of Chavigny, from whom he borrows much with but scant credit, his book is hardly more scientific in approach. Whenever the prophecies don't quite measure up to history, Jaubert blames the careless printers and changes a word here and there. Of those interpretations which are not taken from Chavigny, several involve wishful-thinking additions to make history live up to Nostradamus, i.e., sheer fabrication.[8] Notwithstanding this loose

---

[8]The most noted instance is with reference to 918, credibly applied to the execution of Montmorency in 1632. Jaubert was the first to claim that the name of the executioner was also found in the text. No proof has ever been found that the name of the executioner was indeed Clerepeyne. This item, combined with other elements in the quatrain, caused a German enthusiast to estimate that the chances of the fulfillment of this quatrain by luck were one out of sixty quintillion (nineteen zeros).

handling of the Centuries, Jaubert scrupulously rejects as false not only the Sixains[9] but also the quatrains of Centuries XI and XII.

The work of the next commentator, printed in 1672, is in English. Théophilus de Garencières, author of *The true prophecies or prognostications of Michel Nostradamus,* was a Frenchman who settled in England as a physician. He never quite mastered the English tongue and, accordingly, the crabbed French style of Nostradamus is accompanied by equally crabbed translations and commentaries in English. His text is the false "1568" edition (1649) and to its errors[10] have been added those deriving from poor proofreading.

Not having all the reference books at his disposal that have since done so much to lift the veil from Nostradamus' language, he had to leave many hybrid words or enigmatic names unexplained. His translations are, accordingly, of an "off-the-cuff" and "no-sweat" nature. Besides, he seems to have become rather tired of the whole thing quite often and in one spot he wearily leaves off his commentary in telling the reader he'd like to inform him further but wants to get to bed (see Commentary for 727).

Neither of the next two French commentators is worth much notice. The first was the Chevalier de Jant, keeper of medals for the Duke of Orléans, who in 1673 published *Predictions drawn from the centuries of Nostradamus which seem truly applicable to the present time, and to the war between France and England against the United Provinces.* All commentaries published during the reign of Louis the Great had to reflect his glory, and the Nostradamian ones are no exception. Much of Jant's slim little volume is built around the spurious Sixains, and it is in every sense insignificant.

Into this propaganda barrage the English plunged soon after. In 1689 W. Atwood wrote *Wonderful Predictions of Nostradamus . . . wherein . . . the downfall of France and Rome are delineated.* In 1691 W. Cross came out with *The Predictions of Nostradamus Before the Year 1558,* which highlighted "The Humiliation of the King of France by the present confederacy" and "The Reformation of that Kingdom and the Return of the French Protestants."

The other French commentator of this period who copied Jaubert largely, and whom Buget dismisses with "this one's just a charlatan," was Balthazar Guynaud, Governor of the King's Pages. In 1693 he published *The concordance of the Prophecies of Nostradamus with history from Henry II to Louis the Great.* In 1709 came another edition of it. Both contain the usual elements of copying from Chavigny and Jaubert, apologies for Nostradamus, idealized biographies and a few cracks at original inter-

---

[9]He claims to have seen the original manuscript of them, containing not 58 but 132, in the library of M. Barbotteal, Canon of Amiens.

[10]He also copies some of Jaubert's textual changes to fit interpretations.

pretations for recent events. About half of his book is devoted to "future interpretations." For the most part, they are very logical and sensible interpretations. If they were never fulfilled, it is not Guynaud's fault. The year 1701 found Louis XIV defying most of Europe to enable his grandson, Philip of Anjou, to become King of Spain. On March 4 or 5 the Dukes of Burgundy and Berry were to pass through Salon, the residence of Nostradamus, on the way to join their dynasty-founding brother at the Spanish frontier. For the occasion, a gentleman of Salon who had already established a literary reputation presented the Dukes with a *Résumé of the life of Michel Nostradamus, followed by a new discovery of his quatrains.* This twelve-page booklet by Palamèdes Tronc de Coudoulet had as its heart six quatrains found applicable to the Spanish Succession. However, the work seems to have proved enjoyable to Coudoulet. Two more unpublished manuscripts[11] indicate that he, and later his son, did some original work in adding to the limited biographical information on Nostradamus. Some of the new information was first published by another writer in 1712. It is difficult to establish which of the two did most of the collecting.

As Chavigny was the only interpreter of the 16th century and Jaubert the only really notable one of the 17th, we now come to the only really notable one of the 18th century. In 1710 there appeared *The Key to Nostradamus . . . by a monk.* In spite of the anonymous signature, the author was known to be Jean Leroux, Abbé of Louvichamp. It was not only the affectation of anonymity that he shared with Jaubert. Like Jaubert, he set out to write an immense number of volumes, covering Nostradamus from every angle, of which this was to be the first one. As with Jaubert, the first proved the last.

Leroux, no mean classics scholar, gets off to a splendid start tearing apart the shortcomings of his predecessors with an ever-present holier-than-thou attitude. Guynaud is his particular target. The first key seems to be that you must really know Latin and Greek inside out to understand the Centuries properly. Leroux presents a new thesis, of which not even Chavigny had dreamed. Nothing in the quatrains is ungrammatical and barbaric.

---

[11]The first manuscript was shown Buget by the Comte de Lagoy of Aix. The biographical résumé of 1701 is followed by eighty-four more pages on this phase. After that, twenty-two quatrains are commented upon. However, the enlarged biography has a marginal note *tirée en 1737* and the fourteenth to the twenty-second of the quatrains are associated with events occurring after Coudoulet's death (1722). The inference is that his son completed it.

The second manuscript was shown Buget by Dr. Bossy, former mayor of Salon and great-grandson of Coudoulet. The biographical part shows the influence of Haitze, who died in 1736, mixed with that of the first manuscript. It must have been written before 1745, when Coudoulet's son died. The commentary section is mutilated. The chief importance of this manuscript is that it is the principal source of the anonymous biography of 1789.

Everything represents the application of some established Greek or Latin poetical device. Leroux actually makes a very well-documented case of the thesis that Nostradamus had as his literary model one Franciscus Sylvius, professor at the University of Paris, who in 1528 published *Progymnasmata in artem oratorium.*[12]

But then Leroux sadly goes off the deep end.

The "Clef" is brought to a climax in a series of four "paradoxes," as he terms them. The first demonstrates conclusively (to their author perhaps) that the letter to César is not for César at all, but for the enlightened person who will eventually appear to interpret them, i.e., Mr. Leroux. The second contains equally convincing proof that the letter to Henry II is not intended for its nominal addressee but for Louis XIV. The proof consists in the fact that there is no reason to believe that it was addressed to Henry except that the letter bears his name at the beginning, whereas the numerous cryptic references within the letter to the court of Louis XIV make the facts as plain as day to Leroux. The third and fourth paradoxes prove just as clearly that the Presages and Predictions are not only authentic but are daily being realized. The authenticity of the sixains is proved by the similarity of their style to that of the Centuries, which they resemble as much as they do the poems of Victor Hugo.[13]

In 1711 J. J. Held wrote what appears to be the first German critique of the Centuries. Held belongs to the critical rather than the enthusiastic school of commentators. His book is important chiefly as referring to certain editions of whose existence there remains a great deal of doubt.

In 1712 appeared the first full-length biography, *The Life of Nostradamus,* by Pierre-Joseph de Haitze. He is the source of more than half of the now prevalent biographical information. His connection with the research of the Coudoulet family has already been mentioned. Some of the more critical commentators suspect the source of his information but Buget, in the light of his own research, seems convinced that Haitze was a fairly conscientious and accurate reporter.

In 1715 an English gentleman, apparently seeking to ingratiate himself with the newly-arrived House of Hanover, turned out *The Prophecies of Nostradamus concerning the fate of all the Kings and Queens of Great Britain since the Reformation.* As most of the quatrains which mention England had already been applied to events before his time, D.D., as he called himself, had quite a bit of material to work with. He also included some quatrains that no more concern England than they do Tibet. The keynote is that when the roll is called up yonder, the House of Hanover will still be there.

The next work, dated 1721, was written in French but likewise concerned Britain. One François Geofroy presented *Prophecies of Michel*

---

[12]For more of this, see "Background and Rules of the Game."

[13]From Parker's doctoral thesis "Nostradamus" (Harvard Univ., 1920).

*Nostradamus . . . which predict to us . . . the re-establishment of the king of Great Britain James III on his throne.*

In March, 1720, a gentleman whose identity is still unknown sent to the *Mercure de France* a long "letter" on Nostradamus. For some reason, this letter was not published until the issue of August–November, 1724. The anonymous critic sent documentation to show that Nostradamus was merely a poetic historian, and that his quatrains concerned past events. Although he presents something of a case for this "retroactive prophecy" theory, some of his applications to discredit the prophet are as labored as those of Nostradamus' eulogists. Furthermore, he inadvertently pays Nostradamus great tribute in using as illustrations of his points events which took place *after* the prophecy was written.

In 1775 an English gentleman published what looks like a bull's-eye on the American Revolution (perhaps more on the part of the writer than of Nostradamus). The half century that elapsed between the publication of this work and its predecessor marks the last big gap between works on Nostradamus. Since then, no score of years has passed without a book on Nostradamus. Since the middle of the 19th century, there seems to have been at least one somewhere every decade.

In 1781 the Centuries received the distinction of pontifical condemnation by Pope Pius VI.

*The Life and Testament of Michel Nostradamus* was published anonymously in 1789, on the eve of the cataclysm that was to shake Europe to its very foundations. As we have mentioned, the source is principally, if not entirely, the second of the two unpublished Coudoulet manuscripts. In any event, it was written long before. It contains maladroit giveaways, such as a reference to "Louis XV, at present reigning" (p. 147). The latest event it refers to is the Treaty of the Hague (1720); the author shows no awareness of the nullification of its terms by the Treaty of Vienna (1738). Therefore, it was written somewhere between these two dates. Since the author on page 38 writes of the approach of the dated disasters (1732) of the Preface to César Nostradamus, it can perhaps be placed more specifically in the 1720's. For some strange reason, the author pretends that it is from a manuscript of "Edme Chavigny . . . known as Janus Gallicus," which does Chavigny the double insult of getting his name wrong and confusing him with the title of his book (which referred to Nostradamus). The most interesting part of the book is the résumé of Nostradamus' Testament, long suspect, but now verified and printed in full in this work.

Also in 1789, a German named J. C. Adelung devoted Volume VII of his series on the eerie to Nostradamus.

The next nine works on Nostradamus were written during the era of the French Revolution and Napoleon, and consequently reflect that fact foremost. In 1790 d'Odoucet wrote *The French Revolution, the events which provoked it . . . prognosticated by the prophetic centuries of M. Nostredame.* That same year an anonymous writer came out with *The French Revolution in the prophetic centuries of Nostradamus.* In 1791 Nostradamus was the chief inspiration for *New and old prophecies.* In 1792 came what is the only known Nostradamian work from Slavdom, when there was published in St. Petersburg *The Royalist Almanac, or the Counter-Revolution predicted by Nostradamus for the year . . . 1792,* translated into French verses by the least of his interpreters, Shryalmo.

In 1800 there was printed in Hamburg a highly interesting work by an *émigrée* who can be identified only as Madame H.D. The book was entitled *The future foretold, or concordance of the prophecies of Nostradamus with the past, present and future events of the revolution.* It included no fewer than fifty-two quatrains or sixains applied to the Revolution to that date.

The year 1806 saw a galaxy of four separate works. Dr. Belland wrote the inevitable *Napoleon, first Emperor of the French, predicted by Nostradamus.* A mathematics teacher named Théodore Bouys came out with a highly controversial *New considerations on . . . prophets, and particularly on Nostradamus.* As far as it concerned Nostradamus, Bouys tended to follow Jaubert in making changes of the text or of historical fact, whichever was more convenient, but he also became the principal source of quatrains interpreted for the French Revolution and Napoleon, of which there seem to be quite a few. The chief purpose of the book, however, was to present a theory of his which he confidently expected would revolutionize intellectual history. In brief, it might be summarized as universal clairvoyance.

To this theory Motret replied with a vigorous denial in *Essay to explain two quatrains of Nostradamus.* Motret followed Leroux's idea of there being a method to all the madness and a specific grammatical rule to justify all the apparent barbarities of style. Shortly after this book came out, Destier sprang to Bouys' defense, eulogizing his discovery as the equal of Copernicus', in *Impartial reflections, concerning three works which seem in favor of Nostradamus.*

In 1816 "L.P." presented some Bonaparte nostalgia in the guise of *The true prophecies of Michel Nostradamus in harmony with the events of the Revolution in 1789, 1790 and the years following up to the return of His Majesty Louis XVIII.*

We now pass over all of fifteen years, a span of time not since seen without a work on Nostradamus. Although the next work, by M. Caze, is undated, the title seems to place it in 1831. His work is entitled *Prophecies of Master Michel Nostradamus, in which he announced in 1555 the calamitous events and great mutations which occurred on the earth from 1789 to 1831.*

The year 1839 saw two works. Francis Girault wrote *The past, the*

*present and the future, or predictions, verifications and explanations of
some remarkable prophecies of Michel Nostradamus.* Elie Caisson virtually
copied Belland (1806) with *Napoleon I, emperor of the French, predicted
by Michel Nostradamus.*

Next, 1840 saw the work of Eugène Bareste, who, with Torné and Le
Pelletier, ranks as one of the Big Three of 19th-century commentators and
propagandists. His *Nostradamus* contains a biography, a collection of other
prophecies down through the ages, the text of the Centuries and a rather
brief and insignificant handful of commentaries. The book is chiefly noteworthy for much new biographical material, for which Bareste's enthusiasm
seems to be the only source, and for its inclusion in the text of the now-lost
first edition by Macé Bonhomme (covering the Preface and 353 quatrains).
Bareste also made the first attempt at scientific bibliography, and is thus
the starting point for the much more exhaustive works which followed.
Amongst the "other prophecies" we find the text of the utterly false "prophecies" of "Olivarius," which Bareste, attributing them to Nostradamus,
accepted wholeheartedly, either because he was very naïve, or because he
was the author of one of them.

In 1848 V. E. Charles wrote a critical study of Nostradamus and his
commentators, of the sort later continued by Buget.

In 1849 Eduard Roesch followed the example of his compatriot of
1789, writing a book on Nostradamus (in German) for J. Scheible's series
on the supernatural.

The years 1860–63 saw the very excellent and useful studies of Buget
on the works of Nostradamus and on those of his commentators, published
in successive articles in a literary magazine called *Bulletin du Bibliophile.*
Their greatest value, perhaps, lies in the inclusion of actual texts from the
rarer of then-extant works, such as the Almanac of 1563, the *Orus Apollo*
and *Galen's Paraphrase.*

H. Torné, Curé de la Clotte and Saint-Denis-du-Pin, called himself
Torné-Chavigny, claiming to be descended on his mother's side from the
first commentator. Whether this is true or not, Torné was certainly the
most prolific writer on the prophet since Chavigny, and is one of the most
colorful of all the commentators. He follows Leroux both in being a
researcher and scholar of no mean ability and in believing himself alone
intended by Nostradamus to bring the light.

Between 1862 and 1878, year after year Torné turned out editions, almanacs and articles, dictating to the gods of history what should be their
next moves, and to kings and emperors when they were expected to come
on and off the stage. The inspiration for all his work was his devotion to
the cause of the Comte de Chambord/Duc de Bordeaux, the Bourbon
pretender, of whose imminent return Torné had not one shadow of a doubt.
The monarchical-restoration thesis is a fixation with which most commenta-

tors have been afflicted since Torné's time, only the particular pretender in question varying.[14]

A great believer in publicity, he wrote numerous articles to various publications. He also plagued great scholars and writers like Renan and Hugo, whose peace of mind could not be disturbed by the fact that Torné was likely to drop in at any hour with an armful of Nostradamus texts and, shoving them in front of their eyes, harangue them until they admitted that Nostradamus was the all-seeing infallible. One of his almanacs proudly bears the following quotation on the frontispiece, "'Tell Abbé Torné I'd like to see him again.' VICTOR HUGO." His final triumph, however, seems to have been when Pope Pius IX was led by his writings (and certain events, perhaps) to remark to a visiting prelate, Monseigneur d'Agen, "Napoleon III is indeed the Beast of the Apocalypse."

The year 1863 saw a short, critical essay on Nostradamus by Achille Chereau in *L'Union Médicale*.

In 1867 Anatole Le Pelletier published his monumental two-tome work which, though far from flawless, remains the best-constructed and most impressive propaganda for Nostradamus to date. The first volume contains the usual biographical and background material and the bibliography of Bareste reprinted and supplemented, followed by a well-presented arrangement of about 150 quatrains which he demonstrates to have been confirmed by history. The bulk of these represent only a sifting and improvement of the interpretations of Chavigny, Jaubert, Bouys and others, but they are the most convincing ones to that time. Following this, Le Pelletier could not resist the temptation to do some "future" interpreting, the general line of which was that the heinous activities of Garibaldi in Italy were ushering in the era of the Antichrist and various gentlemen referred to as Saturn, Mars and Jupiter.

The second volume contains "The text of Pierre Rigaud (Lyons, 1558–1566) from the *Editio Princeps* in the Library of Paris; with the variants of Benoist Rigaud (Lyons, 1568) and the supplement of the re-edition of 1605." Which could have been improved but little if true, but it wasn't, as we have seen. Had the Benoist Rigaud he used been genuine, it would have dated thirty-odd years prior to that of "1566," actually printed by Benoist's son *ca.* 1600. However, since the Benoist Rigaud he used was the counterfeit edition of *ca.* 1700, the historically erroneous order comes out right after all. In any case, between the two editions, most of the acceptable variations are covered.

The text is followed by a key to enigmatic personages, which is too

---

[14]Really quite justifiable for anyone believing in Nostradamus' infallibility, since there are many quatrains referring to the achievements of a new Charlemagne named Henry which could not by any stretch of the imagination be considered fulfilled by any of the three Henrys since 1555.

much associated with Le Pelletier's own apocalyptic theses to be of much value. The key is followed by a glossary of the Nostradamian idiom, the first to be undertaken on such a comprehensive scale. Much of it is excellent, but in an effort to prove that there are not only Latin, Old French, Provençal and Greek words but also Spanish, Celtic, Italian and Hebrew he gives many farfetched etymologies that can much more easily be derived from Old French.

In the 20th century, France has, of course, continued to produce more Nostradamus books than any other country, but in the last few decades the competition, if one can call it that, began to grow warmer. The three outstanding names amongst the 20th-century French Nostradamians are those of Larmor, Fontbrune and Ruir. In 1922 Larmor produced the last of the Nostradamian battles of World War I between German Nostradamians (Kniepf and Loog) and French Nostradamians (Nicoullaud, Demar-Latour, Graffont and Larmor). Larmor went on, three years later, to produce what is probably the best all-round book turned out in France this century. Like Le Pelletier's 19th-century work, it has all of the prophecies, a comprehensive glossary and the usual author's selection of interpreted prophecies in historical arrangement. Larmor is much less scholarly than Le Pelletier; his briefer and more casual explanations result in a single volume, instead of Le Pelletier's two volumes. Like Le Pelletier's, the interpretations of Larmor are colored by extreme rightist prejudices. His book has one great physical advantage—good rag paper instead of Le Pelletier's miserable pulp—so poor that few libraries have been able to preserve their copies except on microfilm.

The other two of the "Big Three" of 20th-century French Nostradamians, Fontbrune and Ruir, began their competition in producing books on Nostradamus more than a decade after Larmor. The competition started in the 1930's and was suspended during the period of World War II. After the peace, a sure sign of a return to normalcy in France was a resumption of the Fontbrune–Ruir competition. It continued into the 1950's. The general calibre of both has been about the average, ranging from not unreasonable interpretations to somewhat farfetched ones.

Two other groups of 20th-century French commentators, apart from "traditionalists" like Fontbrune and Ruir, are to be noted. They both have in common a sensational "at last the secret" approach. One group finds the "secret" in some kind of cipher system. The author starts with a handful of widely acknowledged successes of the past, applies a cipher system, sometimes tremendously complicated, and proves that Nostradamus thus even gave the date. Then the cipher is applied to some other quatrain to show that Nostradamus gave a future date for this one (some event dear to the author's heart, like a restoration of the monarchy). These future applications of course did not work out as well as the "already-in-the-bag" ones from the past. This system was applied by Piobb in a 1925 work, and has been applied by Frontenac in *The Secret Key of Nostradamus* (1950). The other "at last the secret" school is not really a Nostradamian one. It is a Nostradamus-debunking group. The leading figure has been Dr. Edgar Leroy of Saint-Rémy, where Nostradamus was born. With the same fanatic devotion to the debasement of Nostradamus that Torné applied to the glory of Nostradamus in the 19th century, Dr. Leroy has been bustling all over Provence, digging into musty archives of various communities, to find dirt on Nostradamus. First, he's found that Nostradamus' ancestors probably weren't royal physicians after all, but just sordid money-grubbers, on one side grain-dealers and on the other side a failure of a doctor who turned tax-collector. Secondly, Dr. Leroy has latched onto the "retroactive prophecy" explanations, apparently believing he was the first to note this element. (Reference to this aspect, which is indeed applicable to some quatrains, but only a small minority, will be found in the section entitled "Inspiration.") Dr. Leroy has delivered lectures on his discoveries, has published articles in academic journals and in 1960 was still working on his *magnum opus*. His one original gimmick regarding inspiration is that Nostradamus was probably over-addicted to wine, and was most likely in a drunken stupor when he wrote the prophecies. He has found a disciple in Raoul Busquet, whose book *Nostradamus, His Family, His Secret* (1950), is based on Dr. Leroy's discoveries and theories.

German interest in Nostradamus has also picked up in the 20th century. Early in the century, two Germans made outstanding contributions. In 1913 Graf Karl von Klinckowström published in a German literary magazine his very valuable work on "The oldest editions of Nostradamus," the most comprehensive to that date. The following decade, in 1926, Dr. Christian Wöllner published *The mystery of Nostradamus*, which is mostly of interest for its astronomical and astrological data. Since there is practically nothing in Wöllner's tables that has been twisted to fit any interpretations, his conclusions would appear worthy of credence (though of course he might have used a different system from Nostradamus' despite his best efforts). Of the forty-odd quatrains that seem to include dates through celestial configurations, Wöllner gives possible dates for more than a dozen. Other German commentators include the ones already referred to in the World War I and postwar period, and more recently (1946) Bartoschek.

Nostradamus books have also appeared in Sweden, Spain, Portugal and in Argentina. In Buenos Aires a novel on Nostradamus by Zevaco and Santanelli (1940) was followed by a radio dramatization (1946).

As for English works on Nostradamus, Le Pelletier was to find his English mouthpiece in Ward as Jaubert found his in Garencières. In 1891 Charles A. Ward published in England his *Oracles of Nostradamus*. Until recently, this book remained the only widely circulated and available book in English. It was reprinted in the United States in 1940. Ward also adopts parts from Garencières (and thus Jaubert) and his predecessor of 1715, D.D. His own contribution consists principally of frequent and various anti-social sentiments, of which the misanthropic Ward relieves himself in fine style. As an English survey of the quatrains on which Nostradamus' reputation was founded, it has perhaps been surpassed by Laver (1942).

A slight foreshadowing of American interest in Nostradamus occurred in the early 1920's. In 1920 Eugene F. Parker presented a thesis on "Michel Nostradamus—Prophet" for a doctorate at Harvard. Unfortunately, it was never published.[15] It includes a bibliography even better than that of Klinckowström, a very interesting analysis of the inspiration for Nostradamus' prophecies and other valuable data. As an appendix, Parker gives the full text of Nostradamus' will, which the reader will find in this book.

In 1923 John W. Cavanaugh published an impressively titled booklet (see list, following), the main subject of which was a quatrain that he applies to the American Revolution. There were also chapters on Nostradamus in Gould's *Oddities* (1928) and Forman's *The Story of Prophecy* (1936).

The real high-water mark of American interest in Nostradamus came in the early 1940's. An increasing number of European writings on the prophet, no doubt intensified by the epic war, inspired a leading American publisher to re-issue Ward's book. A digest of it, appearing in a "pocket magazine," came to the eyes of "idea men" in Culver City, California. According to Carey Wilson,[16] producer of the popular M-G-M Miniatures, he and an associate, Dick Goldstone, got the idea at about the same time.

Four movie shorts were released entitled *Nostradamus, More About Nostradamus, Further Prophecies of Nostradamus* and *Nostradamus IV*. The effect of these movies surpassed the combined effect of the works of Jaubert, Bareste, Torné and Le Pelletier. The degree to which they were inaccurate and exaggerated and distorted facts is quite irrelevant. Millions of Americans became interested in Nostradamus. At least 95 per cent of the Americans since interested in Nostradamus had never heard of him before these shorts appeared.

A ready market for books of the same type was born. Within a very short time the supply caught up with the demand. Writers who had never heard of Nostradamus until they saw the shorts turned out works on the subject within a few months. For the most part, they were only slightly worse than their European counterparts.

In 1941 Lee McCann published *Nostradamus, the Man Who Saw Through Time*. Half the book consists of a fictionalized life of Nostradamus, based on some facts. Nostradamus aside, McCann offers a vast amount of historical background. After the usual smattering of past "successes," Mc-

---

[15]It can be seen in the Archives Room of the Harvard Library. A French translation by Parker of part of it was published in Paris in 1923 as *The legend of Nostradamus and his real life*.

[16]In letters of May 20 and May 27, 1947, to the author, in reply to an inquiry on his significant part in American Nostradamia.

Cann dives into the future. The quatrains are given only in a free translation. Specific dates, mostly in the second half of the 20th century, are given for various quatrains associated with events to come. McCann does not say who computed those dates. Amongst the leading "future" themes is that of the emergence of the foxy Comte de Paris/Duc de Guise as Henry V, the new Charlemagne. In this McCann has been faithfully followed by other American commentators.

Also in 1941 Rolfe Boswell, an editor of a New York newspaper, published *Nostradamus Speaks*. The book follows the usual pattern of biography, background, past "successes" and the author's interpretation of the future. The book is filled with extensive digressions into current events, mostly with quotations from periodicals supposedly verifying Nostradamus. Future predictions include the ever-present new Charlemagne and resurgent Orient themes. Written in a breezy, slangy American style, this book seems assured a place as the most typically American of the English-language works on Nostradamus, and, like McCann's, provides much informative reading. The quatrains used by Boswell are given in both French and English, as all but McCann have done.

In 1941 also the Fellowship Press in Indianapolis put out a booklet called *Nostradamus, Seer and Prophet: Quatrains That Apply to Today*. This poison-pen pamphlet divides its abuse equitably between the Jews and the British in the best Isolationist traditions.

In 1942 there appeared André Lamont's *Nostradamus Sees All: Detailed Predictions Regarding America, Hitler, Mussolini, Franco, Pétain, Stalin, Churchill, the Jews, Etc., With Actual Dates of Forthcoming Events of Importance as Europe's Greatest Prophet Sees Them . . . From 1555 to 1999*. After this staggering title, the reader cannot but be disappointed to find little but a huge collection of quatrains with English translations and only superficial commentaries. The amount of "detail" is questionable, and as for actual dates, they seem to be gathered from Lamont's intuition. Most noteworthy is the inclusion of a translation of both the Preface and the Epistle, usually avoided. The commentaries are very mediocre. The interpreted predictions constitute the largest collection of failures since the time of Torné.

In 1942 appeared also Stewart Robb's *Nostradamus on Napoleon, Hitler, and the Present Crisis*. The first part, on the Revolution and Napoleon, gathered from Le Pelletier, who in turn gathered them from Bouys or Torné, is presented in the most impressive way any collection of quatrains has ever been presented. By comparing similarities of phrases in separated quatrains, by use of diagrams and by supplementing them with well-documented historical quotes and cartoons for "verification," Robb has made a case so excellent that it seems to have convinced many outspoken critics of Nostradamus. It takes more than a hasty perusal to discover the fallacies in his Q.E.D.'s. However, the part of the book dealing with current history, fortunately only a small part, is of no higher calibre than other works of this or any other period, or, what is perhaps more important, of no greater success.

In 1942 also a book was published in England which we consider the best written, most sensible and comprehensive of all the general works on Nostradamus in English. James Laver in *Nostradamus; or, The Future Foretold* maintains a fair balance throughout between faith and skepticism, though he is definitely convinced. In a supplementary section, he presents the hypothesis on Nostradamus' "powers" most tenable in this scientific age. In brief, since many people have had dreams or premonitions of events that happened shortly afterward, and since cases of clairvoyance up to twenty years have been documented, Nostradamus would simply be the greatest clairvoyant of all time, having his premonitions for more than two thousand years instead of twenty years, just a matter of degree.[17] If there is any shortcoming in this book, it is that Laver has fallen into the regrettable habit of some commentators of merely interpreting those lines in a quatrain which prove a point, omitting the more awkward parts. In this case, he omits even the French text of the parts that don't help his interpretation. Laver inspired another British work, a small booklet by Woolf (1944).

In 1943 Hugh Allen brought out what is easily the most ludicrous book ever written on Nostradamus, called *Window in Provence*. By careful study of the text, Allen found passages proving beyond any doubt that it was not Jaubert, Leroux or Torné who was intended as the true revealer. But Allen! Furthermore, the impression that many of the quatrains had already been fulfilled, and that the years up to 3797 would see a steady succession of fulfillments, was quite wrong. Nostradamus actually intended all the predictions for the period 1933 to 1945, many of them for the United States. Accordingly, Allen specified the exact time and manner in which England would again become Catholic and the United States would be invaded and devastated (twice) by various German and Italian forces. The siege of New York by the "Nazi-Fascist-Communist" force was to begin "before sunrise on October 29 or 30, 1942." Alas, this and other dates had already gone by before the book was published! It must be noted, however, that like so many of the off-the-deep-enders, Allen appears to be an excellent scholar and presents quite a bit of interesting research material.

In 1947 there appeared what was essentially a reprint of Garencières' 1672 work, by a New York book-dealer named Henry C. Roberts who had come across the rare old volume. To all the faults of the old translation, Roberts added some "up-to-date" interpretations (plus a few personal revisions in translation) that represented the absolute low point in scholarship in the four centuries since the prophecies were first published. However, it did purport to be a complete translation of all the prophecies and, accordingly, did well enough for a second edition in 1949. In the ensuing years,

---

[17]In a sense, this constitutes only a better-delineated version of Bouys' would-be-earth-shaking theory of 1806, which shook no one then.

Mr. Roberts has appeared on a number of radio and television interview programs in which he has made it rather clear that the man intended by Nostradamus to interpret all his prophecies was not Jaubert, Leroux or Torné. Not even Hugh Allen. But Henry C. Roberts, who might even be the reincarnation of Nostradamus! Ever ready to tell "what Nostradamus had to say" about any current international problem, Mr. Roberts has taken his responsibilities very seriously.

For the future, there would seem to be a strong probability of a new French Nostradamus work built about General de Gaulle, perhaps somehow succeeding in getting the elusive, mighty Henry out of his name. And in the United States, must there not inevitably be a television series in which Nostradamus uses his mystic powers to turn the anguish of the beautiful heroine into radiant joy?

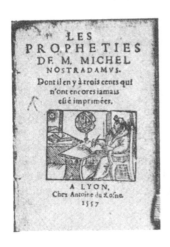

MISCELLANEOUS EARLY EDITIONS

(*Top left*) Title-page of No. 5, the earliest extant edition, which contains the Preface and Quatrains 11–740. Copy in the Lenin Library, Moscow.

(*Top right*) Title-page of the incomplete No. 10, with 10 new "extra quatrains." Copy in the Bibliothèque Nationale, Paris.

(*Bottom left*) First title-page of No. 18, dating between 1590 and 1614, with the same material as the Rigauds. Copy in the Bibliothèque Nationale.

(*Bottom right*) First title-page of No. 20, the enlarged edition of 1605, with the 10 "extra quatrains" of 1589, plus 15 new quatrains and 141 Presages from Almanacs and 58 spurious Sixains. Copy in the Harvard Library.

# Nostradamus Bibliography:
# Chronological List of Original Titles

## A. Works of Nostradamus

### 1. HIS PROPHETIC WORKS

#### a) Earliest Editions of the Centuries (1555-1643)

1. Les Prophéties de Mᵉ Michel Nostradamus. Lyon, chés Macé Bonhomme. M.DLV.
[At end:] Ce present livre a esté achevé d'imprimer le IIII. iour de may M.DLV.

Contains the Preface and first 353 quatrains, reprinted by Bareste in 1840. Copy borrowed from Abbé James by Bareste and described on pp. 253–55, since lost. Cited also by Brunet (*Manuel*, 1863, IV, p. 103).

2. [A 1555 Avignon edition by Pierre Roux, possibly containing Preface and 735 quatrains, mentioned in 1590 edition (see below). But Barthélemy Bonhomme printing shop only one in Avignon in 1552–57, so he is the only possible printer.]

3. [A 1556 Avignon edition mentioned by Held (1711) and in titles of Rouen edition (1649) and Leyden edition (1650). Klinckowström suggests Barthélemy Bonhomme, Macé's brother, as most likely printer. In fact, he is the only possible one (see 2, above).]

4. [A 1556 Lyons edition by Sixte Denyse mentioned by LaCroix du Maine (1584), but there is no record of even the name of this printer.]

5. LES PROPHETIES DE M. MICHEL NOSTRADAMVS.[1] Dont il en y à [*sic*] trois cents[2] qui n'ont encores iamais esté imprimées. [Vignette] A LYON, Chez Antoine du Rosne. *1557*.

---

[1] The distinction of size of type is made only in the titles of these earliest editions (1555–1643), where exact detail is necessary for confirmation that any given copy is genuine, and not a counterfeit.

[2] This advanced orthography makes this edition subject to some suspicion. See footnote 18 in "Nostradamus Bibliography," A1*a*, above. One word is not enough, however, to condemn it as a counterfeit.

Contains Preface and 640 quatrains. Only known copy in the Lenin Library, Moscow. A copy formerly in the State Library at Munich disappeared in 1942. (See reproduction of title-page.)

6. [A 1558 Lyons edition mentioned in the Rouen edition (1649), in the Leyden edition (1650), and Held (1711) and by Adelung (1789). No other proof of existence, so the foregoing may be based on internal date of Epistle.]

7. Les Propheties de M. Michel Nostradamus, dont il y a trois cents qui n'ont encores iamais esté imprimées. A Paris, par Barbe Regnault, *1560.*

Title[3] given by Brunet (*Supplément* II, 1880, p. 35), the only authority for it. Said to contain Preface and seven Centuries. No extant copy known of now.

8. LES PROPHETIES DE M. MICHEL NOSTRADAMVS. [Flower] Dont il y en a trois cens qui n'ont encores iamais esté imprimées. Adioustées de nouueau par ledict Autheur. [Vignette] A LYON, PAR BENOIST RI-GAVD. *1568.* Auec permission.
LES PROPHETIES DE M. MICHEL NOSTRADAMVS. [Flower] Centuries VIII. IX. X. Qui n'ont encores iamais esté imprimées. [Vignette] A LYON, PAR BENOIST RIGAVD.

First part contains Preface and 642 quatrains; second part contains Epistle and 300 quatrains. This edition is the nearest thing to an *editio princeps.* Copy in Musée Arbaud, Aix. (See reproductions of title-pages.) Variants of the title-page:

   *a)* First and second flower differing, as in reproduction.
   *b)* Second flower identical with first.
   *c)* First flower identical with second.
   *d)* No date on first title-page.

Types *b* and *c* cited by Baudrier (*Bibliographie*, III, 1897, p. 257) as belonging to Abbé Rigaux. Type *d* is also in Musée Arbaud, Aix.

*Counterfeit edition 8a:* LES PROPHETIES DE M. MICHEL NOSTRA-DAMVS. Medecin du Roy Charles IX. & l'un des plus excellens Astronomes qui furent iamais. [Portrait] A LYON. *1568.*
LES PROPHETIES DE M. NOSTRADAMVS. Centuries VIII. IX. et X. Qui n'auoient esté premièrement imprimées, et sont en la mesme edition de *1568.*

Printed in 1649 at Paris or Troyes, based on 1605 edition and containing supplement of 1605. Two forged quatrains against Mazarin appear as 742 and 743. Copy in Newberry Library, Chicago. (See reproduction of first title-page.)

---

[3]Brunet does not give the division of sizes of type used.

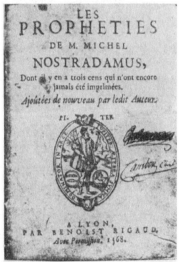

REAL AND FALSE BENOIST RIGAUD EDITIONS

*(Top left)* First title-page of No. 8, the *editio princeps*. Copy in the Musée Arbaud, Aix.

*(Top right)* Its second title-page.

*(Bottom left)* First title-page of No. 8a, the maladroit fake with the material of 1605 and the two anti-Mazarin quatrains dating from 1649.

*(Bottom right)* Title-page of No. 8b, the false edition used by Le Pelletier, dating from *ca.* 1700.

*Counterfeit edition 8b:* LES PROPHETIES DE M. MICHEL NOSTRA-
DAMUS, Dont il y en a trois cens qui n'ont encore jamais été imprimées.
Ajoûtées de nouveau par ledit Auteur. PI [Vignette] TER. A LYON, PAR
BENOIST RIGAUD. Avoc [sic] Permission. *1568.*

Printed *ca.* 1700. Used by Le Pelletier as genuine in 1867. (See reproduction
of title-page.) Variant cited by Baudrier (III, p. 258) with (1) *iamais;* (2)
*Ajoutees;* (3) *JUPI-;* (4) *Avcc.*

9. LES PROPHETIES DE M. MICHEL NOSTRA-damus: Dont il y en
a trois cens qui n'ont encores esté imprimées, lesquelles sont en ceste presente edition. Reueues et additionées par l'Autheur pour l'An mil cinq cens
soixante et vn, de trente neuf articles à la dernier Centurie. [Vignette] A.
Par Pierre Ménier, portier de la porte Sainct Victor.

Printed *ca.* 1588, according to Klinckowström and Parker. The meaning of
"39 articles" is unknown. Contains Preface, 574 successive quatrains, 12
quatrains (4 new, 8 duplicates, etc.) for Century VII and 6 new ones for
Century VIII. Copy in Bibliothèque Mazarine, Paris.

10. LES PROPHETIES DE M. MICHEL NOSTRA-damus: Dont il y
en a trois cens qui n'ont encores esté imprimees, lesquelles sont en ceste
presente edition. Reueues & additionnees par l'Auteur, pour l'An mil cinq
cens soyxante & un, de trente neuf articles à la derniere Centurie. [Vignette]
PARIS, Par Pierrc [sic] Ménier, demeurant à la rue d'Arras, pres la porte S.
Victor. *1589.*

Contains Preface, only 571 successive quatrains, and VII and VIII as above.
Copy in Bibliothèque Nationale, Paris. (See reproduction of title-page.)

11. LES PROPHETIES DE M. MICHEL NOSTRA-damus: Dont il y
en a trois cens qui n'ont encores esté imprimees, lesquels sont en ceste presente edition. Reueues & additionees par l'Autheur, pour l'an mil cinq cens
soixante et un, de trente neuf articles à la dernière Centurie. [Vignette]
A PARIS, Chez Charles Roger Imprimeur, demeurant en la court de Bauiere
pres la porte sainct Marcel. *1589.*

Exact duplication of Ménier's edition. Copy in British Museum.

12. LES PROPHETIES DE M. MICHEL NOSTRA-damus. Dont il y
en a trois cens qui n'ont encores esté imprimees, lesquels sont en ceste
presente edition. Reueues & additionees par l'Autheur, pour l'an mil cinq
cens soixante et un, de trente neuf articles à la dernière Centurie. [Vignette]
A Paris, imprimees pour la veufue Nicolas Rossett, sur [mutilation] Saint
Michel, a la Rose blanche [mutilation] *1588.*

Exact duplicate of Ménier's edition. Copy in British Museum only one known
of; title-page mutilated. True date probably 1589.

13. LES GRANDES ET MERVEILLEVSES PREDICTIONS DE M. MICHEL NO-stradamus, dont il en y a trois cens qui n'ont encores iamais esté imprimées. Esquelles se voit representé vne partie de ce qui se passe en ce temps, tant en Frâce, Espagne, Angleterre, que autres parties du monde. A ANVERS, Par François de Sainct Jaure. *1590.*

[At the end:] Fin des Professies de Nostradamus reimprimées de nouueau sur l'ancienne impression imprimée premièrement en Auignon par Pierre Roux Imprimeur du Légat en l'an mil cinq cens cinquante cinq. Auec privilege du dict Seigneur.

Title given by Klinckowström, who owned a copy. Contains Preface (with unique date June 22, 1555) and 634 quatrains (omitted: 6100, 73, 74, 78, 720 and 722). No copy known of now.

14. LES PROPHETIES DE M. MICHEL NOSTRADAMVS * Dont il y en a trois cens qui n'ont encores iamais esté imprimées. Adioustees de nouueau par le dict Autheur. [Vignette] A LYON, PAR BENOIST RIGAUD. *1594.*

LES PROPHETIES DE M. MICHEL NOSTRADAMUS * Qui n'ont encores iamais esté imprimées. [Vignette] A LYON, PAR BENOIST RI-GAUD. *1596.*

Cited by Baudrier (III, pp. 434 and 443) as being in possession of Abbé Rigaux. No copy known of now.

15. LES PROPHETIES DE M. MICHEL NOSTRADAMVS. [Flower] Dont il y en a trois cens qui n'ont encores iamais esté imprimees. Adioustees de nouueau par ledict Autheur. [Vignette] A LYON, Par les heritiers de Benoist Rigaud. Auec Permission.

LES PROPHETIES DE M. MICHEL NOSTRADAMVS. Centuries VIII. IX. X. Qui n'ont encores iamais esté imprimees. [Vignette] A LYON, Par les heritiers de Benoist Rigaud.

Printed between 1597 and 1601. Copy owned by Klinckowström (described p. 366). Nicoullaud (1914, p. 80) found one in the library of one Canon Jouin. (See reproduction of first title-page.)

16. LES PROPHETIES DE M. MICHEL NOSTRADAMVS. Dont il y en a trois cens qui n'ont encores iamais esté imprimées. Adioustée de nouueau per ledict Autheur. A LYON, PAR JEAN DIDIER.

Undated edition *ca.* 1598. Apparently same layout as earlier Rigaud editions. Copy in M. E. Saltykov-Shchedrin State Public Library of Leningrad, U.S.S.R.

17. NOVVELLE. Prophetie de M. Michel Nostradamus, qui n'ont iamais esté veuës, n'y imprimees, que en ceste presente annee. Dédié av Roy. A PARIS, Pour Sylueste Moreau, Libraire. *1603.* Avec permission.

Contains only Epistle (with "Henry II" removed) and Centuries VIII to X.
Copy in Bibliothèque Nationale.

18. LES PROPHETIES DE M. MICHEL NOSTRADAMVS. °°° Dont
il y en a trois cens qui n'ont encores iamais esté imprimees. Adioustees de
nouueau par ledict Autheur. [Vignette] A LYON, PAR IEAN POYET.

LES PROPHETIES DE M. MICHEL NOSTRADAMVS. °°° Centuries
VIII. IX. X. Qui n'ont encores iamais esté imprimees. [Vignette] A LYON,
PAR IEAN POYET.

Printed between 1590 and 1614 (probably 1602–5). Same layout as Rigaud
editions. Copy in Bibliothèque Nationale. (See reproduction of first title-
page.)

19. LES PROPHETIES DE M. MICHEL NOSTRADAMVS. °°° Dont
il y en a trois cens qui n'ont encores iamais esté imprimees. Adioustées de
nouueau par ledict Autheur. [Vignette] A LYON, Par Pierre Rigavd, ruë
Merciere, au coing de ruë Ferrandiere. Avec permission.

LES PROPHETIES DE M. MICHEL NOSTRADAMVS. °°° Centuries
VIII. IX. X. Qui n'ont encores iamais esté imprimees. [Vignette] A LYON,
Par PIERRE RIGAVD, en ruë Merciere, au coing de ruë Ferrandiere.

Printed between 1580 and 1625, probably 1601–5. Same layout as previous
Rigauds. Used by Le Pelletier as *texte-type* (1867). Copy in Bibliothèque
Nationale. (See reproduction of second title-page.)

*Later Rigaud or counterfeit edition 19a:* LES PROPHETIES DE M.
MICHEL NOSTRADAMVS. Dont il y en a trois cens qui n'ont encores
iamais esté imprimées. Adioustées de nouueau par ledict Aucteur.[4] [Vig-
nette] A LYON, Chez PIERRE RIGAVD, ruë Merciere, au coing de ruë Ferrandiere, à l'enseigne de la Fortune. AVEC PERMISSION.
LES PROPHETIES DE M. MICHEL NOSTRADAMVS. Centuries VIII.
IX. X. Qui n'ont encore iamais esté imprimees. [Vignette] A LYON, Chez
PIERRE RIGAVD, rue Merciere, au coing de ruë Ferrandiere, à l'enseigne
de la Fortune. AVEC PERMISSION.

Printed between 1605 and 1625, if really Rigaud's. If not, 1625–50. Contains
VII-43 and VII-44 and all of supplementary material of 1605. Although the
two main vignettes are not found in previous Rigauds, the last page has the
second vignette of the 1568 edition. Copy in Harvard Library. (See reproduction of first title-page.)

*Counterfeit edition 19b:* LES PROPHETIES DE M. MICHEL NOS-
TRADAMVS, Dont il y en a trois cents qui n'ont jamais été Imprimées.

---

[4]This hyper-archaic spelling is the most suspicious part of the title

**REAL AND FALSE PIERRE RIGAUD EDITIONS**

*(Top left)* First title-page of No. 15, the edition of the Rigaud heirs dating from between 1597 and 1601.

*(Top right)* Second title-page of No. 19, used by Le Pelletier as "1566" but dating from between 1580 and 1625, probably *ca.* 1600.

*(Bottom left)* First title-page of No. 19a, the dubious Fortune edition, dating, if Rigaud, 1605–25; if not, 1625–50. Copy in the Harvard Library.

*(Bottom right)* First title-page of No. 19b, the false edition dating from *ca.* 1700.

Ajoûtées de nouveau par l'Auteur. Imprimées par les soins du Fr. Jean Vallier du Convent de Salon des Mineurs Conven-tuels de Saint François. [Vignette] A LYONS, Par PIERRE RIGAUD, ruë Merciere au coing de ruë Ferrandiere. *1566*. Avec Permission. LES PROPHETIES DE M. MICHEL NOSTRADAMUS, Centuries VIII. IX. X.: Qui n'ont encores jamais été Imprimées par les soins du Fr. Jean Vallier du Convent de Salon des Mineurs Conventuels de Saint François [Vignette] A LYON, Par PIERRE RIGAUD, ruë Merciere au coing de ruë Ferrandière. *1566*. Avec Permission.

Printed *ca.* 1700. Same layout as 1568 and very good text. Ridiculous date the source of Bareste–Le Pelletier illusion about date of Pierre Rigaud. Copy in Bibliothèque Nationale. (See reproduction of first title-page.) Variant with undated title-page cited by Bareste, p. 262.

20. LES PROPHETIES DE M. MICHEL NOSTRADAMVS. Reueuës & corrigées sur la coppie Imprimée à Lyon par Benoist Rigaud. 1568. [Portrait] M.DCV. LES PROPHETIES DE M. MICHEL NOSTRADAMVS. Centurie VIII. IX. X. Qui n'auoient esté premierement Imprimées: et sont en la mesme edition de 1568.

PREDICTIONS ADMIRABLES pour les ans courans en ce siecle. Recueillies des Memoires de feu M. Michel Nostradamvs, vivant Medecin du Roy Charles IX., & l'vn des plus excellens Astronomes qui furent iamais. Presentées au tres-grand Inuincible & tres-clement Prince Henry IIII, vivant Roy de France & de Nauarre. Par Vincent Seue de Beaucaire en Languedoc, dés le 19. Mars 1605, au Chasteau de Chantilly, maison de Monseigneur le Connestable de Montmorency.

Printer possibly Pierre Duruau of Troyes. Contains the new 4 of the 12 of VII and all 6 of VIII from 1589; one extra quatrain for VI and one for X; 2 for XI and 11 for XII as well as 141 Presages and 58 Sixains. Copy in Harvard Library. (See reproduction of first title-page.)

21. LES PROPHETIES DE M. MICHEL NOSTADAMVS [*sic*]. Reueuës et corrigees sur la copie Imprimee à Lyon par Benoist Rigaud en l'an 1568. [Vignette] A TROYES, Par Pierre du Ruau, rue nostre Dame. LES PROPHETIES DE M. MICHEL NOSTRADAMVS. Centvries VIII. IX. X. Qui n'auoient esté premièrement Imprimées: et sont en la mesme edition de 1568.

Same layout as 1605, so date assumed close. However, only dated works of Duruau are from between 1626 and 1629. Copy in Bibliothèque Sainte-Geneviève, Paris. Facsimile reprint by Biblioteca Nacional, Buenos Aires, 1943.

22. LES PROPHETIES DE M. MICHEL NOSTRADAMVS. Dont il y en à trois cens qui n'ont encores iamais esté imprimees. Adioustees de

nouveau par ledict Autheur. [Vignette] A TROYES, Par Pierre Chevillot, l'Imprimeur ordinaire du Roy. Auec permission. LES PROPHETIES DE M. MICHEL NOSTRADAMVS. Centuries VIII. IX. X. Qui n'auoient esté premièrement Impremées: et sont en la mesme edition de 1568.

Printed in 1611 (from dated work with which it was bound, the *Recueil* . . . [of] *Nostradamus le jeune*). Contains all of 1605 material, with variations in arrangement, except extra of VI-100 and XI-56. Copy in Harvard Library.

23. LES PROPHETIES DE M. MICHEL NOSTRADAMVS. Dont il y en a trois cens qui n'ont encores iamais esté imprimee, Trouuez en vne Bibliotecque delaissez par l'Autheur. [Vignette] A TROYES, Par Pierre Chevillot, l'Imprimeur ordinaire du Roy. Auec permission. LES PROPHETIES DE M. MICHEL NOSTRADAMVS. Dont il y en a trois cens qui n'ont esté imprimees, où il se recognoist le passé, et l'aduenir. [Vignette] A TROYES, Par Pierre Chevillot, l'Imprimeur ordinaire du Roy. Auec permission.

Printed between 1605 and 1635, probably *ca.* 1620. According to Klinckowström, contains same material as No. 22, above. Copy in Rutgers University Library.

24. Les Propheties de M. Michel Nostradamus Provencal. Prinses Sur La Copie Imprimée à Lyon, par Benoist Rigaud, 1568. A Marseilles, Par Claude Garcin, Imprimeur du Roy & de la Ville. *M.DC.XXXXIII.*

First dated edition to contain VII-43 and VII-44. Arbitrary omission of parts of 1605 material, no mention of source of two new quatrains. Copy in Harvard Library.

### b) The Almanacs, Prognostications et Al.

1. Prognostication nouuelle et Prediction portenteuse pour l'an M.D.LV, composee par maistre Michel Nostradamus, docteur en médecine, de Salon de Craux en Provence, nommée par Ammianus Marcelinus Saluvium. Lyon, chez Jean Brotot.

Authority: Brunet (*Supplément*, II, p. 35). Dedicated to Joseph des Panisses, Provost of Cavaillon. No copy known of now.

2. La grand' pronostication nouuelle, auec portenteuse prediction pour lan 1557, composee par maistre Michel Nostradamus, docteur en medecine, de Salon de Craux en Prouence, contre ceux qui tant de foys l'ont faict mort. Paris, Jacques Kerver, *1557.*

At back is approbation dated 1556, for Kerver's accuracy. In Paris only he, and in Lyons only Jean Brotot, Antoine Volant and Benoist Odot, are authorized to print and sell. Copy in Musée Arbaud, Aix-en-Provence.

3. Les Significations de l'eclipse qui sera le 16 septembre 1559, laquelle fera sa maligne extension inclusivement jusques en l'an 1560, diligemment obseruee par maistre Michel Nostradamus de Salon de Craux en Prouence, auec une sommaire response à ses détracteurs. Paris, Guil. le Noir.

Authority: Brunet (*Supplément*, II, p. 35). Preface dated 14 August, 1558. No copy known of now.

4. La grant pronostication nouuelle auecques la declaration ample de M.DLIX composée par Mich. Nostradamus, auecques les figures de quatre tems sur les climats 47, 48, 49 et 50. Lyon, Jean Brotot, *1558*.

Authority: Brunet (*Manuel*, IV, 1863, p. 106). A copy belonged to M. de Selle of Paris in 1761. The British Museum has what is apparently an English translation, entitled *The Prognostication of Maister Michael Nostradamus, Doctour in Phisick. In Prouince for the yeare of our Lorde, 1559. With the predictions and presages of every moneth. Antwerpiae.*

5. An excellent Treatise, shewing such perillous and contagious infirmities, as shall issue 1559 and 1560 with the signes, causes, accidents and curation for the health of such as inhabit the 7, 8 and 9 climate; compiled by maister Michel Nostradamus of Salon de Craux in Provence and translated into English at the desire of Laurentius Philotus Tyl. London, by John Daye, *1559*.

Authority: Brunet (*Manuel*, IV, 1863, p. 107).
N.B. It may be that this work should be included in the list of "Professional Works," below.

6. An Almanacke for the yeare of oure Lorde God, 1559. Composed by Mayster Mychael Nostradamus, Doctour of Physic.
[At end:] Imprinted at London by Henry Sutton, for Lucas Harryson, dwellyng in Poules church-yarde, the xx of February, in the yeare of our Lorde, *M.D.LIX.*

Contains Almanac and Presages, but no dedication or Prognostications. Presages included are 34–46, poorly translated. Copy in Huntington Library, San Marino, California.

7. ALMANACH POVR L'AN M.D.LXIII. auec les presages, calculé et expliqué par M. Michel Nostradamus, Docteur en medecine, Astrophile de Salon de Craux en Prouuence. Dedié au tresill. Seign. et tres-excellent capitaine, le S. FRANCOYS FABRICE de SERBELLON, General pour N.S. Pere aux choses de la guerre, en la côté de Venaiscin . . . Imprimé en Avignon, par Pierre Roux.

Excellent summary and quotations by Buget in *Bulletin du Bibliophile*, 1861, pp. 661–76. Dedication dated July 20, 1562. At end Latin verses by Chavigny eulogizing Nostradamus. Copy in Musée Arbaud, Aix-en-Provence.

8. An Almanach For the Yere M.D.LXII. made by maister Michael Nostradamus Doctour of phisike, of Salon of Craux in Prouance. *1562.*

Contains Almanac and Presages, for *1555* and not for 1562, with no dedication or Prognostications. Presages included are 3-12, very poorly translated. Copy in Folger Shakespeare Library, Washington, D.C.

9. Prophétie merveilleuse, commençant ceste presente année et dure jusqu'en l'an de grand mortalité, que l'on dira M.D.LXVIII, an de Bissexte, par Michel Nostradamus. Paris, Guill. de Nyverd.

Authority: Brunet (*Supplément,* II, p. 35). Internal reference to "last year 1565," i.e., printed in 1566. No copy known now.

10. Prognostication ou Révolution avec les présages, pour l'an 1565 . . . par Mi. de Nostradamus. Calculée sur l'orizon de . . . Paris. Lyon, Benoist Rigaud.

Copy in Bibliothèque Nationale (Rés. p. V. 219).

11. Li Presagi et pronostici di M. Michele Nostradamo, quale principiando l'anno M.D. LXV, diligentemente discorrendo di anno in anno fino al 1570 . . . Diligentemente estratti dalli originali francesi, nella nostra italica lingua. In Genova, *1564.*

Copy in Bibliothèque Nationale (Rés. V. 1195).

12. Il Vero Pronostico calcolato dall' eccell^mo astrologo et filosofo M. Michel Nostradamo Francese, il qual narra diligentemente tutte le perverse calamità, che deve incorrere l'anno 1566. In Bologna, per Alessandro Benatio, *1566.*

Copy in Bibliothèque Nationale (Rés. V. 1196).

## 2. HIS PROFESSIONAL WORKS

1. Traicté des fardemens . . . Lyon, *1552.*

Dedication dated April 1, 1552. Although widely cited, and contents often reprinted (under different titles), full title never recorded. No copy known now.

2. Vray et parfaict embellissement de la face . . . Lyon, *1552.*

Reprinted in Antwerp in 1557 by Plantin. Copy in British Museum.

3. Excellent et moult utile Opuscule à touts necessaire qui desirent auoir cognoissance de plusieurs exquises Receptes, divisé en deux parties. La premiere traicte des diverses façons de Fardemens et Senteurs pour illustrer & embellir la face. La seconde nous monstre la façon et maniere de faire

confitures de plusieurs sortes, tant en miel, que succre et vin cuict, le tout mis par chapitres, comme est fait ample mention en la Table. Nouuellement composé par maistre Michel de Nostredame, docteur en Medecine de la ville de Salon de Craux en Prouence, et de nouveau mis en lumiere. A Lyon, par Antoine Volant. *M.D.LV.*

Amply described by Buget (*Bulletin,* 1861, pp. 68–79). First part represents reprint of Nos. 1 and 2, above. Second part contains dedication to brother Jean, also dated 1552. In addition to cited contents, contains love potion, plague-preventive formula, memoirs of travels in Western Europe (1534–44) and praise and abuse for various doctors and druggists. Reprinted with slight variations of title and material in Paris in 1556 by Olivier de Harsy and in 1569 by the widow of Jean Boufons, and in Lyons in 1572 by Benoist Rigaud. Copy in British Museum. Copy formerly in John Crerar Library, Chicago, missing.

4. Singulieres Receptes pour entretenir la santé du corps . . . Poitiers, *1556.*

Apparently similar to parts of foregoing. No copy known of now.

5. La Remede tres-utile contre la peste et toutes fievres pestilentielles, auec la manière d'en guérir; aussi la singulière recepte de l'oeuf dont usoit l'empereur Maximilien premier du nom. Paris, Guillaume Nyverd, *1561.*

Said to be just Chapter 8 of *Opuscule.* No copy known of now.

6. Bastiment de plusieurs receptes, pour faire diverses senteurs et lauements pour l'embellissement de la face, et conseruation du corps en son entier: Aussi de plusieurs confitures liquides, et aultres receptes secrètes et desirés, non encores veues. De l'imprimerie de Guillaume de Nyverd, imprimeur ordinaire du Roy, et libraire à Paris, tenant sa boutique en la Cour du Palais.

Printed shortly before his death in 1566. Contains first part of *Opuscule.* Copy in Bibliothèque Sainte-Geneviève, Paris.

7. Zwey Bücher, darinn warhafftiger, gründtlicher, und volkomner Bericht gegeben wirdt, wie man erstlich einen ungestalten Leib, an Weib- und Mannspersonen ausswendig zieren, schön, und junggeschaffen machen, und allerley wohlrichende, köstliche, krefftige Wasser, Pulfer, Oel, Seyffen, Rauchkertzlin, Bisamkuglen, zü mancherley Gebrechen dienstlich, artlich zubereyten. Und wie man folgents allerley Frücht auff das künstlichest, und lieblichest, in Zucker einmachen, und zur Notturfft auff behalten sol. Erstlich in frantzösischer Sprach von ihm beschriben: Nun aber, unserem Vatterland zü Gütem, in das gemain Tentschauff das trewlichst verdolmetscht, durch Hieremiam Martum. Augsburg, *1573.*

### 3. HIS LITERARY WORKS

1. Orus Apollo, fils de Osiris, roi de Ægipte niliacque, des notes hieroglyphiques, livres deux mis en rithme par epigrammes, œuvre de increedible et admirable erudition et antiquité.

Amply described by Buget (*Bulletin,* 1861, pp. 79–85). Loss of title-page has removed record of printer and date (1551–55). Contains about two thousand lines in 182 Epigrams on ethics, translated into French from 1551 Latin work of Jean Mercier, who translated it from the Greek of Horapollon of Phaenebytis. Horapollon claimed one Phillippus translated it from the original Egyptian, but this is suspect, and the origin may be as late as the 14th century. Copy in Bibliothèque Nationale.

2. Paraphrase de C. Galen sur l'exortation de Menodote, aux estudes des bonnes Artz, mesmement Medecine. Traduict de Latin en Francoys par M. Nostradamus. Lyon, Antoine du Rosne, *1557.*

Well covered by Buget (*Bulletin,* 1861, 394–412). Dedication to Baron de la Garde dated February 17, 1557. Copy in Bibliothèque Mazarine, Paris.

## B. Works of Commentators and Critics

1. La PREMIERE inuective du seigneur Hercule le Francois contre Nostradamus, Traduit du latin (par l.u.c.m.). Lyon, Roux, *1557.*

Probably written by Calvinist Guillaume Farel. See Buget, *Bulletin du Bibliophile,* 1861, pp. 266–68.

2. Le Monstre d'Abus. Composé premierement en Latin par maistre Iean de la Dagueniere, docteur en medecine et matematicien des landes d'anniere. Et despuit traduit et mis en nostre langue Francoyse par le More du Vergier, recteur extraordinaire de l'uniuersité de Mateflon, et protecteur des gondz de la Haioulén. Marinus Nouetus Nucensis. In Nostradamum. Nondum grammaticae calles primordia, et audes. Vim coeli radio suposuisse tuo. A Paris, Pour Barbe Regnault, demourant à la rue S. Iaques, deuant les Mathurins. *1558.* Auec priuilege.

In title, full of cyphers with classical keys, Buget finds Théodore de Bèze, arch-Calvinist. See *Bulletin,* 1861, pp. 241–59.

3. Declaration des abus, ignorances et seditions de Michel Nostradamus, de Salon de Craux en Provence, œuvre tres-utile et profitable à vn chacun. Nouuellement traduit de latin en francois. Auec priuilege. Imprimé en Auignon par Pierre Roux et Jan Tramblay.

Preface by author Laurens Videl dated November 20, 1557. See Buget, *Bulletin*, 1861, pp. 259–66.

4. Les contredicts du Seigneur du Pavillon, les Lorriz, en Gastinois, aux faulses et abbusifues propheties de Nostradamus, et aultres astrologues. A Paris, pour Charles L'Angelier, *1560*.

See Buget, *Bulletin*, 1861, p. 94.

5. William Fulke. Anti-Prognosticon contra inutiles Astrologorum Praedictiones Nostradami . . . London, *1560*.

Copy in the Pennsylvania University library.

6. Conrad Badius. Les vertus de nostre maistre Nostradamus. Geneva, *1562*.

Now lost, this work is known only through Verdier, *Bibliothèque*, 1584, which includes these excerpt lines:

> J'oublioy de dire en un mot
> Qu'il rime comme poix en pot:
> Mais pour un diseur de matines
> Il couppe mal ses feminines.
> Ses vers sont faicts à estriviere
> Fort courts devant et longs derriere,
> Et sont naiz soubs tel horizon
> Qu'il n'y a ny sens ny raison:
> Tellement que ce docte Homere
> Semble estre fils de sotte mere
> Que jadis rimoit en dormant,
> Ou plustot dormoit en rimant.

7. Jean-Aimé de Chavigny, Beaunois. Recueil des présages prosaïques de M. Nostradamus, etc. Œuvre qui se peut dire à la verité les merveilles de notre temps, où se verra à l'œil toute l'histoire de nos troubles et guerres civiles de France, dès le temps mesme qu'elle ont commencé, jusqu'à leur entière fin et periode, non-seulement; mais aussi plusieurs choses rares et singulières, avenues et à venir en l'estat des plus puissants empires, royaumes et principautés qui aujourd'hui lèvent le chef sur la terre: extrait du commentaire d'icelui et réduit en XII livres. . . . Cularonae Allobrogum [Grenoble] *1589*, in fol. MS. Les Propheties revuës et corrigées, avec des Réflexions . . . La Vie de Nostradamus, &c.

Title of this unpublished manuscript cited by Papillon in *Bibliothèque des Auteurs de Bourgogne* (Dijon, 1742). Papillon saw it in the library of M. Boilaud of Dijon.

8. Jean-Aimé de Chavigny. La Première face du Janus françois, contenant sommairement les troubles, guerres civiles et autres choses mémorables, ad-

venues en la France et ailleurs, dès l'an de salut 1534, jusques à l'an 1589, fin de la maison Valésienne. Extraite et colligée des centuries et autres commentaires de M. Michel de Nostredame, iadis conseillier et médecin des rois Henry II, Francoys II et Charles IX. A la fin est adiousté un discours de l'advénement a la couronne de France du roy très-chrestien à present regnant: ensemble de sa grandeur et prosperité à venir. Le tout fait en françois et latin pour le contentement de plusieurs . . . dedié au roy. A Lyon, par les héritiers de Pierre Roussin, *1594*.

Chavigny's most famous work. Includes the Biography of Nostradamus and interpretations of 126 quatrains and 141 Presages, with all the faults of subsequent commentators.

9. [An unpublished manuscript, dated 1594, found by Buget in the Library of Aix, of which he does not give full title (*Bulletin*, 1860, p. 1710). Therein Nostradamus is co-ordinated with prophecies of St. Cataldus and the Tiburtine sibyl about the new Charlemagne, i.e., Henry IV.]

10. Jean-Aimé de Chavigny. Commentaires . . . sur les centuries et prognostications de feu M. Michel de Nostradamus . . . contenant sommairement les troubles, divisions, partialitez et guerres civiles, advenuës tant en ce royaume de France que ailleurs depuis l'an 1534 jusqu' à present. Paris, *1596*.

Unauthorized, pirated reprint of Parts 2 and 5 of 1594 edition. Copy in Richmond Academy of Music.

11. Jean-Aimé de Chavigny. Les pleiades. . . . Divisées en VII Livres, où en l'explication des antiques Propheties, conferées avec les Oracles du celebre et celebré Nostra-Damus, est traicté du renouvellement des siecles, changements des Empires, & avancement du nom Chrestien. Avec les prouesses, victoires et couronnes promises à notre magnanime Prince Henry IIII roy de France & de Navarre. Dedié a Sa Maiesté. Lyon, *1603*.

Represents enlargement of No. 9, above, with five other prophecies added to those two, "co-ordinated" with Nostradamus. Valuable for providing dated excerpts from almanacs. Copy in Harvard Library.

12. [1606 reprint of No. 11, with supplementary *Discours parénetique sur les choses turques* and *Traité du nouveau comète.*]

13. Étienne Jaubert. Eclaircissement des veritables Quatrains de Maistre Michel Nostradamus, Docteur et Professeur en Medecine, Conseiller et Medecin ordinaire des Roys Henry II. François II. & Charles IX. grand Astrologue de son temps, & specialement pour la connoissance des choses futures. *1656*.

Probably printed at Amsterdam. The first and last of an intended series of nineteen, covering 71 quatrains applied to period 1555–60. Although full of inaccuracies, better constructed than Chavigny's and hence the model for all subsequent commentaries. Copies in Harvard Library and New York Public Library.

14. Theophilus de Garencières. The true prophecies; or, Prognostications of Michael Nostradamus, physician to Henry II. Francis II. and Charles IX. kings of France, and one of the best astronomers that ever were. A work full of curiosity and learning. Translated and commented. . . . London, 1672.

The first and last translation till 1947 of all the quatrains. Poor French text and very superficial translation. Copies in Harvard, Williams, Illinois and Michigan college libraries and in Sacramento, New York and Newark public libraries. The Library of Congress has a copy previously Houdini's. Also in many private collections.

15. Chevalier de Jant. Predictions tirées des centuries de Nostredame qui vray semblablement se peuvent appliquer au temps present, & à la guerre entre la France et l'Angleterre, contre les Provinces Unies. . . . [Rouen] 1673.

Copies in Huntington Library (San Marino, California) and in New York Public Library.

16. W. Atwood. Wonderful predictions of Nostradamus. . . . Wherein the grandeur of Their present Majesties, the happiness of England, and downfall of France and Rome, are plainly delineated. With a large preface, shewing, that the crown of England has been not obscurely foretold to Their Majesties William III. and Mary, late prince and princess of Orange; and that the people of this ancient monarchy have duly contributed thereunto, in the present assembly of lords and commons, notwithstanding the objections of men of different extremes. London, 1689.

Copies in Harvard and Texas university libraries; in Boston Athenaeum; in the Peabody Institute of Baltimore.

17. Samuel Cross. The Predictions of Nostradamus Before the Year 1558. Considered in a letter to a Friend. [London, 1691]

Foretelling

The Trial and Death of Charles I.

The Parliamentary and Protectorian Government.

The Burning of London in Sixty-Six.

The Great Plague and Dutch War at the same time.

King James' Departure.

King William and Qu. Maries Reign.

The Humiliation of the King of France by the Present Confederacy.

The Reformation of that kingdom.

And the Return of the French Protestants.

Copy in Harvard Library.

18. Balthazar Guynaud. La concordance des Prophéties de Nostradamus avec l'histoire depuis Henry II jusqu'à Louis le Grand. La vie et l'apologie de cet auteur, ensemble quelques essais d'explications sur plusieurs des ses autres prédictions, tant sur le present que sur l'avenir. Paris, *1693.*

19. Palamèdes Tronc de Coudoulet. Abrégé de la vie de Michel Nostradamus, suivi d'une nouvelle decouverte de ses quatrains. . . . Aix. [*1701.*]

Starting point for the biographies of 1712 and 1789. Two more works, one of which his son completed, contain enlarged biographies. According to Buget, the first manuscript belonged to the Comte de Lagoy of Aix, the second to Dr. Bossy of Salon.

20. Balthazar Guynaud. La concordance des Prophéties de Nostradamus avec l'histoire depuis Henry II jusqu'à Louis le Grand. . . . Novelle Edition, revuë, corrigée & augmentée de nouvelles Prophéties avec leur Explications. Paris, *1709.*

21. [Jean Leroux] La clef de Nostradamus, isagoge ou introduction au véritable sens des Prophéties de ce fameux auteur; avec la critique touchant les sentimens et interpretations de ceux qui ont cy-devant écrit sur cette matière. Ouvrage tres-curieux, Et même tres-utile à toutes les Personnes qui veulent lire ou étudier avec progrés ces sortes de Prophéties. Par un solitaire. Paris, *1710.*

22. Johann Jacob Held. Historischer Bericht von den praetendirten Prophezeuungen . . . Nostradami. . . . [Leipzig] *1711.*

23. Pierre-Joseph de Haitze. La Vie de Nostradamus. Aix, *1712.*

24. D.D. The Prophecies of Nostradamus concerning the fate of all the kings and queens of Great Britain since the Reformation. Now made English. London, *1715.*

25. François Geofroy. Propheties de Michel Nostradamus expliquées, qui nous prédisent les revolutions présentes d'Angleterre & de retablissement du roy de la Grande Bretagne Jaques III sur son trône. Avignon, *1721.*

26. Lettre critique sur la personne et sur les Ecrits de Michel Nostradamus. [In:] *Mercure de France.* Paris, *1724,* pp. 1730–49.

The letter was written in 1720, but seems to have taken four years to get published. The anonymous author is the founder of the "retroactive prophecy" thesis on Nostradamus.

27. Explanation of a prophecy of Nostradamus, in which he predicts the great revolution which is to occur in England and in the English colonies in America. London, *1775.*

28. La Vie et Le Testament de Michel Nostradamus, Docteur en médecine, Astrophile, Conseiller-Médecin ordinaire du Roi; né à Saint-Remy le 14 Décembre 1503, sous le regne de Louis XII. Avec l'explication de plusieurs Prophéties très curieuses. Paris, *1789.*

Apparently taken from the second unpublished Coudoulet manuscript (see No. 19 above), written between 1720 and 1737.

29. Johann Christoph Adelung. Michael Nostradamus, ein Zeichendeuter. [In:] *Geschichte der menschlichen Narrheit, oder Lebensbeschreibungen berümter Schwarzkünstler, Goldmacher, Teufelsbanner, Zeich- und Liniendeuter, Schwärmer, Wahrsager, und anderen philosophischer Unholden.* Leipzig, *1789,* Vol. 7, pp. 105–64.

30. D'Odoucet. Révolution française, les événements qui l'ont provoquée . . . pronostiquées par les Prophétiques centuries de M. Nostradame; avec la clef pour savoir la vrai sens de ses Propheties. *1790.*

31. La Révolution françoise par les prophétiques centuries de Michel Nostradamus. *1790.*

32. Prophétiques anciennes et nouvelles, avec des réflexions sur les rapports parfaits qu'elles ont entres elles. [*1791.*]

33. Shryalmo. Almanach royaliste, ou la contre-Révolution prédite par Michel Nostradamus pour l'année bissexte 1792, traduite en vers francais par le moindre de ses interprètes. . . . St. Petersburg.

34. [Mme H.D.] L'avenir dévoilé, ou concordance des prophéties de Nostradamus avec les événements passés, présents et à venir de la révolution. Suivie d'un grand nombre d'autres prédictions qui s'entendent jusqu'à 3797, et d'événements intéressants prédits par ce prophète, dont l'accomplissement est prouvé par l'histoire d'une manière incontestable. Hamburg, *1800.*

35. Dr. Belland. Napoléon, premier Empereur des Français, prédit par Nostradamus. Paris, *1806.*

36. Théodore Bouys. Nouvelles considérations puisées dans la clairvoyance instinctive de l'homme, sur les oracles, les sibylles, et les prophètes, et particulièrement sur Nostradamus. Paris, *1806.*

37. Motret. Essai d'explication de deux quatrains de Nostradamus, à l'occasion du livre de M. Bouys, intitulé . . . Paris, *1806.*

38. M. Destier. Réflexions impartiales concernant trois ouvrages qui viennent de paraître en faveur de Nostradamus. Paris, *1806.*

39. [Louis Pissot.] Les véritables prophéties de Michel Nostradamus en concordance avec les événements de la Révolution pendant les années 1789, 1790 et suivantes, jusques et y compris le retour de S.M. Louis XVIII. Paris, *1816.*

40. M. Caze. Prophéties de Maître Michel Nostradamus où il a annoncé, en 1555, les événements calamiteux et les grandes mutations survenus sur la terre, depuis 1789 jusqu'en 1831, et où il annonce pour l'avenir de grands changements et de prophètes, avec leurs explication et des observations politiques. Paris.

41. Francis Girault. Le passé, le présent et l'avenir, ou prédictions, vérifications et explications de quelques prophéties remarquables de Michel Nostradamus. Paris, *1839.*

42. Elie Caisson. Napoléon I$^{er}$, empereur des Français, prédit par Michel Nostradamus. Paris, *1839.*

43. Eugène Bareste. Nostradamus. I. Vie de Nostradamus. II. Histoire des oracles et des prophètes. III. Centuries de Nostradamus. IV. Explication des quatrains prophétiques. Paris, *1840.*

Contains a reprint of the now lost Bonhomme edition, i.e., the Preface and first 353 quatrains as they first appeared in 1555.

44. Victor-Emmanuel Charles. Nostradamus et ses commentateurs. [In:] *Études sur la XVI siècle.* Paris, *1848.*

45. Eduard Roesch. Die erstaunlichen Bücher des Grossen Arztes, Sehers und Schicksals-Propheten Nostradamus in's Deutsche übertragen und dem Verständnisse aufgeschlossen. . . . [In J. Scheible's series:] "Bibliothek der Zauber, Geheimniss- und Offenbarungs-Bücher." Stuttgart, *1849.*

46. F. Buget. Étude sur Nostradamus et ses commentateurs. [In:] *Bulletin du Bibliophile et du Bibliothécaire.* Paris, *1860–63.*

In 1860 edition, pp. 1699–1721. In 1861 edition pp. 68–95, 241–68, 383–412, 657–91. In 1862 edition, pp. 761–85. In 1863 edition, pp. 449–73, 513–30, 577–88.

47. H. Torné-Chavigny. Réédition du livre de prophéties de Nostradamus publié en 1566 chez Pierre Rigaud. Lettres à César Nostradamus et à Henri II. Texte de 600 quatrains interprétées du passé, du present et de l'avenir, et placés dans l'ordre chronologique et celle de leur interprétation dans "L'Historie prédite et jugé." Les Dix Centuries et les Présages. Bordeaux, *1862.*

Also a swarm of "almanacs," pamphlets and other works between 1862 and 1878. See No. 50, below.

48. Achille Chereau. Deux mystificateurs du XVI siècle. [In:] *L'Union Médicale. 1863.*

49. Anatole Le Pelletier. Les Oracles de Michel de Nostredame, astrologue, médecin et conseiller ordinaire des rois Henri II, François II et Charles IX. Edition *ne varietur,* comprenant:

1º Le texte-type de Pierre Rigaud (Lyon 1558–1566), d'après l'édition-princeps conservée à la Bibliothèque de Paris, avec les variants de Benoist Rigaud (Lyon, 1568) et les suppléments de la réédition de 1605.

2º Un glossaire de la langue de Nostredame, avec Clef des noms enigmatiques.

3º Une scholie historique des principaux quatrains.

Paris, *1867.*

The Pierre Rigaud of "1566" actually dates from *ca.* 1600. The Benoist Rigaud used herein actually dates from *ca.* 1700, being a counterfeit edition, but it has good text. Copies in Yale and Cincinnati university libraries, also public libraries of Cleveland and New York.

50. H. Torné-Chavigny. Ce Qui Seral d'après le "Grand Prophète," Nostradamus, suivi de l'almanach du "Grand Prophète" pour 1878. Paris. *1877.*

One of many, listed because of the work following.

51. Victor Advielle. Documents inédits sur les prophéties de Nostradamus et sur V. Sève son continuateur; suivis de la critique de l'Almanach-Nostradamus pour 1878. Paris, *1878.*

52. Carl Kiesewetter. Michael Nostradamus und seine Prophezeuunger. [In:] *Sphinx: Monatschrift für . . . Begründung der übersinnlichen Weltanschauung.* Leipzig, *1887.*

53. Charles A. Ward. Oracles of Nostradamus. London, *1891.*

Reprinted in New York in 1940 and subsequently.

54. Tony Kellen. Nostradamus-Bibliographie. [In:] *Börsenblatt für den deutschen Buchhandel.* Leipzig, *1904.*

55. Elisée du Vignois. Notre histoire racontée à l'avance par Nostradamus, interprétation de la lettre à Henry II, des Centuries et des Présages pour les faits accomplis dépuis l'année 1555 jusqu'à nos jours. Paris, *1910.*

56. Dr. Max Kemmerich. Prophezeiungen. Alter Aberglaube oder neue Wahrheit. Munich, *1911.*

57. Eric Karl Borck. Der Prophet Nostradamus. [In:] *Ost und West. 1912.*

58. Graf Karl von Klinckowstrom. Die altesten Ausgaben der "Propheties" des Nostradamus, ein Beitrag zur Nostradamus Bibliographie. [In:] *Zeitschrift fur Bucherfreunde.* Leipzig, *1913.*

Includes pictures of many early editions. Pp. 361–72.

59. Charles Nicoullaud. Nostradamus, Ses Prophéties. Paris, *1914.*

60. A. Demar-Latour. Nostradamus et les événements de 1914–16. Paris, *1915.*

61. Albert Kniepf. Die Weissagungen des altfranzosichen Sehers Michel Nostradamus und der Weltkrieg. Hamburg, *1915.*

62. Adéodat Graffont. La guerre actuelle célébrée en vers antiques ou quelques quatrains de Nostradamus, poète du XVIᵉ siècle, utilisès pour le recit de la grande guerre du XXᵉ siècle. Paris, *1918.*

63. Eugene F. Parker. Michel Nostradamus—Prophet. Doctoral dissertation submitted by Eugene F. Parker. [Cambridge,] *1920.*

An unpublished typescript in the Archives Room, Harvard University.

64. C. L. Loog. Die Weissagungen des Nostradamus; erstmalige Auffindung des Chiffrenschlussels und Enthullung der Prophezeiungen über Europas Zukunft und Frankreichs Gluck und Niedergang, 1555–2200. Pfullingen, *1921.*

65. A. Colin de Larmor. La guerre de 1914–1918 vue en 1555 par M° Nostradamus. La Roche-sur-Yon, *1922.*

66. Eugene F. Parker. La Légende de Nostradamus et sa vie réelle. Paris, *1923.*

An abridged translation, mostly biographical, of No. 63.

67. John W. Cavanaugh. Notre Dame; or, Michel de Nostradamus. He wrote the history of the world divinely 2279 years in advance from the year 1555 to the year 3797, the end of the world, without making a mistake to date, nearly 400 years. New York, *1923.*

68. A. Colin de Larmor. Les merveilleux quatrains de Nostradamus . . . Nantes, *1925.*

This comprehensive work represents a less scholarly, one-volume 20th-century version of Le Pelletier's great two-volume work (No. 49). It contains the complete prophecies, the usual historical selection and Glossary.

69. Dr. Christian Wöllner. Das mysterium des Nostradamus. Leipzig, 1926.
Contains the long-needed astrological background, tables and figures; though unfortunately not complete.

70. G. Lenotre. Prophéties. [In:] *Les Annales Politiques et Littéraires.* January 4, 1926, pp. 90–91.

71. Pierre V. Piobb. Le Secret de Nostradamus et de ses célèbres prophéties du XVI° siècle. Les Prédictions sur la France depuis 1792 et spécialement pour 1927 et les années suivantes. Paris, 1927.
The secret is that Nostradamus didn't really use astrology but numerology, cabalism et al., with Piobb's ciphers applied successfully to "past fulfillments," less successfully to the future.

72. Rupert T. Gould. Nostradamus. [In:] *Oddities: A Book of Unexplained Facts.* New York, 1928.

73. Georg Ljungström. Nostradamus och Anton Johanssons profetior em nu stundande världshändelser, analyserade. Stockholm, 1928.

74. Jean Moura and Paul Louvet. La Vie de Nostradamus. Paris, 1930.

75. Jacques R. Boulenger. Nostradamus. Paris, 1933.

76. Henry James Forman. Nostradamus: Europe's Greatest Prophet. [In:] *The Story of Prophecy in the Life of Mankind From Early Times to the Present Day.* New York, 1936.

77. Dr. E. de Fontbrune. Les Prophéties de Nostradamus dévoilées; lettre à Henry II. Paris, 1937.

78. E. Ruir. Le Grand Carnage d'après les prophéties de Nostradamus de 1938 à 1947; les guerres, les révolutions qui dévasteront l'Europe; retour à la paix; le grand empire français. Paris, 1938.

79. Dr. E. de Fontbrune. Les Prophéties de Maistre Michel Nostradamus. Sarlat, 1939.

80. João Paulo Freire. Profetas e profecias; "Nostradamus" prevê em 1555. Todos os grandes acontecimentos do mundo até 1999. Lisbon, 1939.

81. L. de Gerin-Ricard. As Nostradamus Saw Us. [In:] *The Living Age.* April, 1939.

82. P. Rochetaillée. Prophéties de Nostradamus; clef des centuries; son application à l'histoire de la troisième république. Paris, 1939.

83. Émile Ruir. L'écroulement de l'Europe d'après les prophéties de "Nostradamus"; les invasions, la conversion d'Israel; le regne de Dieu et de l'église du Christ; la fin du monde. Paris, *1939.*

Contains a dedication: "To the Peoples of the Nordic States of North America so that they may prepare themselves for their mission to protect the white race and to save Europe."

84. Charles Reynaud-Plense. Les Vraies Centuries et Prophéties de Michel Nostradamus . . . Colligées des premières éditions imprimées à Lyon en 1558–1605 et, à Troyes en 1611, et à Leyde en 1650, avec sa Vie, et un Glossaire Nostradamique. Salon, *1940.*

Mainly a cheap paperback reprint of the Centuries (which would not be listed here) but also contains some valuable new biographical data, some local illustrations and a Glossary, mostly from Le Pelletier.

85. Norab. What will happen in the near future? For an answer we must turn to "Les vrayes centuries et propheties de Maistre Michel Nostradamus." The prophecies of the ancient French astrologer Michel Nostradamus and the present war. Stockholm, *1940.*

A pro-Nazi propaganda pamphlet distributed in the United States.

86. James Laver. The Predictions of Nostradamus. [In:] *The Spectator.* June 21, *1940.*

87. Miguel Zevaco and Juan Santanelli. Nostradamus. Buenos Aires, *1940.*

A novel.

88. Rolfe Boswell. Nostradamus Speaks. New York, *1941.*

89. Karl E. Krafft. Nostradamus predice el porvenir de Europe. Madrid, *1941.*

90. Lee McCann. Nostradamus, the Man Who Saw Through Time. New York, *1941.*

91. Nostradamus, Seer and Prophet: Quatrains That Apply to Today. Indianapolis, *1941.*

A pro-Nazi propaganda pamphlet based on Norab's (see No. 85).

92. Lionel Sprague de Camp. You Too Can Be a Nostradamus. [In:] *Esquire.* December, *1942.*

93. André Lamont. Nostradamus Sees All; Detailed Predictions Regarding America, Hitler, Mussolini, Franco, Pétain, Churchill, the Jews, etc., With Actual Dates of Forthcoming Events of Importance as Europe's Greatest Prophet Gives Them . . . From 1555 to 1999. Philadelphia, *1942.*

94. James Laver. Nostradamus; or, The Future Foretold. London, *1942* [and 1950 in paperback].

95. Dr. Edgar Leroy. Sur un Quatrain de Nostradamus. [In:] *La Revue d'Arles.* Arles, April/June, *1942.*

Devoting as much diligence in research against Nostradamus as Torné did for him (see No. 47), Dr. Leroy has also published other articles in other Provençal academic journals to prove that (1) Nostradamus' Jewish ancestors were not at all illustrious and (2) Nostradamus' prophecies were composed in a drunken stupor out of personal and historical recollections.

96. Stewart Robb. Nostradamus on Napoleon, Hitler and the Present Crisis. New York, *1942.*

97. Hugh Anthony Allen. Window in Provence. Boston, *1943.*

98. Herman I. Woolf. Nostradamus. London, *1944.*

99. Norbert Bartoschek. Nostradamus und seine berühmten Prophezeiungen; Das Leben und Werk des Astrologischen Sehers von Salon mit einem Ausblick auf 1947. Graz, *1946.*

100. Gracida de Montpellier. Miguel Nostradamus, el médico astrologo. Buenos Aires, *1946.*

The script of a radio drama, apparently based on the novel of 1940 (No. 87).

101. Henry C. Roberts. The Complete Prophecies of Nostradamus. New York, *1947 and 1949.*

Essentially a reprint of Garencières (No. 14), with occasional risible deviations from Garencières' translation, and with many deviations from his interpretations. The incredible ventures into applications to recent history and for coming events represent the ultimate in *non sequitur* interpretations.

102. Émile Ruir. Nostradamus: Ses Prophéties, de nos jours à l'an 2023. Paris, *1947.*

103. Raoul Busquet. Nostradamus, sa famille, son secret. Paris, *1950.*

Based on the local research of Leroy (see No. 95 for the family secret and the personal secret).

104. Jean de Fontbrune. L'étrange XXᵉ siècle vu par Nostradamus. Sarlat, *1950*.

105. Roger Frontenac. La Clef secrète de Nostradamus. Paris, *1950*. The secret key is the same old numbers-game of Piobb (see No. 71).

106. Georges Madeleine. La prochaine guerre mondiale vue par Nostradamus. Toulon, *1952*.

107. Émile Ruir. Nostradamus: les proches et derniers événements. Paris, *1953*.

108. Léon Cristiani. Nostradamus, Malachie et cie. Paris, *1955*.

109. G. Gustafsson. Europas framtid enligt Nostradamus. Stockholm, *1956*.

110. Stewart Robb. Prophecies on World Events by Nostradamus [and] Nostradamus on Napoleon. New York, *1961*.

A rehash, in twin paperback editions, of the traditional collection of "successes." Mr. Robb provides the same impressive scholarship, as well as much the same material, found in his previous work (No. 96 above).

# Background and Rules of the Game

## A. Summary Criticism Through the Ages

It seems fitting to open this section with some diverse opinions on Nostradamus, coming from friend and foe alike. Between the lot of them, they cover all the principal lines of criticism against the prophet. The first which we shall look at, coming from Le Pelletier, one of his principal propagandists, does not differ too greatly from that of many of his scoffers.

> Nostradamus and his works are an enigma. If one looks at them only superficially, one is surprised and intrigued, dazzled and struck by the reflections of the quatrains, attracted and repelled by the cunning irregularity of the plan: the author seems to be playing with his subject and reader who, for his part, replies in kind and promises himself to laugh at the Centuries and at Nostradamus. . . . All is ambiguous in Nostredame: the man, the thought, the style. The man: at once brave and timid, simple and complicated, playful and sinister, clairvoyant and sham, Christian on the surface and pagan perhaps underneath. . . . The thought is no less ambiguous than the man. Everywhere it takes the amphibological form, so familiar to the pagan oracles, so valuable for concealing himself. . . . Finally, the style is as crafty as the thought. Under the external façades of an elementary rime and a polyglot jargon which does not properly belong to any tongue, the author manifests savage poesy, deep erudition and knowledge of all the tongues used by the learned. . . . In the Centuries there lies no visible plan or method; all seems to be thrown together pell-mell in a universal mass of confusion.[1]

In 1625 Gabriel Naudé wrote of the Centuries as follows:

> . . . the Centuries are so ambiguous, and so diverse, obscure and enigmatic, that it is not something to marvel at, if amongst a thousand quatrains, each of which speaks always of five or six different things, and above all of things which happen most ordinarily, one finds sometimes a hemistich which mentions a town in France taken, or the death of a great man in Italy, of a plague in Spain, or of a monster, of a conflagration, of a victory, or of something similar, as if all these things were extraordinary, and as though, if they didn't occur at one period, they couldn't occur at another.[2]

---

[1]*Les Oracles de Nostredame* (Paris, 1867), pp. 8-13.

[2]*Apologie pour tous les grands personnages . . . soupçonnés de magie*, p. 472. But by 1649, when he wrote *Jugement de tout . . . imprimé contre . . . Mazarin*, Naudé had changed his mind, writing, ". . . is it not strange that Nostradamus had predicted the death of this poor prince [Charles I], in this verse that I have read very clearly in one of

In 1915 an English Jesuit named Father Herbert Thurston wrote in a similar vein in a book called *The War and the Prophets:*

> Undoubtedly the unrivalled success of Nostradamus' oracles is due to the fact that, avoiding all orderly arrangement, either chronological or topographical, and refraining almost entirely from categorical statements, it is impossible ever to say that a particular prognostic has missed the mark, whilst among the multitude of political occurrences vaguely outlined, some quite startling coincidences are sure to be observed in the course of years. In other words, Nostradamus provided an ingenious system of divination in which the misses can never be recorded and only the hits come to the surface.[3] For the reputation of the would-be prophet, such conditions are naturally ideal.

Similar to the view that you just can't call Nostradamus' prophecies lies is the one that holds that one can read anything one wants into them. In 1882 Jean Gimon published a book on the history of Salon which included, inevitably, some mention of its most illustrious citizen. His comment on the prophecies seems to best summarize this school of thought:

> The style of the Centuries is so multiform and nebulous that each may, with a little effort and good will, find in them what he seeks. Like airy vapors, they assume, as they unroll, the figures of which the spectator's imagination lends them, and this fact assures this sibylline work of an immense and eternal success with those who are devotees of the marvelous.[4]

But Pierre Gassendi, the great naturalist, had no hesitation in giving Nostradamus the lie. He wrote as follows:[5]

> It will not be amiss for us, here to reflect upon somewhat of *Michael Nostradamus*, my own Comprovincial, that relates to our present argument; for of those so famous *Centuries of Tetrastichs* composed by him, I have another opportunity to speak. I shall give you only a taste of the Astrology he made use of, and if according to that he failed most shamfully in his predictions, I hope we may well beleeve, that he was not inspired by any divine spirit, or Genius, such as might suggest falshoods to him, or put lies in his mouth.
> Being some years since at Salona in company with the worthy person, *Franciscus Bochartius Campinius,* President of the high Court of Justice in

---

his Centuries . . . [949]. It is even more astonishing that he had marked that of the Prince-Prefect. . . . These two events, even had there never been others, could establish the truth of judicial astrology against all those who hold it in scorn as vain and ridiculous."

[3]In line with this theory of hits, Parker in 1920 concluded that "out of a thousand shots (considerably over a thousand when the quatrains containing several prophecies are considered) Nostradamus has scored one direct hit [ascension of Henry IV to the crown] and several ricochets [including the execution of the King of England]."

[4]*Chroniques de Salon* (Aix, 1882).

[5]Taken from pp. 139–141 of *"The Vanity of Judiciary Astrology; or, Divination by the Stars*. Lately written in Latin by that great Schollar and Mathematician, the Illustrious Petrus Gassendus, Mathematical Professor to the King of France. Translated into English by a Person of Quality. London, 1659."

*Province*, and that truly noble Man, *John Baptista Suffredus*, Judge of that City; I remember *Suffredus* showed us the Nativity Scheam of *Antonius Suffredus*, his Father, with the judgements thereupon given, under *Nostradamus his own handwriting*. We were much pleased to enquire of him, concerning his Father, whom we knew well, as not dying till his son was almost arrived at Mans estate. The Father, according to that Scheam, was born in the year *MDXLIII*: on the 13th of *January*, 22. minutes after high Noon, the Altitude of the Pole being supposed to be 44 degrees; which is more by the third part of a degree of the Signes inscribed on the Scheam; but the bare Signes, divided into Houses, after the old *Chaldean* way, beginning at *Aries* pertaining to his *Horoscope;* nor was there any mention of the Five wandering Stars, but only of the Sun referred to the second degree of *Aquarius*, and 36 minutes, and of the Moon related to the sixth degree of *Taurus*, without any minute at all. Now the Son *John Suffredus* being not able to give us any account of those accidents, which *Nostradamus* had foretold should befall the Father in his Youth; as that in the 16th year of his age, he should fall into a dangerous *Dysentery or Bloody Flux;* that he should be invaded with an acute and violent fever, in the 17th year of his Life, and in the 20th fall in Love, and relinquish his studies, &c. I shall relate only such, as he could more certainly inform us of. Among other of the Prophets judgements these are most remarkable. *That he should wear his Beard long, and crisped* (but he alwayes shaved his Chin bare) *that in the middle of his age, his Teeth should be rotten* (but he had very white and firm Teeth to his dying day) *that in his old age he should go almost crooked and double* (but he went to the last upright and straight, as any young man whoever) *that in the 19th year of his Life, he should become exceedingly rich, by inheriting a strangers estate* (but besides what his Father left him, he never had any wealth or estate) *that he should suffer by the treachery of his Brethren*, and again, in the 37th year, *be wounded by his own Mothers son* (but he never had any Brother, nor had his Father more that one Wife) *that he should marry a Forreigner,* (but he married a French woman of Salona) *that in the 27th year, he should be charged with a Bastard Son* (but no Man ever heard of that) *that in the 25th he should be overwhelmed with the Theological Doctrine of some of his Tutors; and that he should be so addicted to Natural Philosophy, and the secrets of Magick, as no man more, as also to Geometry, and Arithmetick, in an extraordinary manner* (when yet it is well known, he never had any particular affection to, or care of any of those Studies, but devoted himself to the knowledge of the Laws, of which *Nostradamus* never dreamt, nor of the Dignity of a Senator, which in that respect was worthily conferred upon him, at *Aix*, in the 25th year of his age) *that in his old age, he should apply himself to Navigation, and Musick* (but he never delighted much in Musick, nor was ever at Sea in his whole Life) *that he should not pass his 75th year* (but he passed not the 54th; of which *Nostradamus* said not a word). And these things I am the more particular in, to the end that Men may judge, what credit is to be given to such predictions.

As the most nearly firsthand evidence of Nostradamus' astrological predictions being tested locally, the above passage represents a rather damning case against our prophet. It has the ring of truth in all respects. The subject's father appears as one of the witnesses of Nostradamus' will. Old man Suffrens seems to have gone out of his way to give Nostradamus the lie at every turn.

The talented Bishop of Pamiers, Henri de Sponde, seemed to hold an opinion of Nostradamus somewhat similar to that of Gassendi. A noted writer, Sponde, concluded his review of the year 1566 in his *Annals*[6] by providing Nostradamus with a mocking epitaph.

This year there died that trifler, so famous throughout the world, Michel Nostradamus, who boasted while he lived that he knew and could foretell future events by the influence of the stars, in whose name afterwards many ingenious men have put forth their imaginings. . . .

César Nostradamus, to whom the Preface was dedicated, was never particularly interested in his father's prophecies other than for providing him, by their fame, with great opportunities for social climbing. He refers to them as "obscure verses, in a sybilline style (to avoid their being profaned by the vulgar)."[7]

It is probably Parker who provides Nostradamus with the most pithy tribute:

All honor, then, to this king of pretenders who has been able to make his bluff good for over three and a half centuries. And the end of his reign is as yet far in the future.[8]

## B. Inspiration

A discussion of the inspiration of Nostradamus breaks down into a discussion of each of two major possibilities. The first possibility is that this very learned scholar was so contemptuous of the ignorance of his age that he wrote his prophetic works as a gigantic hoax or satire. Or, as an alternative, he may have been inspired by a desire for fame and wealth, which he certainly did achieve in far greater proportion than he would have had he remained a mere country doctor. Even if this possibility is accepted as the answer, there still remains the big question of the source from which he drew the material for his prophecies.

The second major possibility is that the man sincerely believed that he had seen the future and was writing of it. If this is true, it remains equally important to discover what was the real source of his prophecies. Divine inspiration? Hereditary clairvoyance? Magic? Astrology? All of these things

---

[6]*Annalium Ecclesiasticorum Eminentissimi Cardinalis Caesaris Baronii* . . . (Pavia, 1682), Vol. III.

[7] *Histoire de Provence* (Lyon, 1614), p. 776.

[8]Unpublished doctoral thesis in Harvard University Archives Room, entitled "Michel Nostradamus—Prophet," 1920.

have been attributed to him at one time or another. Each of them he himself has alluded to in different parts of his writings.

Parker is convinced that the first of the two possibilities is the correct one and gives a very thorough explanation of the "inspiration" of Nostradamus the bluffer.

Nostradamus claims to have been moved to prophecy by divine inspiration but his repeated asseverations fail to prove his statement. Some of his quatrains, which he borrows almost literally from Jamblichus, smack of black magic, but this questionable procedure is no more responsible for his utterances than is his specified pretext, divine inspiration. His actual inspiration is found in a profound scorn for the intelligence of his fellow-men, which he does not hesitate to express in terms that are unquestionable to anyone who is willing to understand his bitter but cleverly expressed sentiments; thus the Centuries take on the form of sharp satire, despite the profound interpretations furnished by the numerous enthusiasts who have essayed to interpret them.

His method of prophecy is tripartite. Firstly, he takes past events and gives them a figurative garb which renders them unrecognizable, putting them in the future tense. Again, he describes a series of well-chosen probabilities, based on contemporary conditions, and treats them likewise. Thirdly, he makes a series of random shots all of which are unlikely but still possible. The language of all the quatrains has the same tone, and all receive an air of plausibility from the mention of actually existing places, while occasionally a specific date is thrown in for good measure. The disguise is so perfect that it is often impossible to say to which of the three classes a quatrain belongs. Of the first group the most remarkable are his account of the sack of Rome by the Imperial army, and that of the contest over the Hungarian succession after the Battle of Mohacz, both events which happened about thirty years before the first edition of the Centuries.[1] In the third group is one very striking prediction, "Senat de Londres mettront a mort leur Roy," which, of course, is always interpreted as forecasting the execution of Charles I. Only one actual prophecy appears in the whole work, namely, the end of the Valois dynasty in France and the accession of Henry IV, concerning which the prophet seems to have had a very definite opinion.[2] This opinion was, very likely, based on physical reasons (Nostradamus was physician in ordinary to the king, Henry II)[3] rather than on astrology or divine inspiration.

[1]This theory was first expounded in an anonymous article in the *Mercure de France* in August and November, 1724. Their author gave many examples of "retroactive prophecies" amongst which are the two cited by Parker.

[2]This one concession on Parker's part is subject to some doubt. Although there is some evidence in the quatrains that he had this conviction, the satisfaction with which he always left Catherine, and the beginning of his prose outline in the Epistle, seem to show that in other instances he played it safe by also predicting greater and greater glory for the House of Valois.

[3]Parker is not at his best here. In another part of his work he says, "This position was . . . an honorary one, involving no residence at court." There is no reason for doubting the paternity of the Duke of Angoulême, the illegitimate son of Charles IX. Only Francis II was sickly.

Such then is the argument of this school of thought. It is a very tempting one, and it further leaves our hero on top with the last laugh. However, it is much too farfetched to be acceptable. Had all his prophecies been written in complete isolation, and discovered only after his death, and had no one known the author, it might be acceptable. But that Nostradamus could have fooled his "disciple" Chavigny, his son, various notables of Salon, the rulers of France and Savoy, several ambassadors and scores of other people with this gigantic "joke" of his is quite ridiculous. Furthermore, the proof of his sincerity lies not only in the Centuries, written indeed to cover a long period of time, but also in the almanacs, written each year for the following year. However, two of the three elements named by Parker do, indeed, show up in various quatrains. They are the element of "retroactive prophecy" and the element of "well-chosen probabilities."[4]

Let us now turn to the probability of Nostradamus' being fundamentally sincere, i.e., really believing he had foreseen future events and was writing of them. Even in this case, the source of his inspiration does not become clear. In various places in his Preface to his son and in his Epistle to Henry II, he refers to having natural powers inherited from his ancestors, to divine inspiration and to adjustment of divine inspiration with astrological computation. Most frequently he refers to the last combination.

He vigorously denounces magic, undoubtedly with his cheek barely able to contain his tongue. Notwithstanding all his protestations, which were for the benefit of a Church which had no objection to prophecy so long as the Dark One was not its source, he was obviously hip-deep in magic. It is fortunate that we know the precise source of all his magical formulas and experiments.

In 1497 that industrious translator and astrologer Marsilio Ficino published in Venice a Latin translation of a classical book on all the magic of the ancient world by Jamblichus, a 4th-century philosopher and Neoplatonist of the Byzantine empire. The book seems to have been quite popular and went through several reprints. One of these was done at Lyons in 1549. There seems little reason to doubt that this was the edition by which Nostradamus was inspired.[5] The two opening quatrains of the Centuries provide his magic formulas for prophesying. They happen to be an almost literal translation from passages of Jamblichus. Buget noted another near-literal translation in the Preface.[6]

We may therefore discard divine inspiration and hereditary powers as

---

[4]Sometimes this element overlaps that of plagiarism from the themes of previous prophets. The ever-present "new Charlemagne" theme may provide a good example.

[5]Buget seems to have been the first to make this valuable discovery. Although he was a "critic," Le Pelletier, an ardent propagandist, enlarged on it in his work of 1867, a few years later.

[6]JAMBLICHUS: *Opera quidem absoluta ducant dii, media angeli, tertia daemones.*

NOSTRADAMUS: *Les œuvres divines, que totalement sont absolues, Dieu les vient parachever: la moyenne qui est au milieu, les anges: la troisième, les mauvais.*

mere vainglorious façades. The two principal foundation stones for his prophecies are magic and astrology. From the evidence we have, it would seem that when the spirit moved him, Nostradamus would go up to his secret study, lock himself in, get out all his magic paraphernalia including brass bowl, tripod and laurel branch, and proceed to go through the demon-evoking formulas prescribed by Jamblichus.

What happened next is a matter of opinion and interpretation. The more superstitious might say that he did actually evoke some sort of spirit. The more modern minds will hold that he induced a state of autohypnosis in which his heated imagination could act. The things which he saw while in this state form the basis of his prophecies. It is not at all unlikely that his subconscious drew, *in part*, on past events familiar to him.

This then is what Nostradamus openly referred to as hereditary powers and divine inspiration, what he actually believed to be the revelation of his demon, and what we would now call the product of his subconscious mind.[7]

Once out of his hypnotic state, it was necessary to determine the inter-relationship, temporal and geographic, of various things that he "saw." For this he turned to judicial astrology, which he had long since mastered. Supposing that he had "seen" an event which seemed to indicate a disaster for an Italian seaport, he might then cast horoscopes for Venice, Genoa, *et al.* If one of these horoscopes reflected an impending calamity, the question was then resolved for him. According to his own claims, through astrology he could fix the temporal relationship between separate events as well, to decide which combination of events should be placed together in individual quatrains. His claim that he could have dated each quatrain, made in the Epistle, is hardly substantiated by the few attempts at actual dates he made. There still remains one to be tested,[8] but on the whole they have served to endanger rather than increase his reputation as a prophet.

The result of this labor so far would be brief notes. The next step was to turn these notes into suitably obscured verses, in the best tradition of oracles if not poets. There is some evidence to indicate that the verses were turned out first in Latin and then translated, almost verbatim, into a language basically French, but with much Latin remaining, not to mention other admixtures. Finally, because there was still some continuity, the verses had to be rearranged. For lack of more exact knowledge, we may assume that each was put on a piece of paper, which was in turn placed in a basket and mixed up with the others. The order in which they were withdrawn was

---

[7]For more than a score of years, the rabid anti-Nostradamian of Saint-Rémy, Dr. Leroy, has been gathering research for a *magnum opus* to prove that the real inspiration for Nostradamus was the grape, and that he was in effect an "old wino" who scribbled down historical and personal recollections just before he passed out dead drunk. Dr. Leroy has already written and read various academic papers to this effect, and inspired the Nostradamus book of Busquet (1950).

[8]One for September, 1999, in 1072.

the order of the Centuries. However, this rule, like most, has an exception: there are a few "series" of consecutive quatrains.

The source of Nostradamus' inspiration has been a very controversial issue amongst commentators and critics down through the ages. Many theories have come forth. At best, there can be no final, positive proof as to what was his inspiration. However, the theory we have presented is most in accord with both the facts available and common sense.

## C. The Nature of the Prophecies

In his Preface, Nostradamus states that his prophecies cover events in Europe and parts of Asia and Africa from 1555 to 3797. However, the occurrence of the date 1792 near the end of his prose outline in the Epistle seems to indicate that in his own mind, he did not actually even think he saw beyond the 20th century. There remains, of course, the possibility that 3797 is not A.D. 3797 but 3,797 years after some other event.[1] This, however, seems rather farfetched. In any event, it has always been assumed that 3797 is Nostradamus' nomination for the Last Year, the end of the world.

Quite naturally enough, most of the quatrains which mention place names mention French names. Nostradamus is first, and above all, the Oracle of France. Some of the more reasonable of the commentators have even gone so far as to claim that if no place name is mentioned, the scene is always France. This, however, is a bit too much of a simplification. For instance, a 16th-century writer, prophet or otherwise, who mentions "the Empire" could mean only the Holy Roman Empire, and not a French empire. After France, the scene of most quatrains is Italy. Thereafter, Iberia, England, the Netherlands, Central Europe, the Balkans, North Africa and the Near East share more or less equally. Of Russia, the Middle and Far East and the Americas there is next to nothing. (For the exact breakdown, see Subject Index.)

No one could rightly claim that the meaning of the quatrains is always quite apparent. However, the common view that they either have no meaning at all, or have a meaning so equivocal that they can be applied to almost anything, is far from true. To a large extent, this view has been strengthened by Nostradamus' greatest propagandists who, in an effort to glorify his name, have twisted many prophecies to an application for which they could never have been intended, thus serving only to discredit him.

Thus we find that if Nostradamus mentions a pestilence, some will say he is referring to a religious war. If he mentions Byzantium, some will say he means Paris and others will claim he is referring to the Habsburg Empire.

---

[1]Le Pelletier proposed 3797 years after Ishmael, which conveniently placed the end of the world soon after, in 1897.

But if we stick to the reasonable view that when he says pestilence he means disease and when he says Byzantium he means Constantinople or Turkey, most of his quatrains will be found generally specific and comprehensible. Although there are indeed some quatrains that are very vague, very general or even meaningless, an overwhelming proportion of them do predict a certain combination of historical events. But alas, not many of the events seem to have occurred since 1555, or are likely to occur any more now.

A rather striking matter in the study of Nostradamus' prophecies is the variation in his outlook as expressed in the prose outline of the Epistle and his outlook as expressed in the quatrains. We have already mentioned that the prose outline seems to indicate greater and greater glories for Catherine's brood, while some of the quatrains seem to indicate his conviction that Henry of Navarre would found a new dynasty on the ashes of the extinct-to-be Valois dynasty. This deviation provides an excellent example of the relative success of each of these two samples of his prophetic powers.

It seems that in the huge mass of predictions that can be found in the prose outline, there is not a single successful prophecy. The dating of two calamities[2] serves to discredit him completely in this work. On the other hand, in the verse quatrains, where he rarely binds himself with any temporal bonds, there occur some successful predictions which, if lucky guesses, are very lucky indeed. This is not to deny that the quatrains also contain some quite clear predictions that were never realized and are never likely to be. Outstanding is the oft-mentioned series involving the new Charlemagne named Henry, of the House of France. Although one cannot say positively that he won't still come, the chances of a French Restoration are now not much better than the chances of the election of a Bolshevik Pope. At best it can be said of Nostradamus as a prophet that he occasionally had a successful "vision" of *what* would happen, but never of *when* anything would happen.

The bulk of the quatrains deal with disasters of various sorts. The disasters include plagues, earthquakes, wars, floods, invasions, murders, droughts, battles and many other themes. Some quatrains cover these in over-all terms; others concern a single person or small group of persons. Some cover a single town, others several towns in several countries. The more intelligent of the commentators have pointed out the helpful method of tying prophecies together by looking for a repetition of the same phrases, or of enigmatic names. By applying this method, we can piece together most of Nostradamus' dream of the career of the new Charlemagne who was never to come, or the theme of the new Arab empire, or that of the removal of the Papacy from Rome. Each of these three examples, it will be noted,

---

[2]1732 as the culmination of upheavals of nature and famine that would practically wipe out the human race; 1792 as the culmination of a long and savage religious persecution.

involves a repetition of history, which has proven uncoöperative and has not repeated itself in these instances. Of these three examples, only the removal of the Papacy from Rome stands any chance of still being fulfilled. Undoubtedly the easiest way for an American to comprehend the style of Nostradamus' quatrains is to examine an "americanized" sample. Most of the supposed imitations of Nostradamus by skeptics have nothing whatsoever in common with his quatrains. If we can imagine a Nostradamus otherwise the same living in the United States in the 1950's, a typical quatrain might run like this (with no attempt at poesy):

> Columbian land thou wilt be much changed
> When the Silver House has the young Seminole:
> Detroit, Duquesne, Amsterdam, mortal strife,
> Pink plot reddened, atomic terror.

The first thing we notice about the verse is that it is tightly packed, full of specific elements, however obscure. An intelligent commentator writing some score years later would be able to point out certain salient facts that might throw light on it. "Columbian land" is of course just a poetic device for America, as in "Hail, Columbia." "The Silver House" is an obscurification of the White House and thus the subject of line 2 is a president. The Seminole Indians live in Florida; therefore, either the President referred to is a native of Florida, or someone actually having Seminole blood is involved.

Fort Duquesne was the ancient name of Pittsburgh. New York was formerly called New Amsterdam. Therefore line 3 concerns bloodshed at three major cities, Detroit, Pittsburgh and New York.

As for line 4, it would be pointed out that the prophet lived in a day when two of the chief subjects were communism and the atomic bomb. These two factors are somehow involved in the last line. Perhaps the meaning is that a project of left-wing liberals would be made use of by deep-dyed "Reds," and that this project would be connected with some atomic weapon.

This would be a sensible interpretation, providing as much information as possible, albeit far from a perfect explanation of what the prophet had in mind.

To match the inane commentators, we would have something like this (with an assurance that all names are purely fictional): The verse refers to Columbus, Ohio. It was fulfilled last year. At about the same time that a hotel that had a ballroom called the Silver Room had a Seminole Indian registered at the hotel, Mr. D. U. Kane (Duquesne), a prominent attorney, got into a fight (mortal strife). His father was from Michigan (Detroit) and his mother's mother came from Belgium, which is next to Holland (Amsterdam). A third event took place the same week: some hoodlums broke up a leftist meeting, and in the terrible confusion that followed, many people thought an atomic bomb had exploded.

## D. *Nostradamus' Rules of the Game*

Until the 19th century, a proper understanding of the prophecies of Nostradamus required an enormous amount of learning, including mastery of Latin, Greek, Old French, classical and medieval geography and some Provençal. In short, the reader was required to have the same knowledge that Nostradamus had.

But in the last hundred years such vast strides have been taken in the cataloguing of human knowledge in convenient reference books that there now remains very little in the text of the prophecies that has not been clarified, or cannot be clarified. When Le Pelletier wrote his edition during the Second Empire, he already had many tools to work with in compiling his Nostradamian glossary. Today we have many more.

Nostradamus states in several places in his Preface and Epistle that he had deliberately obscured his prophecies and veiled them as heavily as possible. Why he did so is no mystery at all, and any reasonable person will think of many reasons: to avoid offense to the authorities of Church and State, which might have involved his own summary liquidation; to avoid the inconceivably wicked, not to mention confusing, sacrilege of threatening to interfere with the fulfillment of God's Will by disclosing it clearly in advance; and perhaps also because of every prophet's quite human desire to reduce the number of his failures to a minimum by use of mysterious and confusing terminology. The important question is then not *why* but *how* Nostradamus goes about this. These seem to be the principal answers:

1. The innumerable glaring examples of Latin syntax seem to offer satisfactory substantiation for the theory that the quatrains were first written in Latin, perhaps from a rough draft in French. What kind of Latin? We find an example in one quatrain that was left in Latin, the "Incantation Against Inept Critics," found at the end of Century VI. Some commentators call it liturgical Latin, others just Low Latin. Jean Leroux in his *Clef* (1712) came forth with something much more specific. He was convinced that Nostradamus had read a book called *Progymnasmata in artem oratorium* by Franciscus Sylvius, professor at the University of Paris. This book, printed in 1528, set forth in the greatest detail how to produce the most elegant Latin. Leroux cites chapter and verse of Sylvius' book for ten instances in which his precepts have been followed in this one quatrain alone.

The French translation of this "elegant" Latin is virtually verbatim. This means that Latin syntax, not French syntax, prevails. It means, for instance, that an ablative absolute construction loses its identity as such in uninflected French, and yet requires the translation of an ablative absolute.

By this theory it would seem that the proper sense of the quatrains could best be derived by translating them back, verbatim, into Latin. In his bilingual *Janus* in 1594, Chavigny did indeed give many of the quatrains in Latin, without, however, much more sense being made by them by any-one. Perhaps Chavigny, excellent classics scholar that he was, did not use the proper Latin. Or perhaps the theory is worthy of but limited applica-tion. In any case, this theory must be kept in mind, even if its application by no means makes the quatrains much clearer.

2. Although the quatrains are nominally translated into French about 5 per cent of the words are not recognizable as French today. About 2.8 per cent of the vocabulary is merely frenchified Latin (with slight changes in the endings) if not pure Latin. Another 2.1 per cent consists of Old French words.[1] The remaining 0.1 per cent consists of words of Greek or Provençal origin.[2] Le Pelletier mentions Spanish, Italian, Celtic and Hebrew as the source of many words, but there is only one Hebrew word (1096), a sentence in Spanish (1025), and nothing from the other two tongues that could not be derived as well or better from Latin or Old French. Perhaps the biggest source of confusion is in connection with words identical with French words, but which the context shows to have another derivation. Thus the word *pont* means "bridge" in French, but we find Nostradamus using it to mean "sea;" from the Greek *pontos,* or "Papacy" from the Latin *pontifex* (and derivatives). Although *pie* means "magpie" in French, Nostradamus used it as a derivative of the Latin *pius,* "pious."

3. Anagrams were all the rage in Nostradamus' day. It is quite reason-able that he should have made use of them. Thus *Chyren* is put for "Henry" (Henryc-us), *Nersaf* for "France," *Rapis* for "Paris," *noir* for *roy,* "king," and *Mendosus* for "Vendosme" (the actual Bourbon sub-branch that came to the throne). In the anagrams latitude is provided by the interchangeability of *y* and *i, u* and *v, s* and *c, i* and *j.* The use of silent *s* instead of a circumflex and similar variations of form in accentation must also be noted. Although the perfect anagram required the use of the same letters, Nostradamus seems to have allowed himself the change of one letter, but never more than one.

Similar to the use of anagrams is the use of enigmas. Prominent amongst these are *Aenobarbe,* which means Bronzebeard but is also the family name of Antichrist Nero, symbol of pagan wickedness; the *Pourceau Mi-homme,* which means "pig-half-man"; and various gentlemen named after Roman gods, like Jupiter, Mars and Saturn.

4. Mythological and historical allusions veil several quatrains. One quat-rain refers to the story of Bellerophon and Proetus, another to that of Jupiter and Phaeton. In the Epistle someone is called a second Thrasibulus, so we must know that this gentleman was the leader of the popular party at Athens who restored the democracy in 403 B.C. and is therefore the symbol of a radical demagogue.

---

[1]As Old French was still much in use in 16th-century writings, it is not quite correct to consider this amongst the deliberate obscurifications of Nostradamus. Furthermore, many words could be derived from either Latin or Old French equally well.

[2]One whole quatrain in Provençal (426) and most of another (444).

5. References to many places are veiled by use of their classical names or origin. Thus we find *Port Phocen* for Marseilles, founded by the Phoceans; *Byzantium* for Constantinople or Istanbul; *Agatha* for Agen; *Lutetia* for Paris; *Bastarnia* for Poland; *Hister* for the Danube; *Pannonia* for Hungary; *Lusitania* for Portugal and many, many others.

6. Nostradamus makes ample use of devices variously considered as grammatical, poetical or rhetorical, and derived chiefly from Latin or Greek usage. Chief amongst these are—

a) ELLIPSIS, the omission of words which are understood. Thus *qui* is used frequently for *ce qui*, "he who."

b) SYNECDOCHE, the part standing for the whole. Thus sword stands for army at times, or Paris may stand for France. A common non-Nostradamiam contemporary example is "the Kremlin" for the U.S.S.R. However, this has been carried too far by some interpreters in twisting simple statements into farfetched images.

c) HYPERBATON, the transposition or inversion of the natural order. This is found throughout. The dividing line between it and the previously mentioned use of Latin syntax is rather blurry.

d) APOCOPE, the omission of the last letter or syllable. In Nostradamus, this amounts to abbreviation. We find *Carpen* for Carpentras, *Ast* for Asti, *Carcas* for Carcassonne, etc.

e) SYNCOPE, the omission of a letter or syllable from the middle of a word. Thus *donra* is used for *donnera*, *lairra* for *laissera*, *monstra* for *monstrera* and *Tamins* for *Tamisiens* (those of the Thames).

f) APHERESIS, the omission of a letter or syllable from the beginning of a word. Thus, *versé* is used for *renversé*, "overthrown."

g) EPENTHESIS, the insertion of a letter or syllable in the middle. Thus we find *Timbre* for *Tibre*, the Tiber River.

h) PROSTHESIS, the insertion of an extra letter at the beginning of a word. Thus, *Aspire* is put for *Spire*, a city in Bavaria.

i) METATHESIS, the transposition of letters or syllables. Thus *Ucetia* is used for *Uticensia*, Latin name for the town of Uzès.

Within this framework, the majority of the words and phrases make sense, and follow some sort of pattern. Nevertheless, Leroux's view that all the quatrains are actually the epitome of polished literature and contain no barbarities is carrying things a bit too far. There are many instances where an adjective does not agree with a noun it obviously modifies and where a plural verb has a singular subject, or vice versa. In this connection, Parker has made a worth-while comment:

The obscurity imparted to the Centuries by the willful use of anagrams, apocopation, prosthesis, epenthesis, and other disfigurations of the written word is intensified by the numerous typographical errors which could not fail to creep into the versions printed from manuscript copies. In some cases the misprint was due to the illegibility of the original; in others it was due to the desire of the compositor to rectify what seemed to him incorrect; in the rest it was due to the ordinary mechanical difficulties to which any printing is subject. Moreover, such is the nature of the work that, in the absence of any original manuscript or authentic corrected edition, it is impossible to establish the true reading for many varying passages, for the logical word, or rather, the obvious one, is by no means necessarily the correct one. . . . As a rule, it is seldom that a slight change will make any considerable difference in the meaning, except for fantastic interpretations.

As Nostradamus himself says, the quatrains are composed out of "a poetic furor, rather than according to the strict rules of poetry." No one will argue this point, for as a poet Nostradamus hardly ranks very high. The meter is basically iambic pentameter, with varying "male" and "female" lengths in the alternating pairs of lines. However, there are instances where, notwithstanding all the crabbed twists, the lines don't scan properly.

Punctuation does not seem to have been particularly dear to his heart. What punctuation there is is probably the work of zealous printers, who manifested wide disagreement. Nostradamus' aversion to punctuation is particularly distressing in the case of the long-drawn-out Preface, and the even longer Epistle.

## E. Rules of the Game in This Edition

As the reader has undoubtedly noticed, about half of this edition consists of French text on the left-hand page and an English translation on the right-hand page. To many, the inclusion of the French in a book for English consumption may seem a waste of paper. Yet such is the nature of these prophecies that no English translation can be considered final, and only a person with some knowledge of French can properly appreciate the meaning or meanings involved in the prophecies. To make this necessary comparison and study possible, the French has been put alongside.

As the earliest editions are neither complete nor available, there is some question as to what should be the text. One solution would seem to be to print the Preface and first 353 quatrains as they appeared in the Bonhomme of 1555 (as reprinted by Bareste in 1840), followed by the next known extant work, the du Rosne of 1557, from 454 on, as far as it goes, viz., 740. After this we might use the Benoist Rigaud of 1568 for 741, 742, the Epistle and the last three Centuries. Finally, we might use the Ménier edition of 1589, Chavigny's *Janus* of 1594, the edition of 1605 and Garcin's edition of 1643 for the supplementary material each of these contains.

Unfortunately, it has proved impossible to obtain a microfilm or photographic copy of the editions of 1557[1] (now only in Moscow) or of 1568, or of the *Janus*. Furthermore, the seeming perfection of this plan is marred by the fact that each of these editions contains some obvious printer's errors,

---

[1] A microfilm of this 1557 edition was at last procured as this book was going to press. It proves to be an extremely poor edition, filled with glaring errors and containing only four credible variants not previously noted (in 341, 532, 691 and 694).

which it would be rather silly to reproduce just for the sake of academic accuracy.

We have therefore done what either is the next-best thing, or is perhaps an even better course to follow. We have derived our text from a careful comparison of the Bonhomme edition of 1555, as reprinted by Bareste, with that of Pierre Rigaud (*ca.* 1600), as reprinted by Le Pelletier, and that of 1605.[2] Each of these has been considered of equal authenticity and no distinction has been made as to which of these three is the source of any particular word. However, in those very rare cases where none of these editions offers a satisfactory version of a dubious word, we have consulted three other early editions, the Fortune Rigaud (19a), Garcin's edition of 1643 (which holds a special place because of its debut of VII-43 and VII-44) and Le Pelletier's false "variations of 1568" (which, however, contains very good text). In these cases, and they are very rare, where a word in our text is not derived from one of the basic three, a footnote has been provided to cite which of the latter three is the origin of it.

In the matter of orthography, this edition represents what appears to be a marked departure from that of previous editions. We have already mentioned the need for the reader with any knowledge of French to consult the French text. In order to make the French text as readable as possible, we have rendered all words which are to be found in a good French dictionary in modern French orthography. All words which are not French and are not to be found in such a dictionary, we have placed in italics, with footnotes showing their origin and meaning. This means that *congnoistre* has become *connaître, vefue veuve, sceu su,* etc. Inevitably, many borderline cases arise.[3] We have followed the simple rule that if there is any doubt whatever as to whether the modern French word that is apparently the same is actually identical, we have avoided making a change, and instead have italicized the word, with a footnote. Thus, *anéantir* has not been substituted for *anichiler,* nor *bouchée* for *boucin,* though in each case the word is similar and the meaning and meter would be unchanged. No changes that involve a change in the number of syllables or in the meter have even been considered.

Besides using them for words not French, or no longer in the French vocabulary, we have used italics for all place names and proper names. As these are not always capitalized in the text, this will be found particularly useful. Once again, wherever there is any doubt, an explanatory footnote has been provided.[4]

---

[2]That is, for the Preface and first 353 quatrains. From there on, Bonhomme drops out, and the Pierre Rigaud and the 1605 form the basis.

[3]It is particularly distressing in cases where the Renaissance spelling coincides with the English, as in *conflict,* now *conflit;* or where the word exists in English, but no longer in French, as with *insuperable* or *neglect.*

[4]Italics are Nostradamus' in only one case. In the Preface and Epistle, illustrative Latin phrases and quotations appeared in italics. As we translated these literally, and placed the English in italics, footnotes are superfluous here.

The basic purpose of the change in orthography is, as we have mentioned, to encourage all readers with any knowledge of French whatever to refer to the original text. We feel that many such readers would not care to struggle with the antiquated spelling which makes many words with which they might be actually familiar quite unrecognizable. We must reiterate that changes have been made only where there was no doubt as to the identity of a word, and that where any doubt exists, the words have been left unchanged, with a footnote.

A translator must always steer between the Scylla of too literal and meaningless translation on one hand, and the Charybdis of too free translation on the other hand. This is particularly true in work of this nature. In general, we have followed a policy of turning the French into reasonably good English when the meaning was unequivocal. However, where the French seems to offer more than one possible meaning, we have either been very literal, or have sought to use English terminology that would allow the same range of possible meanings. Throughout, the idea has been to express in English what Nostradamus seems to have had in mind, no matter how much like absurd nonsense it might sound several centuries later.

Because notes on variants and on the derivation of non-French words cannot but consume much of the footnote space, we have carefully tried to avoid including in this main part of the book anything not directly connected with the text. In the section entitled "Commentaries" will be found other information of interest to the reader. This includes explanations of obscure geographical, mythological or historical proper names, suggestions about enigmas and anagrams, the probable ideas Nostradamus intended to convey in the quatrain or paragraph in question, the chief interpretations of the quatrain to date and other similar information. Some readers may regret that this information has not been placed on the same page, contiguous to the quatrain or paragraph, but the arrangement pursued seems to offer the most orderly and useful arrangement practicable.

Another innovation in this edition lies in the labeling of the quatrain (especially in connection with cross-references and Indexes). For purposes of simplification, we have used Arabic numerals for both Century and quatrain, and have omitted the customary hyphen. Thus 11 is read "one one"; 10100 is read "ten one hundred." Up to 10100 there can be no overlapping or confusion. For the thirteen quatrains in Centuries XI and XII, as well as for the "extra" quatrains (fourteen of them) assigned to Centuries VI, VII, VIII and X, we have used the old-fashioned form. VIII-3 is the third of the six "extra" quatrains in Ménier's edition of 1589 (or that of 1605). No. 124 could only be Quatrain 24 of Century I, since Quatrain 4 of Century XII would be labeled XII-4.

Quatrains of especial interest are preceeded, in their English translation, by a hand (☞) to the left, which in most cases serves also as an indication that reference to the Commentary is advisable.

# NOSTRADAMUS
## and His Prophecies

# Préface
# de
# M. Nostradamus
# à ses Prophéties.

*Ad Caesarem Nostradamum filium*
*Vie et félicité.*

[1] Ton tard avénement, César Nostradame mon fils, m'a fait mettre mon longtemps par continuelles *vigilations*[1] nocturnes *reserer*[2] par écrit toi délaisser mémoire, après la corporelle extinction de ton progéniteur, au commun profit des humains, de ce que la divine essence par Astronomiques révolutions m'ont donné connaissance. [2] Et depuis qu'il a plu au Dieu immortel que tu ne sois venu en naturelle lumière dans cette *terrene*[3] plage, et ne veux dire tes ans qui ne sont encore accompagnés, mais tes mois Martiaux incapables à recevoir dans ton débile entendement ce que je serai contraint après mes jours *définer*:[4] vu qu'il n'est possible te laisser par écrit ce que serait par l'injure du temps oblitéré: car la parole héréditaire de l'occulte prédiction sera dans mon estomac *intercluse*:[5] [3] considérant aussi les aventures de l'humain *definement*[6] être incertaines, et que le tout est régi et gouverné par la puissance de Dieu inestimable, nous inspirant non par bacchante fureur, ne par lymphatique mouvement, mais par astronomiques assertions, *Soli numine divino afflati praesagiunt et spiritu prophetico particularia.* [4] Combien que de longtemps par plusieurs fois j'ai prédit longtemps auparavant ce que depuis est avenu, et en particulières régions, attribuant le tout être fait par la vertu et inspiration divine, et autres félices et sinistres aventures d'accélérée promptitude *prénoncées,*[7] que depuis sont avenues par les climats du monde: ayant voulu taire et délaisser pour cause de l'injure, et non tant seulement du temps présent, mais aussi de la plus grande part du futur, de mettre par écrit, [5] parce que les regnes, sectes et réligions[8] feront changes si opposites, voire au respect du présent diamétralement, que si je venais à *reserer*[9] ce qu'à l'avenir sera, ceux de regne, secte,

---

[1] Latin *vigilatio*, watch.
[2] Latin *reserare*, to disclose, reveal. Variant: *référer.*
[3] Latin *terrenus*, earthly.
[4] Latin *definire*, to designate.
[5] Latin *interclusus*, shut up.
[6] Latin *definitio*, limitation.
[7] Latin *praenunciare*, to predict.
[8] Variant: *régions.*
[9] Latin *reserare*, to disclose, reveal. Variant: *référer.*

# Preface

## of

# M. Nostradamus

## to his Prophecies.

*To Caesar Nostradamus my son*
*Long life and happiness.*

1. Your late arrival, César Nostradamus, my son, has caused me to spend a great deal of time in continual nightly watches so that after my death you might be left a memorial of your father, revealing in writing that which the Divine Spirit has made known to me, through the revolutions of the stars, to the common benefit of mankind.

2. Since it has pleased the immortal God that you should have appeared on this earth but recently, and your years cannot yet be said to be coupled, your weak understanding is incapable of absorbing that which I must needs record of the future. Furthermore, it is impossible to leave you in writing that which would be obliterated by the wear and tear of time. Indeed, the hereditary gift of prophecy will go to the grave with me.

3. Events of human origin are uncertain, but all is regulated and governed by the incalculable power of God, inspiring us not through drunken fury, nor by frantic movement, but through the influences of the stars. *Only those divinely inspired can predict particular things in a prophetic spirit.*

4. For a long time I have been making many predictions, far in advance, of events since come to pass, naming the particular locality. I acknowledge all to have been accomplished through divine power and inspiration. Predicted events, both happy and sad, have come to pass throughout the world with increasing promptness. However, because of the possibility of harm, both for the present and most of the future, I became willing to keep silent and refrain from putting them into writing.

5. For kingdoms, sects and religions will make changes so complete, truly diametrically opposite, that if I came to reveal what will happen in the future, the great ones of the above kingdoms, sects, religions and faiths

réligion, et foi trouveraient si mal accordant à leur fantaisie auriculaire, qu'ils viendraient à damner ce que par les siècles avenir on connaîtra être vu et aperçu. Considérant aussi la sentence du vrai Sauveur, *Nolite sanctum dare canibus nec mittatis margaritas ante porcos ne conculcent pedibus et conversi dirumpant vos.* Qui a été la cause de faire retirer ma langue au populaire, et la plume au papier: [6] puis me suis voulu étendre déclarant pour le commun avénement par abstruses et perplexes sentences les causes futures, même les plus urgentes, et celle que j'ai aperçu, quelque humaine mutation qu'advienne ne scandaliser l'auriculaire fragilité, et le tout écrit sous figure nubileuse, plus que du tout prophétique: [7] combien que, *Abscondisti haec a sapientibus, et prudentibus, id est potentibus et regibus, et enucleasti ea exiguis et tenuibus,* et aux Prophètes par le moyen de Dieu immortel, et des bons Anges ont reçu l'esprit de vaticination, par lequel ils voient les choses lointaines, et viennent à prévoir les futurs avénements; car rien ne se peut parachever sans lui, auxquels si grande est la puissance et la bonté aux sujets, que pendant qu'ils demeurent en eux, toutefois aux autres effets sujets pour la similitude de la cause du bon *genius,*[10] celle chaleur et puissance vaticinatrice s'approche de nous: comme il nous avient des rayons du Soleil, qui viennent jettant leur influence aux corps élémentaires et non élémentaires. [8] Quant à nous qui sommes humains, ne pouvons rien de notre naturelle connaissance et inclination d'engin connaître des secrets abstruses de Dieu le Créateur, *Quia non est nostrum noscere tempora nec momenta, etc.* [9] Combien qu'aussi de présent peuvent avenir et être personnages que Dieu le Créateur a voulu révéler par imaginatives impressions quelques secrets de l'avenir, accordés à l'astrologie judicielle, comme du passé, que certaine puissance et volontaire faculté venait par eux, comme flamme de feu apparait, que lui inspirant on venait à juger les divines et humaines inspirations. Car les œuvres divines, que totalement sont absolues, Dieu les vient parachever: la moyenne qui est au milieu, les anges: la troisième, les mauvais.[11] [10] Mais, mon fils, je te parle ici un peu trop abstrusement; mais quant aux occultes vaticinations que l'on vient à recevoir par le subtil esprit du feu qui quelquefois par l'entendement agité, contemplant le plus haut des astres, comme étant vigilant, même qu'aux prononciations, étant surpris écrits prononçant sans crainte moins atteint d'*invereconde*[12] loquacité: mais quoi? tout procédait de la puissance divine du grand Dieu éternel, de qui toute bonté procède. [11] Encore, mon

---

[10]Latin *genius,* demon presiding at the birth of each man and watching over him.
[11]See "Background and Rules of the Game: Inspiration," footnote 6.
[12]Latin *inverecundus.* shameless.

would find it so little in accord with what their fancy would like to hear, that they would condemn that which future centuries will know and perceive to be true. As the true Saviour said, *Give not that which is holy unto dogs, nor cast your pearls before swine, lest they trample them under their feet and turn and rend you.*[1] This has been the cause of my withholding my tongue from the vulgar and my pen from paper.

6. Later, because of the vulgar advent,[2] I decided to give way and, by dark and cryptic sentences, tell of the causes of the future mutation of mankind, especially the most urgent ones, and the ones I perceived, and in a manner that would not upset their fragile sentiments. All had to be written under a cloudy figure, above all things prophetic.

7. *Thou hast hidden these things from the wise and the prudent, that is, from the powerful and from kings, and hast revealed them to the small and the weak.*[3] And to the Prophets. By means of the immortal God, and his good Angels, they received the spirit of prophecy, by which they see distant things and foresee future events. For nothing can be accomplished without Him whose power and goodness to his creatures is so great that as long as these dwell in them, much as they may be exposed to other influences, on account of their good genius this prophetic heat and power approaches *us.*[4] It approaches us like the rays of the sun, which cast their influence on bodies both elementary and non-elementary.

8. As for ourselves, who are but human, we can discover nothing of the obscure secrets of God the Creator by our own unaided knowledge or by the bent of our ingenuity. *It is not for you to know times or hours, etc.*[5]

9. However, now or in the future there may be persons to whom God the Creator, through fanciful impressions, wishes to reveal some secrets of the future, integrated with judicial astrology, in much the same manner that in the past a certain power and voluntary faculty came over them like a flame, causing them to judge human and divine inspirations alike. For of the divine works, those which are absolute God completes; those which are medial, the angels; and the third kind, the evil spirits.

10. But, my son, I speak to you here a bit too obscurely. Hidden prophecies come to one by the subtle spirit of fire, sometimes through the understanding being disturbed in contemplating the remotest of stars, while remaining alert. The pronouncements are taken down in writing, without fear, without taint of excess verbiage. But why? Because all these things proceeded from the divine power of the great eternal God, from whom all goodness flows.

11. Furthermore, my son, though I have mentioned the name prophet,

---

[1]St. Matthew VII:6.
[2]Best translation of a difficult phrase. See Commentary.
[3]St. Matthew XI:25.
[4]Italics ours. Note sudden switch to first person.
[5]Acts I:7.

fils, que j'aie inséré le nom de prophète, je ne me veux attribuer titre de si haute sublimité pour le temps présent: car qui *Propheta dicitur hodie, olim vocabatur videns:* car Prophète proprement, mon fils, est celui qui voit choses lointaines de la connaissance naturelle de toute créature. Et cas avenant que le Prophète moyennant la parfaite lumière de la Prophétie lui *appaire*[13] manifestement des choses divines, comme humaines: que ce ne se peut faire, vu que les effets de la future prédiction s'étendent loin. [12] Car les secrets de Dieu incomprehensibles, et la vertu *effectrice*[14] contingent de longue étendue de la connaissance naturelle prenant leur plus prochain origine du libéral arbitre, fait apparoir les causes qui d'elles-mêmes ne peuvent acquérir celle notice pour être connues ne par les humains augures, ne par autre connaissance ou vertu occulte comprise sous la convacité du Ciel, même du fait présent de la totale eternité, qui vient en soi embrasser tout le temps. Mais moyennant quelque indivisible éternité, par comitiale agitation *Hiraclienne*,[15] les causes par le céleste mouvement sont connues. [13] Je ne dis pas, mon fils, afin que bien l'entendes, que la connaissance de cette matière ne se peut encore imprimer dans ton débile cerveau, que les causes futures bien lointaines ne soient à la connaissance de la créature raisonnable: si sont nonobstant bonnement la créature de l'âme intellectuelle des causes[16] présentes lointaines, ne lui sont du tout ne trop occultes ne trop *reserées:*[17] [14] mais la parfaite des causes *notice*[18] ne se peut acquérir sans celle divine inspiration: vu que toute inspiration prophétique reçoit prenant son principal principe mouvant de Dieu le créateur, puis de l'heur et de nature. Parquoi étant les causes *indifferentes*,[19] indifferentement produites, et non produites, le présage partie avient, où a été prédit. Car l'entendement créé intellectuellement ne peut voir occultement, sinon par la voix faite au limbe moyennant la exigue flamme en laquelle partie les causes futures se viendront à incliner. [15] Et aussi, mon fils, je te supplie que jamais tu ne veuilles employer ton entendement à telles rêveries et vanités que sèchent le corps et mettent à perdition l'âme, donnant trouble au faible sens: même la vanité de la plus qu'exécrable magie réprouvée jadis par les sacrées écritures, et par les divins canons: [16] au chef duquel est excepté le jugement de l'Astrologie judicielle: par laquelle et moyennant inspiration et révélation divine par continuelles veilles et supputations, avons nos prophéties rédigé par écrit. Et combien que celle occulte Philosophie ne fusse réprouvée, n'ai donc voulu présenter leurs effrénées persuasions: combien que plusieurs volumes qui ont été cachés par longs siècles me sont été manifestés. Mais doutant ce qui aviendrait en ai fait, après la lecture présent à *Vulcan*, que

---

[13]O.F. form of *apparaître*.

[14]O.F. form of *effective*.

[15]Greek *Herakleie*, epileptic (among other meanings).

[16]Variant: *choses*.

[17]Latin *reseratus*, disclosed, revealed. Variant: *réferées*.

[18]Latin *notitia*, concept, knowledge.

[19]Latin *indifferentia*, similarity, equivalence.

I do not wish to assume for myself a title so sublime for the present. For *He who is called a prophet now was once called a seer.* Strictly speaking, my son, a prophet is one who sees things remote from the natural knowledge of men. And it can happen that the prophet, by means of the perfect light of the prophecy appearing before him, thinks he sees things divine as well as human; but this cannot[6] be, for the effects of future prediction extend far.

12. For the incomprehensible secrets of God and their efficient virtue belong to a sphere very remote from human knowledge, deriving their immediate origin from the free will. They bring about the appearance of causes which of themselves could not attract enough attention to be known, neither by human augury, nor by any other hidden knowledge or virtue comprised under the concavity of heaven, even from the present fact of all eternity, which comes in itself to embrace all time. But through some indivisible eternity and by means of epyleptic[7] agitation, the causes are made known by celestial movements.

13. Understand me well, my son. I do not say that the knowledge of this matter cannot yet impress itself upon your feeble brain, nor do I say that very distant events are not within the knowledge of reasoning man. If future events are merely the creation of the intellectual soul out of current events, they are not by any means too greatly hidden from him nor, on the other hand, can they be said to be revealed at all.

14. But the perfect knowledge of events cannot be acquired without divine inspiration, since all prophetic inspiration receives its prime motivating force from God the Creator, then from good fortune and nature. For this reason, the presage occurs in part, where it has been predicted, in proportion to the extent to which similar events have manifested themselves similarly or have failed to manifest themselves. For the human understanding, being created intellectually, cannot see hidden things unless aided by the voice coming from limbo via the thin flame, showing in what direction future events incline.

15. Furthermore, my son, I beg that you will never want to employ your understanding on such dreams and vanities as dry up the body, put the soul in perdition and cause trouble to the weak senses. I caution you especially against the vanity of the more than execrable magic, condemned of yore by the Holy Scriptures and by the Canons of the Church.

16. However, judicial astrology is excepted from this judgment. For it is by this, together with divine inspiration and revelation, and continual nightly watches and calculations, that we have reduced our prophecies to writing. Although this occult Philosophy was not condemned, I did not desire that you should ever be faced with their unbridled promptings. I had at my disposal many volumes which had been hidden for a great many centuries. But dreading what use might be made of them, after reading them I consigned them to the flames. As the fire came to devour them, the

---

[6]One of many negatives that seem out of place in context.
[7]Literally "epyleptic and epyleptic."

cependant qu'il les venait à dévorer, la flamme léchant l'air rendait une clarté insolite, plus claire que naturelle flamme, comme lumière de feu de *clystre*[20] fulgurant, illuminant subit la maison, comme si elle fût été en subite conflagration. Parquoi afin qu'à l'avenir ne fusses abusé *perscrutant*[21] la parfaite transformation tant *séline*[22] que solaire, et sous terre métaux incorruptibles, et aux ondes occultes, les ai en cendres convertis. [17] Mais quant au jugement qui se vient parachever moyennant le jugement céleste cela te veux je manifester: parquoi avoir connaissance des causes futures rejettant loin les fantastiques imaginations qui aviendront, limitant la particularité des lieux par divine inspiration surnaturelle, accordant aux célestes figures les lieux et une partie du temps de propriété occulte par vertu, puissance, et faculté divine, en présence de laquelle les trois temps sont compris par éternité, révolution tenant à la cause passée, présente et future: *quia omnia sunt nuda et aperta etc.* [18] Parquoi mon fils, tu peux facilement nonobstant ton tendre cerveau, comprendre que les choses qui doivent avenir se peuvent prophétiser par les nocturnes et célestes lumières, qui sont naturelles, et par l'esprit de prophétie: non que je me veuille attribuer nomination ni effet prophétique, mais par révélée inspiration, comme homme mortel éloigné non moins de sens au Ciel, que des pieds en terre. *Possum non errare, falli, decipi*: suis pécheur plus grand que nul de ce monde, sujet à toutes humaines afflictions. [19] Mais étant surpris par fois la semaine lymphatiquant, et par longue calculation, rendant les études nocturnes de suave odeur, j'ai composé livres de prophéties, contenant chacun cent quatrains astronomiques de prophéties, lesquelles j'ai un peu voulu raboter obscurement: et sont perpetuelles vaticinations, pour d'ici à l'année 3797. [20] Que possible fera retirer le front à quelques-uns en voyant si longue extension, et par sous toute la concavité de la Lune aura lieu et intelligence: et ce entendant universellement par toute la terre les causes mon fils. Que si tu vis l'âge naturel et humain, tu verras devers ton climat, au propre ciel de ta nativité, les futures aventures prévoir. [21] Combien que le seul Dieu éternel, soit celui seul qui connaît l'éternité de sa lumière, procédant de lui-même: et je dis franchement qu'à ceux à qui sa magnitude immense, qui est sans mesure et incomprehensible, a voulu par longue inspiration mélancolique révéler, que moyennant icelle cause occulte manifestée divinement, principalement de deux causes principales, qui sont comprises à l'entendement de celui inspiré qui prophétise, [22] l'une est qui vient à infuser, éclaircissant la lumière surnaturelle, au personnage qui prédit par la doctrine des astres, et prophétise par inspirée révélation: laquelle est une certaine participation de la divine éternité: moyennant le Prophète vient à juger de cela que son divin esprit lui a donné par le moyen de Dieu le Créateur, et par une naturelle instigation: [23] c'est à savoir que ce que prédit

---

[20]O.F. word for "thunder."
[21]Latin *perscrutare*, to search thoroughly.
[22]Greek *selene*, moon.

flame licking the air shot forth an unusual brightness, clearer than natural fire. It was like the light of lightning thunder, suddenly illuminating the house, as if in sudden conflagration. Thus, so that you might not be led astray in the future in a search for the perfect transformation of silver, or of gold, or of incorruptible metals under the earth, or hidden in the sea, I have reduced them to ashes.

17. But what I do want to make clear to you is the judgment obtained through the calculation of the heavens. By this one has knowledge of future events while rejecting completely all fantastic things one may imagine. With divine and supernatural inspiration integrated with astronomical computations, one can name places and periods of time accurately, an occult property obtained through divine virtue, power and ability. By means of this, past, present and future become but one eternity: *for all things are naked and open.*[8]

18. Thus, my son, notwithstanding your tender brain, you can easily understand that things which are to happen can be prophesied by the lights of the sky at night, which are natural, coupled with the spirit of prophecy. Not that I would assume the name or power of a prophet. It is as a mortal man, whose senses revealed inspiration places no further from Heaven than his feet from the ground. *I cannot fail, err or be deceived,* though I am the greatest sinner in this world, subject to all human afflictions.

19. Many times in the week I am overtaken by an ecstasy; having rendered my nocturnal studies agreeable through long calculation, I have composed books of prophecies, of which each contains one hundred astronomical quatrains of prophecies. I have sought to polish them a bit obscurely. They are perpetual prophecies, for they extend from now to the year 3797.

20. It is possible, my son, that some will raise their eyebrows at seeing such a vast extent of time and treatment of everything under the moon that will happen throughout the earth. But if you attain the natural span of human life, you will come to see, under your own native skies, the fulfillment of future events that I have foreseen.

21. Although the eternal God alone knows the eternity of the light which proceeds from himself, I say frankly to all to whom he has wished to reveal his immense magnitude, immeasurable and incomprehensible as it is, amidst long and melancholy inspiration, that it is a hidden thing, manifested divinely. It is manifested chiefly by two means, which are contained in the understanding of the inspired one who prophesies.

22. One comes by infusion, clearing the supernatural light for the person who predicts by astronomy, making it possible to predict through inspired revelation. The other is a fixed participation of the divine eternity. By means of it, the Prophet comes to judge what has been given him by his divine spirit, through God the Creator and his natural intuition.

23. So that what is predicted, and is true, has an ethereal origin. This

---

[8]Hebrews IV:13.

est vrai, et a pris son origine éthéréement: et telle lumière et flamme exiguë est de toute efficace, et de telle altitude: non moins que la naturelle clarté et naturelle lumière rend les philosophes si assurés que moyenant les principes de la première cause ont atteint à plus profondes abîmes des plus hautes doctrines. Mais à celle fin, mon fils, que je ne vague trop profondément pour la capacité future de ton sens, [24] et aussi que je trouve que les lettres feront si grande et incomparable *jacture*,[23] que je trouve le monde avant l'universelle conflagration avenir tant de déluges et si hautes inondations, qu'il ne sera guère terroir qui ne soit couvert d'eau: et sera par si longtemps que hors mis *enographies*[24] et topographies, que le tout ne soit péri: aussi avant et après telles inondations, en plusieurs contrées les pluies seront si exiguës, et tombera du ciel si grande abondance de feu, et de pierres *candentes*[25] que ne demeurera rien qui ne soit consommé: et ceci avenir en bref, et avant la dernière conflagration. [25] Car encore que la planète de Mars parachève son siècle, et à la fin de son dernier période, si le reprendra il: mais assemblés les uns en Aquarius par plusieurs années, les autres en Cancer par plus longues et continues. Et maintenant que sommes conduits par la Lune, moyennant la totale puissance de Dieu éternel, qu'avant qu'elle aie parachevé son total circuit, le Soleil viendra, et puis Saturne. Car selon les signes célestes le regne de Saturne sera de retour, que le tout calculé, le monde s'approche d'une *anaragonique*[26] révolution: [26] et que de présent que ceci j'écris avant cent septante sept ans trois mois onze jours, par pestilence, longue famine, et guerres, et plus par les inondations le monde entre ci et ce terme préfix, avant et après par plusieurs fois, sera si diminué, et si peu de monde sera, que l'on ne trouvera qui veuille prendre les champs, qui deviendront libres aussi longuement qu'ils sont étés en servitude: [27] et ce quant au visible jugement céleste, qu'encore que nous soyons au septième nombre de mille qui parachève le tout, nous approchons du huitième sphère, où est le firmament de la huitième sphère, qui est en dimension latitudinaire, où le grand Dieu éternel viendra parachever la révolution: où les images célestes retourneront à se mouvoir, et le mouvement supérieur qui nous rend la terre stable et ferme, *non inclinabatur in saeculum saeculi:* hors mis que son vouloir sera accompli, mais non point autrement: [28] combien que par ambiguës opinions excédantes toutes raisons naturelles par songes *Mahométiques,* aussi aucunes fois Dieu le créateur par les ministres de ses messagers de feu en flamme missive vient à proposer aux sens extérieurs, mêmement à nos yeux, les causes de

---

[23]O.F. word for "loss."

[24]A perennial puzzler. Probably syncope for *ethnographies.*

[25]Latin *candens,* burning.

[26]Dubious. Possibly from Greek *anairesin-gonichos,* destruction-engendering, according to Le Pelletier. The Fortune Rigaud has a variant *anaxagorique,* which has two possible meanings: (1) Greek *anax-agora,* sovereign-mob. (2) Anaxagoras, Greek philosopher and tutor of Pericles who predicted the end of the world through fire and water.

light and the thin flame are altogether efficacious, and are of heavenly origin no less than natural light. And it is the latter which renders philosophers so sure of themselves that by means of the principles of the first cause they have penetrated to the innermost cores of the loftiest of doctrines. But an end to this, my son, for I must not stray too far from the future capacity of your senses.

24. I find that letters will suffer a very great and incomparable loss. I find also that before the universal conflagration the world will be deluged by many floods to such heights that there will remain scarcely any land not covered by water, and this will last for so long that everything will perish except the earth itself and the races[9] which inhabit it. Furthermore, before and after these inundations, in many countries the rains will have been so slight, and there will have fallen from the sky such a great abundance of fire, and of burning stones, that nothing will remain unconsumed. And this will occur a short time before the final conflagration.

25. For although the planet Mars will finish its cycle, at the end of its last period, it will start again. Some will assemble in Aquarius for several years, others in Cancer for an even longer time. Now, by means of the supreme power of eternal God, we are led by the Moon; before she has completed her entire circuit, the Sun will come and then Saturn. For according to the signs in the heavens, the reign of Saturn will return; so that, all told, the world is drawing near an anaragonic[10] revolution.

26. From this moment, before 177 years, 3 months and 11 days have passed,[11] by pestilence, long famine, wars and, most of all, by floods, the world will be so diminished, with so few remaining, that no one will be found willing to work the fields, which will remain wild for as long a period as they had been tilled.

27. This is according to the visible judgment of the stars, for although we are now in the seventh millenary,[12] which finishes all, we are approaching the eighth, wherein is located the firmament of the eighth sphere. This is in the latitudinary dimension, whence the great eternal God will come to complete the revolution, and the heavenly bodies will return to their sources, and the upper motion will render the earth stable and fixed for us, *not deviating from age to age,*[13] unless He wills it otherwise.

28. By ambiguous opinions beyond all natural reason, by Mahometan dreams and even sometimes through the flaming missives brought by the angels of fire of God the Creator, there come before exterior senses, even our eyes, predictions of future events or things significant to a future happening.

---

[9]Properly, "topographies and ethnographies(?)." See footnote 24, opposite.
[10]Or "anaxagoric." See footnote 26, opposite.
[11]June 22, 1732, taking into account ten days dropped in 1582.
[12]At variance with views in the Epistle. See commentary on para. 40 of the Epistle.
[13]Psalm CIV:5.

future prédiction, *significatrices*[27] du cas futur [29] qui se doit à celui qui présage manifester. Car le présage qui se fait de la lumière extérieure vient infailliblement à juger partie avec et moyennant le *lume*[28] extérieur: combien vraiment que la partie qui semble avoir par l'oeil de l'entendement, ce que n'est par la lésion du sens imaginatif, [30] la raison est par trop évidente, le tout être prédit par *afflation*[29] de divinité, et par le moyen de l'esprit angélique inspiré à l'homme prophétisant, rendant ointes de vaticinations, le venant à illuminer, lui émouvant le devant de la fantaisie par diverses nocturnes apparitions, que par diurne certitude prophétise par administrations Astronomiques, conjointe de la sanctissime future prédiction, ne consistant[30] ailleurs qu'au courage libre. [31] Viens à cette heure entendre, mon fils, que je trouve par mes révolutions qui sont accordantes à révélée inspiration, que le mortel glaive s'approche de nous maintenant par peste, guerre plus horrible qu'à vie de trois hommes n'a été, et famine, lequel tombera en terre, et y retournera souvent, car les Astres s'accordent à la révolution: et aussi a dit: *Visitabo in virga ferrea iniquitates eorum, et in verberibus percutiam eos.* [32] Car la miséricorde du Seigneur[31] ne sera point *dispergée*[32] un temps, mon fils, que la plupart de mes Prophéties seront accomplies, et viendront être par accomplissement révolues. Alors par plusieurs fois durant les sinistres tempêtes, *Conteram ergo,* dira le Seigneur, *et confringam, et non miserebor,* [33] et milles autres aventures qui aviendront par eaux et continuelles pluies, comme plus à plein j'ai rédigé par écrit aux miennes autres Prophéties qui sont composées tout au long, *in soluta oratione,* limitant les lieux, temps, et le terme préfix que les humains après venus verront, connaissant les aventures avenues infailliblement, comme avons noté par les autres, parlant plus clairement: nonobstant que sous nuée seront comprises les intelligences: *Sed quando submovenda erit ignorantia,* le cas sera plus éclairci. [34] Faisant fin, mon fils, prends donc ce don de ton père Michel Nostradamus, espérant toi déclarer une chacune prophétie des quatrains ici mis. Priant au Dieu immortel, qu'il te veuille prêter vie longue, en bonne et prospère félicité. *De Salon ce 1 de Mars, 1555.*

---

[27]O.F. form of *significatives.*
[28]Latin *lumen,* light.
[29]Latin *afflatus divino,* divine inspiration.
[30]Variant: *considérant.*
[31]Variant: *de Dieu.*
[32]Latin *dispergere,* to spread.

29. These ought to manifest themselves to one who presages anything. For the presage which is made by the exterior light comes infallibly to judge partly with it and by means of the exterior light. Truly, the part which seems to come by the eye of the understanding comes only by the lesion of the imaginative sense.

30. The reason is very evident. All is predicted through divine inspiration, and by means of the angelic spirit with which the man prophesying is inspired, rendering him anointed with prophecies, illuminating him, moving him before his fantasy through diverse nocturnal apparitions. With astronomic calculations certifying the prophesy in the daytime, there is nothing more to the holiest future prediction than free courage.

31. You must see now, my son, that I find by my calculations, which are according to revealed inspiration, that the sword of death is now approaching us, in the shape of pestilence, war more horrible than has been known in three lifetimes, and famine. This famine will fall upon the earth, and return there often, according to the words *I will visit their iniquities with a rod of iron, and will strike them with blows.*[14]

32. For the mercy of the Lord, my son, shall not be extended at all for a long time, not until most of my prophecies will have been accomplished, and will by accomplishment have become resolved. Then several times during the sinister tempests, the Lord will say, *I will trample them, and break them, and not show pity.*[15]

33. And thousands of other events will come to pass, because of floods and continual rains, as I have set forth more fully in writing my other Prophecies, which are drawn out in length, *in prose,*[16] setting forth the places and times so that men coming after may see them, knowing the events to have occurred infallibly. This we have noted in connection with the others, speaking more clearly. For although they are written under a cloud, the meanings will be understood. *When the time comes for the removal of ignorance,* the event will be cleared up still more.

34. I make an end here, my son. Take now this gift of your father, Michel Nostradamus, who hopes to explain to you each prophecy of the quatrains included here. I beseech the immortal God that he will be willing to endow you with long life in good and prosperous happiness.

*From Salon this first of March, 1555.*

---

[14]Resembles Psalm LXXXIX:32, but is not a quotation.
[15]Resembles Isaiah LXIII:3, but is not a quotation.
[16]See Commentary on this dubious claim.

# Centurie I

1. Étant assis de nuit secret étude,
   Seul reposé sur la selle d'airain:
   Flamme exiguë sortant de solitude,
   Fait prospérer[1] qui n'est à croire vain.

2. La verge en main mise au milieu de BRANCHES,[2]
   De l'onde il moulle[3] et le limbe et le pied:
   Un peur et voix frémissant par les manches:
   Splendeur divine. Le divin près s'assied.

3. Quand la litière du tourbillon versée,
   Et seront faces de leurs manteaux couvers,[4]
   La république par gens nouveaux vexée,
   Lors blancs et rouges jugeront á l'envers.

4. Par l'univers sera fait un Monarque,
   Qu'en paix et vie ne sera longuement:
   Lors se perdra la piscature[5] barque,
   Sera régie en plus grand détriment.

5. Chassés seront sans faire long combat,
   Par le pays seront plus fort grevés:
   Bourg et cité auront plus grand débat:
   Carcas.[6] Narbonne auront cœurs éprouvés.

6. L'œil de Ravenne sera destitué,
   Quand à ses pieds les ailes failliront,
   Les deux de Bresse auront constitué
   Turin, Verseil que Gaulois fouleront.

7. Tard arrivé l'exécution faicte,[7]
   Le vent contraire, lettres au chemin prises:
   Les conjurés xiiii. d'une secte,
   Par le Rousseau senez[8] les entreprises.

---

[1]Variant: proférer.
[2]All capitals in original edition.
[3]O.F. form of mouille, which, however, would add one syllable.
[4]Now properly couvertes, which would spoil rime.
[5]Latin piscatura, fishing.
[6]Apocope of Carcassonne.
[7]Properly faite, which would spoil rime.
[8]O.F. senez, wise (Roquefort).

# Century I

☞ 1.  Being seated by night in secret study,
Alone resting on the brass stool:
A slight flame coming forth from the solitude,
That which is not believed in vain is made to succeed.[1]

☞ 2.  With rod in hand set in the midst of Branchus,[2]
With the water he wets both limb and foot:
Fearful, voice trembling through his sleeves:
Divine splendor. The divine seats himself near by.

☞ 3.  When the litter is overturned by the whirlwind,
And faces will be covered by their cloaks,
The republic will be vexed by new people,
Then whites and reds will judge in contrary ways.

☞ 4.  In the world there will be one Monarch
Who will not long be in peace or alive:
Then the fishing bark will be lost,
It will be ruled to its greater detriment.

5.  They will be driven away without much fighting,
They will be very much harried in the country:
Town and city will have a greater debate:
Carcassonne and Narbonne will have their hearts tried.

6.  The eye of Ravenna will be forsaken,
When the wings give way at its feet:
The two of Bresse will have made arrangements in
Turin and Vercelli, which the Gauls will trample.

7.  The arrival late, the execution completed,
The wind contrary, the letters seized en route:
The conspirators fourteen of a sect,
The enterprises by the wise Red-haired One.

[1]Or "is uttered."
[2]Or "of the Branches."

8. Combien de fois prise cité solaire
   Seras, changeant les loix barbares et vaines:
   Ton mal s'approche: Plus seras tributaire,
   Le grand *Hadrie* recouvrira[1] tes veines.

9. De l'*Orient* viendra le cœur *Punique*
   Fâcher *Hadrie* et les hoires *Romulides*,
   Accompagné de la *classe*[2] *Libyque*,
   Trembler[3] *Melites* et proches îles vides.

10. *Serpens*[4] transmis en la cage de fer
    Où les enfants *septains*[5] du Roi sont pris:
    Les vieux et pères sortiront bas de l'enfer,
    *Ains*[6] mourir voir de son fruit mort et cris.

11. Le mouvement de sens, cœur, pieds et mains
    Seront d'accord. *Naples, Leon,*[7] *Sicile:*
    Glaives, feux, eaux: puis aux nobles *Romains,*
    Plongés, tués, morts par cerveau débile.

12. Dans peu *dira*[8] fausse brute fragile,
    De bas en haut élevé promptement:
    Puis en instant déloyale et labile,
    Qui de *Veronne* aura gouvernement.

13. Les exilés par ire, haine intestine,
    Feront au Roi grande conjuration:
    Secret mettront ennemis par la *mine,*[9]
    Et ses vieux siens contre eux sédition.

14. De gent esclave chansons, chants et requètes,
    Captifs par Princes et Seigneurs aux prisons:
    À l'avenir par idiots sans têtes,
    Seront reçus par divines oraisons.

---

[1]Variant: *recourira.*
[2]Latin *classis,* fleet.
[3]Variant: *Temples.*
[4]Apparently *Serpent.* The only alternative is Le Pelletier's farfetched suggestion: Greek *sarpos,* coffin.
[5]Latin *septeni,* the seven.
[6]O.F. word for "before," not to be confused with French *ainsi.*
[7]Variant: *Lyon.*
[8]O.F. *duire,* to lead, govern.
[9]Latin *mina.* threat.

8. How many times will you be taken, solar city,
   Changing the barbarian and vain laws:
   Your evil approaches: You will be more tributary,
   The great "Adria"[1] will re-cover[2] your veins.

☞ 9. From the Orient will come the Punic heart
   To vex "Adria"[1] and the heirs of Romulus,
   Accompanied by the Libyan fleet,
   Malta trembling[3] and the neighboring isles empty.

10. The serpent[4] conveyed in the iron cage
    Where the seven children of the King are taken:
    Their progenitors will come out from their underworld below,
    Before dying seeing of their offspring death and cries.

11. The motion of sense, heart, feet and hands
    Will be in accord. Naples, Leon,[5] Sicily:
    Swords, fires, waters, then the noble Romans
    Submerged, killed, dead because of a weak brain.

12. In a short time a false, frail brute will lead,
    Elevated quickly from low to high:
    Then in an instant disloyal and labile,
    He who will have the government of Verona.

13. The exiles because of anger and intestine hatred
    Will bring a great conspiracy to bear against the King:
    Secretly they will place enemies as a threat,
    And his own old ones against them sedition.

☞ 14. From the slavish[6] people songs, chants and requests,
    For Princes and Lords captives in the prisons:
    In the future such by headless idiots
    Will be received as divine utterances.

[1]Venice, master of both the town of Adria and the Adriatic Sea; or the Adriatic Sea.
[2]Or "will again run through your veins" (i.e., the Adriatic will).
[3]Or "Temples at Malta."
[4]Or "coffin"? See note opposite.
[5]Or "Lyons."
[6]Or "Slavic."

15. *Mars* nous menace par sa force *bellique*,[1]
    Septante fois fera le sang épandre:
    *Auge*[2] et ruine de l'Ecclésiastique
    Et plus ceux qui d'eux rien voudront entendre.

16. Faux à l'étang joint vers le *Sagittaire*
    En son haut *AUGE*[3] de l'exaltation,
    Peste, famine, mort de main militaire:
    Le siècle approche de rénovation.

17. Par quarante ans l'*Iris* n'apparaîtra,
    Par quarante ans tous les jours sera vu:
    La terre aride en siccité croîtra,
    Et grands déluges quand sera aperçu.

18. Par la discorde négligence *Gauloise*
    Sera passage à *Mahomet* ouvert:
    De sang trempé la terre et mer *Senoise*,
    Le port *Phocen* de voiles et nefs couvert.

19. Lors que serpents viendront *circuir*[4] l'*are*,[5]
    Le sang *Troyen* vexé par les *Espaignes:*
    Par eux grand nombre en sera faite tare,
    Chef fuit, caché aux *mares*[6] dans les *saignes*.[7]

20. *Tours, Orléans, Blois, Angers, Reims* et *Nantes*,
    Cités vexées par subit changement:
    Par langues étranges seront tendues tentes,
    Fleuves, dards *Renes* terre et mer tremblement.

21. Profonde argile blanche nourrit rocher,
    Qui d'un abîme ira *lacticineuse*,[8]
    En vain troublés ne l'oseront toucher,
    Ignorant être au fond terre argileuse.

---

[1]Latin *bellicus*, warlike.
[2]Latin *augere*, to increase.
[3]Latin *augere*, to increase. All capitals in original edition.
[4]Latin *circuire*, to encircle.
[5]Latin *ara*, altar.
[6]O.F. *mares*, marsh (Roquefort).
[7]O.F. *saigne*, marsh, swamp.
[8]Latin *lacticineum*, milk-food.

15. Mars menaces us with his warlike force,
    Seventy times will he cause blood to flow:
    Rise and fall for the clergy
    And more for those who will want to hear nothing from them.

16. The scythe joined with the pond[1] towards Sagittarius
    At the high point of its ascendant,
    Plague, famine, death by military hand,
    The century approaches its renewal.

☞ 17. For forty years the rainbow will not appear,
    For forty years it will be seen every day:
    The parched earth will wax more dry,
    And great floods will accompany its appearance.

18. Because of the Gallic discord and negligence
    A passage will be opened to Mahomet:
    The land and sea of Siena[2] soaked in blood,
    The Phocaean port[3] covered with sails and ships.

19. When the serpents will come to encompass the altar,
    The Trojan blood will be vexed by the Spaniards:
    Because of them a great number will be made to suffer for it,
    The chief flees, hidden in the marshes.[4]

20. Tours, Orléans, Blois, Angers, Reims and Nantes,
    Cities vexed through sudden change:
    Tents will be pitched by those of foreign tongues,
    Rivers, darts at Rennes trembling of land and sea.

21. Deep white clay nourishes the rock,
    Which from an abyss will go forth milky,
    Needlessly troubled they will not dare touch it,
    Unaware that the earth at the bottom is clayish.

[1]Or "Saturn in Aquarius."
[2]A probable but not certain translation of *Senoise.*
[3]Always Marseilles, founded by the Phocaeans from Greece.
[4]Literally "in the marshes in the marshes."

22. Ce que vivra et n'ayant aucun sens,
    Viendra léser à mort son artifice:
    *Autun, Chalon, Langres* et les deux *Sens*,
    La grêle et glace fera grand maléfice.

23. Au mois troisième se levant le Soleil,
    Sanglier, Léopard, au champ *Mars* pour combattre:
    Léopard lassé au ciel étend son œil,
    Un Aigle autour du Soleil voit s'ébattre.

24. À cité neuve pensif pour condamner,
    L'oiseau de proie au ciel se vient offrir:
    Après victorie à captifs pardonner,
    *Cremone* et *Mantoue* grands maux aura *souffert*.[1]

25. Perdu, trouvé, caché de si long siècle,
    Sera pasteur demi Dieu honoré:
    *Ains que*[2] la Lune achève son grand siècle,
    Par autres vents[3] sera déshonoré.

26. Le grand du foudre tombe d'heure diurne,
    Mal, et prédit par porteur *postulaire:*[4]
    Suivant présage tombe de l'heure nocturne,
    Conflit *Reims, Londres, Etrusque* pestifère.

27. Dessous le *chaine*[5] *Guien* du ciel frappé,
    Non loin de là est caché le trésor:
    Qui par longs siècles avait été *grappé*,[6]
    Trouvé mourra, l'œil crevé de ressort.

28. La tour de *Boucq* craindra fuste Barbare,
    Un temps, long temps après barque *hesperique:*[7]
    Bétail, gens, meubles, tous deux feront grand tare,
    *Taurus*[8] et *Libra*,[9] quelle mortelle pique!

---

[1] A conspicuous break in rime uniform in all editions.
[2] O.F. for "before."
[3] Variant: *vus*.
[4] Latin *postularius*, demanding, claiming.
[5] O.F. spelling of *chêne* (Saint-Palaye). However, *chaine* is barely possible also.
[6] O.F. *grapper*, gather (Godefroy).
[7] Latin *Hesperius*, of the western land.
[8] Latin *taurus*, bull. Also a sign of the Zodiac.
[9] Latin *libra*, balance. Also a sign of the Zodiac.

22. That which will live without having any sense,
    Its artifice will come to be fatally injured:
    For Autun, Châlon, Langres and the two Sens,
    Hail and ice will cause much evil.

23. In the third month the Sun rising,
    The Boar and Leopard on the field of Mars to fight:
    The tired Leopard raises its eye to the heavens,
    Sees an Eagle playing around the Sun.

24. At the new city contemplating a condemnation,
    The bird of prey comes to offer itself to the heavens:
    After victory pardon to captives,
    Cremona and Mantua will have suffered great evils.[1]

☞ 25. Lost, found, hidden for so long a time,
    The pastor will be honored as a demigod:
    Before the Moon finishes its full period
    He will be dishonored by other winds.[2]

26. The great one of the lightning falls in the daytime,
    Evil predicted by the bearer of demands:
    According to the prediction he falls[3] in the nighttime.
    Conflict at Reims, London, Tuscan plague.

☞ 27. Under the oak tree[4] of Guienne struck from the sky,
    Not far from there is the treasure hidden:
    He who[5] for long centuries had been gathered,
    Found he[6] will perish, his[6] eye put out by a spring.

28. The tower of Bouc will fear the Barbarian foist,[7]
    Then much later, the Hesperian[8] bark:
    Cattle, people, chattels, both cause great waste,
    Bull and Balance,[9] what a mortal quarrel!

---

[1]This translation presupposes that *aura* is an error for *auront*. If the former was really intended, it must read, "At Cremona and Mantua it [he] will have suffered great evils."
[2]Or "Seen by others, he will be dishonored."
[3]Or "another falls" may be the sense intended.
[4]Or "chain" (in the sense of chain of hills).
[5]Or "That which."
[6]Or "it . . . its."
[7]A light galley, propelled by both sail and oar. Possibly synecdoche for "fleet."
[8]Spanish? American? See note opposite and Commentary.
[9]Or "Taurus and Libra."

29. Quand le poisson terrestre et aquatique
    Par forte vague au gravier sera mis,
    Sa forme étrange suave et *horrifique*,[1]
    Par mer aux murs bien tôt les ennemis.

30. La nef étrange par le tourment marin
    Abordera près de port inconnu,
    Nonobstant signes de rameau *palmerin*,[2]
    Après mort, pille: bon avis tard venu.

31. Tant d'ans en *Gaule* les guerres dureront,
    Outre la course du *Castulon* monarque:
    Victoire *incerte*[3] trois grands couronneront,
    Aigle, Coq, Lune, Lion, Soleil en marque.

32. Le grand Empire sera tôt *translaté*[4]
    En lieu petit qui bien tôt viendra croître:
    Lieu bien infime d'exiguë comté
    Où au milieu viendra poser son sceptre.

33. Près d'un grand pont de plaine spacieuse,
    Le grand Lion par forces *Césarées*,[5]
    Fera abattre hors cité rigoureuse,
    Par effroi portes lui seront *reserées*.[6]

34. L'oiseau de proie volant à la sénestre[7]
    Avant conflit fait aux *François parure:*[8]
    L'un bon prendra, l'un ambiguë sinistre,
    La partie faible tiendra par bon augure.

35. Le lion jeune le vieux surmontera
    En champ *bellique*[9] par singulier duel:
    Dans cage d'or les yeux lui crèvera:
    Deux *classes*[10] une, puis mourir, mort cruelle.

---

[1]Latin *horrificus*, frightful.
[2]Latin *palmarius*, of palm.
[3]Latin *incertus*, uncertain.
[4]Latin *translatus*, transferred.
[5]Latin *Caesareus*, imperial.
[6]Latin *reseratus*, unlocked.
[7]Variant: *fenêtre*.
[8]O.F. *pareure*, action of preparing (Godefroy).
[9]Latin *bellicus*, of battle.
[10]Usually Latin *classis*, fleet or army. In this case allegedly from Greek *klasis*, fracture.
See Commentary.

29. When the terrestrial and aquatic fish
    Will be put upon the beach by a strong wave,
    Its form strange, attractive and frightful,
    By sea the enemies very soon at the walls.

30. Because of the stormy seas the strange ship
    Will approach an unknown port,
    Notwithstanding the signals from the branch of palm,
    After death, pillage: good advice given late.

31. The wars in Gaul will last for many years,
    Beyond the course of the monarch of Castulo:[1]
    Uncertain victory will crown three great ones,
    The Eagle, Cock, Moon, Lion, Sun engraved.[2]

32. The great empire will soon be transferred
    To a little place which will very soon come to grow:
    A very lowly place in a petty country
    In the middle of which he will come to lay down his sceptre.

33. Near a great bridge of a spacious plain,
    The great Lion with Imperial forces,
    He will cause a felling outside the austere city,
    Because of fear the gates will be opened to him.

34. The bird of prey flying to the left side,[3]
    Before the conflict preparation made by the French:
    One will take it for good, another for ambiguous or inauspicious,
    The weak party will hold it as a good omen.

35. The young lion will overcome the old one
    On the field of battle in single combat:
    He will put out his eyes in a cage of gold:
    Two fleets[4] one, then to die a cruel death.

[1] A major city of Roman Spain. Probably used here as synecdoche for Spain. See Commentary.
[2] Or possibly "Sun in Leo."
[3] Or "to the window."
[4] Or, according to the popular interpretation, "two fractures," hence "two wounds."

36.  Tard le monarque se viendra repentir
     De n'avoir mis à mort son adversaire:
     Mais viendra bien à plus haut consentir,
     Que tout son sang par mort fera défaire.

37.  Un peu devant que le Soleil s'esconse,[1]
     Conflit donné grand peuple dubieux:[2]
     Profligés,[3] port marin ne fait réponse,
     Pont et sépulcre en deux étranges lieux.

38.  Le Sol[4] et l'Aigle au victeur paraîtront,
     Réponse vaine au vaincu l'on asseure:[5]
     Par cor ne cris harnois n'arrêteront,
     Vindicte,[6] paix par mort si achève à l'heure.

39.  De nuit dans lit le suprême étranglé
     Pour trop avoir séjourné blond élu.
     Par trois l'Empire subrogé[7] exanclé,[8]
     A mort mettra carte, et paquet ne lu.

40.  La trompe fausse dissimulant folie
     Fera Bisance un changement de lois:
     Ira d'Egypte qui veut que l'on délie
     Édit changeant monnaies et alois.

41.  Siège en cité, et de nuit assaillie,
     Peu échappé: non loin de mer conflit:
     Femme de joie, retour fils défaillie,
     Poison et lettres cachées dans le pli.

42.  Le dix Calendes d'avril de fait Gothique
     Resuscité[9] encore par gens malins:
     Le feu éteint, assemblée diabolique
     Cherchant les os du d'Amant et Pselin.[10]

[1] O.F. s'esconser, to set (Godefroy).
[2] Latin dubiosus, doubtful.
[3] Latin profligatus, ruined, overcome.
[4] Latin Sol, Sun.
[5] Properly assure, which would spoil the rime.
[6] Latin vindicta, revenge.
[7] Latin subrogatus, substituted.
[8] Latin exanclatus, enslaved, suffered.
[9] Latin resuscitatus, resuscitated, revived.
[10] Although all editions have this misreading, it should read Démon e Pselin. Latin e is equivalent to de. See Commentary.

36. Too late the monarch will repent
    Of not having put to death his adversary:
    But he will come to consent to a much greater thing,
    That of killing off all his blood.

37. Shortly before the Sun sets,
    Battle is given a great people in doubt:
    Ruined, the marine port makes no reply,
    Bridge and sepulchre in two strange places.

38. The Sun and the Eagle will appear as victor,
    The vanquished is reassured with a vain reply:
    With hue and cry they will not cease arming,
    Revenge, because of death peace made right on schedule.

39. By night the highest one[1] strangled in bed
    Because the blond elect had tarried too long.
    The Empire enslaved by three in substitution,
    Put to death with document and packet unread.

40. The false trumpet concealing madness
    Will bear Byzantium a change of laws:
    From Egypt there will go forth one who wants the withdrawal of
    Edicts debasing the quality of coins.

41. City besieged, and assaulted by night,
    Few escaped: conflict not far from the sea:
    On the return of her son a woman fainting from joy,[2]
    Poison and letters hidden in the fold.

42. The tenth of the Calends of April of Gothic count
    Revived again by wicked folk:
    The fire put out, diabolic assembly
    Searching for the bones of the Demon of Psellus.

[1] Or "last one."
[2] Or "the whore overcome."

43. Avant qu'avienne le changement d'Empire,
    Il aviendra un cas bien merveilleux:
    Le champ[1] mué,[2] le pilier de porphyre
    Mis, *translaté*[3] sus le rocher noueux.

44. En bref seront de retour sacrifices,
    Contrevenants seront mis à martyre:
    Plus ne seront moines, abbés, ni novices:
    Le miel sera beaucoup plus cher que cire.

45. *Secteur*[4] de sectes grand peine au délateur:
    Bête en théâtre, dressé le jeu scénique:
    Du fait antique ennobli l'inventeur,
    Par sectes monde confus et schismatique.

46. Tout auprès d'*Aux*, de *Lectore*[5] et *Mirande*
    Grand feu du ciel en trois nuits tombera:
    Cause aviendra bien *stupende*[6] et *mirande:*[7]
    Bien peu après la terre tremblera.

47. Du lac *Leman* les sermons fâcheront,
    Des jours seront réduits par des semaines,
    Puis mois, puis ans, puis tous défailliront,
    Les Magistrats damneront leur lois vaines.

48. Vingt ans du regne de la Lune passés,
    Sept mil ans autre tiendra sa monarchie:
    Quand le Soleil prendra ses jours lassés
    Lors accomplit et *mine*[8] ma prophétie.

49. Beaucoup, beaucoup[9] avant telles menées
    Ceux d'*Orient* par la vertu lunaire:
    L'an mil sept cent feront grands emmenées,
    Subjugant presque le coin *Aquilonaire*.[10]

---

[1]Variant: *camp.*
[2]O.F. *muer*, to change, move.
[3]Latin *translatus*, transferred. Variant: *transmué* (same meaning).
[4]Latin *sector*, cutter. He who cuts a sect is its founder.
[5]Variant: *Lestore.*
[6]Latin *stupendus*, stupendous.
[7]Latin *mirandus*, marvelous.
[8]O.F. *se miner*, to end (Godefroy). The reflexive would be an improvement also with *accomplit*, but no edition has the reflexive.
[9]Variant: one *beaucoup* only.
[10]Latin *aquilonaris*, northern.

43. Before the change of Empire occurs,
    A very marvelous event will take place:
    The field moved, the pillar of porphyry
    Placed, transferred onto the knotty rock.

☞ 44. In short sacrifices will be resumed,
    Transgressors will be put to martyrdom:
    No longer will there be monks, abbots or novices:
    Honey will be much more expensive than wax.

45. Founder of sects much grief to the accuser:
    Beast in the theater, the pantomine prepared:
    The inventor exalted by the ancient fact,
    The world confused and schismatic because of sects.

46. Very near Auch, Lectoure and Mirande
    Great fire will fall from the sky for three nights:
    A very stupendous and marvelous event will occur:
    Very soon after the earth will tremble.

☞ 47. The sermons from the Lake of Geneva annoying,
    From days they will grow into weeks,
    Then months, then years, then all will fail,
    The Magistrates will damn their useless laws.

48. Twenty years of the reign of the Moon passed,
    Seven thousand years another will hold its monarchy:
    When the Sun will take its tired days
    Then is accomplished and finished my prophecy.

☞ 49. Very much before such intrigues
    Those of the East by the virtue of the Moon:
    The year 1700 they will cause great ones[1] to be carried off,
    Almost subjugating the "Aquilon"[2] corner.

[1]Or "will cause many."
[2]The North[ern Country]. See Commentary for various possibilities.

50. De l'aquatique triplicité naîtra
    D'un qui fera le jeudi pour sa fête:
    Son bruit, los, regne, sa puissance croîtra,
    Par terre et mer aux Orients tempête.

51. Chef d'*Aries, Jupiter* et *Saturne,*
    Dieu éternel quelles mutations!
    Puis par long siècle son malin temps retourne,
    *Gaule* et *Itale* quelles émotions.

52. Les deux malins de *Scorpion* conjoints,
    Le grand Seigneur *meurtri*[1] dans sa salle:
    Peste à l'Eglise par le nouveau Roi joint,
    L'*Europe* basse et Septentrionale.

53. Las! qu'on verra grand peuple tourmenté
    Et la loi sainte en totale ruine,
    Par autres lois toute Chrétienté,
    Quand d'or, d'argent trouve nouvelle mine.

54. Deux révoltes faits du malin *falcigere,*[2]
    De regne et siècles fait permutation:
    Le mobile signe à son endroit si *ingere*[3]
    Aux deux égaux et d'inclination.

55. Sous l'opposite climat *Babylonique,*[4]
    Grande sera de sang effusion,
    Que terre et mer, air, ciel sera inique:
    Sectes, faim, regnes, pestes, confusion.

56. Vous verrez tôt et tard faire grand change,
    Horreurs extrêmes et *vindications,*[5]
    Que si la Lune conduite par son ange,
    Le ciel s'approche des inclinations.

57. Par grand discord la terre tremblera,
    Accord rompu dressant la tête au ciel:
    Bouche sanglante dans le sang nagera,
    Au sol la face ointe de lait et miel.

[1] O.F. *meurtrir,* to murder. In modern French it means only "to bruise."
[2] Latin *falciger,* carrying a scythe.
[3] O.F. *ingere,* intrusive, meddlesome. In modern French, *s'ingéré.*
[4] Latin *Babylonicus,* Babylonian.
[5] O.F. *vindication,* vengeance (Godefroy).

☞ 50. Of the aquatic triplicity[1] there will be born
One who will make of Thursday his[2] holiday:
His[2] fame, praise, rule and power will grow,
By land and sea a tempest to the East.

51. Jupiter and Saturn in the head of Aries,
Eternal God, what changes!
Then for a long age his wicked time returns,
Gaul and Italy, what disturbance.

☞ 52. The two wicked ones[3] conjoined in Scorpio,
The Grand Seignior[4] murdered in his hall:
Plague to the Church by the King newly joined,
Europe low and northerly.

☞ 53. Alas! a great people will one see tormented
And the holy law in utter ruin,
Other laws throughout all Christendom,
When a new mine of gold and silver is discovered.

54. Two revolutions made by the wicked scythe-bearer,[5]
Change made in realm and centuries:
The movable sign[6] so intrusive in its place
To the two equal and like-minded.[7]

55. Under the climate opposite to the Babylonian[8]
There will be great effusion of blood,
The unrighteous will be on land and sea, in air and sky,
Sects, famine, realms, plagues, confusion.

56. You will see great change made soon and late,
Extreme horrors and vengeances.
Because as the Moon is conducted by its angel,
The Sun is approaching its inclinations.

57. Through great dissension the earth will tremble,
Harmony broken lifting its head to heaven:
The bloody mouth will swim in the blood,
On the ground the face anointed with milk and honey.

---

[1] Possibly a planetary configuration is intended here.
[2] Or "its . . . Its."
[3] Saturn and Mars. See Commentary.
[4] A title of the Sultan of Turkey.
[5] Saturn. Two revolutions of Saturn take about fifty-nine years.
[6] Libra.
[7] Or "To the two like-minded ones."
[8] Possibly "Egyptian" is intended, the medieval Caliph of Egypt being often referred to as the Sultan of Babylon.

58. Tranché le ventre, naîtra avec deux têtes,
    Et quatre bras: quelques ans entier vivra:
    Jour qui *Aquiloye*[1] célébrera ses fêtes,
    *Fossen, Turin,* chef *Ferrare* suivra.

59. Les exilés deportés dans les îles,
    Au changement d'un plus cruel monarque
    Seront *meurtris*,[2] et mis deux des *scintilles*,[3]
    Qui de parler ne seront étés *parques*.[4]

60. Un Empereur naîtra près d'Italie,
    Qui à l'Empire sera vendu bien cher:
    Diront avec quels gens il se rallie
    Qu'on trouvera moins prince que boucher.

61. La république misérable *infelice*[5]
    Sera *vastee*[6] du nouveau magistrat:
    Leur grand amas de l'exil maléfice
    Fera *Sueve* ravir leur grand contrat.

62. La grande perte, las! que feront les lettres:
    Avant le cycle de *Latona* parfait,
    Feu, grand déluge plus par ignares sceptres,
    Que de long siècle ne se verra refait.

63. Les fléaux passés diminue le monde,
    Longtemps la paix terres inhabitées:
    Sûr marchera par ciel, terre, mer et onde,
    Puis de nouveau les guerres suscitées.

64. De nuit Soleil penseront avoir vu
    Quand le pourceau demi-homme on verra:
    Bruit, chant, bataille, au ciel battre aperçu,
    Et bêtes brutes à parler l'on *orra*.[7]

---

[1]Aquileia, one of the ten great cities of the Roman Empire, seems intended, but it was already in Nostradamus' time an abandoned village. Possibly Venice, which got its ecclesiastical power, is intended. Le Pelletier suggests Latin *Aquilae lex*, Eagle's law.
[2]O.F. *meurtrir*, to murder. In modern French it means only "to bruise."
[3]Latin *scintilla*, spark.
[4]Latin *parcus*, sparing, moderate.
[5]Latin *infelix*, unhappy.
[6]Latin *vastatus*, ruined.
[7]Lapsed future form of O.F. verb *ouïr*, to hear.

58. The belly cut, it will be born with two heads
And four arms: several years it will live intact:
The day on which Aquileia[1] will celebrate its feasts,
Fossano, Turin, the chief of Ferrara will follow.

59. The exiles transported to the isles,
At the advent of a more cruel monarch,
Will be murdered, and burnt two
Who had not been sparing with their speech.

☞ 60. An Emperor will be born near Italy,
One who will cost his Empire a high price:
They will say that from the sort of people who surround him
He is to be found less prince than butcher.

☞ 61. The miserable unhappy republic
Will be ruined by the new magistrate:
Their great accumulation in wicked exile
Will cause the "Suevi"[2] to tear up their great contract.

62. Alas! What a great loss will letters suffer,
Before the cycle of Latona[3] is completed:
Fire, great deluge more through ignorant rulers
Than will be seen made up for a long time.

☞ 63. The scourges passed the world shrinks,
For a long time peace and populated lands:
One will travel safely by air, land, sea and wave,
Then the wars stirred up anew.

☞ 64. They will think they have seen the Sun at night
When they will see the pig half-man:
Noise, song, battle, fighting in the sky perceived,
And one will hear brute beasts talking.

[1]Or "Venice"? See note 1, opposite, and Commentary.
[2]The Swiss, whose name Nostradamus derives from the Suevi (Swabians), ancestors of the German Swiss.
[3]The moon, by dubious mythology. See Commentary.

65. Enfant sans mains jamais vu si grand foudre:
    L'enfant Royal au jeu d'éteuf blessé.
    Au *puy*[1] *brises*:[2] *fulgures*[3] allant moudre:
    Trois sous les *chaines*[4] par le milieu troussés.

66. Celui qui lors portera les nouvelles,
    Après un peu il viendra respirer.
    *Viviers, Tournon, Montferrant* et *Pradelles,*
    Grêle et tempêtes les fera soupirer.

67. La grande famine que je sens approcher,
    Souvent tourner, puis être universelle,
    Si grande et longue qu'on viendra arracher
    Du bois racine, et l'enfant de mamelle.

68. O quel horrible et malheureux tourment,
    Trois innocents qu'on viendra à livrer.
    Poison suspecte, mal gardé *tradiment:*[5]
    Mis en horreur par bourreaux enivrés.

69. La grande montagne ronde de sept stades,
    Après paix, guerre, faim, inondation,
    Roulera loin abîmant grands *contrades,*[6]
    Mêmes antiques, et grande fondation.

70. Pluie, faim, guerre en *Perse* non cessée,
    La foi trop grande trahira le monarque,
    Par la finie en *Gaule* commencée:
    Secret augure pour à un être *parque.*[7]

71. La tour marine trois fois prise et reprise
    Par *Espagnols, Barbares, Ligurins:*
    *Marseille* et *Aix, Arles* par ceux de *Pise,*
    *Vast,*[8] feu, fer, pillé *Avignon* des *Thurins.*

[1] O.F. *puy,* summit, hill (Saint-Palaye).
[2] O.F. *brises,* breaking, fracture (Godefroy).
[3] Latin *fulgur,* lightning.
[4] O.F. *chaine,* oak (Saint-Palaye). Now *chêne.* However, possibly "chain."
[5] O.F. *tradiment,* betrayal, treason.
[6] Provençal *contrada,* country (Raynouard).
[7] Latin *parcus,* sparing, moderate.
[8] Latin *vastus,* devastated.

☞ 65. Child without hands never was so great a thunderbolt seen:
The royal child wounded at the game of tennis.
On the hill fractures: lightning going to grind:
Three under the oaks[1] trussed up in the middle.

66. He who then will bear the news,
He will shortly after come to rest.
Viviers, Tournon, Montferrand[2] and Pradelles,
Hail and storms will make them sigh.

67. The great famine that I sense approaching,
Often turning, then becoming universal,
So great and long that one will come to pull out
Roots from woods, and babe from breast.

☞ 68. Oh, what a horrible and miserable torment,
Three innocent ones whom one will come to deliver.
Poison suspected, poorly guarded betrayal:
Delivered to horror by drunken executioners.

☞ 69. The great round mountain of seven stades,[3]
After peace, war, famine, flood,
It will roll far sinking great countries,
Even the ancient ones, and of great foundation.

70. Rain, famine, war in Persia not over,
The too great faith will betray the monarch,
Finished there begun in Gaul:
Secret sign for one to be moderate.

71. The marine tower thrice taken and retaken
By Spaniards, Barbarians and Ligurians:[4]
Marseilles and Aix, Arles by those of Pisa.
Devastation, fire, sword, Avignon pillaged by Turinese.

[1]Or "chains."

[2]Montferrand was joined to Clermont in 1731 to form Clermont-Ferrand.

[3]A stade is 606 feet 9 inches, so seven stades amount to 4,247 feet 3 inches. The reference is probably to Vesuvius. See Commentary.

[4]Genoese. The boundaries of the Genoese Republic roughly coincided with those of the ancient Ligurians, and in fact now form the boundaries of the Ligurian province of Italy.

72. Du tout *Marseille* des habitants changée,
    Course et poursuite jusqu'auprès de *Lyon*.
    *Narbonne, Tholouse* par *Bourdeaux* outragée:
    Tués captifs presque d'un million.

73. *France* à cinq parts par *neglect*[1] assaillie,
    *Tunis, Argiels*[2] émus par *Persiens:*
    *Leon, Seville, Barcelone* faillie,
    N'aura la *classe*[3] par les *Venitiens.*

74. Après séjourné vagueront en *Epire:*
    Le grand secours viendra vers *Antioche,*
    Le noir poil crêpe tendra[4] fort à l'Empire:
    Barbe d'airain le rôtira en broche.

75. Le tyran *Sienne* occupera *Savone:*
    Le fort gagné tiendra *classe*[3] marine:
    Les deux armées par la marche d'*Ancone,*
    Par *effrayeur*[5] le chef s'en examine.

76. D'un nom farouche tel proféré sera,
    Que les trois sœurs auront *fato*[6] le nom:
    Puis grand peuple par langue et fait *duira,*[7]
    Plus que nul autre aura bruit et renom.

77. Entre deux mers dressera promontoire
    Que puis mourra par le *mors*[8] du cheval:
    Le sien[9] *Neptune* pliera voile noire,
    Par *Calpre*[10] et *classe*[3] auprès de *Rocheval.*

78. D'un chef vieillard naîtra sens hébété,
    Dégénérant par savoir et par armes:
    Le chef de *France* par sa sœur redouté,
    Champs divisés, concédés aux gendarmes.

[1]Latin *neglectus,* neglect.
[2]Misprint or anagram for *Alger.* Variants: *Argal* (1605), *Argils* (Fortune), *Argel* (1643).
[3]Latin *classis,* fleet.
[4]Variant: *rendra.*
[5]O.F. *effrayeur,* terror (Godefroy).
[6]Latin *fatum,* fate, destiny (dative case).
[7]O.F. *duire,* to lead, govern.
[8]O.F. *mors,* bite (Godefroy). Now, *morsure.*
[9]Although uniform in all editions, probably a misreading of *fier,* as per Garencières' text.
[10]*Calpe,* the classical name for Gibraltar (before the Arab conquest).

72. The inhabitants of Marseilles completely changed,
    Flight and pursuit up to near Lyons.
    Narbonne, Toulouse wronged by Bordeaux:
    Killed and captives nearly a million.

73. France because of negligence assailed on five sides,
    Tunis, Algiers stirred up by Persians:
    Leon, Seville, Barcelona having failed,
    For[1] the Venetians there will be no fleet.

74. After having tarried they will wander into Epirus:
    The great relief will come towards Antioch,
    The black frizzled hair[2] will strive strongly[3] for the Empire:
    Bronzebeard will roast him on a spit.

75. The tyrant of Siena will occupy Savona:
    The fort won he will hold the marine fleet:
    The two armies for the march of Ancona,
    Because of terror the chief examines his conscience about it.

76. With a name so wild will he be brought forth
    That the three sisters will have the name for destiny:
    Then he will lead a great people by tongue and deed,
    More than any other will he have fame and renown.

77. Between two seas he will erect a promontory
    He who will then die by the bite of a horse:
    The proud[4] Neptune will fold the black sail,
    Through Gibraltar and the fleet near "Rocheval."[5]

78. He[6] will be born of an old chief with dulled senses,
    Degenerating in knowledge and in arms:
    The chief of France feared by his sister,
    Fields divided, granted to the troops.

---

[1] Or possibly "From."
[2] Or "The frizzle-haired king," *noir* often being an anagram for *roi* (*roy*).
[3] Or "will make a considerable restoration."
[4] Or "His own," following the uniform reading in our basic texts.
[5] One of the few still-unsolved place names. Le Pelletier calls it "Cape Roche, near Gibraltar," which is two thirds of the way towards Cadiz. It would also be an anagram for *La Roche*, the Rock.
[6] Or "It."

79. *Bazaz, Lectore, Condon, Ausch, Agine*
    Emus par lois, querelle et monopole:
    Car[1] *Bourd Tholouse Bay.* mettra en ruine:
    Renouveler voulant leur *tauropole.*[2]

80. De la sixième claire splendeur céleste
    Viendra tonner si fort en la *Bourgongne:*
    Puis naîtra monstre de très hideuse bête.
    Mars, Avril, Mai, Juin grand *charpin*[3] et rogne.

81. D'humain troupeau neuf seront mis à part,
    De jugement et conseil séparés:
    Leur sort sera divisé en départ,
    *Kappa,*[4] *Thita,*[5] *Lambda,*[6] *mors*[7] bannis égarés.

82. Quand les colonnes de bois grand tremblée,
    D'*Auster*[8] conduite, couverte de *rubriche:*[9]
    Tant videra dehors grande assemblée,
    Trembler *Vienne* et le pays d'*Austriche.*

83. La gent étrange divisera butins,
    Saturne en Mars son regard furieux:
    Horrible *strage*[10] aux *Toscans* et *Latins,*
    *Grecs,* qui seront à frapper curieux.

84. Lune obscurcie aux profondes ténèbres,
    Son frère passe de couleur *ferrugine:*[11]
    Le grand caché longtemps sous les *latebres,*[12]
    Tiédira fer dans la plaie sanguine.

85. Par la réponse de dame, Roi troublé:
    Ambassadeurs mépriseront leur vie:
    Le grand ses frères contrefera doublé,
    Par deux mourront ire, haine et envie.

---

[1]Possibly *Car* for Carcassonne.
[2]Latin *taurobolium*, sacrifice of a bull.
[3]O.F. *charpin* or *charpi*, the rags used to dress wounds. Derived from Latin *carpere*, to tear.
[4]Greek *Kappa*, tenth letter of the Greek alphabet.
[5]Greek *Theta*, eighth letter of the Greek alphabet.
[6]Greek *Lambda*, eleventh letter of the Greek alphabet.
[7]O.F. *mors*, death.
[8]Latin *Auster*, the south wind.
[9]O.F. spelling of *rubrique*, which would change rime.
[10]Latin *strages*, defeat, slaughter. Variant: *étrange*.
[11]Latin *ferruginus*, rusty-colored.
[12]Latin *latebra*, hiding place, retreat, eclipse. Variant: *ténèbres*.

79. Bazas, Lectoure, Condom, Auch, Agen
Moved by laws, quarrel and monopoly:
For[1] Bordeaux Toulouse Bayonne will[2] ruin:
Wishing to renew their bull-sacrifice.

80. From the sixth bright celestial splendor
It will come to thunder very fiercely in Burgundy:
Then of a very hideous beast will be born a monster.
March, April, May, June great tearing and clipping.

☞ 81. Nine will be set aside from the human flock,
Removed from judgment and counsel:
Their fate will be determined on departure,
K., Th., L., dead, banished, astray.

82. When the columns of wood trembling greatly,
Led by the South Wind, covered with red ochre:
A very great assembly will empty outside,
Vienna and the land of Austria will tremble.

83. The strange nation will divide spoils,
Saturn in Mars his aspect furious:
Horrible slaughter of[3] the Tuscans and Latins,
Greeks, who will desire to strike.

84. The Moon hidden in deep shadows,
Her brother passes with a rusty color:
The great one hidden for a long time under the eclipses,[4]
Iron will cool[5] in the bloody wound.

☞ 85. Because of the lady's reply, the King troubled:
Ambassadors will take their lives in their hands:
The great one doubly will imitate his brothers,
Two who will die through anger, hatred and envy.

[1] Or "Carcassonne."
[2] Or "it will."
[3] Or "Horrible and strange to."
[4] Or "hiding places," or "shadows."
[5] Or "He will cool his sword."

86. La grande Reine quand se verra vaincue,
    Fera excès de masculin courage:
    Sur cheval, fleuve passera toute nue,
    Suite par fer: à foi fera outrage.

87. *Ennosigée*[1] feu du centre de terre
    Fera trembler autour de cité neuve:
    Deux grands rochers longtemps feront la guerre,
    Puis *Arethuse* rougira nouveau fleuve.

88. Le divin mal surprendra le grand Prince
    Un peu devant aura femme épousée,
    Son appui et crédit à un coup viendra mince,
    Conseil mourra pour la tête rasée.

89. Tous ceux de *Ilerde*[2] seront dedans[3] *Moselle*,
    Mettant à mort tous ceux de *Loire* et *Seine*:
    Secours[4] marin viendra près d'haute *velle*[5]
    Quand *Espagnols* ouvrira toute veine.

90. *Bourdeaux, Poitiers,* au son de la campane,
    A grande *classe*[6] ira jusqu'à *l'Angon,*
    Contre *Gaulois* sera leur tramontane,
    Quand monstre hideux naîtra près de *Orgon.*

91. Les Dieux feront aux humains apparence,
    Ce qu'ils seront auteurs de grand *conflict:*[7]
    Avant ciel vu serein épée et lance,
    Que vers main gauche sera plus grand *afflict.*[8]

92. Sous un la paix partout sera *clamee,*[9]
    Mais non longtemps *pille*[10] et rébellion,
    Par refus ville, terre et mer entamée,
    Mort et captifs le tiers d'un million.

[1]Latin *Ennosigaeus,* the earthshaker, a surname of Neptune.
[2]Latin *Ilerda, Lerida,* city in Spain.
[3]Variant: *Iler ne seront dans la.*
[4]Variant: *Le cours.*
[5]Latin *vallum,* wall.
[6]Latin *classis,* fleet.
[7]O.F. *conflict,* conflict. Now *conflit..* Preserved for rime.
[8]Latin *afflictus,* cast down, affliction.
[9]O.F. *clamer,* to proclaim.
[10]O.F. *pille,* pillage.

☞ 86. The great Queen when she shall see herself vanquished
Will act with an excess of masculine courage:
On horseback, she will pass over the river entirely naked,
Pursued by the sword: it will mark an outrage to faith.

87. Volcanic fire from the center of the earth
Will cause trembling around the new city:[1]
Two great rocks will make war for a long time.
Then Arethusa[2] will redden a new river.

88. The divine sickness[3] will surprise the great Prince
Shortly before he will have married a woman,[4]
His support and credit will suddenly become slim,
Counsel will perish for the shaven head.

89. All those from Lerida will be in the Moselle,[5]
Putting to death all those from the Loire and Seine:
Marine relief[6] will come near the high wall
When the Spaniards open every vein.

90. Bordeaux, Poitiers at the sound of the tocsin,
With a great fleet one will go as far as Langon,
Their north wind[7] will be against the Gauls,
When a hideous monster will be born near Orgon.

91. The Gods will make it appear to the mortals
That they will be the authors of the great conflict:
Sword and lance before the sky is seen serene,
So that there will be a greater affliction towards the left hand.

92. Under one peace will be proclaimed everywhere,
But not long after pillage and rebellion,
Because of a refusal town, land and sea encroached upon,
Dead and captives one third of a million.

[1]Naples (Greek *Neapolis,* new city).
[2]Possibly Syracuse, near which is located the fountain of Arethusa.
[3]Epilepsy?
[4]Or "he will have a married woman."
[5]Or "from the Iler will not be in the Moselle."
[6]Or "The marine course."
[7]Or "north star."

93. Terre *Italique* près des monts tremblera,
    Lion et Coq non trop confédérés,
    En lieu de peur l'un l'autre s'aidera,
    Seul *Castulon*[1] et *Celtes*, modérés.

94. Au *port Selin*[2] le tyran mis à mort
    La liberté non pourtant recouvrée:
    Le nouveau *Mars* par *vindicte*[3] et *remort*,[4]
    Dame par force de frayeur honorée.

95. Devant moutier trouvé enfant besson
    D'héroïque sang de moine et *vetustique*:[5]
    Son bruit par secte langue et puissance son
    Qu'on dira fort élévé le *vopisque*.[6]

96. Celui qu'aura la charge de détruire
    Temples et sectes, changés par fantaisie:
    Plus aux rochers qu'aux vivants viendra nuire
    Par langue ornée d'oreilles *ressassie*.[7]

97. Ce que fer, flamme n'a su parachever,
    La douce langue au conseil viendra faire:
    Par repos, songe, le Roi fera rêver,
    Plus l'ennemi en feu, sang militaire.

98. Le chef qu'aura conduit peuple infini
    Loin de son ciel, de mœurs et langue étrange:
    Cinq mil en *Crete* et *Thessalie* fini,
    Le chef fuyant sauvé en marine grange.

99. Le grand monarque que fera compagnie
    Avec deux Rois unis par amitié:
    O quel soupir fera la grand *mesnie*,[8]
    Enfants *Narbon* à l'entour, quel pitié.

---

[1]Castulo, one of the great cities of Roman Spain. Now the village of Cazorla.
[2]Greek *selene*, moon or crescent.
[3]Latin *vindicta*, revenge.
[4]O.F. for *remords*, preserved for rime.
[5]Latin *vetustus*, ancient.
[6]Latin *vopiscus*, the healthy survivor of prematurely born twins.
[7]O.F. *ressassie*, dinning, din.
[8]O.F. *mesnie*, family, household, troop.

93. The land of Italy will tremble near the mountains,
    Lion and Cock not too well confederated,
    In place of fear[1] they will help each other,
    Only Castulo[2] and the Celts moderate.[3]

☞ 94. At "Port Selin"[4] the tyrant put to death
    Liberty nevertheless not recovered:
    The new Mars because of vengeance and remorse,
    The Lady honored through force of terror.

☞ 95. A twin child found before the monastery
    One of the ancient and heroic blood of a monk:
    His fame, renown and power through sect and tongue
    Such that one will say the perfect twin has been well raised.

96. He who will have charge of destroying
    Temples and sects, changed through fantasy:
    He will come to do more harm to rocks than to living people
    Because of the din in his ears of a polished tongue.

97. That which fire and sword did not know how to accomplish,
    The smooth tongue in council will come to achieve:
    Through repose, a dream, the King will be made to meditate,
    The enemy more in fire and military blood.

☞ 98. The chief who will have led an infinite people
    Far from skies of their own, of customs and tongue strange:
    Five thousand finished in Crete and Thessaly,
    The chief fleeing saved in a marine barn.

99. The great monarch who will make company
    With two Kings united by friendship:
    Oh, what a sigh will the great host make,
    Children around Narbonne, what a pity.

[1]Possibly "Because of fear."
[2]See note 1, opposite. Probably synecdoche for "Spain."
[3]Or "curbed."
[4]Probably Genoa, chief port of the crescent-shaped Republic of Genoa.

100.  Longtemps au ciel sera vu gris oiseau
      Auprès de *Dole*[1] et de *Toscane* terre:
      Tenant au bec un verdoyant rameau,
      Mourra tôt grand et finira la guerre.

[1]Possibly apheresis of *Mirandole*, Mirandola.

100. For a long time a gray bird will be seen in the sky
Near Dôle[1] and Tuscan land:
Holding in its beak a verdant sprig,
Soon the great one will die and the war will end.

[1] Or possibly Mirandola. See note opposite.

# Centurie II

1. Vers *Aquitaine* par *insuls*[1] *Britanniques*
   De par eux-mêmes grandes incursions.
   Pluies, gelées feront terroirs iniques,
   *Port Selyn*[2] fortes fera invasions.

2. La tête bleue fera la tête blanche
   Autant de mal que *France* a fait leur bien:
   Mort à l'antenne grand pendu sus la branche,
   Quand pris des siens le Roi dira combien.

3. Pour la chaleur solaire sus la mer
   De *Negrepont*[3] les poissons demi cuits:
   Les habitants les viendront entamer
   Quand *Rhod.* et *Gennes* leur faudra le biscuit.

4. Depuis *Monech*[4] jusqu'auprès de *Sicille*
   Toute la plage demeurera désolée:
   Il n'y aura faubourg, cité ni ville,
   Que par Barbares pillée soit et volée.

5. Qu'en[5] dans poisson, fer et lettre enfermée,
   Hors sortira qui puis fera la guerre,
   Aura par mer sa *classe*[6] bien ramée,
   Apparaissant près de *Latine* terre.

6. Auprès des portes et dedans deux cités
   Seront deux fléaux, et onc n'aperçu un tel,
   Faim dedans peste, de fer hors gens boutés,
   Crier secours au grand Dieu immortel.

7. Entre plusieurs aux îles déportés,
   L'un être né à deux dents en la gorge
   Mourront de faim les arbres *esbrotés*,[7]
   Pour eux neuf Roi, nouvel édit leur forge.

[1] Latin *insula*, island. Variant: *insultes*.
[2] Greek *selene*, moon or crescent.
[3] Negroponte, Venetian name for Euboea, their colony in Greece.
[4] Latin *Monoecus*, Monaco.
[5] Possibly Nostradamus' error for *Quand*, overlooked in the 16th-century proofreading
[6] Latin *classis*, fleet.
[7] O.F. *esbrouter*, to strip the leaves of.

# Century II

☞ 1. Towards Aquitaine by the British isles[1]
By these themselves great incursions.
Rains, frosts will make the soil uneven,
"Port Selyn"[2] will make mighty invasions.

2. The blue head will inflict upon the white head
As much evil as France has done them good:
Dead at the sail-yard the great one hung on the branch,
When seized by his own the King will say how much.

3. Because of the solar heat on the sea
Of Euboea the fishes half cooked:
The inhabitants will come to cut them,
When the biscuit will fail Rhodes and Genoa.

☞ 4. From Monaco to near Sicily
The entire coast will remain desolated:
There will remain there no suburb, city or town
Not pillaged and robbed by the Barbarians.

5. That which is enclosed in iron and letter in a fish,[3]
Out will go one who will then make war,
He will have his fleet well rowed by sea,
Appearing near Latin land.

6. Near the gates and within two cities
There will be two scourges the like of which was never seen,
Famine within plague, people put out by steel,
Crying to the great immortal God for relief.

7. Amongst several transported to the isles,
One to be born with two teeth in his mouth
They will die of famine the trees stripped,
For them a new King issues a new edict.

---

[1] Or "insults."

[2] Genoa, chief port of the crescent-shaped republic of Genoa.

[3] 'Garencières' logical correction would make it, "When iron and letter is enclosed in a fish" (with the verb ending not agreeing). This might also allow a conjunction, e.g., "When Mars and Mercury are conjoined in Pisces." See Commentary.

8.  Temples sacrés *prime*[1] façon *Romaine*,
    Rejeteront les *goffes*[2] fondements,
    Prenant leur lois premières et humaines,
    Chassant, non tout, des saints les *cultements*.[3]

9.  Neuf ans le regne le maigre en paix tiendra,
    Puis il *cherra*[4] en soif si sanguinaire:
    Pour lui grand peuple sans foi et loi mourra
    Tué par un beaucoup plus débonnaire.

10. Avant longtemps le tout sera rangé,
    Nous espérons un siècle bien sénestre,
    L'état des masques et des seuls bien changé,
    Peu trouveront qu'à son rang veuille être.

11. Le prochain fils de l'*aisnier*[5] parviendra
    Tant élevé jusqu'au regne des *fors:*[6]
    Son âpre gloire un chacun la craindra,
    Mais ses enfants du regne jetés hors.

12. Yeux closes, ouverts d'antique fantaisie,
    L'habit des seuls seront mis à néant:
    Le grand monarque châtiera leur frénésie,
    Ravir des temples le trésor par devant.

13. Le corps sans âme plus n'être en sacrifice:
    Jour de la mort mis en nativité:
    L'esprit divin fera l'âme félice,
    Voyant le verbe en son éternité.

14. À *Tours, Gien,*[7] gardé seront yeux pénétrants,
    Découvriront de loin la grande sereine:
    Elle et sa suite au port seront entrants,
    Combat, poussés, puissance souveraine.

---

[1]Latin *primus*, first.
[2]O.F. *goffe*, fat, rude, disorderly, unmannerly.
[3]A purely Nostradamian elaboration of *culte*.
[4]O.F. *choir*, to fall. Future tense.
[5]Either *l'aîné* or *l'Aisnier* (*l'Aisné*). See Commentary on the latter.
[6]O.F. *fors*, privileges.
[7]Variant: A. *Tours. Iean.*

☞ 8. Temples consecrated in the original Roman manner,
They will reject the excess[1] foundations,
Taking their first and humane laws,
Chasing, though not entirely, the cult of saints.

☞ 9. Nine years the lean one[2] will hold the realm in peace,
Then he will fall into a very bloody thirst:
Because of him a great people will die without faith and law
Killed by one far more good-natured.

10. Before long all will be set in order,
We will expect a very sinister century,
The state[3] of the masked and solitary ones much changed,
Few will be found who want to be in their place.

11. The nearest[4] son of the elder[5] will attain
Very great height as far as the realm of the privileged:[6]
Everyone will fear his fierce glory,
But his children will be thrown out of the realm.

12. Eyes closed, opened by antique fantasy,
The garb of the monks they will be put to naught:
The great monarch will chastise their frenzy,
Ravishing the treasure in front of the temples.

13. The body without soul no longer to be sacrificed:
Day of death put for birthday:
The divine spirit will make the soul happy,
Seeing the word in its eternity.

14. At Tours, Gien, guarded, eyes will be searching,
Discovering from afar her serene Highness:[7]
She and her suite will enter the port,
Combat, thrust, sovereign power.

[1]The proper translation here is difficult to determine. See note 2, opposite.
[2]Or "vegetarian."
[3]Or "estate."
[4]Or "next," thus, either "elder" or "younger" or "favorite."
[5]Or "of L'Aisnier." See Commentary.
[6]Possibly Poland. See Commentary.
[7]Literally "the great serene [lady]."

15. Un peu devant monarque *trucidé*,[1]
    *Castor Pollux* en nef, astre *crinite*:[2]
    *L'erain*[3] publique par terre et mer vidé,
    *Pise, Ast, Ferrare, Turin* terre interdite.

16. *Naples, Palerme, Sicile, Syracuses,*
    Nouveaux tyrans, *fulgures*[4] feux célestes:
    Force de *Londres, Gand, Bruxelles* et *Suses,*
    Grand hécatombe, triomphe faire *festes.*[5]

17. Le champ du temple de la vierge vestale,
    Non éloigné d'*Ethne*[6] et monts *Pyrénées:*
    Le grand conduit est caché dans la malle,
    *North*[7] jetés fleuves et vignes mâtinées.

18. Nouvelle et pluie subite, impétueuse
    Empêchera subit deux *exercites.*[8]
    Pierre ciel, feux faire la mer pierreuse,
    La mort de sept terre et marin subites.

19. Nouveaux venus, lieu bâti sans défense,
    Occuper place par lors inhabitable:
    Prés, maisons, champs, villes prendre à plaisance,
    Faim, peste, guerre, arpent long labourable.

20. Frères et sœurs en divers lieux captifs
    Se trouveront passer près du monarque:
    Les contempler ses rameaux[9] attentifs,
    Déplaisant voir menton, front, nez, les marques.

21. L'ambassadeur envoyé par birèmes,
    A mi-chemin d'inconnus repoussé:
    De sel renfort viendront quatre trirèmes,
    Cordes et chaînes en *Négrepont*[10] troussé.

---

[1] Latin *trucidare,* to butcher, slaughter.
[2] Latin *crinitus,* bearded.
[3] Latin *eranus,* a fund contributed for mutual protection against want.
[4] Latin *fulgur,* lightning.
[5] O.F. for *fêtes,* preserved for rime.
[6] Can't be Etna in Italy. Possibly anagram for "Elne."
[7] Variant: *North.* (period). Probably O.F. for *nord* but possibly proper or enigmatic name.
[8] Latin *exercitus,* army.
[9] Though uniform in all our basic texts, this appears in Garencières' (and thus in Roberts') text as *deux yeux,* two eyes.
[10] *Negroponte,* Venetian name for Euboea, their colony in Greece.

☞ 15. Shortly before the monarch is assassinated,
Castor and Pollux in the ship,[1] bearded star:[2]
The public treasure emptied by land and sea,
Pisa, Asti, Ferrara, Turin land under interdict.

☞ 16. Naples, Palermo, Sicily, Syracuse,
New tyrants, celestial lightning fires:
Force from London, Ghent, Brussels and Susa,
Great slaughter, triumph leads to festivities.

17. The field of the temple of the vestal virgin,
Not far from Elne[3] and the Pyrenees mountains:
The great tube[4] is hidden in the trunk,
To the north[5] rivers overflown and vines battered.

18. New, impetuous and sudden rain
Will suddenly halt two armies.
Celestial stone, fires make the sea stony,
The death of seven by land and sea sudden.

19. Newcomers, place built without defense,
Place occupied then uninhabitable:
Meadows, houses, fields, towns to take at pleasure,
Famine, plague, war, extensive land arable.

20. Brothers and sisters captive in diverse places
Will find themselves passing near the monarch:
Contemplating them his branches[6] attentive,
Displeasing to see the marks on chin, forehead and nose.

21. The ambassador sent by biremes,
Halfway repelled by unknown ones:
Reinforced with salt four triremes will come,
In Euboea bound with ropes and chains.

[1] Possibly "Gemini in Argo."
[2] Comet.
[3] The nearest possibility. See note 6, opposite.
[4] Or "The great one led."
[5] Subject to some doubt. Enigmatic name "North"? See note 7, opposite.
[6] Offspring? Relations?

22. Le camp *Ascop*[1] d'*Europe*[2] partira,
    S'adjoignant proche de l'île submergée:
    D'*Araon*[3] *classe*[4] phalange pliera,
    Nombril du monde plus grande voix *subrogee*.[5]

23. Palais, oiseaux, par oiseau déchassé,
    Bien tôt après le prince parvenu:
    Combien que[6] hors fleuve ennemi repoussé,
    Dehors saisir trait d'oiseau soutenu.

24. Bêtes farouches de faim fleuves *tranner:*[7]
    Plus part du champ[8] encontre *Hister* sera,
    En cage de fer le grand fera traîner,
    Quand rien[9] enfant de *Germain* observera.

25. La garde étrange trahira forteresse,
    Espoir et ombre de plus haut mariage:
    Garde *décue*,[10] fort prise dans la presse,
    *Loire, Saone, Rosne, Gar.* à mort outrage.

26. Pour la faveur que la cité fera
    Au grand qui tôt perdra champ de bataille,
    Fuis[11] le rang *Pau, Tessin* versera
    De sang, feux, morts, noyés de coup de taille.

27. Le divin verbe sera du ciel frappé,
    Qui ne pourra procéder plus avant:
    Du *reserant*[12] le secret étoupé,
    Qu'on marchera par dessus et devant.[13]

[1]Greek *askopos*, (1) aimless, or (2) obscure, or (3) incredible, or (4) imprudent or unseeing. Variant: *Asop*. Greek *Asopos*, (1) Euboea or (2) Boeotia (Thebes).
[2]Variant: *Eurotte*. Probably Eurotas River, on whose banks lay Sparta.
[3]Greek *araios*, (1) thin, weak, or (2) accursed. Variant: *D'Arton*. Greek *artos*, bread.
[4]Latin *classis*, fleet.
[5]Latin *subrogatus*, substituted.
[6]O.F. *combien que*, although.
[7]Latin *tranare*, to swim across.
[8]Variant: *camp*.
[9]Variant: *Rin*.
[10]Possibly Latin *decisus*, cut down.
[11]Variant: *Puis*.
[12]Latin *reserare*, to unlock, reveal.
[13]Says Le Pelletier (p. 45): "A man of whom one can say 'qu'on marchera par dessus et devant' is one who is found chained to the wall of the bottom of a dungeon . . . or buried at the foot of a wall."

☞ 22. The imprudent[1] army of[2] Europe[3] will depart,
Collecting itself near the submerged isle:
The weak[4] fleet[5] will bend the phalanx,[6]
At the navel of the world[7] a greater voice substituted.

23. Palace birds, chased out by a bird,
Very soon after the prince has arrived:[8]
Although the enemy is repelled beyond the river,
Outside seized the trick[9] upheld by the bird.

☞ 24. Beasts ferocious from hunger will swim across rivers:
The greater part of the region[10] will be against the Hister,[11]
The great one will cause it[12] to be dragged in an iron cage,
When the German[13] child will observe nothing.[14]

25. The foreign guard will betray the fortress,
Hope and shadow of a higher marriage:
Guard deceived,[15] fort seized in the press,
Loire, Saône, Rhône, Garonne, mortal outrage.

26. Because of the favor that the city will show
To the great one who will soon lose the field of battle,
Fleeing[16] the Po position, the Ticino will overflow
With blood, fires, deaths, drowned by the long-edged blow.

27. The divine word[17] will be struck from the sky,
One who cannot proceed any further:
The secret closed up with the revelation,[18]
Such that they will march over and ahead.[19]

[1]Or "invisible," or "aimless," or "incredible." Or, by variant, (1) "Euboean" or (2) "Theban."
[2]Or "from."
[3]Or "Sparta."
[4]Or "accursed."
[5]Or "fleet of bread."
[6]Or vice versa, in true Delphic style.
[7]Rome, in all probability.
[8]Or "upstart prince."
[9]Or "shaft." "Shaft upheld by a bird" would be an arrow (Le Pelletier).
[10]Or "army."
[11]The Lower Danube, in Roman geography. Or "against 'Hister'" (enigmatic name).
[12]Or "him."
[13]Or "the german's," i.e., first cousin's.
[14]Or "the Rhine."
[15]Or "cut down."
[16]Or "Then into."
[17]Or "theologian." See Commentary.
[18]Or "with its revealer."
[19]See note 13, opposite.

28. Le pénultième du surnom du Prophète
    Prendra *Diane* pour son jour et repos:
    Loin vaguera par frénétique tête,
    Et[1] délivrant un grand peuple d'*impos*.[2]

29. L'Oriental sortira de son siège,
    Passer les monts *Apennins* voir la *Gaule:*
    Transpercera le ciel, les eaux et neige,
    Et un chacun frappera de sa gaule.

30. Un qui les dieux d'*Annibal* infernaux
    Fera renaître, *effrayeur*[3] des humains
    Onc plus d'horreur ni plus pire journaux
    Qu'avint viendra par *Babel* aux *Romains*.

31. En *Campanie Cassilin*[4] fera tant
    Qu'on ne verra que d'eaux les champs couverts:
    Devant après la pluie de longtemps
    Hormis les arbres rien l'on verra de vert.

32. Lait, sang grenouilles *escoudre*[5] en *Dalmatie*.
    Conflit donné, peste près de *Balenne:*[6]
    Cri sera grand par toute *Esclavonie*,
    Lors naîtra monstre près et dedans *Ravenne*.

33. Par le torrent qui descend de *Verone*
    Par lors qu'au *Pau* guidera son entrée,
    Un grand naufrage, et non moins en *Garonne*,
    Quand ceux de *Gennes* marcheront leur contrée.

34. L'ire insensée du combat furieux
    Fera à table par frères le fer luire:
    Les départir mort,[7] blessé et curieux,
    Le fier duel viendra en *France* nuire.

---

[1]Variant: *En.*

[2]O.F. *impost*, taxes (now *impôt*). Latin *impos*, not one's own master, powerless, subject.

[3]O.F. *effrayeur*, terror.

[4]Variant: *le Cassilin*. Latin *Casilinum*, a town on the Volturno River near ancient Capua, on whose ruins modern Capua was built. However, the context points to the Volturno River, perhaps as *[fleuve] Cassilin*.

[5]Latin *excudere*, to forge, prepare, compose.

[6]Apparently from Latin *[Trebula] Balliensis*, Treglia, northeast of Capua.

[7]Variant: *Les départir* (*mort* omitted).

☞ 28. The penultimate of the surname of the Prophet
    Will take Diana for his day and rest:[1]
    He will wander far because of a frantic head,
    And[2] delivering a great people from subjection.[3]

☞ 29. The Easterner will leave his seat,
    To pass the Apennine mountains to see Gaul:
    He will transpierce the sky, the waters and the snow,
    And everyone will be struck with his rod.

☞ 30. One who the infernal gods of Hannibal
    Will cause to be reborn, terror of mankind
    Never more horror nor worse of days[4]
    In the past than will come to the Romans through Babel.

31. In Campania the Capuan [river][5] will do so much
    That one will see only fields covered by waters:
    Before and after the long rain
    One will see nothing green except the trees.

32. Milk, frog's blood prepared in Dalmatia.
    Conflict given, plague near Treglia:[6]
    A great cry will sound through all Slavonia,
    Then a monster will be born near and within Ravenna.

33. Through the torrent which descends from Verona
    Its[7] entry will then be guided to the Po,
    A great wreck, and no less in the Garonne,
    When those of Genoa march against their country.

34. The senseless ire of the furious combat
    Will cause steel to be flashed at the table by brothers:
    To part them death, wound,[8] and curiously,
    The proud duel will come to harm France.

[1]I.e., will make Monday his Sabbath. See Commentary.
[2]Or "In."
[3]Or "taxation."
[4]Or "newspapers," according to Le Pelletier. See Commentary.
[5]The Volturno River. See note opposite.
[6]Not certain. See note opposite.
[7]Or "His."
[8]Or "To part them a wound" (no "death").

35. Dans deux logis de nuit le feu prendra,
    Plusieurs dedans étouffés et rôtis.
    Près de deux fleuves pour seul[1] il aviendra:
    *Sol,*[2] *L'Arq,*[3] et *Caper*[4] tous seront amortis.

36. Du grand Prophète les lettres seront prises,
    Entre les mains du tyran deviendront:
    Frauder son Roi seront ses entreprises,
    Mais ses rapines bien tôt le troubleront.

37. De ce grand nombre que l'on envoyera
    Pour secourir dans le fort assiégés,
    Peste et famine tous les dévorera,
    Hormis septante qui seront *profligés.*[5]

38. Des condamnés sera fait un grand nombre
    Quand les monarques seront conciliés:
    Mais à l'un d'eux viendra si mal encombre
    Que guère ensemble ne seront ralliés.

39. Un an devant le conflit *Italique,*
    *Germains, Gaulois, Espagnols* pour le fort:
    Cherra[6] l'école maison de république,
    Où, hormis peu, seront suffoqués morts.

40. Un peu après non point longue intervalle,
    Par mer et terre sera fait grand tumulte:
    Beaucoup plus grande sera *pugne*[7] navale,
    Feux, animaux, qui plus feront d'insulte.

41. La grande étoile par sept jours brûlera,
    Nuée fera deux soleils apparoir:
    Le gros mâtin toute nuit hurlera
    Quand grand pontife changera de terroir.

[1]Variant: *seur (sûr).*
[2]Latin *Sol,* Sun.
[3]Latin *Arquitenens,* or Sagittarius the Archer.
[4]Latin *Caper-cornu* or *Capricornus,* the constellation of Capricorn.
[5]Latin *profligare,* to overwhelm, ruin, destroy.
[6]O.F. *choir,* to fall. Future tense.
[7]Latin *pugna,* battle.

35. The fire by night will take hold in two lodgings,
    Several within suffocated and roasted.
    It will happen near two rivers as one:[1]
    Sun, Sagittarius and Capricorn all will be reduced.

☞ 36. The letters of the great Prophet will be seized,
    They will come to fall into the hands of the tyrant:
    His[2] enterprises will be to deceive his King,
    But his extortions will very soon trouble him.

37. Of that great number that one will send
    To relieve those besieged in the fort,
    Plague and famine will devour them all,
    Except seventy who will be destroyed.

38. A great number will be condemned
    When the monarchs will be reconciled:
    But for one of them such a bad impediment will arise
    That they will be joined together but loosely.

☞ 39. One year before the Italian conflict,
    Germans, Gauls, Spaniards for the fort:
    The republican schoolhouse will fall,
    There, except for a few, they will be choked dead.

40. Shortly afterwards, without a very long interval,
    By sea and land a great uproar will be raised:
    Naval battle will be very much greater,
    Fires, animals, those who will cause greater insult.

☞ 41. The great star will burn for seven days,
    The cloud will cause two suns to appear:
    The big mastiff will howl all night
    When the great pontiff will change country.

[1]Or "near two rivers for sure."
[2]Assuredly the tyrant's, if "the great Prophet" is Nostradamus himself.

42. Coq, chiens et chats de sang seront repus,
    Et de la plaie du tyran trouvé mort,
    Au lit d'un autre jambes et bras rompus,
    Qui n'avait peur mourir de cruelle mort.

43. Durant l'étoile chevelue apparente,
    Les trois grands princes seront faits ennemis:
    Frappés du ciel, paix terre *tremulente*,[1]
    *Pau, Tymbre undans*,[2] serpent sur le bord mis.

44. L'Aigle poussée entour de pavillons
    Par autres oiseaux d'entour sera chassée:
    Quand bruit des *cymbres*,[3] *tubes*[4] et sonnaillons
    Rendront le sens de la dame insensée.

45. Trop le ciel pleure l'Androgyne procrée,
    Près du ciel sang humain répandu:
    Par mort trop tard grand peuple recréé,
    Tard et tôt vient le secours attendu.

46. Après grand trouble[5] humain, plus grand s'apprête
    Le grand moteur les siècles renouvèle:
    Pluie, sang, lait, famine, fer et peste,
    Au ciel vu feu, courant longue étincelle.

47. L'ennemi grand vieil deuil meurt de poison,
    Les souverains par infinis subjugués:
    Pierres pleuvoir, cachés sous la toison,
    Par mort articles en vain sont allégués.

48. La grande *copie*[6] qui passera les monts.
    *Saturne* en l'*Arq*[7] tournant du poisson *Mars:*
    Venins cachés sous têtes de saumons,
    Leur chef pendu à fil de *polemars*.[8]

---

[1] O.F. *tremulente*, trembling (Godefroy).
[2] Latin *undare*, to surge, overflow, inundate.
[3] O.F. *cymble*, cymbal. Metathesis.
[4] Latin *tuba*, trumpet.
[5] Variant (in all since 1555): *troche*, apparently from Greek *trukos*, misery. Nostradamus' revision?
[6] Latin *copia*, troops, army, force.
[7] Latin *Arquitenens*, Sagittarius.
[8] Greek *polemarchos*, one who leads the war.

42. Cock, dogs and cats will be satiated with blood
    And from the wound of the tyrant found dead,
    At the bed of another legs and arms broken,
    He who was not afraid to die a cruel death.

43. During the appearance of the bearded star,[1]
    The three great princes will be made enemies:
    Struck from the sky, peace earth quaking,
    Po,[2] Tiber overflowing, serpent placed upon the shore.

44. The Eagle[3] driven back around the tents
    Will be chased from there by other birds:
    When the noise of cymbals, trumpets and bells
    Will restore the senses of the senseless lady.

☞ 45. Too much the heavens weep for the Hermaphrodite begotten,
    Near the heavens human blood shed:
    Because of death too late a great people re-created,
    Late and soon the awaited relief comes.

46. After great trouble for humanity, a greater one is prepared
    The Great Mover renews the ages:
    Rain, blood, milk, famine, steel and plague,
    In the heavens fire seen, a long spark running.

47. The great old enemy mourning dies of poison,
    The sovereigns subjugated in infinite numbers:
    Stones raining, hidden under the fleece,
    Through death articles are cited in vain.

☞ 48. The great force which will pass the mountains.
    Saturn in Sagittarius Mars turning from the fish:[4]
    Poison hidden under the heads of salmon,
    Their war-chief hung with cord.

[1]Comet.
[2]Translated as "Arno" for a good reason in 1672 but for no reason in 1947. See Commentary.
[3]In the feminine, as used here, a military standard.
[4]Pisces. Supposedly either July 17, 1751, or July 13, 2193. See Commentary.

49. Les conseillers du premier monopole,
    Les conquérants séduits pour la *Melite:*[1]
    *Rodes, Bisance* pour leurs exposant pole:
    Terre faudra les poursuivants de fuite.

50. Quand ceux d'*Hainault,* de *Gand* et de *Bruxelles*
    Verront à *Langres* le siège devant mis:
    Derrière leurs flancs seront guerres cruelles,
    La plaie antique fera pis qu'ennemis.

51. Le sang du juste à *Londres* fera faute,
    Brûlés par foudres de vingt trois les six:
    La dame antique cherra de place haute,
    De même secte plusieurs seront occis.

52. Dans plusieurs nuits la terre tremblera:
    Sur le printemps deux efforts suite:
    *Corinthe, Ephese* aux deux mers nagera:
    Guerre s'émeut par deux vaillants de *luite.*[2]

53. La grande peste de cité maritime
    Ne cessera que mort ne soit vengée
    Du juste sang, par prix damné sans crime
    De la grande dame par feinte n'outragée.

54. Par gent étrange, et de *Romains* lointaine
    Leur grande cité après eau fort troublée:
    Fille sans main, trop different domaine,
    Pris chef, serrure[3] n'avoir été *riblée.*[4]

55. Dans le conflit le grand qui peu valait
    A son dernier fera cas merveilleux:
    Pendant qu'*Hadrie* verra ce qu'il fallait,
    Dans le banquet *pongnale*[5] l'orgueilleux.

[1] Latin *Melita,* Malta.
[2] O.F. *luite,* contest, combat. Now *lutte.* Preserved for rime.
[3] Variant: *ferrure.*
[4] O.F. *ribler,* to lead a wild life, rob, pillage, forage.
[5] O.F. *pongnal,* dagger (Godefroy).

49. The advisers of the first monopoly,
    The conquerors seduced for Malta:
    Rhodes, Byzantium for them exposing their pole:
    Land will fail the pursuers in flight.

50. When those of Hainaut, of Ghent and of Brussels
    Will see the siege laid before Langres:
    Behind their flanks there will be cruel wars,
    The ancient wound will do worse than enemies.

☞ 51. The blood of the just will commit a fault at London,
    Burnt through lightning of twenty threes the six:
    The ancient lady will fall from her high place,
    Several of the same sect will be killed.

52. For several nights the earth will tremble:
    In the spring two efforts in succession:
    Corinth, Ephesus will swim in the two seas:
    War stirred up by two valiant in combat.

☞ 53. The great plague of the maritime city
    Will not cease until there be avenged the death
    Of the just blood, condemned for a price without crime,
    Of[1] the great lady unwronged by pretense.

54. Because of people strange, and distant from the Romans
    Their great city much troubled after water:
    Daughter handless, domain too different,
    Chief taken, lock not having been picked.[2]

55. In the conflict the great one who was worth little
    At his end will perform a marvelous deed:
    While "Adria"[3] will see what he[4] was lacking,
    During the banquet the proud one stabbed.

[1]Or "By."
[2]Or "the ironwork not having been removed."
[3]Venice. See footnote to 18.
[4]Or "it."

56.  Que peste et glaive n'a su *definer*,[1]
     Mort dans le *puys*[2] sommet du ciel frappé:
     L'abbé mourra quand verra ruiner,
     Ceux du naufrage l'écueil voulant *grapper*.[3]

57.  Avant conflit le grand mur tombera,
     Le grand à mort, mort trop subite et plainte,
     Né imparfait: la plupart nagera:
     Auprès du fleuve de sang la terre teinte.

58.  Sans pied ni main par dent aiguë et forte
     Par *globe*[4] au fort de porc[5] et l'aîné né:
     Près du portail déloyal se transporte,
     *Silene*[6] luit, petit grand emmené.

59.  *Classe*[7] *Gauloise* par appui de grande garde
     Du grand *Neptune*, et ses tridents soldats,
     Rougée *Prouence* pour soutenir grande bande:
     Plus *Mars Narbon*, par javelots et dards.

60.  La foi *Punicque* en Orient rompue,
     *Gang*.[8] *Iud*, et *Rosne Loire*, et *Tag* changeront:
     Quand du mulet la faim sera repue,
     *Classe*[7] *espargie*,[9] sang et corps nageront.

61.  *Euge*,[10] *Tamins*,[11] *Gironde* et *la Rochelle*:
     O sang *Troien!* Mars au port de la flèche
     Derrière le fleuve au fort mise à l'échelle,
     Pointes à feu grand meurtre sus la brèche.

62.  *Mabus*[12] puis tôt alors mourra, viendra
     De gens et bêtes une horrible défaite:
     Puis tout à coup la vengeance on verra,
     Cent, main, soif, faim quand courra la comète.

[1]O.F. *definer*, to die, finish, determine.
[2]O.F. *puy*, mountain, hill.
[3]O.F. *grapper*, to seize.
[4]Latin *globus*, mass, crowd, throng.
[5]Variant: *port*.
[6]Greek *Selene*, moon.
[7]Latin *classis*, fleet.
[8]Variant: *Grand*. Another variant, in the 1589 Roger edition, is *Gand* (Ghent).
[9]O.F. *espargier*, to sprinkle, pour (Godefroy).
[10]Latin *Euge*, bravo! excellent!
[11]Possibly syncope of *Tamisiens*, those of the Thames.
[12]A still-unsolved anagram. See Commentary.

56. One whom neither plague nor steel knew how to finish,
    Death on the summit of the hills struck from the sky:
    The abbot will die when he will see ruined
    Those of the wreck wishing to seize the rock.

57. Before the conflict the great wall will fall,
    The great one to death, death too sudden and lamented,
    Born imperfect: the greater part will swim:
    Near the river the land stained with blood.

58. With neither foot nor hand because of sharp and strong tooth
    Through the crowd[1] to the fort of the pork[2] and the elder born:[3]
    Near the portal treacherous proceeds,
    Moon[4] shining, little great one led off.

59. Gallic fleet through support of the great guard
    Of the great Neptune, and his trident soldiers,
    Provence reddened to sustain a great band:
    More at Narbonne,[5] because of javelins and darts.

60. The Punic faith broken in the East,
    Ganges,[6] Jordan,[7] and Rhône, Loire, and Tagus will change:
    When the hunger of the mule will be satiated,
    Fleet sprinkles,[8] blood and bodies will swim.

61. Bravo, ye of "Tamins,"[9] Gironde and La Rochelle:
    O Trojan blood![10] Mars at the port of the arrow[11]
    Behind the river the ladder put to the fort,
    Points to fire great murder on the breach.

62. "Mabus"[12] then will soon die, there will come
    Of people and beasts a horrible rout:
    Then suddenly one will see vengeance,
    Hundred, hand, thirst, hunger when the comet will run.

[1]Or "Across the globe."
[2]Or "of the port."
[3]"The birthplace of the elder"?
[4]Or *Silene* may be an anagram. Indeed, *Selin* is the usual form for moon, when written thus (in Nostradamicized Greek).
[5]Possibly "Mars more at Narbonne," but Narbo-Martius was the proper Roman name for Narbonne.
[6]Or "Great."
[7]Not certain. Apparently the Judaean river, which would be the Jordan. Also possibly, "Great Jew."
[8]Or possibly "sprinkled."
[9]Enigmatic proper name, possibly "[men] of the Thames." See note opposite and Commentary.
[10]The Royal House of France, based on legend of descent from Francus, son of Priam, King of Troy.
[11]Toulon? See Commentary. There is also a town La Flèche, on the Loir (not Loire) R.
[12]A still-unsolved enigmatic proper name. See Commentary.

63. *Gaulois, Ausone* bien peu subjuguera,
    *Pau, Marne* et *Seine* fera *Perme*[1] l'*vrie:*[2]
    Qui le grand mur contre eux dressera,
    Du moindre au mur le grand perdra la vie.

64. Sécher de faim, de soif, gent *Geneuoise,*
    Espoir prochain viendra au défaillir:
    Sur point tremblant sera loi *Gebenoise,*[3]
    *Classe*[4] au grand port ne se peut accueillir.

65. Le parc enclin grande calamité
    Par l'*Hesperie* et *Insubre* fera:
    Le feu en nef peste et captivité,
    *Mercure* en l'*Arq*[5] *Saturne* fanera.

66. Par grands dangers le captif échappé:
    Peu de temps grand la[6] fortune changée.
    Dans le palais le peuple est attrapé,
    Par bon augure la cité assiégée.

67. Le blond au nez fourché viendra commettre
    Par le duel et chassera dehors:
    Les exilés dedans fera remettre,
    Aux lieux marins commettant les plus forts.

68. De l'*Aquilon*[7] les efforts seront grands:
    Sur l'Océan sera la porte ouverte,
    Le regne en l'Île sera *reintegrand:*[8]
    Tremblera *Londres* par voile découverte.

69. Le Roi *Gaulois* par la *Celtique* dextre
    Voyant discorde de la grande Monarchie:
    Sur les trois parts fera fleurir son sceptre,
    Contre la *cappe*[9] de la grande Hiérarchie.

---

[1]Presumably misprint or anagram for *Parme.*
[2]Possibly Latin *urere,* to burn, sting, consume. Or syncope of Latin *urinare,* to submerge in water. Or metathesis of *l'ivré.* Or a play on *Ivrea* in Piedmont or *Ivry* in France
[3]Latin *Gebenna,* the Cevennes mountain chain.
[4]Latin *classis,* fleet.
[5]Latin *Arquitenens,* Sagittarius.
[6]Variants: *a; à.*
[7]Latin *Aquilo,* north wind, north.
[8]O.F. *reintegrande,* the restoration of a lost possession.
[9]O.F. *cappe,* (1) cope (modern *chape*) or (2) cloak (modern *cape*).

☞ 63. The Gauls Ausonia[1] will subjugate very little,
Po, Marne and Seine Parma[2] will make drunk:[3]
He who will prepare the great wall against them,
He will lose his life from the least at the wall.

☞ 64. The people of Geneva drying up with hunger, with thirst,
Hope at hand will come to fail:
On the point of trembling will be the law of him of the Cevennes,
Fleet at the great port cannot be received.

65. The sloping park great calamity
To be done through Hesperia[4] and Insubria:[5]
The fire in the ship, plague and capitivity,
Mercury in Sagittarius Saturn will fade.

66. Through great dangers the captive escaped:
In a short time great his fortune changed.[6]
In the palace the people are trapped,
Through good omen the city besieged.

67. The blond one will come to compromise the fork-nosed one
Through the duel and will chase him out:
The exiles within he will have restored,
Committing the strongest to the marine places.

☞ 68. The efforts of "Aquilon"[7] will be great:
The gate[8] on the Ocean will be opened,
The kingdom on the Isle will be restored:
London will tremble discovered by sail.

☞ 69. The Gallic King through his Celtic right arm
Seeing the discord of the great Monarchy:
He will cause his sceptre to flourish over the three parts,
Against the cope[9] of the great Hierarchy.

---

[1]Poetic name for Italy, in particular southern Italy (in modern times the Kingdom of the Two Sicilies).
[2]Uncertain. See note 1, opposite.
[3]Or "will submerge," or "will burn." Or play on *Ivrea* or *Ivry*. See Commentary.
[4]The Land of the West. Spain? America?
[5]In Roman geography the area around Milan. Thus "the Milanese" or "Lombardy."
[6]Or "the great one has a change of fortune."
[7]The North[ern Country]. See Commentary for the various possibilities.
[8]Or perhaps "window."
[9]Or "cloak." Obviously the Pope.

70. Le dard du ciel fera son étendue,
    Morts en parlant: grande exécution.
    La pierre en l'arbre, la fière gent rendue,
    Bruit, humain monstre, purge expiation.

71. Les exilés en *Sicile* viendront
    Pour délivrer de faim la gent étrange:
    Au point du jour les *Celtes* lui faudront:
    La vie demeure à raison: Roi se range.

72. Armée *Celtique* en *Italie* vexée
    De toutes parts conflit et grande perte:
    *Romains* fuis, ô Gaule repoussée!
    Près du *Thesin*, *Rubicon* pugne[1] incerte.[2]

73. Au lac *Fucin* de *Benac*[3] le rivage,
    Pris de *Leman*[4] au port de *l'Orguion*:[5]
    Né de trois bras prédit *bellique*[6] image,
    Par trois couronnes au grand *Endymion*.

74. De *Sens*, d'*Autun* viendront jusqu'au *Rosne*
    Pour passer outre vers les monts *Pyrénées:*
    La gent sortir de la Marche d'*Anconne:*
    Par terre et mer suivra à grandes trainées.

75. La voix ouïe de l'insolite oiseau,
    Sur le canon du *respiral*[7] étage:
    Si haut viendra du froment le boisseau,
    Que l'homme d'homme sera Anthropophage.

76. Foudre en *Bourgongne* fera cas *portenteux*,[8]
    Que par engin onc ne pourrait faire,
    De leur sénat *sacriste*[9] fait boiteux
    Fera savoir aux ennemis l'affaire.

[1] Latin *pugna*, battle.
[2] Latin *incertus*, uncertain.
[3] Latin *Benacus*, Lake Garda.
[4] Latin *Lemannus*, Lake Geneva.
[5] Still unsolved place name, possibly Orgon in southern France or Orgiano in northern Italy.
[6] Latin *bellicus*, warlike.
[7] O.F. *respiral*, air vent.
[8] Latin *portentosus*, wonderful, revolting, portentous.
[9] O.F. *sacriste*, sexton. In modern French. *sacristain*.

70. The dart from the sky will make its extension,
    Deaths in speaking: great execution.
    The stone in the tree, the proud nation restored,[1]
    Noise, human monster, purge expiation.

71. The exiles will come into Sicily
    To deliver from hunger the strange nation:
    At daybreak the Celts will fail them:
    Life remains by reason: the King joins.

72. Celtic army vexed in Italy
    On all sides conflict and great loss:
    Romans fled, O Gaul repelled!
    Near the Ticino, Rubicon uncertain battle.

73. The shore of Lake Garda to Lake Fucino,[2]
    Taken from the Lake of Geneva to the port of "L'Orguion":[3]
    Born with three arms the predicted warlike image,
    Through three crowns to the great Endymion.[4]

74. From Sens, from Autun they will come as far as the Rhône
    To pass beyond towards the Pyrenees mountains:
    The nation to leave the March of Ancona:
    By land and sea it will be followed by great suites.

75. The voice of the rare bird heard,
    On the pipe of the air-vent floor:[5]
    So high will the bushel of wheat rise,
    That man will be eating his fellow man.

76. Lightning in Burgundy will perform a portentous deed,
    One which could never have been done by skill,
    Sexton made lame by their senate
    Will make the affair known to the enemies.

[1] Or "surrendered."
[2] An ex-lake, as of 1876. See Commentary.
[3] Still unsolved. See note 5, opposite, for possibilities.
[4] Beautiful youth of Greek mythology noted chiefly for (1) being loved by Selene the Moon, and (2) being given the gift of eternal sleep.
[5] "Chimney" is thought to be intended here.

77. Pris arcs feux poix et par feux repoussés:
    Cris, hurlements sur la minuit ouïs:
    Dedans sont mis par les remparts cassés,
    Par *cunicules*[1] les *traditeurs*[2] fuis.

78. Le grand *Neptune* du profond de la mer
    De gent *Punique* et sang *Gaulois* mêlé.
    Les Îles à sang, pour le tardif ramer:
    Plus lui nuira que l'occulte mal célé.

79. La barbe crêpe et noire par engin
    Subjuguera la gent cruelle et fière:
    Le grand *Chyren* ôtera du *longin*[3]
    Tous les captifs par *Seline*[4] bannière.

80. Après conflit du lésé l'éloquence
    Par peu de temps se trame *faint*[5] repos:
    Point l'on n'admet les grands à délivrance:
    Des[6] ennemis sont remis à propos.

81. Par feu du ciel la cité presque aduste:
    L'Urne menace encore *Deucalion:*
    Vexée *Sardaigne* par la *Punique* fuste,
    Après que *Libra*[7] *lairra*[8] son *Phaeton.*

82. Par faim la proie fera loup prisonnier,
    L'assaillant lors en extrême détresse.
    Le né ayant au devant le dernier,
    Le grand n'échappe au milieu de la presse.

83. Le gros trafic d'un grand *Lyon* changé,
    La plupart tourne en *pristine*[9] ruine,
    Proie aux soldats par *pille*[10] vendangé:
    Par *Iura* mont et *Sueve* bruine.

[1]Latin *cuniculus,* underground passage.
[2]Latin *traditor,* traitor.
[3]Latin, *longinquus,* far away.
[4]Greek *Selene,* moon.
[5]O.F. *faint,* (either) lazy, easy, soft, (or) false, feigned.
[6]Variant: *Les.*
[7]Latin *Libra,* the Balance.
[8]O.F. *lairrer,* to quit, leave, abandon.
[9]Latin *pristinus,* pristine, former.
[10]O.F. *pille,* booty, pillage.

77. Hurled back through bows, fires, pitch and by fires:
    Cries, howls heard at midnight:
    Within they are placed on the broken ramparts,
    The traitors fled by the underground passages.

78. The great Neptune of the deep of the sea
    With Punic race and Gallic blood mixed.
    The Isles bled, because of the tardy rowing:
    More harm will it do him than the ill-concealed secret.

☞ 79. The beard frizzled and black through skill
    Will subjugate the cruel and proud people:
    The great "Chyren"[1] will remove from far away
    All those captured by the banner of "Selin."[2]

80. After the conflict by the eloquence of the wounded one
    For a short time a soft[3] rest is contrived:
    The great ones are not to be allowed deliverance at all:
    They are restored by the enemies[4] at the proper time.

☞ 81. Through fire from the sky the city almost burned:
    The Urn threatens Deucalion[5] again:
    Sardinia vexed by the Punic foist,[6]
    After Libra will leave her Phaëthon.[7]

82. Through hunger the prey will make the wolf prisoner,
    The aggressor then in extreme distress.
    The heir having the last one before him,
    The great one does not escape in the middle of the crowd.

☞ 83. The large trade of a great Lyons changed,
    The greater part turns to pristine ruin.
    Prey to the soldiers swept away by pillage:
    Through the Jura mountain and "Suevia"[8] drizzle.

[1]Anagram for "Henry."
[2]The Turkish crescent, which resembles a new moon, or that of "Henry-Selin."
[3]Or "false."
[4]Or "The enemies are restored."
[5]The Noah of Greek mythology. Another Deluge is implied.
[6]A kind of galley. Possibly "fleet" by synecdoche.
[7]An epithet of the Sun in Latin poetry.
[8]Switzerland, the name being derived by Nostradamus from the Suevian (Swabian) ancestors of the German Swiss.

84. Entre *Campaignie, Sienne, Flora, Tuscie,*
    Six mois neuf jours ne pleuvra une goutte:
    L'étrange langue en terre *Dalmatie*
    Courira sus, *vastant*[1] la terre toute.

85. Le vieux plein barbe sous le statut sévère
    À *Lyons* fait dessus l'Aigle *Celtique:*
    Le petit grand trop outre persévère:
    Bruit d'arme au ciel: mer rouge *Ligustique.*[2]

86. Naufrage à *classe*[3] près d'onde *Hadriatique:*
    La terre tremble émue sus l'air en terre mis:
    *Egypte* tremble augment *Mahometique,*
    L'Héraut soi rendre à crier est commis.

87. Après viendra des extrêmes contrées
    Prince *Germain,* dessus le trône doré:
    La servitude et eaux rencontrées,
    La dame serve, son temps plus n'adoré.

88. Le circuit du grand fait ruineux,
    Le nom septième du cinquième sera:
    D'un tiers plus grand l'étrange belliqueux:
    Mouton, *Lutece,*[4] *Aix* ne garantira.

89. Un jour[5] seront demis[6] les deux grands maîtres,
    Leur grand pouvoir se verra augmenté:
    La terre neuve sera en ses hauts êtres,
    Au sanguinaire le nombre raconté.

90. Par vie et mort changé regne d'*Ongrie:*
    La loi sera plus âpre que service:
    Leur grande cité d'hurlements plaintes et crie,
    *Castor* et *Pollux* ennemis dans la lice.

91. Soleil levant un grand feu l'on verra,
    Bruit et clarté vers *Aquilon*[7] tendants:
    Dedans le rond mort et cris l'on ouïra,
    Par glaive, feu, faim, mort les attendants.

[1]Latin *vastare,* to devastate.
[2]Latin *Ligusticus,* Ligurian.
[3]Latin *classis,* fleet.
[4]Latin *Lutetia,* Paris.
[5]Variant: *Du jou.* From O.F. *jou,* yoke
[6]Variant: *damis* (presumably *d'amis* intended).
[7]Latin *Aquilo,* north wind, north.

84. Between Campania, Siena, Florence, Tuscany,
   Six months nine days without a drop of rain:
   The strange tongue in the Dalmatian land,
   It will overrun, devastating the entire land.

85. The old full beard under the severe statute
   Made at Lyon over the Celtic Eagle:
   The little great one perseveres too far:
   Noise of arms in the sky: Ligurian sea[1] red.

86. Wreck for the fleet near the Adriatic Sea:[2]
   The land trembles stirred up upon the air placed on land:
   Egypt trembles Mahometan increase,
   The Herald surrendering himself is appointed to cry out.

☞ 87. After there will come from the outermost countries
   A German Prince, upon the golden throne:
   The servitude and waters met,
   The lady serves, her time no longer adored.

88. The circuit of the great ruinous deed,
   The seventh name of the fifth will be:[3]
   Of a third greater the stranger warlike:
   Sheep,[4] Paris, Aix will not guarantee.

☞ 89. One day the two great masters[5] will be friends,[6]
   Their great power will be seen increased:
   The new land[7] will be at its high peak,
   To the bloody one the number recounted.

☞ 90. Through life and death the realm of Hungary changed:
   The law will be more harsh than service:
   Their great city cries out with howls and laments,
   Castor and Pollux enemies in the arena.

☞ 91. At sunrise one will see a great fire,
   Noise and light extending towards "Aquilon:"[8]
   Within the circle death and one will hear cries,
   Through steel, fire, famine, death awaiting them.

[1]The Gulf of Genoa.
[2]Or "near Venice" (see note on 18).
[3]Or "will he be," or "will it be."
[4]Possibly standing for Reims, the wool-processing center of France. Or Aries the ram (indicating an astrological metaphor).
[5]Or "The two great masters of the yoke."
[6]Or "will be dismissed."
[7]New World?
[8]The North[ern Country]. For various possibilities, see Commentaries for 149 and 268.

92. Feu couleur d'or du ciel en terre vu:
    Frappé du haut né, fait cas merveilleux:
    Grand meurtre humain: pris du grand le neveu,
    Morts de spectacles échappé l'orgueilleux.

93. Bien près du *Tymbre* presse la *Libytine:*[1]
    Un peu devant grande inondation:
    Le chef du nef pris, mis à la *sentine:*[2]
    Château, palais en conflagration.

94. GRAND *Pau,*[3] grand mal pour *Gaulois* recevra,
    Vaine terreur au maritime Lion:[4]
    Peuple infini par la mer passera,
    Sans échapper un quart d'un million.

95. Les lieux peuplés seront inhabitables:
    Pour champs avoir grande division:
    Regnes livrés à prudents incapables:
    Lors les grands frères mort et dissension.

96. Flambeau ardent au ciel soir sera vu
    Près de la fin et principe du *Rosne:*
    Famine, glaive: tard le secours pourvu,
    La *Perse* tourne envahir *Macedoine.*

97. *Romain* Pontife garde de t'approcher
    De la cité que deux fleuves arrose,
    Ton sang viendra auprès de là cracher,
    Toi et les tiens quand fleurira la rose.

98. Celui de sang *resperse*[5] le visage
    De la victime proche sacrifiée:
    *Tonant*[6] en *Leo,* augure par présage:
    Mis être à mort lors pour la fiancée.

[1]Latin *Libitina,* Goddess of Death.
[2]Latin *sentina,* (1) bilge water, (2) dregs of the mob.
[3]Variants: *Grand Paud; GRAN. Pau. Grand* is all capitals in most texts.
[4]Or *Lyon,* the city?
[5]O.F. *respers,* sprinkled.
[6]Latin *Jupiter Tonans,* Jupiter the Thunderer.

☞ 92. Fire color of gold from the sky seen on earth:
    Heir struck from on high,[1] marvelous deed done:
    Great human murder: the nephew of the great one taken,
    Deaths spectacular the proud one escaped.

93. Very near the Tiber presses Death:
    Shortly before great inundation:
    The chief of the ship taken, thrown into the bilge:
    Castle, palace in conflagration.

94. Great Po,[2] great evil will be received through Gauls,
    Vain terror to the maritime Lion:[3]
    People will pass by the sea in infinite numbers,
    Without a quarter of a million escaping.

95. The populous places will be uninhabitable:
    Great discord to obtain fields:
    Realms delivered to prudent incapable ones:
    Then for the great brothers dissension and death.

☞ 96. Burning torch will be seen in the sky at night
    Near the end and beginning of the Rhône:
    Famine, steel: the relief provided late,
    Persia turns to invade[4] Macedonia.

97. Roman Pontiff beware of approaching
    The city that two rivers flow through,
    Near there your blood will come to spirt,
    You and yours when the rose will flourish.

98. The one whose face is splattered with the blood
    Of the victim nearly sacrificed:
    Jupiter in Leon, omen through presage:
    To be put to death then for the bride.[5]

[1] Or "struck by the high-born one."
[2] Subject to some doubt; the variant GRAN. would have some enigmatic significance, while *Pau* is also a city in southwest France (former capital of Navarre) and also appears enigmatically in 679 and 81.
[3] I.e., Venice (see Commentary). The French city of Lyons is unlikely here.
[4] Or "Persia again invades," according to Busquet (1950), who alleges this "turn to" structure is a "provençalism" for "again."
[5] Probably the Church, the "Bride of Christ," is intended here.

99. Terroir *Romain* qu'interpretait augure,
Par gent *Gauloise* par trop sera vexée:
Mais nation *Celtique* craindra l'heure,
*Boreas,*[1] *classe*[2] trop loin l'avoir poussée.

100. Dedans les îles si horrible tumulte,
Rien on n'ouïra qu'une *bellique*[3] brigue,
Tant grand sera des *prédateurs*[4] l'insulte
Qu'on se viendra ranger à la grande ligue.

[1] Latin *Boreas,* North Wind, North.
[2] Latin *classis,* fleet, army.
[3] Latin *bellicus,* of war, warlike.
[4] Latin *praedator,* plunderer.

99. Roman land as the omen interpreted
    Will be vexed too much by the Gallic people:
    But the Celtic nation will fear the hour,
    The fleet[1] has been pushed too far by the north wind.[2]

100. Within the isles a very horrible uproar,
     One will hear only a party of war,
     So great will be the insult of the plunderers
     That they will come to be joined in the great league.

[1]Or possibly "The army."
[2]Or "pushed too far north."

# Centurie III

1. Après combat et bataille navale,
   Le grand *Neptune* à son plus haut beffroi:
   Rouge adversaire de peur viendra pâle,
   Mettant le grand Océan en effroi.

2. Le divin verbe *donra*[1] à la substance,
   Compris ciel, terre, or occulte au lait[2] mystique
   Corps, âme, esprit ayant toute puissance,
   Tant sous ses pieds comme au siège *Celique*.[3]

3. *Mars* et *Mercure*, et l'argent joint ensemble,
   Vers le midi extrême siccité:
   Au fond d'*Asie* on dira terre tremble,
   *Corinthe*, *Ephese* lors en perplexité.

4. Quand seront proches le défaut des lunaires,
   De l'un à l'autre ne distant grandement,
   Froid, siccité, danger vers les frontières,
   Même où l'oracle a pris commencement.

5. Près, loin défaut de deux grands luminaires
   Qui surviendra entre l'Avril et Mars:
   O quel cherté! mais deux grands débonnaires
   Par terre et mer secourront toutes parts.

6. Dans temple clos le foudre y entrera,
   Les citadins dedans leur fort grevés:
   Chevaux, bœufs, hommes, l'onde mur touchera,
   Par faim, soif, sous les plus faibles armés.

7. Les fugitifs, feu du ciel sus les piques:
   Conflit prochain des corbeaux s'ébattants,
   De terre on crie aide, secours *celiques*,[3]
   Quand près des murs seront les combattants.

Syncope of *donnera*.
Variant: *fait*.
O.F. *celique*, celestial, heavenly.

# Century III

1. After combat and naval battle,
   The great Neptune in his highest belfry:
   Red adversary will become pale with fear,
   Putting the great Ocean in dread.

2. The divine word[1] will give to the substance,
   Including heaven, earth, gold hidden in the mystic milk:[2]
   Body, soul, spirit having all power,
   As much under its feet as the Heavenly see.[3]

3. Mars and Mercury, and the silver[4] joined together,
   Towards the south extreme drought:
   In the depths of Asia one will say the earth trembles,
   Corinth, Ephesus then in perplexity.

4. When they will be close the lunar ones[5] will fail,
   From one another not greatly distant,
   Cold, dryness, danger towards the frontiers,
   Even where the oracle has had its beginning.

5. Near, far the failure of the two great luminaries
   Which will occur between April and March.
   Oh, what a loss! but two great good-natured ones
   By land and sea will relieve all parts.

6. Within the closed temple the lightning will enter,
   The citizens within their fort injured:
   Horses, cattle, men, the wave will touch the wall,
   Through famine, drought, under the weakest armed.

7. The fugitives, fire from the sky on the pikes:
   Conflict near the ravens frolicking,
   From land they cry for aid and heavenly relief,
   When the combatants will be near the walls.

[1]Or, according to Garencières, "The theologian." See Commentary.
[2]Or "mystic deed."
[3]The Holy See?
[4]The Moon.
[5]The armies of Islam, with their crescent emblem resembling a new moon.

8. Les *Cimbres* joint avec leurs voisins
   *Depopuler*[1] viendront presque l'*Espagne:*
   Gens amassés *Guienne* et *Limosins*
   Seront en ligue, et leur feront compagne.

9. *Bourdeaux, Roüan* et *la Rochelle* joints
   Tiendront autour la grande mer Océan,
   *Anglois, Bretons,* et les *Flamans* conjoints
   Les chasseront jusqu'auprès de *Roane.*

10. De sang et faim plus grande calamité,
    Sept fois s'apprête à la marine plage:
    *Monech*[2] de faim, lieu pris, captivité,
    Le grand mené *croc*[3] ferrée cage.

11. Les armes battre au ciel longue saison,
    L'arbre au milieu de la cité tombé:
    *Verbine*[4] rogne, glaive, en face tison,
    Lors le monarque d'*Hadrie* succombé.

12. Par la tumeur de *Heb. Po, Tag. Timbre,* et *Rosne*
    Et par l'étang *Leman*[5] et *Aretin,*[6]
    Les deux grands chefs et cités de *Garonne,*
    Pris, morts, noyés: Partir humain butin.

13. Par foudre en l'arche or et argent fondu,
    De deux captifs l'un l'autre mangera:
    De la cité le plus grand étendu,
    Quand submergée la *classe*[7] nagera.

14. Par le rameau du vaillant personnage
    De *France* infime: par le père *infelice*[8]
    Honneurs, richesses travail en son vieil âge,
    Pour avoir cru le conseil d'homme *nice.*[9]

---

[1]Latin *depopulari,* to ravage, plunder, pillage.
[2]Latin *Monoecus,* Monaco.
[3]O.F. adjectival form of modern *croquer,* to crunch; or Latin *croceus,* golden yellow.
[4]Latin *verbena,* sacred bough. Variant: *vermine.*
[5]Latin *Lemannus,* Lake Geneva.
[6]Latin *Aretinus,* of Aretium (modern Arezzo).
[7]Latin *classis,* fleet.
[8]Latin *infelix,* unhappy.
[9]O.F. *nice,* simple, inexperienced, foolish.

8. The Cimbri[1] joined with their neighbors
   Will come to ravage almost[2] Spain:
   Peoples gathered in Guienne and Limousin
   Will be in league, and will bear them company.

9. Bordeaux, Rouen and La Rochelle joined
   Will hold around the great Ocean sea,
   English, Bretons and the Flemings allied
   Will chase them as far as Roanne.

10. Greater calamity of blood and famine,
    Seven times it approaches the marine shore:
    Monaco from hunger, place captured, captivity,
    The great one led crunching[3] in a metaled cage.

11. The arms to fight in the sky a long time,
    The tree in the middle of the city fallen:
    Sacred bough clipped,[4] steel, in the face of the firebrand,
    Then the monarch of "Adria"[5] fallen.

12. Because of the swelling of the Ebro, Po, Tagus, Tiber and Rhône
    And because of the pond of Geneva and Arezzo,
    The two great chiefs and cities of the Garonne,
    Taken, dead, drowned: human booty divided.

13. Through lightning in the arch[6] gold and silver melted,
    Of two captives one will eat the other:
    The greatest one of the city stretched out,[7]
    When submerged the fleet will swim.

14. Through the branch of the valiant personage
    Of lowest France: because of the unhappy father
    Honors, riches, travail in his old age,
    For having believed the advice of a simple man.

---

[1]The first Teutonic invaders of the Roman Empire, who came from modern Denmark.
As they were destroyed in 101 B.C., the reference is obscure. See Commentary.
[2]Meaning either "almost as far as" or "almost all."
[3]Or "yellow."
[4]Or "Vermin itching."
[5]Presumably Venice (see note on 18). See Commentary.
[6]Or "the ark."
[7]Or possibly "hanged."

15. Cœur, vigeur, gloire le regne changera,
    De tous points contre ayant son adversaire:
    Lors *France* enfance par mort subjuguera,
    Un grand Régent sera lors plus contraire.

16. Un prince *Anglois Mars* à son cœur de ciel
    Voudra poursuivre la fortune prospère,
    Des deux duels l'un percera le fiel:
    Haï de lui bien aimée de sa mère.

17. *Mont Auentine* brûler nuit sera vu:
    Le ciel obscur tout à un coup en *Flandres:*
    Quand le monarque chassera son neveu,
    Leurs gens d'Église commettront les esclandres.

18. Après la pluie lait assez longuette,
    En plusieurs lieux de *Reims* le ciel touché:
    Hélas quel meurtre[1] de sang près d'eux s'apprête,
    Pères et fils Rois n'oseront approcher.

19. En *Luques* sang et lait viendra pleuvoir,
    Un peu devant changement de préteur:
    Grande peste et guerre, faim et soif fera voir
    Loin où mourra leur prince et recteur.

20. Par les contrées du grand fleuve *Bethique*[2]
    Loin d'*Ibere* au Royaume de *Grenade*
    Croix repoussées par gens *Mahometiques*
    Un de *Cordube* trahira la *contrade.*[3]

21. Au *Crustamin*[4] par mer *Hadriatique*
    Apparaîtra un horrible poisson,
    De face humaine, et la fin aquatique,
    Qui se prendra dehors de l'hameçon.

22. Six jours l'assaut devant cité donné:
    Livrée sera forte et âpre bataille:
    Trois la rendront, et à eux pardonné:
    La reste à feu et à sang tranche taille.

[1]Variant (in all editions since 1555): *O quel conflict (conflit).* Revised by Nostradamus?
[2]Latin *Baetis,* Guadalquivir River.
[3]Provençal *contrada,* country.
[4]Latin *Crustumius,* the river now known as the Conca.

☞ 15.  The realm will change in heart, vigor and glory,
        In all points having its adversary opposed:
        Then through death France an infancy will subjugate,
        A great Regent will then be more contrary.

☞ 16.  An English prince Mars in his heavenly heart
        Will want to pursue his prosperous fortune,
        Of the two duels one will pierce his gall:
        Hated by him well loved by his mother.

17.  Mount Aventine will be seen to burn at night:
     The sky very suddenly dark in Flanders:
     When the monarch will chase his nephew,
     Then Church people will commit scandals.

18.  After the rather long rain milk,[1]
     In several places in Reims the sky touched:[2]
     Alas, what a bloody murder is prepared near them,
     Fathers and sons Kings will not dare approach.

19.  In Lucca it will come to rain blood and milk,
     Shortly before a change of praetor:[3]
     Great plague and war, famine and drought will be made visible
     Far away where their prince and rector[4] will die.

☞ 20.  Through the regions of the great river Guadalquivir
        Deep in Iberia to the Kingdom of Grenada
        Crosses beaten back by the Mahometan peoples
        One of Cordova will betray his country.

☞ 21.  In the Conca by the Adriatic Sea[5]
        There will appear a horrible fish,
        With face human and its end aquatic,
        Which will be taken without the hook.

22.  Six days the attack made before the city:
     Battle will be given strong and harsh:
     Three will surrender it, and to them pardon:
     The rest to fire and to bloody slicing and cutting.

[1]"Rain of milk"?
[2]Or "the sky touched by Reims."
[3]"Governor" is the most likely here of the many connotations of this title.
[4]Between its Latin, Old French and French meanings, this title may refer to a leader,
university rector, parish curé, instructor or governor.
[5]The Conca flows into the Adriatic at Cattolica. See Commentary.

23. Si *France* passes outre mer *lygustique,*[1]
    Tu te verras en îles et mers enclos:
    *Mahommet* contraire, plus mer *Hadriatique:*
    Chevaux et d'ânes tu rongeras les os.

24. De l'entreprise grande confusion,
    Perte de gens, trésor innombrable:
    Tu n'y dois faire encore tension.[2]
    *France* à mon dire fais que sois *recordable.*[3]

25. Qui au royaume *Nauarrois* parviendra
    Quand le[4] *Sicile* et *Naples* seront joints:
    *Bigorre* et *Landes* par *Foix Loron* tiendra
    D'un qui d'*Espagne* sera par trop conjoint.

26. Des Rois et Princes dresseront simulacres,
    Augures, creux élevés aruspices:
    Corne, victime d'*orée,*[5] et d'azur, d'*acre,*[6]
    Interprétés seront les *extispices.*[7]

27. Prince *Libyque*[8] puissant en Occident
    *Français* d'*Arabe* viendra tant enflammer.
    Savant aux lettres fera condescendant
    La langue *Arabe* en *Français* translater.

28. De terre faible et pauvre *parentelle,*[9]
    Par bout et paix parviendra dans l'empire.
    Longtemps regner une jeune femelle,
    Qu'onc en regne n'en survint un si pire.

29. Les deux neveux en divers lieux nourris:
    Navale *pugne,*[10] terre, pères tombés:
    Viendront si haut élevés *enguerris*[11]
    Venger l'injure, ennemis succombés.

---

[1]Latin *Ligusticus,* Ligurian.
[2]Variant: *extension.* (Latin *tensio* means extension also.)
[3]O.F. *recordable,* memorable.
[4]Variant: *de.*
[5]O.F. *oré,* gilded, of gold.
[6]Latin, *acer,* dazzling. Possibly also a misprint for *ocre.*
[7]Latin *extispicus,* inspector of entrails, soothsayer.
[8]Latin *Libycus,* Libyan, African.
[9]O.F. *parentele,* parentage.
[10]Latin *pugna,* battle.
[11]O.F. *enguerroier,* to make war upon.

23. If, France, you pass beyond the Ligurian Sea,
    You will see yourself shut up in islands and seas:
    Mahomet contrary, more so the Adriatic Sea:
    You will gnaw the bones of horses and asses.

24. Great confusion in the enterprise,
    Loss of people, countless treasure:
    You ought not to extend further there.
    France, let what I say be remembered.

☞ 25. He who will attain to the kingdom of Navarre
    When Sicily and Naples will be joined:[1]
    He will hold Bigorre and Landes through Foix and Oloron
    From one who will be too closely allied with Spain.

26. They will prepare idols of Kings and Princes,
    Soothsayers and empty prophets elevated:
    Horn, victim[2] of gold, and azure, dazzling,[3]
    The soothsayers[4] will be interpreted.

☞ 27. Libyan Prince powerful in the West
    Will come to inflame very much French with Arabian.
    Learned in letters condescending he will
    Translate the Arabian language into French.

☞ 28. Of land weak and parentage poor,
    Through piece[5] and peace he[6] will attain to the empire.
    For a long time a young female to reign,
    Never has one so bad come upon the kingdom.

29. The two nephews brought up in diverse places:
    Naval battle, land, fathers fallen:
    They will come to be elevated very high in making war
    To avenge the injury, enemies succumbed.

[1]"Joined with Navarre"?
[2]Possibly "Victim with horn."
[3]Or possibly "of ochre."
[4]Possibly only "entrails" is intended here.
[5]Or "end."
[6]Or "she."

30. Celui qu'en lutte et fer au fait *bellique*[1]
    Aura porté plus grand que lui le prix:
    De nuit au lit six lui feront la pique,
    Nu sans harnois subit sera surpris.

31. Aux champs de *Mede*, d'*Arabe* et d'*Armenie*
    Deux grandes *copies*[2] trois fois s'assembleront:
    Près du rivage d'*Araxes* la *mesnie*,[3]
    Du grand *Soliman* en terre tomberont.

32. Le grand sépulcre du peuple *Aquitanique*
    S'approchera auprès de la *Toscane*,
    Quand *Mars* sera près du coin *Germanique*
    Et au terroir de la gent *Mantuane*.

33. En la cité où le loup entrera,
    Bien près de là les ennemis seront:
    *Copie*[2] étrange grand pays gâtera.
    Aux murs et *Alpes* les amis passeront.

34. Quand le défaut du Soleil lors sera,
    Sur le plein jour le monstre sera vu:
    Tout autrement on l'interprétera,
    Cherté n'a gardé: nul n'y aura pourvu.

35. Du plus profond de l'Occident d'*Europe*,
    De pauvres gens un jeune enfant naîtra,
    Qui par sa langue séduira grande troupe:
    Son bruit au regne d'Orient plus croîtra.

36. Enseveli non mort apoplectique,
    Sera trouvé avoir les mains mangées:
    Quand la cité damnera l'hérétique,
    Qu'avait leur lois ce leur semblait changées.

37. Avant l'assaut l'oraison prononcée,
    *Milan* pris d'Aigle par embûches deçus:
    Muraille antique par canons enfoncée,
    Par feu et sang à merci peu reçus.

[1] Latin *bellicus*, of war.
[2] Latin *copia*, forces, army.
[3] O.F. *mesnie*, household, following, host.

☞ 30. He who during the struggle with steel in the deed of war
Will have carried off the prize from one greater than he:
By night six will carry the grudge to his bed,
Without armor he will be surprised suddenly.

☞ 31. On the fields of Media, of Arabia and of Armenia
Two great armies will assemble thrice:
The host near the bank of the Araxes,
They will fall in the land of the great Suleiman.[1]

32. The great tomb of the people of Aquitaine
Will approach near to Tuscany,
When Mars will be in the corner of Germany
And in the land of the Mantuan people.

33. In the city where the wolf will enter,
Very near there will the enemies be:
Foreign army will spoil a great country.
The friends will pass at the walls and Alps.

34. When the eclipse of the Sun will then be,
The monster will be seen in full day:[2]
Quite otherwise will one interpret it,
High price[3] unguarded: none will have foreseen it.

35. From the very depths of the West of Europe,
A young child will be born of poor people,
He who by his tongue will seduce a great troop:[4]
His fame will increase towards the realm of the East.

36. Buried apoplectic not dead,
He will be found to have his hands eaten:
When the city will condemn the heretic,
He who it seemed to them had changed their laws.

☞ 37. The speech[5] delivered before the attack,
Milan taken by the Eagle through deceptive ambushes:
Ancient wall driven in by cannons,
Through fire and blood few given quarter.

[1]If we ignore the comma in line 3, the reading may be "Near the bank of the Araxes
the host of the great Suleiman will fall to earth." See Commentary.
[2]At noon?
[3]Or "Scarcity."
[4]Or "many people."
[5]Or "The prayer."

38. La gent *Gauloise* et nation étrange
    Outre les monts, morts, pris et profligés:[1]
    Au mois contraire et proche de vendange,
    Par les Seigneurs en accord rédigés.

39. Les sept en trois mois en concorde
    Pour subjuguer les *Alpes Apennines:*
    Mais la tempête et *Ligure*[2] couarde
    Les *profligent*[1] en subites ruines.

40. Le grand théâtre se viendra redresser:
    Les dés jetés et les rets ja tendus.
    Trop le premier en glas viendra lasser,
    Par arcs *prostrais*[3] de longtemps ja fendus.

41. Bossu sera élu par le conseil,
    Plus hideux monstre en terre n'aperçu,
    Le coup voulant[4] crevera l'œil:
    Le traître au Roi pour fidèle reçu.

42. L'enfant naîtra à deux dents en la gorge,
    Pierres en *Tuscie* par pluie tomberont:
    Peu d'ans après ne sera blé ni orge,
    Pour saouler ceux qui de faim failliront.

43. Gens d'alentours de *Tarn, Loth,* et *Garonne*
    Gardez les monts *Apennines* passer:
    Votre tombeau près de *Rome,* et d'*Anconne,*
    Le noir poil crêpe fera trophée dresser.

44. Quand l'animal à l'homme domestique
    Après grands peines et sauts viendra parler:
    Le foudre à vierge sera si maléfique,
    De terre prise et suspendue en l'air.

45. Les cinq étranges entrés dans le temple,
    Leur sang viendra la terre profaner:
    Aux *Tholosains* sera bien dur exemple
    D'un qui viendra ses lois exterminer.

---

[1]Latin *profligare,* to kill, destroy, overwhelm.
[2]Provençal *ligur,* leaguer; or abbreviation of *Ligurien,* Ligurian.
[3]Latin *prostratus,* overturned, ruined, destroyed.
[4]Variants: *volant; volant Prelat* (1557 edition only).

38. The Gallic people and a foreign nation
    Beyond the mountains, dead, captured and killed:
    In the contrary month and near vintage time,
    Through the Lords drawn up in accord.

39. The seven in three months in agreement
    To subjugate the Apennine Alps:
    But the tempest and cowardly Ligurian,[1]
    Destroys them in sudden ruins.

40. The great theater will come to be set up again:
    The dice cast and the snares already laid.
    Too much the first one will come to tire in the death knell,
    Prostrated by arches already a long time split.

☞ 41. Hunchback will be elected by the council,
    A more hideous monster not seen on earth,
    The willing[2] blow[3] will put out his eye:
    The traitor to the King received as faithful.

42. The child will be born with two teeth in his mouth,
    Stones will fall during the rain in Tuscany:
    A few years after there will be neither wheat nor barley,
    To satiate those who will faint from hunger.

43. People from around the Tarn, Lot and Garonne
    Beware of passing the Apennine mountains:
    Your tomb near Rome and Ancona,
    The black frizzled beard will have a trophy set up.

44. When the animal domesticated by man
    After great pains and leaps will come to speak:
    The lightning to the virgin will be very harmful,
    Taken from earth and suspended in the air.

45. The five strangers entered in the temple,
    Their blood will come to pollute the land:
    To the Toulousans it will be a very hard example
    Of one who will come to exterminate their laws.

---

[1]I.e., Genoan, the Ligurians having been inhabitants of classical Genoa. Or "leaguer.'
See note opposite.
[2]I.e., "intended." Or "flying" or "The Prelate's willing/flying."
[3]Or "shot."

46. Le ciel (de *Plancus* la cité) nous présage
    Par claires insignes et par étoiles fixes,
    Que de son change subit s'approche l'âge,
    Ni pour son bien, ni pour ses maléfices.

47. Le vieux monarque déchassé de son regne
    Aux *Orients* son secours ira *querre:*[1]
    Pour peur des croix pliera son enseigne:
    En *Mytilene* ira par port et terre.

48. Sept cents captifs attachés rudement,
    Pour la moitié meurtrir, donné le sort:
    Le proche espoir viendra si promptement
    Mais non si tôt qu'une quinzième mort.

49. Regne *Gaulois* tu seras bien changé:
    En lieu étrange est *translaté*[2] l'empire:
    En autres mœurs et lois seras rangé:
    *Roüan* et *Chartres* te feront bien du pire.

50. La république de la grande cité
    À grand *rigeur*[3] ne voudra consentir:
    Roi sortir hòrs par trompette cité,
    L'échelle au mur, la cité repentir.

51. *Paris* conjure un grand meurtre commettre
    *Blois* le fera sortir en plein effet:
    Ceux d'*Orleans* voudront leur chef remettre,
    *Angers*, *Troye*, *Langres* leur feront un méfait.[4]

52. En la *Campaigne* sera si longue pluie,
    Et en la *Poüille* si grande siccité.
    Coq verra l'Aigle, l'aile mal accomplie,
    Par Lion mise sera en extrémité.

53. Quand le plus grand emportera le prix
    De *Nuremberg*, d'*Ausbourg*, et ceux de *Basle*
    Par *Agrippine*[5] chef *Frankfort* repris
    Traverseront par *Flamant* jusqu'en *Gale.*

---

[1]O.F. *querre*, to look for, ask.
[2]Latin *translatus*, transferred.
[3]Latin *rigor*, roughness, severity.
[4]Variant: *feront grand forfait.*
[5]Latin *Colonia Agrippina*, Cologne.

46. The sky (of Plancus' city)[1] forebodes to us[2]
Through clear signs and fixed stars,
That the time of its sudden change is approaching,
Neither for its good, nor for its evils.

☞ 47. The old monarch chased out of his realm
Will go to the East asking for its help:
For fear of the crosses he will fold his banner:
To Mitylene he will go through port and by land.

48. Seven hundred captives bound roughly,
Lots drawn for the half to be murdered:
The hope at hand will come very promptly
But not as soon as the fifteenth death.

49. Gallic realm, you will be much changed:
To a foreign place is the empire transferred:
You will be set up amidst other customs and laws:
Rouen and Chartres will do much of the worst to you.

☞ 50. The republic of the great city
Will not want to consent to the great severity:
King summoned by trumpet to go out,
The ladder at the wall, the city will repent.

☞ 51. Paris conspires to commit a great murder
Blois will cause it to be fully carried out:
Those of Orléans will want to replace their chief,
Angers, Troyes, Langres will commit a misdeed[3] against them.

52. In Campania there will be a very long rain,
In Apulia very great drought.
The Cock will see the Eagle, its wing poorly finished,
By the Lion will it be put into extremity.

☞ 53. When the greatest one will carry off the prize
Of Nuremberg, of Augsburg, and those of Bâle
Through Cologne the chief Frankfort[4] retaken
They will cross through Flanders right into Gaul.

[1]Lyons, founded by Lucius Munatius Plancus in 43 B.C.
[2]If we ignore the odd parenthesis, "The sky of the city of Plancus forebodes to us."
[3]Or "a great crime."
[4]"Chief of Frankfort"? "chief of Cologne"?

54. L'un des plus grands fuira aux *Espagnes*
    Qu'en longue plaie après viendra saigner:
    Passant *copies*[1] par les hautes montagnes,
    Dévastant tout, et puis en paix regner.

55. En l'an qu'un œil en *France* regnera,
    La cour sera à un bien fâcheux trouble:
    Le grand de *Blois* son ami tuera:
    Le regne mis en mal et doute double.

56. *Montaubant, Nismes, Auignon, et Besier,*
    Peste, tonnerre, et grêle à fin de *Mars:*
    De *Paris*, pont, *Lyon* mur, *Montpellier,*
    Depuis six cents et sept vingts trois[2] *pars.*[3]

57. Sept fois changer verrez gent *Britannique,*
    Teints en sang en deux cent nonante ans:
    *Franche* non point appui *Germanique.*
    *Aries* doute son pôle *Bastarnan.*[4]

58. Auprès du *Rhin* des montagnes *Noriques*
    Naîtra un grand de gens trop tard venu,
    Qui défendra *Saurome*[5] et *Pannoniques,*[6]
    Qu'on ne saura qu'il sera devenu.

59. Barbare empire par le tiers usurpé,
    La plupart de son sang mettra à mort:
    Par mort sénile par lui le quart frappé,
    Pour peur que sang par le sang ne soit mort.

60. Par toute *Asie* grande proscription,
    Même en *Mysie, Lysie,* et *Pamphilie.*
    Sang versera par absolution
    D'un jeune noir rempli de félonie.

---

[1]Latin *copia*, forces, army.
[2]Variant: *six cent & sept xxiii* (Fortune edition).
[3]O.F. *par,* pair.
[4]Latin *Bastarnae*, Bastarnians (inhabitants of southern Poland and the Ukraine).
[5]Latin *Sauromatia*, Sarmatia (south Russia).
[6]Latin *Pannonicus*. Pannonian.

54. One of the greatest ones will flee to Spain
Which will thereafter come to bleed in a long wound:
Armies passing over the high mountains,
Devastating all, and then to reign in peace.

55. In the year that one eye will reign in France,
The court will be in very unpleasant trouble:
The great one of Blois will kill his friend:
The realm placed in harm and double doubt.

56. Montauban, Nîmes, Avignon and Béziers,
Plague, thunder and hail in the wake of Mars:[1]
Of Paris bridge, Lyons wall, Montpellier,
After six hundreds and seven score three pairs.[2]

☞ 57. Seven times will you see the British nation change,
Steeped in blood in 290 years:
Free[3] not at all its support Germanic.
Aries doubts his "Bastarnian"[4] pole.

☞ 58. Near the Rhine from the Noric mountains
Will be born a great one of people come too late,
One who will defend Sarmatia[5] and the Pannonians,[6]
One will not know what will have become of him.

59. Barbarian empire usurped by the third,
The greater part of his blood he will put to death:
Through senile death the fourth struck by him,
For fear that the blood through the blood be not dead.

60. Throughout all Asia[7] great proscription,
Even in Mysia, Lycia and Pamphilia.
Blood will be shed because of the absolution
Of a young black one[8] filled with felony.

[1] Or "at the end of March."
[2] Or possibly "six hundred and seven twenty-three pairs." The first gives 746 (probably the year 1746 or 2301, i.e., 1555 plus 746). The second would give 653 (1653 or 2208).
[3] Or "Frankish" (i.e., French), with "nation" understood.
[4] Polish? See note opposite.
[5] Greater Lithuania in 1555 (see map).
[6] The Hungarians.
[7] Roman Asia, i.e., Asia Minor.
[8] Or "Of a young king" (*noir* as anagram for *roi*, king).

61. La grande bande et secte *crucigère*[1]
    Se dressera en *Mesopotamie:*
    Du proche fleuve compagnie légère,
    Que telle loi tiendra pour ennemie.

62. Proche del *duero* par mer *Tyrrene*[2] close,
    Viendra percer les grands monts *Pyrénées.*
    La main plus courte et sa *perce*[3] *glose,*[4]
    À *Carcassonne* conduira ses menées.

63. *Romain* pouvoir sera du tout à bas,
    Son grand voisin imiter les vestiges:
    Occultes haines civiles, et débats
    Retarderont aux bouffons leurs folies.

64. Le chef de *Perse* remplira grande *Olchades,*[5]
    *Classe*[6] trirème contre gens *Mahometiques*
    De *Parthe,* et *Mede:* et piller les *Cyclades:*
    Repos longtemps au grand port *Ionique.*

65. Quand le sépulcre du grand *Romain* trouvé,
    Le jour après sera élu Pontife:
    Du Sénat guère il ne sera prouvé
    Empoisonné, son sang au sacré *scyphe.*[7]

66. Le grand Bailli d'*Orleans* mis à mort
    Sera par un de sang vindicatif:
    De mort *merite*[8] ne mourra, ni par sort:
    Des pieds et mains mal le faisait captif.

67. Une nouvelle secte de Philosophes
    Méprisant mort, or, honneurs et richesses
    Des monts *Germains* ne seront limitrophes:
    À les ensuivre auront appui et presses.

[1]Latin *crux-gerens,* cross-bearing, i.e., crusaders.
[2]Variant: *Cyrrene.*
[3]O.F. *perce,* stake, pole; opening.
[4]Variant: *percée gloze.* Derivation uncertain in either case.
[5]Latin *Olcades,* a people living in southeastern Spain, near Cartagena.
[6]Latin *classis,* fleet.
[7]Latin *scyphus,* chalice.
[8]Latin *meritus,* deserved. (*Méritée* would change meter).

61. The great band and sect of crusaders
    Will be arrayed in Mesopotamia:
    Light company of the nearby river,
    That such law will hold for an enemy.

☞ 62. Near the Douro by the closed Tyrian[1] sea,
    He will come to pierce the great Pyrenees mountains.
    One hand shorter and his opening[2] glosses,
    He will lead his traces to[3] Carcassonne.

☞ 63. The Roman power will be thoroughly abased,
    Following in the footsteps of its great neighbor:
    Hidden civil hatreds and debates
    Will delay their follies for the buffoons.

☞ 64. The chief of Persia will occupy great "Olchades,"[4]
    The trireme fleet against the Mahometan people
    From Parthia, and Media: and the Cyclades pillaged:
    Long rest at the great Ionian port.

☞ 65. When the sepulchre of the great Roman is found,
    The day after a Pontiff will be elected:
    Scarcely will he be approved by the Senate
    Poisoned, his blood in the sacred chalice.

☞ 66. The great Bailiff of Orléans put to death
    Will be by one of blood revengeful:
    Of death deserved he will not die, nor by chance:
    He made captive poorly by his feet and hands.

67. A new sect of Philosophers
    Despising death, gold, honors and riches
    Will not be bordering upon the German mountains:
    To follow them they will have power and crowds.

---

[1] In this case, from context, not "Tyrrhenian Sea" (west of Italy) but the Bay of Biscay, discovered by the Tyrian colonizers. See Commentary. Or, per the variant, "Cyrrene Sea," which would make even poorer sense than the Tyrrhenian Sea.

[2] Or "stake." Very uncertain. See note opposite.

[3] Or "conduct his plots at."

[4] Cartagena? See note 5 opposite.

68. Peuple sans chef d'*Espagne*, d'*Italie*
    Morts, *profligés*[1] dedans le Chersonèse:
    Leur *dict*[2] trahi par légère folie,
    Le sang nager partout à la traverse.

69. Grand *exercite*[3] conduit par jouvenceau,
    Se viendra rendre aux mains des ennemis:
    Mais le vieillard né au demi pourceau,
    Fera *Chalon* et *Mascon* être amis.

70. La grande Bretagne comprise d'*Angleterre*
    Viendra par eaux si haut à inonder
    La Ligue neuve d'*Ausonne* fera guerre,
    Que contre eux ils se viendront bander.

71. Ceux dans les îles de longtemps assiégés
    Prendront vigueur force contre ennemis:
    Ceux par dehors morts de faim *profligés*,[1]
    En plus grande faim que jamais seront mis.

72. Le bon vieillard tout vif enseveli,
    Près du grand fleuve par fausse soupçon:
    Le nouveau vieux de richesse ennobli,
    Pris au chemin tout l'or de la rançon.

73. Quand dans le regne parviendra le boiteux,
    Compétiteur aura proche bâtard:
    Lui et le regne viendront si fort rogneux,
    Qu'*ains qu'*[4]il guérisse son fait sera bien tard.

74. *Naples, Florence, Fauence,* et *Imole,*
    Seront en termes de telle fâcherie,
    Que pour complaire aux malheureux de *Nolle*
    Plaint d'avoir fait à son chef moquerie.

75. *Pau, Verone, Vicence, Sarragousse,*
    De glaives loin terroirs de sang humides:
    Peste si grande viendra à la grande gousse,
    Proche secours, et bien loin les remèdes.

---

[1]Latin *profligatus*, overthrown, overcome.
[2]O.F. *dicteur,* dictator (Godefroy). Variant: *duyct* (from *duyre,* to lead?). The mean
ing would be the same.
[3]Latin *exercitus,* army.
[4]O.F. *ains que,* before.

☞ 68. Leaderless people of Spain and Italy
Dead, overcome within the Peninsula:
Their dictator betrayed by irresponsible folly,
Swimming in blood everywhere in the latitude.

69. The great army led by a young man,
It will come to surrender itself into the hands of the enemies:
But the old one born to the half-pig,
He will cause Châlon and Mâcon to be friends.

70. The great Britain including England[1]
Will come to be flooded very high by waters
The new League of Ausonia[2] will make war,
So that they will come to strive against them.

71. Those in the isles long besieged
Will take vigor and force against their enemies:
Those outside dead overcome by hunger,
They will be put in greater hunger than ever before.

72. The good old man buried quite alive,
Near the great river through false suspicion:
The new old man ennobled by riches,
Captured on the road all his gold for ransom.

73. When the cripple will attain to the realm,
For his competitor he will have a near[3] bastard:
He and the realm will become so very mangy
That before he[4] recovers, it will be too late.

74. Naples, Florence, Faenza and Imola,
They will be on terms of such disagreement
As to delight in the wretches of Nola
Complaining of having mocked its chief.

75. Pau, Verona, Vicenza, Saragossa,
From distant swords lands wet with blood:
Very great plague will come with the great shell,[5]
Relief near, and the remedies very far.

---

[1] Or "The great Brittany conceived of England," referring to the French peninsula and province deriving its name from 6th-century refugees from Britain's Saxon invaders.

[2] Ausonia is specifically southern Italy, in which the classical Ausones lived (in early modern political terms, the Kingdom of Naples). It is also a Latin poetical name for Italy in general.

[3] I.e., of dubious legitimacy; or a relative.

[4] Or "it."

[5] Or "husk," or "pod."

76. En *Germanie* naîtront diverses sectes,
    S'approchant fort de l'heureux paganisme,
    Le cœur captif et petites *receptes*,[1]
    Feront retour à payer le vrai dîme.

77. Le tiers climat sous *Aries* compris
    L'an mil sept cent vingt et sept en Octobre,
    Le Roi de *Perse* par ceux d'*Egypte* pris:
    Conflit, mort, perte: à la croix grand opprobre.

78. Le chef d'*Escosse*, avec six d'*Allemagne*
    Pars gens de mer Orientaux captif:
    Traverseront le *Calpre*[2] et *Espagne*,
    Présent en *Perse* au nouveau Roi craintif.

79. L'ordre fatal sempiternel par chaîne
    Viendra tourner par ordre conséquent:
    Du port *Phocen*[3] sera rompue la chaîne:
    La cité prise, l'ennemi quand et quand.

80. Du regne *Anglois* le digne[4] déchassé,
    Le conseiller par ire mis à feu:
    Ses adhérents iront si bas tracer[5]
    Que le bâtard sera demi reçu.

81. Le grand criard sans honte audacieux,
    Sera élu gouverneur de l'armée:
    Le hardiesse de son *contentieux*,[6]
    Le pont rompu, cité de peur pâmée.

82. *Freins*,[7] *Antibol*,[8] villes autour de *Nice*,
    Seront *vastées*[9] fort par mer et par terre:
    Les sauterelles terres et mer vent propice,
    Pris, morts, troussés, pillés sans loi de guerre.

[1]O.F. *recepte*, revenue, returns.
[2]Latin *Calpe*, Gibraltar.
[3]Latin *Phocenses*, Phocaeans, who founded Marseilles.
[4]Variant: *l'indigne*.
[5]O.F. *se tracer*, to efface oneself (Godefroy).
[6]Latin *contentio*, contention, controversy.
[7]Apparently *Fréjus*, misprint for Nostradamus' *Freius*.
[8]Latin *Antipolis*, Antibes.
[9]Latin *vastatus*, devastated, ruined, destroyed.

☞ 76. In Germany will be born diverse sects,
Coming very near happy paganism,
The heart captive and returns small,
They will return to paying the true tithe.

☞ 77. The third climate included under Aries
The year 1727 in October,
The King of Persia captured by those of Egypt:
Conflict, death, loss: to the cross great shame.

☞ 78. The chief of Scotland, with six of Germany
Captive of the Eastern seamen:
They will pass Gibraltar and Spain,
Present in Persia for the fearful new King.

79. The fatal everlasting order through the chain
Will come to turn through consistent order:
The chain of Marseilles[1] will be broken:
The city taken, the enemy at the same time.

☞ 80. The worthy[2] one chased out of the English realm,
The adviser through anger put to the fire:
His adherents will go so low to efface themselves
That the bastard will be half received.

81. The great shameless, audacious bawler,
He will be elected governor of the army:
The boldness of his contention,
The bridge broken, the city faint from fear.

82. Fréjus, Antibes, towns around Nice,
They will be thoroughly devastated by sea and by land:
The locusts by land and by sea the wind propitious,
Captured, dead, bound, pillaged without law of war.

[1] See note 3, opposite, also Epistle, para. 33.
[2] Or "unworthy."

83. Les longs cheveux de la *Gaule Celtique*
    Accompagnés d'étranges nations,
    Mettront captif la gent *Aquitanique*,
    Pour succomber à leur intentions.

84. La grande cité sera bien désolée,
    Des habitants un seul n'y demeurera:
    Mur, sexe, temple et vierge violée,
    Par fer, feu, peste, canon peuple mourra.

85. La cité prise par tromperie et fraude,
    Par le moyen d'un beau jeune attrapé:
    Assault donné *Raubine*[1] près de *L'AVDE*,
    Lui et tous morts pour avoir bien trompé.

86. Un chef d'*Ausonne* aux *Espaignes* ira
    Par mer fera arrêt dedans *Marseille:*
    Avant sa mort un longtemps languira:
    Après sa mort on verra grand merveille.

87. Classe[2] *Gauloise* n'approches de *Corseigne*,
    Moins de *Sardaigne*, tu t'en repentiras:
    *Trestous*[3] mourrez frustrés de l'aide *grogne:*[4]
    Sang nagera: captif ne me croiras.

88. De *Barselonne* par mer si grande armée,
    Toute *Marseille* de frayeur tremblera:
    Îles saisies de mer aide fermée,
    Ton *traditeur*[5] en terre nagera.

89. En ce temps là sera frustrée *Cypres*
    De son secours de ceux de mer *Egée:*
    Vieux *trucidés:*[6] mais par *mesles*[7] et *lyphres*[8]
    Séduit leur Roi, Reine plus outragée.

[1]Variant: *Roubine.*
[2]Latin *classis,* fleet.
[3]O.F. *trestous,* every single one.
[4]O.F. *groing,* cape, promontory (Roquefort).
[5]Latin *traditor,* traitor.
[6]Latin *trucidatus,* slaughtered, massacred, destroyed.
[7]Possibly Greek *melos,* speech. Variant: *masles.* Possibly from O.F. *masle,* cannonball.
[8]Possibly Greek *lypros,* lamentation, supplication. Or possibly O.F. *Lifrelofre,* term of
contempt for Germans used by Rabelais (claiming all their words sounded like that).

83. The long hairs of Celtic Gaul
    Accompanied by foreign nations,
    They will make captive the people of Aquitaine,
    For succumbing to their designs.

84. The great city will be thoroughly desolated,
    Of the inhabitants not a single one will remain there:
    Wall, sex, temple and virgin violated,
    Through sword, fire, plague, cannon people will die.

85. The city taken through deceit and guile,
    Taken in by means of a handsome youth:
    Assault given by the Robine near the Aude,
    He and all dead for having thoroughly deceived.

86. A chief of Ausonia[1] will go to Spain
    By sea, he will make a stop in Marseilles:
    Before his death he will linger a long time:
    After his death one will see a great marvel.

87. Gallic fleet, do not approach Corsica,
    Less Sardinia, you will rue it:
    Every one of you will die frustrated of the help of the cape:
    You will swim in blood, captive you will not believe me.

88. From Barcelona a very great army by sea,
    All Marseilles will tremble with terror:
    Isles seized help shut off by sea,
    Your traitor will swim on land.

89. At that time Cyprus will be frustrated
    Of its relief by those of the Aegean Sea:
    Old ones slaughtered: but by speeches[2] and supplications[3]
    Their King seduced, Queen outraged more.

[1]Ausonia is specifically southern Italy, poetically all Italy (see note to 370 above)
[2]Or "cannonballs."
[3]Or "Germans."

90. Le grand Satyre et Tigre de *Hyrcanie*,
    Don presenté à ceux de l'Océan:
    Un chef de *classe*[1] ira de *Carmanie*,
    Qui prendra terre au *Tyrren Phocean*.

91. L'arbre qu'avait[1a] par longtemps morts séché,
    Dans une nuit viendra à reverdir:
    *Cron*. Roi malade, Prince pied *estaché*,[2]
    Craint d'ennemis fera voile bondir.

92. Le monde proche du dernier période,
    Saturne encore tard sera de retour:
    *Translat*[3] empire devers nation *Brodde*,[4]
    L'œil arraché à *Narbon* par Autour.

93. Dans *Auignon* tout le chef de l'empire
    Fera arrêt pour *Paris* désolé:
    *Tricast*[5] tiendra l'*Annibalique* ire:
    *Lyon* par change sera mal consolé.

94. De cinq cents ans plus compte l'on tiendra
    Celui qu'était l'ornement de son temps:
    Puis à un coup grande clarté *donra*[6]
    Qui par ce siècle les rendra très contents.

95. La loi *Moricque*[7] on verra défaillir:
    Après une autre beaucoup plus séductive:
    *Boristhenes*[8] premier viendra faillir:
    Par dons[9] et langue une plus attractive.

[1]Latin *classis*, fleet.
[1a]Variant (in all editions since 1555): *était*. Revised by Nostradamus?
[2]O.F. *estache*, stump.
[3]Latin *translatus*, transferred.
[4]O.F. *Brode*, brown, black (Roquefort); feeble, decadent (Godefroy).
[5]Possibly Latin *Tricasses*, Troyes; or *Tricastins*, natives of Saint-Paul-Trois-Châteaux.
[6]*Donnera* by syncope.
[7]From *More*, (1) Moor, (2) Sir Thomas More, whose *Utopia* was published (in Latin) in 1516 and was circulating during Nostradamus' days at college.
[8]Latin *Borysthenes*, Dnieper River.
[9]Variant: *Pardons*.

☞ 90. The great Satyr and Tiger of Hyrcania,[1]
    Gift presented to[2] those of the Ocean:
    A fleet's chief will set out from Carmania,[3]
    One who will take land at the "Tyrren Phocaean."[4]

91. The tree which had long been dead and withered,
    In one night it will come to grow green again:
    The Cronian[5] King sick, Prince with club foot,[6]
    Feared by his enemies he will make his sail bound.

92. The world near the last period,
    Saturn will come back again late:
    Empire transferred towards the Dusky[7] nation,
    The eye plucked out by the Goshawk at Narbonne.

93. In Avignon the chief of the whole empire
    Will make a stop on the way to desolated Paris:
    "Tricast"[8] will hold the anger of Hannibal:
    Lyons will be poorly consoled for the change.

94. For five hundred years more one will keep count of him
    Who was the ornament of his time:
    Then suddenly great light will he give,
    He who for this century will render them very satisfied.

☞ 95. The law of More[9] will be seen to decline:
    After another much more seductive:
    Dnieper first will come to give way:
    Through gifts[10] and tongue another more attractive.

[1]The southeastern shore of the Caspian Sea, part of Persia.
[2]Or possibly "by" (in which case, see 378).
[3]The part of Persia at the mouth of the Persian Gulf.
[4]Enigmatic place name, presumably a seaport of Italy or France. Or possibly two ports, Marseilles (Nostradamus' usual Phocaean port) and some Italian port on the Tyrrhenian Sea (west of Italy). See Commentary.
[5]Pertaining to Cronus (Saturn), either as an enigma or in the Greek sense as a nickname for a superannuated old dotard (e.g., "old crone").
[6]Literally "foot stumped." This seems to be the meaning.
[7]Or "Black," or "Decadent."
[8]Possibly Troyes or Saint-Paul-Trois-Châteaux. See note opposite.
[9]I.e., Utopianism, Socialism, Communism, etc. See Commentary. Or "The Moorish law."
[10]Or "Pardons."

96. Chef de *Fossan*[1] aura gorge coupée
    Par le *ducteur*[2] du limier et lévrier:[3]
    Le fait *patré*[4] par ceux du mont *Tarpée*,[5]
    Saturne en *Leo* 13. de Février.

97. Nouvelle loi terre neuve occuper
    Vers la *Syrie, Iudée* et *Palestine*:
    Le grand empire barbare *corruer*,[6]
    Avant que *Phebés*[7] son siècle *determine*.[8]

98. Deux royals frères si fort guerroyeront
    Qu'entre eux sera la guerre si mortelle,
    Qu'un chacun places fortes occuperont:
    De regne et vie sera leur grande querelle.

99. Aux champs herbeux d'*Alein* et du *Varneigne*[9]
    Du mont *Lebron* proche de la *Durance*,
    Camps de deux parts conflit sera si aigre,
    *Mesopotamie* défaillira en la *France*.

100. Entre *Gaulois* le dernier honoré,
    D'homme ennemi sera victorieux:
    Force et terroir en moment exploré,
    D'un coup de trait quand mourra l'envieux.

[1]Variant: *FOVSSAN*.
[2]Latin *ductor*, leader.
[3]O.F. *leurier*, as the word appears in the text, had an original meaning, "hunter of otters."
[4]Latin *patratus*, executed.
[5]Latin *Mons Tarpeius*, Tarpeian Rock on the Capitoline Hill, off which traitors and criminals were thrown.
[6]The nearest to this form is in the Catalan *corroer*, to decay.
[7]Latin *Phoebe*, the Moon.
[8]O.F. *determiner*, to finish.
[9]Lack of rime uniform in all editions. Probably erratum for *Varneigre*.

96. The Chief of Fossano will have his throat cut
By the leader of the bloodhound and greyhound:
The deed executed by those of the Tarpeian Rock,[1]
Saturn in Leo February 13.

97. New law to occupy the new land
Towards Syria, Judea and Palestine:
The great barbarian empire to decay,
Before the Moon completes it cycle.

98. Two royal brothers will wage war so fiercely
That between them the war will be so mortal
That both will occupy the strong places:
Their great quarrel will fill realm and life.

99. In the grassy fields of Alleins and Vernègues
Of the Lubéron range near the Durance,
The conflict will be very sharp for both armies,
Mesopotamia will fail in France.

100. The last one honored amongst the Gauls,
Over the enemy man will he be victorious:
Force and land in a moment explored,
When the envious one will die from an arrow shot.

[1]Possible implications include Romans, Italians, traitors, criminals or republicans.

# Centurie IV

1. Cela du reste de sang non épandu:
   Venise quiert secours être donné:
   Après avoir bien longtemps attendu,
   Cité livrée au premier cor sonné.

2. Par mort la France prendra voyage à faire,
   Classe¹ par mer, marcher monts Pyrenées,
   Espaigne en trouble, marcher gent militaire:
   Des plus grandes Dames en France emmenées.

3. D'Arras et Bourges, de Brodes² grands enseignes,
   Un plus grand nombre de Gascons battre à pied,
   Ceux long du Rosne saigneront les Espaignes:
   Proche du mont où Sagonte s'assied.

4. L'impotent prince fâché, plaints et querelles,
   De rapts et pilles,³ par coqs et par libyques:⁴
   Grand est par terre, par mer infinies voiles,
   Seule Italie sera chassant Celtiques.

5. Croix, paix, sous un accompli divin verbe,
   L'Espaigne et Gaule seront unis ensemble:
   Grande clade⁵ proche, et combat très-acerbe:
   Cœur si hardi ne sera qui ne tremble.

6. D'habits nouveaux après faite la treuve,⁶
   Malice trame et machination:
   Premier mourra qui en fera la preuve,
   Couleur venise insidiation.⁷

7. Le mineur fils du grand et haï Prince,
   De lèpre aura à vingt ans grande tache:
   De deuil sa mère mourra bien triste et mince,
   Et il mourra là où tombe chair lâche.

¹Latin classis, fleet.
²O.F. brode, brown; black; decadent.
³O.F. pille, pillage, plunder.
⁴Latin Libycus, Libyan, African.
⁵Latin clades, disaster.
⁶O.F. treuve, discovery, find.
⁷O.F. insidiation, snare, trap.

# Century IV

1. That of the remainder of blood unshed:
   Venice demands that relief be given:
   After having waited a very long time,
   City delivered up at the first sound of the horn.

☞ 2. Because of death France will take to making a journey,
   Fleet by sea, marching over the Pyrenees Mountains,
   Spain in trouble, military people marching:
   Some of the greatest Ladies carried off to France.

3. From Arras and Bourges[1] many banners of Dusky Ones,[2]
   A greater number of Gascons to fight on foot,
   Those along[3] the Rhône will bleed the Spanish:
   Near the mountain where Sagunto sits.

4. The impotent Prince angry, complaints and quarrels,
   Rape and pillage, by cocks and Africans:[4]
   Great it is by land, by sea infinite sails,
   Italy alone will be chasing Celts.

☞ 5. Cross, peace, under one the divine word accomplished,[5]
   Spain and Gaul will be united together:
   Great disaster near, and combat very bitter:
   No heart will be so hardy as not to tremble.

6. By the new clothes after the find is made,
   Malicious plot and machination:
   First will die he who will prove it,
   Color Venetian trap.[6]

☞ 7. The minor[7] son of the great and hated Prince,
   He will have a great touch of leprosy at the age of twenty:
   Of grief his mother will die very sad and emaciated,
   And he will die where the loose flesh falls.

[1] Though a valid place name, the context suggests that *Bourges* represents metathesis for *Bruges*.
[2] Or "Black ones."
[3] Or possibly "Those from along."
[4] I.e., Frenchmen and Algerians. See Commentary.
[5] Garencières (p. 153) would have it "under an accomplished theologian" (from Greek *theo-logos*, divine word).
[6] Possibly "Trap of Venetian-red color."
[7] From the context, the word apparently indicates "younger" or "youngest."

8.  La grande cité d'assaut prompt *repentin*[1]
    Surpris de nuit, gardes interrompus:
    Les *excubies*[2] et veilles saint *Quintin*
    *Trucidés*,[3] gardes et les portails rompus.

9.  Le chef du camp au milieu de la presse
    D'un coup de flèche sera blessé aux cuisses,
    Lors que *Geneue* en larmes et détresse
    Sera trahie par *Lauzan* et *Souysses*.

10. Le jeune Prince accusé faussement
    Mettra en trouble le camp et en querelles:
    Meurtri le chef pour le soutenement,
    Sceptre apaiser: puis guérir écrouelles.

11. Celui qu'aura *gouvert*[4] de la grande *cappe*[5]
    Sera induit à quelques cas *patrer:*[6]
    Les douze rouges viendront souiller la nappe,
    Sous meurtre, meurtre se viendra perpétrer.

12. Le camp plus grand de route mis en fuite,
    Guère plus outre ne sera pourchassé:
    *Ost*[7] *recampé*[8] et légion réduite,
    Puis hors des *Gaules* du tout sera chassé.

13. De plus grande perte nouvelles rapportées,
    Le rapport fait le camp s'étonnera:
    Bandes unies encontre révoltées:
    Double phalange grand abandonnera.

14. La mort subite du premier personnage
    Aura changé et mis un autre au regne:
    Tôt, tard venu à si haut et bas âge,
    Que terre et mer faudra qu'on le craigne.

[1] Latin *repentinus*, sudden, unexpected.
[2] Latin *excubiae*, guard, watch.
[3] Latin *trucidatus*, slaughtered, massacred.
[4] O.F. *gouvert*, helm, government.
[5] O.F. *cappe*, (1) cope (modern *chape*) or (2) cloak (modern *cape*).
[6] Latin *patrare*, to perform, execute.
[7] O.F. *ost*, expedition, army.
[8] Provençal *recampar*, to collect, gather, reassemble.

8. The great city by prompt and sudden assault
   Surprised at night, guards interrupted:
   The guards and watches of Saint-Quentin
   Slaughtered, guards and the portals broken.

9. The chief of the army in the middle of the crowd
   Will be wounded by an arrow shot in the thighs,
   When Geneva in tears and distress
   Will be betrayed by Lausanne and the Swiss.

10. The young Prince falsely accused
    Will plunge the army into trouble and quarrels:
    The chief murdered for his support,
    Sceptre to pacify: then to cure scrofula.

11. He who will have the government of the great cope[1]
    Will be prevailed upon to perform several deeds:
    The twelve red ones who will come to soil the cloth,
    Under murder, murder will come to be perpetrated.

12. The greater army put to flight in disorder,
    Scarcely further will it be pursued:
    Army reassembled and the legion reduced,
    Then it will be chased out completely from the Gauls.

13. News of the greater loss reported,
    The report will astonish the army:
    Troops united against the revolted:[2]
    The double phalanx[3] will abandon the great one.

14. The sudden death of the first personage
    Will have caused a change and put another in the sovereignty:
    Soon, late come so high and of low age,
    Such by land and sea that it will be necessary to fear him.

---

[1] Or *cloak.* In either case, the Pope is probably intended. See Commentary.
[2] Or "United troops in revolt in opposition."
[3] Or "Both phalanxes."

15.  D'où pensera faire venir famine,
     De là viendra le rassasiement:
     L'œil de la mer par avare canine
     Pour de l'un l'autre *donra*[1] huile, froment.

16.  La cité franche de liberté fait *serve:*[2]
     Des *profligés*[3] et rêveurs fait asile.
     Le Roi changé à eux non si *proterve:*[4]
     De cent seront devenus plus de mille.

17.  Changer à *Beaune, Nuy, Chalons* et *Dijon,*
     Le duc voulant *amander*[5] la *Barree*[6]
     Marchant[7] près fleuve, poisson, bec de plongeon
     Verra la queue: porte sera serrée.

18.  Des plus lettrés dessus les faits célestes
     Seront par princes ignorants réprouvés:
     Punis d'Édit, chassés, comme *scelestes,*[8]
     Et mis à mort là où seront trouvés.

19.  Devant *Roüan d'Insubres* mis le siège,
     Par terre et mer enfermés les passages:
     *D'Haynault,* et *Flandres,* de *Gand* et ceux de *Liege*
     Par dons *laenees*[9] raviront les rivages.

20.  Paix *uberté*[10] longtemps lieu louera:
     Par tout son regne désert la fleur de lis:
     Corps morts d'eau, terre là l'on apportera,
     *Sperant*[11] vain heur d'être là ensevelis.

21.  Le changement sera fort difficile:
     Cité, province au change gain fera:
     Cœur haut, prudent mis, chassé lui habile,
     Mer, terre, peuple son état changera.

---

[1] *Donnera* by syncope.
[2] Latin *servus*, servile, subject.
[3] Latin *profligatus*, profligate, corrupt, dissolute.
[4] Latin *protervus*, violent, vehement.
[5] O.F. *amander*, to better, improve.
[6] O.F. *barré*, motley. The name was applied to the Carmelite monks. A sister order founded in 1452, was reformed by St. Theresa in 1562, after a long fight. See Commentary for further details.
[7] Also the O.F. spelling of *marchand.*
[8] Latin *scelestus*, rogue, scoundrel.
[9] Latin *laena*, cloak, mantle.
[10] Latin *ubertas*, plenty, abundance.
[11] Latin *sperans*, expecting, awaiting.

☞ 15. From where they will think to make famine come,
From there will come the surfeit:
The eye of the sea through canine greed
For the one the other[1] will give oil and wheat.

16. The free city of[2] liberty made servile:
Made the asylum of profligates and dreamers.
The King changed to them not so violent:
From one hundred become more than a thousand.

17. To change at Beaune, Nuits, Châlon and Dijon,
The duke wishing to improve the Carmelite [nun][3]
Marching[4] near the river, fish, diver's[5] beak
Will see the tail: the gate will be locked.

18. Some of those most lettered in the celestial facts
Will be condemned by illiterate princes:
Punished by Edict, hunted, like criminals,
And put to death wherever they will be found.

19. Before Rouen the siege laid by the Insubrians,[6]
By land and sea the passages shut up:
By Hainaut and Flanders, by Ghent and those of Liége
Through cloaked gifts they will ravage the shores.

20. Peace and plenty for a long time the place will praise:
Throughout his realm the fleur-de-lys deserted:[7]
Bodies dead by water, land one will bring there,
Vainly awaiting the good fortune to be buried there.

21. The change will be very difficult:
City and province will gain by the change:
Heart high, prudent established, chased out one cunning,[8]
Sea, land, people will change their state.

[1] Or "For both."
[2] Or "by."
[3] See note five opposite, and Commentary.
[4] Or "Merchant."
[5] I.e., a diving bird. Garencières simplifies to "cormorant."
[6] I.e., "Milanese," the Insubrians being the classical inhabitants of that area, roughly the same as the province of Lombardy.
[7] Or "Throughout his abandoned realm the fleur-de-lys."
[8] The relationship of adjectives, verbs and pronouns here is virtually arbitrary in translation. The meaning is quite obscure.

22. La grande *copie*[1] qui sera déchassée,
    Dans un moment fera besoin au Roi:
    La foi promise de loin sera faussée,
    Nu se verra en piteux désarroi.

23. La légion dans la marine *classe*[2]
    *Calcine*,[3] *Magnes*[4] soufre, et poix brûlera:
    Le long repos de l'assurée place:
    Port *Selyn*,[5] *Hercle*[6] feu les consumera.

24. Ouï sous terre sainte d'âme[7] voix *fainte*,[8]
    Humaine flamme pour divine voir luire:
    Fera des seuls de leur sang terre teinte,
    Et les saints temples pour les impurs détruire.

25. Corps sublimes sans fin à l'œil visibles,
    *Obnubiler*[9] viendront par ces raisons:
    Corps, front compris, sens, chef et invisibles,
    Diminuant les sacrées oraisons.

26. *Lou*[10] *grand eyssame se leuera d'abelhos,*
    *Que non sauran don te siegen venguddos;*
    *De nuech l'embousque, lou gach*[11] *dessous las treilhos*[12]
    *Cieutad trahido per cinq lengos*[13] *non nudos.*

27. *Salon, Mansol*,[14] *Tarascon de SEX.*[15] l'arc,
    Où est debout encore la pyramide:[16]
    Viendront livrer le Prince *Dannemarc*,[17]
    Rachat honni au temple d'*Artemide*.

[1]Latin *copia*, army, troops.
[2]Latin, *classis*, fleet.
[3]Provençal, *Calcina*, lime.
[4]Latin *Magnes*, magnet, loadstone. Or possibly abbreviation for *Magnésie*, used loosely for many oxides of iron and bioxides of manganese, also pyrites and amalgams. All equals "Greek fire."
[5]Greek *selene*, moon or crescent.
[6]Latin *Portus Herculis Monoeci*, Monaco.
[7]Variant: *Dame*.
[8]O.F. *faint*, (1) soft, weak, faint; (2) artificial, false, pretended. Variant: *sainte*.
[9]Latin *obnubilare*, to overcloud, obscure.
[10]Since this quatrain is almost entirely in Provençal, we have transcribed it uncorrected, with footnotes only for disputed words.
[11]Provençal *gach*, (1) sentinel, (2) jay.
[12]Provençal *trelha*, vine. Le Pelletier, seeking to get *Tuileries* out of it (see Commentary) has the French equivalent as an anagram for *Thuileries*. Actually, the French equivalent is *treilles*.
[13]Provençal *lenguos*, babblers (i.e., more than the equivalent of *langues*).
[14]Erratum for *Mausol* (for *Saint-Paul-de-Mausole*, a cloister at Nostradamus' natal Saint-Rémy, subsequently an insane asylum where Van Gogh was confined shortly before his suicide in 1890). Together with the following, probably synecdoche for *Saint-Rémy*.

22. The great army which will be chased out,
    In one moment it will be needed by the King:
    The faith promised from afar will be broken,
    He will be seen naked in pitiful disorder.

23. The legion in the marine fleet
    Will burn lime, loadstone[1] sulfur and pitch:
    The long rest in the secure place:
    "Port Selyn"[2] and Monaco, fire will consume them.

24. Beneath the holy earth of a soul[3] the faint[4] voice heard,
    Human flame seen to shine as divine:
    It will cause the earth to be stained with the blood of the monks,[5]
    And to destroy the holy temples for the impure ones.

☞ 25. Lofty bodies endlessly visible to the eye,
    Through these reasons they will come to obscure:
    Body, forehead included, sense and head invisible,
    Diminishing the sacred prayers.

☞ 26. The great swarm of bees will arise,
    Such that one will not know whence they have come;
    By night the ambush, the sentinel[6] under the vines
    City delivered by five babblers not naked.[7]

☞ 27. Salon, Tarascon, "Mausol,"[8] the arch of "SEX.,"[8]
    Where the pyramid is still standing:[8]
    They will come to deliver the Prince of "Annemark,"[9]
    Redemption reviled in the temple of Artemis.

[1]Or possibly "magnesia" (see note 4 opposite, and Commentary).
[2]Genoa, chief port of the crescent-shaped Republic of Genoa (now the province of Liguria).
[3]Or "Beneath the earth the holy Lady."
[4]Or "false," or "holy."
[5]Literally, "the lone ones."
[6]Or "the jay."
[7]I.e., bribed.
[8]See notes opposite. The two lines add up designating an area bound by three close towns: Saint-Rémy (where Nostradamus was born), Salon (where he passed his final years) and Tarascon (one-time capital of Provence).
[9]If the same as in 641 and 933, "Annemark," or the Mark of Anne, is a clever Nostradamian enigmatic term for the Kingdoms of Bohemia-Moravia and Hungary, which became a Habsburg "mark" or frontier province in 1526 through the marriage to Emperor-designate Ferdinand of their heiress, Anne. (See Commentary and "Historical Background"). Or possibly, contrary to form in 641 and 933, here really "Denmark."

---

[18]Abbreviated first name on ruins of a Roman arch adjacent to Saint-Paul-de-Mausole. See Commentary.
[19]The pyramid-shaped Roman structure, popularly considered a mausoleum, adjacent to the arch, from which Saint-Paul-de-Mausole derived its name. (See Commentary.)
[17]Probably erroneous printer's correction for *d'Annemarc* as it appears in 641 and 933.

28. Lors que *Venus* du *Sol*[1] sera couvert,
    Sous la splendeur sera forme occulte:
    *Mercure* au feu les aura découvert,
    Par bruit bellique sera mis à l'insulte.

29. Le *Sol*[1] caché éclipsé par *Mercure*
    Ne sera mis que pour le ciel second:
    De *Vulcan Hermes* sera faite[2] pâture,
    *Sol*[1] sera vu pur, *rutilant*[3] et blond.

30. Plus onze fois *Luna*[4] *Sol*[1] ne voudra,
    Tous augmentés et baissés de degré:
    Et si bas mis que peu or on coudra:
    Qu'après faim peste, découvert le secret.

31. La Lune au plein de nuit sur le haut mont,
    Le nouveau *sophe*[5] d'un seul cerveau l'a[6] vu:
    Par ses disciples être immortel semond,
    Yeux au midi. En *seins*[7] mains, corps au feu.

32. Ès lieux et temps chair au poisson donnera lieu,
    La loi commune sera faite au contraire:
    Vieux tiendra fort puis ôtée du milieu,
    La *Panta Choina Philon*[8] mis fort arrière.

33. *Iupiter* joint plus *Venus* qu'à la Lune
    Apparaissant de plénitude blanche:
    *Venus* cachée sous la blancheur *Neptune*
    De *Mars* frappée par la *granée*[9] blanche.

34. Le grand mené captif d'étrange terre,
    D'or enchaîné au Roi *CHYREN* offert:
    Qui dans *Ausone, Milan* perdra la guerre,
    Et tout son *ost*[10] mis à feu et à fer.

---

[1] Latin *sol*, sun.
[2] The incorrect feminine is uniform in all editions.
[3] Latin *rutilans*, glowing red.
[4] Latin *luna*, moon.
[5] Latin *sophus*, wise man, sage.
[6] Variant: *la* (i.e., *là*).
[7] Correct as is, or from O.F. *sein*, (1) sign, mark; (2) grease; or O.F. *seins*, holy relics, saints' relics.
[8] Greek *Panta*, in every way; *Choinos*, common, public, social; *Philos*, friend, lover of. Garencières (p. 164) says the phrase is equivalent to Latin *omnia inter amicos communia*.
[9] Variant: *gravée*. Either version is obscure. The nearest are Provençal *granet*, little grain; O.F. *grané*, stew. Le Pelletier cites *gravee* as gravel in "roman" but we have found no authority.
[10] O.F. *ost*, army.

28. When Venus will be covered by the Sun,
    Under the splendor will be a hidden form:
    Mercury will have exposed them to the fire,
    Through warlike noise it will be insulted.

29. The Sun hidden eclipsed by Mercury
    Will be placed only second in the sky:
    Of[1] Vulcan Hermes will be made into food,
    The Sun will be seen pure, glowing red and golden.

30. Eleven more times the Moon the Sun will not want,
    All raised and lowered by degree:
    And put so low that one will stitch little gold:
    Such that after famine plague, the secret uncovered.

31. The Moon in the full of night over the high mountain,
    The new sage with a lone brain has seen it:[2]
    By his disciples invited to be immortal,
    Eyes to the south.[3] Hands in bosoms,[4] bodies[5] in the fire.

☞ 32. In the places and times of flesh giving way to fish,
    The communal law will be made in opposition:
    It will hold strongly the old ones, then removed from the midst,
    Communism[6] put far behind.

33. Jupiter joined more to Venus than to the Moon
    Appearing with white fulness:
    Venus hidden under the whiteness of Neptune[7]
    Struck by Mars through the white stew.[8]

☞ 34. The great one of the foreign land led captive,
    Chained in gold offered to King "Chyren":[9]
    He who in Ausonia,[10] Milan will lose the war,
    And all his army put to fire and sword.

[1]Or "By."
[2]Or "brain seen there."
[3]Or "Eyes at noon."
[4]Or "marks," or "greases," or "holy relics." See note 7, opposite.
[5]Or "body."
[6]Or "Socialism." See note 8, opposite. Literally, "Loving of Everything in Common."
[7]The planet Neptune only if Nostradamus' prophetic powers (and telescopic eyes) are accepted. Neptune, invisible to the naked eye, was not discovered till 1846. See Commentary.
[8]Or "little white grain"? Or "white gravel." (Le Pelletier's dubious version which he would have as the Milky Way, a likely reading in any event.)
[9]Anagram for "Henry."
[10]Italy in general, Kingdom of Naples in particular. See 370 *et al.*

35. Le feu éteint les vierges trahiront
    La plus grande part de la bande nouvelle:
    Foudre à fer, lance les seuls Rois garderont
    *Etrusque* et *Corse*, de nuit gorge *allumelle*.[1]

36. Les jeux[2] nouveaux en *Gaule* redressés,
    Après victoire de l'*Insubre champaigne:*[3]
    Monts d'*Esperie*, les grands liés, troussés:
    De peur trembler la *Romaigne* et l'*Espaigne*.

37. *Gaulois* par sauts, monts viendra pénétrer:
    Occupera le grand lieu de l'*Insubre:*
    Au plus profond son *ost*[4] fera entrer,
    *Gennes, Monech*[5] pousseront *classe*[6] *rubre*.[7]

38. Pendant que Duc, Roi, Reine occupera,
    Chef *Bizant* du captif en *Samothrace:*
    Avant l'assaut l'un l'autre mangera:
    Rebours ferré suivra du sang la trace.

39. Les *Rhodiens* demanderont secours,
    Par le *neglect*[8] de ses hoirs délaissée.
    L'empire *Arabe* révélera[9] son cours,
    Par *Hesperies* la cause redressée.

40. Les forteresses des assiégés serrés,
    Par poudre à feu *profondés*[10] en abîme:
    Les *proditeurs*[11] seront tous vifs serrés,
    Onc aux *sacristes*[12] n'avint si piteux schisme.

---

[1]O.F. *allumelle*, blade, cutting edge.
[2]Correct as is, or O.F. *Jeux*, Jews.
[3]In modern French *campagne;* preserved for rime.
[4]O.F. *ost*, army, expedition.
[5]Latin *Portus Herculis Monoeci*, Monaco.
[6]Latin *classis*, fleet.
[7]Latin *ruber*, red.
[8]Latin *neglectus*, neglect.
[9]Variant: *revalera*. O.F. *revaler*, to lower (one's price).
[10]O.F. *profondé*, sunk.
[11]Latin *proditor*, traitor.
[12]O.F. *sacriste*. sexton.

35. The fire put out the virgins will betray
    The greater part of the new band:
    Lightning in sword and lance the lone Kings will guard
    Etruria[1] and Corsica, by night throat cut.

36. The new sports[2] set up again in Gaul,
    After victory in the Insubrian[3] campaign:
    Mountains of Hesperia,[4] the great ones tied and trussed up:
    "Romania"[5] and Spain to tremble with fear.

37. The Gaul will come to penetrate the mountains by leaps:
    He will occupy the great place of Insubria:[6]
    His army to enter to the greatest depth,
    Genoa and Monaco will drive back the red fleet.

38. While he will engross the Duke, King and Queen
    With the captive the Byzantine chief in Samothrace:
    Before the assault one will eat the other:
    Reverse side metaled will follow the trail of the blood.

39. The Rhodians will demand relief,
    Through the neglect of its heirs abandoned.
    The Arab empire will reveal[7] its course,
    The cause set right again by Hesperia.[4]

40. The fortresses of the besieged shut up,
    Through gunpowder sunk into the abyss:
    The traitors will all be stowed away alive,
    Never did such a pitiful schism happen to the sextons.

[1] I.e., Tuscany.
[2] Or "The new plays," or "The new Jews."
[3] The environs of Milan, i.e., the Milanese or Lombardy.
[4] The Land of the West. Spain? America?
[5] The possessions of Rome, i.e., the Papal States, or the "[Holy] Roman Empire."
[6] Milan. See note 3, above.
[7] Or "will lower."

41. *Gymnique*[1] sexe captive par otage
    Viendra de nuit *custodes*[2] décevoir:
    Le chef du camp déçu par son langage
    *Lairra*[3] à la *gente*,[4] sera piteux à voir.

42. *Geneue* et *Langres* par ceux de *Chartres* et *Dole*
    Et par *Grenoble* captif au *Montlimard*
    *Seysset, Losanne*, par *fraudulente*[5] dol,
    Les trahiront par or soixante marcs.

43. Seront ouïs au ciel les armes battre:
    Celui au même les divins ennemis:
    Voudront loix saintes injustement débattre:
    Par foudre et guerre bien croyant à mort mis.

44. Deux gros de *Mende*, de *Roudés* et *Milhau*
    *Cahours, Limoges, Castres malo sepmano*[6]
    *De nuech l'intrado*,[7] de *Bourdeaux* un *cailhau*[8]
    Par *Perigort* au *toc de la campano*.[9]

45. Par conflit Roi, regne abandonnera:
    Le plus grand chef faillira au besoin:
    Morts, *profligés*[10] peu en réchappera,
    Tous *destranchés*[11] un en sera témoin.

46. Bien défendu le fait par excellence,
    Gardes-toi *Tours* de ta proche ruine:
    *Londres* et *Nantes* par *Reims* fera défense
    Ne passe[12] outre au temps de la bruine.

---

[1]Although uniform in all editions, this meaningless word is obviously a misprint for *gynique*, from Greek *gyne*, female. ( Latin *gymnicus* means gymnastic.)

[2]Latin *custodes*, guards.

[3]Syncope for *laissera*.

[4]Spanish *gente*, people, or variation of equivalent in any Romance language.

[5]Latin *fraudulentus*, fraudulent.

[6]Provençal or Spanish *mala semana*, bad week.

[7]Provençal *De nuech l'intrada*, by night the entry.

[8]Provençal *cailhan*, insult.

[9]Spanish *toque de campana*, peal of the bell.

[10]Latin *profligatus*, ruined, destroyed.

[11]O.F. *destranchés*, cut up.

[12]Variant: *passés* ( i.e., *passés* or *passez*).

☞ 41. Female sex captive as a hostage
   Will come by night to deceive the guards:
   The chief of the army deceived by her language
   Will abandon her to the people, it will be pitiful to see.

42. Geneva and Langres through those of Chartres and Dôle
   And through Grenoble captive at Montélimar
   Seyssel, Lausanne, through fraudulent deceit,
   They will betray them for sixty marks of gold.

43. Arms will be heard clashing in the sky:
   That very same year the divine ones enemies:
   They will want unjustly to discuss the holy laws:
   Through lightning and war the complacent one put to death.

44. Two large ones of Mende, of Rodez and Milhau
   Cahors, Limoges, Castres bad week
   By night the entry, from Bordeaux an insult
   Through Périgord at the peal of the bell.

☞ 45. Through conflict a King will abandon his realm:
   The greatest chief will fail in time of need:
   Dead, ruined few will escape it,
   All cut up, one will be a witness to it.

46. The fact well defended by excellence,
   Guard yourself Tours from your near ruin:
   London and Nantes will make a defense through Reims
   Not passing[1] further in the time of the drizzle.

[1]Or "Do not pass," or "Not passed."

47. Le noir[1] farouche quand aura essayé
    Sa main sanguine par feu, fer, arcs tendus:
    *Trestous*[2] le peuple sera tant effrayé,
    Voir les plus grands par col et pieds pendus.

48. *Planure*[3] *Ausonne* fertile, spacieuse
    Produira taons si tant de sauterelles:
    Clarté solaire deviendra *nubileuse*,[4]
    Ronger le tout, grande peste venir d'elles.

49. Devant le peuple sang sera répandu,
    Que du haut ciel ne viendra éloigner:
    Mais d'un longtemps ne sera entendu,
    L'esprit d'un seul le viendra témoigner.

50. *Libra* verra regner les *Hesperies*,[5]
    De ciel et terre tenir la monarchie:
    D'*Asie* forces nul ne verra péries,
    Que sept ne tiennent par rang la hiérarchie.

51. Un Duc cupide son ennemi ensuivre
    Dans entrera empêchant la phalange:
    Hâtés à pied si près viendront poursuivre,
    Que la journée conflict près de *Gange*.

52. En cité *obsesse*[6] aux murs hommes et femmes,
    Ennemis hors le chef prêt à soi rendre:
    Vent sera fort encontre les gendarmes,
    Chassés seront par chaux, poussière et cendre.

53. Les fugitifs et bannis révoqués:
    Pères et fils grand garnissant les hauts puits:
    Le cruel père et les siens suffoqués:
    Son fils plus pire submergé dans le puits.[7]

---

[1]Here quite possibly an anagram for *roy (roi)*.
[2]O.F. *trestous*, all, every single one.
[3]O.F. *planure*, plain.
[4]Latin *nubilosus*, cloudy.
[5]Latin *Hesperia*, Land of the West.
[6]Latin *obsessus*, besieged.
[7]This is the last verse of the original Bonhomme edition (as reprinted by Bareste). From here on, our text is based on a comparison of two others (the Pierre Rigaud of ca. 1600 and the 1605) instead of the original three texts, unless otherwise noted. For further details, see p. 116.

☞ 47. The savage black one[1] when he will have tried
  His bloody hand at fire, sword and drawn bows:
  All of his people will be terribly frightened,
  Seeing the greatest ones hung by neck and feet.

48. The fertile, spacious Ausonian[2] plain
  Will produce so many gadflies and locusts,
  The solar brightness will become clouded,
  All devoured, great plague to come from them.

49. Before the people blood will be shed,
  Only from the high heavens will it[3] come far:
  But for a long time of one nothing will be heard,
  The spirit of a lone one will come to bear witness against it.[3]

☞ 50. Libra[4] will see the Hesperias[5] govern,
  Holding the monarchy of heaven and earth:
  No one will see the forces of Asia perished,
  Only seven hold the hierarchy in order.

51. A Duke eager to follow his enemy
  Will enter within impeding the phalanx:
  Hurried on foot they will come to pursue so closely
  That the day will see a conflict near Ganges.[6]

52. In the besieged city men and women to the walls,
  Enemies outside the chief ready to surrender:
  The wind will be strongly against the troops,
  They will be driven away through lime, dust and ashes.

53. The fugitives and exiles recalled:
  Fathers and sons great garnishing of the deep wells:
  The cruel father and his people choked:
  His far worse son submerged in the well.

---

[1]Or "The savage king." See note 1, opposite.
[2]The rich Campanian plain, Ausonia being used for the Kingdom of Naples.
[3]Or "he . . . him."
[4]The Balance. See Commentary.
[5]The Lands of the West. Spain? America? See Commentary.
[6]A French town. Also possibly "the Ganges," the Indian river, but this is less likely.

54. Du nom qui onc ne fut au Roi *Gaulois*
    Jamais ne fut un foudre si craintif,
    Tremblant l'*Italie*, l'*Espagne* et les *Anglois*,
    De femme étrangers[1] grandement attentif.

55. Quand la corneille sur tour de brique jointe,
    Durant sept heures ne fera que crier:
    Mort présagée de sang statue teinte,
    Tyran meurtri, aux Dieux peuple prier.

56. Après victoire de *rabieuse*[2] langue,
    L'esprit *tempré*[3] en *tranquil*[4] et[5] repos:
    Victeur sanguin par conflit fait harangue,
    Rôtir la langue et la chair et les os.

57. Ignare envie au grand Roi supportée,
    Tiendra propos défendre lés écrits:
    Sa femme non femme par un autre tentée,
    Plus double deux ni fort ni cris.

58. Soleil ardent dans le gosier *coller*,[6]
    De sang humain arroser terre *Etrusque:*
    Chef *seille*[7] d'eau, mener son fils filer,
    Captive dame conduite en terre[8] *Turque.*

59. Deux assiégés en ardente ferveur:
    De soif éteints pour deux pleines tasses,
    Le fort limé, et un vieillard rêveur,
    Aux *Geneuois* de *Nira*[9] montra trace.

60. Les septs enfants en otage laissés,
    Le tiers viendra son enfant *trucider:*[10]
    Deux par son fils seront d'estoc percés,
    *Gennes, Florence,* les viendra *enconder.*[11]

---

[1]Variant: *étrange* (Fortune edition): *femmes étranges* (Roger, 1589).
[2]Latin *rabiosus*, raving, fierce, mad.
[3]O.F. *tempré*, tempered, moderate (modern *tempéré*). Variant: *tempté* (*tenté*).
[4]Can only be apocope for *tranquillité.*
[5]Variant: *tranquille* (Fortune edition).
[6]O.F. *coller*, to swallow.
[7]O.F. *seille*, pail, bucket, jar.
[8]Variant: *en terre* (Fortune and false "1568" editions).
[9]Enigmatic name uniform in all editions. Original erratum for *Iura*, perhaps?
[10]Latin *trucidare*, to slaughter, massacre.
[11]Of dubious derivation. Possibly Latin *inconditus*, confused, without order, or *incutiere*, to strike against. Variant: *circonder* (Fortune edition) from Latin *circumdare*, to envelop, encompass.

☞ 54. Of the name which no Gallic King ever had
Never was there so fearful a thunderbolt,
Italy, Spain and the English trembling,
Very attentive to a woman and foreigners.[1]

☞ 55. When the crow on the tower made of brick
For seven hours will continue to scream:
Death foretold, the statue stained with blood,
Tyrant murdered, people praying to their Gods.

56. After the victory of the raving tongue,
The spirit tempered[2] in tranquillity and[3] repose:
Throughout the conflict the bloody victor makes orations,
Roasting the tongue and the flesh and the bones.

☞ 57. Ignorant envy upheld before[4] the great King,
He will propose forbidding the writings:
His wife not his wife tempted by another,
Twice two more neither skill[5] nor cries.

58. To swallow the burning Sun in the throat,
The Etruscan land[6] washed by human blood:
The chief pail of water, to lead his son away,
Captive lady conducted into Turkish land.

59. Two beset in burning fervor:
By thirst for two full cups extinguished,
The fort filed, and an old dreamer,
To the Genevans he will show the track from "Nira."[7]

☞ 60. The seven children left in hostage,
The third will come to slaughter his child:
Because of his son two will be pierced by the point,
Genoa, Florence, he will come to confuse[8] them.

---

[1]Or "Very attentive to a foreign woman," or "Very attentive to foreign women."
[2]Or "tempted."
[3]Or "in tranquil."
[4]Or "by."
[5]In view of the many meanings of *fort*, this translation is highly tentative.
[6]I.e., Tuscany.
[7]Unsolved enigmatic place name, or, by erratum, "the Jura," the nearby mountains.
See note opposite.
[8]Or "to envelop," or "to strike against." See note opposite.

61.  Le vieux moqué et privé de sa place,
     Par l'étranger qui le subornera:
     Mains de son fils mangées devant sa face,
     Le frère à *Chartres, Orl*[1] *Roüan* trahira.

62.  Un colonel machine ambition,
     Se saisira de la plus grande armée,
     Contre son Prince *fainte*[2] invention,
     Et découvert sera sous sa ramée.

63.  L'armée *Celtique* contre les montagnards,
     Qui seront sus et pris à la pipée:
     Paysans frais pousseront tôt *faugnars*,[3]
     Précipités tous au fil de l'épée.

64.  Le défaillant en habit de bourgeois,
     Viendra le Roi tenter de son offense:
     Quinze soldats la plupart *Vstagois*,[4]
     Vie dernière et chef de sa chevance.

65.  Au déserteur de la grande forteresse,
     Après qu'aura son lieu abandonné,
     Son adversaire fera si grande prouesse,
     L'Empereur tôt mort sera condamné.

66.  Sous couleur feinte de sept têtes rasées,
     Seront semés divers *explorateurs:*[5]
     Puits et fontaines de poisons arrosées,
     Au fort de *Gennes* humains dévorateurs.

67.  L'an[6] que *Saturne* et *Mars* égaux *combust*,[7]
     L'air fort séché longue *trajection:*[8]
     Par feux secrets d'ardeur grand lieu *adust*,[9]
     Peu pluie, vent chaud, guerres, incursions.

[1]Apocope for *Orléans.*
[2]O.F. *fainte,* false.
[3]Provençal *faugnar,* to press grapes.
[4]O.F. *ustaige,* pirate, corsair, and (by extension) bandit, outlaw.
[5]Latin *explorator,* spy.
[6]Variant: *Lors.*
[7]Latin *combustus,* burned, consumed, ruined, destroyed.
[8]Latin *trajectio,* shooting star, meteor.
[9]Latin *adustus,* burned by the sun, scorched.

61. The old one mocked and deprived of his place,
    By the foreigner who will suborn him:
    Hands of his son eaten before his face,
    His brother to Chartres, Orléans Rouen will betray.

62. A colonel with ambition plots,
    He will seize the greatest army,
    Against his Prince false invention,
    And he will be discovered under his arbor.

63. The Celtic army against the mountaineers,
    Those who will be learned and able in bird-calling:
    Peasants will soon work fresh presses,
    All hurled on the sword's edge.

64. The transgressor in bourgeois garb,
    He will come to try the King with his offense:
    Fifteen soldiers for the most part bandits,
    Last of life and chief of his fortune.

☞ 65. Towards the deserter of the great fortress,
    After he will have abandoned his place,
    His adversary will exhibit very great prowess,
    The Emperor soon dead will be condemned.

66. Under the feigned color of seven shaven heads
    Diverse spies will be scattered:
    Wells and fountains sprinkled with poisons,
    At the fort of Genoa devourers of men.

67. The year that[1] Saturn and Mars are equal fiery,
    The air very dry parched long meteor:
    Through secret fires a great place blazing from burning heat,
    Little rain, warm wind, wars, incursions.

[1] Or "When."

68. En lieu[1] bien proche non éloigné de *Venus*,
    Les deux plus grands de l'*Asie* et d'*Affrique*,
    Du *Ryn* et *Hister*[2] qu'on dira sont venus,
    Cris, pleurs à *Malte* et côté *Ligustique*.[3]

69. La cité grande les exilés tiendront,
    Les citadins morts, meurtris et chassés:
    Ceux d'*Aquilee* à *Parme* promettront,
    Montrer l'entrée par les lieux non tracés.

70. Bien contiguë des grands monts *Pyrenées*,
    Un contre l'Aigle grande *copie*[4] adresser:
    Ouvertes veines, forces exterminées,
    Que jusqu'à *Pau* le chef viendra chasser.

71. En lieu d'épouse les filles *trucidées*,[5]
    Meurtre à grande faute ne sera *superstile*.[6]
    Dedans le puits *vestules*[7] inondées,
    L'épouse éteinte par *hauste*[8] d'*Aconile*.[6]

72. Les *Artomiques*[9] par *Agen* et *l'Estore*,
    À *sainct Felix* feront leur parlement:
    Ceux de *Basas* viendront à la mal'heure,[10]
    Saisir *Condon* et *Marsan* promptement.

73. Le neveu grand par force prouvera
    Le *pache*[11] fait du cœur pusillanime:
    *Ferrare* et *Ast* le Duc éprouvera,
    Par lorsqu'au soir sera le pantomine.

---

[1]Variant: *En l'an*.
[2]Latin *Ister*, Lower Danube.
[3]Latin *Ligusticus*, Ligurian.
[4]Latin *copia*, forces, army.
[5]Latin *trucidatus*, killed, slaughtered.
[6]Uniform misprint in most editions. The Fortune edition has the obvious correction: *superstite . . . Aconite (Aconit)*. O.F. *superstite*, survivor.
[7]Probably misprint for *vestales*. Variant: *vestu (vêtu) les*.
[8]Latin *haustus*, drink.
[9]Obscure etymology. Most likely *Arecomici*, the division of the Volcae with their capital at Nîmes. See Commentary re others.
[10]Not *malheur*, *heur* always being masculine, and without an *e*.
[11]O.F. *pache*, treaty, agreement. Variant: *peché*.

68. In the place[1] very near not far from Venus,[2]
The two greatest ones of Asia and of Africa,
From the Rhine and Lower Danube they will be said to have come,
Cries, tears at Malta and the Ligurian side.[3]

69. The exiles will hold the great city,
The citizens dead, murdered and driven out:
Those of Aquileia[4] will promise Parma
To show them the entry through the untracked places.

70. Quite contiguous to the great Pyrenees mountains,
One to direct a great army against the Eagle:
Veins opened, forces exterminated,
As far as Pau will he come to chase the chief.

71. In place of the bride the daughters[5] slaughtered,
Murder with great error no survivor to be:
Within the well vestals[6] inundated,
The bride extinguished by a drink of Aconite.

72. Those of Nîmes[7] through Agen and Lectoure
At Saint-Félix will hold their parliament:
Those of Bazas will come at the unhappy hour
To seize Condom and Marsan[8] promptly.

73. The great nephew by force will test
The treaty made by the pusillanimous heart:
The Duke will try Ferrara and Asti,
When the pantomine[9] will take place in the evening.

[1]Or "In the year."
[2]Equally obscure as the planet, or as an enigmatic place name. As a place name, Portus Veneris (Portovenere), Venosa and even Venice (which has no etymological connection) remain possible.
[3]I.e., Genoa.
[4]Or "Venice." See notes and Commentary on 158.
[5]Or "the maids." Bridesmaids?
[6]Or possibly "Within the adorned well the."
[7]Somewhat doubtful. See note 9, opposite.
[8]There is a small village by this name in the area. But Mont-de-Marsan is more likely.
[9]Or, in its original Greek meaning, "the comedy."

74. Du *lac Leman* et ceux de *Brannonices:*[1]
    Tous assemblés contre ceux d'*Aquitaine:*
    *Germains* beaucoup encore plus *Souisses,*
    Seront défaits avec ceux d'Humaine.[2]

75. Prêt à combattre fera *defection,*[3]
    Chef adversaire obtiendra la victoire:
    L'arrière-garde fera *defension,*[4]
    Les défaillants morts au blanc territoire.

76. Les *Nibobriges*[5] par ceux de *Perigort*
    Seront vexés, tenant jusqu'au *Rosne :*
    L'associé de *Gascons* et *Begorne*[6]
    Trahir le temple, le prêtre étant au prône.

77. *Selin* monarque l'*Italie* pacifique,
    Regnes unis par Roi Chrétien du monde:
    Mourant voudra coucher en terre *blesique,*[7]
    Après pirates avoir chassé de l'onde.

78. La grande armée de la *pugne*[8] civile,
    Pour de nuit *Parme* à l'étrange trouvée,
    Septante neuf meurtris dedans la ville,
    Les étrangers passés tous à l'épée.

79. Sang Royal fuis, *Monhurt,*[9] *Mas, Esguillon,*
    Remplis seront de *Bourdelois les Landes,*
    *Nauarre, Bygorre* pointes et aiguillons,
    Profonds de faim *vorer*[10] de Liège glands.

[1]Probably Latin *Brannovices,* the people in the environs of Mâcon.

[2]Variant: *ceux du Maine* (Fortune).

[3]Latin *defectio,* (1) desertion; (2) swoon, fainting; (3) disappearance.

[4]O.F. *defension,* defense, resistance, protection.

[5]Variant: *Nictobriges.* In any case, Latin *Nitiobriges,* the people in the environs of Agen.

[6]This lack of rime uniform in all editions. Oddly, this is apparently a variant form of *Bigorre,* which *would* rime.

[7]Medieval Latin *Blesa,* Blois.

[8]Latin *pugna,* combat, contest, battle.

[9]Variant: *Monhuit.*

[10]Latin *vorare.* to devour.

74. Those of Lake Geneva and of Mâcon:[1]
    All assembled against those of Aquitaine:
    Many Germans many more Swiss,
    They will be routed along with those of "Humane."[2]

75. Ready to fight one will desert,[3]
    The chief adversary will obtain the victory:
    The rear guard will make a defense,
    The faltering ones dead in the white territory.

76. The people of Agen[4] by those of Périgord
    Will be vexed, holding as far as the Rhône:
    The union of Gascons and Bigorre
    To betray the temple, the priest giving his sermon.

☞ 77. "Selin"[5] monarch Italy peaceful,
    Realms united by the Christian King of the World:
    Dying he will want to lie in Blois soil,
    After having chased the pirates from the sea.

78. The great army of the civil struggle,
    By night Parma to the foreign one discovered,
    Seventy-nine murdered in the town,
    The foreigners all put to the sword.

79. Blood Royal flee, Monheurt, Mas,[6] Aiguillon,
    The Landes will be filled by Bordelais,
    Navarre, Bigorre points and spurs,
    Deep in hunger to devour acorns of the cork oak.

---

[1]Somewhat doubtful. See note 1, opposite.

[2]An enigmatic term. If "the Humane ones" is the idea intended, one would suspect a dig at the Protestants. If the association is with Humanism, the import would be the same, the Humanists being widely regarded as responsible for the Protestant Reformation. Or possibly "those of Maine."

[3]Or "faint," or "disappear."

[4]Or "Those of Agen." See note 5, opposite.

[5]Enigmatic surname of the victorious conqueror "Chyren" (Henry), the two names being found together in 627. See Commentary.

[6]Probably Le-Mas-d'Agenais.

80. Près du grand fleuve, grande fosse, terre *egeste*,[1]
    En quinze parts sera l'eau divisée:
    La cité prise, feu, sang cris conflit mettre,[2]
    Et la plupart concerne au *collisee*.[3]

81. Pont on fera promptement de nacelles,
    Passer l'armée du grand Prince *Belgique:*
    Dans *profondez*[4] et non loin de *Bruxelles,*
    Outre passés, *detranchez*[5] sept à pique.

82. Amas s'approche venant d'*Esclavonie,*
    L'*Olestant*[6] vieux cité ruinera:
    Fort désolée verra sa *Romanie.*
    Puis la grande flamme éteindre ne saura.

83. Combat nocturne le vaillant capitaine,
    Vaincu fuira peu de gens *profligé:*[7]
    Son peuple ému, sédition non vaine,
    Son propre fils le tiendra assiégé.

84. Un grand d'*Auxerre* mourra bien misérable,
    Chassé de ceux qui sous lui ont été:
    Serré en chaînes, après d'un rude cable,
    En l'an que *Mars, Venus* et *Sol*[8] mis[9] en été.

85. Le charbon blanc du noir sera chassé,
    Prisonnier fait mené au tombereau,
    *More*[10] Chameau sur pieds entrelacés,
    Lors le puîné cillera l'hobereau.

86. L'an que *Saturne* en eau sera conjoint
    Avec *Sol,*[8] le Roi fort et puissant
    À *Reims* et *Aix* sera reçu et oint,
    Après conquêtes meurtrira innocent.

---

[1]Latin *egestus,* drawn out.
[2]Variant: *moeste* (Fortune). From Latin *moestus,* sad.
[3]Possibly *colisée* (Colosseum). Or Latin *collisus,* collision, clash.
[4]Latin *profundatus,* poured forth.
[5]O.F. *detrancher,* to cut in pieces, cut.
[6]Possibly from Greek *oles* (root of *olluo,* to destroy) and possibly *thanatos,* destroying deadly, death-bringing. Thus "destroying-destroying"?
[7]Latin *profligatus,* overthrown, destroyed, ruined, conquered.
[8]Latin *Sol,* Sun.
[9]Variant: *joints* (Fortune).
[10]O.F. *more* (1) Moor *(Maure);* (2) black; (3) vigorous (Godefroy).

80. Near the great river, great ditch, earth drawn out,
    In fifteen parts will the water be divided:
    The city taken, fire, blood, cries, sad conflict,[1]
    And the greatest part involving the colosseum.[2]

81. Promptly will one build a bridge of boats,
    To pass the army of the great Belgian Prince:
    Poured forth inside and not far from Brussels,
    Passed beyond, seven cut up by pike.

☞ 82. A throng approaches coming from Slavonia,
    The old Destroyer[3] the city[4] will ruin:
    He will see his "Romania"[5] quite desolated,
    Then he will not know how to put out the great flame.

83. Combat by night the valiant captain
    Conquered will flee few people conquered:
    His people stirred up, sedition not in vain,
    His own son will hold him besieged.

84. A great one of Auxerre will die very miserable,
    Driven out by those who had been under him:
    Put in chains, behind a strong cable,
    In the year that Mars, Venus and Sun are in conjunction in summer.

85. The white coal will be chased by the black one,
    Made prisoner led to the dung cart,
    Moor[6] Camel on twisted feet,
    Then the younger one will blind the hobby falcon.

☞ 86. The year that Saturn will be conjoined in Aquarius[7]
    With the Sun, the very powerful King
    Will be received and anointed at Reims and Aix,[8]
    After conquests he will murder the innocent.

---

[1] Or "cries conflict to take place."

[2] Or "the collision." If the "colosseum" reading is correct, probably the one at Nîmes. See Commentary.

[3] Translation of a word of uncertain Nostradamian origin. See note 6, opposite.

[4] Or possibly "The Destroyer the old city" if the masculine ending of *vieux* is overlooked.

[5] Always dubious in purport. In this case, "Roman Empire" rather than Papal States seems to be the meaning. See Commentary.

[6] Or "Black," or "Vigorous."

[7] Literally "in the water." The inference is obvious.

[8] Aix-la-Chapelle (Aachen), coronation site for Emperors, 813–1531. Reims was for French kings.

87. Un fils du Roi tant de langues appris,
    À son aîné au regne différent:
    Son père beau[1] au plus grand fils compris,
    Fera périr principal adhérent.

88. Le grand *Antoine* du nom de fait sordide
    De Phtiriase à son dernier rongé:
    Un qui de plomb voudra être cupide,
    Passant le port d'élu sera plongé.

89. Trente de *Londres* secret conjureront,
    Contre leur Roi, sur le pont[2] l'entreprise:
    Lui, satellites la mort dégoûteront,
    Un Roi élu blond, natif de *Frize*.

90. Les deux *copies*[3] aux murs[4] ne pourront joindre,
    Dans cet instant trembler *Milan, Ticin*:[5]
    Faim, soif, *doutance*[6] si fort les viendra poindre
    Chair, pain, ni vivres n'auront un seul *boucin*.[7]

91. Au Duc *Gaulois* contraint battre au duel,
    La nef *Mellele*[8] *Monech*[9] n'approchera,
    Tort accusé, prison perpetuelle,
    Son fils regner avant mort tâchera.

92. Tête tranchée du vaillant capitaine,
    Sera jetée devant son adversaire:
    Sons corps pendu de la *classe*[10] à l'antenne,
    Confus fuira par rames à vent contraire.

93. Un serpent vu proche du lit royal,
    Sera par dame nuit chiens n'aboyeront:
    Lors naître en *France* un Prince tant royal,
    Du ciel venu tous les Princes verront.

[1]Possibly a play on *beau-père*.
[2]Possibly Latin *pontus*, sea.
[3]Latin *copia*, forces, army.
[4]Variant: *mers*.
[5]Latin *Ticinum*, Pavia.
[6]O.F. *doutance*, doubt.
[7]Provençal *boucin*, morsel, mouthful.
[8]This looks like Melilla, which does not fit the context too well. Variants: *Melle le; Mesele* (Fortune); *Meselle* (Garcin).
[9]Latin *Portus Herculis Monoeci*, Monaco.
[10]Latin *classis*, fleet, ship (by the reverse of extension).

87. A King's son learned in many languages,
    Different from his senior[1] in the realm:
    His handsome father[2] understood by the greater son,
    He will cause his principal adherent to perish.

☞ 88. Anthony by name great by the filthy fact
    Of Lousiness wasted to his end:
    One who will want to be desirous of lead,
    Passing the port he will be immersed by the elected one.

☞ 89. Thirty of London will conspire secretly
    Against their King, the enterprise on the bridge:[3]
    He and his satellites will have a distaste for death,
    A fair King elected, native of Frisia.[4]

90. The two armies will be unable to unite at the walls,[5]
    In that instant Milan and Pavia to tremble:
    Hunger, thirst, doubt will come to plague them very strongly
    They will not have a single morsel of meat, bread or victuals.

91. For the Gallic Duke compelled to fight in the duel,
    The ship of Melilla[6] will not approach Monaco,
    Wrongly accused, perpetual prison,
    His son will strive to reign before his death.

92. The head of the valiant captain cut off,
    It will be thrown before his adversary:
    His body hung on the sail-yard of the ship,
    Confused it[7] will flee by oars against the wind.

93. A serpent seen near the royal bed,
    It will be by the lady at night the dogs will not bark:
    Then to be born in France a Prince so royal,
    Come from heaven all the Princes will see him.

[1]Predecessor?
[2]Or possibly "His father-in-law."
[3]Or possibly "on the sea."
[4]The province of Friesland in particular, or Holland in general.
[5]Or "seas." Not very likely.
[6]In view of the doubts about the connotation of Melilla (a Moroccan seaport, Spanish since 1490) or its variants, the proper translation of this line is uncertain.
[7]Or "he."

94. Deux grands frères seront chassés d'*Espagne*,
    L'aîné vaincu sous les monts *Pyrenees*:
    Rougir mer, *Rosne*, sang *Leman*[1] d'*Alemagne*,
    *Narbon*, *Blyterre*,[2] d'*Agath*[3] contaminées.

95. Le regne à deux laissé bien peu tiendront,
    Trois ans sept mois passés feront la guerre:
    Les deux Vestales contre rebelleront,
    *Victor*[4] puîné en *Armonique*[5] terre.

96. La sœur aînée de l'île *Britannique*
    Quinze ans devant le frère aura naissance,
    Par son promis moyennant *verifique*,[6]
    Succédera au regne de balance.

97. L'an que *Mercure, Mars, Venus* rétrograde,
    Du grand Monarque la ligne ne faillir:
    Élu du peuple *l'vsitant*[7] près de *Gaudole*,[8]
    Qu'en paix et regne viendra fort *envieillir*.[9]

98. Les *Albanois*[10] passeront dedans *Rome*,
    Moyennant *Langres demipler*[11] affublés,
    Marquis et Duc ne pardonnent à homme,
    Feu, sang, *morbiles*[12] point d'eau faillir les blés.

99. L'aîné vaillant de la fille du Roi,
    Repoussera si profond les *Celtiques*,
    Qu'il mettra foudres, combien en tel arroi
    Peu et loin, puis profond ès *Hesperique*.[13]

100. Du feu céleste au Royal édifice,
     Quand la lumière de *Mars* défaillira,
     Sept mois grande guerre, mort gent de maléfice
     *Roüan, Eureux* au Roy ne faillira.

[1]Latin *Lemannus*, Lake of Geneva.
[2]Latin *Baeterrae Septimanorum*, Béziers.
[3]Latin *Agatha*, Agde.
[4]Latin *victor*, conqueror, victor.
[5]Probably *Armorica*, Brittany. Variant: *Armenique*.
[6]Nostradamian derivation from Low Latin *verificare*, to verify.
[7]Variant: *Lusitan* (Fortune). Obviously, *Lusitani*, Portuguese.
[8]Variants: *Gagdole; Gandole* (1557). The lack of rime, and excess over the needed single syllable, suggest an erratum. *Gade* for Latin *Gades*, Cadiz, has been an obvious suggestion. Also possible would be *Guarde*, for Guarda, a once-important Portuguese town from which royal princes derived the title Duke of Guarda.
[9]O.F. *envieillir*, to grow old.
[10]Dubious, deriving from Alba or Albania.
[11]A still-unsolved creation of Nostradamus, probably from the Greek. Le Pelletier's suggestion, *demos-pleres*, mob-full or multitude, remains as good as any.
[12]O.F. *morbilles*, smallpox.
[13]Latin *Hesperia*, Land of the West.

94. Two great brothers will be chased out of Spain,
    The elder conquered under the Pyrenees mountains:
    The sea to redden, Rhône, bloody Lake Geneva from Germany,
    Narbonne, Béziers contaminated by Agde.

95. The realm left to two they will hold it very briefly,
    Three years and seven months passed by they will make war:
    The two Vestals will rebel in opposition,
    Victor the younger in the land of Brittany.[1]

☞ 96. The elder sister of the British Isle
    Will be born fifteen years before her brother,
    Because of her[2] promise procuring verification,
    She will succeed to the kingdom of the balance.

97. The year that Mercury, Mars, Venus in retrogression,
    The line of the great Monarch will not fail:
    Elected by the Portuguese people near Cadiz,[3]
    One who will come to grow very old in peace and reign.

98. Those of Alba[4] will pass into Rome,
    By means of Langres the multitude[5] muffled up,
    Marquis and Duke will pardon no man,
    Fire, blood, smallpox no water the crops to fail.

99. The valiant elder son of the King's daughter,
    He will hurl back the Celts very far,
    Such that he will cast thunderbolts, so many in such an array
    Few[6] and distant, then deep into the Hesperias.[7]

100. From the celestial fire on the Royal edifice,
    When the light of Mars will go out,
    Seven months great war, people dead through evil
    Rouen, Evreux the King will not fail.

[1] Or "Armenia." Rather doubtful, unless the quatrain concerns Turkish or Persian princes.

[2] Or "his."

[3] Or "Guarda." Uncertain. See note 8 opposite.

[4] I.e., the troops of the Duke of Alba, generalissimo of Charles V and Philip II. Or "The Albanians," these rugged mountaineers having furnished many mercenaries in the 16th century.

[5] Translation subject to doubt. See note 11, opposite.

[6] "Near"?

[7] The Lands of the West, probably Spain and Portugal.

# Centurie V

1. Avant venue de ruine *Celtique,*
   Dedans le temple deux parlementeront
   Poignard cœur, d'un monté au coursier et pique,
   Sans faire bruit le grand enterreront.

2. Sept conjurés au banquet feront luire,
   Contre les trois le fer hors de navire:
   L'un les deux *classes*[1] au grand fera conduire,
   Quand par le *mal.*[2] Dernier au front lui tire.

3. Le successeur de la Duché viendra,
   Beaucoup plus outre que la mer de *Toscane:*
   *Gauloise* branche la *Florence* tiendra,
   Dans son giron d'accord nautique *Rane.*[3]

4. Le gros mâtin de cité *dechassé,*[4]
   Sera fâché de l'étrange alliance,
   Après aux champs avoir le cerf chassé
   Le loup et l'Ours se *donront*[5] défiance.

5. Sous ombre feinte d'ôter de servitude,
   Peuple et cité l'usurpera lui-même:
   Pire fera par fraude de jeune *pute,*[6]
   Livré au champ lisant le faux poëme.

6. Au Roi l'*Augur*[7] sur le chef la main mettre,
   Viendra prier pour la paix *Italique:*
   À la main gauche viendra changer le sceptre,
   De Roi viendra Empereur pacifique.

7. De Triumvir seront trouvés les os,
   Cherchant profond trésor énigmatique:
   Ceux d'alentour ne seront en repos,
   Ce *concauer*[8] marbre et plomb métallique.

---

[1]Latin *classis,* fleet (or, rarely, ship).
[2]Variant: *le mail,* the mall; the mallet. If *la maille,* the mail, the sense would be better.
[3]Latin *rana,* frog.
[4]O.F. *dechassé,* expelled.
[5]Syncope for *donneront.*
[6]O.F. *pute,* prostitute.
[7]Latin *Augur,* diviner, augur. In this case, apparently, the Pope.
[8]Latin *concavare,* to dig.

# Century V

1. Before the coming of Celtic ruin,
   In the temple two will parley
   Pike[1] and dagger to the heart of one mounted on the steed,
   They will bury the great one without making any noise.

2. Seven conspirators at the banquet will cause to flash
   The iron out of the ship against the three:
   One will have the two fleets[2] brought to the great one,
   When through the evil[3] the[4] latter shoots him in the forehead.

☞ 3. The successor to the Duchy will come,
   Very far beyond the Tuscan Sea:
   A Gallic branch will hold Florence,
   The nautical Frog in its gyron[5] by agreement.

4. The large mastiff expelled from the city
   Will be vexed by the strange alliance,
   After having chased the stag to the fields
   The wolf and the Bear will defy each other.

☞ 5. Under the shadowy pretense of removing servitude,
   He will himself usurp the people and city:
   He will do worse because of the deceit of the young prostitute,
   Delivered in the field reading the false poem.

☞ 6. The Augur[6] putting his hand upon the head of the King
   Will come to pray for the peace of Italy:
   He will come to move the sceptre to his left hand,
   From King he will become pacific Emperor.

☞ 7. The bones of the Triumvir will be found,
   Looking for a deep enigmatic treasure:
   Those from thereabouts will not be at rest,
   Digging for this thing of marble and metallic lead.

[1] Or "Quarrel." The hyperbaton of the original has been abandoned in translating this line.
[2] Or possibly "ships."
[3] Or "When in the mall."
[4] A period (as in the French) would make even less sense here.
[5] A term of heraldry. *Giron* may also mean merely "lap."
[6] By context, apparently the Pope. See note opposite.

8. Sera laissé feu vif, mort caché,
   Dedans les globes horrible épouvantable,
   De nuit à *classe*[1] cité en poudre lâché,
   La cité à feu, l'ennemi favorable.

9. Jusqu'au fond le grand arc *demolue*,[2]
   Par chef captif l'ami anticipé,
   Naîtra de dame front, face chevelue,
   Lors par astuce Duc à mort attrapé.

10. Un chef *Celtique* dans le conflit blessé
    Auprès de cave voyant siens mort abattre:
    De sang et plaies et d'ennemis pressé,
    Et secours par inconnus de quatre.

11. Mer par solaires sûre ne[3] passera,
    Ceux de *Venus* tiendront toute l'*Affrique:*
    Leur regne plus *Saturne* n'occupera,
    Et changera la part *Asiatique.*

12. Auprès du *lac Leman* sera conduite,
    Par *garse*[4] étrange cité voulant trahir:
    Avant son meurtre à *Ausbourg* la grande suite,
    Et ceux du *Rhin* la viendront envahir.

13. Par grande fureur le Roi *Romain Belgique*
    Vexer voudra par phalange barbare:
    Fureur grinçant, chassera gent *Lybique*[5]
    Depuis *Pannons*[6] jusques *Hercules* la hare.[7]

14. *Saturne* et *Mars* en *Leo Espaigne* captive,
    Par chef *Lybique*[5] au conflit attrapé,
    Proche de *Malte, Herodde*[8] prise vive,
    Et *Romain* sceptre sera par Coq frappé.

---

[1]Latin *classis,* fleet.
[2]Apparently a wrong past participle for *démolir,* to demolish.
[3]Variant: *ne* omitted.
[4]O.F. *garse,* young girl.
[5]Latin *Lybicus,* Libyan, African.
[6]Latin *Pannonia* (Upper and Lower).
[7]Latin *ara,* monument.
[8]Dubious word. Most likely *Herod,* were it not for feminine ending on words following (mistake?). Le Pelletier sees an anagram for *Rhodes.*

8. There will be unleashed live fire, hidden death,
   Horrible and frightful within the globes,
   By night the city reduced to dust by the fleet,
   The city afire, the enemy amenable.

9. The great arch demolished down to its base,
   By the chief captive his friend forestalled,
   He will be born of the lady with hairy forehead and face,
   Then through cunning the Duke overtaken by death.

10. A Celtic chief wounded in the conflict
    Seeing death overtaking his men near a cellar:
    Pressed by blood and wounds and enemies,
    And relief by four unknown ones.

11. The sea will not[1] be passed over safely by those of the Sun,
    Those of Venus will hold all Africa:
    Saturn will no longer occupy their realm,
    And the Asiatic part will change.

12. To near the Lake of Geneva will it[2] be conducted,
    By the foreign maiden wishing to betray the city:
    Before its[3] murder at Augsburg the great suite,
    And those of the Rhine will come to invade it.

☞ 13. With great fury the Roman Belgian King
    Will want to vex the barbarian with his phalanx:
    Fury gnashing, he will chase the African people
    From the Pannonias to the pillars of Hercules.[4]

☞ 14. Saturn and Mars in Leo Spain captive,
    By the African chief trapped in the conflict,
    Near Malta, "Herodde"[5] taken alive,
    And the Roman sceptre will be struck down by the Cock.

---

[1]Or "will."
[2]Or "she."
[3]Or "her."
[4]I.e., from Hungary to the Strait of Gibraltar.
[5]Enigmatic name. Herod? The daughter of Herod? Rhodes? See note 8, opposite.

15. En naviguant captif pris grand Pontife,
    Grand après faillir les clercs *tumultués:*[1]
    Second élu absent son bien débiffe,
    Son favori bâtard à mort roué.[2]

16. À son haut prix plus la larme *sabee*,[3]
    D'humaine chair par mort en cendre mettre,
    À l'île *Pharos* par *Croissars*[4] perturbée,[5]
    Alors qu'à *Rhodes* paraîtra dur *espectre*.[6]

17. De nuit passant le Roi près d'une *Androne*,[7]
    Celui de *Cypres*[8] et principal guet:
    Le Roi failli, la main fuit long du *Rosne*,
    Les conjurés l'iront à mort mettre.

18. De deuil mourra l'*infelix*[9] *profligé*,[10]
    Célébrera son *vitrix*[11] l'hécatombe:
    *Pristine*[12] loi, franc édit rédigé,
    Le mur et Prince au septième jour tombe.

19. Le grand Royal d'or, d'airain augmenté,
    Rompu la pache,[13] par jeune ouverte guerre:
    Peuple affligé par un chef lamenté,
    De sang barbare sera couverte terre.

20. Delà les *Alpes* grande armée passera,
    Un peu devant naîtra monstre *vapin*:[14]
    Prodigieux et subit tournera
    Le grand *Tosquan* à son lieu plus *propin*.[15]

[1]O.F. *tumultuer*, to be in a tumult.
[2]Variant: *tué*.
[3]Latin *Sabaeus*, of Saba (the Arabian city famed for frankincense).
[4]O.F. *crois*, crusade. Thus, crusader.
[5]Latin *perturbatus*, troubled, disturbed, unquiet.
[6]Provençal *espectre*, spectre, phantom.
[7]O.F. *androne*, alley.
[8]Variant: *Cipres*.
[9]Latin *infelix*, unhappy.
[10]Latin, *profligatus*, abandoned, overcome.
[11]Latin *victrix*, conqueress.
[12]Latin *pristinus*, former, early, original, primitive.
[13]O.F. *pache*, agreement, treaty.
[14]O.F. *vapin*, scamp, scoundrel, knave.
[15]Latin *propinquus*, near, neighboring.

☞ 15. The great Pontiff taken captive while navigating,
   The great one thereafter to fail the clergy in tumult:
   Second one elected absent his estate declines,
   His favorite bastard to death broken on the wheel.[1]

16. The Sabaean tear[2] no longer at its high price,
   Turning human flesh into ashes through death,
   At the isle of Pharos disturbed by the Crusaders,
   When at Rhodes will appear a hard phantom.

17. By night the King passing near an Alley,
   He of Cyprus and the principal guard:
   The King mistaken,[3] the hand flees the length of the Rhône,
   The conspirators will set out to put him to death.

18. The unhappy abandoned one[4] will die of grief,
   His conqueress will celebrate the hecatomb:
   Pristine law, free[5] edict drawn up,
   The wall and the Prince falls on the seventh day.

19. The great Royal one of gold, augmented by brass,
   The agreement broken, war opened by a young man:
   People afflicted because of a lamented chief,
   The land will be covered with barbarian blood.

20. The great army will pass beyond the Alps,
   Shortly before will be born a monster scoundrel:
   Prodigious and sudden he will turn
   The great Tuscan to his nearest place.

[1] Or "to death slain."
[2] I.e., Frankincense. See note opposite.
[3] Or by lost meanings of *faillir*, "escaped" or "finished" or "fallen."
[4] Or "The unhappy one overcome."
[5] Or "Frank" (i.e., French).

21. Par le trépas du Monarque *Latin*,
    Ceux qu'il aura par regne secourus:
    Le feu luira divisé le butin,
    La mort publique aux hardis encourus.

22. Avant qu'à *Rome* grand aie rendu l'âme,
    *Effrayeur*[1] grande à l'armée étrangère:
    Par escadrons l'embûche près de *Parme*,
    Puis les deux rouges ensemble feront chère.

23. Les deux contents seront unis ensemble,
    Quand la plupart à *Mars* seront conjoint:
    Le grand d'*Affrique* en *effrayeur*[1] tremble,
    DUUMVIRAT[2] par la *classe*[3] déjoint.

24. Le regne et loi sous *Venus* élevé,
    *Saturne* aura sus *Iupiter* empire:
    La loi et regne par le Soleil levé,
    Par *Saturnins*[4] endurera le pire.

25. Le Prince *Arabe Mars, Sol,*[5] *Venus, Lion,*
    Regne d'Église par mer succombera:
    Devers la *Perse* bien près d'un million,
    *Bisance, Egypte ver. serp.*[6] *invadera.*[7]

26. La gent esclave par un heur martial,
    Viendra en haut degré tant élevée:
    Changeront Prince, naîtra un provincial,
    Passer la mer *copie*[8] aux monts levée.

27. Par feu et armes non loin de la *marnegro,*[9]
    Viendra de *Perse* occuper *Trebisonde:*
    Trembler *Pharos,*[10] *Methelin,*[11] *Sol*[5] *alegro,*[12]
    De sang *Arabe* d'*Adrie* couvert onde.

[1] O.F. *effrayeur*, terror, fright.
[2] In capitals thus in original.
[3] Latin *classis*, fleet.
[4] Latin *Saturnius*, of Saturn.
[5] Latin *Sol*, Sun.
[6] Possibly apocope of Latin *vera serpens*, true serpent.
[7] Latin *invadere*, to invade.
[8] Latin *copia*, forces, army.
[9] Italian *marne(g)ro*, Black Sea.
[10] Variant: *Phato.*
[11] Apparently Nostradamian version of *Mytilene.*
[12] Either O.F. *alegre*, joyful, or Italian *allegro*, brisk.

21. By the death of the Latin Monarch,
    Those whom he will have assisted through his reign:[1]
    The fire will light up again the booty divided,
    Public death for the bold ones who incurred it.

22. Before the great one has given up the ghost at Rome,
    Great terror for the foreign army:
    The ambush by squadrons near Parma,
    Then the two red ones will celebrate together.

23. The two contented ones will be united together,
    When for the most part they will be conjoined with Mars:
    The great one of Africa trembles in terror,
    Duumvirate disjoined by the fleet.

24. The realm and law raised under Venus,
    Saturn will have dominion over Jupiter:
    The law and realm raised by the Sun,
    Through those of Saturn it will suffer the worst.

25. The Arab Prince Mars, Sun, Venus, Leo,[2]
    The rule of the Church will succumb by sea:
    Towards Persia very nearly a million men,
    The true serpent[3] will invade Byzantium and Egypt.

26. The slavish[4] people through luck in war
    Will become elevated to a very high degree:
    They will change their Prince, one born a provincial,
    An army raised in the mountains to pass over the sea.

27. Through fire and arms not far from the Black Sea,
    He will come from Persia to occupy Trebizond:
    Pharos, Mytilene to tremble, the Sun joyful,[5]
    The Adriatic Sea covered with Arab blood.

[1]Or "throughout his realm."
[2]Presumably meaning when Mars, the Sun and Venus are conjoined in Leo.
[3]Questionable. See note 6, opposite.
[4]Or "Slavic."
[5]Or "brisk."

28. Le bras pendu et la jambe liée,
    Visage pâle, au sein poignard caché,
    Trois qui seront jurés de la mêlée
    Au grand de *Gennes* sera le fer lâché.

29. La liberté ne sera recouvrée,
    L'occupera noir,[1] fier, vilain, inique,
    Quand la matière du pont[2] sera *ouvrée*,[3]
    D'*Hister*,[4] Venise fâchée la république.

30. Tout alentour de la grande cité,
    Seront soldats logés par champs et villes:
    Donner l'assaut *Paris, Rome* incité,
    Sur le pont[2] lors sera faite grande *pille*.[5]

31. Par terre *Attique* chef de la sapience,
    Qui de présent est la rose du monde:
    Pont[6] ruiné, et sa grande prééminence
    Sera *subdite*[7] et naufrage des ondes.

32. Où tout bon est, tout bien Soleil et Lune
    Est abondant, sa ruine s'approche:
    Du ciel s'avance *varier*[8] ta fortune,
    En même état que la septième roche.

33. Des principaux de cité rebellée
    Qui tiendront fort pour liberté ravoir:
    *Detrancher*[9] mâles, *infelice*[10] mêlée,
    Cris, hurlements à *Nantes* piteux voir.

34. Du plus profond de l'Occident *Anglois*
    Où est le chef de l'île *Britannique*
    Entrera *classe*[11] dans *Gyronde* par *Blois*,[12]
    Par vin et sel, feux cachés aux barriques.

---

[1]Possibly an anagram for *roi*.
[2]Quite possibly here apocope of *pontife*.
[3]O.F. *ouvrer*, (1) to open, (2) to create, execute.
[4]Latin *Ister*, Danube.
[5]O.F. *pille*, pillage.
[6]Possibly apocope for *pontificat*.
[7]Latin *subditus*, subjected.
[8]Per the original 1557 edition. Variant (in all others): *vaner* (*vanner*).
[9]O.F. *detrancher*, to cut up.
[10]Latin *infelix*, unhappy.
[11]Latin *classis*, fleet.
[12]*Blaye* rather than *Blois* is called for by the context.

☞ 28. His arm hung and leg bound,
Face pale, dagger hidden in his bosom,
Three who will be sworn in the fray
Against the great one of Genoa will the steel be unleashed.

29. Liberty will not be recovered,
A proud, villainous, wicked black one[1] will occupy it,
When the matter of the bridge[2] will be opened,[3]
The republic of Venice vexed by[4] the Danube.

30. All around the great city
Soldiers will be lodged throughout the fields and towns:
To give the assault Paris, Rome incited,
Then upon the bridge[2] great pillage will be carried out.

31. Through the Attic land fountain of wisdom,
At present the rose of the world:
The bridge[5] ruined, and its great pre-eminence
Will be subjected, a wreck amidst the waves.

32. Where all is good, the Sun all beneficial and the Moon
Is abundant, its ruin approaches:
From the sky it advances to change[6] your fortune.
In the same state as the seventh rock.

☞ 33. Of the principal ones of the city in rebellion
Who will strive mightily to recover their liberty:
The males cut up, unhappy fray,[7]
Cries, groans at Nantes pitiful to see.

☞ 34. From the deepest part of the English West
Where the head of the British isle is
A fleet will enter the Gironde through Blois,[8]
Through wine and salt, fires hidden in the casks.

[1] Or "wicked king."
[2] Or possibly "the pontiff" or "the pontificate," i.e., the Papacy.
[3] Or "will be built."
[4] Or "from."
[5] Or possibly "the pontificate," i.e., the Papacy.
[6] Or "to winnow," according to the very dubious prevailing variant.
[7] Or "unhappy mixture." In connection with this translation, see Commentary for an interesting interpretation.
[8] Blaye? See note 12, opposite.

35. Par cité franche de la grande mer *Seline*,[1]
    Qui porte encore à l'estomac la pierre,
    *Angloise classe*[2] viendra sous la bruine
    Un rameau prendre, du grand ouverte guerre.

36. De sœur le frère par *simulte*[3] *faintise*[4]
    Viendra mêler rosée en minéral:
    Sur la *placente*[5] donné à vieille tardive,
    Meurt le goûtant sera simple et rural.

37. Trois cents seront d'un vouloir et accord,
    Que pour venir au bout de leur atteinte,
    Vingt mois après tous et *record*[6]
    Leur Roi trahi simulant haine feinte.

38. Ce grand monarque qu'au mort succédera,
    Donnera vie illicite lubrique:
    Par nonchalance à tous concédera,
    Qu'à la *parfin*[7] faudra la loi *Salique*.

39. Du vrai rameau de fleur-de-lis issu,
    Mis et logé héritier d'*Hetrurie:*
    Son sang antique de longue main tissu,
    Fera *Florence* fleurir en l'armoiries.

40. Le sang royal sera si très mêlé,
    Contraints seront *Gaulois* de l'*Hesperie:*
    On attendra que terme soit coulé,
    Et que mémoire de la voix soit périe.

41. Né sous les ombres et journée nocturne,
    Sera en regne et bonté souveraine:
    Fera renaître son sang de l'antique urne,
    Renouvelant siècle d'or pour l'airain.

[1]Greek *selene*, moon or crescent.
[2]Latin *classis*, fleet.
[3]O.F. *simulte*, quarrel.
[4]O.F. *faintise*, deceit, dissimulation.
[5]Latin *placenta*, cake.
[6]O.F. *record*, memory.
[7]O.F. *parfin*, end.

35. For the free city of the great Crescent[1] sea,
    Which still carries the stone in its stomach,
    The English fleet will come under the drizzle
    To seize a branch, war opened by the great one.

36. The sister's brother through the quarrel and deceit
    Will come to mix dew in the mineral:
    On the cake given to the slow old woman,
    She dies tasting it she will be simple and rustic.

37. Three hundred will be in accord with one will
    To come to the execution of their blow,
    Twenty months after all memory[2]
    Their king betrayed simulating feigned hate.

☞ 38. He who will succeed the great monarch on his death
    Will lead an illicit and wanton life:
    Through nonchalance he will give way to all,
    So that in the end the Salic law will fail.

☞ 39. Issued from the true branch of the fleur-de-lys,
    Placed and lodged as heir of Etruria:[3]
    His ancient blood woven by long hand,
    He will cause the escutcheon of Florence to bloom.

40. The blood royal will be so very mixed,
    Gauls will be constrained by Hesperia:[4]
    One will wait until his term has expired,
    And until the memory of his voice has perished.

41. Born in the shadows and during a dark day,
    He will be sovereign in realm and goodness:
    He will cause his blood to rise again in the ancient urn,
    Renewing the age of gold for that of brass.

---

[1]Probably the Bay of Biscay, shaped like a crescent moon. The city may be La Rochelle.

[2]The grammar here is particularly confusing.

[3]I.e., the Duchy of Florence (Duchy of Tuscany, 1569–1860).

[4]The Land of the West. Spain? America?

42. *Mars* élevé en son plus haut beffroi,
    Fera retraire les *Allobrox*¹ de *France:*
    La gent *Lombarde* fera si grand effroi,
    À ceux de l'Aigle compris sous la Balance.

43. La grande ruine des sacrés ne s'éloigne,
    *Prouence, Naples, Sicille, Seez* et *Ponce:*
    En *Germanie*, au *Rhin* et la *Cologne,*
    Vexés à mort par tous ceux de *Magonce.*²

44. Par mer le rouge sera pris de pirates,
    La paix sera par son moyen troublée:
    L'ire et l'avare commettra par feint acte,
    Au grand Pontife sera l'armée doublée.

45. Le grand Empire sera tôt désolé
    Et *translaté*³ près d'*arduenne silue:*⁴
    Les deux bâtards par l'aîné décollé,⁵
    Et regnera *Aenobarbe*,⁶ nez de *milve.*⁷

46. Par chapeaux rouges querelles et nouveaux schismes
    Quand on aura élu le *Sabinois:*
    On produira contre lui grands sophismes,
    Et sera *Rome* lésée par *Albanois.*

47. Le grand *Arabe* marchera bien avant,
    Trahi sera par les *Bisantinois:*
    L'antique *Rodes* lui viendra au-devant,
    Et plus grand mal par *austre Pannonois.*⁸

48. Après la grande affliction du sceptre,
    Deux ennemis par eux seront défaits:
    *Classe*⁹ d'*Affrique* aux *Pannons*⁸ viendra naître,
    Par mer et terre seront horribles faits.

---

¹Latin *Allobrox*, classical inhabitants of Savoy.
²Latin *Maguntiacum*, Mayence or Mainz.
³Latin, *translatus*, transferred.
⁴Latin *Ardvenna Silva*, the Ardennes Forest.
⁵Uniformly in singular in all editions.
⁶Latin *Aenobarbus*, Redbeard. Also Nero's family name.
⁷Latin *milvus*, kite (a bird of the hawk family).
⁸Latin *Pannonii*, Pannonians, inhabitants of classical Hungary.
⁹Latin *classis*. fleet.

42. Mars raised to his highest belfry
Will cause the Savoyards to withdraw from France:
The Lombard people will cause very great terror
To those of the Eagle included under the Balance.

43. The great ruin of the holy things[1] is not far off,
Provence, Naples, Sicily, Sées[2] and Pons:[2]
In Germany, at the Rhine and Cologne,
Vexed to death by all those of Mainz.

44. On sea the red one will be taken by pirates,
Because of him peace will be troubled:
Anger and greed will he expose through a false act,
The army doubled by the great Pontiff.

45. The great Empire will soon be desolated
And transferred to near the Ardennes:
The two bastards beheaded[3] by the oldest one,
And Bronzebeard[4] the hawk-nose will reign.

46. Quarrels and new schisms by the red hats
When the Sabine will have been elected:
They will produce great sophisms against him,
And Rome will be injured by those of Alba.[5]

47. The great Arab will march far forward,
He will be betrayed by the Byzantinians:
Ancient Rhodes will come to meet him,
And greater harm through the Austrian Hungarians.

48. After the great affliction of the sceptre,
Two enemies will be defeated by them:[6]
A fleet from Africa will appear before the Hungarians,[7]
By land and sea horrible deeds will take place.

[1]Or possibly "of the clergy."
[2]Probable but not positive. The context permits of no certainty.
[3]See note 5, opposite.
[4]Or possibly "Nero." See note 6, opposite.
[5]Or "by the Albanians." See 498.
[6]Or "by each other," or "by themselves."
[7]A small strip of the Adriatic around Fiume was left to Austrian Hungary after the Turkish conquest.

49. Nul de l'*Espagne*, mais de l'antique *France*
    Ne[1] sera élu pour la tremblante nacelle,
    À l'ennemi sera faite *fiance*,[2]
    Qui dans son regne fera peste cruelle.

50. L'an que les frères du lis seront en âge,
    L'un d'eux tiendra la grande *Romanie*:
    Trembler les monts, ouvert *Latin* passage,
    *Pache*[3] marcher contre fort d'*Armenie*.

51. La gent de *Dace*, d'*Angleterre*, *Polonne*
    Et de *Boësme* feront nouvelle ligue:
    Pour passer outre d'*Hercules* la colonne,
    *Barcins*,[4] *Tyrrens*[5] dresser cruelle brigue.

52. Un Roi sera qui *donra*[6] l'opposite,
    Les exilés élevés sur le regne:
    De sang nager la gent *caste*[7] *hypolite*,[8]
    Et fleurira longtemps sous telle enseigne.

53. La loi du *Sol*[9] et *Venus contendus*,[10]
    Appropriant l'esprit de prophétie:
    Ni l'un ni l'autre ne seront entendus,
    Par *Sol*[9] tiendra la loi du grand *Messie*.

54. Du *Pont Euxine*,[11] et la grande *Tartarie*,
    Un Roi sera qui viendra voir la *Gaule*,
    Transpercera *Alane* et l'*Armenie*,
    Et dedans *Bisance lairra*[12] sanglante gaule.

[1]This negative does not go with the context here.
[2]O.F. *fiance*, assurance, promise.
[3]O.F. *pache*, accord, agreement, treaty. Or possibly the Turkish title *pasha*, governor.
[4]Latin *Barcino*, Barcelona.
[5]Latin *Tyrrheni*, Tyrrhenians (ancestors of Etruscans and Tuscans). Or possibly *Tyrii*, Tyrian, and thus applicable to any port believed by Nostradamus to have originated as a Phœnician colony.
[6]Syncope of *donnera*.
[7]Latin *castus*, chaste, pure.
[8]Greek *hypolitos*, rather poor, little or mean.
[9]Latin, *Sol*, Sun.
[10]O.F. *contendre*, to dispute, struggle, contend.
[11]Latin *Pontus Euxinus*, the Black Sea.
[12]O.F. *lairre*. to leave. abandon.

☞ 49. Not from Spain but from ancient France
Will one be elected for the trembling bark,[1]
To the enemy will a promise be made,
He who will cause a cruel plague in his realm.

☞ 50. The year that the brothers of the lily come of age,
One of them will hold the great "Romania":[2]
The mountains to tremble, Latin passage opened,
Agreement[3] to march against the fort of Armenia.

☞ 51. The people of Dacia,[4] England, Poland
And of Bohemia[5] will make a new league:
To pass beyond the pillars of Hercules,
The Barcelonans and Tuscans[6] will prepare a cruel plot.

52. There will be a King who will give opposition,
The exiles raised over the realm:
The pure poor people[7] to swim in blood,
And for a long time will he flourish under such a device.

53. The law of the Sun and of Venus in strife,
Appropriating the spirit of prophecy:
Neither the one nor the other will be understood,
The law of the great Messiah will hold through the Sun.

☞ 54. From beyond the Black Sea and great Tartary,
There will be a King who will come to see Gaul,
He will pierce through "Alania"[8] and Armenia,
And within Byzantium will he leave his bloody rod.

[1]I.e., the Papacy, the Bark of St. Peter.
[2]Used as a synonym of "Roman Empire." Or possibly the Papal States.
[3]Or possibly "Pasha."
[4]Probably intended for Transylvania, now part of Rumania (whose boundaries approximate those of Dacia) but in Nostradamus' time an intrinsic part of Hungary. See Commentary.
[5]Or, in modern terms, Czechoslovakia.
[6]Or "Tyrians," referring to a people believed by Nostradamus to be descended from Phœnicians.
[7]Mendicant friars?
[8]The land inhabited by the Alans, between the Don, the Volga and the Caucasus.

55.  De la *Felice Arabie contrade*,[1]
     Naîtra puissant de loi *Mahometique:*
     Vexer l'*Espagne, conquester*[2] la *Grenade,*
     Et plus par mer à la gent *Ligustique.*[3]

56.  Par le trépas du très-vieillard Pontife
     Sera élu *Romain* de bon âge,
     Qui sera dit que le siège débiffe,
     Et long tiendra et de piquant ouvrage.

57.  Ira de mont *Gaulfier*[4] et *Auentin,*
     Qui par le trou avertira l'armée:
     Entre deux rocs pris le butin,
     De *SEXT. mansol*[5] faillir la renommée.

58.  De l'aqueduc d'*Vticense*[6] *Gardoing,*
     Par la forêt et mont inaccessible,
     *Emmy*[7] du pont sera tranché[8] au poing
     Le chef *nemans*[9] qui tant sera terrible.

59.  Au chef *Anglois* à *Nimes* trop séjour,
     Devers l'*Espagne* au secours *Aenobarbe:*[10]
     Plusieurs mourront par *Mars* ouvert ce jour,
     Quand en *Artois* faillir étoile en barbe.

60.  Par tête rase viendra bien mal élire,
     Plus que sa charge ne porte passera:
     Si grande fureur et rage fera dire,
     Qu'à feu et sang tout sexe tranchera.

61.  L'enfant du grand n'étant à sa naissance,
     Subjuguera les hauts monts *Apennis:*
     Fera trembler tous ceux de la balance,
     Et des monts feux[11] jusqu'à *Mont Senis.*

[1]Provençal *contrada,* country.
[2]O.F. *conquester,* to conquer, win.
[3]Latin *Ligusticus,* Ligurian.
[4]Variant: *Gaufier.* Correct form is *Gaussier,* a hill near Saint-Rémy.
[5]Erratum for *Mausol.* See note on 427 and Commentary.
[6]Latin *Castrum Uceciense,* Uzès. *Uticensis* is actually the adjectival form of Utica,
near Carthage in North Africa, impossible here.
[7]O.F. *emmy,* in the middle of. Variant: *Ennemi.*
[8]Variants: *taché, tâché* (false "1568").
[9]Latin *Nemausus,* Nîmes.
[10]Latin *Aenobarbus,* Redbeard. Also Nero's family name.
[11]The Greek equivalent of *feu, pyr,* is the root of Pyrenees.

☞ 55. In the country of Arabia Felix[1]
There will be born one powerful in the law of Mahomet:
To vex Spain, to conquer Grenada,
And more by sea against the Ligurian people.[2]

56. Through the death of the very old Pontiff
A Roman of good age will be elected,
Of him it will be said that he weakens his see,
But long will he sit and in biting activity.

☞ 57. There will go from Mont Gaussier and "Aventin,"[3]
One who through the hole[4] will warn the army:
Between two rocks will the booty be taken,
Of Sextus' mausoleum[5] the renown to fail.

☞ 58. By the aqueduct of Uzès over the Gard,
Through the forest and inaccessible mountain,
In the middle of[6] the bridge there will be cut in[7] the fist
The chief of Nîmes who will be very terrible.

☞ 59. Too long a stay for the English chief at Nîmes,
Towards Spain Redbeard[8] to the rescue:
Many will die by war opened that day,
When a bearded star[9] will fall in Artois.

60. By[10] the shaven head a very bad choice will come to be made,
Overburdened he will not pass the gate:
He will speak with such great fury and rage,
That to fire and blood he will consign the entire sex.[11]

61. The child of the great one not by his birth,
He will subjugate the high Apennine mountains:
He will cause all those of the balance to tremble,
And from the Pyrenees to Mont Cenis.

[1]The part of Arabia now divided between Yemen and the Aden Protectorate.
[2]I.e., the Genoese.
[3]Mont Gaussier is a spur of the small Alpine range. "Aventin" may be a name used in Nostradamus' boyhood at Saint-Rémy, not to be located now. See Commentary.
[4]Or "Through the Trou," one of the ancient gates of Saint-Rémy. See Commentary.
[5]See note on 427 and Commentary regarding this Saint-Rémy landmark.
[6]Or "The enemy from."
[7]Or "Cut off by," or "Endeavor by."
[8]Or possibly "Nero."
[9]I.e., a comet, by poetic license. More realistically, a meteorite.
[10]Or "In."
[11]Or "both sexes."

62. Sur les rochers sang on verra pleuvoir,
    *Sol*[1] Orient, *Saturne* Occidental:
    Près d'*Orgon* guerre, à *Rome* grand mal voir,
    Nefs *parfondrées,*[2] et pris le *Tridental.*

63. De vaine *emprinse*[3] l'honneur indue plainte,
    Galiotes errants par *latins,* froids, faim, vagues
    Non loin du *Tymbre* de sang la terre teinte,
    Et sur humains seront diverses *plagues.*[4]

64. Les assemblés par repos du grand nombre,
    Par terre et mer conseil contremandé:
    Près de l'*Antonne*[5] *Gennes, Nice* de l'ombre
    Par champs et villes le chef *contrebandé.*[6]

65. Subit venu l'*effrayeur*[7] sera grande,
    Des principaux de l'affaire cachés:
    Et dame en braise[8] plus ne sera en vue,
    Ce peu à peu seront les grands fâchés.

66. Sous les antiques édifices vestaux,
    Non éloignés d'aqueduc ruiné:[9]
    De *Sol*[1] et Lune sont les luisants métaux,
    Ardente lampe *Traian* d'or buriné.[9]

67. Quand chef *Perouse* n'osera sa tunique
    Sens[10] au couvert tout nu s'*expolier:*[11]
    Seront pris sept fait Aristocratique,
    Le père et fils morts par pointe au collier.

[1]Latin *Sol,* Sun.
[2]O.F. *parfondrer,* to sink to the bottom (Godefroy).
[3]O.F. *emprinse,* enterprise, project.
[4]O.F. *plague,* wound, plague.
[5]Variant: *Autonne.* The 1589 Roger has *Automne.* A still unsolved proper noun. The closest compromises between the geography required by context and the sound are *Antibes* and *Mentone.*
[6]O.F. *contrebander,* to be in revolt (Sainte-Palaye).
[7]O.F. *effrayeur,* terror.
[8]Variant: *brasse* (O.F. word meaning "beer" or "brewery").
[9]*Ruine* and *burine* appear without accents in both the Rigaud and the 1605. Nevertheless, the accents given in the Fortune and here are made necessary by context, grammar and meter all. Variant: *butine (butiné).*
[10]Variant: *sans.*
[11]Latin *exspoliare,* to plunder, strip. Not from *expoliare.*

62. One will see blood to rain on the rocks,
    Sun in the East, Saturn in the West:
    Near Orgon war, at Rome great evil to be seen,
    Ships sunk to the bottom, and the Tridental[1] taken.

63. From the vain enterprise honor and undue complaint,
    Boats tossed about among the Latins,[2] cold, hunger, waves
    Not far from the Tiber the land stained with blood,
    And diverse plagues will be upon mankind.

64. Those assembled by the tranquillity of the great number,
    By land and sea counsel countermanded:
    Near "Antonne"[3] Genoa, Nice in the shadow
    Through fields and towns in revolt against the chief.[4]

65. Come suddenly the terror will be great,
    Hidden by the principal ones of the affair:
    And the lady on the charcoal[5] will no longer be in sight,
    Thus little by little will the great ones be angered.

66. Under the ancient vestal edifices,
    Not far from the ruined aqueduct:
    The glittering metals are of the Sun and Moon,[6]
    The lamp of Trajan engraved with gold burning.[7]

67. When the chief of Perugia[8] will not venture his tunic
    Sense under cover to[9] strip himself quite naked:
    Seven will be taken Aristocratic deed,
    Father and son dead through a point in the collar.

[1]One who wields the trident, the ruler of the seas. The "Neptune" of 259?
[2]Garencières' "Latin seas" seems a reasonable improvement here.
[3]Unsolved enigmatic place name. Autun? Mentone? Antibes? Or by Roger's (1589) variant, not a place name at all but "Near autumn."
[4]Or "the chief in revolt."
[5]Or "in the beer" or "in the brewery."
[6]I.e., gold and silver.
[7]Or "The golden lamp of Trajan burning, pillaged."
[8]I.e., the Pope.
[9]Or "Without any cover and."

68. Dans le *Danube* et du *Rhin* viendra boire
    Le grand Chameau, ne s'en repentira:
    Trembler du *Rosne*, et plus fort ceux de *Loire*,
    Et près des *Alpes* Coq le ruinera.

69. Plus ne sera le grand en faux sommeil,
    L'inquiétude viendra prendre repos:
    Dresser phalange d'or, azur et vermeil
    Subjuguer *Afrique* la ronger jusqu'os.

70. Des régions sujettes à la Balance,
    Feront troubler les monts par grande guerre,
    Captifs tout sexe dû et tout *Bisance*,
    Qu'on criera à l'aube terre à terre.

71. Par la fureur d'un qui attendra l'eau,
    Par la grande rage tout l'*exercite*[1] ému:
    Chargé des nobles à dix-sept bateaux,
    Au long du *Rosne* tard messager venu.

72. Pour le plaisir d'édit voluptueux,
    On mêlera le poison dans la foi:[2]
    *Venus* sera en cours si vertueux,
    Qu'offusquera du Soleil tout aloi.

73. Persécutée sera de Dieu l'Eglise,
    Et les saints Temples seront *expoliez*,[3]
    L'enfant la mère mettra nue en chemise,
    Seront *Arabes* aux *Pollons* ralliés.

74. De sang *Troyen* naîtra cœur *Germanique*
    Qui deviendra en si haute puissance:
    Hors chassera gent étrange *Arabique*,
    Tournant l'Eglise en *pristine*[4] prééminence.

75. Montera haut sur le bien plus à dextre,
    Demeurera assis sur la pierre carrée,
    Vers le midi posé à sa sénestre,
    Bâton tortu en main bouche serrée.

[1]Latin *exercitus,* army.
[2]Variant: *Loi.*
[3]Latin *exspoliare,* to plunder, pillage.
[4]Latin *pristinus,* former, original, pristine.

68. In the Danube and of the Rhine will come to drink
    The great Camel, not repenting it:
    Those of the Rhône to tremble, and much more so those of the Loire,
    And near the Alps the Cock will ruin him.

69. No longer will the great one be in his false sleep,
    Uneasiness will come to replace tranquillity:
    A phalanx of gold, azure and vermilion arrayed
    To subjugate Africa and gnaw it to the bone,

70. Of the regions subject to the Balance,
    They will trouble the mountains with great war,
    Captives the entire sex[1] enthralled and all Byzantium,
    So that at dawn they will spread the news from land to land.

71. By the fury of one who will wait for[2] the water,
    By his great rage the entire army moved:
    Seventeen boats loaded with the noble,
    The messenger come late along the Rhône.

72. For the pleasure of the voluptuous edict,
    One will mix poison in the faith:[3]
    Venus will be in a course so virtuous
    As to becloud the whole quality of the Sun.

☞ 73. The Church of God will be persecuted,
    And the holy Temples will be plundered,
    The child will put his mother out in her shift,
    Arabs will be allied with the Poles.

☞ 74. Of Trojan blood[4] will be born a Germanic heart
    Who will rise to very high power:
    He will drive out the foreign Arabic people,
    Returning the Church to its pristine pre-eminence.

75. He will rise high over the estate more to the right,
    He will remain seated on the square stone,
    Towards the south facing to his left,
    The crooked staff in his hand his mouth sealed.

[1]Or "both sexes."
[2]Or possibly "wait at."
[3]Or "the Law."
[4]Of the House of France, based on the legend of descent from Francus, a son of
Priam, King of Troy.

76. En lieu libre tendra son pavillon,
    Et ne voudra en cités prendre place:
    *Aix, Carpen*[1] *l'Isle Volce Mont*[2] Cauaillon,
    Par tous ces lieux abolira sa trace.

77. Tous les degrés d'honneur Ecclésiastique
    Seront changés en *dial*[3] *quirinal:*[4]
    En *Martial*[5] *quirinal flaminique,*[6]
    Puis un Roi de *France* le rendra *vulcanal.*[7]

78. Les deux unis ne tiendront longuement,
    Et dans treize ans au Barbare Satrape:
    Aux deux côtés feront tel *perdement,*[8]
    Qu'un bénira la Barque et sa *cappe.*[9]

79. La sacrée pompe viendra baisser les ailes,
    Par la venue du grand législateur:
    Humble haussera, vexera les rebelles,
    Naîtra sur terre aucun émulateur.

80. *Logmion*[10] grande *Bisance* approchera,
    Chassée sera la *Barbarique*[11] Ligue:
    Des deux lois l'une l'*estinique*[12] lâchera,
    Barbare et franche en perpétuelle brigue.

81. L'oiseau royal sur la cité solaire,
    Sept mois devant fera nocturne augure:
    Mur d'Orient cherra tonnerre éclair,
    Sept jours aux portes les ennemis à l'heure.

[1]Apocope for *Carpentras.*
[2]Uncertain. Perhaps apocope for *Montfavet.*
[3]Latin *Dialis,* of Jupiter.
[4]Latin *Quirinalis,* of Quirinus.
[5]Latin *Martialis,* of Mars.
[6]Latin *Quirinalis flamen,* priest of Quirinus.
[7]Latin *Vulcanalis,* of Vulcan.
[8]O.F. *perdement,* loss.
[9]O.F. *cappe,* (1) cope (modern *chape*) or (2) cloak (modern *cape*).
[10]Uniform error for *L'Ogmion.* Ogmios was the Celtic Hercules.
[11]Latin *Barbaricus,* Barbarian, Barbaric.
[12]Latin *ethnicus,* heathen, pagan.

76. In a free place[1] will he pitch his tent,
    And he will not want to lodge in the cities:
    Aix, Carpentras, L'Isle,[2] Vaucluse "Mont,"[3] Cavaillon,
    Throughout all these places will he abolish his trace.

77. All the degrees of Ecclesiastical honor
    Will be changed to that of Jupiter and Quirinus:[4]
    The priest of Quirinus[5] to one of Mars,
    Then a King of France will make him one of Vulcan.

78. The two will not remain united for very long,
    And in thirteen years to the Barbarian Satrap:
    On both sides they will cause such loss
    That one will bless the Bark and its cope.[6]

☞ 79. The sacred pomp will come to lower its wings,
    Through the coming of the great legislator:
    He will raise the humble, he will vex the rebels,
    His like will not appear on this earth.

☞ 80. Ogmios[7] will approach great Byzantium,
    The Barbaric League will be driven out:
    Of the two laws the heathen one will give way,
    Barbarian and Frank[8] in perpetual strife.

☞ 81. The royal bird over the city of the Sun,[9]
    Seven months in advance it will deliver a nocturnal omen:
    The Eastern wall will fall lightning thunder,
    Seven days the enemies directly to the gates.

[1]Or possibly "In the open air."
[2]Probably L'Isle-sur-la-Sorgue.
[3]Possibly Montfavet, a village near the other places. See note opposite.
[4]Or "Of Quirinus will be changed to that of Jupiter."
[5]The Sabine Mars, God of the Roman state, identified with Romulus.
[6]Or "cloak." In any event, the Papacy seems clearly intended, the Bark being the Bark of St. Peter.
[7]The Celtic Hercules (sometimes also identified with Mercury). See Commentary.
[8]Or "freeman."
[9]Probably Rome. Possibly Paris.

82. Au *conclud*[1] *pache*[2] hors de la forteresse,
    Ne sortira celui en désespoir mis:
    Quand ceux d'*Arbois*, de *Langres*, contre *Bresse*,
    Auront monts[3] *Dolle bouscade*[4] d'ennemis.

83. Ceux qui auront entreprise subvertir,
    Nonpareil regne, puissant et invincible:
    Feront par fraude, nuits trois avertir,
    Quand le plus grand à table lira Bible.

84. Naîtra du gouffre et cité *immesurée*,[5]
    Né de parents obscurs et ténébreux:
    Qui la puissance du grand Roi révérée,
    Voudra détruire par *Roüan* et *Eureux*.

85. Par les *Sueues* et lieux circonvoisins,
    Seront en guerre pour cause des nuées:
    Camp[6] marins locustes et cousins,
    Du *Leman*[7] fautes seront bien dénuées.

86. Par les deux têtes, et trois bras séparés,
    La cité grande sera par eaux vexée:
    Des grands d'entr'eux par exil égarés,
    Par tête *Perse Bisance* fort pressée.

87. L'an que *Saturne* hors de servage,
    Au franc terroir sera d'eau inondé:
    De sang *Troyen* sera son mariage,
    Et sera sûr d'*Espagnols circundé*.[8]

88. Sur le sablon par un hideux déluge,
    Des autres mers trouvé monstre marin:
    Proche du lieu sera fait un refuge,
    Tenant *Sauone* esclave de *Turin*.

---

[1]Nostradamus' own abbreviated noun form of O.F. *concluder*, to conclude.
[2]O.F. *pache*, treaty, agreement.
[3]Variant: *mons*.
[4]Apheresis for *embuscade*.
[5]O.F. *immesuree*, unmeasured.
[6]Variant: *Gamp*.
[7]Latin *Lemannus*, Lake of Geneva.
[8]Latin *circumdare*, to enclose, encircle, confine.

82. At the conclusion of the treaty outside the fortress
Will not go he who is placed in despair:
When those of Arbois, of Langres against Bresse
Will have the mountains of Dôle an enemy ambush.

83. Those who will have undertaken to subvert,
An unparalleled realm, powerful and invincible:
They will act through deceit, nights three to warn,
When the greatest one will read his Bible at the table.

84. He will be born of the gulf and unmeasured city,
Born of obscure and dark family:
He who the revered power of the great King
Will want to destroy through Rouen and Evreux.

85. Through the Suevi[1] and neighboring places,
They will be at war over the clouds:
Swarm of marine locusts and gnats,
The faults of Geneva will be laid quite bare.

86. Divided by the two heads and three arms,
The great city will be vexed by waters:
Some great ones among them led astray in exile,
Byzantium hard pressed by the head of Persia.

87. The year that Saturn is out of bondage,
In the Frank[2] land he will be inundated by water:
Of Trojan blood[3] will his marriage be,
And he will be confined safely by the Spaniards.

88. Through a frightful flood upon the sand,
A marine monster from other seas found:
Near the place will be made a refuge,
Holding Savona the slave of Turin.

---

[1]The Swiss, whose name Nostradamus derives from the Suevi (Swabians), ancestors of the German Swiss.

[2]Or "free." Probably Franche-Comté, the province of eastern France formerly belonging to the Habsburgs.

[3]Of the House of France, based on the legend of descent from Francus, son of King Priam of Troy.

89. Dedans *Hongrie* par *Boheme, Nauarre,*
    Et par bannière saintes[1] séditions:
    Par fleurs-de-lis pays portant la barre,
    Contre *Orleans* fera émotions.

90. Dans les *cyclades*, en *perinthe* et *larisse,*
    Dedans *Sparte* tout le *Peloponnesse:*
    Si grande famine, peste par faux *connisse,*[2]
    Neuf mois tiendra et tout le chersonèse.

91. Au grand marché qu'on dit des mensongers,
    Du tout Torrent[3] et champ *Athenien:*
    Seront surpris par les chevaux légers,
    Par *Albanois Mars, Leo, Sat.* un[4] *versien.*[5]

92. Après le siége tenu dix-sept ans,
    Cinq changeront en tel révolu terme:
    Puis sera l'un élu de même temps,
    Qui des *Romains* ne sera trop conforme.

93. Sous le terroir du rond globe lunaire,
    Lors que sera dominateur *Mercure:*
    L'île d'*Escosse* fera un luminaire,
    Qui les *Anglois* mettra à déconfiture.

94. *Translatera*[6] en la grande *Germanie,*
    *Brabant* et *Flandres, Gand, Bruges,* et *Bolongne:*
    La trêve feinte, le grand Duc d'*Armenie*
    Assaillira *Vienne* et la *Cologne.*

95. Nautique rame invitera les ombres,
    Du grand Empire lors viendra *conciter:*[7]
    La mer *Aegée* des *lignes*[8] les encombres
    Empêchant l'onde *Tirrenne defflottez.*[9]

[1]Variant: *faintes* (i.e., *feintes*).
[2]Doubtful. Possibly Greek *konis*, dust, ashes. Or Latin *connissus*, striven against exerted.
[3]Uniformly capitalized in all editions, although it does not appear to be a proper noun.
[4]Uniform error for *en* or *au.*
[5]Nostradamian adjustment of *verseau* to get his rime.
[6]O.F. *translater*, to transfer.
[7]O.F. *conciter*, to excite, provoke, move, stir up.
[8]O.F. *ligne*, wood.
[9]Latin *defluere*, to cease flowing, to deviate.

89. Into Hungary through Bohemia, Navarre,
    And under that banner holy[1] insurrections:
    By the fleur-de-lys region carrying the bar,[2]
    Against Orléans they will cause disturbances.

90. In the Cyclades, in Perinthus[3] and Larissa,
    In Sparta and the entire Peloponnesus:
    Very great famine, plague through false dust,[4]
    Nine months will it last and throughout the entire peninsula.

91. At the great market that they call that of liars,
    Of the entire Torrent[5] and field of Athens:
    They will be surprised by the light horses,
    By those of Alba[6] when Mars is in Leo and Saturn in Aquarius.

92. After the see has been held seventeen years,
    Five will change within the same period of time:
    Then one will be elected at the same time,
    One who will not be too conformable to the Romans.

☞ 93. Under the land of the round lunar globe,
    When Mercury will be dominating:
    The isle of Scotland will produce a luminary,
    One who will put the English into confusion.

☞ 94. He will transfer into great Germany
    Brabant and Flanders, Ghent, Bruges and Boulogne:
    The truce feigned, the great[7] Duke of Armenia
    Will assail Vienna and Cologne.

95. The nautical oar[8] will tempt the shadows,
    Then it will come to stir up the great Empire:
    In the Aegean Sea the impediments of wood
    Obstructing the diverted Tyrrhenian Sea.

[1] Or "feigned."
[2] The three lilies with a diagonal bar running from one corner to another formed the arms of the Duke of Bourbon. The three lilies with a diagonal bar merely in the center formed the arms of junior branches and sub-branches, such as Vendôme (which got the throne), Condé, Conti.
[3] Known by its Turkish name of Eski Eregli for many centuries.
[4] Or "ashes," or "exertions." See note opposite regarding the uncertainty of derivation.
[5] Something of a puzzler. Why capitalized? Exact meaning?
[6] Or "the Albanians."
[7] Or "Grand."
[8] Or possibly "frog" (if *rame* is erratum for *rane;* see 53).

96. Sur le milieu du grand monde la rose,
    Pour nouveaux faits sang public épandu:
    À dire vrai, on aura bouche close,
    Lors au besoin viendra tard l'attendu.

97. Le né difforme par horreur suffoqué,
    Dans la cité du grand Roi habitable:
    L'édit sévère des captifs révoqué,
    Grêle et tonnerre, *Condom* inestimable.

98. À quarante-huit degré climatérique,
    À fin de *Cancer* si grande sécheresse:
    Poisson en mer, fleuve, lac cuit hectique,
    *Bearn, Bigorre* par feu ciel en détresse.

99. *Milan, Ferrare, Turin,* et *Aquilleye,*
    *Capue, Brundis* vexés par gent *Celtique:*
    Par le Lion et phalange *aquilée,*[1]
    Quand *Rome* aura le chef vieux *Britannique.*

100. Le boute-feu par son feu attrapé,
     De feu du ciel à *Calcas*[2] et *Cominge:*
     *Foix, Aux, Mazere,* haut vieillard échappé,
     Par ceux de *Hasse,* des *Saxons* et *Turinge.*

[1]O.F. *aquilé,* curved like an eagle's beak, eagle-like.
[2]Variant: *Cartas.* Obviously, apocope for *Carcassonne.*

96. The rose upon the middle of the great world,
For new deeds public shedding of blood:
To speak the truth, one will have a closed mouth,
Then at the time of need the awaited one will come late.

☞ 97. The one born deformed suffocated in horror,
In the habitable city of the great King:
The severe edict of the captives revoked,
Hail and thunder, Condom inestimable.

98. At the forty-eighth climacteric degree,
At the end of Cancer very great dryness:
Fish in sea, river, lake boiled hectic,
Béarn, Bigorre in distress through fire from the sky.

99. Milan, Ferrara, Turin and Aquileia,[1]
Capua, Brindisi vexed by the Celtic nation:
By the Lion and his eagle's[2] phalanx,
When the old British chief Rome will have.

100. The incendiary trapped in his own fire,
Of fire from the sky at Carcassonne and the Comminges:
Foix, Auch,[3] Mazères, the high old man escaped,
Through those of Hesse and Thuringia, and some Saxons.

[1]Or "Venice." See note for 158.
[2]Probably used as a synonym for "imperial."
[3]Or possibly the village of Aux-et-Aussat, but Auch is more likely.

# Centurie VI

1. Autour des monts *Pyrenees* grand amas
   De gent étrange secourir Roi nouveau:
   Près de *Garonne* du grand temple du *Mas*,
   Un *Romain* chef le craindra dedans l'eau.

2. En l'an cinq cent octante plus et moins,
   On attendra le siècle bien étrange:
   En l'an sept cent et trois cieux en témoins,
   Que plusieurs regnes un à cinq feront change.

3. Fleuve qu'éprouve le nouveau né *Celtique*
   Sera en grande de l'Empire discorde:
   Le jeune Prince par gent ecclésiastique,
   Ôtera le sceptre[1] *coronal*[2] de concorde.

4. Le *Celtique* fleuve changera de rivage,
   Plus ne tiendra la cité d'*Agripine:*
   Tout transmué hormis le vieil langage,
   *Saturne, Leo, Mars, Cancer* en rapine.

5. Si grande famine par onde pestifère,
   Par pluie longue le long du pôle arctique:
   *Samarobryn*[3] cent lieues de l'hémisphère,
   Vivront sans loi exempt de politique.

6. Apparaîtra vers le Septentrion
   Non loin de *Cancer* l'étoile chevelue:
   *Suze, Sienne, Boëce, Eretrion,*
   Mourra de *Rome* grand, la nuit disparue.

7. *Norneigre*[4] et *Dace*, et l'île *Britannique*,
   Par les unis frères seront vexés:
   Le chef *Romain* issu de sang *Gallique*
   Et les *copies*[5] aux forêts repoussées.

[1] Variant: *Le sceptre ôté.*
[2] Latin *coronalis*, pertaining to a crown.
[3] Latin *Samarobriva*, Amiens? However, this does not fit the context. Variant: *Samato bryn.*
[4] Allowing for variation by spelling, and misprint, probably *Norvège*, Norway, is intended here.
[5] Latin *copia*, forces, army, troops.

# Century VI

1. Around the Pyrenees mountains a great throng
   Of foreign people to aid the new King:
   Near the great temple of Le Mas[1] by the Garonne,
   A Roman chief will fear him in the water.

☞ 2. In the year five hundred eighty[2] more or less,
   One will await a very strange century:
   In the year seven hundred and three[2] the heavens witness thereof,
   That several kingdoms one to five will make a change.

3. The river that tries the new Celtic heir
   Will be in great discord with the Empire:
   The young Prince through the ecclesiastical people
   Will remove[3] the sceptre of the crown of concord.

☞ 4. The Celtic river will change its course,
   No longer will it include the city of Agrippina:[4]
   All changed except the old language,
   Saturn, Leo, Mars, Cancer in plunder.[5]

☞ 5. Very great famine through pestiferous wave,
   Through long rain the length of the arctic pole:
   "Samarobryn"[6] one hundred leagues from the hemisphere,
   They will live without law exempt from politics.

6. There will appear towards the North
   Not far from Cancer the bearded star:[7]
   Susa, Siena, Boeotia, Eretria,
   The great one of Rome will die, the night over.

☞ 7. Norway[8] and Dacia[9] and the British Isle
   Will be vexed by the united brothers:
   The Roman chief sprung from Gallic blood
   And his forces hurled back into the forests.

[1] Undoubtedly Le-Mas-d'Agenais, which contains many Roman ruins.
[2] 1580 and 1703, of course.
[3] Or "Deprived."
[4] Cologne, originally Colonia Agrippina, named after Nero's mother.
[5] Possibly "Saturn in Leo, Mars in Cancer in plunder."
[6] Amiens? A space-station astronaut named Sam R. O'Brien? See note opposite and Commentary.
[7] A comet.
[8] Somewhat doubtful. See note 4, opposite.
[9] Probably intended for Transylvania, now part of Rumania (whose boundaries approximate those of ancient Roman Dacia) but in Nostradamus' time an intrinsic part of Hungary.

8. Ceux qui étaient en regne pour savoir,
   Au Royal change deviendront appauvris:
   Uns exilés sans appui, or n'avoir,
   Lettrés et lettres ne seront à grand prix.

9. Aux sacrés temples seront faits scandales,
   Comptés seront par honneurs et louanges:
   D'un que l'on grave d'argent d'or les médailles,
   La fin sera en tourments bien étranges.

10. Un peu de temps les temples des couleurs
    De blanc et noir des deux entremêlées:
    Rouges et jaunes leur *embleront*[1] les leurs,
    Sang, terre, peste, faim, feu d'eau *affollée*.[2]

11. Des sept rameaux à trois seront réduits,
    Les plus aînés seront surpris par morts,
    *Fratricider*[3] les deux seront séduits,
    Les conjurés en dormant seront morts.

12. Dresser *copies*[4] pour monter à l'empire,
    Du *Vatican* le sang Royal tiendra:
    *Flamans, Anglois, Espagne* avec *Aspire*,[5]
    Contre l'*Italie* et *France* contiendra.

13. Un *dubieux*[6] ne viendra loin du regne,
    La plus grande part le voudra soutenir:
    Un *Capitole* ne voudra point qu'il regne,
    Sa grande charge ne pourra maintenir.

14. Loin de sa terre Roi perdra la bataille,
    Prompt échappé poursuivi suivant pris,
    Ignare pris sous la dorée maille,
    Sous feint habit, et l'ennemi surpris.

[1]O.F. *embler*, to take, remove, carry off.
[2]O.F. *affollé*, murdered, crippled, wounded.
[3]Nostradamus' own verbal form of *fratricide*.
[4]Latin *copia*, forces, troops, army.
[5]Probably prosthesis of *Spire*, Speyer or Spires, an imperial city in the Palatinate. Or Germany, whose language is full of aspirates.
[6]Latin *dubiosus*, doubtful.

8. Those who were in the realm for knowledge
   Will become impoverished at the change of King:
   Some exiled without support, having no gold,
   The lettered and letters will not be at a high premium.

9. In the sacred temples scandals will be perpetrated,
   They will be reckoned as honors and commendations:
   Of one of whom they engrave medals of silver and of gold,
   The end will be in very strange torments.

10. In a short time the temples with colors
    Of white and black of the two intermixed:
    Red and yellow ones will carry off theirs from them,
    Blood, land, plague, famine, fire extinguished by water.

☞ 11. The seven branches will be reduced to three,
    The elder ones will be surprised by death,
    The two will be seduced to fratricide,
    The conspirators will be dead while sleeping.

☞ 12. To raise forces to ascend to the empire
    In the Vatican the Royal blood will hold fast:
    Flemings, English, Spain with "Aspire"[1]
    Against Italy and France will he contend.

13. A doubtful one will not come far from the realm,
    The greater part will want to uphold him:
    A Capitol[2] will not want him to reign at all,
    He will be unable to bear his great burden.

☞ 14. Far from his land a King will lose the battle,
    At once escaped, pursued, then captured,
    Ignorant one taken under the golden mail,
    Under false garb, and the enemy surprised.

---

[1]Speyer? The Palatinate? Germany? See note opposite.
[2]Originally the citadel of Rome. Possibly synecdoche for "Pope."

15. Dessous la tombe sera trouvé le Prince,
    Qu'aura le prix par dessus *Nuremberg:*
    L'*Espagnol* Roi en *Capricorne* mince,
    Feint et trahi par le grand *Vvitemberg.*

16. Ce que ravi sera du jeune *Milve,*[1]
    Par les *Normans* de *France* et *Picardie:*
    Les noirs du temple du lieu de *Negrisilve*[2]
    Feront auberge et feu de *Lombardie.*

17. Après les limes brûlés les asiniers,[3]
    Contraints seront changer d'habits divers:
    Les Saturnins brûlés par les meuniers,
    Hors la plupart qui ne sera couverte.

18. Par les *Phisiques*[4] le grand Roi délaissé,
    Par sort non art de l'*Ebrieu*[5] est en vie,
    Lui et son genre au regne haut poussé,
    Grace donnée à gent qui *Christ* envie.

19. La vraie flamme engloutira la dame,
    Qui voudra mettre les Innocents à feu:
    Près de l'assaut l'*exercite*[6] s'enflamme,
    Quand dans *Seville* monstre en bœuf sera vu.

20. L'union feinte sera peu de durée,
    Des uns changés réformés la plupart:
    Dans les vaisseaux sera gent endurée,
    Lors aura *Rome* un nouveau Léopard.

21. Quand ceux du pôle arctique unis ensemble,
    En Orient grand *effrayeur*[7] et crainte:
    Élu nouveau, soutenu le grand *tremble,*[8]
    *Rodes, Bisance* de sang Barbare teinte.

[1]Latin *milvus,* kite or glede, a kind of hawk.
[2]Latin, *silva nigra,* a black forest (suitably Nostradamicized).
[3]Variant: *le rasiniers.*
[4]O.F. *phisique,* medicine. Here metonymy for "physicians."
[5]O.F., *Ebrieu,* Jews.
[6]Latin *exercitus,* army.
[7]O.F. *effrayeur,* terror.
[8]O.F. *tremble,* trembling.

☞ 15. Under the tomb will be found a Prince
Who will be valued above Nuremberg:
The Spanish King in Capricorn[1] thin,
Deceived and betrayed by the great Wittenberg.

16. That which will be carried off by[2] the young Hawk,
By the Normans of France and Picardy:
The black ones of the temple of the Black Forest place
Will make an inn and fire of Lombardy.

17. After the files the ass-drivers[3] burned,
They will be obliged to change diverse garbs:
Those of Saturn burned by the millers,
Except the greater part which will not be covered.

☞ 18. The great King abandoned by the Physicians,
By fate not the Jew's art he remains alive,
He and his kindred pushed high in the realm,
Pardon given to the race which denies Christ.

19. The true flame will devour the lady
Who will want to put the Innocent Ones to the fire:
Before the assault the army is inflamed,
When in Seville a monster in beef will be seen.

20. The feigned union will be of short duration,
Some changed most reformed:
In the vessels people will be in suffering,
Then Rome will have a new Leopard.

☞ 21. When those of the arctic pole are united together,
Great terror and fear in the East:
Newly elected, the great trembling supported,[4]
Rhodes, Byzantium stained with Barbarian blood.

---

[1]The Sun enters Capricorn on December 22, if that is the import here.

[2]Or "from."

[3]A rather odd word in this context, but the French word has no other meaning. The variant might be correct as a compound form of *raisin*, "grape," but in all texts it has only the singular article *le*, which makes the whole variant highly doubtful. Le Pelletier, however, accepting the variant, takes the word as a Nostradamian invention based on *ras*, shaven ones, after deriving *limes* from O.F. *lime*, penance; thus he would have this line: "After the penances the priests burned." Garencières takes *limes* as a misprint for *livres*, books.

[4]Or possibly "The newly elected one upheld the great one trembles."

22. Dedans la terre du grand temple *celique*,[1]
    Neveu à *Londres* par paix feinte meurtri:
    La barque alors deviendra schismatique,
    Liberté feinte sera *au corn' et cry*.[2]

23. D'esprit de regne *numismes*[3] décriés,
    Et seront peuples émus contre leur Roi:
    Paix fait[4] nouveau, saintes lois empirées,
    *RAPIS*[5] onc fut en si très dur arroi.

24. *Mars* et le sceptre se trouvera conjoint,
    Dessous *Cancer* calamiteuse guerre:
    Un peu après sera nouveau Roi oint,
    Qui par longtemps pacifiera la terre.

25. Par *Mars* contraire sera la monarchie
    Du grand pêcheur en trouble ruineux:
    Jeune noir[6] prendra la hiérarchie,
    Les *proditeurs*[7] iront jour bruineux.[8]

26. Quatre ans le siège quelque peu bien tiendra,
    Un surviendra libidineux de vie:
    *Rauenne* et *Pyse*, *Veronne* soutiendront,[9]
    Pour élever la croix de Pape envie.

27. Dedans les Îles de cinq fleuves à un,
    Par le croissant du grand *Chyren Selin:*[10]
    Par les bruines de l'air fureur de l'un,
    Six échappés, cachés fardeaux de lin.

28. Le grand *Celtique* entrera dedans *Rome*,
    Menant amas d'exilés et bannis:
    Le grand Pasteur mettra à mort tout homme,
    Qui pour le coq étaient aux *Alpes* unis.

[1]O.F. *celique*, celestial, heavenly.
[2]Archaic form of *à cor et à cri*, with horn and voice.
[3]Latin *numisma*, coin. Variant: *munismes*, possibly from Latin *munimen*, defense, rampart.
[4]Variant: *saint*.
[5]Anagram for *Paris*.
[6]Possibly an anagram here for *roi (roy)*.
[7]Latin *proditor*, traitor.
[8]O.F. *bruineux*, rainy.
[9]Lack of rime uniform in all editions. Presumably Nostradamus meant to write *soutiendra*.
[10]Greek *selene*, moon or crescent.

☞ 22. Within the land of the great heavenly temple,
Nephew murdered at London through feigned peace:
The bark will then become schismatic,
Sham liberty will be proclaimed everywhere.

23. Coins depreciated[1] by the spirit of the realm,
And people will be stirred up against their King:
New peace made,[2] holy laws become worse,
Paris was never in so very severe an array.

24. Mars and the sceptre will be found conjoined
Under Cancer[3] calamitous war:
Shortly afterwards a new King will be anointed,
One who for a long time will pacify the earth.

☞ 25. Through adverse Mars[4] will the monarchy
Of the great fisherman[5] be in ruinous trouble:
The young red black one[6] will seize the hierarchy,[7]
The traitors will act on a day of drizzle.

26. For four years the see will be held with some little good,
One libidinous in life will succeed to it:
Ravenna, Pisa and Verona will give support,
Longing to elevate the Papal cross.

27. Within the Isles of five rivers to one,
Through the expansion[8] of the great "Chyren Selin":[9]
Through the drizzles in the air the fury of one,
Six escaped, hidden bundles of flax.

28. The great Celt will enter Rome,
Leading a throng of the exiled and banished:
The great Pastor will put to death every man
Who was united at the Alps for[10] the cock.

[1] Or possibly "The defenses undermined."
[2] Or "Peace a new saint."
[3] I.e., when Mars and Jupiter are conjunct in Cancer.
[4] I.e., bad luck in war, or some astrological configuration.
[5] St. Peter.
[6] Or "The young red king."
[7] In its original Greek meaning, the presidency of the sacred rites, i.e., the Papacy.
[8] Or "crescent."
[9] Note that this otherwise insignificant quatrain is the first of only two (the other being 854) in which we find clearly combined (in 279 both appear but not combined) the two names of "Henry of the Crescent," i.e., *Chyren* (anagram for *Henry*) and *Selin* (crescent). See Commentary for 477.
[10] Or possible "against"?

29. La veuve sainte entendant les nouvelles,
    De ses rameaux mis en *perplex*[1] et trouble:
    Qui sera *duit*[2] appaiser les querelles,
    Par son *pourchas*[3] des rases fera comble.

30. Par l'apparence de feinte sainteté,
    Sera trahi aux ennemis le siège:
    Nuit qu'on *cuidait*[4] dormir en sûreté,
    Près de *Brabant* marcheront ceux de *Liege*.

31. Roi trouvera ce qu'il désirait tant,
    Quand le Prélat sera repris à tort:
    Réponse au Duc le rendra malcontent,
    Qui dans *Milan* mettra plusieurs à mort.

32. Par trahison de verges à mort battu,
    Pris surmonté sera par son désordre:
    Conseil frivole au grand captif *sentu*,[5]
    Nez par fureur quand *Berich*[6] viendra mordre.

33. Sa main dernière par *Alus*[7] sanguinaire,
    Ne se pourra par la mer garantir:
    Entre deux fleuves craindre main militaire,
    Le noir[8] l'*ireux*[9] le fera repentir.

34. De feu volant[10] la machination,
    Viendra troubler un grand chef assiégé:
    Dedans sera telle sédition,
    Qu'en désespoir seront les *profligez*.[11]

35. Près de *Rion*,[12] et proche à blanche laine,
    *Aries, Taurus, Cancer, Leo,* la *Vierge*,
    *Mars, Iupiter,* le *Sol*[13] ardera grande plaine,
    Bois et cités lettres cachés au cierge.

[1]Apocope of *perplexité*.
[2]O.F. *duire*, to teach, instruct.
[3]O.F. *pourchas*, pursuit.
[4]O.F. *cuider*, to think, believe, persuade oneself.
[5]Archaic past participle of *sentir*.
[6]If not from Berrichon (man from Berry), an enigma. Variant: *Berlch*.
[7]Still unsolved proper name, possibly an anagram (for "Saul"?).
[8]Possibly an anagram for *roi*, king.
[9]O.F. *ireux*, angry, furious, irritated.
[10]Variant: *voulant*.
[11]Latin *profligatus*, profligate, abandoned, dissolute.
[12]Probably a misprint for *Trion*, from Latin *Triones*, the Bears (Ursa Major and Minor).
[13]Latin *Sol*, Sun.

29. The saintly widow hearing the news,
    Of her offspring placed in perplexity and trouble:
    He who will be instructed to appease the quarrels,
    He will pile them up by his pursuit of the shaven heads.

30. Through the appearance of feigned sanctity
    The siege[1] will be betrayed to the enemies:
    In the night when they trusted to sleep in safety,
    Near Brabant will march those of Liège.

31. The King will find that which he desired so much
    When the Prelate will be blamed unjustly:
    His reply to the Duke will leave him dissatisfied,
    He who in Milan will put several to death.

32. Beaten to death by rods for treason,
    Captured he will be overcome through his disorder:
    Frivolous counsel held out to the great captive,
    When "Berich"[2] will come to bite his nose in fury.

33. His last hand through "Alus"[3] sanguinary,
    He will be unable to protect himself by sea:
    Between two rivers he will fear the military hand,
    The black and irate one[4] will make him rue it.[5]

34. The device of flying[6] fire
    Will come to trouble the great besieged chief:
    Within there will be such sedition
    That the profligate ones will be in despair.

35. Near the Bear[7] and close to the white wool,[8]
    Aries, Taurus, Cancer, Leo, Virgo,
    Mars, Jupiter, the Sun will burn a great plain,
    Woods and cities letters hidden in the candle.

[1] Or "see."
[2] Or "Berlch." Or "the Berry man" (Duke of Berry?). See note opposite.
[3] Unidentified proper name, probably an anagram (for "Saul"?).
[4] Or possibly, by anagram, "The irate king."
[5] Or possibly "The black one [or king] will make the irate one rue it."
[6] Or "intended."
[7] Somewhat doubtful. See note 12, opposite.
[8] Probably this means the Milky Way.

36. Ni bien ni mal par bataille terrestre,
    Ne parviendra aux confins de *Perouse,*
    Rebeller *Pise, Florence* voir mal être,
    Roi nuit blessé sur mulet à noire housse.

37. L'œuvre ancienne se parachevera,
    Du toit cherra sur le grand mal ruine:
    Innocent fait mort on accusera,
    *Nocent*[1] caché taillis à la bruine.

38. Aux *profligez*[2] de paix les ennemis,
    Après avoir l'*Italie superée:*[3]
    Noir[4] sanguinaire, rouge, sera commis,
    Feu, sang verser, eau de sang colorée.

39. L'enfant du regne par paternelle prise
    *Expolier*[5] sera pour le délivrer:
    Auprès du lac *Trasimen* l'azur prise,[6]
    La troupe otage par trop fort s'enivrer.

40. Grand de *Magonce*[7] pour grande soif éteindre,
    Sera privé de sa grande dignité:
    Ceux de *Cologne* si fort le viendront plaindre,
    Que le grande *groppe*[8] au *Rhin* sera jeté.

41. Le second chef du regne *d'Annemarc,*
    Par ceux de *Frize* et l'Île *Britannique,*
    Fera *despendre*[9] plus de cent mille marc,
    Vain exploiter voyage en *Italique.*

42. À *Logmyon*[10] sera laissé le regne,
    Du grand *Selin,*[11] qui plus fera de fait:
    Par les *Itales* étendra son enseigne,
    Regi sera par prudent contrefait.

[1] Latin *nocens,* harmful, noxious, guilty.
[2] Latin *profligatus,* abandoned, dissolute, profligate.
[3] Latin *superatus,* subdued, conquered, vanquished.
[4] Possibly again an anagram for *roy (roi).*
[5] Variant (Fortune and false "1568"): *Expolié,* undoubtedly correct. Latin *exspoliatus,* stripped clean, pillaged, plundered, deprived.
[6] Le Pelletier suggests brightly that this meaningless phrase may represent a prankish play on *la surprise.*
[7] Latin *Maguntiacum,* Mayence or Mainz.
[8] Low Latin *groppa,* rump, haunches.
[9] O.F. *despendre,* to spend.
[10] Uniform misprint for *l'Ogmion.* Ogmios was the Celtic Hercules.
[11] Greek *selene,* moon or crescent.

36. Neither good nor evil through terrestrial battle
Will reach the confines of Perugia,
Pisa to rebel, Florence to see an evil existence,
King by night wounded on a mule with black housing.

37. The ancient work will be finished,
Evil ruin will fall upon the great one from the roof:
Dead they will accuse an innocent one of the deed,
The guilty one hidden in the copse in the drizzle.

38. The enemies of peace to the profligates,
After having conquered Italy:
The bloodthirsty black one,[1] red, will be exposed,
Fire, blood shed, water colored by blood.

39. The child of the realm through the capture of his father
Will be plundered to deliver him:
Near the Lake of Perugia the azure captive,[2]
The hostage troop to become far too drunk.

☞ 40. To quench the great thirst the great one of Mainz
Will be deprived of his great dignity:
Those of Cologne will come to complain so loudly
That the great rump will be thrown into the Rhine.

☞ 41. The second chief of the realm of "Annemark,"[3]
Through those of Frisia[4] and of the British Isle,
Will spend more than one hundred thousand marks,
Exploiting in vain the voyage to Italy.

☞ 42. To Ogmios will be left the realm
Of the great "Selin,"[5] who will in fact do more:
Throughout Italy will he extend his banner,
He will be ruled by a prudent deformed one.

[1]Or possibly "The bloodthirsty king."
[2]Or possibly "the surprise." See note 6, opposite.
[3]Hungary and Bohemia-Moravia. See note for 427 and Commentary.
[4]The province of Friesland in particular or Holland in general.
[5]The enigmatic hero. See 627 above and others (per Index).

43. Longtemps sera sans être habitée,
    Où *Signe* et *Marne* autour vient arroser:
    De la *Tamise* et martiaux tentée,
    Déçus les gardes en *cuidant*[1] repousser.

44. De nuit par *Nantes* l'Iris apparaîtra,
    Des arts marins susciteront la pluie:
    *Arabiq*[2] gouffre grande *classe*[3] *parfondra,*[4]
    Un monstre en *Saxe* naîtra d'ours et truie.

45. Le gouverneur du regne bien savant,
    Ne consentir voulant au fait Royal:
    *Mellile classe*[3] par le contraire vent
    Le remettra à son plus déloyal.

46. Un juste sera en exil renvoyé,
    Par pestilence aux confins de *Nonseggle,*[5]
    Réponse au rouge le fera dévoyé,
    Roi retirant à la Rane[6] et à l'Aigle.

47. Entre deux monts les deux grands assemblés
    Délaisseront leur *simulte*[7] secrète:
    *Brucelle* et *Dolle* par *Langres* accablés,
    Pour à *Malignes* exécuter leur peste.

48. La sainteté trop feinte et *seductive,*[8]
    Accompagné d'une langue diserte:
    La cité vieille, et *Parme* trop hâtive,
    *Florence* et *Sienne* rendront plus desertes.

[1] O.F. *cuider,* to think, believe, persuade oneself.
[2] Variant: *Vrabiq* (the Gulf of Urabá or Darien east of Panama).
[3] Latin *classis,* fleet.
[4] O.F. *parfondrer,* to plunge to the bottom.
[5] Unsolved place name.
[6] Latin *rana,* frog. Variant: *Rame.*
[7] O.F. *simulte,* quarrel.
[8] Archaic form of *séduisant.*

43. For a long time will she remain uninhabited,
    Around where the Seine and the Marne she comes to water:
    Tried by the Thames[1] and warriors,
    The guards deceived in trusting in the repulse.

☞ 44. By night the Rainbow will appear for Nantes,
    By marine arts they will stir up rain:
    In the Gulf of Arabia[2] a great fleet will plunge to the bottom,
    In Saxony a monster will be born of a bear and a sow.

45. The very learned governor of the realm,
    Not wishing to consent to the royal deed:
    The fleet at Melilla through contrary wind
    Will deliver him to his most disloyal one.

46. A just one will be sent back again into exile,
    Through pestilence to the confines of "Nonseggle,"[3]
    His reply to the red one will cause him to be misled,
    The King withdrawing to the Frog and the Eagle.

47. The two great ones assembled between two mountains
    Will abandon their secret quarrel:
    Brussels and Dôle overcome by Langres,
    To execute their plague at Malines.

48. The too false and seductive sanctity,
    Accompanied by an eloquent tongue:
    The old city, and Parma too premature,
    Florence and Siena they will render more desert.

[1]Or "by La Tamise" (a town in Flanders near Antwerp).
[2]Or possibly "the Gulf of Uraba" (in Colombia, South America).
[3]Still unsolved proper name.

49. De la partie de *Mammer*[1] grand Pontife,
    Subjuguera les confins du *Danube:*
    Chasser la croix, par fer *raffe ni riffe*,[2]
    Captifs, or, bagues plus de cent mille *rubes*.[3]

50. Dedans le puits seront trouvés les os,
    Sera l'inceste commis par la marâtre:
    L'état changé, on querra bruit et los,
    Et aura *Mars* attendant pour son astre.

51. Peuple assemblé, voir nouveau *expectacle*,[4]
    Princes et Rois par plusieurs assistants,
    Piliers faillir, murs: mais comme miracle
    Le Roi sauvé et trente des instants.

52. En lieu du grand qui sera condamné,
    De prison hors, son ami en sa place:
    L'espoir *Troyen* en six mois joint, mort né,
    Le *Sol*[5] à l'urne seront pris fleuves en glace.

53. Le grand Prélat *Celtique* à Roi suspect,
    De nuit par cours sortira hors du regne:
    Par Duc fertile à son grand Roi *Bretaine*,[6]
    *Bisance* à *Cypres* et *Tunes insuspect*.[7]

54. Au point du jour au second chant du coq,
    Ceux de *Tunes*, de *Fez*, et de *Bugie*,
    Par les *Arabes* captif le Roi *Maroq*,
    L'an mil six cent et sept, de Liturgie.

55. Au calmé Duc en *arrachant*[8] l'*esponce*,[9]
    Voile *Arabesque* voir, subit découverte:
    *Tripolis*, *Chio*, et ceux de *Trapesconce*,
    Duc pris, *Marnegro*[10] et la cité déserte.

---

[1]Either from (1) *Mamers*, the Sabine and Oscan name for Mars, or (2) *Mamertini*, the inhabitants of Messina in Sicily.

[2]Provençal *de rifla ou de raffa*, by hook or by crook.

[3]Properly *rubis*, ruby or rubies, but left in its one-syllable original form for meter and rime.

[4]Prosthesis of *spectacle*.

[5]Latin *Sol*, Sun.

[6]Variant: *Bretagne*.

[7]O.F. *insuspect*, unsuspected. Note this quatrain rimes *a b b a* instead of the usual *a b a b*.

[8]Low Latin *aracare*, to draw up, contract.

[9]Provençal *esponcio*, promise, obligation.

[10]Italian *Marne(g)ro*, Black Sea.

☞ 49. The great Pontiff of the party of Mars[1]
Will subjugate the confines of the Danube:
The cross to pursue, through sword hook or crook,
Captives, gold, jewels more than one hundred thousand rubies.

50. Within the pit will be found the bones,
Incest will be committed by the stepmother:[2]
The state changed, they will demand fame and praise,
And they will have Mars attending as their star.

☞ 51. People assembled to see a new spectacle,
Princes and Kings amongst many bystanders,
Pillars walls to fall: but as by a miracle
The King saved and thirty of the ones present.

☞ 52. In place of the great one who will be condemned,
Outside the prison, his friend in his place:
The Trojan hope in six months joined, born[3] dead,
The Sun in the urn[4] rivers will be frozen.

53. The great Celtic Prelate suspected by the King,
By night in flight he will leave the realm:
Through a Duke fruitful for his great British King,[5]
Byzantium to Cyprus and Tunis unsuspected.

☞ 54. At daybreak at the second crowing of the cock,
Those of Tunis, of Fez and of Bougie,
By the Arabs the King of Morocco captured,
The year sixteen hundred and seven, of the Liturgy.

55. By the appeased Duke in drawing up the contract,
Arabesque sail seen, sudden discovery:
Tripolis, Chios, and those of Trebizond,
Duke captured, the Black Sea and the city a desert.

[1]Or "of Messina."
[2]Or possibly "mother-in-law."
[3]Or "heir."
[4]I.e., Aquarius.
[5]Or "Breton King."

56.  La crainte armée de l'ennemi *Narbon*
     Effrayera si fort les *Hesperiques:*
     *Parpignan* vide par l'aveugle d'*arbon*,[1]
     Lors *Barcelon* par mer *donra*[2] les piques.

57.  Celui qu'était bien avant dans le regne,
     Ayant chef rouge proche à la hiérarchie,
     Âpre et cruel, et se fera tant craindre,
     Succédera à sacrée monarchie.

58.  Entre les deux monarques éloignés,
     Lorsque le *Sol*[3] par *Selin*[4] clair perdue:
     *Simulté*[5] grande entre deux indignés,
     Qu'aux Îles et *Sienne* la liberté rendue.

59.  Dame en fureur par rage d'adultère,
     Viendra à son Prince conjurer non de dire:
     Mais bref connu le vitupère,
     Que seront mis dix-sept à martyre.

60.  Le Prince hors de son terroir *Celtique*
     Sera trahi, déçu par interprète:
     *Roüan, Rochelle* par ceux de l'*Armorique*[6]
     Au port de *Blaue* déçus par moine et prêtre.

61.  Le grand tapis plié ne montrera,
     Fors qu'à demi la plupart de l'histoire:
     Chassé du regne loin âpre apparaîtra,
     Qu'au fait *bellique*[7] chacun le viendra croire.

62.  Trop tard tous deux les fleurs seront perdues,
     Contre la loi serpent ne voudra faire:
     Des Ligueurs forces par *gallots*[8] confondues,
     *Sauone, Albingue* par *monech*[9] grand martyre.

[1]Dubious. If geographical, there is an Arbon in Switzerland, and two Arbonnes in France.
[2]Syncope of *donnera.*
[3]Latin *Sol,* Sun.
[4]Greek *selene,* Moon or crescent.
[5]Latin *simultas,* rivalry, enmity.
[6]Latin *Armorica,* Brittany.
[7]Latin *bellicus,* warlike.
[8]O.F. *gallot,* Gallic or French. Sometimes used for French-speaking Bretons.
[9]Latin *Portus Herculi Monoecis,* Monaco.

56. The dreaded army of the Narbonne enemy
    Will frighten very greatly the "Hesperians":[1]
    Perpignan empty through the blind one of Arbon,[2]
    Then Barcelona by sea will take up the quarrel.

57. He who was well forward in the realm,
    Having a red chief close to the hierarchy,[3]
    Harsh and cruel, and he will make himself much feared,
    He will succeed to the sacred monarchy.

58. Between the two distant monarchs,
    When the clear Sun is lost through "Selin":[4]
    Great enmity between two indignant ones,
    So that liberty is restored to the Isles and Siena.

59. The Lady in fury through rage of adultery,
    She will come to conspire not to tell her Prince:
    But soon will the blame[5] be made known,
    So that seventeen will be put to martyrdom.

60. The Prince outside his Celtic land
    Will be betrayed, deceived by the interpreter:
    Rouen, La Rochelle through those of Brittany
    At the port of Blaye deceived by monk and priest.

61. The great carpet folded will not show
    But by halves the greatest part of history:[6]
    Driven far out of the realm he will appear harsh,
    So that everyone will come to believe in his warlike deed.

62. Too late both the flowers will be lost,
    The serpent will not want to act against the law:
    The forces of the Leaguers confounded by the French,
    Savona, Albenga through Monaco great martyrdom.

[1]The inhabitants of the Land of the West. Spaniards? Americans?
[2]Dubious. The name of a town in the canton of Thurgau, Switzerland. Or possibly Arbonne, the name of a village in Basses-Pyrénées. See Commentary.
[3]I.e., having as patron a cardinal close to the Pope.
[4]Or "through the Moon." See Commentary.
[5]"The culprit"?
[6]Or "of its history."

63. La dame seule au regne demeurée,
    D'unique éteint premier au lit d'honneur:
    Sept ans sera de douleur éplorée,
    Puis longue vie au regne par grand heur.

64. On ne tiendra *pache*[1] aucun arrêté,
    Tous recevants iront par tromperie:
    De paix et trêve, terre et mer protesté,
    Par *Barcelonne classe*[2] pris d'industrie.

65. Gris et *bureau*[3] demie ouverte guerre,
    De nuit seront assailis et pillés:
    Le *bureau*[3] pris passera par la *serre*,[4]
    Son temple ouvert, deux au plâtre *grillez*.[5]

66. Au fondement de la nouvelle secte,
    Seront les os du grand *Romain* trouvés,
    Sépulcre en marbre apparaîtra couverte,
    Terre trembler en Avril, mal *enfoüez*.[6]

67. Au grand Empire parviendra tout un autre,
    Bonté distant plus de félicité:
    Regi par un issu non loin du *peautre*,[7]
    *Corruer*[8] regnes grande *infelicité*.[9]

68. Lorsque soldats fureur séditieuse,
    Contre leur chef feront de nuit fer luire:
    Ennemi d'*Albe* soit par main furieuse,
    Lors vexer *Rome* et principaux séduire.

69. La pitié grande sera sans loin tarder,
    Ceux qui donnaient seront contraints de prendre:
    Nus affamés de froid, soif, se bander,
    Les monts passer commettant grand esclandre.

[1]O.F. *pache*, peace, agreement.
[2]Latin *classis*, fleet.
[3]Variant form of O.F., *burel*, brown.
[4]O.F. *serre*, (1) lock, (2) saw, (3) prison.
[5]O.F. *griller*, to slip, slide.
[6]O.F. *enfouer*, to bury (modern *enfouir*).
[7]O.F. *peautre*, bed, pallet; place of prostitution.
[8]Latin *corruere*, to fall to the ground.
[9]Latin *infelicitas*, misfortune, ill luck.

☞ 63. The lady left alone in the realm
By the unique one extinguished first on the bed of honor:
Seven years will she be weeping in grief,
Then with great good fortune for the realm long life.

64. No peace agreed upon will be kept,
All the subscribers will act with deceit:
In peace and truce, land and sea in protest,
By Barcelona fleet seized with ingenuity.

65. Gray and brown in half-opened war,
By night they will be assaulted and pillaged:
The brown captured will pass through the lock,[1]
His temple opened, two slipped in the plaster.

☞ 66. At the foundation of the new sect,
The bones of the great Roman will be found,
A sepulchre covered by marble will appear,
Earth to quake in April, poorly buried.

67. Quite another one will attain to the great Empire,
Kindness distant more so happiness:
Ruled by one sprung not far from the brothel,
Realms to decay great bad luck.

68. When the soldiers in a seditious fury
Will cause steel to flash by night against their chief:
The enemy Alba[2] acts with furious hand,
Then to vex Rome and seduce the principal ones.

☞ 69. The great pity will occur before long,
Those who gave will be obliged to take:
Naked, starving, withstanding cold and thirst,
To pass over the mountains committing a great scandal.

[1]Or "saw," or "prison."
[2]I.e., probably the Duke of Alba, Habsburg generalissimo.

70. Au chef du monde le grand *CHIREN*[1] sera,
    *PLVS OVTRE*[2] après aimé, craint, redouté:
    Son bruit et los les cieux surpassera,
    Et du seul titre Victeur fort contenté.

71. Quand on viendra le grand Roi *parenter*[3]
    Avant qu'il ait du tout l'âme rendue:
    Celui qui moins le viendra lamenter,
    Par Lions, Aigles,[4] croix couronne vendue.

72. Par fureur feinte d'émotion divine,
    Sera la femme du grand fort violée:
    Juges voulant damner telle doctrine,
    Victime au peuple ignorant immolée.

73. En cité grande un moine et artisan,
    Près de la porte logés et aux murailles,
    Contre *Modene*[5] secret, cave disant,
    Trahis pour faire sous couleur d'épousailles.

74. La *dechassée*[6] au regne *tournera*,[7]
    Ses ennemis trouvés des conjurés:
    Plus que jamais son temps triomphera,
    Trois et septante à mort trop assuré.

75. Le grand Pilote par Roi sera mandé,
    Laisser la *classe*[8] pour plus haut lieu atteindre:
    Sept ans après sera *contrebandé*,[9]
    Barbare armée viendra *Venise* craindre.

[1]Variant: *Chyren*. Either way, anagram for *Henri*.
[2]Only the 1605 has preserved the capitals, as it should be, from PLVS VLTRA CAROL' QUINT, device of Charles V.
[3]Latin *parentare*, to give the last rites to the dead.
[4]The 1605 has quite a variant for a line and a half: *On le verra bien tôt apparenter/ D'Aigles, Lions, . . .*
[5]Variant: *Moderne*.
[6]O.F. *dechasser*, to chase out, expel.
[7]O.F. *tourner*, to return.
[8]Latin *classis*, fleet.
[9]O.F. *contrebander*, to be in rebellion (Sainte-Palaye).

☞ 70. Chief of the world will the great "Chyren"[1] be,
     *Plus Ultra* behind,[2] loved, feared, dreaded:
     His fame and praise will go beyond the heavens,
     And with the sole title of Victor will he be quite satisfied.

   71. When they will come to give the last rites to the great King
     Before he has entirely given up the ghost:
     He who will come to grieve over him the least,
     Through Lions, Eagles,[3] cross crown sold.

☞ 72. Through feigned fury of divine emotion
     The wife of the great one will be violated:
     The judges wishing to condemn such a doctrine,
     She is sacrificed a victim to the ignorant people.

   73. In a great city a monk and artisan,
     Lodged near the gate and walls,
     Secret speaking emptily against Modena,[4]
     Betrayed for acting under the guise of nuptials.

☞ 74. She chased out will return to the realm,
     Her enemies found to be conspirators:
     More than ever her time will triumph,
     Three and seventy to death very sure.

☞ 75. The great Pilot will be commissioned by the King,
     To leave the fleet to fill a higher post:
     Seven years after he will be in rebellion,
     Venice will come to fear the Barbarian army.

---

[1]Anagram for *Henri* (Henry). See Commentary.

[2]I.e., Charles V will play second fiddle to him. See note 2, opposite.

[3]Or "They will very soon see him related by marriage with Eagles, Lions," etc.

[4]Or possibly *Moderna/Moderne*, conceivably the name of a section of some town in the Latin world.

76. La cité antique d'*antenoree*[1] *forge,*[2]
    Plus ne pouvant le tyran supporter:
    Le manche[3] feint au temple couper gorge,
    Les siens le peuple à mort viendra bouter.

77. Par la victoire du déçu *fraudulente,*[4]
    Deux *classes*[5] une, la révolte *Germaine:*[6]
    Le chef meurtri et son fils dans la tente,
    *Florence, Imole* pourchassés dans *Romaine.*[6]

78. Crier victoire du grand *Selin*[7] croissant:
    Par les *Romains* sera l'Aigle *clamé,*[8]
    *Ticcin,*[9] *Milan* et *Gennes* n'y *consent,*
    Puis par eux-mêmes *Basil*[10] grand réclamé.

79. Près de *Tesin* les habitants de *Loire,*
    *Garonne* et *Saone, Seine, Tain* et *Gironde:*
    Outre les monts dresseront promontoire,
    Conflit donné, *Pau granci,*[11] submergé onde.

80. De *Fez* le regne parviendra à ceux d'*Europe,*
    Feu leur cité, et lame tranchera:
    Le grand d'*Asie* terre et mer à grande troupe,
    Que bleus, pers, croix à mort *dechassera.*[12]

81. Pleurs, cris et plaintes, hurlements, *effrayeur,*[13]
    Cœur inhumain, cruel noir et transi:
    *Leman*[14] les Îles, de *Gennes* les majeurs,
    Sang épancher, *frofaim*[15] à nul merci.

---

[1]Latin *Antenoreus,* of Antenor, the legendary founder of Padua.
[2]O.F. *forge,* product, handiwork, construction, creation.
[3]Variant (Fortune and false "1568"): *manchet (manchot,* one-armed).
[4]Latin *fraudulentus,* deceitful, fraudulent.
[5]Latin *classis,* fleet.
[6]Variant: *Germanie,* so perhaps *Romaine* is erratum for *Romanie.*
[7]Greek *selene,* moon or crescent.
[8]O.F. *clamer,* to demand. Latin *clamare,* to proclaim.
[9]Latin *Ticinum,* Pavia.
[10]Greek *Basileus,* king, prince, lord, captain.
[11]Erratum for *grandi;* or Tuscan *grancito,* snatched, seized, hooked.
[12]O.F. *dechasser,* to drive out, expel.
[13]O.F. *effrayeur,* terror.
[14]Latin *Lemannus,* Lake of Geneva.
[15]Variant: *fromfaim.* Insoluble barbaric word, with infinite combination of possibilities. Perhaps *froment-faim.*

76. The ancient city the creation of Antenor,[1]
    Being no longer able to bear the tyrant:
    The feigned handle[2] in the temple to cut a throat,
    The people will come to put his followers to death.

77. Through the fraudulent victory of the deceived,[3]
    Two fleets one, German revolt:
    The chief murdered and his son in the tent,[4]
    Florence and Imola pursued into "Romania."[5]

78. To proclaim the victory of[6] the great expanding "Selin":[7]
    By the Romans will the Eagle be demanded,
    Pavia, Milan and Genoa will not consent thereto,
    Then by themselves the great Lord[8] claimed.

79. Near the Ticino the inhabitants of the Loire,
    Garonne and Saône, the Seine, the Tain and Gironde:
    They will erect a promontory beyond the mountains,
    Conflict given, Po enlarged,[9] submerged in the wave.

80. From Fez the realm will reach those of Europe,
    Their city ablaze and the blade will cut:
    The great one of Asia by land and sea with a great troop,
    So that blués and perses[10] the cross will pursue to death.

81. Tears, cries and laments, howls, terror,
    Heart inhuman, cruel, black and chilly:
    Lake of Geneva the Isles, of Genoa the notables,
    Blood to pour out, wheat famine[11] to none mercy.

[1]I.e., Padua, whose legendary founder was Trojan Prince Antenor.
[2] Or "one-armed one."
[3]Or "Through the victory of the fraudulent deceit."
[4]Or "The chief and his son murdered in the tent."
[5]Either (1) Romagna, or (2) the Papal States, or (3) the "[Holy] Roman Empire."
[6]Or possibly "over."
[7]Or "crescent Moon."
[8]Or "King" or "Captain." See note opposite.
[9]Or "Pau seized." See Commentary for fantastic interpretation here.
[10]A color variously defined as bluish gray, sky blue and bluish green.
[11]Very dubious and tentative. See note 15, opposite.

82. Par les déserts de lieu libre et farouche,
    Viendra errer neveu du grand Pontife:
    Assomé à sept avec lourde souche,
    Par ceux qu'après occuperont le *Cyphe*.[1]

83. Celui qu'aura tant d'honneur et caresses
    À son entrée en la *Gaule Belgique:*
    Un temps après fera tant de rudesses,
    Et sera contre à la fleur tant *bellique*.[2]

84. Celui qu'en *Sparte Claude*[3] ne peut regner,
    Il fera tant par voie séductive:
    Que du court, long, le fera *araigner*,[4]
    Que contre Roi fera sa perspective.

85. La grande cité de *Tharse* par *Gaulois*
    Sera détruite, captifs tous à Turban:
    Secours par mer du[5] grand *Portugalois*,
    Premier d'été le jour du sacre *Vrban*.

86. Le grand Prélat un jour après son songe,
    Interprété au rebours de son sens:
    De la *Gascogne* lui surviendra un *monge*,[6]
    Qui fera élire le grand prélat de *Sens*.

87. L'élection faite dans *Frankfort*,
    N'aura nul lieu, *Milan* s'opposera:
    Le sien plus proche semblera si grand fort,
    Qu'outre le *Rhin* ès *mareschs*[7] chassera.

88. Un regne grand *demourra*[8] désolé,
    Auprès de l'*Hebro* se feront assemblées:
    Monts *Pyrenees* le rendront consolé,
    Lorsque dans Mai seront terre tremblées.

[1]Latin *Scyphus*, chalice, cup, goblet.
[2]Latin *bellicus*, warlike.
[3]Latin *claudus*, lame.
[4]O.F. *araigner*, to accuse.
[5]Variant: *au*.
[6]Provençal *monge*, monk.
[7]O.F. *maresqs*, marshes.
[8]O.F. *demourer*, to remain, to be left (modern *demeurer*).

82. Through the deserts of the free and wild place,
    The nephew of the great Pontiff will come to wander:
    Felled by seven with a heavy club,
    By those who afterwards will occupy the Chalice.

☞ 83. He who will have so much honor and flattery
    At his entry into Belgian Gaul:
    A while after he will act very rudely,
    And he will act very warlike against the flower.

84. The Lame One, he who lame could not reign in Sparta,
    He will do much through seductive means:
    So that by the short and long, he will be accused
    Of making his perspective against the King.

☞ 85. The great city of Tarsus by the Gauls
    Will be destroyed, all of the Turban captives:
    Help by sea from[1] the great one of Portugal,
    First day of summer Urban's consecration.[2]

86. The great Prelate one day after his dream,
    Interpreted opposite to its meaning:
    From Gascony a monk will come unexpectedly,
    One who will cause the great prelate of Sens to be elected.

☞ 87. The election made in Frankfort
    Will be voided, Milan will be opposed:
    The follower closer will seem so very strong
    That he will drive him out into the marshes beyond the Rhine.

88. A great realm will be left desolated,
    Near the Ebro an assembly will be formed:
    The Pyrenees mountains will console him,[3]
    When in May lands will be trembling.

[1]Or "to."
[2]Or possibly "St. Urban's Day."
[3]Or "it."

89. Entre deux *cymbes*[1] pieds et mains attachés,
    De miel face oint, et de lait *substanté*:[2]
    Guêpes et mouches, *fitine*[3] amour fâchés,
    *Poccilateur*[4] *faucer*,[5] *Cyphe*[6] tenté.

90. L'*honnissement*[7] puant abominable,
    Après le fait sera félicité:
    Grande excuse[8] pour n'être favorable,
    Qu'à paix *Neptune* ne sera incité.

91. Du conducteur de la guerre navale,
    Rouge effréné, sévère, horrible grippe,
    Captif échappé de l'aîné dans la balle:[9]
    Quand il naîtra du grand un fils *Agrippe*.

92. Prince[10] de beauté tant *venuste*,[11]
    Au chef menée, le second fait trahi:
    La cité au glaive de poudre face aduste,
    Par trop grand meurtre le chef du Roi haï.

93. Prélat avare d'ambition trompé,
    Rien ne sera que trop viendra *cuider*:[12]
    Ses messagers et lui bien attrapé,
    Tout au rebours voit qui le bois fendrait.

94. Un Roi *iré*[13] sera aux *sedifragues*,[14]
    Quand interdits seront harnois de guerre:
    Le poison teint au sucre par les *fragues*,[15]
    Par eaux meurtris, mort, disant terre terre.[16]

[1]O.F. *cymbe*, boat.
[2]Low Latin *substantare*, to sustain.
[3]Greek *phitus*, father.
[4]Latin *pocillator*, cup-bearer.
[5]O.F. *faucer*, to falsify.
[6]Latin *scyphus*, chalice, cup, goblet.
[7]O.F. *honnissement*, disgrace.
[8]Variant: *excusé*.
[9]Per the original 1557 edition. All others have the erratum *baste*.
[10]Variant: *Prince sera*. As this line scans short, this, or Garencières' *Princesse*, may
represent the original draft.
[11]Latin *venustus*, winning, graceful, comely.
[12]O.F. *cuider*, to think, believe, persuade oneself.
[13]O.F. *iré*, angry.
[14]Insoluble Nostradamian concoction. Most likely from *sedem-frangere*, which allows
of many translations. Literally, to break a seat.
[15]Latin *fraga*, strawberries.
[16]Per 1557 edition. See note 6 opposite.

89. Feet and hands bound between two boats,[1]
    Face anointed with honey, and sustained with milk:
    Wasps and flies, paternal love vexed,
    Cup-bearer to falsify, Chalice tried.

90. The stinking abominable disgrace,
    After the deed he will be congratulated:
    The great excuse for not being favorable,
    That Neptune will not be persuaded to peace.

91. Of the leader of the naval war,
    Red one unbridled, severe, horrible whim,
    Captive escaped from the elder one in the bale,
    When there will be born a son to the great Agrippa.[2]

92. Prince of beauty so comely,
    Around his head a plot, the second deed betrayed:[3]
    The city to the sword in dust the face burnt,
    Through too great murder the head[4] of the King hated.

93. The greedy prelate deceived by ambition,
    He will come to reckon nothing too much for him:
    He and his messengers completely trapped,
    He who cut the wood sees all in reverse.

94. A King will be angry with the see-breakers,[5]
    When arms of war will be prohibited:
    The poison tainted in the sugar for the strawberries,
    Murdered by waters, dead, saying land, land.[6]

[1]Possibly used for "troughs," the ensuing being an old Persian torture, according to Garencières. See Commentary.

[2]Possibly implying a reincarnation of Marcus Vipsanius Agrippa (63–12 B.C.), Roman statesman and generalissimo, son-in-law of Augustus, grandfather of Caligula, great-grandfather of Nero, a model of the finest type of Roman leader.

[3]Le Pelletier would have it (see Commentary): "Against his head a plot, made second, betrayed." Garencières would have it: "A Princess of an exquisite beauty/Shall be brought to the general. . . ."

[4]Or "chief."

[5]Many other translations are possible, but all equal Protestants.

[6]This translation is derived from the text of the original 1557 edition. All others, instead of *terre terre*, have *serre serre*.

95. Par détracteur calomnie à puîné,
    Quand iront faits enormes et martiaux:
    La moindre part *dubieuse*[1] à l'aîné,
    Et tôt au regne seront faits *partiaux*.[2]

96. Grande cité à soldats abandonnée,
    Onc n'y eut mortel tumulte si proche:
    O quelle hideuse calamité s'approche,
    Fors une offense n'y sera pardonnée.

97. Cinq et quarante degrés ciel brûlera,
    Feu approcher de la grande cité neuve:
    Instant grande flamme éparse sautera,
    Quand on voudra des *Normans* faire preuve.

98. Ruiné aux *Volsques* de peur si fort terribles,
    Leur grande cité teinte, fait pestilent:
    Piller *Sol*,[3] Lune et violer leurs temples:
    Et les deux fleuves rougir de sang coulant.

99. L'ennemi docte se trouvera[4] confus,
    Grand camp malade, et défait par embûches,
    Monts *Pyrenees* et *Poenus*[5] lui seront faits refus,
    Proche du fleuve découvrant antiques cruches.[6]

LEGIS CANTIO CONTRA INEPTOS CRITICOS[7]

100. *Qui legent hosce versus, maturè censunto,*
     *Profanum vulgus et inscium ne attrectato:*
     *Omnesque Astrologi, Blennis,*[8] *Barbari procul sunto,*
     *Qui aliter facit, is rite sacer esto.*[9]

[1]Latin *dubiosus,* doubtful.
[2]O.F. *partial,* partisan.
[3]Latin *Sol,* Sun.
[4]Variant: *se tournera.*
[5]Latin *Alpes Poeninae,* Pennine Alps.
[6]Variant: *roches.*
[7]Since the entire verse is in Latin (Low Latin), it is here impossible to give a footnote for every non-French word.
[8]Greek *blennos,* simpleton, blockhead.
[9]For the other 6100 (or VI-100) see "Extra Quatrains," following Century X.

95. Calumny against the cadet by the detractor,
    When enormous and warlike deeds will take place:
    The least part doubtful for the elder one,
    And soon in the realm there will be partisan deeds.

96. Great city abandoned to the soldiers,
    Never was mortal tumult so close to it:
    Oh, what a hideous calamity draws near,
    Except one offense nothing will be spared it.

97. At forty-five degrees the sky will burn,
    Fire to approach the great new city:
    In an instant a great scattered flame will leap up,
    When one will want to demand proof of the Normans.

98. Ruin for the Volcae[1] so very terrible with fear,
    Their great city[2] stained, pestilential deed:
    To plunder Sun and Moon[3] and to violate their temples:
    And to redden the two rivers flowing with blood.

99. The learned enemy will find himself[4] confused,
    His great army sick, and defeated by ambushes,
    The Pyrenees and Pennine Alps will be denied him,
    Discovering near the river ancient jugs.[5]

INCANTATION OF THE LAW AGAINST INEPT CRITICS

100. *Let those who read this verse consider it profoundly,*
    *Let the profane and ignorant herd keep away:*
    *And far away all Astrologers, Idiots and Barbarians,*
    *May he who does otherwise be subject to the sacred rite.*

[1]The classical inhabitants of Languedoc. The Languedocians.
[2]Probably Toulouse.
[3]I.e., gold and silver.
[4]Or "will turn around."
[5]I.e., funeral urns. Or, per the variant, "ancient rocks."

# Centurie VII

1. L'Arc du trésor par *Achilles* déçu,
   Aux procrées[1] su la quadrangulaire:
   Au fait Royal le *comment*[2] sera su,
   Corps vu pendu au vu de populaire.

2. Par *Mars* ouvert *Arles* le[3] *donra*[4] guerre,
   De nuit seront les soldats étonnés:
   Noir, blanc à l'inde dissimulées en terre,
   Sous la feinte ombre traîtres *verrez*[5] et sonnés.

3. Après de *France* la victoire navale,
   Les *Barchinons*,[6] *Saillimons*,[7] les *Phocens*:[8]
   *Lierre*[9] d'or, l'enclume serré dedans la balle,
   Ceux de *Ptolon*[10] au fraud seront *consens*.[11]

4. Le Duc de *Langres* assiégé dedans *Dole*,
   Accompagné d'*Autun* et *Lyonnois*:
   *Geneue, Ausbourg*, joint ceux de *Mirandole*,
   Passer les monts contre les *Anconnois*.

5. Vin sur la table en sera répandu,
   Le tiers n'aura celle qu'il prétendait:
   Deux fois du noir[12] de *Parme* descendu,
   *Perouse* à *Pise* fera ce qu'il *cuidait*.[13]

6. *Naples, Palerme*, et toute la *Sicille*,
   Par main Barbare sera inhabitée:
   *Corsique, Salerne* et de *Sardeigne* l'Île,
   Faim, peste, guerre, fin de maux *intentée*.[14]

---

[1]Variant: *procès*.
[2]Latin *commentum*, invention, contrivance.
[3]Variant: *ne*.
[4]Syncope of *donnera*.
[5]O.F. *verrer*, to sweep? Possibly correct as second person, plural, of the future tense of *voir*.
[6]Latin *Barchinona*, Barcelona.
[7]Variants: *Salinons; Saillinons* (Garcin). Still unidentifiable.
[8]Latin *Phocenses*, Phocaeans, founders of Marseilles.
[9]All right as stands; or O.F. *lierre*, robber.
[10]Either anagram, or approximation of *Ptolémée* or *Ptolemais* (Acre).
[11]O.F. *consens*, a party to.
[12]Probably again an anagram for *roy/roi*.
[13]O.F. *cuider*, to believe, think.
[14]Latin *intentatus*, stretched out, extended.

# Century VII

1. The Ark of the treasure through Achilles deceived,
   To the procreated ones[1] the quadrangular known:
   The invention will be known by the royal deed,
   Body seen hung in the sight of the people.

2. Opened by Mars Arles will give him[2] battle,
   By night will the soldiers be astonished:
   Black and white concealing indigo on land,
   Under the feigned shadow traitors swept and[3] sounded.

3. After the naval victory of France,
   Those of Barcelona, the "Saillimons,"[4] those of Marseilles:
   Golden ivy, incus[5] enclosed in the ball,
   Those of "Ptolon"[6] will be a party to the fraud.

4. The Duke of Langres besieged in Dôle,
   Accompanied by Autun and those of Lyons:
   Geneva, Augsburg, allied those of Mirandola,
   To pass over the mountains against those of Ancona.

5. Of the wine on the table some will be spilled,
   The third one will not have that which he[7] claimed:
   Twice descended from the black one[8] of Parma,
   Perugia will do to Pisa that which he[9] believed.

6. Naples, Palermo and all Sicily,
   Through Barbarian hand it will be uninhabited:
   Corsica, Salerno and the Isle of Sardinia,
   Famine, plague, war, end of evils remote.

[1] Posterity? Or, by variant, "In the documents."
[2] Or "it." Or, by variant, "will not give."
[3] Or possibly "you will see traitors."
[4] Or "Salinons." Still unidentified. Le Pelletier derives this word from *Saillien*, which he claims means "Provençal," apparently referring to the classical inhabitants of the Salon area, the Salians (a Ligurian tribe).
[5] Or possibly "Robber of gold, anvil."
[6] Ptolemy? Ptolemy's land, i.e., Egypt? Acre (Ptolemais)?
[7] Or "The third . . . it."
[8] Or possibly "the king."
[9] Or "it."

7. Sur le combat des grands chevaux légers,
   On criera le grand croissant *confond:*[1]
   De nuit tuer monts, habits de bergers,
   Abîmes rouges dans le fossé profond.

8. *Florira,*[2] fuis, fuis le plus proche *Romain,*
   Au *Fesulan*[3] sera conflit donné:
   Sang épandu, les plus grands pris à main,
   Temple ni sexe ne sera pardonné.

9. Dame à l'absence de son grand capitaine,
   Sera priée d'amour du Vice-Roi:
   Feinte promesse et malheureuse *estreine,*[4]
   Entre les mains du grand Prince *Barrois.*

10. Par le grand Prince limitrophe du Mans
    Preux et vaillant chef du grand *exercite:*[5]
    Par mer et terre de *Gallots*[6] et *Normans,*
    *Calpre*[7] passer *Barcelonne* pillé l'île.

11. L'enfant Royal *contemnera*[8] la mère,
    Oeil, pieds, blessés, rude, *inobeissant:*[9]
    Nouvelle à dame étrange et bien amère,
    Seront tués des siens plus de cinq cents.

12. Le grand puîné fera fin de la guerre,
    Aux Dieux assemble les excusés:
    *Cahors, Moissac* iront loin de la *serre,*[10]
    Refus *Lestore,* les *Agenois* rasés.

13. De la cité marine et tributaire
    La tête rase prendra la satrapie:
    Chasser sordide qui puis sera contraire,
    Par quatorze ans tiendra la tyrannie.

[1] O.F. *confondu,* destroyed, by apocope.
[2] Variant: *Flora.* Either way, Florence is denoted.
[3] Latin *Faesulae,* Fiesole.
[4] O.F. *estrenne,* luck; success in love (Sainte-Palaye).
[5] Latin *exercitus,* army.
[6] O.F. *Gallot,* French, used especially for the French-speaking Bretons by Brittany's Breton-speaking inhabitants.
[7] Latin *Calpe,* Gibraltar.
[8] Latin *contemnare,* to despise, disdain.
[9] O.F. *inobeissant,* disobedient.
[10] O.F. *serre,* prison, confinement.

7. Upon the struggle of the great light horses,
   They will proclaim the great crescent destroyed:
   To kill by night mountains, shepherds' garb,
   Red gulfs in the deep ditch.

8. Florence, flee, flee the approaching Roman,
   At Fiesole will battle be given:
   Blood shed, the greatest ones taken by hand,
   Neither temple nor sex will be spared.

☞ 9. The Lady in the absence of her great captain
   Will be wooed by the Viceroy:
   Feigned promise and unfortunate luck,[1]
   In the hands of the great Prince of Bar.[2]

10. By the great Prince bordering on Le Mans,
    Doughty and valiant chief of the great army:
    By land and sea with Bretons[3] and Normans,
    To pass Gibraltar and Barcelona the isle sacked.

☞ 11. The royal child will scorn his mother,
    Eye, feet wounded, rude, disobedient:
    Strange and very bitter news to the lady,
    More than five hundred of her[4] followers will be killed.

12. The great cadet will put an end to the war,
    Before the Gods he assembles the pardoned:
    Cahors and Moissac will go far from the confinement,
    At Lectoure refusal, those of Agen shaved.

☞ 13. From the marine and tributary city
    The shaven head will take the satrapy:
    To chase the sordid one who will then be against him,
    For fourteen years he will hold the tyranny.

[1] Or "success."
[2] A possession of the House of Lorraine (or Guise). See Commentary.
[3] Literally, French-speaking Bretons of eastern Brittany (Nantes, Rennes, *et al.*)
[4] Or "his."

14. Faux exposer viendra topographie,
Seront les cruches des monuments ouvertes:
Pulluler secte, sainte philosophie,
Pour blanches noires, et pour antiques vertes.

15. Devant cité de l'*Insubre* contrée,
Sept ans sera le siège devant mis:
Le très grand Roi y fera son entrée,
Cité puis libre hors des ennemis.

16. Entrée profonde par la grande Reine faite
Rendra le lieu puissant inaccessible:
L'armée des trois Lions sera défaite,
Faisant dedans cas hideux et terrible.

17. Le Prince rare de pitié et clémence
Viendra changer par mort grande connaissance:[1]
Par grand repos le regne travaillé,
Lorsque le grand tôt sera étrillé.

18. Les assiégés coloreront leurs *paches*,[2]
Sept jours après feront cruelle issue:
Dans repoussés, feu, sang Sept mis à l'hache
Dame captive qu'avait la paix tissue.

19. Le fort *Nicene* ne sera combattu:
Vaincu sera par *rutilant*[3] métal.
Son fait sera un long temps débattu,
Aux citadins étrange épouvantal.

20. Ambassadeurs de la *Toscane* langue,
Avril et Mai *Alpes* et mei passer:
Celui de veau[4] exposera l'harangue,
Vie *Gauloise* ne venant effacer.

[1] The 1605 edition goes 'way off again here: *Après avoir la paix aux siens baillé:* Line 3 is 2 of above; line 4 is 3 of above. This gives the normal *a b a b* rime instead of the unusual *a a b b* rime above.

[2] O.F. *pache*, treaty, pact, agreement.

[3] O.F. *rutiler*, to shine.

[4] Le Pelletier thinks this is a play on *Vaud*, the Swiss canton.

☞ 14. They will come to expose the false topography,
     The jugs[1] of the tombs will be opened:
     Sect and holy philosophy to multiply,
     Black for white, and the unripe for the ancient.

15. Before the city of the Insubrian region,[2]
     The siege will be laid for seven years:
     The very great King will enter therein,
     City then free its enemies out.

16. The deep entry made by the great Queen
     Will render the place powerful and inaccessible:
     The army of the three Lions will be defeated,
     Causing within a hideous and terrible event.

17. The Prince rare in pity and mercy
     Will come to change through death great knowledge:[3]
     Through great tranquillity the realm attended to,
     When the great one soon will be fleeced.

18. The besieged will color their pacts,
     Seven days after they will make a cruel sortie:
     Hurled back inside, fire, blood, Seven put to the ax
     The Lady who had woven the peace captive.

19. The fort of Nice will not be engaged:
     It will be conquered by shining metal.
     Which deed will be discussed a long time,
     To the citizens strange and frightful.

☞ 20. Ambassadors of the Tuscan tongue,
     In April and May to pass the Alps and sea:
     He of the calf[4] will deliver the oration,
     About not coming to wipe out the Gallic life.

[1] I.e., funeral urns.
[2] I.e., Lombardy, whose chief city is Milan.
[3] Or, as per the 1605, "After having given peace to his followers:" Lines 3 and 4 of the 1605 are lines 2 and 3 of above.
[4] Or possibly (according to Le Pelletier) "He of Vaud." See Commentary.

21. Par pestilente inimitié *Volsique*,[1]
    Dissimulée chassera le tyran:
    Au pont de *Sorgues* se fera le trafic
    De mettre à mort lui et son adhérent.

22. Les citoyens de *Mesopotamie*[2]
    *Irez*[3] encontre amis de *Tarraconne:*[4]
    Jeux, rites, banquets, toute gent endormie,
    Vicaire au *Rosne*, pris cité, ceux d'*Ausone*.

23. Le Royal sceptre sera contraint de prendre,
    Ce que ses prédécesseurs avaient engagé
    Puisque l'anneau on fera mal entendre,
    Lorsqu'on viendra le palais saccager.

24. L'enseveli sortira du tombeau,
    Fera de chaînes lier le fort du pont:
    Empoisonné avec œufs de Barbeau,
    Grand de *Lorraine* par le Marquis *du Pont*.

25. Par guerre longue tout l'*exercite*[5] épuiser,
    Que pour soldats ne trouveront pécune,
    Lieu d'or, d'argent, cuir on viendra *cuser*,[6]
    *Gaulois* airain, siège, croissant[7] de Lune.

26. Fustes et galères autour de sept navires,
    Sera livrée une mortelle guerre:
    Chef de *Madric* recevra coup de *vires*,[8]
    Deux échappées, et cinq menées à terre.

[1]From *Volcae*, classical inhabitants of the territory corresponding to Languedoc.
[2]Greek *Meso-potamos*, between rivers (or seas).
[3]Latin *iratus*, angry.
[4]Variants: *Tarocconne; Tarragonne*. Either from Latin *Tarraco, Tarragona* (in Catalonia) or *[Hispania] Tarraconensis*, the northeastern half of Roman Iberia.
[5]Latin *exercitus*, army.
[6]Latin *cusare (cudere)*, to coin money.
[7]Variant: *signe croissant*.
[8]O.F. *vire*. arrow. dart.

21. By the pestilential enmity of Languedoc,
    Dissimulated the tyrant will be driven out:
    On the bridge of Sorgues will be made the bargain
    To put to death him and his adherent.

☞ 22. The citizens of "Mesopotamia"[1]
    Angry with their friends of Catalonia:[2]
    Games, rites, banquets, a whole people lulled to sleep,
    Vicar at the Rhône, city taken, those of Ausonia.[3]

23. The royal sceptre will be obliged to take
    That which his predecessors had pledged
    Since they will pretend not to understand about the ring,
    When they will come to sack the palace.

☞ 24. The buried one will come out from his tomb,
    He will cause the fort[4] of the bridge to be bound with chains:
    Poisoned with Barbel roe,
    The Great One of Lorraine by the Marquis du Pont.[5]

25. Through long war the entire army exhausted,
    So that they will not find money for the soldiers,
    Instead of gold and silver, they will come to coin leather,
    Gallic brass, see, crescent Moon.[6]

26. Foists and galleys around seven ships,
    A mortal war will be fought:
    The Chief of Madrid will receive a wound from arrows,
    Two escaped, and five brought to land.

[1]The Land Between Rivers (see note opposite). With two possible exceptions (361 and 399) used by Nostradamus not for the classical territory between the Tigris and the Euphrates rivers (in modern Iraq) but for a French territory, probably Avignon and the surrounding Venaissin County (between the Rhône and Durance rivers). See Commentary.

[2]This seems the best translation, between the lesser one of "Tarragona" (a mere town) and the greater one of "northern and eastern Spain." In all likelihood, Nostradamus thought the Roman province corresponded to Catalonia, though it actually covered three-fourths of modern Spain.

[3]Southern Italy (in Nostradamus' day the Kingdom of Naples).

[4]Or "the strong one."

[5]I.e., Marquis of Pont-à-Mousson, a title borne by the younger sons of the Duke of Lorraine.

[6]Or "Gallic brass, crescent Moon stamp."

27.  Au *cainct*[1] de *Vast* la grande cavalerie,
     Proche à *Ferrage*[2] empêchée au bagage:
     Prompt[3] à *Turin* feront tel volerie,
     Que dans le fort raviront leur otage.

28.  Le capitaine conduira grand *proie*,[4]
     Sur la montagne des ennemis plus proche:
     Environné par feu fera telle voie,
     Tous échappés, *or*[5] trente mis en broche.

29.  Le grand Duc d'*Albe* se viendra rebeller,
     À ses grands pères fera le *tradiment*:[6]
     Le grand de *Guise* le viendra *debeller*,[7]
     Captif mené et dressé monument.

30.  Le sac s'approche, feu grand sang épandu,
     *Po*, grands fleuves, aux bouviers l'entreprise:
     De *Gennes*, *Nice*, après long attendu,
     *Foussan*, *Turin*, à *Sauillan* la prise.

31.  De *Languedoc*, et *Guienne* plus de dix
     Mille voudront les *Alpes* repasser:
     Grands *Allobroges*[8] marcher contre *Brundis*,
     *Aquin* et *Bresse* les viendront rechasser.

32.  Du mont Royal naîtra d'une *casane*,[9]
     Qui cave, et compte viendra tyranniser:
     Dresser *copie*[10] de la marche *Millane*,
     *Fauene*, *Florence* d'or et gens épuiser.

[1]O.F. *caint*, belt, waist.
[2]Variant (Garcin): *Ferrare*. This is undoubtedly the correct one.
[3]Variant: *Pompe*.
[4]O.F. *proie*, herd, flock.
[5]Although uniform in all editions, this must be erratum for *hors*.
[6]O.F. *tradiment*, treason.
[7]Latin, *debellare*, to completely conquer, vanquish, subdue.
[8]Latin *Allobroges*, the inhabitants of Savoy.
[9]Low Latin *casana*, bank.
[10]Latin *copia*, forces, troops, army.

27. At the belt[1] of Vasto[2] the great cavalry,
    Near Ferrara impeded by the baggage:
    Suddenly[3] at Turin they will carry on such robbery,
    That in the fort they will ravage their hostage.

28. The captain will lead a great flock,
    On the mountain closer to the enemy:
    Surrounded by fire he will cut such a path,
    All escaped except thirty put on the spit.

☞ 29. The great Duke of Alba will come to rebel,
    He will betray his great ancestors:
    The great one of Guise will come to vanquish him,
    Led captive and a monument erected.

30. The sack approaches, fire, great shedding of blood,
    Po, great rivers, enterprise for the cow-keepers:[4]
    Of Genoa, Nice, after a long wait,
    Fossano, Turin, at Savigliano the capture.

31. From Languedoc and Guienne more than ten
    Thousand will want to pass over the Alps again:
    The great Savoyards to march against Brindisi,
    Aquino and Bresse will come to drive them back.

32. Of a bank of the royal mount[5] will be born
    One who boring and calculating will come to tyrannize:
    To prepare a force in the confines of Milan,
    To drain Faenza and Florence of gold and men.

[1]Wall?
[2]Somewhat uncertain. See Commentary.
[3]Or "Pomp."
[4]Or "clowns."
[5]Or possibly "Montereale."

33. Par fraude regne, forces *expolier*,[1]
    La *classe*[2] *obsesse*,[3] passages à l'*espie:*[4]
    Deux feints amis se viendront rallier,
    Éveiller haine de longtemps assoupie.

34. En grand regret sera la gent *Gauloise*,
    Cœur vain, léger croira témérité:
    Pain, sel, ni vin, eau, venin ni cervoise,
    Plus grand captif, faim, froid, nécessité.

35. La grande pêche viendra plaindre, pleurer,
    D'avoir élu, trompés seront en l'âge:
    Guère avec eux ne voudra demeurer,
    Déçu sera par ceux de son langage.

36. Dieu, le ciel tout le divin verbe à l'onde,
    Porté par rouges sept rases à *Bizance:*
    Contre les oints trois cents de *Trebisconde*
    Deux lois mettront, et horreur, puis crédence.

37. Dix envoyés, chef de nef mettre à mort,
    D'un averti en *classe*[5] guerre ouverte:
    Confusion chef l'un se pique et mord,
    *Leryns, stecades*[6] nefs, cap dedans la *nerte.*[7]

38. L'aîné Royal sur coursier voltigeant,
    Piquer viendra si rudement courir:
    Gueule, lippée, pied dans l'étreinte plaignant,
    Traîné, tiré, horriblement mourir.

39. Le conducteur de l'armée *Françoise*,
    *Cuidant*[8] perdre le principal phalange:
    Par sus pavé de l'avoine et d'ardoise,
    Soi *parfondra*[9] par *Gennes* gent étrange.

[1]O.F. *expolier*, to despoil, strip, plunder.
[2]Latin *classis*, fleet.
[3]Latin *obsessus*, blockaded.
[4]O.F. *espie*, spy.
[5]Latin *classis*, fleet.
[6]Latin *Stoechades*, Isles of Hyères.
[7]O.F. *nerte*, black; or Greek *nerthe*, beneath, underneath.
[8]O.F. *cuider*, to think, believe, persuade oneself.
[9]O.F. *parfondrer*, to undermine.

33. Through guile the realm stripped of its forces,
The fleet blockaded, passages for the spy:
Two feigned friends will come to rally,
Hatred long dormant to awaken.

34. In great grief will the Gallic people be,
Vain and light of heart they will trust in rashness:
No bread, salt, wine, water, venom[1] or ale,
Greater captivity, famine, cold, need.

35. The great fishery will come to complain and weep
Over the choice it has made, deceived about his age:
He will want to remain with them scarcely at all,
He will be deceived by those of his own tongue.

36. God, heaven all the divine word in the waves,
Carried by seven red shaven heads to Byzantium:
Against the anointed three hundred from Trebizond
Will set two laws, and horror, then credence.

37. Ten sent to put to death the captain of the ship,
Warned by one open war in the fleet:
Confusion, the chief and another prick and bite one another,
At the Lérins and Hyères islands ships, prow into the darkness.[2]

38. The elder royal one upon a prancing steed,
To spur so rudely it will come to run off:
Mouth, mouthful, foot sparing in the embrace,
Dragged, pulled, to die horribly.

39. The leader of the French army,
Expecting to ruin the principal phalanx:
Upon the pavement of oats and slate,
The foreign people will undermine themselves through Genoa.

[1] A strange usage here. Possibly used for hard liquor.
[2] Or "the bottom"?

40. Dedans tonneaux hors oints d'huile et graisse
    Seront vingt un devant le port fermés:
    Au second guet par mort feront prouesse
    Gagner les portes, et du guet assomés.

41. Les os des pieds et des mains enserrés,
    Par bruit maison longtemps inhabitée,
    Seront par songes *concavant*[1] déterrés,
    Maison salubre et sans bruit habitée.

42. Deux de poison saisis nouveaux venus
    Dans la cuisine du grand Prince verser:
    Par le *souillard*[2] tous deux au fait connus,
    Pris qui *cuidait*[3] de mort l'aîné vexer.[4]

[1] O.F. *concaver*, to dig.
[2] O.F. *souillard*, scullion (Sainte-Palaye).
[3] O.F. *cuider*, to think, believe, persuade oneself.
[4] See "Extra Quatrains" following Century X for additions to this Century printed after 1568.

40. Within casks anointed outside with oil and grease
There will be twenty-one shut up before the port:
At the second watch through death they will perform a feat
To win the gates, and be felled by the watch.

41 The bones of the feet and of the hands locked up,
Because of the noise the house long uninhabited,
Digging in dreams they will be dug up,
House healthy and inhabited without noise.

☞ 42. Two newly arrived in possession of poison
To pour out in the kitchen of the great Prince:
Through the scullion both caught in the act,
Seized he who thought to vex the elder one with death.

# [Épître]

À L'*Invictissime*,[1]
Très-Puissant et Très-Chrétien
*Henri*, Roi de *France* Second:
Michel Nostradamus,
très-humble et très-obéissant serviteur et sujet,
Victoire et Félicité.

[1]Pour icelle souveraine observation que j'ai eu, ô très-Chrétien et très-victorieux Roi, depuis que ma face étant longtemps *obnubilus*[2] se présente au devant de la déité de votre Majesté *immesurée*,[3] depuis en ça j'ai été perpétuellement ébloui, ne désistant d'honorer et dignement vénérer icelui jour que premièrement devant icelle je me présentai, comme à une singulière Majesté tant humaine. Or cherchant quelque occasion par laquelle je pusse manifester le bon cœur et franc courage, que moyennant icelui mon pouvoir eusse fait ample extension de connaissance envers votre sérénissime Majesté. Or voyant que par effets le déclarer ne m'était possible, [2] joint avec mon singulier désir de ma tant longue *obtenebration*[4] et obscurité, être subitement éclaircie et transportée au devant de la face du souverain œil, et du premier Monarque de l'Univers, tellement que j'ai été en doute longuement à qui je viendrais consacrer ces trois Centuries du restant de mes Prophéties parachevant la *milliade*,[5] et après avoir longuement *cogité*[6] d'une téméraire audace, ai pris mon adresse envers votre Majesté, n'étant pour cela étonné, comme raconte le *gravissime*[7] auteur *Plutarque* en la vie de *Lycurgue*, que voyant les offres et présents qu'on faisait par sacrifices aux temples des dieux immortels d'icelui temps, et à celle fin que l'on ne s'étonnât par trop souvent dédits frais et mises, ne s'osaient présenter aux temples. Ce nonobstant voyant votre splendeur Royale, accompagnée d'une incomparable humanité, ai pris mon adresse, non comme aux Rois de *Perse*, qu'il n'était nullement permis d'aller à eux, ni moins s'en approcher. [3] Mais à un très-prudent, à un très-sage Prince, j'ai consacré mes nocturnes et prophétiques supputations, composés plutôt d'un naturel instinct, accompa-

[1]Latin *invictissimus*, most invincible.
[2]Latin *obnubilus*, cloudy.
[3]Latin *immensuratus*, unmeasured.
[4]Latin *obtenebratio*, darkness.
[5]O.F. *milliade*, thousand.
[6]Latin *cogitare*, to meditate.
[7]Latin *gravissimus*, most grave.

# [Epistle]

## To the Most Invincible,
## Most Powerful and Most Christian
## Henry, King of France the Second:
## Michel Nostradamus,
### his very humble and very obedient servant and subject,
### Wishes Victory and Happiness.

1. Ever since my long-beclouded face first presented itself before the immeasurable deity of your Majesty, O Most Christian and Most Victorious King, I have remained perpetually dazzled by that sovereign sight. I have never ceased to honor and venerate properly that date when I presented myself before a Majesty so singular and so humane. I have searched for some occasion on which to manifest high heart and stout courage, and thereby obtain even greater recognition of Your Most Serene Majesty. But I saw how obviously impossible it was for me to declare myself.

2. While I was seized with this singular desire to be transported suddenly from my long-beclouded obscurity to the illuminating presence of the first monarch of the universe, I was also long in doubt as to whom I would dedicate these last three Centuries of my prophecies, making up the thousand. After having meditated for a long time on an act of such rash audacity, I have ventured to address Your Majesty. I have not been daunted like those mentioned by that most grave author Plutarch, in his Life of Lycurgus, who were so astounded at the expense of the offerings and gifts brought as sacrifices to the temples of the immortal gods of that age, that they did not dare to present anything at all. Seeing your royal splendor to be accompanied by such an incomparable humanity, I have paid my addresses to it and not as to those Kings of Persia whom one could neither stand before nor approach.

3. It is to a most prudent and most wise Prince that I have dedicated my nocturnal and prophetic calculations, which are composed rather out of a natural instinct, accompanied by a poetic furor, than according to the strict

gné d'une fureur poétique, que par règle de poésie, et la plupart composé
et accordé à la calculation Astronomique, correspondant aux ans, mois et
semaines des régions, contrées, et de la plupart des villes et cités de toute
l'*Europe*, comprenant de l'*Afrique*, et une partie de l'*Asie* par le changement
des régions, qui s'approchent la plupart de tous ces climats, et composé
d'une naturelle *faction*:[8] [4] répondra quelqu'un qui aurait bien besoin de
soi moucher, le rythme être autant facile, comme l'intelligence du sens est
difficile. Et parce, ô très-*humanissime*[9] Roi, la plupart des quatrains prophétiques sont tellement scabreux, que l'on n'y saurait donner voie ni moins
aucuns interpréter, [5] toutefois espérant de laisser par écrit les ans, villes,
cités, régions où la plupart aviendra, même de l'année 1585 et de l'année
1606, commençant depuis le temps présent, qui est le quatorzième de Mars
1557, et passant outre bien loin jusqu'à l'avènement, qui sera après au
commencement du septième millénaire profondément supputé, tant que
mon calcul astronomique et autre savoir s'a pu étendre, où les adversaires de
*Jésus-Christ* et de son Église commenceront plus fort de pulluler, [6] le
tout a été composé et calculé en jours et heures d'élection et bien disposées,
et le plus justement qu'il m'a été possible. Et le tout *Minerva libera et non
invita*, supputant presque autant des aventures du temps avenir, comme
des âges passés, comprenant de présent, et de ce que par le cours du temps
par toutes régions l'on connaîtra avenir, tout ainsi nommément comme il est
écrit, n'y mêlant rien de superflu, combien que l'on dit: *Quod de futuris non
est determinata omnino veritas.* [7] Il est bien vrai, Sire, que pour mon
naturel instinct qui m'a été donné par mes *avites*,[10] ne[11] cuidant présager et
ajustant et accordant icelui naturel instinct avec ma longue supputation uni,
et vidant l'âme, l'esprit, et le courage de toute cure, solicitude, et fâcherie
par repos et tranquillité de l'esprit. Le tout accordé et présagé l'une partie
*tripode aeneo.* [8] *Combien qu*[12]ils sont plusieurs qui m'attribuent ce qu'est
autant à moi, comme de ce que n'en est rien, Dieu seul éternel, qui est
*perscrutateur*[13] des humains courages, *pie*,[14] juste, et miséricordieux, en est
le vrai juge, auquel je prie qu'il me veuille défendre de la calomnie des
méchants, qui voudraient aussi calomnieusement s'enquérir pour quelle
cause tous vos *antiquissimes*[15] progéniteurs Rois de *France* ont guéri des
écrouelles, et des autres nations ont guéri de la morsure des serpents, les
autres ont eu certain instinct de l'art divinatrice; et d'autres cas qui seraient
longs ici à raconter. [9] Ce nonobstant ceux à qui la malignité de l'esprit

---

[8]Latin *factio*, making, doing.
[9]Latin *humanissimus*, most humane.
[10]Latin *avites*, ancestors.
[11]*Me* would seem in order, but *ne*, which makes no sense, is uniform in all editions.
[12]O.F. *combien que*, although.
[13]Latin *perscrutator*, a thorough searcher.
[14]Latin *pius*, pious. *Pie* in French means magpie.
[15]Latin *antiquissimus*, most ancient.

rules of poetry. Most of them have been integrated with astronomical calculations corresponding to the years, months and weeks of the regions, countries and most of the towns and cities of all Europe, including Africa and part of Asia, where most of all these coming events are to transpire. They are composed in a natural manner.

4. Indeed, someone, who would do well to blow his nose, may reply that the rhythm is as easy as the sense is difficult. That, O Most Humane king, is because most of the prophetic quatrains are so ticklish that there is no making way through them, nor is there any interpreting of them.

5. Nevertheless, I wanted to leave a record in writing of the years, towns, cities and regions in which most of the events will come to pass, even those of the year 1585 and of the year 1606, reckoning from the present time, which is March 14, 1557, and going far beyond to the events which will take place at the beginning of the seventh millenary,[1] when, so far as my profound astronomical calculations and other knowledge have been able to make out, the adversaries of Jesus Christ and his Church will begin to multiply greatly.

6. I have calculated and composed all during choice hours of well-disposed days, and as accurately as I could, all when *Minerva was free and not unfavorable.*[2] I have made computations for events over almost as long a period to come as that which has already passed, and by these they will know in all regions what is to happen in the course of time, just as it is written, with nothing superfluous added, although some may say, *There can be no truth entirely determined concerning the future.*

7. It is quite true, Sire, that my natural instinct has been inherited from my forebears, who did not believe in predicting,[3] and that this natural instinct has been adjusted and integrated with long calculations. At the same time, I freed my soul, mind and heart of all care, solicitude and vexation. All of these prerequisites for presaging I achieved in part *by means of the brazen tripod.*

8. There are some who would attribute to me that which is not mine at all. The eternal God alone, who is the thorough searcher of human hearts, pious, just and merciful, is the true judge, and it is to him I pray to defend me from the calumny of evil men. These evil ones, in their slanderous way, would likewise want to inquire how all your most ancient progenitors, the Kings of France, have cured the scrofula, how those of other nations have cured the bite of snakes, how those of yet other nations have had a certain instinct for the art of divination and still others which would be too long to recite here.

9. Notwithstanding those who cannot contain the malignity of the evil

---

[1] For possible dates of this event, see Commentary on para. 40.

[2] Horace used *invita Minerva* to mean contrary to one's natural abilities.

[3] A very strange phrase, but capable of no other translation.

malin ne sera compris par le cours du temps après la *terrene*[16] mienne
extinction, plus sera mon écrit qu'a mon vivant, cependant si à ma supputation des âges je faillais, on ne pourrait être selon la volonté d'aucuns.
Plaira à votre plus qu'impériale Majesté me pardonner, protestant devant
Dieu et ses Saints, que je ne prétends de mettre rien quelconque par écrit
en la présente Épître, qui soit contre la vraie foi Catholique, conférant les
calculations Astronomiques, jouxte mon savoir: [10] car l'espace du temps de
nos premiers, qui nous ont précédé sont tels, me remettant sous la correction
du plus sain jugement, que le premier homme *Adam* fut devant *Noé* environ
mille deux cent quarante deux ans, ne computant les temps par la supputation des *Gentils*, comme a mis par écrit *Varron:* mais tant seulement selon
les sacrées Écritures, et selon la faiblesse de mon esprit, en mes calculations
Astronomiques. Après *Noé*, de lui et de l'universel déluge, vint *Abraham*
environ mille huitante ans, lequel a été souverain Astrologue selon aucuns,
il inventa premier les lettres *Chaldaïques:* après vint *Moyse* environ cinq
cent quinze ou seize ans et entre le temps de *David* et *Moyse*, ont été cinq
cent septante ans là environ. Puis après entre le temps de David, et le
temps de notre Sauveur et Rédempteur *Iésus-Christ*, né de l'unique Vierge,
ont été (selon aucuns Chronographes) mille trois cent cinquante ans:
pourra objecter quelqu'un cette supputation n'être veritable, parce qu'elle
diffère à celle d'*Eusèbe*. Et depuis le temps de l'humaine Rédemption
jusqu'à la séduction détestable des *Sarrazins,* ont été six cent vingt et un
an, là environ, depuis en ça l'on peut facilement colliger quels temps sont
passés, [11] si la mienne supputation n'est bonne et valable par toutes
nations, parce que tout a été calculé par le cours céleste, par association
d'émotion infuse à certaines heures délaissées, par l'émotion des mes antiques
progéniteurs: Mais l'injure du temps, ô sérénissime Roi, requiert que tels
secrets événements ne soient manifestés, que par énigmatique sentence,
n'ayant qu'un seul sens et unique intelligence, sans y avoir rien mis d'ambigue ni amphibologique calculation: mais plutôt sous *obnubilée*[17] obscurité
par une naturelle infusion approchant à la sentence d'un des mille et
deux Prophètes, qui ont été depuis la création du monde, jouxte la supputation et Chronique Punique de *Ioël, Effundam spiritum meum super omnem
carnem et prophetabunt filii vestri et filiae vestrae.* Mais telle Prophétie
procédait de la bouche du Saint Esprit qui était la souveraine puissance
éternelle, adjointe avec la céleste à d'aucuns de ce nombre ont prédit de
grandes et émerveillables aventures. [12] Moi en cet endroit je ne m'attribue
nullement tel titre, ja à Dieu ne plaise, je confesse bien que le tout vient de
Dieu, et lui en rends grâces, honneur et louange immortelle, sans y avoir
mêlé de la divination que provient à *fato*, mais à *Deo*, à *natura*,[18] et la
plupart accompagnée du mouvement du cours céleste, tellement que voyant
comme dans un miroir ardent, comme par vision *obnubilee*,[17] les grands

---

[16]Latin *terrenus*, earthly.

[17]Latin *obnubilus*, cloudy.

[18]These last three italicized words are Nostradamus' (or his first printer's) italicizations.

spirit, as time elapses after my death, my writings will have more weight than during my lifetime. Should I, however, have made any errors in my calculation of dates, or prove unable to please everybody, I beg that your more than Imperial Majesty will forgive me. I protest before God and his Saints that I do not propose to insert any writings in this present Epistle that will be contrary to the true Catholic faith, whilst consulting the astronomical calculations to the best of my ability.

10. Such is the extent of time past, subject to correction by the most learned judgment, that the first man, Adam, came 1,242 years before Noah (not reckoning by such Gentile calculations as Varro[4] used, but simply by the Holy Scriptures, as best my weak understanding and astronomical calculations can interpret them). About 1,080 years after Noah and the universal flood came Abraham, who, according to some, was a first-rate astrologer and invented the Chaldean alphabet. About 515 or 516 years later came Moses, and from his time to that of David about 570 years elapsed. From the time of David to that of our Saviour and Redeemer, Jesus Christ, born of the unique Virgin, 1,350 years elapsed, according to some chronographs. Some may object that this calculation cannot be true, because it differs from that of Eusebius.[5] From the time of the human redemption to the detestable heresy of the Saracens about 621 years elapsed. From this one can easily add up the amount of time gone by.[6]

11. Although my calculations may not hold good for all nations, they have, however, been determined by the celestial movements, combined with the emotion, handed down to me by my forebears, which comes over me at certain hours. But the danger of the times, O Most Serene King, requires that such secrets should not be bared except in enigmatic sentences having, however, only one sense and meaning, and nothing ambiguous or amphibological inserted. Rather are they under a cloudy obscurity, with a natural infusion not unlike the sentential delivery of one of the 1,002 Prophets who have existed since the creation of the world, according to the calculation and Punic Chronicle of Joel: *I will pour out my spirit upon all flesh and your sons and daughters will prophesy.*[7] But such Prophecy proceeded from the mouth of the Holy Ghost who was the sovereign and eternal power, together with the heavens, and caused some of them to predict great and marvelous events.

12. As for myself, I would never claim such a title, never, please God. I readily admit that all proceeds from God and render to Him thanks, honor and immortal praise. I have mixed therewith no divination coming from fate. All from God and nature, and for the most part integrated with celestial movements. It is much like seeing in a burning mirror, with clouded vision,

---

[4]Marcus Terrentius Varro (116–27 B.C.), author of quasi-historical works with fictitious chronologies.

[5]Bishop Eusebius of Cæsarea (260–340), ecclesiastical historian.

[6]About 4,758 years before Christ. See Commentary.

[7]Joel II:28.

événements tristes, prodigieux, et calamiteuses aventures qui s'approchent par les principaux *culteurs*.[19] Premièrement des temples de Dieu, secondement par ceux qui sont terrestrement soutenus s'approcher telle décadence, avec mille autres calamiteuses aventures, que par le cours du temps on connaîtra avenir. [13] Car[20] Dieu regardera la longue stérilité de la grande dame, qui puis après concevra deux enfants principaux: mais elle périclitant, celle qui lui sera ajoutée par la témérité de l'âge de mort périclitant dedans le dix-huitième ne pouvant passer le trente-sixième qu'en délaissera trois mâles, et une femelle, et en aura deux, celui qui n'en eut jamais d'un même père, [14] des trois frères seront telles differences, puis unies et accordées, que les trois et quatre parties de l'*Europe* trembleront; par le moindre d'âge sera la Monarchie Chrétienne soutenue, et augmentée: sectes élevées, et subitement abaissées, Arabes reculés, Royaumes unis, nouvelles lois promulguées: [15] des autres enfants le premier occupera les Lions furieux couronnés, tenant les pattes dessus les armes[21] intrépides. [16] Le second *se profondera*[22] si avant par les *Latins* accompagné, que sera faite la seconde voie tremblante et furibonde au *mont Iouis*[23] descendant pour monter aux *Pyrénées*, ne sera translaté à l'antique Monarchie, sera faite la troisième inondation de sang humain, ne se trouvera de longtemps Mars en Carême. [17] Et sera donnée la fille pour la conservation de l'Église Chrétienne, tombant son dominateur à la paganisme secte des nouveaux infidèles, elle aura deux enfants, l'un de fidelité, et l'autre d'infidelité par la confirmation de l'Église Catholique. [18] Et l'autre qui à sa grande confusion et tarde repentance la voudra ruiner, seront trois régions par l'extrême différence des ligues, c'est-à-savoir la *Romaine*, la *Germanie*, *l'Espagne*, qui feront diverses sectes par main militaire, délaissant le 50 et 52 degrés d'hauteur, [19] et feront tous hommage des religions lointaines aux régions de l'*Europe* et de Septentrion de 48 degrés d'hauteur, qui premier par vaine timidité tremblera, puis les Occidentaux, Méridionaux et Orientaux trembleront, telle sera leur puissance, que ce qui se fera par concorde et union *insuperable*[24] des conquêtes belliques. [20] De nature seront égaux, mais grandement diffé-

---

[19]Latin *cultor*, worshipper.
[20]Here the PROSE PROPHECY begins.
[21]Variant: *armets* (in Fortune and false "1568" editions).
[22]Latin *se profundare*, to run forth.
[23]Latin *Mons Jovis*, Great St. Bernard.
[24]O.F. *insuperable*, invincible, insuperable.

the great events, sad, prodigious and calamitous events that in due time will fall upon the principal worshippers. First, upon the temples of God; secondly, upon those who, sustained by the earth, approach such decadence. Also a thousand other calamitous events which will be known to happen in due time.

13. For God will take notice of the long barrenness of the great dame, who thereupon will conceive two principal children. But she will be in danger, and the female to whom she will have given birth will also, because of the temerity of the age, be in danger of death in her eighteenth year, and will be unable to live beyond her thirty-sixth year. She will leave three males, and one female, and of these two will not have had the same father.

14. There will be great differences between the three brothers, and then there will be such great co-operation and agreement between them that the three and four parts of Europe will tremble. The youngest of them will sustain and augment the Christian monarchy,[8] and under him sects will be elevated, and suddenly cast down, Arabs will be driven back, kingdoms united and new laws promulgated.

15. The oldest one will rule the land whose escutcheon is that of the furious crowned lions with their paws resting upon intrepid arms.[9]

16. The one second in age, accompanied by the Latins, will penetrate far, until a second furious and trembling path has been beaten to the Great St. Bernard Pass. From there he will descend to mount the Pyrenees, which will not, however, be transferred to the French crown. And this third one will cause a great inundation of human blood, and for a long time Lent will not include March.[10]

17. The daughter will be given for the preservation of the Christian Church. Her lord will fall into the pagan sect of the new infidels. Of her two children, one will be faithful to the Catholic Church, the other an infidel.

18. The unfaithful son, who, to his great confusion and later repentance, will want to ruin her, will have three widely scattered regions, namely, the Roman, Germany and Spain, which will set up diverse sects by armed force. The 50th to the 52d degree of latitude will be left behind.

19. And all will render the homage of ancient religions to[11] the region of Europe north of the 48th parallel. The latter will have trembled first in vain timidity but afterwards the regions to its west, south and east will tremble. But the nature of their power will be such that what has been brought about by concord and union will prove insuperable by warlike conquests.

20. In nature they will be equal, but very different in faith.

---

[8]The monarchy of the Most Christian King (France) or the monarchy of Christ (the Papacy). Probably the first.
[9]Or "intrepid helmets."
[10]Or Mars. Either version leaves the meaning obscure.
[11]Or possibly "in."

rents de foi. [21] Après ceci la Dame stérile de plus grande puissance que
la seconde sera reçue par deux peuples, par le premier obstiné par celui qui
a eu puissance sur tous, par le deuxième [22] et par le tiers qui étendra ses
forces vers le circuit de l'*Orient* de l'*Europe* aux *pannons*[25] l'a *profligé*[26] et
succombé, et par voile marine fera ses extensions, à la *Trinacrie*,[27] *Adriati-*
*que* par *Mirmidons* et *Germaniques* du tout succombé, et sera la secte
Barbarique du tout des *Latins* grandement affligée et déchassée. [23] Puis le
grand Empire de l'*Antéchrist* commencera dans la *Atila* et *Zerses* descendre
en nombre grand et innumerable, tellement que la venue du Saint Esprit
procédant du 48 degré, fera transmigration, déchassant à l'abomination de
l' *Antéchrist:* faisant guerre contre le Royal qui sera le grand Vicaire de
*Iesus-Christ*, et contre son Église, et son regne *per tempus, et in occasione*
*temporis.* [24] Et précédera devant une éclipse solaire le plus obscur et le
plus ténébreux, qui soit été depuis la création du monde jusqu'à la mort et
passion de *Iesus-Christ*, et de là jusqu'ici, et sera au mois d'Octobre que
quelque grande translation sera faite, et telle que l'on cuidera le pesanteur
de la terre avoir perdu son naturel mouvement, et être abîmée en perpé-
tuelles ténèbres, [25] seront précédents au temps vernail, et s'en ensuivant
après d'extrêmes changements, permutations de regnes, par grands tremble-
ments de terre, avec pullulation de la neuve *Babylone*, fille misérable
augmentée par l'abomination du premier holocauste, et ne tiendra tant seulement que septante trois ans, sept mois, [26] puis après en sortira de la tige
celle qui avait demeuré tant longtemps stérile, procédant du cinquantième
degré, qui renouvellera toute l'Église Chrétienne. Et sera faite grande paix,
union et concorde entr'uns des enfants des fronts égarés, et séparés par
divers regnes; et sera faite telle paix, que demeurera attaché au plus profond
*barathre*[28] le suscitateur et promoteur de la martiale faction par la diversité
des Religieux, et sera uni le royaume du Rabieux, qui contrefera le sage.[27]
Et les contrées, villes, cités, regnes, et provinces qui auront laissé les premières voies pour se délivrer, se captivant plus profondément, seront secrètement fâchés[29] de leur liberté, et parfaite religion perdue, commenceront de
frapper dans la partie gauche, pour retourner à la dextre, et remettant la
sainteté *profligée*[30] de longtemps avec leur *pristin*[31] écrit, [28] qu'après le
grand chien sortira le plus gros mâtin, qui fera destruction de tout, même
de ce qu'auparavant sera été perpétré, seront redressés les temples comme
au premier temps, et sera restitué le Clerc à son *pristin*[31] état, et comm-

---

[25]Pannonia, Upper and Lower. See quatrains 513, 548, 815 and 928.
[26]Latin *profligare*, to overthrow, kill, ruin.
[27]Latin poetical name for Sicily ( Trinacria ).
[28]Latin *barathron*, pit, hell.
[29]Variant: *lâchés*.
[30]Latin *profligatus*, ruined, overcome.
[31]Latin *pristinus*, original, former, earliest.

21. After this the barren Dame, of greater power than the second, will be received by two of the nations. First, by them made obstinate by the one-time masters of the universe. Second, by the latter themselves.

22. The third people will extend their forces towards the circuit of the East of Europe where, in the Pannonias, they will be overwhelmed and slaughtered. By sea they will extend their Myrmidons[12] and Germans to Adriatic Sicily. But they will succumb wholly and the Barbarian sect will be greatly afflicted and driven out by all the Latins.

23. Then the great Empire of the Antichrist will begin where once was Attila's empire and the new Xerxes will descend with great and countless numbers, so that the coming of the Holy Ghost, proceeding from the 48th degree, will make a transmigration, chasing out the abomination of the Antichrist, who will have made war upon the Royal Pope and upon the Christian Church, and whose reign will be *for a time and to the end of time.*

24. This will be preceded by a solar eclipse more dark and gloomy than any since the creation of the world, except that after the death and passion of Jesus Christ. And it will be in the month of October than the great translation will be made and it will be such that one will think the gravity of the earth has lost its natural movement and that it is to be plunged into the abyss of perpetual darkness.

25. In the spring there will be omens, and thereafter extreme changes, reversals of realms and mighty earthquakes. These will be accompanied by the procreation of the new Babylon, miserable daughter enlarged by the abomination of the first holocaust. It will last for only seventy-three years and seven months.

26. Then there will issue from the stock which had remained barren for so long, proceeding from the 50th degree, one who will renew the whole Christian Church. A great peace will be established, with union and concord between some of the children of opposite ideas, who have been separated by diverse realms. And such will be the peace that the instigator and promoter of military factions, born of the diversity of religions, will remain chained to the deepest pit. And the kingdom of the Furious One, who counterfeits the sage,[13] will be united.

27. The countries, towns, cities, realms and provinces which will have abandoned their old customs to gain liberty, but which will in fact have enthralled themselves still more, will secretly have wearied of their liberty. Faith lost in their perfect religion, they will begin to strike to the left, only to return to the right. Holiness, for a long time overcome, will be replaced in accordance with the earliest writings.

28. Thereafter the great dog, the biggest of curs, will go forth and destroy all, the same old crimes being perpetrated again. Temples will be set up again as in ancient times, and the priest will be restored to his original posi-

---

[12]Macedonian tribe metamorphosed from ants by Jupiter. Probably used for Spaniards.
[13]Possibly a reference to Henry VIII. See Commentary.

encera à *meretriquer*[32] et *luxurier*,[33] faire et commettre mille forfaits. [29] Et étant proche d'une autre désolation, par lors qu'elle sera à sa plus haute et sublime dignité, se dresseront des potentats et mains militaires, et lui seront ôtés les deux glaives, et ne lui demeurera que les enseignes, desquelles par moyen de la curvature qui les attire, le peuple le faisant aller droit, et ne voulant se condescendre à eux par le bout opposite de la main aiguë, touchant terre, voudront stimuler [30] jusqu'à ce que naîtra d'un rameau de la stérile de longtemps, qui délivrera le peuple univers de celle servitude bénigne et volontaire, soi remettant à la protection de *Mars*, spoliant *Iupiter* de tous des honneurs et dignités, pour la cité libre, constituée et assise dans une autre exiguë *Mezopotamie*. Et sera le chef et gouverneur jeté du milieu et mis au lieu de l'air, ignorant la conspiration des conjurateurs avec le second *Trasibulus*, qui de longtemps aura manié tout ceci. [31] Alors les immondicités, les abominations seront par grande honte objectées et manifestées aux ténèbres de la lumière *obtenebree*,[34] cessera devers la fin du changement de son regne, et les chefs[35] de l'Église seront en arrière de l'amour de Dieu, et plusieurs d'entr'eux *apostatiseront*[36] de la vraie Foi, et des trois sectes, celle du milieu, par les culteurs d'icelle, sera un peu mis en décadence. La prime totalement par l'*Europe*, la plupart de l'*Afrique* exterminée de la tierce, moyennant les pauvres d'esprit, qui par insensés élevés par la luxure libidineuse adultéreront. [32] La plèbe se levera soutenant, déchassera les adhérents des législateurs, et semblera que les regnes affaiblis par les *Orientaux* que Dieu le Créateur aie délié *Satan* des prisons infernales, pour faire naître le grand *Dog et Doham*,[37] lesquels feront si grande fraction abominable aux Églises que les rouges ni les blancs sans yeux ni sans mains plus n'en jugeront, et leur sera ôtée leur puissance. [33] Alors sera faite plus de persécution aux Églises que ne fut jamais. Et sur ces entrefaites naîtra pestilence si grande, que des trois parts du monde plus que les deux défaudront. Tellement qu'on ne saura ne connaîtra les appartenants des champs et maisons, et naîtra l'herbe par les rues des cités plus haute que les genoux. Et au Clergé sera faite toute désolation et usurpe-

---

[32]Latin *meretricari*, to deal with harlots.
[33]Latin *luxuriare*, to live in luxury.
[34]Latin *obtenebratus*, obscured.
[35]Variant: *clefs*.
[36]O.F. *apostatiser*, to apostatize.
[37]Variant: *Dohan*.

tion, and he will begin his whoring and luxury, and will commit a thousand crimes.

29. At the eve of another desolation, when she[14] is atop her most high and sublime dignity, some potentates and warlords will confront her, and take away her two swords, and leave her only the insignia, whose curvature attracts them. The people will make him[15] go to the right and will not wish to submit themselves to those of the opposite extreme with the hand in acute[16] position, who touch the ground, and want to drive spurs into them.

30. And hereupon it is that there is born of a branch long sterile one who will deliver the people of the world[17] from this benevolent slavery to which they had voluntarily submitted. He will put himself under the protection of Mars, stripping Jupiter[18] of all his honors and dignities, and establish himself in the free city in another scant Mesopotamia.[19] The chief and governor will be cast out from the middle and hung up, ignorant of the conspiracy of one of the conspirators with the second Thrasibulus,[20] who for a long time will have directed all this.

31. Then the impurities and abominations, with a great shame, will be brought out and manifested in the shadows of the veiled light, and will cease towards the end of the change in reign. The chiefs of the Church will be backward in the love of God, and several of them will apostatize from the true faith. Of the three sects, that which is in the middle, because of its own partisans, will be thrown a bit into decadence. The first one will be exterminated throughout all Europe and most of Africa by the third one, making use of the poor in spirit who, led by madmen to libidinous luxury, will adulterate.

32. The supporting common people will rise up and chase out the adherents of the legislators. From the way realms will have been weakened by the Easterners, it will seem that God the Creator has loosed Satan from the prisons of hell to give birth to the great Dog and Doham,[21] who will make such an abominable breach in the Churches that neither the reds nor the whites without eyes or hands will know what to make of it, and their power will be taken from them.

33. Then will commence a persecution of the Churches the like of which was never seen. Meanwhile, such a plague will arise that more than two thirds of the world will be removed. One will be unable to ascertain the true owners of fields and houses, and weeds growing in the streets of cities will rise higher than the knees. For the clergy there will be but utter desolation.

---

[14]"She," it would seem, can refer only to this perverted church.

[15]Presumably the great dog-cur-Jupiter individual.

[16]Meaning either "sharp" or of an angle less than 90 degrees.

[17]Literally "universal people," which may refer to the French, in the way that "great" usually seems to.

[18]Presumably the villain of para. 28.

[19]Possibly the Venaissin enclave with Avignon. See Commentary.

[20]The classical "people's friend" who restored the Athenian democracy.

[21]Apparently a Nostradamian version of Gog and Magog.

ront les martiaux ce que sera retourné de la cité du Soleil de *Melite*[38] et
des îles *Stechades*,[39] et sera ouverte la grande chaîne du port qui prend sa
dénomination au bœuf marin. [34] Et sera faite nouvelle incursion par les
maritimes plages, voulant le *saut Castulum*[40] délivrer de la première reprise
*Mahometane.* Et ne seront du tout leurs[41] assaillements vains, et au lieu
que jadis fut l'habitation d'*Abraham*, sera assaillie par personnes qui auront
en vénération les *Jovialistes*. Et icelle cité d'*Achem* sera environnée et
assaillie de toutes parts en très-grande puissance de gens d'armes. Seront
affaiblies leurs forces maritimes par les Occidentaux. Et à ce regne sera
faite grande désolation, et les plus grandes cités seront dépeuplées et ceux
qui entreront dedans seront compris à la vengeance de l'ire de Dieu. [35]
Et demeurera le sépulcre de tant grande vénération par l'espace de
longtemps sous le serein à l'universelle vision des yeux du Ciel, du Soleil,
et de la Lune. Et sera converti le lieu sacré en hebergement de troupeau
menu et grand et adapté en substances profanes. O quelle calamiteuse
affliction sera par lors aux femmes enceintes: [36] et sera par lors du
principal chef Oriental la plupart ému par les Septentrionaux et Occidentaux
vaincu et mis à mort, *profligez*[42] et le reste en fuite, et ses enfants de plusieurs femmes emprisonnés, et par lors sera accomplie la prophétie du Royal
Prophète: *Ut audiret gemitus compenditorum, ut solveret filios interempto-
rum.* [37] Quelle grande oppression que par lors sera faite sur les Princes
et Gouverneurs des Royaumes, même de ceux qui seront maritimes et
Orientaux, et leurs langues entremêlées à grande société: la langue des
*Latins* et des *Arabes* par la communication *Punique*, et seront tous ces Rois
Orientaux chassés, *profligés*,[42] exterminés, non du tout par le moyen des
forces des Rois d'Aquilon, et par la proximité de notre siècle par le moyen
des trois unis secrètement cherchant la mort et *insidies*[43] par embûches l'un
de l'autre, et durera le renouvellement de Triumvirat sept ans, que la
renommée de telle secte fera son étendue par l'univers, et sera soutenu le
sacrifice de la sainte et immaculée Hostie, [38] et seront lors les Seigneurs
deux en nombre d'Aquilon, victorieux sur les Orientaux, et sera en iceux
fait si grand bruit et tumulte bellique, que tout icelui Orient tremblera de la
frayeur d'iceux frères, non frères *Aquilonaires*.[44] [39] Et parce, Sire, que par

---

[38]Latin *Melita*, Malta.
[39]Latin *Stoechades*, Isles of Hyères.
[40]Latin *Saltus Castulonensis*, the Sierra Moreña in southern Spain.
[41]Variants: *de leurs; du tout.*
[42]Latin *profligatus*, overwhelmed, overthrown.
[43]Latin, *insidia*, ambush.
[44]Latin *Aquilonaris*, of the North, of the North Wind, Northern.

The warlords will usurp what is returned from the City of the Sun,[22] from Malta and the Isles of Hyères. The great chain of the port which takes its name from the marine ox[23] will be opened.

34. And a new incursion will be made by the maritime shores, wishing to deliver the Sierra Moreña from the first Mahometan recapture. Their assaults will not all be in vain, and the place which was once the abode of Abraham[24] will be assaulted by persons who hold the Jovialists[25] in veneration. And this city of "Achem"[26] will be surrounded and assailed on all sides by a most powerful force of warriors. Their maritime forces will be weakened by the Westerners, and great desolation will fall upon this realm. Its greatest cities will be depopulated and those who enter within will fall under the vengeance of the wrath of God.

35. The sepulchre, for long an object of such great veneration, will remain in the open, exposed to the sight of the heavens, the Sun and the Moon. The holy place will be converted into a stable for a herd large and small, and used for profane purposes. Oh, what a calamitous affliction will pregnant women bear at this time.

36. For hereupon the principal Eastern chief will be vanquished by the Northerners and Westerners, and most of his people, stirred up, will be put to death, overwhelmed or scattered. His children, offspring of many women, will be imprisoned. Then will be accomplished the prophecy of the Royal Prophet, *Let him hear the groaning of the captives, that he might deliver the children of those doomed to die.*[27]

37. What great oppression will then fall upon the Princes and Governors of Kingdoms, especially those which will be maritime and Eastern, whose tongues will be intermingled with all others: the tongue of the Latins, and of the Arabs, via the Phoenicians. And all these Eastern Kings will be chased, overthrown and exterminated, but not altogether, by means of the forces of the Kings of the North, and because of the drawing near of our age through the three secretly united in the search for death, treacherously laying traps for one another. This renewed Triumvirate will last for seven years, and the renown of this sect will extend around the world. The sacrifice of the holy and immaculate Wafer will be sustained.

38. Then the Lords of "Aquilon" [the North], two in number, will be victorious over the Easterners, and so great a noise and bellicose tumult will they make amongst them that all the East will tremble in terror of these brothers, yet not brothers, of "Aquilon" [the North].

---

[22]Probably Rome is meant.

[23]Marseilles (Port Phocen, Latin *phoce*, sea calf). See 379.

[24]Possibly Shechem (Neapolis). The sudden switch from Spain to the Holy Land as the subject is quite strange.

[25]Probably the followers of the above-mentioned Jupiter.

[26]Certainly not Achin in Sumatra. Either a Hebraic anagram for *Shechem*, capital of the Kingdom of Israel, 933-722 B.C., or *Acre*.

[27]Resembles Psalm CII:20 but is not a quotation.

ce discours je mets presque confusément ces prédictions, et quand ce
pourra être et l'avènement d'iceux, pour le dénombrement du temps qui
s'ensuit, qu'il n'est nullement, ou bien peu, conforme au supérieur, lequel
tant par voie Astronomique, que par autres, même des sacrées Écritures, qui
ne peuvent faillir nullement, que si je voulais à chaque quatrain mettre le
dénombrement du temps, se pourrait faire: mais à tous ne serait agréable, ne
moins les interpréter, jusqu'à ce, Sire, que votre Majesté m'aie octroyé
ample puissance pour ce faire, pour ne donner cause aux calomniateurs de
me mordre. [40] Toutefois, contant les ans depuis la création du monde
jusqu'à la naissance de *Noé* sont passés mille cinq cent et six ans, et depuis
la naissance de *Noé* jusqu'à la parfaite fabrication de l'Arche, approchant
de l'universelle inondation, passèrent six cents ans (si les dons[45] étaient
solaires ou lunaires, ou des dix[46] mixtions) je tiens ce que les sacrées
Écritures tiennent qu'étaient solaires. Et à la fin d'iceux six cents ans, *Noé*
entra dans l'Arche, pour être sauvé du déluge: et fut icelui déluge universel
sur la terre, et dura un an et deux mois. Et depuis la fin du déluge jusqu'à
la nativité d'*Abraham*, passa le nombre des ans de deux cent nonante cinq.
Et depuis la nativité d'*Abraham* jusqu'à la nativité d'*Isaac* passèrent cent
ans. Et depuis *Isaac* jusqu'à *Iacob* soixante ans, dès l'heure qu'il entra
en *Egypte* jusqu'à l'issue d'icelui passèrent cent trente ans. Et depuis
l'entrée de *Iacob* en Egypte jusqu'à l'issue d'icelui passèrent quatre cent
trente ans. Et depuis l'issue d'*Egypte* jusqu'à l'édification du Temple faite
par *Salomon* au quatrième an de son regne passèrent quatre cent octante,
ou quatre-vingts ans. Et depuis l'édification du Temple jusqu'à *Iesus Christ*,
selon la supputation des *Hiérographes*[47] passèrent quatre cent nonante ans.
Et ainsi par cette supputation que j'ai faite, colligée par les sacrées lettres,
sont environ quatre mille cent septante trois ans et huit mois, peu ou moins.
Or de *Iesus Christ* en ça par la diversité des sectes, je le laisse, [41] et
ayant supputé et calculé les présentes prophéties, le tout selon l'ordre de la
chaîne qui contient sa révolution, le tout par doctrine Astronomique, et
selon mon naturel instinct, et après quelque temps et dans icelui comprenant depuis le temps que Saturne tournera entrer à sept du mois d'Avril
jusqu'au 25[48] d'Août, Jupiter à 14 de Juin jusqu'au 7 d'Octobre, Mars
depuis le 17 d'Avril jusqu'au 22 de Juin, Vénus depuis le 9 d'Avril jusqu'au
22 de Mai, Mercure depuis le 3 de Février jusqu'au 24 dudit. En après
du 1 de Juin jusqu'au 24 dudit, et du 25 de Septembre jusqu'au 16 d'Octobre,
Saturne en Capricorne, Jupiter en Aquarius, Mars en Scorpion, Vénus en
Pisces, Mercure dans un mois en Capricorne, Aquarius et Pisces, la Lune en
Aquarius, la tête du Dragon en Libra: la queue à son signe opposite suivant

---

[45]A rather strange misprint for *ans*, uniform in all early editions.
[46]An equally strange misprint for *deux*, likewise in all editions. This whole parenthesis,
including the latter bracket, is odd.
[47]Greek *Iero-graphia*, sacred writings.
[48]Variant: *15*.

39. By this discourse, Sire, I present these predictions almost with confusion, especially as to when they will take place. Furthermore, the chronology of time which follows conforms very little, if at all, with that which has already been set forth. Yet it was determined by astronomy and other sources, including the Holy Scriptures, and thus could not err. If I had wanted to date each quatrain, I could have done so. But this would not have been agreeable to all, least of all to those interpreting them, and was not to be done until Your Majesty granted me full power to do so, lest calumniators be furnished with an opportunity to injure me.

40. Anyhow, I count the years from the creation of the world to the birth of Noah as 1,506, and from the birth of Noah to the completion of the Ark, at the time of the universal deluge, as 600 (let the years be solar, or lunar, or a mixture of the ten)[28] I hold that the Sacred Scriptures use solar years.[29] And at the end of these 600 years, Noah entered the Ark to be saved from the deluge. This deluge was universal, and lasted one year and two months. And 295 years elapsed from the end of the flood to the birth of Abraham, and 100 from then till the birth of Isaac. And 60 years later Jacob was born. 130 years elapsed between the time he entered Egypt and the time he came out. Between the entry of Jacob into Egypt and the exodus, 430 years passed. From the exodus to the building of the Temple by Solomon in the fourth year of his reign, 480 years. According to the calculations of the Sacred Writings, it was 490 years from the building of the Temple to the time of Jesus Christ. Thus, this calculation of mine, collected from the holy writ, comes to about 4,173 years and 8 months, more or less.[30] Because there is such a diversity of sects, I will not go beyond Jesus Christ.

41. I have calculated the present prophecies according to the order of the chain which contains its revolution, all by astronomical doctrine modified by my natural instinct. After a while, I found the time when Saturn turns to enter on April 7 till August 25,[31] Jupiter on June 14 till October 7, Mars from April 17 to June 22, Venus from April 9 to May 22, Mercury from February 3 to February 24. After that, from June 1 to June 24, and from September 25 to October 16, Saturn in Capricorn, Jupiter in Aquarius, Mars in

---

[28]Were the French text corrected, it would read "two."
[29]See Commentary on this serious error.
[30]Less: 4,098. See Commentary on para. 40.
[31]Or August 15.

une conjonction de Jupiter à Mercure avec un quadrin aspect de Mars à Mercure, et la tête du Dragon sera avec une conjonction du Soleil à Jupiter, l'année sera pacifique sans éclipse, [42] et non du tout, et sera le commencement comprenant ce de ce que durera et commençant icelle année sera faite plus grande persécution à l'Église Chrétienne, que n'a été en *Afrique*, et durera cette ici jusqu'à l'an mille sept cent nonante deux que l'on cuidera être une rénovation de siècle: [43] après commencera le peuple *Romain* de se redresser, et de chasser quelques obscures ténèbres, recevant quelque peu de leur *pristine*[49] clarté, non sans grande division et continuels changements. *Venise* en après en grande force et puissance levera ses ailes si très haut, ne distant guère aux forces de l'antique *Rome.* [44] Et en icelui temps grandes voiles *Bisantines* associées aux *Ligustiques*,[50] par l'appui et puissance *Aquilonaire*[51] donnera quelque empêchement que des deux *Cretenses*[52] ne leur sera la foi tenue. Les arcs édifiés par les antiques Martiaux, s'accompagneront aux ondes de *Neptune.* En l'*Adriatique* sera faite discorde grande, ce que sera uni sera séparé, approchera de maison ce que paravant était et est grande cité, comprenant le *Pempotam*[53] la *Mesopotamie*[54] de l'*Europe* à quarante-cinq et autres de quarante-un, quarante-deux et trente-sept.[55] [45] Et dans icelui temps et en icelles contrées la puissance infernale mettra à l'encontre de l'Église de *Iesus Christ* la puissance des adversaires de sa loi, qui sera le second Antéchrist, lequel persécutera icelle Église et son vrai Vicaire, par moyen de la puissance des Rois temporels, qui seront par leur ignorance séduits par langues qui trancheront plus que nul glaive entre les mains de l'insensé. [46] Le susdit regne de l'Antéchrist ne durera que jusqu'au *definement*[56] de ce né près de l'âge, et de l'autre à la cité de *Plancus*,[57] accompagné de l'élu de *Modone Fulcy*,[58] par *Ferrare*, maintenu par *Liguriens Adriatiques*, et de la proximité de la grande *Trianacrie*:[59] Puis

[49]Latin *pristinus*, early, ancient, original.
[50]Latin *Ligusticus*, Ligurian.
[51]Latin *Aquilonaris*, of the North, of the North Wind.
[52]Latin *Cretenses*, natives of Crete.
[53]Variant: *Pompotam.* From either (1) Greek *pan*, all, and Latin *potens*, powerful; or (2) Greek *pan*, all, and *potamos*, river, sea, in contrast to:
[54]Greek *meso-potamos*, between rivers (or seas).
[55]Variant: *Quarante-sept* (Le Pelletier's "false 1568" edition).
[56]O.F. *definement*, end, death.
[57]Lyon, founded by Lucius M. Plancus in 43 B.C. (see 346).
[58]Very doubtful meaning and derivation. *Modona*, uniform in all editions, is probably Modena, which no copyist dared correct. There is, indeed, a Greek seaport called Modon but it would not fit the context. *Fulcy* is possibly from Greek, *fule*, tribe. Thus House of Modena, or House of Este. See Commentary.
[59]Latin *Trinacria*, poetical name for Sicily.

Scorpio, Venus in Pisces, Mercury for a month in Capricorn, Aquarius and Pisces, the Moon in Aquarius, the Dragon's head in Libra: its tail in opposition following a conjunction of Jupiter and Mercury with a quadrature of Mars and Mercury, and the Dragon's head coinciding with a conjunction of the Sun and Jupiter. And the year without an eclipse peaceful.

42. But not everywhere. It will mark the commencement of what will long endure. For beginning with this year the Christian Church will be persecuted more fiercely than it ever was in Africa,[32] and this will last up to the year 1792, which they will believe to mark a renewal of time.[33]

43. After this the Roman people will begin to re-establish themselves, chasing away some obscure shadows and recovering a bit of their ancient glory. But this will not be without great division and continual changes. Thereafter Venice will raise its wings very high in great force and power, not far short of the might of ancient Rome.

44. At that time the great sails of Byzantium, allied with the Ligurians[34] and through the support and power of "Aquilon" [the Northern Realm], will impede them so greatly that the two Cretans will be unable to maintain their faith. The arks[35] built by the Warriors of ancient times will accompany them to the waves of Neptune. In the Adriatic great discord will arise, and that which will have been united will be separated. To a house will be reduced that which was, and is, a great city, including the "Pampotamia" and "Mesopotamia"[36] of Europe at 45, and others of 41, 42 and 37[37] degrees.

45. It will be at this time and in these countries that the infernal power will set the power of its adversaries against the Church of Jesus Christ. This will constitute the second Antichrist, who will persecute that Church and its true Vicar, by means of the power of three temporal kings who in their ignorance will be seduced by tongues which, in the hands of the madmen, will cut more than any sword.

46. The said reign of the Antichrist will last only to the death of him who was born at the beginning of the age and of the other one of Lyon, associated with the elected one of the House of Modena[38] and of Ferrara, maintained by the Adriatic Ligurians[39] and the proximity of great Sicily. Then the Great St. Bernard will be passed.

---

[32]Presumed to be the Vandal persecution (439–534).

[33]See Commentary on this much-noted date.

[34]I.e., a Turco-Genoese alliance.

[35]Or "arches."

[36]See notes 53 and 54 on opposite page. Both may refer to Avignon, between the Rhône and the Durance rivers, and the 14th-century capital of Christendom. (In 10100 "Pampotamia" is England.) See Commentary.

[37]Or 47.

[38]A very tentative translation. See note opposite.

[39]The Genoese of the Adriatic are presumably the Venetians.

passera le *mont Jovis*,[60] [47] Le *Gallique ogmium*,[61] accompagné de si grand nombre que de bien loin l'Empire de sa grande loi sera présenté, et par lors et quelque temps après sera épanché profusément le sang des Innocents par les *nocents*[62] un peu élevés: alors par grands déluges, la mémoire des choses contenues de tels instruments recevra innombrable perte, même les lettres: qui sera devers les *Aquilonaires* par la volonté Divine, [48] et entre une fois lié *Satan*. Et sera faite paix universelle entre les humains, et sera délivré l'Église de *Iesus Christ* de toute tribulation, *combien que*[63] par les *Azostains*[64] voudrait mêler dedans le miel du fiel, et leur pestifère séduction; et cela sera proche du septième millénaire, que plus le sanctuaire de *Iesus Christ* ne sera *conculqué*[65] par les Infidèles, qui viendront de l'*Aquilon*, le monde approchant de quelque grande conflagration, *combien que*[63] par mes supputations en mes Prophéties, le cours du temps aille plus loin. [49] Dedans l'Épître que ces ans passés ai dedié à mon fils *César Nostradamus*, j'ai assez apertement déclaré aucuns points sans présage. Mais ici, ô Sire, sont compris plusieurs grands et merveilleux avènements, que ceux qui viendront après le verront. [50] Et durant icelle supputation Astrologique, conférée aux sacrées lettres, la persécution des gens Ecclésiastiques prendra son origine par la puissance des Rois *Aquilonaires*,[66] unis avec les Orientaux. Et cette persécution durera onze ans, quelque peu moins, que par lors défaillira le principal Roi *Aquilonaire*,[66] [51] lesquels ans accomplis surviendra son uni Méridional, qui persécutera encore plus fort par l'espace de trois ans les gens d'Église par la séduction Apostatique, d'un qui tiendra toute puissance absolue à l'Église militante, et le saint peuple de Dieu, observateur de sa loi, et tout ordre de religion sera grandement persécuté et affligé, tellement que le sang des vrais Écclésiastiques nagera partout, [52] et un des horribles Rois temporels par ses adhérents lui seront données telles louanges, qu'il aura plus répandu du sang humain des Innocents Écclésiastiques, que nul ne saurait avoir du vin: et icelui Roi commettra des forfaits envers l'Église incroyables, coulera le sang humain par les rues publiques et temples, comme l'eau par pluie impétueuse, et rougiront de sang les plus prochains fleuves, et par autre guerre navale rougira la mer, que le rapport d'un Roi à l'autre lui sera dit: *Bellis rubuit navalibus aequor*. [53] Puis dans la même année et les suivantes s'en ensui-

---

[60]Latin *Mons Jovis*, Great St. Bernard.
[61]Ogmios, Celtic deity identified with Hercules or Mercury.
[62]Latin *nocens*, guilty.
[63]O.F. *combien que*, although.
[64]Variants: *Azos tains; Azos rains; Azoarains* (Le Pelletier's "1568"). Azotus (Ashdod) in Philistaea is the most likely source.
[65]Latin *conculcare*, to step upon, tread on.
[66]Latin *Aquilonaris*, of the North, Northern.

47. The Gallic Ogmios[40] will be accompanied by so great a number that the Empire of his great law will extend very far. For some time thereafter the blood of the Innocent will be shed profusely by the recently elevated[41] guilty ones. Then, because of great floods, the memory of things contained in these instruments will suffer incalculable loss, even letters. This will happen to the "Aquiloners" [the Northern People] by the will of God.

48. Once again Satan will be bound, universal peace will be established among men, and the Church of Jesus Christ will be delivered from all tribulations, although the Philistines[42] would like to mix in the honey of malice and their pestilent seduction. This will be near the seventh millenary,[43] when the sanctuary of Jesus Christ will no longer be trodden down by the infidels who come from "Aquilon" [the North]. The world will be approaching a great conflagration, although, according to my calculations in my prophecies, the course of time runs much further.

49. In the Epistle that some years ago I dedicated to my son, César Nostradamus, I declared some points openly enough, without presage. But here, Sire, are included several great and marvelous events which those to come after will see.

50. During this astrological supputation, harmonized with the Holy Scriptures, the persecution of the Ecclesiastical folk will have its origin in the power of the Kings of "Aquilon" [the North], united with the Easterners. This persecution will last for eleven years, or somewhat less, for then the chief King of "Aquilon" will fall.

51. Thereupon the same thing will occur in the South, where for the space of three years the Church people will be persecuted even more fiercely through the Apostatic seduction[44] of one who will hold all the absolute power in the Church militant. The holy people of God, the observer of his law, will be persecuted fiercely and such will be their affliction that the blood of the true Ecclesiastics will flow everywhere.

52. One of the horrible temporal Kings will be told by his adherents, as the ultimate in praise, that he has shed more of human blood of Innocent Ecclesiastics than anyone else could have spilled of wine. This King will commit incredible crimes against the Church. Human blood will flow in the public streets and temples, like water after an impetuous rain, coloring the nearby rivers red with blood. The ocean itself will be reddened by another naval battle, such that one king will say to another, *Naval battles have caused the sea to blush.*

53. Then, in this same year, and in those following, there will ensue the

---

[40] See note 61, opposite.
[41] Or "half-educated."
[42] See note 64 opposite for possible derivations.
[43] By Nostradamus' quaint addition, about 1826. See Commentary on para. 40.
[44] A possible reference to an antipope.

vra la plus horrible pestilence, et la plus merveilleuse par la famine précédente et si grandes tribulations que jamais soient avenues telles depuis la première fondation de l'Église Chrétienne, et par toutes les régions *Latines*, demeurant par les vestiges en aucunes contrées des *Espagnes*. [54] Par lors le tiers Roi *Aquilonaire*[67] entendant la plainte du peuple de son principal titre, dressera si grande armée, et passera par les détroits de ses derniers *avites*[68] et bisaïeuls, qu'il remettra la plupart en son état, et le grand Vicaire de la *cappe*[69] sera remis en son *pristin*[70] état: mais désolé, et puis du tout abandonné, et tournera être *Sancta Sanctorum* détruite par Paganisme, et le vieux et nouveau Testament seront déchassés et brûlés, [55] en après l'Antéchrist sera le prince infernal, encore par la dernière fois trembleront tous les Royaumes de la Chrétienté, et aussi des infidèles, par l'espace de vingt cinq ans, et seront plus grièves guerres et batailles, et seront villes, cités, châteaux et tous autres édifices brûlés, désolés, détruits, avec grande effusion de sang vestal, mariées, et veuves violées, enfants de lait contre les murs des villes *allidez*[71] et brisés, et tant de maux se commettront par le moyen de *Satan*, prince infernal, que presque le monde universel se trouvera défait et désolé: et avant iceux avènements aucuns oiseaux insolites crieront par l'air: *Hui, hui,* et seront après quelque temps évanouis. [56] Et après que tel temps aura duré longuement, sera presque renouvelé un autre regne de *Saturne*, et siècle d'or: Dieu le Créateur dira entendant l'affliction de son peuple Satan sera mis et lié[72] en l'abîme du *barathre*[73] dans la profonde fosse: et adonc commencera entre Dieu et les hommes une paix universelle, et demeurera lié environ l'espace de mille ans, et tournera en sa plus grande force, la puissance Ecclésiastique, et puis tourne[74] délié.

[57] Que toutes ces figures sont justement adaptées, par les divines lettres aux choses célestes visibles, c'est-à-savoir, par *Saturne, Iupiter* et *Mars* et les autres conjoints, comme plus à plein par aucuns quatrains l'on pourra voir. J'eusse calculé plus profondément, et adapté les uns avec les autres: Mais voyant, ô sérénissime Roi, que quelqu'uns de la censure trouveront difficulté, qui sera cause de retirer ma plume à mon repos nocturne: [58] *Multa etiam, ô Rex omnium potentissime, praeclara et sane in brevi ventura, sed omnia in hac tua epistola innectere non possumus, nec volumus: sed ad intelligenda quaedam facta, horrida fata, pauca libanda sunt, quamvis tanta sit in omnes tua amplitudo et humanitas homines, deosque pietas, ut solus amplissimo et Christianissimo Regis nomine, et ad quem summa totius reli-*

---

[67]Latin *Aquilonaris,* of the North, Northern.
[68]Latin *avites,* ancestors.
[69]O.F. *cappe,* hood.
[70]Latin *pristinus,* ancient, former, original.
[71]Latin *allidare,* to throw upon.
[72]Variant: *jeté.*
[73]Latin *barathron,* pit, hell.
[74]Variant: *tout.*

most horrible pestilence, made more stupendous by the famine which will have preceded it. Such great tribulations will never have occurred since the first foundation of the Christian Church. It will cover all Latin regions, and will leave traces in some countries of the Spanish.[45]

54. Thereupon the third King of "Aquilon" [the North], hearing the lament of the people of his principal title, will raise a very mighty army and, defying the tradition of his predecessors, will put almost everything back in its proper place, and the great Vicar of the hood[46] will be put back in his former state. But desolated, and then abandoned by all, he will turn to find the Holy of Holies[47] destroyed by paganism, and the old and new Testaments thrown out and burned.

55. After that Antichrist will be the infernal prince again, for the last time. All the Kingdoms of Christianity will tremble, even those of the infidels, for the space of twenty-five years. Wars and battles will be more grievous and towns, cities, castles and all other edifices will be burned, desolated and destroyed, with great effusion of vestal blood, violations of married women and widows, and sucking children dashed and broken against the walls of towns. By means of Satan, Prince Infernal, so many evils will be committed that nearly all the world will find itself undone and desolated. Before these events, some rare birds will cry in the air: *Today, today,* and some time later will vanish.

56. After this has endured for a long time, there will be almost renewed another reign of Saturn, and golden age. Hearing the affliction of his people, God the Creator will command that Satan be cast into the depths of the bottomless pit, and bound there. Then a universal peace will commence between God and man, and Satan will remain bound for around a thousand years, and then all unbound.

57. All these figures represent the just integration of Holy Scriptures with visible celestial bodies, namely, Saturn, Jupiter, Mars and others conjoined, as can be seen at more length in some of the quatrains. I would have calculated more profoundly and integrated them even further, Most Serene King, but for the fact that some given to censure would raise difficulties. Therefore I withdraw my pen and seek nocturnal repose.

58. *Many events, most powerful of all Kings, of the most astounding sort are to transpire soon, but I neither could nor would fit them all into this epistle; but in order to comprehend certain horrible facts, a few must be set forth. So great is your grandeur and humanity before men, and your piety before the gods, that you alone seem worthy of the great title of the Most Christian King, and to whom the highest authority in all religion should be deferred.*

---

[45]In Nostradamus' day, almost all Western Europe but France.
[46]Almost certainly the Pope.
[47]Presumably Rome.

*gionis auctoritas deferatur dignus esse videare.* [59] Mais tant seulement je vous requiers, ô Roi très-clément, par icelle votre singulière et prudente humanité, d'entendre plutôt le désir de mon courage, et le souverain étude que j'ai d'obéir à votre sérénissime Majesté, depuis que mes yeux furent si proches de votre splendeur solaire, que la grandeur de mon labeur n'atteint ne requiert. De *Salon* ce 27 de Juin 1558.

*Faciebat Michaël Nostradamus Salonae Petrae Provinciae.*

59. But I shall only beseech you, Most Clement King, by this singular and prudent humanity of yours, to understand rather the desire of my heart, and the sovereign wish I have to obey Your Most Serene Majesty, ever since my eyes approached your solar splendor, than the grandeur of my labor can attain to or acquire. From Salon, this 27th of June, 1558.

*Done by Michel Nostradamus at Salon-de-Crau in Provence.*

# Centurie VIII

1. PAV, NAY, LORON plus feu qu'à sang sera,
   Laude[1] nager, fuir grand aux surrez:[2]
   Les agassas[3] entrée refusera,
   Pampon,[4] Durance les tiendra enserrés.

2. Condon et Aux et autour de Mirande,
   Je vois du ciel feu qui les environne:
   Sol[5] Mars conjoint au Lion, puis Marmande
   Foudre, grande grêle, mur tombe dans Garonne.

3. Au fort château de Vigilanne et Resuiers
   Sera serré le puîné de Nancy:
   Dedans Turin seront ards[6] les premiers
   Lorsque de deuil Lyon sera transi.

4. Dedans Monech[7] le Coq sera reçu,
   Le Cardinal de France apparaîtra:
   Par Logarion[8] Romain sera déçu,
   Faiblesse à l'Aigle, et force au Coq naîtra.

5. Apparaîtra temple luisant orné,
   La lampe et cierge à Borne et Bretueil:
   Pour la Lucerne le Canton détourné,
   Quand on verra le grand Coq au cercueil.

6. Clarté fulgure[9] à Lyon apparente
   Luisant, print[10] Malte, subit sera éteinte:
   Sardon,[11] Mauris[12] traitera décevante,
   Geneue à Londes à Coq trahison feinte.

[1]O.F. laude, praise.

[2]Greek, surrous, confluence, flowing together. (Latin Confluentes, Coblenz? Latin Confluens, Münster?)

[3]Provençal agassa, magpie. A synonym for the French spelling, agace, is pie, which is also French for "Pius." See Commentary.

[4]Dubious. Possibly from Greek pamponeros, all-depraved, most villainous.

[5]Latin Sol, Sun.

[6]Possibly from Latin ardere, to burn.

[7]Latin Portus Herculi Monoecis, Monaco.

[8]Variants: Logathion; Legation (Fortune), most plausible.

[9]Latin fulgur, lightning.

[10]Uniform in all editions, and thus prend rather than pris, in modern orthography, although the latter fits the context better.

[11]Several possible derivations, especially Sardinia.

[12]Probably derived from Saint-Maurice, patron saint of the French-speaking Alpine areas and of Savoy; many towns are named after him.

# Century VIII

☞ 1. PAU, NAY, OLORON[1] will be more of fire than blood,
To swim in praise, the great one to flee to the confluence:[2]
The magpies[3] he will refuse entry,
"Pampon,"[4] the Durance will keep them confined.

2. Condom and Auch and around Mirande,
I see fire from the sky encompassing them:
Sun and Mars conjoined in Leo, then at Marmande
Lightning, great hail, wall falls into the Garonne.

☞ 3. In the strong castle of "Vigilanne" and "Resviers"[5]
The cadet of Nancy will be confined:
Within Turin the first ones will be burned[6]
When Lyons will be numbed by grief.

☞ 4. The Cock will be received into Monaco,
The Cardinal of France will appear:
By the Roman Legation will he be deceived,
Weakness for the Eagle and strength for the Cock will develop.

5. A glittering ornate temple will appear,
The lamp and candle at Borne and Breteuil:
For Lucerne the Canton[7] turned aside,
When one will see the great Cock in his tomb.

6. Lightning brightness at Lyons visible
Shining, Malta is taken, suddenly it will be extinguished:
"Sardon,"[8] Maurice will treat deceitfully,
Geneva at London to the Cock feigned treason.

---

[1]Although all towns are in Béarn (southwest France), the capitalization and context offers some justification for a more fanciful reading by anagram. For the NA.PAU.LO.N. RO.Y. interpretation, see Commentary.

[2]Or possibly "to Coblenz" or "to Münster." See note opposite.

[3]Or possibly "the piuses/Piuses." See note opposite and Commentary.

[4]Possibly "The All-Depraved Ones." See note opposite.

[5]An uncertain pair of place names. Most likely is "San Vigilio and the Riviera." Other possibilities are "Rubbiera and Vignola" and "Vigevano and Revera." See Commentary.

[6]Somewhat uncertain in the context. See note opposite.

[7]Or "For the Canton of Lucerne."

[8]"Sardinia" is an obvious possibility, but is not a certain translation for this enigmatic name.

7. *Verceil, Milan donra*[1] intelligence,
Dedans *Ticin*[2] sera faite la plaie:
Courir par *Seine* eau, sang, feu par *Florence*,
Unique choir d'haut en bas faisant *maye*.[3]

8. Près de *Linterne*[4] dans de tonnes fermés.
*Chiuaz* fera pour l'Aigle la menée,
L'élu chassé lui ses gens enfermés,
Dedans *Turin* rapt épouse emmenée.

9. Pendant que l'Aigle et le Coq à *Sauone*
Seront unis, Mer, *Levant* et *Ongrie*:
L'armée à *Naples, Palerne, Marque d'Ancone*,
*Rome, Venise* par Barbe horrible cri.

10. Puanteur grande sortira de *Lausanne*,
Qu'on ne saura l'origine du fait,
L'on mettra hors toute la gent lointaine,
Feu vu au ciel, peuple étranger défait.

11. Peuple infini paraîtra à *Vicence*
Sans force, feu brûler la basilique:
Près de *Lunage*[5] défait grand de *Valence*,
Lorsque *Venise* par *morte*[6] prenda pique.

12. Apparaîtra auprès de *Buffalore*
L'haut et *procere*[7] entré dedans *Milan*,
L'Abbé de *Foix* avec ceux de saint *Morre*
Feront la fourbe habillés en vilain.

13. Le croisé frère par amour effrénée
Fera par *Praytus Bellerophon* mourir,
*Classe*[8] à milans[9] la femme forcenée,
Bu le breuvage, tous deux après périr.

<hr>

[1]Apocope for *donnera*.
[2]Latin *Ticinum*, Pavia.
[3]O.F. *maye*, kneeding-trough; *maie (ma aïe)*, help me! (Roquefort).
[4]Latin *Linternum*, now Foce di Patria, or Focia, near Naples.
[5]Dubious. Probably Lunigiana.
[6]Apparently the only place where *mort* is spelled thus, but with no special significance discernible.
[7]Latin *procerus*, tall.
[8]Latin *classis*, fleet.
[9]Variant: *mil ans*.

7. Vercelli, Milan will give intelligence,
   Within Pavia the wound[1] will be made:
   To run in the Seine water, blood, fire through Florence,
   Unique one to fall from high to low while calling for help.[2]

8. Near Focia enclosed in some tuns,
   Chivasso will plot for the Eagle,
   The elected one driven out he and his people shut up,
   Within Turin rape bride led away.

9. While the Eagle and the Cock at Savona
   Will be united, Sea, Levant and Hungary:
   The army at Naples, Palermo, March of Ancona,
   Rome, Venice by the Beard[3] great outcry.

10. A great stench will come out of Lausanne,
    Such that one will not know the source of the fact,
    They will put out all the remote people,
    Fire seen in the sky, foreign people defeated.

11. Countless people will appear at Vicenza
    Without force, fire to burn the basilica:
    Near "Lunage"[4] the great one of Valenza[5] defeated,
    When Venice through death will take up the quarrel.

12. He will appear near Buffalora,
    The high and tall one entered into Milan,
    The Abbot of Foix with those of Saint-Maur[6]
    Will do mischief dressed like serfs.

13. The crusader brother through unbridled love
    Will cause Bellerophon to die through Proetus,[7]
    Fleet like hawks[8] the woman gone mad,
    The potion drunk, both thereupon to perish.

[1]Or "the plague."
[2]Or "while kneeding."
[3]Or "because of Barbary." Also possibly apheresis of "Aenobarbe," one of Nostradamus' enigmatically named subjects (see 545, 559 *et al.*).
[4]Probably the Lunigiana Valley (southeast of Genoa).
[5]Or possibly Valence (in France), or Valencia (in Spain).
[6]The legendary founder of the Benedictine Order in Gaul, after whom several monasteries and towns are named.
[7]According to the legend, Bellerophon delivered to Proetus a letter requesting his own death. See Commentary.
[8]Or "Fleet of a thousand years."

14. Le grand crédit, d'or et d'argent l'abondance
    Fera aveugler par *libide*[1] l'honneur,
    Sera connu d'adultère l'offense,
    Qui parviendra à son grand déshonneur.

15. Vers *Aquilon*[2] grands efforts par hommasse,
    Presque l'*Europe* et l'Univers vexer,
    Les deux eclipses mettra en telle chasse,
    Et aux *Pannons*[3] vie et mort renforcer.

16. Au lieu que *HIESON*[4] fait sa nef fabriquer,
    Si grand déluge sera et si subite,
    Qu'on n'aura lieu ni terre s'attaquer,
    L'onde monter *Fesulan*[5] *Olympique.*

17. Les bien aisés subit seront démis,
    Par les trois frères le monde mis en trouble,
    Cité marine saisiront ennemis,
    Faim, feu, sang, peste, et de tous maux le double.

18. De *FLORE* issue de sa mort cause,
    Un temps devant par jeune et vieille boire,
    Car les trois lis lui feront telle pause,
    Par son fruit sauve comme chair crue moire.

19. À soutenir la grande *cappe*[6] troublée,
    Pour l'éclaircir les rouges marcheront:
    De mort famille sera presque accablée,
    Les rouges rouges le rouge assommeront.

20. Le faux message par élection feinte,
    Courir *par vrben*[7] rompue *pache*[8] arrête:[9]
    Voix acheté, de sang chapelle teinte,
    Et à un autre l'empire contracte.[9]

[1]Latin *libido,* unlawful or inordinate desire, passion, longing.
[2]Latin *Aquilo,* the north wind, north.
[3]Latin *Pannonis,* a Pannonian, inhabitant of classical Hungary.
[4]Variant: *HIERON.* Each appears in capitals in the original.
[5]Usually Latin *Faesulae,* Fiesole, which however makes no sense in the Grecian setting of this verse. The closest compromise between context and text is *Pharsalus,* but that is not too close.
[6]O.F. *cappe,* (1) cope (modern *chape*) or (2) cloak (modern *cape*).
[7]Latin *per urbem,* through the city.
[8]O.F. *pache,* pact, peace, agreement.
[9]The original orthography (*arreste . . . contraicte*) rimes only slightly better. The obviously correct reading appears only in: Variant (Garcin): *arrêté . . . contracté.*

14. The great credit, the abundance of gold and silver
    Will cause honor to be blinded by lust,
    Known will be the offense of the adulterer,[1]
    Which will occur to his[1] great dishonor.

☞ 15. Great exertions toward "Aquilon"[2] by the mannish woman,
    To vex Europe and almost all the world,
    She will put the two eclipses into utter route,
    And reinforce life and death for the Pannonians.[3]

16. At the place where Jason[4] had his ship built,
    There will be a flood so great and so sudden
    That one will have no place or land to fall upon,
    The waves to mount Olympian "Fesulan."[5]

☞ 17. Those well off will suddenly be removed,
    Through the three brothers the world put in trouble,
    The enemies will seize the marine city,
    Famine, fire, flood, plague and all evils doubled.

18. The cause of her death issued from Florence,[6]
    Once before by young and old to drink,
    For the three lilies will force her to quite a pause,
    Through her offspring safe as raw meat is watered.

19. To uphold the great troubled cope,[7]
    To clear it up the reds will march:
    A family will be almost ruined by death,
    The red red ones will knock down the red one.

20. The false message about the sham election,
    To run through the city peace broken stopped:
    Voice bought, chapel stained with blood,
    And to another one the empire contracted.

[1]Or "the adulteress . . . her."
[2]The North[ern Country].
[3]Or "the Magyars." Or "the Pannonias" (i.e., Austria and Hungary).
[4]Or possibly Jerome. Jason set out from Iolcos, near modern Volo on the Bay of Volo.
[5]"Fiesole" (see note opposite) does not go with the Greek setting. "Pharsalus"? Or possibly "to mount Thessalian Olympus." See Commentary.
[6]Or "Issued from Florence cause of her death."
[7]Or "cloak." Either way, the Papacy is implied.

21. Au port de *Agde* trois fustes entreront,
    Portant l'infect, non foi et pestilence:
    Passant le pont mil milles *embleront*,[1]
    Et le pont rompre à tierce résistance.

22. *Gorsan, Narbonne,* par le sel avertir
    *Tucham,* la grâce[2] *Parpignan* trahie,
    La ville rouge n'y voudra consentir,
    Par haute vol drap gris vie faillie.

23. Lettres trouvées de la Reine les coffres,
    Point de souscrit sans aucun nom d'auteur:
    Par la *police*[3] seront cachés les offres,
    Qu'on ne saura qui sera l'amateur.

24. Le lieutenant à l'entrée de l'huis
    Assommera le grand de *Parpignan:*
    En se *cuidant*[4] sauver à *Montpertuis,*
    Sera déçu bâtard de *Lusignan.*

25. Cœur de l'amant ouvert d'amour furtive
    Dans le ruisseau fera ravir la Dame:
    Le demi mal contrefera lascive,
    Le père à deux privera corps de l'âme.

26. De *Caton es*[5] trouvés en *Barcelonne,*
    *Mys*[6] découverts lieu retrouvé et ruine:
    Le grand qui tient ne tient voudra *Pamplonne,*
    Par l'*abbage*[7] de *Montferrat* bruine.

27. La voie *auxelle*[8] l'une sur l'autre *fornix*[9]
    Du *muy deser*[10] hormis brave et genêt,
    L'écrit d'Empereur le *fenix*[11]
    Vu à celui ce qu'a nul autre n'est.

---

[1]O.F. *embler*, to carry off.

[2]Variant (Le Pelletier's false "1568"): *grande.*

[3]O.F. *police*, (1) government or (2) ruse.

[4]O.F. *cuider*, to think, believe, persuade oneself.

[5]Although uniform in all editions, quite likely erratum for *os.* The only possible derivation: O.F. *es*, planks, boards.

[6]This odd orthography uniform in all editions. Significance?

[7]Variant (false "1568" and Fortune): *abbaye.*

[8]Latin *auxiliarus*, auxiliary.

[9]Latin *fornix*, (1) arch or (2) brothel.

[10]Probably *le Muy désert.*

[11]Latin *Phoenix*, (1) Phoenician or (2) the Phoenix, five-hundred-year-old bird.

21. Three foists will enter the port of Agde,
    Carrying the infection, not faith and[1] pestilence:
    Passing the bridge they will carry off millions,
    And to break the bridge resistance by a third.

22. Coursan, Narbonne, through the salt to warn
    Tuchan, the grace[2] Perpignan betrayed,
    The red town will not want to consent thereto,
    In high flight a gray cloth life ended.

☞ 23. In the Queen's coffers letters found,
    No signature without any name of their author:
    The offers will be concealed by the government,[3]
    So that they will not know who the lover is.

24. The lieutenant in the doorway
    Will knock down the great one of Perpignan:
    In thinking to save himself at "Montpertuis"[4]
    The bastard of Lusignan will be deceived.

☞ 25. The heart of the lover opened by furtive love
    Will cause the Lady to be ravished in the brook:
    The lustful woman will feign half a hurt,
    The father will deprive the body of each of its soul.

26. The bones[5] of Cato found in Barcelona,
    Placed, discovered, place refound and ruin:
    The great one who holds and does not hold it[6] will want Pamplona,
    For the abbey of Montserrat drizzle.

27. The auxiliary way one arch upon the other[7]
    Of Le Muy deserted except for the brave one and his jennet,
    The writing of the Phoenix[8] Emperor[9]
    Seen by him that which by none other is.

[1]Context would seem to require "but."
[2]Or possibly "her Grace of/by." Or possibly "the great."
[3]Or "by the ruse."
[4]Probably the Pass of Perthus in the Pyrenees (south of Perpignan).
[5]See note opposite with respect to original word.
[6]Or "them."
[7]I.e., an aqueduct.
[8]Or "the Phoenician" (which includes Carthaginian).
[9]In its original Latin sense "Commander" or "General."

28. Les simulacres d'or et d'argent enflés,
    Qu'après le rapt au feu furent jetés,
    Au découvert éteints tous et troublés,
    Au marbre écrits, prescrits interjetés.

29. Au quart pilier l'on *sacre*[1] à *Saturne*,
    Par tremblant terre et déluge fendu:
    Sous l'édifice *Saturnin* trouvée urne,
    D'or *Capion* ravi et puis rendu.

30. Dedans *Tholouse* non loin de *Beluzer*,[2]
    Faisant un puits loin, palais de spectacle:
    Trésor trouvé un chacun ira vexer,
    Et en deux *locs*[3] tout et près *delvasacle*.[4]

31. Premier grand fruit le Prince de *Pesquiere*,
    Mais puis viendra bien et cruel malin:
    Dedans *Venise* perdra sa gloire fière,
    Et mis à mal par plus jeune *Celin*.[5]

32. Garde-toi Roi *Gaulois* de ton neveu,
    Qui fera tant que ton unique fils
    Sera meurtri à *Venus* faisant vœu,
    Accompagné de nuit que trois et six.

33. Le grand naîtra de *Veronne* et *Vicence*,
    Qui portera un surnom bien indigne,
    Qui à *Venise* voudra faire vengeance,
    Lui-même pris homme du guet et signe.

34. Après victoire du Lion au Lion,
    Sus la montagne de *Ivra Secatombe*,[6]
    *Delues*[7] et *brodes*[8] septième million,
    *Lyon*, *Vlme*[9] à *Mansol*[10] mort et tombe.

[1]O.F. *sacrer*, to dedicate.
[2]Dubious. Provençal *belousar*, to dig. Or *beluze*, used in central France for a schist (a type of rock formation).
[3]O.F. *locs*, places.
[4]Variants: *des vesacle; de la vasacle* (Fortune).
[5]Apparently a variant of *Selin*. Greek *selene*, moon or crescent.
[6]Uniform in all editions but obviously a misprint for *hécatombe*.
[7]Derivation uncertain. Possibly from Latin *diluvies*, flood; desolation; destruction.
[8]O.F. *brode*, black; brown; decadent.
[9]If not the German city, possibly a play on Latin *ulmus*, elm.
[10]Misprint for *Mausol* (for *Saint-Pol-de-Mausole*). See note on 427 and Commentary.

☞ 28. The images bloated by gold and silver,
      Which after the rape were thrown into the fire,
      At the discovery all dulled and troubled,
      On the marble inscriptions, prescripts inserted.

☞ 29. At the fourth pillar where they dedicate to Saturn,
      Split by earthquake and flood:
      Under the Saturnin edifice[1] an urn found,
      Of gold carried off by Caepio and then restored.[2]

☞ 30. Within Toulouse not far from "Beluzer,"[3]
      Digging a deep pit, palace of spectacle:[4]
      The treasure found will come to vex everyone,
      And all in two places and near the Basacle.[5]

31. First great fruit the[6] Prince of Peschiera,
      But then will come one[7] very cruel and evil:
      Within Venice he will lose his proud glory,
      And put to evil by the more youthful "Selin."[8]

32. Gallic King, beware of your nephew,
      He who will do so much that your only son
      Will be murdered making a vow to Venus,
      Accompanied at night by three and six.

33. The great one will be born of Verona and Vicenza,
      He who will bear a very unworthy surname,
      He who at Venice will want to take vengeance,
      He himself taken by a man of the watch and sign.

34. After the victory of the Lion over the Lion,
      Upon the Jura mountain great slaughter,
      Floods[9] and dusky ones seventh million,
      Lyons,[10] Ulm[11] at the Mausoleum[12] death and tomb.

---

[1]The Church of Saint-Saturnin (St. Sernin) in Toulouse.
[2]Q. S. Caepio, after plundering the Volcae temple at Toulouse, was routed by the Cimbri at Orange. The gold was never found. See Commentary.
[3]"The digging"? "the schist"? An anagram? A lost local name?
[4]Probably an outdoor theater.
[5]The mill section of Toulouse.
[6]Or possibly "of the"?
[7]Or possibly "he will become"?
[8]Enigmatic name. See note opposite and note on 477.
[9]Or "Destruction."
[10]Or possibly "Lion" again.
[11]The German city is somewhat doubtful here. Possibly "Elm." (See note opposite.)
[12]At Nostradamus' natal Saint-Rémy. See note and Commentary on 427.

35. Dedans l'entrée de *Garonne* et *Bayse*
    Et la forêt non loin de *Damazan,*
    Du *mar saues*[1] gelées, puis grêle et bise,
    *Dordonnois gelle*[2] par erreur de *mesan.*[3]

36. Sera commis contre oindre *aduché*[4]
    De *Saulne* et *Sainct Aulbin* et *bel l'œuvre*[5]
    Paver de marbre de tours *loins*[6] épluché
    Non *Bleteran* résister et chef-d'œuvre.

37. La forteresse auprès de la *Tamise*
    Cherra par lors le Roi dedans serré:
    Auprès du pont sera vu en chemise
    Un devant mort, puis dans le fort barré.

38. Le Roi de *Bloys* dans *Auignon* regner
    Une autre fois le peuple *emonopolle*[7]
    Dedans le *Rosne* par murs fera baigner
    Jusqu'à cinq le dernier près[8] de *Nolle.*

39. Qu'aura été par Prince *Bizantin,*
    Sera *tollu*[9] par prince de *Tholouse:*
    La foi de *Foix* par le chef *Tholentin*
    Lui faillira, ne refusant l'épouse.

40. Le sang du Juste par *Taur*[10] et *la Dorade,*[11]
    Pour se venger contre les *Saturnins,*
    Au nouveau lac plongeront la *mainade,*[12]
    Puis marcheront contre *Albanins.*

---

[1]O.F. *mar*, sea (Sainte-Palaye); O.F. *save*, discovery (Godefroy).

[2]Apparently an O.F. form of *gelée*, frost. Left in its original form to avoid adding an extra syllable.

[3]Apparently metathesis of Latin *mensa*, month (done to get a rime).

[4]Provençal *aducha*, brought.

[5]Variant: *Belœuvre.*

[6]O.F. *loin*, distant.

[7]Probably from Greek *aima*, blood, + ? No sensible compounds are too close: Le Pelletier's *aimapnoos*, bloodthirsty, or *aimatopotes*, blood-drinker. Perhaps "bloody" will do.

[8]Variant: *perse.*

[9]O.F. *tollu*, taken away (Roquefort).

[10]Church of Saint-Saturnin-du-Taur in Toulouse.

[11]Church of Sainte-Marie-de-la-Daurade in Toulouse.

[12]Provençal *mainada*, (1) band, (2) child, people, servants.

35. Within the entry of the Garonne and Baïse
And the forest not far from Damazan,
Discoveries of the sea frozen, then hail and cold,
In the Dordonnais frost through error of month.

36. It will be committed against the anointed brought
From Lons-le-Saunier, Saint-Aubin and beautiful work[1]
To pave with marble picked from distant towers
Not to resist Bletterans and masterpiece.

☞ 37. The fortress near the Thames
Will fall when the King is locked up within:
Near the bridge in his shirt will be seen
One confronting death, then barred in the fort.

38. The King of Blois to reign in Avignon
Once again the people bloody[2]
He will cause to bathe by the walls in the Rhône
Up to five the last one near[3] "Nolle."[4]

39. He who will have been for the Byzantine Prince,
He will be taken away by the Prince of Toulouse:
The faith of Foix through the chief of Tolentino
Will fail him, not refusing the bride.

40. The blood of the Just for Taur and La Daurade,[5]
To avenge itself against the Saturnines,[6]
In the new lake[7] they will immerse the band,[8]
Then they will march against those of Alba.[9]

---

[1] Or "Belœuvre," an enigmatic place name not located near the other places.
[2] Dubious. See note 7, opposite.
[3] Or "the last perse of." Perse is a color variously defined as sky blue, grayish blue, or blue green.
[4] Here apparently enigmatic proper name, rather than Nola in Italy. Possibly anagram for *Oulle*, a waterfront section of Avignon. Or possibly metaplasm of *Noël*, Christmas.
[5] The Churches of Saint-Saturnin-du-Taur and Sainte-Marie-de-la-Daurade in Toulouse.
[6] Either "the Saturnine ones," "those of Saturn," or "those of Saint-Saturnin."
[7] Based on an old Toulouse legend. See Commentary on 829.
[8] Or "the child," or "the household."
[9] The troops of the Duke of Alba, Habsburg generalissimo of Charles V and Philip II. Or possibly "the Albanians," these rugged mountaineers having furnished many 16th-century mercenaries.

41. Élu sera Renard ne sonnant mot,
    Faisant le saint public vivant pain d'orge,[1]
    Tyranniser après tant à un *cop*,[2]
    Mettant à pied des plus grands sur la gorge.

42. Par avarice, par force et violence
    Viendra vexer les siens chef *d'Orleans*,
    Près saint *Memire*[3] assaut et résistance,
    Mort dans sa tente diront qu'il dort léans.

43. Par le *decide*[4] de deux choses bâtards,
    Neveu du sang occupera le regne,
    Dedans *lectoyre*[5] seront les coups de dards,
    Neveu par peur pliera l'enseigne.

44. Le procrée naturel *dogmion*,[6]
    De sept à neuf du chemin détourner:
    À Roi de longue et ami au mi-homme.
    Doit à *Nauarre* fort de *Pau* prosterner.

45. La main écharpe et la jambe bandée,
    Longs[7] puîné de *Calais* portera,
    Au mot du guet la mort sera tardée,
    Puis dans le temple à Pâques saignera.

46. *Pol mensolee*[8] mourra trois lieues du *rosne*,
    Fuis les deux prochains *tarasc destrois*:[9]
    Car *Mars* fera le plus horrible trône,
    De Coq et d'Aigle de *France* frères trois.

[1]Possibly from *faire ses orges*, to feather his nest.
[2]O.F. spelling of *coup* (preserved for rime).
[3]A non-existent name. For an interpretation, Le Pelletier renders it *Saint-Méri*.
[4]Latin *decidere*, to fall.
[5]Presumably *Lectoure*. To get Sedan out of it, see Commentary.
[6]Uniform in all editions. For *d'Ogmion*, of Ogmios, the Celtic Hercules.
[7]Plural in all editions. Anagram? Garencières thinks for *Louis*.
[8]From *Saint-Paul-de-Mausolée*, a convent at Saint-Rémy.
[9]O.F. *destrois*, (1) oppressed, (2) narrow pass.

☞ 41. A Fox will be elected without saying a word,
    Playing the saint in public living on barley bread,[1]
    Afterwards he will very suddenly tyrannize,
    Putting his foot on the throats of the greatest ones.

42. Through avarice, through force and violence
    The chief of Orléans will come to vex his followers,
    Near "Saint-Memire"[2] assault and resistance,
    Dead in his tent they will say that he sleeps within.

☞ 43. Through the fall of two illegitimate things,
    The Nephew by blood will occupy the realm,
    Within Lectoure[3] there will be blows by lances,
    The Nephew through fear will fold his standard.

44. The natural offspring of Ogmios,[4]
    To turn aside from the road from seven to nine:
    To the King of long and friend to the half-man.
    It behooves Navarre to destroy the fort of Pau.

45. His hand in a sling and his leg bound,
    Far[5] the younger brother from Calais will reach,[6]
    Upon the watchword the death will be delayed,
    Then he will bleed in the temple at Easter.

46. He will die at St.-Paul-de-Mausole[7] three leagues from the Rhône,
    The two nearest oppressed[8] Tarascon[9] fled:
    For Mars will make the most horrible throne,
    Of Cock and of Eagle of France three brothers.

[1]Or possibly "feathering his own nest."
[2]Still unidentified enigmatic place name. For "Saint-Méri" interpretation, see Commentary.
[3]For the Sedan interpretation, see Commentary.
[4]The Celtic Hercules. See Commentary.
[5]Or, as an anagram, "Longs." Louis?
[6]Or possibly "will carry Calais."
[7]A convent at Nostradamus' natal Saint-Rémy, subsequently an insane asylum (where the painter Van Gogh was confined shortly before his suicide in 1890). See note for 427 and Commentary.
[8]Or "the narrow place of."
[9]Dubious but probable. The town is named after a monster, the Tarasca.

47. Lac *Trasmenien* portera témoignage,
    Des conjurés serrés dedans *Perouse:*
    Un *despolle*[1] contrefera le sage,
    Tuant *Tedesque*[2] *sterne*[3] et *minuse*.[4]

48. *Saturne* en *Cancer*, *Iupiter* avec *Mars*,
    Dedans Février *Chaldondon*[5] *saluaterre*,[6]
    *Sault Castallon*[7] assailli de trois *pars*,[8]
    Près de *Verbiesque* conflit mortelle guerre.

49. *Satur* au bœuf *iouë* en l'eau, *Mars* en flèche,
    Six de Février mortalité donnera,
    Ceux de *Tardaigne*[9] à *Bruge* si grande brèche,
    Qu'à *Ponteroso* chef *Barbarin*[10] mourra.

50. La pestilence l'entour de *Capadille*,[11]
    Une autre faim près de *Sagont* s'apprête:
    Le chevalier bâtard de bon sénile,
    Au grand de *Thunes* fera trancher la tête.

51. Le *Bisantin* faisant oblation,
    Après avoir *Cordube* à soi reprise:
    Son chemin long repos *pamplation*,[12]
    Mer passant proie par la *Colongna*[13] prise.

52. Le Roi de *Bloys* dans *Auignon* regner,
    D'*Amboise* et *seme*[14] viendra le long de *Lyndre:*
    Ongle à *Poitiers* saintes ailes ruiner,
    Devant *Boni*.[15]

[1]Variant (Fortune): *despollé*. O.F. *despollé*, fool (according to Le Pelletier).
[2]O.F. *Tudesque*, Teuton, German.
[3]O.F. *esterner*, to destroy, overthrow, rout.
[4]O.F. *menuser*, to cut to pieces.
[5]Dubious enigma. Possibly from Latin *Chaldaeus*, Chaldean, soothsayer.
[6]From Latin *salva terra*, safe land. Or the name of a place (Salvatierra?).
[7]Probably Latin *Saltus Castulonensis*, Sierra Moreña.
[8]O.F. *pars*, sides.
[9]Error for *Sardaigne;* or Tardenois district, southeast of Soissons.
[10]O.F. *barbarin*, barbarian. Or *Barberini*, Roman name (including Urban VIII).
[11]Latin *Capillada*, Capellades (thirty miles northwest of Barcelona).
[12]Dubious derivation. Apparently from Latin *pampinatio*, lopping of vines.
[13]From *Colonnes d'Hercule*, the Pillars of Hercules, i.e., Strait of Gibraltar.
[14]Variant: *semer*. Possibly *seme* is an erratum for *seine*. O.F. *seme*, weak.
[15]Unfinished. Le Pelletier found "an apocryphal edition of the Centuries, printed without the date and without the editor's name," completed with *Devant Bonieux viendra la guerre éteindre*.

47. The Lake of Perugia will bear witness
    To the conspirators locked up within Perugia:
    A fool will imitate the sage,
    Killing routs and cuts to pieces German.

☞ 48. Saturn in Cancer, Jupiter with Mars,
    In February "Chaldondon Salvaterre,"[1]
    The Sierra Moreña assailed from three sides,
    Near "Verbiesque"[2] conflict mortal war.

49. Saturn in Taurus, Jupiter in Aquarius, Mars in Sagittarius,
    Sixth of February[3] will bring mortality:
    Those of "Tardaigne"[4] at Bruges so great a breach,
    That the Barbarian[5] chief will die at "Ponteroso."[6]

☞ 50. The pestilence around Capellades,
    Another famine approaches Sagunto:
    The knight bastard of the good old man,
    He will cause the great one of Tunis to lose his head.

51. The Byzantine making an oblation,
    After having taken Cordoba to himself again:
    His road long rest vines lopped,
    On sea passing prey taken by the Pillar.[7]

52. The King of Blois to reign in Avignon,
    From Amboise and "Seme"[8] he[9] will come the length of the Indre:
    Claw at Poitiers holy wings to ruin,
    Before Boni . . .[10]

[1]Possibly "the Soothsayer at Salvatierra." See note opposite.
[2]Unsolved place name, presumably near Sierra Moreña. Le Pelletier's suggestion, the Roman city Urbiaca (Molina, or Checa), is quite distant.
[3]According to Wöllner, from 1555 to 3797, only in 1736.
[4]"Sardinia" or "the Tardenois." See note opposite.
[5]Or possibly "the Barberini."
[6]Unsolved place name, of which the etymology is "red bridge."
[7]The Pillar(s) of Hercules, i.e., the Strait of Gibraltar.
[8]Or "Semer," which would amount to unidentified enigmatic place names in either case. Or "the Seine."
[9]Or "From Amboise the weak one."
[10]Or, according to the so-called apocryphal version (see note opposite), "Before Bonnieux he will come to extend the war."

53. Dedans *Bolongne* voudra laver ses fautes,
    Il ne pourra au temple du soleil:
    Il volera faisant choses si hautes,
    En hiérarchie n'en fut onc un pareil.

54. Sous la couleur du traité mariage,
    Fait magnanime par grand *Chyren selin*:[1]
    *Quintin, Arras* recouvrés au voyage,
    D'*Espagnols* fait second banc *macelin*.[2]

55. Entre deux fleuves se verra enserré,
    Tonneaux et caques unis à passer outre:
    Huits ponts rompus chef à tant enferré,
    Enfants parfaits sont jugulés en *coultre*.[3]

56. La bande faible la terre occupera,
    Ceux du haut lieu feront horribles cris:
    Le gros troupeau d'*estre*[4] coin troublera,
    Tombe près *Dinebro*[5] découverts les *escris*.[6]

57. De soldat simple parviendra en empire,
    De robe courte parviendra à la longue:
    Vaillant aux armes en Église où plus pire,
    Vexer les prêtres comme l'eau fait l'éponge.

58. Regne en querelle aux frères divisé,
    Prendre les armes et le nom *Britannique*:
    Titre *Anglican* sera tard avisé,
    Surpris de nuit mener à l'air *Gallique*.

59. Par deux fois haut par deux fois mis à bas,
    L'Orient aussi l'Occident faiblira:
    Son adversaire après plusieurs combats,
    Par mer chassé au besoin faillira.

---

[1] Greek *selene*, moon or crescent.
[2] From Latin *macellum*, meat market. By context, "butcher."
[3] O.F. *coultre*, knife.
[4] In this case, rather than *être*, probably O.F. *estre*, outer.
[5] Variant: *D. nebro.*
[6] O.F. *escris*, cries. Somewhat dubious: erratum for *escripts (écrits)?*

☞ 53. Within Boulogne[1] he will want to wash away his errors,
    To the temple of the sun he cannot:
    He will fly away doing things very mighty,
    In the hierarchy there was never one to equal him.

54. Under the color of the marriage treaty,
    Magnanimous deed by[2] the great "Chyren Selin":[3]
    Saint-Quentin and Arras recovered in the trip,
    Of[4] the Spanish a second butcher's bench made.

55. He will find himself shut up between two rivers,
    Casks and barrels joined to pass beyond:
    Eight bridges broken the chief run through many times,
    Perfect children have their throats cut on the knife.

56. The weak band will occupy the land,
    Those of the high place will utter horrible cries:
    The large herd of the outer corner will be troubled,
    Near "Dinebro"[5] it falls[6] the cries[7] discovered.

☞ 57. From simple soldier he will attain to empire,
    From short robe he will attain to the long:
    Valiant in arms in the Church the very worst,
    To vex the priests as water does the sponge.

☞ 58. Realm in quarrel divided between the brothers,
    To take the arms and the name of Britain:
    The Anglican title will be advised too late,
    Surprised by night off to the Gallic air.

59. Twice high twice lowered,
    The East also the West will weaken:
    Its adversary after several struggles,
    Routed by sea will fail in the pinch.

[1]Or "Within Bologna."
[2]Or "for."
[3]The enigmatic "Henry of the Crescent." See notes on 477 and 627 and Commentary.
[4]Or "By."
[5]Interpretations for this enigma vary from Embrun (Ebredunum) to Edinburgh (phonetic Edinbro). See Commentary.
[6]Or "Five hundred fall near the Ebro" (*nebro for l'Ebro*).
[7]Just barely possible: "the inscriptions."

60. Premier en *Gaule*, premier en *Romanie*,
    Par mer et terre aux *Anglois* et *Paris*,
    Merveilleux faits par cette grand *mesnie*,[1]
    Violant,[2] *terax*[3] perdra *le NORLARIS*.[4]

61. Jamais par le *descouurement*[5] du jour,
    Ne parviendra au signe *sceptrifere*:[6]
    Que tous ses sièges ne soient en séjour,
    Portant au coq don du TAG[7] *armifere*.[8]

62. Lorsqu'on verra *expiler*[9] le saint temple,
    Plus grand du *Rhosne* leurs sacrés profaner:
    Par eux naîtra pestilence si ample,
    Roi fait[10] injuste ne fera condamner.

63. Quand l'adultère blessé sans coup aura
    Meurtri la femme et le fils par dépit:
    Femme assommée l'enfant étranglera:
    Huit captifs pris, s'étouffer sans répit.

64. Dedans les îles les enfants transportés,
    Les deux de sept seront en désespoir:
    Ceux du *terrouer*[11] en seront supportés,
    Nom pelle pris des ligues fui l'espoir.

65. Le vieux frustré du principal espoir,
    Il parviendra au chef de son empire:
    Vingt mois tiendra le regne à grand pouvoir,
    Tyran, cruel en délaissant un pire.

[1]O.F. *mesnie,* family, household, followers, troops.
[2]Or possibly, should be corrected to *Violent*.
[3]From a compound of which the basis is Greek *ther,* wild beast (thus *therarchos,* keeper of wild beasts; *therates,* hunter).
[4]Anagram for *Lorraine*.
[5]O.F. *descouvrement,* discovery.
[6]Latin *sceptrifer,* sceptre-bearing.
[7]Variant (Fortune and Garcin): *TA C.* Capitals in all editions. Possibly from Greek *tagma,* regular body of soldiers, legion.
[8]Latin *armifer,* bearing weapons, armed, warlike.
[9]Latin *expilare,* to pillage, rob, plunder.
[10]Variant: *fuit.*
[11]O.F. *terrouer,* soil, ground, land (modern *terroir*).

☞ 60. First in Gaul, first in "Romania,"[1]
By land and sea against the English and Paris,
Marvelous deeds by that great troop,
Violating,[2] the wild beast[3] will lose Lorraine.

☞ 61. Never by the light of day
Will he attain to the sceptre-bearing sign:
Until all his sieges are at rest,
Bearing to the cock the gift of the armed legion.[4]

62. When the holy temple will be seen plundered,
The greatest one of the Rhône profaning their sacred things:
Through[5] them will appear a very copious pestilence,
The King is unjust he will not have them condemned.[6]

63. When the adulterer wounded without a blow will have
Murdered his wife and son out of spite:
Wife knocked down he will strangle the child:
Eight captives taken, to choke without respite.

64. Within the Isles the children transported,
Two out of seven will be in despair:
Those of the soil will be supported by it,
The name shovel[7] taken the hope of the leagues faded.

☞ 65. The old one disappointed in his principal hope,
He will attain to the head of his empire:
Twenty months he will hold the realm with great power,
Tyrant, cruel in giving way to one worse.

[1]Either (1) [Holy] Roman Empire; (2) Romagna; or (3) Papal States (territory of Rome).
[2]Or, barely possible, "Violent."
[3]Not certain. Various compound translations are possible. See note 3, opposite.
[4]An uncertain translation. Also possibly "of the warlike Tagus."
[5]Or "For."
[6]Or "The King flees the wrong/The King flees unjustly he will not be condemned."
[7]The thought behind this provocative phrase has never been solved. Garencières sees the two words as a quasi-anagram for *Montpellier.*

66. Quand l'écriture *D.M.*[1] trouvée,
Et cave antique à lampe découverte:
Loi, Roi, et Prince *Vlpian* éprouvée,
Pavillon Reine et Duc sous la couverte.

67. *PAR. CAR. NERSAF,*[2] à ruine grande discorde,
Ni l'un ni l'autre n'aura élection:
*Nersaf*[3] du peuple aura amour et concorde,
*Ferrare, Collonne*[4] grande protection.

68. Vieux Cardinal par le jeune[5] déçu,
Hors de sa charge se verra désarmé:
*Arles* ne montres double soit aperçu,
Et *Liqueduct*[6] et le Prince embaumé.

69. Auprès du jeune le vieux ange baisser,
Et le viendra surmonter à la fin:
Dix ans égaux aux plus vieux rebaisser,
De trois deux l'un huitième séraphin.

70. Il entrera vilain, méchant, infame,
Tyrannisant la *Mesopotamie:*[7]
Tous amis fait d'adulterine dame,
Terre horrible noir de physionomie.

71. Croîtra le nombre si grand des astronomes
Chassés, bannis et livres censurés:
L'an mil six cent et sept par sacrées[8] *glomes,*[9]
Que nul aux sacres ne seront assurés.

[1]Probably nothing more than the Latin *D.M. (Diis Manibus),* the equivalent of "Here lies" on tombstones. But ingenious attempts have been made to connect this with the more perplexing one of 984.

[2]Probably apocope for Carcassonne and Paris, anagram for *France.*

[3]Anagram of *France.* See above.

[4]Either the Roman family Colonna, or Cologne *(Colonia Agrippina).*

[5]Variant: *jeusne (jeûne).*

[6]Perplexing Nostradamian compound. Le Pelletier, for a fancy interpretation, would have it derived *Ille aqua ductus,* he who is driven by water. Reynaud-Plense produces a Latin verb, *liqueducere,* to rot.

[7]Greek *meso-potamos,* between rivers (or rarely, seas). Certainly not the Asiatic territory in this quatrain.

[8]Variant: *sacre.*

[9]Latin, *glomus,* body of people, assembly.

66.  When the inscription D.M.[1] is found,
     And the ancient cave with a lamp is discovered:
     Law, King and Prince Ulpian[2] tried,
     In the pavilion the Queen and Duke under the covering.

67.  Paris, Carcassonne, France to ruin in great discord,
     Neither the one nor the other will be elected:[3]
     France will have the love and concord of the people,
     Ferrara, Colonna[4] great protection.

☞ 68.  The old Cardinal deceived by the young one,[5]
     He will find himself out of his dignity disarmed:
     Arles do not show that the duplicate is perceived,
     Both "Liqueduct"[6] and the Prince embalmed.[7]

69.  Beside the young one the old angel to fall,
     And he will come to rise above him in the end:
     Ten years equal in most things, the old one to fall again,
     Of three two one the eighth seraphin.[8]

70.  He will enter ugly, wicked, infamous,
     Tyrannizing over "Mesopotamia":[9]
     All friends made by the adulterine lady,
     Land horrible black of physiognomy.

☞ 71.  The number of astronomers[10] will become very great
     Driven out, banished and their books censured:
     The year 1607 by holy assemblies,[11]
     Such that none will be safe from the holy ones.

[1]Equivalent to "Here lies . . ." See note opposite.
[2]Either (1) Domitius Ulpianus, Roman jurist, murdered A.D. 230, or (2) Emperor Trajan (Marcus Ulpius Trajanus). Vaguely possible: (3) Hadrian as Trajan's Prince (i.e., heir).
[3]Or "will have an election."
[4]Or possibly "Cologne."
[5]Or possibly "through the fast."
[6]Dubious. "The Rotted One"? "He Borne by Water"? See note 6, opposite, and Commentary.
[7]The context favors this translation, though *embaumé* is singular in all editions.
[8]The Franciscans were more formally called the Seraphic Order.
[9]Probably Avignon and the surrounding Venaissin County, between the Rhône and Durance rivers, a papal possession until 1791.
[10]The context would seem to indicate that astrologers are designated.
[11]Or "assemblies for the consecration."

72. Champ *Perusin* ô l'énorme défaite,
    Et le conflit tout auprès de *Rauenne:*
    Passage sacre lorsqu'on fera la fête,
    Vainqueur vaincu cheval manger l'aveine.[1]

73. Soldat Barbare le grand Roi frappera,
    Injustement non éloigné de mort,
    L'avare mère du fait cause sera,
    Conjurateur et regne en grand remords.

74. En terre neuve bien avant Roi entré,
    Pendant sujets lui viendront faire accueil:
    Sa perfidie aura tel rencontré,
    Qu'aux citadins lieu de fête et recueil.

75. Le père et fils seront meurtris ensemble,
    Le *prefecteur*[2] dedans son pavillon:
    La mère à *Tours* du fils ventre aura enflé,
    *Caiche*[3] verdure de feuilles papillon.[4]

76. Plus *Macelin*[5] que Roi en *Angleterre,*
    Lieu obscur né par force aura l'empire:
    Lâche sans foi sans loi saignera terre,
    Son temps s'approche si près que je soupire.

77. L'antechrist trois bien tôt annihilés,
    Vingt et sept ans sang durera sa guerre:
    Les hérétiques morts, captifs exilés,
    Sang corps humain eau rougie grêler terre.

78. Un *Bragamas*[6] avec la langue torte,
    Viendra des dieux le[7] sanctuaire:
    Aux hérétiques il ouvrira la porte,
    En suscitant l'Église militaire.

[1]Variant: *la venne.* Le Pelletier would make this "flesh," from Latin *venatio,* game.
[2]Low Latin *Praefectorius,* Count. But also equivalent to many other offices.
[3]Variant: *cache.* Possibly from Provençal *caicha,* chest, box, coffer.
[4]All right as stands, or O.F. *papillon,* small bit of paper (Sainte-Palaye).
[5]Latin *macellum,* meat market. Nostradamian usage as "butcher."
[6]O.F. *bragamas,* broadsword. Derivative: Provençal *Braimanso,* a soldier of fortune.
[7]Variant (Fortune): *piller le.*

72. Oh, what an enormous defeat on the Perugian field,
    And the conflict very near to Ravenna:
    Holy passage when they will celebrate the feast,
    Conqueror vanquished horse to eat the oats.[1]

73. A Barbarian soldier will strike the great King,
    Unjustly not far from death,
    The covetous mother will be the cause of the deed,
    Conspirator and realm in great remorse.

74. A King entered very far into the new land,
    While his subjects come to welcome him:
    His perfidy will have such an effect
    That for the citizens a replacing of feast and reception.

75. The father and son will be murdered together,
    The count[2] within his pavilion:
    The mother at Tours will have her belly swelling with a son,
    Chest[3] verdure with tiny sheets of paper.[4]

76. More Butcher than King in England,
    Born of obscure place he will have the empire through force:
    Base without faith without law he will bleed the land,
    His time approaches so near that I sigh.

77. The Antichrist[5] three very soon annihilated,
    Seven and twenty years of blood will his war last:
    The heretics dead, captives exilea,
    Blood human body water reddened on land to hail.

78. A Soldier of Fortune[6] with twisted tongue
    Will come to pillage the sanctuary of the gods:
    To the heretics he will open the gate,
    Thus stirring up the Church militant.

[1] Or possibly "to eat horse's flesh"? See note 1, opposite.
[2] Or many other possible titles, amounting to "leader."
[3] Or possibly "Hides"?
[4] Or possibly "of leaves butterfly"?
[5] Or possibly "By the Antichrist"? Or "Of the Antichrist"?
[6] Le Pelletier would have it "A Bully."

79. Qui par fer père perdra né de *Nonnaire*,[1]
    De *Gorgon* sur là sera sang *perfetant*:[2]
    En terre étrange fera si tout de taire,
    Qui brûlera lui-même et son enfant.

80. Des innocents le sang de veuve et vierge,
    Tant de maux faits par moyen *se*[3] grand Rouge:
    Saints simulacres trempés en ardent cierge,
    De frayeur crainte ne verra nul qui bouge.

81. Le neuf empire en désolation,
    Sera changé du pôle *aquilonaire*:[4]
    De la *Sicile* viendra l'émotion,
    Troubler l'*emprise*[5] à *Philip.* tributaire.

82. Ronge long sec faisant du bon valet,
    À la parfin n'aura que son *congie*:[6]
    Poignant poison, et lettres au collet,
    Sera saisi échappé en *dangie*.[6]

83. Le plus grand voile hors du port de *Zara*,
    Près de *Bisance* fera son entreprise:
    D'ennemi perte et l'ami ne sera,
    Le tiers à deux fera grand pille et prise.

84. *Paterne* ouïra de la *Sicile* cri,
    Tous les *aprests*[7] du gouffre de *Trieste*,
    Qui s'entendra jusqu'à la *Trinacrie*,[8]
    De tant de voiles fui, fui l'horrible peste.

[1]Low Latin *nonneria*, nunnery.
[2]Apheresis of Latin *superfetans*, conceiving again (while pregnant).
[3]O.F. *se*, for (1) *si* or (2) *son*.
[4]Latin *aquilonaris*, northern.
[5]O.F. *emprise*, enterprise.
[6]Odd Nostradamian variants for *congé . . . danger*.
[7]O.F. *aprest*, preparation.
[8]Latin *Trinacria*, poetic term for Sicily.

☞ 79. One who born of the nunnery the father through steel destroyed,
 Gorgon's blood thereupon will be conceiving anew:
 In foreign land much will he do all to keep silent,
 He who will burn himself and his child.

80. The blood of the innocent of widow and virgin,
 So many evils committed by means of the very great Red One:
 Holy images dipped in burning wax,
 Frightened by terror none will be seen to move.

☞ 81. The new empire in desolation,
 It will be changed by the northern pole:[1]
 From Sicily will come the disturbance,
 To trouble the enterprise tributary to Philip.

82. Spare, tall, dry playing the good valet,
 In the end he will have only his leave:
 Keen poison, and letters in his collar,
 He will be seized escaped into danger.

83. The greatest sail out of the port of Zara,
 Near Byzantium will he[2] carry out his[2] enterprise:
 Loss of enemy and the friend will not take place,
 The third upon both will inflict great plunder and capture.

84. Paterno will hear a cry from Sicily,
 In the Gulf of Trieste all the preparations,
 Which will be heard as far as Sicily,
 From so many sails fled, the horrible plague fled.

[1]Or "by the north pole [country]."
[2]Or "it . . . its."

85.  Entre *Bayonne* et *sainct Iean de Lux*
     Sera posé de *Mars* la *promotoire:*[1]
     Aux *Hanix*[2] d'*Aquilon Nanar*[3] ôtera *lux,*[4]
     Puis suffoqué au lit sans *adjutoire.*[5]

86.  Par *Arnani Tholoser Ville*[6] *Franque,*
     Bande infinie par le mont *Adrian:*
     Passe rivière, *Hutin*[7] par pont la *planque*[8]
     *Bayonne* entrer tous *Bichoro*[9] criant.

87.  Mort conspirée viendra en plein effet,
     Charge donnée et voyage de mort:
     Élu, créé, reçu par siens défait.
     Sang d'innocence devant soi par remords.

88.  Dans la *Sardaigne* un noble Roi viendra,
     Qui ne tiendra que trois ans le royaume,
     Plusieurs couleurs avec soi conjoindra,
     Lui-même après soin sommeil *marrit*[10] *scome.*[11]

89.  Pour ne tomber entre mains de son oncle,
     Qui ses enfants pour regner *trucidez:*[12]
     *Orant*[13] au peuple mettant pied sur *Peloncle*[14]
     Mort et traîné entre chevaux bardés.

90.  Quand des croisés un trouvé de sens trouble,[15]
     En lieu du sacre verra un bœuf cornu:
     Par vierge porc son lieu lors sera comble,[15]
     Par Roi plus ordre ne sera soutenu.

[1]Either for *promontoire* (which should, however, be masculine), or as a feminine of *promoteur* (which properly is *promotrice*).
[2]Dubious. Possibly Greek *aniketos*, unconquerable; or Latin *Hamaxaeci*, the nomads of northeastern Europe; or Latin *annixus*, effort.
[3]Possibly Latin *nonaria*, prostitute. Variant: *Nanat*.
[4]Latin *lux*, light.
[5]O.F. *adjutoire*, aid, assistance.
[6]Variant: *Isle*.
[7]O.F. *hutin*, quarrel, dispute, hostility, combat.
[8]O.F. *planque*, plank (modern *planche*).
[9]According to Reynaud-Plense, the war cry of Navarre.
[10]O.F. *marrir*, to afflict, to be afflicted.
[11]Latin *scomma*, a taunt, jeer, scoff.
[12]Latin *trucidare*, to massacre, slaughter.
[13]Latin *orans*, arguing, pleading.
[14]Dubious. Possibly from *Pellonia*, goddess who puts enemy to flight.
[15]Although uniform in all editions, probably errata for *troublé . . . comblé*.

85. Between Bayonne and Saint-Jean-de-Luz
    Will be placed the promontory of[1] Mars:
    For the Unconquerables[2] of "Aquilon"[3] "Nanar"[4] will remove the
    Then suffocated in bed without assistance.                    [light,

86. Through Ernani, Tolosa and Villafranca,
    Infinite band through the Sierra de San Adrian:
    Passes river, Combat the plank for a bridge
    To enter Bayonne all crying Bichoro.[5]

87. Death conspired will come into full execution,
    Charge given and voyage of death:
    Elected, created, received, defeated by his followers.
    Blood of innocence before him in remorse.

☞ 88. A noble King will come into Sardinia,
    One who will hold the kingdom only three years.
    He will join several colors to himself,
    He himself after care slumber scorn afflicts.

89. In order not to fall into the hands of his uncle,
    Who his children slaughtered in order to reign:
    Pleading with the people putting his foot on "Peloncle"[6]
    Dead and dragged between barded horses.

90. When one of the crusaders is found with his senses troubled,
    In the place of the holy one will see a horned ox:
    Through the virgin pig its[7] place then will be filled,
    By the King order will no longer be maintained.

[1]Or possibly "she who promoted."
[2]Or "Efforts."
[3]The North[ern Country].
[4]Or "Nanat." From either word: "the Whore"?
[5]The war cry of Navarre (or at least Bigorre), according to Reynaud-Plense.
[6]Pellonia, the goddess of victory? See note 14 opposite.
[7]Or "her," or "his."

91. Parmi[1] les champs des *Rodanes*[2] entrées
    Où les croisés seront presque unis,
    Les deux brassières en *pisces* rencontrées,
    Et un grand nombre par déluge punis.

92. Loin[3] hors du regne mis en hasard voyage
    Grand *ost*[4] *duira*[5] pour soi l'occupera:
    Le Roi tiendra les siens captif otage,
    À son retour tout pays pillera.

93. Sept mois sans plus obtiendra prélature,
    Par son décès grand schisme fera naître:
    Sept mois tiendra un autre la préture,
    Près de *Venise* paix, union renaître.

94. Devant le lac où plus cher fut *getté*[6]
    De sept mois, et son *ost*[4] déconfit
    Seront *Hispans* par *Albanois gastez*,[7]
    Par délai perte en donnant le conflit.

95. Le séducteur sera mis en la fosse,
    Et attaché jusqu'à quelque temps:
    Le clerc uni le chef avec sa *crosse*,[8]
    Piquante droite *attraira*[9] les contents.

96. La synagogue stérile sans nul fruit
    Sera reçue entre les infidèles:
    De *Babylon* la fille du poursuit,
    Misère et triste lui tranchera les ailes.

97. Aux fins du *Var*[10] changer les *pompotans*,[11]
    Près du rivage les trois beaux enfants naître:
    Ruine au peuple par âge compétent,
    Regne au pays changer plus voir croître.

[1]Variant: *Frymy*.
[2]Latin *Rhodanus*, the Rhône, or (by metonymy) dwellers by the Rhône. Or *Rhodius*, of Rhodes, Rhodians.
[3]Variant (1605): *LOIN* (suggesting anagram for *Lion*).
[4]O.F. *ost*, army.
[5]O.F. *duire*, to lead.
[6]O.F. *getter*, to put down.
[7]O.F. *gaster*, to devastate, destroy, pillage, torment, fatigue.
[8]All right as is, or O.F. *crosse*, abbey.
[9]O.F. *attraire*, to attract, draw.
[10]Variant (1605): *VAR*.
[11]Compound of Greek *pan*, all, and Latin *potens*, powerful, thus "All-powerful," according to most interpretations.

91. Entered amidst the fields beside the Rhône[1]
    Where the crusaders will be almost united,
    Mars and Venus[2] met in Pisces,
    And a great number punished by flood.

☞ 92. Far[3] beyond his realm set on a hazardous journey
    He will lead a great army and take possession of it for himself:
    The King his followers[4] captive and hostage will hold,
    Upon his return he will plunder the entire country.

93. Seven months, no more he will obtain the prelacy,
    Through his death a great schism will arise:
    Seven months another will hold the governorship,
    Near Venice peace, union to arise again.

☞ 94. Before the lake where the dearest one[5] was put down
    For seven months, and his army routed
    There will be Spaniards destroyed through those of Alba,[6]
    Loss through delay in giving battle.

95. The seducer will be placed in the dungeon,
    And bound for some time:
    The scholar joined the chief with his crozier,
    The sharp right will attract the contented ones.

☞ 96. The synagogue sterile without any fruit
    Will be received by the infidels:
    The daughter of the persecuted of Babylon,
    Miserable and sad her wings will be clipped.[7]

97. At the limits of the Var to change the All-powerful,
    Near the bank the three beautiful children to be born:
    Ruin to the people by competent age,
    In the country the realm to change seen growing more.[8]

[1] Or "of the Rhodians."
[2] Literally "The two leading-strings." Le Pelletier cites a legend of Venus having been bound to husband Mars by a thread produced by Vulcan.
[3] "The Lion"?
[4] Or "kindred."
[5] Suggests a play on words, such as a name *Carissimo*.
[6] I.e., the troops of the Duke of Alba, generalissimo of Charles V and Philip II.
[7] Or "Misery and sadness will clip her wings."
[8] Or possibly "no more."

98.  Des gens d'Église sang sera épanché,
     Comme de l'eau en si grande abondance:
     Et d'un long temps ne sera retranché,
     *Ve ve*[1] au *clerc*[2] ruine et doléance.

99.  Par la puissance des trois Rois temporels,
     En autre lieu sera mis le saint Siège:
     Où la substance de l'esprit corporel,
     Sera remise et reçus pour vrai siège.

100. Pour l'abondance de larme répandue,
     Du haut en bas par le bas au plus haut:
     Trop grande foi par jeu vie perdue,
     De soif mourir par abondant défaut.

[1]Latin *vae*, alas, woe.
[2]O.F. *clerc*, clerk, scholar, clergyman.

98. The blood of the Church people will be poured out,
In as great abundance as water:
And for a long time it will not be stopped,
Woe, woe for the clergy ruin and wailing.

☞ 99. Through the power of the three temporal Kings,
The Holy See will be put in another place:
Where the substance of the corporal spirit
Will be restored and received as the true see.

100. For the abundance of tears shed,
From high to low through the low one to the highest:
Faith too great through play life lost,
To die through abundant deficiency of thirst.[1]

---

[1]As Le Pelletier suggests, this probably boils down to "drowned" (or even "To drink himself to death").

# Centurie IX

1. Dans la maison du traducteur de *Bourc*,[1]
   Seront les lettres trouvées sur la table,
   Borgne, roux, blanc, chenu tiendra de cours,
   Qui changera au nouveau Connétable.

2. Du haut du mont *Auentin* voix ouïe,
   Videz, videz de tous les deux côtés:
   Du sang des rouges sera l'ire *assomie*,[2]
   D'*Arimin Prato, Columna*[3] *debotez*.[4]

3. La *magna vaqua*[5] à *Rauenne* grand trouble,
   Conduits par quinze enserrés à *Fornase*:
   À Rome naîtra deux monstres à tête double,
   Sang, feu, déluge, les plus grands à l'espace.

4. L'an ensuivant découvertes par déluge,
   Deux chefs élus, le premier ne tiendra:
   De fuir ombre à l'un d'eux le refuge,
   Saccagée case qui premier maintiendra.

5. Tiers doigt du pied au premier semblera
   À un nouveau monarque de bas haut,
   Qui *Pyse* et *Lucques* Tyran occupera
   Du précédent corriger le défaut.

6. Par la *Guienne* infinité d'*Anglois*
   Occuperont par nom d'*Anglaquitaine*:
   Du *Languedoc Ispalme*[6] *Bourdelois*,
   Qu'ils nommeront après *Barboxitaine*.[7]

---

[1]Probably Bourg, north of Bordeaux, whose inhabitants are called *Bourcais*.

[2]O.F. *assomir*, to appease (Godefroy).

[3]Original form of the name of the great Colonna clan of Rome.

[4]O.F. *debouter*, to drive out, expel.

[5]Latin *magna vacca*, great cow. Magnavacca is the name of a valley and tiny port (renamed Porto di Garibaldi) between Ravenna and Ferrara, and also, according to *The Catholic Encyclopedia*, the name of a former canal in the same area.

[6]Variants: *1. palme; Ipsalme* (Fortune). In any case, an enigmatic place name.

[7]Possibly derived from *Barbe-Occitanie*, *Barbe* being the enigmatic *Aenobarbe* and *Occitanie* the medieval name for Languedoc or the whole Mediterranean coast.

# Century IX

☞ 1. In the house of the translator of Bourg,
The letters will be found on the table,
One-eyed, red-haired, white, hoary-headed will hold the course,
Which will change for the new Constable.

2. From the top of the Aventine hill a voice heard,
Be gone, be gone all of you on both sides:
The anger will be appeased by the blood of the red ones,
From Rimini and Prato, the Colonna expelled.

3. The "great cow"[1] at Ravenna in great trouble,
Led by fifteen shut up at Fornase:
At Rome there will be born two double-headed monsters,
Blood, fire, flood, the greatest ones in space.[2]

4. The following year discoveries through flood,
Two chiefs elected, the first one will not hold:
The refuge for the one of them fleeing a shadow,
The house which will maintain the first one plundered.

☞ 5. The third toe will seem first
To a new monarch from low high,
He who will possess himself as Tyrant of Pisa and Lucca,
To correct the fault of his predecessor.

☞ 6. An infinity of Englishmen in Guienne
Will settle under the name of Anglaquitaine:
In Languedoc, "Ispalme,"[3] Bordelais,
Which they will name after "Barboxitaine."[4]

---

[1]With this translation, an enigmatic name. Or "[The] Magnavacca." See note 5, opposite.

[2]I.e., hanged.

[3]A still-unsolved place name, possibly an erratum for *Lapalme*, near Narbonne. See note 6, opposite, for possible variants.

[4]Possibly meaning "the Occitania (southwest France) of the [Bronze]beard." See note opposite.

7. Qui ouvrira le monument trouvé,
   Et ne viendra le serrer promptement,
   Mal lui viendra, et ne pourra prouver
   Si mieux doit être Roi *Breton* ou *Normand*.

8. Puîné Roi fait son père mettra à mort,
   Après conflit de mort très *inhonneste*:[1]
   Écrit trouvé, soupçon *donra*[2] remords,
   Quand loup chassé pose sur la couchette.

9. Quand lampe ardente de feu inextinguible
   Sera trouvé au temple des Vestales:
   Enfant trouvé feu, eau passant par crible:
   Périr eau *Nymes*, *Tholose* choir les halles.

10. Moine moinesse d'enfant mort exposé,
    Mourir par ourse, et ravi par *verrier*,[3]
    Par *Fois* et *Pamyes* le camp sera posé,
    Contre *Tholose Carcas*[4] dresser fourrier.

11. Le juste à tort à mort l'on viendra mettre,
    Publiquement et du milieu[5] éteint:
    Si grande peste en ce lieu viendra naître,
    Que les jugeants[6] fuir seront contraints.

12. Le tant d'argent de *Diane* et *Mercure*,
    Les simulacres au lac seront trouvés:
    Le figurier cherchant argile neuve,
    Lui et les siens d'or seront abreuvés.

13. Les exilés autour de la *Sologne*,
    Conduits de nuit pour marcher en l'*Auxois*,
    Deux de *Modene truculent*[7] de Bologne,
    Mis découverts par feu de *Burançois*.

[1] O.F. *inhonneste*, dishonest.
[2] Syncope for *donnera*.
[3] Probably Nostradamian variant of Latin *veres*, boar (French *verrat*), rather than *verrier*, glazier.
[4] Apocope for *Carcassonne*.
[5] Variants: *Publiquement du lieu; Publiquement du lieu fera* (Fortune).
[6] This gerund form seems to be Nostradamus' own variant, not being recorded in any dictionary we have seen.
[7] Latin *truculentus*, ferocious, harsh, cruel.

7. He who will open the tomb found,
   And will not come to close it promptly,
   Evil will come to him, and one will be unable to prove
   If it would be better to be a Breton or Norman King.

8. The younger son made King will put his father to death,
   After the conflict very dishonest death:
   Inscription found, suspicion will bring remorse,
   When the wolf driven out lies down on the bedstead.

9. When the lamp burning with inextinguishable fire
   Will be found in the temple of the Vestals:
   Child found fire, water passing through the sieve:
   To perish in water Nîmes, Toulouse the markets to fall.

10. The child of a monk and nun exposed to death,
    To die through a she-bear, and carried off by a boar,[1]
    The army will be camped by Foix and Pamiers,
    Against Toulouse Carcassonne the harbinger to form.

11. Wrongly will they come to put the just one to death,
    In public and in the middle extinguished:[2]
    So great a pestilence will come to arise in this place,
    That the judges will be forced to flee.

12. So much silver of Diana and Mercury,
    The images will be found in the lake:
    The sculptor looking for new clay,
    He and his followers will be steeped in gold.

13. The exiles around Sologne,
    Led by night to march into Auxois,
    Two of Modena for Bologna cruel,
    Placed discovered by the fire of Buzançais.

[1]Somewhat uncertain. See note opposite.
[2]Or "Publicly in the place [they will cause him to be (Fortune)] extinguished."

14. Mis en *planure*[1] chaudrons d'*infecteurs,*[2]
    Vin, miel et huile, et bâtis sur fourneaux:
    Seront plongés, sans mal dit malfaiteurs,
    Sept *fum*[3] extant au canon des *borneaux.*[4]

15. Près de *Parpan*[5] les rouges détenus,
    Ceux du milieu *parfondres*[6] menés loin:
    Trois mis en pièces, et cinq mal soutenus,
    Pour le Seigneur et Prélat de *Bourgoing.*

16. De *Castel Franco* sortira l'assemblée,
    L'ambassadeur non plaisant fera schisme:
    Ceux de *Ribiere* seront en mêlée,
    Et au grand gouffre dénieront l'entrée.

17. Le tiers premier pis que ne fit *Neron,*
    Videz vaillant que sang humain répandre:
    R'*edifier*[7] fera le *forneron,*[8]
    Siècle d'or mort, nouveau Roi grand esclandre.

18. Le lis *Dauffois*[9] portera dans *Nansi,*
    Jusqu'en *Flandres* Électeur de l'Empire:
    Neuve *obturee*[10] au grand *Montmorency,*
    Hors lieux prouvés délivre à *clere*[11] peine.

19. Dans le milieu de la forêt *Mayenne,*
    *Sol*[12] au Lion la foudre tombera:
    Le grand bâtard issu du grand du *Maine,*
    Ce jour *Fougeres* pointe en sang entrera.

[1]O.F. *planure,* plain, flat surface.
[2]Latin *infector,* dyer.
[3]O.F. *fum,* smoke.
[4]Dubious. There is a village name Borneaux in Haute-Loire. Variant: *bordeaux.*
[5]Syncope for *Parpignan* (Perpignan).
[6]O.F. *parfondre,* to completely ruin (Godefroy).
[7]Archaic reiterative of *édifier* (for *réédifier*).
[8]O.F. *forneron,* baker's boy. Hardly likely here. Le Pelletier takes it as "synonymous with *fourneau*" (variant thereof?).
[9]Assumed to be syncope of *Dauphinois.*
[10]Low Latin *obturatum,* stopper. Figure of speech for "prison."
[11]O.F. *cler,* illustrious, celebrated.
[12]Latin *Sol.* Sun.

14. Dyers' caldrons put on the flat surface,
    Wine, honey and oil, and built over furnaces:
    They will be immersed, innocent, pronounced malefactors,
    Seven of Borneaux[1] smoke still in the cannon.

15. Near Perpignan the red ones detained,
    Those of the middle completely ruined led far off:
    Three cut in pieces, and five badly supported,
    For the Lord and Prelate of Burgundy.

16. Out of Castelfranco will come the assembly,
    The ambassador not agreeable will cause a schism:
    Those of Riviera[2] will be in the squabble,
    And they will refuse entry to the great gulf.

☞ 17. The third one first does worse than Nero,
    How much human blood to flow, valiant, be gone:
    He[3] will cause the furnace[4] to be rebuilt,
    Golden Age dead, new King great scandal.

☞ 18. The lily of the Dauphin will reach into Nancy,
    As far as Flanders the Elector of the Empire:
    New confinement for the great Montmorency,
    Outside proven places delivered to celebrated punishment.

19. In the middle of the forest of Mayenne,
    Lightning will fall, the Sun in Leo:
    The great bastard issued from the great one of Maine,
    On this day a point will enter the blood of Fougères.

---

[1] Or "Bordeaux." This word is of very uncertain derivation and may not even be a proper name (uncapitalized in the original French).

[2] Probably the Genoese. The translation is not quite certain, but it is the most probable of the various possibilities. See Commentary.

[3] Or "It."

[4] Somewhat dubious. See note opposite.

20. De nuit viendra par la forêt de *Reines*,
    Deux *pars*[1] *voltorte*[2] *Herne*[3] la pierre blanche,
    Le moine noir[4] en gris dedans *Varennes:*
    Élu *cap.*[5] cause tempête, feu, sang, tranche.

21. Au temple haut de *Bloys* sacré *Salonne*,
    Nuit pont de *Loyre*, Prélat, Roi *pernicant:*[6]
    *Curseur*[7] victoire aux marais de la *lone*,[8]
    D'où prélature de blancs *abormeant.*[9]

22. Roi et sa cour au lieu de langue *halbe*,[10]
    Dedans le temple vis à vis du palais:
    Dans le jardin Duc de *Mantor*[11] et d'*Albe*,
    *Albe* et *Mantor*[11] poignard langue et palais.

23. Puîné jouant au frais dessous la *tonne*,[12]
    Le haut du toit du milieu sur la tête,
    Le père Roi au temple saint *Salonne*,
    Sacrifiant sacrera *fum*[13] de fête.

24. Sur le palais au *rochier*[14] des fenêtres,
    Seront ravis les deux petits royaux:
    Passer *aurelle*[15] *Luthece*,[16] *Denis* cloîtres,
    Nonnain, *Mallods*[1.] avaler verts noyaux.

[1]O.F. *pair, par,* couple (Godefroy).
[2]Possibly compounded of O.F. *volte,* route, and *tort,* detour (Godefroy).
[3]Probably anagram for *Reine.*
[4]Probably anagram for *roi/roy.*
[5]Probably apocope for *Capet.*
[6]Latin *pernecare,* to kill or slay outright; or *pernix,* swift.
[7]O.F. *curseur,* runner, messenger. Variant: *Cuiseur.* O.F. *cuiseur,* deep imprint, mark, impression.
[8]Provençal *lona,* pool, pond (any still water).
[9]Latin *aboriri* or *abortare,* to miscarry. From which Provençal *abouriment,* destruction.
[10]Probably metathesis of O.F. *hable,* sharp, clever (modern *habile*).
[11]Variants: *Montor; Mantou* (Garcin).
[12]O.F. *tonne,* arbor.
[13]O.F. *fum,* smoke.
[14]A derivative of *roche,* used for various mechanical devices. Here the context seems to point to its meaning "balcony."
[15]Latin *Aurelianum,* Orléans.
[16]Latin *Lutetia,* Paris.
[17]Dubious. O.F. *malots,* flies; *malois,* wicked, detestable. Latin *malum,* apple. Anagram?

☞ 20. By night will come through the forest of "Reines,"[1]
Two couples roundabout route Queen the white stone,
The monk king in gray in Varennes:
Elected Capet causes tempest, fire, blood, slice.

☞ 21. At the tall temple of Saint-Solenne[2] at Blois,
Night Loire bridge, Prelate, King killing outright:[3]
Crushing[4] victory in the marshes of the pond,
Whence prelacy of whites miscarrying.

☞ 22. The King and his court in the place of cunning tongue,
Within the temple facing the palace:
In the garden the Duke of Mantua[5] and Alba,
Alba and Mantua[5] dagger tongue and palace.

☞ 23. The younger son playing outdoors under the arbor,
The top of the roof in the middle on his head,
The father King in the temple of Saint-Solenne,[2]
Sacrificing he will consecrate festival smoke.

☞ 24. Upon the palace at the balcony[6] of the windows,
The two little royal ones will be carried off:
To pass Orléans, Paris, abbey of Saint-Denis,
Nun, wicked ones[7] to swallow green pits.[8]

---

[1]No forest exists by this name. The original word, in its old spelling, is *forest*, which Le Pelletier would have derived from Latin *foris*, gate, which would yield the translation "through the gates of queens." See Commentary on this famous quatrain.

[2]The Cathedral of Blois, renamed in 1730 L'Eglise de Saint-Louis.

[3]Or "King swift."

[4]Or "Runner."

[5]Or "Mantor." Or "Montor." See Commentary.

[6]Uncertain. See note 14, opposite.

[7]Or "flies"? or "Mallods"? Very uncertain.

[8]Or possibly "Nun, to swallow cores of green apples."

25.  Passant les ponts venir près des rosiers,[1]
     Tard arrivé plus tôt qu'il *cuidera*,[2]
     Viendront les *noves*[3] *Espagnols* à *Besiers*,
     Qu'icelle chasse *emprinse*[4] cassera.

26.  *Nice* sortie sur nom[5] des lettres âpres,
     La grande *cappe*[6] fera présent non sien:
     Proche de *Vultry* aux murs de vertes capres,
     Après *plombin*[7] le vent à bon escient.

27.  De bois la garde, vent clos rond pont sera,
     Haut le reçu frappera le Dauphin,
     Le vieux *teccon*[8] bois unis passera,
     Passant plus outre du Duc le droit confin.

28.  Voile *Symacle*[9] port *Massiliolique*,[10]
     Dans *Venise* port marcher aux *Pannons*:
     Partir du gouffre et *sinus*[11] *Illirique*,
     *Vast*[12] à *Socille*, *Ligurs* coups de canons.

29.  Lorsque celui qu'à nul ne donne lieu,
     Abandonner voudra lieu pris non pris:
     Feu neuf[13] par *saignes*,[14] *bitument*[15] à *Charlieu*,
     Seront *Quintin*, *Balez*[16] repris.

30.  Au port de *Puola* et de *sainct Nicolas*,
     Périr *Normande* au gouffre *phanatique*:[17]
     *Cap.*[18] de *Bisance* rues crier hélas,
     Secours de *Gaddes*[19] et du grand *Philippique*.

[1]Variant: *de* (in which case *rosiers* as a proper name).
[2]O.F. *cuider*, to think, believe.
[3]O.F. *nove*, new (modern *nouveau*).
[4]O.F. *emprinse*, enterprise.
[5]Le Pelletier thinks this should be read as *surnom*.
[6]O.F. *cappe*, (1) cope (modern *chape*) or (2) cloak (modern *cape*).
[7]O.F. *plombin*, leaded, leaden. Or perhaps for *Piombino*.
[8]O.F. *tecon*, a game like football, rather unlikely here. Perhaps from Greek *tekton*, craftsman.
[9]Greek *symmachos*, leagued or allied with, ally, auxiliary.
[10]Latin *Massilioticus*, of Marseilles.
[11]Latin *sinus*, gulf, bay.
[12]Low Latin *vastum*, destruction.
[13]Variant: *nef*.
[14]O.F. *saigne*, marsh, swamp.
[15]O.F. *bitument*, bitumen (modern *bitume* has one syllable less).
[16]Anagram for *Calez* (Calais). Jaubert "corrects" the line to: *Seront Guines, Calais Oye repris.*
[17]Latin *Sinus Flanaticus*, Gulf of Quarnero.
[18]Probably apocope for *Capet*.
[19]Latin *Gades*. Cadiz.

25. Passing the bridges to come near the rosebushes,[1]
Arrived late sooner than he will believe,
The new Spaniards will come to Béziers,
So that this chase the enterprise will break.

26. Departed from Nice under the name[2] of the harsh letters,
The great cope[3] will bestow a gift not his own:
Near Voltri at the walls of green capers,
After leaden[4] the wind in good earnest.

☞ 27. The forester, the wind will be close round the bridge,
The received one high will strike the Dauphin,
The old craftsman[5] will pass the level woods,[6]
Going far beyond the rightful confines of the Duke.

☞ 28. Allied Fleet from the port of Marseilles,
In the port of Venice to march to the Pannonias:[7]
To leave from the gulf and bay of Illyria,[8]
Destruction to Sicily, cannon shots for the Ligurians.[9]

29. When he who gives place to none
Will want to abandon a place taken yet not taken:
New fire[10] through swamps, bitumen at Charlieu,
Saint-Quentin and Calais will be recaptured.

☞ 30. At the port of Pola and of San Nicolo,
Norman to perish in the Gulf of Quarnero:
Capet in the streets of Byzantium to cry alas,
Help from Cadiz and the great Philip.

[1] Or "near Rosiers."
[2] Or "Nice surname."
[3] Or "The great cloak." In either case, probably the Pope.
[4] Or possibly "Beyond Piombino"?
[5] Not quite certain. See note 8, opposite.
[6] Or possibly "will pass the forest with company."
[7] Classical territories corresponding to Hungary and eastern Austria.
[8] I.e., the Adriatic.
[9] The inhabitants of classical Genoa. The name is still used.
[10] Or "Fire ship," or possibly "Ship afire."

31. Le tremblement de terre à *Mortara*,
    *Cassich*[1] *sainct George* à demi *perfondrez*,[2]
    Paix assoupie la guerre éveillera,
    Dans temple à Pâques abîmes *enfondrez*.[3]

32. De fin porphyre profond colonne trouvée,
    Dessous la *laze*[4] écrits *capitolin*:[5]
    Os poil retors *Romain* force prouvée,
    *Classe*[6] agiter au port de *Methelin*.

33. *Hercules* Roi de *Rome* et *d'Annemarc*,[7]
    De *Gaule* trois *Guion*[8] surnommé,
    Trembler l'*Italie* et l'un[9] de *sainct Marc*,
    Premier sur tous monarque renommé.

34. Le part *soluz*[10] *mary*[11] sera mitré,
    Retour conflit passera sur la tuile:
    Par cinq cents un trahir sera titré
    *Narbonne* et *Saulce*[12] par couteaux[13] avons d'huile.

35. Et *Ferdinand* blonde sera *descorte*,[14]
    Quitter la fleur, suivre le *Macedon*:
    Au grand besoin défaillira sa route,
    Et marchera contre le *Myrmidon*.

36. Un grand Roi pris entre les mains d'un jeune,
    Non loin de Pâques confusion coup *cultre*:[15]
    *Perpet*.[16] captifs temps! que foudre en la hune,
    Lorsque trois frères se blesseront et meurtre.

[1]Probably from Greek *Cassiterides*, the tin islands (name given to Cornwall and the Scilly Islands) from *kassiteros*, tin.
[2]O.F. *parfondrer*, to sink to the bottom (Godefroy).
[3]O.F. *enfondrer*, to rip open (Sainte-Palaye).
[4]Greek *laz*, foot, base.
[5]Latin *Capitolinus*, pertaining to the Capitol [of Rome].
[6]Latin *classis*, fleet.
[7]See note 2, opposite.
[8]O.F. *guion*, guide, chief, leader.
[9]Variant: *l'onde*.
[10]O.F. *solu*, free, untied, single; or *solz*, alone.
[11]O.F. *marir*, to be afflicted, to be vexed (Sainte-Palaye).
[12]Salces near Narbonne, or Mayor Sauce of Varennes? See Commentary.
[13]Variants: *contaux*; *coutaux* ("1568"); *cauteaux* (Fortune); *couraux* (Garcin). Le Pelletier suggests Latin *custos*, guard, keeper.
[14]O.F. *descorte*, detached, in disagreement (Godefroy). All editions have apparently improper feminine endings on *blonde* and *descorte*.
[15]Latin *culter*, knife.
[16]Probably apocope of Latin *perpetualis*, everlasting (or any more modern version of the same, in O.F., French, etc.).

31. The trembling of land at Mortara,
    Tin St. George[1] half sunk to the bottom,
    Drowsy peace the war will awaken,
    In the temple at Easter abysses ripped open.

32. A deep column of fine porphyry found,
    Under the base inscriptions of the Capitol:
    Bones twisted hair Roman force tried,
    Fleet to stir at the port of Mytilene.

☞ 33. Hercules King of Rome and of "Annemark,"[2]
    With the surname of the chief of triple Gaul,[3]
    Italy and the one[4] of St. Mark[5] to tremble,
    First monarch renowned above all.

☞ 34. The single[6] part afflicted will be mitred,
    Return conflict to pass over the tile:[7]
    For five hundred one to betray[8] will be titled
    Narbonne and Salces[9] we have oil for knives.[10]

☞ 35. And fair Ferdinand will be detached,
    To abandon the flower, to follow the Macedonian:[11]
    In the great pinch his course will fail,
    And he will march against the Myrmidons.[12]

36. A great King taken by the hands of a young man,
    Not far from Easter confusion knife thrust:
    Everlasting captive times what lightning on the top,
    When three brothers will wound each other and murder.

[1]The Tin Islands of St. George (patron of England since the 14th century)? See Commentary.

[2]Hungary and Bohemia-Moravia. See note for 427 and Commentary.

[3]I.e., the surname of the one-time (58-49 B.C.) ruler of Gaul, *Caesar* or *Imperator*, title borne by the (Holy) Roman Emperor. See Commentary.

[4]Or "the wave."

[5]Venice, whose patron is St. Mark.

[6]Or possibly "The solitary."

[7]For the "Tuileries" reading of this line, see Commentary.

[8]Or possibly "one traitor."

[9]The surname Sauce? See Commentary on this remarkable quatrain.

[10]Or possibly, as Garencières suggests, "by the quintal" (using the 1605 *contaux* as a Nostradamian derivative from Arabic *qíntar*).

[11]Probably the Spaniard is intended.

[12]Achilles' tribe, renowned for their unquestioning obedience to all commands. Probably intended by Nostradamus interchangeably with "the Macedonian."

37. Pont et moulins en Décembre versés,
    En si haut lieu montera la *Garonne:*
    Murs, édifices, *Tolose* renversés,
    Qu'on ne saura son lieu autant matrone.

38. L'entrée de *Blaye* par *Rochelle* et l'*Anglois,*
    Passera outre le grand *Aemathien:*[1]
    Non loin d'*Agen* attendra le *Gaulois,*
    Secours *Narbonne* déçu par entretien.

39. En *Arbissel* à *Veront* et *Carcari,*
    De nuit conduits pour *Sauone* attraper:
    Le vif *Gascon Turby* et *la Scerry:*
    Derrière mur vieux et neuf palais gripper.

40. Près de *Quintin* dans la forêt *bourlis,*[2]
    Dans l'Abbaye seront *Flamends* ranchés:[3]
    Les deux puînés de coups mi-étourdis,
    Suite oppressée et garde tous hachés.

41. Le grand *CHYREN* se saisir d'*Auignon,*
    De *Rome* lettres en miel plein d'amertume:
    Lettre ambassade partir de *Chanignon,*
    *Carpentras* pris par duc noir rouge plume.

42. De *Barcelonne,* de *Gennes* et *Venise,*
    De la *Secille* peste *Monet*[4] unis:
    Contre Barbare *classe*[5] prendront la vise,
    Barbare poussé bien loin jusqu'à *Thunis.*

43. Proche à descendre l'armée *Crucigere,*[6]
    Sera guettée par les *Ismaëlites,*
    De tous côtés battus par nef *Rauiere,*[7]
    Prompt assaillis de dix galères élites.

---

[1]Latin *Emathia,* poetic synonym for Macedonia (or Thessaly).
[2]Dubious. Possibly O.F. *boulé, deceived.* Proper name?
[3]Variant (Fortune): *tranchés.* Probably the correct form.
[4]Although uniform in all editions, probably erratum for *Monech,* from Latin *Portus Herculi Monoecis,* Monaco.
[5]Latin *classis,* fleet.
[6]Latin *crucem-gerens,* bearing a cross, Crusader.
[7]O.F. *raviere,* impetuosity.

37. Bridge and mills overturned in December,
The Garonne will rise to a very high place:
Walls, edifices, Toulouse overturned,
So that none will know his place like a matron.

38. The entry at Blaye for La Rochelle and the English,
The great Macedonian will pass beyond:
Not far from Agen will wait[1] the Gaul,
Narbonne help beguiled through conversation.

39. In Albisola to "Veront"[2] and Carcara,
Led by night to seize Savona:
The quick Gascon La Turbie and L'Escarène:
Behind the wall old and new palace to seize.

40. Near Saint-Quentin in the forest deceived,[3]
In the Abbey the Flemish will be cut up:
The two younger sons half-stunned by blows,
The rest crushed and the guard all cut to pieces.

☞ 41. The great "Chyren"[4] will seize Avignon,
From Rome letters in honey full of bitterness:
Letter and embassy to leave from "Chanignon,"[5]
Carpentras taken by a black duke with a red feather.

☞ 42. From Barcelona, from Genoa and Venice,
From Sicily pestilence Monaco[6] joined:
They will take their aim against the Barbarian fleet,
Barbarian driven 'way back as far as Tunis.

43. On the point of landing the Crusader army
Will be ambushed by the Ishmaelites,[7]
Struck from all sides by the ship Impetuosity,[8]
Rapidly attacked by ten elite galleys.

[1]Or "he will await."
[2]Not Verona, all the other places being to the west of Albisola and close. Still unsolved.
[3]Or possibly "the forest of 'Bourlis.'"
[4]Anagram for *Henry (Henri)*.
[5]Unsolved place name, or enigmatic proper name.
[6]Not quite certain. See note 4, opposite.
[7]Biblical name for the Arabs, who themselves recognize Ishmael, son of Abraham and Hagar, as their ancestor.
[8]This seems to suggest that Nostradamus is perhaps here seeking to name the flagship of a fleet.

44. Migrez, migrez de *Geneue trestous*,[1]
    Saturne d'or en fer se changera,
    Le contre *RAYPOZ*[2] exterminera tous,
    Avant l'avent le ciel signes fera.

45. Ne sera seul jamais de demander,
    Grand *MENDOSVS*[3] obtiendra son empire:
    Loin de la cour fera contremander
    *Piedmont, Picard, Paris, Tyrron*[4] le pire.

46. Videz, fuyez de *Tolose* les rouges,
    Du sacrifice faire expiation:
    Le chef du mal dessous l'ombre des courges:
    Mort étrangler *carne omination.*[5]

47. Les soussignés d'indigne délivrance,
    Et de la *multe*[6] auront contre avis:
    Change monarque mis en péril *pence*,[7]
    Serrés en cage se verront vis à vis.

48. La grande cité d'Océan maritime,
    Environnée de marais en cristal:
    Dans le solstice *hyemal*[8] et la *prime*,[9]
    Sera tentée de vent *espouvantal.*[10]

49. *Gand* et *Bruceles* marcheront contre *Anuers*,
    Sénat de *Londres* mettront à mort leur Roi:
    Le sel et vin lui seront à l'envers,
    Pour eux avoir le regne en désarroi.

[1]O.F. *trestous*, every single one.

[2]Anagram. Le Pelletier sees it for Paris, Raynaud-Plense for Zopyra, who betrayed Babylon to Darius. Variant: *FAYPOZ*.

[3]Latin *mendosus*, full of faults, erroneous. Also an anagram for Vendôme, the Bourbon branch which won the throne in 1594.

[4]Variants: *Tyrhen; Tyrton* (Fortune). Probably from Latin *Tyrrheni*, Etrurians (thus Tuscan, Florentine).

[5]Latin *carnis ominatio*, prognostic of flesh.

[6]Latin *multus*, many, i.e., mob.

[7]O.F. *pense*, thought. Or possibly, if Nostradamus had a smattering of English, Anglo-Saxon *pence* (pennies).

[8]Latin *hiemalis*, of winter.

[9]O.F. *prime*, Spring (Godefroy).

[10]O.F. *espouvantal*, frightful.

44. Leave, leave Geneva every last one of you,
    Saturn will be converted from gold to iron,
    "Raypoz"[1] will exterminate all who oppose him,
    Before the coming the sky will show signs.

45. None will remain to ask,
    Great "Mendosus"[2] will obtain his dominion:
    Far from the court he will cause to be countermanded
    Piedmont, Picardy, Paris, Tuscany[3] the worst.

46. Be gone, flee from Toulouse ye red ones,[4]
    For the sacrifice to make expiation:
    The chief cause of the evil under the shade of pumpkins:
    Dead to strangle carnal prognostication.

47. The undersigned to an infamous deliverance,
    And having contrary advice from the multitude:
    Monarch changes put in danger over thought,[5]
    Shut up in a cage they will see each other face to face.

48. The great city of the maritime Ocean,
    Surrounded by a crystalline swamp:
    In the winter solstice and the spring,
    It will be tried by frightful wind.

☞ 49. Ghent and Brussels will march against Antwerp,
    The Senate of London will put to death their King:
    Salt and wine will overthrow him,
    To have them the realm turned upside down.

[1]"Zopyra"? "Faypoz"? See note opposite, and Commentary.
[2]Or perhaps "Vendôme the Faulty."
[3]Not quite certain. See note 4, opposite.
[4]Or "flee from the red ones of Toulouse."
[5]Or possibly "over pennies."

50. *MENDOSVS*[1] tôt viendra à son haut regne,
    Mettant arrière un peu les *Norlaris:*[2]
    Le rouge blême, le mâle à l'interrègne,
    Le jeune crainte et frayeur *Barbaris.*[3]

51. Contre les rouges sectes se banderont,[4]
    Feu, eau, fer, corde par paix se minera:[5]
    Au point mourir ceux qui machineront,
    Fors un que monde surtout ruinera.

52. La paix s'approche d'un côté, et la guerre,
    Onc ne fut la poursuite si grande:
    Plaindre homme, femme sang innocent par terre,
    Et ce sera de *France* à toute bande.

53. Le *Neron* jeune dans les trois cheminées,
    Fera de pages vifs pour *ardoir*[6] jeter:
    Heureux qui loin sera de tels menées,
    Trois de son sang le feront mort guetter.

54. Arrivera au port de *Corsibonne,*[7]
    Près de *Rauenne,* qui pillera la dame:
    En mer profonde légat de la *Vlisbonne,*[8]
    Sous roc cachés raviront septante âmes.

55. L'horrible guerre qu'en l'Occident s'apprête,
    L'an ensuivant viendra la pestilence
    Si fort horrible que jeune, vieux, ni bête,
    Sang, feu *Mercure, Mars, Iupiter* en *France.*

56. Camp près de *Noudam* passera *Goussanville,*
    Et à *Maiotes*[9] laissera son enseigne:
    Convertira en instant plus de mille,
    Cherchant les deux remettre en chaîne et *legne.*[10]

---

[1]Latin *mendosus,* full of faults, erroneous. Also an anagram for Vendôme, the Bourbon branch which won the throne in 1594.

[2]Anagram for *Lorraine.*

[3]Apparently Nostradamian variant of *Barbare,* to make the rime.

[4]O.F. *se bander,* to league together, conspire (Sainte-Palaye).

[5]O.F. *se miner,* to destroy, ruin (Sainte-Palaye); to weaken (Godefroy).

[6]O.F. *ardoir,* to burn.

[7]*Porto Corsini,* the port of Ravenna.

[8]Presumably from Latin *Olisipo,* Lisbon (*Olisipona* under Goths).

[9]Either an erratum for *Mantes* (or an unsolved place name) or, as Le Pelletier suggests, from Greek *memaotes,* eager soldiers.

[10]Provençal *legna,* firewood.

☞ 50. "Mendosus"[1] will soon come to his high realm,
Putting behind a little the Lorrainers:
The pale red one, the male in the interregnum,
The fearful youth and Barbaric terror.

☞ 51. Against the red ones sects[2] will conspire,
Fire, water, steel, rope through peace will weaken:
On the point of dying those who will plot,
Except one who above all the world will ruin.

52. Peace is nigh on one side, and war,
Never was the pursuit of it so great:
To bemoan men, women innocent blood on the land,
And this will be throughout all France.

53. The young Nero in the three chimneys
Will cause live pages to be thrown to burn:
Happy those who will be far away from such practices,
Three of his blood will have him ambushed to death.

54. There will arrive at Porto Corsini,
Near Ravenna, he who will plunder the lady:
In the deep sea legate from Lisbon,
Hidden under a rock they will carry off seventy souls.

55. The horrible war which is being prepared in the West,
The following year will come the pestilence
So very horrible that young, old, nor beast,
Blood, fire Mercury, Mars, Jupiter in France.

56. The army near Houdan will pass Goussainville,
And at "Maiotes"[3] it will leave its mark:[4]
In an instant more than a thousand will be converted,
Looking for the two to put them back in chain and firewood.

[1] Or possibly "Vendôme the Faulty."
[2] Or "Against the red sects they."
[3] At Mantes? Or possibly "And to the Eager Soldiers."
[4] Or possibly "he will show his standard."

57.  Au lieu de *DRVX* un Roi reposera,
     Et cherchera loi changeant d'Anathème:
     Pendant le ciel si très fort tonnera,
     Portée neuve Roi tuera soi-même.

58.  Au côté gauche à l'endroit de *Vitry*,
     Seront guettés les trois rouges de *France*:
     Tous assomés rouge, noir non meurtri,
     Par les *Bretons* remis en assurance.

59.  À *la Ferté* prendra la *Vidame*,
     *Nicol* tenu rouge qu'avait produit la vie:
     La grande *Loyse* naîtra qui fera *clame*,[1]
     Donnant *Bourgongne* à *Bretons* par envie.

60.  Conflit Barbare en la Cornette noire,
     Sang épandu, trembler la *Dalmatie*:
     Grand *Ismael* mettra son promontoire,
     *Ranes*[2] trembler secours *Lusitanie*.

61.  La *pille*[3] faite à la côte marine,
     En *cita nova* et parents amenés:
     Plusieurs de *Malte* par le fait de *Messine*,
     Étroit serrés seront mal guerdonnés.

62.  Au grand de *Cheramon agora*,
     Seront croisés par rang tous attachés,
     Le *pertinax*[4] *Oppi*,[5] et *Mandragora*,[6]
     *Raugon*[7] d'*Octobre* le tiers seront lâchés.

63.  Plaintes et pleurs, cris et grands hurlements,
     Près de *Narbon* à *Bayonne* et en *Foix*:
     O quels horribles calamités changements,
     Avant que *Mars* révolu quelques fois.

[1]Latin *clam*, secretly.
[2]Latin *rana*, frog.
[3]O.F. *pille*, pillage, plunder.
[4]Latin *pertinax*, long-lasting.
[5]Greek *opion*, opium.
[6]Greek *mandragoras*, mandrake.
[7]Unsolved place name or derivative from Greek. Possibly *roge*, rent, cleft; or the Rogonis River (modern, Bender-rik).

57. In the place of "Drux"[1] a King will rest,
    And will look for a law changing Anathema:
    While the sky will thunder so very loudly,
    New entry the King will kill himself.

58. On the left side at the spot of Vitry,
    The three red ones of France will be awaited:
    All felled red, black one not murdered,
    By the Bretons restored to safety.[2]

59. At La Ferté-Vidame he will seize,[3]
    Nicholas held red who had produced his life:
    The[4] great Louise who will act secretly one will be born,
    Giving Burgundy to the Bretons through envy.

60. Conflict Barbarian in the black Headdress,
    Blood shed, Dalmatia to tremble:
    Great Ishmael[5] will set up his promontory,
    Frogs to tremble Lusitania aid.

61. The plunder made upon the marine coast,
    In Cittanova and relatives brought forward:
    Several of Malta through the deed of Messina
    Will be closely confined poorly rewarded.

62. To the great one of Ceramon-agora,[6]
    The crusaders will all be attached by rank,
    The long-lasting Opium and Mandrake,
    The "Raugon"[7] will be released on the third of October.

63. Complaints and tears, cries and great howls,
    Near Narbonne at Bayonne and in Foix:
    Oh, what horrible calamities and changes,
    Before Mars has made several revolutions.

[1]Dreux may be intended. See Commentary.
[2]Or possibly "By the Bretons reassured."
[3]Or possibly "At La Ferté he will seize the Vidame" (in which case La Ferté could still be La Ferté-Vidame, or one of the twenty-three others).
[4]Or possibly "To the"?
[5]The son of Abraham and Hagar, recognized by the Arabs as their ancestor.
[6]In modern times, probably the Turkish town of Ushak.
[7]Dubious. "The Cleft"? "The Bender"? See note 7, opposite.

64. L'*AEmathion*[1] passer monts *Pyrenées,*
En Mars *Narbon*[2] ne fera résistance:
Par mer et terre fera si grande menée,
*Cap.*[3] n'ayant terre sûre pour *demeurance.*[4]

65. Dedans le coin de *Luna* viendra rendre,
Où sera pris et mis en terre étrange:
Les fruits immûrs seront à grand esclandre,
Grand vitupère, à l'un grande louange.

66. Paix, union sera et changement,
États, offices, bas haut, et haut bien bas:
Dresser voyage, le fruit premier tourment,
Guerre cesser, civil procès, débats.

67. Du haut des monts à l'entour de *Lizere,*
Port à la roche *Valent* cent assemblés:
De *Chasteau neuf Pierre late* en[5] *donzere,*
Contre le *Crest, Romans, foy*[6] assemblés.

68. Du mont *Aymar*[7] sera noble obscurcie,
Le mal viendra au joint de *Saone* et *Rosne:*
Dans bois cachés soldats jour de *Lucie,*
Qui ne fut onc si horrible trône.

69. Sur le mont de *Bailly* et *la Bresle*
Seront cachés de *Grenoble* les fiers:
Outre *Lyon, Vien* eux si grande grêle,
*Langoult*[8] en terre n'en restera un tiers.

[1]Latin *Emathius,* Macedonian.
[2]Possibly Latin *Narbo Martius,* Narbonne.
[3]Probably apocope of *Capet.*
[4]O.F. *demeurance,* residence.
[5]Although uniform in all editions, possibly erratum for *et.*
[6]Le Pelletier thinks this should be read "Foix," but the latter is quite distant (all the places here being in L'Isère). Probably it is just *foi,* to line up "Crest" and "Romans" with the Catholic Faith.
[7]Le Pelletier suggests Greek *aima,* bloodshed and thus slaughter. Garencières sees a play on *Montélimar,* equally sensible.
[8]Apparently Nostradamian variant of *langouste,* locust in Old French, lobster in the modern.

64. The Macedonian to pass the Pyrenees mountains,
    In March Narbonne[1] will not offer resistance:
    By land and sea he will carry on very great intrigue,
    Capetian[2] having no land safe for residence.

65. He will come to go into the corner of "Luna,"[3]
    Where he will be captured and put in a strange land:
    The unripe fruits will be the subject of great scandal,
    Great blame, to one great praise.

66. There will be peace, union and change,
    Estates, offices, low high and high very low:
    To prepare a trip, the first offspring torment,
    War to cease, civil process, debates.

67. From the height of the mountains around the Isère,
    One hundred assembled at the haven in the rock Valence:
    From Châteauneuf, Pierrelatte, in[4] Donzère,
    Against Crest, Romans, faith assembled.

68. The noble of "Mount Aymar"[5] will be made obscure,
    The evil will come at the junction of the Saône and Rhône:[6]
    Soldiers hidden in the woods on Lucy's day,[7]
    Never was there so horrible a throne.

69. On the mountain of Sain-Bel and L'Arbresle[8]
    The proud ones of Grenoble will be hidden:
    Beyond Lyons and Vienne on them a very great hail,
    Lobster[9] on the land not a third thereof will remain.

---

[1]Or "In Narbonne." See note 2, opposite.
[2]Uncertain but probable.
[3]The possibilities here are numerous. Possibly Lunigiana.
[4]Or possibly "and"?
[5]Or possibly "Montélimart"? Or "by the mountain of slaughter"?
[6]I.e., at Lyons.
[7]December 13 is the day of St. Lucy.
[8]The most likely of the several possible combinations.
[9]Or "Locust."

70. Harnois tranchants dans les flambeaux cachés,
    Dedans *Lyon*, le jour du Sacrement,
    Ceux de *Vienne* seront *trestous*[1] hachés,
    Par les cantons *Latins Mascon* ne ment.

71. Aux lieux sacrés animaux vu à *trixe*,[2]
    Avec celui qui n'osera le jour:
    À *Carcassonne* pour disgrâce propice,
    Sera posé pour plus ample séjour.

72. Encore seront les saints temples pollus,
    Et *expillez*[3] par Sénat *Tholosain*:
    *Saturne* deux trois cycles révolus,
    Dans Avril, Mai, gens de nouveau levain.

73. Dans *Fois* entré Roi *ceiulee*[4] Turban,
    Et regnera moins évolu *Saturne*:
    Roi Turban blanc *Bizance* cœur *ban*,[5]
    *Sol*,[6] *Mars*, *Mercure* près *la hurne*.[7]

74. Dans la cité de *Fertsod*[8] homicide,
    Fait, et fait *multe*[9] bœuf *arant*[10] ne *macter*:[11]
    Retour encore aux honneurs d'*Artemide*,
    Et à *Vulcan* corps morts *sepulturer*.[12]

75. De l'*Ambraxie* et du pays de *Thrace*
    Peuple par mer, mal et secours *Gaulois*:
    Perpétuelle en *Prouence* la trace,
    Avec vestiges de leur coutume et lois.

[1]O.F. *trestous*, every single one, all.
[2]Greek *thrix*, hair, wool.
[3]Latin *expilare*, to plunder, pillage, rob.
[4]Variant ("1568" and Fortune): *cerulee* from Latin *caeruleus*, blue.
[5]O.F. *ban*, punishment, exile, banishment (and many other meanings).
[6]Latin *Sol*, Sun.
[7]Nostradamian elongation of *l'urne* to get another syllable in.
[8]Dubious. The second syllable can only be from *Sodom*. The first may be Latin *fertus* rich, fertile, or apocope of one of the twenty-four La Fertés in France.
[9]Latin *multus*, many.
[10]Latin *arare*, to plow.
[11]Latin *mactare*, to sacrifice.
[12]O.F. *sepulturer*, to bury.

70. Sharp weapons hidden in the torches.
    In Lyons, the day of the Sacrament,[1]
    Those of Vienne will all be cut to pieces,
    By the Latin Cantons[2] Mâcon does not lie.

71. At the holy places animals seen with hair,[3]
    With him who will not dare the day:
    At Carcassonne propitious for disgrace,
    He will be set for a more ample stay.

72. Again will the holy temples be polluted,
    And plundered by the Senate of Toulouse:
    Saturn two three cycles completed,
    In April, May, people of new leaven.[4]

73. The Blue Turban King entered into Foix,
    And he will reign less than an evolution of Saturn:
    The White Turban King Byzantium heart banished,
    Sun, Mars and Mercury near Aquarius.[5]

74. In the city of "Fertsod"[6] homicide,
    Deed, and deed many oxen plowing no sacrifice:
    Return again to the honors of Artemis,
    And to Vulcan bodies dead ones to bury.

75. From Ambracia[7] and the country of Thrace
    People by sea, evil and help from the Gauls:
    In Provence the perpetual trace,
    With vestiges of their custom and laws.

[1] Assumed to mean Corpus Christi day, celebrated on the first Thursday after Trinity Sunday, with many processions.
[2] Possibly the Grisons, where almost all of the Ladin-speaking and Romansch-speaking Swiss live.
[3] Or "wool." Sheep being shorn?
[4] I.e., the Protestants, in dispute over the Eucharist.
[5] Literally "near the urn." Another conjunction is obviously intended here.
[6] "Rich Sodom"? "La Ferté-'Sodome' "?
[7] Modern Arta.

76. Avec le noir[1] *Rapax*[2] et sanguinaire,
    Issu du *peaultre*[3] de l'inhumain *Neron:*
    *Emmy*[4] deux fleuves main gauche militaire,
    Sera meurtri par Jeune *chaulveron.*[5]

77. Le regne pris le Roi conjurera,[6]
    La dame prise à mort jurés à sort:
    La vie à Reine fils on déniera,
    Et la *pellix*[7] au fort de la *consort.*[8]

78. La dame *Grecque* de beauté *laydique,*[9]
    Heureuse faite de *procs*[10] innombrable:
    Hors *translatee*[11] au regne *Hispanique,*
    Captive prise mourir mort misérable.

79. Le chef de *classe*[12] par fraude stratagème,
    Fera timides sortir de leurs galères:
    Sortis meurtris chef renieur de chrême,
    Puis par l'embûche lui rendront le salaire.

80. Le Duc voudra les siens exterminer,
    Envoyera les plus forts lieux étranges:
    Par tyrannie *Bize* et *Luc* ruiner,
    Puis les Barbares sans vin feront vendanges.

81. Le Roi rusé entendra ses embûches,
    De trois quartiers ennemis assaillir:
    Un nombre étrange larmes de coqueluches,
    Viendra *Lemprin*[13] du traducteur faillir.

[1]Here probably again an anagram for *roi/roy.*
[2]Latin *rapax,* rapacious.
[3]O.F. *peaultre,* pallet; brothel.
[4]O.F. *emmi,* between.
[5]Nostradamian diminutive of *chauve,* bald.
[6]Variant: *conviera.*
[7]Latin *pellex,* concubine, kept mistress.
[8]O.F. *consorte,* wife (Godefroy).
[9]Latin *Laidis,* of Lais, the most beautiful woman of Corinth, or Nostradamian agglutinative of *laid,* ugly.
[10]Latin *procus,* suitor.
[11]Latin *translatus,* transferred.
[12]Latin *classis,* fleet.
[13]Possibly from Greek *lampros,* brilliancy, splendor, grandeur.

76. With the rapacious and blood-thirsty king,[1]
    Issued from the pallet of the inhuman Nero:
    Between two rivers military hand left,
    He will be murdered by Young Baldy.[2]

☞ 77. The realm taken the King will conspire,[3]
    The lady taken to death ones sworn by lot:
    They will refuse life to the Queen and son,[4]
    And the mistress at the fort of the wife.

☞ 78. The Greek lady of ugly beauty,[5]
    Made happy by countless suitors:
    Transferred out to the Spanish realm,
    Taken captive to die a miserable death.

79. The chief of the fleet through deceit and trickery
    Will make the timid ones come out of[6] their galleys:
    Come out, murdered, the chief renouncer of chrism,
    Then through ambush they will pay him his wages.

80. The Duke will want to exterminate his followers,
    He will send the strongest ones to strange places:
    Through tyranny to ruin Pisa and Lucca,
    Then the Barbarians will gather the grapes without vine.

81. The crafty King will understand his snares,
    Enemies to assail from three sides:
    A strange number tears from hoods,[7]
    The grandeur[8] of the translator will come to fail.

[1]Or possibly "black one"?
[2]Or possibly "Baldy will be murdered by a Young Man."
[3]Or possibly "will make advances."
[4]Or possibly "to the Queen's son."
[5]Or "of the beauty of Lais."
[6]Or possibly "with."
[7]I.e., monks (probably).
[8]Not certain. See note 13, opposite.

82. Par le déluge et pestilence forte,
    La cité grande de long temps assiégée:
    La sentinelle et garde de main morte,
    Subite prise, mais de nulle outragée.

83. *Sol* vingt de *Taurus* si fort terre trembler,
    Le grand théâtre rempli ruinera:
    L'air, ciel et terre obscurcir et troubler,
    Lors l'infidèle Dieu et saints *voguera*.[1]

84. Roi exposé parfera l'hécatombe,
    Après avoir trouvé son origine:
    Torrent ouvrir de marbre et plomb la tombe,
    D'un grand *Romain* d'enseigne *Medusine*.[2]

85. Passer *Guienne, Languedoc* et le *Rosne,*
    D'*Agen* tenant de *Marmande* et *la Roole:*
    D'ouvrir par foi *parroy*,[3] *Phocen*[4] tiendra son trône,
    Conflit auprès *sainct Pol de Mauseole*.[5]

86. Du *bourg Lareyne* parviendront droit à *Chartres,*
    Et feront près du pont *Anthoni* pause:
    Sept pour la paix cauteleux comme Martres,
    Feront entrée d'armée à *Paris* close.

87. Par la forêt du *Touphon*[6] essartée,
    Par ermitage sera posé le temple:
    Le Duc d'*Estampes* par sa ruse inventée,
    Du *mont Lehori* prélat *donra*[7] exemple.

[1]Variant (Fortune): *voquera.* From Latin *vocare,* to call upon, invoke.
[2]Dubious. Possibly from Latin *Medusaeus,* of Medusa (whose serpent-topped head turned all onlookers to stone) or her offspring, the flying horse Pegasus. Or possibly, as Lee McCann suggested, the anagram of *Deus in Me* (which would tie in with *D.M.* in 866).
[3]O.F. *parroy,* the seashore (Sainte-Palaye); *parroi,* wall, partition (Roquefort).
[4]For *Port Phocen,* common Nostradamian epithet for Marseilles, founded by Phocaeans.
[5]Variant: *de Manseole.*
[6]Dubious. Garencières mentions a Forêt du Torfou some thirty miles from Paris. There is a Torfou, but no forest by that name. Le Pelletier suggests Greek *tophion,* plaster quarry. It could also be derived from the French word *touffe,* tuft, clump.
[7]Syncope of *donnera.*

82. By the flood and fierce pestilence,
    The great city for long besieged:
    The sentry and guard dead by hand,
    Sudden capture but none wronged.

83. Sun twentieth of Taurus[1] the earth will tremble very mightily,
    It will ruin the great theater filled:
    To darken and trouble air, sky and land,
    Then the infidel will call upon God and saints.

☞ 84. The King exposed will complete the slaughter,
    After having discovered his origin:
    Torrent to open the tomb of marble and lead,
    Of a great Roman with "Medusine" device.[2]

85. To pass Guienne, Languedoc and the Rhône,
    From Agen holding Marmande and La Réole:
    To open through faith the wall,[3] Marseilles will hold its[4] throne,
    Conflict near Saint-Paul-de-Mausole.[5]

86. From Bourg-la-Reine they will come straight to Chartres,
    And near Pont d'Antony they will pause:
    Seven crafty as Martens for peace,
    Paris closed by an army they will enter.

87. In the forest cleared of the Tuft,[6]
    By the hermitage will be placed the temple:
    The Duke of Étampes through the ruse he invented
    Will teach a lesson to the prelate of Montlhéry.

[1]The Sun enters Taurus on April 20. The "twentieth" may be to confirm this, or signify twenty days later, i.e., May 10.
[2]"Device of Medusa"? "Device of Pegasus"? "Device of 'Deus in Me'"?
[3]Or "seashore."
[4]Or "his."
[5]A convent, subsequently an insane asylum (where the painter Van Gogh was confined shortly before his suicide in 1890), outside Nostradamus' birthplace, Saint-Rémy.
[6]Uncertain. "In the cleared Forest of Torfou"? See note opposite.

88.  *Calais, Arras,* secours à *Theroanne,*
     Paix et semblant simulera l'*escoute:*[1]
     *Soulde*[2] d'*Alobrox*[3] descendre par *Roane,*
     Détourné peuple qui défera la *routte.*[4]

89.  Sept ans sera *Philipp.*[5] fortune prospère,
     Rebaissera des *Arabes*[6] l'effort:
     Puis son midi perplexe rebours affaire,
     Jeune *ogmion* abîmera son fort.

90.  Un capitaine de la Grande *Germanie*
     Se viendra rendre par simulé secours
     Au Roi des Rois aide de *Pannonie,*
     Que sa révolte fera de sang grand cours.

91.  L'horrible peste *Perynté* et *Nicopolle,*
     Le Chersonèse tiendra et *Marceloyne:*[7]
     La *Thessalie vastera*[8] l'*Amphipolle,*
     Mal inconnu, et le refus d'*Anthoine.*

92.  Le Roi voudra en cité neuve entrer,
     Par ennemis *expugner*[9] l'on viendra:
     Captif libre faux dire et perpétrer,
     Roi dehors être, loin d'ennemis tiendra.

93.  Les ennemis du fort bien éloignés,
     Par chariots conduit le bastion:
     Par sur[10] les murs de *Bourges* égrenés,
     Quand *Hercules* battra l'*Haemathion.*[11]

94.  Faibles galères seront unies ensemble,
     Ennemis faux le plus fort en rempart:
     Faibles assailies *Vratislaue* tremble,
     *Lubecq* et *Mysne* tiendront barbare part.

---

[1] O.F. *escoute,* spy (Roquefort).
[2] O.F. *soulde,* pay (especially for soldiers, and by extension:) mercenary soldiers.
[3] Latin *Allobrox,* the inhabitants of classical Savoy.
[4] O.F. *route,* rout (Godefroy).
[5] Variant: *PHILIP* (no period).
[6] Variant: *BARBARES.*
[7] Assumed by both Garencières and Le Pelletier to be for *Macedoine.*
[8] Latin *vastare,* to destroy, devastate, ruin.
[9] Latin *expugnare,* to storm, capture, reduce, subdue, violate.
[10] Undoubtedly for *par-dessus.*
[11] Latin *Emathius.* Macedonian.

88. Calais, Arras, help to Thérouanne,
    Peace and semblance the spy will simulate:
    The soldiery of Savoy to descend by Roanne,
    People who would end the rout deterred.

☞ 89. For seven years fortune will favor Philip,
    He will beat down again the exertions of the Arabs:[1]
    Then at his noon[2] perplexing contrary affair
    Young Ogmios[3] will destroy his stronghold.

90. A captain of Great Germany
    Will come to deliver through false help
    To the King of Kings the support of Pannonia,[4]
    So that his revolt will cause a great flow of blood.

91. The horrible plague Perinthus[5] and Nicopolis,[6]
    The Peninsula[7] and Macedonia will it fall upon:
    It will devastate Thessaly and Amphipolis,[8]
    An unknown evil, and from Anthony refusal.

92. The King will want to enter the new city,
    Through its[9] enemies they will come to subdue it:[9]
    Captive free falsely to speak and act,
    King to be outside, he will keep far from the enemy.

93. The enemies very far from the fort,
    The bastion brought by wagons:
    Above the walls of Bourges crumbled,
    When Hercules the Macedonian will strike.

94. Weak galleys will be joined together,
    False enemies the strongest on the rampart:
    Weak ones assailed Bratislava trembles,
    Lübeck and Meissen will take the barbarian side.

[1] Or "Barbarians."
[2] This presumably means his middle age. Or possibly "his south."
[3] The Celtic Hercules.
[4] Classical Hungary.
[5] Modern Eski Eregli.
[6] Modern Preveza.
[7] The reference may be either to the (Thracian) Chersonese (the classical name for the Gallipoli peninsula) or to the Peloponnesus.
[8] Near the modern Salonika.
[9] Or "his . . . him."

95. Le nouveau fait conduira l'*exercite*,[1]
    Proche *apamé*[2] jusqu'auprès du rivage:
    Tendant secours de *Millannoile*[3] élite,
    Duc yeux privé à *Milan* fer de cage.

96. Dans cité entrer *exercit*[4] déniée,
    Duc entrera par persuasion:
    Aux faibles portes *clam*[5] armée amenée,
    Mettront feu, mort, de sang effusion.

97. De mer *copies*[6] en trois parts divisées,
    À la seconde les vivres failliront,
    Désespérés cherchant champs *Helisees*,
    Premiers en brèche entrés victoire auront.

98. Les affligés par faute d'un seul teint,
    *Contremenant*[7] à partie opposite:
    Aux *Lygonnois*[8] mandera que contraint
    Seront de rendre le grand chef de *Molite*.[9]

99. Vent Aquilon[10] fera partir le siège,
    Par murs jeter cendres, chaux et poussière:
    Par pluie après, qui leur fera bien *piege*,[11]
    Dernier secours encontre leur frontière.

100. Navale *pugne*[12] nuit sera *superée*,[13]
     Le feu aux *naves*[14] à l'Occident ruine:
     Rubriche neuve, la grande nef colorée,
     Ire à vaincu, et victoire en bruine.

[1]Latin *exercitus*, army.
[2]Greek *apamao*, to cut off.
[3]Both Garencières and Le Pelletier agree again that this can only be for *Milanoise*
(Milanais).
[4]Latin *exercitus*, army.
[5]Latin *clam*, secretly.
[6]Latin *copia*, troops, forces, army.
[7]Probably an erratum for *contrevenant*.
[8]Either *Lyonnais* or from *Lingones*, classical tribe around Langres.
[9]Dubious. Possibly from Greek *molos*, war, or Latin *Melita*, Malta.
[10]Latin *Aquilon*, north, north wind.
[11]Provençal *piegi*, worse.
[12]Latin *pugna*, battle.
[13]Latin *superatus*, conquered, overcome.
[14]Latin *naves*, ships.

95. The newly made one[1] will lead the army,
    Almost cut off up to near the bank:
    Help from the Milanais elite straining,
    The Duke deprived of his eyes in Milan in an iron cage.

96. The army denied entry to the city,
    The Duke will enter through persuasion:
    The army led secretly to the weak gates,
    They will put it to fire and sword, effusion of blood.

97. The forces of the sea divided into three parts,
    The second one will run out of supplies,
    In despair looking for the Elysian Fields,
    The first ones to enter the breach will obtain the victory.

98. Those afflicted through the fault of a single one stained,
    The transgressor in the opposite party:
    He will send word to those of Lyons[2] that compelled
    They be to deliver the great chief of "Molite."[3]

99. The "Aquilon"[4] Wind will cause the siege to be raised,
    Over the walls to throw ashes, lime and dust:
    Through rain afterwards, which will do them much worse,
    Last help against their frontier.

100. Naval battle night will be overcome,
     Fire in the ships to the West ruin:
     New trick, the great ship colored,
     Anger to the vanquished, and victory in a drizzle.

[1]Or "The new fact."
[2]Or "of Langres."
[3]"Chief of War"? "chief of Malta"? See note opposite.
[4]The North[ern Country], or in this case perhaps merely the north wind.

# Centurie X

1. À l'ennemi, l'ennemi foi promise
   Ne se tiendra, les captifs retenus:
   Pris *preme*[1] mort, et le reste en chemise,
   Damné le reste pour être soutenus.[2]

2. Voile galère voile de nef cachera,
   La grande *classe*[3] viendra sortir la moindre:
   Dix *naves*[4] proches le tourneront pousser,
   Grande vaincue unies à soi joindre.

3. En après cinq troupeau ne mettra hors,
   Un *fuytif*[5] pour *Penelon*[6] lâchera:
   Faux murmurer, secours venir par lors,
   Le chef le siège lors abandonnera.

4. Sur la minuit conducteur de l'armée
   Se sauvera subit évanoui:
   Sept ans après la fame non blamée,
   À son retour ne dira onc oui.

5. *Albi* et *Castres* feront nouvelle ligue,
   Neuf *Arriens Lis bon* et *Portugues*:
   *Carcas*,[7] *Tholose* consommeront leur brigue,
   Quand chef neuf monstre[8] de *Lauragues*.

6. *Sardon*[9] *Nemaus*[10] si haut déborderont,
   Qu'on *cuidera*[11] *Deucalion*, renaître:
   Dans le colosse la plus part fuiront,
   *Vesta* sépulcre feu éteint apparaître.

---

[1]O.F. *preme*, next, neighboring, close, near.

[2]The 1605 goes off on its own tack here again with *Donnant le reste pour être secourus*. This obviously does not rime as well.

[3]Latin *classis*, fleet.

[4]Latin *navis*, ship.

[5]O.F. *fuitif*, fugitive (Roquefort).

[6]Dubious enigma. Le Pelletier suggests an anagram for *Polone*, Poland, which is fairly reasonable.

[7]Apocope of *Carcassonne*.

[8]Le Pelletier notes that "some editions have *ira* here," but none of the five we have referred to has this.

[9]Probably an erratum for the *Gardon* (or *Gard*) river.

[10]Latin *Nemausus*, Nîmes.

[11]O.F. *cuider*, to think, believe.

# Century X

1. To[1] the enemy, the enemy faith promised
   Will not be kept, the captives retained:
   One near death captured, and the remainder in their shirts,
   The remainder damned for being supported.[2]

2. The ship's veil[3] will hide the sail galley,
   The great fleet will come the lesser one to go out:[4]
   Ten ships near will turn to drive it back,
   The great one conquered the united ones to join to itself.

3. After that five[5] will not put out the flock,
   A fugitive for "Penelon"[6] he will turn loose:
   To murmur falsely then help to come,
   The chief will then abandon the siege.

☞ 4. At midnight the leader of the army
   Will save himself, suddenly vanished:
   Seven years later his reputation unblemished,
   To his return they will never say yes.[7]

5. Albi and Castres will form a new league,
   Nine Arians[8] Lisbon and the Portuguese:
   Carcassonne and Toulouse will end their intrigue,
   When the chief new monster[9] from the Lauraguais.

6. The Gardon will flood Nîmes so high
   That they will believe Deucalion reborn:
   Into the colossus[10] the greater part will flee,
   Vesta tomb[11] fire to appear extinguished.

[1]Or possibly "By."
[2]Or, according to the 1605, "Giving the remainder to be relieved."
[3]Or "sail."
[4]Or possibly "The great fleet the lesser one will cause to come out."
[5]Probably meaning a ruler the fifth of his name.
[6]Poland? See note 6, opposite.
[7]The context would seem to make more likely "they will say naught but yes."
[8]Contemporary equivalents of either (1) the ancient heretics who held that Christ was not of the same substance as God; or (2) the Aryan people, speaking the parent language of the Indo-Europeans and dwelling in the vicinity of what is now Afghanistan.
[9]Or possibly, according to Le Pelletier's mysterious variant, "When the new chief will go out."
[10]The famous amphitheater of Nîmes, surviving from Roman times.
[11]Probably meaning a tomb with an "eternal flame" such as that kept by the priestesses of Vesta.

7. Le grand conflit qu'on apprête à *Nancy*,
   *L'Aemathien*[1] dira tout je soumets:
   *L'Isle Britanne* par vin, sel en souci,
   *Hem. mi.*[2] deux *Phi.*[3] longtemps ne tiendra *Mets.*

8. Index et pouce *parfondera*[4] le front,
   De *Senegalia* le Comte à son fils propre:
   La *Myrnamée*[5] par plusieurs de *prin*[6] front,
   Trois dans sept jours blessés *more.*[7]

9. De *Castillon*[8] *figuieres* jour de brume,
   De femme infame naîtra souverain prince:
   Surnom de chausses *perhume*[9] lui posthume,
   Onc Roi ne fut si pire en sa province.

10. Tache de meurtre, enormes adultères,
    Grand ennemi de tout le genre humain:
    Que sera pire qu'aieuls, oncles ni pères,
    En fer,[10] feu, eaux, sanguin et inhumain.

11. Dessous *Ionchere* du dangereux passage,
    Fera passer le posthume sa bande:
    Les monts *Pyrens* passer hors son bagage,
    De *Parpignan* courira duc à *Tende.*

12. Élu en Pape, d'élu sera moqué,
    Subit soudain ému prompt et timide:
    Par trop bon doux à mourir provoqué,
    Crainte éteinte la nuit de sa mort guide.

[1]Latin *Emathius,* Macedonian.
[2]The possibilities here are many. O.F. *hemi,* half; or *emmi,* between?
[3]Almost certainly apocope for *Philip.*
[4]Latin *perfundere,* to moisten, wet, sprinkle.
[5]Latin *Mimnermia,* (a surname of) Venus, is the most likely derivation.
[6]O.F. *prin,* thin, small, delicate; *de prin front,* in short order.
[7]Variants: *mort; morts* ("1568," Garcin and Fortune). None rimes properly; *more* comes closest but it is not a variant form of *mort,* and neither of its O.F. meanings (marsh; minever fur) fits.
[8]Spanish *Castillo,* castle. Figueras is a sort of Spanish Verdun.
[9]Curious enigma. Possibly from Latin *per humum,* on the ground.
[10]Variant: *Enfer.*

☞ 7. The great conflict that they are preparing for Nancy,
The Macedonian will say I subjugate all:
The British Isle in anxiety over wine and salt,
"Hem. mi."[1] Philip[2] two Metz will not hold for long.

8. With forefinger and thumb he will moisten the forehead,
The Count of Senigallia to his own son:
The Venus[3] through several of thin forehead,[4]
Three in seven days wounded dead.

☞ 9. In the Castle of Figueras[5] on a misty day
A sovereign prince will be born of an infamous woman:
Surname of breeches[6] on the ground will make him posthumous,
Never was there a King so very bad in his province.

10. Stained with murder and enormous adulteries,
Great enemy of the entire human race:
One who will be worse than his grandfathers, uncles or fathers,
In steel,[7] fire, waters, bloody and inhuman.

11. At the dangerous passage below Junquera,
The posthumous one will have his band cross:
To pass the Pyrenees mountains without his baggage,
From Perpignan the duke will hasten to Tende.

12. Elected Pope, as elected he will be mocked,
Suddenly unexpectedly moved prompt and timid:
Through too much goodness and kindness provoked to die,
Fear extinguished guides the night of his death.

[1]"Half"? "Between"? See note 2, opposite.
[2]Or possibly "Between two Philips." See Commentary.
[3]Not quite certain, but most likely. See note 5, opposite.
[4]"Small brain"? Or "several in short order."
[5]The famous fortress, the Castillo de San Fernando, was built only in the 18th century, but doubtless some fort existed there before. It is now a prison. See Commentary.
[6]Or "stockings."
[7]Or "Hell."

13. Sous la pâture d'animaux ruminants,
    Par eux conduits au ventre[1] *herbipolique:*[2]
    Soldats cachés, les armes bruit menant,
    Non loin tentés de cité *Antipolique.*[3]

14. *Vrnel Vaucile*[4] sans conseil de soi-même,
    Hardi timide, par crainte pris vaincu:
    Accompagné de plusieurs *putains*[5] blêmes,
    À *Barcellonne* au *Chartreux*[6] convaincu.

15. Père duc vieux d'ans et de soif chargé,
    Au jour extrême fils déniant l'aiguière:
    Dedans le puits vif mort viendra plongé,
    Sénat au fil[7] la mort longue et légère.

16. Heureux au regne de *France,* heureux de vie,
    Ignorant sang mort fureur et rapine:
    Par nom flatteurs[8] sera mis envie,
    Roi dérobé, trop de foi en cuisine,

17. Le Reine *Ergaste*[9] voyant sa fille blême,
    Par un regret dans l'estomac enclos:
    Cris lamentables seront lors d'*Angolesme,*
    Et au germain mariage forclos.

18. Le rang *Lorrain* fera place à *Vendosme,*
    Le haut mis bas, et le bas mis en haut:
    Le fils de *Mamon*[10] sera élu dans *Rome,*
    Et les deux grands seront mis en défaut.

19. Jour que sera par Reine saluée,
    Le jour après le salut, la prière:
    Le compte fait raison et *valbuée,*[11]
    *Paravant*[12] humble onc ne fut si fière.

---

[1]Possibly an erratum for *vente.*
[2]Possibly a compound of Latin *herba,* grass, and Greek *poleo,* to sell, or *polis,* city. Variant: *Helbipolique.*
[3]Latin *Antipolis,* Antibes.
[4]*Urnel* may be an erratum for Urgel. O.F. *vaucele,* valley. The two words may also be intended as an anagram.
[5]O.F. *putain,* prostitute, whore.
[6]*Chartreux* means Carthusian monk, while *Chartreuse* refers to a Carthusian convent, but the context seems to point to the latter.
[7]Possibly a play on *fils* should be understood here.
[8]Variant (Fortune): *flatteur,* most likely correct.
[9]Latin *ergastulum,* workhouse, penitentiary; *ergastulus,* convict. Variant: *étrange.*
[10]Variant: *Hamon.*
[11]Unsolved etymology, or corrupted text. Le Pelletier suggests *valable.*
[12]Apheresis for *auparavant.*

13. Beneath the food of ruminating animals,[1]
Led by them to the belly of the fodder city:[2]
Soldiers hidden, their arms making a noise,
Tried not far from the city of Antibes.

☞ 14. "Urnel Vaucile"[3] without a purpose of his own,
Bold, timid, through fear overcome and captured:
Accompanied by several pale whores,
Convinced[4] in the Carthusian convent at Barcelona.[5]

☞ 15. Father duke old in years and choked by thirst,
On his last day his son denying him the jug:
Into the well plunged alive he will come up dead,
Senate to[6] the thread[7] death long and light.

☞ 16. Happy in the realm of France, happy in life,
Ignorant of blood, death, fury and plunder:
For a flattering name[8] he will be envied,
A concealed[9] King,[10] too much faith in the kitchen.

☞ 17. The convict[11] Queen seeing her daughter pale,
Because of a sorrow locked up in her breast:
Lamentable cries will come then from Angoulême,
And the marriage to the first cousin impeded.

☞ 18. The house of Lorraine will make way for Vendôme,
The high put low, and the low put high:
The son of Mammon[12] will be elected in Rome,
And the two great ones will be put at a loss.

19. The day that she will be hailed as Queen,
The day after the benediction the prayer:
The reckoning is right and valid,[13]
Once humble never was one so proud.

[1] I.e., beneath the hay in a cart, drawn by oxen.
[2] Dubious. Or possibly "to the fodder-selling market."
[3] Llanos (plain) de Urgel? An anagram? See Commentary.
[4] Or "Convicted."
[5] At Monte Allegro, a few miles from Barcelona. Or "by the Carthusian."
[6] Or possibly "Senate the son to"? See note 7, opposite.
[7] I.e., has him strangled (or hanged).
[8] Or "Flatterers for his name."
[9] "Retired"?
[10] Or "A King robbed."
[11] Or "The foreign/strange."
[12] Or "Hamon" (probably Amon, the Egyptian sun god, with whom Jupiter was eventually identified and merged, i.e., pagans, i.e., heretics, i.e., Huguenots). See Commentary.
[13] By no means certain. See note 11, opposite.

20. Tous les amis qu'auront tenu parti,
    Pour rude en lettres mis mort et saccagé:
    Biens publiés par fixe grand *neanty*,[1]
    Onc *Romain* peuple ne fut tant outragé.

21. Par le dépit du Roi soutenant moindre,
    Sera meurtri lui présentant les bagues:
    Le père au fils voulant noblesse poindre,
    Faint comme à *Perse* jadis firent les *Magues*.

22. Pour ne vouloir consentir au divorce,
    Qui puis après sera connu indigne:
    Le Roi des Îles sera chassé par force,
    Mis à son lieu qui de roi n'aura signe.

23. Au peuple ingrat faites les remonstrances,
    Par lors l'armée se saisira d'*Antibe:*
    Dans l'arc *Monech*[2] feront des doléances,
    Et à *Freius* l'un l'autre prendra *ribe*.[3]

24. Le captif prince aux *Itales*[4] vaincu
    Passera *Gennes* par mer jusqu'à *Marseille:*
    Par grand effort des *forens*[5] *survaincu*,[6]
    Sauf coup de feu, baril liqueur d'abeille.

25. Par *Nebro*[7] ouvrir de *Bisanne*[8] passage,
    Bien éloignés *el tago fara muestra:*[9]
    Dans *Pelligouxe*[10] sera commis l'outrage,
    De la grande dame assise sur l'orchestra.

26. Le successeur vengera son beau frère,
    Occuper regne sous ombre de vengeance:
    Occis obstacle son sang mort vitupère,
    Longtemps *Bretaigne* tiendra avec la *France*.

[1]O.F. *neantir*, to annihilate.
[2]Latin *Portus Herculi Monoecis*, Monaco.
[3]Provençal *riba*, bank, shore, edge.
[4]To conform to an imaginative interpretation, perhaps derived from Latin *Aethalia*, Elba.
[5]O.F. *forain*, foreigner (Godefroy).
[6]Latin *supervinco*, to conquer, overcome.
[7]Almost certainly an anagram for the Ebro River. Or merely erratum for *l'Ebro*.
[8]Dubious. The closest would seem *Bézenas (Pézenas)*, on the French side of the Pyrenees. Variant: *Brisanne*.
[9]A sudden burst of Spanish, *El Tago fara muestra*, the Tagus will make a demonstration.
[10]Unsolved enigmatic place name.

20. All the friends who will have belonged to the party,
For the rude in letters put to death and plundered:
Property up for sale at fixed price the great one annihilated.
Never were the Roman people so wronged.

21. Through the spite of the King supporting the lesser one,
He will be murdered presenting the jewels[1] to him:
The father wishing to impress nobility on the son
Does as the Magi did of yore in Persia.[2]

☞ 22. For not wishing to consent to the divorce,
Which then afterwards will be recognized as unworthy:
The King of the Isles will be driven out by force,
In his place put one who will have no mark of a king.

23. The remonstrances made to the ungrateful people,
Thereupon the army will seize Antibes:
The complaints will place Monaco in the arch,
And at Fréjus the one will take the shore from the other.

☞ 24. The captive prince conquered in Italy[3]
Will pass Genoa by sea as far as Marseilles:
Through great exertion by the foreigners overcome,
Safe from gunshot, barrel of bee's liquor.

25. Through the Ebro to open the passage of "Bisanne,"[4]
Very far away will the Tagus make a demonstration:
In "Pelligouxe"[5] will the outrage be committed,
By[6] the great lady seated in the orchestra.

26. The successor will avenge his brother-in-law,
To occupy the realm under the shadow of vengeance:
Obstacle slain his blood for the death blame,
For a long time will Brittany[7] hold with France.

---

[1]Or "treasures."

[2]Possibly this is a reference to the election (A.D. 309) of Shapur the Great, posthumous son of Hormisdas II of Persia, as king by the nobles while still in his mother's womb.

[3]Or, according to an imaginative interpretation, "Elba." See note opposite and Commentary.

[4]Or "Brisanne." Probably Bézenas (Pézenas).

[5]Another unsolved enigmatic place name.

[6]Or possibly "To."

[7]Or "Britain."

27. Par le cinquième et un grand *Herculés*
    Viendront le temple ouvrir de main *bellique*:[1]
    Un *Clement, Iule* et *Ascans* reculés,
    L'épée, clef, aigle, n'eurent onc si grand pique.

28. Second et tiers qui font prime musique
    Sera par Roi en honneur sublimée:
    Par grasse et maigre presque demi étique,
    Rapport de *Venus* faux rendra déprimée.

29. De *POL MANSOL*[2] dans caverne *caprine*[3]
    Caché et pris extrait hors par la barbe:
    Captif mené comme bête mâtine
    Par *Begourdans*[4] amenée près de *Tarbe*.

30. Neveu et sang du saint nouveau venu,
    Par le surnom soutient arcs et couvert:
    Seront chassés mis à mort chassés nu,
    En rouge et noir convertiront leur vert.

31. Le saint Empire viendra en *Germanie*,
    *Ismaëlites* trouveront lieux ouverts:
    Ânes voudront aussi la *Carmanie*,
    Les soutenants de terre tous couverts.

32. Le grand empire chacun an[5] devait être,
    Un sur les autres le viendra obtenir:
    Mais peu de temps sera son regne et être,
    Deux ans aux *naves*[6] se pourra soutenir.

[1]Latin *bellicus*, of war.
[2]Erratum for *POL MAUSOL* (Saint-Paul-de-Mausole). See note for 427 and Commentary.
[3]Latin *caprinus*, pertaining to goats.
[4]Inhabitants of Bigorre.
[5]Uniform in all editions, but Le Pelletier thinks it an erratum for *en*, and Garencières also renders it this way.
[6]Latin *navis*, ship.

☞ 27. Through the fifth one and a great Hercules
They will come to open the temple by hand of war:
One Clement, Julius and Ascanius[1] set back,
The sword, key, eagle, never was there such great animosity.

28. Second and third which make prime music
By the King to be sublimated in honor:
Through the fat and the thin almost half emaciated,
By the false report of Venus to be debased.

29. In a cave of Saint-Paul-de-Mausole[2] a goat[3]
Hidden and seized pulled out by the beard:
Led captive like a mastiff beast
By the Bigorre people brought to near Tarbes.

30. Nephew and blood of the new saint come,[4]
Through the surname he will sustain arches and roof:
They will be driven out put to death chased nude,
Into red and black will they convert their green.

31. The Holy Empire will[5] come into Germany,[6]
The Ishmaelites[7] will find open places:
The asses will want also Carmania,[8]
The supporters all covered by earth.

32. The great empire, everyone would be of[9] it,
One will come to obtain it over the others:
But his realm and state[10] will be of short duration,
Two years will he be able to maintain himself on the sea.[11]

---

[1]All three names apparently refer to Pope Clement VII (Giulio de' Medici, probably descended from one Ascanio de' Medici), and this whole quatrain, the prime instance of "retroactive prophecy," concerns the Sack of Rome (1527). See Commentary.

[2]The convent outside Saint-Rémy (Nostradamus' birthplace), subsequently an insane asylum where the painter Van Gogh was confined shortly before he shot himself (1890). See note on 427 and Commentary. In this case probably synecdoche for Saint-Rémy.

[3]Or possibly "a goatherd" (or even a wild "goat-boy" raised by goats?).

[4]Or "of the saint newly-created."

[5]Or "The Holy Empire, he will."

[6]If the Holy Empire is the Holy Roman Empire, more likely "It/He will come into Germany and the Holy Empire," the two being virtually synonymous.

[7]The Arabs, who recognize as their ancestor Ishmael, son of Abraham.

[8]The Persian province at the mouth of the Persian Gulf; or an anagram.

[9]Or possibly "would have."

[10]Or "reign and life."

[11]Literally "in his ships."

33. La faction cruelle à robe longue,
    Viendra cacher sous les pointus poignards:
    Saisir *Florence* le Duc et lieu *diphlongue,*[1]
    Sa découverte par immûrs et *flaugnards.*[2]

34. *Gaulois* qu'empire par guerre occupera,
    Par son beau-frère mineur sera trahi:
    Pour cheval rude voltigeant traînera,
    Du fait le frère longtemps sera haï.

35. Puîné royal flagrant d'ardent *libide,*[3]
    Pour se jouir de cousine germaine:
    Habit de femme au temple d'*Arthemide,*
    Allant meurtri par inconnu du *Maine.*

36. Après le Roi du souche guerres parlant,
    L'île *Harmotique*[4] le tiendra à mépris:
    Quelques ans bons rongeant un et pillant,
    Par tyrannie à l'île changeant *pris.*[5]

37. L'assemblée grande près du lac de *Borget,*
    Se rallieront près de *Montmelian:*
    Marchant plus outre pensifs feront projet,
    *Chambry, Moriane* combat *Sainct Iulian.*

38. Amour allègre non loin pose le siège,
    Au saint barbare seront les garnisons:
    *Ursins*[6] *Hadrie* pour *Gaulois* feront *pleige,*[7]
    Pour peur rendus de l'armée aux *Grisons.*

39. Premier fils veuve malheureux mariage,
    Sans nuls enfants deux Îles en discord:
    Avant dix-huit incompétant âge,
    De l'autre près plus bas sera l'accord.

[1]Dubious. Erratum for *diphtongue,* or Greek *diph-logos,* double word.
[2]Provençal *flaugnard,* sycophant, flatterer, wheedler.
[3]Latin *libido,* lust.
[4]Dubious. Possibly from Greek *armostikos,* fitted for joining together, or *armostos* joined together, adjusted.
[5]O.F. *pris,* estimation, worth. Similar to modern *prix.*
[6]Almost certainly the Orsini, the great medieval clan of Rome.
[7]O.F. *pleige,* security, guarantee.

33. The cruel faction in the long robe
    Will come to hide under the sharp daggers:
    The Duke to seize Florence[1] and the diphthong[2] place,
    Its discovery by immature ones and sycophants.

☞ 34. The Gaul who will hold the empire through war,
    He will be betrayed by his minor brother-in-law:
    He will be drawn by a fierce, prancing horse,
    The brother[3] will be hated for the deed for a long time.

☞ 35. The younger son of the king flagrant in burning lust
    To enjoy his first cousin:
    Female attire in the Temple of Artemis,[4]
    Going to be murdered by the unknown one of Maine.

36. Upon the King of the stump speaking of wars,
    The United[5] Isle will hold him in contempt:
    For several good years one gnawing and pillaging,
    Through tyranny in the isle esteem[6] changing.

37. The great assembly near the Lake of Bourget,
    They will meet near Montmélian:
    Going beyond the thoughtful ones will draw up a plan,
    Chambéry, Saint-Jean-de-Maurienne, Saint-Julien combat.

38. Sprightly love lays the siege not far,
    The garrisons will be at the barbarian saint:[7]
    The Orsini and "Adria"[8] will provide a guarantee for the Gauls,
    For fear delivered[9] by the army to the Grisons.[10]

☞ 39. First son, widow, unfortunate marriage,
    Without any children two Isles in discord:
    Before eighteen, incompetent age,
    For the other one the betrothal will take place while younger.[11]

[1] Or "To seize Florence, the Duke."
[2] Or "the double word." A diphthong place might well be Fiesole (Latin *Faesula*) near Florence.
[3] The context would seem to require "brother-in-law" again.
[4] Or "of Diana."
[5] Not quite certain. See note 4, opposite. Probably England is intended.
[6] Or possibly "prices."
[7] I.e., a place named after a "barbarian saint."
[8] Venice, master of the town of Adria and of the Adriatic Sea.
[9] Or possibly "fear of being delivered"?
[10] Or possibly "to the Grisons in the army"?
[11] One of the predictions that made Nostradamus famous. See Commentary.

40.  Le jeune né au regne *Britannique,*
     Qu'aura le père mourant recommandé:
     Icelui mort *LONOLE*[1] donnera *topique,*[2]
     Et à son fils le regne demandé.

41.  En la frontière de *Caussade* et *Charlus,*
     Non guère loin du fond de la vallée:
     De *ville franche* musique à son de luths,
     Environnés *combouls*[3] et grand *mittée.*[4]

42.  Le regne humain d'Angélique[5] géniture,
     Fera son regne paix union tenir:
     Captive guerre demi de sa clôture,
     Longtemps la paix leur fera maintenir.

43.  Le trop bon temps, trop de bonté royale,
     Faits et défaits prompt, subit, négligence:
     Léger croira faux d'épouse loyale,
     Lui mis à mort par sa bénévolence.

44.  Par lors qu'un Roi sera contre les siens,
     Natif de *Bloys* subjuguera *Ligures,*
     *Mammel,*[6] *Cordube* et les *Dalmatiens,*
     Des sept puis l'ombre à Roi étrennes et lémures.

45.  L'ombre du regne de *Nauarre* non vrai,
     Fera la vie de sort illégitime:
     La vœu promis incertain de *Cambray,*
     Roi *Orleans* donnera mur légitime.

[1]Dubious anagram, or enigmatic proper name. Ward ingeniously suggests it as an anagram of OLE NOL, a phonetic pronunciation of Cromwell's nickname. Le Pelletier can only suggest an anagram of a Greek verb (meaning to destroy)!

[2]Probably from O.F. *topiquer,* to dispute, quarrel (Roquefort).

[3]Greek *kumbalon,* cymbalon.

[4]Dubious. There are numerous possible derivations with the root *mit-*. Le Pelletier suggests Greek *mitos,* string of a musical instrument.

[5]Variant ("1568" and Garcin): *Anglique.*

[6]Uncertain. Memel on the Baltic? Mammola in southern Italy?

☞ 40. The young heir to the British realm,
Whom his dying father will have recommended:
The latter dead "Lonole"[1] will dispute with him,
And from the son the realm demanded.

41. On the boundary of Caussade and Caylus,
Not at all far from the bottom of the valley:
Music from Villefranche to the sound of lutes,
Encompassed by cymbals and great stringing.[2]

☞ 42. The humane[3] realm of Anglican[4] offspring,
It[5] will cause its[5] realm to hold to peace and union:
War half-captive in its[5] enclosure,
For long will it[5] cause them to maintain the peace.

☞ 43. Too much good times, too much of royal goodness,
Ones made and unmade, quick, sudden, neglectful:
Lightly will he believe falsely of his loyal wife,
He put to death through his benevolence.

44. When a King will be against his people,
A native of Blois will subjugate the Ligurians,[6]
Memel,[7] Cordoba and the Dalmatians,
Of the seven then the shadow to the King handsel and ghosts.

45. The shadow of the realm of Navarre untrue,
It will make his life one of fate unlawful:
The vow made in Cambrai[8] wavering,
King Orléans will give a lawful wall.

---

[1]Ward would have it "Ole Nol" Cromwell. See Commentary.
[2]Rather dubious. See note 4, opposite.
[3]Or "The human."
[4]Or "Angelic," in which case "The human realm of Angelic offspring."
[5]Or "He . . . his . . . his . . . he."
[6]I.e., the Genoese.
[7]Uncertain. Possibly also Mammola? See note opposite.
[8]A reference to the Peace of Cambrai of 1529, whereby the French renounced their claims to Flanders.

46. Vie sort mort de l'or vilaine[1] indigne,
    Sera de *Saxe* non nouveau électeur:
    De *Brunsuic* mandra d'amour signe,
    Faux le rendant au peuple séducteur.

47. De *Bourze* ville à la dame Guirlande,
    L'on mettra sur la trahison faite:
    Le grand prélat de *Leon* par *Formande*,[2]
    Faux pèlerins et ravisseurs défaite.

48. Du plus profond de l'*Espagne* enseigne,
    Sortant du bout et des fins de l'*Europe:*
    Troubles passant auprès du pont de *Laigne,*
    Sera défaite par bande sa grande troupe.

49. Jardin du monde auprès de cité neuve,[3]
    Dans le chemin des montagnes cavées:
    Sera saisi et plongé dans la Cuve,
    Buvant par force eaux soufre envenimées.

50. La *Meuse* au jour terre de *Luxembourg,*
    Découvrira *Saturne* et trois en l'urne:
    Montagne et plaine, ville, cité et bourg,
    *Lorraine* déluge, trahison par grande urne.

51. Des lieux plus bas du pays de *Lorraine*
    Seront des basses *Allemagnes* unis:
    Par ceux de siège *Picards, Normans, du Maisne,*
    Et aux cantons se seront réunis.

[1]The feminine ending apparently an erratum, but uniform in all editions, is somewhat perplexing. (See how Garencières worked it out, note 1, opposite.)

[2]Probably Formentera, the smallest of the Balearic Islands.

[3]Probably a reference to Greek *nea polis,* new city, the etymology of Naples.

46. In life, fate and death a sordid, unworthy man of gold,[1]
He will not be a new Elector of Saxony:
From Brunswick he will send for a sign of love,
The false seducer delivering it[2] to the people.

☞ 47. At the Garland lady of the town of Burgos,[3]
They will impose[4] for the treason committed:
The great prelate of Leon through "Formande,"[5]
Undone[6] by false pilgrims and ravishers.

48. Banners of the deepest part of Spain,
Coming out from the tip and ends of Europe:
Troubles passing near the bridge of "Laigne,"[7]
Its great army will be routed by a band.

☞ 49. Garden of the world near the new city,[8]
In the path of the hollow mountains:
It will be seized and plunged into the Tub,
Forced to drink waters poisoned by sulfur.

50. The Meuse by day in the land of Luxemburg,
It will find Saturn and three in the urn:[9]
Mountain and plain, town, city and borough,
Flood in Lorraine, betrayed by the great urn.

51. Some of the lowest places of the land of Lorraine
Will be united with the Low Germans:
Through those of the see Picards, Normans, those of Maine,
And they will be joined to the cantons.

---

[1]Garencières has an extraordinary translation for this line: "The living receives his death from gold, infamous slut." An apparently prudish Roberts (1947) changes this to "The living die of too much gold, an infamous villain," having apparently missed the whole point about the feminine ending.

[2]Or "him."

[3]Apparently the Cathedral of San Estéban at Burgos (see Commentary). Alternatively, Bourges in France might be intended but for the Spanish setting (with the reference to Leon, of which Burgos was the capital and archiepiscopal seat).

[4]I.e., impose a severe penalty.

[5]Probably the island of Formentera (see note opposite). Not certain.

[6]Unless the feminine ending is an erratum in the French, this word apparently modifies the subject of line 1.

[7]Unsolved place name. The context would suggest a town or river near the Spanish border. There is a Laignes River, and also the Aisne (French L'Aisne) but they are far distant (although the Aisne is near the *northern* border).

[8]Naples (see note opposite) near the fertile fields of Campania.

[9]I.e., Saturn and three other planets conjoined in Aquarius.

52. Au lieu où *Laye* et *Scelde* se marient,
    Seront les noces de longtemps maniées:
    Au lieu d'*Anuers* où la *crappe*[1] *charient,*[2]
    Jeune vieillesse *consorte*[3] *intaminee.*[4]

53. Les trois *pellices*[5] de long[6] *s'entrebattront,*
    La plus grande moindre demeurera à l'écoute:
    Le grand *Selin*[7] n'en sera plus patron,
    Le nommera feu *pelte*[8] blanche route.

54. Née en ce monde par concubine furtive,
    À deux haut mise par les tristes nouvelles:
    Entre ennemis sera prise captive,
    Et amenée à *Malings* et *Bruxelles.*

55. Les malheureuses noces célébreront
    En grande joie mais la fin malheureuse,
    Mari et mère *nore*[9] dédaigneront,
    Le *Phybe*[10] mort et *nore*[9] plus piteuse.

56. Prélat royal son baissant trop tiré,
    Grand flux de sang sortira par sa bouche:
    Le regne Angélique[11] par regne respiré,[12]
    Longtemps mort vif en *Tunis* comme souche.

57. Le soulevé ne connaîtra son sceptre,
    Les enfants jeunes des plus grands honnira:
    Onc ne fut un plus *ord*[13] cruel être,
    Pour leurs épouses à mort noir[14] bannira.

[1]O.F. *crappe*, siftings, chaff.
[2]O.F. *charier*, to convey, carry, travel, go, proceed.
[3]O.F. *consorte*, wife.
[4]Latin *intaminatus*, undefiled.
[5]Latin *pellex*, concubine, kept mistress.
[6]Variant: *loin.*
[7]Greek *Selene*, Moon or crescent.
[8]Latin *pelta*, a small shield used by the Thracians.
[9]O.F. *nore*, daughter-in-law.
[10]Latin *Phoebus*, Apollo. To get *François II* out of this, see Commentary.
[11]Variant: *Anglicque (Anglique).*
[12]O.F. *respirer* (for *respiter*), to save, pull out of danger (Roquefort).
[13]O.F. *ord*, impure, dirty, base, filthy.
[14]Here again probably an anagram for *roi/roy.*

52. At the place where the Lys and the Scheldt unite,[1]
    The nuptials will be arranged for a long time:
    At the place in Antwerp where they carry the chaff,
    Young old age wife undefiled.

53. The three concubines will fight each other for a long time,[2]
    The greatest one the least will remain to watch:
    The great "Selin"[3] will no longer be her patron,
    She will call him fire shield white route.

54. She born in this world of a furtive concubine,
    At two raised high by the sad news:
    She will be taken captive by her enemies,
    And brought to Malines and Brussels.

55. The unfortunate nuptials will be celebrated
    In great joy but the end unhappy:
    Husband[4] and mother will slight the daughter-in-law,
    The Apollo[5] dead and the daughter-in-law more pitiful.

56. The royal prelate his bowing too low,
    A great flow of blood will come out of his mouth:
    The Anglican[6] realm a realm pulled out of danger,
    For long dead as a stump alive in Tunis.

57. The uplifted one will not know his sceptre,
    He will disgrace the young children of the greatest ones:
    Never was there a more filthy and cruel being,
    For their wives the king will banish them to death.[7]

[1]I.e., at Ghent.

[2]Or "each other from afar."

[3]Again Nostradamus' enigmatic "Henry-Selin" or "Henry of the Crescent." See notes for 627, 854 *et al.*

[4]Of course this could be taken at face value as *Mary*, for an English or Scottish queen or princess, but this is not too likely. The original reads *Mary*.

[5]To get "Francis II" as a translation, see Commentary.

[6]Or "Angelic." See notes on 1042.

[7]Or "For their wives he will banish them to black death."

58. Au temps du deuil que le félin monarque
    Guerroyera le jeune *AEmathien:*[1]
    *Gaule* branler, péricliter la barque,
    Tenter *Phossens*[2] au Ponant entretien.

59. Dedans Lyon vingt-cinq d'une haleine,
    Cinq citoyens *Germains, Bressans, Latins:*
    Par-dessus noble conduiront longue traîne,
    Et découverts par abois de mâtins.

60. Je pleure *Nisse, Mannego, Pize, Gennes,*
    *Sauone, Sienne, Capue, Modene, Malte:*
    Le dessus sang et glaive par étrennes,
    Feu, trembler terre, eau, malheureuse *nolte.*[3]

61. *Betta,*[4] *Vienne, Emorte,*[5] *Sacarbance,*[6]
    Voudront livrer aux Barbares *Pannone:*
    Par pique et feu enorme violence,
    Les conjurés découverts par matrone.

62. Près de *Sorbin*[7] pour assaillir *Ongrie,*
    L'héraut de *Brudes*[8] les viendra avertir:
    Chef *Bizantin, Sallon* de *Sclauonie,*
    À loi d'*Arabes* les viendra convertir.

63. *Cydron, Raguse,* la cité au saint *Hieron,*
    Reverdira le *medicant*[9] secours:
    Mort fils de Roi par mort de deux *heron,*[10]
    L'*Arabe, Hongrie* feront un même cours.

[1]Latin *Emathius,* Macedonian.
[2]Latin *Phocenses,* the Phocaeans, who founded Marseilles.
[3]Uncertain derivation. Possibly from Latin *noluntas,* nolition, unwillingness.
[4]Probably from Latin *Baetis,* the Guadalquivir, or *Baetica,* one of the Roman provinces of Spain.
[5]Probably from *Augusta Emerita,* Merida. Variant: *Emorre.*
[6]Latin *Scarbantia,* modern Sopron.
[7]Probably a reference to the early medieval Sorbian March, against the Slavic Sorbs, in Saxony around Leipzig.
[8]Probably epenthesis of *Bude* (Buda, capital of Turkish Hungary).
[9]Latin *medicans,* healing, curing.
[10]Probably a false plural ending (for rime) of *héros.*

☞ 58. In the time of mourning the feline monarch
Will make war upon the young Macedonian:
Gaul to shake, the bark[1] to be in jeopardy,
Marseilles to be tried in the West a talk.

59. Within Lyons twenty-five of one mind,
Five citizens, Germans, Bressans, Latins:[2]
Under a noble one they will lead a long train,
And discovered by barks of mastiffs.

60. I weep for Nice, Monaco, Pisa, Genoa,
Savona, Siena, Capua, Modena, Malta:
For the above blood and sword for a New Year's gift,
Fire, the earth to tremble, water, unfortunate nolition.[3]

☞ 61. "Betta,"[4] Vienna, "Emorte,"[4] Sopron,
They will want to deliver Pannonia[5] to the Barbarians:
Enormous violence through pike and fire,
The conspirators discovered by a matron.

62. Near "Sorbia"[6] to assail Hungary,
The herald of "Brudes"[7] will come to warn them:
Byzantine chief, Salona of Slavonia,[8]
He will come to convert them to the law of the Arabs.

63. Cydonia,[9] Ragusa,[10] the city of St. Jerome,[11]
With healing help to grow green again:
The King's son dead because of the death of two heroes,
Araby and Hungary will take the same course.

[1]I.e., the Papacy, the Bark of St. Peter.
[2]Possibly "Ladins," referring to the Ladin-speaking Grisons, the politically active inhabitants of southeast Switzerland. Ladin, or Romansch, the canton's official language, is the least significant of all the surviving Romance languages.
[3]Rather uncertain. See note opposite.
[4]Probably the Guadalquivir River (or Valley) and Merida near by: by synecdoche, Spain. See note opposite.
[5]Classical Hungary.
[6]Corresponding to Saxony. See note 7, opposite.
[7]Probably "Buda." See note opposite.
[8]Literally, the "Salon of Slavonia," a play on *Salon-de-Provence*. Salona (now Solin) is actually in Dalmatia, not Slavonia.
[9]Modern Canea is built on the site of this ancient Cretan center.
[10]Now Dubrovnik.
[11]Dubious. St. Jerome was born in Stridon (thought to be modern Tesanj in Bosnia) and passed many years at the long-defunct Aquileia (near Venice).

64.  Pleure *Milan*, pleure *Lucques, Florence,*
     Que ton grand Duc sur le char montera:
     Changer le siège près de *Venise* s'avance,
     Lorsque *Colonne* à *Rome* changera.

65.  O vaste *Rome* ta ruine s'approche,
     Non de tes murs, de ton sang et substance:
     L'âpre par lettres fera si horrible coche,
     Fer pointu mis à tous jusqu'au manche.

66.  Le chef de *Londres* par regne l'*Americh,*
     L'Île d'*Escosse tempiera*¹ par gelée:
     Roi *Reb*² auront un si faux *Antechrist,*
     Que les mettra *trestous*³ dans la mêlée.

67.  Le tremblement si fort au mois de Mai,
     *Saturne, Caper,*⁴ *Iupiter, Mercure* au bœuf:
     *Venus* aussi, *Cancer, Mars* en *Nonnay,*⁵
     Tombera grêle lors plus grosse qu'un œuf.

68.  L'armée de mer devant cité tiendra,
     Puis partira sans faire longue allée:
     Citoyens grand *proye*⁶ en terre prendra,
     Retourner *classe*⁷ prendre grande *emblee.*⁸

69.  Le fait luisant de neuf vieux élevé,
     Seront si grands par *Midi, Aquilon:*⁹
     De sa sœur propre grandes *alles*¹⁰ levé,
     Fuyant meurtri au buisson d'*Ambellon.*¹¹

70.  L'œil par objet fera telle excroissance,
     Tant et ardente que tombera la neige:
     Champ arrosé viendra en décroissance,
     Que le primat succombera à *Rege.*

---

¹From Latin *temperare*, to soften, rule, govern, order. Variant (Fortune): *temptera* (modern *tentera*).
²Dubious. Possibly apocope for *rebelle.*
³O.F. *trestous*, every single one.
⁴Latin *Caper*, goat, for *Caper-cornu (Capricornus)*, Capricorn.
⁵Probably for *Nonne* or *Nonnain*, nun = virgin = Virgo.
⁶O.F. *proye*, flock.
⁷Latin *classis*, fleet.
⁸O.F. *emblee*, robbery, thievery.
⁹Latin *Aquilo*, north wind, north.
¹⁰O.F. *alle*, trip, alacrity, crowd.
¹¹Dubious. Le Pelletier lists *Ambellinus*, Amiens. We have found no such name for Amiens. The closest is *Ambianum*. Probably the village of Ambel.

64. Weep Milan, weep Lucca and Florence,
As your great Duke climbs into the chariot:
The see to change it advances to near Venice,
When at Rome the Colonna[1] will change.

65. O vast Rome, thy ruin approaches,
Not of thy walls, of thy blood and substance:
The one harsh in letters will make a very horrible notch,
Pointed steel driven into all up to the hilt.

☞ 66. The chief of London through the realm of America,[2]
The Isle of Scotland will be tried[3] by frost:
King and "Reb"[4] will face an Antichrist so false,
That he will place them in the conflict all together.

67. A very mighty trembling in the month of May,
Saturn in Capricorn, Jupiter and Mercury in Taurus:
Venus also, Cancer,[5] Mars in Virgo,[6]
Hail will fall larger than an egg.

68. The army of the sea will stand before the city,
Then it will leave without making a long passage:
A great flock of citizens will be seized on land,
Fleet to return to seize it great robbery.

69. The shining deed of the old one exalted anew,[7]
Through the South and "Aquilon"[8] they will be very great:
Raised by his own sister great crowds,
Fleeing, murdered in the thicket of "Ambellon."[9]

70. Through an object the eye will swell very much,
Burning so much that the snow will fall:
The fields watered will come to shrink,
As the primate succumbs at Reggio.

[1]A great clan of medieval Rome, rival of the Orsini.
[2]The possible interpretations of this fascinating line are many.
[3]Or "will be softened."
[4]"Rebel"? See note opposite.
[5]Or possibly "And Venus in Cancer."
[6]Wollner calculated that this would happen only in April, 1929, and May, 3755, within the period 1558–3797.
[7]Or possibly "of the new old one exalted," with some sort of play on names.
[8]The North[ern Country]. Or here possibly just "North."
[9]Ambel? Amiens? See note opposite.

71. La terre et l'air geleront si grand eau,
    Lorsqu'on viendra pour Jeudi vénérer:
    Ce qui sera jamais ne fut si beau,
    Des quatres parts le viendront honorer.

72. L'an mil neuf cent nonante neuf sept mois,
    Du ciel viendra un grand Roi d'*effrayeur:*[1]
    Ressusciter le grand Roi d'*Angolmois,*[2]
    Avant après *Mars* regner par bonheur.

73. Le temps présent avec le passé,
    Sera jugé par grand Jovialiste:
    Le monde tard lui sera lassé,
    Et déloyal par le clergé juriste.

74. Au révolu du grand nombre septième,
    Apparaîtra au temps jeux d'Hécatombe:
    Non éloigné du grand âge millième,
    Que les entrés[3] sortiront de leur tombe.

75. Tant attendu ne reviendra jamais,
    Dedans l'*Europe* en *Asie* apparaîtra:
    Un de la ligue issu du grand *Hermés,*
    Et sur tous Rois des Orients croîtra.

76. Le grand Sénat décernera la *pompe,*[4]
    À l'un qu'après sera vaincu, chassé:
    Des adhérents seront à son de trompe,
    Biens publiés, ennemis *dechassez.*[5]

77. Trente adhérents de l'ordre de *quirettes*[6]
    Bannis, leurs biens donnés ses adversaires:
    Tous leurs bienfaits seront pour démérites,
    *Classe*[7] *espargie,*[8] délivrés aux Corsaires.

[1]O.F. *effrayeur,* terror.
[2]Variant: *d'Angoulmois.* Not the Angoumois district in west-central France (which has never produced a King of Terror) but probably an anagram of O.F. *Mongolois,* Mongols. The anagram serves to avoid the extra syllable that would be required by *Roi des Mongolois.*
[3]Syncope of *enterrés.* Or correct as is. Similar meaning either way.
[4]Latin *pompa,* (triumphal) parade.
[5]O.F. *dechasser,* to expel, drive out.
[6]Variant (Fortune): *quirites.* Latin *Quirites,* Roman citizens in their civil as opposed to their military capacity. Low Latin *quirites,* renowned warriors.
[7]Latin *classis,* fleet.
[8]O.F. *espargier,* to sprinkle, spill, disperse.

71. The earth and air will freeze a very great sea,[1]
When they will come to venerate Thursday:
That which will be never was it so fair,[2]
From the four parts they will come to honor it.[2]

☞ 72. The year 1999, seventh month,
From the sky will come a great King of Terror:
To bring back to life the great King of the Mongols,[3]
Before and after Mars to reign by good luck.

73. The present time together with the past
Will be judged by the great Jovialist:[4]
The world too late will be tired of him,
And through the clergy oath-taker disloyal.

74. The year of the great seventh number accomplished,
It will appear at the time of the games of slaughter:
Not far from the great millennial age,
When the buried will go out from their tombs.

75. Long awaited he will never return
In Europe, he will appear in Asia:
One of the league issued from the great Hermes,
And he will grow over all the Kings of the East.

76. The great Senate will ordain the triumph
For one who afterwards will be vanquished, driven out:
At the sound of the trumpet of his adherents there will be
Put up for sale their possessions, enemies expelled.

77. Thirty adherents of the order of "Quirites"[5]
Banished, their possessions given their adversaries:
All their benefits will be taken as misdeeds,
Fleet dispersed,[6] delivered to the Corsairs.

[1] Or "stream" or "lake." Literally, "water."
[2] Or "He who will be never was there one so fair . . . him."
[3] I.e., Genghiz Khan. See derivation in note opposite.
[4] An adherent of Jove or Jupiter, hence a pagan, hence a heretic and probably hence, according to Nostradamus' views, the Protestant Calvin. See Commentary.
[5] I.e., two contrary possible meanings, "citizens" or "warriors." See note 6, opposite.
[6] Or "sprinkled," i.e., sunk.

78. Subite joie en subite tristesse,
    Sera à *Rome* aux graces embrassées:
    Deuil, cris, pleurs. *larm.*[1] sang, excellent liesse,
    Contraires bandes surprises et troussées.

79. Les vieux chemins seront tous embellis,
    L'on passera à *Memphis somentrée:*[2]
    Le grand *Mercure* d'*Hercules* fleur de lis,
    Faisant trembler terre, mer et contrée.

80. Au regne grand du grand regne regnant,
    Par force d'armes les grandes portes d'airain:
    Fera ouvrir, le Roi et Duc joignant,
    Fort[3] démoli, nef à fond, jour serein.

81. Mis trésor temple citadins *Hesperiques,*
    Dans icelui retiré en secret lieu:
    Le temple ouvrir les liens faméliques,
    Repris, ravis, proie horrible au milieu.

82. Cris, pleurs, larmes viendront avec couteaux,
    Semblant fuir, donneront dernier assaut,
    L'entour parcs planter profonds plateaux,
    Vifs repoussés et meurtris *de prinsaut.*[4]

83. De batailler ne sera donné signe,
    Du parc seront contraints de sortir hors:
    De *Gand* l'entour sera connu l'enseigne,
    Qui fera mettre de tous les siens à morts.

84. La naturelle à si haut haut non bas,
    Le tard retour fera marris contents:
    Le *Recloing*[5] ne sera sans débats,
    En employant et perdant tout son temps.

[1]Uniform in all editions, but its purport (the period) is dubious.
[2]O.F. *somentir,* to fail, miss, escape suddenly (Godefroy), does not seem to fit here. Possibly from Greek *symmetros,* resembling, like.
[3]Variant: *Port.*
[4]O.F. *de prinsaut,* firstly, in the first place, at once, instantly.
[5]Derivation uncertain. Possibly from Latin *recolligo,* to regain, to recover, to be reconciled.

78. Sudden joy to sudden sadness,
It will occur at Rome for the graces embraced:
Grief, cries, tears, weeping, blood, excellent mirth,
Contrary bands surprised and trussed up.

79. The old roads will all be improved,
One will proceed on them to the modern Memphis:[1]
The great Mercury of Hercules fleur-de-lys,
Causing to tremble land, sea and country.

80. In the realm the great one of the great realm reigning,
Through force of arms the great gates of brass
He will cause to open, the King and Duke joining,
Fort[2] demolished, ship to the bottom, day serene.

☞ 81. A treasure placed in a temple by "Hesperian"[3] citizens,
Therein withdrawn to a secret place:
The hungry bonds to open the temple,
Retaken, ravished, a horrible prey in the midst.

82. Cries, weeping, tears will come with knives,
Seeming to flee, they will deliver a final attack,
Parks around to set up high platforms,
The living pushed back and murdered instantly.

83. The signal to give battle will not be given,
They will be obliged to go out of the park:
The banner around Ghent will be recognized,
Of him who will cause all his followers to be put to death.

84. The illegitimate girl so high, high, not low,
The late return will make the grieved ones contented:
The Reconciled One[4] will not be without debates,
In employing and losing all his time.

---

[1]Somewhat dubious (see note 2, opposite). Memphis was the ancient capital of the Pharaohs, to which Nostradamus would seem to be likening the capital of this enigmatic ruler, alias "Ogmios." See Commentary.
[2]Or "Port."
[3]"Of the Western Land." Spanish? American?
[4]Somewhat uncertain. See note opposite.

85. Le vieil tribun au point de la *trehemide*,[1]
    Sera pressé captif ne délivrer:
    Le *vueil*,[2] non *vueil*,[2] le mal parlant timide,
    Par légitime à ses amis livrer.

86. Comme un griffon viendra le Roi d'*Europe*,
    Accompagné de ceux d'*Aquilon*:[3]
    De rouges et blancs conduira grande troupe,
    Et iront contre le Roi de *Babylon*.

87. Grand Roi viendra prendre port près de *Nisse*,
    Le grand empire de la mort si en fera:
    Aux *Antipolles*[4] posera sa génisse,
    Par mer la Pille tout évanouira.

88. Pieds et Cheval à la seconde veille,
    Féront entrée *vastient*[5] tout par la mer:
    Dedans le poil[6] entrera de *Marseille*,
    Pleurs, cris, et sang, onc nul temps si amer.

89. De brique en marbre seront les murs *reduicts*,[7]
    Sept et cinquante années pacifiques:
    Joie aux humains, renoué l'*aqueduict*,[7]
    Santé, grands fruits, joie et temps *melifique*.[8]

90. Cent fois mourra le tyran inhumain,
    Mis à son lieu savant et débonnaire,
    Tout le Sénat sera dessous sa main,
    Fâché sera par malin téméraire.

91. Clergé *Romain* l'an mil six cents et neuf,
    Au chef de l'an feras élection:
    D'un gris et noir de la Compagne[9] issu,
    Qui onc ne fut si malin.

---

[1]Derivation uncertain. Possibly from Greek *trachoma*, roughness. Le Pelletier suggests a sensible but etymologically distant Latin *tremor*, trembling.
[2]O.F. *vueil*, wish, will, power.
[3]Latin *Aquilon*, north, north wind.
[4]Latin *Antipolis*, Antibes.
[5]Variant (Fortune): *vastant*. Latin *vastare*, to devastate.
[6]Le Pelletier sees this as an erratum for *port*; Garencières gives it as *port*.
[7]Modern *réduits . . . aqueduc;* original preserved for rime.
[8]Latin *mellificus*, honey-making. (Nostradamus probably had in mind *mellifluus*.)
[9]Variant: *Compagnie*. Probably for *Campanie*, Campania.

85. The old tribune on the point of trembling,[1]
    He will be pressed not to deliver the captive:
    The will, non-will, speaking the timid evil,
    To deliver to his friends lawfully.

☞ 86. Like a griffin will come the King of Europe,
    Accompanied by those of "Aquilon":[2]
    He will lead a great troop of red ones and white ones,
    And they will go against the King of Babylon.[3]

87. A Great King will come to take port near Nice,
    Thus the death of the great empire will be completed:
    In Antibes will he place his heifer,
    The plunder by sea all will vanish.

88. Foot and Horse at the second watch,
    They will make an entry devastating all by sea:
    Within the port[4] of Marseilles he will enter,
    Tears, cries, and blood, never times so bitter.

89. The walls will be converted from brick to marble,
    Seven and fifty pacific years:
    Joy to mortals, the aqueduct renewed,
    Health, abundance of fruits, joy and mellifluous times.

☞ 90. A hundred times will the inhuman tyrant die,
    In his place put one learned and mild,
    The entire Senate will be under his hand,
    He will be vexed by a rash scoundrel.

☞ 91. In the year 1609, Roman clergy,
    At the beginning of the year you will hold an election:
    Of one gray and black issued from Campania,
    Never was there one so wicked as he.

[1]Or "of the roughness." Very uncertain. See note opposite.
[2]The North[ern Country].
[3]The Sultan of Egypt, in medieval chronicles, was often referred to as the King of Babylon; which may be relevant to Nostradamus' meaning here.
[4]Or "the nap" or some part of Marseilles, whose name, in French, includes the sound *poil*. See note opposite.

92. Devant le père l'enfant sera tué,
    Le père après entre cordes de jonc:
    *Geneuois* peuple sera évertué,
    Gisant le chef au milieu comme un tronc.

93. La barque neuve recevra les voyages,
    Là et auprès transféreront l'Empire:
    *Beaucaire, Arles* retiendront les otages,
    Près deux colonnes trouvées de Porphyre.

94. De *Nismes*, d'*Arles*, et *Vienne contemner*,[1]
    N'obéir à l'édit *Hespericque*:
    Aux *labouriez*[2] pour le grand condamner,
    Six échappés en habit séraphique.

95. Dans les *Espaignes* viendra Roi très-puissant,
    Par mer et terre subjuguant le Midi:
    Ce mal fera, rebaissant le croissant,
    Baisser les ailes à ceux du Vendredi.

96. Religion du nom des mers vaincra,
    Contre la secte fils *Adaluncatif*:[3]
    Secte obstinée déplorée craindra
    Des deux blessés par *Aleph*[4] et *Aleph*.[4]

97. Trirèmes pleines tout âge captifs,
    Temps bon à mal, le doux pour amertume:
    Proie à Barbares trop tôt seront hâtifs,
    Cupide de voir plaindre au vent la plume.

98. La splendeur claire à pucelle joyeuse,
    Ne luira plus, longtemps sera sans sel:
    Avec marchands, rufiens, loups odieuse,
    Tout pêle-mêle monstre universel.

[1]Latin *contemnere*, to scorn, despise, set at naught.
[2]O.F. *labourier*, to be tormented.
[3]Still unsolved anagram or obscure derivative. Le Pelletier suggests Latin *adalligatus*, attached to.
[4]Hebrew *aleph*, the letter *a*. Arabic is close—*alif*.

92. Before his father the child will be killed,
    The father afterwards between ropes of rushes:
    The people of Geneva will have exerted themselves,
    The chief lying in the middle like a log.

93. The new bark will take trips,
    There and near by they will transfer the Empire:
    Beaucaire, Arles will retain the hostages,
    Near by, two columns of Porphyry found.

94. Scorn from Nîmes, from Arles and Vienne,
    Not to obey the "Hesperian"[1] edict:
    To the tormented to condemn the great one,
    Six escaped in seraphic garb.[2]

95. To the Spains[3] will come a very powerful King,
    By land and sea subjugating the South:
    This evil will cause, lowering again the crescent,
    Clipping the wings of those of Friday.[4]

96. The Religion of the name of the seas will win out
    Against the sect of the son of "Adaluncatif":[5]
    The stubborn, lamented sect will be afraid
    Of the two wounded by A and A.

97. Triremes full of captives of every age,
    Good times for bad, the sweet for the bitter:
    Prey to the Barbarians hasty they will be too soon,
    Anxious to see the feather wail in the wind.

98. For the merry maid the bright splendor
    Will shine no longer, for long will she be without salt:
    With merchants,[6] bullies, wolves odious,
    All confusion universal monster.

[1]"Of the Western Land." Spanish? American?
[2]I.e., Franciscans, properly called the Order of Seraphim.
[3]Including the Spanish possessions in Europe outside Spain.
[4]The Mahometans, whose sabbath is Friday.
[5]Unlike most unsolved Nostradamia, this would seem definitely capable of solution but it is still unsolved. *Calif* is a likely component of it. See Commentary.
[6]Mercenary soldiers?

99. La fin le loup, le lion, bœuf, et l'âne,
   Timide *dama*[1] seront avec mâtins:
   Plus ne cherra à eux la douce manne,
   Plus vigilance et custode aux mâtins.

100. Le grand empire sera par *Angleterre,*
   Le *pempotam*[2] des ans plus[3] de trois cents;
   Grandes *copies*[4] passer par mer et terre,
   Les *Lusitains* n'en seront pas contents.

[1]Latin *dama,* deer.
[2]Probably hybrid of Greek *pan,* all, and Latin *potens,* powerful, thus, the all-powerful one, or Greek, *potamos,* river (rarely, sea), thus all-seas.
[3]Variant: *des ans (plus* omitted).
[4]Latin *copia,* forces.

99. The end of wolf, lion, ox and ass,
    Timid deer they will be with mastiffs:
    No longer will the sweet manna fall upon them,
    More vigilance and watch for the mastiffs.

☞ 100. The great empire will be for[1] England,
    The all-powerful one[2] for more than three hundred years:[3]
    Great forces to pass by sea and land,
    The Lusitanians[4] will not be satisfied thereby.

[1]Or "in" or "through" or "by."
[2]Or "The all-seas."
[3]Or "for three hundred years."
[4]The inhabitants of classical Portugal, i.e., Portuguese.

# Duplicate and Fragmentary Centuries[1]

## Centurie VI

100. Fille de l'*Aure*,[2] asile du mal sain,
  Où jusqu'au ciel se voit l'amphithéâtre:
  Prodige vu, ton mal est fort prochain,
  Seras captive, et des fois plus de quatre.

## Centurie VII

43. Lorsqu'on verra les deux licornes,
  L'une baissant, l'autre abaissant,
  Monde au milieu, plier aux bornes
  S'enfuira le neveu riant.

44. Alors qu'un *bour*[3] sera[4] fort bon,[3]
  Portant en soi les marques de justice,
  De son sang lors portant long nom
  Par fuite injuste recevra son supplice.

73. Renfort de sièges *manubis*[5] et *maniples*[6]
  Changé le sacre et passe sur le prône,
  Pris et captifs n'arrête les prés triples
  Plus par fond mis élevé, mis au trône.

80. L'Occident libre les Îles *Britanniques*
  Le reconnu passer le bas, puis haut
  Ne content triste *Rebel corss.*[7] *Escotiques*
  Puis rebeller par plus et par nuit chaud.

---

[1]For pertinent details, see "Nostradamus Bibliography." The 1605 edition is the basic text for all but VII-43 and VII-44, of which the Fortune and Garcin are taken equally as the source. Nostradamus' authorship is not absolutely certain.

[2]Latin *aura*, breeze.

[3]Obviously a play on *Bourbon*.

[4]Variant: *fera*.

[5]Latin *manubiae*, plunder.

[6]Latin *manipulus*, maniple.

[7]Probably apocope of *rebelles corsaires*.

# Duplicate and Fragmentary Centuries

## Century VI

100. Daughter of the Breeze, asylum of the unhealthy,
Where the amphitheater is seen on the horizon:
Prodigy seen, your evil is very near,
You will be captive, and more than four times.

## Century VII

43. When one will see two unicorns,
The one lifting, the other lowering,
World in the middle, to bend to the limit
The nephew will run away laughing.

☞ 44. When a Bourbon will really be[1] good,
Bearing in his person the marks of justice,
Bearing then the longest name of his blood
Through flight unjustly he will receive his punishment.

73. Reinforcement of sieges plunder and maniples[2]
The holy one changed and passes over the sermon,
Taken and captives it does not stop the triple meadows,
Put in the uttermost depths, raised, put on the throne.

☞ 80. The West free the British Isles
The recognized one to pass low, then high
Discontented sad Rebel Scottish corsairs
Then to rebel much more and by warm night.

[1] Or "will really do."
[2] A Roman military unit with from 60 to 120 men.

82. Le stratagème *simulte*[1] sera rare
    La mort en voie rebelle par contrée:
    Par le retour du voyage Barbare
    Exalteront la protestante entrée.

83. Vent chaud, conseils pleurs, timidité,
    De nuit au lit assailli sans les armes:
    D'oppression grande calamité,
    L'épithalame converti pleurs et larmes.

## Centurie VIII

1. Seront confus plusieurs de leur attente,
   Aux habitants ne sera pardonné:
   Qui bien pensaient persévérer l'attente,
   Mais grand loisir ne leur sera donné.

2. Plusieurs viendront, et parleront de paix,
   Entre Monarques et seigneurs bien puissants:
   Mais ne sera accordé de si près,
   Que ne se rendent plus qu'autres obéissants.

3. Las quelle fureur! hélas quelle pitié,
   Il y aura entre beaucoup de gens:
   On ne vit onc une telle amitié,
   Qu'auront les loups à courir diligents.

4. Beaucoup de gens voudront parlementer,
   Aux grands seigneurs qui leur feront la guerre:
   On ne voudra en rien les écouter,
   Hélas! si Dieu n'envoie paix en terre.

5. Plusieurs secours viendront de tous côtés,
   De gens lointains qui voudront résister:
   Ils seront tout à coup bien hâtés,
   Mais ne pourront pour cette heure assister.

6. Las quel désir ont Princes étrangers,
   Garde toi bien qu'en ton pays ne vienne:
   Il y aurait de terribles dangers
   Et en maintes contrées, même en la *Vienne*.

[1]O.F. *simulte,* quarrel.

82. The stratagem in the quarrel will be uncommon
    The death en route in the country rebellion:
    On the return from the Barbarian voyage
    They will exalt the Protestant entry.

83. Wind warm, counsels, tears, timidity,
    By night in bed assailed without arms:
    Great calamity from oppression,
    The wedding song converted, weeping and tears.

## Century VIII

1. Several will be confused in their waiting,
   Pardon will not be given the inhabitants:
   Those who thought well of persisting in the waiting,
   But not much spare time will be given them.

2. Several will come, and will speak of peace,
   Between Monarchs and very powerful lords:
   But it will not be accorded so soon,
   Unless they become more obedient than the others.

3. Alas what a fury! Alas what a pity
   Will there be between people:
   Never did one see such a friendship
   As the wolves will have diligent in running.

4. Many people will want to come to terms
   With the great lords who will bring war upon them:
   They will not want to hear anything of it from them,
   Alas! if God does not send peace to the earth.

5. Varieties of aid will come from all sides,
   From distant people who will want to resist:
   Suddenly they will be much urged on,
   But they will be unable to assist at that hour.

6. Alas, what ambition foreign Princes have,
   Take careful heed lest they come into your country:
   There should be terrible dangers
   And in many countries, even in Vienna.

## Centurie X

100. Quand le fourchu sera soutenu de deux paux,
   Avec six demi-corps[1] et six ciseaux ouverts:
   Le très-puissant Seigneur, héritier des crapauds,
   Alors subjuguera, sous soi tout l'univers.

## Centurie XI

91. Meysnier, Manthi, et le tiers qui viendra,
   Peste et nouveau insulte, enclos troubler:
   Aix et les lieux fureur dedans mordra,
   Puis les Phocens[2] viendront leur mal doubler.

97. Par ville franche, Mascon en désarroi,
   Dans les fagots seront soldats cachés:
   Changer de temps en prime[3] pour le Roi,
   Par de Chalon et Moulins tous hachés.

## Centurie XII

4. Feu, flamme, faim, furt,[4] farouche, fumée,
   Fera faillir, froissant fort, foi faucher:
   Flis[5] de Denté toute Prouence humée,
   Chassé de regne, enragé sans[6] cracher.

24. Le grand secours venu de la Guyenne,
   S'arrêtera tout auprès de Poictiers:
   Lyon[7] rendu par Mont Luel et Vienne,
   Et saccagés partout gens de métiers.

36. Assaut farouche en Cypre se prépare,
   La larme à l'œil, de ta ruine proche:
   Byzance classe,[8] Morisque si grande tare,
   Deux différents, le grand vast[9] par la roche.

[1]Le Pelletier sees as erratum for cors. Meaning is same either way.
[2]Latin Phocenses, Phocaeans, who founded Marseilles.
[3]O.F. prime, spring.
[4]O.F. furt, secretly (Roquefort); robber (Godefroÿ).
[5]O.F. flis, arrow. Le Pelletier thinks it an erratum for fils.
[6]Le Pelletier thinks this an erratum for sang.
[7]All right as is, or should be changed to Lion.
[8]Latin classis, fleet.
[9]Low Latin vastum. devastation.

## Century X

☞ 100. When the fork will be supported by two stakes,
With six half-bodies and six open scissors:[1]
The very powerful Lord, heir of the toads,[2]
Then he will subject the entire world to himself.

## Century XI

91. "Meysnier, Manthi"[3] and the third one that will come,
Plague and new affront, to trouble the enclosure:
The fury will bite in Aix and the places thereabout,
Then those of Marseilles will want to double their evil.

97. Through Villefranche, Mâcon in disorder,
Soldiers will be hidden in the bundles:
In the spring times to change for the King,
In Châlon and Moulins all cut to pieces.

## Century XII

4. Fire, flame, hunger, robber,[4] wild smoke,
It will cause to fail, striking hard, to destroy faith:
Arrow[5] of "Denté"[6] all Provence sucked up,
Driven out of the realm, enraged without spitting.[7]

24. The great relief come from Guienne,
It will halt quite near Poitiers:
Lyons[8] surrendered through Montluel and Vienne,
And tradesmen will be plundered everywhere.

36. A ferocious attack is being prepared in Cyprus,
Tear in my eye, for your imminent ruin:
Byzantine and Moorish fleet very great loss,
Two different ones, the great devastation by the rock.

[1] I.e., MCCCCCCXXXXXX, or 1660.
[2] Presumably a reference to the device used by the Merovingians.
[3] Dubious. Possibly "Meusnes, Manthelan."
[4] Or "secret" ("secret, wild smoke").
[5] Or possibly "Son."
[6] Unsolved enigmatic name.
[7] Or possibly "enraged blood to spurt."
[8] Or possibly "The Lion."

52. Deux corps, un chef, champs divisés en deux,
    Et puis répondre à quatre non ouïs:
    Petits pour grands, *apertius*[1] mal pour eux,
    Tour d'*Aigues* foudre, pire pour *Eussouis*.

55. Tristes conseils, déloyaux, cauteleux,
    Avis méchant, la Loi sera trahie:
    Le peuple ému, farouche, querelleux,
    Tant bourg que ville, toute la paix haïe.

56. Roi contre Roi et le Duc contre Prince,
    Haine entre iceux, dissension horrible:
    Rage et fureur sera toute province,
    *France* grande guerre et changement terrible.

59. L'accord et *pache*[2] sera du tout rompue:
    Les amitiés pollues par discorde:
    L'haine éveillie, toute foi corrompue,
    Et l'espérance. *Marseille* sans concorde.

62. Guerres, débats, à *Blois* guerre et tumulte,
    Divers aguets, aveux *inopinables*:[3]
    Entrer dedans *Chasteau Trompette*, insulte,
    *Chasteau du Ha*, qui en seront *coulpables*.[4]

65. À tenir fort par fureur contraindra,
    Tout cœur trembler. *Langon* avent terrible:
    Le coup de pied mille pieds se rendra,
    *Guirond. Guaron*, ne furent plus horribles.

---

[1]Probably from Latin *apertus*, open, clear.
[2]O.F. *pache*, peace, agreement.
[3]O.F. *inopinable*, unforeseen, incredible (Godefroy).
[4]Latin *culpabilis*, worthy of blame, criminal.

52. Two bodies, one head, fields divided in two,
    And then to reply to four unheard ones:
    Little ones for great ones, clear evil for them,
    Lightning at the tower of Aiguesmortes, worse for "Eussouis."[1]

55. Sad counsels, disloyal, cunning,
    Wicked advice, the Law will be betrayed:
    The people stirred, wild, quarrelsome,
    In borough as in town, the entire peace hated.

56. King against King and the Duke against Prince,
    Hatred between them, horrible dissension:
    Rage and fury throughout every province,
    In France great war and horrible change.

59. The accord and peace will be broken everywhere:
    Friendships polluted by discord:
    Hatred awakened, all faith corrupted,
    And hope. Marseilles without concord.

62. Wars, debates, at Blois war and tumult,
    Diverse watches, unexpected avowals:
    To enter into Château Trompête,[2] affront,[3]
    Château du Hâ,[2] those who will be to blame for it.

65. Through fury he will force the fort to hold,
    Every heart to tremble. At Langon a terrible arrival:
    The kick will become a thousand kicks,
    Gironde, Garonne, never more horrible.

[1]Unsolved enigmatic name. Anagram?
[2]Fortresses of Bordeaux.
[3]Or "attack."

69.  *EIOVAS*[1] proche éloigner, lac *Leman,*
     Fort grands apprêts, retour, confusion:
     Loin des neveux, du feu grand *Supelman,*[2]
     Tous de leur suite.[3]

71.  Fleuves, rivières de mal seront obstacles,
     La vieille flamme d'ire non apaisée:
     Courir en *France;* ceci comme d'oracles,
     Maisons, manoirs, Palais, secte rasée.

[1]A very obvious anagram for *Savoie* (Savoy), spelled backwards.

[2]A fascinating problem is posed here. Can this be *Superman? Super* is, of course, simple Latin. According to Roquefort, the Germanic *mann* or *man* did come into the French vocabulary through the Normans. He also cites Barbazon as quoting Bochard and Bord that the word was also ancient Celtic. A third theory he cites would have the word derived from Latin *manens,* inhabitant. But one way or another, it *is* cited by Roquefort as part of the Old French vocabulary. On the other hand, it may simply be an anagram.

[3]Generally thought to be incomplete.

69. Savoy near to go far, Lake of Geneva,
    Very great preparations, return, confusion:
    Far from the nephews of the late great "Supelman,"[1]
    All of their following . . .

71. Rivers, streams will be obstacles to evil,
    The old flame of anger unappeased:
    To run in France; this as of oracles,
    Houses, manors, Palace, shaven sect.

[1]"Superman"? See note 2, opposite. Inasmuch as three years before the 1605 edition appeared the Duke of Savoy made a sensational "last try" to capture Geneva, this verse is not above suspicion. Garencières, applying it to his famous "Escalade," sees *Supelman* as Henry IV, but explains neither the derivation, the relationship (there were no Condés or Contis involved) nor the "late" (Henry lived eight years beyond it).

# Présages tirés de ceux faits par M. Nostradamus, es années 1555. & suivantes jusqu'en 1567.[1]

## *1555.*

*D'un présage sur la dite année.*

1.  D'Esprit divin l'âme présage atteinte,
    Trouble, famine, peste, guerre courir:
    Eaux, siccités, terre et mer de sang teinte,
    Paix, trève, à naître Prélats, Princes mourir.

*De l'Épître luminaire sur la dite année.*

2.  La mer *Tyrrhene*, l'Océan par la garde,
    Du grand *Neptun* et ses tridents soldats:
    *Prouence* sûre par la main du grand *Tende*,
    Plus *Mars Narbon* l'héroïque *de Vilars*.

*Janvier.*

3.  Le gros airain qui les heures ordonne,
    Sur le trépas du Tyran cassera:
    Pleurs, plaintes et cris, eaux, glace pain ne donne
    V.S.C. paix, l'arme passera.

*Février.*

4.  Près du *Leman*[2] la frayeur sera grande,
    Par le conseil, cela ne peut faillir:
    Le nouveau Roi fait apprêter sa bande,
    Le jeune meurt faim, peur fera faillir.

---

[1] As with the Sixains, the 1605 edition is the direct text, but the Presages have been edited in the same manner as the Centuries. For the background of the Presages, see pp. 48–49.

[2] Latin *Lemannus*, Lake of Geneva.

# Presages drawn from those made by M. Nostradamus in the years 1555 and subsequent ones up to 1567.

## 1555.

1. The soul touched by the divine Spirit presages,
   Trouble, famine, plague, war to follow:
   Floods, droughts, land and sea stained with blood,
   Peace, truce, Prelates to be born, Princes to die.

*From the luminary Epistle on the said year.*

2. The Tyrrhenian Sea, the Ocean through the care
   Of the great Neptune and his trident soldiers:
   Provence safe because of the hand of the great Tende,
   More Mars at Narbonne[1] the heroic de Villars.

*January.*

3. The large brazen one which decrees the hours,
   Upon the death of the Tyrant it will wear out:
   Tears, laments and cries, waters, ice bread does not give
   "V.S.C."[2] peace, the army will pass.

*February.*

4. Near the Lake of Geneva the terror will be great,
   Through the counsel, that cannot fail:
   The new King has his band prepare,
   The young one dies, famine, fear will cause failure.

[1] Or "More at Narbonne" (Latin *Narbo Martius*).
[2] Thought to be Philip II *(Charles V Successeur)*.

*Sur Mars.*

5. O *Mars* cruel, que tu seras à craindre,
   Plus est la Faux avec l'Argent conjoint:
   *Classe,*[1] *copie,*[2] eau, vent l'*ombriche*[3] craindre,
   Mer terre trève. L'ami à *L.V.* s'est joint.

*Avril.*

6. De n'avoir garde seras plus offensé,
   Le faible fort, l'inquiet pacifique:
   La faim on crie, le peuple est oppressé,
   La mer rougit, le Long fier et inique.

*Mai.*

7. Le cinq, six, quinze, tard et tôt l'on séjourne,
   Le né sans fin: les cités révoltées:
   L'héraut de paix vingt et trois s'en retourne,
   L'ouvert cinq serre, nouvelles inventées.

*Juin.*

8. Loin près de l'Urne le malin tourne arrière,
   Qu'au grand *Mars* feu donnera empêchement:
   Vers l'Aquilon au midi la grande fière,
   *FLORA*[4] tiendra la porte en *pensement.*[5]

*Juillet.*

9. Huit, quinze et cinq quelle déloyauté.
   Viendra permettre l'*explorateur*[6] malin:
   Feu du ciel foudre, peur, frayeur Papauté,
   L'Occident tremble, trop serre vin Salin.

*Août.*

10. Six, douze, treize, vingt parler à la Dame,
    L'aîné sera par femme corrompu:
    *Dijon, Guyenne* grêle, foudre l'entame,
    L'insatiable de sang et vin repu.

[1]Latin *classis*, fleet.
[2]Latin *copia*, forces, army, troops.
[3]Dubious. Probably Nostradamization of *ombrage*.
[4]Probably for Florence (Latin *flora*, flower).
[5]O.F. *pensement*, thought; pensive air.
[6]Latin *explorator*, spy.

5. O cruel Mars, how thou art to be feared,
   More is the Scythe[1] conjoined with the Silver:[2]
   Fleet, forces, water, wind the shadow[3] to fear,
   Truce by land and sea. The friend has joined "L.V."[4]

6. Thou wilt be injured more for not having care,
   The weak strong, the uneasy peaceful:
   They will cry famine, the people are oppressed,
   The sea reddens, the Tall One proud and unjust.

7. The five, six, fifteen, late and soon they remain,
   The heir without end: the cities revolted:
   The herald of peace twenty and three returns,
   Locks up the opened five, news invented.

8. Far near the Urn[5] the wicked one[6] turns back,
   So that fire will provide an obstacle for the great Mars:
   Towards the North to the south the great proud female,
   Florence[7] the gate[8] in thought will hold.

9. Eight, fifteen and five what disloyalty.
   The wicked spy will come to be allowed:
   Fire from the sky, lightning, fear, Papal terror,
   The West trembles, too much pressing the wine salty.

10. Six, twelve, thirteen, twenty to speak to the Lady,
    The older one will be corrupted by a woman:
    Dijon, Guienne hail, lightning cuts it,
    The insatiable one satiated with blood and wine.

[1] I.e., Saturn.
[2] I.e., Mercury or the Moon.
[3] Somewhat dubious. See note 3, opposite.
[4] Possibly "LVther." He had died in 1546.
[5] I.e., Aquarius.
[6] I.e., Saturn.
[7] Or "The Flower."
[8] Or "the Porte" (the Turkish Sultan).

*Septembre.*

11.  Pleurer le ciel à il cela fait faire,
     La mer s'apprête, *Annibal* fait ses ruses:
     *Denys* mouille, *classe*[1] tarde, ne taire,
     N'a su secret, et à quoi tu t'amuses.

*Octobre.*

12.  *Venus Neptune* poursuivra l'entreprise,
     Serrés pensifs, troublés les opposants:
     *Classe*[1] en *Adrie*, cités vers la *Tamise*,
     Le quart bruit blessé de nuit les reposants.

*Novembre.*

13.  Le grand du ciel sous la Cape donnera,
     Secours, *Adrie* à la porte fait offre:
     Se sauvera des dangers qui pourra,
     La nuit le Grand blessé poursuit le coffre.

*Décembre.*

14.  La porte exclame trop frauduleuse et feinte,
     La gueule ouverte, condition de paix:
     *Rosne* au cristal, eau, neige, glace teinte,
     La mort, mort, vent, par pluie cassé faix.

## *1557.*

*Janvier.*

15.  L'indigne orné craindra la grande fournaise,
     L'élu premier, des captifs n'en retourne:
     Grand bas du monde L'*Irale*[2] non à l'aise
     *Barb. Ister*,[3] *Malte*. Et le *Buy*[4] ne retourne.

*Mai.*

16.  Conjoint ici, au ciel *appert*[5] dépêsche,
     Prise, laissée, mortalité non sûre:
     Peu pluie, entrée, le ciel la terre sèche,
     De fait, mort, pris, arrivé à mal heure.

[1] Latin *classis*, fleet.
[2] Dubious. As place name unsolved. Possibly O.F. *iral*, in anger (Godefroy).
[3] Latin *Hister*, Danube.
[4] O.F. *buy*, empty.
[5] Latin *apertus*, open, manifest.

*September.*

11. The sky to weep for him made to do that,
    The sea is being prepared, Hannibal performs his tricks:
    Denis soaks, fleet delays, does not keep silent,
    Has not known the secret, and at which you are amused.

*October.*

12. Venus Neptune the enterprise will pursue,
    Pensive ones confined, those in opposition troubled:
    Fleet in the Adriatic,[1] cities towards the Thames,
    The fourth noise wounded those reposing by night.

*November.*

13. The great one of the sky under the cloak will give
    Aid, Venice[2] makes an offer to the Porte:
    He who can will save himself from the dangers,
    By night the Great One wounded the chest pursues.

*December.*

14. The Porte cries out too fraudulent and false,
    The mouth open, condition of peace:
    Rhône in ice, water, snow, ice stained,
    The death, death, wind, through rain burden broken.

## 1557.

*January.*

15. The unworthy one embellished will fear the great furnace,
    The elected one first, not returning some of the captives:
    Great bottom of the world, the Angry Female[3] not at ease,
    "Barb."[4] Danube, Malta. And the Empty One does not return.

*May.*

16. Conjoined here, in the sky despatch manifest,
    Taken, abandoned, mortality uncertain:
    Little rain, entry, the sky the earth dries,
    In fact, death, taken, arrived at a bad hour.

---

[1] Or "Fleet at Venice" (for which *Adrie* seems to be generally used, Venice having been perennial mistress of the Adriatic).
[2] See note 1, above.
[3] Or, as an unidentified place name, "Irale."
[4] Probably apocope for "Barbary" or "The Barbarians."

17.  Victeur naval à *Houche*,[1] *Anuers* divorce,
     Né grand, du ciel feu, tremblement haut *brule*:[2]
     *Sardaigne* bois, *Malte, Palerme, Corse,*
     Prélat mourir, l'un frappe sus la Mule.

18.  L'héraut errant du chien au Lion tourne,
     Feu ville ardra, pille, prise nouvelle:
     Découvrir fustes, Princes pris, on retourne,
     *Explor.*[3] pris *Gall.*[4] au grand jointe pucelle.

19.  De la grande Cour banni, conflit, blessé,
     Élu, rendue, accusé, *mat.*[5] mutins:
     Et feu cité *Pyr.*[6] eaux, venins, pressé
     Ne voguer onde, ne fâcher les *latins.*

20.  Mer, terre aller, foi, loyauté rompue,
     Pille, naufrage, à la cité tumulte:
     Fier, cruel acte, ambition repue,
     Faible offensé, le chef du fait *inulte.*[7]

21.  Froid, grand déluge, de regne *dechassé,*[8]
     *Niez,*[9] discord, *Trion*[10] Orient mine:
     Poison, mis siège, de la Cité chassé,
     Retour *felice,*[11] neuve secte en ruine.

[1]Dubious. Possibly Hoek in Belgium, or Hoek-van-Holland.
[2]O.F. *brulée*, action of burning; *brulas*, pillage; *brule*, wood(s).
[3]Probably apocope of Latin *explorator*, spy.
[4]Dubious. Possibly apocope for Latin *Gallia*, Gaul.
[5]Dubious apocope, possibly of *matois.*
[6]Apocope of *Pyrénées.*
[7]Latin *inultus*, unpunished.
[8]O.F. *dechasser*, to expel.
[9]O.F. *niez*, nephew, grandson; idiot (Godefroy).
[10]Latin *Triones*, Constellation of the Great Bear and the Little Bear.
[11]Latin *felix*, happy.

*June.*

17. Naval victor at "Houche,"[1] at Antwerp divorce,
    Great heir, fire from the sky, trembling, high woods:[2]
    Sardinia woods, Malta, Palermo, Corsica,
    Prelate to die, strikes the one on the Mule.

*July.*

18. The wandering herald turns from the dog to the Lion,
    Fire will burn a town, pillage, new capture:
    To discover foists, Princes captured, they return,
    Spy captive Gaul[3] the maiden joined to the great one.

*August.*[4]

19. Banished from the great Court, conflict, wounded,
    Elected, surrendered, accused, cunning[5] rebels:
    And fire for the Pyrenees city,[6] waters, venoms, pressed
    Not to sail the wave, not to vex the Latins.

*September.*

20. Sea, land to go, faith, loyalty broken,
    Pillage, wreck, tumult in the city:
    Proud, cruel act, ambition satiated,
    Weak one injured, the author of the deed unpunished.

*October.*

21. Cold, great flood, expelled from the realm,
    Nephew,[7] discord, Bear face East:
    Poison, siege laid, driven out of the City,
    Happy return, new sect in ruins.

[1]Hoek? Hoek-van-Holland?

[2]Or "burning," or "pillage."

[3]This double-apocope phrase is naturally very very dubious as regards meaning and translation.

[4]This Presage should cover the catastrophic French defeat at Saint-Quentin (August 10, 1557).

[5]At best little more than a guess. See note 5, opposite.

[6]Probably Perpignan.

[7]Or "Grandson," or "Idiot."

22.  Mer close, monde ouvert, cité rendue,
     Faillir le Grand, élu nouveau grande brume:
     *Floram patere*,[1] entrer camp, foi rompue,
     Effort fera sévère à blanche plume.

23.  Tutelle à *Veste*, guerre meurt, *translatée*,[2]
     Combat naval, honneur, mort, prélature:
     Entrée décès, *France* fort augmentée,
     Élu passé, venu à la mal'heure.

## 1558.

24.  Puîné Roi fait funèbre épithalame,
     Sacrés émus festins, jeux, *soupi*[3] Mars:
     Nuit larme[4] on crie, hors on conduit la Dame,
     L'arrêt et *pache*[5] rompu de toutes *pars*.[6]

25.  Vaine rumeur dedans la hiérarchie,
     Rebeller *Gennes:* courses, insultes, tumultes:
     Au plus grand Roi sera la monarchie,
     Élection, conflit, couverts, *sepultes*.[7]

26.  Par la discorde défaillir au défaut,
     Un tout à coup le remettra au sus:
     Vers l'Aquilon seront les bruits si haut,
     Lésions, pointes à travers, par-dessus.

27.  La mer *Tyrrhene* de différente voile,
     Par l'Océan seront divers assauts:
     Peste, poison, sang en maison de toile,
     *Presults*[8] Légats émus marcher mer haut.

---

[1]Latin *floram patere*, the flower to open (or, possibly, Florence, etc.). In italics in the original text, which made Piobb (1927) regard it as "the key to the mystery."

[2]O.F. *translater*, to transfer.

[3]Aphaeresis for *assoupi*.

[4]Le Pelletier thinks this should be *l'arme*, i.e., *aux armes*.

[5]O.F. *pache*, peace, agreement.

[6]O.F. *par*, side.

[7]From Latin *sepultus*, buried.

[8]Latin *praesul*, president, prefect; public dancer.

*November.*

22. Sea closed, world opened, city surrendered,
    The Great One to fail, newly elected great mist:
    Florence[1] to open, army to enter, faith broken,
    A severe effort will be made by the white feather.

*December.*

23. Guardianship for Vesta,[2] war dies, transferred,
    Naval combat, honor, death, prelacy:
    Entry death, France greatly augmented,
    Elected one passed, come to a bad end.

## 1558.

*January.*[3]

24. The Younger King makes a mournful wedding song,
    Holy one stirred up feasts, games, Mars quieted:
    By night tears[4] they cry, they lead the Lady outside,
    The arrest and peace broken on all sides.

*March.*

25. Vain rumor within the hierarchy,
    Genoa to rebel: flights, offenses, tumults:
    The monarchy will be for the greater King,
    Election, conflict, coverings, burials.

*April.*

26. Through discord in the absence to fail,
    One suddenly will put him back on top:
    Towards the North the noises will be very loud,
    Injuries, points across, above.

*May.*

27. Of different sail on the Tyrrhenian Sea,
    On the Ocean there will be diverse assaults:
    Plague, poison, blood in the house of cloth,
    Presidents, Legates stirred up to march high seas.

[1] Or possibly just "Flower."
[2] The Roman Mother-Goddess of the Earth. Used chiefly in regard to the Vestal Virgins, and thus perhaps for the Virgin.
[3] This Presage should cover the French recapture of Calais (January 6, 1558), last British possession in France.
[4] Or, according to Le Pelletier, "arms" ("to arms").

*Juin.*

28.  Là où la foi était sera rompue,
     Les ennemis les ennemis paîtront:
     Feu ciel pleuvra, ardra, interrompue,
     Nuit entreprise. Chefs querelles mettront.


*Juillet.*

29.  Guerre, tonnerre, maints champs *depopulez*,[1]
     Frayeur et bruit, assaut à la frontière:
     Grand Grand failli, pardon aux Exilés,
     *Germains, Hispans.*[2] par mer *Barba.*[3] bannière.


*Août.*

30.  Bruit sera vain, les défaillants troussés,
     Les Rases pris: élu le *Pempotan:*[4]
     Faillir deux Rouges et quatre bien croisés,
     Pluie *empeschable*[5] au Monarque *potent.*[6]


*Octobre.*

31.  Pluie, vent, *classe*[7] Barbare *Ister,*[8] *Tyrrhene,*
     Passer *holcades,*[9] *Ceres,*[10] soldats munies:
     Réduits bien faits par *Flor.*[11] franchie *Sienne,*
     Les deux seront morts, amitiés unies.


*Novembre.*

32.  *Venus* la belle entrera dedans *FLORE.*[12]
     Les Exilés secrets lairront[13] la place:
     Veuves beaucoup, mort de Grand on déplore,
     Ôter du regne, le Grand Grand ne menace.

[1]Latin *depopulatus*, depopulated.
[2]From Latin *Hispania*, Spain.
[3]Apocope of *Barbare*.
[4]Apparently a hybrid of Greek *pan*, all, and Latin *potens*, powerful, thus all-powerful (see Epistle, para. 44; 897, 10100).
[5]O.F. *empeschable*, troublesome, intrusive, tiresome, inconvenient.
[6]Latin *potens*, powerful.
[7]Latin *classis*, fleet.
[8]Latin *Ister*, Danube.
[9]Latin *Olcades*, a tribe dwelling in southeastern Spain; or *Orcades*, the Orkney Islands.
[10]Latin *Ceres*, Goddess of Corn and fruits. The latter by metonymy.
[11]Apocope of *Flora*, Flower, used for Florence, apparently.
[12]Latin *Flora*, Flower, apparently used for Florence.
[13]O.F. *lairrer*. to abandon.

*June.*

28. There where the faith was it will be broken,
    The enemies will feed upon the enemies:
    The sky to rain fire, it will burn, interrupted,
    Enterprise by night. Chiefs will make quarrels.

*July.*

29. War, thunder, many fields depopulated,
    Terror and noise, assault on the frontier:
    The Great Great One fallen, pardon for the Exiles,
    Germans, Spaniards by sea the Barbarian banner.

*August.*

30. The noise will be vain, the faltering ones trussed up,
    The Shaven Ones taken: the All-powerful One[1] elected:
    The two Red Ones and four true crusaders to fail,
    Rain inconvenient for the powerful Monarch.

*October.*

31. Rain, wind, Barbarian fleet, Danube, Tyrrhenian Sea,
    To pass the Orkneys,[2] grain, soldiers provided:
    Retreats well executed by Florence, Siena crossed,
    The two will be dead, friendships joined.

*November.*

32. Venus the beautiful will enter Florence.
    The secret Exiles will abandon the place:
    Many widows, they will lament the death of a Great One,
    To remove from the realm, the Great Great One does not threaten.

[1]Used for England in 10100. See also note 4, opposite.
[2]Dubious. For other possibility, see note 9, opposite.

*Décembre.*

33.  Jeux, festins, noces, mort Prélat de renom,
     Bruit, paix de trève pendant l'ennemi mine:
     Mer, terre et ciel bruit, fait du grand *Brennon,*
     Cris or, argent, l'ennemi l'on ruine.

## *1559.*

*Sur la dite année.*

34.  Peur, glas grand pille, passer mer, croître regne,
     Sectes, sacrés outre mer plus polis:
     Peste, chaud, feu, Roi d'Aquilon l'enseigne,
     Dresser trophée, cité d'*HENRIPOLIS.*

*Janvier.*

35.  Plus le Grand n'être, pluie, au char, le cristal.
     Tumulte ému, de tous biens abondance:
     Rasés, Sacrés, neufs, vieux *espouvental,*[1]
     Élu ingrat, mort, plaint, joie, alliance.

*Février.*

36.  Grain corrompu, air pestilent, locustes,
     Subit cherra, noue nouvelle naître:
     Captifs ferrés, légers, haut bas, *onustes,*[2]
     Par ses os mal qu'à Roi n'a voulu être.

*Mars.*

37.  Saisis au temple, par sectes longue brigue,
     Élu ravi au bois forme querelle:
     Septante *pars*[3] naître nouvelle ligue,
     De là leur mort, Roi apaisé nouvelle.

*Avril.*

38.  Roi salué *Victeur,*[4] *Impereateur,*[5]
     La foi faussée, le Royal fait connu:
     Sang *Mathien,*[6] Roi fait *supereatur,*[7]
     De gent superbe humble par pleurs venu.

[1] O.F. *espouvental,* frightful.
[2] Latin *onustus,* loaded, burdened, full.
[3] O.F. *pair, par,* pair; *part, par,* side (Godefroy).
[4] Latin *Victor,* conqueror.
[5] Latin *Imperator,* Master, General (or Emperor).
[6] Dubious. Possibly aphaeresis of *Aemathien* (see Index for others in Centuries), from Latin *Emathius,* Macedonian. Or possibly from *mal de Saint-Mathelin,* epilepsy.
[7] Latin *superator,* conqueror.

33. Games, feasts, nuptials, Prelate of renown dead,
    Noise, peace of truce while the enemy undermines:
    Noise on sea, land and sky, deed by the great Brennus,[1]
    Cries gold, silver, the enemy they ruin.

## 1559.

*On the said year.*

34. Fear, knell, great pillage, to pass the sea, realm to grow,
    Sects, holy ones more polite beyond the sea:
    Plague, warmth, fire, banner of the King of "Aquilon,"[2]
    To prepare a trophy, city of "Henripolis."[3]

*January.*

35. The Great One to be no longer, rain, in the chariot, the crystal.
    Tumult stirred up, abundance of all goods:
    Shaven Ones, Holy Ones, new ones, old ones, frightful,
    Ingrate elected, death, lament, joy, alliance.

*February.*

36. Grain spoiled, air pestilent, locusts,
    Suddenly it will fall, new pasturage to arise:
    Captives put in irons, light ones, high low, burdened,
    Through his bones evil to the King he did not wish to be.

*March.*

37. Seized in the temple, through sects long intrigue,
    Elected ravished in the woods forms a quarrel:
    Seventy pairs new league to be born,
    From there their death, King appeased news.

*April.*

38. King hailed as Conqueror and Master,[4]
    Faith broken, the royal deed known:
    Macedonian[5] blood, King made conqueror
    Of a proud people become humble through tears.

[1] The Celtic chief who conquered Rome in 390 B.C.

[2] The North[ern Country].

[3] Somewhat redundant, since *polis* is Greek for city. Thus "city of Henry's city." Most likely Paris (for Henry II) is intended.

[4] "Emperor" is rather unlikely here.

[5] Or possibly "Epileptic." See note 6, opposite.

*Mai.*

39. Par le dépit noces, épithalame,
    Par les trois parts Rouges, Rasés partis:
    Au jeune noir[1] remis par flamme l'âme,
    Au grand *Neptune Ogmius* convertis.

*Juin.*

40. De maison sept par mort mortelle suite,
    Grêle, tempête, pestilent mal, fureurs:
    Roi d'Orient d'Occident tous en fuite,
    Subjuguera ses jadis *conquereurs.*[2]

*Juillet.*

41. *Predons*[3] pillés chaleur, grande sécheresse,
    Par trop non être, cas non vu, inouï:
    À l'étranger la trop grande caresse,
    Neuf pays Roi, l'Orient ébloui.

*Août.*

42. L'Urne trouvée, la cité tributaire,
    Champs divisés, nouvelle tromperie:
    L'*Hispan*[4] blessé faim, peste, militaire,
    *Moq*[5] obstiné, confus, mal, rêverie.

*Septembre.*

43. Vierges et veuves, votre bon temps s'approche,
    Point ne sera ce que l'on prétendra:
    Loin s'en faudra que soit nouvelle approche,
    Bien aisés pris, bien remis, pis tiendra.

*Octobre.*

44. Ici dedans se parachevera,
    Les trois Grands hors le *BON-BOURG*[6] sera loin:
    Encontre d'eux l'un d'eux conspirera,
    Au bout du mois on verra le besoin.

[1]Here again, as often in the Centuries, probably anagram for *roi/roy.*
[2]O.F. *conquereur*, conqueror.
[3]Latin *praedo*, plunderer, robber.
[4]Latin *Hispania*, Spain.
[5]O.F. *moque*, mockery (Godefroy).
[6]A rather obvious play on *Bourbon.*

*May.*

39. Through spite nuptials, wedding song,
    For the three parts Red Ones, Shaven Ones parted:
    For the young black one[1] the soul restored by fire,
    Converted to the great Neptune Ogmios.[2]

*June.*

40. Mortal sequence in death of the house seven,
    Hail, tempest, pestilent evil, furies:
    King of the East[3] all of the West in flight,
    He will subjugate his former conquerors.

*July.*[4]

41. Plunderers[5] pillaged heat, great drought,
    Through too much not being, event unseen, unheard of:
    For the foreigner the too great affection,
    New country King, the East dazzled.

*August.*

42. The Urn found, the city tributary,
    Fields divided, new deceit:
    Spain wounded famine, plague, military,
    Mockery obstinate, confused, evil, reverie.

*September.*

43. Virgins and widows, your good time approaches,
    It will not at all be that which they pretend:
    Far it will be necessary that the approach for it be new,
    The very comfortable ones taken, completely restored, it will hold
    worse.

*October.*

44. Here within it will be completed,
    The three Great Ones outside the Bourbon will be far:
    Against them one of them will conspire,
    At the end of the month they will see the need.

[1]Or, more likely, "For the young king."

[2]The Celtic Hercules. Also an enigmatic name used by Nostradamus (see General Index).

[3]Presumably Suleiman the Magnificent (1520–1566), who was, however, involved in only the most desultory war with Ferdinand in Hungary, 1551–62. No big victories or big defeats for anyone.

[4]This Presage should cover the death of King Henry II in a tournament (July 10, 1559).

[5]Pirates?

45. Propos tenus, noces recommencées,
    La Grande Grande sortira hors de *France:*
    Voix à *Romagne* de crier non lassée,
    Reçoit la paix par trop feinte assurance.

46. La joie en larmes viendra captiver *Mars,*
    Devant le Grand seront émus Divins:
    Sans sonner mot entreront par trois *pars,*[1]
    *Mars* assoupi, dessus glace *troutent*[2] vins.

## *1560.*

47. Journée, diète, intérim, ne concile,
    L'an paix prépare, peste, faim schismatique:
    Mis hors dedans, changer ciel, domicile,
    Fin du congé, révolte hiérarchique.

48. Rompre diète, l'antique sacré ravoir,
    Dessous les deux, feu par pardon s'ensuivre:
    Hors d'armes Sacre: long Rouge voudra avoir,
    Paix du *neglect,*[3] l'Élu *le Vefue*[4] vivre.

49. Fera *paroir*[5] élu de nouveauté,
    Lieu de journée, sortir hors des limites:
    La bonté feinte de changer cruauté,
    Du lieu suspect sortiront *trestous*[6] vite.

50. Du lieu élu Rases n'être contents,
    Du Lac *Leman* conduite non prouvée:
    Renouveler on fera le vieil temps,
    *Espeuïllera*[7] la trame tant couvée.

---

[1] O.F. *par,* side.
[2] From Provençal *troutar,* to run.
[3] Latin *neglectus,* neglected.
[4] Rather dubious. Either *le Veuf* or *la Veuve,* but not *le Veuve.*
[5] Aphaeresis of *apparoir.*
[6] O.F. *trestous,* every single one, all.
[7] Very dubious. O.F. *espewirer,* to frighten, or Provençal *espelhar,* to strip, despoil.

*November.*

45. Talks held, nuptials begun again,
    The Great Great female will go out of France:
    Voice in Romagna not weary of crying out,
    Receives the peace through too false assurance.

*December.*

46. The joy in tears will come to captivate Mars,
    Before the Great One Divine Ones will be stirred up:
    Without saying a word they will enter from three sides,
    Mars quieted, wines run on ice.

## 1560.

*January.*

47. Day, diet, interim, no council,
    The year peace is being prepared, plague, famine schismatic:
    Put outside inside, sky to change, domicile,
    End of the leave, revolt in the hierarchy.

*February.*

48. Diet to break up, the ancient holy one to recover,
    Under the two, fire through pardon to follow:
    Consecration without arms: the tall Red One will want to have,
    Peace of neglect, the Elected One Widower to live.[1]

*March.*

49. To be made to appear elected with novelty,
    Place of day-labor, to go beyond the boundaries:
    The feigned goodness to change to cruelty,
    They will all go out quickly from the suspect place.

*April.*

50. The Shaven Ones will not be satisfied with the place chosen,
    Led from the Lake of Geneva unproven:
    They will cause the old times to be renewed,
    They will strip[2] the plot so well hatched.

[1] Or "the Elected One a Widow to live."
[2] Or possibly "They will frighten of."

*Mai.*

51. *Pache*[1] *Allobrox*[2] sera interrompu,
    Dernière main fera forte levée:
    Grand conjuré ne sera corrompu,
    Et la nouvelle alliance approuvée.

*Juillet.*

52. Longue *crinite*[3] léser le Gouverneur,
    Faim, fièvre ardente, feu et de sang fumée:
    À tous états Joviaux grand honneur,
    Sédition par Rases allumée.

*Août.*

53. Peste, faim, feu et ardeur non cessée,
    Foudre, grande grêle temple du ciel frappé:
    L'édit, arrêt, et griève loi cassée,
    Chef inventeur ses gens et lui happé.

*Septembre.*

54. Privés seront Rases de leurs harnois,
    Augmentera leur plus grande querelle:
    Père *Liber*[4] déçu *fulg.*[5] *Albonois,*
    Seront rongées sectes à la moelle.

*Octobre.*

55. Sera reçue la requête décente,
    Seront chassés et puis remis au sus:
    La Grande Grande se trouvera contente,
    Aveugles, sourds seront mis au dessus.

*Novembre.*

56. Ne sera mis, les Nouveaux *dechassez.*[6]
    Noir[7] et de *LOIN*[8] et le Grand tiendra fort:
    Recourir armes. Exilés plus chassés,
    Chanter victoire, non libres réconfort.

[1] O.F. *pache*, peace, agreement.
[2] Latin *Allobrox*, the Allobroges, inhabitants of classical Savoy.
[3] Latin *crinitus*, comet.
[4] Latin *Liber*, the Italian deity associated with Bacchus as god of wine.
[5] Apocope of Latin *fulgur*, lightning.
[6] O.F. *dechasser*, to expel.
[7] Probably anagram for *roi/roy* again.
[8] Capitals probably indicate anagram, for *Lion*, or *Lyon*.

51. Savoy peace will be broken,
    The last hand will cause a strong levy:
    The great conspirator will not be corrupted,
    And the new alliance approved.

52. A long comet to injure the Governor,
    Hunger, burning fever, fire and reek of blood:
    Jovial Ones[1] to all estates in great honor,
    Sedition stirred up by Shaven Ones.

53. Plague, famine, fire and ardor incessant,
    Lightning, great hail, temple struck from the sky:
    The edict, arrest, and grievous law broken,
    The chief author he and his people caught.

54. The Shaven Ones will be deprived of their arms,
    It will increase their quarrel much more:
    Father Liber[2] deceived lightning Albanians,[3]
    Sects will be gnawed to the marrow.

55. The modest petition will be received,
    They will be driven out and then restored on top:
    The Great Great female will be found content,
    Blind ones, deaf ones will be put uppermost.

56. He will not be placed, the New Ones expelled.
    Black One[4] and of Lyons[5] and the Great One will hold stoutly:
    To have recourse to arms. Further exiles driven out,
    To sing of victory, not free, consolation.

---

[1]Probably meaning the followers of Jupiter, i.e., pagans, i.e., heretics, i.e., Huguenots.
Nostradamus resents the toleration at first extended to them.

[2]Or "Bacchus." Possibly the implication is that someone is being made drunk.

[3]Widely used as mercenaries. Or "those of Alba," meaning possibly the troops of the
Duke of Alba.

[4]Or "King." See note 7, opposite.

[5]Or "and of the Lion."

57.  Les deuils laissés, suprêmes alliances,
     Rase Grand mort, refus fait en à l'entrée:
     De retour être bienfait en *oubliance*,[1]
     La mort du juste à banquet perpétrée.

## 1561.

*Sur la dite année.*

58.  Le Roi Roi n'être, du Doux la *pernicie*,[2]
     L'an pestilent, les émus *nubileux*:[3]
     Tien' qui tiendra[4] des grands non *letitie*:[5]
     Et passera terme de *cavilleux*.[6]

*Mars.*

59.  Au pied du mur le cendré *cordigeré*,[7]
     L'enclos livré foulant cavalerie:
     Du temple hors *Mars* et le *Falcigeré*,[8]
     Hors, mis, démis, et sus la rêverie.

*Avril.*

60.  Le temps purgé, pestilente tempête,
     Barbare insulte, fureur, invasion:
     Maux infinis par ce mois nous apprête,
     Et les plus Grands, deux moins, *d'irrision*.[9]

*Mai.*

61.  Joie non longue, abandonné des siens,
     L'an pestilent, le plus Grand assailli:
     La Dame bonne aux champs *Elysiens*,
     Et la plupart des biens froid non cueilli.

[1]O.F. *oubliance*, oblivion, forgetfulness.
[2]Latin *pernicies*, destruction, ruin, disaster, calamity.
[3]Latin *nubilosus*, cloudy.
[4]Le Pelletier suggests this is from Latin *teneat qui tenebit*, the equivalent of "every man for himself."
[5]Latin *laetitia*, joy.
[6]Latin *cavillator*, jeerer, mocker.
[7]Low Latin *Cordiger*, Franciscan.
[8]Latin *falciger*, carrying a scythe (an attribute of Saturn).
[9]Latin *irrisio*, mockery.

*December.*[1]

57. The mourning abandoned, supreme alliances,
    Great Shaven One dead, to the entry refusal given:
    Upon return benefits to be in oblivion,
    The death of the just one perpetrated at a banquet.

## 1561.

*On the said year.*

58. The King King not to be, calamity for the Clement One,[2]
    The year pestilent, the beclouded stirred up:
    For the great ones every man for himself no joy:
    And the term of jeerers will pass.

*March.*

59. At the foot of the wall the ashy Franciscan.
    The enclosure delivered the cavalry trampling:
    Outside the temple Mars and Saturn,
    Outside, appointed, dismissed, and upon the reverie.

*April.*

60. The times purged, pestilential tempest,
    Barbarian offense, fury, invasion:
    For this month infinite evils prepared for us,
    And the Greatest Ones, two less, of mockery.

*May.*

61. Joy not long, abandoned by his followers,
    The year pestilent, the Greatest One assailed:
    The good Lady in the Elysian Fields,
    And the greater part of the good things cold unpicked.

[1]This Presage should cover the death in that month of King Francis II, the sickly husband of Mary, Queen of Scots.

[2]Very curious. Le Pelletier makes a very good case for referring this to the assassination of Henry III by Jacques Clément, ignoring the time element (August, 1589, instead of 1561). More likely, even if we grant the *Doux-Clément* pun, is that Nostradamus thought that Pius IV would die and be succeeded by a Clement VIII.

*Juin.*

62. Courses de *LOIN*,[1] ne s'apprêter conflits,
    Triste entreprise, l'air pestilent, hideux:
    De toutes parts les Grands seront *afflits*,[2]
    Et dix et sept assaillir vingt et deux.

*Juillet.*

63. Repris, rendu, épouvanté du mal,
    Le sang par bas, et les faces hideuses:
    Aux plus savants l'ignare *espouuental*,[3]
    Porte, haine, horreur, tomber bas la piteuse.

*Août.*

64. Mort et saisi, des nonchalants le change,
    S'éloignera en s'approchant plus fort:
    Serrés unis en la ruine, grange,
    Par secours long étonné le plus fort.

*Octobre.*

65. Gris, blancs et noirs, *enfumez*[4] et *froquez*,[5]
    Seront remis, démis, mis en leurs sièges:
    Les ravisseurs se trouveront moqués,
    Et les Vestales serrées fortes *riegges*.[6]

## *1562.*

*Sur la dite année.*

66. Saison d'hiver, *ver*[7] bon, sain, mal été,
    Pernicieux automne, sec, froment rare:
    Du vin assez, mal yeux, faits, molesté,
    Guerre, *mutin*,[8] séditieuse tare.

*Janvier.*

67. Désir occulte pour le bon parviendra,
    Religion, paix, amour et concorde:
    L'épithalame du tout ne s'accordra,
    Les haut qui bas, et haut mis à la corde.

[1]Capitals probably indicate anagram for *Lion* or *Lyon*.
[2]O.F. *aflit*, afflicted, thrown down (Roquefort).
[3]O.F. *espouvental*, frightful.
[4]O.F. *enfumer*, to disguise, hide.
[5]Provençal *frocar*, to break, to be put out of combat.
[6]Provençal *riege*, grill, bars, grating.
[7]O.F. *ver*, spring.
[8]O.F. *mutin*, sedition, mutiny.

*June.*

62. Flights of a Lion,[1] not to prepare for conflicts,
    Sad enterprise, the air pestilential, hideous:
    From all sides of the Great Ones will be afflicted,
    And ten and seven to assail twenty and two.

*July.*

63. Retaken, surrendered, frightened by the evil,
    The blood below, and the faces hideous:
    To the most learned ones the ignorant one frightful,
    Gate,[2] hatred, horror, the pitiful female to fall low.

*August.*

64. Dead and seized, the change of the careless ones,
    It will go far away in approaching much more:
    United ones in the ruin, barn,
    Through long help the hardiest one astonished.

*October.*

65. Gray, white, and black ones, hidden and broken,
    They will be replaced, dismissed, put in their sees:
    The ravishers will find themselves mocked,
    And the Vestals confined behind strong bars.

## 1562.

*On the said year.*

66. Season of winter, good spring, sound, bad summer,
    Pernicious autumn, dry, wheat rare:
    Of wine enough, bad eyes, deeds, molested,
    War, sedition, seditious waste.

*January.*

67. Hidden desire for the good will succeed,
    Religion, peace, love and concord:
    The wedding song will not be in accord entirely,
    The high ones low, and high put to the rope.

[1]Or possibly "from Lyons."
[2]Or "Porte." i.e.. the Turkish Sultan.

*Février.*

68.  Pour Rases Chef ne parviendra à bout,
     Édits changés, les serrés mis au large:
     Mort Grand trouvé, moins de foi, bas debout.
     Dissimulé, transi frappé à *bauge*.[1]

*Mars.*

69.  Ému de *LOIN*,[2] de *LOIN*[2] près minera,
     Pris, captive, pacifié par femme:
     Tant ne tiendra comme on barguignera,
     Mis non passés, ôter de rage l'âme.

*Avril.*

70.  De *LOIN*[2] viendra susciter pour mouvoir,
     Vain découvert contre peuple infini:
     De nul connu le mal pour le devoir,
     En la cuisine trouvé mort et fini.

*Mai.*

71.  Rien d'accordé, pire plus fort et trouble,
     Comme il était, terre et mer *tranquiller*:[3]
     Tout arrêté ne vaudra pas un double,
     Dira l'inique, Conseil d'*anichiler*.[4]

*Juin.*

72.  *Portenteux*[5] fait, horrible et incroyable,
     *Typhon*[6] fera émouvoir les méchants:
     Qui puis après soutenus par le cable,
     Et la plupart exilés sur les champs.

*Juillet.*

73.  Droit mis au trône du ciel venu en *France*,
     Pacifié par Vertu l'Univers:
     Plus sage[7] épandre, bien tôt tourner change,
     Par les oiseaux, par feu, et non par *vers*.[8]

---

[1] O.F. *bauge*, hut (Godefroy); heap (Roquefort). Possibly erratum for *barge*, a perfectly good word that would rime.
[2] Capitals probably indicate anagram for *Lion* or *Lyon*.
[3] O.F. *tranquiller*, to quiet (Godefroy).
[4] O.F. *anichiler*, to ruin, destroy (Roquefort).
[5] Latin *portentosus*, portentous.
[6] O.F. *typhon*, rash, bold.
[7] Le Pelletier thinks this an erratum for *sang*.
[8] Dubious. Possibly from Latin *vir*, man.

68. For the Shaven Ones the Chief will not reach the end,
    Edicts changed, the confined ones set at large:
    Great One found dead, less of faith, standing low.
    Dissimulated, chilled struck in the hut.[1]

69. Moved by Lyon,[2] near Lyon[2] he will undermine,
    Taken, captive, pacified by a woman:
    He will not hold as well as they will hesitate,
    Placed unpassed, to remove the soul from rage.

70. From Lyon[2] he will come to arouse to move,
    Vain discovery against infinite people:
    Known by none the evil for duty,
    In the kitchen found dead and finished.

71. Nothing in accord, trouble worse and more severe,
    As it was, land and sea to quiet:
    All stopped it will not be worth a double,
    The wicked one will speak, Counsel of destruction.

72. Portentous deed, horrible and unbelievable,
    The Bold One will cause the wicked ones to be stirred up:
    Those who then afterwards supported by the rope,
    And the greater part exiled on the fields.

73. Right enthroned come from the sky into France,
    The Universe pacified by Virtue:
    Wiser to scatter,[3] sooner change to come,
    For[4] the birds, for[4] fire, and not for[4] men.[5]

---

[1]Or "in a heap." Or (by erratum, see note 1, opposite) possibly "in a haystack."
[2]Or "the Lion."
[3]Or possibly "Blood to be shed" (see note 7, opposite).
[4]Or "through."
[5]Uncertain. See note 8, opposite.

*Août.*

74. Les colorés, les Sacres malcontents,
    Puis tout à coup par Androgynes allègres:
    De la plupart voir, non venu le temps,
    Plusieurs d'entre eux feront leur soupes maigres.

*Septembre.*

75. Remis seront en leur pleine puissance,
    D'un point d'accord conjoints, non accordés:
    Tous defiés, plus aux Rases fiance,
    Plusieurs d'entre eux à bande débordés.

*Octobre.*

76. Par le légat du terrestre et marin,
    La grande Cape à tout s'accommoder:
    Être à l'écoute tacite LORVARIN,[1]
    Qu'à son avis ne voudra accorder.

*Novembre.*

77. D'ennemi vent empêchera la troupe,
    Le plus grand point mis avant difficile:
    Vin de poison se mettra dans la coupe,
    Passer sans mal de cheval gros fusil.

*Décembre.*

78. Par le cristal l'entreprise rompue.
    Jeux et festins, de LOIN[2] plus reposer:
    Plus ne fera près des Grands sa *repue*,[3]
    Subit catarrhe l'eau bénite arroser.

## *1563.*

*Sur la dite année.*

79. Lever sain, sang, mais ému, rien d'accord,
    Infinis meurtres, captifs, morts, prévenus:
    Tant d'eau et peste, peu de tout, sonnés cors,
    Pris, morts, fuites, grands devenir, venus.

[1]Anagram for *Lorraine*, fairly obvious.
[2]Capitals probably indicate anagram for *Lion* or *Lyon*.
[3]O.F. *repue*, meal (Sainte-Palaye).

*August.*

74. The colored ones, the discontented Holy Ones,
Then suddenly through the gay Hermaphrodites:
Of the greater part to see, the time not come,
Several amongst them will make their soups weak.

*September.*

75. They will be restored to their full power,
Conjoined at one point of accord, not in accord:
All defied, more betrothed to the Shaven Ones,
Several amongst them outflanked in a band.

*October.*

76. For the legate of land and sea,
The great Cape[1] will accommodate himself to all:
Silent Lorraine to be listening,
He whose advice they will not agree with.

*November.*

77. The wind will impede the enemy troop,
For the greatest one difficult to advance at all:
Wine with poison will be put in the cup,
To pass the great gun without horse-power.

*December.*

78. Because of the crystal[2] the enterprise broken.
Games and feasts, in Lyons[3] to repose more:
No longer will he take his meal near the Great Ones,
Sudden catarrh blessed water to wash him.

## *1563.*

*On the said year*

79. To restore health, blood, but stirred up, nothing in accord,
Infinite murders, captives, deaths, warned:
So much water and plague, little of all, horns sounded,
Taken, deaths, flights, to become great, come.

[1] Quite possibly a play on "Capet."
[2] I.e., ice.
[3] Or "a Lion."

*Janvier.*

80. Tant d'eau, tant morts, tant d'armes émouvoir,
    Rien d'accordé, le Grand tenu captif:
    Que sang humain, rage, fureur n'avoir:
    Tard pénitent peste, guerre motif.

*Février.*

81. Des ennemis *mort*[1] de langue s'approche,
    Le Débonnaire en paix voudra réduire:
    Les obstinés voudront perdre la proche,
    Surpris, captifs, et suspects fureur nuire.

*Mars.*

82. Pères et mères morts de deuils infinis,
    Femmes à deuil, la pestilente monstre:
    Le Grand plus n'être, tout le monde finir,
    Sous paix, repos, et *trestous*[2] à l'encontre.

*Avril.*

83. En débats Prince et Chrétienté émue,
    *Gentils*[3] étranges, siège à *CHRIST* molesté:
    Venu très mal, prou bien, mortelle vue.
    Mort Orient peste, faim, mal traité.

*Mai.*

84. Terre trembler, tué prodige, monstre,
    Captifs sans nombre, faire défaite, faite:
    D'aller sur mer aviendra malencontre,
    Fier contre fier mal fait de contrefaire.

*Juin.*

85. L'injuste bas fort l'on molestera,
    Grêle, inonder, trésor, et gravé marbre:
    Chef de *suard*[4] peuple à mort tuera,
    Et attachée sera la lame à l'arbre.

[1]O.F. *mort*, bite.
[2]O.F. *trestous*, every single one, all.
[3]O.F. *gentil*, noble (Sainte-Palaye).
[4]Dubious. Probably from Latin *Suada*, Goddess of Persuasion. Or from *Suardones*, inhabitants of classical Brunswick (or Lüneburg, or Hanover).

*January.*

80. So much water, so many deaths, so many arms to stir up.
Nothing in accord, the Great One held captive:
What has not human blood, rage, fury,
Repentant too late plague, war the cause.

*February.*

81. The bite of the enemy's tongue approaches,
The Good-natured One to peace he will want to reduce:
The obstinate ones will want to lose the kinswoman,
Surprised, captives, and suspects fury to injure.

*March.*

82. Fathers and mothers dead of infinite sorrows,
Women in mourning, the pestilent monster:[1]
The Great One to be no more, all the word to end,
Under peace, repose and all in opposition.

*April.*

83. Princes and Christendom stirred up in debates,
Foreign nobles, Christ's see[2] molested:
Become very evil, much good, mortal sight.
In the East death, plague, famine, bad treaty.

*May.*

84. Land to tremble, prodigy killed, monster,
Numberless captives, to do, undone, done:
To go by sea mishap will occur,
Proud against proud one evil done in disguise.

*June.*

85. The unjust one low they will molest him terribly,
Hail, to flood, treasure, and marble engraved:
Chief of Persuasion[3] people to death will kill,
And the blade will be attached to the tree.

[1]Apparently a female monster. See Presage 82 opposite.
[2]I.e., the Papacy.
[3]Dubious. Possibly "of Brunswick." See note 4, opposite.

86.  De quel non mal? inexcusable suite,
     Le feu non duel, le Légat hors confus:
     Au plus blessé ne sera faite luite,
     La fin de Juin le fil coupé de *fus*.[1]

87.  Bons finement affaiblis par accords,
     *Mars* et Prélats unis n'arrêteront:
     Les Grands confus par dons *incidez*[2] corps,
     Dignes indignes biens indues saisiront.

88.  De bien en mal le temps se changera,
     Le *pache*[3] d'*Aust*,[4] des plus Grands espérance:
     Des Grands *deul*[5] *LVIS* trop plus trébuchera,
     Connus Rases pouvoir ni connaissance.

89.  Voici le mois par maux tant à douter,
     Morts, tous saigner peste, faim, quereller:
     Ceux du rebours d'exil viendront noter,
     Grands, secrets, morts, non de *contreroller*.[6]

90.  Par mort mort mordre, conseil, *vol*,[7] pestifère,
     On n'osera Marins[8] assaillir:
     *Deucalion* un dernier trouble faire,
     Peu de gens jeunes: demi-morts tressaillir.

91.  Mort par dépit fera les autres luire,
     Et en haut lieu de grands maux avenir:
     Tristes concepts à chacun viendront nuire,
     Temporel digne, la Messe parvenir.

[1]O.F. *fus*, (1) fire, (2) wood, (3) spindle.
[2]Latin *incidere*, to cut open.
[3]O.F. *pache*, peace, agreement.
[4]Apocope for either *Austriche*, Austria, or *Auster*, South Wind.
[5]Either O.F. for *deuil* or, as Le Pelletier suggests, erratum for *seul*.
[6]O.F. *contreroler*, to criticize, to censure (Sainte-Palaye).
[7]O.F. *vol*, robbery, pillage, plunder.
[8]All right as is, or perhaps should be *Marines*.

*July.*

86. Of what not evil? inexcusable consequence,
    The fire not double, the Legate outside confused:
    Against the worse wounded the struggle will not be waged,
    The end of June the thread cut by fire.[1]

*August.*

87. Good ones acutely weakened by agreements,
    Mars and Prelates united will not stop:
    The Great Ones confused by gifts bodies cut open,
    Worthy ones unworthy ones undue goods will seize.

*September.*

88. From good to evil the times will change,
    The peace in the South,[2] hope of the Greatest Ones:
    Of the Great Ones only[3] Louis[4] too much more will stumble,
    Shaven Ones recognized neither power nor recognition.

*October.*

89. Here is the month for evils so many as to be doubted,
    Deaths, plague to bleed all, famine, to quarrel:
    Those of the reverse of exile will come to observe,
    Great Ones, secrets, deaths, not to criticize.

*November.*

90. Through death death to bite, counsel, plunder, pestiferous,
    They will not dare to attack seamen:[5]
    Deucalion a final trouble to cause,
    Few young people: half-dead to give a start.

*December.*

91. Dead through spite he will cause the others to shine,
    And in a high place some great evils to occur:
    Sad conceptions will come to harm each one,
    Temporal worthy, the Mass to succeed.

[1] Or "wood"; or possibly "the thread of the spindle cut."
[2] Or possibly "the peace of Austria."
[3] Or possibly "grieving."
[4] The most famous Louis of the day was Prince Louis I de Condé (1530–69), brother of Anthony of Navarre, uncle of Henry IV, Huguenot leader assassinated in 1569 at the Battle of Jarnac.
[5] Or possibly "to attack fleets."

# 1564.

92. L'an sextil pluies froment abonder, haines,
    Aux hommes joie, Princes Rois en divorce:
    Troupeau périr, mutations humains,
    Peuple *affoulé:*[1] et à poison sous l'écorce.

93. Temps fort divers, discorde découverte,
    Conseil *belliq,*[2] changement pris, changé:
    La Grande n'être, conjurés par eau perte,
    Grande *simulté,*[3] tous au plus Grand rangé.

94. Déluge grand, bruit de mort conspirée,
    Renoué siècle, trois Grands en grande discorde:
    Par boute-feux la concorde empirée,
    Pluie empêchant, conseils malins d'accord.

95. Entre Rois haines on verra apparaître,
    Dissensions et Guerres commencer:
    Grand Changement, nouveau tumulte croître,
    L'ordre plebée on viendra offenser.

96. Secret *coniur,*[4] conspirer populaire,
    La découverte en machine émouvoir:
    Contre les Grands, *[5]
    Puis *trucidé*[6] et mises sans pouvoir.

97. Temps inconstant, fièvres, peste, langueurs,
    Guerres, débats, temps désolé sans feindre:
    Submersions, Princes à mineurs rigueurs,
    *Felices*[7] Rois et Grands, autre mort craindre.

---

[1]O.F. *affouler,* to become mad; to step on, oppress, vex, murder.
[2]Latin *bellicus,* of war, warlike.
[3]Latin *simultas,* enmity, hostility, dissension, animosity.
[4]O.F. *conjur,* conspiracy (Godefroy).
[5]This is exactly as it appears in the 1605. We can only assume that at this point the Censor found a bit more than the Church would take from M. Nostradamus.
[6]Latin *trucidere,* to slaughter.
[7]Latin *felix,* happy.

# 1564.

*On the said year.*

92. The year sextile rains wheat to abound, hatreds,
For men joy, Princes and Kings divorced:
Flock to perish, human mutations,
People oppressed: and under the crust poisoned.

*January.*

93. Times very diverse, discord discovered,
Counsel of war, change made, changed:
The Great Female not to be, conspirators through water loss,
Great dissension, for[1] the great one all ranged.

*February.*

94. Great flood, noise of death conspired,
Age renewed, three Great Ones in great discord:
Through incendiaries the concord aggravated,
Rain impeding, wicked counsel of agreement.

*March.*

95. Between Kings one will see hatreds appear,
Dissensions and Wars to begin:
Great Change, new tumult to grow,
The plebeian order they will come to injure.

*April.*

96. Secret conspiracy, rabble to conspire,
The discovery in the device to move:
Against the Great Ones, . . .[2]
Then slaughtered and put without power.

*May.*

97. Times inconstant, fevers, plague, languors,
Wars, debates, times desolated without pretending:
Submersions, Princes to minors severities,
Happy Kings and Great Ones, other death to fear.

[1]Or "against."
[2]Apparently censored here. See note 5, opposite.

*Juin.*

98.  Du lieu feu mis la peste et fuite naître,
     Temps variant, vent, la mort de trois Grands:
     Du Ciel grands foudres, état des Rases paître,
     Vieil près de mort bois peu dedans *vergans*.[1]

*Juillet.*

99.  En péril monde et Rois féliciter,
     Rases émus par conseil ce qu'était
     L'Église Rois pour eux peuple irriter,
     Un montrera après ce qu'il n'était.

*Août.*

100. Déluge près, peste bovine, neuve.
     Secte fléchir, aux hommes joie vaine:
     De loi sans loi, mis au devant pour preuve,
     Appât, embûche: et décus couper veine.

*Septembre.*

101. Tout inonder, à la Rasée perte,
     Vol de mur, mort, de tous biens abondance:
     Échappera par manteau de couvertes,
     Des neufs et vieux sera tournée chance.

*Octobre.*

102. La bouche et gorge en *fervides*[2] pustules,
     De sept Grands cinq, tous distillante nuire:
     Pluie si longue, à non mort tournent bulles,
     Le Grand mourir, qui *trestous*[3] faisait luire.

*Novembre.*

103. Par bruit de feu Grands et Vieux défaillir.
     Peste assoupie, une plus grande naître:
     Peste de l'*Ara*,[4] foin caché, peu cueillir,
     Mourir troupeau fertile, joie hors prêtre.

*Décembre.*

104. Allègre point, douce fureur au Sacre,
     Enflés trois quatre et au côté mourir:
     Voie défaillir, n'être à demi au sacre,
     Par sept et trois, et par quinte courir.

---

[1]Dubious. Either O.F. *vergon*, twig, or Latin *vergere*, to bend.
[2]Latin *fervidus*, burning.
[3]O.F. *trestous*, every single one, all.
[4]Latin *ara*. altar.

98. In the place fire placed the plague and flight will arise,
    Times fickle, wind, the death of three Great Ones:
    From the Sky great thunderbolts, to feed upon the estate of Shaven
                          Ones,
    Old One near death wood scarce in twigs.[1]

99. The world in peril and Kings to congratulate,
    Shaven Ones stirred up by counsel that which was
    The Church Kings for them people to irritate,
    One will show afterwards what he was not.

100. Flood near, bovine plague, new.
    Sect to bend, for men vain joy:
    Of law without law, placed in front for proof,
    Bait, ambush: and deceived to cut a vein.

101. To flood all, loss for the Shaven Female,
    Wall flight, death, abundance of all goods:
    He will escape through a coat of coverings,
    The luck of new ones and old ones will be changed.

102. The mouth and throat in burning pustules,
    Five of seven Great Ones, the distillant to harm all:
    Rain so long, not to death blisters turn,
    The Great One to die, he who made all to shine.

103. Through noise of fire Great Ones and Old Ones to fail.
    Plague quieted, a greater female to be born:
    Plague of the Altar, hidden hay, to pick little,
    Fertile flock to die, joy beyond the priest.

104. Gay point, sweet fury at the Consecration,
    Swelled up three four and on the side to die:
    Way to fail, not to be by half at the consecration,
    For seven and three, and for fifth to run.

[1] Or "in bending."

## 1565.

*Sur la dite année.*

105.  Pire cent fois cet an que l'an passé,
      Même au plus Grands du regne et de l'Église:
      Maux infinis, mort, exil, ruine, cassé,
      À mort Grande être, peste, plaies et bille.[1]

*Janvier.*

106.  Neiges, rouillures, pluies et plaies grandes,
      Au plus Grands joie, pestilence *insopie*:[2]
      Semences, grains beaucoup, et plus de bandes,
      S'apprêteront, *simulté*[3] n'amortie.

*Février.*

107.  Entre les Grands naître grande discorde,
      Le Clerc *procere*[4] un grand cas brassera:
      Nouvelles sectes mettre en haine et discorde,
      Tout peuple guerre et change offensera.

*Mars.*

108.  Secret *coniur*,[5] changement périlleux,
      Secrètement conspirer factions:
      Pluies, grands vents, plaies par orgueilleux,
      Inonder *flumes*,[6] pestifères actions.

*Avril.*

109.  Pulluler peste, les Sectes s'entrebattre,
      Temps modéré l'hiver peu de retour:
      De messe et prêche grièvement se débattre,
      Inonder fleuves, maux, mortels tout autour.

*Mai.*

110.  Au menu peuple par débats et querelles,
      Et par les femmes et défunts grande guerre:
      Mort d'une Grande, célébrer écrouelles,
      Plus grandes Dames expulsées de terre.

---

[1]This obviously does not rime with *Eglise. Bise* would both rime and make sense. Besides the many meanings of *bille* (if correct), it can also be a variant spelling of *bile,* with additional meanings possible.

[2]Latin *insopitus,* sleepless, wakeful.

[3]Latin *simultas,* dissension, hostility, enmity.

[4]Latin *procer,* noble; *procerus,* tall.

[5]O.F. *conjur,* conspiracy (Godefroy).

[6]Latin *flumen,* river.

# *1565.*

105. A hundred times worse this year than the year passed,
     Even for the Greatest Ones of the realm and of the Church:
     Infinite evils, death, exile, ruin, broken,
     The Great Female to death to be, plague, wounds and log.[1]

*January.*

106. Snow, rust, rain and great plagues,
     For the Greatest Ones joy, pestilence sleepless:
     Seeds, grains plentiful, and more of bands,
     They will prepare themselves, hostility unallayed.

*February.*

107. Among the Great Ones great discord to arise,
     The tall[2] Cleric will plot a great event:
     New sects to place in hatred and discord,
     War and change to injure all people.

*March.*

108. Secret conspiracy, perilous change,
     Factions to conspire secretly:
     Rains, great winds, plagues for proud ones,
     Rivers to overflow, pestiferous actions.

*April.*

109. Plague to multiply, the Sects to fight each other,
     Times moderated winter little return:
     Of mass and meeting house grievously to debate,
     Rivers to overflow, evils, mortals all around.

*May.*

110. People in debates and quarrels over trivia,
     And over women and deceased great war:
     Death of a Great Female, to celebrate king's evil,
     More great Ladies expelled from the land.

[1]For other possibilities, see note 1, opposite.
[2]Or "noble."

*Juin.*

111. Viduité tant mâles que femelles,
     De grands Monarques la vie péricliter:
     Peste, fer, faim, grand péril pêle-mêle,
     Troubles par changes, pettis Grands *conciter.*[1]

*Juillet.*

112. Grêle, rouillure, pluies et grandes plaies,
     Préserver femmes, seront cause du bruit:
     Mort de plusieurs peste, fer, faim par *haies,*[2]
     Ciel sera vu quoi dire qu'il reluit.

*Août.*

113. Point ne sera le grain à suffisance,
     La mort s'approche à neiger plus que blanc:
     Stérilité, grain pourri, d'eau *bondance,*[3]
     Le grand blessé, plusieurs de mort de flanc.

*Septembre.*

114. Guère de fruits, ni grain, arbres et arbrisseaux,
     Grand *volataille,*[4] *procere*[5] stimuler:
     Tant temporel que prélat *leonceaux,*[6]
     *TOLANDAD*[7] vaincre, *proceres*[5] reculer.

*Octobre.*

115. Du tout changé, persécuter l'un quatre,
     Hors maladie, bien loin mortalité:
     Des quatre deux plus ne viendront débattre,
     Exil, ruine, mort, faim, perplexité.

*Novembre.*

116. Des grands le nombre plus grands ne sera tant.
     Grands changements, commotions, fer, peste:
     Le peu devis: prêtés, payés, comptant,
     Mois opposite gelée fort moleste.

[1] Latin *concitare*, to stir up, incite.
[2] O.F. *haie*, hatred.
[3] Aphaeresis of *abondance*.
[4] Dubious. Possibly Nostradamian variant for *volatile*.
[5] Latin *procere*, noble; *procerus*, tall.
[6] O.F. *leoncel*, young lion.
[7] Anagram for *D'Andelot*, brother of Admiral Coligny, Huguenot leader.

*June.*

111. In widowhood as many males as females,
     The life of great Monarchs to be in danger:
     Plague, steel, famine, great peril pell-mell,
     Troubles, through changes, little Great Ones to incite.

*July.*

112. Hail, rust, rains and great plagues,
     To preserve women, they will be the cause of the noise:
     Death of several plague, steel, famine through hatreds,
     The sky will be seen which is to say that it will light up again.

*August.*

113. The grain will not be at all sufficient,
     The death approaches to snow more than white:
     Sterility, grain rotted, abundance of water,
     The great one wounded, several of death on the flank.

*September.*

114. Scarcity of fruits, nor grain, trees and shrubs,
     Great fowl,[1] tall[2] to spur on:
     As temporal as the little-lion-like prelate,
     D'Andelot to conquer, tall[2] ones to draw back.

*October.*

115. Everything changed, one to persecute four,
     Malady outside, mortality very far:
     Of the four two will come to debate no more,
     Exile, ruin, death, famine, perplexity.

*November.*

116. The number of the great ones greater will not be as many.
     Great changes, commotions, steel, plague:
     The small estimate: lent, paid, counting,
     Contrary month frost molests greatly.

[1]Somewhat dubious. See note 4, opposite.
[2]Or "noble."

*Décembre.*

117.  Forte gelée, glace plus que concorde.
      Veuves matrones, feu, *deploration:*[1]
      Jeux, ébats, joie, *Mars citera*[2] discorde,
      Par mariages bonne expectation.[3]

## *1566.*

*Sur la dite année.*

118.  Aux plus grands mort, *jacture*[4] d'honneur, et violence.
      Professeurs de la foi, leur état et leur secte:
      Aux deux grandes Églises divers bruit, décadence,
      Maux voisins querellants serfs d'Églises sans tête.

*Janvier.*

119.  Perte, *jacture*[4] grande, et non sans violence,
      Tous ceux de la foi, plus à religion,
      Les plus Grands perdront vie, leur honneur et chevance
      Toutes les deux Églises, la coulpe à leur faction.

*Février.*

120.  À deux fort Grandes *naistres*[5] perte pernicieuse,
      Les plus Grands feront perte, biens, d'honneur, et de vie,
      Tant grands bruits couriront, l'urne trop odieuse.
      Grands maladies être, prêche, messe en envie.

*Mars.*

121.  Les servantes des Églises leur Seigneurs trahiront,
      D'autres Seigneurs aussi par l'indivis des champs:
      Voisins de prêche et messe entre eux querelleront,
      Rumeurs, bruits augmenter à mort plusieurs couchants.

*Avril.*

122.  De tous biens abondance terre nous produira,
      Nul bruit de guerre en France, hors mis séditions:
      Homicides, voleurs par voie on trouvera,
      Peu de foi, fièvre ardente, peuple en émotion.

[1]O.F. *deploration,* a kind of poetic lament (Sainte-Palaye).
[2]Latin *citare,* to incite.
[3]Le Pelletier thinks that from here on the Presages are not the work of Nostradamus, pointing out the differences in style, syntax and "inspiration." These are indeed recognizable in some, but many still contain typical Nostradamian hybrid words and phrases.
[4]O.F. *jacture,* loss.
[5]O.F. *naistre,* birth (Godefroy).

117. Severe frost, ice more than concord,
Widows, matrons, fire, lament:
Games, frolics, joy, Mars to stir up discord,
Through marriages good expectation.

## 1566.

*On the said year.*

118. For the greatest ones death, loss of honor and violence.
Professors of the faith, their estate and their sect:
For the two great Churches diverse noise, decadence,
Evil neighbors quarreling serfs of the Church without a head.

*January.*

119. Loss, great loss, and not without violence,
All those of the faith, more for religion,
The Greatest Ones will lose their life, their honor and substance
Both the Churches, the fault in their faction.

*February.*

120. For the two very Great Ones births pernicious loss,
The Greatest Ones will cause loss, goods, of honor, and of life,
As much great noises will run, the urn very odious,
Great maladies to be, meeting house, mass in envy.

*March.*

121. The servants of the Churches will betray their Masters,
Of other Masters also by the undivided of the fields:
Neighbors of meeting house and mass will quarrel amongst them,
Rumors, noises to grow several reposing to death.

*April.*

122. Abundance of all blessings, the earth will produce for us,
No noise of war in France, seditions put outside:
Murderers, robbers one will find en route,
Little faith, burning fever, people in upheaval.

*Mai.*

123. Entre peuple discorde, inimitié brutale,
    Guerre, mort de grands Princes, plusieurs parts d'*Italie:*
    Universelle plaie, plus fort occidentale,
    *Tempore*[1] bonne et pleine, mais fort sèche et tarie.

*Juin.*

124. Les bleds trop n'abonder, de toutes autres fruits force,
    L'été, printemps humides, hiver long, neige, glace:
    En armes l'Orient, la *France* se renforce,
    Mort de bétail prou miel, aux assiégés la place.

*Juillet.*

125. Par pestilence et feu fruits d'arbres périront,
    Signe d'huile abonder. Père *Denys* non guère:
    Des grands mourir, mais peu d'étrangers *sailliront*,[2]
    Insulte, marine Barbare, et dangers de frontières.

*Août.*

126. Pluies fort excessives, et de biens abondance,
    De bétail prix juste être, femmes hors de danger:
    Grêles, pluies, tonnerres: peuple abattu en *France*,
    Par mort travailleront, mort peuple corriger.

*Septembre.*

127. Armes, plaies cesser, mort de séditieux,
    Le père *Liber*[3] grand non trop abondra:
    Malins seront saisis par plus malicieux,
    *France* plus que jamais *victrix*[4] triomphera.

*Octobre.*

128. Jusqu'à ce mois durer la sécheresse grande,
    À l'*Itale* et *Prouence*, des fruits tous à demi:
    Le Grand moins d'ennemis prisonnier de leur bande,
    Aux écumeurs, pirates, et mourir l'ennemi.

[1] Latin *tempora*, times.
[2] Aphaeresis of *assailliront*.
[3] Latin *Liber*, God of Vines, identified with Bacchus.
[4] Latin *victrix*, she that is victorious, conqueress.

*May.*

123. Between people discord, brutal enmity,
     War, death of great Princes, several parts of Italy:
     Universal plague, more very western,
     Good and full times, but very dry and exhausted.


*June.*

124. The grains not to abound too much, abundance of all other fruits,
     The summer, spring humid, winter long, snow, ice:
     The East in arms, France gathers its strength,
     Death of cattle much honey, the place to the besieged.


*July.*[1]

125. Through pestilence and fire fruits of trees will perish,
     Signs of oil to abound. Father Denis[2] not scarce:
     Some great ones to die, but few foreigners will attack,
     Offense, Barbarian fleet, and dangers at the frontiers.


*August.*

126. Rains very excessive, and of blessings abundance,
     Price of cattle to be just, women out of danger:
     Hail, rain, thunder: people dejected in France,
     Through death they will work, death people to punish.


*September.*

127. Arms, plagues to cease, death of seditious ones,
     Father Bacchus[3] great not too much will he abound:
     Wicked ones will be seized by more wicked ones,
     France more than ever victorious will triumph.


*October.*

128. Up to this month will the great drought endure,
     For Italy and Provence, all fruits to half:
     The Great One less of enemies prisoner of their band,
     For the rovers, pirates, and the enemy to die.

[1]This Presage might be expected to have some passing reference to Nostradamus' own death (July 2, 1566).

[2]This is obviously some sort of metonymy, but we have been unable to find for what. St. Denis is the patron of France and sometimes in poetry identified with the King, but the context here would seem to indicate his patronage of some crop.

[3]See note 3, opposite.

*Novembre.*

129. L'ennemi tant à craindre retirer en *Thracie*,
     Laissant cris, hurlements, et pille désolée:
     Laisser bruit mer et terre, religion *mutrie*,[1]
     Joviaux mis en route, toute secte *affoulée*.[2]

## 1567.

*Sur le dite année.*

130. Mort, maladie aux jeunes femmes, rhumes,
     De tête aux yeux malheur marchands de terre:
     De mer *infaust*,[3] *semes*[4] mal, vin par brumes,
     Prou huile trop de pluie, aux fruits moleste, guerre.

*Janvier.*

131. Prison, secrets: ennuis, entre proches discorde,
     La vie on donnera, par mal divers catarrhes:
     La mort s'en ensuivra, poison fera concorde,
     Frayeur, peur, crainte grande, voyageant *lairra*[5] d'*arres*.[6]

*Février.*

132. Prisons par ennemis occultes et manifestes,
     Voyage ne tiendra, inimitié mortelle:
     L'amour trois, *simulté*[7] secret publiques fêtes,
     Le rompu ruiné, l'eau rompra la querelle.

*Mars.*

133. Les ennemis publics, noces et mariages,
     La mort après, l'enrichi par les morts:
     Les grands amis se montrer au passage,
     Deux sectes jargonner, de surpris tard remords.

[1]Dubious. Possibly from O.F. *mutre*, murder.
[2]O.F. *affouler*, to oppress.
[3]Latin *infaustum*, misfortune.
[4]Probably Nostradamian noun form of *semer* (for *semences*).
[5]O.F. *lairrer*, to release, abandon.
[6]O.F. *arre*, pledge, guarantee, security (Sainte-Palaye).
[7]Latin *simultas*, hostility, dissension, enmity.

*November.*

129. The enemy so much to be feared to retire into **Thrace**,
Leaving cries, groans, and pillage desolated:
To leave noise on land and sea, religion murdered,
Jovial Ones[1] put to route, every sect oppressed.

## *1567.*

*On the said year.*

130. Death, malady for young women, colds,
From head to the eyes misfortune merchants of land:
By sea misfortune, seeds bad, wine in mists,
Much oil too much rain, molests the fruits, war.

*January.*

131. Prisons, secrets: annoyances, discord between relatives,
They will give life, through evil diverse catarrhs:
Death will ensue, poison will cause concord,
Terror, fear, great fear, traveling will release from pledges.

*February.*

132. Prisons for enemies hidden and open,
Travel will not hold, mortal enmity:
Love three, secret hostility public feasts,
The broken ruined, the water will end the quarrel.

*March.*

133. The enemies public, nuptials and marriages,
Death after, he grown rich through the deaths:
The great friends will show themselves in the passage,
Two sects to jabber, from surprise remorse later.

[1]Probably meaning the worshippers of Jove, i.e., pagans, i.e., heretics, i.e., Protestants.

*Avril*

134. Par grandes maladies, religion fâchée,
     Par les enfants et *legats*[1] d'Ambassade:
     Don donné à indigne, *nouulle*[2] loi lâchée,
     Biens de vieux pères, Roi en bonne *contrade*.[3]

*Mai.*

135. Du père au fils s'approche: Magistrats dits sévères,
     Les grandes noces, ennemis *garbelans:*[4]
     De *latens*[5] mis avant, par la foi d'*improperes,*[6]
     Les bons amis et femmes contre tels grommelants.

*Juin.*

136. Par le trésor, trouvé l'héritage du père:
     Les Rois et Magistrats, les noces, ennemis:
     Le public malveillant, les Juges et le Maire,
     La mort, peur et frayeur; et trois Grands à mort mis.

*Juillet.*

137. Encore la mort s'approche, don Royal et *legat,*[7]
     On dressera ce qu'est, par vieillesse en ruine:
     Les jeunes hoirs de soupçon nul *legat,*[7]
     Trésor trouvé en plâtres et cuisine.

*Août.*

138. Les Ennemis secrets seront emprisonnés,
     Les Rois et Magistrats y tiendront la main sûre:
     La vie de plusieurs, santé maladie yeux, nez,
     Les deux grands s'en iront bien loin à la male heure.

*Septembre.*

139. Longues langueurs de téte noce, ennemi,
     Par Prélat et voyage, songe du Grand terreur:
     Feu et ruine grande trouvé en lieu oblique,
     Par torrent découvert sortie *noues*[8] erreurs.

[1]Here apparently O.F. *legat*, legacy, gift.
[2]Dubious. For either *nouvelle* or *nulle*.
[3]Provençal *contrada*, country.
[4]Low Latin *garbellare*, to sift, hence by usage to mangle, mutilate.
[5]Latin *latens*, concealed, hidden.
[6]Latin *improperus*, slow; *improperium*, taunt, reproach.
[7]O.F. *legat*, legacy, gift.
[8]O.F. *nove*. new.

*April.*

134. Through great maladies, religion vexed,
Through the children and gifts of the Embassy:[1]
Gifts given to an unworthy one, new[2] law relaxed,
Goods of old fathers, King in good country.

*May.*

135. From the father it approaches the son: Magistrates called severe,
The great nuptials, enemies mutilating:
Hidden put in front, through the faith of slow ones,[3]
The good friends and women against such grumblings.

*June.*

136. Through the treasure, the estate of the father found:[4]
Kings and Magistrates, the nuptials, enemies:
The public malevolent, the Judges and Mayor,
Death, fear and terror; and the three Great Ones put to death.

*July.*

137. Again death approaches, Royal gift and legacy,
They will prepare what is, through old age in ruins:
The young heirs in suspicion of no legacy,
Treasure found in plasters and kitchen.

*August.*

138. The secret Enemies will be imprisoned,
Kings and Magistrates will hold there a safe hand:
The life of several, health eye malady, nose,
The two great ones will go away very far at the bad hour.

*September.*

139. Long languors in the head nuptial, enemy,
Through Prelate and trip, dream of the Great One terror:
Fire and ruin great one found in the oblique place,
Discovered by torrent new errors to come out.

[1] All mention of "Embassy" hereafter apparently refers to Nostradamus' "mission" for the King towards the end of his life (see "Biography of Nostradamus").
[2] Or "no."
[3] Or "of reproaches."
[4] A great part of the remaining Presages seems to contain Nostradamian autobiography, both past and attempted prophetic.

*Octobre.*

140. Les Rois et Magistrats par les morts la main mettre,
     Jeunes filles malades, et des Grands corps enfle:
     Tout par langueurs et noces, ennemis serfs au maître.
     Les publiques douleurs, le Composeur tout enfle.

*Novembre.*

141. Du retour d'Ambassade, don de Roi; mis au lieu
     Plus n'en fera: sera allé à DIEU:
     Parents plus proches, amis, frères du sang,
     Trouvé tout mort près du lit et du banc.

*October.*

140. The Kings and Magistrates to place their hand through death,
Young girls sick, and of the Great Ones body swells:
All through languors and nuptials, enemies serfs for the master.
The public mourning, the Author all swelled up.

*November.*[1]

141. On his return from the Embassy, the King's gift, put in place
He will do no more: he will be gone to God:
Close relatives, friends, brothers by blood,
Found entirely dead near the bed and bench.

[1]This Presage, for November, 1567, predicts Nostradamus' death, which actually took place seventeen months earlier.

# Indexes to the Prophecies

## A. General Index

This index is to the Centuries—i.e., the Preface, the Epistle and the quatrains. Reference is made to the Presages only in connection with enigmatic proper names. References to the Preface and the Epistle are also limited, chiefly to proper names.

Quotation marks indicate that the term is enigmatic; a question (?) that it is uncertain; parentheses that the term is a paraphrase; and *italics* that it is a classical name.

The references are *not* to book page numbers, but to the numbers of the quatrains, as explained at the end of the section "Rules of the Game in This Edition," preceding the prophecies. "E" precedes the number of a paragraph in the Epistle, and "P" the number of a paragraph in the Preface.

# B. Index of Subjects: A Summary Breakdown of the Quatrains

The categories are arranged in the approximate order of interest to the English-speaking reader. A citation in parentheses indicates that this quatrain has already been cited in a previous category, but has been considered equally applicable to one or more additional ones. However, as the intention is to *minimize* the number of duplicate citations, such duplicate citations have been applied only where considered *equally* applicable to more than one.

The total of citations not in parentheses equals the total of quatrains in the prophecies—i.e., 969—and it is against this total that percentages are calculated, to the nearest one half of one per cent. Where a calculation including also the citations in parentheses would be appreciably greater, this alternate percentage is given in parentheses, having been calculated against 1,119, the total of *all* citations.

## 1. GEOGRAPHICAL SETTING SPECIFIED OR IMPLIED (63%)

*England and Scotland: 4%*
Domestic
   126, 251, 316, 357, 380, 489, 496, 593, 622, 837, 858, 876, 949, 107, 1022, 1039, 1040, 1066

(615), 640, 649, (677), (687), (74),
815, (933), 935, 990, 994, 1031, 1046,
(1051), 1061, 1062, 1063, (VIII-6)

*Iberia (Spain and Portugal): 2½% (5%)*
(173), 177, (260), (38), 320, 354, 362,
(368), (375), 42, (43), (45), (436),
(494), 497, (513), (514), (551),
(555), (587), (612), (615), 619,
645, 664, 688, 710, (722), 726, 826,
848, 850, 851, (886), 894, (930),
(935), (942), (954), 960, (964), 978,
(989), (105), (107), 109, 1011, 1014,
1025, (1044), 1047, 1048, (1058),
(1061), 1095

*Northern and Eastern Europe (Scandinavia,
Poland and East, Balkans): 3% (4%)*
149, 152, 174, 198, 23, 221, 222, (232),
(249), 252, (260), (284), 33, 347,
389, 395, 438, 439, 482, 516, 527,
(547), (551), 554, 570, 573, (580),

586, 590, 591, (66), (67), 621, (653),
(815), (816), 883, (928), (930),
932, (960), (975), 991, (1044),
(1062), (1063), 1086, XII-36.

*Moslem World of North Africa and Asia:
3% (7%)*
(19), (118), 140, (149), (152), (170),
(173), (174), (229), 286, 296, (320),
327, 331, 359, 360, 361, 364, 377,
(378), 390, 397, (439), 450, (458),
(468), 511, (513), (514), (516), 519,
523, 525, (527), (547), (548), (550),
(554), (555), (568), 569, (573),
(574), (578), (580), (586), (594),
(621), (653), 654, 655, (675), 680,
(76), 736, (848), (850), (851), 859,
896, (942), 943, (960), 962, (973),
(980), (989), (1031), (1056), (1061),
(1062), (1063), 1075, (1077), (1095),
1096, 1097, VII-82, (XII-36).

## 2. GEOGRAPHICAL SETTING NOT SPECIFIED (37%)

In a substantial proportion, the implied setting is probably France. Most
of the categories hereunder can of course also be applied to most of the quatrains that *do* have setting indicated.

*Empires, Wars, Murders and Disasters: 19%*
116, 117, 132, 133, 137, 138, 141, 150,
159, 160, 162, 167, 168, 169, 176, 187,
192, 22, 26, 27, 29, 211, 218, 219, 228,
230, 235, 237, 238, 240, 242, 244, 246,
247, 248, 253, 255, 267, 275, 277, 278,
280, 291, 292, 295, 298, 2100, 31, 36,
37, 313, 322, 328, 329, 330, 333, 335,
341, 348, 350, 371, 373, 381, 384, 385,
398, 410, 413, 414, 420, 422, 426, 440,
443, 445, 447, 449, 452, 453, 455, 456,
462, 465, 471, 475, 480, 483, 492, 52,
54, 58, 518, 526, 536, 537, 538, 545,
552, 560, 571, 579, 581, 583, 62, 611,
614, 629, 633, 634, 659, 661, 665, 667,
674, 684, 691, 692, 693, 695, 696, 697,
77, 711, 716, 718, 725, 728, 733, 740,
817, 820, 827, 841, 855, 856, 857, 864,
865, 874, 887, 889, 892, 94, 98, 911,
917, 936, 947, 951, 953, 955, 965, 966,
976, 977, 979, 981, 982, 983, 992, 996,
997, 999, 9100, 101, 102, 103, 104,
1010, 1019, 1021, 1032, 1042, 1057,
1068, 1071, 1072, 1076, 1082, 1089,
1090, 1098, VII-73, VII-83, VIII-4,
VIII-5, X-100, XII-55

*Religious and Social Turmoil: 2%*
13, 114, 115, 144, 145, 153, 196, 28, 210,
212, 213, 326, 367, 424, 425, 553, 572,
(573), (622), 669, 672, 877, 878, 880,
898, (972)

*Discovery of Tombs and Treasures: 1%*
125, 127, (365), 57, 566, (615), 666,
714, (85), (826), (828), (829), (830),
866, (94), 97, (98), (99), 912, (932),
984, (106), 1074, (1093)

*Monsters and Prodigies: 1%*
129, 143, (158), 164, (180), (190),
(232), (321), 334, (588), (644), (93)

*Nostradamus Personal: 1%*
11, 12, 142, 236, (34), 394, 6100

*Miscellany: 13%*

Especially interesting: 4%
135, 139, 163, (164), 165, 181, 185,
186, 188, 195, 245, 270, 289, 336, 344,
46, 47, 415, 418, 432, 441, 457, 488,
55, 65, 618, 637, 651, 652, 79, 713,
738, 742, 863, 871, 873, 879, 882, 1081

Not especially interesting although reasonably clear: 6%
17, 110, 113, 121, 123, 130, 136, 148,
155, 157, 187, 191, 197, 220, 223, 256,

## C. Geographical Names in the Prophecies

The grouping under subtitles is according to contemporary boundaries. A question (?) means uncertain; parentheses indicate the modern equivalent of Nostradamus' nomenclature; *italics* indicate an ancient name. For the numbers of quatrains in which these names occur, see the General Index.

### 1. FRANCE

## 2. ITALY & ADJACENT ISLES

Cittanova
(Conca R.)
Cremona
Elba
*Etruria*
Faenza
Ferrara
Fiesole
Florence
(Focia)
Fornase
Fossano
Genoa
Imola
Lake Arezzo
Lake Fucino
Lake Garda
Lake of Perugia
Liguria
*Liternum*
Lombardy
Lucca
Lunigiana(?)
Magnavacca
Malta
Mantua
Messina

Milan
Mirandola
Modena
Mortara
Mount Aventine
Naples
Nola
Padua
Palermo
Parma
Paterno
(Pavia)
Perugia
Peschiera
Piedmont
Piombino(?)
Pisa
Po R.
Pola
(Porto Corsini)
Prato
(Quarnero, Gulf of)
Ravenna
Reggio
Rimini
Riviera
Romagna(?)

Rome
Salerno
San Nicolo(?)
Sardinia
Savigliano
Savona
Senigallia
Sicily
Siena
Susa
Syracuse
Tiber R.
Ticino R.
Tolentino
(Treglia)(?)
Trieste
Turin
Tuscany
Tyrrhenian Sea
Valenza
Vasto(?)
Venice
Vercelli
Verona
Vicenza
Voltri(?)

## 3. IBERIA (SPAIN & PORTUGAL)

Barcelona
Burgos
Cadiz
(Capellades)(?)
*Castulo*
Catalonia
Cordoba
Douro R.
Ebro R.
Ernani
Figueras

(Formentera I.)(?)
(Gibraltar)
Grenada
Guadalquivir R.
Junquera
Leon
Lerida
Lisbon
Madrid
Montserrat
Pamplona

Sagunto
(San Adrian, Sierra de)
Saragossa
Seville
(Sierra Moreña)
Tagus R.
Tarragona(?)
Tolosa
(Urgel, Llanos de)(?)
Villafranca

## 4. CENTRAL EUROPE (GERMANY, AUSTRIA, HUNGARY CZECHOSLOVAKIA, SWITZERLAND, &c.)

Aachen (Aix)
Alps
Augsburg
Austria
Bâle/Basel
Black Forest
Bohemia

Bratislava
Brunswick
Buda
Cologne
Danube
Frankfurt
Geneva

Germany
Grisons Canton
Hesse
Hungary
Iler(?)
Lausanne
Lübeck

Lucerne | *Pannonia* | *Suevia*
Mainz | Pennine Alps | Swabia(?)
Meissen | Rhine R. | Thuringia
Memel(?) | Saxony | Ulm(?)
Noric Mts. | Sopron *(Scarbantia)* | Vienna
Nuremberg | *Sorbia* | Wittenberg

## 5. THE NORTH SEA AREA (BRITISH ISLES, BELGIUM, HOLLAND, SCANDINAVIA, &c.)

Antwerp | Flanders | Lys R.
Brabant | Frisia | Mechlin (Malines)
British Isles | Ghent | Norway (?)
Bruges | Hainaut | Scheldt R.
Brussels | Liège | Scotland
Denmark(?) | London | Thames R.
England | Luxembourg |

## 6. EASTERN EUROPE (POLAND, RUSSIA, BALKANS, AEGEAN SEA)

*Ambracia* | Dalmatia | (Preveza)
*Amphipolis* | Danube R. | (Quarnero, Gulf of)
(Arta) | (Dnieper R.) | Ragusa
Athens | Epirus | Rhodes
Attica | (Eski Eregli) | (Roumania)
Black Sea | *Eretria* | *Salona*
Boeotia | Euboea | Samothrace I.
*Boristhenes* | Greece | San Nicolo(?)
*Byzantium* | Larissa | *Sarmatia*
Chios I. | Macedonia | Slavonia
(Constantinople) | Mytilene | Sparta
Corinth | *Nicopolis* | (Split)
Crete I. | Peloponessus | Thessaly
Cyclades Is. | *Perinthus* | Thrace
Cyprus | Pola | Trieste
*Dacia* | (Poland) | Zara

## 7. ASIA & NORTH AFRICA

*Alania* | *Ephesus* | Palestine
Algiers | Fez | *Pamphilia*
Antioch | *Hyrcania* | Persia
Arabia | Jordan R. | Pharos I.
Araxes R. | Judea | Susa(?)
Armenia | Levant | Syria
Babylon | Libya | Tarsus
*Barbary* (Algeria) | *Lycia* | *Tartary*
Bougie | *Media* | Trabzond (Trebizond)
*Carmania* | Memphis | Tripolis
*Ceramon-agora* | Mesopotamia | Tunis
Cyprus I. | Morocco | Turkey
Egypt | *Mysia* |

## 8. WESTERN HEMISPHERE

America                           Gulf of Uraba (Gulf of Darien) (?)

# D. Unsolved, Uncertain or Enigmatic Proper Names

For the numbers of the quatrains in which these names occur, see the General Index.

| | | |
|---|---|---|
| Achem | Denté | Medusine |
| Achilles | Dinebro | Memire, St. |
| Adaluncatif | D.M. | MENDOSUS |
| Agrippa | DRVX | Mercury |
| Alba/Albanois/Albanians | Emorte | Mesopotamia |
| Alus | Eussouis | Meysnier |
| Ambellon | Ferdinand | Modone Fulcy |
| Angolmois | Fertsod | Molite |
| Annemarc, d' | Fesulan Olympique | Monet |
| Antipolles | Flora | Mont |
| Antonne./Autonne | Formande | Montpertuis |
| Aquilon | Gallots | Nanar |
| Aquiloye | Gaudole | Nebro |
| Arbon, d' | HA(M)/HO(M) | Nero |
| Arriens | Hanix | Nicholas |
| Artomiques | Henry | Nira |
| Aspire | Hercules | Nolle |
| Ausonia | Hermes | Nonseggle |
| Aventin (in Provence) | Herne | Norlaris |
| Aymar, mont | Herodde | Norneigre |
| Azostains | Hesperia | North |
| Balenne | Humaine | Ogmios |
| Barbaris | Ispalme | Olchades |
| Barboxitaine | Iud. | Orguion |
| Belœuvre | Jupiter | Pampon |
| Beluzer | K | Pampotamia |
| Ferich/Berlch | L | PAR. CAR. NERSAF |
| Betta | Laigne | PAU NAY LORON |
| Boni | Lectoyre | Pelligouxe |
| Borneaux | Logarion/Logathion | Peloncle |
| Bourc | Lonole | Penelon |
| Bourze | Louise | Perme |
| Brannonices | Luna | Philip |
| B(r)isanne | Lunage | Ponteroso |
| Brode (nation) | Lygonnois | Ptolon |
| Capadille | Mabus | Raugon |
| Cassich saint George | Magnavacca | Raviere |
| Castulo | Maiotes | RAYPOZ |
| Chaldondon salvaterre | Mammel | Reines, Forest of |
| Chanignon | Mammer | Resviers |
| Chyren(-Selin) | Manthi | Rion |
| Cimbri | Mantor et d'Albe | Rocheval |
| Cydron | Mauris | Rodanes |

Romaigne/Romania
Saillimons
Salvaterre
Samarobryn
Sardon
Saulce
Seez et Ponce
Selin
Seme

Senoise
Sorbin
Suevi
Tamins
Tardaigne
Th
Torrent
Touphon, Forêt du
Tricast
Tyrren Phocean

Tyrron/Tyrhen
Uhne
Ulpian
Urnel Vaucile
Vast
Verbiesque
Veront
Vigilanne
Vultry

# E. Unsolved or Uncertain Barbarisms

abormeant, 921
auaragonic/anaxagoric, P25
apamé, 995
ards, 83
asiniers, les, 617
Bichoro, 886
borneaux, 914
bourlis, 940
Bragamas, 878
brodes, 834
ca(i)che, 875
cailhau, 444
capitole, 613
chaulveron, 976
connisse, 590
contaux, 934
Contremenant, 998
cout(e)aux, 934
Delves & brodes, 834
demipler, 498
diphlongue, 1033
emonopolle, 838
enconder, 460
es, 826
frofaim, 681
gelle, 835
granci, 679
gravee blanche, 433
halbe, 922
Harmotique, 1036
Hem. mi. deux Phi., 107
herbipolique/helbipolique, 1013
hypolite, 552
larm, 1078
legne, 956
Lemprin, 981
Liqueduct, 868
lyphres, 389
mainade, 840
mallods, 924

marsaves/mar saues, 835
maye, 87
medicant, 1063
mesan, 835
mesles, 389
mittee, 1041
Molite, 998
More, 485
Myrnamee, 108
nerte, 737
nolte, 1060
Nonnay, 1067
Olestant, 482
pamplation, 851
pampon, 81
papillon, 875
pelte, 1053
pence, 947
perce glose, 362
perhume, 109
Reb, 1066
Recloing, 1084
rochier, 924
sedifragues, 694
soluz, 934
somentrees, 1079
Supelman, XII-69
surrez, 81
TAG, 861
tauropole, 179
teccon. 927
terax, 860
trehemide, 1085
Vstagois, 464
valbuee, 1019
vaner, 532
verrier, 910
ver. serp., 525
vestules, 471

# F. Time Specifications in the Prophecies

## 1. BY PRECISE DATES

| Year | Quatrain, Etc. |
|---|---|
| 1580 | 62 |
| 1607 | 871 |
| 1607 of the Liturgy | 654 |
| 1609 | 1091 |
| 1660 | X-100 |
| 1700 | 149 |
| 1703 | 62 |
| 1727, in October | 377 |
| 1732 (in June) | Preface, para. 26 |
| 1792 | Epistle, para. 42 |
| 1999, seventh month | 1072 |
| 3797 | Preface, para. 19 |

## 2. BY NUMBER OF YEARS

Presumably the number should be added to 1555.

| Interval | Quatrains |
|---|---|
| 1 month (or greater lunar cycle of 36 years?) | 162, 397 |
| 59 years (2 revolutions of Saturn) | 154 |
| 177 years (6 revolutions of Saturn) | 172 |
| 290 years | 357 |
| 300 years | 10100 |
| 500 years | 394 |

## 3. BY PLANETARY CONFIGURATIONS

Parentheses indicate not written that precisely, but probable. A question (?) indicates perhaps not an actual configuration but, rather, enigmatic characters or substances.

290 Castor and Pollux enemies in the arena (?)

215 Castor and Pollux in Argo

151 Jupiter and Saturn in the head of Aries (Wöllner, pp. 44–45: October 19, 1583; December 13, 1702; September 2, 1995)

298 Jupiter in Leo

433 Jupiter joined more to Venus than to the Moon

624 Mars and Jupiter conjoined in Cancer (Wöllner, p. 59: June 21, 2002)

33 Mars and Mercury and (Moon) conjoined

25 (Mars and Mercury conjoined in Pisces)(?)

891 (Mars and Venus conjoined in Pisces)

591 (Mars in Leo, Saturn in Aquarius)

525 Mars, Sun and Venus conjoined in Leo (McCann, p. 412: August 2, 1987)

484 Mars, Venus and Sun conjoined in summer

593 Mercury dominating (Wöllner, p. 52: 1720–56, 1972–2008, etc.)

265 Mercury in Sagittarius, Saturn will fade (Wöllner, p. 60: December 13, 1604; December 25, 1839; December

# Historical Background of the Prophecies

## A. *The Historical Setting*

In considering the historical setting against which Nostradamus wrote his prophecies, one should keep in mind both the key dates of Nostradamus' life and the years when his prophecies were written and published. It will be recalled from the Biography of Nostradamus that he was born in 1503 and had his general education just before and just after 1520, his education after 1525 being primarily medical. After many years of wandering and practicing medicine in different communities (including a protracted stay at Agen with a wife and children until they were carried off by the plague), Nostradamus settled down in Salon from 1547 until his death in 1566. His prophetic quatrains were composed probably between 1554 and 1558, and published in three cumulative editions, the last one in 1568 after his death. (A relatively small additional number were published still later.)

The foremost European ruler of Nostradamus' day was the Emperor Charles V, whose empire exceeded Charlemagne's. In effect, Charles "hit the jackpot" in the dynastic game, having inherited different pieces of his empire from his father and from each of his grandfathers. His empire included, in one form or another, virtually all of Western and Central Europe except the British Isles, Portugal, Denmark and the Scandinavian countries, France and Switzerland. With his son Philip married to his niece Mary, Queen of England, it might even have seemed after 1554 that England would become part of the empire. Overseas in America, Asia and Africa, Charles had further possessions which exceeded many times the total of his European possessions.

A decent man by nature, and also industrious, Charles would have been well contented merely to reign over such a vast and diverse empire. But when Charles became ruler of the Spanish Empire in 1516 and of the Holy Roman Empire in 1519, he was plunged into the middle of one of the most exciting half centuries in European history, with clashes of every conceivable sort, political, religious, social and economic. Wars of every kind were virtually unending, and the period had more cloak-and-dagger intrigue than any other half century in European history.

First, Charles was plunged into a perpetual struggle with the Kings of France, a struggle mainly centered in Italy and fought in a series of wars called the Italian Wars (1494–1559). Charles more than held his own in this struggle.

Second, there was the struggle with the armies of Islam, which it behooved Charles as Holy Roman Emperor to conduct with especial vigor. The principal adversary here was of course the Sultan of the Turks, who had been pushing deeper and deeper into the Balkans ever since the 14th century, when they were first invited by the Byzantine Emperor to help him against the Serbs. In 1453 the Turks had conquered Constantinople itself and overthrown the Byzantine.Empire. During Charles' reign they got as far as Hungary, where they overthrew the Hungarian monarchy (1526), and were soon pressing towards Vienna itself. As part of a sort of pincers movement against Europe, the Turks during Charles' reign also swept into Syria and Egypt, while their faithful vassal, Khaireddin, established a strong naval power based on Algeria (called Barbary) and used his corsairs to ravage the coasts of Charles' empire. Against the Turks Charles was less successful, but the Turks in turn faced a "second front" fight against the Persians throughout this period.

Having his hands full enough with these two persistent enemies, who soon developed an alliance against him (their mutual emnity to Charles apparently overshadowing the gulf between Christian and Moslem), Charles was to face yet another great battle, within his own Holy Roman Empire, or Germany, after the Protestant Reformation was begun by Luther (1517).

At first committed to extirpating this heresy from his dominions, Charles soon discovered how thoroughly it was involved with patriotic German feelings, as well as local politics, and finally had to yield almost completely in this, his least-successful struggle. In Charles' later days, the religious picture was further complicated when yet another reform movement, substantially different from Luther's, was initiated by the Frenchman John Calvin.

At just the time that the Centuries were written, Charles V began his abdications, deliberately dissolving his empire in the same piecemeal fashion in which he had acquired it. In all minds, doubtless also that of Nostradamus, there was the question of whether the divisions would remain as ordered by Charles, or whether, because of the quarrels of his heirs or the cupidity of neighbors, things would work out differently.

Charles' son Philip had received Spain's possessions on the mainland of Italy in 1554 as well as the Netherlands, and was married to Queen Mary of England, with the title King of England, which he retained till Mary's death in 1558. At just the time the first edition of the Centuries was published (May, 1555), Mary had announced to the world that her baby would be born. This heir to the Tudors and the Habsburgs turned out to be a figment of Mary's hysterical imagination; but it is an interesting subject for speculation how such an heir might have changed the course of history, and Nostradamus may have been amongst those who speculated. Philip rounded out his empire by receiving from his father in 1556 Spain, the Spanish islands in the Mediterranean, including Sicily, and the Spanish possessions overseas. His uncle, Ferdinand, who had acquired the Kingdom of Bohemia and what was left by the Turks of Hungary, and had ruled Germany for Charles V, was given the hereditary Habsburg possessions in Central Europe; and when Charles made his final abdication, the one as Emperor (1558), Ferdinand was expected to be elected Emperor to succeed him. Or would Philip contest this, and risk everything to gain everything, the whole mighty empire of his father? Certainly the Ottoman sultans reacted in this all-or-nothing fashion in the face of wills whereby they were supposed to share power with brothers.

We have now seen the situation in 1555 in the various parts of Charles' empire: Spain, the Netherlands, and the area covering the modern Germany, Austria, Czechoslovakia and Hungary, with England and most of Italy also included in the sphere. To the southeast, the Turks were in control of almost the whole Balkans. To the east lay the relatively unimportant state of Poland-Lithuania and, bordering on it, backward and feudal states of Eastern Europe, including Muscovy. Of the most northerly states, Denmark possessed Norway, but had recently lost Sweden. None of these states, however, played any great role in this period.

Of other states more westerly, Portugal played no role in European affairs at the time, being concerned entirely in her vast overseas empire, built up in competition with the Spanish. The Swiss were also independent, although they had played an active role in the Italian Wars with their mercenaries. In Italy, most of the petty states swung back and forth as puppets between the two giants. With the Spanish in control of Sicily and southern Italy as well as Lombardy in the North, and the French occupying Piedmont and Savoy, the only independent states of any consequence were the Papal States, which behaved as an ordinary important power in the game of power politics, and the Venetian Republic, whose strength was being ever reduced by the loss of eastern territories to the Turks and the consequent decrease in annual revenues.

The chief state outside the empire of Charles V was, of course, France. The general prosperity of the country had been threatened by the constant wars of its ambitious Valois kings, which usually ended with costly defeats, most recently (1557) at Saint-Quentin. Furthermore, France had its own Luther in the person of Calvin, and although he had fled to Geneva to build there his theocratic state, he took advantage of being on the French borders and remained in constant contact with the troublesome Huguenots (French Calvinists), whose aristocratic leaders seized upon the religious issue as a pretext for self-serving political struggle against the power of the French crown. Between the time the first edition of the Centuries was published (1555) and the death of Nostradamus (1566), the Wars of Religion (1562–98) broke out in France, giving France a foretaste of the Thirty Years' War that was to come to Germany in the following century. However, there may have been in Nostradamus' mind ideas that the King of France would emerge as the ultimate victor, if the heirs of Charles V fell out amongst themselves, and thus far too powerful to be opposed by the Huguenots.

All these areas will be found referred to in greater detail in the following pages under "Chronology of Significant Dates." Let us here note in summary that in the exciting period in which Nostradamus reached his mature years, all of the following were pre-eminent factors in history:

1. Defense against the powerful onslaughts of the Turks on land and sea, with the Turks themselves under Persian attack.
2. The unceasing duel between the French and the colossal Habsburg empire, which seemed about to add even England to the rest, or to break up completely.
3. The breaking up of the unity of Christendom in the face of the "heresies" of the Lutherans and the Calvinists, this threat becoming interwoven with political strife.
4. The migration of Europeans into the Western Hemisphere and, to a lesser extent, to the East.

The extent to which Nostradamus' prophecies, in prose and poetry, reflected awareness of these factors, and the extent to which his prognostications on how they would develop did or did not coincide with things as they actually turned out, will be noted in the Commentary section.

## B. Chronology of Significant Dates

### *(1453–1871, but especially 1492–1566)*

Dated events are given in the greatest detail for the period of Nostradamus' life (1503–66) and for the preceding quarter century, vivid in the memory of those who taught him and talked to him. The detail increases in proximity to the period in which the Centuries were written (1554–58) and is especially significant as providing material upon which Nostradamus drew during his trances, deliberately or unconsciously, depending upon which of the several theories is credited. After 1558, dates are principally of interest as providing possible material for the Presages (up to 1567) and thereafter in connection with various widely repeated interpretations by Nostradamian commentators. Events of significance to Nostradamus personally are given in brackets.

1453 Ottoman Turks capture Constantinople and put an end to the ancient Byzantine Empire (originally the Eastern Roman Empire).

1461 The Hundred Years' War between France and England ends as the English are driven out of all their possessions in France except Calais. The French kings are tempted to use the national energies aroused in the long struggle for further expansion of France, or for more thrones for Valois princes.

1492 Columbus discovers the New World, subsequently America.

The Spaniard Rodrigo Borgia is elected Pope as Alexander VI (1492–1503). With his own great talents, together with the useful marriages of his daughter Lucrezia and the military and political genius of his brilliant and amoral son Cesare (the model for Machiavelli's *The Prince*), Pope Alexander makes the Papacy a political Great Power.

The Spanish, united by the marriage of Isabella of Castile to Fer-

## MAP OF NOSTRADAMUS' EUROPE

## GENEALOGY OF THE HOUSE OF FRANCE

### CAPET, VALOIS, ANJOU-LORRAINE, BURGUNDY

### BOURBON

*Note that this genealogy chart continues over four pages.*

## GENEALOGY OF THE HOUSE OF HABSBURG IN GERMANY AND SPAIN

MAP C

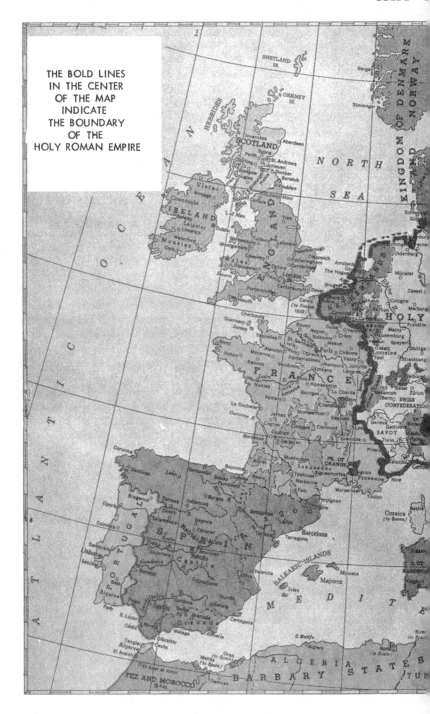

THE BOLD LINES
IN THE CENTER
OF THE MAP
INDICATE
THE BOUNDARY
OF THE
HOLY ROMAN EMPIRE

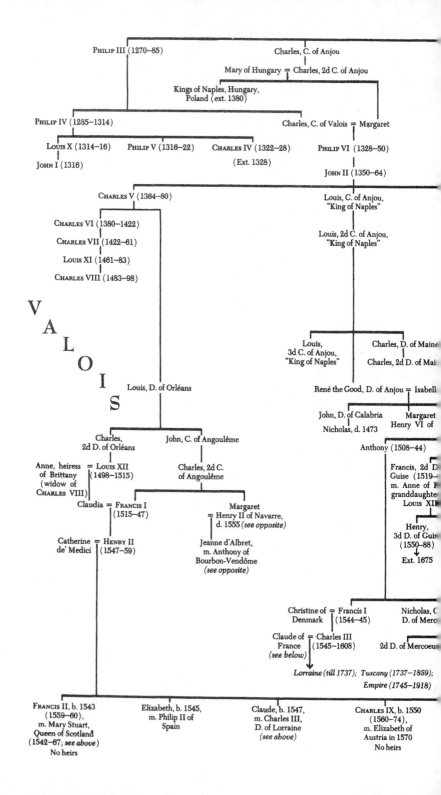

PHILIP III (1270–85)

Charles, C. of Anjou

Mary of Hungary = Charles, 2d C. of Anjou

Kings of Naples, Hungary,
Poland (ext. 1380)

PHILIP IV (1285–1314)

Charles, C. of Valois = Margaret

LOUIS X (1314–16)    PHILIP V (1316–22)    CHARLES IV (1322–28)    PHILIP VI (1328–50)

JOHN I (1316)                                    (Ext. 1328)

JOHN II (1350–64)

CHARLES V (1364–80)

Louis, C. of Anjou,
"King of Naples"

CHARLES VI (1380–1422)

Louis, 2d C. of Anjou,
"King of Naples"

CHARLES VII (1422–61)

LOUIS XI (1461–83)

CHARLES VIII (1483–98)

**V
A
L
O
I
S**

Louis, D. of Orléans

Louis,
3d C. of Anjou,
"King of Naples"

Charles, D. of Maine

Charles, 2d D. of Mai

René the Good, D. of Anjou = Isabell

John, D. of Calabria        Margaret

Nicholas, d. 1473        Henry VI of

Charles,
2d D. of Orléans

John, C. of Angoulême

Anthony (1508–44)

Charles, 2d C.
of Angoulême

Francis, 2d D
Guise (1519–
m. Anne of
granddaughte
LOUIS XII

Anne, heiress = LOUIS XII
of Brittany    (1498–1515)
(widow of
CHARLES VIII)

Claudia = FRANCIS I
(1515–47)

Margaret
= Henry II of Navarre,
d. 1555 (see opposite)

Henry,
3d D. of Guis
(1550–88)
↓
Ext. 1675

Catherine = HENRY II
de' Medici    (1547–59)

Jeanne d'Albret,
m. Anthony of
Bourbon-Vendôme
(see opposite)

Christine of = Francis I
Denmark    (1544–45)

Nicholas, (
D. of Merc

Claude of = Charles III
France    (1545–1608)
(see below)

2d D. of Mercoeur

Lorraine (till 1737); Tuscany (1737–1859);
Empire (1745–1918)

FRANCIS II, b. 1543
(1559–60),
m. Mary Stuart,
Queen of Scotland
(1542–67; see above)
No heirs

Elizabeth, b. 1545,
m. Philip II of
Spain

Claude, b. 1547,
m. Charles III,
D. of Lorraine
(see above)

CHARLES IX, b. 1550
(1560–74),
m. Elizabeth of
Austria in 1570
No heirs

## 1: The House of France:
Capet, Valois, Bourbon, Anjou-Lorraine & Burgundy

**ABBREVIATIONS**

(Kings of France are in CAPITALS;
dates in parentheses indicate life dates,
except for sovereigns, whose reigns are
indicated)

Archb. = Archbishop     Gen. = General
b. = born     Gov. = Governor
C. = Count     M. = Marquis
D. = Duke     = or m. = married to
d. = died     P. = Prince
Ext. = Extinct in

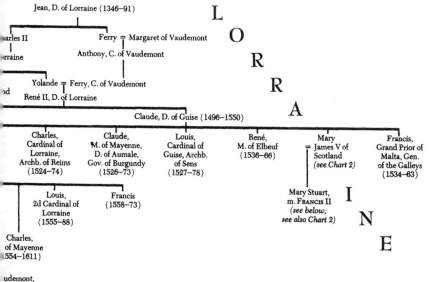

ilip the Bold, = Margaret, heiress of
of Burgundy | Flanders and Artois

John the Fearless

Philip the Good

Charles the Bold

Mary = Emperor Maximilian (1493–1519):

See Chart 2, "The House of Habsburg in Germany & Spain"

## BURGUNDY

Jean, D. of Lorraine (1346–91)

arles II

rraine

Ferry = Margaret of Vaudemont

Anthony, C. of Vaudemont

Yolande = Ferry, C. of Vaudemont

René II, D. of Lorraine

Claude, D. of Guise (1496–1550)

| | | | | | |
|---|---|---|---|---|---|
| Charles, Cardinal of Lorraine, Archb. of Reims (1524–74) | Claude, M. of Mayenne, D. of Aumale, Gov. of Burgundy (1526–73) | Louis, Cardinal of Guise, Archb. of Sens (1527–78) | René, M. of Elbeuf (1536–66) | Mary = James V of Scotland (see Chart 2) | Francis, Grand Prior of Malta, Gen. of the Galleys (1534–63) |

Louis, 2d Cardinal of Lorraine (1555–88)

Francis (1558–73)

Mary Stuart, m. FRANCIS II (see below; see also Chart 2)

Charles, of Mayenne (1554–1611)

udemont, (1524–77)

Louise, m. HENRY III (see below)

LORRAINE

| | | |
|---|---|---|
| Alexander, b. 1551: HENRY III (1574–89), m. Louise of Lorraine (see above) No heirs | Margaret, b. 1553, m. HENRY IV No heirs | Hercules (Francis), b. 1554, d. 1584, D. of Alençon, D. of Anjou, "Protector of the Netherlands" |

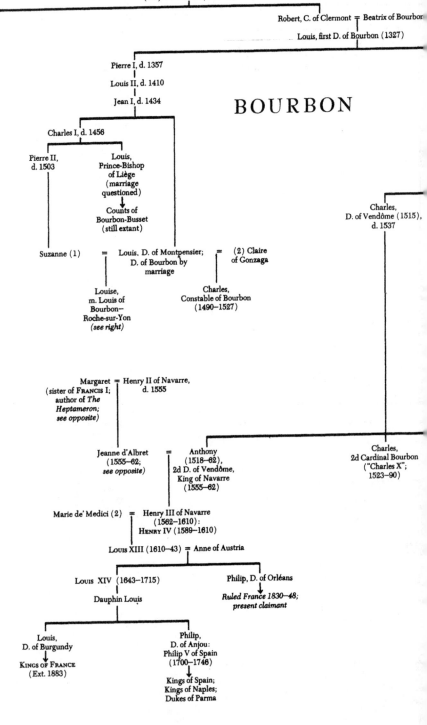

(ST.) LOUIS IX (1226–70)

Robert, C. of Clermont = Beatrix of Bourbon

Louis, first D. of Bourbon (1327)

Pierre I, d. 1357

Louis II, d. 1410

Jean I, d. 1434

# BOURBON

Charles I, d. 1456

Pierre II, d. 1503

Louis, Prince-Bishop of Liège (marriage questioned)

↓

Counts of Bourbon-Busset (still extant)

Charles, D. of Vendôme (1515), d. 1537

Suzanne (1) = Louis, D. of Montpensier; D. of Bourbon by marriage = (2) Claire of Gonzaga

Louise, m. Louis of Bourbon—Roche-sur-Yon *(see right)*

Charles, Constable of Bourbon (1490–1527)

Margaret = Henry II of Navarre, (sister of FRANCIS I; d. 1555 author of *The Heptameron; see opposite*)

Jeanne d'Albret (1555–62; *see opposite*) = Anthony (1518–62), 2d D. of Vendôme, King of Navarre (1555–62)

Charles, 2d Cardinal Bourbon ("Charles X"; 1523–90)

Marie de' Medici (2) = Henry III of Navarre (1562–1610): HENRY IV (1589–1610)

LOUIS XIII (1610–43) = Anne of Austria

LOUIS XIV (1643–1715)

Dauphin Louis

Philip, D. of Orléans

*Ruled France 1830–48; present claimant*

Louis, D. of Burgundy

KINGS OF FRANCE (Ext. 1883)

Philip, D. of Anjou: Philip V of Spain (1700–1746)

Kings of Spain; Kings of Naples; Dukes of Parma

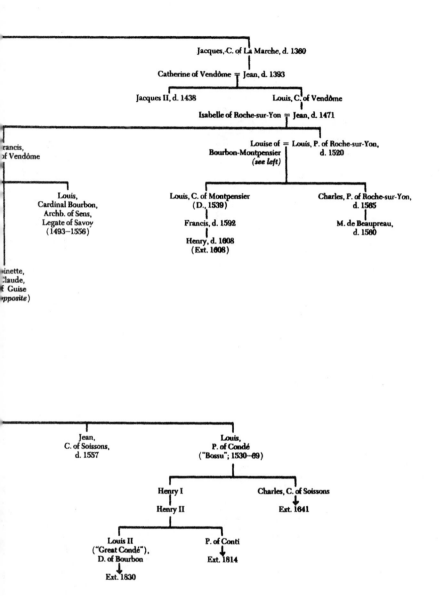

Jacques, C. of La Marche, d. 1360

Catherine of Vendôme = Jean, d. 1393

Jacques II, d. 1438          Louis, C. of Vendôme

Isabelle of Roche-sur-Yon = Jean, d. 1471

Francis,
of Vendôme

Louise of = Louis, P. of Roche-sur-Yon,
Bourbon-Montpensier          d. 1520
(*see left*)

Louis,
Cardinal Bourbon,
Archb. of Sens,
Legate of Savoy
(1493–1556)

Louis, C. of Montpensier
(D., 1539)

Charles, P. of Roche-sur-Yon,
d. 1565

Francis, d. 1592

M. de Beaupreau,
d. 1560

Henry, d. 1608
(Ext. 1608)

inette,
Claude,
f Guise
*pposite*)

Jean,
C. of Soissons,
d. 1557

Louis,
P. of Condé
("Bossu"; 1530–69)

Henry I          Charles, C. of Soissons

Henry II          Ext. 1641

Louis II          P. of Conti
("Great Condé"),
D. of Bourbon          Ext. 1814

Ext. 1830

# 2: The House of Habsburg in Germany & Spain,

Showing Its Connections With Burgundy & England

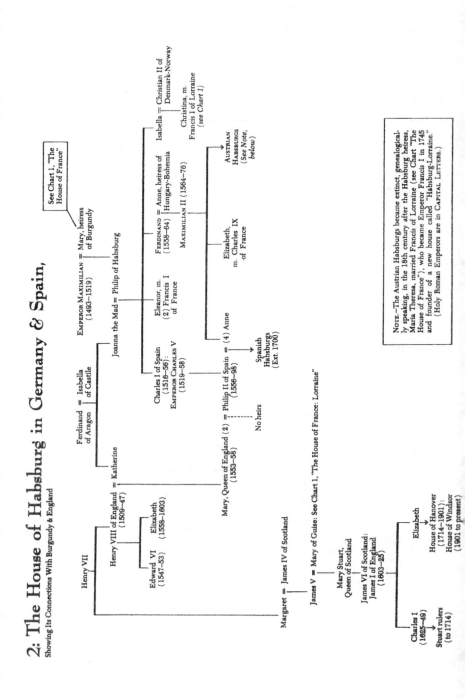

See Chart 1, "The House of France"

Henry VII

Ferdinand of Aragon = Isabella of Castile

EMPEROR MAXIMILIAN (1493–1519) = Mary, heiress of Burgundy

Isabella = Christian II of Denmark-Norway

Henry VIII of England (1509–47) = Katherine

Joanna the Mad = Philip of Habsburg

Eleanor, m. (2) Francis I of France

FERDINAND = Anne, heiress of Hungary-Bohemia (1558–64): MAXIMILIAN II (1564–76)

Christina, m. Francis I of Lorraine (see Chart 1)

Edward VI (1547–53)    Elizabeth (1558–1603)

Charles I of Spain (1516–56): EMPEROR CHARLES V (1519–58)

AUSTRIAN HABSBURGS (See Note, below)

Elizabeth, m. Charles IX of France

Mary, Queen of England (1553–58) (2) = Philip II of Spain (4) Anne (1556–96)

No heirs

Spanish Habsburgs (Ext. 1700)

Margaret = James IV of Scotland

James V = Mary of Guise: See Chart 1, "The House of France: Lorraine"

Mary Stuart, Queen of Scotland

James VI of Scotland: James I of England (1603–25)

Charles I (1625–49)

Elizabeth

House of Hanover (1714–1901): House of Windsor (1901 to present)

Stuart rulers (to 1714)

NOTE.—The Austrian Habsburgs became extinct, genealogically speaking, in the 18th century after the Habsburg heiress, Maria Theresa, married Francis of Lorraine (see Chart "The House of France"), who became Emperor Francis I in 1745 and founder of a new house called "Habsburg-Lorraine." (Holy Roman Emperors are in CAPITAL LETTERS.)

dinand of Aragon, complete the expulsion of the Moors from Europe by the conquest of Granada, the last Moorish state in Europe. Persecution of Moors and Jews refusing conversion.

1493 Charles VIII of France (1483–98) gives the French provinces of Roussillon and Cerdagne to Spain (1493–1659) as a bribe for approval of French acquisition of Brittany and the pending French invasion of Italy.

1494 Charles VIII invades Italy to claim the Kingdom of Naples, thus beginning the Italian Wars (1494–1559), a sort of World War involving all the various states of Italy, France, Spain, the Empire (Germany), Switzerland, England and even the Turks and Algerians.

Piero de' Medici, strong man of Florence (Tuscany), surrenders all Tuscan fortresses to Charles, and is then exiled, along with his whole family, in a democratic revolution. The Dominican monk Savonarola becomes the new strong man and inaugurates a Puritan-type theocracy. Florence turns against Charles VIII, who captures Florence and takes away Pisa and other Florentine possessions.

1495 The French enter Naples. Pope Alexander forms a league against them with Emperor Maximilian I, Ferdinand of Spain (ruler of Sicily), Milan and Venice. The French are driven out of Italy.

1497 Savonarola excommunicated by Pope Alexander for denouncing Church corruption. Savonarola excommunicates Pope Alexander.

1498 Florence (Tuscany) threatened by interdict. Savonarola arrested in coup, confesses under torture to being a false prophet, is tried for heresy and schism and then hanged.

1499 A new invasion of Italy by Louis XII of France (1498–1515), who has inherited both his second cousin's kingdom and his widow, Anne. Louis claims Milan (Lombardy) and occupies it after driving out the dark-complected Ludovico the Moor, a wicked uncle who had seized it from his infant nephew.

1500 Ludovico (the Moor) Sforza, having used his great wealth to buy himself Swiss mercenaries, returns to Milan. The French defeat the Swiss at Novara and carry Ludovico off to confinement in France.

1501 Louis XII leads another French invasion of southern Italy to claim Naples, this time in alliance with the Spanish and with the blessing of the Pope, who uses the occasion to have his son Cesare conquer a new state for himself in central Italy. The Spanish quarrel with the French, defeat them and force the surrender of a whole French army. The French are driven out of all Italy but Milan and Genoa. The Spanish now remain masters of Naples as well as Sicily.

1503 Cesare Borgia lures all his enemies to a friendly conference at Sinigaglia and has them all strangled. (A cardinal at seventeen, Cesare had resigned at twenty-one after being suspected of complicity in the murder of his brother and was sent off to France as his father's envoy to King Louis. Greatly impressed by Cesare, King Louis made him Duke of Valentinois in France and married him to a sister of the King of Navarre, where he fled after being driven out by his father's successors. )

[1503 Nostradamus born at Saint-Rémy in Provence.]

1508 League of Cambrai formed to partition Venetian possessions in Italy. Emperor Maximilian promises to legalize French occupation of Milan in return for support; the Pope and the Spanish are also members.

1509 Spanish colonies founded on Gulf of Uraba on the northern coast of South America and on many other coastal sites of Central and South America throughout the 16th century.

Henry VIII becomes King of England (1509–47), and England once again plays an active part in Europe's wars and intrigues.

The French defeat the Venetians. The Emperor takes Verona, Vicenza and Padua; the Pope takes Ravenna, Rimini, Faenza and other Venetian outposts in central Italy; the Spanish take Brindisi, Otranto and other Venetian outposts in southern Italy.

1510 The allies fall out. The Pope switches sides and joins Venice, which has been aided by a revolt against the Germans in Vicenza and has succeeded in retaking Padua. Ferdinand of Spain neutral.

1511 The Pope forms a Holy League to expel the French from Italy; in the League he has Venice, Spain and even Henry VIII of England, who can keep French troops engaged in the North, attacking from Calais.

The Spanish complete a succession of victories in North Africa, making Oran, Bougie, Tripoli and other cities into protectorates.

1512 The French defeat the Holy League with great victories at Brescia, and, most of all, on Easter Sunday at Ravenna, where their great leader, Gaston of Foix, dies in battle.

Emperor Maximilian and the Swiss, both alarmed at French successes, join the Holy League. The Swiss storm Milan, which Maximilian gives to his namesake, Ludovico's son, Maximilian Sforza. The Swiss remain in control of Milan.

Florence is forced by the Spanish to take back the Medici. Machiavelli, a prominent diplomat and the republic's defense secretary (who inaugurated conscription for a citizen militia) is arrested for plotting against the Medici, tortured, imprisoned and forced into retirement. He takes to writing, including *The Prince* (1532).

Selim the Grim becomes Sultan after forcing his father, Bayazid II, to abdicate, then poisoning him. Selim goes on to defeat his brothers in war, then has them strangled.

1513 The Swiss defeat the French at Novara, avenging their defeat in 1500. The French are again driven out of most of Italy, and are invaded from the North by an Anglo-German coalition. After a French defeat at Guinegate (also called the Battle of the Spurs, from the flight of French cavalry), Louis XII concludes peace.

1514 Selim the Grim begins forty years of war with Persia (1514–55), which is to represent a Turkish second front in relation to fighting in Europe. Great Turkish victory at Chaldiran in Mesopotamia.

1515 Francis I, cousin and son-in-law of Louis XII, becomes King of France (1515–47) and at once resumes war in Italy. This time the French are allied with England and Venice against the Emperor, the Pope, Spain, Milan, Florence and the Swiss. French artillery and Venetian cavalry win a great victory over the Swiss and Milanese at Marignano. Peace concluded 1515–16 with the Swiss, who pledge "eternal alliance" with France, and with the Pope, who further, in the Concordat of Bologna, recognizes the right of the King to choose all bishops and abbots, in return for acknowledgment of some fiscal and theological claims of the Pope.

Emperor Maximilian concludes a double marriage treaty with the King of Hungary and Bohemia whereby Maximilian's grandson Ferdinand, as husband of Anne of Hungary and Bohemia, becomes the heir to these states if Anne's brother Louis dies without issue.

1516 Ferdinand of Spain dies and Charles of Burgundy (later Charles V) becomes King of Spain. Charles makes peace with Francis, who gives up claim to Naples but retains Milan. Charles' grandfather, Emperor Maximilian, allows Venice to ransom back her cities.

Francis I returns to France, including amongst his Italian acquisitions the brilliant painter and scientist, one-time protégé of Cesare Borgia, Leonardo da Vinci (1452–1519), whose scientific drawings included plans for flying machines.

Egypt joins the Persians against the Turks. The Turks win a great victory near Aleppo, and

1517 The Turks push their conquests into Egypt, Syria and Arabia.

Martin Luther nails his 95 Theses to the door of the castle church at Wittenberg and begins the Protestant Reformation.

[1517 Nostradamus goes to Avignon, the papal enclave in France, for his secondary education.]

1519 The Lesbian adventurer (from the island of Lesbos, that is) Khaireddin, known as Barbarossa, takes Algiers from the Spanish in the name of the Sultan and lays the foundations for the Barbary empire in North Africa as a Mediterranean power. Khaireddin evacuates the persecuted Moors from Spain, and they contribute many skills, as the Huguenots are to do later under similar circumstances of persecution and exile.

Sir Thomas More publishes his *Utopia*, concerning an ideal state where everything is ordered by the rulers for the general good of the citizens.

Emperor Maximilian dies and his grandson Charles, who has inherited from his other grandfather the Spanish Empire in Europe and overseas and from his father modern Holland and Belgium and parts of modern France, inherits the Habsburg territories in Central Europe and becomes the leading candidate for election as Emperor. With huge loans from German bankers, to be repaid by Spanish gold from America, Charles outbids Francis I of France and Henry VIII of England in bribing the Electors and becomes Emperor Charles V, ruler of more European territory than any monarch between Charlemagne and Napoleon.

1520 Suleiman the Magnificent becomes Turkish Sultan (1520–66) but leaves most of ruling during his first years to a Greek named Ibrahim Pasha.

1521 The Turks capture Belgrade and push on to round out their complete conquest of the Balkans, also making frequent raids into Italy, Austria and Hungary.

Henry VIII secures the title "Defender of the Faith" for England's rulers from the Pope for his erudite treatise against Luther.

1522 Rhodes, the headquarters for Christian pirates preying upon Turkish shipping, is captured by the Turks after help from the West fails to arrive. The Knights of St. John are evacuated and set up by Charles V on Malta, where they become the Knights of Malta.

The austere Dutch tutor of Charles V, Adrian of Utrecht, is elected Pope as Adrian VI. Unsuccessful in his attempts to get Charles and Francis to end their wars and join against the Turks, he is equally unsuccessful in his attempts to curb the luxury and abuses of the Church. The last non-Italian pope to date, he dies after twenty months, amidst universal rejoicing by the Italians.

[1522–25 Nostradamus studies medicine at Montpellier.]

1522 Charles V puts his brother Ferdinand in charge of German affairs and resumes the Habsburg–Valois wars, driving the French out of Milan (except the citadel) and Genoa, and giving Milan to Francesco Sforza, last of the Sforza dynasty.

1523 Charles of Bourbon, Constable of France (titular leader of France's armed forces), goes over to Emperor Charles V.

A French expedition to Italy under Bonnivert meets with disaster.

1524–25 The Peasants' War in Germany, together with the related Anabaptist movement, adds communistic social revolt to the religious revolt and briefly unites Catholic and Protestant princes in Germany. The rebels are extirpated with great ferocity.

1524 Charles sends an expedition to invade Provence (Nostradamus' home province).

Francis crosses the Mont Cenis Pass of the Alps in a new invasion of Italy, with the Pope as an ally. Milan is retaken.

[1525–29 Nostradamus leaves Montpellier to fight the plague in Narbonne, Carcassonne, Toulouse, Bordeaux and then goes back to Avignon.]

1525 The French suffer their worst defeat in more than a century at the Battle of Pavia. The Spanish under the Marquis of Pescara and the renegade Duke of Bourbon capture King Francis and carry him off to Spain.

1526 Francis is forced to sign the Treaty of Madrid, giving up all his claims in Italy and to territories north of France, and promising to cede French Burgundy to Charles V. Francis repudiates the treaty as soon as he is set at liberty and forms the League of Cognac with the Pope, Henry VIII, Venice, Milan and Florence.

The entire Hungarian army is wiped out by the Turks in the Battle of Mohacs and the twenty-year-old King Louis is killed. In accordance with the marriage treaty of 1515, Charles' brother Ferdinand claims Bohemia and Hungary, but his claim to Hungary is contested by the nobles of Transylvania, who elect John Zapolya as King John I. Civil war follows, and after John is defeated by Ferdinand (1527) he retires to Transylvania and Ferdinand is crowned King of Hungary.

1527 The pro-Habsburg Medici are again expelled from Florence and a republic is again formed.

Charles V sends an army under the Constable of Bourbon against Pope Clement VII. The Constable is killed in the attack and the mutinous and underpaid army, consisting mostly of German Lutheran mercenaries, perpetrates the Sack of Rome. The Pope is a prisoner.

The French seize Genoa with the aid of Andrea Doria. The French army under Marshal Lautrec, supported by the Genoese navy, sets out for Rome to rescue the Pope. The Pope suddenly comes to terms with the Emperor.

1528 The French army and the Genoese fleet, with nothing further to do at Rome, instead besiege Naples. Doria quarrels with Lautrec, breaks his alliance with France and goes over to Charles V, becoming Admiral of the Imperial Navy. The French, with plague following after the Genoese desertion, retire to France.

1529 The Treaty of Cambrai (also called "The Ladies' Peace," having been negotiated by Charles' aunt, Margaret, and Francis' mother, Louise of Savoy) restores the terms of the Treaty of Madrid, except that Francis can pay an indemnity of two million crowns instead of ceding Burgundy. (In 1530 Francis marries Charles' sister Eleanor.)

[1529–32 Nostradamus gets his doctorate at Montpellier and joins the faculty, which in 1530 gives Rabelais a bachelor's degree.]

1529 John of Transylvania appeals to Sultan Suleiman for aid against Ferdinand. Suleiman invades Hungary and Austria and besieges Vienna. John also defeats Ferdinand, surrenders his crown to Suleiman and receives it back as a Turkish vassal. Transylvania becomes a peaceful Protestant state under Moslem protection, but sporadic fighting continues in western Hungary between the Turks and the Germans.

1530 Charles V crowned as Roman Emperor at Bologna by Pope Clement.

Charles V makes Alessandro de' Medici hereditary Duke of Florence.

1531 Charles V has his brother Ferdinand crowned at Aachen as King of the Romans (i.e., King of Germany).

Khaireddin's Algerian corsairs plunder the Mediterranean shores of Charles V's empire while the Turks on land again invade Ferdinand's Hungary, but retire because of threats on the Persian front.

[1532 Nostradamus resigns from the faculty at Montpellier and wanders in southwest France, including Bordeaux, La Rochelle and Toulouse. In Toulouse he gets a letter from Scaliger at Agen, and

1533–38 Nostradamus is at Agen, practicing medicine, with a wife and two children. His wife and children die in 1537 in a plague.]

1533 Suleiman concludes a truce with Ferdinand whereby Ferdinand can keep part of Hungary and his title in return for tribute. However, Suleiman continues the naval war against Ferdinand's brother, the Emperor. Khaireddin captures Tunis from its Habsburg puppet ruler.

Henry VIII of England declares null and void his marriage to Charles V's aunt, Catherine of Aragon, who had failed to produce a surviving male heir. He secretly marries the pregnant Anne Boleyn, but to his great disappointment, the baby turns out to be a girl, the future Queen Elizabeth.

1534 Henry VIII promulgates the Act of Supremacy whereby the King of England is the head of the Church in England. The ritual remains unchanged for the time being.

Suleiman victorious on all fronts. The Turks capture Bagdad and take Mesopotamia from the Persians, while Khaireddin's corsairs ravage Sicily and southern Italy.

Francis I sends Jacques Cartier to explore Canada in preparation for French colonization.

1535 Spectacular expedition of Charles V to Tunis. Khaireddin is defeated in a naval battle by Doria, and the Spanish recapture Tunis (and retain it till 1570). A three-day sack follows. The Duke of Alba makes his first appearance on the stage of history, where he is to be a key figure for forty years.

Italian Wars begin again with the death of the last Sforza ruler of Milan. Charles V claims Milan as King of Italy and is credited with the *bon mot* "King Francis and I are in complete agreement; we both want Milan."

John Calvin, in seclusion at Angoulême about a hundred miles from Nostradamus at Agen (there is no record of a meeting, though it is not impossible), completes his theological masterwork, *Institutes of the Christian Religion,* whose tenets are to hold sway from Transylvania to Massachusetts, but in the immediate future are to be most important in Switzerland, France, Scotland and Holland.

1536 King Francis concludes a formal alliance with Sultan Suleiman against Charles V, invades Savoy and Piedmont and captures Turin. Suleiman renews his attack against the Habsburgs in Hungary, while Khaireddin obligingly again ravages the coasts of Italy.

Calvin is invited to Geneva to set up a theocracy, but in 1538 is driven out in a revolt headed by the Libertine party.

Henry VIII has Anne Boleyn executed for adultery and declares Elizabeth a bastard, which is to be confirmed subsequently by various popes.

1538 The Truce of Nice restores peace between Francis and Charles, confirming the Treaty of Cambrai, except that the French retain most of their conquests in Savoy and Piedmont (until 1559).

The Pope forms a Holy League with the Emperor and Venice against the Turks. Charles V tries unsuccessfully to buy Khaireddin. The Venetians are defeated at sea, and are forced to yield more of their overseas empire and to pay an indemnity.

Mount Vesuvius stages a spectacular eruption with unusual variations.

[1538–45 Nostradamus, saddened by the death of his wife and children and by his quarrel with Scaliger, and apparently also in some sort of trouble with the Inquisition, resumes his wandering, this time over a wider area of southwest Europe than before.]

1540 The Jesuits, founded in 1534, are recognized by the Pope.

John I of Transylvania dies, and his three-month-old son is crowned as John II amidst counterclaims from Ferdinand.

1541 The Turks again invade Hungary, to protect little John this time. Buda captured and, like Rome in 1527 and Tunis in 1535, is delivered to an epic sack. In Transylvania the mother of little John becomes regent, but real power falls into the hands of an adventurous Italian monk named George Martinuzzi.

Andrea Doria makes an unsuccessful attempt to capture Algiers from Khaireddin.

Calvin invited back to Geneva and makes sure this time it's to stay. His theocracy becomes absolute and totalitarian, including secret police. He remains in complete control till his death (1564) and Geneva becomes the Protestant Rome—or, in the eyes of any clairvoyant Catholics, a Protestant Moscow.

1542 Francis, outraged at Charles' having invested his fifteen-year-old son, the future Philip II, as Duke of Milan, begins his fourth war with Charles. This time Suleiman is again with Francis while Charles has Henry VIII as an ally. The co-operation of Islam with the Most Christian King is closer than ever as Khaireddin's fleet of Algerian corsairs joins the French in the bombardment and capture of Nice. In the Southwest, Alba defends Perpignan against French attack. A French victory at Ceresole is followed by an invasion of France, while Suleiman is faithfully invading Hungary and Austria.

The Universal Inquisition is established by the Pope.

Catherine de' Medici, after nine years of childless marriage to the future Henry II, conceives the future Francis II, the first of ten children, thus apparently saving the Valois dynasty from the threat of extinction (which occurs nevertheless in 1589).

1544 Treaty of Crespy is signed to cement relations between Charles and Francis by marriage. Francis' son, the Duke of Orléans, is to marry either Charles' daughter, with Burgundy (Holland, Belgium and Franche-Comté) as a dowry, or Charles' niece, with Milan as a dowry, in return for which Francis is to return Savoy and Piedmont to the Duke of Savoy.

1545 The Duke of Orléans suddenly dies, thus apparently voiding the whole treaty.

Francis authorizes the first organized persecution of French Protestants.

The Council of Trent begins, ushering in the Counter-Reformation.

[1545 Nostradamus practices medicine at Marseilles.

1546 Nostradamus achieves spectacular success in fighting the plague at Aix.

1547 Nostradamus settles down in Salon and gets married again, although absenting himself awhile to fight a plague at Lyons.]

1547 Francis I dies, allegedly of syphilis. Henry II inherits his father's kingdom, France, as well as his one-time mistress, Diane de Poitiers (now forty-eight years old).

Henry VIII dies and under the regency for the young Edward VI (1547–53) Protestant doctrines are introduced into England (1549).

Ivan the Terrible, aged seventeen, takes over power in Muscovy from his regency and has himself crowned Tsar, in succession to the Byzantine Caesars or Tsars, and begins the great expansion of Muscovy, subsequently the Russian Empire.

Spectacular conspiracy in Genoa led by Fieschi against the Doria tyranny. Andrea Doria's nephew is murdered and Andrea forced to flee, but the conspiracy collapses when Fieschi is accidently drowned. Andrea Doria is restored as Doge.

1548 Another conspiracy at Genoa against Doria, again unsuccessful.

Suleiman the Magnificent again invades Persia.

[1550 Nostradamus alleged to have turned out the first of his Almanacs, commencing his career as prophet. However, there is no bibliographical record of any before 1555.]

1551 Transylvania once more comes into the spotlight as Martinuzzi develops dreams of grandeur, deposes John and his mother and recognizes Ferdinand as King of a united Hungary. Martinuzzi becomes a cardinal, but subsequently is assassinated on orders of Ferdinand when he is suspected of treason. Martinuzzi's action brings renewal of war by the Turks, which continues in desultory fashion till 1561.

1552 The Persians attack the Turks, who respond with another ravaging invasion of Persia.

Henry II of France, in alliance with the Protestant Elector of Saxony, goes to war with Charles V, and the French capture Metz, Toul and Verdun. The Duke of Guise enters the stage, where he and his relatives are to hold key roles for half a century, defending Metz against attempts by the Duke of Alba to recapture it.

[1552 Nostradamus publishes the first edition of his best-selling *Moult Utile Opuscule* ("Very Useful Little Treatise"), a book of cosmetic, gastronomic and medical recipes, allegedly written at the request of Nostradamus' one Protestant friend, Jeanne d'Albret, mother of the future Henry of Navarre.]

1553 Suleiman has his son Mustafa strangled.

Calvin at Geneva has Michael Servetus, brilliant theologian and physician, burned for heresy, having captured him after Servetus had escaped from a prison of the Catholic Inquisition.

Edward VI dies and is succeeded by his half sister, Mary ("Bloody Mary"), as Queen of England (1553–58). A marriage treaty is concluded whereby Mary is to marry her cousin Philip, Charles V's son and heir, who is to have the title King of England, though without the powers or the right to succeed Mary. This treaty, in addition to Mary's restoration of Catholicism, produces rebellion.

1554 The rebellion against Mary reaches its peak and fails. Several nobles are executed. Mary marries Philip (July 26), who has been made King of Naples as a wedding gift by his father. The thirty-eight-year-old Queen falls madly in love with her twenty-seven-year-old husband.

Suleiman makes peace with Persia, retaining Mesopotamia.

Dragut, the successor of Khaireddin, attacks Habsburg outposts in North Africa.

[1554 Nostradamus' Centuries believed to have been started on March 23, 1554.

1555, MARCH 1: Nostradamus completes the Preface to his Centuries and sends it to his Lyons publisher, who shows May 4 as the date of the printing of this first edition (with 353 quatrains). In the same year, Nostradamus also publishes an enlarged edition of his recipe book of 1552, and the first of his authenticated Almanacs.]

1555, APRIL 30: London crowds gather at Westminster awaiting description of Queen Mary's baby, whose impending birth she has ordered proclaimed following upon previous advices as to her pregnancy. Philip and other intimates put off during May and June breaking the news to Mary that her baby is imaginary.

MAY 25: Henry II of Navarre (not to be confused with the contemporary Henry II of France) is killed in a riding accident and his son-in-law, Anthony, Duke of Bourbon-Vendôme, becomes King of Navarre, giving the House of Bourbon the first of many thrones.

SEPTEMBER: Philip, his nerves frayed by the months with his hysterical wife, pleads important royal business and leaves England. In Germany, Charles V concludes the Peace of Augsburg, permitting any German prince to choose the Lutheran faith (but not the Calvinist) for his state and his people.

OCTOBER: Philip gets the Netherlands officially from his father, who abdicates as Duke of Burgundy October 25.

DECEMBER: Pope Paul IV forms a new league to settle Italian affairs in the face of Charles' impending abdication, so as to remove the Spanish. The French, the Pope and Ferrara are to conquer Milan and Naples from the Spanish, each to be ruled by a French prince with the Pope as his suzerain. Also, the Medici are again to be driven out of Florence and the republic restored. Charles of Guise, Cardinal of Lorraine, signs for France.

1556, JANUARY: Charles V abdicates as ruler of Spain, giving Philip Spain and her possessions in Italy and overseas. Ferdinand is confirmed as ruler of Germany, although Charles holds off abdicating as Emperor.

FEBRUARY: The Constable of France, Anne de Montmorency, rival of the Guise, frustrates their plans in Italy by concluding the Truce of Vaucelles with Spain.

MARCH: Persecution of Protestants in England reaches its climax. More than three hundred burned at the stake for heresy.

[JULY: Nostradamus travels to Paris at royal command and confers with Catherine de' Medici.]

SEPTEMBER: Alba, Spanish commander in Italy since 1552, is ordered to move against Pope Paul to counter his intrigues, which have now led to persecution of pro-Spanish clique in Rome.

NOVEMBER: Guise crosses the Alps with his army and marches on Naples but fails to get the promised support of the Pope. Guise is forced back and Alba marches to the outskirts of Rome.

[1557 An enlarged second edition of Nostradamus' Centuries is published, with 287 additional quatrains.]

1557, MARCH: Philip returns to England, and after giving Mary the "second honeymoon" treatment, persuades her to enter the war against France. He is less successful in persuading Elizabeth to marry his protégé, Duke Emmanuel-Philibert of Savoy.

MAY: Montmorency orders Guise to leave Italy at once and return to France in the face of the Spanish build-up in the North. Guise finds excuses to procrastinate, hoping somehow still to beat Alba in Italy.

JULY: Philip leaves Mary and England forever (though in the time of the Spanish Armada in 1588 he has hopes of returning there under other circumstances). An English herald dashes off to France to locate King Henry and deliver a declaration of war.

AUGUST 10: The Spanish under the Duke of Savoy inflict a catastrophic defeat on the French at Saint-Quentin. Montmorency is a prisoner.

OCTOBER: Guise rushes back to France and is appointed Lieutenant-General of the Realm.

1558, JANUARY: Guise takes Calais, the last English possession in France and England's sacrifice to its Queen's romantic passion.

MARCH: Charles V abdicates as Emperor, remaining in the monastery at Yuste, to which he had retired in 1556, and dies later in the year.

APRIL: The Dauphin is married to Mary Stuart, Queen of Scotland and niece of the Duke of Guise.

[JUNE 27: Nostradamus signs the Epistle to Henry II, which serves as a preface to the third, enlarged edition of his *Centuries*, containing three hundred more quatrains, although apparently it is not published until 1568.]

NOVEMBER: Queen Mary of England dies. Elizabeth becomes Queen and the terribly unstable English now go Protestant again.

1559, APRIL: The Treaty of Cateau-Cambresis puts an end to the Italian Wars and to the Habsburg–Valois duel. The French keep Calais, Metz, Toul and Verdun but restore Savoy and Piedmont to Philip's protégé, the Duke of Savoy.

JULY: During a tournament in celebration of the marriage of the Duke of Savoy to Henry II's sister, Henry is killed by the Captain of the Scottish Guard, the Count of Montgomery, a lance penetrating his brain in the course of a joust. The sickly Dauphin becomes Francis II and his wife, Mary Stuart, already a queen at the age of six, takes the title Queen of Scotland and England.

[OCTOBER: The Duke of Savoy and his bride visit Nostradamus at Salon.]

1560 Maximilian, Ferdinand's son, agrees to abandon his Lutheran proclivities, which had produced the threat of a Protestant Holy Roman Emperor. (In the face of this possibility, Philip had plans to succeed his uncle Ferdinand as Holy Roman Emperor.)

The Conspiracy of Amboise by the French Huguenots—led by the Bourbon Prince of Condé, supported by Elizabeth and Calvin, and aimed at abducting King Francis at the castle of Amboise and arresting the Catholic leaders, the Duke of Guise and his brother, the Cardinal—is foiled when the Guise are forewarned. Widespread massacre of Huguenots. Francis dies in December just before his eighteenth birthday and is succeeded by his brother, his mother serving as regent.

1561 The Colloquy of Passy takes place, a Catholic-Calvinist debate between the Cardinal of Lorraine and, for the Calvinists, Calvin himself and his chief lieutenant, Théodore de Bèze.

1562 Beginning of the Wars of Religion (1562–98), an all-pervasive civil war and time of troubles for France in which politics and religion are inextricably mixed.

Anthony of Navarre killed in battle. His nine-year-old son Henry, the future Henry IV, becomes King of Navarre.

Maximilian elected King of the Romans (i.e., King of Germany) and also King of Bohemia. The following year he is elected King of Hungary, thus precluding all doubts about his succeeding Ferdinand.

1563  The Duke of Guise is assassinated after his victory over the Huguenots at Dreux.

1564  Emperor Ferdinand dies and is succeeded by Maximilian. Calvin also dies.

[1564  The regent, Catherine de' Medici, visits Nostradamus at Salon, along with her Court and her son, Charles IX. Nostradamus also sees the eleven-year-old King of Navarre, third in line now for the throne, and predicts he will be King of France.]

1565  Unsuccessful siege of Malta by the Turks.

1566  Suleiman the Magnificent dies.

[1566  Nostradamus dies.]

1567  Alba sent to the Netherlands in the face of the impending Revolt of the Netherlands (1568–1648).

1570  The Algerians retake Tunis from the Habsburgs. Cyprus is besieged.

1571  The Holy League formed by the Papacy and, including the Pope, Spain and Venice, achieves an epic naval victory over the Turks at Lepanto under Charles V's bastard son, Don John of Austria; but the victory is not followed up.

1572  The marriage of Henry of Navarre to Charles IX's sister Margaret is followed by the St. Bartholomew's Day Massacre of Huguenots throughout France. Henry saves himself by abjuring Calvinism, but subsequently returns to Protestant faith when at liberty, after virtual imprisonment (1572–76).

1573  The Venetians, despite the Lepanto victory, lose Cyprus to the Turks, retaining only Crete (Candia) and the Ionian Islands of their once great eastern empire. However, Don John retakes Tunis for the Spanish, but it is lost again the following year.

1574  Charles IX dies at twenty-four. His brother, elected King of Poland the previous year, deserts Poland and rushes back to France to become Henry III (1574–89).

1576  The Holy League is formed by the Duke of Guise and his brothers (sons of the great military leader) to unite all French Catholics against the Protestants. It aims especially at excluding Henry of Navarre from the succession and also to advance Guise power at the expense of the King. A three-cornered struggle develops between the King, the Guise and the Huguenots, with the King switching between the two sides and his brother, the Duke of Alençon, also being used by the Guise.

1578  King Sebastian of Portugal is killed in a "crusade" against the Moors, leaving no heirs. Philip of Spain sends the aged Duke of Alba, removed from the Netherlands in 1573 after years of bloody terror, on his last mission for the House of Habsburg, to conquer Portugal. Lisbon is captured and a general massacre by Alba's troops follows (1580). Alba dies in 1582.

1582  Francis of Alençon, frustrated in his efforts to woo Queen Elizabeth, accepts invitation by William the Silent to become Protector of the

Netherlands. Attempting to secure absolute power, he becomes universally disliked and is expelled.

1584 Alençon dies and Henry of Navarre is the heir to the French throne. Guise and the Catholic League step up their popular movement and secure control of most French cities.

1588 Henry III, outraged at being expelled from Paris by its pro-Guise citizens, secures the assassination of the Duke of Guise at Blois, together with a brother. The other brother, Mayenne, assumes leadership of the League and becomes the arch-foe of Henry of Navarre.

1589 Henry III, having fled to the camp of Henry of Navarre at Saint-Cloud outside Paris, is assassinated by a young Catholic fanatic, Jacques Clément.

Henry of Navarre, now legally King of France, devotes five years to fighting his domestic enemies, who are soon divided along lines of the more patriotic versus the more Catholic, when the Spanish enter France again to aid the Catholics.

1594 Henry of Navarre, after several victories, abjures Protestantism again, and with his famous cynical remark, "Paris is well worth a Mass," enters Paris and is subsequently crowned King, as Henry IV, commencing the Bourbon dynasty.

1594–1610 Henry devotes his tremendous energy to rebuilding France, is thoroughly successful and becomes the most popular king in French history. He is assassinated in 1610.

1610–43 Louis XIII, Henry's infant son, is King. His mother, Marie de' Medici, a distant cousin of Catherine, is regent (1610–24). In 1624 Richelieu becomes chief minister and puts down several conspiracies, including the one involving Montmorency, concluded with Montmorency's execution (1632). After establishing strong royal power at home, Richelieu enters the Thirty Years' War. France replaces Spain as the strongest power in Europe.

1643–1715 Louis XIV. Again France has an infant, a mother as regent and a cardinal (Mazarin) as the real ruler, until Louis XIV comes of age. Rebellion against Mazarin is frequent, especially the Fronde (1649).

1649 Charles I of England, grandson of Mary Stuart, is executed as the conclusion of the Civil War. Cromwell, the leader of the rebel army in the Civil War, becomes Protector and virtual dictator.

1660 Restoration of the Monarchy in England under Charles I's son, Charles II (1660–85). His brother, James II (1685–88), is expelled in the Glorious Revolution (1688).

1661 Louis XIV assumes personal control in France, and plunges France into wars of ever-increasing cost.

1701–14 The War of the Spanish Succession is fought to support the claim of Louis' grandson to establish a new dynasty in Spain, to succeed the defunct Spanish Habsburgs.

1715–74 Louis XV, the third king in a row to succeed to the throne as an infant. General indifference by the good-natured King to growing problems and rising discontent.

1774–92 Louis XVI is King of France. In 1789 the French Revolution breaks out. In 1791 the King and the Queen attempt to flee France, are recognized and seized at Varennes and return to Paris as prisoners.

1793 Louis XVI executed. The Reign of Terror follows, under Robespierre.

1795 Robespierre is arrested and executed and succeeded by the Directory. France is at war with her neighbors on all frontiers.

1799–1814 Napoleon Bonaparte seizes control of France, first as Consul, subsequently as Emperor. Wars continue all over Europe, with the French at first generally victorious and in control of the largest empire since Charlemagne's time, then confronted with a number of defeats after the disastrous Russian Campaign (1812–13).

1814 Napoleon is exiled to Elba. Louis XVI's brother becomes King as Louis XVIII, the title Louis XVII having belonged to the Dauphin, who is believed to have died in prison.

1815 Napoleon returns from Elba for his Hundred Days. Louis XVIII flees. Napoleon is defeated at Waterloo by a European coalition, and exiled to St. Helena, where he dies in 1821.

1824 Louis XVIII (1814–24) is followed by Charles X (1824–30). Less-easy-going than his brother, Charles tries to restore strong royal power, leading to the Revolution of 1830.

1830–48 Louis-Philippe, a distant cousin of the last three kings, is elected King with a liberal program.

1848 Revolution breaks out again, this time as part of a general European revolution, with social and economic factors involved along with the political. Napoleon's nephew, Louis-Napoleon, is elected President under a republican constitution.

1851 Louis-Napoleon overthrows the republic in a coup and, after bloody repression of the opposition, comes out in complete control.

1852–70 Louis-Napoleon re-establishes the Napoleonic Empire with himself as Napoleon III.

1870 War with Prussia. Napoleon III and his army capitulate at the Battle of Sedan. The war continues, the Emperor a prisoner.

1871 Paris surrenders and peace, at a heavy price, follows later in the year. The foundations of the Third Republic are laid, and France has apparently seen the last of French kings and emperors. The German Empire is revived, and Germany replaces France as the strongest power in Europe.

# Commentaries

## *The Preface to César Nostradamus*

The bulk of this Preface consists of Nostradamus' account of how he came to prophesy. Such is the nature of his involved structures that it may strike the reader as sheer gibberish and leave him no better informed than before he started to read it.

To make it as comprehensible as possible, we have taken great liberties in breaking up sentences pages long into short sentences. The paragraphs are a further arbitrary subdivision, based as nearly as possible on breaks in the chain of thought. They are also essential for Index references, though the latter have been kept to a minimum (proper names only) for the Preface and the Epistle.

Great care has been taken not to read anything into the translation that is not implied in the original French; but in the writings of Nostradamus the dividing line between a translation of verbatim gibberish and unjustifiable paraphrasing is a very thin one indeed.

1. This is clear enough. César was but a few months old at the time.

2. Here we already run into confusion. He is writing a preface to written prophecies, yet states that he cannot leave in writing that which might perish. The only answer would seem that he feared a single manuscript might be destroyed, but in book form, with many copies, its existence would remain assured.

3. Ever in danger of falling under the suspicion of the ecclesiastical authorities, Nostradamus makes repeated references to the omnipotence of God, to whom he owes everything—i.e., not to the cohorts of Satan.

4. This is a clear-enough reference to his past success with almanacs, and his natural fear of conflict with authority over more ambitious predictions.

5. Here we find a very specific and reasonable explanation of his reluctance. Regardless of what proportion of his predictions have been fulfilled, or will be fulfilled, there are some very specific ones. A classic example remains "The senate of London will put their king to death," which Henry VIII, dead scarcely a decade, would have scarcely enjoyed reading. Of this sentence, Parker (1920) writes, "It would hardly be an exaggeration to say that this is the most scandalous utterance which passed by the censors in the 16th Century."

6. It is difficult to conceive of any other meaning underlying this phrase besides what Le Pelletier calls "the coming to power of the common people" and Ward "the vulgar advent." This would mean that Nostradamus did at least foresee the epic social cataclysm which we know as the French Revolu-

tion. From this it does not by any means follow that he foresaw correctly the time or manner of its coming. The chronological outline of the Epistle does not add to his reputation in this respect.

7. Here we have what might be called background. He begins by speaking of the Biblical Prophets in the third person and concludes by including himself as a recipient of the "divine heat."

8. Time out again for the acknowledgment of God's omnipotence.

9. The days of the Prophets are not yet passed. The meaning of the three varieties of divine works is a problem for the metaphysician.

10. A fairly lucid outline of his prophetic technique: (1) star-gazing in a semi-trance; (2) the magic demon in the thin flame; (3) fearless taking of notes.

11. Lest he be considered sacreligious, he declines to call himself a prophet—yet. And more metaphysics.

12. Very involved Nostradamian theory, of which the gist would seem: if you're inspired by God, and work yourself into the right sort of trance, you can read the future from the stars.

13. More occult philosophy and gibberish.

14. Another acknowledgment for God, another explanation of how to prophesy. For "good fortune" read "magic," and for "nature" "astrology." The "thin flame" continues to recur, apparently being the magical environment for his "demon," or "genius."

15. Retreat and self-protection again. Tongue in cheek, he tells his son never, never to have anything to do with that dreadful thing called magic. If he were put on trial, this passage would undoubtedly serve as the backbone of his defense. The Church of that day did not object so much to what an astrologer predicted as to his getting his information from an unauthorized source (such as Satan). If it was from Satan, his immortal soul would have to be saved; i.e., he would have to be burned at the stake.

16. This is perhaps the most important section of the Preface. He has no reluctance about admitting his dependence on judicial astrology. With this, divine inspiration and "nightly watches and calculations" (doubletalk for magic), he was able to write his prophecies. "Sheer vandalism," writes one commentator horrified at the destruction of those priceless books, probably received from Grandfather Jean de Saint-Rémy. Guesses as to what the destroyed works consisted of include *De Daemonibus* by the Byzantine Michael Psellus, *De mysteriis Aegyptiorum* by Jamblichus, the semi-legendary Keys of Solomon and the legendary Kabbala.

17. Despise not judicial astrology. If César were to become interested in it, he would have the paternal blessing. He did not.

18. A careful, modest retreat into humility again.

19. Since Nostradamus both calls his prophecies perpetual prophecies and states that they extend until the year 3797, he states in effect that this will be the year when the roll is called up yonder. Of course, not every commentator will accept this as A.D. 3797. Since by chronology 3,797 years since

Creation must have long since passed, the varying interpretations require arbitrary starting points. Le Pelletier (1867) brightly decided it must be 3797 years after Ishmael, whom he placed at 1906 B.C. But 1891 came and went. If nothing happens in 3797, it will at once be assumed that he meant 3797 years after 1555. What the commentators of 5352 will think up remains a problem for them. McCann (1942, p. 288) notes that the sum of crowns left in his will (3,444) and the number of quatrains in the first edition (353) just equals this number. "These number oddities," she observes astutely, "may be only coincidental, but there are a great many curious such correspondencies."

20. Don't pay any attention to what others say. You'll see.

21. More hcmage to God, more gibberish.

22. The gist of this would seem that the chosen prophet is prepared for his work by direct divine inspiration, and by the sending of a divine mentor, i.e., angel, demon, genius, etc.

23. Prophecy, like logical science, is infallible, since God is the source of each.

24. We get a prose outline of his idea of the shape of things to come, to some extent an abbreviation of the prose outline written three years later in the Epistle. But there is conflict on many points. For instance, in paragraph 27 he states that he is in the seventh millennium; by 1558 his calculations led him to conclude that the seventh millennium did not start until much later (probably *ca.* 1826). The net result of both outlines is conclusively to invalidate any claim to his infallibility, which the non-chronological order of the quatrains would have left invulnerable (except for the few dated quatrains). After a reading of either outline, the best that can be said for him is that he foresaw some events, but was completely confused about the period and order of their occurrence.

Universal fire, drought, flood and destruction of learning are among the disasters foreseen. Great as the ravages of Europe have been, it would take more than poetic license to justify this somber prediction, at least yet.

25. More astrological gibberish. The purport of "anaragonic" has never been conclusively settled. Inasmuch as the 17th-century variant "anaxagoric" has a sounder etymological background, without any suspiciously lucid meaning, it can be accepted as equally valid.

26. Nostradamus here made the disastrous mistake of naming an exact date, beyond all dispute. June 22, 1732, was to mark the climax of the shattering upheavals that would all but wipe out the human race. As a matter of fact, after the close of the War of the Spanish Succession in 1713, Europe had several decades of relative peace and prosperity.

27. More astrological gibberish, somewhat similar to that of Roussat (General Bibliography, 1550).

28. A return to the "origin of prophets" theme.

29. More metaphysics and "occult philosophy."

30. And yet more. Always there remains the vague suspicion that Nos-

tradamus is satirizing certain metaphysicians, but the suspicion does not seem justified.

31. These dire predictions serve as a prototype for many quatrains.

32. With all these somber predictions hanging over his head, it is remarkable that César lived to the ripe old age he did.

33. There is a great deal of doubt about what works Nostradamus refers to here. The only prose prophecies known of are the prognostication sections of his almanacs. Chavigny wrote of "Twelve Books," which were probably no more than the almanacs for twelve years (see "Nostradamus Bibliography"). If these ever really existed, Nostradamus must have destroyed them. Or else he is inventing their existence for any of several possible reasons.

34. César makes no mention that his father ever fulfilled the promise.

## Century I

1. Only with quatrain 3 do we have the first real prophecy; 1 and 2 are devoted to "prophetic background." To these verses Jaubert devotes sixteen pages. We have here as the necessary elements (1) the night, (2) study of forbidden literature, (3) solitude and (4) a brass stool or tripod (traditionally used by the Delphic Oracle). Again we have the "thin flame" (mentioned several times in the Preface), suggesting either divine inspiration or magic.

2. There are somewhat varying interpretations of the metaphors in this verse. The rod may refer to the laurel branch used by the ancient oracles, or simply to his pen. Jaubert sees the branches as either the twigs on the laurel branch, or as a metaphor for the fingers between which he inserts the pen. Le Pelletier suggests a third idea, supported by the capitalization (BRANCHES). Branchus was the name of a Greek youth given the gift of prophecy by Apollo, and having his own temple and cult. The water may be the sacred water in which he dips the laurel branch, or, by metaphor, ink. The limb and foot may refer to the hem of his robe (Latin, *limbus*), or to his arm and foot or, by metaphor, to the edges of his paper. By Le Pelletier's Branchus interpretation, it is the Greek youth actually wetting the hem of his robe and his feet.

The third line, according to Jaubert, is intended to get from the Greek to the Biblical Prophets. According to Le Pelletier, it is actually the voice of the divine mouthpiece, the heaven-sent Branchus, a crude blend of Greek and Christian lore. The last line Jaubert sees as a purely metaphorical reference to divine inspiration, while Le Pelletier sees it as a description of the actual presence of his "genius" Branchus.

Le Pelletier further ties the salient points of this quatrain with various sentences from the Epistle (paras. 14–16) and, with even greater ingenuity, shows the marked similarities between the procedure in these two quatrains and that in Jamblichus' *De mysteriis Aegyptiorum* (pp. 66, 67 and 191).

3. The litter being a symbol of the aristocracy, this verse can be applied with some justification to the "vulgar advent" referred to in paragraph 6 of the Preface. Le Pelletier sees the second line as a reference to the hypocrisies of the revolutionaries. Unfortunately, the application of reds and whites to revolutionaries and reactionaries does not seem to go back beyond the Revolution. Garencières has the less glamorous, but probably correct solution with "The French wear white scarves, and the Spaniards red ones." Thus the Spaniards are somehow to enter into this social upheaval.

4. There are two elements here, a universal ruler or emperor, generally at war and dying young, and disaster for the Papacy (the Bark of St. Peter). There is an obvious implication of the first element being the cause of the second. The forces of Charles V had sacked Rome in 1527. While Charles did spend most of his reign in warfare, he lived reasonably long (fifty-eight). (The fact that the sack preceded the Centuries does not rule out its significance here, in line with the "past-events-in-Nostradamus'-unconscious-mind" theory.) The only other close fulfillment came with Napoleon, who died somewhat younger (fifty-two) and held the Pope captive from 1809 to 1814—which not even Charles had dared do. A still better fulfillment may yet come.

5. The background for this verse probably lies in the religious wars about to break out. Up to the last line, all is general, and of it history provided no resounding confirmation. At best, when Carcassonne declared for the Catholic League, the Protestants seized part of the town. Both towns are in southwest France.

6. Ravenna having formed part of the Papal States since 1509, the current Pope would seem intended. All the other places belonged to the Duke of Savoy, but were then (1555) under French occupation. Bresse was occupied from 1535 to 1559, then recaptured in 1595 and ceded to France in 1601. Turin was occupied by the French 1506–62, 1640 and 1798–1814. Vercelli was occupied 1553–56, 1704, and 1798–1814.

7. The "sect" is always likely to refer to Calvinists. The scene would seem routine 16th-century intrigue.

8. This is in the nature of an ode to Rome, the sun being identified with Christianity and, more specifically, with the Church in the Centuries. A fate worse than the Sack of 1527 is forecast. Venice either will be responsible or will be of great aid—opposite alternatives made possible by doubt about one letter!

9. The Punic heart signifies the spirit of Carthage, come to take vengeance on Rome in the person of the Sultan. The Libyan fleet is the navy of the Algerian corsairs. The quatrain came closest to fulfillment with the siege of Malta in 1565. But Venice, though at war with the Turks 1570–73, 1645–69 and 1684–99, and though losing most of her colonies, was never directly threatened. Likewise, Rome's woes came from Christians; she was never directly attacked by the Turks. Roberts (1947) finds this verse "a re-

markably prophetic description of the role of Emperor Haile Selassie in World War II. . . ."

10. If we can accept Le Pelletier's *sarpos*, his interpretation is fairly credible. In 1610 the remains of Henry III, last Valois king, were moved to the Valois sepulchre at Saint-Denis. But Henry was not the last of Catherine's brood of seven to die or to be interred there. Margaret, first wife of Henry IV, lived until 1615. Lines 3 and 4 are supposed to refer to the emotions of the Valois ghosts upon beholding this tragic spectacle. Actually, from its use elsewhere, "serpent" is probably one of Nostradamus' nasty epithets for a Calvinist leader.

11. Naples, Leon and Sicily were all parts of the Spanish Habsburg Empire. Apparently the latter is to make an attack upon Rome, facilitated by the mistakes of a "weak brain," presumably the current Pope. In a very mild manner, under the Duke of Alba, this occurred a year after the quatrain was published. It was never fulfilled in the bloody and violent manner delineated.

12. This entire quatrain seems to be intended solely for Verona. Since Verona had belonged to Venice since 1405, a podesta, or captain, must be the subject. The podestas, theoretically, were changed every year or two, precluding any possibility of such tyranny (and after 1562 their place was taken by a council of proveditors). However, one Jacopo Sansebastiani held the post of Captain of Verona from 1539 to 1562. Perhaps he incurred Nostradamus' wrath.

13. This one is quite credibly applied by Jaubert to the Conspiracy of Amboise (1560). All the factions disgruntled by the advent to power of the Guise (notably the Bourbon and Montmorency clans) joined in a conspiracy to kill the Guise and, by seizing the person of Francis II, regain power and "save France." The advance intrigue brought a "leak" and the plot failed dismally. The wording, however, is sufficiently general that the quatrain may fit other palace plots of history as well.

14. Jaubert applies this to the Huguenots of Nostradamus' day, seeking to reform the Catholic ritual, then being punished by the government. Le Pelletier applies it to the Revolution, with the Princes and Lords on the receiving end of the captivity. Since the words "slave" and "Slav" are etymologically one and the same, there remains a third application, to the Slavic people, which would give the Russian instead of the French Revolution. Hugh Allen (1943), for reasons best known to himself, applies it to Father Divine and his "Harlem heaven."

15. A very general quatrain, containing but two clear elements. The first is seventy wars, which one could compute in any century without much trouble. The second is the oft-reiterated "woe to the clergy" theme.

16. The Roman god Saturn is depicted with a scythe, and thus provides Nostradamus with suitably obscure material. Wöllner fixes this planetary configuration on September 13, 1699. Undoubtedly somewhere in that year there was plague, famine, etc. To Roberts (1947) this tells that "In 1999 . . .

between November 23rd and December 21st, the climactic War of Wars shall be unleashed."

17. No forty-year drought and forty-year rain and flood has been recorded since 1555—if ever.

18. Jaubert connects this prophecy with events of 1555–56, close to publication day, but with enough clearance to reflect some glory on Nostradamus. To divert the Habsburgs during his invasion of Italy in 1555, Henry II called upon his Turkish ally, Suleiman the Magnificent. The Sultan obliged by sending the pirate Dragut to ravage the island of Elba and besiege Piombino, near Siena. Siena itself was a French ally (with a French garrison, which surrendered to the Florentines on April 22, 1555). At the same time, according to Jaubert, a fleet was being assembled in Marseilles to get supplies to the French troops on Corsica since 1553 (which detail may be a fiction).

If there is a catch, it is that the first line hardly suggests that the French wanted this Moslem attack. Jaubert's only explanation is that the French commander, Marshal de Brissac, had many enemies and thus did not get proper co-operation. In consequence, the French were hard-pressed in northern Italy, and the Turks were free to do far more damage than their "allies" had intended.

19. When there is doubt about the subject of a base epithet, it's usually the Huguenots, so we may take them as the serpents, pressing hard on the Catholic altar. The reference to Trojan blood, found in several places in the Centuries (and also in Nostradamus' verse for Duchess Margaret: see "Biography of Nostradamus"), is probably derived from the medieval legend of the French kings being descended from a new addition to the Trojan myth, Francus, son of Priam. Thus, when the French are internally weakened, the Spanish will press hard from their borders, which indeed happened during the Interregnum of 1589–94.

This still leaves the very specific last line up in the air. Jaubert, applying the verse to the war of 1556–59, claims that after the Battle of Saint-Quentin, Coligny, one of the French leaders, fled and hid in the marshes near the battlefield until found by the Spaniards. Not only have we found no proof of this, but Huguenot activity at this period was still insignificant.

20. All of the cities in line 1, save Reims, are on the Loire River. Most of these cities witnessed several foreign occupations: by the Russians and Prussians in 1815, by the Prussians in 1871 and 1940 and to some extent by the Americans in 1917–19 and 1944–45. But there does not seem to have been any earthquake at Rennes since 1555.

21. This rather curious verse is pure local history, though no confirmation of its occurrence has been made. It would seem to predict that in some locality there will be much ado about this mysterious natural phenomenon which will baffle the superstitious inhabitants. It is in a class with 1014 and 1041 in suggesting an event that Nostradamus actually witnessed, and became imbedded in his subconscious.

22. This verse can be taken literally or metaphorically. Garencières gives an interesting literal interpretation (about the only one he didn't steal from Jaubert). He claims that in 1613 there was removed from one Columba Chatry of Sens a petrified embryo (of which there are many instances in medical annals). The metaphorical applications are infinite. All the towns are in or near the Duchy of Burgundy. The second Sens is probably the small town near Louhans. To Roberts (1947) all this is a "forecast of the use of supersonic weapons."

23. This prophecy could be applied to any epic battle taking place in March, in which four elements, designated as Sun, Boar, Leopard and Eagle, take part. It is perhaps pertinent that the Sun Rising, with the motto *Non dum in auge*, was the first device taken by Charles V. If one of the factors, the Sun stands for the Church (papal forces). The Eagle stands for the Empire. The other two are uncertain. (The British leopards are not too likely here.)

24. The number of European towns whose name means "new city" is great. The most notable is Naples (Nea-polis). The bird of prey is probably a synonym for the Imperial eagle. Mantua remained an independent state until 1708, when the Austrians seized it and held it till 1859. Cremona belonged to the Habsburgs 1525–1859. To Roberts (1947) this plainly forecasts "the War Criminal trials at NU-Rem-Burg *[sic! sic! sic!]*."

25. This rather interesting verse probably predicts the discovery of the tomb of one of the Church Fathers, perhaps of St. Peter. But after one month interest will be transferred elsewhere. Roberts (1947) finds this to foreshadow the "worship of Louis Pasteur."

26. A rather lucid and far-ranging series of specific predictions. The distribution of conflict and plague between France, England and Italy remains uncertain.

27. Guienne is an ancient province of southwestern France. Many interpretations can be made as to the identity of the treasure. (A similar reference is found in 97.) Treating it as Nostradamus' tomb (a ridiculous proposition, since the latter is very definitely in Salon-de-Provence), Carey Wilson used this quatrain as the basis for a scene in one of his movie shorts on Nostradamus. The result caught the imagination of many movie-goers.

28. Here we have the first instance of the provocative Hesperia. It would clearly be the Spaniards, were it not for 450, which predicts the "monarchy of heaven and earth" for the Hesperians. At a time when Spanish power was supreme everywhere, this is hardly a prediction. Hesperia, the Land of the West, was used by the Greeks for Italy and by the Romans for Spain. One cannot but reflect that it would have been an ideal name for the New World. Thus, though probably the Spanish are intended, there is some slight justification for reading "American" in (if Nostradamus be granted prophetic powers). Bouc is a port near Marseilles.

Although in modern geopolitics Britain has been the Balance *par excellence*, the sign was unfortunately associated not with her but with Austria. Turkey was amongst the areas Taurus was supposed to influence, so that we have here but a reference to the Habsburg–Ottoman struggle, with a period in which the Moslems are no longer French allies.

29. A very general prediction that the washing-ashore of some odd amphibian creature will serve as an omen of impending invasion from the sea. The quatrain has also been taken as forecasting various craft of amphibious warfare. Roberts (1947) finds it "a clear account of the D-Day Invasion of the Normandy beaches."

30. Another general one, which may well enough have been fulfilled.

31. *Castulo* appears several times in different forms. The simple meaning, as the ancient Iberian city (near present Linares), hardly seems to fit, except as synecdoche for Spain. On the other hand, Le Pelletier's fanciful derivation from *castula*, the name of the undergarment worn by Roman women (hence the Goddess of Liberty and the French Revolution), is a bit too much to swallow. Yet if the Spanish are indeed designated, the prophecy would mean that Spanish forces will still be fighting in France after their King (Charles I, or Emperor Charles V) is dead. The division of the metaphors amongst the three great ones must needs be arbitrary.

Le Pelletier sees it as concerning the struggle between three dynasties (1804–71). The Bonapartist is the Imperial Eagle, the Orleanist the Cock and the Moon (symbols, respectively, of the Revolution and infidelity) and the Bourbon the monarchical Lion and most Christian Sun. All very ingenious. (His version for the last line thus runs "Eagle, Cock-Moon, Lion-Sun as marks.")

32. This lucid little prophecy has been applied to both Charles V and Napoleon I. Charles V had already started his piecemeal abdication in 1554 (see "Historical Background"). But neither the monastery of Yuste, to which Charles retired in 1555 (shortly after the verse was published) nor Elba experienced any great growth. Of course, Nostradamus may have foreseen a more spectacular retirement. To Roberts (1947) it predicts quite clearly that "Great Japan will degenerate into a minor power, with the Emperor abdicating the throne."

33. The spacious plain is most likely Lombardy, and the Lion the commander of the Imperial forces. The most austere city of the day was Calvin's Geneva (1541–64). The bridge is probably a pass to the north. Putting all these elements together, Nostradamus' hatred of Calvinism seems to have induced this hopeful prophecy of the fall of Geneva. The attack is to come from the south, possibly the Great St. Bernard Pass.

34. Bird of prey is probably synonymous with eagle. The left having no political or social significance in the 16th century, it probably refers to France's geographical left which, facing the traditional enemy, is the Low Countries. The verse thus touches on the background of another Franco-Imperial war, in which the Emperor will send troops into the Low Countries while the French are torn by disagreement.

35. Few commentators have dared to question the application of this quatrain to the tragic and dramatic death of Nostradamus' sovereign in a

joust with the Count of Montgomery, Captain of the Scottish Guard, on July 10, 1559. The standard interpretation has Montgomery as the young lion and Henry II as the old lion, because both used lions as their emblems. But Buget (1863) points out that Henry II (age forty) was probably only six years older than his adversary (whose exact age is uncertain), that neither one actually used a lion as an emblem, and that the helmet of the King was neither of gold nor gilded. One might further add that with *classe* meaning "fleet" everywhere else in its many occurrences in the Centuries, it is rather suspicious to use a Greek derivation here. And certainly there was no union of fleets in 1559. And, in fact, a tournament is not "the field of battle."

Buget's concluding comment (1863, p. 455) on this quatrain, which may be said to have made Nostradamus famous, is "There is not, then, as far as I can see, a single word in this quatrain which is applicable to the unhappy end of this prince."

The final judgment must lie somewhere between these two extremes. Indeed, poetic license would make only lines 1 and 2 substantially acceptable. Line 3 is more dubious. The wound not only did not put out the royal eye, but hardly touched the eye itself. A splinter lodged above his right eye and broke the veins of the pia mater. Line 4 is a complete failure. There was only one wound (unless an abscess be counted) even for the fancy Greek derivation, and certainly no union of fleets. The most important of all reasons for rejecting this interpretation is, as we shall see, that Nostradamus had big things in store for Henry II as the new Charlemagne.

36. Clear enough. The nearest fulfillment seems to have been when Henry III had his adversary, the Duke of Guise, murdered, as well as his brother, at Blois (December 23, 1588). But this was far from exterminating the House of Guise. According to Guynaud (1693), Henry missed the opportunity of putting to death Mayenne, the real troublemaker, so that he was obliged to aim later at the extermination of the whole House of Guise. Bouys (1806, p. 56) applies it to Louis XVI and the Duke of Orléans. To Roberts (1947) it refers to Napoleon and Toussaint L'Ouverture, the Negro warlord of Haiti, of all things.

37. The scene here is limited only in that it must be on the sea. The last line is a bit too obscure for all but the most arbitrary of suggestions.

38. The Sun is likely to be the Papacy and the Eagle the Empire, but the text leaves uncertain whether the struggle is between the two, or between them and a third power.

39. This quatrain has been applied to the suspicious deaths of two princes, Don Carlos of Spain (1568) and Louis of Bourbon-Condé (1830). Each interpretation is full of loopholes. In the case of the first, the blond elect was Carlos' stepmother, of whose relations with her stepson Philip II was very suspicious. But it has never been proven that Carlos died an unnatural death. Furthermore, the blond elect is not female, and the rest fits poorly.

Le Pelletier's application to the last of the Condé is somewhat better.

The Prince was found hanged (though hardly in bed). According to Le Pelletier (who is far from unprejudiced) he was "done in" because he favored the hero of the 19th-century Nostradamians, the Duke of Bordeaux (alias the Count of Chambord). Le Pelletier further insists that Condé was blond, and that he had written a will in favor of Bordeaux, which was hidden and replaced by an earlier one in favor of Louis-Philippe's son, the Duke of Aumale. The slavery of line 3 he sees as referring to the regimes of the Orléanists, the Republicans and the Bonapartists after Condé's death.

40. In this verse we are in big-time geopolitics, involving the Ottoman Empire and Egypt. But what is the false trumpet concealing madness? The debasing of coins by edict was an old trick of Christian sovereigns which may well enough have been imitated by the Sublime Porte. But it was not until the 19th century that the Egyptians rebelled, and then it was not over the coinage.

41. Jaubert applies this to events during the French invasion of Italy in 1556–57, with rather dubious authenticity. Line 2 is rather general while lines 3 and 4 (for which Jaubert has intricate explanations) defy historical records. Boswell (1941, p. 208) applies it to events in 1940: Dunkirk and the Fall of France, the whore being the Third Republic and the poison and letters Nazi indoctrination of prisoners.

42. Le Pelletier ties this one up with 11 and 12 as part of the autobiographical material. He claims that inasmuch as Good Friday was the best occasion for magical evocations, this verse tells on exactly which night Nostradamus evoked his "demon" in accordance with the rites prescribed by Psellus in *De Daemonibus*. But what with the change of calendar and the mysterious "Gothic count" (which some commentators insist means that Nostradamus foresaw the calendar change and is thus designating the Old Style), it is difficult to tell the date intended. In the years immediately preceding 1555, Good Friday came on April 15 in 1552, on March 31 in 1553 and on March 23 in 1554. Since the calends was the first day of the Roman month, the tenth would presumably be April 10. If, however, as some commentators would have it, the date designates ten days *before* the calends, March 23, 1554, works out very nicely. This would then be the date on which Nostradamus wrote his first quatrain.

43. The change of Empire probably refers to nothing more than a new Emperor, the death of his predecessor having been foreshadowed by the mysterious movements of a pillar of porphyry.

44. Le Pelletier applies this one to the abolition of the worship of God and the establishment of the Cult of Reason on November 10, 1793, followed by the Festival of the Supreme Being on June 8, 1794. The Constitution accepted by the King on July 14, 1790, had provided for the dissolution of all ecclasiastical orders and a civil constitution for the clergy. Refractory priests can certainly be said to have been persecuted. There being so little demand for church candles, the price may well have dropped greatly. On the whole, this prophecy was fairly well fulfilled.

45. This verse is less a prophecy than a tirade against schismatics and heretics who have broken the unity of the Church. Whatever lines 2 and 3 mean, they probably refer to Calvin (rather than Luther).

46. All three towns are in proximity to one another in the Department of Gers in southwest France. Perhaps meteorites are intended.

47. This quatrain provides proof that even a fairly specific prediction can be applied more than once. There is little reason to doubt that Nostradamus intended it as a tirade and wishful-thinking prophecy against Calvin's theocracy at Geneva. However, it has been applied with far more success to the debacle of the League of Nations between 1931 and 1939.

48. This rather incomprehensible bit of cosmology may provide some people with information about the end of the world, but we are not amongst them. Wöllner calculated that Nostradamus used 4184 B.C. as Creation Year, which would appear to place this verse at A.D. 2816. Roberts (1947) has it much simpler: in the year 7000 the Sun will destroy the Earth.

49. Just what state Nostradamus had in mind for Aquilon, the North Wind, is another mystery. Chavigny, supposedly his disciple, is no help in writing that Aquilon "has a very long and large extent, such that it could be called another world, if we include all Germany, Poland, Lithuania, Livonia, Gothia, Sweden, Norway, Scandia, the isles of the Ocean and come to Muscovy, the two Sarmatias, up to the columns of Alexander and even the Caspian Sea, and take Scythia on this side of Mount Imaus, otherwise called Great Tartary; all this is part of Aquilon as well as other provinces that I do not mention." In current geography, Scandinavia, Germany, Poland and Russia.

Indeed, in the war with Austria of 1682–99, the Turks made great advances, carrying them to the gates of Vienna in 1683. But then followed their long retreat from Europe. Almost by way of a direct slap in the face for our prophet, it was in 1699 that the Treaty of Karlowitz obliged Turkey to give up most of her territory north of the Balkans. Furthermore, in the very year 1700 the Turks lost Azov to the Russians (though later winning it back to hold again, 1710–39). The prophecy is thus quite clear, and quite a clear failure.

Roberts (1947) as usual gets a remarkable message out of it. "In the year 2025, by ritual, China, having completed her industrial and economic expansion, will absorb almost the whole of western Russia and Scandinavia."

50. Whether or not such was Nostradamus' intention, this prophecy fits the United States quite nicely, certainly better than any other national candidate. The United States is surrounded by three seas, has a unique Thursday feast in Thanksgiving and has of late, at least in the 1940's, fulfilled lines 3 and 4. Which, while most interesting, does not preclude the probability that the verse was intended for an individual, in which case the aquatic triplicity would concern the astrological configurations at the time of his birth. The Thursday motif is found also in 1071.

51. The actual prophecy involved is completely general, and limited only

by the occasions on which the configuration of line 1 occurs. According to Wöllner, the configuration occurred twice, on October 19, 1583, and December 13, 1702, and will again on September 2, 1995. The 1702 date found Italy and France involved in the War of the Spanish Succession and thus would fulfill the prophecy quite well. The Nazi Norab (1941) finds that it will occur again on September 12, 1994. Perhaps he and Wöllner could compromise on February 25, 1995.

52. The two wicked ones are Mars and Saturn, both malign in astrological usage. According to Wöllner, the configuration has occurred (from 1555 to the fall of the Ottoman Empire) in the following years: 1572, 1602, 1660, 1662, 1690, 1720, 1748, 1777, 1779, 1807, 1809, 1837, 1867 and 1895. The only sultan to be removed upon one of these dates was Selim III in 1807. But although deposed in 1807, he was strangled only in 1808. This is close, and furthermore, the other lines were fulfilled nicely at this time. Napoleon, who had brought the Church back to power in France, at the same time kept Pius VII a prisoner and otherwise asserted his authority violently. In 1807 he was at the height of his power, Austria, Prussia and Russia having been defeated in turn. Only the Russians managed to maintain any semblance of an independent policy.

53. Le Pelletier applies this one to the Creation of Assignats on December 19, 1789. The confiscated property of the Church became security for the government notes. Inflation and economic chaos followed "overproduction" of the notes. The other lines go well enough with the period, and the interpretation is quite credible.

54. If we add fifty-nine years (two revolutions of Saturn) to 1555, we find this prophecy covering the period 1555–1614. This period certainly saw great changes, including that of a dynasty (or at least of branches thereof). The mobile sign is Libra the Balance, which influenced Austria in geopolitical astrology. More Habsburg skullduggery is thus suggested, at the expense of the enigmas of line 4.

55. The climate here is probably astrological rather than meteorological, but either way it remains a mystery. The airborne reference in line 3 is noteworthy. According to Hugh Allen (1943, p. 101), "Here again, we find the use of Babylon as a metaphor for Paris. As France is the most Occidental country of continental Europe, so Russia is the most Oriental." Clear?

56. The cosmology here is somewhat similar to that of 148.

57. Le Pelletier applies this well enough to the French Revolution and the execution of Louis XVI. To Roberts (1947) it represents a "clear and forthright prediction" of the Japanese attack on Pearl Harbor and the Japanese Co-prosperity Sphere.

58. The first two lines may be interpreted as the Caesarean removal of a human monster, or as an allegory. Jaubert sees it as the former, referring to the birth of a two-headed child recorded by César Nostradamus, and trusting that it had four arms also. The last two lines he applies rather unconvincingly to the wars of 1555–57.

Le Pelletier makes the allegorical interpretation. The belly cut is the House of Bourbon, whose head was removed in 1793. The two heads are the royal members after 1815, i.e., Louis XVIII and Charles X. The four arms are the uncrowned Dukes of Normandy, Berry, Angoulême and Bordeaux, following the Imperial Law of Napoleon, extending to Piedmont and the Papal States. The interpretation breaks down on the inadequate explanation of the last two lines. The reading of Piedmont for Fossano is reasonable, but Ferrara was not annexed by the Papacy until 1598. Since 1208 it had been a duchy under the Este dynasty.

There are a few other possible leads to what Le Pelletier makes the Eagle's law. Aquila, one of St. Paul's most faithful converts, is commemorated in the Roman martyrology on *July* 8. On July 13, 1031, the Patriarch of Aquileia consecrated its cathedral. The city then was a smaller reproduction of the ancient metropolis, destroyed by Attila in 452 and the Lombards in 590. Venice, founded by its refugees in 452, took over its power, and in 1451 its patriarchate.

59. Little can be said of this clear but insignificant prophecy. Le Pelletier applies it to the Second Republic, when Lamartine gave way to the dictatorship of General Cavaignac (1848) and some radicals were sent to the Marquesas Islands in the Pacific. Roberts (1947) finds that it refers to Hitler's cremation of Jews.

60. Hailed as a magnificent prediction of the birth of Napoleon, it can be applied equally well to a Holy Roman Emperor (which Nostradamus probably meant) Ferdinand II (1619–37), born at Graz, about ninety miles from Italy, and surrounding himself with a person like Wallenstein in the Thirty Years' War, which certainly cost the Empire dearly.

61. This is another prophecy of doom for Calvin's republic at Geneva, with the Swiss of Geneva revoking their previous invitation to Calvin to impose on them his theocratic absolutism. They had indeed banished him in 1538, but after his recall in 1541, he retained absolute power until his death in 1564.

62. Latona in classical mythology was the mother of Apollo and Diana, respectively identified with the sun and the moon. In poetry the lady is occasionally used in place of her daughter. Wöllner's charts show one "great cycle" of the moon between 1288 and 1648, with the next one coming only after 3797 (in 3808) and several lesser cycles of 252 years, ending in 1576, 1828, 2080, etc.

63. Since this prophecy includes travel by air amongst the blessings of postwar peace, its application would seem limited to the 20th century, and after, and as such is rather interesting.

64. No commentator has gotten any really bright idea as to the identity of the pig-half-man, who appears in 369 (as the half-pig) and perhaps also in 844 (as the half-man). Le Pelletier rather capriciously applies it to one of his pet villains, Signor Garibaldi. Fighting in the sky sounds very modern; perhaps Nostradamus had "signs in the heavens" in mind. Or perhaps scien-

tific developments of 1960 offer a solution: a Soviet illuminated, giant, propaganda-transmitting satellite balloon constructed in the image of the porcine Big Brother of the Soviet Animal Farm, Nikita Khrushchev.

65. This one is certainly thoroughly specific and detailed, but no attempt at confirmation of it has ever been made, i.e., the hands of a prince on a tennis court burned off by a lightning bolt.

66. Viviers and Tournon are in Ardèche, Pradelles just over the border in Haute-Loire, in east-central France. Montferrand, in the Puy-de-Dome, did not join with Clermont (to become Clermont-Ferrand) until 1731. A rather pointless quatrain.

67. A rather typical specimen of Nostradamian terror, similar to much in the Preface and Epistle.

68. Many interpretations are in order for this rather general one, including perhaps the July 16, 1918, murder of whichever three members of the Romanov family are considered innocent.

69. This quatrain' probably predicts, like 1049, another terrible eruption of Mount Vesuvius, a round mountain about 4,000 feet in height. There have been about eighteen eruptions since the prophecy was written, but none as terrible as implied here, or as the one in A.D. 79, which buried Pompeii and Herculaneum.

70. This quatrain is fairly specific. There have been several occasions on which France and Persia were at war at the same time, but as France was usually allied with the Turks, and Persia an enemy of the Turks, they were on different sides. There does not seem to have been any fulfillment of it, at least not yet.

71. The marine tower may be the tower of Bouc referred to in 128. We know of no time at which the Spaniards, Algerians (the Barbarian corsairs) and Genoese all made attacks in that area since 1555. "Those of Pisa" probably designates the Tuscans, Pisa having been sold to Florence in 1405. Turin was the capital of the Duchy of Savoy. With at least thirteen variable factors, this prophecy is extremely specific and would have reflected great glory on Nostradamus, had it ever been fulfilled. It never was.

72. Very lucid and quite specific, but with no conceivable historical verification. The setting is southern France. The casualty figures could be correct only in modern times.

73. A rather far-ranging quatrain, including French, Spaniards, Venetians, Algerians and Persians. How Nostradamus fitted in what is apparently a Persian *drang nach West* with his Neo-Arab Empire can only be guessed at. The only time since 1555 that France was assailed on five sides was 1813–14, and then only by Europeans.

74. And yet another colorful and action-packed prophecy (however inscrutable). The stage extends from northwest Greece to Syria (all part of Turkey till the 19th century). Two enigmatic characters mentioned again elsewhere (see Index) are found here. The subject is quite possibly a new Crusade, a theme found in many quatrains. However, line 3 may indicate a

new Turkish onslaught on the Empire, which did occur in 1683. Barbarossa (Redbeard) was the nickname of the 12th-century Emperor, Frederick I, and of a Turkish family which took over leadership of the Algerian corsairs (most active *before* Nostradamus wrote). There is also some indication Nostradamus applied this name to young Philip of Spain, with a reddish-blond beard.

75. Savona was a sort of autonomous protectorate of the Genoese Republic. Siena was a free city that had long resisted the Florentine yoke and allied itself with France, which sent a garrison. On April 22, 1555 (probably after the quatrain was written) the French garrison surrendered to the Florentines. Ancona had belonged to the Papal States since 1532.

76. Le Pelletier is at his most ingenious in applying this verse to Napoleon. In his very name he sees his destiny, derived from the Greek, *neapolluon*, "certain destroyer." To prove that his insertion of the extra *e* is not arbitrary, he cites the inscription on the Vendôme Column:

NEAPOLIO. IMP. AUG.
MONUMENTUM, BELLI, GERMANICI
ANNO MDCCCV.

Certainly the prophecy fits Napoleon well enough. Hugh Allen (1943, p. 601) sees it for our own Henry Wallace!

77. The outstanding promontory between two seas is Gibraltar. The fortifications were first constructed in the 15th century by Juan Bautista Calvi and El Fratiano, and improved in the 16th century by Daniel Speckle, but none of these is known to have died of the bite of a horse (but may have). Line 3 is based on the myth of Theseus. The black sail was the customary insignia of the ship carrying the human sacrifice for the Cretan Minotaur. Theseus promised his father to replace it with a white one if he returned successful. In the rejoicing, he forgot his promise. When the old man saw the black sail from the Acropolis, he flung himself into the sea. In 259 and in the Presages, Neptune appears to be the Moslem navy, so that the quatrain in effect predicts a Moslem victory, i.e., putting away the black sail of bad fortune, in the vicinity of Gibraltar. Actually, they did poorly at sea after this time (1555). See also 31.

78. Marshal Pétain has of late been a candidate for this quatrain, but the case is none too good. It is too general to be of much note.

79. A rather typical Nostradamian quatrain, involving a number of French towns and at least one barbarism. All the towns are in the Southwest, and all except Bayonne on or near the Garonne. According to one theory, widely disputed, Condom gave its name to a famous rubber article. The connection of the bull-sacrifice (bullfight?) is not clear.

80. Line 1 apparently indicates some cosmo-astrological subdivision of the heavens, from which a hail of meteorites will fall.

81. This is one of those very unusual type of quatrains, with no con-

ceivable application in the intervening centuries since it was written, but with at least a potential application now on the horizon. It ties in with 65 in suggesting pioneer astronauts of one sort or another. By this interpretation, the voyage would be rather unsuccessful, and especially fatal to three whose names begin, respectively, with K, L and Th.

82. This one is highly obscure, notwithstanding the last line.

83. Greek victories over Italians seem to be suggested by lines 3 and 4. The first time this occurred since the 6th century was in 1940. The German machinations take care of line 1 well enough, but it is doubtful if the conjunction (if such it is) occurred that year.

84. The Moon undergoes an eclipse, the Sun looks reddish. The rest is incomprehensible, apparently allegorical or metaphysical.

85. Le Pelletier (from Guynaud, and he from Chavigny) applies this one to the closing Valois days. Catherine will not approve of Henry III having the Guises murdered (December 23, 1588). The envoys from Paris and the deputies to the Estates-General at Blois will remonstrate with the King against the deed. The Duke of Mayenne assumes the leadership previously exercised by his two brothers, taking the title of Lieutenant-General of the Realm, and acting as chief of the League (1589–94). The last line is applied to the murder itself, the anger, hatred and envy being that of Henry III.

86. One of the most colorful of the quatrains, even if never fulfilled. Probably Mary Stuart came closest to fulfilling it (to date). In May, 1568, she escaped from captivity, and, after being defeated a second time by her half-brother Murray, fled to England. However, she seems to have been quite fully clothed during her flight, and did not pass the border river on horseback (but by ferry).

87. It is fairly certain that Nostradamus is here predicting an eruption of Vesuvius, and earthquake around Naples. Vesuvius is twelve miles from Naples. The third line can mean practically anything. Arethusa was a nymph who was chased by Alpheus from Greece to the island of Ortygia off Syracuse in Italy. When she called on Diana to save her from the fate worse than death, Diana obliged by transforming her into a fountain. Another version has her changed in Greece into a stream which passed under the sea and came out a fountain in Sicily. As there is nothing of blood in the legend, Nostradamus' inference is difficult to see. Boswell (1941, p. 349) finds that it is New York that will be destroyed by this earthquake.

88. The divine sickness may be epilepsy, or, as Le Pelletier would have it, the disease based on "whom the gods would destroy they first make mad." He applies it to Napoleon, translating it as divine anger. In 1808 Napoleon was at his peak. Then followed the Spanish revolt, his divorce and remarriage to Marie-Louise of Austria and the Russian fiasco. Even before the last event, such shrewd characters as Talleyrand were withdrawing support. The shaven head is justified by his short hair in contrast to the long hair and wigs of the rulers of the *ancien régime*.

89. This simply predicts that the Spanish will overrun France. But neither in 1557 nor in 1589-93 did they come very far beyond the borders.

90. Langon is thirty miles southeast of Bordeaux, on the Garonne. Orgon is about thirteen miles north of Nostradamus' Salon. The tocsin was an alarm bell, a signal of danger. The prophecy is thus quite clear and specific, involving an invasion, a French defeat and the birth of a monster at the same time. There are two scenes, the Southwest and Provence. The monster is probably another two-headed baby or such.

91. This is so vague and general as to be worthless.

92. Jaubert applies this one to the late Valois period, starting with the peace of 1559. Pillage and rebellion did indeed follow in the Civil Wars of 1562-94. The refusing town is La Rochelle, which put up a stout defense against the crown in 1572-73. The figure in line 4 Jaubert considers about correct for the casualty rate in the wars, which is highly dubious.

There was a limit to what Le Pelletier, writing under the Second Empire, could say; otherwise he might have anticipated another interesting interpretation, referred to by Boswell (1941). Line 1 he applies to Napoleon's slogan, *L'empire, c'est la paix*. Lines 2-4 are applied to the Franco-Prussian War, nominally begun over the refusal of the King of Prussia to agree to the humiliating demands presented by the French. On line 4 Boswell really goes to work. Juggling casualty figures from several publications, he comes out with the exact total of 333,333. The *Encyclopaedia Britannica* gives French casualties as 156,000 dead, 143,000 wounded and disabled and 720,000 surrendered. (Boswell chooses only certain key battles.)

To Roberts (1947) it shows that "The sneak attack on Pearl Harbor, by the Japanese, ushered the U.S. into World War II, resulting in 350,000 American casualties."

93. The mountains are certainly the Alps. The Cock was the symbol of the ancient Gauls. (Nostradamus used it for obscurity; the French Revolutionists adopted it.) The Lion may refer to Venice, with her Lion of St. Mark, or to other powers. "Celts" is probably used synonymously with French and Gauls. *Castulo* still remains an enigma (see 131).

94. This quatrain probably predicts the murder of Andrea Doria (1468-1560), tyrant of Genoa and Admiral of the Imperial Fleet. It never occurred (though his nephew Gianettino had been the victim of such a murder in 1547 in the course of an attempted pro-French coup). The identity of "the new Mars" of line 3 and the lady of line 4 is less readily apparent.

95. A perfectly clear and comprehensible prophecy. An illustrious leader who is one of twins sired by a monk is by no means a generality bound to occur sooner or later. Had it occurred, it would have reflected great credit on Nostradamus. Making use of Dumas' version of *The Man in the Iron Mask*, Larmor (1925, p. 160) applies this one to Louis XIV, born at Saint-Germain opposite the monastery of Loges. But he denies that the twin became the Man in the Iron Mask. Rather, the latter was the son of Dowager Queen Anne and Cardinal Mazarin.

96. Here we have a persecutor whose heart is softened by the blandishments of some wily character. Rather general.

97. This quatrain has been applied to the revocation of the Edict of Nantes by Louis XIV in 1685, whereby most Protestants were driven out of France. Line 1 would refer to the unsuccessful attempts at extermination in the 16th century. Louis' morganatic wife, the hyper-pious Madame de Maintenon, is known to have added her tongue to the voices advising Louis to take this fatal step.

98. Another very lucid prophecy that does not seem to have been fulfilled. The only time since 1555 that any distant nation had an expeditionary force fighting in both Thessaly and Crete was in 1940. But the British casualties were a good deal larger than 5,000 and nothing is known to have occurred to justify the last line (though the meaning of "marine barn" is rather obscure). To Roberts (1947) this tells of the escape of Adolf Hitler in a submarine. Crete was Venetian till the Turkish conquest of 1645–69. Thessaly had been held by the Turks since 1393. In 1821 the Egyptians were in Crete but not in Thessaly.

99. Much too general for any interpretation. Narbonne is in southwest France.

100. The great bird is assumed to be the dove of peace. The verse would thus seem to fit any peace ending a Franco-Italian war shortly after the death of a leader. Dôle is in Burgundy; Mirandola, if this be intended by apheresis, is about thirty miles north of Tuscany.

## Century II

1. This quatrain predicts two very specific events. The first is a new English overrunning of France (like that of the 14th century). The second is a series of conquests by Genoa. But Genoa never reversed the decline it had already fallen into in Nostradamus' day, although it was able to get back Corsica in 1559, when its tyrant, Doria, switched back to the French side.

2. The meaning of blue and white heads is completely obscure. Perhaps it refers to a plume or ornament worn on the helmet of warriors, or to the livery of the great houses. The white would then be identified with France.

3. A sea made so hot that the fish within it are almost cooked is a rather quaint idea. It occurs again in 598. Euboea is an island northeast of Athens. The biscuit probably refers to sea biscuit or hardtack. The relationship between the three places is difficult to see. Rhodes belonged to the Turks from 1522 to 1912, Euboea from 1470 to 1831.

4. A very simple prediction that the Barbary corsairs would become worse than ever. Perhaps Garencières, confused about his dates, lets the cat out of the bag. "This prophecy," writes he, "hath been once already fulfilled, when the famous Pyrate Barbarossa, being sent by the grand Seignor, to help the French king against the Emperour Charles the V, in his return

home, plundered all that Coast, and carried away an innumerable multitude of people into slavery." All of which happened ten years before the quatrain was written.

5. Seeing a possible configuration in line 1, the pro-Nazi Norab (1941) finds that it will next occur on March 23, 1996. "Latin land" would properly be the land of Latium, extending from just north of Rome to north of Capua, along Italy's west coast. But the term may be used loosely. If it has not yet been fulfilled, it is hardly likely that any ships of 1996 will be using oars. Roberts (1947) finds that it applies to General Mark Clark's secret mission to North Africa (*sic!*) in 1942. There have been other recent interpretations with "iron fish" representing a submarine.

6. This one is too general to be of any note.

7. "The isles" here probably refers to some of those along the southern coast of France, long used for dangerous prisoners, political or otherwise. To Roberts (1947) it foretells the rise of a great Australian leader. There are records in medical annals of babies born with two teeth, including, allegedly, Louis XIV (see Gould and Pyle, pp. 242–43).

8. Le Pelletier, apparently inventing a meaning of *goffe*, applies this one, like 144, to the Feast of the Supreme Being on June 8, 1794, which Robespierre considered more workable than the Goddess of Reason of the extremists. As a matter of fact, even with the proper meaning of *goffe* established, Le Pelletier's version holds fairly well. Nostradamus seems to be predicting another of the long succession of "back to the simple way of the Apostles" reform movements, using classical-style churches, rejecting all the fancy rites of the Catholic Church and returning to the simplest precepts of Christ, the Apostles, and others. Such was undoubtedly the justification given by Robespierre's clerical henchmen. However, the verse was in all likelihood intended for Protestants.

9. This prophecy appears general, but it actually requires for fulfillment the concurrence of at least three specific factors. First, there must be a ruler noted for his thinness, or for being a vegetarian. Second, he must plunge his country into a war disastrous for either his own country or the country attacked (the old ambiguous Delphic trick). Third, his chief opponent must be noted for his easygoing nature. Hitler and Roosevelt make one of the best possible combinations, but it breaks down on the time element. The best effort has been to claim that Hitler really came into power when the elections of 1930 made the Nazis the second-largest party, but this is a good bit to swallow. To Hugh Allen (1943) the subject is the "war-monger," Franklin D. Roosevelt himself, with the handy dates November, 1932–November, 1941. Republican readers, take note.

10. This quatrain is fairly general, but line 3 has the "woe to the clergy" theme again, which was not however fulfilled at the turn of the century (1600). The last line is likely to be fulfilled in any period, most of all in the 20th century.

11. Garencières gives an interesting but rather dubious interpretation

which, as usual, he stole from Jaubert (p. 428). "This is an Horoscope, for the interpretation of which we are beholding to Mr. Mannessier of Amiens, who saith that the Father of the Lords l'Aisniers went to Nostradamus his friend, to know his childrens fortune, who sent him these four lines for an answer." He then gives very unconvincing details.

However, it is possible that "the realm of the privileged" refers to Poland, notorious for the already-archaic privileges of its turbulent nobility. When Nostradamus wrote, the last King of the Jagellon dynasty, Sigismund II, was without heir. Nostradamus may well have meant to predict that a French prince would eventually be chosen King—which is exactly what did happen (1573). However, it is difficult to apply the third line to Edward of Anjou (Henry III). He was the third son of a second son. If Nostradamus' meaning was such, it was further nullified by the fact that the French prince in question never had any children, and slipped away in 1574 to become King of France. Guynaud (1693) saw it in this sense, after making a few "corrections." *Fors* becomes *forts* (strong) and *l'aisnier L'anric* (for Henry). Line 4 he takes to simply mean that the dynasty will die out.

12. Other than that this prophecy is of the religious sphere, little can be said of it.

13. Le Pelletier concludes his future-interpreting verses by applying this one to Judgment Day. Line 1 he applies to the sacraments, the rest to eternal life in the Kingdom of Heaven, all of which may quite well have been what Nostradamus had in mind.

14. Like Tours, Gien is on the Loire, but it is more than one hundred miles further up the river. The verse would seem to concern rebellion against the authority of a French queen who is regent. If it be granted that Nostradamus did indeed foresee the imminent death of Henry II, the verse may have been intended for Catherine de' Medici.

15. One of the more specific verses, involving several variable elements. In line 1 we have a monarch assassinated. Line 2 probably indicates a configuration prevailing at the time, though it may have a more complex meaning. In line 3 we have a mighty war effort. The last line tells of three separate states being placed under interdict: Florence or Tuscany (Pisa), Savoy (Turin and Asti) and Ferrara. It is of course possible that just the cities are under interdict, with no synecdoche involved, but this would be unusual. There is some further doubt about the subject in that while Asti had nominally belonged to Savoy since 1538, it was not until 1575 that the Duke really established his authority there. And in the case of Pisa, Nostradamus may have foreseen that the French would free it of the Florentine yolk. In any case, the prophecy was never fulfilled. None of the cities or states has been under interdict since. The nearest thing to fulfillment (retroactively) had come under Pope Julius II: From August 9, 1510, to July 4, 1512, Alfonso, Duke of Ferrara, was *threatened with* an interdict. And on July 18, 1512, an interdict was laid on all cities adhering to the *Council of Pisa*. Perhaps these facts were in Nostradamus' subconscious. Once again, a very un-

fortunate failure of a highly specific quatrain the fulfillment of which would have brought the prophet great glory.

16. Le Pelletier applies this one to his own day. Line 1 signifies the Kingdom of the Two Sicilies, all the places named being the chief cities of that kingdom. Line 2 refers to the revolutionists of 1859, drawing upon themselves the ire of heaven for their anti-Bourbon activities. In line 3 they are given moral support by England (London) and Belgium (Ghent and Brussels) and physical support by Garibaldi's troops from Piedmont (Susa). This application is probably as close as the quatrain can be brought to fulfillment, for the simultaneous interplay of forces from Savoy, England and the Low Countries in the Two Sicilies is hardly frequent (and never really happened). What Nostradamus apparently had in mind was trouble for Philip of Spain. In 1554 Charles V gave him Milan, and later Naples (but not until 1556 Sicily) and married him to Queen Mary of England. At just about the time Nostradamus wrote, Philip received the Netherlands. According to this quatrain, it would seem that Charles V's Viceroy of Sicily is to try to take Naples away from Philip in the chaos following Charles V's departure from the scene, with Philip trying to hold his own with forces from his various dominions: England (London), the Netherlands (Ghent and Brussels) and the satellite Savoy (Susa). Such an attempt to deprive Philip of Naples did actually occur in 1556, but it originated with the Pope, who invited the French to drive out the Spanish and set up a French prince as King (see "Historical Background").

17. Another one of those odd, strictly local quatrains, suggesting an event that Nostradamus once witnessed. The problem is to discover what field (near Elne?) had in classical times a temple of Vesta or Diana (equally acceptable as the chaste goddess). *Elne* is an anagram for *Ethne* only by using the Greek alphabet, wherein *th* is one letter. Elne is, however, in the shadow of the Pyrenees. It is rather useless to try to interpret line 3. As for line 4, Elne lies between the Réart and the Tech, each of which flows east into the Mediterranean.

18. This one is perfectly clear and, by virtue of the last line, very specific. It requires the concurrence of three highly unusual events: (1) a fierce rainstorm impeding a battle; (2) prodigious droppings from the sky; (3) the sudden and approximately simultaneous death of seven important figures "by land and sea." Although the odds against the concurrence of these factors are great, it could just as well take place in a thousand years as in past years.

19. Far too general to be of any worth, and resembling the Presages.

20. This verse has been applied quite reasonably by Jaubert (1656) to the capture of Huguenots of varying social degree in a raid in the rue Saint-Jacques in Paris in September, 1557. Henry II then went to look at them, accompanied by his children, and was annoyed to see that they had not been taken without wounds having been inflicted. However, the quatrain is probably sufficiently general to bear other applications.

21. Biremes are vessels with two banks of oars, triremes with three banks.

Though sailing ships came into ever greater use in the great oceans, galleys continued to be used in the Mediterranean for a century. However, most were single-banked. Salt seems to be used in many places in the Centuries. In this sense, its probable meaning is wit, good sense, wisdom, etc. Euboea is a large island northeast of Athens, taken by the Turks from the Venetians in 1480, then lost to the Kingdom of Greece in 1831.

22. The large number of variants and classical words makes it difficult to clarify this quatrain. It probably belongs to the "New Crusades" theme of Nostradamus (or, if the variants are accepted, to some sort of internal Greek struggle). In another verse (931), Nostradamus appears to predict that Britain would drop below sea level, in which case the "submerged isle" rendezvous may indicate the English Channel area. The last line probably refers to a change of Popes.

23. Courtiers are most likely indicated by the palace birds. The other bird may be an eagle. The quatrain is really hopelessly vague.

24. With *Hister* as an anagram for "Hitler," this quatrain was long held by contemporary Nostradamians to forecast the fate of Hitler. It must be admitted that it is difficult to see what the Danube being dragged in an iron cage could refer to.

25. The guard here probably refers to foreign mercenaries, such as the Swiss or the Albanians. "Higher marriage" suggests more pay in the service of a ruler for whose benefit their treachery would be. But then, in the 20th-century lingo, the traitors are double-crossed. Since the use of mercenaries came to an end in France (the probable scene) in 1792, this verse would have to have been fulfilled by then.

26. The Ticino River flows into the Po east of Pavia. The second line concludes with aposiopesis, as do many.

27. Writes Garencières, "By the Divine Word . . . you must understand a Divine or Theologian, called in Greek Theologos, which signifieth a Divine Word." This is plausible, though the whole verse is very obscure.

28. A very intriguing prophecy. If by "the Prophet" he modestly refers to himself, we have *NostraDAmus*. If he refers to the Islamic one, we have *MaHOmet* (or *MoHAMmed*). Diana is the goddess of the moon, and the day of the moon is Monday. It would then appear that the subject of the verse is to make Monday his Sabbath. Even with the choice of three sets of initials, this quatrain can be termed highly specific. Hugh Allen (1943) applies this one to himself!

29. One of the "conquering Orient" theme. The invader comes to France by way of Italy. Probably intended for an Arab or Persian, the Turks being France's chief ally and friend in Nostradamus' day. Is aerial navigation intended in line 3? In this age, the rod would suggest a "secret weapon." Bouys (1806, p. 82) sees this one for Napoleon (Corsica being east of France [*sic!*]). Other commentators derive the appelation from his Egyptian campaign.

30. Le Pelletier vents his wrath on Voltaire & Co. for this one. Voltaire,

he says, renews Hannibal's hatred against Rome (this time the Roman Church), a hatred which Hannibal had called upon the infernal gods to witness. In *Journaux,* Le Pelletier finds a miraculous etymological prophecy (the daily newspapers being foreshadowed by the Encyclopedists). Actually, the verse is probably intended for an Antichrist. Babel was a city referred to in the Bible (Gen. XI:9) as the scene of a confusion of languages. It is also Hebrew for Babylon, which has become a synonym for voluptuous living, and occurs as such in 1096. Paris may indeed be intended.

31. In Roman times, Casilinum was a city three miles from ancient Capua. Modern Capua was built on the site of Casilinum, and it is probably to this city, or its river, that Nostradamus is referring. Campania province extended along the west coast from north of Capua to south of Salerno. Nothing is really predicted except a terrible flood of the Volturno River, which has doubtless occurred many times.

32. Dalmatia is the eastern shore of the Adriatic. The ancient Trebula Balliensis is now a tiny village eight miles northeast of Capua. Perhaps Capua is once again intended. Ravenna is a historic city of central Italy. The ancient province of Slavonia is bounded by the Drave, Danube, Theiss and Save rivers, and is now in northern Yugoslavia. It was part of the Kingdom of Hungary before and after the Turkish conquest. This prophecy thus extends to both sides of the Adriatic, with all fairly clear except for the obscure concoction mentioned in line 1.

33. Verona (which belonged to Venice), is on the Adige River, which may be the torrent mentioned here. It flows into the Adriatic parallel to the Po, about ten miles away. This is another ambitious verse, covering three 16th-century states: France and the Republics of Venice and Genoa.

34. Since the duel in question is to affect France, it is more than likely that the brothers are meant to be French princes. Such a mortal hatred existed between Henry III and the Duke of Alençon; with poetic license, the mutual intrigues might be said to constitute a duel. But there was no duel in the actual sense delineated here.

35. Another strictly local one, but quite specific. Although there are many towns at the confluence of two rivers, Lyons is the most perfect and most notable example in France. The last line would appear to give the date of the prophecy: on December 22 the Sun comes out of Sagittarius into Capricorn. Garencières insists that "This Prophecy was fulfilled about 90 years ago (c. 1582)" and cites Paradin's third book of the history of Lyons, chapter 22.

36. Torné-Chavigny (1870's) is convinced that in this verse Nostradamus sympathetically foresaw the trouble he got into with the Imperial authorities in 1858. However, it does seem quite possible that Nostradamus is indeed referring to his own writings here, the tyrant being some powerful enemy of Nostradamus seeking to undermine his influence with the King.

37. A perfectly clear little prophecy. It sounds general, but can anyone cite even one case in which it was fulfilled since 1555?

38. Jaubert applies this to the Truce of Vaucelles (1556) between Henry II and Philip II, which implied concerted action against the Protestants, including those in Philip's England. The truce was soon broken by Henry II, on the pretext of helping the Pope. However, the verse is general enough to allow other interpretations, including Hitler and Stalin (1939–41).

39. The third line makes this verse exceedingly interesting, but it is difficult to see what Nostradamus had in mind. In the 16th century the only place where German (Austrian), French and Spanish interests clashed was in the Grisons Canton and Valtelline Pass of Switzerland. The Habsburgs wanted to connect the Austrian and Spanish dominions through it; the French were as anxious to keep them apart. Perhaps the name "schoolhouse of the republic" is applied to the Swiss Confederation in general. Nostradamus would be most likely to apply it to the didactic Calvin's theocratic republic at Geneva. To Roberts (1947) this quatrain tells that "One year before Italy enters World War III, Paris will be overwhelmed by a terrific onslaught of atomic . . . rockets." Hugh Allen (1943) makes this helpful contribution: "March 18, 1937: An explosion of natural gas . . . destroyed the Consolidated Public School at New London, Texas. . . ."

40. This one is hopelessly vague and general.

41. All sorts of prodigies are to take place when a Pope dies (or, perhaps, is forced to move the papal seat from Rome). It is perhaps worth noting that nuclear explosions have been likened to a "second sun."

42. A quatrain equally gory and obscure.

43. This is a highly specific verse, requiring the concurrence of five factors: (1) a comet; (2) strife between three rulers; (3) a flood of the Po; (4) a flood of the Tiber; (5) some sort of sea serpent being washed up on the shore. Jaubert writes that on March 1, 1556, a "blazing star" was seen for three months. Henry II and Pope Paul IV went to war against Philip II. On October 14, 1557, peace was made. The next day, the Tiber had one of its biggest floods. When the flood receded, he claims, a serpent of prodigious size was seen (for which we have only Jaubert's not impartial word). This still leaves the Po, which he insists is a misprint for the Arno *(sic!)*, flooded at the same time. As an amusing postscript to this little change, started by Jaubert, we note the following chain of events: Garencières (1672), in order to delight his readers with Jaubert's interpretation, translates *Pau* as Arno. Roberts (1947), faithfully copying Garencières' deliberate mis-translation, throws away the whole basis for it, substituting for the Arno sea serpent of 1556 a more timely comment on the imminent reappearance of Halley's Comet "due in 1985."

44. Le Pelletier makes an interesting application of this one to France in 1813–14. The Eagle is of course Napoleon, driven back by the Allies. The senseless lady is the France which broke her ancient monarchical ties, first as the Republic, then as the Empire. We can only add that while the Eagle is indeed the symbol of Emperor and Empire, Nostradamus probably had the Holy Roman Empire in mind, rather than a future French empire, in

which case the verse might be applied to the latter part of the Thirty Years' War (*ca.* 1642).

45. In line 2 we have another suggestion of aerial warfare, for which apparently a hermaphrodite ruler is responsible. None such known of to date.

46. During the course of any long war, some sort of comet or meteoric display is likely to be seen, so that this verse is really quite general. It can probably be applied to World War I or II as well as any.

47. Another blend of the very specific and very obscure.

48. According to Wollner (p. 62), the configuration mentioned is very rare, and subject only to two occurrences mentioned in the period 1555–3797. The mountains are likely to refer to the Alps. When we consider the limitation of the dates, and the quite unique method of giving poison, this verse ranks as one of the most daring and specific. There now remains only one chance of fulfillment, in July, 2193.

49. Rhodes is the strategic island in the eastern Mediterranean. Byzantium is the ancient name for Constantinople (now Istanbul), and, by synecdoche, Turkey. The meaning is rather obscure.

50. Ghent was the chief city of Flanders, Brussels of Brabant. Flanders, Brabant and Hainaut were the richest provinces of the Netherlands, here apparently providing troops for a Habsburg attack on Langres, a key city near the 16th-century frontier. Line 3 might indicate that Nostradamus foresaw the revolt of the Netherlands in 1568. Line 4 is rather obscure.

51. This verse obviously refers to the struggle of Catholics and Protestants in England. Real Protestant doctrines were first introduced in 1549. Then in 1553 Mary Tudor succeeded Edward VI, restored the Catholic bishops, and in 1554 married Philip of Spain. A persecution of Protestants was beginning just when Nostradamus wrote the quatrain. But the exact meaning remains obscure.

A popular interpretation has "the blood of the just" as the martyrs of the English Revolution, avenging themselves through the Great Fire of 1666 (twenty threes plus six). The ancient lady is then St. Paul's Cathedral, the others of the same sect the other churches destroyed with it. It is indeed possible that "twenty threes the six" was intended for 66. But it would be more likely that Nostradamus foresaw a Protestant restoration under Elizabeth in 1566, not having foreseen Mary's death in 1558, with the peaceful succession of Elizabeth and return of Protestantism at that time.

52. This quatrain, together with the preceding and following ones, has been held to form part of a trio. From 1665 to 1667 England was at war with Holland. These two are likened to Corinth and Ephesus, though the significance of the latter pair is a mystery. (It occurs also in 33.) There was no particular connection between them. The former was in Greece, the latter in Asia Minor opposite the isle of Samos, near modern Smyrna. Both belonged to the Ottoman Empire in Nostradamus' day.

53. This one, of course, is interpreted as forecasting the Great Plague of April, 1665. The vengeance required was for Charles I, sold by the Scots

for £400,000 to Parliament on January 30, 1647, and condemned on January 27, 1649. According to our interpretation of 251, with which this one seems to be tied, the plague would be in the 1560's and the great lady of line 4 Queen Mary. (Also in 186?)

54. All that stands out amidst the obscurity here is that, following a flood, Rome will be attacked by a people from a distant country (which would seem to preclude French, Spanish or German invaders).

55. This one requires the concurrence of three factors, of which two are certainly not commonplace. First we have a bit of heroism by some despised person, resulting in his death. Second, we have an assassination at a banquet (in the best traditions of Renaissance Italy). The third factor, activity by Venice, was fairly common at all times. According to Hugh Allen (1943, p. 538) this quatrain foretells the siege of New York City by the Nazi-Fascist-Communist forces *(sic!)* in 1942, and the gallant death in battle of Mayor LaGuardia.

56. This one is quite specific, in an obscure sort of way.

57. Nothing can be clarified in this one.

58. Another of those both very specific and very obscure. The meaning may be that a baby that has lost a foot and a hand to a wild beast is to be carried at night to the gates of the fort of Nancy, whose device was a porcupine, in French *porc-épic*.

Torné-Chavigny (1870's) has an elaborate application for Napoleon, after Waterloo. Fleeing to Rochefort, unable to obtain passage to America, he surrendered to British Admiral Hotham. His bad luck Torné lays to treachery by his subordinates. The phrase "little great one" appears in another verse applied to Napoleon (285). Out of *Silene luit* Torné somehow or other gets an anagram for St. Helena.

59. Line 2 of this quatrain appears also in Presage 2, entitled "From the luminary Epistle on the said year [1555]," as does much of line 4. Apparently it refers to Turkey, then the dominant naval power in the Mediterranean. The trident soldiers may be the Turkish equivalent of marines, or troops of their French allies. Line 3 Jaubert applies to the strain put upon the resources of Provence when Toulon became the base for both the French army and the Turkish fleet, co-operating against the Habsburgs in 1558. The date is Jaubert's, and what he is referring to took place in the 1540's. Dragut did not work as closely with the French as Barbarossa had done. Jaubert admits that he knows of nothing to justify the strife in Narbonne at the time.

60. Presumably "the Punic faith" refers to Islam, perhaps because both were enemies of Rome. Line 2 takes us from India to the Atlantic without telling much of the common denominator. Line 3 is completely obscure, while line 4 appears to predict a naval disaster. The verse probably belongs to the "New Crusades" theme.

61. A very rich quatrain. The meaning of *Tamins*, however, remains uncertain. Grammatically, it is quite valid to consider it as syncope of *Tamisiens*, but there is something a bit too modern about English soldiers fighting

side by side with French soldiers, as this verse suggests. Aside from the centuries of mutual hostility, England seemed about to become part of the Habsburg Empire. There is a town of Tamines on the Sambre, about twenty miles northeast of Charleroi, in modern Belgium (and then in Brabant). The Trojan blood is that of the House of France (see 119). The meaning of "the port of the arrow" remains uncertain also. There is a town La Flèche on a tributary of the Loire, but that hardly makes it a port. Toulon derives its name from Telo-Martius. *Telum* means "spear" or "lance" and poetically could do for arrow, but *telum* is not the origin of the *Telo* (which, however, Nostradamus may not have known). La Rochelle had been a Protestant stronghold since 1554, but there is no arrow in its arms. The Gironde is the name given to the estuary of the Garonne, about thirty miles from La Rochelle. It is perhaps worth noting that on October 28, 1628, La Rochelle, in revolt against the government, was taken by Richelieu, after a siege of fourteen months and the dispatching of three fleets from England to save the Huguenots. But the picture of Nostradamus cheering the Protestants on is an impossible one.

62. This one all depends on the meaning of *Mabus*. In his list of Nostradamus' successful name-predictions, Jaubert identifies it with one Captain Ampus (the interpretation was to come in one of his later books, which never appeared). The only Ampus we find is a Henri de Castellane, Marquis d'Ampus, whose chief claim to immortality appears to be that he married one Marie de Villars-Brancas in 1613. But at least the name is genuine.

63. The Russian city of Perm (now Molotov—or is it still?) was not founded until 1568, and not named Perm till the 17th century, so that is presumably ruled out. If Parma, it was seized by the Papacy in 1511, and on August 26, 1545, made into an hereditary duchy by Pope Paul III, in favor of his bastard, Pierluigi Farnese, whose son Ottavio was married to Charles V's illegitimate daughter Margaret, by whom he became father of one of the key figures of the late 16th century in the Netherlands and France, Alexander Farnese, Duke of Parma. In connection with the latter, and the juxtaposition of Parma and *l'vrie*, an interesting interpretation can be built. In 1590 Parma, having succeeded in separating the Belgian part of the Netherlands from the revolting Dutch and preserving it for his uncle, Philip II of Spain, was ordered to France to help the Catholic League against Henry of Navarre. In 1590 he was defeated by Henry at *Ivry*, a Norman village, the site of Henry's gallant order: "If you lose your standards, follow my white plume." Although he did advance further into France thereafter, all hopes of subjugating the French Protestants soon vanished, since the introduction of foreign troops rallied even Catholics to the side of Henry of Navarre (whose capital was Pau—suggesting in this context that the ever-ambiguous French word *Pau* might be left in this case as the city instead of being rendered as the Italian river Po). Parma, who might be said to have served Philip in his capacity as King of Naples (Ausonia), died in 1592 after receiving a wound at the Battle of Rouen. Doubtless it could be shown somehow

that he responsible for the wound might properly be called "least at the wall."

Boswell (1941, p. 204) applies the last line to the death of André Maginot (builder of France's supposedly impregnable wall to the east in the 1930's), due to typhoid fever contracted from tainted oysters, and the entrance of Italy into World War II.

64. This one is probably another of those hopefully predicting the imminent doom of Calvin. Unfortunately, Calvin was born nowhere near the Cevennes mountains. However, his chief lieutenant, Théodore de Bèze (Beza), was born at Vézelay, which is in that area. Since Beza is considered the most likely author of the famous distich at Nostradamus' expense (see "Biography of Nostradamus"), our prophet's wrath against him probably equaled that against Calvin. In any case, the phrase proved most justified, since the roots of Calvinism grew so deep in the Cevennes that a full-scale revolt against Louis XIV took place here after the revocation of the Edict of Nantes (1685). The last line poses the question of what concern Geneva could have with a fleet, unless it be a lake fleet bringing supplies from some ally on the Lake of Geneva.

65. Again we have the problem of the meaning of *Hesperia* (see 128). Insubria is definitely the Milanese, which the Spanish held from 1535 to 1713. According to Wöllner, the dates for the configuration, whatever it is, are December 13, 1604, December 25, 1839, December 7, 2044, December 17, 2281, and December 1, 2486.

66. Le Pelletier applies this one ably to the Hundred Days (April 20 to June 22, 1815). Napoleon, captive at Elba, escapes from the danger of the British cruiser guarding him. His fortune changes in both directions. Line 3 really taxes Le Pelletier's ingenuity and he rises to the occasion: On April 23, in the Tuileries, Napoleon signed the act giving France a constitution, thus seducing or tricking the French people. But to France's good fortune, Paris is soon besieged by the Allied armies.

67. With a very farfetched rearrangement of words, Le Pelletier applies this one to the second restoration of Louis XVIII *(par le duel* [sic!]). The real meaning, it would seem, is that the fork-nosed victim having killed an important person in a duel, his blond enemy (probably a French prince or king) is at last able to remove him from power, and restore to power a disgraced faction he favors. The adherents of the fork-nosed one are then confined to some islands like those off southeast France. All of which is a perfectly logical plot, and not in the least Nostradamus' fault if it apparently never happened.

68. The meaning of *Aquilon* remains a puzzle similar to that of *Hesperia*. Even Nostradamus' supposed disciple, Chavigny, had only the vaguest idea (see 149). Le Pelletier sees it here for the French expedition to Ireland ("situated to the north of England") in 1689–91, on behalf of ex-King James II. The greatest power in the North in 1555 was Denmark. Sweden's career was just beginning. But Germany and England (and Scotland) are not to

be ruled out either. Today, of course, Russia would be the most popular choice (and Le Pelletier in his Glossary saw it as such already in 1866). Line 2 does, indeed, suggest Czar Peter's demand for a "window on the sea." The only restoration in England since 1555 was that of the Stuarts in 1660. Nostradamus probably had in mind a Catholic restoration after reverses (see 251). The nearest fulfillment for line 4 occurred in June, 1667, when the Dutch fleet sailed up the Thames in a raid. Somehow or other Bouys (1806) got out of this a prophecy that his Emperor would successfully conquer Britain.

69. Le Pelletier sees this one for Napoleon. The Celtic right arm is the French army. He reunites the three estates, in discord since the Revolution, notwithstanding the protests of Louis XVIII, head of the royal hierarchy. More likely the prophecy concerns further French aggression in Italy, with the three parts concerning any three Italian territories, possibly the three Habsburg territories of Naples, Sicily and Milan. The latter line would refer to the opposition of the Pope. The great monarchy would be the Holy Roman Empire, always subject to discord, but beginning in Nostradamus' day, especially to religious strife. Furthermore, there was a prospect of strife in the immediate future between Charles V's son Philip and his brother Ferdinand over the division of Charles' vast empire (see "Historical Background").

70. Le Pelletier sees this one for Napoleon also. The scene is the Battle of Waterloo (June 18, 1815). The dart from the sky is the vengeance of heaven. Line 2 refers to the general slaughter, just touching on the unmentionable *mot de Cambronne* (for which the United States now has its equivalent in the word of McAuliffe at Bastogne). Le Pelletier rises nobly now to the big problem: the stone stands for a primitive stone ax, poetically cutting down the Bonaparte dynastic tree. Ingenious, if it can be swallowed. France surrenders, expiates, is purged, etc., as the famous monster passes off the scene.

71. Another of the detailed but obscure variety. The exiles are probably a pro-French faction, suddenly abandoned by the French.

72. The Rubicon was the stream north of Rimini which formed the boundary between Cisalpine Gaul and Italy. It is identified with an insignificant modern stream called the Fiumicino. It is probably intended here in a figurative sense, referring to the occasion when Gallic Proconsul Julius Caesar crossed it. Thereafter he had either to defeat his enemies, or be executed as a traitor. This quatrain is supposed to form another prize exhibit for the "retroactive prophecy" school. The anonymous critic of 1724 discovered that it was a perfect description of the Battle of Pavia (1525), line 3 hinting of the strategy employed by the Imperial forces. The Ticino flows into the Po just below Pavia. However, the battle was hardly uncertain. The French suffered their worst defeat since Agincourt, including the capture of King Francis.

73. Lake Fucino was about sixty-five miles east of Rome. We say *was* because it was drained in 1876. Lake Garda is in northeastern Italy. The

former lake was in the Kingdom of the Two Sicilies, the latter in the Republic of Venice. The port of "L'Orguion" remains a mystery. Orgon in Provence, twenty miles north of Nostradamus' Salon, is but on the Durance River. The "three crowns" probably refers to the triple tiara of the Popes. The great Endymion is probably intended for Henry II, lover of Diane de Poitiers (Diana the Moon), who used the moon as her device. Those are the pieces, but to fit them together still remains a problem. Through a felicitous erratum, Roberts (1947) tells his readers that "Nostradamus [Garencières] confessed his inability to interpret this obscure stanza." Allen (1943) writes, "Endymion was the lad whom the goddess Silene threw into a perpetual slumber that she might caress him at will. It is a metaphor for the U.S.A."

74. The geography is very confusing here. Sens and Autun are two cities of northeast France more than one hundred miles apart. But the Rhône is not on the way from them to the Pyrenees. Perhaps "Pyrenees" is a slip for "Alps." Apparently this one concerns another invasion of Italy. The March of Ancona extended along the Italian east coast from south of Rimini to north of Giulianova.

75. This quatrain is easily one of the most completely obscure, at least in the first two lines, which have no apparent connection with the last two.

76. The senate is presumably the Parliament of Burgundy, inflicting some punishment, physical or psychological, on the subject of the quatrain. The actual meaning is quite obscure.

77. This one apparently concerns the defense of a city against a siege. After a valiant defense, the besieged are betrayed by traitors who escape. All rather general.

78. In 259 we saw that Neptune is probably used for the Moslem fleet. Line 2 is in keeping with the joint Franco-Turkish operations of the day. "Punic" is the adjective for Carthage, on the site of whose ancient empire the Barbary corsairs held sway. Their leader, Barbarossa, was Admiral of the Turkish fleet. The isles may refer to any of those in the western Mediterranean: Majorca, Minorca, Malta, Corsica, Sardinia, etc. Line 4 is quite obscure.

Jaubert applies it to events in the second half of 1558 (his date), when the Turkish fleet, instead of helping the French in northwest Italy, attacked Minorca. On July 10 they took Ciudadela, killing or enslaving the entire population. The tardy rowing, according to Jaubert, was justified in that the Turks had been bribed to delay in coming to co-operate with the French. This delay was supposed to have completely demoralized the French.

79. This one, according to the anonymous critic of 1724, is another exhibit for Nostradamus as the "retroactive prophet." In 1551 Dragut of Algiers captured Tripoli from the Knights of Malta. Gabriel d'Aramon, ambassador to the Porte from 1546 to 1553, after a report to the King in 1551, returned to Turkey aboard Dragut's flagship. There he is supposed to have used his influence to get those of the Knights who were French released. If there

is a catch to this, it is in the application to the Turks of *Seline,* which in 477 we will see to refer probably to Henry II himself (like Chyren). However, it is possible that Nostradamus uses the word in both ways in different places.

80. Jaubert applies this one to the Constable of Montmorency. After the French disaster at Saint-Quentin on August 10, 1557, the Constable, wounded in the hip and a prisoner, was allowed to give his parole and go back and forth to negotiate the peace. Jaubert gets around *faint* by changing it to *saint,* thus getting the holy rest of Cateau-Cambresis (1559). But the peace was neither a soft one nor a false one. It was a hard one for France, and a comparatively long one. Since no edition has the variant *saint,* that remains the range of possible meanings. With the last lines, Jaubert tries again: Philip II refused to consider having his many noble prisoners ransomed, setting them free *gratis* after the peace. The real meaning would seem that the eloquent one obtains good treatment for the prisoners for (not *in*) a short time.

81. There is always doubt about what Nostradamus had in mind for "fire from the sky." Had he written in the 20th century, it would obviously refer to some sort of aerial bombardment. Deucalion was the Greek Noah, so that in line 2 another Great Flood is predicted. Line 3 refers to an Algerian raid on Sardinia. Line 4 is a very rich one. Phaéthon was the youth who in Greek mythology was allowed for a day to drive the chariot of Phoebus (Apollo) the Sun God. He was on the point of setting the world on fire when Zeus struck him down with a thunderbolt. Philip II, while still Infante (and thus before 1555) took as his device the chariot of Phoebus, with the motto *Jam illustrabit omnia* ("Soon it will light all") (Palliser, p. 250). The youth at the reins could be taken as Apollo, Phaethon or Philip II. While Libra influenced Austria rather than England in geopolitical astrology, there was a slight bit of justification for regarding the ruler of England as the Balance already in 1555. On the field of the Cloth of Gold (1520) Henry VIII had used the inscription *Cui adhereo praeest* (Palliser, p. 379), meaning "He to whom I adhere prevails." If this is correct, Nostradamus might be here tying the other events with the death of Mary Tudor (England's ruler when he wrote), queen since 1553 and wife of Philip since 1554. She did indeed die soon, in 1558.

82. As clear as an obscure prophecy can be.

83. This one seems to predict a sack of Lyons, like that of Rome in Nostradamus' youth (1527). Something of this order occurred in October, 1795, when troops of the Revolution put down a counter-revolutionary uprising at Lyons, after a two months' siege, with a devastation of the city and a massacre of its inhabitants. We do not know if at this time there was a widespread drizzle in southeast France and Switzerland.

84. The area specified for this immense drought extends along the west coast of Italy, roughly from Pisa to Salerno. As the Venetians still held

Dalmatia in 1555 as a sort of island in the Turkish Empire, Nostradamus is probably predicting that Dalmatia will eventually fall to the Turks too. It never did. Or possibly the Arab or Persian invaders, mentioned so often, are intended.

85. We already mentioned in 258 that "little great one" was applied to Napoleon. It is somewhat more difficult to apply this one. It has been tied up with Marshal Ney. He had no actual beard, but as a poetic device for "stout-hearted" it could do for him whom Napoleon called the bravest of the brave. When Napoleon arrived at Lyons (March 10) during the Hundred Days, Ney marched to Lons-le-Saunier, in order to bar Napoleon's passage and carry out his vow to bring him back in an iron cage. But so great was the enthusiasm for the Emperor amongst his officers and men that Ney went over to him on March 17. But this took place at Auxerre, not Lyons. The minor details work out all right, but the last phrase provides a real stumbling block. There was no bloody activity in the Gulf of Genoa in 1815. Whatever Nostradamus meant by the verse, it is noteworthy that the prefix of Celtic seems to identify the Eagle definitely with the French, instead of the Germans as usual. If the Eagle is intended for a great warrior, rather than Emperor, it was undoubtedly intended for Nostradamus' contemporary, the Duke of Guise, who led the French armies against Charles V. And in those days there was always blood in the Gulf of Genoa.

86. Another of the detailed but very obscure variety. Line 3 seems rather meaningless, since the Turks had already taken Egypt (1517). Anyhow, Egypt had been Moslem since the 8th century. Perhaps he means that a further Turkish expansion will be based on Egypt. If the line can be applied to Egyptian imperialism, this occurred in 1769–73, in the 1820's, and is probably due again in the 20th century. Little can be said of line 4, other than that Mercury was the messenger or herald of the gods.

87. This rather general prophecy has been applied to such divergent characters as Gustavus Adolphus, George I of England and Adolf Hitler. Here is Garencières' application to the first:

> This Prophecy is concerning Gustavus Adolphus, King of Swedeland, who is called German Prince, because his Ancestors came out of Germany, he came out of a remote Countrey, that is Swedeland, he came upon a gilded throne, that is a Ship gilded, he shall make slavery and waters meet, because as soon as he was Landed he began to conquer, and to subdue that Lady (viz. Germanica) that was no more worshipped since as she was before.

88. Another of the very detailed and very obscure ones. With regard to the last line, it is probably no coincidence that Reims and Aix-la-Chapelle (Aachen) are something of opposite numbers. From 813 to 1531 all emperors were crowned at Aix, while Reims is the traditional site of French coronations. The same combination occurs again in 486.

89. Probably this can be applied to nothing Nostradamus may have had

in mind as well as it can be and has been applied, under one of the variants, to the Anglo-American Entente of 1941, with the Atlantic Charter meeting of Churchill and Roosevelt, and American industry switching to heavy war production, the statistics of which seemed foolish boasting to the bloody Hitler.

90. This quatrain has been viewed as another specimen of "retroactive prophecy," applying quite nicely to the Battle of Mohacs (1526). The Magyars were routed by the Turks and the last King killed. Line 2 is applied to the inability of the many political factions to unite against enslavement by the Turks. Line 3 is applied to Pest, which the Turks sacked in 1526. The last line refers to the disputed succession: John Zapolya was elected in Transylvania and Ferdinand of Habsburg at Pressburg. They fought a civil war for two years. Zapolya was defeated and appealed to Sultan Suleiman in 1528. Castor and Pollux were the twins of Greek mythology who faced a terrible problem: one was mortal and the other immortal. After Castor's death, Zeus decreed that they be reunited by living in the upper and lower worlds on alternate days. This might well be a play on one being King, the other not. The case is a good one, but not exclusive of a future fulfillment as well. Doubtless applications have been made to events of October, 1956.

91. This one might some day be applied to the explosion of U.S. H-bombs in Russia in World War III.

92. Le Pelletier applied several nephew quatrains to Napoleon III, as gingerly as he could. Had he written five years later than he did, he wouldn't have hesitated to apply this one to the Battle of Sedan, as Torné did later. Line 1 is the German artillery. The nearest fulfillment for line 2 was that the Prince Imperial displayed great coolness when a bullet struck the earth near his feet while visiting the lines at Saarbrücken on August 2, 1870, an incident which the press played up much. Lines 3 and 4 work out nicely. Napoleon III, after wandering around the field of battle in the vain hope of being struck by a bullet, was captured in the general capitulation of September, 1870. But the quatrain being fairly general, there are probably other equally valid applications.

93. Le Pelletier includes this one amongst his "future interpretations." The chief of the ship (Bark of St. Peter) is the Pope. The castle is that of San Angelo, the palace the Vatican. He thinks that the Pope will literally be thrown into the dregs—which may indeed be what Nostradamus had in mind.

94. Another of the detailed but obscure variety. Most noteworthy is the figure in the last line, a very modern casualty list. With the doubt about the beginning, and with the Pau vs. Po as well as the Lyons vs. Lion uncertainty, any interpretation is rather hopeless. If "Lion" is the right reading, it probably refers to Venice, the great maritime power. One of the chief sights of Venice is the Winged Lion of St. Mark, her patron.

95. This one is hopelessly vague and general.

96. The beginning of the Rhône is at the foot of the Furka Pass, a few

miles from the source of the Rhine. Its end is of course in the Mediterranean west of Marseilles. Apparently in the whole area between these two points some prodigy is to be seen in the heavens. It is line 4 which is most interesting. Persia was never part of the Ottoman Empire, and was almost continually at war with it, as of yore with the Roman Empire. Nostradamus seems to have foreseen that some Persian Shah was to inflict such a shattering defeat on the Turks as to open the way for an invasion of the Balkans.

97. This prophecy warns a Pope that he and his (probably meaning nephew-cardinals) will be assassinated, probably by an Orsini conspiracy, the rose being the chief device of that turbulent clan. There is no way of telling what city is referred to.

98. Jaubert sees this one as the saga of a jealous lover who kills his rival. The whole thing would seem to fit the classical world better than the Renaissance world. However, it may go with the preceding one.

99. With the word "omen" occurring again, there is a possibility that this one is supposed to go with its predecessor. Jaubert applies it to 1556. The Gallic people are the mercenaries of Montluc, serving the Pope against the Duke of Alba, and behaving very badly. At that time, the fleet of the Baron de la Garde was supposed to have been driven north into the harbor of Saint-Florent in Corsica, and was thus unable to provide the much-needed assistance. Jaubert fails to say what disaster this brought. (Indirectly the French effort here may be said to have weakened them in the North, where the Spanish inflicted the ruinous defeat of Saint-Quentin the next year.)

Le Pelletier's version is as ingenious as usual:

> The Roman Territory, which the sovereign Pontiffs governed spiritually (that the Augur [Roman priest] interpreted) will be trampled under the feet of the French people. But this nation fears the hour of heavenly vengeance, when a mortal cold will make it regret having hurled its army too far, in the frozen steppes of Russia.

100. This would appear to refer to the inhabitants of the western Mediterranean isles (Balearics, Sardinia, Corsica, etc.) becoming so outraged at the constant raids by the corsairs as to organize a great league and expedition to exterminate them. This sounds like a good idea, but it never occurred—at least not exactly that way. But that was the general idea of the League which resulted in the epic Battle of Lepanto in 1571.

## Century III

1. If, as we saw in 259, Neptune is used for the Turko-Algerian fleet, this verse would seem to predict a great Turkish naval victory over the Spaniards, whose color was red. (See also 177.) The only great clash of the century had just the opposite result, when the Moslems were defeated at the Battle of Lepanto in 1571. However, they continued to ravage the western Mediterranean for the rest of the century.

2. This bit of sublime mysticism and metaphysics seems rather incomprehensible, but Garencières is chock-full of ideas about it:

> I desire the judicious Reader, and chiefly if he be given to the Hermetick Philosophy, to take a special notice of this Stanza, for in it is contained the secret of the Elixir or Philosophers Stone . . . by the Divine word you must not understand the second portion of the Trinity, but a Doctor in Divinity or a Theologian, called in Greek Theologos, or Divine Word . . . shall give to the substance, that is, to Gold. . . . Heaven and Earth, that is all the Celestial and Terrestrial qualities lurking in the Gold, which is hid in the mystical milk, that is the Azoth, or Mercury of the Philosophers. Body, Soul, Spirit, having all power, that is, the three principles, of which the Philosophers say their stone is compounded . . .

3. "Those that shall desire to be better and further informed, may come to me, and they shall have all the satisfaction I can afford them," writes Garencières for this one. The first line probably represents a configuration, rather than further mysticism. The odd combination of Corinth and Ephesus appears also in 252. And the familiar subjects of earthquake and drought are found here.

4. Jaubert takes the first line as indicating a year when a solar and lunar eclipse come close to each other. He finds that in 1556 there was a solar eclipse on November 1, followed by a lunar one on November 16. He quotes one Belleforest as confirming that there was no rain from April to August, and that an extremely cold winter began in December. The danger at the frontier came with the Spanish invasion of Picardy. The last line he believes refers to the heretics at Salon, who bothered Nostradamus so much. Indeed, it must be either Salon or Saint-Rémy, his birthplace. But his troubles with the Protestants did not take place until the 60's.

5. Garencières believes that this one refers to eclipses also. The date in line 2 is rather confusing. As it stands, it could be any month. One must assume that he means between the calends of March and April, or any time during March. The verse remains very vague and general.

6. Lightning striking a church has doubtless occurred more than once. Gould and Pyle (p. 727) record a case at Châteauneuf on July 11, 1819. Nine were killed and eighty-two wounded amongst the congregation.

7. An interesting interpretation of this one has been for the Fall of France in 1940, with the "fire from the sky on the pikes" being aerial attacks on soldiers armed with bayonets. By the same token, the heavenly relief is applied to air support. The quatrain is, however, rather vague.

8. To speak of depopulating the country of the conquistadors was then quite a daring prophecy, but it is impossible to see whom Nostradamus would have accomplishing this. Denmark was known as the Cimbric Chersonese. The Cimbri, either a German or Celtic people, moved along the east bank of the Rhine until in 113 B.C. they crossed the Rhône and ravaged Gaul. In the process, they defeated two Roman armies. Upon advancing into Spain,

they suffered defeat. Retreating to northern France, they suffered further defeats from the Gauls. Next they teamed up with the Teutones (who gave the Germanic people their name). The Teutones were to attack Italy from southern Gaul while the Cimbri attacked via the Alps. But in 102 B.C. Marius, the great soldier-statesman of the Roman Republic, defeated the Teutones at Aix and the Cimbri at Vercelli. This was supposedly the last of them. But Nostradamus apparently has some inside information as to what racial stock they became identified with. The Danes would hardly seem eligible. Since the Angles and the Saxons came from approximately the same territory, the English may be intended. Limousin and Guienne, contiguous provinces near the Spanish border, are apparently to provide allies for the northern invaders.

9. Bordeaux and La Rochelle are comparatively close and go together quite well, but Rouen is far to the north. Roanne is on the upper Loire, near the eastern frontier. By reason of the names of places and peoples, the verse is quite detailed, but the plot remains obscure.

10. This quatrain seems intended primarily for Monaco, already in Nostradamus' day a more or less independent city-state under the House of Grimaldi. The last line could refer to any ruler of Monaco in a time of disaster.

11. This one would seem to tell of the prodigies that will mark the death of a great ruler. The monarch of Venice (unless Nostradamus foresaw a change in government) would be the Doge of Venice. But it would seem strange for Nostradamus to be so concerned with the death of a doge. With a translation of "Hadrian," to whom Henry IV is likened, line 1 has been explained by Guynaud. According to him, a story appeared in the *Mercure Français* of 1619 to the effect that a ghostly army of ten to twelve thousand armed spirits were beheld marching around the skies over Angoumois at about the time Henry was assassinated (1610). The verse is full of details, but they are incomprehensible details. In line 1 we have once again what sounds like modern aerial combat.

12. Widespread floods are forecast here. The Ebro and Tagus are in Spain (and Portugal) the Po and Tiber in Italy, and the Rhône in France. The "pond of Geneva" is in Switzerland and Arezzo (the city—there is no lake) east of Siena in Italy. The two greatest cities of the Garonne are Bordeaux and Toulouse. The throwing together of all these distant geographical entities makes the quatrain quite a puzzler.

13. Another of the very detailed and very obscure variety. Except for the hanging in line 3, all the events are unlikely ones. Line 4 suggests submarines; God knows what Nostradamus really had in mind for it. To Allen (1943, p. 254), the two captives are "probably Churchill and George VI. . . . You will see what supposedly will happen to George VI when he escapes from the calaboose, in the next chapter."

14. Other than that "branch" probably means offspring, we can offer little here.

15. Le Pelletier applies this one quite convincingly to the minority of Louis XV. After the bloody glory of Louis XIV, France "went to the dogs" under his nephew, the Regent of Orléans. It is the Regent or no one for this quatrain, since all the other regents (1555–1848) were women (Catherine for Charles IX, Marie for Louis XIII and Anne for Louis XIV). A woman could not be designated by the *un* in line 4.

16. A lucid prophecy, and a very imaginative one, considering the great dearth of English princes since the death of Edward VI in 1553. In fact, there wasn't to be another till James VI of Scotland became James I of England (1603), at which time the future Charles I was three. We have here a near Richard the Lion-Hearted, or Black Prince. Neither the Stuarts nor the Hanoverians have provided anyone to fulfill it. Allen (1943, p. 274) applies it to the future of one of the few Englishmen he seems to like, the Duke of Windsor (formerly Edward VIII).

17. Mount Aventine was one of the seven hills of Rome, and here probably represents Rome by synecdoche. The second line concerns an eclipse visible in Flanders. The occurrence at the same time of these two rare events, and the two additional less rare events of lines 3 and 4, is so unlikely as to make this one of the more daring prophecies.

18. Even with the specific mention of Reims, this one is hopelessly obscure and general.

19. The frequent mention of a rain of milk is puzzling. (See the preceding quatrain also.) Lucca was a duchy between Modena and Tuscany. "Praetor" may refer to the Gonfalonier of Lucca. It would be only an arbitrary guess to try to identify the rector in line 4. Instances of a rain of blood have been recorded by Charles Fort (pp. 40, 304, 583, 599).

20. This is a refreshingly detailed, specific and comprehensible quatrain (even if never fulfilled). The Kingdom of Grenada, the last Moorish outpost in Iberia, was conquered in 1492. It lay south of the Guadalquivir, while Cordova is on its northern bank. Nostradamus apparently foresaw a Moorish comeback, aided by the treachery of a grandee of Cordova.

21. Another of the strangely local, yet extremely specific quatrains. It is thoroughly exact and comprehensible. We are told that at the point where the Conca River flows into the Adriatic, which is by the village of Cattolica, a sort of mermaid will be caught, and that it will not be caught with a hook. The only uncertain factor is whether this ever occurred before or after it was written. Garencières writes that a creature taken for a mermaid was seen by one Gesuerus near Rome in 1523, and by Rondeletius in 1531. As far as the records of Cattolica go, we are informed by the present chief of Cattolica's Tourist Board, Dr. Riciputi, that there is no record in the archives of Cattolica of such a mermaid, or even a manatee (letter of August 8, 1960).

22. A rather general one. Writes Garencières (1672):

Most men that have knowledge in History, interpret this of the City of Magdeburg in Germany, that was destroyed with Fire and Sword by the Earl of

Tilly, General for the Emperour against Gustavus Adolphus, King of Swedeland. For the like devastation and cruelty was never heard of in Europe.

23. Garencières, stealing from Jaubert as usual, has it that "The Author directeth his speech to the French Fleet that went to Corsica in the year 1555." This sounds valid enough, but the rest is rather unconvincing: the Venetians are supposed to have been prevented by the Turks from helping. Actually, the Turks were French allies and the Venetians neutral. The last line, which suggests starvation, is applied to a feast upon receipt of the news of peace. More likely it is a prediction of actual disaster.

24. This one goes well with the preceding one: a further warning to France not to embark on over-ambitious expeditions. Jaubert applies it to the general French reverses of 1556–57 in Italy and Picardy.

25. Another very detailed, yet rather meaningless one as far as significance goes. Naples and Sicily had been joined on and off for many centuries. After a separation, they were rejoined by Spain in 1504, then separated for the last time during a two-year interval, in the middle of which this prophecy was written. In 1554 Charles V gave his son Philip Naples (for a wedding present so that he could marry Queen Mary of England as a king and not just a prince), while holding back Sicily until 1556. At just about the time this prophecy was published (it went into the presses on May 4, 1555, the date found in the first edition), Anthony of Vendôme became King of Navarre upon the death of his father-in-law (May 25, 1555). He therefore did not qualify for this quatrain, Naples and Sicily still being separated. Accordingly, the first to qualify was his son, who became King of Navarre in 1562 and finally King Henry IV of France in 1594 ("Paris is well worth a mass"). All of the places mentioned in line 3 were parts of the House of Navarre's realm, held in fief from the French King. In 1562 the King, Charles IX, was only twelve, but under the Regency of his mother Catherine de' Medici, his government was indeed working closely with the Spanish. All in all, a 100% success but with very little of any substance involved.

26. This one, though somewhat obscure, is rather interesting. Nostradamus seems to be taking a guess at the ultimate development of Lutheranism and Calvinism, seeing them deifying rulers. Line 2 probably refers to leaders like his old enemy Théodore de Bèze.

27. A rather colorful quatrain. The subject must be a potentate of northwest Africa, perhaps of Morocco, or of Barbary (Algeria and Tunisia). Although strictly speaking Libya is only a small area west of Egypt, Nostradamus seems to use it loosely for North Africa. In view of the frequent cooperation of that day between pashas like Barbarossa and Dragut and the French, there is nothing very fantastic in the cultural entente delineated here. A dictionary cannot be meant—there already were several, since 1505.

28. Although very general, this one may mark a consciously successful prediction. Since *empire* is not capitalized, it may mean "dominion," rather than refer to the German Emperor. If so, and if the first two lines refer to

a male person different from the female one labeled as such in the latter part, the quatrain probably predicts the advent of Elizabeth to the English throne (1558), and the King of Navarre to the French throne (1594). They ruled simultaneously for only a few years (1594–1603). The Court of Navarre was known for its poverty-stricken simplicity. Since Elizabeth remained Protestant even after Mary came to the throne (1553), she would rate Nostradamus' epithet in line 4. She reigned long enough—forty-five years. Since a female could not rule France (except as regent), the whole verse could not apply to France. But it could all apply to England, with lines 1–2 referring to the lowly origin of Elizabeth's mother, Anne Boleyn, and to Elizabeth's poverty in her youth.

Guynaud divides the verse between Elizabeth and Pope Sixtus V, natural son of a servant girl.

29. The most famous nephews of Nostradamus' day were those of Constable Montmorency: Admiral Coligny, Cardinal Châtillon and d'Andelot. But there is nothing to prove that this verse was intended for two of them. Papal nephews are always a good bet.

30. Le Pelletier applies this one to the arrest of Montgomery (see 135). After the tragedy in which he slew Henry II, he became a Huguenot leader in Normandy. After an incredibly adventurous career, one that Hollywood has overlooked, he came to the end of his rope in 1574. After holding out for sixteen days with 150 men against 10,000, he surrendered at Domfront on May 25. He was promised immunity, but this was violated. Taken to Paris, he was condemned and executed on June 27. However, the circumstances were not as dramatic as those of lines 3 and 4. He came into the hands of his enemies through negotiation, not by seizure in bed. However, the grudge is well enough applied to Catherine's vow to have his head.

31. This one is certainly quite detailed. Unfortunately, it was never fulfilled. One of the armies is obviously that of the Turks. The other might refer to that of the New Crusaders, predicted elsewhere. But to give Nostradamus the benefit of the doubt, let us say he refers only to the Persians, intermittently at war with the Turks during most of the reign of Suleiman (1520–66). Although the wording of the last two lines makes either a Turkish victory or defeat possible, the latter seems most likely. The scene covers an immense area: Armenia is east of the Black Sea, Media southeast of Armenia and Arabia several hundred miles south of both. There was indeed a great battle of the Araxes in 1514, but the Battle of Chaldiran was a great Turkish victory. Fighting continued, with constant raids by the Turks, until the general peace of 1555. Much of the fighting took place in "Armenia" and "Media" but none in Arabia. Nor were there any epic battles. Furthermore, the Turks were successful at all times. The first great Persian victory came at Lake Van in 1603. It might be said that with poetic license "the host of the great Suleiman" could designate the Turkish army, even after his death. But even so, no Persian victory, from that of Lake Van on, was on the

Araxes. A shrewd perversion of the meaning has been used in one interpretation: the great Turkish defeat by the Christian navy in 1571 took place at Lepanto, only a few miles from the classical Greek promontory of Araxus.

32. Another highly specific one. French disaster is predicted for a time when there is fighting in three areas. An expedition composed mainly of Gascons (as was Montluc's in the early 1550's) will meet disaster in Tuscany. There will also be fighting in Franche-Comté, where the Empire extended like a wedge between France and the Swiss. (There was fighting here in the 1590's and 1630's; it became French in 1678.) The third scene will be the Duchy of Mantua in northeastern Italy. Jaubert applies it to events of July–September, 1557, when Gascons were sent from Corsica to fight under Montluc and Guise around Rome. Of line 4 he writes that the Duke of Ferrara sent his son Alfonso d'Este to invade Mantua at the time. The best he can do for line 3 is to apply it to the Duke of Savoy's attempt to retake Mariembourg, captured by the Duke of Nevers in 1555.

33. Jaubert interprets this one also for the same period. The wolf is the Spaniard. The city, Jaubert decides, is Neptune, a town near Rome which Alba took while the French were near by. The French are the friends (to the Pope), but also the enemies (to Alba) and, third, the foreign army (to the Italians, whose country Jaubert concedes they devastated on their way). All of which is extremely involved and equally tenuous.

34. This one is rather vague and obscure. Only the solar eclipse and the monster are comprehensible. Line 4 would seem to indicate a drought or famine.

35. Le Pelletier applies this one to Napoleon Bonaparte—which is probably as good an application as any, though it is sufficiently general to be applicable to many other notables, including Hitler. Had he not already died (in 1552) it might also have been applied to St. Francis Xavier.

36. This one is rather obscure. The first two lines suggest the horror of burial of a person merely unconscious and not dead, as has happened (Gould and Pyle, pp. 519–22). The last two lines are probably a bit of wishful thinking that the Genevans would turn on Calvin. Roberts (1947) finds that "The escape of Hitler from embattled Berlin is here foreshadowed."

37. Le Pelletier applies this one to 1859. On January 1, Napoleon III, before the whole diplomatic corps, made some remarks to the Austrian ambassador that let the secret of the Franco-Piedmontese treaty out. The Austrians lost Lombardy (Milan) by the Treaty of Zurich (October 17) after the Emperor's series of deceptive moves. For the ancient wall, Le Pelletier can offer only Austria itself. The prophecy has also been interpreted for Napoleon I, who took Milan on May 15, 1796, and again on June 2, 1800. An especially famous speech occurred prior to the first occasion, when Napoleon took command of the Army of Italy:

> Soldiers, you are ill-fed and half naked. The government owes you much, but it can do nothing for you. Your patience, your courage, do honor to you, but

obtain for you neither advantage nor glory. I am going to lead you to the most fertile plains in the world; you will find there great cities, rich provinces; you will find there honor, glory and wealth. Soldiers of Italy, will you be wanting in courage?

38. Jaubert applies this one to the peace between the Pope and the Spanish on September 23, 1557. According to Jaubert, this is one month from vintage time. By this agreement, the Pope's French and Swiss forces under the Duke of Guise were left to fend for themselves.

39. Seven rulers are here in agreement for the division of Italy. Their arrangements are upset by their faint-hearted Genoese colleague. There were several leagues in the 16th century, especially the "Holy Leagues" formed in 1510 and 1576, but none of note in 1555, so the "Ligurian" reading is probably correct.

40. This one is hopelessly obscure.

41. Le Pelletier interprets this one for the murder of Louis of Condé on March 13, 1569.

> Prince Louis of Condé, small and hunch-backed, will be elected commander-in-chief by the council of Calvinist notables. Never was there seen on earth a more unworthy scoundrel. Montesquiou, in shooting him in cold blood (willingly) in the head, at the Battle of Jarnac, in 1569, will put an end to the incessant rebellions of this traitor who, twice before (in 1560 and in 1562) had obtained a pardon, by swearing loyalty to Charles IX.

This one seems to mark a completely successful application.

42. The reference to being born with two teeth is found also in 27—see its commentary regarding instances of this. The two prodigies are to serve as an omen of a great famine.

43. Both the Lot and the Tarn are tributaries of the Garonne. The gist of this quatrain is similar to that of 332. Ancona is on the east coast of central Italy, part of the former Papal States. In 174 and 279, "black frizzle beard" seemed to be the Turk, but here it is difficult to see how the Turk could prove the nemesis of a French force in central Italy. Le Pelletier interprets it for the fate of the Papal Zouaves (who he claims were recruited chiefly in southwest France). They were almost annihilated on September 18, 1860, at the Battle of Castelfidardo by the troops of Victor Emmanuel, who did indeed have a black beard, though of dubious frizzilosity.

44. This prophecy would seem to concern that great day when talking dogs are available. At the same time a virtuous maiden is to be hurled into the air by a bolt of lightning. But Le Pelletier has made something more ingenious out of it. Nostradamus foresaw that the French would call the trigger of the musket, perfected about 1630, after great pains, the *chien*. The leap is the recoil. *Foudre à vierge* is derived from a "latinism," *fulmen a virgâ*, for saltpeter, loaded with a ramrod into the barrel of the gun. The last line is supposed to refer to an explosion in the air, whatever that can mean with

reference to a musket shot. Writes Ward, Le Pelletier's British alter ego, of *chien:*

> This anticipation of the slang term of manufacture, a hundred years before the thing itself was used or named, seems to show an intimacy with what would be called matters of chance, that is inconceivable and beyond all comprehensibility.

Ward then goes on to reveal that he almost split his sides laughing at the naïveté displayed by Guynaud (1693) in *his* interpretation: Guynaud actually thought Nostradamus meant just what he wrote.

45. This one is quite clear. Five persons seeking the right of sanctuary in one of Toulouse's churches (apparently Nostradamus' favorite churches; they appear frequently) are slaughtered there by their pursuer, who will be tyrannizing over Toulouse. Something like this may well have happened during the Revolution.

46. The parenthesis in line 1 is rather confusing, but it is uniform in all texts. Apparently the verse marks another prophecy of doom for Lyons, similar to that of 283.

47. Another rather clear and specific one. A Christian ruler, unable to retain power, will seek help from the Sultan. During the struggle over the Hungarian succession, this is exactly what John Zapolya (John I) did (1528). But the rest differs. Restored to power, he will arouse such hatred for being a Turkish puppet that he will be forced to flee again. He takes refuge on Mytilene, an island off northwest Asia Minor, otherwise known as Lesbos.

48. To Roberts (1947) this is "an example of Nazi brutality to both civilians and combatants in World War II."

49. This verse is especially interesting as showing that *empire,* with a small *e,* can refer to France, rather than the Holy Roman Empire. Rouen was in Normandy, Chartres in the Orléanais. This is probably intended to provide a clue to the titles of the notables responsible for the disaster. The wording is such that it may yet be fulfilled.

50. The outstanding city-republics of the 16th century were Geneva, Genoa and Venice. There may be a connection with the *cité rigoreuse* of 133, in which case Geneva would be the certain subject, and line 3 might refer to an appeal to the King of France. Le Pelletier applies it to the Day of Barricades (May 12, 1588), when a popular insurrection in Paris, on behalf of Guise and the League, obliged Henry III to flee to Blois. "Later," writes Pelletier, "when Paris will be besieged by Henry III (ladder at the wall), it will repent of its rebellion." Actually, Henry fled to the camp of Henry of Navarre at Saint-Cloud, with no serious siege involved at that time. He was murdered there on July 31, 1589.

51. This one Le Pelletier (from Guynaud, and he probably from Chavigny) applies to the celebrated murder of the Guises on December 23, 1588.

Henry III is supposed to have plotted the murder at Paris. It was carried out in the Château of Blois. Upon hearing news of the murder, Orléans rose against Balzac d'Entragues, Henry's governor of Orléans, upon which Charles of Lorraine, Duke of Mayenne, one of the leaders of the League, took it over. The last line he interprets as three cities remaining loyal to Henry III, though admitting that the records are confused on that score. This is untrue. According to the local histories, Angers and Langres were definitely in with the League, and Troyes maintained a benevolent neutrality, so that some other interpretation would have to be found for line 4.

52. Campania is a province in western Italy, extending from north of Capua to south of Salerno. Apulia is in the east, just above the heel. As they are in the same latitude, and nearly contiguous, the meteorological variations mentioned here are a bit unlikely. The Cock, chief emblem of the Gauls, was adopted by the Revolutionists again, thus tearing the veil off at least one of Nostradamus' enigmas. The Eagle, besides being one of the devices of Charles V, always stands for empire. The Lion may refer to Venice's Lion of St. Mark.

53. Another of the very detailed and very obscure variety. In 1555 Nuremberg was a free city, Augsburg a bishopric, Bâle a Swiss canton, Cologne an archbishopric and Frankfort a free city. The only thing that all these places had in common is their being at least nominally a part of the Empire. The verse probably means nothing more than that shortly after a new Emperor is elected, the Imperial forces will invade France from the north.

54. Insofar as some detail can be found to fit the first line, this verse is general enough to be applied to any invasion of Spain from France via the Pyrenees. The two principal occasions were 1703–13 and 1808–13. Minor ones occurred in the 1640's, 1794–95 and 1822.

55. Le Pelletier applies this one to France 1559–89, notwithstanding the fact that the text clearly limits it to one year:

> After the year (1559) that Henry II will have lost an eye (from the blow of Montgomery), the court of France will be in great confusion. Henry III (the Great One of Blois) will convoke the Estates-General at Blois (1588), and will cause the Duke of Guise to be assassinated there, after having partaken of the holy sacrament with him, in sign of reconciliation and friendship. Then the kingdom, desolated and uncertain, will be divided into two opposing parties: the royalists on one side, and the Leaguers or Catholics on the other.

56. Another of the detailed and obscure variety. All the towns in line 1 are in southernmost France, though in scattered areas. Montpellier, about halfway from Béziers to Nîmes, was where Nostradamus got his doctorate. Nothing can be made of line 3. It is uncertain whether a date is indicated in line 4, and if so, whether it is 1653, 1746, 2208 or 2301.

57. This is certainly one of the most interesting of the quatrains. The period for fulfillment would seem 1555–1845. Some commentators start with Henry VIII's "revolution" of 1534. Ward's order for the changes is—

1. Protestant reversion under Elizabeth in 1558.
2. Stuart succession in 1603.
3. Commonwealth and Protectorate in 1649.
4. Restoration in 1660.
5. Glorious Revolution in 1688.
6. Hanoverian Succession in 1714.
7. Reform Bill in 1832.

He gives as optional omitting No. 7 and making No. 3 into two revolutions.

In Nostradamus' time, Britain was regarded as the most unstable of countries, in marked contrast to her more recent aura of conservatism and respectability. Line 3 is very interesting. It is always translated as "French," in contrast to "British," but it can also mean "free," so we see no reason to drag France into the prophecy. More likely it refers to British claims of national freedom from papal control, made vociferously clear by Henry VIII and under Edward VI. Nostradamus is probably saying simply that they'll be very far from having real freedom. The reference to Germanic support remains a real puzzler. Perhaps an alliance with the Lutherans is envisaged.

According to geopolitical cosmology, Aries presided over Britain, Germany, Denmark, Poland, Palestine and Syria. It is here always interpreted for Poland. The area inhabited by the classical Bastarnae coincided quite closely with the boundaries of Poland-Lithuania (as of 1555). All of which leads up to an application of line 4 to the partitions of Poland in the late 18th century.

Jaubert in 1656 admits he has counted only four changes. For line 3 he has a bright suggestion: the Germanic support that France (*franche*) will get will come through Louis XIV's having become Emperor. Reading *double* for *doute* in line 4, he gives an elaborate bit of cosmology to show that Aries will have doubled its pole in exactly 1845.

58. The classical Noricum corresponded roughly to the ancient Duchy of Austria, the Habsburg heartland. The Sarmatians lived in what is now southern Russia, but what was in Nostradamus' day Lithuania, united with the Polish crown since 1447. Apparently Nostradamus is predicting that a Habsburg prince, or some other Austrian, will become a Polish king or generalissimo, and defend it and Hungary (which he will have liberated) against the Turks or other enemies. The Polish dynasty expired in 1572; its last king, in Nostradamus' day, was without an heir. Curiously, the prophecy was fulfilled in reverse: From 1682 to 1699 Austria and Poland were allied in a war against the Turks, but it was the Polish King, John Sobieski, who defended the Austrians, by saving Vienna from the Turks in 1683. However, the Austrians under Charles of Lorraine conquered Hungary 1685–87 and were able to hold it till the Peace of 1699 recognized the cession. The quatrain has also been applied to the Austrian Hitler, with line 3 fulfilled 1944–45.

59. "Barbarian empire" properly would refer to that of the corsairs of North Africa (Barbary), but may be used for that of the Turks in general.

In interpretations dealing with France, *tiers* has been gleefully applied to the Third Estate, but that is hardly feasible here. Bouys (1806, p. 55) applies it to the French Revolution, evading the touchy issue of why the Bourbon dynasty should be the Barbarian Empire. Probably the prophecy is entirely for Turkey: a third son will seize the throne in a palace coup, putting many of his brothers to death, in the best Ottoman tradition. The fate of a younger brother or nephew is mentioned in the obscure words of line 3. The last line suggests that a son of one of the original victims will cause him some trouble.

60. Another prophecy for the Turks, possibly referring to the above usurper. The provinces in line 2 were all parts of classical Asia Minor. The gist would seem to be that the massacres of the bloody young Sultan will extend to Asia Minor.

61. Rather vague, except for the "New Crusades" theme. Mesopotamia, which was taken by the Turks from the Persians at about the time the Centuries were written (1555), is the land between the Tigris and the Euphrates (or between any two rivers). In other places it seems to be used for some French territory, possibly Avignon and the Venaissin enclave of the Popes.

62. This is an extremely interesting quatrain, very specific and very obscure at the same time. The sea mentioned in line 1 would ordinarily be identified with the Tyrrhenian Sea, but this is off the west coast of Italy and thus nowhere near the setting of this quatrain. The same word appears elsewhere, in rather odd context, and the solution would seem to be that Nostradamus read some book about the early Phoenician voyagers from Tyre and means to refer to them. The name of the mysterious Basque nation in northeast Spain has the same etymology as that of the Bay of Biscay, which is closed on three sides and is probably the sea intended. Indeed, one of the Bay's biggest ports, Bordeaux, is supposed to have originated as a Phoenician colony. Apparently some leader, perhaps one of the oriental conquerors, described in line 3 cryptically, is to launch an attack from a point between where the Douro River rises, in the mountains around Burgos, and the Bay of Biscay, effecting a crossing of the Pyrenees into France near the Bay of Biscay, then moving into the ancient city of Carcassonne.

63. This line has been applied to the Fascist regime much better than it could be for anything Nostradamus probably had in mind, Hitler being a neighbor of Mussolini after 1938. It would seem difficult to apply it to the 16th-century Papal States, which had no neighbor more powerful than Venice or Tuscany, unless the viceregal government of the Two Sicilies is made synonymous with full Habsburg might. It is possible that Roman refers to the Empire, rather than the Papacy, in which case the meaning might be that the Imperial Habsburgs would plays second fiddle to the Spanish branch, which was a neighbor in the Netherlands and northern Italy. This indeed happened, but it must be remembered that when the verse was written (not earlier than 1554 and not later than 1556), the division of Charles V's Empire was still somewhat uncertain. There was much question as to whether the divisions of 1555–56 would "stick."

64. The chief of Persia here may be the invader of 362, and is probably the same as the character in 296 and 586. It must be admitted that Spain does not seem to fit in too well with the geographical context, but the only Olcades lived there, near Cartagena in the Southeast. The trireme fleet is a fleet of ships with three banks of oars, likely to be Spanish or Venetian. Parthia and Media confirm the nationality of the invader, both being provinces of classical Persia. The Cyclades Islands are between Greece and Crete. The Ionian Sea is between Greece and Sicily, so that many ports are eligible: Syracuse, Catania, Otranto, Brindisi, Ragusa, Modona/Navarino, etc. After pillaging, the Persian rests at one of these ports, with the trireme fleet presumably destroyed.

65. This one is strictly for the Papacy. The finding of the tomb of a great Roman (lay or clerical? St. Peter? see also 615, 666, 984) will serve as an omen that the election of a Pontiff will take place on the next day. "The Senate" refers to the College of Cardinals. The last line is somewhat obscure, but we may gather that one way or another he is to be murdered.

66. Le Pelletier has an interesting interpretation for this one.

Jérôme Groslot, Bailiff of Orléans, will be arrested on November 9, 1561, and condemned, by the tribunal of the Inquisition, to be beheaded, for having wanted to deliver this town to the Calvinists. However, he will not die the death he had earned and he will not submit to his fate: but, having been poorly guarded, he will flee.

Unfortunately, a reading of the history of Orléans discloses several flaws in Le Pelletier's dates, beyond the primary flaw that line 1 has him clearly put to death. Jérôme opened the gates on April 13, 1562, and he was not condemned until November 9, 1569. What is most noteworthy is that the office of bailiff had been hereditary in the Groslot family since 1530, so that the prophecy is indeed clearly for a Groslot. (E. Bimbenet, *Histoire de la ville d'Orléans,* III, Orléans, 1887.)

67. This one should be applicable to most monastic orders. Line 3 is somewhat obscure, telling where they *don't* come from. Possibly the sect will begin in Germany, but then spread far beyond. Nostradamus perhaps anticipated a spectacular comeback for the Anabaptists, who had been more or less wiped out twenty years earlier.

68. This is a rather startling quatrain. We deal with Italy and Spain as national units. There is no reason to question *dict* as leader or dictator, Roman titles having much currency amidst the 16th-century rediscovery of classical lore. It does indeed all have a very modern sound. The only possible 16th-century interpretation is that Nostradamus is referring to Italians and Spaniards on an expedition against the Turks on, perhaps, the Greek peninsula. But this is far more forced than the one which fits currently, or potentially, in a 20th-century setting.

69. All is vague or obscure. The half-pig occurs elsewhere (164 and as half-man in 844). Perhaps the basis lies in a wrong version of the etymology

of "Milan." According to the legend, it derived its name from the discovery of a biformed pig (half pig and half sheep) at its first foundation. Mâcon and Châlon were in Burgundy.

70. According to Garencières, this one was fulfilled 1603–7. Line 1 he applies to the union of England and Scotland in 1603, line 2 to a flood in Somerset during January, 1607, which attained proportions 10 leagues long, 2 leagues wide and 12 feet high. The last two lines he applies to a renewal in 1606 of the Holy League of 1526 (France, Venice and the Papacy). But this is none too convincing. Line 2 may well be another instance of Nostradamus' conviction (222, 931) that Britain would "go under," literally. Most likely Nostradamus is predicting that while England or Brittany is suffering a tidal flood, there will be a renewal of the Italian Wars and intrigues that occupied so large a place in the 16th century.

71. Although the isles were probably meant for the Mediterranean isles (Corsica, Malta, etc.), the verse has been quite nicely applied to the British with respect to the Germans in World Wars I and, to some extent, II.

72. Although rather vague, and very parochial, this one is quite colorful.

73. Le Pelletier cannot refrain from applying this one to his Messiah, the Duke of Bordeaux (alias the Count of Chambord). Accordingly, he really succeeded to the throne on August 16, 1830, when Grandfather Charles X was sent off to Scotland. The competing near-bastard is none other than Louis-Philippe, of the "illegitimate" House of Orléans (quite legitimately descended from a brother of Louis XIV). Hugh Allen (1943, p. 510) sees this one, somehow or other, for Al Smith and Franklin D. Roosevelt.

74. Faenza and Imola were in the Papal States, while Florence and Naples were the chief cities, respectively, of Tuscany and the Two Sicilies. Nola is about seventeen miles east of Naples: nothing much has happened there since Hannibal was defeated, and Augustus died. However, something other than this ancient city may be intended.

75. Pau was in French Navarre, Saragossa in Spain and Verona and Vicenza in the Venetian Republic, making a strange combination. Perhaps all are to suffer invasion by the Oriental.

76. This one is probably intended for some extreme sect like that of the Anabaptists (or perhaps merely Lutherans). It has been applied quite nicely to National Socialism. The last line predicts that the erring Germans in question will go back to paying their tithe to the Catholic Church.

77. On this one Nostradamus really stuck his neck out. In 357 we found Aries presiding over Bastarnia (Poland-Lithuania). But, as we saw, it presides also over Syria and Palestine, the scene here. There was indeed a peace concluded in October, 1727, between the Turks and the Persians. Ashraf, usurping Shah of Persia, had defeated the Turks, but in return for recognition of his dynasty, he gave back Erivan, Tauris and Hamadan, and recognized the Sultan as legitimate successor of the Caliph. But even if the Turks are made "those of Egypt" by synecdoche (having conquered Egypt in 1517), they did not, by any stretch of the imagination, capture (or even de-

feat) the Persian ruler. Nor did this oriental diplomacy bring any particular shame to Christendom. It is impossible to see how this could ever have been, unless the Persians were seen as converted allies. Aside from the date, in the three centuries of intermittent warfare between the Turks and the Persians, no Shah was ever captured. And if "Egypt" is taken literally, there has been no war between Egypt and Persia since 1555 (or in fact since the 6th century B.C.), though there may well be one in the future. So this one must be considered a well-dated failure, although Roberts (1947) converts the date to "2025, under a special chronology enumerated by Nostradamus."

78. This one is extremely lucid, rich and colorful. Apparently some oriental expedition is to get to the North Sea and one way or another obtain as prisoners six German notables and the ruler of Scotland. Then they will sail around Spain, through the Strait of Gibraltar, and be brought before the new Cyrus.

79. Lines 1 and 2 are rather hopelessly obscure. The breaking of the chain of Marseilles (chains or booms being used as harbor defenses until very recently) occurs in the Epistle also. The last line suggests a Pyrrhic victory for the invader.

80. The variant of the subject, in line 1, makes an interpretation very difficult. Le Pelletier, using the "worthy" version, applies it to the fall of Charles I. Line 2 is applied to Strafford, thrown to the Parliamentary wolves in 1640. Line 3 becomes the treacherous Scottish army, which sold Charles to Parliament on January 30, 1647, for their back pay. The bastard of line 4 is of course Cromwell, received only as Protector, and not as full King.

The quatrain could probably be applied better to James II in 1688. He could fulfill either variant, being legally the worthy one, and privately quite unworthy. And he was chased out literally. However, it is not necessarily indicated that Nostradamus had in mind an English sovereign (as in 949). It might refer to some Protestant or Catholic prelates, in the seesaw struggle going on in Nostradamus' day. People were literally "put to the fire" then. The bastard of line 4 might have been intended for Elizabeth, frequently, and not unjustly, termed as such by her enemies, and so declared officially by Pope Paul IV. Several weeks did indeed elapse between the time she was conceived and the time of the wedding of Henry VIII and Anne Boleyn. In this case, "the worthy one" might have been intended for Philip of Spain, since 1554 husband of Queen Mary.

81. Jaubert makes a rather unconvincing application of this one to Francis of Vendôme, appointed Colonel of Infantry in 1557. It is so general as to be applicable to many rambunctious generalissimos. It could probably be applied best to the Catholic Generalissimo in the Thirty Years' War, Wallenstein.

82. Both Fréjus and Antibes are coastal towns southwest of Nice. Whether the devastation of line 2 is by locusts or by war is hard to tell. The invader by land could be the Emperor, the Duke of Savoy still being a refugee from his French-occupied land when this was written. The locusts in line 3

may be used figuratively for myriads of destructive invaders; an extreme, modern interpretation has been for airplanes.

83. This one is rather confusing. Celtic Gaul, or France, is here with a foreign ally enslaving Aquitaine, also part of France. Perhaps Aquitaine is seen as the British colony of 96. Le Pelletier elsewhere has it that the long hairs is used by Nostradamus for the Frankish nobility. To Roberts (1947) it is all clear. "The intellectuals [*sic!*] of Northern France, with the support of foreign agents, shall stamp out and imprison their opponents that favor the opposition view."

84. Le Pelletier applies this one to the extinction of Paris in his set of apocalyptic interpretations. Whatever city it is that is to suffer this fate, it is certainly an extreme fate.

85. The Robine is a stream, tributary to the Aude, extended to become a canal (in the Narbonne-Perpignan area). The city mentioned is likely to be one of these two. The prophecy is fairly clear.

86. This one is rather simple. A ruler or notable of either any Italian state, or the Two Sicilies in particular, will stop in Marseilles en route to Spain. But he will get no further than Marseilles, dying there. This could certainly have happened easily enough, but we know of no fulfillment of it.

87. Jaubert makes a very poor interpretation of this one to a French fleet under the Baron de la Garde in 1556. Le Pelletier's is more ingenious. In 1655, according to his version, the squadron of de la Ferrière went down to the last ship in a storm in the area specified. The "captive" is the master pilot Jean de Rian, a former galley slave.

88. Le Pelletier (from Guynaud) has a bright interpretation of this one for events of February 17, 1596.

> A Spanish fleet of twelve galleys, commanded by Charles Doria and sent by Philip II to help the Leaguers, will seize the isles of Château d'If and Ratonneau and will shut off all help for Marseilles by sea. Charles de Casau (the traitor), consul, who wanted to deliver the town to the Spanish, will be killed with a sword-thrust by Pierre Libertat, and the body of this traitor will be dragged by the populace in the gutters.

89. The last line is both detailed and incomprehensible. The last Lusignan King of Cyprus died in 1474 but a daughter married the Duke of Savoy and passed on the title to her descendants, one of whom is perhaps seen by Nostradamus as having regained Cyprus under Venetian aegis. Venice held Cyprus from 1489 to 1571, when the Turks completed its conquest. The verse might perhaps be accepted as a prediction that the Turks would capture it. "Those of the Aegean" probably refers to the Venetians, who held most of the Aegean isles till 1566. Line 2 was fulfilled quite well. According to the *Encyclopedia of World History*, after the Sultan declared war on Venice (1570), "Spain joined Venice in the war, but the two allies were unable to cooperate successfully and their fleets delayed the relief

of Cyprus until too late." After capturing Famagusta on August 3, 1571, after a siege of eleven months and six assaults, the Turks inflicted their usual carnage. But beyond this point, the prophecy is inapplicable. In the future, Cyprus may have its own king and queen again, in which case the quatrain may get another chance.

90. This one may tie in with 378. It appears to relate also to the new Cyrus. Both Carmania and Hyrcania were provinces of classical Persia. We have here a Persian expedition setting out from the Persian Gulf, but there being no Suez Canal then, it could not be entirely a naval one. The geography of the last line is uncertain. "Phocaean" is always used elsewhere for Marseilles, but Marseilles is not on the Tyrrhenian Sea. Was Marseilles another port Nostradamus associated with early Phoenician colonists from Tyre? (See Commentary on 362 in this connection.) It is, however, possible that two places are designated—a Tuscan port, and Marseilles—the Persian landing at each in succession.

91. Le Pelletier applies this one to the posthumous birth of his Messiah, the Duke of Bordeaux, on September 29, 1820. Owing to a fall from a horse, he was a cripple. The interpretation for the rest is rather unconvincing.

92. This one is rather obscure, an odd blend of the apocryphal and of the most specific details. Line 4 is obscure, while line 3 depends on the meaning of the *nation Brodde*. In all probability, it refers to the dark-tinted Spaniards. "Empire" is more likely the German Empire than the French nation. But the "empire transferred" phrase appears more than once— whatever it refers to.

93. Another of the detailed and obscure variety. Avignon belonged to the Papacy until 1791. All that we can guess at for Hannibal is "arch-enemy of Rome." Saint-Paul-Trois-Châteaux is a small town a few miles north of Orange on the east bank of the Rhône, while Troyes is a major city southeast of Paris, from which "troy" weight gets its name.

94. This one is rather vague. Perhaps Nostradamus meant it for himself. Roberts (1947), for reasons known best to himself, sees it as foretelling that "Sir Francis Bacon . . . shall be disclosed in a new light."

95. For the reader in the second half of the 20th century, this is one of the most interesting of all the prophecies of Nostradamus—one full of portentous meaning for this era, after having had none from the 16th to the 20th centuries. We now have the generic name "communism" to apply to the utopian ideologies of which Sir Thomas More's *Utopia* is the common ancestor. Undoubtedly this work, published in Latin when Nostradamus was in the midst of his education, was read by him. The prophecy implies a widespread success of this ideology prior to its decline, and mentions that the decline will start where the Dnieper is located. This is the principal river of the Ukraine. In Nostradamus' day it was one of the most backward parts of Europe, part of the Polish-Lithuanian state for three hundred years, and hardly an area Nostradamus would choose for the locale involving

any contemporary movement of this nature, such as the Anabaptists. Accordingly, it is not unreasonable to speculate on a possible 20th-century fulfillment of this prophecy, involving the Soviet Ukraine and perhaps its chief city (which is on the Dnieper), Kiev. The nature of the more seductive law and the more attractive tongue are subjects for further speculation. Another "decline of communism" prophecy is found in 432.

96. Le Pelletier, on the basis of the date, triumphantly applies this one to the assassination of his Messiah's father, the Duke of Berry, on February 13, 1820. But getting him to be the Chief of Fossano, and getting Louvel, his assassin, to be a leader of bloodhounds and greyhounds, is a bit too ridiculous. Furthermore, Wöllner finds that this was not one of the February 13's when the configuration occurred. The years, for seven centuries, are 1565, 1595, 1624, 1654, 1683, 1713, 1742, 1771, 1801, 1830, 1860, 1889, 1919, 1948, 1977, 2007, 2036, 2066, 2095, 2124 and 2154. Fossano was in the Duchy of Savoy, and it is probably a Duke of Savoy whose assassination is portrayed here. The assassin would seem to be something akin to a "master of the hunt." The meaning of line 3 is probably that the conspirators are either traitors or Romans.

97. This one belongs to the "New Crusades" theme. Once again (as in the 12th century), Christendom is to possess the eastern shore of the Mediterranean. The barbarian empire is probably that of the Turks here. Wöllner has it that the first completion of a cycle of the moon after 1555 was in 1576 (next, 1828, 2080, 2332, etc.). However, if this prophecy was not fulfilled as soon as Nostradamus intended, it was at least fulfilled in 1917–20 by the French and British.

98. This prophecy is fairly simply, though never fulfilled. It came closest with respect to Henry III and the Duke of Alençon (1574–84), and Louis XIII and the Duke of Orléans *ca.* 1632, but in neither case was the plotting quite that strong. The anonymous critic of 1724, the exponent of the "retroactive prophecy" theory, explains that this verse is merely an enigmatic history of the struggle between the sons of Suleiman (1558–59, according to him)—which results in quite a compliment for our prophet, since the quatrain was in print in 1555!

99. The battleground is clearly specified here. Alleins and Varnègues are two villages a few miles northeast of Salon, Nostradamus' home town. The Lubéron Mountains are on the north side of the Durance River. From the Epistle there is much reason to believe that Mesopotamia refers to a European state, probably Avignon and the Venaissin enclave of the Popes.

100. This one is general enough to be applied to any great general who had previously been out of favor. Recently it has been applied to General de Gaulle, with line 4 applied to the assassination of Admiral Darlan (December 24, 1942).

# *Century IV*

1. This one might be applied to the Turkish attack on Cyprus (1570–73) and to the war over Crete (1645–64). Venice got little or no help. The chief city of Cyprus, Famagusta, fell to the Turks on August 3, 1571, after a siege of eleven months. But the verse is too general to reflect much glory on Nostradamus.

2. As Le Pelletier shows, this verse was fairly well fulfilled in the War of the Spanish Succession.

> In 1700, as a result of the will of Charles II, Philip V, grandson of Louis XIV, will mount the throne of Spain. But Austria, England, Holland, Prussia, Portugal and Savoy will form a coalition to support the pretensions of Archduke Charles: the fleets of France will take to the sea; her armies will pass over the Pyrenees; Spain, divided into two camps, will be trampled by the feet of soldiers. This terrible war will arise from the rights conferred on the House of Bourbon by the marriage of the two Infantas of Spain, eldest daughters of Philip III and of Philip IV, with the Kings of France Louis XIII and Louis XIV.

However, the interpretation of the last line is rather forced.

It is worth noting the interpretation Guynaud gives in his edition of 1693 (seven years *before* the event). His interpretation of the last line, far more in accord with Nostradamus' probable meaning, is the only part not fulfilled:

> This could be understood as a King of Spain coming to die without children, and this Kingdom, following the Laws of the Estate, falling into the female line; France, i.e., the King, will put armies on foot, by sea as well as by land, and that he will march at their head, to sustain his rights and make it clear that this Kingdom belongs to him legitimately, as the nearest successor; so well that the army will march by land across the Pyrenees against the Spaniards, who at this time will be greatly divided; thereafter, things will quiet down because there will be found some Spanish princess of marriageable age whom one of our Princes will marry with great advantages and will lead off with him to France.

3. The meaning of *Brodes* remains uncertain, but as the context calls for Spaniards, it is probably a reference to the dark complexions of many of the Spanish soldiers of Moorish descent. Arras was in Artois, north of the French border until 1659. But Bourges is in the very heart of France; it must be either an erratum or metathesis for Bruges in Flanders, which the context calls for. Thus, line 1 would simply refer to another Habsburg invasion from the North, as indeed occurred about two years after the verse was written, climaxed by the Battle of Saint-Quentin (1557). Line 2 denotes that most of the French troops opposing them will be Gascons. Lines 3 and 4, however, suggest a French invasion of Spain, which did

not come off for another century. Or perhaps merely a naval engagement in denoted. Sagunto, halfway down the east coast of Spain, is at the foot of a spur of the Peñas de Pajarito, though it is difficult to see what significance that could have in the prophecy.

4. Inasmuch as the cocks are the French (the cock was the chief emblem of the Gauls), and the Libyans their infidel allies (specifically, the Algerian corsairs), the impotent prince must be a Habsburg ruler, or one of his satellites, such as the Medici Duke of Florence. Indeed, Duke Cosimo had been entrusted with the defense of Elba and contiguous territories. When they were ravaged by the corsair Dragut in 1555, he undoubtedly was told off by Charles V or the Duke of Alba. The last line, however, is quite confusing. It suggests that while the French will suffer reverses in Italy, they will be successful elsewhere. If, as it seems, Nostradamus intended the quatrain for the immediate future, it turned out just the opposite: the French held their own in Italy and suffered disastrous defeat in the North.

5. This quatrain represents one of the boldest of prophecies. A conquest of one country by the other was not to be considered, and a merger of Spain and France would seem equally impossible. Nowhere near the horizon in Nostradamus' day, it is still not on the horizon in the 20th century. Or perhaps only a military alliance is indicated. Possibly the verse belongs to the somewhat apocryphal era of the World Emperor and Antichrist. Indeed, the last two lines suggest the Antichrist.

6. This one is rather hopelessly obscure. "The new clothes" may refer to a new order of monks. It is not certain that the city of Venice is called for in the last line. There is a color called Venetian red which has a yellowish-brown appearance.

7. A very lucid and precise prophecy, but if there was ever a fulfillment of it, the secret has been well guarded.

8. Unfortunately, nothing happened at the Battle of Saint-Quentin (two years after publication) to justify this verse, and neither Jaubert nor Le Pelletier attempted it. It fell by storm after a seventeen-day siege. But at least Nostradamus gets credit for prophesying the capture of Saint-Quentin (August 10, 1557).

9. Geneva was an independent state, since 1536 a theocratic republic under John Calvin and a sort of world headquarters for all Protestants. One of many Nostradamian prophecies on the doom of Calvin, this one apparently has it that the Genevans are to be the last Calvinist holdouts, after Lausanne and other Swiss Calvinist centers have again seen the light of Rome.

10. A fairly lucid and very colorful quatrain, of which we know of no fulfillment. The chief must be the commander of the army, who makes the mistake of supporting the Prince. A new king is denoted in line 4. Only the Kings of France and England were credited with curing scrofula by their touch (especially on their coronation day).

11. Another of the detailed yet obscure variety. A Pope will be talked into taking some drastic action, which will be either opposed or carried out by twelve cardinals. Most likely, the twelve cardinals will be hostile, and after causing the Pope to be killed, will commit further murders (a sort of Papal Committee of Public Safety or Politburo).

12. This one is very general, and probably capable of many interpretations, of which the most recent would be the German invasions of France in World Wars I and II. The plural *Gaules* suggests the ancient Roman provinces outside modern France bearing that name, such as Transpadane Gaul (Lombardy) and Cispadane Gaul (between the Po and the Rubicon), later lumped as Cisalpine Gaul.

13. Garencières here gives one of the few interpretations not stolen from Jaubert. He applies it to the 1580's when a rumor spread through the army of the Duke of Parma of a great defeat, leaving them so demoralized that the Dutch succeeded in capturing Antwerp for a short time. The double phalanx he applies to infantry and cavalry, which is none too convincing. The classical Macedonian phalanx, 16 men deep and 50 across, would total 800. Double would be 1,600. On the whole, the verse is rather general.

14. Another general prophecy, designed to fit any ruler who, coming to power very young, surprises his contemporaries by proving an able leader and conqueror. Alexander of Macedon and Charles XII of Sweden are both good examples. Larmor (1925) applied it to 1661, when the successive deaths of Cardinal Mazarin and his royal mistress, Queen Anne, made Louis XIV at last sole ruler. Bouys (1806) applied it to Louis XVI and Napoleon I. To Hugh Allen (1943) it somehow or other showed that Roosevelt would die in January, 1944, and be succeeded by Henry Wallace.

15. Whatever Nostradamus may have had in mind, this one fits nothing so well as World War II: lines 1 and 2 to be applied to Britain. The Germans hoped to starve her out, but instead she became the seat of an incredibly large concentration of food as well as other commodities. "The eye of the sea" is a perfectly good figure for the periscope of Nazi U-boats. In line 4, of course, we have American aid.

16. Europe being full of free cities in the 16th century, one can only guess at which one Nostradamus had in mind. If France is the scene, the leading candidate would be Orange, which gave its name to the Dutch dynasty, and was not annexed by France until 1713. In our prophet's day, it had been inherited by the future William the Silent in 1544 and was a refuge for Protestants, for whom the epithets of line 2 may well be intended. In that case, "the King" would refer to Henry II or a successor.

17. It may or may not be pertinent to mention some facts about the Carmelites here. The first Carmelite order of nuns was founded in 1452. St. Theresa had a vision, which led her to seek to reform the order in 1554. Had Nostradamus gotten wind of this comparatively obscure Spanish news? If the answer is positive, the line would suggest her finding a patron in a powerful duke. It was not until 1562 that she succeeded with her

"Discalced Carmelite Nuns of the Primitive Rule of St. Joseph." However, the gibberish of lines 3–4 seem to have no connection therewith. All the towns were in Burgundy, eastern France.

18. This one clearly enough predicts a persecution of astrologers, which does not seem to have come off in such an extreme manner. There is a similar prediction in 871.

19. Rouen was taken by the troops of the Duke of Parma (aiding the Guises against Henry of Navarre) on April 16, 1592, but without much of a siege. It is highly unlikely that there were sizable Milanese contingents in his forces; however, since Milan was amongst the Spanish dominions, it is not impossible. Rouen was again taken without much of a siege by the Germans in 1870 and 1940, and by the Americans in 1944, but never, never by the Italians. Liège, Hainaut and Flanders, were all amongst the provinces of the Netherlands. Ghent is a city in Flanders. Since the Netherlands, or at least the southern part thereof, continued to belong to the Habsburgs till 1795, any Habsburg invasion from the North would fulfill lines 3–4. While the prophecy is clear enough, it has never been borne out.

20. This one is too hopelessly vague for any interpretation. Although the fleur-de-lys was the emblem of the French kings, it was also used by many other families.

21. This rather vague prophecy has been applied quite nicely to the French scene between 1940 and 1944, with lines 1 and 2 referring to the Fall of France and Pétain's centralized decentralization, line 3 to de Gaulle, and line 4 to the whole scene. However, it could serve the Interregnum of 1589–94 equally well. Henry of Navarre goes in for de Gaulle, and shares line 3 with the Duke of Parma or some exiled potentate of the League. The change would then refer to that of dynasty, or really of branch (Bourbon for Valois-Angoulême).

22. The political action here is rather confusing. Apparently a certain king, after quarreling with an ally, and demanding the withdrawal of the latter's forces, suddenly begs that troops be furnished him again. But one of them breaks a promise and the King is left to his fate without any power. A fairly logical chain of events, it may have occurred on more than one occasion.

23. Whatever formula is to be envisaged by line 2, it is perhaps Nostradamus' recipe for "Greek Fire," the great secret weapon of the Byzantines, used in one form or another for over a thousand years. The possible meanings of magnesia are nearly infinite. To Pliny it was hematite, to the Greek alchemists a pyrite, to the Latin alchemists an alloy of tin and mercury. In modern chemistry, it is magnesium oxide. Which did Nostradamus have in mind? In line 4 we have the mysterious *Port Selin* again, identified as Genoa. Here and at Monaco, fires will be set. By the Algerian pirates? It just so happened that Monaco was one of the few vulnerable places along this coast untouched by the corsairs since Nostradamus' day. As for

line 3, Toulon was used by Barbarossa as a base while aiding the French against the Emperor in Italy in the 1540's.

Jaubert changes *Hercle* to *chercher*, states that Port Selin is any port on the ocean, and applies the verse to an action by some Dieppe ships against the Spaniards in November, 1555. Line 3, more convincingly, he applies to Calais, held so peacefully by the English from 1347 to 1558. According to Roberts (1947), "A terrific assault by a great fleet equipped with weapons employing potent chemical agents shall attack a country which has long enjoyed peace and security. They shall attack the great Port of LES N.Y. [*sic!*] but shall be repulsed by weapons even more terrible."

24. The general purport of this very obscure quatrain seems to be the persecution of the Church, instigated by some sort of fanatically anticlerical regime. A fairly decent fulfillment might be found in France during the Terror.

25. Le Pelletier makes rather an interesting interpretation for this one.

When the perfection of optical instruments will have permitted one to distinguish stars beyond the range of the eye, which one will assume to be worlds, gravitating endlessly in the depths of the sky, one will draw from this discovery rationalizations hostile to religious beliefs. The materialists, subordinating the soul to the body and recognizing neither God nor superior spirits, will deliver a blow to traditional worship.

Since the telescope was not invented until 1610, this would be a prophecy within a prophecy.

26. Le Pelletier makes a fairly good case for applying this one to the Eighteenth Brumaire (November 9), the 1799 *coup d'état* of Bonaparte. The bees were indeed taken by Napoleon as the emblem of his dynasty. "Five babblers" is not a bad term for the Directory, which gave way to Napoleon's Consulate. But unfortunately there was no ambush at night. (Le Pelletier explains that the coup was prepared on the previous night.) Furthermore, *treilhos/treilles* means very specifically vines, and there is not the slightest justification for distorting it to *tuiles*. However, the application is probably as good as any that will ever be made for this obscure verse. Why it should have been written in Provençal is the most obscure point of all.

27. Few quatrains require more research than this one. In the first place, we have *Mansol*, another of the great Nostradamian mystery words, appearing elsewhere as *Mausole* and *Saint Pol de Mauseole*. It is the latter which provides the key, and it is not unlikely that the *n* is a misprint for *u*, copied from the initial erratum.

Just outside the confines of Saint-Rémy, where Nostradamus was born, there are two great Roman monuments, side by side. One is a mausoleum (by popular belief, though not according to archeologists), perhaps the most famous one in Provence. Its shape roughly resembles that of a pyramid. The other is an arch of triumph. On the mausoleum is the following inscription: SEX. L.M. JULIEI C.F. PARENTIBUS SUEIS. Various scholars have taken cracks at filling it in, and Nostradamus' version is recorded amongst them (Abbé Paulet, *Saint-Rémy de Provence*, Avignon, 1907), proving his familiarity with it. His version ran *Sextus Lucius Manlius Juliae Istam Columnam Fecit Parentibus Sueis.*

In the late 4th century, near this spot, there lived a hermit who became St. Paul. After he went off to become Bishop of Trois-Châteaux (renamed Saint-Paul-Trois-Châteaux), the people of Glanum, as Saint-Rémy was then called, built a priory and named it after him. But because there was also a convent in Saint-Rémy named for St. Paul, the one outside came to be called that of Saint-Paul-de-Mausole, after the nearby monument. Nostradamus undoubtedly spent many hours here with his grandfather during his impressionable years, and uses the name of the priory to refer to his birthplace, in his continual lust for obscurity.

The solution to line 3 is less certain. The clues are found in later instances of Nostradamus' use of "Annemark," from which it appears to be his ingenious short word to designate the Kingdoms of Bohemia and Hungary, both of which became hereditary crown lands of the Austrian Habsburgs in 1526, when the King of Hungary and Bohemia, Louis II, fell in battle against the Turks (see "Historical Background"). By a treaty previously arranged by the fathers of the parties concerned, Louis' sister Anne became the heiress and thus brought these territories to her husband Ferdinand, brother of Charles V, who in 1531 was elected "King of the Romans" i.e., King of Germany, and was expected to succeed Charles V shortly as Emperor. Ferdinand was thus the first *King* of this "Annemark" (or frontier provinces of Anne) and Maximilian, son of Ferdinand and Anne, would be the *Prince* of Annemark (and in 641 Nostradamus, looking ahead, has him as the "second chief of 'Annemark'"). From his astrological rigmarole, and perhaps from rumors he'd heard of Maximilian's Lutheran leanings, Nostradamus seemed to decide that Maximilian would turn Protestant. In any event, because of events involved with this, or for some other reason, Maximilian, twenty-eight years old when the prophecy was written, is to be confined in a prison in this area at some time in the future, which in due course brings an army bent upon rescuing him. As it turned out, no such thing ever happened, and Maximilian "straightened out," abandoning his Lutheran leanings in 1560. He was "elected" King of Bohemia in 1562, King of Hungary in 1563 (thus rounding out "Annemark") and in 1564 Holy Roman Emperor. We shall return to these facts about Maximilian subsequently, since Nostradamus seemed to give him much attention.

Getting back again to the details of the quatrain, the last line involves ruins of a temple of Diana (such as the one at Nîmes) in this area, but it is unlikely that the prince is supposed to be confined there. A more likely place would be the Castle of Tarascon, often used as a prison.

28. As Garencières suggests, 428, 429, 430, 431 and 433 may all be intended to refer to the discovery of the "philosopher's stone," for the transmutation of lesser metals into gold. The Sun stands for gold. Otherwise it is incomprehensible.

29. Reading Sun as gold, Vulcan as fire, and Hermes as identical with Mercury, we have a continuation of 428. For alchemists only.

30. The Moon is probably used here for silver.

31. The hero of this one is the great "philosopher" who makes the discovery. Line 4 is hopelessly obscure, but suggests that our hero comes to some sort of violent end.

32. Another extremely fascinating quatrain, associated with 395 in predicting the decline of communism. Since there is no bizarre Ukrainian setting for this one, there exists the possibility of Nostradamus' foreseeing communist trends amongst some local and contemporary group, presumably one of the Protestant sects. In this connection, Larmor (1925, p. 153) writes of "Protestant Communists" being the subject of the prophecy. The first and third lines are thoroughly obscure.

33. This one is certainly similar to 428–31, and may belong to the cycle (which suggests that perhaps 432 does also). Or it may indeed refer to a celestial configuration. What is most curious is that Neptune, which now seems perfectly well in place amongst all these planets, was not discovered and named until 1846—which leaves Le Pelletier triumphant. Since this planet is not visible to the naked eye, it could hardly be obscuring Venus, or in fact be intended here at all. What did Nostradamus use "Neptune" for? Aquarius?

34. Another very rich and pregnant one. King "Chyren" is, of course, King Henry, and notwithstanding all wishful thinking that Nostradamus meant the Chyren-Selin ones for a Charlemagne of the distant future, the evidence is overwhelming that he meant it for his own Henry II (see Index for other references). The French and the Habsburgs had been fighting over Italy for more than half a century, with many changes of fortune. Here the Habsburg ruler or one of his Italian satellites (such as the Medici Duke of Florence) is to go down in defeat before Henry II in both Milan and Naples (the two areas claimed by France), have his army wiped out and be brought a captive in golden chains to Henry—a fanciful bit of prophetic chauvinism. The Ausones dwelt in what became the Kingdom of Naples. In any event, no captive since 1555 has been put in gold chains to be presented to any King Henry.

35. The virgins in line 1 are apparently suggested by those of ancient Rome, charged with eternal vigilance in guarding the sacred flame of Vesta. Etruria is the classical equivalent of Tuscany. Line 3 suggests a "secret weapon." Both Tuscany and Corsica were fair game for the French then, Tuscany being ruled by an ally of the Emperor, and Corsica belonging to his fairly faithful Genoa. But the prophecy is too obscure for much to be made of it.

36. Another of the rich and detailed, but obscure, variety. Whatever line 1 may mean, the French did not again enjoy victory in a campaign around Milan till 1796. Lines 3 and 4 suggest further French victories in Spain and central Italy (or Germany if "Roman Empire" is intended). Once again, the nearest this verse came to fulfillment was in the time of Napoleon.

37. Whatever Nostradamus may have intended it for, this verse was quite well fulfilled in 1800. Genoa was besieged by the Austrians and finally surrendered on June 4. The British fleet, which had been helping with a blockade, made an attack on Monaco on May 23. This is fine if the British fleet can be called a red fleet; unfortunately, except where used for cardinals, red designates the Spanish, whose color it was, with Nostradamus. In May, Napoleon made his dramatic passage of the Great St. Bernard Pass with 40,000 men. On June 2 he took Milan. Nostradamus may have had something like this is mind, with the Duke of Guise for Napoleon, and the Spanish fleet for the British.

38. Samothrace is an island just west of the Dardanelles. The Byzantine chief is the Sultan, or a great Turkish leader.

39. After the surrender of Rhodes to the Turks (1522), Charles V installed the Knights of St. John on Malta (1530). Nostradamus is probably writing of them here. Unless the verse is a "retroactive prophecy" for 1522, we must assume that it concerns Malta. The long-expected siege came in 1565. "Arab empire" might perhaps be merely a poetic device for the Turks or Algerians, but elsewhere our prophet seems to foresee a really distinct new Arab Empire. Line 4 might be vaguely considered a foreshadowing of the victory over the Turks at the Battle of Lepanto (1571), to which Spain contributed the most.

40. Too general for any interpretation.

41. A rich and colorful quatrain, though far from clear. Apparently a woman held as hostage will put one over on her guards, then on the general. But when the general discovers that he has been duped, he hands her over to the mob, to meet a horrible death. Hugh Allen (1943, p. 608) somehow or other sees this one as an American officer of German descent allowing a captive Hitler to escape.

42. The great distances separating the places herein, with no common denominator, make this verse rather incomprehensible. Geneva and Lausanne were Calvinist centers in Switzerland; Langres was in Burgundy, Dôle in Franche-Comté, Chartres in the Orléanais and Montélimar in Dauphiny. There are twin towns on opposite sides of the Rhône, below Geneva, named Seyssel. When the quatrain was written, both legally belonged to the Duke of Savoy, but were under French occupation. The one on the west bank, to which Nostradamus probably refers, became French with the annexation of Bresse in 1605. The one on the east bank did not become French till the annexation of Savoy in 1860. The mark is usually considered to equal half a pound.

43. Jaubert quotes César Nostradamus to the effect that in 1557 prodigies were seen in the heavens. Line 2 he reads "divine enemies," which becomes "enemies of the divine," and hence Protestant heretics. That year the Protestants began showing greater strength, and a raid in the rue Saint-Jacques of Paris netted many captives. For line 3, Jaubert tells of how d'Andelot had the effrontery in 1558 to start preaching Protestant theology to Henry II. Line 4 he reads as Protestant revenge against the faithful (believing well). All of which fits fairly well, but the quatrain is general enough to allow of other interpretations, including ones involving modern aerial warfare.

44. The big puzzler about this one is the reason for the dashes of Spanish and Provençal. Little can be offered except in regard to place names. Castres and Mende were in Languedoc, Limoges in the Limousin, all the other places in Guienne. But all are in southwest France.

45. This quatrain has a rather modern ring to it, suggesting Napoleon I (Waterloo) or Napoleon III (Sedan) or Kaiser Wilhelm II. A good 16th-century possibility would be Sebastian, King of Portugal. He went on a "crusade" against the Moors. On August 4, 1578, his army was wiped out at the Battle of Kasr Al-Kabir, and he himself was "missing in action."

46. Nantes is in Brittany, Tours in Touraine, Reims in Champagne. Nantes and Tours are both on the Loire, Reims quite far away to the northeast. The bringing in of London makes this one quite international, and utterly incomprehensible. Perhaps it ties in with 261.

47. Le Pelletier gives the classic interpretation of this one, for St. Bartholomew's Day (August 24, 1572). The savage king is Charles IX, who merited the epithet in many ways. A great hunter, he delighted in cutting off the heads of asses and pigs he met on the way, with one blow. "Drawn bows" Le Pelletier somehow sees for arquebuses, and points out that Charles IX sat in the Louvre, taking pot shots at the fleeing Huguenots from his window. With regard to line 4, after Admiral Coligny had been killed and dragged through the streets by the mob, he was hung up by one foot.

One might think that Garencières belonged to the 20th century from where he goes for his interpretation (in 1672): "Since the Author did write there had been such a Tyrant in the world, namely, John Basilides, great Duke of Russia, in the year 1572. Read Paul Osburne in his Life." The person to whom he refers, curiously *using the same year* as for the French interpretation, is better known as Ivan the Terrible.

48. Ausonia, properly, would correspond to the Kingdom of Naples. The most notable plain in southern Italy is that of Campania on the west coast. Nothing more seems to be predicted here than the coming of countless swarms of insects to devour the products of the plain.

49. This one is hopelessly vague and obscure.

50. This is an extremely fascinating quatrain. According to Pearce, the

only two European states that Libra influenced were Austria and Savoy, so that the prophecy may be that Austria would see a separate Spain (separated after the death of Charles V), as distinct from the conglomerate empire of Charles V, become supreme. Austria did indeed become a sort of junior partner to the arrogant Spaniards. Line 3 suggests calamity for the Turks, which did not occur (the Battle of Lepanto had no long-range significance). It may be that the monarchy of heaven goes with line 4 to mean a succession of seven Spanish Popes. This has never occurred. Since 1523 there have been only Italian Popes.

For the less conservative-minded, the contemporary possibilities of applying it to the United States are fairly obvious, with line 2 suggesting an American Pope and line 3 some rather widespread use of H-bombs.

51. The French town of Ganges is in Languedoc, about twenty-five miles north of Montpellier.

52. Allen (1943, p. 536) is sure that this one refers to the siege of New York City by the "Nazi-Fascist-Communist forces" in late 1942; Mayor LaGuardia is the subject of line 2.

53. This one is too vague to be of any significance. It is a typical specimen of one type of Nostradamian quatrain.

54. Bouys (1806, p. 83) first applied this one to Napoleon, and this application can't be beaten. To a lesser extent it could be applied to Napoleon III. It is unlikely ever again to fit anyone else so well. Since Nostradamus' time, the Napoleons have been the only crowned rulers of France with a new name (otherwise the score is Louis 6 [counting Louis-Philippe: 7], Henry 2, Charles 2, Francis 1). Lines 2 and 3 were very clearly fulfilled by Napoleon I but not Napoleon III. Line 4 is applicable to either Napoleon I or III, in either variant, as well as to many other rulers. Napoleon I had his Creole and his Pole, Napoleon III his Spaniard.

55. This one is very clear and very specific. Two events will serve as an omen that a tyrant will be murdered. The first one is a crow sitting on a brick tower and screeching for seven hours. The second is a statue starting to bleed. Fantastic as the latter sounds, every once in a while, even in the 20th century, it is claimed that some famous relic was seen to give forth blood (frequently helped by the mechanisms installed by priests to please their miracle-loving flocks).

56. This one is too vague and obscure to be of much note. What clear elements there are were probably more nearly fulfilled by Hitler than any other famous leader, "raving tongue" being a highly suitable epithet for the Fuhrer.

57. One cannot but wonder whether the writings referred to are Nostradamus' Centuries, being maligned by an enemy before Henry II. In that case line 3, obviously indicating a royal mistress, would refer to Diane de Poitiers. A similar prediction appears in 79. Line 4 is hopelessly obscure.

58. *The New York Times* writer who reviewed Roberts' book (1947) chose this one as most typical, either of Nostradamus or of Roberts' (in this case Garencières') interpretations. We offer the latter, "Molten gold shall be poured into a throat and human blood shall flow. Because of this, a great water carrier shall make his son effeminate *(lead his son to spin)*, and a captive lady shall be exiled."

59. This thoroughly obscure verse is noteworthy chiefly for containing one of the few still unsolved proper names, "Nira." It probably has some sort of connection with Calvin.. As we stated, it is probably nothing more than an erratum for "IVRA" (Jura). Some modern-minded interpreters have raised the totally irrelevant point that it is a perfect anagram for Iran (Persia). There is no hint that it is connected with the "Persian conqueror" theme.

60. *Otage* appears in its O.F. form of *hostage*, which leads Le Pelletier to identify it with a "roman" word, *hostaige*, "house," of which we find no trace. He thus applies it to the seven children left by Henry II in the House of Valois. The third, instead of being the third of the seven hostages, is the Third Estate, represented by the proto-Revolutionary Council of Sixteen, which Le Pelletier accuses of having sent Jacques Clément to murder Henry III (August 1, 1589). Line 3 he applies quite nicely to Henry's murder of the Guise brothers (December 23–24, 1588). Line 4 really taxes the old boy. Genoa becomes Duke Charles-Emmanuel I of Savoy, "Genoa being an important town in his States" (in the 19th century, but not in the 16th). Florence turns into Alexander Farnese, Duke of Parma, because Parma was founded by the Etruscans, or ancient Tuscans, and Florence is the capital of Tuscany. These two leaders both made war against Henry of Navarre during the Interregnum (1589–94), which fact Le Pelletier applies to the last line, ignoring the singular form of the verb, and making further devious claims too absurd to waste space on.

61. Line 1 would apply very nicely to Marshal Pétain, but not so the rest. Just what picture line 3 is intended to convey is a perplexing question. Chartres and Orléans were both in the Orléanais and Rouen in Normandy. The prophecy may have been intended for old Constable Montmorency, to be replaced in power by the Guise, "foreigners" from Lorraine.

62. Garencières felt quite strongly about this one. "I never saw the late Tyrant Cromwell better painted to the life, than in the three first verses." The first permanent rank of colonel (really Colonel-General of Infantry) was created in 1547, and the post was given to Admiral Coligny, who may be the intended subject and, from a Catholic point of view, fulfilled it pretty well, becoming the leader of the Huguenot armies. But we know of no fulfillment of line 4, unless somehow associated with the St. Bartholomew's Day Massacre (August 24, 1572), of which he was the first victim.

63. Another very specific prophecy. The French army will run into

trouble amongst mountain peasants famous for their bird-calling abilities. Either Savoyard or Swiss peasants are probably intended. In the course of French expansion, and especially during the Napoleonic Wars, the prophecy was fulfilled either way, though not as drastically as line 4 suggests. Larmor (1925, p. 164) applies it to Marshal Villars' struggle (1702–4) against the Camisard (Protestant peasant) rebels of the Cevennes, who pioneered in guerilla warfare.

64. Another of the detailed yet obscure variety.

65. This quatrain can be applied quite nicely to Napoleon III. He was indeed condemned for the Franco-Prussian War and the disaster it brought to France. He died soon after (1873). Lines 1 and 2 can be applied well enough to his surrender of Sedan to the Prussians (September 1, 1870). The Prussians in turn fulfilled line 3 well enough.

66. Of the detailed yet obscure variety. Seven shaven heads presumably refer to seven clerics of one sort or another.

67. Probably the configuration delineated here is nothing more than a conjunction of Saturn and Mars, which is very common.

68. This one is quite rich and colorful. Line 1 may mean that the prophecy will be fulfilled when the earth in its orbit around the sun (or vice versa, the point being then in dispute) comes very close to the planet Venus. Or, alternatively, a town with a name derived from Venus may be intended. The greatest one of Asia is probably the Sultan. The greatest one of Africa in the 16th century was the Beylerbey of Algiers, a position held by the Barbarossas, and then by Dragut. Line 3 is quite incomprehensible. Line 4 suggests the attacks made by the Algerian corsairs against Malta and the Ligurian coast during much of the 16th century. The great Siege of Malta took place in 1565, almost a decade after the verse was written. Nice, which might be considered on the Ligurian coast, suffered its great siege by the Turks (as French allies) in 1546. Except for a brief raid on the eve of Pentecost, 1556, there was no further siege of Nice till those by the French in July, 1623, May, 1691, and April, 1705. Genoa is the chief port of Liguria proper. This prophecy may yet have a fulfillment in the future that will accomplish the difficult task of involving both line 2 and line 3.

69. Aquileia, a great city of the late ancient and early medieval period, was already reduced to little more than a village in the 16th century. As Venice was founded by its citizens, and fell heir to its power (see Commentary for 158), the Venetians may be intended here. Parma, which belonged to the Papacy since 1511, was made into a hereditary duchy on August 26, 1545, by Pope Paul III, for his bastard, Pierluigi Farnese. Little can be offered as to the meaning behind the obscurities.

70. The Eagle is the symbol for the Emperor and the Empire. Until 1556, the Emperor held Spain too. Until 1659, Spain extended north of the Pyrenees to include Roussillon, of which Perpignan was the chief city. Although this verse was probably written after the partition of Charles' Empire (1555–56), Spain may be intended here. Pau, the capital of the King-

dom of Navarre, is also just north of the Pyrenees, but more than one hundred miles west of Roussillon.

71. For all the work involved in solving the involved bits of etymology, this verse remains hopelessly obscure and worthless. Aconite is a classic poison, distilled from monkshood or wolfsbane.

72. Garencières thinks that *Artomiques* is derived from *artos*, Greek for "bread," and thus denotes the Protestants, using leavened bread in communion. This is rather farfetched, but not impossible. But more likely the word is an erratum on the part of Nostradamus or the printer, derived from the Arecomici, one of the two tribes forming the great Volcae nation in ancient Gaul. Their chief city was Nîmes, so that this probably is nothing more than a fancy obscurification for "those of Nîmes." Agen, Lectoure and Condom are all towns close together in Guienne, quite a distance west of Nîmes. Saint-Félix, a village about twenty-five miles southeast of Toulouse, was indeed once the seat of an assembly, that of the proto-Protestant Albigensians, in 1167. Marsan was the name of a tiny viscounty, whose capital, Mont-de-Marsan, is still an important town. If the latter itself is intended, it lies about thirty-five miles west of Condom. A vague suspicion that the whole quatrain represents a "retroactive prophecy" of the Albigensian period is not entirely out of order.

73. Le Pelletier can't resist applying any "nephew" quatrain to his Emperor (always as tactfully as possible). This is the last of his "historical" (as opposed to "future") interpretations.

Napoleon III will force the recognition of the treaty [Treaty of Zurich, October 17, 1859] which he will have previously made possible through his prudence. The King of Piedmont (Duke of Asti), master of a part of the Papal States [Ferrara], will be grateful when the drama reaches its conclusion.

When Nostradamus wrote, Asti was under French occupation, while Ferrara, though nominally a papal fief, was not annexed by the Papacy for about another half century. One of Le Pelletier's silliest.

74. Mâcon, assuming it is intended here, is about seventy-five miles west of Geneva, and was in Burgundy. Aquitaine, the large province in southwest France (one is tempted to say a French Texas), was more or less synonymous with Guienne. The last line probably indicates a defeat for the allied Protestant army composed of treacherous Frenchmen, Swiss and Germans.

75. This one has been applied to the Battle of Waterloo in 1815, with Grouchy the deserter of line 1, Wellington the chief adversary, the rear guard the Imperial Guard, and the last line the White Terror. But the quatrain is rather elastic.

76. The ancient county of Périgord was on the northern border of the Agenais. Each is about two hundred miles west of the Rhône. The Gascons are the inhabitants between the Garonne and the Pyrenees. Bigorre, of which Tarbes was the capital, was a county of Gascony and belonged to the House of Navarre. Agen was the first town in which Nostradamus settled

down and married. Since Bigorre became a Calvinist stronghold, some sort of religious war might be seen in lines 3 and 4. In spite of the many place names, the verse is an obscure one.

77. This one is very important as a key to Nostradamus' theories about the course of European history. The evidence is unfortunately very overwhelming that Nostradamus' new Charlemagne, "Henry-Selin," is none other than his own King, the utterly insignificant Henry II. He held his mistress, Diane de Poitiers, in such high esteem that he made wide use of the crest *H-D* in all sorts of forms and in all sorts of places. *Selene* is simply the Greek equivalent of Diana, so that Nostradamus' designation has the same meaning (Henry-Selene instead of Henry-Diana). However, his mistress's name was only one reason for Henry's identification with the moon. Henry actually adopted the moon as his device, in natural contrast to the use of the sun by Emperor Charles V. Indeed, Henry had one crest combining an H with a crescent, thus:

It is difficult to reconcile the ridiculous predictions that Nostradamus made for this royal mediocrity with his many more logical ones. There was a limit to the demands for flattery, and the manner in which he obscured the name leaves some doubt as to whether anyone recognized the designation as being for Henry before his death (1559). After his death, the loyalty of Nostradamians to the master's infallibility precluded mention of this perfectly obvious fact (obvious to Henry's contemporaries).

The prediction is fairly clear. Henry will subdue Italy, unite Christendom, and become Emperor (involving the removal of Emperor Ferdinand; even were this verse written before Charles' abdication [1556], Ferdinand had been crowned King of Rome, the Imperial equivalent of Prince of Wales, in 1531). In line 4 he will wipe out the piratical corsairs of Barbary, a rather treacherous move considering that they were allies of long standing. Line 3 tells that he will be interred at Blois, the equivalent of Windsor for the Valois dynasty. Everything turned out as contrary as could be. Henry was disastrously defeated a few months after the verse was first published (1557). The French were booted out of Italy, and lost all their hard-won gains like Savoy. Henry himself was killed in a tournament in 1559, and, contrarily, was buried at Saint-Denis, just outside Paris.

78. Parma was a duchy in northern Italy (see 469). It is uncertain which army is referred to in line 1. The foreigners referred to are probably the Spanish, Parma being generally a French ally then.

79. This one is much like 476, in that though it is crammed full with place names, the meaning remains quite obscure. All the towns in line 1 are in the Agenais, west of Agen. Monheurt is about five miles northwest of Aiguillon, while Le-Mas-d'Agenais is about six miles northwest of Monheurt. Nostradamus' familiarity with these villages undoubtedly dates back to his

residence there (*ca.* 1536). Landes, one of the few ancient *pays* to be salvaged as a department, is west of the Agenais. The Bordelais, the peninsula at the base of which stands Bordeaux, was in turn north of Landes. Navarre was in the extreme southwest corner of France, while Bigorre, which belonged to Navarre's King, was just to the east of Navarre. All action is thus in the Southwest.

80. The action in lines 1–3 must have taken place in the course of many wars, and has recently been applied quite nicely to the Maginot Line and the Fall of France. The only limiting detail occurs in line 4. If the word *collisee* merely means "clash," we have no clue. But if it means *colosseum*, the scene is much limited. The word is synonymous with amphitheater. The most famous remains of a Roman amphitheater are in Rome, and the action may be set here. If set in France, the most famous specimen is at Nîmes, while lesser ones are at Arles and Fréjus.

81. Most interesting about this one is the phrase "Belgian Prince." Today the word "Belgian" does not cause much notice, but in the 16th century it was as archaic as Lusitanian or Pannonian. There was only one possible candidate when Nostradamus wrote: Philip II, who had been given this territory in 1554 by his father, Emperor Charles V. The quatrain probably concerns an attack on northern France, which occurred a few months after the writing. The bridge of boats is probably for passing over the Scheldt.

82. Slavonia is a distinctly limited province of the northern Balkans, between the Drave and Save rivers. But by treating the word as a poetic term for Slavdom, Le Pelletier is able to apply it to Russia, and thus refers it to Napolean's retreat from Moscow in 1812–13. The best that can be said for this application (which was improved upon by Robb in 1942) is that there is none other particularly clear. In the 16th century (and until 1699) the Turks held Slavonia. The verse in that setting would have to tell of an Emperor suffering such a great defeat in the course of a campaign against the Turks that they would invade the Empire, leading to a revolt (of German princelings). If lines 2 and 3, as it seems, refer to the same person, the defeated Emperor would be the Destroyer, rather than the Turk—which hardly makes sense in the context. However, the meaning of *Olestant* is by no means certain.

Garencières' interpretation for this incomprehensible but interesting verse reminds one of the interpretations of his 20th-century "rewrite man":

> That great troop from Sclavonia shall be the Venetians because they possess most part of that country [confused with Dalmatia]. The old Olestant is their Duke, because he is not chosen unless he is very old [*sic!*].

From which the rewrite man himself gets even more confused, and Roberts (1947) makes it: "A Russian advance to the West shall be slowed up by an attack by an Olestant (Duke [*sic!*]). But he will thus meet his ruin and his country will be made desolate."

83. This one is quite clear and specific, but we know of no application

of it. Some elements in it suggest the preceding quatrain. The last line certainly had a good chance for fulfillment in the cloak-and-dagger 16th century: an heir turns on his father and besieges or imprisons him.

84. Auxerre was in Burgundy, about one hundred miles east of Orléans. The prophecy is very precise, since the conjunction of line 4 is a rare one, even without the further limitation of summer. We have been unable to find any notable of Nostradamus' day who was a native of Auxerre.

85. Another of the detailed but utterly obscure variety.

86. A very rich and meaningful prophecy, limited in time by the fairly rare conjunction of lines 1–2. Reims was the traditional coronation site for Kings of France, while Aix (Aachen) was where German Kings (in most cases the Holy Roman Emperor or his heir with the title "King of the Romans") were crowned from 813 to 1531. In the final case, it was as King of the Romans (i.e., King of Germany) that Ferdinand was crowned here, his brother Charles V having been crowned Holy Roman Emperor in 1530 at Bologna, Italy. In other words, the verse predicts that the same individual will rule both France and Germany, as did Charlemagne. In view of his other prophecies for Henry II, the quatrain probably means that Henry will become Emperor.

87. While lines 1, 2 and 4 fit Henry III well enough (line 4 referring to his murder of the Guises in 1588), line 3 would have little significance for him. His father would be Henry II; his father-in-law Nicholas of Lorraine, a complete nonentity.

88. This one may have been an embarrassingly precise prophecy for some 16th-century potentate. Phthiriasis (pediculosis) is a rather vague kind of illness caused by lice. Although lines 3 and 4 are obscure, Anthony and the lice stand out clearly enough. The most notable Anthony of the day was Henry IV's father, Duke of Bourbon-Vendôme and King of Navarre (1555–62). He did not become a really important figure till a few years after the quatrain was published, but he was a king (since May, 1555). From 1559 till his death he was one of the most important factors determining France's destiny. However, there is no record of his lousiness. Gould and Pyle (p. 821) mention a number of famous men reportedly "eaten of worms" or lice, and while not including Anthony, they do include, surprisingly, one of Nostradamus' favorite characters, Philip II of Spain.

89. Somehow or other, all Nostradamus' predictions involving England are very clear and lucid. An extremely good case can be made for applying this one to the Glorious Revolution of 1688–89. William III, having no intention of being double-crossed by his English supporters if things went badly, insisted that the great lords who proposed his "liberating" England should put it in writing. Ward (1891) cites the *Gentleman's Magazine* as saying that twenty-nine signatures were affixed to the document. (According to most accounts, however, only the names of Shrewsbury, Devonshire, Danby, Lumley, Compton, Russell and Sydney were on it.) If *pont* is taken for sea, which is not too farfetched, there was indeed a constant flurry of conspirators going

back and forth across the Channel before William finally sailed with his expedition. Line 3 applies well enough to James II and his reactionary clique, who, finding themselves without military support (because of the timely desertion of Winston Churchill's illustrious ancestor, the future Duke of Marlborough), decided they'd just as soon not become martyrs. William III is not recorded as having been fair (one meek interpretation has it that he had been in his youth), but he certainly was from Frisia, the classical name for Holland, and still the name of one of its provinces. Another point for Nostradamus is that there was no conceivable Dutch candidate for the English throne in his own day.

90. Pavia is about twenty miles south of Milan. Each is to suffer a horrible drought while being fought over, presumably by the French and the Spanish.

91. Jaubert applies this one to events of 1555–56. Line 1 he refers to the Duke of Nemours (presumably not the French General, also known as Gaston de Foix, who was killed in 1512) being challenged by the Marquis of Pescara (presumably not the famous general who had died in 1525) to break a lance. Jaubert wrestles with line 2 in typical fashion, changing *Mellele* to *Mole*, and then pointing out that de la Mole did not dare bring his fleet near Monaco during the course of his operations. Lines 3 and 4 he applies to some petty intrigue in Savoy. With Roberts (1947) the same confusion occurs as we saw with 243: he copies Garencières' revision of *Mellele* to *Mole*, as per Jaubert, then throws away the interpretation requiring this brazen change, producing instead a magnificent *non sequitur* about *The Man in the Iron Mask*. *Mellele* is apparently nothing but Melilla, the North African port held by Spain since 1490, though it is difficult to fit it in with the context. Line 4 is not unlike the fourth line of 483.

92. Perhaps this is meant for the same valiant captain mentioned in 483. Using heads as trophies was quite common in ancient times and still occurs every now and then, as in Greece in 1947. Roberts (1947) tells us that "This quatrain caused confusion in the mind of Nostradamus [*sic!*—a frequent error for "Garencières"]. To us, there is an obvious reference to radio in it. . . ."

93. Garencières points out that this prodigy is supposed to have occurred to Queen Olympia of Macedonia before the birth of Alexander the Great. Le Pelletier applies it to the birth of his Messiah, the Duke of Bordeaux, on September 9, 1820. The serpent is Louis-Philippe, whose rank entitled him to free access, protesting that the posthumous prince is illegitimate (which would make the Orléans branch the legitimate successor to the throne after the abdication of Charles X in 1830).

94. A very specific quatrain. As Philip II had no brothers, there was no apparent application in Nostradamus' time (Don John, however, was a bastard half-brother). The quatrain may be related to 470. Narbonne and Agde are both ports near the Spanish border. Béziers lies between them. Line 3 seems to predict, once again, woes for Calvin's Geneva. At least five separate prophecies are thus to be found in this quatrain: (1) exile for two Spanish princes or grandees; (2) defeat of one of them in Roussillon; (3) an attack

against Geneva; (4) plague spreading from Agde (see also 821) to Narbonne and Béziers; (5) a bloody sea fight.

95. The Imperial realm was left to two at just about the time this quatrain was written, when Charles V divided his Empire between son Philip and brother Ferdinand. But they did not, as Nostradamus seems to be predicting here (and elsewhere), go to war against each other. Line 3 remains obscure. Possibly two royal nuns are referred to. The meaning of line 4 hinges upon the still uncertain meaning of *Armonique*. Apparently the Vestals are to fight each other, something which is rather difficult to visualize. Vestals were classically Roman priestesses attending the sacred fire of the goddess Vesta.

96. Another very interesting and pregnant quatrain. Although Elizabeth was born only four years before Edward VI (1533 and 1537, respectively) and was the younger sister in relation to Mary, the reigning Queen when Nostradamus wrote, it is possible that Nostradamus did indeed have her in mind and was merely misinformed on his dates. Line 3 is obscure, but must have something to do with Elizabeth's Protestant religion. Line 4 is most interesting in that it seems to tie Nostradamus' often-mentioned enigmatic "Libra" or "the Balance" with England, notwithstanding that in geopolitical astrology it is supposed to pertain only to Austria and Savoy (at least in Europe—see 281). However, it is perhaps somewhat relevant to this point, and what Nostradamus may have had in mind, that in 1555 Philip, as titular King of England, was trying to persuade his sister-in-law Elizabeth to marry Philip's young protégé, Emmanuel Philibert, Duke of Savoy. Perhaps confounding Nostradamus, Elizabeth turned him down (she later did the same to King Charles IX of France, although Nostradamus also predicted she'd marry him—see "Biography of Nostradamus"), and the Duke of Savoy went on to inflict a crushing defeat on France at Saint-Quentin (1557), marry the sister of Henry II of France (July, 1559) and visit Nostradamus at Salon (October, 1559).

97. A highly specific quatrain, limited in time by the configuration in line 1. It seems to concern the Portuguese succession, with the rather odd point of a Portuguese king being elected in Spain. When Nostradamus wrote the verse, there was no apparent crisis of heirs. But Sebastian I, who came to the throne in 1557, was killed in a crusade against the Moors (1578). His brother, a cardinal, ruled for two years. There being then no clear legitimate male heir, Philip II, having several claims in the female line, sent Alba to conquer the country. Philip seized the throne and ruled Portugal till his death (1621), and was followed by his son, Philip III. In 1640 the Portuguese revolted against Spain. But there was no election in Cadiz (Spain) or even in Guarda (Portugal) of either Philip (in 1580) or of John IV (in 1640).

98. This quatrain contains several obscure or confusing elements. The first centers upon *Albanois*, with its choice of possible meanings. In this case (but not in all the others), the troops of the Duke of Alba seem most

likely. Garencières has it that "the people of Albania lying between the Venetian Territories, and Grecia, shall come to Rome." Langres was in Champagne near the northeastern border. It may here be used for the same "Duke of Langres" found in 74. The rest remains obscure, except for the many disasters.

99. It is very uncertain in this verse whether the French are winning or losing. Perhaps each in turn. Line 1 should be clear, but does not suggest anyone. In line 2 the French are hurled back by this hero, who in line 3 invades Spain(?). The only power which could potentially have fought both France and Spain was then an Empire separated from Spain (as it was after 1556). In 495 we saw that Nostradamus seemed to foresee that the division of the Empire would lead to war between the two parts. Ferdinand, Emperor in 1558, was only the second son of Joanna, daughter of Ferdinand and Isabella. But his son and heir Maximilian would fit, being the elder son of Anne, daughter and heiress of the King of Hungary and Bohemia (see 427).

100. Another specimen of the detailed yet obscure variety. The chief royal edifice in Paris in Nostradamus' day was the Louvre. The Tuileries was just being built. More widely used was Saint-Germain, outside Paris. "Celestial fire" may refer to a fire started by lightning, or fire reflecting the "anger of the gods." Line 2 must mean either just after a war ends, or when French military strength collapses (as in 1557). Rouen and Evreux are both in Normandy, and their odd combination is found also in 584.

# Century V

1. This one is rather general, and one can probably find some interpretation for it each time there has been a "Celtic ruin." A perfectly reasonable interpretation of late has been for the Fourth Partition of Poland (1939). The temple is the Kremlin in Moscow, the two are Ribbentrop and Molotov, arranging for the murder of Poland, whose ever-turbulent aristocracy might be considered denoted in line 3. This deal in the East was not without effect on the Fall of France (1940), since the Germans were able to turn all their forces westward.

2. Another of the detailed yet hopelessly obscure variety.

3. A very interesting prophecy, though the exact meaning is not quite clear. (See also the similar 539.) The Medici had left Florence in 1494, were restored in 1512, expelled again in 1527, restored again in 1530, when Charles V appointed Alexander as hereditary ruler. In 1537 Cosimo became Duke of Florence and in 1569 Grand Duke of Tuscany. Here our prophet seems to be predicting that Medici rule will come to its final conclusion, to be replaced by that of a French prince. As a matter of fact, while Nostradamus probably meant the prophecy for the 16th century, it was twice ful-

filled later. In 1737 the Medici died out, upon which Duke Francis of Lorraine (which might be considered a Gallic branch—see Genealogical Chart) became Grand Duke. When he became Emperor, the House of Lorraine became the House of Habsburg-Lorraine, but Tuscany continued in the family until 1859 (except for French control during the Revolution). From 1801 to 1805 Tuscany became the Kingdom of Etruria, and was given as a sop to the Spanish Bourbons, which were really a Gallic branch. The prophecy was thus vaguely fulfilled by the House of Lorraine in 1737, and the House of Bourbon in 1801. As for the nautical frogs, Le Pelletier cites a myth in which Bacchus transformed the earliest inhabitants of Tuscany, the Tyrrhenians, into frogs. Probably the reference is to the standard of mythical Merovingian King Pharamond—three toads of gold on a field of azure.

4. The whole prophecy concerns intrigues of Renaissance Italy. The problem lies in applying the devices to the appropriate individuals. Only the Bear is clear, being the device of the great Orsini clan of Rome. Perhaps the wolf refers to their perpetual arch-rivals, the Colonna. The dog has been used by the House of Sforza, particularly by Duke Francesco of Milan (d. 1466) but the family died out in 1535, at least in the ducal branch. The stag was the device of the notorious Constable of Bourbon, but he was killed during the Sack of Rome (1527). Perhaps this one is really another of the "retroactive prophecy" group.

5. This one is rather vague, and undoubtedly many interpretations can be made for it, especially in Renaissance Italy. A rather recent application has been to Adolf Hitler, removing Germany from the servitude of Versailles. The young prostitute is of course Marianne, the corrupt Third Republic, and somehow or other line 4 brings in *Mein Kampf*. Larmor (1925, p. 150) is such an arch-legitimist as to apply this to the "usurpation" of the French throne by Henry of Navarre in 1589, whereafter he shut up his former wife and quondam partner, Marguerite of Valois, in an Auvergne castle, where, according to Larmor, "she divided her time between reading the Bible and debauchery."

6. This one is quite clear and simple, belonging to the wishful-thinking group that would have Henry II become Emperor. The Pope, anxious for peace to be restored in Italy, makes the King of France Emperor. Another bit of "prophetic imperialism."

7. Another rather simple and meaningful one. The two most famous triumvirates in history were in the Roman Empire. The personnel of the first consisted of Gaius Julius Caesar, Gnaeus Pompeius and M. Licinius Crassus; the second consisted of Gaius Julius Caesar Octavianus (Augustus), Marcus Antonius and Marcus Lepidus. The discovery of the bones of one of these six would seem prophesied here. Otherwise, the points are obscure.

8. In this verse we find predicted a horrible "new weapon," a city burnt to the ground by it and by the action of a ship and an enemy convinced of the necessity of making peace. The quatrain thus probably fits nothing so well as the action of the United States against Japan, with ships and atom

bombs, in the latter half of 1945. World War III may see a much better fulfillment.

9. Roberts confesses that "These words are too veiled in obscurity for either Nostradamus or myself to render a clear interpretation." Le Pelletier, however, is less modest than "Nostradamus" (Garencières) and with a few farfetched twists applies it to the Orsini conspiracy (January 14, 1858). The great arch is the peristyle of the Opéra, damaged by the bomb intended for Emperor Napoleon III. The chief is Hébert, head of the secret police, who captured in advance (*sic!*) Orsini's fellow conspirator Pieri. The lady of line 3 is Demagoguery, while the hairiness refers to that typical characteristic of leftist "agitators." In line 4 he takes "Duke" back to its original meaning as "leader," and thus commoner Orsini becomes eligible.

10. This one is applied to the same event. Napoleon III is the Celtic chief, slightly wounded in the eye by glass. *Cave* is derived from *cavea*, "theater," and thus, lo and behold, we have the Opéra itself. The last line Le Pelletier would have "saved from four by unknown ones." The four are then identified as Orsini, Pieri, Rudio and Gomez, and the unknown ones as the gods watching over their precious Emperor. (Le Pelletier is so carried away here as to forget that he is supposed to hate the Emperor for standing in the way of the Bourbon Pretender.)

11. The Sun was a device much used by Charles V and Philip II, but it is also used by Nostradamus to stand for Christendom or the Church. "Those of Venus" probably refers to the corsairs of Barbary. The corsairs, acknowledging the Sultan as their overlord, carved out their empire at the expense of both the Habsburgs, who had North African bases, and the previous dynasty from the Arab caliphate. Saturn probably refers to a member of the latter. The Turks are sure to be intended somehow in the very general line 4.

12. All that is clear in this detailed but obscure medley of prophecies is trouble for Calvin's Geneva, a theme to which Nostradamus keeps returning gleefully. Augsburg is almost three hundred miles from Geneva. Perhaps some clue to its mention here lies in the fact that in 1530 the Lutheran theologian Melancthon presented Charles V with the so-called Confession of Augsburg at the Imperial Diet held there. On September 25, 1555, the religious Peace of Augsburg put a temporary halt to the German religious wars. By it, all princes or free cities could choose Lutheranism, but not Calvinism, for their territories. An imperial attack upon the still-outcast Calvinists is probably intended in the last line.

13. A very interesting quatrain. The first line would seem intended for a successor of Charles V. But while Charles was both Roman Emperor and ruler of the classical Belgium (as Duke of Burgundy), his multiple abdications had begun before this was written (see "Historical Background"). As Emperor he was succeeded by his brother Ferdinand, who suffered defeat when he tried to drive the Turks out of Hungary, and ended up paying tribute to them. Anyhow, Ferdinand did not fall heir to "Belgium" (given

to Charles' son Philip of Spain in 1555). The Imperial title and rule of the [Belgian] Netherlands was combined again only between 1713 and 1795. Either Nostradamus foresaw Ferdinand or Philip reuniting the Empire of Charles V, or saw Henry II succeeding to the whole thing, after suitable fighting. The prophecy was equally lacking in fulfillment on the sea. If anyone did the chasing, it was Dragut and his corsairs. By 1556 they had the whole North African coast, and in 1565 occurred the great Siege of Malta. However, it is also possible the quatrain is part of the "New Oriental Conquerors" theme, the Turks having been succeeded in Europe by other invaders, including African ones.

14. This is a rather dazzling prophecy with its sweeping statements of events on a grand scale. When the configuration in line 1 takes place (unfortunately not covered by Wöllner), Spain will be conquered. By whom? Apparently, by one of the successors of Barbarossa, the Bey of Algiers. In the 1550's it was Dragut who was clearly the "African chief." Perhaps it is not the conquest of all Spain that is intended (quite a large order when Spanish power was at its peak), but merely of the rest of the Spanish forts in North Africa. Most of these by 1556 had been lost by the Habsburgs. With reference to line 2, Dragut himself was perhaps trapped in the conflict, when he perished in the Siege of Malta (1565). Line 3 is completely obscure. What place is "near Malta"? The only answer would seem a ship at sea. What is the derivation of *Herodde?* The primary poetic meaning of Herod would be "enemy of Christ," in which case it might be used loosely for any Moslem leader. But the feminine ending complicates the matter further. Just to show what one can do with the word, the League in the 1580's made the anagram *vilain Herodes* out of "Henri de Valois" (Henry III). Line 1 would seem to predict that the French would inflict a shattering defeat upon either the Emperor (Roman Emperor) or the Pope (ruler of Rome). Neither was to be fulfilled properly till the time of Napoleon.

15. Another very daring prophecy, with a Pope captured on the high seas (although it may be a reference to steering the Bark of St. Peter). The Papacy falls into chaos. Line 3 may refer to his frightened successor hiding himself, or merely tell that the same Pope will be the second of his name. The last Pope of whom this was true was Marcellus II, Pope for a few weeks in 1555 (probably before the verse was written). The last Pope famous for his bastards was Paul III (1534–49), who set one of them up as Duke of Parma. One of two possible forms of death can be seen for this bastard. The only popes actually taken captive since 1555 were Pius VI (who died at Valence in France in 1799) and Puis VII (Napoleon's captive at Fontainebleau, 1809–14).

16. Frankincense is one of the most widely used of incenses, but just how this fact fits into line 2 is none too clear. The island of Pharos, with its famous lighthouse, forms part of the harbor of Alexandria. Egypt had belonged to the Turks since 1517, Rhodes since 1522. "The Crusaders" may

refer to nothing more than some Christian pirates attacking Alexandria. One of the chief reasons that the Turks attacked Rhodes in 1522 was that it had become the headquarters for Catalan and Maltese pirates making raids in Egyptian waters. This quatrain is thus not above suspicion of falling into the "retroactive" class. Or it may belong to the "New Crusade" group.

17. Certainly a highly dramatic quatrain. The attempted assassination of a king seems to be the subject. Line 2 is obviously data on the assassin, but from there on it is uncertain whether the conspirators are after the King or the unsuccessful assassin. The presence of the Rhône clearly places this one in France. Venice got Cyprus in the 15th century, when the House of Lusignan died out, and held it until 1571.

18. Little can be made of this one. With regard to the female conqueror, it is noteworthy that many women rulers were on the stage, or in the wings, in the middle of the 16th century: Bloody Mary, Elizabeth, Catherine de' Medici, Jeanne of Navarre, Margaret of Parma (in the Netherlands) and Mary Stuart. Even in the Orient Sultan Suleiman's Russian wife Roxelana exerted tremendous power behind the scenes.

19. This one is rather obscure. Properly, Barbarians refers to the Barbary corsairs of Algeria, but Nostradamus seems to use it for Turks or other Moslems more generally in places.

20. Only two factors stand out amidst the obscurities here. The first is a French invasion of Italy. The second is that the ruler of Florence will be expelled. Although this did not occur again in the 16th century, when it was probably intended, it did in the 19th, as Le Pelletier points out. In 1859 the French engaged the Austrians in northern Italy while the ruler of Tuscany was driven out by a revolution. As for the "monster scoundrel," Le Pelletier is only too happy to apply the epithet to Garibaldi, who, by his attempt to conquer the sacrosanct Papal States, became Le Pelletier's nominee for the Antichrist. For those who prefer the retroactive solution, the verse was quite nicely fulfilled in 1512, when, as we noted in 53, the Medici were again kicked out, and a French expedition under the Napoleon of that day, Gaston de Foix, Duke of Nemours (see 491), won a great victory at Ravenna against the Spanish and Papal forces. And again in 1527 (more important, since Nostradamus was of a mature age then) the Medici were kicked out, and again a French expedition overran Lombardy.

21. It is rather uncertain whom Nostradamus refers to by the "Latin Monarch." Technically, it would be the ruler of Latium, which, since it was entirely within the Papal States, would indicate the Pope. However, some other Italian ruler may be intended. Of late, of course, Mussolini and the Fascists have been favored in interpretations. In any event, those who amassed great wealth under the subject of this verse will have it stripped from them and will suffer public execution.

22. As a Pope lies dying, a foreign army (probably the Spanish or the Imperial) will suffer a terrible defeat near Parma, in northern Italy. This

will cause two cardinals to rejoice. Fairly simple and reasonable, but did it ever occur?

23. Line 1 may or may not contain the beginning of a configuration. While Saturn and Mars are traditionally of malevolent influence, those may be two beneficial ones in contrast. Otherwise, the line must needs concern two leaders well pleased with themselves, and their alliance, which is for war (as are most alliances). The great one of Africa would be Dragut or a successor as Bey of Algiers or Tunis. In our prophet's day, they were generally allied with France against the Emperor, so the Bey is perhaps the other half of the Duumvirate here. The Habsburg fleet was under the Genoese Nelson, Andrea Doria, until his death (1560).

24. We found Venus and Saturn in 511. Although Venus is apparently used for the Infidel, the usage of Saturn remains uncertain. A configuration, at face value, remains possible, but less likely here. The Sun is used both as the emblem of Charles V (and Philip) and as standing for the Church of Christendom. Like everything else, here its meaning is obscure.

25. In complete contrast to the above comes this breath-taking and daring barrage of predictions. At a time when the configuration in line 1 takes place, a new Arab Empire will arise. Four separate lines of attack are mentioned: (1) against Persia, (2) against Egypt, (3) against Constantinople (Byzantium), and (4) against the naval forces of Christendom. For the "retroactive" school, all this happened in the 7th century. The conquest of Persia (but not with a million men) took place A.D. 635–50. Egypt was taken in 639. Most of the Arab conquests had been part of the Byzantine empire, but it was not until 673 that Constantinople was attacked. However, in 655 the Arab fleet inflicted a crushing defeat on the Imperial Byzantine fleet. According to Lee McCann (1942) the configuration will take place on August 21, 1987.

26. The words "Slav" and "slave" being etymologically one and the same, either reading is valid here. It is not certain that the Russians were regarded as Slavs in the 16th century, so that application may not be permissible. Most likely one of the Balkan peoples would be required to fulfill the Slav version. The quatrain may represent a prediction that one of the subject people of the Balkans would rise against the Turks with such success as to be able to invade Turkey-in-Asia. This did not occur until the 19th century, and then line 4 was not fulfilled. The closest it came to fulfillment was when the Greeks, only partially Slav, landed troops at Smyrna (1919) and remained there until 1922. And the Greeks did indeed change their King then. Constantine, exiled in 1917, was recalled in 1920 and exiled again in 1922. Though of a German house, Constantine was born right in Athens, but his rival, Premier Venizelos, was a Cretan.

With the translation "slavish" rather than "Slavic," this quatrain has been applied to the successes of the "common herd" in the armies of the French Revolution. Line 3 is of course applied to Napoleon, born in Corsica one year after it became French. Line 4 is applied rather poorly to Napoleon's expedition against Egypt, though it is doubtful if most of the Army of Egypt came from France's few mountainous districts.

27. It is uncertain here whether the conquerors are the Arabs of 525 (and elsewhere), or yet another oriental conqueror in the Persians (see Index for further references). Trebizond, in the northeastern corner of Asia Minor, was never taken by the Arab conquerors of the first millennium, and held out against the Turks till 1461. The island of Pharos forms part of the harbor of Alexandria. Mytilene, otherwise known as Lesbos, is an island off northwestern Asia Minor, taken by the Turks in 1462. The "joyful Sun" perhaps refers to the delight of Christendom at the crumbling of the Ottoman Empire. In this quatrain Nostradamus is again found foreseeing the imminent collapse of the Turks in the face of attack by the Arab-Egyptians, Persians and a new Charlemagne, probably in the person of Henry II. Line 4 suggests the natural consequence: the victors to fight amongst themselves.

28. Le Pelletier (1867) infers rather delicately that he would like to see this assassination fulfilled by a scion of the House of Savoy. A few decades later, King Humbert of Italy was assassinated (July 29, 1900). It is doubtful if the assassin, an unemployed smith named Acciarito, would fit the very detailed inscription of lines 1–2. Since Savoy held Genoa only since 1815, Nostradamus could hardly have intended it for a Savoy. In Nostradamus' day the great one of Genoa was certainly Andrea Doria, Grand Admiral of the Imperial Fleet and tyrannical Doge of Genoa, whose assassination Nostradamus also appeared to predict in 194. The assassin was to have one arm in a sling.

Hugh Allen (1943, p. 406) spares no pains to stick his neck out here, with a super-intuitive interpretation.

> Here you have prognosticated the assassination of the King-Emperor, Victor-Emmanuel III , on Easter Sunday, April 5, 1942, at approximately 11.00 A.M. on that day, or on April 25, 1942.

29. This somewhat general and highly obscure quatrain has had a number of interpretations, one most recently involving Mussolini and intrigues of his to secure a connection via Austria with his ally Hitler in the period 1934–38. Hitler is seen as denoted by *Hister* as an anagram. If the verse is taken more literally, Venice was not seriously threatened from the direction of the Danube from the time the prophecy was written until the time of the French Revolution, when Napoleon, after using it for bait in his dealings with the Austrians, put a finish to it. The possibilities of Nostradamus' probable meaning are multiplied when we consider that in some cases (531, for instance) the word *pont* is used for the Papacy.

30. This quatrain seems to predict a sack of Rome by the French, to match that of the Habsburgs in 1527. "Rome incited" may refer to a "fifth column," easy enough to find amidst the Roman feuds. In line 4, whether the pontiff or a bridge is referred to as in the preceding quatrain, the meaning is fairly clear. The only chance of fulfillment for this quatrain came

during the Revolution. The French twice took Rome (in February of 1797 and of 1808). As for the pillage, the Pope was forced to cede part of his States in February of 1797; while on May 17, 1809, the Papal States were incorporated into France. Here is Le Pelletier's version:

Towards the time (September 4, 1797) when the executive Directory, in violation of the Constitution which had expressly forbidden it, will have encamped some troops around Paris, with the aim of combatting the counter-revolution, a Frenchman, General Berthier, will take Rome by assault, under the pretext of avenging the death of General Duphot, killed in an insurrection (Rome incited): the Sovereign Pontiff, in the person of Pius VI, dispossessed of his States and arrested in his palace, will then undergo a great pillage.

31. If the "Attic land" is to be taken literally, it refers to the southeastern tip of Greece proper, north of the Peloponnesus, where Athens is located. However, Nostradamus is probably referring to his own France, as cultural heir of Athens. In fact, one of the court poets of the Pleiad may well have used this figure. In spite of this legacy, France is to commit the heinous crime of destroying the Papacy, "wreck" referring to the Bark of St. Peter. Note that this is the third quatrain in succession in which *pont* is possibly used for the Papacy.

32. This one may perhaps be the third of a trio on the "doom of Rome" theme. "From the sky" gives a 20th-century sound to the quatrain. The reference in line 4 remains obscure.

33. An ingenious application of this one came out of the French Revolution. As Le Pelletier gives it:

Nantes, having been the seat of the Vendean insurrection, in 1793, against the National Convention, will be delivered to the bloody repression of the proconsul Carrier. The men will be beheaded; under the name of "republican marriages," the odious coupling of victims who will be thrown into the Loire will be perpetrated.

With the reading "unhappy mixture," he refers to Carrier's grim trick of tying women and priests together, putting the couples on barges on the Loire, then sinking the barges. On the whole, this interpretation stands up very well.

34. This one is certainly worthy of notice. While it is possible that Nostradamus is merely referring to the west coast of England, this is hardly likely. One interpretation allows of Nostradamus' having foreseen the anglicization of North America (which hadn't yet begun in his day). Another might be that he foresaw another Hundred Years' War, when the English for many decades held most of the west coast of France. There are other quatrains suggesting this.

The Gironde is the estuary of the Garonne. Blois is several hundred miles away. Not only is it not on the Garonne, or the Gironde; it is not even on the sea. It does not fit at all. Perhaps it denotes a person, being the seat of the Capetian branch then ruling France. It may also be an erratum for Blaye. Wine and salt seem to be used metaphorically. One interpretation is that they are the traditional bases for taxation. Another one has it that salt stands for wit and intelligence, wine for emotion and energy. The hidden fire may refer to a real weapon of war, or may represent a metaphor. The interpretation which would have the English West as North America, seat of a British ruler, may yet be fulfilled.

35. Although the crescent is elsewhere associated with the new Charlemagne ("Henry-Selin" or Henry of the Crescent) or with Genoa ("Port Selin"), we must start here with the fact that there was nothing of an English fleet in the Mediterranean in Nostradamus' day. Holding no particular brief for consistency, Nostradamus is here apparently using the crescent image for the Bay of Biscay, which is indeed shaped like a crescent, and a very likely area in which a hostile English fleet might be operating. La Rochelle, with a long history involving the special status of a "free city," derived its name from *rupes*, "rock" (thence, *Rupella*), because of the large quantities of rocks gathered there. "Branch" may refer to any of the numerous offshoots of the House of France (see Genealogical Table) being used as a valuable political prisoner. Like the preceding quatrain, this one seems to belong to a series involving protracted war with English invaders.

36. One of the detailed but obscure variety, apparently concerning the poisoning of a woman (ruler?) by her brother. The method of poisoning is specified with incomprehensible Nostradamian obscurity. Since Nostradamus was a first-class pharmacist, some pharmacist may find a clue here. In Latin *rosarius* referred to a poison extracted from the laurel rose.

Hugh Allen (1943) who manages to liquidate almost the entire British royal family before he gets done, sees this as a prophecy of the murder of Dowager Queen Mary of England and adds helpfully, "there may be amongst those present some individuals who had already assisted at the simple, rural and ghoulish murder of Queen Mary's cousins at Ekaterinburg."

37. Garencières comment (1672) on this very general one, shortly after the turmoil of Civil War, Cromwellian dictatorship and Restoration, is very amusing:

> The difficulty of meeting in any Countrey three hundred men of one mind, hath perswaded me that our Author writ this for England, but by reason there hath been since a general pardon, I will keep my mind to myself.

38. Although there is no denying that it is very general, this one turned out to be a bull's-eye for Louis XV. The great monarch (actually called *le grand monarque*) is of course Louis XIV. The details of his great-grandson's licentious life are known well enough. The famous *Après nous, le déluge* can be seen in line 3. There are two interpretations for the failure of the Salic

Law. In its broader sense, it simply referred to the succession. Le Pelletier applies it to the fall of the monarchy. However, it was popularly associated with the minor clause barring women from ruling France. In this sense, the great political power of Pompadour and du Barry constituted a violation of the Salic Law.

39. This quatrain is practically a paraphrase of 53, predicting the advent of a scion of the House of France to the rule of Tuscany. As we mentioned, while this never occurred in the 16th century (for which Nostradamus probably intended it), it was fulfilled to some extent with the House of Lorraine (descended from French kings only in the female line), and almost perfectly in 1801–5. On March 21, 1801, Napoleon set up Louis of Bourbon-Parma as King of Etruria. After his death in 1803, his widow, Marie-Louise, became regent for the infant Louis II. However, she was so negligent that on October 23, 1807, Napoleon set the family up in a new creation around Oporto called "Northern Lusitania." In March, 1809, Etruria was formally incorporated into France. Lines 3–4 seem to refer to some triviality about arms, perhaps merely the "blooming" effect of adding the royal flower of France to the Tuscan arms.

40. This one is both general and obscure. Hesperia is most likely Spain, though the reader who chooses to see it as American may do so.

41. From Le Pelletier on, this one has always been associated with the new Charlemagne, "Chyren-Selin," and is accorded in each case to the prevailing pretender of the moment. As we have seen elsewhere (477), the new Charlemagne is probably none other than Henry II. Nostradamus certainly would never have intended this one for Henry II, who was not born in any shadows.

42. Mars here may refer to war in general or to a great French military leader (Gaston de Foix in the 1500's, François de Guise in the 1550's, etc.). Nostradamus must be given credit for real prediction here, since when he wrote it was the French who held Savoy, instead of the other way around. As it turned out, the only really notable Savoyard invasion was during the Interregnum (1589–94). Except during the Revolution, Lombardy remained under the Habsburgs till 1859, under the Spanish till 1713. The Milanese was the first section of Charles V's empire entrusted to Philip II. The quatrain is apparently in line with Nostradamus' conviction that the death of Charles V would be followed by a war between brother Ferdinand and son Philip. According to geopolitical astrology, the Balance affected only two European states, Austria and Savoy. Thus, in short, Philip is to bring terror to the Austrian half of the empire.

43. Notwithstanding the great abundance of place names, this one remains obscure. The places are certainly far-spread. If *Seez et Ponce* is indeed Sées and Pons, the former is the seat of a venerable bishopric in Normandy, while the latter is about sixty miles north of Bordeaux. Besides these places, we have Provence in the southeast, Naples and Sicily in Italy, the

Rhine and Cologne in Germany. And the villain is presumably the German Archbishop of Mainz. Perhaps Nostradamus thought that the Archbishop would turn Protestant and make Mainz the Protestant center of Germany. Another possible interpretation involves Mainz being Gutenberg's city and the original center for printing books, with all the dangers inherent in them.

44. With Nostradamus, the "red one" seems to refer always either to the Spaniard, or to a cardinal, distinguished by his red hat. Here the capture of a cardinal by the Barbary corsairs threatens the peace. The Pope strengthens his army (and the 16th-century popes had real armies).

45. This quatrain, like 542 and many others, is probably also in line with the "War of the Imperial Succession" theme. Here Ferdinand is seen as getting the worst of it, forced to move from Germany and Austria to the Netherlands. The Ardennes touches several provinces of the Netherlands. Line 3 would seem to refer to Philip's killing off his father's bastards (Don John, Margaret of Parma, etc.). The last line remains uncertain, since Philip had neither a red beard nor a hawk nose. However, according to Prescott's biography (I, p. 39), his hair was light yellow in his youth, and Philip was still in his twenties when the prophecy was written. As it happened, none of this occurred. The empire was divided peacefully according to Charles' plan and will. It was to Philip, and not Ferdinand, that the Netherlands fell. Finally, Don John and Margaret were given great honors and high offices by their grim half-brother.

46. This one is for the Papacy. A cardinal who will be from the Sabine country (northeast of Rome in the environs of Rieti) will be elected Pope, but a group of cardinals will refuse to acknowledge his election. At the same time, Rome will suffer from the "Albanois," whose identity remains uncertain. The troops of the Spanish Duke of Alba would seem a good possibility here. Garencières takes it quite literally: "Rome shall be endamaged by the Albanians, which are a Warlike people, and for the most part subject to the Common-wealth of Venice."

47. Another prophecy on the "New Arab Empire" theme (see 525, 527 and Index for others), and a very obscure one. The Byzantines are the Turks, whose capital was originally called Byzantium. Rhodes is the strategic Mediterranean island off southwest Turkey, captured from the Knights of St. John by the Turks (1522). Apparently Rhodes is to be the base for a fleet which will inflict a great deal of damage on the Arabs. The last line refers to the fact that after the Turkish conquest of Hungary, the Emperor retained a narrow strip of western and northern Hungary, for which he paid tribute. The inhabitants of this strip are the "Austrian Hungarians." It included an outlet on the Adriatic in the vicinity of Fiume (now Rijeka).

48. The "great affliction of the sceptre" is probably another reference to the "War of the Imperial Succession" theme. Line 2 is rather cryptic. Line 3 predicts a corsair fleet at Fiume (now Rijeka).

49. Another one for the Papacy. A French Pope will be elected, rather

than a Spanish one. Actually, only Italian Popes have been elected since Nostradamus' day (specifically, since 1522). "The enemy" probably refers to the Spanish, traditional French enemy of the 16th century.

50. The brothers of the lily are princes of the House of France. As we saw elsewhere, Nostradamus foresaw Henry II becoming Emperor, so that the verse may be intended for his four sons. The future Francis II was born in 1542, the future Charles IX in 1550, the future Henry III in 1551 and the future Francis of Alençon (christened Hercules) in 1554. Perhaps one of them is here seen as succeeding his father as Emperor. In line 3 the mountains are undoubtedly the Alps, with the Latin passage referring to Rome. In this and other respects, the verse calls to mind paragraphs 16 and 17 of the Epistle. We look in vain for some territory in Europe designated as "Armenia." (See also 594.) The last line seems to take us to Asia.

51. Dacia was the ancient Roman province corresponding to modern Rumania. In the 16th century it consisted of three principalities, each autonomous under Turkish sovereignty. Of the three, Moldavia and Wallachia played no active roles in the international scene, but Transylvania did, and it is undoubtedly the last that Nostradamus has in mind here. Here it is in league with the Poles, the Czechs and the English, a very modern-sounding combination (especially with the English 'way in there). Bohemia had belonged to the Habsburgs since 1526. The purpose of the league is not stated; were it not for the presence of the English, war against the infidel would seem the answer. This is really only the first of two separate prophecies. The second one is even more obscure: Spaniards (or Catalonians) from Barcelona and Italians from Tuscany (or unidentified descendants of Phoenician colonists ["Tyrians"]) will co-operate to get past the Strait of Gibraltar. Against whom? The Spaniards held Gibraltar until it was taken by the British (July 24, 1704). On the other side, they got Ceuta with the rest of the Portuguese Empire (1580), and retained it even when Portugal regained its independence (1640). The Portuguese had Ceuta since 1415. Perhaps Nostradamus foresaw both Gibraltar and Ceuta under control of the resurgent Moslems.

52. Except for line 3, the victim of which would seem the mendicant order of friars, this quatrain remains both obscure and general.

53. The Sun here would seem to represent Christianity or Christendom, rather than the device of Charles V and Philip II. In 524 and 525 we saw Venus probably used for the Moslems. This quatrain is thus rather general and worthless, predicting war between Christendom and Islam, and that Christendom will prevail. The reference to the spirit of prophecy is quite obscure.

54. The name of Tartary was given loosely to the whole of Central Asia, from the Caspian to China. From this area came the Huns of Attila, Genghiz Khan, Tamerlane and the Turks. It is to produce another conqueror, who will be headed for France. (See also 1072.) In lines 3–4 we appear to have his route. The Armenians lived south of the Caucasus and the Alanians north

of it. Unless the conqueror is making a great detour, he comes through Persia, passes east of the Black Sea, then follows around the sea to the Balkan Peninsula and Constantinople.

55. This one is a thoroughly clear, simple and lucid prophecy. A great Moslem ruler will come out of Arabia Felix. He will avenge the recent expulsion of the Moors by reconquering Grenada for Islam and fighting the Spaniards, as did his 7th-century ancestors. The Kingdom of Grenada, the last Moorish outpost in Spain, fell in 1492. By sea the Arab will move against the Genoese.

56. Another one just for the Papacy, of a rather general nature. A very old Pope will be succeeded by a youngish one who, though arousing much enmity, remains Pope long and accomplishes much.

57. To some interpreters, there is just one noteworthy thing here: *mont Gaulfier* can be nothing but Montgolfier, the name of the brothers who invented the balloon in the late 18th century. The fact that this doesn't fit the context at all proves of no importance: the quatrain is applied to a hodgepodge of events in the 1790's (the Battle of Fleurus, in which the balloon was used for scouting, in 1794; the capture of Rome; the captivity of Pope Pius VI; etc.). The real setting appears to be in Nostradamus' natal Saint-Rémy. From 427 we can see that the *SEXT. mansol* refers to the famous mausoleum, whose inscription begins with *SEX*. This mausoleum is at the foot of Mont Gaussier. "The hole" probably refers to the Porte du Trou, the gate of Saint-Rémy which is nearest to the area. These are the pieces, but to fit them together still remains a problem. Another problem is that there is nothing now in the area resembling the name of the Aventine, originally one of the Seven Hills of Rome, but in Nostradamus' time a desolated area outside the city proper, containing monasteries and cemeteries, and obviously not intended. Possibly it was a name formerly applied to a local mountain. Line 4 would seem to suggest either that the famous ruins at Saint-Rémy would be destroyed, or that their mystery would be cleared up.

58. "Aqueduct" refers to the most famous ruins of a Roman aqueduct in France, extending from Uzès to Nîmes. The prophecy has been applied to an exploit of the Duke of Rohan in September, 1627 (by Larmor in 1925 and more extensively by Boswell in 1941). Another religious revolt had taken place. His Calvinist co-religionists at Nîmes were besieged. To get support to them, Rohan moved artillery over the aqueduct. The rather obscure event of line 3 is applied to his pioneers having cut part of the supports of the bridge over the Gard to widen the path for the cannon. Line 4 is taken care of by the fact that Rohan was made general of the party upon his arrival at Nîmes. Certainly Nostradamus seems to have had some such exploit on the aqueduct in mind.

59. This is a very dramatic quatrain. Nîmes, in southeastern France, would certainly be an odd place for an "English chief." Perhaps this one belongs to the "New Hundred Years' War" theme. In 545 we saw the possibility that *Aenobarbe* was intended for Philip II, titular King of Eng-

land 1554–58. A great war will begin the day that a meteor falls in Artois, then the southernmost of the provinces of the Netherlands (French after 1659).

60. Le Pelletier applies this one to Napoleon in 1813-15, with a rather free translation of line 2:

> France will have made in the person of Bonaparte, a man with short hair, a choice which will become very disastrous for it: it will undergo a burden heavier than its forces can bear. Napoleon will be animated by such a warlike fury that it will be feared that the male sex will be completely exterminated on the field of battle.

The two principal elections having been for Emperor and Pope, this verse must have been intended for one or the other. Popes, however, were more likely to have shaven heads than emperors. Actually both may be involved: a Pope may have the opportunity to settle a rival claim to the Imperial title by offering one of them a Papal Coronation.

61. Line 1 seems to suggest an adopted son. Mont Cenis, containing one of the passes to Italy, was in Savoy. In 1859 it became part of the border line between France and Italy. The Apennines run down the length of Italy. According to Pearce, only two European states were under the influence of Libra the Balance: Savoy and Austria. Probably Austria is intended here. The prophecy is rather general, telling that the adopted son of a French ruler will vex the Habsburgs in Spain and Italy, and conquer Italy. Nearest to fulfill it seems to have been Josephine's son, Eugène de Beauharnais, who was made Viceroy of Italy by Napoleon. But it was Daddy who did the conquering.

62. Another of the detailed but obscure variety. Line 1 may be taken as a prodigy, or as a figure for the blood of those wounded in a naval battle spurting onto the rocks. Line 2 is more likely a metaphor than a configuration. The Sun stands for Christendom and Saturn probably for the Antichrist or something along that line. Orgon is an insignificant town about twenty miles north of Nostradamus' Salon, seeming strangely out of place amidst the big doings here. In line 4 "the Tridental" refers to the power holding the sovereignty of the Mediterranean, in Nostradamus' day, the Turks (and their Algerian vassals).

63. This one is rather general and obscure. The general subject is probably a disastrous French expedition to Italy, a theme which appears elsewhere also.

64. This one is hopelessly obscure and tending to gibberish. In line 3 we have Genoa and Nice clearly enough, but the identity of *Antonne* remains a mystery. *Mentone* is probably closest in sound, but not in etymology. *Antibes* is derived from Antipolis, but that is hardly closer. The unique variant of one early printer provides an easy way out: "autumn."

65. This one would seem hopelessly general and obscure, but Roberts (1947) is immediately struck by its message: "Consternation shall seize the

betrayers of the people when they perceive the growing strength of the masses and their insistence upon a voice in their destiny."

66. The vestals were the priesteses of Vesta. The fact that they were required to be virgins allows poetic association with that first of chaste goddesses, Diana. Therefore Garencières' (i.e., Jaubert's) note is interesting: the Convent of Saint-Sauveur-de-la-Fontaine at Nîmes was built on the ruins of a temple of Diana. Garencières states that the ruins of a basilica built by Hadrian to the Empress Plotina, his stepmother, were still to be found at Nîmes. Thus Nostradamus predicts that a lamp from the Temple of Plotina, made of gold and silver, will have found its way to the near-by Temple of Diana, where it will be dug up in modern times. This is specific enough, though rather unlikely with respect to the "still burning" feature, which is included also in 99, a similar prophecy.

67. Perugia having been part of the Papal States since 1534, this one undoubtedly concerns the Pope. The rather obscure wording indicates nothing very clearly, so we offer Le Pelletier's rather imaginative interpretation:

> When Sixtus V will not dare to excommunicate Henry III, for fear that the Church of Rome (already stripped, in 1534, by the schism of England) would be rendered entirely naked by a French schism, there will be an end to the posterity of Henry II, through a memorable event: Henry III will perish, as his father Henry II, through a thrust directed at the throat.

Although Henry and Catherine did indeed have seven children, Henry was not the last to die. Margaret, first wife of Henry IV, lived on until 1615.

68. "The great Camel" probably refers to the Arab leader mentioned elsewhere (see General Index), the Camel being considered a typically Arabian creature. It might also refer to a hunchback. Apparently, though he will have swept all aside in Germany, he has a less smooth time with the French. The latter, after being in great fear of him, bring about his downfall.

69. Le Pelletier applies this one to an ever more uneasy Louis-Philippe, trying to strengthen his shaky position at home through the conquest of Algeria (1830-48). Somehow or other Le Pelletier gets the Tricolor out of line 3, glibly stating that *phalange* means "standard," which it certainly doesn't. But the verse is far too obscure to be able to tell what Nostradamus really meant.

70. According to Pearce (see General Bibliography), the only European states influenced by Libra the Balance were Austria and Savoy. If Austria be intended here, she is apparently allowed to get in on the overthrow of the Turkish Empire, presumably under the French Emperor. Rather vague.

71. This quatrain sounds interesting, but is far too general for much interpretation. Attempts have been made to apply it to various of the frustrated would-be conquerors of Britain: Parma, Napoleon, Hitler, etc. However, it obviously points to a fleet at Marseilles, not on the English Channel.

72. The rather general poetic language allows elasticity of application. Jaubert and Le Pelletier make a perfectly good case for applying it to the

Edict of Poitiers (September 17, 1577) whereby the King legalized Calvinist worship. It was voluptuous since it allowed marriage for the clergy. Thereby the Catholic Sun was legally beclouded, poison was put in the true faith, and Venus (heretic, infidel, etc.) was made to seem virtuous, instead of heretical and illegal.

73. This one is very specific and very colorful, with three separate elements: (1) a persecution of the Church; (2) an ungrateful royal child (Louis XIII did something like this to Marie de' Medici in *ca.* 1620), and (3) the Poles going in with the Arab invaders of Europe.

74. Another rather general one, with Henry II, or one of his progeny, becoming Emperor. "Trojan blood" is based on a legend of descent from "Francus, son of Priam of Troy," for the French rulers. It was begun by the Merovingians. King Dagobert was wont to sign a deed *ex nobilissimo et antiquo Trojanorum reliquiarum sanguine nati* (see *Encyclopaedia Britannica*). This verse has caused all sorts of fancy interpretations, with very different ideas for "foreign Arabic people." It rarely occurs to a commentator that when Nostradamus said Arabs he might mean just that. The new Charlemagne, after driving the Infidel invader from Europe, will restore the Church to its power of yore.

75. This one bids fair to taking the prize for the most obscure one. It is an example of what many unjustly regard as typical of all Nostradamus' quatrains. The only clue is in line 4: the crooked staff is the traditional bishop's staff.

76. This one is rather vague except for the places, and not all of them are clear. The towns are fairly close to each other in Nostradamus' home area in Provence.

77. Another interesting but utterly obscure one. Here is Le Pelletier's version:

> All the dissident churches of the world will be reformed according to the Roman rite: the Great Pastor himself, at the same time Pontiff *(flaminique)*, Citizen *(quirinal)* and Warrior *(martial)*, will seem clothed in an impenetrable armor, through the protection of the King of the Franks.

78. This one at first seems very specific, but the meaning is not clear. The Barbarian Satrap is probably Dragut, Beylerbey of Tunis, or a successor, satrap of the Turkish Sultan. However, from 1535 to 1570 the ruler of Tunis itself was a nominal vassal of the Habsburg Emperor, so that it might also refer to him. In the last line we find the Pope and the Papacy at last appreciated by all. Line 1 may connect this one with the Duumvirate of 523.

79. While no good son of Rome would think of applying this one to Napoleon, it has nevertheless been applied quite well as such. All the rather general qualifications fit Napoleon well. He treated the Popes and the clergy as the Byzantine Emperors treated the Patriarch. He was a great legislator, nominally (the Code Napoléon). He made titled aristocrats out of the lowborn. He stamped out rebellion ruthlessly. Some of his admirers may agree

with line 4. But to Roberts (1947), "The Advent of Abraham Lincoln is plainly prophesied here."

80. Ogmios in Celtic mythology was the equivalent of Hercules (or to some extent, of Mercury). According to McBain (*Celtic Mythology and Religion*, p. 66):

> Lucian speaks of a sort of Gaulish Hercules, represented as an old man drawing a large multitude after him by cords fastened to their ears and his tongue, and he was their god of letters and eloquence, and they called him Ogmios.

It would be very interesting to find in what 16th-century book our prophet picked up this rather rare deity. In 642 this character appears to be the successor, presumably as Emperor, of the new Charlemagne, "Henry-Selin." In connection with the probability that "Henry-Selin" is none other than Nostradamus' own thoroughly mediocre and soon-to-die Henry II, it is worth noting that his youngest son, born 1550, was christened Hercules and only later in life (after this prophecy was written) did his name get changed to Francis. He grew up to become the Duke of Alençon and Anjou, equally ugly in body and character. After being used by various factions during the Wars of Religion against his royal brothers, he went off to woo Queen Elizabeth of England. After she turned him down, calling him "her frog," he sailed off to the Netherlands to accept the offer made by the Dutch leader, William the Silent, that he become their ruler under the title "Protector of the Netherlands." Alienating all with his high-handed efforts to establish absolute power, his brutality and his treachery, he was kicked out by the Dutch in 1583 and died the following year, a total loss to the French, to the Dutch and to Nostradamus.

81. The royal "bird" is undoubtedly the eagle. It will appear over Rome (capital of the Sun of Christendom) as an omen that seven months later disaster will strike. By applying the latter to Paris, a fair case has been made (by Boswell, 1941, pp. 201–2) for the Fall of France, with the Maginot Line and the Blitzkrieg seen in line 3. The royal bird becomes a lone night plane appearing over Paris on November 13, 1939. The seven days of line 4 are applied to June 5–11, 1940.

82. Langres was in Champagne, Dôle and Arbois in Franche-Comté. The latter remained legally Spanish until 1678. Bresse was not legally annexed by France from Savoy until 1601. All the places are thus in the environs of the 16th-century eastern frontier. The military action envisaged here is hard to see.

83. This quatrain, at the same time general yet sharp, should have a number of popular applications in the 20th century. The Bible in line 4 is probably meant literally, and is associated with the hated Calvinists. Thus some Calvinist leader is probably denoted here.

84. Rouen and Evreux, both in Normandy, are coupled also in 4100 and may have some meaning together never appreciated. Lines 1–2 should denote something specifically, but don't. This one is certainly very general. "Ac-

cording to Trotsky," writes Allen (1943, p. 375), "Stalin's mother was a neurotic afraid of her shadow and his father was a brutal old soak," whatever significance that may have here.

85. This one can be applied to nothing Nostradamus intended as well as to the failure of the League of Nations and World War II. It is remarkable how many of the quatrains mentioning Geneva with obvious reference to Calvin's theocracy seem to fit circumstances in the 20th century, especially with the implications here of aerial warfare.

86. Le Roux (1710) has applied this one to a flooding of the Seine in Paris: the heads were the Fauxbourgs St. Bernard and St. Victor, the arms the left and right banks and the islands in the middle. The data of line 3 can be substantiated at any time in any country. The Turks were hard-pressed by the Persians in the first quarter of the 17th century and the first half of the 18th. But all the fighting was over how much of the former Persian territories the Turks would be able to hold on to. At no time did the Turks come close to near disaster and invasion, as Nostradamus seemed to foresee.

87. It is uncertain whether line 1 denotes a configuration or a metaphor. The context makes the second more likely. Some sort of non-Catholic (probably Protestant rather than Moslem), freed from captivity, will be "inundated," whatever that means. He will marry a French princess (see 574 re Trojan blood) and then will be imprisoned by the Spanish.

88. Savona, west of Genoa, belonged to the Republic of Genoa. The latter did indeed become the "slave of Turin" in 1815, when it was given to the House of Savoy. But the rest is less clear.

89. Very detailed, but very obscure. Possibly it tells of a Crusade via Bohemia into Hungary under the leadership of a member of one of the branches of the House of France (possibly that of Bourbon-Vendôme of Navarre). Duke of Orléans was the title of Henry II until the death of his brother made him Dauphin—which may or may not provide a clue to line 4.

90. This one is fairly clear, predicting that for nine months a famine and a plague (whose identity is veiled in the obscure meaning of *connisse*) will devastate the southern Balkans and the islands off the coast. Larissa was the chief city of Thessaly in northern Greece, while Sparta is in the Peloponnesian peninsula at the southern end. Perinthus was near the eastern tip of Thrace, fifty miles west of Byzantium. It has remained Turkish since the 15th century, under the name of Eski Eregli. The Cyclades (Andros, Tinos, Naxos, *et al.*) are the islands southeast of Greece.

91. Another of the detailed but obscure variety. The scene would seem to be Athens, but the identity of the market and the Torrent is not clear. In line 4, the time of the prophecy is limited by a configuration. And again we have the elusive "Albanois," in this case more likely the Albanians than the troops of the Spanish generalissimo. Perhaps this one goes with the "New Crusade" theme.

92. This quatrain is obviously intended for the Papacy, but Le Pelletier

can't resist applying it to Louis-Philippe, with the five his Orléanist princes. The personage of lines 3–4 is none other than Prince-President Bonaparte (later Napoleon III). Actually, the prophecy is very simple. A Pope whose pontificate has lasted for seventeen years will be succeeded by five others, in the same space of seventeen years. The seventh Pope will then be a great churchman with many enemies. This might well have been fulfilled, but never was.

93. Nostradamus probably meant this one for a Scottish king who would restore Catholicism in England by fire and sword. However, if the astrology of lines 1–2 can be reconciled, the quatrain was fulfilled by Charles I, born at Dunfermline in Scotland in 1600 (three years before the Stuarts got the throne). He certainly did throw the English into confusion.

94. A very rich and dramatic quatrain. Flanders and the Brabant were both provinces in the Habsburg Netherlands. Bruges and Ghent are both in Flanders. (Flanders and Brabant were indeed parts of various German empires, 1713–95, 1914–18 and 1940–44.) Boulogne, however, was in northern France. This may be another reflection of Nostradamus' confusion about the legacy of Charles V. He seems to have foreseen that out of the war which would ensue between Ferdinand and Philip, Ferdinand would be strong in the Netherlands. As it happened, there was no war and the Netherlands went to Philip. The Emperor is seen as enjoying enough success to annex the Netherlands into the Empire, and to try to extend the boundaries to France. "The Grand Duke of Armenia" is probably intended for one of the oriental conquerors foreseen as fighting over the Turkish Empire (possibly the one in 554). Cologne brings him rather near France. The name appears in an apparently European setting also in 550.

95. It seems more than likely that this one ties up with 53, with both being either *nautique rane* or *rame*. But whom this designates remains uncertain. Lines 3–4 suggest some marvelous but quite incomprehensible feats of engineering. The Aegean Sea is between Greece and Asia Minor, the Tyrrhenian between Sicily and Tuscany.

96. The rose was one of the chief devices of the great Orsini clan, involved here in some intrigue at Rome (middle of the great world). But the intrigue involved is quite obscure. Roberts (1947) here shows his profound learning: "Nostradamus predicts the coming of a great world leader, and by a simple play on words as expressed in the first line, we have his name: rose and world (*Welt*, in German), combined to make Roosevelt." (The *velt*, if it is worth pursuing this nonsense, comes from Dutch *veld*, field.)

97. With a bit of imagination, this one might be applied to *The Man in the Iron Mask*. Line 2, if not referring to Paris, does not tell much. Line 3 might be applied to the revocation of the Edict of Nantes (1685). Condom is a small town in Guienne in the Southwest, which, according to one theory, gave its name to a well-known rubber article.

98. If this refers to the 48th degree of latitude, it passes near Rennes, Le Mans, Orléans and Langres. "The end of Cancer" probably means the

date at which the sun leaves that sign of the Zodiac (about June 21). The drought will be so great from the prodigious heat that fish will be cooked as they swim (a prodigy we found in 23). Béarn and Bigorre were contiguous counties of the Southwest belonging to the House of Bourbon-Navarre. What Nostradamus had in mind for "fire from the sky" is not clear. In the 20th century it would make much sense.

99. These cities cover every corner of Italy, to show how complete French activity in Italy will be. The conqueror is presumably Henry II after he has become Emperor. The identity of the British chief referred to in line 4 at Rome is not clear. An interpretation of this verse for the time of Napoleon (which is not unreasonable) does have an answer to this problem: Cardinal York, last of the Stuarts, who died in Rome in 1807.

100. And again we have "fire from the sky." All the places of lines 2–3 are in southwest France. Comminges is an ancient county east of Bigorre. There is no town by that name. Mazères is about twenty miles north of Foix. The last lines refer to the German states, which is real prophecy, since enemy troops in France in the 16th century were generally Spaniards, and in that area there have probably never been many Germans, not even in 1940–44.

# Century VI

1. Le-Mas-d'Agenais is a small town on the Garonne, with many Roman and even pre-Roman ruins. Nostradamus lived at Agen in the 1530's. The most famous temple in the environs is one dedicated to the Gallic sun god Vermetis. The new King would seem to be that of either France or Spain. The Roman chief is probably a prelate of the Church of Rome. (Neither the Pope nor the Emperor would be likely to enter this locale.)

2. Nostradamus stuck out his neck on dates here and for once did quite nicely. In 1580 France was torn by civil wars (specifically, by the so-called Seventh War, which began and ended in 1580), and her future looked gloomy. But 1703 saw the mighty France of Louis XIV defying Europe in the War of the Spanish Succession. A very ingenious interpretation has been found for line 4. The Kingdom of Spain, as inherited by Louis XIV's grandson Philip V ("to five") actually consisted of several states beyond Spain, such as the Two Sicilies, the Netherlands, the Milanese and many kingdoms in Asia and America. Roberts (1947), however, is not satisfied with these dates here, and reveals that "Nostradamus commences his count of time from A.D. 325, the date of the Council of Nicaea."

3. The river is probably the Rhine. According to Garencières, "the ancient Frenchmen when they had a King newly born, they used to put him upon a Target to make him swim up on that River, to try whether by his swimming he was lawfully begotten or no. . . ." This young King, under the

influence of the clergy, will be in conflict with the Empire. Line 4 remains rather obscure.

4. In this case the river is definitely the Rhine, and this prophecy may go with the preceding one. It is a very specific and daring one: the Rhine will change its course in such a manner that it will no longer wash Cologne. So far this has not happened. To make it yet more specific, we have a configuration in line 4 (though the usage of *en rapine* remains a mystery). Line 3 seems clear, but the thought behind it is difficult to understand.

5. Of all the prophecies of Nostradamus, there is probably none more completely inapplicable to his own period, or to the whole four centuries to the 1960's, than this one. Suddenly, it has an excellent chance of a very impressive fulfillment. A league was generally about 2.5 miles, sometimes as much as 4.5 miles. In 846, Nostradamus' league equals 2.7 miles. Now, there is only one way one can get 270 miles from the hemisphere, and that is upwards into space. And note that there is real meaning to "hemisphere," since anyone a certain distance away from merely the "earth" on one side would be many times that distance away from the other side of the earth at any given moment. Since we can eliminate any thought of the whole city of Amiens in France being 270 miles out in space, we are entitled to be imaginative in suggesting to whom or to what the word *Samarobryn* might apply. Supposing that we give Nostradamus the benefit of the doubt for an occasional genuine and correct burst of clairvoyance, might we not here have a prophecy of a space-station thought by Nostradamus, rightly or wrongly, to be about 270 miles from the earthly hemisphere? And might we not consider that in the course of this vision Nostradamus overheard a name associated with this pioneer venture into space, a name such as Sam R. O'Brien, the sound of which, as it struck his French ear, he transcribed as "Samarobryn"?

In addition to the space reference (in which connection see also 181) we have cryptic references to other matters sounding rather contemporary: activity in the arctic of a strange sort in line 2, and in line 1 perhaps a hint of bacteriological warfare.

6. "The North" in line 1 may refer to the North of the European map or of the celestial map. In the constellation of Cancer will be seen a comet. This will be an omen that at dawn a Pope (probably) will have died. Line 3 presents an odd assortment of geography. Susa is in Piedmont in northwest Italy; Siena is in central Italy, south of Florence. The first belonged to the House of Savoy, the second to the Duchy of Tuscany. Boeotia was the province in southeastern Greece which contained Thebes. Eretria (now Aletria) was on the large island of Euboea, east of Boeotia. Both belonged to the Turks from the 15th to the 19th centuries, but had been held by Venice the previous century.

7. Another ambitious and modern-sounding geopolitical amalgamation. In 551 we found Dacia to be used for Transylvania, in odd combination with

Britain. It appears that Norway is to be added here. (The Scandinavian unity broke up when Sweden became independent [1523]. Norway, however, remained under the Danish crown till 1815. Next it went to Sweden, becoming independent only in 1905—with a Danish King.) The only common denominator of these three areas would seem that they represented the northern, eastern and western extremities of 16th-century Christendom. Even these will be threatened by the "united brothers." Line 3 probably refers to a pope or an emperor of French origin.

8. This is one of several quatrains bemoaning the fate of the learned after a royal patron of arts is succeeded by a less cultured boor.

9. This one is rather general and must have been fulfilled many times.

10. A very obscure quatrain. The colors may be associated with the characteristic garb of various monastic orders.

11. Le Pelletier gives a rather impressive version of this one for the period 1575–88:

> When the seven surviving children of Henry II will be reduced to the three youngest (in 1575 Henry III, Queen Margaret of Navarre and Francis of Alençon), Henry III and the Duke of Alençon will engage in a fratricidal war. The Guise, conspiring with the Leaguers against Henry III, will find death while being lulled into a false security (in 1588).

However, it's general enough to have other applications.

12. This one is about as detailed, clear, specific and colorful a prophecy as one can find. What is most remarkable is that the geopolitical line-up is in completely modern terms. (There was no Italy until 1870, while the Flemings—acceptable today as synecdoche for Belgium—were completely dependent on the Habsburgs.) We find three main elements: (1) an attempt at gaining the Imperial throne by conquest; (2) a Pope of Capetian blood; (3) an alliance between the Habsburgs and the English against Italy and France. The first and third factors were fulfilled well enough in the time of Napoleon, but the second one does not seem ever to have been fulfilled. All popes since 1523 have been Italian.

13. Le Pelletier hopefully applies this one to the impending doom of the new Savoy King of Italy, Victor Emmanuel:

> A despot, pretending to be a liberal (a doubtful one), will not be far from being crowned King of all Italy: he will receive a majority of the votes; but the republican party (allusion to the Capitol, ancient rampart of the republicans of Rome) will be opposed to his government, and he will be unable to sustain the great burden he had assumed.

Undoubtedly to Le Pelletier's chagrin, Italy did not dissolve again.

14. It is a rather curious fact that one can find support for romantic versions of several of the leading "historical mysteries" in the Centuries. Quatrain 597 could be taken as support for the theory of the Man in the Iron Mask being the twin brother of Louis XIV (see Dumas). Later, we will find

quatrains that could support the escape of Louis XVII. This one could be applied quite nicely to the escape of King Sebastian I of Portugal. Educated by the Jesuits, he was consumed with the idea of a crusade against the infidel. Against the advice of the Pope and the King of Spain, and the fact that crusades were plainly out of date, Sebastian attacked the King of Fez in Morocco in 1578. On August 4, at the Battle of Kasr Al-Kabir, his army was completely obliterated. He was supposed to have been killed, but rumors of his survival persisted, and produced various pretenders. This quatrain would thus tell that he had changed armor with a faithful friend, to be captured in his place. Line 4 would suggest that the Moors discovered that they had not killed the King, but preferred to let that impression prevail.

Hugh Allen (1943, p. 608) sees this as referring to Hitler fleeing in disguise after losing a battle.

15. Another prize example of the specific but obscure variety. Nuremberg came into the 16th-century scene only in 1532, when the Religious Peace of Nuremberg permitted the Protestants the free exercise of their religion until a new council could be called in 1533. Nuremberg had been the first Imperial city to throw its lot in with the Protestants. It is probably used here for Lutheranism. It was at Wittenberg that the Reformation began when Luther nailed his 95 Theses to the door of the local court church (October 31, 1517). Luther himself cannot be referred to, since he had died in 1546. But either the ruler of Wittenberg (Maurice, Elector of Saxony, who had ended his long loyalty by attacking Charles V in 1552) or a Lutheran leader will deliver a terrible blow to the King of Spain around New Year's. This will worry him so much that he will become thin. At around the same time, the tomb of some faithful son of Rome will be found. (Constantine? Clovis? St. Peter? A Church Father?)

16. Another of the very detailed but very obscure variety. "Normans of France and Picardy" is rather meaningless, Picardy having been part of France since the 13th century. Perhaps it should read "Normans and Picards of France," Picardy being contiguous to Normandy. Apparently the French, under a young Hawk (or Eagle) are the villains of this piece. Line 3 takes us to Germany, the Black Forest running east of the Rhine from Basel to Baden. Presumably the Benedictines ("Black Monks") of the Convent of Herrenalb are intended, this being the only Benedictine monastery in the area.

17. This one is hopelessly obscure.

18. This one is very lucid and meaningful. It could have happened but never did. It is quite dramatic. A French king lies dying. The great physicians of the realm have given up hope for him. A Jew is called in as a last resort. After poking around, he confidently predicts that the King will recover. When he does recover, the Jew is given credit. The grateful King loads honors upon him, and extends great privileges to his Jewish brethren. Perhaps there is a retroactive touch in this one, suggesting Nostradamus' grandfather and "Good King René" (1409–80) of Provence.

19. This one is very general, and should be applicable to any fanatical queen. It is more than likely that at the same time that she exercises her fanaticism, some army will become inflamed, will make an attack, and that in the bullfighting of Seville, an especially large bull will be noted.

20. Also very general and obscure. Line 3 probably refers to galley slaves, line 4 to a new Pope (with a lion in his coat of arms; in heraldry, a leopard is a lion walking to the left, with its head turned to its left facing the viewer). Perhaps the leopard is the same as the one in 123.

21. A rather rich and colorful quatrain. Line 1 is very provocative. The only 16th-century states with any parts within the Arctic Circle were Sweden and Denmark's Norway. Neither of these would seem likely to cause terror in the East. Now, of course, we have the U.S. and the U.S.S.R. A newly elected Pope or emperor, lines 3–4 would indicate, throws in his support, whereupon "Barbarians" invading Constantinople and the island of Rhodes are slaughtered. The name Barbarians is applied properly to the corsairs of the North African Barbary states, but Nostradamus seems at times to use it more widely for any subjects of the Sultan.

22. This one is quite specific and lucid. From the context, the land of the great heavenly temple would appear to be England. The reason is best known to Nostradamus. In line 2 the nephew of some ruler (of Scotland?) is induced to come to London to make peace, only to be murdered treacherously. There is no reason why this should not have occurred, but apparently it hasn't. At the same time, there will be a schism in the Church of Rome (the Bark of St. Peter). Line 4 probably refers to the "religious nationalism" of the 16th century, manifested chiefly in the Germanic states as liberty from Rome, which Nostradamus of course considers a sham liberty.

Le Pelletier has a quaint version for the Second Empire. The nephew, of course the Emperor, is murdered by the ruinous terms of a trade treaty with Britain (January 23, 1860). On November 24, the sham "Liberal Empire" began when Napoleon stepped down as dictator and extended the powers of the legislature. The schism is the plunder of the Papal States by the Italian nationalists.

23. Although this one sounds very detailed, it is really full of general and frequently applicable factors: inflation, political unrest, a peace, religious controversy, trouble in Paris, etc. The anonymous critic of 1724 sees it for the 1560's (thinking Nostradamus wrote it after the event, and thus paying him a fine compliment). Le Pelletier sees it for the French Revolution and Napoleon.

24. According to Wollner (1926, p. 59), the configuration of lines 1–2 will take place only on June 21, 2002. It is fairly general: there will be a terrible war; then the world will be pacified by a newly crowned king (French?).

25. This one is for the Papacy and fairly clear. The Papacy will run into great trouble when its troops are defeated. This happened in 1796–1815 and 1860–70, and before then, and will possibly happen again. Just what is meant

by the *jeune noire rouge*, who seizes the Papacy, is not clear. The politico-social significance of red dates from the 19th century. With Nostradamus it means Spaniard or cardinal. Thus we have a young black cardinal, or a young cardinal-king (not impossible: Portugal was ruled by one from 1578 to 1580). In line 4 we find that the foul deed will be perpetrated on a rainy day.

26. Another one for the Papacy. After holding his see for four years, a good Pope will die, to be succeeded by a worldly one. Lines 3 and 4 are somewhat obscure, but apparently reflect which states will back the Pope in some sort of conflict. Ravenna was one of the semi-autonomous Legations, ruled by a Cardinal-Legate. Pisa belonged to Tuscany and Verona to the Venetian Republic.

27. The reference in line 1 is obscure, seemingly the British Isles. There is no special incidence of five rivers flowing to one there. If not the British Isles, the Isles are likely to be those of the Mediterranean. In any case, they are involved in the career of "Henry-Selin" (see 477). The rest is even more obscure.

28. The great Celt may be Henry-Selin, or his heir, "Ogmios" (the Celtic Hercules—see 580). The cock refers to the device used by the ancient Gauls. In lines 3–4 it is not clear whether he is an ally or an enemy of the great Celt. He may be the royal Pope of 612. Jaubert applies it to the campaign of the Duke of Guise in 1557, with the exiles and banished from Milan and Naples. He gets around line 3 by telling how the Pope took under his protection all those French clients to protect them from the Duke of Alba after Guise was recalled to France (1557). Le Pelletier gets around the problem by applying the cock to Savoy (hoping that it would be fulfilled in the near future), with the great Celt the miserable Duke of Bordeaux, Le Pelletier's Messiah.

29. Le Pelletier gives a fairly reasonable interpretation for this one:

Catherine de' Medici will hear the sad laments of her sons plunged into perplexity and troubles. Henry III, whom she will have brought back from Poland, in order to appease the civil discord, will increase the trouble through his alliance with Henry IV and the Huguenots against the Catholic League, and above all by the murder of the Cardinal, brother of the Duke of Guise, killed by his order on December 24, 1588.

30. Liège, besides being a city, was a province (or, more specifically, a bishopric) east of Brabant in the Netherlands. Some sort of struggle between the two provinces is predicted here. The quatrain is rather vague.

31. This one almost sounds like a 20th-century gossip column. It is clear enough, except for the identity of the participants.

32. The form of execution appears to be an ancient Roman one. The rest is obscure, and *Berich/Berlch* remains a complete mystery.

33. A very obscure quatrain, to whose meaning a clue may lie in *Alus*, either an anagram or a derivative of some Greek word. Hugh Allen (1943) finds plenty of meaning in it:

Alus is an anagram for Saul, who beat the Philistines, but, experiencing God's displeasure, fell on his sword on seeing his three sons die. The analogy is striking. Downing Street, having sent the somewhat Machiavellian Sir Stafford Cripps to the USSR to unleash the Russian Bear on Germany, will ultimately bring about Hitler's downfall, but that will be cold comfort to Downing Street, for meanwhile, according to the quatrain, the three countries in the British Isles, England, Scotland and Wales, will be . . . destroyed and the British Empire at an end and Russia will be in at the finish.

34. Nothing Nostradamus could have had in mind could have provided as neat an explanation as the 20th-century effect of bombings on any of various states compelled to surrender. Line 3 would go nicely with a "fifth column." But the wording is quite general.

35. The path of something across the celestial map seems to be traced here. Little can be discerned amidst the obscurities except drought on a great plain (of Lombardy?).

36. Notwithstanding the place names, this one remains obscure. Perugia was part of the Papal States, Florence and Pisa part of the Duchy of Tuscany. Pisa was sold to Florence in 1405, and appears to be rebelling here. Line 4 is quite specific, concerning the wounding of a king.

37. A very specific little prophecy. From some ancient edifice, being rebuilt, a stone falls down upon a "great one," and he is killed. An innocent person is accused of responsibility for the calamity, while the real culprit is hidden in a copse during a downpour of rain. It may seem so general that it has been fulfilled often, but we would be content to know of a single fulfillment.

38. Rather vague, general and obscure. "Profligates" occurs so often that one wonders if Nostradamus had some specific group in mind.

39. Lake Trasimene is west of Perugia in central Italy, and was in the Papal States. The action is rather dramatic.

40. The great dignity of the great one of Mainz refers to the Archbishop of Mainz as one of the Electors of the Empire. A perfectly clear and simple prophecy, it never quite happened. Mainz was conquered by the French during the Revolution. By a secret clause of the Treaty of Campoformio (October 17, 1797) it was ceded to France by the Emperor. But the Elector continued to hold the territory on the right bank of the Rhine, and remained an Elector until the formal end of the Holy Roman Empire (August 6, 1806). "The great thirst" probably means that another state will be greedy for the electoral title. The Archbishop of Cologne, here complaining, was also an Elector. His dignity was indeed abolished three years before the end of the Empire (February, 1803).

Roberts (1947) is at his gruesome best on this one:

> The German populace shall feel the loss of their great prestige and shall mourn the loss of their leader, Schickel-GROPPE (Hitler), even to the point of making his name synonymous with the German National Symbol, the River Rhine.

41. In 427 we saw that the Prince of "Annemark" was probably the future Emperor Maximilian II, nephew of Charles V. The Frisians were the inhabitants of classical Holland and the name still applies to a northerly maritime province. The mark was an old weight of gold and silver, equivalent to eight ounces. Those are the pieces, but the way they fit is uncertain. Possibly the common denominator was Protestantism, since England had already been mixed up with it, and Holland was another increasingly important center—or at least the northern portion of the Netherlands, since Holland was not yet independent. As for Maximilian, it seems from various prophecies that Nostradamus, hearing the rumors of his tendencies towards Lutheranism, expected him to turn Protestant. Anyhow, Maximilian, by the time of this prophecy perhaps supposed to be King of Hungary and Bohemia (which he actually became in 1562–63), is persuaded by the Hollanders and the Britishers to spend fifty thousand pounds (of gold?) on an invasion of Italy that proves in vain. It should also be pointed out that when the prophecy was written, both Frisia and England had the same ruler in the person of Philip of Spain, titular King of England and ruler of all the Netherlands. It is perhaps also worth noting that in 489 a Frisian is elected King of England.

42. Ogmios was the Celtic equivalent of Hercules (or to some extent, of Mercury). Since *Selin* is Henry II, it might refer to one of his children (especially his youngest son, christened Hercules but later Francis—see 580). Although Henry was supposed to have already conquered Italy, this hero seems to be required to do the job again.

43. Notwithstanding the place names, this one is rather vague and obscure. The Marne runs in an arc parallel to the Seine in Champagne and flows into it above Paris. Thus both really wash Paris and it may be Paris that is here "uninhabited." Line 3 may refer to the Thames (and thus the English) or to the town of La Tamise about twenty miles west of Antwerp.

44. One of the most fascinating and intriguing of the quatrains, covering a wide span of territory. We find four separate predictions:

(1) Something that looks like a rainbow is observed at Nantes by night.
(2) An artificial manner of producing rain is discovered (fulfilled in 1947).
(3) A great fleet meets disaster, with a choice by variants between Arabia and South America for the scene. Actually South America has the edge, since there is no real Gulf of Arabia. To the west of Arabia there is the Red Sea, to the east the Persian Gulf and to the south the Arabian *Sea*. The Gulf of Urabá was in Nueva Andalusia, now part of Colombia. Settlements were established in 1509–10 along its shores and were probably known to Nostradamus.
(4) A monster, half bear and half sow, is born in Saxony (the ancient German province of which Leipzig is the capital).

It is interesting to note that this quatrain could just as easily be fulfilled, in all its details, in the 20th century as in the 16th.

45. Melilla, on the Mediterranean coast of Morocco, was captured by the Spanish in 1490 and has been Spanish ever since. Everything else in the quat-

rain is obscure. Boswell (1941, p. 169) has a lengthy interpretation of this one for the Spanish Civil War.

46. While the first line does suggest an application to Louis XVIII during the Hundred Days, there is nothing in the rest to help this application along. *Nonseggle* remains unsolved, notwithstanding Le Pelletier's laborious efforts to get Saint-Cloud out of it. "The red one" is likely to indicate a cardinal. While the Eagle is always used for the Emperor or the Empire, the reference to the Frog (perhaps the same as the "nautical frog," appearing elsewhere) remains a mystery.

47. Notwithstanding the farflung place names, this one is quite obscure. Brussels and Malines (Mechlin) were both in Brabant, in the Netherlands. Langres was in Champagne, Dôle in Franche-Comté (Spanish till 1674). Therefore Brussels and Dôle, both in the Spanish realm, may stand for Spain being overcome by France (Langres).

48. Parma was a duchy in northern Italy, ruled by the descendants of a Pope's bastard. Florence and Siena were both parts of the Medici Duchy of Tuscany. The words are intriguing, but obscure.

49. A papal crusade against the Moslem invaders appears to be indicated here.

50. This one is rather obscure.

51. This one has a plot somewhat similar to that of 637. But in this case there is no fatality. Though the quatrain is clear enough in its details, we know of no fulfillment of it.

52. One of the more popular "historical mysteries" centers around the question of whether the son of Louis XVI and Marie-Antoinette actually died in prison in 1795 or escaped. This quatrain, as well as 972, could be applied very nicely to the details of an escape. One of the escape theories indeed centers around the substitution of a deaf mute for the young King. We have already seen "Trojan" used for the House of France. Nicollaud (1914, p. 139) thinks that "Trojan hope" refers to a Trojan horse kind of ruse and that Louis XVII was smuggled out in a coffin. The drama of line 3 is rather obscure. It may refer either to the death of the fake Dauphin six months after the substitution, or to the death of the real Dauphin. The Sun is in Aquarius from mid-February to mid-March, which is at a time when many rivers are frozen. If applied to the Dauphin, who was reported dead on June 8, 1795, the prophecy would then be for January of 1795.

53. Line 1 presumably refers to a French cardinal. Yet the anonymous D.D. (1715) made an ingenious effort to get Marlborough out of the "fruitful Duke," which also requires getting "Queen" out of "King." Equally ridiculous efforts were made to get French place names out of line 4. The fact remains that a Prince of the Church appears to be taking refuge with the Infidel. The route is in the shape of a U: to Constantinople (possibly by land), then to Tunis in North Africa via the island of Cyprus. The relationship between the French Cardinal and the British King and Duke remains difficult to see.

54. Nostradamus really stuck his neck out on this one. It is quite clear and

simple when taken at its face value. It bears out the theory that Nostradamus foresaw the imminent fall of the Ottoman Empire, at the hands of a new Charlemagne in Europe (Henry II) and in Asia at the hands of new Persian and Arab empires. Just how imminent is seen by the date 1607. While elaborate theses have been evolved regarding how many years to add on for the Liturgy, it is quite likely that the word is merely used for scanning and rime, in much the same way as *Anno Domini*, and is thus to be taken as 1607. Boswell (1941, p. 325) would add 355 to 374 (the dates when Auxentius, who developed the Liturgy, was Bishop of Milan). Tunis was the great citadel of the Barbarians, captured by the Spanish in 1535 and lost to the corsairs again in 1570. Bougie, about four hundred miles west of Tunis along the coast, was also a vital corsair base. Fez, however, was inland, and the capital of the Moorish Kingdom of Fez. The Moors, however, unlike their eastern neighbors, were never even nominally subject to the Turks. But they had been conquered by the Arabs in the second half of the 7th century, and this is to occur again, with their King captured. (One such king did die in battle, against Sebastian of Portugal at Kasr Al-Kabir [August 4, 1578].) A nice, clear failure.

55. All that stands clear amidst the obscurities of this verse is the Arab fleet (Arabesque sail), which may tie this one in with the previous one. Trebizond (now Trabzon) is near the northeastern corner of Asia Minor, on the Black Sea. After an illustrious history as Constantinople's great rival, it fell to the Turks in 1462. Tripolis (modern Tirebolu) is about fifty miles west along the Black Sea coast. Either of these can qualify for the Black Sea city of line 4, though a third place, such as Varna or Sinope, may be intended. Chios is an island off western Asia Minor, in the Aegean.

56. All is fairly clear in this one except the *arbon*. Arbon on Lake Constance in Switzerland could hardly qualify. There is a tiny village of Arbonne in southern France, but it is far west of the scene. Apparently it is the Spaniards here who are taking a beating, in their trans-Pyrenees domains. It must be remembered that Roussillon, with its capital at Perpignan, remained Spanish until 1659. Narbonne is about forty miles north of Perpignan. Barcelona, in Spain proper, here sending relief, lies about one hundred miles south of Perpignan. There was one great siege of Perpignan, in 1542, and a minor one in 1597.

57. This one is entirely for the Papacy. It tells of a cruel and hated protégé of a cardinal (or possibly a cardinal himself), who manages to get himself elected Pope. It is so general as to be applicable to practically any Pope the reader does not like.

58. This quatrain seems to be clearly for Nostradamus' own day. Charles V took the Rising Sun as his device at the age of eighteen. His son, Philip II, also adopted it while young, in the form of the chariot of Apollo. Henry II, to oppose this Habsburg device, as well as to honor his mistress Diana (Roman moon goddess) took the Moon as his device. Nostradamus is thus predicting once again a triumph of Henry over the Habsburgs. At the time the

quatrain was probably written, Siena was held by a French garrison, and the French were also engaged in an effort to conquer Corsica. It would seem that Nostradamus' usual patriotism is absent here, and that liberty refers to the withdrawal of the French. The two distant monarchs are most likely Henry and Charles, each far from the scene. An eclipse remains a possibility in line 2, but is less likely in this case. (Jaubert can only find a new moon for the period in question.) Line 3 probably refers to satellites of Charles and Henry.

Jaubert, under the impression that *simulte* had something to do with friendship, tells how the Marquis de Marignan, who was besieging Siena, repeatedly sent food and drink to the French commander, Blaise de Montluc. As Jaubert points out, line 4 was fulfilled. The French garrison surrendered Siena on April 21, 1555 (possibly before the quatrain was written), and by the Peace of 1559 withdrew from Corsica. But line 2 was never fulfilled: Charles and Philip triumphed over Henry. If the restoration of liberty meant that the French would win out at Siena and Corsica, then nothing in the quatrain was fulfilled.

59. This one seems to be concerned entirely with royal scandal and court gossip. Only the detail of line 4 limits its application.

60. This one is rather dramatic but a bit obscure. Italy is the most likely scene for lines 1–2. The places in lines 3–4 are scattered all over France. Rouen is in Normandy on the Seine, La Rochelle just south of Brittany, Blaye on the Gironde about twenty-five miles north of Bordeaux.

61. Much too vague and general to be of any worth.

62. The leagues of the early 16th century were usually of various Italian states against the French or the Spanish. Although there does not seem to have been any in existence when Nostradamus wrote, it is apparently a league against the French that he refers to here. But the French triumph. Savona and Albenga were ports west of Genoa, and belonging to Genoa. Monaco, then as now, was an independent state under the Grimaldis, but was completely under Spanish domination and bound by treaty (1524) to fight in all Spanish wars against the French.

63. Both Jaubert and Le Pelletier agree on applying this one to Catherine de' Medici. Although this interpretation is of necessity at variance with the predictions of Henry II living to become the new Charlemagne, it is an impressive one. Henry died on July 10, 1559, of wounds received on July 1. Catherine remained in mourning until August 6, 1566 (a month after Nostradamus' death). Her regency and power lasted throughout the reigns of her sons Francis II and Charles IX, but she lost most of it under her favorite son, Henry III (1574–89). She died in 1589 at the age of seventy. As for the remarkable seven years, the possibility should not be overlooked that Catherine, who undoubtedly had a copy of the Centuries, applied this one to herself and fulfilled it co-operatively, though Nostradamus may have meant it otherwise.

64. This quatrain is so general as to be applicable to almost any period

from Nostradamus' day to the reader's. Not even the detail of line 4 sets much of a limit: fulfillment can probably be found in the background of any war in which Spain was involved.

65. This prophecy concerns a bitter rivalry between two monastic orders, probably both Franciscan branches. Gray was the regular Franciscan color, but some of the Franciscans turned up in a hue closer to brown. While the details of the battle are obscure, they are hardly vague. One wonders again if this was not something that had already occurred and became imbedded in our prophet's subconscious, etc.

66. The new sect is presumably another Protestant one. At the same time that it is founded, an earthquake in April will turn up the tomb of a great Roman (classical or clerical?). Several quatrains are devoted to this prediction (see Index).

67. A rather general one about a cold-hearted and notoriously unlucky emperor. His chief adviser, it seems, will have been born in a rather shady environment.

68. It seems fairly certain that "Alba" refers to the Duke of Alba (Alva), in which case the quatrain was meant for the immediate future. It would seem that Alba suppresses a revolt in the Spanish army with quick ruthlessness (as he tried later in the Netherlands). But Jaubert applies it to events of 1556. Pope Paul IV, having lightly decided to take a firm stand against Spain, persecuted the Spanish party in Rome and raised a motley army. The Spanish party appealed to Alba, busy up north against the French. He responded, with great diplomacy as well as military sagacity. He intrigued to cause friction in the papal forces until the soldiers began to revolt against the incompetent papal nephews and cardinals who commanded them. Meanwhile Alba continued to win over adherents in Rome as well as to capture towns in its environs. Which, while very interesting, varies from Nostradamus' apparent meaning.

69. This one Jaubert applies also to events of 1556. Because Guise paid his soldiers better, the troops of Marshal Brissac deserted to the other French army. Brissac found himself without any more money for his troops, which in the winter had to be disbanded. Starving, they proceeded to plunder Piedmont (including the mountains of Montferrat). While assinine, this interpretation is backed up by the "before long." Though Le Pelletier does not have the latter behind him, his interpretation is much more convincing:

> The condition of the French clergy will soon (1792) become pitiful. These men who distributed their immense wealth to the poor [*sic!*] will be obliged to beg for their bread. Stripped, proscribed, wandering, dying of the cold, of hunger, of thirst, they will pass over the Alps in bands and will take refuge in Italy, causing everywhere a great scandal.

It is far more likely that Nostradamus indeed meant it for a persecution of the clergy.

70. This one is perfectly clear. It represents the last word as a eulogy of

his King by Nostradamus. Charles V's motto *Plvs Ovltre* went with the device of a crowned eagle straddling the Pillars of Hercules. Here it is predicted that the fame of Charles V will become as nothing compared with that which Henry II will achieve when he becomes Emperor. Le Pelletier, with more justice, applies it to Henry IV (arbitrarily separating it from the other *Chyren* verses, applied to his Messiah, the Duke of Bordeaux).

Roberts (1947) gives *Chyren* a new title. "The nations will organize a super-government covering the entire world. The president will be named Henry."

71. Using the 1605 version, with additional "modifications" of his own, Jaubert applies this one to the almost simultaneous death of Henry II and the double marriage of his sister to the Duke of Savoy and his daughter to Philip II. Line 4 is undoubtedly intended to designate the notables who bear the devices mentioned. Jaubert finds them all in the arms of Savoy.

72. One of the more imaginative interpretations for this dramatic and colorful quatrain was to the Czarina Alexandra and Rasputin in the period 1912–17.

73. This one is quite obscure and worthless.

74. Le Pelletier applies this one allegorically to the French Revolution. Except that the first line makes it somewhat untenable, the quatrain could be applied quite nicely to Queen Elizabeth, who died in 1603 at the age of seventy. But she was never chased out. However, it is quite likely that this quatrain ties in with the 73 years and 7 months of the Epistle, paragraph 25.

75. The classical interpretation for this one, as Le Pelletier gives it, is as follows:

Gaspard de Coligny, raised to the rank of Admiral (great Pilot) by Henry II in 1552, will resign his post in 1559, upon the death of the King, to put himself at the head of the Calvinist party. Named first Lieutenant-General of the Calvinists in 1562, he will be at the peak of his rebellion in 1567, and the principal instigator of the Civil War. These events will occur at the same time that Venice will fear the victorious arms of Sultan Selim II, who will seize the island of Cyprus from them in 1570.

While Nostradamus may indeed have intended this one for Admiral Coligny, line 2 suggests the Admiral going to a higher royal post, rather than resigning the one which he held. Line 4 suggests a threat to Venice itself, and not just the loss of a colony. The corsairs did indeed make raids all over the Adriatic throughout the 16th century.

76. This prophecy is entirely for the city of Padua in northeastern Italy. As it belonged to Venice, the tyrant is presumably a Venetian podesta. He is assassinated in a church, and thereafter his henchmen meet the same fate. It is specific enough, but did it ever happen?

77. This one is quite obscure and general. Even "German revolt" need mean nothing more than a revolt against the authority of the Emperor, with

which the 16th and 17th centuries were filled. Florence was the capital of the Duchy of Tuscany, Imola part of the Papal States. *Romaine* may be papal Romagna, in which Imola was located, or the "Roman Empire."

78. All that stands out clearly here is a victory of Henry-Selin (Henry II, see 477). There will be some dispute about it, involving the factors of lines 2 and 3. Line 4 probably indicates the Sultan, one of whose titles was "Grand Seignior" (to Europeans). Perhaps a captive sultan, very valuable as a political prisoner, is intended (suggesting the famous Sultan Jem of the late 15th century). Pavia was part of the Spanish Milanese and Genoa an independent republic under Habsburg domination.

79. The Ticino joins the Po at Pavia. The other rivers cover all France and probably just stand for the French. All of which makes the quatrain a rather general prediction of that common phenomenon, a French invasion of Lombardy.

If there is anything specific it is in the last line. Having established in 81 that Pau is Napoleon, Stewart Robb (1942) makes this one "great Napoleon submerged." The precise Tuscan derivation of *granci* in no way impairs this, giving "Napoleon hooked, submerged." All of which refers to an incident at the Battle of Lodi (May 10, 1796). During the storming of the bridge over the Adda, Napoleon fell into the water (submerged) but was pulled out (hooked) before he could drown. Thus we would see that Nostradamus took note of General Bonaparte before his contemporaries did.

80. In 654 we found the King of Fez captured by the Arabs, so presumably it is the Arabs who go on from here to Europe, probably Spain. The rest is vague or obscure.

81. This rather vague collection of horrors seems to concern the coming of the Antichrist. The geography is quite scattered. We have the Lake of Geneva in Switzerland, Genoa in Italy and the Isles uncertain, but more likely those of the Mediterranean (Corsica, Sardinia, Malta, etc.) than of Britain.

82. Another of the detailed but obscure variety.

83. This quatrain was fulfilled twice in the 16th century, and is similar to 874. Upon Charles V's abdication (1556), Philip was at first well received in the Netherlands. But his tactlessness and bigotry alienated the people and in 1568 the revolt broke out. In 1580 the Duke of Alençon, youngest of Catherine's four sons, was invited to become "Protector." (See 580.) Being tactless, ambitious and sensitive about being a mere figurehead, Francis made a savage attempt to capture Antwerp from his "loyal subjects." Were the flower to be found in the arms of Antwerp, the case would be perfect. But, alas, there is no sort of flower in its arms. If line 4 is held as a parallel prophecy, independent of the rest, we could return to Philip, who, besides causing revolt in the Netherlands, was very warlike against the lilies of France, in the person of Henry of Navarre in the years 1589–98.

Le Pelletier has yet another idea. He seeks to apply it to the second Belgian revolt, against the Dutch in 1830–31. Louis, Duke of Nemours, one of Louis-Philippe's talented sons, was invited to be King. Unlike Philip and Francis, he was in no way rude, so Le Pelletier resorts to an absurd out: he had been rude to the real French heir, the Duke of Bordeaux, when his father usurped the throne in the previous year. This Le Pelletier calls *hyperbaton*.

84. It is not known for whom Nostradamus intended this one. Were it not for the inapplicability of line 4, it might well be applied to Franklin D. Roosevelt, pretty well assured of his place as the most famous cripple in history. Line 1 refers to the fact that in Sparta children with any imperfection were killed; least of all could one of them be king. The one here apparently merely conspires against the King. Probably Talleyrand came closest to fulfilling it, if we can substitute Emperor for King.

85. This one is quite a simple and interesting quatrain. Tarsus is in southeastern Asia Minor. The victorious army of the new Charlemagne (Henry II), having overthrown the Turkish Empire in Europe, will cross over into Asia. By sea they get help from the King of Portugal, then one of the greatest European sea powers. Only line 4 is confusing. Two St. Urbans have their day. Pope Urban I's is commemorated on May 25. That of St. Urban, Bishop of Langres, is on January 23. The first day of summer, June 21, is far from either of them. There are twelve other St.Urbans, but their days are obscure, if existent. By the other possible reading, it may be that a new Pope named Urban is to be consecrated on that day.

86. The great prelate of Sens must needs be the Archbishop of Sens, one of the original twelve archbishoprics of Gaul. The great prelate of line 1 may or may not be the same as the archbishop of line 4. Gascony is in southwest France.

87. This daringly plain quatrain is probably another on the theme of war between Philip and Ferdinand over Charles V's international estate. The nominal election which resulted in the coronation of Ferdinand as King of the Romans (King of Germany) took place in Cologne (1531). His coronation was in Aachen. Finally, his coronation as Emperor took place at Frankfurt (March 24, 1558). In 1542 Philip had been invested with Milan by Charles V. Thus the quatrain tells that after Charles' death, Philip will not recognize his uncle as Emperor. In line 4 Philip is successful and drives Ferdinand out of Germany (into the Netherlands: see 545). As it turned out, no such strife developed but Philip did persist until 1562 in intrigues that would result in his succeeding Ferdinand as Emperor.

88. This one may or may not have a connection with 545 and 687 through line 1. The Ebro River is in northern Spain. The rest is vague or obscure.

89. For this hopelessly obscure-sounding conglomeration, Le Pelletier has a bright interpretation:

Napoleon I, after having been consecrated as Emperor of the French by the sovereign Pontiff Pius VII, will be chained doubly at the isles of Elba and

St. Helena (between two boats). The Emperor, in despair after the refusal of the Allied sovereigns to ratify the treaty by which he consented to abdicate in favor of his son, will try in vain to kill himself, during the night of April 12 or 13, 1814, in taking a poison prepared badly by his surgeon, Ivan.

Garencières' suggestion that lines 1–2 (and part of 3) refer to an old Persian torture has been combined with Le Pelletier's version to have Napoleon suffering a living death in exile comparable in agony to the Persian torture. Quite possibly Garencières' version is to be taken literally. It appears also in the Decameron of Boccaccio.

90. In Presage 2 "Neptune" is confirmed as being used for the Turks, then the greatest sea power in the Mediterranean.

91. Another of the detailed but obscure variety. In Nostradamus' time, line 1 would refer to the Baron de la Garde, or to de la Mole, chief naval commanders in the Mediterranean. Line 3 is rather specific drama. Agrippa may be a new Vipsanius Agrippa, or may refer to a contemporary whose first name was Agrippa (not too rare in the classics-worshipping atmosphere of the Renaissance).

92. The obscurities of this quatrain are further confused by the possible variants. Le Pelletier (from Bouys) applies it as follows:

Louis XVI, a Prince of remarkable beauty, will be the victim of plots directed against his power; he will be reduced to a subordinate position by the National Convention, which will arrogate to itself the right to judge him; he will find himself betrayed and abandoned by his followers. Paris, the city of the sword of murder, will char his remains in quicklime, in order that the head of this King, which they will have hated until his death, will not become later the venerated relic of so great a crime.

93. A too ambitious cleric meets his end. Line 4, though quite intriguing, remains obscure.

94. A typical specimen of the completely obscure sort of quatrains, full of typical Nostradamian etymological concoctions. "The see-breakers" (if that is the correct derivation) undoubtedly refers to the Protestants, who broke up the unity of the See of Rome. Typical also is the explanation of Roberts (1947): "After a trial, held against the treaty breakers, they shall be executed saying, 'We came very close' " (based on misreading of an erratum).

95. The cadet is the younger brother, or younger branch, of a royal family. All is quite general and obscure.

96. This one is quite general and can be applied to almost any sack of a city (as long as an explanation can be found for line 4). Jaubert applies it to the Sack of Saint-Quentin (August 27, 1557), saying that the only thing the city was spared was the torch. Le Pelletier sees it for Paris in the apocalyptic days.

97. The only towns in Western Europe of any size on the 45th parallel are Valence in France and Piacenza and Pola in Italy (Pola in Yugoslavia from 1947). The largest towns near it are Lyons, Bordeaux, Turin, Milan

and Genoa. The classic new city is Naples, derived from *Neapolis,* but that does not seem too likely here. The chief element of this quatrain seems to be an epic fire. Boswell (1941, p. 159) gave a rather clever application of this one to the great explosion at Halifax on October 6, 1917, which caused great fires and heavy loss of life. Halifax is indeed on the 45th parallel, but was not founded until 1749. For those who suspected sabotage, some suspicion centered on a Norwegian grain ship, the *Imo,* in the harbor. "Normans" and "Norwegians" have the same etymology, like "slaves" and "Slavs."

98. There is something very strange about this quatrain. It smacks of a classical setting. The Volcae were the great Gallic nation whose adventurous warriors conquered most of southern Europe and part of Asia in the late 4th and early 3rd centuries B.C. According to legend they carried back enormous treasure in gold and silver to their temples at Toulouse, all of which involves other legends and historical facts (of which we shall see more in 828–30). Toulouse was conquered and plundered by a Roman army under Consul Caepio in 106 B.C., after it had revolted to the Cimbri. It lies on the Garonne, near the Touch and the tiny Hers. The quatrain resembles a verse on events of 105 B.C. more than a prophecy. (See also 828, 829 and 830.)

99. It is probable that the learned enemy to be annihilated is the Spaniard. The Pennine Alps are the section between the Great St. Bernard and St. Gothard passes in Switzerland. Line 4 is obscure.

100. Here we have in medieval Latin our prophet's famous "Incantation Against Inept Critics." It is surprising that Astrologers are included amongst the objectionables. Line 4 is taken to designate a curse. The verse is of further note in connection with the theory that all the quatrains were written in Latin first. If they were, we have here a sample of the kind of Latin used.

## *Century VII*

1. Detailed but obscure. The Achilles in line 1 may refer to some contemporary who bore that first name (just as we found an Agrippa in 691). In classical mythology, of course, Achilles was one of the great heroes of the Trojan War, invulnerable to wounds in all parts of his body save his heel. Most famous, perhaps, of all Achilles' in French history was Achille Bazaine, Marshal of France, whose defeatism and incapacity contributed much to the French disaster of 1870. Garencières (1672) comes up with Achille de Harlay, President of the Parliament of Paris, who contributed to the downfall of the Italian adventurer Concini (favorite of Queen Regent Marie as Marshal d'Ancre) by accusing him of misuse of funds. Concini was assassinated in 1617, in the quadrangular of the Louvre, according to Garencières, who further claims that his body was hung up afterwards.

2. Arles is in Provence near the mouth of the Rhône. Everything else is quite obscure. Hugh Allen (1943, p. 346) comes forth with the following

explanation: "Bolshies in black-face. Or could the sweet-scented Aryans be playing end-man?"—whatever that means.

3. In most of the obscure verses, at least the proper names are clear. But not so here. France is France, the Phocaeans are the Marseillais and the Barchinons are probably the Barcelonans. But the identity of the Saillimons remains a mystery. Perhaps the closest etymologically was Salinae, thought to be the village of Castellane in Provence, but definitely not on the sea. Then there is also Le Pelletier's suggestion of the Salians. Only dubious suggestions can be made for *Ptolon* on the basis of its resemblance to Ptolemy. Garencières (1672) and thus Roberts (1947) quite casually changed the reading to Toulon, of which it may indeed be a contortion.

4. Here again we have a far-flung geographical hodgepodge. Langres was in Champagne in the east, under the administration of its bishop (who might perhaps be considered its duke). From 1528 to 1561 the latter office was held by Claude de Longwy, Cardinal de Givry. The Duke of Guise was hereditary seneschal of Champagne and like Longwy belonged to the House of Lorraine. So perhaps Guise is intended. Dôle was in Franche-Comté, Spanish until 1678. Autun was in Burgundy, west of Franche-Comté, and Lyons south of Burgundy in the Lyonnais. Geneva was an independent state in Switzerland. Augsburg was a bishopric in southwest Germany, famous chiefly as the scene of the Diet which produced the Augsburg Confession (1530). Mirandola was an independent Italian principality until 1710, while Ancona belonged to the Pope. Thus the verse may mean that the Duke of Guise, with soldiers from Burgundy, the Lyonnais, etc., is besieged in Dôle during an attack upon the Spanish. At the same time, troops from the Empire, from Geneva and from northern Italy will invade the Papal States.

5. Perugia belonged to the Papacy, Pisa to Tuscany. Parma was made into a Duchy by Pope Paul III in favor of his bastard Pierluigi Farnese (August 26, 1545). On the extinction of the Farnese, Parma passed to the Bourbons (1731–1859). Beyond these facts, nothing can be offered for this obscure one.

6. This rather general verse merely predicts that Sicily and southern Italy (Kingdom of the Two Sicilies), as well as Corsica and Sardinia, will be ravaged by the corsairs from the Barbary Coast. This was partially fulfilled in many raids during the 16th century.

7. This detailed but obscure verse apparently concerns some victory over the Turks (whose emblem was the crescent). "Red gulfs" of line 4 undoubtedly means rivers of blood. Line 3 suggests some infiltration by troops disguised as shepherds in a mountainous region.

8. Fiesole is just a few miles northeast of Florence, a virtual suburb. The verse seems to forecast a sack of Florence by papal troops.

9. This is a very daringly documented prediction. The nearest thing to a Viceroy in France would have been either the Constable or the Lieutenant-General. When Nostradamus wrote, Montmorency held the former post and

the Duke of Guise the latter. Line 4 makes Guise the leading candidate. The title Duke of Bar actually existed. It was held by the eldest son of the Duke of Lorraine after his marriage. As the Duke was then a child, there was none. Guise, of a cadet branch, also happened to be born in the very Castle of Bar. As no one would be very likely to try to seduce Catherine, the reference must be to the famous royal mistress, Diane de Poitiers. Thus she is accused of playing while the royal cat is away (undoubtedly engaged in becoming the new Charlemagne). If this is the correct interpretation, it proves Nostradamus was no age-snob: Diane was already in her late fifties when this was written.

10. Le Mans was the chief city of Maine in northwest France. The next most important city was Mayenne, which belonged to the Guise. In Nostradamus' time, the title belonged to Guise's brother Claude, Marquis of Mayenne and Duke of Aumale (1526–73), Governor of Burgundy. He fought at Metz in 1552 and later at Calais, Dreux, Saint-Denis and Montcoutour, but he never reached the heights Nostradamus seems to have foreseen for him, including an invasion of Spain and North Africa. The isle in line 4 is probably one of the Balearics.

11. One of the more imaginative applications of this rather obscure quatrain has been to the Prince Imperial. Against the protests of his mother, the former Empress Eugénie, Louis joined the British expedition against the Zulus and was killed by them on June 1, 1879. However, the death occurred during a routine reconnaissance, and there were only about one hundred deaths during the entire campaign, so that the five hundred is left in the air. It is more likely that line 4 refers to the actual followers of a queen mother being killed in the course of a struggle for power with her royal son. Such a struggle did occur once since Nostradamus wrote, between Louis XIII and Marie de' Medici, in which struggle, according to Garnecières, more than five hundred of Marie's followers were killed.

12. The cadet is the younger brother, or descendant of the younger brother, of a ruler. The reference might be to a scion of the Guise (cadets of Lorraine). All the towns are fairly close to each other in Guienne in southwest France.

13. Le Pelletier gives the popular application of this one to Napoleon:

Bonaparte (the shaven head) will retake Toulon (marine city) from the English who will have rendered it tributary. He will overthrow the Directory (the sordid one) and will put an end to the Republic, whose partisans will thereupon become hostile to him. He will enjoy absolute power for fourteen years (November 9, 1799, to April 13, 1814).

In a footnote, Le Pelletier notes that some interpreters prefer to apply the "sordid" to the English, which is equally satisfactory.

14. Le Pelletier gives an interesting interpretation for this one too:

A decree of the National Assembly, of December 22, 1789, will arbitrarily change, under the name of departments, the ancient provincial districts of

France; the sepulchres of the Kings of France, at Saint-Denis, will be violated and their ashes will be scattered to the winds; the anti-Christian sects will multiply, and an impious philosophy will take the place of religion; that which is black will pass for white and the novelties will prevail over the old national traditions.

15. A very clear prophecy of a seven-year siege of Milan (rather a fantastic length of time). The King is presumably the French King "liberating" the city from its Spanish master.

16. The great Queen is probably Mary Tudor, whose forces still held Calais until it was taken by the Duke of Guise (January 7, 1558). Through the marriage of the Queen, England was for a time an ally of Spain against France. Three lions (technically leopards, which were only lions with their heads turned) formed part of the arms of England. This quatrain might be held as a successful prediction of the capture of Calais.

17. This one is hopelessly vague and obscure.

18. Detailed, but obscure. Apparently some treacherous enemy who is besieged will pretend to sue for peace and then a week later will make a savage attack, which results in disaster for him. As for line 4, such female activity was not unprecedented in that day. The Peace of Cambrai (1529) was called the "Ladies' Peace" because it was negotiated by the mother of Francis I and the aunt of Charles V.

19. A rather general prophecy that Nice would fall to an enemy through bribery rather than by direct attack. This may well have been fulfilled twice (once before the quatrain was written). In 1543, after sustaining a long siege by the French and Turks, Nice was forced by the peace terms to submit to pillage. It was captured by the French in 1691 and 1705. But there is no proven case of bribery in any of these captures. Boswell (1941, p. 206) applies it to the Maginot Line (Fort of Victory, from Greek *nike*, "victory").

20. If line 3 is indeed "He of Vaud," the subject can be assumed from Lausanne, the only important city in the Vaud and a Calvinist center. The subject may be Théodore de Bèze, Calvin's lieutenant, professor of Greek here from 1549 to 1558. McCann (1942) makes it "He of the Calf," and thus Hitler, born under Taurus. The gist of the quatrain seems to be that Tuscany, though a great threat to France, tries to reassure the French of its good intentions. This sounds so absurd that a fairly good case can be made for taking Tuscany as Italy by synecdoche, in which case the verse came closest to fulfillment in the period 1938–40.

21. The Sorgues River is in Vaucluse, between Avignon and Carpentras. The only town of any size it washes is Sorgues, so that the bridge is probably here. It was in the Venaissin County, which belonged to the Papacy from 1274 to 1791. Languedoc was a large province to the west of the Rhône.

22. Mesopotamia is used several times by Nostradamus, but it is still not certain what territory he had in mind. It is obvious that he is not referring

to the original territory in Asia; some European area must be sought. The Venaissin, lying between the Rhône and the Durance, where they form a small angle, seems the best answer. Tarragona is a port of Catalonia in northeast Spain. The vicar of line 4 probably refers to the Pope. The only fulfillment came in 1799, when Pope Pius VI was taken to Valence and died there. Ausonia seems to be used for the Kingdom of the Two Sicilies. The application to the 1790's seems the best possible. The French invaded Catalonia in 1795. Nostradamus may have had in mind the Roman province Hispania Tarraconensis, considering it as corresponding roughly to Catalonia, rather than the city of Tarragona. If the first part of line 4 is applied to the death of Pius VI at Valence in 1799, there is also an application for the second part. Repelling a Neapolitan attack made on France's satellite Roman Republic in November, 1798, a French army under General Championnet recaptured Rome and then went on to the Kingdom of Naples in January, 1799.

23. A very specific but obscure bit of prophetic gossip that seems to involve the pawning of part of the crown jewels. The sacking of the palace may be figurative, referring to the repaying of creditors from ornaments of the palace. Hugh Allen (1943, p. 280) hopefully designates Buckingham Palace as the scene.

24. Line 1 and 2 are quite obscure, but 3 and 4 are fairly comprehensible. The Barbel is a European fresh-water fish with barbels on its upper jaw. The Great One of Lorraine is probably the Duke (in Nostradamus' time young Charles III, carried off by the French to be reared at the French court). The Pont is undoubtedly Pont-à-Mousson. The title Marquis of Pont-à-Mousson really existed. Emperor Charles IV made it into a sovereign principality under the Duke of Bar. The title was borne by the heir to the Duchy of Bar. After Bar passed to the House of Lorraine (1431), the title was given to younger sons of the Duke of Lorraine. Apparently the Duke is to be poisoned by the Marquis, i.e., by a younger son. This could hardly be called a vague prophecy!

25. A rather ingenious ideas is suggested here. A government with no more gold or silver resorts to coining leather to pay its soldiers after an exhaustive war. Not much can be made of line 4.

26. Jaubert applies this one to a naval battle of November, 1555, when some privateers from Dieppe attacked a Spanish fleet in the Channel. He derives *vire* from *virer*, a nautical term for tacking. He uses it as synonymous with ships, which could be derived equally well by treating it as an aphaeresis of *navires*. According to Jaubert, the French ships concentrated on the Admiral's flagship. Six other Spanish galleons came to help him, but they nevertheless succeeded in capturing the Admiral and four other notables, and took them to Dieppe. This interpretation gains strength in that the events probably took place in 1555 before the verse was published (1557).

27. Garencières' note here is one of despair.

I could not find what he meaneth by this place Vast, which being the Key of all the rest, I could proceed no further, but I am constrained to go to bed, and leave this for tonight, among *Insolubilia de Alliaco*.

Our sympathies are with Garencières. The Vasto in Italy is near Chieti in the Kingdom of the Two Sicilies, quite a way from Ferrara or Turin. There is a possibility that the first line represent a play on Saint-Vaast (both the name of a monastery near Arras, and a port near Cherbourg, as well as nine other villages, all in northern France), but here the distance is even greater. Another possible inspiration might lie in some event in the life of the great Habsburg general, Alfonso II of Avalos, Marquis of Vasto (1502-44). From 1537 he was Governor and Captain-General of Milan. In 1543 he took Mondovi, but suffered defeat at Cerisoles in 1544, and retired to Asti. He died at Vigevano. One of these places might be intended. Ferrara was a duchy under the House of Este, seized in 1597 by their nominal lord, the Pope. Turin in Savoy was under French occupation during much of the 16th century.

28. The only obscure part of this verse concerns "on the spit." It probably means "run through."

29. Nothing could be much more clear and lucid than this quatrain. The Duke of Guise was the principal French general of the day and Alba the principal Spanish one. But Guise never triumphed over Alba, and least of all led him off captive anywhere. It is uncertain what Nostradamus had in mind for a rebellion and betrayal by Alba. That he would go over to Henry II would seem rather unlikely. Jaubert tries to interpret lines 2 for the Pope and his cardinals; which is rather weak. (From 1555 to 1557 Alba had to fight the Pope as a French ally.)

30. Nice, Fossano, Turin and Savigliano were all in Piedmont, but all except Nice had been lost to the Duke of Savoy when Nostradamus wrote. Genoa was an independent republic under Habsburg domination.

31. Another geographical hodgepodge is found here. Languedoc and Guienne were provinces of southwest France. Bresse was a province north of Lyons belonging to Savoy till 1601. Brindisi is near the "foot" of the Italian east coast. Both Brindisi and Aquino were in the Kingdom of Two Sicilies. The action is very obscure.

32. Inasmuch as the root of Medici power lay in the family bank, this one may have been intended for a Medici. It may be that the section of Florence they came from was called Montereale or Monreale. There is a Monreale in Sicily, the seat of an archbishopric, but it is not too likely here. There are many other possible interpretations as well. Milan belonged to the Habsburgs. Philip was invested with it in 1542. Faenza was in the north of the Papal States, Florence the capital of Medici Tuscany. The action is very obscure.

33. This rather general one must have been fulfilled many times, not least among which is prior to the Fall of France in 1940, line 3 to be applied to the Germans and the Russians, line 4 to Anglo-French relations.

34. Like its predecessor, this one could be applied to the Fall of France and France under the Germans (1940–44).

35. Le Pelletier (from Guynaud) makes a rather neat application of this one to Henry III as King of Poland, on the basis of Poland being notorious for electing its kings in a reckless manner (*pêche*). But when our prophet wrote, Poland had its own respectable dynasty. When it died out, Henry was expected to found a new dynasty. Only when he ran off to become King of France (1574) did the practice get under way. However, the only alternative is a Pope, and the wording makes that unlikely, even with the fishing tie (Fisherman, Bark of St. Peter, Fisherman's Ring, etc.). As Le Pelletier would have it:

> Poland will complain and weep of having elected, in the person of the Duke of Anjou, a King whose unexpected arrival on the throne of France, after the premature death of Charles IX, will destroy the computation which it had made on the respective ages of the two brothers; he will not remain long with the Poles. This prince will perish of a violent death and at the hands of his compatriots.

36. The red shaven heads are presumably cardinals, on a misson to Constantinople. To convert the Sultan? Trebizond (modern Trabzon) is on the Black Sea in northeastern Asia Minor.

37. A rather dramatic quatrain, with an attempt to assassinate an admiral or naval commander. The Isles of Lérins are off the southern coast of France between Cannes and Antibes. The Isles of Hyères are off Hyères, east of Toulon.

38. Notwithstanding the rather dubious wording of line 3, both Jaubert (probably from Chavigny) and Le Pelletier apply this to an accident in which a royal personage pulled the reins so tight on a runaway horse as to cut its mouth, upon which the maddened horse threw the Prince. His foot caught in the stirrup, he was dragged to a horrible death. What is quite remarkable is that each suggests a different candidate. Jaubert claims it for Henry II of Navarre (May 25, 1555, and probably before the verse was written—it was first published in 1557), Le Pelletier for the eldest son and heir of Louis-Philippe (July 13, 1842). However, we have been unable to find an account of Henry's death, while the details of Crown Prince Ferdinand's death vary somewhat in other accounts. A third possible application involved the death of the heir of the Prince of Bourbon–Roche-sur-Yon (1560) under somewhat similar circumstances.

39. This one is rather general and thoroughly obscure.

**40.** **A bit of drama of** Trojan horse tactics to capture a seaport is found here. Apparently they succeed in entering the town, only to be struck down by the guards.

41. A bit of local drama, suggesting a haunted house. Garencières writes that he happened to hear of the fulfillment of this one at a place he calls

"Lapacodier, four leagues from Lyons," in 1624. According to him, the drama came to a climax when a captain and twelve soldiers were lodged in this house. In the process of proving it, he takes great liberties with his translation.

42. This one is very clear, specific and colorful. Two conspirators join the kitchen staff of a great prince for the purpose of poisoning him. Just as they are on the point of succeeding, the kitchen boy discovers them. Only one is mentioned as being captured, so it is perhaps to be understood that the other one gets away.

## *The Epistle to Henry II*[1]

The debate begins even before we get to the first paragraph. Many of the commentators whose chief interest in Nostradamus centers upon the Capetian Messiah theme refuse to concede that *Henri Roi de France Second* refers to Henry II, to whom Nostradamus had indeed been presented. Instead, they follow Leroux (1710) in suggesting that *Second* is derived from *secundus*, meaning either "following" or "favorable." Leroux ends up by getting Louis XIV out of Henry II, but more recently the beneficiary has been "Henry V." This nonsense is too foolish to merit further discussion.

1. The opening paragraph contains the inevitable flowery sentiments, prerequisite in addressing an absolute monarch. He refers to his visit to the Court at Saint-Germain-en-Laye in the latter half of 1556, or about half a year previously.

2. The mention of "Milliade" suggests that a "millennium" of ten "centuries" was the ultimate goal, and casts suspicion on the fragmentary Centuries XI and XII.

3. No man of letters has ever argued the point that the quatrains are not according to the strict rules of poetry. This theme of natural inspiration (including hereditary gift, magic and trances, and divine inspiration) followed by astronomical and astrological calculations as the source of his prophecies occurs again and again.

The area which the prophecies cover is set forth plainly: all Europe (but the further east, the less), Africa (only the Mediterranean coast) and part of Asia (west of India). The one mention of America by name (1066) is in a quatrain of which the setting is really Britain. That the *Hesperia* references are intended for America remains a highly tenuous proposition.

4. Nostradamus himself makes the alarming statement that his quatrains can't be interpreted. However, few seem to have been alarmed.

5. It is rather curious that our prophet tells us here that he began the

---

[1]The Introduction to the Commentary on the Preface, and the Commentary on paragraph 24 of the Preface, serve also as an introduction to the Commentary on the Epistle and should be referred to again at this point.

Epistle on March 14, 1557. At the end it is dated June 27, 1558: a total of fifteen months, however intermittent, consumed on the Epistle. The two dates, 1585 and 1606, are typical of his usual failure (or bad luck, as the reader prefers) with dates. It would be hard to find two less significant dates. French commentators are obliged to fall back on such unimpressive data as the Pope formally barring the House of Bourbon-Vendôme from the succession (1585) and the head of that branch, Henry IV, being at the apogee of his power (1606). On the other hand, an American commentator reveals that in 1585 a law was passed in England prescribing death for all Catholic priests, while in 1606 the London Company (which established the first American colony) was chartered. More will be said on the seventh millenary in paragraph 40.

6. The length of time for which his predictions run is mentioned in the Preface to Caesar as being till the year 3797, a total of 2,242 years. Yet, as we will see later, the prose outline in this Epistle loses even the little detail it has at what must have been intended in about the 20th century.

7. Natural instinct plus astrology again. The information as to how he went into his trance is similar to that contained in the first quatrain (11).

8. The lavish sentiments into which Nostradamus breaks out every now and then are judiciously divided between God, the Catholic Church and Henry II. Here God gets his share. By rather devious logic he also informs the King that his (Nostradamus') enemies are likely to be the King's enemies also.

9. Contrary to his hope (if not prophecy), the balance between devotees and mocking critics is approximately the same even today as it was in his own day. The protest here, one of several necessarily with tongue in cheek, was for the benefit of the ecclesiastical censor whose permission was prerequisite before his works could be printed.

10. If we add up the figures here, we find that the world was created in 4758 B.C. The final estimate of pre-Darwinian Bible experts was 4004 B.C. Since the seventh millenary or millennium would start six thousand years later, we find that it would have started already in A.D. 1242, or more than three hundred years before Nostradamus wrote. This would indeed agree with his statement in the Preface, paragraph 27, that "we are now in the seventh millenary." But it is quite at odds with his *predictions* placed at the commencement of the seventh millennium, as in paragraph 40. However, a more harmonious chronology, substantially different, is to be found later in the Epistle. We can only guess what is behind this absurd discrepancy. That all these numbers are just part of a master-cipher, as some faithful commentators suggest, is a bit too farfetched.

11. Here we have once again the hereditary-instinct-plus-astrology theme. Almost all readers will take issue with the statement that his enigmatic sentences have only "one sense and meaning and nothing ambiguous or amphibological." He compares his style with that of the Hebrew prophets

though, as Le Pelletier writes, it has far more in common with that of the oracles of Greece and Egypt. The reference to Joel's Punic Chronicle is puzzling, since "Punic" refers to Carthage or Phoenicia.

12. All praise and credit modestly, and wisely, goes to God. This is for the French branch of the Inquisition, in case they ever start proceedings against him on the grounds of holding special favor with Satan. The burning mirror comes close to suggesting the legendary magic mirror of his patroness, Catherine de' Medici, to which De France devotes an entire chapter (see General Bibliography at end, 1911). A bit of prediction is included here, and it is extremely interesting. The first element is obviously a persecution of the Church. But can the second element be conceded as the Revolution? "Sustained by the earth" and "who approach such decadence" are two phrases highly applicable to the French aristocracy on the eve of the Revolution. A fairly good case can be made here, and elsewhere, for Nostradamus' having really foreseen something equivalent to the Revolution.

13. Here beginneth the prose outline of history according to Nostradamus, lasting uninterrupted through paragraph 38, and continuing again further on. Many commentators, finding sentences and phrases here and there applying nicely to events of their own day, have sought to make out that the order was intended by Nostradamus to be shuffled, as in the verses. But there is no justification for such a theory, and Nostradamus is not to be saved from criticism through such a loophole.

After a great number of events, and a good deal more than half the outline, we have the year 1792. We must therefore conclude that the point of departure is right in his own day. There is some reason to interpret "the great dame" as the most obvious, a queen of France, but there is also some justification for the ideological approach. For instance, we find her offspring being received by three nations—which indeed suggests a religion or something similar.

The ideological interpretations variously feature as the star the Church, France, the French Revolution, Democracy, *et al.* Of late, Communism and Fascism have entered in prominent roles. If the meaning is indeed allegorical, Calvinists and Lutherans would be far more likely candidates. In any event, no interpretation, ideological or genealogical, has held water all the way through. Just what Nostradamus had in mind will probably never be known.

If "the great dame" so long barren is merely a queen of France, one must first consider a possible application to the reigning Queen, Catherine de' Medici, Nostradamus' patroness. However, with seven children (plus three who died soon after birth), could she have been considered barren? As a matter of fact, yes.

Catherine had been married to the Duke of Orléans (later Dauphin, then Henry II) for *nine years* without conceiving. Both King Francis I and her husband were seriously considering arranging for a divorce from this barren Florentine. At this turning point in her life, Catherine was saved only by her own shrewdness and the gallantry of Francis I. When she heard the rumors of divorce, Catherine went right to the King and told him sweetly that she'd be the last person in the world to stand in the way of France's needs, and upon his command she would retire to a nunnery or, if he pleased, serve the lady who replaced her. To this her gallant father-in-law replied:

> Since God has willed that you should be my daughter-in-law and wife of the Dauphin, I do not wish to make any change and perhaps it will please Almighty God in this matter to grant to you and to me the gift we long for so much. (Van Dyke, *Catherine* [New York, 1927].)

The Almighty, or France's best surgeons, granted the King's wish as follows:

Saturday, January 19, 1543: The future Francis II born.
Friday, April 12, 1545: Elizabeth, who married Philip II of Spain, born.
Saturday, November 12, 1547: Claude, who married Charles of Lorraine, born.
Sunday, February 3, 1549: Louis, who died in 1550, born.
Friday, June 27, 1550: The future Charles IX born.
Saturday, September 20, 1551: Edward-Alexander (future Henry III) born.
Sunday, May 14, 1553: Margaret, first wife of Henry IV, born.
Monday, March 18, 1554: Hercules, the future Francis of Alençon, born.
June 24, 1556: Twin girls who died a few weeks after their birth born.

As all these children had been born before Nostradamus wrote, there is no reason why any two should be singled out as the two principal ones. The two eldest would be Francis and Elizabeth, and it is just barely possible that the prophecy is concerned with the supposed descendants of Elizabeth. Until 1559, it was Don Carlos of Spain whom she was supposed to marry. Then there was a sudden change and she was married off to her fiancé's father (Philip II) instead.

Or it may be remembered that the next Queen after Catherine was already sure to be Mary Stuart. After a long betrothal, she was married to the Dauphin in April, 1558. How long she might have remained childless (and then of course through the fault of her sickly husband: all Europe's sovereigns and pretenders can trace their lineage to her) cannot be known, since Francis died in December, 1560.

Whichever Queen is intended, she is to have two children, presumably a son and a daughter. The daughter will in turn have three sons and one daughter. (It is also barely possible that the two daughters may be the same, and that the three brothers are sons, rather than grandsons, of the Queen. This involves regarding the statement that she would have "two principal children" as meaning that only one son and one daughter are important, and the other two brothers insignificant. Though dubious, this would be as valid as disregarding five of Catherine's children.)

14. If the three brothers are indeed intended as the grandsons of Mary,

the earliest date at which they could be acting would be about 1610 (figuring Mary barren till 1565, her grandchildren born in the 1580's). Nostradamus begins by forecasting the destiny of the youngest. He will be King of France, a strange inheritance for the *youngest* son. Obviously his father (or his mother's husband—we have seen a note on her infidelity) is not King of France. The attributes of this ruler are not unlike those of the great "Chyren-Selin" (Henry II), of whose glory nothing is to be found here. The latter is one of the most noteworthy differences between the "line" in the quatrains and that in the Epistle. "Arabs" may be used for Moslems, and thus Turks, or really for the new Arab conquerors touched upon in the quatrains.

15. If it was indeed Mary whom Nostradamus intended for the original barren Queen, it must be remembered that she was also Queen of Scotland (since 1542, when she was six). It would be natural that one of her sons inherit the Scottish throne. The arms of Scotland featured a crowned lion sitting on a crowned helmet, with a sword in its right paw and a mace in its left paw. Yet it would be strange for the eldest son to take one of Europe's least important realms.

16. The second son will perform the famous feat of Hannibal, to take his army across the St. Bernard Pass into Italy. Napoleon Bonaparte did this in 1800, and seems to have been the only other military leader of note in history to do so. (In fact, Napoleon accomplished many of Nostradamus' fantastic odds and ends intended for royalty.) His being accompanied by the Latins (properly the inhabitants of Latium, the area around Rome) suggests that perhaps the invasion is the other way, from Italy into France. Support is given this interpretation by the appearance of the Pyrenees next, far more likely to follow an invasion of France than an invasion of Italy. While one of his brothers appears to be King of France and another King of Scotland, we have no clear indication about this warrior's title. Perhaps his bastardy is too clearly established. But "Lent will not include March/Mars" remains baffling.

17. As for the daughter, she will sacrifice herself in a marriage in the interests of Catholic unity. Most likely it is to an emperor or an emperor's son. But it will have been in vain, for her husband will become one of the new infidels, i.e., a Protestant. With mention of her children, we come into the fourth generation and presumably approach the middle of the 17th century.

18. One of her sons is a good Catholic, the other a Protestant. The latter accedes to great power. The Roman realm probably means "Roman Empire" (Holy Roman Empire), but could be used for Italy. As Emperor, he will rule much that Charles V did, at least both Germany and Spain. As there was no reference to the cuckold husband of the barren dame's daughter and the nominal ancestor of all these figures, it may well have been a Habsburg prince like Don Carlos. Apparently this new Charles V is to be a Protestant

one, and we are confronted with the astonishing idea of a Protestant Spain. The area between the 50th and 52d degrees, specified as not being included in his empire, is the southern Netherlands, classical and modern Belgium.

It must be conceded that the temptation to apply all this to military Fascism in Italy, Spain and Germany in the 1930's is a very strong one.

19. Although, obviously, many religions are to be found north of the 48th parallel, the latter is approximately the southern boundary of only one— Germany. In so many ways is this particular section applicable to the Nazi empire that it is most unfortunate to have to try to decipher what Nostradamus really had in mind. Both a return to the worship of Germanic gods and great German military power seem to be predicted here. Probably Nostradamus foresaw a united, militant Germany emerging from the chaos initiated by Luther.

20. This is indeed a very pithy little sentence, and probably fits Fascism and Communism in the 20th century much better than whatever Nostradamus had in mind. Who is being compared? It is possibly the faithful child (of whom nothing has been said) and the infidel one, who has perverted the Holy Roman Empire into Protestantism, a theme found also in the quatrains.

21. The sudden re-emergence of the barren Dame is startling, and is almost enough to make a convincing case for the ideological approach. Certainly being received by two nations does suggest a religion. The one-time masters of the universe are the Romans. The Spaniards, one of whose most renowned national traits is obstinacy and stubbornness, may perhaps trace this trait back to the time of their intercourse with the Romans. Perhaps it is the wife of the Protestant Emperor and mother of the unfaithful son converting the Spaniards and Italians back to Catholicism, leaving her son only Germany.

22. In paragraph 18 we found the unfaithful son having three regions, the Roman, Germany and Spain. The third people here are probably the Germans, for the Romans and Spaniards have been referred to above. The Germans will spread to the land of the Slavs and Magyars, but will meet disaster in Hungary. In the quatrains, we find the Macedonian used for the Spaniard. Therefore the Myrmidon (the name of a Macedonian tribe) can likewise be identified with the Spaniard. These will be allied with the Germans (as indeed they were during most of the 16th century). After a defeat in Hungary, they will concentrate in an attack on Sicily. But here the Protestant Imperials will meet their final defeat.

23. In Hungary (classical Upper and Lower Pannonia) they are defeated by either the Turks or some other Asiatic power which has replaced the Turks. Indeed, in the quatrains we find that Nostradamus foresaw the imminent collapse of the Turkish Empire, under pressure from resurgent Arab and Persian empires. Attila was the leader of the Huns, who gave Hungary their name. After his defeat of the heretics, the Moslem leader is able to found his "Empire of the Antichrist." Xerxes was the Persian Emperor (485–65 B.C.) who invaded Greece in 480 B.C. but was turned back. The 48th degree passes near Brest, Rennes, Le Mans, Orléans, Langres, Munich, Vienna and many

other cities which would be happy to play host to the Holy Ghost. Paris, the choice of some commentators, is nearer the 49th degree. The new Xerxes, or Antichrist No. 1, will make war upon a Pope of royal, presumably Capetian, blood. To this Pope there are many references in the quatrains. What do "the Holy Ghost" and "transmigration" refer to? Le Pelletier thinks that these are the personification of wisdom and force, and that *dechassera* means "to give way to." Thus, the Holy Ghost decides that it doesn't have a chance and goes back to heaven. Although this is rather absurd, no sure solution can be provided.

It is quite noteworthy that France has been left out of the picture almost since the beginning, so that the 48th degree may refer to one of the French cities named, whence will come a great new French ruler, inspired by the Holy Ghost, to rally Christendom after the setbacks it has suffered from both the heretics and the infidel. But this would be a foreshadowing of paragraph 26.

24. These great events will be accompanied by an extraordinary eclipse. Between 1557 and 1792, there were only six total eclipses of the sun visible in France:

(1) October 12, 1605. Total only near Pyrenees.
(2) June 10, 1630. Band of totality NW-SE from Brest to Nice.
(3) January 27, 1683. Band of totality W-E, Paris to Lyon.
(4) May 12, 1706. Band of totality SW-NE through Lyons.
(5) May 22, 1724. Band of totality NW-SE from Normandy through Paris to Venice.
(6) April 1, 1764. Band of totality SW-NE through Brussels, Paris and La Rochelle.

Of all these, the context calls for one of the first three, since the action appears to be in the 17th century. The first one is eliminated as hardly touching France. That of 1683 covered the very heart of France, and also happened to be of the longest duration. It also comes just seventy-three years (see para. 25) after our estimate of the time of the action in paragraph 14 (1610). All of which, again, presupposes Nostradamus' having had accurate astronomical data.

25. The reversal of realms and the new Babylon have, understandably enough, suggested the Revolution to many commentators. "Holocaust" means literally "wholly burned" and probably refers to the destruction by fire of large numbers of human beings. Much labor has been expended on the seventy-three years and seven months. Of late a favorite trick has been to make the period of the Third Republic add up to this figure, which involved World War II being followed by a Bourbon restoration. The first holocaust was thus the First Republic, and the new Babylon the Third Republic.

Though all hope of fulfillment of this interpretation has now vanished, the real meaning remains as uncertain as ever. Most likely the new Babylon is Protestant Germany. It is rather interesting that during this period there was indeed a holocaust going on in the Thirty Years' War (1618–48).

It is difficult to judge whether this period is to come at the beginning or the end of the seventy-three years. Since the context scarcely indicates a jump of seventy-three years to paragraph 26, it is most likely at the end. If this is correct, the first holocaust would refer to the activities of the Protestant emperors, beginning in paragraph 17, which were placed *ca.* 1610. This, as we saw, fits well enough with the eclipse of 1683. If Nostradamus did not, however, have accurate astronomical data, it is perhaps necessary to add seventy-three years to *ca.* 1630, which would bring us into the beginning of the 18th century.

26. The only Western European city of significance on or very close to the 50th parallel is Mayence or Mainz. However, Reims, the traditional site of French coronations, is about halfway between the 49th and the 50th, and remains a possibility. It is perhaps worth noting also that Guise, from which the great house took its name, is almost on the 50th parallel. In any case, the great sovereign is undoubtedly French. He will drive back the hosts of Islam ( see para. 23 ), restore the Pope and Christendom and establish universal peace. Militant Protestantism will be subdued. The reference to the Furious One who counterfeits the sage may or may not be to Henry VIII. He was certainly furious enough. By setting himself up as head of the Church of England, he might be said to have counterfeited the sage. That his kingdom would be united is more likely to indicate a restoration to Catholicism, or annexation by France, rather than a union with Scotland.

27. Since the personage of paragraph 26 seems to be the same as that of paragraph 30, we must assume that paragraphs 27–29 between them represent a "flashback" to the horrible conditions that this great ruler will eliminate. In the chaos brought by the Protestants and the Moslems, central government will have broken down. What Nostradamus is predicting in this connection is just about what happened in Germany after the Treaty of Westphalia ( 1648 ). Many petty states will have established their "liberty." As the political meaning of "right" and "left" dates from the 19th century, Nostradamus' meaning remains a mystery.

28. Here we have another villain. He may still be the Antichrist Xerxes of paragraph 23, or some Protestant villain. Pagan-type temples will be set up and the priests will be made servile, debased and encouraged to rather unchaste behavior.

29. Certain elements in this paragraph sound quite applicable to the 20th century, while others remain equally obscure for any century. Much depends on what the "she" refers to. Perhaps it is the perverted church. Le Pelletier ( 1867 ) could not resist applying this to the removal of Pope Pius IX's temporal power a few years before he wrote. It is certainly not difficult to read "communists" into "those of the opposite extreme [left] with the hand in acute position" ( clenched fist: the reader may note that it is impossible to form an acute angle with his hand without presenting a fist ). But what could one possibly read into touching the ground, curvature, etc?

30. We return again to the savior of Christendom. The Jupiter-Mars reference is obscure. In its simplest form, putting himself under the protection of Mars would seem to mean "putting his faith in the sword." Jupiter is probably to be understood as the chief pagan god, and thus the leader of the pagans and heretics, perhaps the same as the "great cur." In "Mesopotamia" we have one of the more interesting Nostradamian enigmas. It appears also in the quatrains. The most likely candidate is the Venaissin enclave, in the angle between the Durance and Rhône rivers, in which Avignon is located. It belonged to the Papacy from 1274 to 1791, and was thus a free city in relation to France. Nostradamus went to college there, and according to some recent research, it was the ancestral home of his grain-selling paternal forebears. In Nostradamus' day the chief and governor was the Papal Legate, usually a cardinal. The intrigue connected with the "second Thrasibulus" is rather complicated.

31. Suddenly there is no further word about the savior of Christendom. Dark days come again. The Church decays, apostasy is rampant. The identity of the three sects remains obscure. The three principal Protestant sects of Nostradamus' day were the Lutherans, the Calvinists and the Anglicans. But none of these had any hold in Africa. Yet if the division is Catholics, Protestants and Moslems, it seems inconceivable that Nostradamus would refer to the Catholics as a sect. Perhaps it is Christians, Neo-Pagans and Moslems. The 20th-century commentators since the 1930's have, of course, made it Democracy, Fascism and Communism.

32. Once again a 20th-century interpretation could find further support, the legislators referring to doctrinaires who try to change mankind by decrees. In paragraph 22 we found "East" used for the East of Europe; it might be used in this sense again. The Easterners could be Slavs, Magyars or the Moslem overlords of the Balkans. Perhaps the Moslems are the most likely here. In the quatrains "the red ones" refer either to cardinals (red hats) or to the Spaniards (whose color it was). Here neither application seems too good. But the association of red with radical and white with conservative postdates the French Revolution. Dog and Doham are assumed to be an odd Nostradamian variant for the Gog and Magog of the Revelation.

33. By all possible counts, we are now in the 18th century. In paragraph 26 of the Preface, we find June, 1732, as the culmination of a long series of horrors ("pestilence, long famine, wars . . . floods, the world will be so diminished, with so few remaining, that no one will be found willing to work the fields, which will remain wild for as long a period as they had been tilled . . ."). This period is probably the same. Two-thirds of mankind are wiped out by plague and desolation is everywhere. The Church is persecuted once again. The combination of place names appearing here is certainly odd: Malta, Rome, Hyères Islands (near Toulon) and Marseilles. The chain of the port of Marseilles still existed as late as the 19th century.

34. From here through paragraph 38 the setting is in the Near East and

smacks in part of the Crusades and in part of the Armageddon cycle of the Revelation. We begin, oddly, in Spain. The *Saltus Castulonensis*, which appears again in 848, was about equivalent to the Sierra Morena in southern Spain. It formed part of the boundary between Christian and Moslem Spain in the 12th century. The Mahometan recapture suggests a new Moslem invasion of Spain, confirmed in several of the quatrains. But what connection there is between the two areas is puzzling. It might be noted, however, that in the 11th century the Crusades in Spain served as a prelude to the more famous Crusades in the Near East.

The various abodes of Abraham were Ur, Haran, Shechem, Bethel and Hebron. Of these Shechem is of course closest to *Achem* and perhaps might be derived by some sort of Hebraic anagram. If *Achem* might be considered different from the city of Abraham, Acre is a likely choice. In Egyptian it is Aka, in Assyrian Akku, in Hebrew Akko, in Greek Ake, in Latin Acce, in Arabic Akka and to the Crusaders it was Accon. Amidst all these variants, *Achem* is not too much different. It might also be worth noting that Shechem is but thirty miles south of Armageddon (Mount Megiddo). The Jovialists are probably the followers of Jupiter (alias Jove), the neo-pagan leader of paragraph 30, who redeem themselves in this way.

35. There is no reason to doubt that the sepulchre is the sepulchre of Christ and the holy place Bethlehem.

36. There may or may not be a distinction between *Septentrionaux* and *Aquilonaires,* both meaning "Northern Ones." The "Aquilon" country presents an oft-repeated enigma in the Centuries, not clear even to Nostradamus' disciple (see Commentary on 149); the Westerners are probably the French and/or the Spanish. This 18th-century Crusade would appear to be a smashing success.

37. This paragraph is filled with obscurities, including even philological theories. We find Kings of the North in the plural. If one is the German King, who is the other? He might be the ruler either of Scandinavia, of Britain or of Poland-Lithuania. The Triumvirate would then be formed of each of these Northern Kings plus the Western (French and/or Spanish) King. Even while co-operating, the three plot against each other. One is reminded of Philip Augustus and Richard the Lion-hearted in the Third Crusade.

38. Again we have the two Northern Kings and further references to their complete triumph over Islam.

39. The prophetic narrative is interrupted here. As we may judge by the few examples, it is just as well that Nostradamus did not date everything. He plainly tells us that the following chronology does not check with the previous one, a most extraordinary admission. We have also a hint here as to how earnestly he sought to co-ordinate his conclusions with those of St. John in the Revelation. His remark that dating the prophecies would be agreeable "least of all to those interpreting them" has much point to it.

40. Hugh Allen (1943) is amazed that Nostradamus, a learned Jew, did

not know that all Jewish calculations involved lunar months. McCann (1942) thinks this enough to prove he was not really of Jewish origin. Not only does the chronology not check with that of paragraph 10, but Nostradamus' addition is a bit off, unless Jacob was 212 years old when he went into Egypt. (Jacob's age at this point is the biggest obstacle in adding up the second group of figures.) However, allowing this age in order for it all to add up to Nostradamus' 4,174 years, we would have the following comparison between the two chronologies (to which we have added a third column for some historical estimates):

| | *Para. 10* | *Para. 40* | *Historians'* |
|---|---|---|---|
| Adam created | 4758 B.C. | 4174 B.C. | |
| Noah born | — | 2668 B.C. | |
| One-year flood over | 3516 B.C. | 2067 B.C. | |
| Abraham born | 2436 B.C. | 1772 B.C. | |
| Isaac born | — | 1672 B.C. | |
| Jacob born | — | 1612 B.C. | |
| Jacob into Egypt | — | 1400 B.C. | |
| "Time of Moses" | 1920 B.C. | — | |
| Exodus | *same?* | 970 B.C. | *ca.* 1225 B.C. |
| David born | 1350 B.C. | — | *ca.* 1040 B.C. |
| Solomon king | — | 494 B.C. | *ca.* 970 B.C. |
| Temple built | — | 490 B.C. | |
| 7th Millenary begins | 1242 A.D. | 1826 A.D. | |

The start of the 7th Millenary in 1826 would fit fairly well with mention of 1792 (paragraph 48) as being shortly before the beginning of the new millenary. It would, however, be in contradiction to the statement in the Preface (paragraph 27) that "we are now in the seventh millenary," although this statement would be supported by the first chronology (paragraph 10) by which the 7th Millenary had begun three centuries earlier (in A.D. 1242). One of many discrepancies in Nostradamus' outpourings, relatively minor in comparison to the totally different dynastic prophecies as between the Epistle and the quatrains or, one might add, between different groups of quatrains.

41. This astrological rigmarole seems rather incomprehensible. The answer may lie in the date 1792 in the next paragraph. In 1550 another famous astrologer, Richard Roussat, published a book to show that the world was coming to an end in the not too distant future. It included the following sentence (p. 86), "Now, I say that we are immediately approaching the future renovation of the world in around 243 years. . . ." Copying from the work of a still earlier (1531) astrologer, Pierre Turrel, he referred also to "a marvelous conjunction that the astrologers say will occur around 1789, with ten revolutions of Saturn . . . with very great and wonderous mutations and altercations . . . even of sects and laws . . . Antichrist." Nostradamus probably read these books, was much impressed and on his own calculated the exact "chart" of the sky when this would happen. But to throw a monkey

wrench into this theory, Wöllner (p. 29) claims that it occurred only on January 1, 1606 (see that date in para. 5).

42. Apparently Nostradamus differed slightly with these gentlemen. One saw 1789 as the key year, the other 1793. Nostradamus saw things starting earlier, with 1792 as the culmination. While 1792 was indeed the year that the monarchy finally ended, the Republic was proclaimed and even a new calendar attempted, these events do not have much connection with what Nostradamus writes. He predicts a savage persecution of the Church between the year to which paragraph 41 applies and 1792. What persecution there was began rather than ended in 1792. He comes closest to a bull's-eye with the reference to a renewal of time, since the Republicans introduced their calendar then as symbolic of the new era for mankind.

Naturally the date did not go unnoticed in the year 1792. A contemporary magazine *(Journal historique et littéraire,* Vol. I [February 1, 1792], p. 233) mentions that the following was printed in a royalist newspaper called the *Journal de la ville:*

> New Year's gift for the Jacobins, drawn from Page 18 of the letter of Nostradamus to Henry II, dated from Salon, June 27, 1558, printed in the Prophecies of the same author, Lyon edition by Pierre Rigaud.
>
> "Plus grande persecution sera fait à l'Eglise chrétienne . . . et continuels changements."
>
> N.B. This copy of Nostradamus, in which this prediction is found, will remain exposed in our office for eight days, so that the curious will be able to verify it for themselves.

The editor of the magazine then goes on to explain how, though Nostradamus is generally conceded to be a fraud, he might have been divinely inspired for just this one marvelous prophecy.

43. It is rather ironical that during the very period Nostradamus predicts that Venice will attain to the might of ancient Rome, Napoleon snuffed out the last remnants of the dying Venetian Republic (1796). However, with the Romans he came a little closer, for in February, 1798, the French occupied Rome and set up a Roman Republic. But there was little glory for the Romans in this puppet state.

44. Whatever its meaning, this is an extremely interesting section. The Genoese, ancient rival of the Venetians, will be allied with the Turks (or whoever holds Constantinople then) and the Germans in opposing Venetian expansion. Since Crete belonged to Venice until 1669, and thus when Nostradamus wrote, the two Cretans are probably two Venetian leaders. The warriors of ancient times are probably the Romans. While Neptune seems to be used by our prophet for the Turk (see Presage 2), what his arches or arks refer to remains a puzzler. Perhaps "the waves of Neptune" refers to the Aegean Sea. Venice will apparently lose her possessions on the shores of the Adriatic. The final part of this paragraph is the most perplexing of all. In paragraph 30 *Mesopotamia* seems to be Avignon or the Venaissin. In quatrain

10100, we find *Pampotamia,* whether "all-water" or "all-powerful," to be England. For the degrees, we can only list the following possibilities:

45: Bordeaux, Lyons, Turin, Milan, Pavia, Venice.
41: Oporto, Salamanca, Madrid, Barcelona, Naples.
42: Rome.
37: Cadiz, Seville and Sicily.
47: Nantes, Angers, Tours, Dijon.

Avignon is near 44, and Britain above 50. How all these elements tie together remains an insoluble problem.

45. In paragraph 23 we had Antichrist No. 1. Here we have Antichrist No. 2. Again the Papacy is attacked. The setting is probably the early 19th century, and here Nostradamus came pretty close: on July 6, 1809, Napoleon had Pope Pius VII arrested. He was taken prisoner, first to Savona, and in 1812 to Fontainebleau. But far from fiercely persecuting the Church, Napoleon made it an instrument of his policy. Nor could the "three temporal kings" be fitted in here.

46. The various possible translations of this perplexing paragraph make any interpretation difficult. *Modona* is probably Modena by a misprint and not by a classical derivation, for the Latin was *Mutina.* The House of Este, which held both Modena and Ferrara, had one of the most lavish courts in Europe in Nostradamus' day. Its Duke Hercules was the father-in-law of the "French Mars," the Duke of Guise, and Captain-General of the Franco-Papal forces of the 1550's. It is quite possible that a scion of this house is intended. However, the Estes lost Ferrara to the Papacy in 1597, and the House expired at the beginning of the 19th century. Perhaps he is to be elected Pope, with Venetian support. Somehow Sicily has to be worked in too. We have yet another reference (see para. 16) to a repetition of Hannibal's deed of crossing the Great St. Bernard. Napoleon, just prior to this time (1800) did do that.

47. Here we have the Gallic Ogmios, who appears four times in the quatrains and there is apparently meant for the youngest son of Henry II—see 580). According to Edwardes and Spence (1912),

Ogmios was a continental Celtic deity of agriculture. He is equated by the Roman authors with Mercury, and is represented, like him, with club and lion-skin. Strangely enough, he also possessed the qualities of a god of eloquence, and is depicted as drawing men after him, their ears being attached to his tongue by golden threads.

Commentators have variously tagged Ogmios as the French Republic, the French nation or Napoleon. Here he seems less a hero than an agent of persecution. Again we have the northern people.

48. Nostradamus informs us that we are on the eve of the seventh millenary. In paragraph 40 we found the most likely of the possible starting points for this to be 1826. There is a brief Golden Age. The Philistines are

perhaps Protestants. The infidels from the northern realm are perhaps the militant German Protestants whom we have found throughout the prophecy (Russian Communists, according to more recent interpretations; it is amusing how many of the predictions and epithets intended by Nostradamus for the Calvinists, since become the epitome of conservative capitalists, seem to apply so nicely to Communists).

49. Another slight break. One may dispute just how "openly" the points were declared in the Preface.

50. The "universal peace" seems to have come to an end. Another persecution of the Church is initiated by the kings of "Aquilon," united with the Moslems. It ends with the fall of an "Aquilon" king.

51. The South is probably Italy. Persecution, antipope and schism are all implied here. Apostatic seduction may mean the Protestants capturing the Papacy.

52. Here we have a gory picture of the cruelty of one of the villains, of either the North or the South. Also implied is an epic naval battle of the calibre of Salamis, Actium, Lepanto, Trafalgar, Midway, etc.

53. At the same time, the most terrible plague and famine of the Christian Era will take place. "Latin regions" probably refers to all the regions with language and culture of Roman origin—France, Spain, Italy, Portugal, etc.

54. The third "Aquilon" King turns out to have a good heart after all. He sees the light and restores the Papacy to its former glory. But in the meantime, his erstwhile followers have destroyed Rome.

55. Here we have Antichrist No. 3 (mentioned also in quatrain 877?). He is apparently the worst of the three. A lurid picture of his gruesome reign is given.

56. We are now well into the 20th century. All detail comes to an end (though there is indeed a quatrain dated July, 1999). If we take "a long time" as being at least half a century, we have a new Golden Age starting in the early 21st century, ironically enough. After "peace on earth and good will towards men" from about A.D. 2050 to 3000, Satan appears again.

57. Nostradamus solemnly affirms that the only reason he did not extend his predictions further was because "some given to censure would raise difficulties."

58. With a bit of elegant Latin, tribute is again paid to Henry II.

59. The lush tribute and humility close the Epistle. The final date marks a passing of fifteen months since the earlier date, March 14.

## *Century VIII*

1. This is one of the most interesting of the quatrains. Pau and Nay, just as they stand, are towns in ancient Béarn. Oloron is the name of another town in that province of southwest France. Each of the towns is within fifteen miles of the other two. And yet the context does seem to indicate a person rather than an area. On this basis, the imaginative Torné (1860-70's) decided that they were intended as a clever and deceptive anagram for *Napaulon Roy* or Napoleon-King. Out of *agassas*, as indicated, he eventually got "Pi-uses," which went well enough with the imprisonment of Popes Pius VI and Pius VII. The confluence of line 2 would refer to Valence at the confluence of the Rhône and Isère, where Pius VI was taken to die (1798-99). However, he did not flee there, but was taken as prisoner. Pius VII was taken to Savona in 1809 and to Fontainebleau in 1812. Neither was thus confined near the Durance. Stewart Robb (1942, p. 25) took over this interpretation, and for the mysterious *Pampon, Durance* got "great bridge Durance." The latter was supposed to be a synonym for France, or southeast France. "Such precision," writes Robb, "is not guesswork; it is prescience."

If we go back to the original point that a person does indeed seem intended, it must be noted that all the places are in Béarn. The latter was the heartland of the Kingdom of Navarre; Henry IV was to be referred to contemptuously as *le Béarnais*. In all probability, the first line was meant for his father, Anthony of Vendôme (1518-62), King of Navarre (1555-62) by marriage with Jeanne d'Albret. Henry himself was born at Pau in Béarn in 1553, or two to five years before the verse was written. Could Nostradamus have been making this prediction for the infant? Great things are predicted for the House of Bourbon-Vendôme in 945, 950 and 1018 but they may be intended for either Anthony or Henry. In the "Biography of Nostradamus" we saw that by 1564 our prophet did indeed seem to foresee Henry's becoming King. For the rest, the magpies may indeed have been intended as a play on the papal name Pius, common enough in the 16th century. The Pope when Nostradamus was born (1503) was Pius III. The first papal election after the prophecy was written (*ca.* 1557) resulted in the election in 1559, of Pius IV, and he was followed (1566-72) by St. Pius V (the last pope to be canonized). Since 1775 Pius has been the name of most popes. Although, as we noted, the setting may be indicated in line 2 to be Münster or Coblenz, the mention of the Durance in line 4 suggests Avignon, which belonged to the Papacy till 1791, and was near the confluence of the Rhône and Durance rivers.

2. Condom, Auch and Mirande are all in the modern Department of Gers in the Southwest. Marmande is in the same area to the north, about fifty miles up the Garonne from Bordeaux. The wall may be falling here, or at another Garonne city, such as Bordeaux, Agen or Toulouse.

3. Another extremely interesting one, both detailed and obscure. To get

any existing combination of place names out of *Vigilanne* and *Resuiers* some
sort of violence must be done to each of them. All possible combinations are
in Italy. The Lake Garda one seems the most likely. An old castle built by
the Scaligers of Verona is on the promontory of Sermione on the southern
end of the Lake. (Nostradamus' quondam friend, Julius Caesar Scaliger,
claimed to be descended from the Veronese tyrants, and to have been born
in this castle, though both claims are doubted.) Another castle dating back
to the time of Charlemagne stands at Malcesino. It was sketched by Goethe
in the 18th century and was the seat of the Venetian *Capitano del Lago*.
Finally, on the Isle of Garda, between the Riviera and San Vigilio, there was
an old Franciscan monastery, bought by St. Francis himself (1220), in which
someone might have been confined. If the two place names thus designate
the Garda area, we have three possible prison sites.

Nancy was the capital of Lorraine. The cadet of Nancy is thus the cadet
(younger brother or branch) of Lorraine. This leaves two possibilities. The
Duke of Lorraine when Nostradamus wrote was the young Charles III. The
younger brother of his grandfather became the first Duke of Guise. The
younger brother of his father was Nicholas, Count of Vaudemont and Duke
of Mercœur, father-in-law of Henry III. He was quite active when Nostradamus wrote and did not die till 1577. If he is intended, it is the cadet himself. If Guise is intended, it would be the son of the original cadet.

Putting all this together, we have the probable meaning that the Duke of
Mercœur will be confined in one of the castles of Lake Garda in northeastern
Italy. Turin, in the Duchy of Savoy, was under French occupation when
Nostradamus wrote. Any interpretation of line 3 depends upon the meaning
of the uncertain *ards*.

4. This quatrain concerns the struggle for power between the French and
the Spanish forces on the Ligurian coast. Monaco already had its nominal
independence under the Grimaldis, but was bound by treaty (1524) to assist
the Spanish in all wars against France. Nostradamus predicts that the "protection" of Spain will be replaced by that of France—which did not finally
occur until 1641. The French Cardinal most active in Italian intrigue in Nostradamus' day was Charles, second Cardinal of Lorraine (1524–74), Archbishop of Reims and brother of Guise, who was responsible for the Franco-
Papal Treaty of 1556. For the common *Logarion* we can offer nothing, but the
corrected *Legation* provides several possibilities. In France there was a viceregal Legate at Avignon, and another Legate as ambassador. The latter at
that time was the very active Cardinal Caraffa, nephew of Paul IV. Finally,
some Italian cities belonging to the Papacy were called Legations, since their
governors were Cardinals-Legate. Anyhow, one of these Cardinals-Legate is
here deceiving the enthusiastic Frenchmen, as probably occurred often in
his life. In spite of the deception, the Habsburg position in Italy will weaken
and that of France will strengthen. Actually, history proved just the opposite.
Monaco was bound even closer to Spain when a Spanish garrison took over

in 1605 (to remain till 1641), while the French were driven out of Italy in 1559.

5. Line 1 suggests the discovery of some ancient Roman or Celtic temple. There are two Breteuils, but neither has a Borne near it. One is in Normandy, about twenty miles southwest of Evreux. (However, there is a Bernay near by.) The second Breteuil is also in northern France, about ten miles west of Montdidier. There is a Borne in Ardèche. Line 3 is probably a prediction that the Canton of Lucerne would be subjugated, but that did not occur. At the same time, a French King, or great leader, will die.

6. Malta was an independent state under the Knights of St. John until the French Revolution. The only people likely to attack it would be the Turks, who did so in 1565. According to the popular legend, St. Maurice was the leader of the Theban Legion which was twice decimated, and then annihilated, by order of Emperor Maximian, for refusing to massacre fellow Christians. The scene was Martigny, near Geneva, in 286. The cult of this saint is strong in Savoy and western Switzerland but we find no confirmation for Le Pelletier's claim that St. Maurice was *the* patron saint of Savoy. Le Pelletier further sees *Sardon* as Sardinia, and thus has them both indicating the House of Savoy, which held both regions. But Sardinia was not added until long after Nostradamus' time (1720).

As far as persons named Maurice in the 16th-century scene are concerned, the picture is not promising. The great Maurice of Saxony (who was deceptive enough, having betrayed Charles V in 1552) had died in 1553. His grandson, Maurice of Holland, was not even born till 1567.

Line 4 is quite international. Geneva was not only Calvin's headquarters but also the center of international Calvinism, the Red Menace of the 16th century. Apparently some representative of Calvin is to be sent to London to plot joint action against the French. As Bloody Mary was then on the throne, the English were helping her husband Philip against the French. However, it must be conceded that the prospect of fiercely Catholic Mary negotiating with the heretic is an incredible one. If the prophecy was meant for the more distant future, Nostradamus may have foreseen the advent of Elizabeth, in which case such negotiations would be less surprising. As it happened, Elizabeth *was* to be implicated with Calvin in the Conspiracy of Amboise (1560).

7. Vercelli and Pavia were both in the Duchy of Milan, which, after changing hands between the French and the Habsburgs, finally came to rest with the latter, from before the Centuries were written until the 19th century. Line 3 covers quite a wide area, the Seine being in northern France and Florence in central Italy. Line 4 is quite obscure.

8. Linternum or Liternum was a Roman town northwest of Naples. The village of Foce di Patria or Focia now occupies its site, yet it is not likely that an insignificant village is the subject. The meaning thus remains obscure. Chivasso is a few miles northeast of Turin, and was occupied by the French when Nostradamus wrote. It is to be involved in a plot on behalf of the Em-

peror. Line 3 may refer to the leader of the Chivasso plot being exiled after a siege, or to some other Italian town.

9. Another one covering quite a bit of territory. Savona, part of the Genoese Republic, is to be the scene of a strange spectacle, an alliance between the Emperor and the French. The Levant involves the Turks. Most of Hungary was occupied by the Turks; the Habsburgs paid tribute for the buffer strip they retained. Naples and Palermo were both in the Habsburg Kingdom of Two Sicilies, while the March of Ancona was in the Papal States. Perhaps a Moslem invasion of Italy is to cause a sudden union of Christian forces (though the French were constantly encouraging their Turkish allies to attack Italy to divert the Habsburgs).

10. Lausanne was in the Canton of Vaud, north of Lake Geneva. In 1536 it was conquered by Berne, its quondam "ally." The "stench" probably has some Calvinist meaning, since Lausanne went Calvinist and its professor of Greek was de Bèze, Calvin's lieutenant. A modern interpretation applies the stench to the once frequent meetings of Marxists there.

11. Vicenza was in the Venetian Republic, Valenza in the Habsburg Duchy of Milan. Valence may of course be the French town at the confluence of the Rhône and the Isère. Had the prophecy been written half a century earlier (or if it is "retroactive"), the great one of Valence would undoubtedly be Caesar Borgia, who had been given the title of Duke of the Valentinois by the King of France. Curiously, he had also been made Bishop of Valencia in Spain by his papal father. In Nostradamus' time the Valentinois title was borne by Henry's mistress, Diane de Poitiers. (In 1642 it was given to the Prince of Monaco and has since been borne by his heir-apparent [currently Grace Kelly's son].) The basilica is that of the Cathedral of Vicenza by Andrea Palladio, called "one of the finest works of the Renaissance" (*Britannica*). Vicenza had belonged to Venice since 1404. Lunigiana was the name of the strategic valley in eastern Liguria, in which Pontremoli and Sarzana are the chief towns.

12. Buffalora is a village west of Milan so insignificant that we must assume Nostradamus had been there himself to have heard of it. As St. Maurus was the founder of the Benedictine Order in Gaul, we can assume that "those of Saint-Maur" means Benedictine monks. The abbey at Foix was the 9th-century Abbey of St. Volisianus, belonging to the Augustinians.

13. This quatrain involves a classical myth. After having her advances repelled by guest Bellerophon, Anteia persuaded her husband Proetus, King of Argos, to send Bellerophon on a mortal mission. He was to carry a sealed message to Iobates, King of Lycia. The message asked Iobates to have Bellerophon killed. Iobates thereupon sent him off to kill a monster called the Chimaera. With the aid of the flying horse Pegasus, he succeeded. In this case, apparently, the cuckolded husband is more successful. Hereupon the woman poisons him and herself.

14. Lines 1 and 2 appear to constitute a general lament, similar to Cato's

*O tempora, o mores.* The great riches of the Spanish mines in America were flooding Europe and causing a general inflationary rise of prices throughout most of the 16th century. Monetary lust is apparently to be bound closely with sexual lust.

15. This quatrain may be bound up with the great German expansion forecast in the Epistle, paragraph 22. In that case the mannish woman would be Germania. The more recent applications of this verse to the Nazi empire may thus not be far from Nostradamus' meaning. See Commentary on 149 for the range of possibilities on "Aquilon."

16. This quatrain is most puzzling with respect to its locale. *Fesulan* can only come from *Fesulae* (Fiesole) in central Italy. Jason, of the Golden Fleece myth, obviously had nothing to do with Italy. *Olympique* must refer to Mount Olympus in Thessaly. Of course it may be that the flood, which first strikes Volo, will involve a general rise in sea level extending to Italy as well, but the mention of such limited and small localities seems to preclude this fantastic interpretation. Fiesole is 970 feet above sea level, Olympus is 9,570 feet.

If, by the other variant, St. Jerome (Eusebius Sophronius Hieronymus) is chosen, we have no place name connected with his life that fits well. He lived at Aquileia, Treves, Alexandria, Rome, Antioch and Bethlehem (where he built a monastery and died). Furthermore, building a ship has no particular meaning for St. Jerome's life, so the Jason reading is probably correct.

If we decide that the flood is purely for Thessaly in Greece, we find that Mount Olympus is about sixty miles northwest of ancient Iolcus. Pharsalus is about forty miles west of Iolcus, but it is on a famous plain, and could hardly be called "Olympic." The only solution would seem to be the heretical one that Nostradamus was mixed up somewhere on his geography or mythology.

17. Le Pelletier sews this one up for the French Revolution:

> The Clergy and the Nobility will, in one night (May 4, 1789) be deprived of their titles and possessions; the world will be turned upside down because of the attacks directed against the monarchical principle, represented then by three royal brothers: Louis XVI, Louis XVIII and Charles X; the English will seize Toulon; famine, revolt, massacres and impieties will increase.

The only catch is that the three brothers are in all likelihood those mentioned in the Epistle, paragraph 14, whose setting would appear to be the early 17th century.

18. Except for the mention of Florence, capital of the Medici Duchy of Tuscany, and the three lilies, undoubtedly referring to the emblem of France, this quatrain is rather hopelessly obscure. The Medicis were particularly skillful with poisons.

19. In 578, we have fairly conclusive proof that *cappe* refers to the Pope, and has nothing to do with Capet. But Le Pelletier has an interpretation along the latter lines:

The French people will not support the great Capetian family shaken by the Revolution: Republicans of all shades will join to annihilate them; they will be almost completely destroyed; then the Mountain (red red ones) will guillotine the Girondins (red ones).

Actually, the quatrain concerns some disputed papal election. Red ones being either cardinals or Spaniards, the red, red ones must be Spanish cardinals. Popes often followed their elections by installing their relatives in important posts in the Church and the government. Thus, when the Pope whose election is disputed is killed, his powerful family will lose all influence, or perhaps will be exterminated literally. The Spanish cardinals are able to assert their will against the Franco-Italian faction.

20. The election here appears to concern a Holy Roman Emperor. "Voice bought" suggests the bribery which usually characterized the elections. The false election is apparently to be followed by a brief civil war, concluded with the murder of the "Pretender."

21. Agde is a seaport in southwestern France, between Narbonne and Marseilles. A foist is a long, low, light ship propelled by either sail or oar. Millions is a rather large estimate for the total number of victims of a plague. Line 4 is quite obscure.

22. Coursan is about ten miles northwest of Narbonne, Tuchan about twenty-five miles southwest and Perpignan about thirty miles south. Perpignan was in the County of Roussillon, which, though north of the Pyrenees, belonged to the Spanish till 1659. Tuchan must have been just inside the French border. Since red was the Spanish color, the red town is probably Perpignan. (As if to give Nostradamus' fame a shot in the arm, there are today many Communist strongholds in that part of France.) Apparently the French learn in advance of a surprise attack from Perpignan by the Spanish. The gray cloth may perhaps signify one of the "gray monks," i.e., the Franciscans. The rest is pretty obscure.

23. A quite specific and very colorful little prophecy of royal scandal. If any queen ever did fulfill it, the leading candidates would be Margaret in the 1590's, Marie in the 1610's, Anne in the 1630's and 1640's and Marie-Antoinette in the 1770's or 1780's.

24. Two widely separated locales are involved here. Perpignan was in Spanish Roussillon, in southwest France. Lusignan, the seat of the great medieval family which provided Kings of Jerusalem and ruled Cyprus till 1489, is about twenty miles southwest of Poitiers. But by Nostradamus' time the family was supposed to have been completely extinct. The French branch died out in 1308. The "oriental" branch passed its titles on to the House of Savoy in 1485, so that "bastard of Lusignan" might indicate the bastard of Savoy. The latter title would indeed make sense, for Nostradamus' patron, the Count of Tende, Governor of Provence, though not himself a bastard was the son of the "Grand Bastard of Savoy." If such is the meaning, the Lusignan locale is out and the action is entirely in Roussillon. In that case

*Montpertuis* is probably the Perthus Pass in the Pyrenees, south of Perpignan. Perhaps the idea is that Tende, after inflicting a defeat on the Spanish in Roussillon, finds himself trapped in the Pyrenees with the Spanish between him and France. Roussillon was indeed Spain's "doorway" into France.

25. Another saga of lust and scandal, presumably royal, with a fairly clear plot: virgin ravished in brook, deserted, gets revenge.

26. None of the scions of the famous Roman family died in Barcelona, so it is odd that any Catonic bones should be found there. C. Porcius Cato, the grandson of the Censor, was the only one to die in Spain, and it was at Tarragona. The Benedictine Abbey of Our Lady of Montserrat was about twenty-five miles west of Barcelona and famous for its splendid library. Pamplona was the capital of the Kingdom of Navarre in northern Spain (which lost all connections with French Navarre in 1512). It is uncertain whether the subject of line 3 is French or Spanish.

27. The setting of this one seems to be in Provence. Le Muy is about eight miles west of Fréjus. A near-by Roman aqueduct brought water from the Siagne to Fréjus. A jennet is a small Spanish horse. Line 3 may refer to Hannibal (Punic commander) or to Marius (Phoenix commander, because of his many "comebacks").

28. In this verse, taken together with 29 and 30, we have one of the most interesting of the prophecies. To understand it, we must look at its background. Part of the background is history, part local legend. In the 4th and 3rd centuries B.C. the Gauls went on the warpath. In 390 they sacked Rome. In 279 they invaded Greece and crossed over into Asia. After ravaging it for forty-six years, they settled down in the province that became known as Galatia. But the inhabitants of Toulouse liked to look at the story differently. It was their own Volcae-Tectosages that had gone out and conquered the world, and then returned home laden with the riches of the classical world.

According to the local story, their plundering had included the sacrilege of despoiling the Oracle of Apollo at Delphi. Soon after they returned, a great plague spread over the land. When they consulted their local oracle (which apparently operated as a branch office of Delphi) they were told that it was punishment for their sacrilege, and that the plague would cease only when they had thrown their treasures into a mysterious "sacred lake." Some scholars believe that the lake may simply have been a pit.

This is the first of the two strands. Whether or not they had indeed retained some of their riches, or whether, as the more prosaic version goes, all the gold mined in the Pyrenees was sent to Toulouse because it had the chief temples, Toulouse did have much gold. When the Germanic Cimbri invaded Gaul, the Volcae broke their alliance with Rome and allied themselves with the invaders. The Roman Consul Caepio, sent to fight the Cimbri, used this as an excuse to plunder Toulouse (106 B.C.). A year later, he was responsible for one of the most calamitous defeats in Roman military history, when the Cimbri wiped out the Roman armies at Orange. The local inhabitants considered it divine punishment for his sacrilege. The gold never reached Rome. Either Caepio had it hidden somewhere, or it was stolen while on the way to Marseilles for shipment to Rome. Caepio himself was impeached, expelled from the Senate and convicted for embezzlement and misconduct.

Actually, these two stories are rather unconnected. The prophecies concern mainly the first story, except for the name of the consul, which can only be explained by the second story.

It was definitely part of the Toulouse tradition that the Church of Saint-Saturnin-du-Taur had been built on the site of the "sacred lake." It therefore followed that somewhere under, or near, the church the wealth of the ancient world lay hidden (Cayla and Paviot, *Histoire de Toulouse,* p. 22). Nostradamus accepted this and here predicts its discovery.

The rape of line 2 may refer to that of Delphi by the Gauls, or that of Toulouse by the Romans. The two seem to have been blended confusedly in Nostradamus' mind. The fire is apparently a variant of the sacred lake or sacred pit. Line 4 is rather obscure.

29. Line 1 apparently tells the exact spot where the first "lead" will be found, though it is difficult to see what a "pillar dedicated to Saturn" would be doing in a Christian church. Line 4 demonstrates Nostradamus' confusion of the two stories. There is no reason to believe that, whatever may have happened to Caepio's gold, it was returned to its original place. The only way this could have happened would be under the "robbery en route to Marseilles" theory, if the thieves were devout patriots of Toulouse.

30. The name of Bazacle occurs in several places in Toulouse. It was the name of a castle which protected the bridge and principal gate, and also the name of the busy milling section of Toulouse. However, the name *Beluzer* is more difficult to place. The answer is probably still to be found. Quatrain 829 suggests that the discovery is due to eruptions of nature, but here it is suggested that the discovery is the result of some workmen digging. Perhaps both. Line 3 suggests a natural result. The two places of line 4 may mean that two different discoveries are involved. The distance between the Bazacle and the Church of Saint-Saturnin is about half a mile.

31. Inasmuch as Peschiera in northeastern Italy belonged to Venice, it could not have a prince. A key may lie in the fact that the fortifications built there for Venice in the early 16th century were under the direction of a della Rovere, which family ruled the Duchy of Urbino (1508–1624). The most likely solution is that Nostradamus was mixed up about the identity of the place. There may also be some connection with the Habsburg general, victor at Pavia (1525), the Marquis of Pescara. We have seen elsewhere (477) that Selin is probably Henry II. In 1557 Henry was thirty-eight, which hardly makes him a youth, but is still comparatively young for a king.

32. A dramatic and quite lucid prophecy but there does not appear to have ever been any application of it.

33. This one is entirely for the Venetian Republic, to which both Verona

and Vicenza belonged. The two towns are about thirty miles apart. The character in line 4 would seem to be a guard.

34. The Jura Mountains run through Franche-Comté, which belonged to the Habsburgs till 1674. A great battle is to be fought there with the Spaniards, to whom "dusky ones" probably refers, because of the dark complexion of many of the Moorish-descended soldiers. Seven million, however, is a figure that sounds more in place in the 20th century than in the 16th. Someone denoted by "Ulme" is to die at Saint-Rémy (for derivation, see 427).

35. The setting for this one is southwest France. The Blaïse joins the Gelise at Lavardac; the common stream flows into the Garonne at Aiguillon, a few miles east of Damazan. The Dordonnais, which survives in the Department of Dordogne, lay to the north of modern Gers.

36. Lons-le-Saunier, Saint-Aubin and Bletterans were but a few miles apart in Franche-Comté, which belonged to the Habsburgs till 1674. But the identity of the beautiful work or "Belœuvre" remains uncertain.

37. We have already noted that all Nostradamus' quatrains dealing with England are remarkably lucid and, what is more, come very close to seeming like bulls'-eyes. This one is no exception. After his defeat and captivity elsewhere, Charles I was taken to Windsor Castle, overlooking the Thames (December 23, 1648). (Quite possibly, however, Nostradamus had the Tower of London in mind.) He was imprisoned there till January 19, 1649. When he was removed (the castle could not be said to have fallen, since it had been in Parliamentary hands), it was to stand trial. On January 30, dressed in a white shirt, Charles was beheaded. Afterwards he was buried in St. George's Chapel at Windsor. Unfortunately, Westminster Bridge, which would be near enough to the scene of execution for "near the bridge," does not seem to have been built till 1750. In both Nostradamus' day and Charles', the only bridge was London Bridge, about two miles down the Thames from the scene of the execution. According to Garencières, Charles' bloody shirt was hung on a pike on London Bridge, but this sounds somewhat suspect. No matter what Nostradamus had in mind, the quatrain is undoubtedly connected with "The senate of London will put their King to death" in 949.

38. Little can be made of this one. Blois, on the Loire below Orléans, was the Windsor of the Valois dynasty. This new King may be the one of paragraph 30 in the Epistle, who establishes himself in "the free city in another scant Mesopotamia." The Avignon identification for "Mesopotamia" would be further borne out with *Nolle* an anagram for Avignon's Oulle. Whether near the Oulle, or near Christmas, five are to be executed by drowning.

39. The identity of the three persons mentioned here has been most effectively obscured. Though the Byzantine Prince is either the Sultan or a high Moslem leader, one can only guess at the others. The Prince of Toulouse may be its Archbishop, or one of its hereditary governors of the Montmorency family. Tolentino is about twenty-five miles southwest of Ancona, in the Papal States since 1445. Its chief is presumably the Pope. Foix in southwestern France belonged to the House of Navarre.

40. This one is set in Toulouse. Line 1 alludes to two churches, that of Saint-Saturnin-du-Taur and that of Sainte-Marie-de-la-Dorade. In line 2, "the Saturnines" probably refers to Calvinists who have perpetrated some outrages upon these churches. "The new lake" is a reference to the mythical "sacred lake" of ancient Toulouse (see 828). It is possible that there is a still undiscovered key to the use of *Albanois* and *Albanins*. The Spanish army of the Duke of Alba remains a good possibility. The inhabitants of Toulouse would then be obliged to fight both Huguenots and Spaniards beleaguering them.

41. This rather general one has been applied to several notables, perhaps best of all to Napoleon III. He was indeed a fox and was elected President in 1848 without saying very much. Line 3 he accomplished very well with the coup which prepared the way for the Second Empire (December 2, 1851). Line 4 he also fulfilled well enough, but then almost any ruler can be accused of the same. Le Pelletier must have had a terrible time trying to figure out some way he could apply this to the Emperor without getting his book banned and himself jailed. Torné, writing after the Fall of the Empire, made a typical contribution for line 2. He quotes from a letter sent him by a reader in Montauban ( *Lettres du Grand Prophète,* p. 101):

> I said to M.D. . . . . His Majesty's pantler: "You should bake him a cake with the finest flour." "You're quite mistaken, Napoleon III eats only barley bread," he said to me seriously.

42. We have been unable to find any trace of either a saint or a place called Saint-Memire. Le Pelletier, of course, knew that this one must refer to the hated Louis-Philippe as soon as he saw "chief of Orléans" and managed to work out something for the rest:

> By his greed and by the abuse he will make of his power, Louis-Philippe will alienate those who had carried him to the throne. There will be an assault and combat, against the republicans, near and in the Church of Saint-Méri (June 5 and 6, 1832). Orléans, after his victory, will not show any more energy at all, and will seem henceforth asleep and as if dead in his palace.

When there were no descendants of a previous duke, the title Duke of Orléans was bestowed on the second son of the King. Henry II had borne it, and Charles IX had probably already received it when Nostradamus wrote. The only other possible meaning of Orléans' chief would be its bailiff or governor. The family of Groslot held both offices more or less perpetually (on good behavior, which ended when they became Huguenots in the 1560's). Lines 1 and 2 suggest the lingo Nostradamus usually uses for Calvinists. In line 4 we see that when the chief is killed, his followers find it necessary to conceal his death for a time.

43. Here we have what is surely the most remarkable of all Le Pelletier's interpretations. It must be remembered that his book was published in 1867, under the Second Empire of Napoleon III.

Following the overthrowal of the two illegitimate governments of Louis-Philippe of Orléans and of the National Assembly of 1848, Napoleon III, the great nephew of the founder of the Napoleonic dynasty, will mount the throne of France. At a later date* there will be, within Lectoyre,† a battle in which the imperial Nephew because of fear will have the standard folded.‡

[Le Pelletier's footnotes:] *This epoch is indeterminate and nothing now (1866) makes it foreseeable.

†Enigma. The name of Lectoure, town in the department of Gers, comes naturally to mind. Nevertheless, the word Lectoyre might, in one of the many tongues familiar to Nostradamus (Hebrew, Greek, Latin, Celtic, Provençal, Spanish and Italian) have a connotation not yet perceived, and which will be revealed after the event itself, as happens in a number of predictions.

‡What standard? This presents an enigma which will not be cleared up until—if ever—an ulterior event, humanly impossible to foresee. The inversion of subjects and of realm, familiar to oracles, permit transposing to the passive of that which appears to be active (as happened to Croesus, King of Lydia, to whom the Delphic Oracle had replied that in passing the Halys, he would overthrow a great empire: from which Croesus had believed himself able to conclude that he would overthrow the Persian Empire while, on the contrary, he overthrew his own), and vice versa, they permit transposing to the active that which appears to be passive. There are thus grounds for believing that this refers to the imperial nephew, who will cause the banner of his enemies to be folded by the terror of his arms. It could nevertheless mean the contrary, and the calculated ambiguity of the text have as its object to veil, until its realization, a check to the fortunes of the imperial arms [*sic!*].

With all these nervous "not-that-I-mean-the-Emperor-will-be-defeated" apologies, Le Pelletier, in the name of Nostradamus, scored a bull's-eye. That left one big question: how to get Sedan out of *lectoyre?*

Le Pelletier's English alter ego, Ward (1891), offered an answer.

After much difficulty and searching I have at last come upon two old maps. . . . In one of these the embattled town of Sedan is given as seated on the right bank of the Meuse, while on the left bank is shown an extensive territory named Grand Torcy and Petit Torcy. . . . In a more modern map it appears as Le Grand Torcy. Now Lectoyre is the precise anagram, letter for letter, of Le Torcey, though the commoner [*sic!*] spelling is without the second *e*, Le Torcy. If we are to reckon this as being a chance coincidence, my only further comment will be, that such chance as this is quite as miraculous as any miracle in the world could be.

In brief, as Ward could have found without all these old maps, Le Torcy is a suburb of Sedan. Did any fighting take place at Le Torcy? The interesting answer is given by one Colonel Maude in his article on Sedan in the *Encyclopaedia Britannica:*

The only part which its [Sedan's] defenses played, or might have played, in the ensuing battle lay in the strategic possibilities of the fine and roomy bridge-head of Torcy, covering an elbow bend of the Meuse whence the whole

French army might have been hurled between the German III. and Meuse armies, had there been a Napoleon to conceive and execute this plan.

The white flag was hoisted first on Sedan's church, then on its citadel. The formal surrender of the Emperor took place at the Castle of Bellevue in Donchery, about two miles west of Torcy.

44. Ogmios was a Celtic deity, variously considered the equivalent of Mercury and of Hercules. (See 580.) Le Pelletier takes it as the symbol of the French people. Anyhow, it is used by Nostradamus several times in both quatrains and the Epistle. Pau was the birthplace of the founders of the most recent dynasties of both France and Sweden, Henry IV and Bernadotte. It was the capital of the Bourbon Kingdom of Navarre, which must be somehow intended in line 4. The fort is the famous Castle of Pau, in which Henry IV was born. Nostradamus seems to want it destroyed. An extremely obscure quatrain, despite all the names.

45. An interpretation of this one must needs depend upon the weighty question of whether Nostradamus "cheated" or not. On January 6, 1558, the Duke of Guise captured Calais from the English, who had held it since 1347. This was probably after Nostradamus had completed all the prophecies, but before he had finished the Epistle, and certainly before publication. Guise was of course of the cadet line of Lorraine, but the rest had no special connection with the capture. Line 4 had no conceivable connection with Guise. If Nostradamus wrote the prophecy before the capture, as seems likely, it must have revolved around one of two things: an English expedition to help their Spanish allies, or a prediction of the capture of Calais (not necessarily by Guise) being followed by further advances (which Guise did not fulfill). The conqueror would then be assassinated in a church on Easter (a theme found in 836 also). Boswell (1941) mentions an application to the capture of Calais in 1596 by Christian de Savigny, Lord de Rosne, a renegade Frenchman working for Archduke Albert's Habsburg army. But the details of this capture fit no better.

46. Le Pelletier gives the popular fanciful version of this one. *Pol* is Greek for "great"; *mensolee* is derived from Latin and ends up as "celibate." The Great Celibate is of course the Pope, so this predicts the death of Pope Pius VI at Valence (which is on the Rhône and not three leagues from it). The rest is derived from Greek or history to fit the times. What are the less colorful possibilities? *Pol mensolee* comes from Saint-Paul-de-Mausolée outside Saint-Rémy (see 427), which is just three leagues from the Rhône. Either someone is to die here, or the celebrated monuments themselves are to be destroyed. Tarascon is the three leagues distance to the Rhône, being on the river at its nearest point. The Cock stands for France and the Eagle for the Empire. The three brothers are probably those mentioned in the Epistle, paragraph 14. Cautions Roberts (1947), "Paul Mensolee is warned to avoid the road to Mt. Tarare as they are infested with thieves and murderers."

47. Lake Trasimeno is west of Perugia in central Italy. Both were in the Papal States. According to Roberts, this one is a "reference to the victory of Hannibal. . . ."

48. This quatrain bids fair to containing the greatest number of twisted and incomprehensible obscurities. According to Wöllner (p. 63), in the period 1555–3797 the conjunction specified will never take place but will come closest on February 1, 2769. This is odd, as the two elements seem rather commonplace. As for *Chaldondon salvaterre,* one might as well give up.

Boswell (1941, p. 156), copied, without credit, by McCann (1942, pp. 341–42), explains it this way:

> The first line is mere astrological rigmarole for warring powers in an era of misery which 1914–18 certainly was. On February 3, 1917, answering Germany's declaration of total submarine warfare, the United States severed diplomatic relations with Berlin. Chaldean is a deft, Nostradamic touch epitomizing Woodrow Wilson, architect of the League of Nations, that modern Leaning Tower of Babble at Geneva. The clairvoyant word-twister added *don* to Chaldon, making another pun, President Wilson having been a college don [*sic!*] before he entered politics.
>
> The last word of the second line, salvaterre, is telescoped from the Latin *salus* (safety) and *terrae* (of the earth). [Translation: In February the Chaldean gives the Earth safety.] The first word of the next line, sault, has been taken as deriving from the Latin *saltus* (fall) while the next, *castallon,* is cognate with *castallum* (strong point). [Translation: The stronghold falls.]
>
> *Verbiesque* is a typical Nostradamic anagram, which is unravelled into three parts, as he hints slyly in the preceding line. These are V, the Roman numeral for five; *erbies,* transformed into Serbie by transposing the terminal *s* to the front of the cryptogram, making the perfectly good French name for Serbia; and *que* (what).
>
> The "stronghold" of the third line is Germany, chief of the Central Powers, which occupied such a naturally defendable position, but which had to fight a war on three fronts—eastern, southern and western, a nightmare for any general staff. The V, or five, stands for the five powers originally involved in the dispute over Serbia in 1914—France, Belgium, Russia, Germany and Austria.
>
> All this seems a bit cryptic. . . .

In the face of this ingenious analysis, which would have warmed Nostradamus' heart, it is sad to have to identify the locale as southern Spain. It appears also in the Epistle in connection with the New Crusade. There is a Salvatierra near by, but nothing for *Chaldondon* or *Verbiesque.* Closest to the latter is probably the Verbices, the name of a classical tribe near Tangier in North Africa (for "Moors"?).

49. According to Wöllner, this conjunction occurred in 1736, and won't occur again until long after 3797. The prophecy certainly wasn't fulfilled then. According to McCann (1942), it occurs on February 6, 1971. Bruges was in

Flanders in the Spanish Netherlands. The identity of its assailants remains subject to confusion. Sardinia belonged to the Spanish until 1713, so that a Sardinian attack would in effect mean civil war in the Spanish realm. If the Tardaigne reading is correct, the Tardenois was a small *pays* southeast of Soissons. While there is a tiny village named Ponterosso eight miles north of Genoa, the name more likely represents some sort of enigma here, or perhaps a bridge in Bruges, which as "the Venice of the North" has more than fifty of them. *Barbarin* may refer either to the Moslem Barbarians or to the famous Roman family of Barberini, which produced many cardinals and Pope Urban VIII (who died right in Rome). But in either case it would be difficult to see why an attack against the Spanish would cause his death elsewhere.

50. This quatrain represents a substantial success for Nostradamus that seems to have been missed by all the interpreters to date. In 1573 Don John of Austria, the knightly bastard of Charles V, who when the prophecy was written could aptly be called "the good old man," recaptured Tunis for his half-brother, Philip of Spain. Tunis had been captured by the Habsburgs in 1535 and held till 1570, when it was taken by the Algerian corsairs. It is certainly more than likely that upon his victory, Don John cut off the head of the ruler who had been installed by the Algerians. Finally, although we have no information on a famine, there was indeed a pestilence in Spain, in the years 1570 and 1574, and presumably to some extent in between (see Gould and Pyle, p. 901).

51. The Byzantine is the Turk, or a leader of whatever people holds Byzantium (Constantinople). This quatrain seems to be part of the "New Arab Empire" theme, involving a new invasion of Spain. An "oblation" is a religious offering, here in gratitude to Allah for his favor in the capture of Cordoba. Cordoba, in southern Spain, was the seat of an Arab Caliphate from 756 to 1031, and of petty Moslem states till 1236. Line 3 may be intended to suggest drunkenness and carelessness, leading to his capture at sea off Gibraltar.

52. Line 1, it will be noted, is an exact repetition of line 1 in 838. Amboise is about twenty-five miles down the Loire from Blois. The Indre flows into the Loire at about another twenty-five miles down, below Tours. Poitiers lies about seventy-five miles to the south. *Seme* remains subject to doubt. Apparently the censor felt obliged to cut short whatever sense line 4 might have made. Le Pelletier's suggestion, Bonnieux, is none too likely, being in Vaucluse about three hundred miles to the southeast. Much more likely is the monastery of Bonnes-Vaux, a few miles south of Poitiers. A thoroughly obscure quatrain.

53. The scene of this one may be Bologna in the Papal States or Boulogne, south of English Calais. If the temple of the sun is the same as the great heavenly temple in 622 (in England), the setting is definitely in the North, and quite a bit of justification is given Ward and Robb's application to Napoleon. They explained that Westminster Abbey is built on the site of the Temple of Apollo (the sun god), shaken down by an earthquake in A.D. 154. Bouys (1806) sees the temple of the sun as a reference to Napoleon's past

failure in Egypt. Boulogne was still a potential jumping-off point for the invasion of England when he wrote. However, since "the hierarchy" has an ecclesiastical connotation, an Italian setting would seem more likely. Le Pelletier tries to harmonize these two points by using Boulogne with reference to Louis-Napoleon's attempted coup of 1840, but applying line 2 to Italy after he became Emperor. Although it is not impossible that the quatrain was intended for a Cardinal-Legate of Bologna who aspired to the Papacy, a strong argument for Boulogne lies in its identity of spelling with the name in 594.

54. The setting for this one is certainly not very far distant from the time Nostradamus wrote. Henry-Selin, as we have seen (477), is Henry II. Saint-Quentin and Arras in northern France had seen humiliating Spanish invasion (1557). They were probably both in Spanish hands when Nostradamus wrote the quatrain. Line 4 rings with jingoistic revenge. At that time, a marriage between Henry's daughter Elizabeth and Philip II's son, Don Carlos, was in the offing. Before it took place, Bloody Mary died and Philip married her himself (1559). It was probably this marriage which was to see Henry II's magnanimity.

55. Lines 1–3 give fairly specific details of a battle. Line 4 is quite obscure.

56. This one also concerns some battle. The locale depends upon the meaning of *Dinebro*. D.D. (1715) made a rather ingenious interpretation of it for the Battle of Dunbar, twenty-five miles east of Edinburgh (Edinbro). Charles II landed in Scotland in 1650. The Scottish force (those of the high place, or highlanders) under Leslie was more numerous than Cromwell's force, but they took up a poor position. Accordingly, the "weak band" routed the Scots on September 3. As for line 4, it is explained that Cromwell captured all the papers of the Scottish War Office. Farfetched as the "Edinburgh" derivation may be, it is probably no more so than an "Embrun" one would be. There is yet another possibility: the Ebro River in Spain with the "D" representing 500.

57. This is one of several quatrains scrambled over by the boosters (or vilifiers) of Napoleon and Cromwell. According to Garencières:

I never knew nor heard of any body to whom this Stanza might be better applied, then to the late Usurper Cromwell, for from a simple soldier, he became to be Lord Protector, and from a Student in the University be became a graduate in Oxford, he was valliant in Arms, and the worse Churchman that could be found; as for vexing the priests, I mean the Prelatical Clergy, I believe none went beyond him.

We hasten to add that the punctuation and spelling are Garencières'. Le Pelletier (from Bouys) has a smoother version:

From simple lieutenant, which he had at first been (1785), Bonaparte will attain to Empire. He will exchange his consular robe for the Imperial mantle. Valiant in battles; but less skillful in his direction of ecclesiastical affairs, which he will want to regulate, he will vex the Catholic clergy, as water does the sponge, by raising and lowering them in turn.

Bouys (1806) handled the last line more gently. Water "renders it more voluminous and more beautiful. Thus has Napoleon treated the priests: he has
cleaned them, he has purified them. . . ."

58. This one seems to be all for England, and while fairly clear, none of
the interpretations to date has done too well. As there was no male successor
(let alone two) to the English throne in sight when Nostradamus wrote
(other than titular King Philip), this is at least a truly long-range prophecy.
The subject seems to be a civil war between brothers, with the compromise
in line 3 having something to do with the Anglican Church established under
Edward VI (1547–53). One of them flees to France. Probably the nearest it
came to fulfillment was in November and December of 1688, between James
II and his son-in-law (not brother), William of Orange. Since one of the
biggest causes of discontent was religious (the Catholic King had even arrested the Archbishop of Canterbury and six other prelates in 1687), it is
quite possible that some follower suggested that the only way to save himself
would be for James to return to the Anglican faith, or to make some sort of
great gesture to the Church of England. Not having done so, James took to
the Gallic air on December 11.

59. This one says just about the same as 525. For line 4 here, we have in
line 2 of 525 "The rule of the Church will succumb by sea."

60. A very interesting quatrain. Perhaps it was intended for Henry II.
He was King of France, and Nostradamus seemed to think he would conquer
Italy and become Emperor (see Henry-Selin quatrains). He was fighting the
English (allied with Spain through the marriage of Mary Tudor and Philip
II). However, the coupling of Paris with the English, as if Paris were also
to be an enemy of this ruler, is extremely odd. Line 4 is obscure. Probably it
meant that before he lost the Empire itself, the former Emperor (Ferdinand?
Philip?) would lose to France Lorraine (nominally part of the Empire). On
the other hand, "Lorraine" may have reference to a scion of the House of
Lorraine (or its cadet branch of Guise).

There have been attempts to apply this one to Napoleon III, who did
indeed cause France to lose Lorraine (allowing Nostradamus' having foreseen that France would have annexed it), but the rest does not stand up too
well. Napoleon I, whom some parts fit well enough, neither won nor lost
Lorraine.

61. This one may have been intended for the ambitious Duke of Guise.
Le Pelletier has an interesting interpretation, which allows a sly dig at the
expense of his sovereign (Napoleon III):

> Never will a Napoleonic Emperor reach the throne openly and in direct
> line. Always will he take his first steps in the shadow of the republican flag,
> and he will scarcely conceal his aim, acknowledging that he owes his position
> to the love of battle with which he had inspired the French people.

By the other and less likely reading, the Tagus is an Iberian river that flows into the Atlantic in Portugal. It does not seem too unreasonable to associate line 4 with the modern monster of "universal conscription," born of the French Revolution, which had such a deep effect on French and all European history. The cock, emblem of the ancient Gauls, was used by Nostradamus as an obscure reference to France but lost its obscurity when the Revolutionaries adopted it.

62. A rather general one about sacrilege, pestilence and an unjust King.

63. Here we go from geopolitics to some family scandal.

64. While most commentators have assumed that Nostradamus uses "Isles" always to refer to the British Isles, it is far more likely that he had in mind those of the Mediterranean (Balearics, Corsica, Sardinia, etc.). However, this one has been applied quite well to Britain under siege by the Nazis in World War II. The whole quatrain is rather obscure, and line 4 most of all. One cannot but suspect some deep and hidden meaning or derivation in *pelle*.

65. If this rather general one is considered to be set in France, it was probably best fulfilled by Marshal Pétain. On July 10, 1940, a rump session of the French Assembly invested Pétain with plenary powers until a new constitution should be promulgated. After ever-increasing German pressure for collaboration, he virtually handed over all power to Laval in April, 1942. There are many possible ideas for the frustration of line 1 for Pétain: restoration of the monarchy, the defeat of Britain, amongst others.

66. *D.M.* is probably just the ancient *Diis Manibus,* with which most inscriptions on Roman tombs began. Jaubert has a very unconvincing interpretation for 1555, involving the capture of Vulpiano in northern Italy by the Duke of Aumale. It is a rather vague verse, though with the adultery in line 4, presumably royal, quite unambiguous.

67. The meaning of this one is rather dependent on the proper interpretation of the cryptic geography. But it is probably correct as shown. Carcassonne was in Languedoc in the Southwest. In line 3, however, *Nersaf* does not read too well as "France." Ferrara was a duchy belonging to the House of Este, whose Duke was the father-in-law of Guise and nominal commander-in-chief of the Franco-Papal forces fighting the Spanish in 1557. The great Colonna clan of Rome was firmly on the Spanish side at this time. Otherwise all is obscure.

68. Whatever its meaning, this quatrain contains an immense amount of tightly packed prophecy. Le Pelletier's version (mostly stolen from Guynaud) is very interesting:

Old (57) Cardinal Richelieu will be supplanted by the young (22) Cinq-Mars, his former protégé, who will cause him to lose the favor of Louis XIII and to resign his office; but he will receive, some time afterwards, from the town of Arles, a copy of the treaty negotiated by Cinq-Mars on March 13, 1642, with Spain, in the name of Monsieur, the brother of Louis XIII; and he will have this treaty shown to the King, who will at once recall the Cardinal. Richelieu will then go up the Rhône, from Tarascon to Lyons, sick and lying on his bed, on a boat, leading with him as prisoners Cinq-Mars and de Thou; then he will go down the Seine, in the same manner, from Fontainebleau to Paris, where he will die two months after, on December 4, 1642. On the following May 14 Louis XIII will die also, and both will be embalmed, according to ancient custom.

This very interesting interpretation requires line 3 to run "If Arles does not," etc, but that is possible. Of Reynaud-Plense's etymology we can find no trace. Arles is in Provence at the mouth of the Rhône.

69. Parts of this suggest the preceding interpretation. It definitely seems to concern the rivalry of favorites. Line 4 is rather obscure, but *seraphin* is probably used for "Franciscan."

70. The locale of this one depends upon the interpretation of "Mesopotamia." From the context elsewhere, it is probably Avignon, above the confluence of the Rhône and Durance, which run almost parallel near their junction. If this be correct, the villain may be the Cardinal-Legate governing it in the name of the Pope. Larmor (p. 159) takes Mesopotamia as the Île de France and applies it to Mazarin. Warns Roberts (1947): "The country near Babylon shall be terrorized by a person of the Negro race."

71. This would appear to be one of the dated failures. It simply predicts a persecution of astrologers by the Inquisition in 1607. Some commentators have insisted that it was fulfilled when astrology was censored by a Council of Malines in that year. It seems that some commentator just made this fact up, and was thereupon copied by successors. There was no such council in that year. There is a similar prophecy in 418.

72. Both Perugia and Ravenna were in the Papal States, but Ravenna is about one hundred miles north of Perugia. The anonymous critic of 1724 applies it to the victory of Gaston de Foix at Ravenna in 1512, another one of his "retroactive" accusations.

73. Properly, a Barbarian soldier would be one of the corsairs from Barbary (Algeria). However, it may be used broadly for Moslems, or perhaps even for Spaniards on occasion, in a burst of French patriotism (especially since the Moslems were French allies).

74. The new land suggests the new world, and has opened all sorts of interesting speculations on this one. Boswell (1941, p. 347) saw it as another case of "Perfidious Albion." The meaning seems to be of a monarch visiting a possession newly acquired. In this sense, the verse may tie in with 683, and it might be considered as having been fulfilled by Philip II or Francis of Alençon in the Netherlands.

75. This is a very rich and meaningful quatrain, all being clear enough except the jargon of line 4. A king and a crown prince will be murdered together. The personage of line 2 is perhaps responsible for it. At the same time, the pregnant wife of either the King or the Prince will be at Tours. The odds against this joint assassination with a pregnant widow at Tours must

run into the millions. Alas, without even worrying about pregnant widows, no French king and dauphin were ever assassinated together. Of the sixteen French monarchs (fourteen kings and two emperors) since 1557, only five died in any fashion resembling murder (Henry II, III and IV and Louis XVI and XVII). Only in the case of Louis XVI and Louis XVII was there any proximity in the time of the "murders" (twenty-nine months). It can be argued that Nostradamus did not specify that it must be King and Dauphin. But at the opposite extreme, it was undoubtedly fulfilled by many a father-and-son pair from Tours. Outside France, a notable king-and-crown-prince assassination occurred when Carlos I and Louis-Philippe of Portugal were assassinated in Lisbon (February 1, 1908). But alas, no pregnant widow at Tours.

76. Even Le Pelletier lets England have this one, Cromwell of course being the candidate. There is some question about the nearness of time, which was in fact more than forty years. Cromwell lived 1599–1658.

77. Since three apparently separate Antichrists appear in the Epistle, it is tempting to call this one Antichrist No. 3 and tie him in with the character in paragraph 55 of the Epistle. However, the verb is plural in line 1, presenting something of an obstacle.

78. Nothing can be contributed here. It is fairly clear and was probably fulfilled many times in France during the Wars of Religion (1562–98) and in Germany during the Thirty Years' War (1618–48).

79. A rather colorful and tightly packed series of predictions, but smothered in obscurities. The Gorgon was one of three snaky-haired sisters, whose ugliness turned the beholder to stone. A gorgon is thus a fantastically repulsive woman. Hugh Allen (1943, p. xii) applies this one to himself, for reasons best known to himself.

80. This one may have a fulfillment Nostradamus never had in mind. "The Reds" seem to be used by Nostradamus to denote one of two groups: Spaniards (their color) or cardinals (for their red hats). However, it must be admitted that in some cases neither seems to fit too well. Yet the politico-social meaning dates from the 19th century.

81. The Philip here probably refers to no one more enigmatic than the contemporary Philip II. Nostradamus seems to have foreseen a Habsburg civil war between Philip and Uncle Ferdinand over the division of Charles V's empire. Here a great insurrection against Philip's authority is predicted as starting in Sicily.

82. A rather detailed but still very obscure prophecy dealing with a dangerous Jeeves. These odd bits of trivia keep on popping up strangely amidst the masses of quatrains dealing with events of mighty geopolitical significance.

83. Zara is a venerable seaport on the Dalmatian coast, now part of Yugoslavia. Venice held it when Nostradamus wrote, having acquired it in the infamous Fourth Crusade (1202). Venice had agreed to take the Crusaders to Egypt for 85,000 marks and half the booty. When the Crusaders could not

raise the money, they captured Zara for her instead (from the Hungarians). Upon which Pope Innocent III *excommunicated the entire Crusade.* The unperturbed Crusaders went on to capture and sack Constantinople (1204), setting up Romania, or the Latin Empire of the East. This is about the only important appearance of Zara on the stage of history, and the details of this quatrain bear a suspicious resemblance to the above details of history.

84. Paterno is the name both of a small town north of Rome and of a town about ten miles northwest of Catania in Sicily. In addition, there was a Roman city named Paternum in southern Italy, on the Gulf of Taranto, about forty miles north of Croton. Trieste is at the head of the Adriatic east of Venice. It belonged to the German Habsburgs, while the Two Sicilies belonged to the Spanish branch. This quatrain may tie in with 881.

85. Though interesting, this quatrain is filled with enigmas. Bayonne and Saint-Jean-de-Luz are about ten miles apart in the extreme southwest corner of France. The general purport of this verse depends on the meaning of various enigmas: *Aquilon* (see 149), *Hanix* and *Nanar*. Le Pelletier (1867) had the audacity to interpret this one (with only the flimsiest justification) as predicting the death of the Prince Imperial (the son of Napoleon III). He was subsequently slain in Africa fighting Zulus (1879).

86. This one is set in the extreme southwest corner of France, in and near Bayonne. The three towns of line 1 and the mountain of line 2 are all near each other southwest of the western tip of the Pyrenees in Spain. The only river between these Spanish towns and Bayonne, north of the Pyrenees, is the Bidassoa in Spain. The Adour, on which Bayonne is located, is north of the city, while the Nivelle is east of it. We have never seen confirmation that *Bichoro* was the war cry of Navarre, but it is quite possible. The original Navarre extended north of the Pyrenees into France and south in Spain. Here invaders from Spain seem to be using the war cry of the French Navarre, separate since 1515.

87. Le Pelletier (from Bouys) interprets this one for the fate of Louis XVI:

> The conspiracy formed against Louis XVI, to take away from him his crown and his life, will be fully carried out; the office of constitutional King which will have been imposed upon him, and his attempted flight to Varennes, will cause his death: He will be dethroned and put to death by his own subjects, by the very same ones who will have elected, received and acclaimed him as a constitutional King; his innocent blood will become the object of eternal remorse by the French people who will have shed it.

88. Sardinia was held by Spain from 1296 to 1713. After seven years under Austria, it went to the House of Savoy, its Duke becoming "King of Sardinia." Therefore the Kingdom of Sardinia, which had no meaning until the 18th century, suggests real prophecy on Nostradamus' part (unless it be understood as synecdoche for the Spanish Empire). Accordingly, Le Pelletier's application of it to a scion of the House of Savoy is not too unreasonable.

Charles Emmanuel IV, King of an old line, despoiled by the French Republic of his continental possessions, will retire to the isle of Sardinia, where he will reign three years (1798 to 1802); then he will abdicate in favor of his brother Victor Emmanuel I, and after many cares, he will go to live obscure, sad and humiliated, at Rome, where he will die in 1819, as a Jesuit.

This appears to have been the only time in modern history when Sardinia had its own resident king rather than a mere titular king.

89. The general purport of this quatrain is fairly clear. "Barded horses" are horses with armor. The most uncertain element is the identity of *Peloncle*.

90. An extremely perplexing quatrain. Here is Garencières' explanation:

By the crossed is understood some order of Knighthood who for the most part wear that Badge, one of which being mad, and seeing in a Church a Horny Ox come, by a Virgin Hog shall be kept from harm, or rescued by a Hog or Sow that was a Virgin, and it seems crossed the said Oxe, that he should not gore the Knight, that then such order of Knighthood shall be no more maintained nor upheld by the King of that Countrey, wherein such thing shall happen.

Though this meaningless gibberish is indeed ridiculous, we can offer nothing much more sensible. However, the mention of a crusader does place this quatrain with others of the "New Crusade" theme.

91. The configuration of line 3 provides a limit on the time setting of this one. The geographical setting is the valley of the Rhône in southern France. Presumably the crusaders are standing up against a Moslem counterattack.

92. A very clear, dramatic and meaningful quatrain, though we know of no application of it. Some reader who is a historian may think of one, and let us hope it wouldn't turn out to be a "retroactive" application.

93. This one is probably intended for the Papacy. The death of a Pope and a new schism are included here. The two rivals will come to an understanding near Venice (Padua?). That two Popes in succession would rule the Church for only seven months would not seem too likely, though once since 1558 there have been three Popes in the same year. In 1590, after the death of Sixtus V, Urban VII was elected, only to die after two weeks. Gregory XIV was then elected, only to die in ten months. But schism there was none.

94. The general meaning of this one depends on the meaning of the enigmatic *Albanois*. Here it can only be the Spanish troops of the Duke of Alba, if Nostradamus thought that the Duke of Alba would turn against Spain (for which, however, there is some justification in 729). Or perhaps it's merely that Spanish disaster is to result from Alba's delays. "Albanians" is not too likely, though there were many Albanian mercenaries in various armies. Ward (from D.D.) derives it from "Albion" and "Albanies," and applies it to the English attack on Cadiz Bay by Essex, Howard and Raleigh (June, 1596). Line 1 becomes "where much treasure is stranded" because the heavy

ships were unable to move about in defense; they had come from a seven months' voyage. Cadiz Bay is a lake because the name is derived from the Punic *Gaddir*, "an enclosed place." Had they given battle at once, instead of procrastinating in typical Spanish manner, concludes Ward, they might have averted the disaster that overtook them: forty galleons and thirteen warships destroyed. This interpretation requires Nostradamus to have foreseen the duel between Spain and England. When he wrote they were close allies. England's Queen was the daughter of a Spanish princess and wife of Spain's King.

95. This quatrain is both too obscure and too general to be worth much attention.

96. This quatrain appears to predict that in the wake of persecution of Jews in Catholic lands, the Jews will flee to the Moslems. This was taking place to a substantial extent at about the time this prophecy was written, when thousands of Jews accepted the hospitality of Sultan Suleiman the Magnificent and settled in Constantinople, Salonika and Adrianople after expulsion from Spain and Italy. One of these Jews, Don Joseph Nassi, who arrived in Constantinople in 1553, became a powerful figure. In 1566 (the year of Nostradamus' and Suleiman's death), he was created Duke of Naxos and became one of the principal advisers of Selim II.

Boswell (1941, p. 326) sees the quatrain as predicting the conversion of Islam to Judaism. McCann (1942, p. 387) explains the quatrain with just five words: "Leon Blum's tenure of office."

97. If the *pompotans* here is the same as the *pempotam* of 10100, we know that it is England. The Var flows into the Mediterranean between Cannes and Nice. In Nostradamus' day, the legal border between France and Savoy just about coincided with the Var, though Savoy was occupied by the French for many decades. The quatrain is an obscure one, and it is doubtful if England is intended. Roberts (1947), having tried to pronounce "Var," made a great discovery, and casting Garencières to the winds, translates this as "finish of the War" *(sic!)*.

98. A general lament over the persecution of the clergy, a favorite Nostradamian theme.

99. This theme on the power of the three temporal Kings, etc., is found also in paragraph 45 of the Epistle. According to our chronology, it was intended for the early 19th century. To where is the Holy See to be moved? Perhaps back to Avignon.

100. This one is much too vague to be noteworthy, and belongs to the gibberish category from which mockers of Nostradamus are fond of quoting.

# *Century IX*

1. Another of the very specific and yet obscure variety. One of the best known of the 16th-century scholars engaged in translations of the classics was Étienne de la Boétie (1530–63), the intimate friend of Montaigne, who was mixed up in a fracas with Anne de Montmorency, Constable of France (the chief of France's armed forces). The tyranny of the Constable in suppressing rebellion at Bordeaux had inspired the precocious La Boétie in 1548 to write *La servitude volontaire* or *Contr'un*. Though not published till 1570, it had a wide circulation in manuscript, and has since become one of the sacred scriptures of democracy (in English translation it is entitled *Anti-Dictator*). Our prophet made use of the title (or perhaps it's coincidence) in the Epistle (para. 30). Montmorency had been Constable since 1538 and apparently Nostradamus foresaw that the unwonted forbearance that Montmorency had shown the eighteen-year-old idealist would not be maintained by Montmorency's successor (possibly foreseen by Nostradamus as Anne's zealous son Henry bent on avenging the insult to the family honor). As it happened, Montmorency held his post till his death in 1567 (though his powers were largely given to the more able Guise with the title "Lieutenant-General of the Realm"). Thereafter only three other men received the title Constable: Henry de Montmorency (his son) in 1593 (he to whom the Sixains were dedicated, also the father of the alleged subject of one of Nostradamus' most famous quatrains—918); Charles de Luynes, the favorite of Louis XIII, in 1621, just before his death; and finally, in 1622, the near-octogenerian Duke of Lesdiguières, as a reward for abjuring Protestantism after a lifetime as a Huguenot leader and general. The prophecy was not fulfilled as intended, and could not have been, since La Boétie died four year before the first change of Constable. All further chance of fulfillment ended in 1626 with the death of France's last Constable, who, curiously enough, was already alive and in his adolescence when the prophecy was written.

2. This one is all for Italy. The Aventine was one of the Seven Hills of Rome, in Nostradamus' day having mostly churches and monasteries. Possibly it is merely synecdoche for Rome here. The red ones of line 3 are cardinals. Prato is eleven miles northwest of Florence, and had belonged to the Duchy of Tuscany (or Florence) since 1512. Rimini, on the Adriatic, had belonged to the Papacy since 1528. The Colonna family shared honors with its great rival, the Orsini, as Rome's first family (and still does at the Vatican). In Nostradamus' day, they were faithful to the Spanish, and thus were deeply involved in the anti-Spanish moves by Pope Paul IV that precipitated war in 1556.

3. Magnavacca was the name of a canal between Ravenna and Ferrara, and also the name of a port south of the mouths of the Po (renamed Porto di Garibaldi). Translated, it would be "Great Cow," which must needs be

classified as an enigma. It has been suggested that it indicates the Pope, but we see no special reason for that. Fornase is the name of a village about ten miles west of Venice. Thus both the Papal States and the Venetian Republic seem to be involved, but the action is quite incomprehensible, except for the hanging-parties and the two-headed creatures.

4. Elsewhere we have reference to various "discoveries" through flood: the treasure of Toulouse, the tomb of the Great Roman, etc. The chiefs of line 2 may be rival Popes or Emperors, more likely the former, with a new schism involved.

5. Pisa had belonged to Florence since 1509. Lucca, which Nostradamus not illogically saw as being absorbed by Florence, happened to retain its independence till the Revolution. "Tyrant" probably refers to the Medici Duke of Tuscany, a Habsburg minion when our prophet wrote. (See also 980.) Le Pelletier gets something French out of it:

> The National Assembly of 1848 (the second Third Estate)—a copy of the National Convention of 1792 (first Third Estate)—will be trampled by a new Emperor, Louis-Napoleon Bonaparte raised, like the first one, from low to high, by vote of the people. This Prince, the same one who in his youth (1831) will have directed the revolutionary movement of Tuscany, in mounting the throne will take the name of Napoleon III, in order to make up for the deficiency of the son of Napoleon I (Napoleon II, Duke of Reichstadt), dead at Vienna on July 22, 1832.

Unsatisfactory everywhere, this becomes ridiculous in its attempted application to line 3.

6. Lines 1 and 2 were fairly well fulfilled in parts of the 12th, 13th, 14th and 15th centuries, but have never been repeated since. Languedoc was the province between Guienne and the Rhône. The Bordelais is the peninsula at the base of which Bordeaux stands. It was one of the centers of English domination of southern France. *Ispalme* is perhaps Lapalme, near Narbonne, through a typographical error, while *Barboxitaine* can only be viewed as an enigma designating "The 'Beard's' southwest France." If the Beard is "Bronzebeard," he is also to be found in this area in 559.

7. Another one on the discovery of a tomb. The last line suggests one of the bright sayings attributed to the Egyptian sphinx. This prophecy may refer to the same little drama covered in 127.

8. An over-ambitious crown prince seeks to push his feeble father off the throne. It sounds reasonable, but we know of no fulfillment of it involving murder and those odd details of the rest of the verse.

9. The lamp is usually assumed to be a so-called perpetual lamp of the Romans, though the existence of such a device in tombs, etc., seems to be somewhat apocryphal (referred to also in 566). However, it is fitting enough that perpetual flames should be found in Vestal temples. While the location is uncertain, Nostradamus may be referring to the ruins at Nîmes, which were popularly held to be a temple of Diana. A terrible flood at Nîmes is predicted

in line 4. Such a flood occurred on September 9, 1557 (in dangerous proximity to the probable date of composition of the verse) as a result of a cloudburst lasting from 1 to 8 P.M. The water reached six feet in places and otherwise fulfilled Nostradamus' provisions, even to uncovering the monuments. A *History of Nîmes* (Ménard, 1874) cites this verse in connection with it. The dire calamity of Toulouse, about 140 miles northwest of Nîmes, has a very modern sound.

10. A rather colorful and curious quatrain, set in southwest France. Pamiers is about twenty miles north of Foix, Toulouse about fifty miles north of Foix and Carcassonne about fifty miles northeast of Foix. Half the quatrain is devoted to parochial scandal and tragedy, half to big military activities.

11. This one is fairly clear and fairly general. After someone is unjustly condemned and executed, a great plague occurs, causing those that sent him to death to flee. It has been applied to England with the Great Plague (1665–66) as divine punishment for the execution of Charles I (1649).

12. This one may be related to the "treasure in Toulouse" theme (see 828–30).

13. The setting for this quatrain is far-flung in France and Italy. Sologne was the region on the southern bank of the Loire, from its bend at Orléans to about one hundred miles up the Loire past Blois. Auxois was a small region west of Dijon with its center at Semur, about one hundred miles east of Sologne. Buzançais is just south of the Sologne. Line 3 takes us to Italy, to Modena, ruled by the Este Duke of Ferrara since 1288. In 1452 it became a duchy, and in 1598 the Este capital when the Pope seized Ferrara. Bologna was ruled by a Cardinal-Legate on behalf of the Pope.

14. Another of the gibberish category and a strong competitor for the title of most obscure.

15. Perpignan was the chief city of Roussillon, which belonged to the Spanish until 1659. Red was the color of the Spaniards. Some Franco-Spanish struggle near the Pyrenees seems to be involved. As for line 4, if it refers to the Governor of Burgundy in Nostradamus' day, that office was held by Guise's brother, the Duke of Aumale, from 1550 until his death in 1573. Perhaps Nostradamus has him identified with one of his clerical brothers, the Cardinal of Lorraine, or of Guise. Burgundy was divided between the archbishoprics of Sens and Lyons. It had four bishops: at Châlon, Autun, Mâcon and Auxerre.

16. Seeing the name of two of Spain's dictators, i.e., Primo de Rivera and Francisco Franco, so plainly set forth, few commentators of the 1930's or 1940's are inclined to look two prophetic gift horses in the mouth. The unfortunate fact remains that there are several Castelfrancos and a Riviera in *Italy;* the only question is which one Nostradamus had in mind. The Castelfranco west of Modena is closest (about one hundred miles) to Liguria (the Riviera; the application of the name to the French coast is a misnomer). Other Castelfrancos are southeast of Ferrara and northeast of Vicenza. Ap-

parently the Genoese of Liguria will object to something and close the Gulf of Genoa to shipping.

17. Le Pelletier makes an interesting application of this one to the French Revolution:

> The National Convention (the third first) will be more cruel than Nero was: behold how much generous blood it will cause to be shed! It will erect the scaffold which will devour the Clergy and Nobility at the *place* called that of the Revolution, opposite the Tuileries Palace, where formerly there were tile kilns. Age of Steel! New dynasty! [Footnote: The Napoleonic!] Great scandal!

The Tuileries does indeed get its name from the tile kiln on whose site it was built. Furthermore, it is not impossible that Nostradamus did have the Third Estate in mind for *tiers* (see Preface, para. 6).

18. Largely on the basis of lines 3 and 4, this is one of Nostradamus' most acclaimed quatrains. As Le Pelletier gives it:

> Louis XIII [footnote: The first French King to bear the title of Dauphin since the publication of Century IX] will enter Nancy, in 1633, and will penetrate to Flanders, in 1635, to uphold the cause of the Elector of Trèves, prisoner of the Spaniards. At about the same time (in 1632), the great Montmorency, charged with rebellion against his sovereign, will be confined in the prison of the newly-built Hôtel de Ville at Toulouse; then he will be delivered to a soldier named Clerepeyne, who will behead him in the courtyard of the prison, outside the place named for his execution.

There are unfortunately a few catches to this. Louis XIII may have been the first Dauphin since publication date (1568, not 1566, as Le Pelletier thought, based on his false edition), but not since it was written (*ca.* 1557), which would be what counts. The future Francis II was Dauphin when Nostradamus wrote. It may have been meant for a future Dauphin, but as Dauphin, and not as King.

Secondly, the Elector of Trier, Philip Christopher von Sötern (1623–52) was indeed arrested by the Spanish (March 26, 1635) and taken to Tervuren, near Brussels. But it was through the intercessions of Pope Urban VIII that he was taken to Vienna. The French took no particular interest in him till their entrance into the Thirty Years' War in the 1640's, whereupon they demanded his release. The alleged connection between the Elector and the French attack against Louvain is dubious. Line 2 might be applied to the Elector's "trip" into captivity.

Next we come to Montmorency, if we allow this chronological regression (leaving the quatrain with no real unity of the elements). It is true enough that Montmorency's punishment was celebrated. It was the talk of the day. Long in search of an example to show the turbulent French nobility who was master, Richelieu made use of this *premier baron* of France (grandson of the Constable of Nostradamus' day and son of the one mentioned in the dedication of the Sixains) to serve his purpose. Montmorency was involved in a revolt by the King's nitwit brother Gaston. Richelieu ignored all the pleas for clemency that poured in from all corners of France.

Le Pelletier's note that he was executed privately in the courtyard as a special concession to his family is valid enough. The note that as another concession he was executed by a soldier instead of the public executioner is subject to more doubt. But his claim that the very name of this soldier was Clerepeyne is without any foundation whatever. In a letter of August 4, 1947, the Archivist of Toulouse confirmed to us that a most exhaustive search on his part through the archives of Toulouse does not yield the name of the executioner of Montmorency. It all comes from a section of Jaubert's book (1656) in which he mentions the names of future personages recorded by Nostradamus, amongst which he includes (p. 18) "the executioner of M. de Montmorency named Clerepeyne." Le Pelletier quotes de Jant, Garencières, Leroux and Motret as "confirming" this, but each of them merely copied this assertion, which was probably pure fabrication. The execution took place only twenty-four years before his book was published, and if Jaubert had *bona fide* inside information, he would probably have mentioned it.

19. Mayenne was in the province of Maine in northwest France. It belonged to House of Guise and gave the Duke of Aumale the title Marquis of Mayenne. The forest a few miles west of the city is quite extensive (nine by two miles). Fougères is about twenty-five miles west of Mayenne. It was the seat of a great family which died out in 1256, and also a possession of Diane de Poitiers, Henry II's mistress (previously his father's). From 1552 to 1576 the appanage of Maine belonged to Edward Alexander, Duke of Anjou (later Henry III). Only three houses or titles can be identified with Maine: Mayenne, Fougères and Laval. Line 4 apparently tells the fate of a scion of the Fougères family, extinct as it was.

20. This one is another of Nostradamus' most famous. As Le Pelletier gives it:

A royal couple, Louis XVI, abandoned by his people (monk) and dressed in gray, and Marie-Antoinette, this precious stem of the line of Hugh Capet [*sic!*], dressed in white, will enter Varennes during the night of June 21 or June 22, 1791, after having secretly left the Tuileries, the preceding night, through a secret door (Latin, *fores*, gate) in the Queen's apartments, and after having changed their route, at the outskirts of Sainte-Menehoulde, as a result of having lost their way. The transformation of this Capetian, of this absolute King, into a constitutional King of the French, will cause a horrible revolution, the fire of civil and foreign war, great shedding of blood, and beheading by the slice of the guillotine.

Of the weak points, the first lies in line 1. The only justification for making *forest* (the original form for *forêt*) into *fores* is the apparent lack of any Forêt de Reines in France. As a matter of fact, there really is a small forest called Forêt de la Reine in that general area, but it is on the far side of Varennes, over fifty miles to the southeast. It would not be on the route from Paris to Varennes, even allowing for a poorly-chosen roundabout route, being in the Department of Meurthe-et-Moselle *(Encyclopédie universelle du XXe siècle,* 1908, Vol. X). Nevertheless, Bouys (1806, p. 57) unabashedly writes that "Reines is the name of the forest traversed by the great road which leads to Varennes and which Louis XVI took." The forest in question is a well-known one, the Argonne. Perhaps some scholar can find a derivation of *Argonne* from some word meaning "queen" in some language.

In line 2, *deux pars* obviously means two couples, and not *a* couple, but one could add Mme de Tourzel and Count Fersen. Le Pelletier's derivation of *voltorte,* making it "crossroads," is rather dubious. But it is substantially true that the party took a poor route to Montmedy. (Bouys notes that the correct route to Montmedy goes through Châlons and Clermont-en-Argonne.) That the Queen was dressed in white is highly unlikely. Le Pelletier as an alternate quotes Mme de Campan to the effect that the Queen's hair had turned quite white after the harrowing experience, but this does not make her white-haired during the trip.

In line 3, rather than account for the monk by the fact that Louis had been left alone, some commentators prefer to insist that his drab gray garb and broad-brimmed hat made him resemble a Carmelite monk. As for Varennes, there are twenty-six towns by that name in France, but the one which this event made famous was no more insignificant than any of the others.

Line 4 perhaps stands up best of all, especially the final word (as suggesting the guillotine).

21. This one seems to be set entirely in Blois and is the first of an apparent series of three. The Church of Saint-Solenne (Cathedral of Blois) appears again in 923, tending to confirm that the intervening one goes with these other two. Nostradamus' association of a future king or dynasty with Blois is seen also in the twice-repeated line "The King of Blois will reign in Avignon." The quatrain is full of dramatic details, with the usual obscurity. The King and a prelate are involved in murder at Blois while fighting takes place in marshes outside the city.

22. The key to this one lies in the meaning of the enigmatic titles of *Mantor* and *Albe.* If the *Mantou* reading is right, suggesting Mantua, it is perhaps more than chance that the same Duke ruled in Mantua, capital of the Duchy of Mantua, and Alba in the Marquisate of Montferrat (whose capital, however, was Casale). Montferrat, given to Mantua in 1536 by Charles V, was divided into Upper and Lower Montferrat; Alba was the chief city of Upper Montferrat. The ruler from 1550 to 1587 was Guglielmo Gonzaga. There was indeed a plot to assassinate him (1567) but it was at Casale and not at Blois. The only member of the family to be mixed up in French history was his younger brother, who inherited the Duchy of Nevers, but did not fulfill the quatrain any better. The palace referred to would probably be the famous Château of Blois. But the cathedral does not face the chateau.

Allen (1943) points out that *Montoro* is one of the titles of the Dukes of Alba. However, it came into the family only in 1688.

23. The Church of Saint-Solenne places this one, like 921, in Blois again. The younger son of this tragedy is presumably a prince. Putting together the remarkable wealth of details in these three quatrains, which represent one of the best arguments against Nostradamus' supposed vagueness (but not against his lack of "success"), we have the following: While a King (of France?), accompanied by high prelates and other members of his court, is in a part of the Cathedral of Blois referred to as "the place of the cunning tongue," and involved with something where incense is used, he and the prelate are stabbed by a dagger. His younger son, playing outdoors in the arbor, is struck on the head by a loosened part of the roof. A duke, whose titles involve, by synecdoche or anagram, the names Mantor and Alba (as would be the case with any of the Gonzaga Dukes of Mantua between 1536, when they were invested by Charles V with the Marquisate of Montferrat [Alba being the capital of Upper Montferrat], and 1631, when they lost it to Savoy), is in the garden of either the Cathedral or the Château of Blois, and is involved in the plot, as is a religious faction associated with the color white. At about the time of this assassination, a crushing victory is gained in a battle in a nearby swampy area. All this is certainly specific enough, but unless there's a restoration of the monarchy, its chances for fulfillment have passed. However, should there ever be a restoration of the monarchy in France, we can certainly expect that any time the royal family visits Blois, the royal security forces will be keeping a pretty sharp eye on any visiting Duke of Alba, who qualifies for the Duke of 922, as of when the Montoro title passed into the family (1688). The present Dukes, by the way, still very active in the affairs of Spain, are descended from the Duke who is the subject of so many quatrains of Nostradamus only by marriages of female descendants of the 16th-century Alba; traced in the customary male line, they descend from a bastard of James II of England, the Duke of Berwick, who became a Spanish general and fought against the English in the War of the Spanish Succession.

24. Saint-Denis is five miles north of Paris (more in the 16th century). Orléans is about seventy-five miles southwest. The only clear element here is the kidnapping of two children of a king. It may possibly represent a continuation of the exciting drama in the preceding three, since Orléans is on the way from Blois to Paris.

25. If we are to take Rosiers as a place name, one is in northern France near Angers and another in the South, near Tulle in Corrèze. There are also several towns called Rosières, two called Rosier and one La Rosière. What Nostradamus meant by "new Spaniards" is a most interesting point. Béziers is on the Spanish invasion route about fifty miles northeast of the pre-1659 border. The river is probably the one that has become part of the Canal du Midi.

26. Voltri is on the Mediterranean between Genoa and Savona. It belonged

to Genoa. If Piombino is intended in line 4, it lies further down the coast opposite Napoleon's Elba. Nice belonged to Savoy till 1860 (except during the Revolution; it was one of the few places left to Savoy when Nostradamus wrote). Line 2 refers to the Pope (see 578).

27. This rather colorful quatrain could be viewed as a Nostradamian confirmation of the escape of the Dauphin (Louis XVII), reported dead on June 8, 1795. Though there is tightly packed drama here, its meaning is far from clear.

28. The setting for this one is far-flung indeed. The subject might seem to be an attack against the Turks, who held most of Hungary (Pannonia). "The gulf and bay of Illyria" is just a fancy name for the Adriatic Sea. It is also possible that the Allied Fleet represents a Franco-Turkish combination against the Habsburgs, quite frequent when this was written. Since Sicily belonged to the Habsburgs and Genoa was constantly subject to their pressure, this theory is perhaps more likely. It would then involve an initial attack against the Habsburg outlet on the Adriatic in the Trieste-Fiume area.

29. All lines but the last are thoroughly obscure. Charlieu is on the Sornin, a tributary of the Loire, about forty miles northwest of Lyons. There is also a famous old abbey by that name near Besançon. Saint-Quentin had been captured by the Spanish on August 10, 1557 (perhaps a matter of weeks before this was written). Calais had been held by the English since 1347; it was recaptured for France by the Duke of Guise on January 6, 1558. (He also captured the two other nearby places in Jaubert's "corrected" version.) Therefore, this verse was probably written after August 10, 1557, and (unless Nostradamus was "cheating") before January 6, 1558. The capture of Calais was quite sudden and unexpected, so that if this prophecy is honest, it deserves credit. But Saint-Quentin was to be "recaptured" only by the general settlement of 1559.

30. This one is set entirely in the Balkans, all places now part of Yugoslavia. Pola is a venerable port on the west coast of the Istrian peninsula at the head of the Adriatic. In 1947 it went to Yugoslavia. San Nicolo (if this be the right reading) lies across the bay from Capodistria on the north of the peninsula. The Gulf of Quarnero is the gulf on which Fiume (now Rijeka) is located. Cadiz is the great port of southern Spain; the Philip mentioned as sending help against what appears to be a new Fourth Crusade may well be meant for Philip II, especially if it is intended to tie in with 928 as predicting a Franco-Turkish attack on the inner citadel of the Habsburgs from the south, with the Spanish help being against the French.

31. Mortara in northern Italy is about thirty-five miles southwest of Milan. If it is indeed Britain that is intended in line 2, it seems that Nostradamus is predicting that the British Isles would "go under" literally, a rather drastic outcome for an earthquake one thousand miles away. More likely a statue of St. George at Mortara, with tin in it, is involved.

32. Mytilene is another name for Lesbos off the west coast of Asia Minor,

and also the name of its chief city. Roman inscriptions are probably implied in line 2. The first part of line 3 probably refers to the opening of a tomb, the second part to an attack on the Papacy. Larmor (1925, p. 146) claims that in 1588 "an enormous obelisk of rose granite" was found by workmen in the Basilica of St. Peter in Rome. As for line 4, "At this date, a Venetian squadron invaded the isle of Lesbos and its capital."

33. Le Pelletier applies this one to Napoleon, getting around the "Denmark" obstacle by saying that the Bonaparte family originally came from Denmark, to which nonsense he devotes a huge footnote without much conviction. Robb (1942, p. 71) polishes up Le Pelletier as usual, and adds this shattering quote to cinch the point: "'Napoleon . . . was ruler of Denmark.' Walter Lippman, *Herald Tribune*, November 26, 1940."

What this quatrain really seems to amount to is a dazzling horoscope for Henry II's infant son Hercules, later Francis of Alençon (see 580). He gets himself elected "King of the Romans," i.e., King of Germany, and also King of "Annemark," i.e., King of Hungary and Bohemia (see 427). All of this just line 1. Then, per line 2, he gets elected Caesar-Imperator, i.e., Holy Roman Emperor. Now the first monarch in Christendom, he moves against Venice and Italy to round out the whole Empire, France having been his to begin with. Of course, this might have been intended by Nostradamus to be fulfilled by marriage as well as by war if heir-apparent Maximilian had no surviving children other than a daughter, wedded to Hercules/Francis. As it turned out, although one daughter of Maximilian's did indeed marry Charles IX, the older brother of Hercules/Francis, Maximilian also had nine sons. Concerning how far away Hercules ended up from these glorious heights, we refer the reader back to the Commentary on 580. His name was changed from Hercules to Francis by Catherine de' Medici on the advise of a numerologist who was apparently no fan of Nostradamus'.

34. This one goes with 920 and is another of the most celebrated ones. As Le Pelletier gives it:

> Louis XVI alone will have the affliction to find himself clothed in the red cap by the populace, on June 20, 1792, upon his return from Varennes. The Marseillais Federates, five hundred of them, will direct the attack of the people, on August 10 of the same year, against the Tuileries Palace. Amongst the traitors who contribute powerfully to the ruin of Louis XVI, there will stand out, in the ranks of the nobility, the Count of Narbonne, his Minister of War; and amongst the people, a son and grandson of chandler-grocers, named Sauce, procureur-syndic of the commune of Varennes, who will cause him to be arrested in this town.

Le Pelletier derives *avons* from *avus*, "grandfather," so that for him the last line reads "Narbonne and Saulce grandfathers of oil amongst the guards." If we examine line 4 merely from the point of mundane geography, we find a village of Salces about fifteen miles north of Perpignan. It was the victim of a sudden attack by the Spanish from Roussillon in 1542. It cannot, however, be denied that *Saulce* seems closer to "Sauce" (or "Sausse," as it appears too) than to "Salces," and indeed the straight geographical reading makes no particular sense.

35. The principal Ferdinand when Nostradamus wrote was the new Emperor, brother of Charles V and uncle of Philip II. It seems that he is to ally himself with Spain first, then turn against the Spaniards, coming back to the Ferdinand-Philip duel theme. According to a 20th-century interpretation, it is applied to Ferdinand of Bulgaria, with the Macedonian, the German and the Myrmidons, the Greeks, in World War I.

36. Jaubert makes a rather ridiculous application of this one to the Bourbon brothers: King Anthony of Navarre, Louis of Condé and the Cardinal of Bourbon ("Charles X") in the 1560's. Le Pelletier's is slightly better:

> The King of France, Henry III, at Saint-Cloud, in his camp, will be taken by the hand of a young religious Jacobin (Jacques Clément, age twenty-five) who, just after receiving the holy sacraments, and wrongly considering his crime as an act agreeable to God, will strike him in the abdomen with one knife thrust. This outrage will be committed at a time when the Parisians, surrounded by Henry III, will see the vengeance of this prince ready to strike their ramparts; and this murder will cause the last of the three brothers, sons of Henry II and Catherine de' Medici, who will have successively worn the crown of France, to lose his life.

One big shortcoming of this interpretation is that "near Easter" cannot be explained by the sacraments. The murder took place on August 1, 1589. The three brothers here are probably the same as those found in 817, 846 and the Epistle, paragraph 14.

37. The subject here is clearly a flood on the Garonne, affecting especially Toulouse (and thus similar to 99). The reference to the matron in line 4 is puzzling; perhaps "midwife" is intended.

38. The geography is a bit confused here. Blaye is near the mouth of the Gironde (the estuary of the Garonne) north of Bordeaux. La Rochelle is about forty miles north of the estuary. Agen is about one hundred miles up the Garonne. Narbonne is on the Mediterranean, more than two hundred miles southeast of Agen. Apparently an Anglo-Spanish invasion, with help from the independent-minded commune of La Rochelle, is concerned here. This is hinted in various other quatrains and reasonably enough if this was written while Philip was still titular King of England. Le Pelletier, who insists on deriving *Aemathien* from the name of a mythological character who opened the gates of the morning to the Sun (ergo, Sun King), applies this one to events of 1702–4.

> Louis the Great will feel easy when he will have constructed, in 1689, the Pate de Blaye, to close the entrance of the Gironde to the English, leagued with the French Calvinists of La Rochelle against the Revocation of the Edict of Nantes. As for the Camisards, in revolt in the Cevennes, they

will await the help from Agen and Narbonne promised them by their co-religionists: relief that will be rendered impossible after the submission in 1704 of Jean Cavalier, their principal leader, following a conference at Nîmes with Marshal Villars.

39. All the places here are on the Riviera, involving military intrigue, under some Gascon raider, between Genoa and Savona. *Veront* alone has not been identified (Verona is unlikely). Perhaps the closest is the village of Vorazzo or Voragine. L'Escarène and La Turbie are north of Monaco, in the former Duchy of Savoy; Albisola, Savona and Carcara were in the Republic of Genoa. The Pass of Carcara (Cardibona) is about ten miles northwest of Albisola.

40. Jaubert gives an interpretation based on an admitted guess that as a preliminary to their attack on Saint-Quentin in 1557, the Spaniards seized the Abbey of Vermandois in the forest of the same name, which he states was formerly called Bourlis. He concludes this combination of conjecture and downright falsification (Bourlis) with "This quatrain has not been clarified entirely to my satisfaction. Something must be left for the keen wits." Some sort of revenge against the Spanish and their Flemish mercenaries seems envisaged here by our patriotic prophet, shortly after the humiliation of Saint-Quentin (August 10, 1557). But the details are quite obscure.

41. Since we have seen that Chyren and Chyren-Selin refer to Henry II (477), this is a prophecy of no little daring: Henry II will seize Avignon, which had belonged to the Papacy since 1348 (and was to be retained until 1791). It had indeed been seized briefly in 1536 (under Henry's father, Francis I). It was to be occupied again 1663–64, 1688 and 1768–74. Line 2 reflects the not unnatural papal indignation. The meaning of line 3 is obscured by the perplexing *Chanignon*. Carpentras is about fifteen miles northeast of Avignon and was also part of the papal possessions, comprising the so-called Venaissin enclave.

42. This prophecy was substantially fulfilled in the epic battle of Lepanto on October 7, 1571, when the allied fleet of Spain (including such satellites as Monaco and Genoa), Venice and the Papacy inflicted a crushing defeat on the Turkish fleet, consisting mostly of the ships of the Algerians from the Barbary area. In 1573 the leader at this victory, Don John of Austria, went on to recapture Tunis. The Algerians had taken it from Spain in 1570. After losing it to Don John in 1573, they retook it in 1574.

43. This one may go with the preceding one if the scene of the intended landing is Tunis. The Christians are to meet disaster. (They didn't in 1573).

44. Geneva in Nostradamus' day was noteworthy chiefly as Calvin's seat, i.e., the Protestant Rome. Either Nostradamus is warning the victims of a purge by Calvin, or else is taking pity on the hated Calvinists, warning them that they will be exterminated by Philip II, who used the name Zopyra in one of his devices. The device consisted of two sceptres passed in saltire through a crown over an open pomegranate, with the motto *Tot Zopiro* (as many of

Zopyros). According to Mrs. Paliser (pp. 251–52), it originated in the following manner:

> One day Philip being asked of what he would like as large a number of as the seeds of a pomegranate, answered he would like as many of Zopyros, that is, as many faithful friends, alluding to the well-known story of Zopyro, who, by cutting off his nose and ears, wounding himself and pretending to be a fugitive, delivered Babylon into the power of his sovereign Darius.

Of course, one question remains: Could word of this have gotten to Nostradamus by the gossip route? To Roberts (1947) it is "Startling! Nostradamus here foretells the advent of atomic power."

45. Though convinced that *Mendosus* was intended for Henry IV, Le Pelletier refrains from trying to tackle this one. The fact remains that *Mendosus* is a pretty sure anagram for *Vendôme*, in which case the quatrain may have been intended for either Henry IV or his father, King Anthony of Navarre, also Duke of Vendôme. Line 4 is extremely obscure. Piedmont was the Italian territory of the House of Savoy. Picardy was the northernmost province of France.

46. Only two elements are at all clear here: the scene is Toulouse and "red ones" probably refers to the Spaniards, whose colors were red and yellow. The rest is close to gibberish.

47. One of the detailed but obscure variety. Jaubert made an attempt to apply it to France under Francis II (1559–60).

48. With no geographical limitation at all, this one is hopelessly vague. According to Allen (1943, p. 83), "the crystalline water is Central Park [in New York City]. There is no doubt whatever this was what Nostradamus meant." Boswell (1941, p. 348) sees it for the destruction of Tokyo by fire from Russian chemical bombs.

49. Line 2 makes this one of Nostradamus' most distinguished prophecies. Lines 3 and 4 can be worked out, though with less distinction. But line 1, alas, presents an insurmountable object. As Le Pelletier gives it:

> At the time of the war of Philip IV, master of the southern part of the Netherlands (Ghent, Brussels and Antwerp), against revolted Holland, the Long Parliament of England will condemn its King, Charles I, to death; force and wisdom (wine and salt) will have failed this King, and his Kingdom will fall into anarchy.

Le Pelletier's interpretation of wine and salt may be the intended one, but we think they are more likely to signify taxation, being two basic taxable items. This would not spoil the interpretation, and in fact might help.

However, Le Pelletier's claim that the Spanish tried right up to the Treaty of Westphalia (1648) to subdue the Netherlands is quite without foundation. There had been little fighting for many years, and when there was, the Dutch were the aggressors. The best that can be done for the line is that by a treaty of January 30, 1648, the Spanish, anxious to get the Dutch out of the war, gave them the key towns of Maestriot, Bois-le-Duc, Berg-op-Zoom, Breda and Hulst. But best of all, for the Dutch and Nostradamus, they closed the Scheldt, which brought wealth to Amsterdam and ruin to Antwerp. In other words, Antwerp was ruined by its own ruler.

Ward has a somewhat labored version, "Philip IV . . . will move Ghent and Brussels toward Antwerp against Holland." Garencières is also interesting: "The first Verse signifieth, that at that time there was no good intelligence between the cities of Flanders and Brabant, as I remember very well that there was not, but upon what score, I have forgotten."

50. This time Le Pelletier is willing to place *Mendosus* as Vendôme.

> Henry IV, this Vendôme-Heretic who will have thrice changed his religion, will rapidly attain to the throne to which the Salic Law will give him the right, setting aside the Lorraine princes who will claim it, the old Cardinal of Bourbon, the Duke of Mayenne, Lieutenant-General of the Realm during the Interregnum, the young Duke of Guise, son of Balafré and the ferocious Philip II, King of Spain.

The best tribute to the success of this prophecy is that one tends to suspect its validity, but it was indeed in print by 1568. If there is anything unsatisfactory in the application, it lies in the *Barbaris*. The anonymous 1789 book (Coudoulet's) applies the epithet to the Marquis of Pont-à-Mousson, later Duke of Lorraine, another would-be candidate for the throne. But words with that root usually refer to the Algerians, or the Turks anyhow, with Nostradamus.

51. Here neither the cardinals nor the Spaniards reading for "reds" makes as much sense as the modern politico-social meaning does. In fact, nothing Nostradamus could have had in mind could fit this verse as well as conditions in Europe between World Wars I and II. In line 1 we would have Fascism, Naziism, Anti-Comintern, etc., in line 2 even the Cordon Sanitaire (rope) amongst other expedients in which faith was put. Line 3 would refer to all the red-terrified statesmen of the West, of which most became appeasers. The exception became the subject of line 4; few would deny Hitler the terminology.

52. Both Jaubert and Le Pelletier agree in applying this one to the Peace of Cateau-Cambresis (April 13, 1559), as a result of which the King was supposed to turn from fighting the Spaniards to liquidating the heretics in his own kingdom. Le Pelletier explains it thus:

> The peace of France with Spain approaches on one side, and the Civil War of the Catholics with the Calvinists approaches on the other: never will one have seen a struggle so relentless. Pity the men, the women, the innocent children whose blood will flow in torrents: for, Catholics or Protestants, it will be French blood that is shed on all sides.

53. The historical novelist Rafael Sabatini writes of at least one prince of the Italian Renaissance wont to throw a pageboy into the fireplace in a

fit of anger. Writes Garencières, "this fact savoureth so much of bestial cruelty that I cannot believe any Christian Prince can ever be guilty of it."

54. An invader of the Papal States will land at Porto Corsini, eight miles northeast of Ravenna, and will plunder someone or something referred to as "the lady." A Cardinal-Legate from Portugal is involved in line 3. The rest is rather obscure.

55. Jaubert takes this to be a prediction of the Spanish onslaught, resulting in the disaster at Saint-Quentin (August 10, 1557). But the verse was probably written after that date. The quatrain has also been applied to World War I and influenza epidemics thereafter. The configuration should limit the time.

56. Houdan and Goussainville are both west of Paris. The second about nine miles northeast of Dreux, the first about twelve miles. But *Maiotes* remains unidentified, unless it is an erratum for nearby Mantes. The meaning of *legne* is also uncertain. The general subject seems to be an attack upon Paris.

57. One cannot be quite certain about Dreux. The capitalization makes it necessary to wonder, while there is no other bit of geographia to confirm the setting of this quatrain. If it be Dreux, it lies fifty miles west of Paris in Normandy (which would not be far from the scene of the preceding quatrain). In line 2 it seems that the King is to be excommunicated by the Pope.

58. There are several Vitrys, of which the most important are Vitry-le-François in Champagne, about twenty miles southeast of Paris and Vitry-sur-Seine, a few miles south of Paris. If we are to limit the red ones to cardinals or Spaniards, the former would seem more likely here.

59. La Ferté-Vidame is about twenty-five miles southeast of Dreux. If the two names are not to be joined, it must be noted that the Vidame was the representative of a bishop in temporal and military matters. Only the following bishoprics still retained a Vidame: Amiens, Beauvais, Cambrai, Châlons, Chartres, Laon, Le Mans, Meaux, Reims, Rouen, Sens and Senlis. The Vidame of La Ferté was that of Chartres. The principal Nicholas of the day was Nicholas of Lorraine, Count of Vaudemont and Duke of Mercœur, uncle of young Charles III of Lorraine, who like his Guise kin chose to fish in the troubled French waters. He indeed had a daughter named Louise, born in 1553, who was to marry Henry III, the last Valois king. Line 3 suggests that Louise will give birth to a bastard in some retreat. But nothing in the life of either came close to fulfilling the obscurities here. Both Louise and Henry III were children when the prophecy was written.

60. This one seems to involve an Arab invasion of the Balkans, another of the "Neo-Arab Empire" theme. Dalmatia, on the eastern shores of the Adriatic, belonged to Venice. Lusitania was the classical name for Portugal. The obscure reference to the frogs is probably connected with the "frog's blood . . . in Dalmatia" of 232.

61. Cittanova, if this be the right heading, is about twenty-five miles

northeast of the Straits of Messina. Malta had been the seat of the Knights of St. John since 1530. Both Cittanova and Messina were part of the Habsburg Kingdom of the Two Sicilies and Malta a protectorate of theirs. The protagonists are probably Spanish adventurers and Algerian corsairs.

62. A very curious and cryptic quatrain. Ceramon-agora was actually the name of a Greek town in Asia Minor, the site of which is thought to be occupied by modern Usak. It was about seventy-five miles northeast of Sardis, capital of Croesus' Lydia. Mandrake and opium were herbs with many mysterious usages.

63. This one is set on the French side of the Pyrenees. Bayonne is on the Atlantic on the western end, Narbonne on the Mediterranean on the eastern end. Foix is about seventy-five miles west of Narbonne, in between. If the revolutions of Mars are to be taken literally, each one takes 687 days.

64. Since Macedonian is a Nostradamian epithet for Spaniards, this one forecasts an invasion of France from the south. Narbonne was a sort of frontier town with respect to Spanish Roussillon. Le Pelletier's "Sun God" reading (see 938) obliges him to see the invasion going the other way, in the War of the Spanish Succession.

> Louis XIV will cause his troops to pass over the Pyrenees again and, instead of exterminating them, will treat with the Camisards in revolt in Narbonne, and will make desperate efforts by land and sea when the Capetian (Philip V), his grandson, will be forced by the Imperials to leave Spain.

The chief trouble with this is that there were no Camisards at Narbonne. Le Pelletier can only explain that Narbonne was also a quondam Protestant center.

65. The only specific element in this very vague and very general one is the *Luna*, and that is rather obscure. The valley of Lunigiana, of which the chief cities are Pontremoli and Sazana, remains a likelihood. However, the Land of the Moon might be the Empire of the Crescent (Turkey).

66. The setting of this one is a "postwar period," but it is sufficiently general to be applicable to many such periods.

67. This one is set chiefly in the Department of Drôme, part of ancient Dauphiné. The Isère flows into the Rhône at Valence. Romans is about ten miles northeast of Valence, Crest about fifteen miles southeast. Pierrelatte is about forty-five miles down the Rhône from Valence. Châteauneuf, north of Avignon, is in the Department of Vaucluse, south of Drôme. Donzère is five miles north of Pierrelatte. Most of the towns were in the papal enclave of Venaissin. Though there are mountains fairly close, none are close enough to Valence to justify the epithet applied in line 2. If it is the *pays* of Valentinois that is intended, it included Crest, Romans and possibly Pierrelatte but not Châteauneuf or Donzère, and was quite mountainous. A third possibility is that a town in the Valentinois other than Valence is intended. Religious strife is the subject.

68. Only two factors are clear here: Lyons and December 13. The identity of _Mont Aymar_ is still a matter of conjecture; the closest thing (in sound) in the environs is Montélimar. This may be another "sack of Lyons" prophecy, which was to some extent fulfilled in 1793 by the soldiers of the Revolution.

69. Dauphiny is the setting for this one. Sain-Bel and L'Arbresle are about three miles apart, on opposite sides of a mountain about twelve miles northwest of Lyons. Vienne is down the Rhône from Lyons, Grenoble southeast of Vienne on the Isère. Tempting as it might be to apply the cryptic line 4 to the British redcoats, there is no justification for it.

70. This one is set in southeastern France also. Vienne is about thirty miles down the Rhône from Lyons, Mâcon fifty miles up the Saône from Lyons. If the Latin cantons are indeed the Grisons, they are located in southeastern Switzerland, quite a distance from this setting. However, some other non-Germanic canton may be intended.

71. All is obscure here except Carcassonne, which was in Languedoc in southwestern France. As Garencières says, "Whether the Author did understand himself here I know not, I am sure I do not."

72. Another of the many quatrains dealing with religious strife at Toulouse. The Senate of line 2 refers to its Parliament. Apparently Nostradamus sees this body falling into Calvinist hands, then authorizing the violation of Catholic churches. For line 3 we can only mention that a revolution of Saturn takes 29.5 years. If "six revolutions" is intended, that would be 177 years, which would coincide with the figure in the Preface, paragraph 26.

73. Turbans being associated with oriental potentates, we must assume that this quatrain involves Moslem invasions. Foix in the Southwest is to be a Moslem principality for nearly thirty years. The relationship of the character in line 3 to Byzantium (Constantinople) is not clear. The configuration of line 4 should date this prophecy clearly, but Wöllner skipped it. According to McCann (1942) it occurs on February 18, 1981.

74. Another of the leading contenders for the title of most obscure. The setting as well as the action is a mystery, until someone figures out where _Fertsod_ is. Torné-Chavigny took it as Paris (Rich Sodom).

75. The setting of this one seems to be divided between France and Greece. Ambracia (Arta) in western Greece was quite distant from Thrace in the Northeast. Perhaps both are used as synecdoche for Greece. Provence in southeastern France was where Nostradamus was born, lived and died. McCann (1942, p. 16) sees this as the Greeks in trouble seeking aid from Provence, on which the ancient Greek colonists left such a heavy stamp.

76. Another reference to the "new Nero." If line 2 is to be taken literally, this quatrain involves his offspring. As practically any city in Europe is between two rivers, the locale is none too specific. However, Avignon and the Venaissin enclave seem to be intended elsewhere by Mesopotamia, which means "between rivers." Larmor (1925, p. 148) applies it to Henry III. Nero

is his great-grandfather, Piero II of Florence, ally of Caesar Borgia and enemy of Pope Sixtus IV.

77. Le Pelletier explains this interesting quatrain as follows:

> The National Convention, usurper of the prerogatives of royalty, will pretend that it is convicting the King, a prisoner, of treason; Marie-Antoinette, a prisoner, will be condemned to death by a jury chosen by lot; they will cause the young Dauphin to lose his life, in delivering him to the cobbler Simon, charged with killing him slowly; then the National Convention, decimating itself, will send its members to the Conciergerie, and from there to the scaffold, where they will undergo the fate of their victims (consort—same fate).

Le Pelletier's version is especially weak in line 4. The Convention is a prostitute (rather than concubine) because it prostituted justice. *Consort* means "same fate," a ridiculous derivation. Another ingenious stab was made more literally, based on the fact that Mme du Barry was supposed to have been in the Conciergerie at the same time as the Queen (though wife and mistress of different kings). As it was, du Barry was not taken to the Conciergerie but to the prison of Sainte-Pelagie. But the fascinating "jury" reference leads Bouys (1806, p. 70) to exclaim that calling this chance is "to push obstinacy too far. When all the academicians, when all the philosophers persist in this obstinacy, we will always say that it is more astonishing than the prophecy itself."

78. The most ingenious application that has been made for this one, perhaps, is that in which the Greek lady is taken as Democracy. Line 4 would apply to its death beginning in 1936 in Spain. Larmor (1925, p. 157) applies it to Marie de' Medici because she was of beauty "comparable to that of the Greek courtesan Lais." In 1631 she went into exile to Brussels, indeed then a Spanish possession, but her death in 1642 was at Cologne.

79. There was some hope of applying this one to Admiral Darlan in the period 1940–42, but it didn't work out too well. Chrism is the consecrated oil used by the Church at baptisms, confirmations, etc. A renouncer thereof is presumably a Protestant. Elements of it seem applicable to Admiral Coligny, the Huguenot leader who was the first victim of the St. Bartholomew's Day Massacre (1572), but others again have loopholes. It involves an admiral active in war, religion and politics, to which Coligny has come closest in French history. The first part suggests ending a naval mutiny by false promises, followed by execution of the gullible.

80. Pisa was annexed by Florence in 1406. Lucca managed to maintain its independence from Florence until the Revolution. The Duke is probably a Medici Duke of Florence (Tuscany). The Barbarians are probably corsairs from Algeria. When Nostradamus wrote, they were wont to raid the dominions of the Emperor and his satellites on behalf of their French allies (for profit as well). See similar prophecy in 95.

81. This one is a bit too vague to be of much note. Perhaps the translator mentioned in line 1 is the same as that of 91.

82. Another rather vague one: a great city besieged suffers from flood and plague; it is captured in a sudden surprise attack (probably at night) but great restraint is exercised and it is not plundered.

83. A somewhat apocalyptic flavor seems present in this one beyond the earthquake and eclipse.

84. Another quatrain dealing with the discovery of a great Roman's tomb. Perhaps the key lies in the meaning of the cryptic *Medusine*. One imaginative suggestion has been as an anagram of *Deus in me*, suggesting St. Peter. This one is probably connected with 866.

85. Guienne was the large province of southwest France. Languedoc lay between Guienne and the Rhône. All the towns of line 3 are on the Garonne in Guienne. Marmande is about thirty miles downstream from Agen, La Réole ten miles below Marmande. Marseilles is just east of the mouth of the Rhône, at quite a distance from the above. Saint-Rémy, Nostradamus' birthplace (see 427), is about forty miles northwest of Marseilles. How these two areas tie together is uncertain.

86. This one, like so many in Century IX, is set in northern France. Chartres is about fifty miles southwest of Paris. Bourg-la-Reine, just a few miles south of Paris, and Pont d'Antony, three miles further, might be considered en route. Le Pelletier applies the quatrain to the capitulation of Paris on July 3, 1815.

> The generals of the seven nations in coalition against Napoleon [footnote: England, Austria, Prussia, Russia, Sweden, Spain and Portugal], under the pretext of re-establishing peace, but secretly desirous of weakening France, will, by virtue of the capitulation of July 3, 1815, enter a Paris stripped of troops and evacuated by the French army, which will retreat to Chartres, to take up positions beyond the Loire, passing on the way Bourg-la-Reine and Pont d'Antony, beneath which it was camped.

For line 4, Le Pelletier gets "emptied" out of it through Latin *exclusus*— which is as labored as the whole translation.

87. And yet another set in northern France. Montlhéry is about twenty miles southwest of Paris and Étampes about ten miles further. There is a Torfou about halfway between them, but we find neither forest nor hermitage there. The title is not an empty one, for when the verse was written it belonged to the King's mistress, Diane de Poitiers. In fact, it seemed to have a permanent connection with royal mistresses, having previously belonged to Diane's predecessor, Anne de Pisseleu, and belonging later to Henry IV's Gabrielle d'Estrées. But it would be difficult to fit in any of these ladies. The prelate of line 4 probably goes with the elusive hermitage.

88. As Jaubert points out, this quatrain presents a curious problem with regard to time. The setting for the events would be 1557. Calais had belonged to the English since 1347. Arras was about sixty miles to the south-

east and Therouanne (leveled by Charles V in 1553) between it and Calais, both in Artois (Spanish till 1659). Since the King of Spain was also titular King of England (1554–58), all three were subject to Philip II in this period.

With the capture of Calais by Guise (January 8, 1558) and with the death of Mary later in the year, Philip lost all claim to Calais. On February 5, 1556, the Truce of Vaucelles between France and Spain had gone into effect. Therefore, unless Nostradamus was "cheating," the quatrain was written between the beginning of the Truce and the Spanish attack of 1557, culminating in the French fiasco of August 10.

Line 3 presents another problem. By the Treaty of Cateau-Cambresis in 1559, the western borders of Savoy were only thirty-five miles from Roanne. But at this time Savoy was almost completely occupied by the French. Quite possibly the Savoy garrison was rushed north after Saint-Quentin, and Savoy might have been in a position to invade France. But if Nostradamus wrote this after August 10, then he was cheating on lines 1–2.

It must also be noted that the realmless Emmanuel Philibert of Savoy was one of Philip's leaders in the North, and he might be designated by Savoy (for his army, which was attacking Mariembourg in the Northeast). But Roanne was several hundred miles distant.

If Nostradamus intended the whole quatrain for the more distant future, he would have to have foreseen the English co-operating with the Spaniards for many years (either through Mary's living longer or through a marriage of her successor with Philip).

89. If Philip II is intended, this would perhaps predict disaster for him in 1562. However, in the Epistle we found Ogmios in the early 19th century. Unless Ogmios refers to a nation, dynasty or other non-individual being, this Philip would have to come at the same time (presupposing logic in Nostradamus, a rash step). Whoever this Philip is, he is to have great success against the Moslems.

Curiously, Le Pelletier's interpretation is for the very period in which we placed Ogmios in the Epistle:

> Fortune will favor Louis-Philippe for the first seven years of his reign (1830–1838); he will subdue the Arabs and consolidate the French domination of Algeria. Then the middle of his reign (1839–1840) will be troubled, over the Eastern Question, the outcome of which will cover him with shame (July 15, 1840); and finally (February 24, 1848) the French people, proclaiming again the Republic (young Ogmios), will dethrone him in Paris, his capital, surrounded by him with fortifications.

Aside from the question of whether it bears any resemblance to what Nostradamus had in mind, this application is quite solid.

90. The *Grossdeutschland* of line 1 gives this one a very modern sound. "Greater Germany" would be a perfectly valid translation. A curious interpretation of recent times was for Rudolf Hess. Allowing the British monarch as the King of Kings, it never quite got around Pannonia. Except for the nar-

row strip in the west for which the Habsburgs paid tribute, and the autono-mous principality of Transylvania, Hungary belonged to the Turks. "The King of Kings" must designate either the Emperor or the King of France.

91. This one seems to be set entirely in Greece. Perinthus was in Thrace in the Northeast, Nicopolis (Preveza) in Epirus in the West, with Macedonia between Epirus and Thrace. Thessaly was east of Epirus. Amphipolis, near modern Salonika, was in Macedonia. It is perhaps worth mentioning that the leading Anthony of the day was Anthony Duke of Vendôme, King of Navarre, father of Henry IV.

92. The new city may be one literally built recently, or one whose name means that (Naples from Neapolis, or Cittanova, etc.).

93. With the appearance of *Aemathien* again, in a slightly variant form, Le Pelletier is obliged to work it out again for Louis XIV.

> When the Peace of the Pyrenees concluded with Spain in 1659 will have pushed back the frontiers of France, Vauban will have perfected the earth-works bastion; the Château de la Grosse Tour, at Bourges, which com-manded the walls of the city, will fall into ruin (in 1651): then (in 1666) Louis XIV will undertake a labor of Hercules, in digging the canal of Languedoc, destined to join the Mediterranean to the Atlantic.

If we now see what Nostradamus had in mind, we have the following more likely elements: a mobile siege weapon, such as the Romans used, being brought into play against a fort weakly garrisoned by the "enemy," whose main forces will be distant. Apparently the city is Bourges in the heart of France, so the intended enemy must be Calvinist rather than Habs-burg. At the time of this assault against Bourges, some French leader desig-nated as Hercules (perhaps the fourth son of Henry II—see 580) will de-liver a great blow against the Spaniard.

94. The setting for this one is central Europe. The city of line 3 appears to be Bratislava. It is ironic that Nostradamus gave Pressburg its ancient Slavic name by way of obscurity; today it is called Bratislava again and Pressburg is forgotten. It was part of Habsburg buffer strip of Hungary. They regarded it as Hungary's capital during the Turkish occupation of Budapest (1541–1784). It remained the seat of the Magyar Parliament until 1845. Lübeck was an Imperial Free City on the Baltic. Meissen in Saxony is on the Elbe, just north of Bohemia. Since they are more than two hundred miles apart, and seem to have no connection whatsoever, they are perhaps synecdoche for a rebellious Germany, allied with the Moslems against the Austrian Habsburgs.

95. Except for the colorful line 4, this one is rather vague. The Milanese belonged to the Habsburgs till 1859. Boswell (1941, p. 275) was inspired to comment, "Fascism's Fat Boy would look even more like a chimpanzee in an iron cage."

96. This rather vague one must have been fulfilled many times. Only in line 3 is there any element not commonplace.

97. One of the detailed but obscure variety. Apparently we begin with a naval battle and end up with a land battle ("breech" hardly being a term applicable to naval warfare). The Elysian Fields, however they may be intended here, formed the heaven of Greek mythology.

98. If "Chief of War" be the proper translation of line 4, it is perhaps noteworthy that this was the title dug up for Joan of Arc by Charles VII (1429). The verse is most obscure.

99. *Aquilon* may be taken literally as the North Wind, or as an enigmatic country, for which the candidates stretch from Britain to Russia (see 149). The quatrain appears to deal with the relief of some vital fort that is besieged.

100. With the colored ship suggesting camouflage, this one has been applied to the Battle of Jutland in World War II. But as between Britain and Germany, Britain was the West. More likely this one goes with 525 and 859 as predicting a calamity for Christendom resulting from a great naval victory of the Moslems—a Lepanto in reverse.

## *Century X*

1. This rather vague but fairly clear quatrain had some degree of fulfillment under the Vichy regime, when the Germans failed to make collaboration a two-way proposition. There are doubtless many other possible applications.

2. This one is frequently tied with 9100, as possessing the same hint of naval camouflage. It could probably do equally well for a smoke screen. In any event, it seems to concern an epic naval battle.

3. So much obscurity prevails here that its meaning would probably not be clarified greatly even if we could be certain about *Penelon.*

4. Ward (1891) applied this one quite nicely to England and the Battle of Worcester (September 3, 1651). After his defeat, Charles II fled to France in disguise (via Scotland and enough romance to supply material for many books). With the death of his conqueror, Oliver Cromwell, exactly seven years later (September 3, 1658), his return became only a matter of time (two years, as it turned out). However, it is probably general enough to allow French fulfillments also.

5. Albi and Castres are about twenty-five miles apart, in southwest France. Carcassonne and Toulouse are about fifty miles apart. The Lauraguais was a *pays* around the town of Castelnaudary, between Albi, Castres and Toulouse. All the places were in Languedoc. Just how the Portuguese come into this, and the identity of the "new Arians," are two unsolved questions. It is perhaps worth noting that Albi was the center of the Albigensians who were wiped out by a "Crusade" instigated by Innocent III. Beginning as a reaction of the lower classes against clerical corruption, it was taken

up by the nobles in order to appropriate church lands. The "Crusade" lasted from 1208 to 1213. Possibly there were some Portuguese adventurers amongst the Crusaders; the Albigensians might be considered a new manifestation of the ancient Arian "heretics." Another exhibit for the "retroactive prophecy" school of thought?

6. Like 99, this one was fulfilled on September 9, 1557, when a storm lasting from 5 A.M. to 9 P.M., according to Jaubert, combined with a flood of the Gardon. According to Menard's *History of Nîmes* (1874), the storm lasted from 1 to 9 P.M., without any flood of the Gardon being involved. Indeed, Menard (who incidentally mentions this verse) confirms Jaubert with regard to the uncovering of antiquities. However, this does not reflect much credit on Nostradamus, since it is uncertain whether this verse was written before the date of the flood (certainly very close to that date). In any event, it was not in print by then. The Gard is about five miles from Nîmes.

7. Once again, seeing *Aemathien* (see 938), Le Pelletier feels obliged to work this out for the reign of Louis XIV.

> The Treaty of Westphalia, concluded with the Emperor in 1648, under the reign of Philip IV, King of Spain and before the War of the Spanish Succession, an enterprise in the interests of Philip V, grandson of Louis XIV [between Philips, *sic!*], will cede Metz to France and cause it to lose definitely its ancient title of imperial city.
>
> England, a prey to the horrors of Revolution, will decapitate in 1649 its legitimate King, Charles I, who will have lacked force and wisdom [wine and salt, see 949] in the government of his state.
>
> Nancy will be taken in 1660 by the French, who will drive out its Duke, Charles IV, raze its fortifications and incorporate it into France.
>
> It will be then (in 1661) that Louis XIV, relieved of the tutelage of Mazarin, will begin to rule himself and will put into effect his famous maxim, "The State, that's me."

The greatest weakness of this labored interpretation is that it has no unity, stretching over at least thirteen years, and with two farfetched Philips fifty years apart.

However, if we regard the Macedonian simply as the Spaniard, the quatrain predicts an attack by Philip II (*deux Phi.*) against French-occupied Lorraine, whose Duke was a captive at the French court. Although Metz was not finally ceded until 1648, it was captured in 1552 and remained in French control thereafter. Nor do we find any evidence for Nancy's violent fate in 1660. It was rather on February 28, 1661, that the French restored Nancy to its Duke after a twenty-seven-year occupation (it was again occupied 1670–77). In one respect, however, Le Pelletier cannot be contradicted: the wine and salt used again in connection with England does tie this to 949.

8. Senigallia, or Sinigaglia, was above Ancona in the Papal States. In 1474 Pope Sixtus IV erected it into a fief for his nephew Giovanni della

Rovere. When the latter's son inherited the Duchy of Urbino in 1508, Senigallia was absorbed into Urbino, which the family ruled until 1624. The prophecy thus would seem to be intended for a scion of the della Roveres.

However, in connection with the baptism inferred in line 1, a recent commentator made a great discovery. When on June 15, 1856, the Prince Imperial, son of Napoleon III, was baptized, his godfather was Pope Pius IX. The Pope was the son of Count Mastai-Ferretti of Senigallia. Venus is assumed to be Empress Eugénie. But line 4 is not to be handled as readily.

9. This is a very detailed and rather fascinating verse. It appears to concern the birth of one of the Antichrists. Figueras is on the Spanish side of the Pyrenees near the Mediterranean and was briefly the Loyalist capital in 1939. In the 18th century the citadel of San Fernando was built up to be an impregnable fortress against the French. (As it turned out, it never bothered the French much. It's now a prison.) Line 3 suggests that the Antichrist's father will be killed by someone whose name means "stocking [or breeches] on the ground." We have six very specific details:

(1) The exact place of his birth, down to the very building
(2) The weather at the time of his birth
(3) The fact that he will be a posthumous child
(4) A strong hint as to the name of his father's slayer
(5) The fact that his father will be a king or sovereign ruler
(6) A hint that his mother will be a virtual whore

Line 4 might be considered to provide another detail, but there is probably no ruler about whom someone did not make this statement.

10. This one may or may not refer to the posthumous one of 109. General as it is, it could be applied to many a ruler by his enemies. It is perhaps worth noting that the Venetian ambassador Mocenigo applied the epithet of line 2 to Napoleon Bonaparte. It does smack of the Antichrist, and might well be intended as part of a series of three, including 109 and 1011.

11. This one undoubtedly concerns the Catalonia-born posthumous of 109, which might support the inclusion of 1010 also. La Junquera is on the Spanish side of the Perthus Pass, about twelve miles north of Figueras. Crossing the Pyrenees at this point, the Duke goes via Perpignan (Spanish till 1659) to Tenda (incorporated into France as Tende in 1947), about thirty-five miles northeast of Nice.

12. This one seems to be entirely for the Papacy. Except for the obscurities of line 4, it is a clear characterization of some unfortunate pontiff. Garencières applies it to one Cardinal Santa Severina who died of grief two months after his election (1591) was declared illegal. His successor, Innocent IX, also died in two months.

13. Leroux (1710) chooses this one to show that with enough learning and logic, one can extract from a Nostradamian quatrain the exact details of a future event. He devotes page after page to the drama of soldiers hidden

in a haywagon on the way to a market in Antibes, and their adventures en route. All of which may be perfectly well what Nostradamus did have in mind.

14. This one seems to be set entirely in Catalonia in northeastern Spain. An extensive area, known as the Llanos de Urgel, is adjacent to the town of Urgel. Yet a person does seem to be intended here, rather than a place. This is another of those odd, petty local dramas that pop up every now and then amidst the quatrains devoted to mighty battles, the fall of empires, Popes and kings. On a hunch, we wrote to the Carthusian monastery of Monte Allegro, seven miles west of Barcelona, to ask if their records disclosed any such drama in the period 1536–46 (when Nostradamus might have been a witness of it during his extensive and untraced travels). We received the following reply from someone whose signature is illegible but looks like "Monsieur Jaricot":

*Cartuja de Montalegre, May the 8th 1947*
DEAR SIR:

We are in receipt of your letter of April 28th: The Writer happens to be French, to know English and to be thoroughly acquainted with the history of this House and begs to state:

1) No such name as Urnel Vaucile appears on the list of religious which is kept in the archives and is quite complete.

2) The sense of the quatrain seems to be rather that a man of the world, light-headed and of changing dispositions, had led a bad life, but overcome by fear (of Hell) was converted (by the grace of God) and entered a cloister. Vaincu par la crainte (des châtiments). "Convaincu" means convinced rather than convicted and therefore "converted."

3) It seems probable that (in this case at any rate) the names are fictitious and that such a prophecy is very commonplace.

For which gratuitous interpretation we are grateful, notwithstanding disappointment in finding no confirmation of the "retroactive" hunch.

15. Here we have everything included from the crime to the punishment. After denying his dying father a bit of water, the cruel son gives him an excess of it (in a well), whereupon one of the Parliaments (Toulouse's?) has him strangled or hanged.

16. This one seems to provide a characterization of some French king. Le Pelletier makes a good case for applying it to Louis XVIII.

Happily re-established on the throne of France, and happy during his life, Louis XVIII will not die a violent death and, unlike his brothers, he will not be the victim of criminal outrages. He will be given the flattering surname of *Désiré*. This prince will be guilty of not occupying himself enough with public affairs and of loving good cheer (i.e., food) too much.

Bouys (1806) applies lines 1–3 to Napoleon and line 4 to Louis XVI.

17. Another rather successful prophecy. As Le Pelletier gives it:

Marie-Antoinette, a prisoner and reduced to working with her hands like a slave, will see Madame Royale (her daughter) pale with grief caused by the misfortunes of her family. There will then be, in the prison of the Temple, lamentable cries from the young princess who will be Duchess of Angoulême through a marriage in name only with Louis-Antoine de Bourbon, Duke of Angoulême, her first cousin, to whom she will have been engaged in 1787.

The couple was not actually joined in wedlock until 1799. If we can allow a duke's title to be applied to his betrothed, the application is fairly good. Angoulême is about sixty miles northeast of Bordeaux. The title Count of Angoulême was borne by Francis I before he became King.

18. This is easily one of the most completely and indisputably successful of Nostradamus' prophecies. It could not have been intended for anyone but Henry of Navarre (or possibly his father, Anthony). As Le Pelletier gives it:

> The House of Lorraine will be eclipsed by Henry IV, Duke of Vendôme; Mayenne, chief of this house and Lieutenant-General of the Realm, will be defeated and Henry IV, who was derisively calle *le petit Béarnais,* will be elevated from low to high. This heretic prince (the son of Mammon) will (thanks to his abjuration) be accepted in Rome as King of France in preference to his rivals, and the two Pretenders [footnote: The Duke of Guise and Mayenne, son and brother *(sic)* of the great Duke Francis] will not mount the throne.

Clear as this is, there is an implied conflict with the prophecies of glory for Henry II and his youngest son (see Commentary on 477 and 580). If "Amon" is the right reading, the reference is probably an oblique one to Jove, to whose pagan worshippers the Protestants are compared in several prophecies. Henry IV was the Huguenot leader, excommunicated by the Pope.

19. Perhaps this one was intended for Elizabeth, who was the heir of Bloody Mary, childless when Nostradamus wrote (and till her death).

20. This very interesting quatrain can be applied quite nicely to post-Fascist Italy. Little application of it could be made in Nostradamus' day, unless to the so-called Spanish Party of cardinals and Roman potentates (their Spanish patrons presumed to be culturally backward). But even if the King of France were to triumph, such drastic occurrences would not be in accord with 16th-century custom.

21. This is one of the detailed but obscure variety, colorful but incomprehensible.

22. Here it seems more than likely that the British Isles rather than the Spanish-held isles of the Mediterranean are intended. Yet the only British kings since 1558 with even the remotest potentialities for fulfillment are Charles I, Charles II, James II and Edward VIII. In the first three cases, the divorce must be taken figuratively, as the divorce of royal title and power, and in the last case, which involved actual divorce, the line-up was somewhat different. An application to either Charles I or Charles II (the latter

between 1649 and 1651) would give the last line to Oliver Cromwell. An application to James II would give the last line to William III. To strict legitimists, either might be justified. However, Nostradamus probably had a real divorce in mind, in the best traditions of Henry VIII. Perhaps the implication is that the English will blame Philip for the childless state of Queen Mary and, when he refuses to be replaced, he is seized in a palace coup. As it turned out, Mary died in 1558, just after the quatrain was probably written.

23. This one is set on the French and Italian Riviera. Antibes is about thirty miles northeast of Fréjus and in Nostradamus' day was near the Savoyard border. Monaco is about the same distance beyond Antibes. It was already an independent principality under the Grimaldis, but under smothering Spanish "protection."

24. By deriving *Itales* from *Aethalia*, classical name for Elba, and by making numerous other distortions, Le Pelletier manages to apply this one to the Hundred Days of Napoleon Bonaparte (1815).

> Napoleon, who was a closely guarded prisoner on the isle of Elba, will escape by sea on March 1, 1815, from the residence which will have been assigned to him, and will land at Cannes, near Marseilles, going across the Gulf of Genoa. He will be overcome again by an energetic effort of the foreign armies, at Waterloo, where he will seek death without being able to find it, and where the bees of the empire will spill all their honey.

The interpretation gets fouled on line 1 and Marseilles. Being well over one hundred miles away, Cannes is hardly "near Marseilles." It is noteworthy, however, that the bees, actually taken by Napoleon for his emblem, appear in another quatrain more successfully applied to Napoleon (426).

25. This one seems to be set in Spain, though two places remain uncertain. *Bisanne*, if Bézenas (Pézenas) north of Narbonne, would be on the classic Spanish invasion route into France. The Ebro River is in northeastern Spain, the Tagus in central Spain and Portugal. Garencières again gets very personal here.

> Here once more I lost my Spectacles, and could not see through, therefore I had rather be silent than coin less, I shall only tell you, that Orchestra in Latine is the seat wherein noble Personages sit at the beholting of Stageplays.

26. All is rather vague here except for the intriguing last line. The big question is: Brittany or Britain? In the case of the former, the line would involve Brittany's pretenses of being joined to France merely by a personal union with the King of France. When the Duke of Brittany died in 1488, the Empire, Spain and England joined in a coalition to preserve its independence. But by marrying the heiress Anne in 1491, and buying off Spain with Roussillon, Charles VIII managed to acquire control of Brittany. When he died in 1498 without an heir, another crisis came. It was solved when

Charles' successor (second cousin once-removed) became Louis XII and married Anne himself. This time Anne had only a daughter, named Claudia. She married Louis' cousin, who became Francis I. Their heir was Nostradamus' Henry II.

If Britain be intended, this is quite a prophecy. Although France and England were to enjoy fairly friendly relations before their great duel of 1689–1815, their friendly relations began only with the accession of Elizabeth; when Nostradamus wrote they were at war. If the prophecy means political union, it is even more extreme.

27. This quatrain is doubtless Exhibit A in the case of the exponents of the "retroactive prophecy" interpretation of Nostradamus, which, like other extremist views, falls apart when a generalization is drawn from the appearances of a minor portion of the whole. But in this case there can be little question. In 1527, while Charles V was at war with Pope Clement VII, an Imperial army, composed largely of Lutheran Germans and commanded by a renegade royal French prince, the Constable Duke of Bourbon, perpetrated the infamous Sack of Rome, the devastation of which is supposed to have compared not unfavorably with that of the Vandals (A.D. 455). According to this quatrain, the fifth one would be Charles V and Hercules the Constable, the epithet being rated on a personal basis. All the names in line 3 apparently apply to Pope Clement VII, the first two being obvious, the third less obvious. In line 4, the key applies to the Pope (Keys of St. Peter— to the Kingdom of Heaven), the eagle to the Emperor, and the sword to the somewhat independent army. In line 2, the temple has been variously interpreted as the city of Rome or, more allegorically, the temple of Janus.

28. Far too obscure for any reasonable interpretation.

29. Another of the extremely detailed but obscure variety. The setting of *Pol Mansol* is just outside Saint-Rémy, Nostradamus' birthplace (see 427). The entire quatrain seems to be devoted to a goat (or a wild goat-boy?) being captured outside Saint-Rémy and made a mascot by natives of Tarbes, chief city of Bigorre—an odd subject for a prophecy. Bigorre was in the Southwest, about 250 miles away, and belonged to the House of Navarre. Presumably, they are on a visit to Saint-Rémy. Perhaps all this involves a childhood memory, dredged out of his subconscious mind.

30. With reference to the word nephew, Le Pelletier makes the following note in his glossary:

> The commentator, following the general rule which prevails in the composition of this glossary, has noted here *indiscriminately* the numbers of all quatrains which contain the word Nephew, although many of these quatrains are unintelligible, or amphibological, or clearly foreign to His Majesty, the Emperor.

In another note, however, he suggests that since the new saint was obviously Napoleon I (Pius VII made August 15 the fête of St. Napoleon, martyred under Diocletian, in honor of the Emperor), the nephew of the same must be

Napoleon III. With a great deal of figurative application, the quatrain can be applied to the administration (presidential) and reign (imperial) of Louis-Napoleon.

31. We have here four distinct factors, whose interrelationship is perplexing. The Empire and Germany were approximately synonymous, the Empire including also claims to sovereignty in northern Italy (usurped anyhow by the Spanish). The Arabs and the Persians were apparently seen by Nostradamus as rivals in the plunder of the Ottoman Empire and in an attack on Central Europe from the Balkans.

32. Clear enough as far as the language goes.

33. Only line 3 has any clarity and its meaning is obscured by doubt about the "diphthong" place. If Fiesole, it is only three miles northeast of Florence and now essentially a suburb. Like 95 and 980, it seems to concern a tyrannical Medici Duke of Florence (Tuscany).

34. Robb (1942) makes a fairly good case for applying this one to Napoleon Bonaparte and Joachim Murat, King of Naples. Murat, the great cavalry leader of the Revolutionary armies, was married to Napoleon's younger sister, Caroline. He made the mistake of not remaining a consistent traitor. He betrayed Napoleon in 1814, but sided with him in 1815. He was shot on October 13, 1815. Robb (p. 41) seeks to clinch the case with a direct quote from the Emperor:

> The conduct of the King of Naples is infamous, and that of the Queen has no word to describe it. I hope to live long enough to take vengeance, for myself and for France, on such ingratitude.

According to Robb (in a letter to *The New York Times* dated January 4, 1942), this quatrain served to make a Nostradamian convert of the illustrious Professor Jacques Barzun of Columbia University, since become its Dean and Provost. In addition, wrote Robb, Professor Siceloff of the Mathematics Department calculated that the chances of fulfillment of this prophecy by a lucky hit were "about zero." (Published in a privately printed pamphlet *Letters on Nostradamus, et Al.*)

35. A scandal-mongering prophecy in a very clear, specific and colorful quatrain involving royal lust. If the murderer of line 4 is supposed to be a great notable, he might be a Duke of Maine or a Duke of Mayenne (in Maine). The former title was one of those borne by the future Henry III, too young to have any potential when Nostradamus wrote. The latter title belonged to a brother of the Duke of Guise named Claude (1526–73), Governor of Burgundy and son-in-law of Diane de Poitiers, Henry II's mistress. The title passed to his nephew, Charles, second son of Guise and arch-foe of Henrys III and IV. Maine was a province in northwest France, of which Le Mans, Mayenne, Laval, Alençon and Fougères were the chief cities.

36. If this one was intended for England, it might be seen as a successful prophecy of England's duel with Philip II (if some justification can be found

for terming him "King of the root"). Line 3 would rather suggest Drake, Hawkins, Raleigh, Essex and other glorified pirates of Britain's pre-virtuous days.

37. All these places were in the Duchy of Savoy and all but one are now in that department. The Lake of Bourget is about five miles north of Chambéry. Montmélian is about eight miles and Saint-Jean-de-Maurienne about thirty miles southeast of Chambéry. Saint-Julien in Upper Savoy is on the border a few miles south of Geneva. According to Larmor (1925, p. 151), this was fulfilled *ca.* 1597–1600, when the Duke of Savoy concentrated an army at Montmélian for an invasion of France but was defeated by Henry IV at Saint-Julien. After which, according to Larmor, Henry captured Chambéry and Saint-Jean-de-Maurienne.

38. The epithet of line 1 has been considered particularly suited to Henry of Navarre. Laver (1942) translates it as "Light o' love." The setting seems to be in northern Italy and Switzerland. The cryptic place name in line 2 should be identifiable but isn't. There is a Barbarano (not St.) twelve miles south of Vicenza. Perhaps the reference is to December 4, feast day of St. Barbara. Since their rivals, the Colonna, took the Spanish side, the Orsini tended to take the French side in Italian intrigues. The Grisons Canton in southeastern Switzerland possessed the strategic Valtelline Pass, vital to the Habsburgs as linking their German and Italian possessions. The records of the Grisons (see Jecklin in General Bibliography B) disclose a great deal of correspondence with the French about an alliance or protectorate. Henry II sought to renew the Franco-Swiss alliance of 1516, which included the Grisons, in the 1550's. In 1602 they signed a treaty giving the French right of passage, causing the Spanish to seize the Valtelline in 1609. But Henry IV took no action then. Larmor (1925, p. 151), puts forward a dubious fulfillment: Henry, the *vert galant,* had established his headquarters at Saint-Cloud (St: Clodoald) after his victory at Arques (September 21, 1589). Thereafter, because the Swiss Oursons (which we have been unable to identify) at Berne agreed to support Henry, Paris was terrified by fear of an army *(sic!)* of Grisons (who had no connection with Berne) and thus surrendered to him. All of which is history according to Larmor.

39. According to De France (1911) this quatrain was quoted by the Venetian ambassador in a despatch on the occasion of Francis II's swooning illness (November 20, 1560). As Le Pelletier gives it:

Francis II, eldest son of Henry II, will die in the flower of his age, less than 18 years old [footnote: Francis lived 17 years 10 months 15 days]; he will leave Mary Stuart without children, after an unfortunate marriage which will have lasted less than two years. His death will give rise to great discord between Elizabeth and Mary Stuart, Queens of England and Scotland. Charles IX, his younger brother, will be engaged at a still younger age to Elizabeth of Austria. [Footnote: Charles was engaged to her at the age of 11, though married only in 1570.]

All of which sounds quite convincing, but as it was not in print till 1568, some skeptics will remain suspicious (which at least is a great tribute to the prophecy). Unfortunately, the record in the French National Library to which De France refers is an 18th-century copy rather than the original. This does not, however, in any way throw suspicion on it.

40. Most commentators are certain that Charles I and Cromwell are intended here. Le Pelletier's version embraces half a century of Stuart history.

> After the death of James VI, King of Scotland, son of Mary Stuart (this child, whom his father, before perishing assassinated by Bothwell, will have recommended to the loyalty of the Scottish lords and who in 1603 will have mounted the throne of England under the name of James I), the usurper Cromwell will seduce the English people through his cunning speeches, and he will cause his son, Charles I, to lose his crown and life.

Le Pelletier seems unable to decide whom to have dying, Lord Darnley or James I. How to get Cromwell out of *Lonole?* Le Pelletier connects it with a Greek verb meaning *to destroy*. Ward (1891) has a much simpler solution: it is a phonetic anagram for Cromwell's nickname Old Noll (Ole Nol).

41. Another of the very odd microscopically local quatrains. Only Villefranche(-de-Rouergue) in Aveyron is of any size. Caylus is about fifteen miles to the southwest. Caussade lies at a slightly lesser distance to the southwest of Caylus. The two are separated by the Lère River, a tributary of the Garonne, and by a range of hills called the Crèzes. The whole thing is set about fifty miles east of our prophet's one-time home at Agen. Like 1014 and 1029, it suggests some event which Nostradamus witnessed once and which popped up in his mind during one of his prophetic trances. There is little in the nature of a prediction, with mere music involved.

42. If the "Anglican" reading is taken for line 1, this quatrain works out rather nicely as forecasting a *Pax Anglosaxonica*. In a sense, this quatrain was fulfilled by the *Pax Britannica* of the 19th century. Those who would include America must needs place it later.

43. It is perhaps quite a tribute to this quatrain that Garencières saw it much the same as Le Pelletier, though he wrote almost two hundred years earlier. According to Garencières:

> This is concerning another King, who through his too much goodness, simplicity and negligence, shall make and unmake those about him, and being fickle, shall believe false reports, made concerning his own wife; and at last by his too much goodness, shall be put to death.

Le Pelletier (from Bouys) saw this one as a perfect characterization of Louis XVI and explained it as follows:

> Louis XVI will be put to death because he will have applied himself too little (because of his lack of ability) to the affairs of State, because of his weakness, his irresolution, the untimely irascability of his character, his negligence, the lightness with which he will have put faith in the calumnious reports

against the honor of the Queen, and above all, because of his excessive kindness, which will leave him defenseless before his enemies.

All of which is quite convincing, and stands up well to the facts.

44. This one may be connected with the two quatrains containing the line "The King of Blois to reign in Avignon" (838 and 852). There is also a possibility of the "retroactive" element. The County of Blois was acquired in 1397 by the Orléans branch of the House of Valois, which got the French throne in 1498 (and died out in 1589). Blois held somewhat the same place with them as Windsor with the British royal family. French subjugation of the Ligurians or Genoans occurred several times in the early 16th century, with many occasions when the hostility between ruler and subjects provided an excuse for war. However, none of these occasions seems to have involved the far-flung places cited in line 3. Cordoba is in Spain. Dalmatia, on the eastern shore of the Adriatic, was a Venetian island (figuratively) in the Turkish Balkans. The third place may indeed be Memel, founded in 1252 by the Teutonic Order and an important member of the Hanseatic League. The other possibility, Mammola in southern Italy, is unlikely in view of its insignificance. As for line 4, it would appear to be a good example of Nostradamian gibberish.

45. There are several interesting elements in this quatrain, though it is difficult to see how they fit together. Lines 1 and 2 are sufficiently general to be applied to the adventure-packed careers of either Duke Anthony of Bourbon-Vendôme, King of Navarre, or his young son, the future Henry IV (b. 1553). Jaubert points out the fitness of the "untrue" since the real Kingdom of Navarre was in Spain. The Treaty of Cambrai (1529), by which the King of France renounced his claims to Naples, Artois and Flanders, was broken in 1556 by the French, who were decisively beaten (1557). The *Orleans* in line 4 may represent an allusion, of dubious purport, to Henry II (Duke of Orléans before he became King), or to the city itself. Jaubert (1656) makes a very unconvincing application of the quatrain to events of 1560, pointing out that Charles IX had also been Duke of Orléans before becoming King in that year.

46. This one seems to be set entirely in Germany. The primary fact about the villain of line 1 seems to be that he won't be a new Elector of Saxony. There were two great Electors in Nostradamus' day, Frederick the Wise (1486–1525), who had been a supporter of Luther from the beginning, and Maurice, who, though a Lutheran, refrained from joining the fight against Charles V until 1552, and thus long retained a decisive role as the balance of German politics. The Duchy of Brunswick was to the northwest of the Electorate. Inasmuch as it played no significant role in the 16th century, the reference is a curious one. The verse probably has some connection with Luther, presumably a retroactive one, since Luther had been dead ten years.

47. A rather colorful but incomprehensible quatrain. *Bourze* must be either Bourges in central France or Burgos in northwestern Spain. Since

garlands were a common architectural device, the reference is probably to some cathedral or other public building. The Cathedral of San Esteban at Burgos is famous for its infinity of architectural flourishes, some of which might be considered garlands. We know of no suitable candidate at Bourges. The Province of Leon in Spain, a former kingdom, had two archbishoprics, one at Burgos and the other at Santiago de Compostela. The great prelate is presumably the Archbishop of Burgos, apparently punished for treason by toughs disguised as pilgrims. Formentera, if that be the right reading, is the fourth-largest of the Balearic islands, east of Spain, but its connection with the drama is incomprehensible.

48. This one seems to concern a commonplace event of the 16th century, a battle between the French and the Spanish. The only detail lies in the geography of line 2, and it is uncertain. The town of Laignes, which is also the source of a stream of the same name, lies about forty-five miles northwest of Dijon. It was also about forty miles from the borders of Franche-Comté, which belonged to the Spanish but was supposedly neutralized. It was two hundred miles from the northern border, and many more from the southern one. But if the Aisne River is the correct reading, it was only about forty miles from the Spanish Netherlands, and in the very area that the Spanish penetrated in the invasion of 1557, culminating in the French disaster at Saint-Quentin. The Spanish were hardly routed then (August 10, 1557, probably a few weeks or months before the quatrain was written).

49. Jaubert (1656) explains that this quatrain represents a reply to one Monsieur Jardin about the future of his son Cosme (Greek *cosmos,* world). The name is chiefly associated with the Medici Cosimo. Aside from this nonsense, the quatrain is predicting a new eruption of Vesuvius, about fifteen miles from the most famous of "new cities," Naples *(Nea-polis,* new city). "Garden of the world" refers to the lava-enriched, fertile Campanian plain between Naples and Vesuvius. Quatrain 187 seems to predict the same. Though Vesuvius has erupted often, notably in 1631, its lava has never bothered Naples. Boswell (1941, pp. 349–50) sees the prophecy as involving the Palisades in New Jersey, the new city being New York.

50. The Meuse came within two miles of the southwest border of Luxembourg, as it was in Nostradamus' day, at a point just below Sedan. Luxembourg was one of the provinces of the Spanish Netherlands. In a vague sort of way, line 2 seems to provide a configuration to date this quatrain, which predicts a tremendous flood in Lorraine, through which the Meuse flows.

51. Rather comprehensive geopolitics are involved here. The Palatinate and the Bishopric of Strassburg were chief amongst the states contiguous to the Duchy of Lorraine. The bishopric corresponded roughly to Alsace. As it happened, the French occupied Lorraine several times and finally annexed it in 1766, having absorbed most of Alsace by 1681. The Germans did of course get Lorraine twice (1871–1919 and 1940–44). The see of line 3 may refer to Strassburg or to the Papacy. The relationship to the new state of the variety

of Frenchmen in line 3 is obscure. Picardy was near the border but Normandy and Maine were far south of it. In line 4 the new state seems to be joined by the cantons of the Swiss Confederation. It would seem odd that the French are to favor this change. Charles the Bold of Burgundy was attempting to achieve an approximation of this geopolitical creation when he was defeated and killed (1477). Since then, there has been no similar try, although most of the areas were included in Napoleon's empire.

52. This one is set in the Spanish Netherlands. *Leye* is the way the Flemish spell the River Lys. A long-drawn-out marriage takes place at Ghent in Flanders. Then the rather obscure events of lines 3–4 take place at Antwerp in Brabant, involving a young wife left "intact" by her aged bridegroom. Another odd parochial one!

53. If "Selin" in line 3 does indeed refer to Henry II (see 427), some rivals of Diane de Poitiers would seem to be involved here. The epithet hurled by the enraged cast-off mistress of line 4 is completely obscure (though intriguing).

54. This one seems to be devoted to the career of a mistress's daughter. One daughter of Diane de Poitiers was married to the Duke of Aumale (brother of Guise) and another to the Duke of Bouillon. Neither could fulfill this. Diane de France (1538–1619), a bastard of Henry II, was also supposed to be Diane's daughter but opinion seems to hold that her mother was really an Italian peasant girl named Philippa Duc. Larmor (1925, p. 157) applies it to Marie de' Medici, who fled from Richelieu to Brussels in 1631. However, this breaks down on line 1, inasmuch as her mother was the Duchess of Florence (Joan of Austria). Larmor can only suggest that the Duchess was neglected by her husband for his mistress, Blanche Capello, but that hardly makes the mistress Marie's mother. Malines/Mechlin was a lordship about fifteen miles north of Brussels, capital of Brabant and the Netherlands.

55. This one may perhaps go with the unfortunate nuptials of 1052. The anonymous critic of 1724 has a very bright suggestion for this one. *Phy (phi)* is the first letter in Greek for the Greek spelling of Francis. *Be* stands for *beta,* the second letter of the Greek alphabet, and thus produces Francis II. By this he means to discredit Nostradamus (as a "retroactive prophet"), but actually pays him a fine compliment, since all evidence points to this Century's being written in 1557 or early 1558 (though it was indeed not in print till 1568). This involves seeing *Mary* (the original old spelling) as Mary Stuart and not as "husband." Mary and Francis were married in 1558. In 1559 Francis became King and in 1560 he died. It is quite true that no love was lost between Catherine de' Medici and her daughter-in-law, who called her a "merchant's daughter."

56. Three separate events seem to be involved here. Lines 1–2, if merely taken literally, tell the circumstances under which a prelate of royal blood will die ("hemorrhage of the throat," per Dr. Garencières). In line 3, England will have a close escape from some great danger. At Tunis, which from

1535 to 1570 was ruled by a Moslem puppet of the Habsburgs, someone who seemed to be "out of the picture" will suddenly become a force to be reckoned with again. Writes Allen (1943, p. 552), "it is my view that Mussolini read this quatrain and set off the fireworks labelled 'Tunisia' in order to defeat the prophecy by going there while he still had some of his buttons."

57. This villainous king is probably one of the Antichrists.

58. This was probably written after Charles V abdicated but before he died (1558). Therefore the time of mourning might be after his imminent death. The young Macedonian (Spaniard) would be Philip II (b. 1527) and the feline monarch his uncle, Emperor Ferdinand. We have seen elsewhere (545 *et al.*) that Nostradamus seemed to foresee a life-and-death struggle between them for the whole of Charles V's empire. At the time, France (especially Marseilles) and the Papacy are to have their troubles. Le Pelletier must needs apply all *Aemathien* quatrains to Louis XIV (see 938) and this one is no exception:

> At the time that the court of France will be in mourning for Louis XIII, dead in 1643, the astute Philip IV, King of Spain, will make war on the young King, a minor, in order to profit from the confusion of the Regency. France will then be shaken, from 1648 to 1653, by the Civil War called the Fronde; and Rome will be endangered by nascent Jansenism. On March 2, 1660, Louis XIV will enter by a breach into Marseilles, which will then return to its allegiance; and he will go to the western extremity of France, to the Isle of the Conference, on the Bidassoa, to conclude there with Philip IV the so-called Peace of the Pyrenees and his marriage with the Infanta Maria Theresa of Austria, daughter of the King of Spain.

Except for the fact that he requires a period of seventeen years to handle all these events, with no unity whatsoever, the interpretation is a skillful one.

59. According to Jaubert (1656), this was fulfilled on September 5, 1560, by a Calvinist plot under Condé. The mastiffs are the zealous Catholics on guard against the Protestant wolves. Bressans would be natives of Bresse, a province of Savoy north of Lyons which did not become French till 1601. Latins properly would be natives of Latium, the province around Rome, but members of the politically active Grisons' canton, with their Latin language, might be more probable in the context. While the plot Jaubert refers to really took place, there is no record of any foreign elements participating in it.

60. The afflictions here are set in various parts of Italy. Nice was in Savoy, Monaco and Malta independent Habsburg protectorates, Modena an independent duchy, Savona and Genoa in the Genoese Republic, Pisa and Siena in the Duchy of Tuscany and Capua in the Habsburg Kingdom of the Two Sicilies.

61. This colorful quatrain has a very extensive setting. Merida and the Guadalquivir River are both in southern Spain. Vienna was of course the capital of the hereditary Habsburg possessions. Sopron was in the buffer strip of Hungary that Ferdinand was allowed to retain for payment of tribute

to the Turks. Line 2 is rather confusing. The Turks had all of Hungary except for the above-mentioned strip and the autonomous dependency of Transylvania. Though the Barbarians are properly the Algerians from Barbary, they may be used for some other Moslem people who overthrow the Turkish Empire (Arabs or Persians) and are here engaged in the conquest of Hungary.

62. Another quatrain on a Moslem conquest of Hungary. The medieval Sorbian March extended south from the Elbe below Wittenberg. Together with the land inhabited by the Sorbs themselves, it formed the future Electorate of Saxony. Between it and Hungary lay the Erzgebirge Mountains, Bohemia and Moravia. Buda was in Turkish Hungary. Line 3 involves a Turkish sultan or leader (or whoever rules Constantinople at the time). After Salona, the ancient capital of Dalmatia, was destroyed by the Avars (639), its inhabitants founded Spalato (Split) near by. Salona itself was not completely deserted until the 12th century. In 1420 the Venetians acquired Spalato. It is uncertain in line 4 whether "the Arabs" is to be taken literally, or whether "the law of the Arabs" simply means Islam.

63. Possibly this one goes with the preceding two. Again the Arabs, Hungary and Dalmatia are involved. But one place (Cydonia) is uncertain and another essentially unidentified, while lines 2–3 are quite obscure.

64. This one seems to suggest that Milan, Lucca and Florence would have the same duke. Actually, the Duchy of Milan belonged to the Spanish, while Florence was in the Duchy of Tuscany and Lucca remained independent. Perhaps the quatrain is concerned with anti-papal activities of ambitious Philip II, ruler of Milan, who used the chariot of Apollo as one of his devices and exercised great influence over the Duke of Tuscany. By taking the chariot as the imperial throne, it has been pointed out that a Duke of Tuscany did indeed become Emperor twice. In 1737 Duke Francis of Lorraine swapped Lorraine for Tuscany, and in 1745 became Emperor as husband of Maria Theresa. In 1790 this happened again, when Duke Leopold succeeded his brother as Emperor. Line 3 suggests that the Papacy will be forced to move, perhaps to Ravenna (elsewhere it is back to Avignon). Perhaps it is the Spanish and their faithful Italian adherents, the Colonna clan of Rome, who force the "move." Garencières takes it as predicting that the Duke of Tuscany would become King of an enlarged realm, with its capital at Venice.

65. A rather general one of some future sack of Rome, perhaps going with the preceding one with the finger pointed at Philip of Spain.

66. This is one of the few quatrains with any future potentialities remaining. It may be connected with VII–80. It is interesting to see two early interpretations of it. Wrote Garencières (1672):

> I conceive this Prophecy can be appropriated to no body better than Oli. Cromwell, who is called here *the Chief of London* by *Reign* of America, that is, by Reign of confusion [*sic!*], whose projects and treasons were all brought to nought, by the victorious Mars of the ever renowned General *Monck,* who came with his army from *Scotland* to *London* in the Winter time, he is called

a false Antichrist, because he was an enemy to King and Reb. that is Respublica or Commonwealth.

In 1710 Leroux (p. 42) saw it this way:

> . . . a King of England, whom Nostradamus designates by the name of Chief of London because he will be only the Chief of the Parliament of London and not Chief of the Church, as he will falsely and sacriligiously call himself . . . will seize the lands of America which are dependent or will be dependent on England, where he will have himself proclaimed King.

Boswell (1941), translating *par* as "out of," gets the American Revolution of 1776 out of it, alleging a Great Freeze in Scotland that year.

67. A rather worthless quatrain, since nothing is predicted but earthquake and hail. However, according to Wollner's reckoning, the configuration is a very rare one.

68. A fleet stands off a city, leaves, comes back to take captives and to pillage. The Barbary corsairs must have done all this quite frequently in Nostradamus' day.

69. The only specific element in this very vague one is in line 3, and remains quite uncertain. Le Pelletier's *Ambellinus* for Amiens is a figment of his imagination, the name being derived from *Ambianensis*. Ambel, an insignificant village near Grenoble, is indeed on a wooded mountain.

70. All is vague and obscure again but for the last line. It probably refers to the Archbishop of Reggio, in Italy's toe.

71. Sunday is the holy day of Christians, Saturday of Jews, Friday of Moslems. But Thursday? One interpretation points the finger at the United States, with its unique national holiday of Thanksgiving Thursday. A similar theme is found in 150.

72. Since this is the only dated one (not counting configurations), with a date still to come, it is of great interest. In September, 1999, a "King of Terror" will come. "From the sky," if taken literally, would be both real prophecy and a justification for putting some credence in its possibilities of fulfillment. Line 3 must needs hold the key to all of it. If *Angolmois* is Angoumois (capital, Angoulême), we presumably have a reference to the House of Angoulême, which provided France with Francis I, his son Henry II and his grandsons Francis II, Charles IX and Henry III, though the name "Valois" was left officially. Yet neither Francis nor Henry would seem to qualify as a King of Terror, nor is there any such in the history of the region. Unless some third possible meaning is discovered, it must be noted that *Angolmois* is an anagram for *Mongolois*, which would give us Genghiz Khan, highly suitable as a King of Terror. Line 4 is rather general. Mars is of course the god of war. This quatrain will probably be a favorite in Peking.

73. A Jovialist must needs be a follower of Jove or Jupiter, the chief god of the pagan Romans. We find the name in the Epistle, paragraph 34, probably designating neo-pagans (as Nostradamus saw Protestants ending up).

The quatrain has been applied to both Rabelais and Voltaire, but was probably meant for Calvin. Jaubert (1656) saw both this one and the preceding one as apocalyptic. In connection with line 4 it is perhaps worth noting that *Huguenot* is a frenchification of the German *eidgenossen,* meaning "oathmate," hence comrade.

74. This one is clearly apocalyptic. Could Nostradamus' quatrains be arranged according to the order of their intended fulfillment, it would come last or very close to the end. The seventh number is probably the seventh millennium, the source of much confusion in the Preface and the Epistle. Nostradamus' alleged clairvoyance is to extend to the resurrection on Judgment Day.

75. Does this refer to Jesus Christ? "The great Hermes" may be synonymous with "Ogmios," variously considered the Hercules and the Mercury of the Celts (see 580). Mercury and Hermes are the same.

76. All is fairly clear here except the state in which it is set.

77. This one may go with the preceding one. It has probably been applied to post-Fascist Italy, in which case the corsairs (Barbary pirates) would probably turn out to be the Russians, who received a large part of the Italian navy.

78. Some sort of disaster for Rome seems to be predicted here again.

79. As in 1075, we find the mysterious "Ogmios" (see 580 and 642). With both Mercury and Hercules present, there is no doubt. Some King of France must be intended, with lines 1–2 referring to the prosperity of France during his reign. In the Epistle, we place the setting of "Ogmios" (if a non-repetitive individual rather than a nation or the like) in the 19th century. The fleurs-de-lys was the emblem of the Kings of France.

80. A very vague and very obscure quatrain.

81. This is another of the more interesting quatrains. Since gold was pouring into Spain from the New World in the 16th century, this might be taken literally: a hoard secreted in a great Spanish cathedral. But in line 3 we are faced with the perplexing question of how a bond (band, cord, shackle, chain, etc.) can be hungry. An imaginative interpretation of this one involves economic chaos in the United States and a riot at Fort Knox, Kentucky, site of the greatest hoard of gold in the history of the world.

82. The general subject of this obscure one seems to be a siege, involving tricky strategy and bloody triumph.

83. Little can be said of this one, except that Ghent was in Flanders in the Spanish Netherlands, now Belgium.

84. Almost all of this is obscure. Perhaps line 1 shows it to be intended for Elizabeth Tudor, considered a bastard by the Catholics, and so pronounced by Pope Paul IV, as indeed she was in a strictly technical sense.

85. Another of the detailed but obscure variety. Recently, it has been applied to Marshal Pétain and his negotiations with the Germans (1940–43) on prisoners of war as slave labor.

86. This one is probably intended for the great King who would overthrow the Antichrist, "red ones" referring to the Spanish and "white ones" to the French (according to their battle colors). Once again we have the mysterious *Aquilon*, which can refer to any northern state (see 149 for the extensive list proposed by Nostradamus' disciple Chavigny). Garencières saw it for Gustavus Adolphus in the 17th century and Le Pelletier, in 1867, saw *Aquilon* for Russia and the "King of Europe" for Louis XVIII, of all people:

> Louis XVIII will come like a bird of prey, accompanied by the Russians, and leading a great army of Englishmen (in red uniforms) and of Austrians (in white uniforms); all together will march against Napoleon, the King of Paris.

This quatrain may be part of the "New Crusades" group since, as noted, Babylon was a name used for Egypt (see Decameron X, 9).

87. This may be another on Nostradamus' theme of a war-to-the-death between Philip II and his uncle Ferdinand over Charles V's empire. Nice was in Savoy, one of the few places not occupied by the French when Nostradamus wrote. If *Antipolles* is Antipolis, Antibes is about twelve miles southwest of Nice, and was near the Savoy border.

88. This one is set in Marseilles and seems to forecast a fierce attack against the great port.

89. The subject of this one seems to be the prosperity of France under some great king. It has been applied to the reign of Louis XIV from 1643 (he did not begin to rule till 1661) to 1701, when he began a war which really cost France heavily (as his previous wars had not).

90. Le Pelletier applies this one to Napoleon at St. Helena and France under the Restoration:

> The Emperor, whose dictatorial powers will have caused, through his long wars, a great shedding of human blood, will die a hundred times of grief at St. Helena, wherein the English will overwhelm him with abuses. His palace will be taken by Louis XVIII, a wise and kindly King who will find, in the two Chambers set up by the Charter of 1815, an absolute devotion to his person; but the audacious murder of the Duke of Berry by a scoundrel named Louvel on February 13, 1820, will plunge this prince into grief.

Bouys (1806, p. 80) applies it to Robespierre, Napoleon and "Georges" (Cadoudal?). It is particularly apt for Robespierre, who, in an attempt to commit suicide, blew off half his face, and spent a none too comfortable twenty-four hours before he was guillotined. But would "learned and mild" be appropriate epithets for Napoleon?

91. A very clear and simple prophecy for the Papacy. In 1609 will be elected a Pope who will be a native of Campania (the province between Capua and Salerno on the west coast of Italy) and who had been a monk (of what order is uncertain; the gray monks were the Franciscans and the black monks the Benedictines). Unfortunately, Paul V remained Pope from

1605 to 1621. Pierre de l'Estoile (1878 edition, IX, 218) records that in February, 1609, courtiers of Rome and Paris were in a dither waiting for Paul V to die co-operatively.

McCann (1942, p. 112) gives a loving excuse for this failure with the following explanation:

> The year, during Nostradamus' lifetime, began in France with the Spring Equinox. Sixtus V was elected to the Papacy in 1585, and the election was held April 2. If 24 is added to the number of the year, it gives 1609, just one of the prophet's little subtleties which make life difficult for his interpreters.

Per Roberts (1947) 1609 must be added to 325 to give 1934, "the year Hitler was granted full power."

92. Another detailed but obscure quatrain. Geneva was the seat of the "Protestant Pope," Calvin. Perhaps Nostradamus hopefully foresaw his being lynched by a mob of outraged and austerity-weary Genevans.

93. The bark referring to that of St. Peter, we have the equivalent of "new Papacy." Perhaps this one concerns the theme of the Papacy being forced to leave Rome, found several times. The transfer-of-the-Empire theme appears elsewhere also, notably in 132 and 545. Beaucaire is a few miles up the Rhône from Arles, but on the opposite bank. Porphyry is a rare kind of rock formation.

94. Nîmes was in Languedoc. Arles, in Provence, lies about fifteen miles to the southeast. Vienne, in Dauphiny, is about 140 miles up the Rhône from Arles. A Spanish invasion seems to be involved.

95. This rather general one might be considered vaguely fulfilled by Philip II, though his accomplishments against the Moslems were rather limited: persecution of the Moors, futile expeditions to North Africa and a share in the Battle of Lepanto (1571).

96. This quatrain is a most stimulating puzzler, which should have been solved by now but hasn't been. Perhaps the Arabian Gulf is the clue to line 1. The name of Mahomet's father was Abdullah. Being a posthumous son, he was brought up by his grandfather Abd Al-Muttalib and his uncle, Abu Talib. But none of these is quite an anagram for Adaluncatif. The rather irrelevant fact has been introduced that it is an anagram for "The Year One of the Calif" in French. *Aleph* is the Hebrew *a*, to which the Arabic *alif* is close. It must be noted that only line 1 or 2, and not both, can refer to orthodox Islam. Perhaps line 2 refers to a divergent sect, which is to be stamped out. The Shi'ites, for instance, supported the descendants of Mahomet's daughter Fatima as opposed to elected (soon hereditary) unrelated caliphs. Her husband was Ali, son of Abu Talib (alias Abd Manaf), who in turn was the son of Abd Al-Muttalib. Ali took the surname of Abu Turab. But none of these will yield *Adaluncatif*. The Shi'ite sect was officially established in Persia in 1502 and underwent persecutions 1722–29 and 1736–47. Since most Moslem names begin with A, line 4 provides the least problem in this one.

97. Other than to note that Barbarians were properly Algerians from Barbary, but used loosely for Moslems, we can offer little for this very vague and obscure quatrain.

98. Since the Third Republic was personified as "Marianne," this rather general one might be well applied to France 1940–44. Le Pelletier's reading of "salt" as wisdom seems valid enough. Garencières' version is really none too different: "This is concerning a famous beauty, who in her latter age shall prostitute herself to all comers."

99. Garencières had a brainstorm for this utterly obscure one: "This signifieth that the Europeans shall be fed no more with Manna, as the Jews were in the Desert, but shall pass to the Land of Promise, that is of peace and quietness."

100. Much has been made of the fact that the last of the Centuries proper deals with England's great future. McCann (1942, p. 378) explained it thus:

> There is something deeply symbolic in the fact that this verse is the closing one of the Centuries. It is as if there were an implication that the end of England would be the end of the world as we know it. . . . The civilized world today has a similar feeling about England and her relationship to all that is held free and precious.

Garencières in 1672 interpreted the verse thus:

> This is a favourable one for England, for by it the Empire, or the greatest Dominion of Europe is promised to it, for the space of above three hundred years, at which the Portuguese or Spaniards shall much repine.

Two centuries later (1867) Le Pelletier gave it this way:

> England will hold the rule of the seas for more than three hundred years, from the reign of Elizabeth, who created its navy: then great armies will destroy its power by land and sea; the Portuguese, allied with the English, will not rejoice at that (because, doubtless, great upheavals or battles will take place, then, in Portugal).

It is still uncertain whether the *pempotam*, which appears in varying forms in the Epistle, paragraph 44, and in 897, means "all-powerful" or "all-seas." It is certain that a great future is predicted for England, but Garencières and Le Pelletier demonstrate that it is not certain in what manner Nostradamus saw this greatness taking shape. There are further disagreements as to how the Portuguese fit in. Even on the innocuous line 3 there is disagreement: does it refer to English forces or to the forces that will end her greatness? This ambiguity is of course in the best traditions of prophecy.

# *Duplicate and Fragmentary Centuries*

## CENTURY VI

100. This quatrain is obviously a long-range prophecy for some town. But what town? Le Pelletier believes it is Orange, where there is indeed a ruined amphitheater, and on whose name *L'Aure* would be a play. But we find no confirmation of his statement that there is always a breeze there. On the other hand, according to the *Encyclopaedia Britannica,* "Avignon is subject to violent winds, of which the most disastrous is the mistral. . . ." But Avignon, alas, has no theatrical ruins. The other towns besides Orange which have ruins of amphitheaters are Nîmes, Arles, Fréjus and Tours. According to Le Pelletier, the Orange reading would have brought fulfillment. It was the nominal property of William the Silent, leader of the revolting Netherlands. In 1561 the Calvinists took it. In 1562 the Catholics took it. In 1573 it fell to an adventurer named Glandage. In March, 1660, Louis XIV demolished its fortifications. In 1701, with the death of William III and extinction of the House of Orange proper, Louis settled a disputed claim by giving it to Francis Louis of Bourbon-Conti. On May 14, 1731, the latter "bequeathed" it to France.

## CENTURY VII

43. Seeking to apply as many "nephew" quatrains as possible to Napoleon III, Le Pelletier applies this one to his desertion of the Italians with the Treaty of Zurich (October 17, 1859), and gives highly unconvincing data for the other details. The two unicorns probably refer to two persons each of whom used unicorns in his arms. But we have not found any likely candidates. Line 3 is very obscure.

44. This one, of course, must be applied to the execution of Louis XVI (January 21, 1793). As Le Pelletier gives it:

> When a very good Bourbon will sit on the throne of France, bearing the hand of justice and a name longer than that of any other King of his line, this Prince, because of his flight to Varennes, will be unjustly condemned to the extreme penalty.

The long name, explains Le Pelletier, is long because there was no other French king to that time who was the sixteenth of his name. The applications stands up well enough. Whether Nostradamus' or not, it was in print at least 150 years before its "fulfillment."

73. Except for the very interesting last phrase "put on the throne" (which perhaps mean that the verse should be worked out for Henry of Navarre), all is obscure here.

80. This very curious quatrain has been applied to the American Revolu-

tion, John Paul Jones and the rise of the United States. If the plural in line 3 is just for uniformity with the *Britanniques*, the characterization is not a bad one of Jones, who raided the English coast in April, August and September, 1778. Garencières agrees with this in 1672, having it "Scottish Pirates shall be, who shall rebel." However, the relationship between the West and the British Isles in line 1 is somewhat anomalous. Possibly it is connected with 1066.

82. Though they are the subject of numerous quatrains, this is the only one in which the word *Protestant* appears. Barbarian properly refers to an Algerian corsair, but may be used for Moslems in general.

83. This quatrain seems to concern a bride deprived of her husband on her wedding night.

### CENTURY VIII

1. It is rather remarkable that all six of these can be applied with various degrees of aptness to the period between World Wars I and II. They are somewhat suspiciously lucid for Nostradamus. This one might be entitled *Sitzkrieg und Blitzkrieg*.

2. Here we can place appeasement. Somehow or other Roberts (1947) gets out of this ". . . relations between powerful industrialists and leaders of labor organizations shall not be settled soon, unless a greater spirit of cooperation develops."

3. This one is rather vague. Line 4 might be applied to the Roosevelt-Churchill friendship and its adverse effects on the wolves of the Rome-Berlin Axis.

4. Here we have appeasement again.

5. Could this one be applied to the United States and Lend-Lease?

6. Vienna was the first victim of the Nazi juggernaut. Of course, *Vienne* might refer equally well to the town in Dauphiny.

### CENTURY X

100. This remarkable prophecy came rather close to fulfillment as specified. As Le Pelletier gives it:

> On March 10, 1661 (the morning after the death of Cardinal Mazarin), the great King, Louis XIV, the heir of the lilies [footnote: The toads were the ancient insignia of France, under the first Merovingians; and the fleurs-de-lis were not substituted for them until the reign of Clovis, son of Childeric I and founder of the Christian Monarchy of the Frankish Kings], who will then be reigning in France, will seize the reins of State with a firm hand and will subject all to himself.

By this, line 4 would have to be taken as a statement of intentions rather than of fact. It is interesting to see Jaubert's comment (1656, p. 74) on the verse, written four or five years before it was to take place:

By this quatrain the King of France would appear to be Emperor of the World in 1660. One may indeed hope for this, but it does not seem likely to be accomplished; however, the true Nostradamus seems to predict that he ought to be Emperor soon. May God will it for the maintenance of his Church, and of this very Christian Kingdom.

Jaubert also points out that the verse was doctored up previously to yield the date 1593, with the last line changed to "The great King of the toads will route his enemies," all for the greater glory of Henry of Navarre.

## CENTURY XI

91. The setting of lines 3–4, obscure as they are, is clearly in Provence, but the location of the distorted names of line 1 is subject to more doubt. If Meusnes, it is located east of Saint-Aignan, while Manthelan is about thirty miles to its southwest.

97. This one is set in eastern France. Villefranche is about twenty miles down the Saône from Mâcon. Moulins, capital of the old Duchy of Bourbon, is about seventy miles west of Mâcon. Châlon-sur-Saône is about fifty miles north of Mâcon.

## CENTURY XII

4. All is completely obscure here but Provence. Could *Denté* be the Italian poet? The style suggests a Presage Nostradamus had left over from an Almanac.

24. The setting for this one is quite far-flung. Guienne was the huge province of the Southwest. Poitiers lay to the north of it. Montluel, ten miles east of Lyons, was in Bresse and thus legally part of Savoy till 1601. Vienne is about twenty miles down the Rhône from Lyons.

36. This one was fulfilled suspiciously well. Famagusta on Cyprus fell on August 6, 1571. Nicosia fell after a forty-five-day siege; twenty thousand men were put to the sword by the Turks. On October 7, the Ottoman navy suffered disaster at the epic Battle of Lepanto, in the rock-girt Gulf of Corinth. The Moslem fleet consisted of a large contingent under Uluch Ali, Dey of Algiers.

52. Aiguesmortes is a once-great seaport, from which Louis IX embarked on his Crusades, located on the western mouth of the Rhône. There is an Essoyes, but it is far to the north, about twenty-five miles southeast of Troyes in Champagne.

55. A quatrain that reads like a typical Presage from the Almanacs.

56. The subject here is undoubtedly the civil wars of religion.

59. Another one on the 16th-century religious struggles in France.

62. Château Trompête and Château du Hâ were both at Bordeaux in the Southwest. Blois, about 210 miles northeast of Bordeaux, seems to have been

seen by Nostradamus as the seat of a great new king. It was closely associated with the reigning house of Nostradamus' day (see 1044).

65. The Gironde is the estuary of the Garonne River. Langon is about twenty-five miles up the Garonne from Bordeaux.

69. This one is easily the most interesting of the fragmentary Century XII. It obviously concerns another of the frequent attempts of the Duke of Savoy to subjugate and annex Geneva, just over their northern borders. From 1451 to 1522 the House of Savoy had controlled the city through its Bishop, who always happened to be a scion of the House of Savoy.

The last attempt by Savoy to take Geneva was in a daring raid on the night of December 11, 1602. Under the pretext that Henry IV was about to send Marshal Lesdiguières to capture it, the Duke of Savoy dispatched an expedition of two thousand men under an adventurer named d'Albigny. Ladders were put up during the night, but the Genevans roused themselves in time to fight off the invaders. However, there was nothing in history to explain either *Supelman* or the nephews. Part of the last line seems to have been eliminated by the censor, for reasons we will never know.

71. This utterly obscure verse may perhaps concern the religious wars of the 16th century.

# MISCELLANY

# The Letter to Jean Morel[1]

Monsieur ce sabmedi xxix$^{me}$ novembre 1561. i'ay ⸗voz lettres receues de paris le xii$^{me}$ doctobre de la presente annee. Et voy que selon quil me semble voz lettres sont plaines d'estomach, de querelle et de indignation que vous avez alencontre de moy, que ne puys scavoir la cause pourquoy. Ou$^2$ ce que vous plaignez de ce que moy estant a paris m'en allant voyre faire la reverence a la maiesté de la Royne me prestatez deux nobles a la roze et douze escuz, qui est chose iuste equitable et veritable, et en cella vous monstrates ce qui estoit et perpetuellement apert de estre, que moy ne vous connoissant ne vous a moy que par renommee. Et devez entendre, Seigneur, que tout incontinent que ie feuz arrivé a la cour apres avoir parlamente quelque peu a la maiesté de la Royne, ie luy diz mesme la noblesse vostre et vostre plus que Caesaree liberalité de ce que maviez presté. Et ce ne fut pas une foys que le diz a sa ma$^{tie}$ mais asseurez vous que il feut reiteré par moy de plus de quatre foys. Et ie suis marry que maiez en telle estimation que ie ne suys pas tant ignorant que je ne scache: quod benefacta malé locata male facta arbitror. Mais ie congnoys que par vostre lettre vous parlez de colere et de indignation: et selon quil me semble sans avoir ample notice de moy. Et de ce que vous distez m'avoir escript par quelque Cappitaine d'Aix. Asseurez vous, Seigneur, que ie n'ay receu iamais lettre de vous que cesteicy, que ie cuydoys fermement veoir ce que javoys dict a la maiesté de la Royne, que vous feut esté satisfaict, Sed de minimis a eulx.$^3$ Mais pour venir au poinct comme il est juste et tres raisonnable que vous soyiez satisfaict que il faut que vous asseuriez que en cest endroict et en tous aultres ie me veoiz aultant homme de bien non tant seullement en vostre endroict mais aussi en tous aultres comme vous vous estez monstré noble et heroique. Et veritablement ie pensois men aller estre a la court que jestois mandé pour y aller. Mais aussy a l'opposite par daultres contremandé de n'y aller poinct et ce ne feust pas esté sans vous demander ny vous satisfaire amplement. Dernierement il y avoit chez Monsieur le Baron de la garde ung jeune gentilhomme paige qui se disoit estre vostre privigne que souvent ie luy diz et luy fiz offre quil m'apprint de voz nouvelles que ie vous eusse satisfaict amplement du tout.

---

[1]Catalogued as *Fonds latin* No. 8589 in the French National Library, though hardly Latin. The text given below represents an exact transcript of the original, taken from a photostatic reproduction in the translator's possession. The main source of confusion is the interchangeability of *s* and *z*, *j* and *i*, *v* and *u*. We have tried to stick to the original in each word, although the writer himself varies his orthography at random.

[2]This word is somewhat uncertain, owing to illegibility.

[3]A contorted Franco-Latin version of the Latin proverb *De minimis non curat praetor* (The magistrate does not concern himself with trifles).

# The Letter to Jean Morel

SIR,[1]

This Saturday, the 29th of November, 1561, I received your letters sent from Paris the 12th of October of this year. I seem to note that your letters are full of the offense, quarrel and indignation that you have against me for I know not what reason.

You complain that when I was in Paris and went off to pay reverence to Her Majesty the Queen, you lent me two rose nobles and twelve crowns, which is just, fair and true, and with that you state what was so and remains perpetually so, that I did not know you nor you me, other than by reputation.

I would have you understand, Sir, that immediately after I had arrived at the court and had spoken for a short time to Her Majesty the Queen, I especially mentioned to her the nobility and more than imperial liberality with which you had made me the loan. And this was not the only time that I spoke to her about this matter; I assure you that it was mentioned again on four later occasions. I am grieved that you hold such a poor opinion of me as to think I am so ignorant as not to know that *benefits unwisely conferred are considered misdeeds.*

But from your letter I recognize that you are speaking in anger and indignation and, so it seems to me, without knowing much about me.

Now with regard to what you say you have sent me through a certain captain from Aix. Rest assured, Sir, that I have never received any letter from you other than this one, that I firmly believed that as a result of what I had said to Her Majesty the Queen you had been satisfied. *But with trifles,* etc.

But to come to the point. It is just and very reasonable that you be satisfied. You must understand that in this matter and in all others I stand as a man of good character not only towards you but also towards all others. As indeed you showed yourself to be truly noble and heroic.

I thought my going to the court was by command. But there were also counterorders from others not to go there at all, and this was not without asking you and satisfying you fully.[2]

Recently, there was with Monsieur le Baron de la Garde a young gentleman page who professed to be your stepson, so that I often spoke to him and asked him for news of you, in order to be fully satisfied about everything.

---

[1] In order to make this letter as readable as possible, liberties have been taken with the translation and division of sentences and paragraphs. At the same time, great care has been taken not to violate Nostradamus' meaning, where it is clear. Where the meaning is not clear, the translation is more nearly literal.

[2] This paragraph is completely incomprehensible. One is reminded of certain quatrains.

Mais jamais il ne men parla. Combien que bien souvent ie luy en tins propos. Quand a ce que m'escripviez que je m'en vins de paris, hospite insalutato, asseurez vous quil vous plaist de ainsy escripre que ie ne pensois pas a cella et de moy ne de mon naturel ie ne scay que cest affronter ne affronterie telles imperfections me v–s[4] ne me sont nullement ni ne m'appartiennent mais sont esloingnés totalement de mon naturel de ma qualité et condition. Mais iestois malade pour bonne recompense que ieuz de la court, ie y devins malade, Sa Maiesté du Roy me bailla cens escuz. La Royne men bailla trente et voila une belle somme pour estre venu de deux cens lieues y avoir despendu cens escuz, j'en ai trente. Mais ce n'est pas cella: que apres que ie feuz arrivé a Paris du retour de sainct germain une fort honneste grande femme que ie ne scay quelle estoit a son apparence demonstroit estre dame grandement honneste et dame d'honneur quelle que fut qui me vint veoir le seoir que ie feuz arrivé et me tint aulcuns propos ie ne scaurois dire quelz estoient, et print congé qui estoit assez nuict. Et le lendemain matin me vint veoir et apres que sa noblesse m'eust tenu quelques propos tant de ses affaires particulieres que aultrement. A la parfin elle me dist que Messieurs de la Iustice de Paris me debvoient venir a trouver pour me interroger de quelle science ie faisois et presageois ce que je faisois. Ie luy diz par response quilz ne prinsent pas de peine de venir pour telz affaires, que ie leur ferois place, que aussy ie avois delibere mon partir le matin pour men retourner en Provence ce que ie feiz. Et que ce feust pour vous frustrer ie ny pensy aulcunement. Mais quoy vous pourrez avoir de moy telle sinistre estimation quelle quil vous plaira, si suis certaigne le connoistrez en brief. Et si suis grandement desplaisant que plus tost ne men avez escript que plus tost raison vous seroit estre faicte, et si vous dyz que ne vous viz iamais que par lettre et si ne connoy, que par vostre aspect de phisiognomie propter conniventêis oculos que vostre singuliere preudhomye, honté, foy, probité, doctrine, et erudition. Mais vous penserez que avec toutes telles parolles que ie vous escriptz quil feust suffisant pour vostre satisfaction. Non est. Ie vous enuoye cydedans vostre lettre deux petitz billetz quil vous plaira de les bailler que tout incontinent que vous les aurez delivrez ie suis asseuré que vostre argent vous sera delivré et promptement. Lung est a Mademoiselle de Sainct Remy et laultre a Monsieur de Fizes. Et de ce ie vous supplye ne voulloir faillir les leur delivrer. Car par apres, deux jauray response si les ayans receues quil ny aura faulte aulcune. Et il y a plusieurs aultres de Paris et de la court que de plus grande somme ne me voudroient esconduire, et si en aulcune chose de ce monde ie vous puys faire service ie vous supplyerois bien fort quil vous pleust de me voulloir emploier soit pour vous ou pour quelqu'ungs de voz amys que vous pouvez tenir pour asseuré de vous fyer a moy aultant que homme qui soit en ce monde. Et si nestoient les tumultes qui journellement sont pour le faict de la religion ie me

---

[4]The two (or possibly three) middle letters are illegible.

But of this matter he never spoke to me, although very often I mentioned it to him.

With regard to what you wrote, that I left Paris snubbing my friend, rest assured that, though you may be pleased thus to write, I did not think in that fashion, that it is not in my nature, that I do not know how to insult, nor of insult, and that such imperfections are not mine and do not belong to me but are quite alien to my nature, quality and condition.

As a matter of fact, as a fine reward for having gone to court, I became sick, whereupon His Majesty the King sent me one hundred crowns. The Queen sent me thirty. There you have a fine sum for having come two hundred leagues: having spent a hundred crowns, I made thirty crowns out of it.

But that's beside the point. After I had returned to Paris from Saint-Germain,[3] a very striking great lady, whose identity I do not know, but who by her appearance seemed to be a very virtuous and honorable lady, came to see me the night I returned and spoke to me for some time, I couldn't say of what, and took leave quite late.

The next morning she came to see me again. After Her Ladyship had conversed with me about her affairs with more intimacy than before, she finally told me that the Gentlemen from the Justice of Paris intended to find me in order to question me about the science of which I made use and how I predicted what I did. I told her by way of reply that they need not take the trouble to come on such a mission, that I would save them the trouble and that I had planned to leave the next morning for return to Provence, which indeed I did.

That this would disappoint you did not occur to me at the time at all. But although you can have as poor an opinion of me as you please, I am certain you will know it soon.[4] And I am very sorry that you did not write to me sooner so that you might have been given satisfaction sooner. And I tell you that though I see you only by letter and do not cultivate your acquaintance, yet when I shut my eyes I recall your physical appearance, your singular honesty, goodness, faith, probity, learning and erudition.

But you will consider that all these words that I write you I consider sufficient to satisfy you. Not so. I send you herewith two little notes. If it will please you to make use of them, I feel sure that as soon as you will have delivered them your money will be delivered to you promptly. One is to Mademoiselle de Saint-Rémy and the other to Monsieur de Fizes. And I beg that you will not hesitate to deliver them. For I will expect word from both of having received them, so that there will be no mistake. And there are several others in Paris and at the court who would not refuse me a much greater sum.

---

[3] No mention of the traditional Blois visit! (See "Biography of Nostradamus.")
[4] Another seemingly ill-balanced and incomprehensible thought.

serois mis en chemyn et ce ne feust pas esté sans m'enquerre de vous amplement. J'attendz voz lettres expostulissement, desquelles je suis asseuré que la
response que vous me ferez que vous serez satisfaict. Jespere daller a la court
tant que pour amener mon filz Caesar Nostradamus aux estudes et pour satisfaire a quelques personnaiges qui me pryent d'y voulloir aller ce que ie feray.
Ce pendant ie vous supplye le plus tost quil vous plaira de mescrire de voz
nouvelles. Et ie ne failliray de m'employer a vostre faveur tout le service quil
me sera possible de faire, et le connoistrez plus amplement par effect aultant
affectueusement que ie me recommande Monsieur de Morel a vostre bonne
grace. Priant dieu quil vous doinct sancté vye longue accroissement d'honneur et laccomplissement de voz nobles et heroiques vertus. De Salon de
Craux en Provence ce dernier octobre.1561. Vostre humble obeissant serviteur, prest a vous obeyr.

M. Nostradamus[5]

Monsieur ie vous envoye a deux que ie suis asseuré que le premier que
vous demanderez a vostre premiere instance on ne fauldra de vous satisfaire
comme est de raison, il vous plaira de men escripre de tout.

Vostre humble et obeyssant serviteur<br>
prest a vous obeyr<br>
M. Nostradamus[6]

---

[5]Written in the hand of the writer of the letter. Notary public? Chavigny?

[6]Written in a weak and faltering hand, so illegible that it was crossed out. Nostradamus'? It is barely conceivable that Nostradamus himself wrote the letter, and that the
scrawl is an effort by young César (age six) to imitate his father's signature.

If in any way in the world I can be of service to you, I beseech you very emphatically that you will be pleased to make use of me, whether it be for yourself or for any of your friends. You may rest assured that you can rely on me as much as on any man in this world.

And were it not for the tumults which take place daily because of religion, I would be on the road, and this would not take place without my inquiring of you fully.

I await your letters most anxiously, being certain your reply will tell me you are satisfied. I hope to go to court both to set my son Caesar Nostradamus at his studies and to satisfy several personages who beg me to come there, which I will do.

However, I beg you to write me your news as soon as possible. And I will not fail to employ in your favor all the services of which I am capable and demonstrate more fully by deed how affectionately I recommend myself, Monsieur de Morel, to your good grace.

Begging God that he give you health, long life, increase of honor and the fruition of your noble and heroic virtue, From Salon de Craux in Provence this last day of October *[sic!]*, 1561, Your humble and obedient servant, ready to obey you,

M. NOSTRADAMUS

P. S. Sir, I send you the two [notes], although I am sure that, upon your first demand with the first one, you will not fail to be appropriately satisfied. Write to me as fully as it may please you.

Your humble and obedient servant<br>ready to obey you<br>M. NOSTRADAMUS[5]

---

[5]See note 6 opposite on signatures.

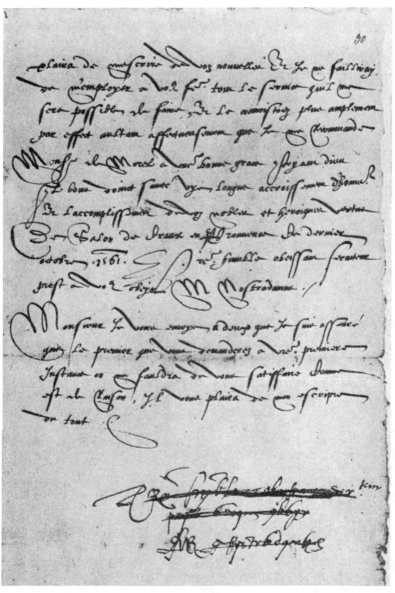

Last page, with signatures, of the five-page letter to Jean Morel.

# [Épître]

## A mes venerables Seigneurs Messieurs les Chanoines de l'Eglise Cathedrale de l'antiquiss. cité D'aurange[1]

Venerables Seigneurs par la interrogations faites sur certains Sacrilege nombre entre les rauissements *de furto et de thesauro abscondito non celato* que iouxte la figure astronomique erigée si dessus comme voyez emplement manifestant le fait du rauissement sacré qui a été par le consentement de deux de vos freres de l'eglise, même qui auparauant votre conseil priué tenu, que vous fites par plusieurs fois quest ce que l'on feroit de votre argenterie qui dit vne opinion qui en dit ung aultre, qui disoit de len porter en Auignon qui disoit le porter en aultre part, puis deux furent dopinion de la vendre puis qu'ainsi etoit. et *dividere preda canoniis* qui de presant sont *veluti milites.* Cette opinion ne feut pas prouuée bonne Saincte ne loüable que furent plusieurs que ny le acorderent combien quil y en auoit quelques ioyeux qui tenoient cella a la parfin ne feut acordée ne vng point ne autere mais feut du tout aresté quelle se metroit a la maison d'vng de vos messieurs la emfermée, comme feut fait mal agreable a quelques vng. Car vne opinion tenoit qu'il falloit fondre et metre en lingots et la vendre pour prouoir a vng Cheseung pour le temps presants. puis sortirent deux et trois qui dirent que ceci possible ne dureroit guierres, que l'Eglise Romaine seroit deliurée de tels euenements sinistres et feut enfermée que guierres ny a demeuré que deux de ceux la qui etoit dopinion de la vendre fondre et aliener secretement auecques vng aultre et netoient que trois et de l'Eglise fraternelle et ont raui se que sans faulte auecques vne intention de derober le tout et non sans le consentement du custode, *quia ouem lupo commisisti* que tout ainsi que Iesus Christ par quelques temps auoit commis son troppeau a longs rauissants de son Eglise, aussi sous vmbre de foy et de preudhomye aués commis votre arganterie sacrée et dediée pour le sacré ornement de votre temple iadis offert par les Roys monarques et souuerains dominateurs de la terre comme vray obseruateur de foy et de religion mais

---

[1]The text of this letter is transcribed literally from a photographic reproduction of a copy made in 1714 of the original letter. The copy is in a fine script and thoroughly legible, but Nostradamus' syntax and general intelligibility are so bad that we have had to take great liberties with the translation in many places so as to render it at least moderately readable and comprehensible. Nostradamus' Latin quotations have been italicized. For the background of this letter, see page 29.

# [Letter]

## To my venerable Lords Messieurs the Canons of the Cathedral Church of the most ancient city of Orange

VENERABLE LORDS: with respect to your inquiry concerning the specified and enumerated sacrilegious thefts, *concerning theft and hoard hidden but not concealed.*

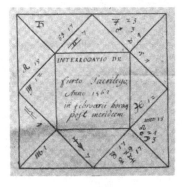

According to the astronomical figure drawn above, you will see fully that it shows that the theft of the sacred objects has been perpetrated with the collusion of two of your brothers of the Church—indeed, ones who have previously extended to you private counsel on several occasions as to what had befallen your silver. One of them gave his opinion that it had been taken to Avignon, the other that it had been taken some other place. Both were of the opinion that it had been sold, as indeed was their intention.

*Booty to be divided among canons* who are at present *like soldiers.*

This opinion was not rendered as good and godly and commendable. Several would not agree with it, although some others were pleased though in the end not agreed on one point or the other. But all was halted as the silver was put in the house of one of your people and locked up; which was not done agreeably to some. One opinion held that it was necessary to melt it down into bars and sell it, storing it for the present in the home of one of them.

Then two or three came forth to say that this could not possibly be for scarcely any length of time, since the Roman Church would be involved in most sinister events. It was locked up, although with but two of them remaining of the opinion that it should be sold melted down and plotting secretly with one another.

There were only three, and they brothers of the Church, and they have ravished that which was without fault with the intention of stealing everything and not without the collusion of the custodian, *for you entrusted the sheep to the wolf.* As indeed Jesus Christ for some time committed His flock to long plunderings of His Church, also under the shadow of faith and of probity, as you have committed your silver, sacred and dedicated as it is to the sacred ornamentation of your temple, donated in ages past by Kings, monarchs, lordly sovereigns of the earth as true observers of the faith and of religion.

notez mes venerables Seigneurs que si en bref ceux qui sont de votre compagnie qui nont ignoré le iour et la nuit que le sacré rauissement a été fait,
qu'il leur viendra le plus grand malheur ·sur eulx et sur toute leur famille que
iamais aduient. en oultre que la pestilence s'aproche de votre cité et dedans
sarapans aux plus grands que iamais ne se apesera de votre cité et du contenu
dedans vos meurs, que cela ne soit restitué et remis le tout qu'il a été pillié
non tant seulement dans le lieu et entre les mains de ceux qui en auoit garde,
mais aussi qu'il le retournent dans le temple et que leur souuienne *de argento
cholosano,* et qu'il ne obiettent point vedette—*commilitones quomodo dii
propicii sint sacerdotes,* mais ont dira que lon voit comme Dieu prent la
vengence de ceux qui ont profané le saint temple et que ont raui ce que par
ancieneté auoit été offert par les obseruateurs de la religion chretienne. parquoy que cette mienne letre soit lüe a la presence de tous vos messieurs, et
quelle ne soit ouuerte que tous ne y soient, que lors incontinent la face des
consentants changera de haute vergoigne et de confussion qu'il auront ne se
pourront contenir. parquoy gardez ce mien ecript par vn parfait temoignage
de verité, pour en temoigner auec le temps et assurez vous mes venerables
Seigneurs si ceux qui sont rauie ne se deliberent par vne voye ou par autre
de la rendre qu'il mouront de la plus malheurese mort plus longue et d'vng
grandissime rage, et fureur incensée que iamais ne se separera deux que le
tout ne soit restitué et remis a leur ancien repositoire et lors ainsi vous le
verrés. Ie suis marri que la brebis a été commise au loup tant pour la obseruer
que pour la diuiser que pour messaige faire. ce que ie vous escris c'est iouxte
la iugement astronomique protestant de ne offencer personne de ce monde,
*humanus sum possum errare falli et decipi,* toutesfois il ne peut etre que dans
votre cité il ny ait quelqung à la doctrine astronomique arriuant—a la
iudiciere que par la figure iugera s'il entent que mon dire contient verité. mes
messieurs ne vous fachiez de rien que en bref tout se trouuera, que si ainsi
nest assurez vous que leur malheureux destinée saproche de ceux qui
ont le sacrilege perpetré par execrable forfait. aultre chose pour le presant ne
vous puis decrire. Dieu vous veille restituer en votre premier etat. Combien
qu'il en y a plusieurs qu'ils seroient deplaisant si leur faloit tourner porter
laulmusse et ceux et ceux [*sic!*] qui sont proche de vous et vng qui ne se
voudra pas trouuer acompagnié d'vng aultre de meme façon. Dieu de mal
vous garde, de Sallom ce 4$^{me}$ febrier 1562.

> *faciebat M. Nostradamus*
> *Salonæ petræ in prouincia*
> *iiii februarii M.D.L.XII*

pour copie dont l'original est dans les archives de l'Eglise Cathedrale de cette
ville . . .
    *Avrange le 19$^e$ juin 1714.*

But note, my venerable Lords, that unless by those of your company who are not without knowledge of the day and the night when the theft of the sacred objects was perpetrated there be restored and replaced in full what was stolen, not only in its place and into the hands of those entrusted with its custody, but also returned into the temple, remembering *the silver chalice*, there will fall upon them the greatest misfortune that ever befell anyone, on them and on their family; and furthermore, pestilence will approach your city and within its ramparts as great as ever covered your city or was contained within your walls, and let them not object to the above. *Priests are like comrades of propitious gods.*

But they will see, as it is said, that God takes his vengeance on those who have profaned His holy temple and who have stolen what in ages past was donated by the observers of the Christian religion.

Therefore, let this letter of mine be read in the presence of all your people, as if not opened until all are present, and then without fail the faces of those in collusion will change with great shame and confusion that they will be unable to repress.

Therefore, keep this my letter as a complete witness of the truth, time to come to bear witness to it, and rest assured, my venerable Lords, if that which was stolen is not brought back one way or another, that they will die the most miserable death, more lingering and more violent and of more inconceivable intensity than ever before occurred—unless everything is restored and replaced in its ancient repository, and thus you will find it to be.

I am grieved that the sheep has been entrusted to the wolf, as much to take note of it as to devise what message to send about it.

What I write you is according to astronomical judgment and, I protest, lacking in offense to anyone in this world. *I am human and can err, be wrong and be deceived;* nevertheless, be there anyone in your city familiar with the astronomical doctrine extending to the judicial, by the figure let him judge if he understands not that my saying contains the truth.

Have no fear whatever, sirs, but that shortly all will be found, and that if it be not thus, rest assured that their unhappy destiny approaches for those who have perpetrated sacrilege by their execrable crime.

Further I cannot write you for the present. God watch over you to restore you to your first state. Although there are several who would be displeased if they had to wear again the amice, several of them near you, and one there is who will not want to find himself accompanied by another of the same type.

God guard you from evil. From Salon this 4th of February, 1562.

M. NOSTRADAMUS
*Salon-de-Crau in Provence*

# Testament de Michel Nostradamus[1]

L'an à la Nativité de Notre Seigneur mil cinq cens soixante six et le dix-septiesme du mois de juin. Comme ne soit chose plus certaine qu'est la mort, n'est chose plus incertaine que l'heure d'icelle; pour ce est-il qu'en la présence de moy Joseph Roche notaire Royal et tabellion juré de la présente ville de Sallon, Diocèse d'arles, et des temoins ci-après nommés, fut présent en sa personne Mᵉ Michel Nostradamus, Docteur en médecine et Astrophile de la ditte ville de Sallon, Conseiller et Medecin ordinaire du Roy, lequel considérant et estant en son bon entendement, bien portant et voyant, et entendant, combien que en tout ne soit affoibly, causant son ancien eage et certaine maladie corporelle, de laquelle il est à présent destenu, voulant pourveoir, et pendant qu'il est en vie, des ses biens que Dieu le Créateur-luy a donnés et prestés en ce mortel monde, à celle fin que après son decez et trespas sur iceuz biens n'y ayt question, procès, et différens, pour ce ledᵗ Mᵉ Michel Nostradamus, de son bongré, pure et franche volonté, propre mouvement et délibération a fait, ordonné et establi, et par ces présentes fait, ordonne et etablit son testament nuncupatif, disposition et ordonnance finale à la forme et manière que s'ensuit: et premièrement, comme bon, vray chrestien et fidelle, a recommandé son ame à Dieu le Créateur, le priant que quand sera son bon plaisir de l'appeler, que luy plaise colloquer son ame au Royaume éternel de Paradis, et pour ce que après l'ame, le corps est la chose plus digne de ce siècle, ledᵗ testateur a vollu, quand son ame sera séparée de son corps, que icelluy soit porté en sépulture dans l'Église du Couvent de Sᵗ Francoys dudᵗ Sallon, et entre la grand porte d'icelle et l'autel de Sᵗᵉ Marthe, là ou a vollu estre faicte une tombe ou monument contre la muraille; et a vollu sondᵗ corps estre accompagné avecques quatres cierges, d'une livre la pièce; et a vollu aussi toutes ses obsèques et funérailles estre faictes à la discretion de ses gaigiers cy-après nommés; et aussy a légué, vollu, et ordonné incontinent que soit baillé à treize pauvres six souls pour chascun, une fois tant seulement après son décès; et aussi a legué aux Frères de l'Observance de Sᵗ Pierre de Canon un escu une fois tant seulement, payable incontinent après son trespas; et aussi a legué a la Chapelle de Nostre Dame des Pénitents-Blancs dudᵗ Sallon un escu payable une fois tant seullement incontinent après son décès; et aussi a legué aux Frères Mineurs du Couvent de Sᵗ Francoys, deux escus une fois tant seullement, payables incontinent après son trespas; et aussi a légué à Magdeleine Besaudine fille

[1]Taken from Parker's thesis (see "Nostradamus Bibliography"). The thesis carries a note that it was copied on December 17, 1918, by Henry Dayre, archivist-librarian of Arles, from the original copy in the *fonds Bonnemant*, No. 298, of the Catalogue of Manuscripts of the Municipal Library of Arles, under the division *Testaments Curieux*. The above text shows many variations of orthography, which points either to M. Dayre's lack of accuracy, or to the loose and changing rules of 16th-century orthography.

# Last Will and Testament of Michel Nostradamus

The year of Our Lord one thousand five hundred and sixty-six and the seventeenth day of the month of June. Just as there is nothing more certain than death, nothing is more uncertain than its hour. For this reason it is that in the presence of myself, Joseph Roche, royal notary and sworn scrivener of the present town of Salon, Diocese of Arles, and of the witnesses hereinafter named, there was present in his person Master Michel Nostradamus, Doctor in medicine and Astrophile of the said town of Salon, Counselor and Physician-in-Ordinary of the King.

The latter, considering and being in his full understanding, resting well and seeing and understanding, and although all-told not being weakened, because of his ancient age and certain bodily illness, by which he is at present confined, wishes to provide while he is alive for his possessions that God the Creator has given him and lent him for this mortal world, to the end that after his decease and passing, there will be no question, process and difference over these possessions.

Therefore the said M. Michel Nostradamus of his own mind, pure and free will, by his own movement and deliberation, has made, ordered and established, and by these presents makes, orders and establishes his noncupative will, disposition and final ordinance in the form and manner that follows:

Firstly, as a good, true and faithful Christian, he has recommended his soul to God the Creator, begging Him that when it will be His good pleasure to call him, that it may please Him to collect his soul into the eternal Kingdom of Paradise.

Because after the soul the body is the most worthy thing at this time, the said testator has willed that when his soul has departed from his body, the latter will be carried to burial in the Church of the Convent of St. Francis of the said Salon, and between its great door and the altar of St. Martha, where he has willed that a tomb or monument be erected against the wall. He has willed that his said body be accompanied by four candles, of one livre each, and he has willed also that all his obsequies and funeral rites be conducted at the discretion of his executors hereinafter named.

He has also bequeathed, willed and ordered incontinent that six sous be given to each of thirteen beggars, one time only after his death. He has also bequeathed to the Friars of the Observance of Saint-Pierre-de-Canon one crown once only, payable incontinent after his death. He has also bequeathed to the Chapel of Notre Dame des Pénitents-Blancs of the said Salon one crown payable once only incontinent after his death. He has also bequeathed to the Friars Minor of the Convent of St. Francis two crowns once only, payable incontinent after his death.

de Loys Besaudine son germain, la somme de dix escus d'or pistollets, lesquelles a vollu luy estre baillés quand elle sera colloquée en mariage, et non autrement; tellement que si lad^te Magdeleine venoit à mourir avant qu'estre colloquée en mariage, a vollu led^t testateur le présent legat estre nul; et pareillement a légué et laissé led^t de Nostradamus testateur à Damoyselle Magdeleine Nostradamus sa fille légitime et naturelle et de Damoyselle Anne Ponsarde sa femme commune, la somme de six cens escus d'or sol, payable une fois tant seullement le jour qu'elle sera colloquée en mariage; et pareillement a légué et lègue à Damoyselles Anne et Diane de Nostradamus ses filles légitimes et naturelles et de la ditte Anne Ponsarde sa femme commune, et à chascunes d'elles, la somme de cinq cens escus d'or pistollet, payable à chascune d'elles le jour que seront colloquées en mariage, et cas advenant que lesd^tes Damoyselles Magdeleine, Anne et Diane sœurs, ou une d'elle vint à mourir en pupillarité, ou autrement, sans heoirs légitimes et naturels, aud^t cas a substitué à chascune desd^tes Magdeleine, Anne et Diane, ses héritiers ci-après nommés; et aussi a légué et laissé à la ditte Damoyselle Anne Ponsarde sa femme bien aimée la somme de quatre cens escus d'or pistollets, lesquels led^t testteur a vollu estre expédié à la ditte Damoyselle Anne Ponsarde incontinent après la fin et trespas dud^t testateur; et desquels quatre cens escus lad^e Ponsarde en jourira tant qu'elle vivra veuve, et en son nom dud^t testateur; et cas advenant que lad^e Ponsarde vienne è se remarier, aud^t cas led^t testateur a vollu lesd^ts quatre cens escus estre restitués à ses heoirs ci-après nommés; et si lad^e Ponsarde ne vient à soy remarier aud^t cas led^t testateur a vollu qu'elle puisse léguer et laisser lesd^ts quatre cens escus à un des enfans dud^t testateur, tel ou tels que bon lui semblera pourveu toutes fois qu'elle ne les puisses laisser à autres qu'auxd^ts enfans dud^t testateur; et pareillement a légué et lègue à lad^e Ponsarde sa femme le usage et habitation de la tierce partie de toute la maison dudit testateur laquelle tierce partie lad^e Ponsarde prendra à son choix et de laquelle en jourira tant qu'elle vivra, et veuve en nom dud^t testateur; et aussi a légué a lad^e Ponsarde une caisse de noyer dicte la Grand Caisse, estant à la salle de la maison dud^t testateur, ensemble l'autre petite joignant ycelles près du lict, et aussi le lict estant à lad^e salle, avecques sa bassaque, matelats, coultre, traversier, couverte de tapisserie, les cortines et rideaux estans aud^t lict, et aussy six linceuls, quatre toailhes, douze serviettes, demi-douzaine de plats, demi-douzaine d'assiettes, demi-douzaine d'écuelles, deux pichieres une grande et une petite, une eyguedière et une salière, le tout d'estaing, et d'autres meubles de maison que luy sera nécessaire selon sa qualité, trois boutes pour tenir son vin, et une petite pyle quarrée estant dans la cave, lesquels meubles après la fin de lad^te Ponsarde, ou cas advenant qu'elle vint à se remarier, a vollu torner à ses heoirs cy-après nommés; et pareillement a légué et lègue

He has also bequeathed to Madeleine Besaudine, daughter of Louis Besaudine his first cousin, the sum of ten gold pistolets, which he has willed be given her when she becomes married, and not otherwise, so that if the said Madeleine dies before she is married, the said testator has willed that the present legacy be null and void.

Likewise the said de Nostradamus, testator, has bequeathed and left to Miss Madeleine Nostradamus the legitimate and natural daughter of himself and of Madame Anne Ponsarde his common wife, the sum of six hundred gold crowns, payable once only the day that she becomes married.

Likewise he has bequeathed and bequeaths to Misses Anne and Diana de Nostradamus the legitimate and natural daughters of himself and of the said Anne Ponsarde his common wife, and to each of them, the sum of five hundred gold crown-pistolets, payable to each one of them the day that they become married. And in the event the said Misses Madeleine, Anne and Diana, sisters, or one of them, die in pupillarity, or otherwise, without legitimate and natural heirs, in the said case he has substituted for each of the said Madeleine, Anne and Diana his heirs hereinafter named.

He has also bequeathed and left to the said Madame Anne Ponsarde, his beloved wife, the sum of four hundred gold crown-pistolets, which the said testator has willed be dispatched to the said Ponsarde incontinent after the end and death of the said testator. These four hundred crowns the said Ponsarde will enjoy as long as she lives a widow in the name of the said testator. In the event that the said Ponsarde comes to remarry, in the said event the said testator has willed that the said four hundred crowns be restored to his heirs hereinafter named. If the said Ponsarde does not come to remarry, in the said case the said testator has willed that she can bequeath and leave the said four hundred crowns to one of the children of the said testator, to whichever one or ones will seem proper to her, provided always that she cannot leave them to anyone other than the said children of the said testator.

Likewise he has bequeathed and bequeaths to the said Ponsarde his wife the use of and abode in a third of the entire house of the said testator, which third part the said Ponsarde will take as she chooses, and which she will enjoy as long as she lives as a widow in the name of the said testator. He has also bequeathed to the said Ponsarde a walnut chest, called the Great Chest, located in the hall of the house of the said testator, together with the little one next to it near the bed, as well as the bed located in the said hall, with its mattress cover, mattresses, spring, bolster, tapestry cover, and the curtains and drapes located in the said bed; also six winding sheets, four towels, twelve napkins, a half-dozen dishes, a half-dozen plates, a half-dozen porringers, two pitchers large and small, a cup and a salt cellar, all of pewter. And of the other movables of the house which will be necessary for her according to her station, three casks to hold her wine, and a little square bowl located in the cellar, which movables after the death of the said Ponsarde, or in case she remarries, he has willed to return to his heirs hereinafter named.

ledt testateur à ladte Anne Ponsarde sa femme toutes ses robes, habillements, bagues, et joyaux, pour d'yceux en faire à tous ses plaisirs et volontés, et aussy a prélégué ledt testateur tous et un chascuns ses livres à celluy de ses fils qui profitera plus à l'etude, et qui aura plus de la fumée de la lucerne; lesquels livres, ensemble toutes les lettres missives que se trouveront dans la maison dudit testateur, ledt testateur n'a vollu aucunement estres inventorissées ne mis par description, ains estre serrés en paquets et banastes, jusques à ce que celluy que les doit avoir soit de l'eage de les prendre et mis et serrés dans une chambre de la maison dudt testateur; et aussy a prélégué à Caesar de Nostradamus son fils légitime et naturel et de ladte Damoyselle Ponsarde sa femme commune, la maison où ledt testateur habite; item luy a prélégué sa cape, qu'a ledit testateur d'argent surdoré, et aussy les grosses cadières de bois et de fer, demeurant toutes fois le légat fait à lade Ponsarde sa femme en sa force et vertu, tant qu'elle vivra veuve, et en son nom, ledt testateur; et laquelle maison demeurera en commun et indivis, quand pour regard de l'usage entre lade César, Charles et André ses frères, jusques à ce que tous lesds frères soyent de l'eage de vingt-cinq, après lequel temps toute lade maison sera entièrement dudt César, pour en faire à son plaisir et vollonté, demeurant toutefois le legat fait à lade Ponsarde sa mère, pour le regard de lade maison, en sa force et vertu; et aussy a prélégué et prélègue audt Charles de Nostradamus son fils légitime et naturel et de ladte Ponsarde so femme commune, la somme de cent escus d'or pistollets, une fois tant seullement, lesquels cent escus ledt Charles porra prendre sur tout l'héritage, avant que partir, quand sera de l'eage de vingt-cinq ans; et aussy a prélégué audt André de Nostradamus son fils légitime et naturel et de lade Ponsarde sa femme commune, la somme de cent escus d'or pistollets, une fois tant seullement, lesquels cent escus ledt André porra prendre sur son héritage, avant que partir, quand sera, comme dict est, de l'eage de vingt-cinq ans; et en tous et un chascuns ses autres biens, meubles et immeubles, présents et advenir, droits, noms, actions, dettes, a fait ses héritiers unversels, nommés de sa bouche par leurs noms et surnoms, lesdts César, Charles et André de Nostradamus ses enfants légitimes et naturels et de ladte Ponsarde sa femme commune, par égales parts et portions en les substituant de l'un à l'autre, s'ils viennent à mourir en pupillarité, ou autrement sans heoirs légitimes et naturels; et si ladte Anne Ponsarde sa femme estoit enceinte, et fit un fils ou deux, les a fait heritiers également comme les autres, avec semblable substitution; et si elle faisoit une ou deux filles leur a légué a ycelle et

Likewise the said testator has bequeathed and bequeaths to the said Anne Ponsarde, his wife, all his robes, clothes, rings and jewels, so that she may take of them all that she wills and pleases.

The said testator has also left by preference legacy each and all of his books to that one of his sons who will profit most by study, and who will have drunk the most of the smoke of the lamp. These books, together with all the letters that will be found in the house of the said testator, the said testator has willed not to be catalogued at all, nor placed by their description, but to be tied up in parcels and baskets, until the one who is to have them is of age to take them, and that they be placed and locked up in a room of the house of the said testator.

He has also left by preference legacy to César de Nostradamus his legitimate and natural son, and of the said Madame Ponsarde his common wife, the house in which the said testator lives. Likewise, he has left him by preference legacy the cape which the said testator has double-gilded with silver, and also the large chair of wood and iron, the legacy made to the said Ponsarde his wife remaining at all times in force and virtue, as long as she remains a widow in the name of the said testator. This house will remain in common undivided as regards usage between the said César and Charles and André his brothers, until all the said brothers are of the age of twenty-five, after which time all of the said house will belong entirely to the said César, to do with as he may please and will, there remaining in force and virtue at all times the legacy made to the said Ponsarde his mother, with regard to the said house.

He has also left by preference legacy and leaves by preference legacy to the said Charles de Nostradamus his legitimate and natural son, and of the said Ponsarde his common wife, the sum of one hundred gold crown-pistolets, once only, which hundred crowns the said Charles can take as his entire heritage, before leaving, when he reaches the age of twenty-five.

He has also left by preference legacy to the said André de Nostradamus, his legitimate and natural son, and of the said Ponsarde his common wife, the sum of one hundred gold crown-pistolets, once only, which hundred crowns the said André can take for his heritage before parting when he reaches, as is stated, the age of twenty-five.

Each and all of his other possessions, movable and immovable, present and future, rights, names, actions, debts he has left to his heirs at large, named from his mouth by their names and surnames, the said César, Charles and André de Nostradamus the legitimate and natural children of himself and of Anne Ponsarde his common wife, in equal parts and portions interchangeable, if they come to die in pupillarity, or otherwise, without legitimate and natural heirs.

If the said Anne Ponsarde his wife should be pregnant, and give birth to one or two sons, he has made them heirs equally with the others, with similar substitution; and if she gives birth to one or two daughters, he has be-

chascune d'ycelles la somme de cinq cens escus, a mesme paye et substitution que les autres; et si a vollu led[t] testateur que sesd[ts] enfans et filles ne se puissent colloquer en mariage que ce ne soit de consentement et bon volloir de lad[e] Ponsarde leur mère, et des plus proches parents dud[t] testateur; et cas advenant que tous vinssent à mourir sans heoirs légitimes ou naturels, a substitué au dernier, lesd[ts] Damoyselles Magdeleine, Anne et Diane de Nostradamus des sœurs, et filles dud[t] testateur, et pour ce que led[t] testateur voit son héritage consister la plus part en argent comptant et dettes a vollu led[t] testateur led[t] argent comptant et dettes quand seront exigés, estre mis entre les mains de deux ou trois marchands solvables, à gain et proffits honnestes; et aussy pour ce que a vu ses enfans estre en bas eage et pupillarité constitués leur a pourveu de tuteresse et administraresse testamentaire de leurs personnes et biens, lad[e] Damoyselle Anne Ponsarde sa femme, de laquelle spécialement se confia, pourveu qu'elle soit tenue de faire bon et loyal inventaire, ne vollant toutesfois qu'elle puisse estre constrainte de vendre aucuns meubles ne utensiles de maison dud[t] héritage et a tant qu'elle vivra veuve au nom dud[t] testateur, deffendant faire alliénation de meubles en quelque sorte que ce soit, ains que soient gardés et puis divisés auxd[ts] enfans, quand seront d'eage; laquelle tuteresse prendra et recourrera les proffits dud[t] argent que sera esté mis entre mains desd[ts] marchands, pour dud[t] proffit s'en norrir elle avec sesd[ts] enfans, chausser, vestir et pourveoir de ce que sera necessaire sellon leur qualité, sans que desd[ts] fruits elle soit tenue d'en rendre aucun compte ains seullement pourveoir sesd[ts] enfans comme dict est; deffendant expressement led[t] testateur que sesd[ts] héritiers ne puissent demander leur part de leurd[t] héritage, en ce que concernera en argent, qu'ils ne soient de l'eage de vingt-cinq ans; et touchant aux légats faits à sesd[ts] filles, se prendront sur les fonds de l'argent que sera esté mis entre les mains desd[ts] marchands, quand elles viendront soy colloquer en mariage, suyvant les susdits légats; vollant en oultre led[t] testateur que aucun de ses frères dud[t] testateur aie et ne puisse avoir aucun maniement et charge dud[t] héritage, ains en a laissé le toutal régiment et gouvernement d'icelluy et de la personne de sesd[ts] enfans a la susditte Damoyselle Anne Ponsarde sa femme, et fait ses gaigiers et executeurs du présent son testament Pallamèdes Marc escuyer sire de Chasteauneuf, et sire Jacques Suffren bourgeois dud[t] Sallon, auxquels etc. cassant etc. et tout incontinent led[t] Nostradamus a dict et declaré, en présence des tesmoins ci-après nommés avoir en comptant la somme de trois mil quatre cens quarante quatre escus et dix sols, lesquels a exhibés et monstrés réellement en présence desd[ts] tesmoins susnommés et en espèces ci-après espécifiées, premièrement en trente six nobles à la Rose; ducats simple cent et un; Angelots, septante neuf; doubles ducats,

queathed to each of them the sum of five hundred crowns, with the same payment and substitution as the others.

The said testator has willed that his said sons and daughters cannot be married without the consent and approval of the said Ponsarde their mother, and of the nearest relatives of the said testator. In case all die without legitimate or natural heirs, he has substituted for the latter the said Misses Madeleine, Anne and Diana de Nostradamus their sisters, and daughters of the said testator.

The said testator, realizing that his estate consists mostly of cash and debts, has willed that the said cash and debts when collected be placed in the hands of two or three solvent merchants, for gain and honest profit.

And because he realizes his children to be of low age and in pupillarity, he has provided them with a guardian and testamentary administratrix of their persons and possessions, in the person of the said Anne Ponsarde, his wife, to whom they are especially entrusted. It is provided that she be held to keep a good and true inventory, and at all times she can be constrained from selling any movables or utensils of the house of the said heritage for as long as she lives a widow in the name of the said testator. She is forbidden to alienate movables in any way whatever while they are being held for and then divided amongst the said children, when they come of age.

This guardian will take and withdraw the profits from the said money that will be placed in the hands of the said merchants, and from the said profit she will provide for herself along with her children, to shoe them, clothe them and provide them with what will be necessary according to their station. Excepting the said fruits, she will be held to render an account thereof solely to provide for her said children as is stated.

The said testator expressly forbids his said heirs from demanding their share of the said heritage, as far as the money is concerned, before they reach the age of twenty-five. Concerning the legacies made to his said daughters, they will be taken from the funds of the money which will be placed in the hands of the said merchants, when they will come to be married, according to the said legacies.

The said testator wills furthermore that none of the brothers of the said testator can have any handling and charge of the said heritage. He has left the entire rule and government of it and of the persons of his said children to the said Madame Anne Ponsarde his wife.

He has made the executors of his present testament Pallamèdes Marc, Esq., lord of Châteauneuf, and the Hon. Jacques Suffren, burgher of the said Salon, to whom, etc., abrupt, etc., and all incontinent the said Nostradamus has spoken and declared, in the presence of the witnesses hereinafter named, that he has in cash the sum of three thousand four hundred and forty-four crowns and ten sous, which he has exhibited and shown, actually, in the presence of the said witnesses above-named and in the species hereinafter specified. Firstly, rose nobles 36; simple ducats 101; Angelots 79; double

cent vingt et six; escus vieux, quatre; lyons d'or en forme d'escus vieux, deux; un escu du Roy Louys; une médaille d'or vallant deux escus; florins d'Allemagne, huict; imperiales, dix; marionnetes, dix sept; demy-escus sol, huict; escus sol, mil quatre cent dix neuf; escus pistollets, douze cents; trois pièces d'or dittes Portugaise, vallant trente six escus; que reviennent toutes les susd^{tes} sommes d'argent comptant réduites ensemble, lad^{te} somme de trois mil quatre cens quarante quatre escus et dix sols, et aussy a fait apparoir, tant par son livre, que par obliges et cedules, que gaiges, qu'il a de dettes la somme de mil six cens escus, lesquelles sommes d'argent comptant ont été mises dans trois coffres sive caisses estans dans la maison ded^t de Nostradamus, les clefs dequelles sont esté bailhées, l'une à Pallamedes Marc sire de Chasteauneuf, l'autre à sire Jacques Suffren bourgeois dud^t Sallon, qu'ils ont reçues réellement, après avoir esté mis l'argent dans lesd^tes caisses par iceux mesmes. Fait et passé aud^t Sallon, en l'estude de la maison de M^r Nostradamus, testateur, en présence de sires Joseph Raynaud borgeoys, Martin Manson consuls, Jehan Allegret trésorier, Pallamedes Marc escuyer sire de Chasteauneuf, Guillaime Giraud, noble Arnaud d'Amiranes, Jaumet Viguier escuyer, et Frère Vidal de Vidal, Gardien du Couvent de S^t Francoys dud^t Sallon, tesmoins à ce appellés, que se sont soussignés excepté led^t Raynaud. Ainsi signé: Michel Nostradamus, Martin Manson *consul;* Jehan Allegret *trésorier,* Fr. Vitalis *gardien tesmoing,* Balthezar d'Amirane *tesmoin,* P. Marc *tesmoin,* J. de Viguier, Guilhaume Giraud. Roche *notaire.*

## Codicil du mesme

L'an à la Nativité de Nostre Seigneur mil cinq cens soixante six, et le dernier jour du mois de juin, sachent tous presents et advenir que les presentes verront, que par devant et en la presence de moy Joseph Roche notaire Royal et Tabellion juré de la presente ville de Sallon, Diocèse d'Arles, soussigné, et des tesmoins ci-après nommés, fut present en sa personne M^r M^e Michel Nostradamus Docteur en medecine, Astrophile, Conseiller et Medecin ordinaire du Roy, lequel considerant et reduisant en sa memoire, comme il a dit, avoir fait son dernier testament nuncupatif prins et receu par moy dit et soussigné notaire sur l'an présent et le dix sep^e jour du present mois de juin, auquel, entre autres choses contenues en icelluy, auroit fait ses héritiers César, Charles et André de Nostradamus ses enfans; et pour ce que à ung chascun est licite et permis de droit codiciller et faire ses codicils après son testament, par lesquels à sond^t testament puisse adjouster ou diminuer, ou autrement de tout en tout abolir pour ce led^t M^e Michel de Nostradamus, vollant faire ses codicils, et de present codicillant, et adjoustant à sond^t testament a légué et lègue aud^t Cesar de Nostradamus son fils bien aimé, son Astrolabe de leton, ensemble son gros anneau d'or avecques la corneline y

ducats 126; old crowns 4; gold lions in the form of old crowns 2; a crown of King Louis; a gold medal worth 2 crowns; German florins 8; imperials 10; marionettes 17; half-crowns 8; crowns 1,419; crown-pistolets 1,200; 3 pieces of gold said to be Portuguese, worth 36 crowns. So that all the said sums of cash together come to the said sum of 3,444 crowns and 10 sous. He has also made it clear, by his book as well, that by obligations and notes of hand, and guarantees, he has debts to the sum of 1,600 crowns. These sums of cash have been placed in three coffers or chests located in the house of the said de Nostradamus, the keys of which have been entrusted, the one to Palla-mèdes Marc, lord of Châteauneuf, the other to the Hon. Jacques Suffren, burgher of the said Salon, which they have actually received, after the money had been placed in the said chests by themselves.

Done and passed in the said Salon, in the study of the house of Master Nostradamus, testator, in the presence of the honorables Joseph Raynaud burgher, Martin Manson consul, Jehan Allegret treasurer, Pallamèdes Marc esquire lord of Châteauneuf, Guillaume Giraud, the noble Arnaud d'Ami-ranes, Jaumet Viguier, Esq., and Friar Vidal de Vidal, Superior of the Convent of St. Francis of the said Salon, witnesses named here, who are undersigned except for the said Raynaud.

Signed thus: MICHEL NOSTRADAMUS, MARTIN MANSON *consul;* JEHAN ALLEGRET *treasurer;* FRIAR SUPERIOR VIDAL *witness,* BALTHEZAR D'AMIRANE *witness,* P. MARC *witness,* J. DE VIGUIER, GUILHAUME GIRAUD. ROCHE, *notary.*

## Codicil of the Same

The year of Our Lord one thousand five hundred and sixty-six, the last day of the month of June. Know all present and to come by these presents that before and in the presence of myself, Joseph Roche, royal notary and sworn scrivener of the present town of Salon, Diocese of Arles, undersigned, and of the witnesses hereinafter named, there was present in person Master Michel Nostradamus, Doctor in medicine, Astrophile and Physician-in-Ordinary of the King.

The latter, considering and reducing in his memory, as he has said, has made his last nuncupative will taken and received by me, the said and undersigned notary in the present year on the seventeenth day of the present month of June, at which time among other things contained therein, he made his heirs César, Charles and André de Nostradamus his children.

Because the right to codicile and to make his codicils after his will is legal and is permitted to everyone, so that he can add to or withdraw from his said will, or otherwise entirely abolish it, the said M. Michel de Nostradamus, wishing to make his codicil, and at present codicilling, and adding to his said will, has bequeathed and bequeaths to the said César de Nostradamus, his beloved son, his brass Astrolabe, together with his large gold ring with

enchassée et ce oultre et par dessus le prelegat à luy fait par ledit de Nostradamus son pere à sond$^t$ testament; et aussy a legué et legue à Damoyselle Magdeleine de Nostradamus sa fille légitime et naturelle, outre ce que luy a esté legué par sond$^t$ testament, savoir est deux coffres de bois noyer estant dans l'estude dud$^t$ codicillant, ensemble les habillements, bagues, et joyaux que lad$^e$ Damoyselle Magdeleine aura dans lesd$^{ts}$ coffres, sans que nul puisse voir ny regarder ce que sera dans yceux; ains dud$^t$ legat l'en a fait maistresse incontinent après le décès dud$^t$ collicitant; lequel legat lad$^e$ Damoyselle pourra prendre de son autorité, sans qu'elle soit tenue de les prendre par main d'autruy ny consentement d'aucuns; et en toutes et chascunes les autres choses contenues et déclarées à sond$^t$ testament led$^t$ M$^e$ Michel de Nostradamus codicillant a approuvé, ratiffié, et confirmé, et a vollu et veut ycelles valloir et avoir tousjours perpetuelle valleur et fermesse; et aussi a vollu et veut ycelluy codicillant ce present codicil et tout le contenu en ycelluy avoir vertu et fermesse par droit de codicil, et autres, et par droit de tout autre dernière vollonté, et par la meilleure forme et manière que faire se pourra, et a requis et requiert moy soussigné notaire et tesmoins cy-après nommés, estre records de sond$^t$ present codicil; lesquels tesmoins il a bien connus et nommés par leurs noms; et lesquels tesmoins ont aussy connu led$^t$ codicillant; dont et de quoy led$^t$ M$^e$ de Nostradamus codicillant a vollu acte en estre fait à ceux à qui de droit appartiendra par moy dit et soussigné notaire. Faict, et passé, et publié aud$^t$ Sallon, et dans la maison dud$^t$ codicillant, en presence de sire Jehan Allegret trésorier, M$^e$ Anthoine Paris docteur en médecine, Jehan Girard dit de Bessoune, Guillem Eyraud appotiquaire, et M$^e$ Gervais Berard chirurgien dud$^t$ Sallon, tesmoin à ce requis et appellés. Lesquels codicillant et tesmoins se sont soussignés, excepté led$^t$ Giraud tesmoin, qui a dit ne savoir ecrire. Ainsi signés: M. Nostradamus, Jehan Allegret, Gervais Berard, A. Paris, Guillem Eyraud. Roche *notaire.*

the corneline set in it and this above and beyond the preference legacy made in his favor by the said Nostradamus, his father, in his said will.

He has also bequeathed and bequeaths to Miss Madeleine de Nostradamus, his legitimate and natural daughter, beyond that which has been bequeathed to her by his said will, two walnut coffers which are in the study of the said codicillant, together with the clothes, rings and jewels that the said Miss Madeleine will find in the said coffers, without anyone being permitted to see or look at that which will be therein. Thus by the said legacy she has been made mistress of it incontinent after the death of the said codicillant. This legacy the said Mademoiselle can take as her authority, without being held back from taking them by the hand of another nor for the consent of anyone.

In each and all of the other things contained and declared in his said will the said M. Michel de Nostradamus codicillant has approved, ratified and confirmed and has willed and wills these to stand and to have always perpetual value and strength. This codicillant has willed and wills this present codicil, and others, and by right of all other last will, and by the best form and manner that can be attained, and has required and requires me the undersigned notary and the witnesses hereinafter named, to remember his said present codicil. These witnesses he has known well and named by their names. These witnesses have also known the said codicillant. The said M. de Nostradamus codicillant has willed the act to be done through them and by them, to whom by right it belongs, and by me the said and undersigned notary.

Done and passed, and published in the said Salon, and in the house of the said codicillant, in the presence of the Hon. Jehan Allegret, treasurer; M. Antoine Paris, doctor in medicine; Jehan Giraud, surnamed de Bessoune; Guillaume Eyraud, apothecary, and M. Gervais Berard, surgeon of the said Salon, witnesses requested and called here. Which codicillant and witnesses are undersigned, except for the said witness Giraud, who has said he does not know how to write.

Signed thus: M. Nostradamus, Jehan Allegret, Gervais Berard, A. Paris, Guillem Eyraud. Roche *notary*.

# Prophecies Falsely Attributed to Nostradamus

## A. *Sixains* (1605)[1]

AVTRES PROPHETIE DE M MOSTRADA-
MVS, POVR LES
*ans courans en ce siecle.*

  I.  Siecle nouueau, alliance nouuelle,
      Vn Marquisat mis dans la nacelle,
      A qui plus fort des deux l'emportera,
      D vn Duc d'vn Roy, gallere de Florance,
      Port à Marseil, Pucelle dans la France,
      De Catherine fort chef on rasera.

 II.  Que d'or d'argent fera despendre,
      Quand Comte voudra Ville prendre,
      Tant de mille & mille soldats,
      Tuez, noyez, sans y rien faire,
      Dans plus forte mettra pied terre,
      Pigmée ayde des Censuarts.

III.  La Ville sans dessus dessous,
      Renuersée de mille coups
      De canons: & forts dessous terre:
      Cinq ans tiendra: le tout remis,
      Et lasche à ses ennemis,
      L'eau leur fera apres la guerre.

IIII. D'vn rond, d'vn lis, naistra vn si grand Prince,
      Bien tost, & tard venu dans sa Prouince,
      Saturne en Libra en exaltation:
      Maison de Venus en descroissante force,
      Dame en apres masculin soubs l'escorse,
      Pour maintenir l'heureux sang de Bourbon.

  V.  Celuy qui la Principauté,
      Tiendra par grande cruauté,
      A la fin verra grand phalange:
      Par coup de feu tres dangereux,
      Par accord pourroit faire mieux,
      Autrement boira suc d'Orange.

 VI.  Quand de Robin la traistreuse entreprise,
      Mettra Seigneurs & en peine vn grand Prince,
      Sceu par la Fin, chef on luy tranchera:
      La plume au vent, amye dans Espagne,
      Poste attrapé estant dans la campagne,
      Et l'escriuain dans l'eauë se jettera.

---

[1]Reprinted exactly as they appeared for the first time, in the edition of 1605 (for the background of the Sixains, see pp. 49–50). All the original orthography and printer's errors have been left as they first appeared.

# Prophecies Falsely Attributed to Nostradamus

## A. *Sixains* (1605)

I. New century, new alliance,
   A Marquisate put in the bark,
   To him who the stronger of the two will carry it off,
   Of a Duke and of a King, galley of Florence,
   Port at Marseilles, the Damsel in France,
   The chief fort of Catherine will be razed.

II. How much gold and silver will have to be spent
    When the Count will desire to take the town,
    Many thousands and thousands of soldiers,
    Drowned, killed, without doing anything there,
    In stronger land will he set foot,
    Pygmy aid by the Copy-holders.

III. The Town without above below,
     Overturned by a thousand shots
     From cannons: and fortifications underground:
     Five years will it hold: everything delivered up,
     And left for its enemies,
     The water will make war upon them afterwards.

IIII. Of a circle, of a lily, there will be born a very great Prince,
      Very soon, and late come into his Province,
      Saturn in Libra in exaltation:
      The House of Venus in decreasing force,
      The Lady thereafter masculine under the bark,
      In order to maintain the happy Bourbon blood.

V. He who the Principality
   Will hold through great cruelty,
   He will see his great phalanx at its end:
   By very dangerous gunshot,
   By agreement he could do better,
   Otherwise he will drink Orange juice.

VI. When the treacherous enterprise of Robin
    Will cause Lords and a great Prince trouble,
    Known by Lafin, his head will be cut off:
    The feather in the wind, female friend to Spain,
    The messenger trapped while in the country,
    And the scribe will throw himself into the water.

VII.    La sangsuë au loup se ioindra,
        Lors qu'en mer le bled defaudra,
        Mais le grand Prince sàns enuie,
        Par ambassade luy donra
        De son bled pour luy donner vie,
        Pour vn besoin s'en pouruoira.

VIII.   Vn peu deuant l'ouuert commerce,
        Ambassadeur viendra de Perse,
        Nouuelle au franc pays porter:
        Mais non receu, vaine esperance,
        A son grand Dieu sera l'offance,
        Feignant de le vouloir quitter.

IX.     Deux estendars du costé de l'Auuergne,
        Senestre pris, pour vn temps prison regne,
        Et vne Dame enfans voudra mener,
        Au Censuart mais descouuert l'affaire,
        Danger de mort murmure sur la terre,
        Germain, Bastille frere & sœur prisonnier.

X.      Ambassadeur pour vne Dame,
        A son vaisseau mettra la rame,
        Peur prier le grand medecin:
        Que de l'oster de telle peine,
        Mais en ce s'opposera Royne,
        Grand peine auant qu'en veoir la fin.

XI.     Durant le siecle on verra deux ruisseaux,
        Tout vn terroir inonder de leurs eaux,
        Et submerger par ruisseaux et fontaines:
        Coups & Monfrin Beccoyran, & ales,
        Par le gardon bien souuant trauaillez,
        Six cens & quatre alez, & trente moines.

XII.    Six cens & cinq tres grand' nouuelle,
        De deux Seigneurs la grand querelle,
        Proche de Genaudan sera,
        A vne Eglise apres l'offrande
        Meurtre commis, prestre demande
        Tremblant de peur se sauuera.

XIII.   L'auanturier six cens & six ou neuf,
        Sera surpris par fiel mis dans vn œuf,
        Et peu apres sera hors de puissance
        Par le puissant Empereur general
        Qu'au monde n'est vn pareil ny esgal,
        Dont vn chascun luy rend obeïssance.

VII. The leech will attach itself to the wolf,
When the grain will sink into the sea,
But the great Prince without envy,
Through his embassy he will give him
Of his own grain to give him life,
He will provide himself with it for time of need.

VIII. Shortly before the opening of commerce,
An ambassador will come from Persia,
To bring news to the Frank land:
But unreceived, vain hope,
It will be an offense to his great God,
Pretending to desire to abandon him.

IX. Two standards from the direction of Auvergne,
The left one taken, for a time prison rule,
And a Lady will want to lead her child
To the Copy-holder but the affair is discovered,
Danger of death and murmur throughout the land,
German, brother and sister prisoner in the Bastille.

X. The Ambassador for a Lady
To his vessel will put the oar,
To beseech the great physician
That he relieve her of such pain,
But to this a Queen will be opposed,
Great pain before seeing the end of it.

XI. During the century one will see two streams
Flood an entire land with their waters,
And to be submerged by streams and fountains:
Shots at Montfrin Bouçoiron and Alais,
Very often troubled by the Gardon,
Six hundred and four, and thirty monks.

XII. Six hundred and five very great news,
The great quarrel of the two Lords,
It will take place near Gevaudan,
At a Church after the offering
Murder committed, the priest begs
Trembling with fear he will flee.

XIII. Six hundred and six or nine, the adventurer
Will be surprised by gall put in an egg,
And shortly afterwards he will be out of power
Through the powerful Emperor-General
To whom the world has not an equal,
Of which each will render him obedience.

XIIII.  Au grand siege encor grands forfaits,
Recommançans plus que iamais
Six cens & cinq.sur la verdure,
La prise & reprise sera,
Soldats és champs iusqu'en froidure
Puis apres recommencera.

XV.  Nouueau esleu patron du grand vaisseau,
Verra long temps briller le cler flambeau
Qui sert de lampe à ce grand territoire,
Et auquel temps armez sous son nom,
Ioinctes à celles de l'heureux de Bourbon
Leuant, Ponant, & Couchant sa memoire.

XVI.  En Octobre six cens & cinq.
Pouruoyeur du monstre marin,
Prendra du souuerain le cresme,
Ou en six cens & six, en Iuin,
Grand' ioye aux grands & au commun,
Grands faits apres ce grand baptesme.

XVII.  Au mesme temps vn grand endurera,
Ioyeux mal sain, l'an complet ne verra,
Et quelques vns quiseront de la feste,
Feste pour vn seulement, à ce iour,
Mais peu apres sans faire long seiour,
Deux se donront l'vn à l'autre de la teste.

XVIII.  Considerant la triste Philomelle
Qu'en pleurs & cris sa peine renouuelle,
Racoursissant par tel moyen ses iours,
Six cens & cinq, elle en verra l'issuë,
De son tourment, ia la toille tissuë,
Par son moyen senestre aura secours.

XIX.  Six cens & cinq, six cens & six & sept,
Nous monstrera iusques à l'an dix sept,
Du boute feu l'ire, hayne & enuie,
Soubz l'olivier d'assez long temps caché,
Le Crocodril sur la terre a caché,
Ce qui estoit mort, sera pour lors en vie.

XX.  Celuy qui a par plusieurs fois
Tenu la cage & puis les bois,
R'entre à son premier estre
Vie sauue peu apres sortir,
Ne sesçachant encor congnoistre,
Cherchera sujet pour mourir.

XIIII. At the great siege great crimes again,
Starting again worse than ever
Six hundred and five in the spring,
There will take place the capture and recapture,
Soldiers in the fields until winter
Then afterwards it will begin again.

XV. The newly elected master of the great vessel,
He will see shining for a long time the clear flame
Which serves this great territory as a lamp,
And at which time armed under his name,
Joined with the happy ones of Bourbon
East, West and West his memory.

XVI. In October six hundred and five,
The purveyor of the marine monster
Will take the unction from the sovereign,
Or in six hundred and six, in June,
Great joy for the common and the great ones alike,
Great deeds after this great baptism.

XVII. At the same time a great one will suffer,
Merry, poor health, he will not see the completion of the year,
And several who will be at the feast,
Feast for one only, on this day,
But shortly afterwards without delaying long,
Two will knock their heads together.

XVIII. Considering the sad Nightingale
Who with tears and laments renews her anguish,
By such means making her days shorter,
Six hundred and five, she will see the end of it,
Of her torment, the cloth already woven,
By means of it sinister aid will she have.

XIX. Six hundred and five, six hundred and six and seven,
It will show us up to the year seventeen,
The anger, hatred and jealousy of the incendiary,
For a long enough time hidden under the olive tree,
The Crocodile has hidden on the land,
That which was dead will then be alive.

XX. He who several times has
Held the cage and then the woods,
He will return to his first state
His life safe shortly afterwards to depart,
Still not knowing how to know,
He will look for a subject in order to die.

XXI.   L'autheur des maux commencera regner
       En l'an six cens & sept sans espargner
       Tous les subiets qui sont à la sangsuë,
       Et puis apres s'en viendra peu à peu,
       Au franc pays r'allumer son feu,
       S'en retournant d'où elle est issuë.

XXII.  Cil qui dira, descouurissant l'affaire,
       Comme du mort, la mort pourra bien faire
       Coups de poignards par vn qu'auront induit,
       Sa fin sera pis qu'il n'aura fait faire
       La fin conduit les hommes sur la terre,
       Gueté par tout, tant le iour que la nuit.

XXIII. Quand la grand nef, la prouë & gouuernal,
       Du franc pays & son esprit vital,
       D'escueils & flots par la mer secoüée,
       Six cens & sept, & dix cœur assiegé
       Et des reflus de son corps affligé,
       Sa vie estant sur ce mal renoüée.

XXIIII. Le Mercurial non de trop longue vie,
       Six cens & huict & vingt, grand maladie,
       Et encor pis danger de feu & d'eau,
       Son grand amy lors luy sera contraire,
       De tels hazards se pourroit bien distraire,
       Mais bref, le fer luy fera son tombeau.

XXV.   Six cens & six, six cens & neuf,
       Vn Chancelier gros comme vn bœuf,
       Vieux comme le Phœnix du monde,
       En ce terroir plus ne luyra,
       De la nef d'oubly passera,
       Aux champs Elisiens faire ronde.

XXVI.  Deux freres sont de l'ordre Ecclesiastique,
       Dont l'vn prendra pour la France la picque,
       Encor vn coup si l'an six cens & six
       N'est affligé d'vne grande maladie,
       Les armes en main iusques six cens & dix,
       Gueres plus loing ne s'estendant sa vie.

XXVII. Celeste feu du costé d'Occident,
       Et du Midy, courir iusques au Leuant,
       Vers demy morts sans point trouuer racine,
       Troisiesme aage, à Mars le Belliqueux,
       Des Escarboucles on verra briller feux,
       Aage Escarboucle, & à la fin famine.

XXXV.   Dame par mort grandement attristée,
Mere & tutrice au sang qui la quittée,
Dame & Seigneurs, faits enfans orphelins,
Par les aspics & par les Crocodilles,
Seront surpris forts Bourgs, Chasteaux Villes
Dieu tout puissant les garde des malins.

XXXVI.   L grand rumeur qui sera par la France,
Les impuissans voudront auoir puissance,
Langue emmiellée & vrays Cameleons,
De boutefeux, allumeurs de Chandelles,
Pyes & geyes, rapporteurs de nouuelles
Dont la morsure semblera Scorpions.

XXXVII.   Foible & puissant seront en grand discord,
Plusieurs mourront auant faire l'accord
Foible au puissant vainqueur se fera dire,
Le plus puissant au ieune cedera,
Et le plus vieux des deux decedera,
Lors que l'vn d'eux enuahira l'Empire.

XXXVIII.   Par eauë, & par fer, & par grande maladie,
Le pouuoyeur à l'hazer de sa vie
Sçaura combien vaut le quintal du bois,
Six cens et quinze, ou le dixneufiesme,
On grauera d'vn grand Prince cinquiesme
L'immortel nom, sur le pied de la Croix.

XXXIX.   Le pouruoyeur du monstre sans pareil,
Se fera veoir ainsi que le Soleil,
Montant le long la ligne Meridienne,
En poursuiuant l'Elephant & le loup,
Nul Empereur ne fit iamais tel coup,
Et rien plus pis à ce Prince n'aduienne.

XL.   Ce qu'en viuant le pere n'auoit sceu,
Il acquerra ou par guerre ou par feu
Et combatra le sangsuë irritée,
Ou iouyra de son bien paternel
Et fauory du grand Dieu Eternel
Aura bien tost sa Prouince heritée.

XLI.   Vaisseaux, galleres auec leur estendar,
S'entrebattront prés du mont Gilbattar
Et lors sera fors faits à Pampelonne,
Qui pour son bien souffrira mille maux,
Par plusieurs fois soustiendra les assaux,
**Mais à la fin vnie à la Couronne.**

XXI.   The author of the evils will begin to reign
In the year six hundred and seven without sparing
All her subjects who belong to the leach,
And then afterwards she will come little by little
To the Frank country to relight her fire,
Returning whence she has come.

XXII.   He who will tell, revealing the affair,
As with death, death will be able to do well
Blows of daggers which will have been incited by one,
His end will be worse than he will have devised to make
The end leads the men on land,
Watched for everywhere, as much by day as by night.

XXIII.   When the great ship, the prow and rudder
Of the Frank land and its vital spirit,
By the sea shaken over reef and billow,
Six hundred and seven and ten, heart besieged
And afflicted by the ebbings of its body,
Upon this evil its life being renewed.

XXIIII.   The Mercurial not of too long a life,
Six hundred and eight and twenty, great sickness,
And yet worse danger from fire and water,
His great friend will then be against him,
With such hazards he could divert himself well enough,
But in brief, the sword will cause his death.

XXV.   Six hundred and six, six hundred and nine,
A Chancellor large as an ox,
Old as the Phoenix of the world,
In this world will shine no more,
He will pass with the ship of oblivion,
To the Elysian Fields to make his round.

XXVI.   Two brothers are of the Ecclesiastical order,
One of them will take up the pike for France,
Another blow if in the year six hundred and six
He is not afflicted with a great malady,
Arms in his hand up to six hundred and ten,
Scarcely much further does his life extend.

XXVII.   Celestial fire from the Western side,
And from the South, running up to the East,
Worms half dead without finding even a root,
Third age, for Mars the Warlike,
One will see fires shining from the Carbuncles,
Age a Carbuncle, and in the end famine.

XXVIII. L'an mil six cens & neuf ou quatorziesme,
Le vieux Charon fera Pasques en Charesme,
Six cens & six, par escript le mettra
Le Medecin, de tout cecy s'estonne,
A mesme temps assigné en personne
Mais pour certain l'vn d'eux comparoistra.

XXIX. Le Griffon se peut aprester
Pour à l ennemy resister,
Et renforcer bien son armée,
Autremenr l'Elephant viendra
Qui d'vn a bord le surprendra,
Six cens & huict, mer enflammée.

XXX. Dans peu de temps Medecin du grand mal,
Et la sangsuë d'ordre & rang inegal,
Mettront le feu à la branche d'Oliue,
Poste courir, d'vn & d'autre costé,
Et par tel feu leur Empire accosté,
Se r'alumant du franc finy saliue.

XXXI. Celuy qui a, les hazards surmonte,
Qui fer, feu, eauë, n'a iamais redouté,
Et du pays bien proche du Basacle,
D'vn coup de fer tout le monde estouné,
Par Crocodil estrangement donné,
Peuple raui de veoir vn tel spectacle.

XXXII. Vin à foison, tres bon pour les gendarmes',
Pleurs & souspirs, plainctes cris & alarme—
Le Ciel fera ses tonnerres pleuuoir
Feu, eau & sang, le tout meslé ensemble,
Le Ciel de sol, en fremit & en tremble,
Viuant n'a veu ce qu'il pourra bien veoir.

XXXIII. Bien peu apres sera tres-grande misere,
Du peu de bled, qui sera sur la terre,
Du Dauphiné, Prouence & Viuarois,
Au Viuarois est vn pauure presage,
Pere du fils, sera entropophage,
Et mangeront racine & gland du bois.

XXXIIII. Princes & Seigneurs tous se feront la guerre,
Cousin germain le frere auec le frere,
Finy l'Arby de l'heureux de Bourbon,
De Hierusalem les Princes tant aymables,
Du fait commis enorme & execrable,
Se ressentiront sur la bourse sans fond.

XXVIII. The year one thousand six hundred and nine or fourteen,
The old Charon will celebrate Easter in Lent,
Six hundred and six, in writing he will place it
The Physician, by all this is astonished,
At the same time summoned in person
But for certain one of them will appear.

XXIX. The Griffon is able to prepare himself
For resisting the enemy,
And to reinforce well his army,
Otherwise the Elephant will come
He who will suddenly surprise him,
Six hundred and eight, the sea aflame.

XXX. In a short while the Physician of the great disease,
And the leech of the unequal rank and order,
They will set fire to the Olive branch,
Post running, from one side and another,
And by means of such fire their Empire approached,
Being rekindled by the Frank saliva finished.

XXXI. He who has overcome the hazards,
Who has ne'er dreaded sword, fire, water,
And of the country very close to Toulouse,
By a blow of steel the entire world astonished,
Strangely given by the Crocodile,
People delighted to see such a spectacle.

XXXII. Wine in abundance, very good for the troops',
Tears and sighs, complaints, groans and alarm
The Sky will cause its thunderbolts to rain
Fire, water and blood, all mixed together,
Sun's heaven, shaking and trembling from it,
That which can be seen clearly no living person has
e'er seen.

XXXIII. Very soon after there will be very great misery,
From the scarcity of grain, which will be on the land
Of Dauphiny, Provence and Vivarais,
To Vivarais it is a poor prediction,
Father will eat his own son,
And from the woods they will eat root and acorn.

XXXIIII. Princes and Lords will all make war against one another,
First cousin brother against brother,
Araby by the happy ones of Bourbon finished,
The Princes of Jerusalem very agreeable,
Of the heinous and execrable deed committed,
They will feel the effects on the bottomless purse.

XXXV. The Lady greatly saddened by death,
Mother and guardian to the blood which has
abandoned her,
The Lady and Lords, children made orphans,
By the slanderers and by the Crocodiles,
Strong Towns and Castle Cities will be surprised
God almighty guards them from the wicked ones.

XXXVI. The great rumor which will be throughout France,
The powerless will want to have power,
Honeyed tongue and true Chameleons,
Of incendiaries, lighters of Candles,
Magpies and jays, reporters of news,
Of whom the bite will be like that of Scorpions.

XXXVII. The weak and the powerful will be in great discord,
Several will die before agreement is reached
The weak one will speak up to the powerful conqueror,
The most powerful one will give way to the young one,
And the older of the two will pass away,
When one of them will invade the Empire.

XXXVIII. By water, and by steel, and by great illness,
The purveyor at the risk of his life
Will know the worth of the hundredweight of wood,
Six hundred and fifteen, or nineteenth,
Of a great fifth Prince one will engrave
The immortal name, on the foot of the Cross.

XXXIX. The purveyor of the unparalleled monster,
He will see himself even as the Sun,
Mounting the length of the Meridian line,
In pursuing the Elephant and the wolf,
No Emperor ever delivered such a blow,
And nothing worse happens to this Prince.

XL. He who his father alive did not know,
He will gain either by war or by fire
And will battle with the irritated leech,
Or will enjoy his paternal endowment
And favored by the great Eternal God,
He will come into his Province very soon.

XLI. Vessels and galleys with their standards,
They will engage in combat near the rock of Gibraltar
And then there will be heinous crimes at Pamplona,
Which for its benefit will suffer a thousand hurts.
Several times it will sustain assaults,
But in the end united to the Crown.

XLII.   La grand' Cité où est le premier homme,
       Bien amplement la ville ie vous nomme,
       Tout en alarme, & le soldat és champs
       Par fer & eauë, grandement affligée,
       Et à la fin des François soulagée,
       Mais ce sera dés six cens & dix ans.

XLIII.   Le petit coing, Prouinces mutinées
       Par forts Chasteaux se verront dominées,
       Encor vn coup par la gent militaire,
       Dans bref seront fortement assiegez,
       Mais ils seront d'vn tres-grand soulagez,
       Qui aura fait entrée dans Beaucaire.

XLIIII.   La belle rose en la France admirée,
       D'vn tres-grand Prince à la fin desirée,
       Six cens & dix, lors naistront ses amours
       Cinq ans apres, sera d'vn grand blessée,
       Du trait d'Amour, elle sera enlassée,
       Si à quinze ans du Ciel reçoit secours.

XLV.   De coup de fer tout le monde estonné,
       Pa Crocodil estrangement donné,
       A vn bien grand, parent de la sangsue,
       Et peu apres sera vn autre coup
       De guet à pens, commis contre le loup,
       Et de tels faits on ne verra l'issuë.

XLVI.   Le pouruoyeur mettra tout en desroute,
       Sansuë & loup, en mon dire n'escoute
       Quand Mars sera au signe du Mouton
       Ioint à Saturne, & Saturne à la Lune,
       Alors sera ta plus grande infortune,
       Le Soleil lors en exaltation.

XLVII.   Le grand d'Hongrie, ira dans la nacelle,
       Le nouueau né fera guerre nouuelle
       A son voisin qu'il tiendra assiegé,
       Et le noireau auec son altesse,
       Ne souffrira, que par trop on le presse,
       Durant trois ans ses gens tiendra rangé.

XLVIII.   Du vieux Charron on verra le Phœnix,
       Estre premier & dernier des fils,
       Reluyre en France, & d'vn chascun aymable,
       Regner long temps auec tous les honneurs
       Qu'auront iamais eu ses precesseurs
       Dont il rendra sa gloire memorable.

XLII. The great city where the first man is,
Quite amply am I naming the town to you,
All in alarm, and the soldier in the fields
Through fire and water, greatly afflicted,
And in the end relieved by the French,
But this will be from six hundred and ten years.

XLIII. The little corner, Provinces mutinous
Will see themselves dominated by strong Castles,
Another blow by the military people,
In brief they will be strongly besieged.
But they will be relieved by a very great one,
Who will have made an entry into Beaucaire.

XLIIII. The beautiful rose admired in France,
In the end desired by a very great Prince,
Six hundred and ten, then her love will come
Five years after, she will be wounded by a great one,
By the arrow of Love, she will be entwined,
If by fifteen years she receives assistance from Heaven.

XLV. The entire world astonished by blow of steel,
Strangely given by the Crocodile,
To a very great one, relative of the leech,
And shortly after there will be another blow
By foul play, committed against the wolf,
And of such deeds one will not see the result.

XLVI. The purveyor will put all to route,
Leech and wolf, he does not heed my word
When Mars will be in the sign of Aries
Joined to Saturn, and Saturn to the Moon,
Then your greater misfortune will take place,
The Sun then in exaltation.

XLVII. The great one of Hungary, he will go into the bark,
The new heir will make new war
Against his neighbor whom he will hold besieged,
And the dark one with her highness
Will not allow him to be pressed too much,
For three years he will keep his people arrayed.

XLVIII. One will see the Phoenix of old Charon
To be first and last of the sons,
To rekindle in France, and loved by everyone,
To reign a long time with all the honors
That will ever have been had by his predecessors
Whose glory he will render memorable.

XLIX.  Venus & Sol, Iupiter & Mercure
       Augmenteront le genre de nature
       Grande alliance en France se fera,
       Et du Midy la sangsue de mesme,
       Le feu esteint par ce remede extreme,
       En terre ferme Oliuer plantera.


    L.  Vn peu deuant ou apres l'Angleterre
        Par mort de loup. mise aussi bas que terre,
        Verra le feu resister contre l'eau,
        Le r'alumant auecques telles force
        Du sang humain, dessus l'humaine escorse
        Faite de pain, bondance de cousteau.


   LI.  La Ville qu'auoit en ses ans
        Combatu l'iniure du temps,
        Qui de son vainqueur tient la vie,
        Celuy qui premier l'a surprist,
        Que peu apre François reprist
        Par combats encor affoiblie.


  LII.  La grand Cité qui n'a pain à demy,
        Encor vn coup la sainct Barthelemy,
        Engrauera au profond de son ame,
        Nismes, Rochelle, Geneue & Montpellier,
        Castres, Lyon, Mars entrant au Belier,
        S'entrebattront le tout pour vne Dame.


 LIII.  Plusieurs mourront auant que Phœnix meure,
        Iusques six cens septante est sa demeure,
        Passé quinze ans, vingt & vn, trente neuf,
        Le premier est subiet à maladie,
        Et le second au fer, danger de vie,
        Au feu à l'eau, est subiect à trente-neuf.


LIIII.  Six cens et quinze, vingt, grand Dame mourra,
        Et peu apres vn fort long temps plouura,
        Plusieurs pays, Flandres & l'Angleterre,
        Seront par feu & par fer affligez,
        De leurs voisins longuement assiegez,
        Contraints seront de leurs faire la guerre.


   LV.  Vn peu deuant ou apres tres-grand' Dame,
        Son ame au Ciel, & son corps soubs la lame,
        De plusieurs gens regrettée sera,
        Tous ses parens seront en grand' tristesse,
        Pleurs & souspirs d'vne Dame en ieunesse,
        Et à deux grands, le dueil delaissera.

XLIX. Venus and the Sun, Jupiter and Mercury
Will augment the forms of nature:
A great alliance will be made in France,
And the leech in the South the same,
The fire put out by this extreme remedy,
In farmland will he plant the Olive Tree.

L. Shortly before or after England
By the death of the wolf, likewise put low as the earth,
Will see fire resisting water,
Relighting it with immense force
Of human blood, upon the human crust
Made with bread, abundance of knife.

LI. The town which had in its years
Fought against the ravages of time,
Which holds its life from its conqueror,
The one who first surprised it,
Which shortly after the French took again
Again weakened by struggles.

LII. The great City which has not bread by halves,
Yet another blow St. Bartholomew
Will engrave in the depths of its soul,
Nîmes, La Rochelle, Geneva and Montpellier,
Castres, Lyons, Mars entering into Aries,
All fighting each other for a Lady.

LIII. Many will die before the Phoenix dies,
Up to six hundred and seventy is its span,
Gone by fifteen years, twenty-one, thirty-nine,
The first is subject to malady,
And the second to steel, in danger of life,
To fire and water is he subject at thirty-nine.

LIIII. Six hundred and fifteen, twenty, the great Lady will die,
And shortly after it will rain for a very long time,
Several countries, Flanders and England,
They will be afflicted by fire and sword,
Long besieged by their neighbors,
They will be obliged to make war against them.

LV. Shortly before or after a very great Lady,
Her soul to Heaven, and her body under the blade,
She will be regretted by many people,
All her relatives will be in great sadness,
Tears and sighs by a Lady in her youth,
And by two great ones, the mourning will be abandoned.

LVI.   Tost l'Elephant de toutes parts verra
       Quand pouruoyeur au Griffon se ioindra,
       Sa ruine proche, & Mars qui tousiours gronde:
       Fera grands faits aupres de terre saincte,
       Grands estendars sur la terre & sur l'onde,
       Si la nef a esté de deux freres enceinte.

LVII.  Peu apres l'aliance faicte,
       Auant solemniser la feste,
       L'Empereur le tout troublera,
       Et la nouuelle mariée,
       Au franc pays par sort liée,
       Dans peu de temps apres mourra.

LVIII. Sangsuë en peu de temps mourra,
       Sa mort bon signe nous donra,
       Pour l'accroissement de la France,
       Alliance se trouueront,
       Deux grands Royaumes se ioindront,
       François aura sur eux puissance.

## B. The Anti-Mazarin Pair (1649)[1]

Quant Innocent tiendra le lieu de Pierre,
Le Nizaram cicilien (se verra
En grands honneurs) mais après il cherra
Dans le bourbier d'une civille guerre.

Latin en Mars, Sénateurs en crédit,
Par une nuict Gaule sera troublée.
Du grand Croesus l'Horoscope prédit,
Par Saturnus, sa puissance exillée.

[1] In the false edition, predated 1568 (See "Nostradamus Bibliography"), these two appeared as 42 and 43 in the seventh Century. being followed by the real 42 as 44.

LVI. Soon the Elephant will see on all sides
When the purveyor joins himself to the Griffon,
His ruin near, and Mars who roars every day:
He will perform great deeds near holy land,
Great standards on land and sea,
If the ship has been encompassed by two brothers.

LVII. Shortly after the alliance is made,
Before the feast is solemnized,
Everything will trouble the Emperor,
And the new bride,
Bound to France by chance,
Shortly after she will die.

LVIII. The leech in a short time will die,
His death will provide us with a good sign,
For the enlargement of France,
They will find each other in alliance,
Two great Kingdoms will join together,
The French will have power over them.

## B. The Anti-Mazarin Pair (1649)

When Innocent will hold the place of Peter,
The Sicilian Nizaram (he will be seen
In great honors) but after he will fall
In the slough of a civil war.

Latin in Mars, Senators in repute,
For one night Gaul will be troubled.
Of the great Croesus the Horoscope predicted,
By Saturn, his power exiled.

## C. The Prophecy of Olivarius (1820)[1]

Prophétie extraite d'un vieux livre de prophéties de Philippe-Dieu-
donné-Noel Olivarius, imprimé en 1542; soustrait pendant la révolution chez les cidevant Bénédictins de . . .

La Gaule *itale* verra naître non loin de son sein un être supernaturel. Cet
homme sortira tout jeune de la mer, viendra prendre langue et mœurs chez
les Celtes-Gaulois; s'ouvrira, encore jeune, à travers mille obstacles chez les
soldats, un chemin, et deviendra leur premier chef.

Ce chemin sinueux lui baillera force peines. S'enviendra guerroyer près
de son natal pays par un lustre et plus; outre mer sera vu guerroyant avec
grande gloire et valeur et guerroyera de nouveau l'Italie, donnera des lois aux
Germains, pacifiera troubles et terreurs aux Gaulois-Celtes, et sera nommé
ainsi non *roi*, mais peu après appelé *imperator*, par grand enthousiasme populaire; bataillera partout dans l'Empire; déchassera princes, seigneurs, rois
par deux lustres et plus; puis élevera de nouvels princes et seigneurs à vie,
et parlant sur son estrade, criera: Peuples, ô sidera! ô sacra!

Sera vu avec armée forte de quarante-neuf fois vingt mille piétons armés,
qui porteront armes à cornets de fer; il aura sept fois sept fois sept mille
chevaux montés d'hommes qui porteront, plus que les premiers grande épée
ou lance et corps d'airain; il aura sept fois sept fois deux mille hommes qui
feront jouer machines terribles, vomiront et soufre et feu et mort. La toute
suppute de son armée sera de quarante-neuf fois vingt-neuf mille, portera
en dextre main une aigle, signe de la victoire à guerroyer; donnera maints
pays aux nations, et à chacun paix; s'en viendra dans la grande ville, ordon-
nant force grandes choses: édifices, ponts, ports de mer, aqueducs, canaux;
fera à lui tout seul, par grandes richesses, autant que tous Romains et tous
dans les dominations des Gaules.

Aura femme par deux, et fils un seul; s'en ira guerroyant jusqu'où se croi-
sent les lignes longitude et latitude, cinquante-cinq mois; là ses ennemis
brûleront par feu la grande ville, et lui y entrera et sortira avec siens de dessous cendres, force ruines; et les siens n'ayant plus ni pain ni eau, par grande
et décide froidure, qui seront si malencontres, et que les deux tierces parties
de son armée périront, et en plus par demie l'autre, lui n'étant plus en sa
domination.

Lors le plus grand homme, abandonné, trahi par les siens amis, pour-
chassé à son tour par grande perte jusque dans sa grande ville, et déchassé
par grande population européenne, à la sienne place sera mis les rois du
vieil sang de la Cap.

Lui, contraint à l'exil dans la mer dont est devenu si jeune, et proche de
son natal lieu y demeurera par onze lunes avec quelques-uns des siens, vrais
amis et soldats, qui, n'étant plus que sept fois sept fois sept fois deux fois de

---

[1]This first appeared in *Mémoires historiques et secrets de l'impératrice Joséphine* by
Mlle M. A. Le Normand (Paris, 1820, Vol. II, pp. 470-73). Napoleon was supposed to
have carried it about him. It was given further notice by Bareste in 1839 and 1840, and
Torné-Chavigny several decades later. Both sought to add the prophecy to Nostradamus'
works.

## C. The Prophecy of Olivarius (1820)

Prophecy extracted from an old book of prophecies of Philippe-Dieudonné-Noël Olivarius, printed in 1542; confiscated during the revolution from the former Benedictines of . . .

*Italic* Gaul will see born not far from its heart a supernatural being. This man will come out from the sea quite young and will come to acquire the language and customs of the Celtic Gauls; he will open for himself, while still young, a way through a thousand obstacles with his soldiers, and will become their first chief.

This sinuous road will give him many troubles. He will come to wage war near his native land for five years and more; he will be seen waging war beyond the sea with great glory and valor and will again wage war in Italy, will give laws to the Germans, will calm the troubles and terrors among the Celtic Gauls, and will thus be named not *king*, but shortly after called *emperor*, through great popular enthusiasm; he will battle everywhere in the Empire; he will drive out princes, lords, kings for ten years and more; then he will elevate new princes and lords for life, and speaking on his platform, will cry: Peoples, O stars! O gods!

He will be seen with a strong army of forty-nine times twenty thousand armed foot soldiers with steel horns; he will have seven times seven times seven thousand horses mounted by men who will bear, more than the first ones a great sword or lance and bodies of brass; he will have seven times seven times two thousand men who will ply terrible engines, which will vomit forth sulphur and fire and death. The total count of his army will be forty-nine times twenty-nine thousand and he will carry in his right hand an eagle, the emblem of victory in warfare; he will give many lands to the nations, and to each one peace; he will come into the great city, ordering many great things: edifices, bridges, seaports, aqueducts, canals; he will do this by himself alone, through great riches, as great as all the Romans' and all within the domination of the Gauls.

He will have a wife twice, and a single son; he will go forth waging war as far as where the lines of longitude and latitude cross, fifty-five months; there his enemies will burn the great city with fire, and there will he enter and depart with his men from amidst ashes and many ruins; and his men no longer having bread or water, because of great and decisive cold which will be so fatal that two thirds of his army will perish, and more than half of the remainder being no longer under his control.

Then the very great man, abandoned, betrayed by his own friends, pursued in his turn with great loss right into his great city, and driven out by the great European population, will be replaced by the kings of the ancient blood of the Capet.

He, forced into exile in the sea from which he came so young, and near his native land will remain there for eleven moons with some of his own true friends and soldiers, who, being no more than seven times seven times seven

nombre, aussitôt les onze lunes parachevées, que lui et les siens prendre navires et venir mettre pied sur terre Celte-Gauloise, et lui cheminer vers la grande ville où s'être assis le roi du vieil sang de la Cap, qui se lève, fuit, emportant à lui ornemens royaux, pose chose en son aulienne domination; donne aux peuples force lois admirables. Ains, déchassé de nouveau par trinité population européenne, après trois lunes et tiers de lune, est remis à la sienne place le roi du vieil sang de la Cap; et lui cru mort par ses peuples et soldats qui, dans ce tems, garderont pénates contre leurs cœurs.

Les peuples et les Gaulois, comme tigres et loups, s'entre-dévoreront. Le sang du vieil roi de la Cap sera le jouet de noires trahisons; les malencontreux seront décus, et par fer et par feu seront occis, le *lis* maintenu; mais les derniers rameaux du vieil sang seront encore menacés, ains guerroyeront entre eux.

Lors un jeune guerrier cheminera vers la grande ville, il portera lion et coq sur son armure: ains la lance lui sera donnée par grand prince d'Orient. Il sera secondé merveilleusement par peuple guerrier de la Gaule-Belgique, qui se réuniront aux Parisiens pour trancher troubles et réunir soldats, et les couvrir tous de rameaux d'oliviers, guerroyant encore avec tant de gloire sept fois sept lunes, que trinité populations européenne, par grande crainte et cris et pleurs, offrant leurs fils et épouses en ôtages, et ployant sous les lois saines et justes, et aimées de tous. Ains paix durant vingt-cinq lunes.

Dans *Lutetia,* la Seine, rougie par sang, suite de combats à outrance, étendra son lit par ruine et mortalité, séditions nouvelles de malencontreux *maillotins.* Ains seront pourchassés du palais des rois par l'homme valeureux, et par après les immenses Gaules déclarées par toutes les nations grande et mère-nation; et lui, sauvant restes échappés du vieil sang de la Cap, règle les destinées du monde, dictant conseil souverain de toute nation et de tout peuple, pose base de fruit sans fin, et meurt.

times two in number, as soon as eleven moons have passed, will with him take ships and will come to set foot on Celtic-Gallic land, and will walk towards the great city where sitteth the king of the ancient blood of the Capet, who arises, flees, carrying with him royal ornaments [whereupon] he sets everything under his aulian control, giving to the people many admirable laws. Then, driven out again by the trinity of the European population, after three and a third moons, the king of the ancient blood of the Capet is put back in his place; and he believed dead by his people and soldiers who, in this time, will guard their homes against their hearts.

The nations and the Gauls, like tigers and wolves, will devour each other. The blood of the old king of the Capet will be the sport of black treasons; the unfortunate ones will be deceived, and by fire and sword slain, the *lily* upheld; but the last branches of the ancient blood will again be threatened and will wage war against each other.

Then a young warrior will walk towards the great city, bearing upon his armor a lion and a cock: then the lance will be given him by the great prince of the East. He will be seconded marvelously by the warrior people of Belgian Gaul, who will join the Parisians to resolve the troubles and unite soldiers, covering them all with olive branches, waging war again with so much glory for seven times seven moons that the trinity of the European population, through great fear and cries and tears, will offer their sons and wives as hostages and submit to sane and just laws, cherished by all. Then peace for twenty-five moons.

In *Paris*, the Seine, reddened by blood, after combats at its mouth, will extend its bed through ruin and mortality and new seditions of unfortunate *infants*. Then they will be pursued from the palace of the kings by the valorous man, and afterwards the mighty Gauls will be recognized by all nations as the great mother-nation; and he, sparing the rest escaped from the ancient blood of the Capet, rules the destinies of the world, dictating the sovereign counsel of every nation and all people and sets down with endless offspring, and dies.

# D. The Prophecy of Orval (1839)[1]

... la fameuse prophetie dite d'*Orval*, écrite
en 1544, par Philippe Olivarius.[2]

En ce temps-là un jeune homme venu d'outre-mer dans le pays du Celte-Gaulois se manifestera par conseil de force; mais les Grands ombragés l'envoieront guerroyer dans l'isle de la captivité. La victoire le ramènera au pays premier. Les fils de Brutus, moult stupides, seront à son approche: car il les dominera, et prendra nom Empereur.

Moult hauts et puissans rois sont en crainte vraie, car l'aigle enlève moult sceptres et moult couronnes. Piétons et cavaliers portant aigles sanglantes, avec lui courrent autant de moucherons dans les airs; et toute l'europe est moult ébahie, aussi moult sanglante, car il sera tant fort que Dieu sera cru guerroyer avec lui.

L'Église de Dieu se console tant peu en oyant ouvrir encore ses temples à ses brebis tout plein égarées, et Dieu est béni.

Mais c'est fait, les lunes sont passées. Le Vieillard de Sion crie à Dieu de son cœur moult endolori par peine cuisante, et voilà que le puissant est aveuglé pour péché et crimes. Il *quitte*[3] la grande ville avec une armée si belle que oncques ne se vit jamais si telle. Mais point de guerrier ne tiendra bon devant la force du temps, et voilà que la tierce part de son armée et encore la tierce part a péri par le froid du Seigneur puissant. Mais deux lustres sont passés d'après le siècle de la désolation, comme j'ai dit à son lieu. Tout plein fort ont crié les veuves et les orphelins, et voilà que Dieu n'est plus sourd.

Les Haults abaissés reprennent force et font ligue pour abattre l'homme tant redouté. Voici venir avec eux le vieux sang des siècles qui reprend place et lieu en la grande Ville: ce pendant que l'homme dit moult abaissé va au pays d'outre-mer d'où il étoit advenu.

Dieu seul est grand; la lune onzième n'a pas lui encore. et le fouet sanguinolent du Seigneur revient en la grande ville; et le vieux sang quitte la grande ville.

Dieu seul est grand; il aime son peuple et a le sang en haine; la cinquième lune a relui sur maints guerroyers d'Orient; la Gaule est couverte d'hommes et de machines de guerre: c'est fait de l'homme de mer. Voici encore venir le vieux sang de la Cap.

[1] It first appeared in *L'Oracle pour 1840* .. by Henri Dujardin (Paris, 1839), with the note that it had been copied in 1823 from a little booklet *printed* at Luxembourg in 1544. It was reprinted in Bareste's work of 1840 (pp. 218–23), whence we have copied it exactly.

[2] Such is Bareste's heading, presumably a quote from Dujardin. Bareste admitted he couldn't find the book of 1544 and made no mention of having even seen the reprint of 1823.

[3] Bareste (or Dujardin) inserted this word for a "poorly printed and illegible word in the original."

# D. The Prophecy of Orval (1839)

... the famous prophecy attributed to Orval,
written in 1544, by Philippe Olivarius.

At that time a young man come from beyond the sea into the country of
the Celtic Gauls will make himself known through counsel of force; but the
Great Ones overshadowed will send him to wage war in the isle of the captivity. Victory will lead him back to the first country. The sons of Brutus,
very stupid, will be at his service: for he will dominate them, and take the
name Emperor.

Many high and powerful kings are in true fear, for the eagle carries off
many sceptres and many crowns. Infantry and cavalry carrying bloody
eagles run with him as plentiful as gnats in the air; and all Europe is much
amazed, also very bloody, for he will be so strong that God will be thought
to wage war with him.

The Church of God consoles itself very little in hearing its temples opened
again to its sheep quite fully strayed, and God is blessed.

But it is done, the moons have passed. The Elder of Zion cries to God
with his heart grieving much from a sharp pain, and behold the powerful
one blinded for sin and crimes. He leaves the great city with an army so
magnificent that the likes of it was never seen. But no warrior will stand well
before the force of time, and behold, the third part of his army and another
third perished through the cold of the powerful Lord. But ten years have
passed since the age of desolation, as I have said in its place. Quite fully
loudly have the widows and orphans cried out, and behold, God is no longer
deaf.

The High Ones humbled take force again and make a league to bring
down the man so redoubtable. Behold coming with them the old blood of
the centuries which takes its place again in the great City: this while the man
considered thoroughly humbled goes to the land beyond the sea whence he
had come.

God alone is great; the eleventh moon has him no longer, and the san-
guineous whip of the Lord returns to the great City; and the old blood leaves
the great city.

God alone is great; he loves his people and hates blood; the fifth moon
has lighted again on many warriors from the East; Gaul is covered with men
and machines of war: the man from the sea is done for. Behold coming again
the old blood of the Capet.

Dieu veut la paix et que son saint nom soit béni. Or, paix grande et *florissante*[4] sera au pays de *céleste* Gaulois. La fleur blanche est en honneur moult grand; la maison de Dieu chante moult saints cantiques. Cependant les fils de Brutus oyent avec ire la fleur blanche et obtiennent réglement puissant: ce pourquoi Dieu est encore moult fâché à cause de ses élus et pour ce que le saint jour est encore moult profané. Pourtant Dieu veut éprouver le retour à lui par 18 fois 12 lunes.

Dieu seul est grand; il purge son peuple par maintes tribulations; mais toujours les mauvais auront fin.

Sus donc, lors une grande conspiration contre la fleur blanche chemine dans l'ombre par vue de compagnie maudite; et le pauvre vieux sang de la Cap quitte la grande Ville, et moult gaudissent les fils de Brutus. Oyez comme les servants de Dieu crient tout fort à Dieu et que Dieu est sourd par le bruit des ses flèches qu'il retrempe en son ire pour les mettre au sein des mauvais.

Malheur au céleste Gaulois! le coq effacera la fleur blanche, et un grand s'appelle le Roi du peuple. Grande commotion se fera sentir chez les gens, parceque la couronne sera posée par des mains d'ouvriers qui auront guerroyé dans la grande ville.

Dieu seul est grand; le règne des mauvais sera vu croître; mais qu'ils se hâtent: voilà que les pensées du céleste Gaulois se choquent et que grande division est dans l'entendement. Le Roi du peuple en abord vu moult foible et pourtant contre ira bien des mauvais. Mais il n'étoit pas bien assis, et voilà que Dieu le *jette bas.* . . .

Hurlez fils de Brutus, appelez sur vous les bêtes qui vont vous dévorer! Dieu grand! quel bruit d'armes! Il n'y a pas encore un nombre plein de lunes, et voici venir maints guerroyers.

C'est fait: la montagne de Dieu désolée a crié à Dieu; les fils de Juda ont crié à Dieu de la terre étrangère, et voilà que Dieu n'est plus sourd. Quel feu va avec ses flèches! Dix fois six lunes et puis encore six fois dix lunes ont nourri sa colère. Malheur à toi grande ville! Voici des rois armés par le Seigneur; mais déjà le feu t'a égalée à la terre. Pourtant tes justes ne périront pas: Dieu les a écoutés. La place du crime est purgée par le feu; le grand ruisseau a conduit, toutes rouges de sang, ses eaux à la mer; et la Gaule vue comme délabrée va se rejoindre.

Dieu aime la paix. Venez jeune prince; quittez l'isle de la captivité; joignez le lion à la fleur blanche.

Ce qui est prévu Dieu le veut; le vieux sang des siècles terminera encore de longues divisions. Lors un seul pasteur sera vu dans la céleste Gaule. L'homme puissant par Dieu s'assoyra bien; moult sages réglements appelleront la paix. Dieu sera cru d'avec lui tant prudent et sage sera le rejeton de la Cap.

Grâce au père de la miséricorde la sainte Sion rechante dans ses temples un seul Dieu grand! Moult brebis égarées s'en viennent boire au ruisseau vif:

---

[4]All words in italics, according to Bareste, are logical guesses for illegible words. This brilliant device is almost sufficient to make the 1544 story convincing.

God desires peace and that his holy name be blessed. Accordingly, great and flourishing peace will come to the land of heavenly Gaul. The white flower is in very great honor; the house of God sings many holy songs. However, the sons of Brutus hear with anger the white flower and obtain powerful rule: therefore God is again very angry on behalf of his chosen ones and because the holy day is again greatly profaned. Nevertheless God is willing to try his return for eighteen times twelve moons.

God alone is great; he purges his people by many tribulations; but always the bad ones will have their end.

Now then, then a great conspiracy against the white flower proceeds in the shadow in sight of the cursed company; and the poor old blood of the Capet leaves the great City, and the sons of Brutus rejoice greatly. Listen as the servants of God cry out very loudly to God and God is so deaf because of the noise of his arrows that he grows stronger in his anger to place them in the bosom of the evil ones.

Woe to heavenly Gaul! the cock will erase the white flower, and a great one calls himself the King of the people. Great commotion will make itself felt by the people, because the crown will be set by the hands of workers who will have warred in the great city.

God alone is great; the kingdom of the evil ones will be seen to grow; but let them hasten: behold the thoughts of the heavenly Gaul clashing with each other and there is great division in understanding. The King of the people at once seen very weak and yet he will go against the good of the evil ones. But he was not well seated, and behold, God hurls him down. . . .

Howl, ye sons of Brutus, call down upon yourselves the beasts who are going to devour you! Great God! what a clash of arms! There are no longer a full number of moons, and behold many warriors coming.

It is done: the desolated mountain of God has cried out to God; the sons of Judah have cried out to God from the foreign land, and behold, God is no longer deaf. What fire goes with his arrows! Ten times six moons and then further six times ten moons have fed his anger. Woe to you, great city! Behold the kings armed by the Lord; but already fire has leveled you with the earth. Yet your just ones will not perish: God has listened to them. The place of the crime is purged by fire; the great stream has led, all red with blood, its waters to the sea; and Gaul seen shattered sets out to reunite itself again.

God loves peace. Come, young prince; leave the isle of captivity; join the lion to the white flower.

That which is foreseen God wills; the old blood of the ages will terminate again with long divisions. Then a single pastor will be seen in heavenly Gaul. The powerful man will be well assured by God; many wise laws they will call peace. So prudent and wise will the scion of the Capet be that God will be believed to be with him.

Thanks to the father of pity the holy Zion sings again in his temples a single great God! Many strayed sheep come to drink of it in the running

trois princes et rois mettent bas le manteau de l'erreur et oyent clair en la foi de Dieu.

En se temps-là un grand peuple de la mer reprendra vraie croyance en deux tierces parts. Dieu est encore béni pendant quatorze fois six lunes et six fois treize lunes. Dieu est saoûl d'avoir baillé des miséricordes, et ce pourtant il veut pour ses bons prolonger la paix encore pendant dix fois douze lunes.

Dieu seul est grand. Les biens sont faits; les saints vont souffrir. L'homme du mal arrive de deux sangs, et prend croissance. La fleur blanche s'obscurcie pendant dix fois six lunes et six fois vingt lunes, puis disparoit pour ne plus paroitre.

Moult maux, guère de bien en ce temps-là, moult villes périssent par le feu. Sus donc Israel vient à Dieu tout de bon.

Sectes maudites et sectes fidèles sont en deux parts bien marquées. Mais c'est fait; lors, Dieu seul sera cru, et la tierce part de la Gaule et encore la tierce part et demie n'a plus de croyance.

Comme aussi tout de même des autres gens.

Et voilà déjà six fois trois lunes et quatre fois cinq lunes que tout se sépare, et le siècle de fin a commencé.

Après un nombre non plein de lunes, Dieu combat par ses deux justes et l'homme du mal a le dessus. Mais c'est fait le haut Dieu met un mur de feu qui obscurcit mon entendement et je n'y vois plus. Qu'il soit loué à jamais!

stream: three princes and kings cast off the mantle of error and hear clear in the faith of God.

At that time a great people of the sea will take back their true belief in two third parts. God is again blessed for fourteen times six moons and six times thirteen moons. God is through with having extended pity and yet he wants his good ones to prolong the peace for ten times twelve moons more.

God alone is great. The good deeds are done; the holy ones are going to suffer. The man of evil comes from two bloods, and grows in power. The white flower is obscured for ten times six moons and six times twenty moons, then disappears never to be seen again.

Many evils, scarcely any good at that time, many towns perish by fire. Now then Israel comes to God all good.

Cursed sects and faithful sects are well marked in two parts. But it is done; then, God alone will be believed, and the third part of Gaul and again the third part and half no longer has belief.

Quite the same also with other peoples.

And behold already six times three moons and four times five moons and then all is separated, and the age of the end has begun.

After a number not full of moons, God fights through his two just ones and the man of evil has the upper hand. But it is done, the high God places a wall of fire which obscures my understanding and I see no more. May he be praised forever.

# General Bibliography

## A. Works Connected With Nostradamus[1]

1506. [Albumazar (Abu-Maaschar).] *Introductorium in Astronomiam.* Venice.

1549. Jamblichus. *De mysteriis Aegyptiorum, Chaldaeorum, Assyriorum. Proclus in Platonicum Alcibiadem de anima atque Daemone. Porphyrius de Divinis atque Daemonibus. Psellus de Daemonibus. Mercurii Trismegisti Pimander, ac ejusdem Asclepius.* Lyons.

1550. Richard Roussat. *Livre de l'Estat et Mutation des Temps, prouvant par authoritez de l'Escripture saincte, et par raisons astrologales la fin du Monde estre prochaine.* Lyons.

Venons à parler de la grande et merueilleuse conionction que messieurs les Astrologues disent estre à venir enuiron les ans de nostre Seigneur mil sept cens octante et neuf auec dix révolutions Saturnales: et oultre enuiron vingt cinq ans apres, sera la quatrieme et derniere station de l'altitudinaire Firmament. Toutes ces choses imaginees et calculees, concluent les susdictz astrologues que, si le Monde jusques a ce & tel temps dure (qui est à Dieu seul congnu) de tres grandes et merueilleuses, & espouuentables mutations et alterations seront en cestuy vniuersel Monde: mesmement quant aux sectes et loyx. [P. 162.]

Maintenant donc je di que nous sommes en l'instant, & approchons de la future renouation du Monde, ou de grâdes alterations ou d'iceluy l'anichilation, enuiron deux cens quarante troys ans selon la côune supputation des Hysteriographes, en prenant à la date de la côpilation de ce présent traicté: laquelle date est posé et escripte à la fin d'iceluy. [P. 86.]

... quinzieme iour du moys de Febrier, l'an de grace mil cinq cens quarante huict. [P. 180.]

1569. "M. de Nostradamus le jeune." *Predictions pour vingt ans.* . . . Rouen.

1571. "M. de Nostradamus le jeune." *Prédictions des choses plus mémorables qui sont à advenir depuis cette présente année jusques à l'an mil cinq cens quatre vingt et cinq.* Troyes.

1571. "M. Anthoine Crespin Nostradamus." *Epistre (en vers) dédie au très-hault et très-chrestien Charles IX, roy de France . . . d'une signe admirable d'une comette apparue au ciel, ensemble l'interprétation du tremblement de terre de Ferrare et du déluge de Hollande, Anvers et de Lyon, que suyvront leurs effectz jusques en l'année 1584.* Paris.

1575. "Nostradamus le Ieune." *Recueil des révélations et propheties de Saincte Brigide, Sainct Cirile et plusieurs autres saincts et religieux personnages (par Fr. Gruget de Loche). Les augmentations de plusieurs révélations et prophéties extraictes de diuers liures.* . . . Venice.

---

[1]The previous bibliography ("Nostradamus Bibliography") consists of works by Nostradamus and those solely or principally about him. This bibliography consists of other works consulted or referred to, connected with Nostradamus only incidentally.

1584. François Grudé de la Croix Du Maine. *Premiere volume de la Bibliothèque françoise . . . qui est un catalogue général de toutes sortes d'autheurs qui ont escrit en françois depuis cinq cents ans plus jusques à ce jour.* Paris.

1614. César de Nostradame. *L'Histoire et Chronique de Provence . . . où passent de temps en temps et en bel ordre les Anciens Poëtes, Personnages et familles Illustres qui y ont fleury depuis 600 ans, oultre plusieurs races de France, d'Italie, Hespagne etc., comme aussi les plus signales combats et faits d'armes qui s'y ont passés.* Lyons.

1616–20. Théodore-Agrippa d'Aubigné. *L'Histoire universelle. . . .* Maillé.

1625. Gabriel Naudé. *Apologie pour tous les grands personnages qui ont esté faussement soupconnez de magie. . . .* Paris.

[*Ca.* 1650.] Gabriel Naudé. *Jugement de tout ce qui a esté imprimé contre le cardinal Mazarin depuis le 6 janvier jusqu'à la déclaration du 1ᵉʳ avril 1649.* Paris.

1659. [Pierre Gassendi.] *The Vanity of Judiciary Astrology or Divination by the Stars.* Lately written in Latin by that Great Schollar and Mathematician, the Illustrious Petrus Gassendus, Mathematical Professor to the King of France. Translated into English by a Person of Quality. London.

1664. Honoré Bouche. *La Chorographie ou description de Provence et l'histoire chronologique. . . .* Aix.

1666. Jean-Scholastique Pitton. *Histoire de la ville d'Aix.* Aix.

1682. Henri de Sponde. *Annalium Ecclesiasticorum Eminentissimi Cardinalis Caesaris Baronii Continuation ab Anno M.CXCVII Quo Is Desiit ad Finem M.DC.XLVI.* Pavia. (Vol. III, p. 327.)

1694. Jean François de Gaufridi. *Histoire de Provence.* Aix.

1767. Jean Astruc. *Memoires pour servir à l'histoire de la Faculté de médecine de Montpellier. . . .* Paris.

1792. *Journal Historique et Littéraire.* Paris. (Vol. I, p. 233.)

1820. Marie-Adelaide Le Normand. *Mémoires historiques et secrets de l'impératrice Joséphine.* Paris.

1834. Georges-Bernard Depping. *Les Juifs dans le moyen-âge. . . .* Paris.

1835. *Revue des Lyonnais.* Lyon. (Vol. II.)

1835. [Claude de l'Aubespine.] *Archives Curieuses de la France.* Paris. (Series I, Tome III, p. 295.)

Inclytissimus Gallorum rex Henricus christianissimus erit regum quorundam imperator, ante supremos cineres ad rerum culmina perveniet, foelicissimamque ac viridem senectam, uti colligitur ex Sole Venere et Luna horoscopantibus et potissimum Sole in suo trono partiliter suppotato. In civitatibus Arieti subjectis maximum sortietur dominium, si forte superaverit suae aetatis annos 56, 63, 64, ad annos 69 menses 10 dies 12, facili ac foelici tramite [variant: coelici transite] perducetur. A Gaurico observata quinquennio ante ipsius genitura, monuerat eum per literas, ne circiter unum et quadragesimum aetatis annum vitaret duellum, astra minari vulnus in capite, quod vel coecitatem vel mortem continuo afferet.

1838. "Collection de Documents Inédits sur l'Histoire de France." *Relations des Ambassadeurs Vénitiens sur les Affaires de France au XVI siècle.*

Paris. (*Relazione dell' eccelentissimo G. Michiel, ambassador, che ritornò dalla sua legazione l'anno 1561.* Venice. 1561. [P. 425.])

1839. Henri Dujardin. *L'Oracle pour 1840 et les années suivantes; ou, Recueil de prophéties anciennes et modernes.* . . . Paris.

1848. Henri Dujardin. *Deuxième supplément à l' "Oracle pour 1840" contenant un mémoire sur l'authenticité de la prophétie d'Orval, par la personne qui, en 1823, tira cette pièce d'un livre imprimée en 1544.* . . . Paris.

1863. Jacques-Charles Brunet. *Manuel du Libraire et de l'Amateur de Livres.* Paris. (Fifth Edition, Vol. IV. Also Supplement of 1880, Vol. II.)

1865. *Négociations diplomatiques de la France avec Toscane.* Paris.

1869. [Pierre de Bourdeille, Seigneur de Brantôme.] *Oeuvres Complètes.* (Edited by Ludovic Lalanne.) Paris.

1878. [Pierre de l'Estoile.] *Journal des choses advenus durant le regne de Henry III.* Paris.

1880. *Les Correspondants de Peiresc.* Marseilles. (Vol. II: *César Nostradamus.* Edited by Tamizey de Larroque.)

1882. Jean L.-M. Gimon. *Chroniques de la ville de Salon.* Aix.

1909. "Collection de Documents Inédits sur l'Histoire de France." *Lettres de Catherine de Médicis.* Paris. (Vol. X, p. 145.)

> . . . et pasant par Salons, avons veu Nostradamus, qui promest tou playn de bien au Roy mon filz, et qu'il vivera aultant que vous, qu'il dist aurés avant mourir quatre vins et dis ans . . .

1909. Dr. Walter Bormann. *Die Nornen.* Leipzig.

1911. Eugène De France. *Catherine de Médicis, ses astrologues et ses magiciens-envoûteurs.* . . . Paris.

1913. Jean de Nostredame. *Chronique de Provence.* Paris. (First publication of a 16th-century manuscript of Michel's brother.)

1915. Father Herbert J. Thurston. *The War and the Prophets.* London.

1927. Paul Van Dyke. *Catherine.* New York.

## B. Works Not Connected With Nostradamus

This Bibliography, unlike the others, is presented alphabetically inasmuch as the chronological order would have no significance for these reference works.

*Atlante Internazionale del Touring Club Italiano.* Milan, 1929.

Baedeker, Karl. [Handbooks on France, Italy and Spain.] Leipzig, v.d.

Bagot, Richard. *Lakes of Northern Italy.* Leipzig, 1908.

Baudrier, Henri. *Bibliographie Lyonnaise. Recherches sur les Imprimeurs, Libraires, Relieurs et Fondeurs de Lettres de Lyon au XVIᵉ Siècle.* Lyons, 1897.

Beaulieux, Charles. *Les accents et autres signes auxiliaires dans la langue française.* Paris, 1927.

Bimbenet, E. *Histoire de la ville d'Orléans.* Orléans, 1807.

Breban, M. Corrard de. *Recherches sur l'Établissement et l'Exercise de l'Imprimerie à Troyes*. Paris, 1873.

Catel, Guillaume de. *Mémoires de l'histoire du Languedoc*. Toulouse, 1633.

*Catholic Encyclopedia, The*. New York, 1907–12.

Cayla and Paviot. *Histoire de Toulouse*. Toulouse, 1839.

*Diccionario Enciclopédico Hispano-Americano*. Barcelona, 1887–98.

Edwardes, M., and L. Spence. *A Dictionary of Non-Classical Mythology*. London, 1912.

*Enciclopedia Italiana*. Milan, 1929–37.

*Encyclopedia of Islam, The*. London, 1913–38.

*Fort, Books of Charles*, New York, 1941. (One-volume collected works.)

Godefroy, Frédéric. *Dictionnaire de l'Ancienne Langue Française*. Paris, 1881–95.

Gould, George M., and Walter L. Pyle. *Anomalies and Curiosities of Medicine*. New York, 1896. Reprinted 1956.

Graesse, Jean G. T. *Orbis Latinus*. Berlin, 1922.

——. *Trésor de Livres Rares et Précieux ou Nouveau Dictionnaire Bibliographique*. Berlin, 1922.

*Grande Encyclopédie, La*. Paris, 1886–1902.

Guilhe, Henry-Charles. *Études sur l'Histoire de Bordeaux*. Bordeaux, 1835.

Honnorat, S. J. *Dictionnaire de la Langue d'Oc, Ancienne et Moderne*. Digne, 1946–47.

*Inventaire-Sommaire des Archives Communales Antérieures à 1790. Ville de Lyon*. Paris, 1865.

Jecklin, Fritz. *Materielen sur Standes- und Landesgeschichte, Mem. III Bünde (Graubünden) 1464–1803*. Bâle, 1903.

Langer, William L. (ed.). *An Encyclopedia of World History*. Boston, 1940 and 1948.

McBain, O. *Celtic Mythology and Religion*. Stirling, 1917.

MacCulloch, Canon J. A. M. *Mythology of all Races*. Boston, 1923.

Maigne d'Arnis, W. H. *Lexicon Manuale ad Scriptores Mediae et Infimae Latinitatis*. Paris, 1866.

Ménard, M. *Histoire de la Ville de Nîmes*. Nîmes, 1874.

Mussey, Jean. *La Lorraine Ancienne et Moderne*. Nancy, 1712.

*New Catholic Encyclopedia, The*. New York, 1929.

*Nouvelle Biographie Générale*. Paris, 1853–70.

*Nouveau Petit Larousse. Illustré Dictionnaire Encyclopédique*. Paris, 1940.

Paliser, Mrs. Bury. *Historical Devices, Badges and War-Cries*. London, 1870.

Pansier, P. *Histoire du Livre et de l'Imprimerie à Avignon du XIVᵐᵉ au XVIᵐᵉ Siècle*. Avignon, 1922.

Papillon, Abbé Philibert. *Bibliothèque des auteurs de Bourgogne*. Dijon, 1742.

Paulet, Abbé L. *Saint-Rémy de Provence*. Avignon, 1907.

Pearce, A. J. *Text-book of Astrology.* London, 1889.

Peck, H. T. *Harper's Dictionary of Classical Literature and Antiquities.* New York, 1897.

Roquefort, J. B. B. *Glossaire de la Langue Romaine.* Paris. 1808.

Sainte-Palaye, Jean-Baptiste la Curne de. *Dictionnaire de l'Ancien Langage Français.* Paris, 1875–82.

Shepherd, William R. *Historical Atlas.* Leipzig, 1921.

Smith, William. *Dictionary of Greek and Roman Geography.* Boston, 1854.

(Also various French, Latin and Greek dictionaries, and various editions of the *Encyclopaedia Britannica.*)

# Index
## Of Historical and Eminent Persons

This index refers, by conventional page number, to persons mentioned by the author (including quotations from other commentators) and, for the most part, applies to the Biography, Historical Background and Commentaries sections. It should not be confused with the "Indexes to the Prophecies," which refer to Nostradamus' prophecies themselves, by quatrain number or paragraph number. With but very few exceptions, there is no duplication.

G indicates that the name is to be found on one or both of the genealogical charts at pages 552–53.

# A CATALOG OF SELECTED DOVER
# BOOKS IN ALL FIELDS OF INTEREST

CONCERNING THE SPIRITUAL IN ART, Wassily Kandinsky. Pioneering work by father of abstract art. Thoughts on color theory, nature of art. Analysis of earlier masters. 12 illustrations. 80pp. of text. 5⅜ x 8½.                   23411-8 Pa. $4.95

ANIMALS: 1,419 Copyright-Free Illustrations of Mammals, Birds, Fish, Insects, etc., Jim Harter (ed.). Clear wood engravings present, in extremely lifelike poses, over 1,000 species of animals. One of the most extensive pictorial sourcebooks of its kind. Captions. Index. 284pp. 9 x 12.                   23766-4 Pa. $14.95

CELTIC ART: The Methods of Construction, George Bain. Simple geometric techniques for making Celtic interlacements, spirals, Kells-type initials, animals, humans, etc. Over 500 illustrations. 160pp. 9 x 12. (Available in U.S. only.)        22923-8 Pa. $9.95

AN ATLAS OF ANATOMY FOR ARTISTS, Fritz Schider. Most thorough reference work on art anatomy in the world. Hundreds of illustrations, including selections from works by Vesalius, Leonardo, Goya, Ingres, Michelangelo, others. 593 illustrations. 192pp. 7⅛ x 10¼.                   20241-0 Pa. $9.95

CELTIC HAND STROKE-BY-STROKE (Irish Half-Uncial from "The Book of Kells"): An Arthur Baker Calligraphy Manual, Arthur Baker. Complete guide to creating each letter of the alphabet in distinctive Celtic manner. Covers hand position, strokes, pens, inks, paper, more. Illustrated. 48pp. 8¼ x 11.       24336-2 Pa. $3.95

EASY ORIGAMI, John Montroll. Charming collection of 32 projects (hat, cup, pelican, piano, swan, many more) specially designed for the novice origami hobbyist. Clearly illustrated easy-to-follow instructions insure that even beginning papercrafters will achieve successful results. 48pp. 8¼ x 11.        27298-2 Pa. $3.50

THE COMPLETE BOOK OF BIRDHOUSE CONSTRUCTION FOR WOODWORKERS, Scott D. Campbell. Detailed instructions, illustrations, tables. Also data on bird habitat and instinct patterns. Bibliography. 3 tables. 63 illustrations in 15 figures. 48pp. 5¼ x 8½.                   24407-5 Pa. $2.50

BLOOMINGDALE'S ILLUSTRATED 1886 CATALOG: Fashions, Dry Goods and Housewares, Bloomingdale Brothers. Famed merchants' extremely rare catalog depicting about 1,700 products: clothing, housewares, firearms, dry goods, jewelry, more. Invaluable for dating, identifying vintage items. Also, copyright-free graphics for artists, designers. Co-published with Henry Ford Museum & Greenfield Village. 160pp. 8¼ x 11.                   25780-0 Pa. $12.95

HISTORIC COSTUME IN PICTURES, Braun & Schneider. Over 1,450 costumed figures in clearly detailed engravings–from dawn of civilization to end of 19th century. Captions. Many folk costumes. 256pp. 8⅜ x 11¾.        23150-X Pa. $12.95

STICKLEY CRAFTSMAN FURNITURE CATALOGS, Gustav Stickley and L. & J. G. Stickley. Beautiful, functional furniture in two authentic catalogs from 1910. 594 illustrations, including 277 photos, show settles, rockers, armchairs, reclining chairs, bookcases, desks, tables. 183pp. 6½ x 9¼.                          23838-5 Pa. $11.95

AMERICAN LOCOMOTIVES IN HISTORIC PHOTOGRAPHS: 1858 to 1949, Ron Ziel (ed.). A rare collection of 126 meticulously detailed official photographs, called "builder portraits," of American locomotives that majestically chronicle the rise of steam locomotive power in America. Introduction. Detailed captions. xi+ 129pp. 9 x 12.                          27393-8 Pa. $13.95

AMERICA'S LIGHTHOUSES: An Illustrated History, Francis Ross Holland, Jr. Delightfully written, profusely illustrated fact-filled survey of over 200 American lighthouses since 1716. History, anecdotes, technological advances, more. 240pp. 8 x 10¾.
25576-X Pa. $12.95

TOWARDS A NEW ARCHITECTURE, Le Corbusier. Pioneering manifesto by founder of "International School." Technical and aesthetic theories, views of industry, economics, relation of form to function, "mass-production split" and much more. Profusely illustrated. 320pp. 6⅛ x 9¼. (Available in U.S. only.)                          25023-7 Pa. $10.95

HOW THE OTHER HALF LIVES, Jacob Riis. Famous journalistic record, exposing poverty and degradation of New York slums around 1900, by major social reformer. 100 striking and influential photographs. 233pp. 10 x 7⅞.
22012-5 Pa. $11.95

FRUIT KEY AND TWIG KEY TO TREES AND SHRUBS, William M. Harlow. One of the handiest and most widely used identification aids. Fruit key covers 120 deciduous and evergreen species; twig key 160 deciduous species. Easily used. Over 300 photographs. 126pp. 5⅜ x 8½.                          20511-8 Pa. $3.95

COMMON BIRD SONGS, Dr. Donald J. Borror. Songs of 60 most common U.S. birds: robins, sparrows, cardinals, bluejays, finches, more–arranged in order of increasing complexity. Up to 9 variations of songs of each species.
Cassette and manual 99911-4 $8.95

ORCHIDS AS HOUSE PLANTS, Rebecca Tyson Northen. Grow cattleyas and many other kinds of orchids–in a window, in a case, or under artificial light. 63 illustrations. 148pp. 5⅜ x 8½.                          23261-1 Pa. $7.95

MONSTER MAZES, Dave Phillips. Masterful mazes at four levels of difficulty. Avoid deadly perils and evil creatures to find magical treasures. Solutions for all 32 exciting illustrated puzzles. 48pp. 8¼ x 11.                          26005-4 Pa. $2.95

MOZART'S DON GIOVANNI (DOVER OPERA LIBRETTO SERIES), Wolfgang Amadeus Mozart. Introduced and translated by Ellen H. Bleiler. Standard Italian libretto, with complete English translation. Convenient and thoroughly portable–an ideal companion for reading along with a recording or the performance itself. Introduction. List of characters. Plot summary. 121pp. 5¼ x 8½.
24944-1 Pa. $3.95

TECHNICAL MANUAL AND DICTIONARY OF CLASSICAL BALLET, Gail Grant. Defines, explains, comments on steps, movements, poses and concepts. 15-page pictorial section. Basic book for student, viewer. 127pp. 5⅜ x 8½.
21843-0 Pa. $4.95

THE CLARINET AND CLARINET PLAYING, David Pino. Lively, comprehensive work features suggestions about technique, musicianship, and musical interpretation, as well as guidelines for teaching, making your own reeds, and preparing for public performance. Includes an intriguing look at clarinet history. "A godsend," *The Clarinet,* Journal of the International Clarinet Society. Appendixes. 7 illus. 320pp. 5⅜ x 8½. 40270-3 Pa. $9.95

HOLLYWOOD GLAMOR PORTRAITS, John Kobal (ed.). 145 photos from 1926-49. Harlow, Gable, Bogart, Bacall; 94 stars in all. Full background on photographers, technical aspects. 160pp. 8⅜ x 11¼. 23352-9 Pa. $12.95

THE ANNOTATED CASEY AT THE BAT: A Collection of Ballads about the Mighty Casey/Third, Revised Edition, Martin Gardner (ed.). Amusing sequels and parodies of one of America's best-loved poems: Casey's Revenge, Why Casey Whiffed, Casey's Sister at the Bat, others. 256pp. 5⅜ x 8½. 28598-7 Pa. $8.95

THE RAVEN AND OTHER FAVORITE POEMS, Edgar Allan Poe. Over 40 of the author's most memorable poems: "The Bells," "Ulalume," "Israfel," "To Helen," "The Conqueror Worm," "Eldorado," "Annabel Lee," many more. Alphabetic lists of titles and first lines. 64pp. 5$\frac{3}{16}$ x 8¼. 26685-0 Pa. $1.00

PERSONAL MEMOIRS OF U. S. GRANT, Ulysses Simpson Grant. Intelligent, deeply moving firsthand account of Civil War campaigns, considered by many the finest military memoirs ever written. Includes letters, historic photographs, maps and more. 528pp. 6⅛ x 9¼. 28587-1 Pa. $12.95

ANCIENT EGYPTIAN MATERIALS AND INDUSTRIES, A. Lucas and J. Harris. Fascinating, comprehensive, thoroughly documented text describes this ancient civilization's vast resources and the processes that incorporated them in daily life, including the use of animal products, building materials, cosmetics, perfumes and incense, fibers, glazed ware, glass and its manufacture, materials used in the mummification process, and much more. 544pp. 6⅛ x 9¼. (Available in U.S. only.) 40446-3 Pa. $16.95

RUSSIAN STORIES/PYCCKNE PACCKA3bl: A Dual-Language Book, edited by Gleb Struve. Twelve tales by such masters as Chekhov, Tolstoy, Dostoevsky, Pushkin, others. Excellent word-for-word English translations on facing pages, plus teaching and study aids, Russian/English vocabulary, biographical/critical introductions, more. 416pp. 5⅜ x 8½. 26244-8 Pa. $9.95

PHILADELPHIA THEN AND NOW: 60 Sites Photographed in the Past and Present, Kenneth Finkel and Susan Oyama. Rare photographs of City Hall, Logan Square, Independence Hall, Betsy Ross House, other landmarks juxtaposed with contemporary views. Captures changing face of historic city. Introduction. Captions. 128pp. 8¼ x 11. 25790-8 Pa. $9.95

AIA ARCHITECTURAL GUIDE TO NASSAU AND SUFFOLK COUNTIES, LONG ISLAND, The American Institute of Architects, Long Island Chapter, and the Society for the Preservation of Long Island Antiquities. Comprehensive, well-researched and generously illustrated volume brings to life over three centuries of Long Island's great architectural heritage. More than 240 photographs with authoritative, extensively detailed captions. 176pp. 8¼ x 11. 26946-9 Pa. $14.95

NORTH AMERICAN INDIAN LIFE: Customs and Traditions of 23 Tribes, Elsie Clews Parsons (ed.). 27 fictionalized essays by noted anthropologists examine religion, customs, government, additional facets of life among the Winnebago, Crow, Zuni, Eskimo, other tribes. 480pp. 6⅛ x 9¼. 27377-6 Pa. $10.95

FRANK LLOYD WRIGHT'S DANA HOUSE, Donald Hoffmann. Pictorial essay of residential masterpiece with over 160 interior and exterior photos, plans, elevations, sketches and studies. 128pp. 9¼ x 10¾. 29120-0 Pa. $14.95

THE MALE AND FEMALE FIGURE IN MOTION: 60 Classic Photographic Sequences, Eadweard Muybridge. 60 true-action photographs of men and women walking, running, climbing, bending, turning, etc., reproduced from rare 19th-century masterpiece. vi + 121pp. 9 x 12. 24745-7 Pa. $12.95

1001 QUESTIONS ANSWERED ABOUT THE SEASHORE, N. J. Berrill and Jacquelyn Berrill. Queries answered about dolphins, sea snails, sponges, starfish, fishes, shore birds, many others. Covers appearance, breeding, growth, feeding, much more. 305pp. 5¼ x 8¼. 23366-9 Pa. $9.95

ATTRACTING BIRDS TO YOUR YARD, William J. Weber. Easy-to-follow guide offers advice on how to attract the greatest diversity of birds: birdhouses, feeders, water and waterers, much more. 96pp. 5³⁄₁₆ x 8¼. 28927-3 Pa. $2.50

MEDICINAL AND OTHER USES OF NORTH AMERICAN PLANTS: A Historical Survey with Special Reference to the Eastern Indian Tribes, Charlotte Erichsen-Brown. Chronological historical citations document 500 years of usage of plants, trees, shrubs native to eastern Canada, northeastern U.S. Also complete identifying information. 343 illustrations. 544pp. 6½ x 9¼. 25951-X Pa. $12.95

STORYBOOK MAZES, Dave Phillips. 23 stories and mazes on two-page spreads: Wizard of Oz, Treasure Island, Robin Hood, etc. Solutions. 64pp. 8¼ x 11. 23628-5 Pa. $2.95

AMERICAN NEGRO SONGS: 230 Folk Songs and Spirituals, Religious and Secular, John W. Work. This authoritative study traces the African influences of songs sung and played by black Americans at work, in church, and as entertainment. The author discusses the lyric significance of such songs as "Swing Low, Sweet Chariot," "John Henry," and others and offers the words and music for 230 songs. Bibliography. Index of Song Titles. 272pp. 6½ x 9¼. 40271-1 Pa. $10.95

MOVIE-STAR PORTRAITS OF THE FORTIES, John Kobal (ed.). 163 glamor, studio photos of 106 stars of the 1940s: Rita Hayworth, Ava Gardner, Marlon Brando, Clark Gable, many more. 176pp. 8⅜ x 11¼. 23546-7 Pa. $14.95

BENCHLEY LOST AND FOUND, Robert Benchley. Finest humor from early 30s, about pet peeves, child psychologists, post office and others. Mostly unavailable elsewhere. 73 illustrations by Peter Arno and others. 183pp. 5⅜ x 8½. 22410-4 Pa. $6.95

YEKL and THE IMPORTED BRIDEGROOM AND OTHER STORIES OF YIDDISH NEW YORK, Abraham Cahan. Film Hester Street based on *Yekl* (1896). Novel, other stories among first about Jewish immigrants on N.Y.'s East Side. 240pp. 5⅜ x 8½. 22427-9 Pa. $7.95

SELECTED POEMS, Walt Whitman. Generous sampling from *Leaves of Grass*. Twenty-four poems include "I Hear America Singing," "Song of the Open Road," "I Sing the Body Electric," "When Lilacs Last in the Dooryard Bloom'd," "O Captain! My Captain!"—all reprinted from an authoritative edition. Lists of titles and first lines. 128pp. 5³⁄₁₆ x 8¼. 26878-0 Pa. $1.00

THE BEST TALES OF HOFFMANN, E. T. A. Hoffmann. 10 of Hoffmann's most important stories: "Nutcracker and the King of Mice," "The Golden Flowerpot," etc. 458pp. 5⅜ x 8½. 21793-0 Pa. $9.95

FROM FETISH TO GOD IN ANCIENT EGYPT, E. A. Wallis Budge. Rich detailed survey of Egyptian conception of "God" and gods, magic, cult of animals, Osiris, more. Also, superb English translations of hymns and legends. 240 illustrations. 545pp. 5⅜ x 8½. 25803-3 Pa. $13.95

FRENCH STORIES/CONTES FRANÇAIS: A Dual-Language Book, Wallace Fowlie. Ten stories by French masters, Voltaire to Camus: "Micromegas" by Voltaire; "The Atheist's Mass" by Balzac; "Minuet" by de Maupassant; "The Guest" by Camus, six more. Excellent English translations on facing pages. Also French-English vocabulary list, exercises, more. 352pp. 5⅜ x 8½. 26443-2 Pa. $9.95

CHICAGO AT THE TURN OF THE CENTURY IN PHOTOGRAPHS: 122 Historic Views from the Collections of the Chicago Historical Society, Larry A. Viskochil. Rare large-format prints offer detailed views of City Hall, State Street, the Loop, Hull House, Union Station, many other landmarks, circa 1904-1913. Introduction. Captions. Maps. 144pp. 9⅜ x 12¼. 24656-6 Pa. $12.95

OLD BROOKLYN IN EARLY PHOTOGRAPHS, 1865-1929, William Lee Younger. Luna Park, Gravesend race track, construction of Grand Army Plaza, moving of Hotel Brighton, etc. 157 previously unpublished photographs. 165pp. 8⅞ x 11¾. 23587-4 Pa. $13.95

THE MYTHS OF THE NORTH AMERICAN INDIANS, Lewis Spence. Rich anthology of the myths and legends of the Algonquins, Iroquois, Pawnees and Sioux, prefaced by an extensive historical and ethnological commentary. 36 illustrations. 480pp. 5⅜ x 8½. 25967-6 Pa. $10.95

AN ENCYCLOPEDIA OF BATTLES: Accounts of Over 1,560 Battles from 1479 B.C. to the Present, David Eggenberger. Essential details of every major battle in recorded history from the first battle of Megiddo in 1479 B.C. to Grenada in 1984. List of Battle Maps. New Appendix covering the years 1967-1984. Index. 99 illustrations. 544pp. 6½ x 9¼. 24913-1 Pa. $16.95

SAILING ALONE AROUND THE WORLD, Captain Joshua Slocum. First man to sail around the world, alone, in small boat. One of great feats of seamanship told in delightful manner. 67 illustrations. 294pp. 5⅜ x 8½. 20326-3 Pa. $6.95

ANARCHISM AND OTHER ESSAYS, Emma Goldman. Powerful, penetrating, prophetic essays on direct action, role of minorities, prison reform, puritan hypocrisy, violence, etc. 271pp. 5⅜ x 8½. 22484-8 Pa. $8.95

MYTHS OF THE HINDUS AND BUDDHISTS, Ananda K. Coomaraswamy and Sister Nivedita. Great stories of the epics; deeds of Krishna, Shiva, taken from puranas, Vedas, folk tales; etc. 32 illustrations. 400pp. 5⅜ x 8½. 21759-0 Pa. $12.95

THE TRAUMA OF BIRTH, Otto Rank. Rank's controversial thesis that anxiety neurosis is caused by profound psychological trauma which occurs at birth. 256pp. 5⅜ x 8½. 27974-X Pa. $7.95

A THEOLOGICO-POLITICAL TREATISE, Benedict Spinoza. Also contains unfinished Political Treatise. Great classic on religious liberty, theory of government on common consent. R. Elwes translation. Total of 421pp. 5⅜ x 8½. 20249-6 Pa. $10.95

MY BONDAGE AND MY FREEDOM, Frederick Douglass. Born a slave, Douglass became outspoken force in antislavery movement. The best of Douglass' autobiographies. Graphic description of slave life. 464pp. 5⅜ x 8½. 22457-0 Pa. $8.95

FOLLOWING THE EQUATOR: A Journey Around the World, Mark Twain. Fascinating humorous account of 1897 voyage to Hawaii, Australia, India, New Zealand, etc. Ironic, bemused reports on peoples, customs, climate, flora and fauna, politics, much more. 197 illustrations. 720pp. 5⅜ x 8½. 26113-1 Pa. $15.95

THE PEOPLE CALLED SHAKERS, Edward D. Andrews. Definitive study of Shakers: origins, beliefs, practices, dances, social organization, furniture and crafts, etc. 33 illustrations. 351pp. 5⅜ x 8½. 21081-2 Pa. $12.95

THE MYTHS OF GREECE AND ROME, H. A. Guerber. A classic of mythology, generously illustrated, long prized for its simple, graphic, accurate retelling of the principal myths of Greece and Rome, and for its commentary on their origins and significance. With 64 illustrations by Michelangelo, Raphael, Titian, Rubens, Canova, Bernini and others. 480pp. 5⅜ x 8½. 27584-1 Pa. $10.95

PSYCHOLOGY OF MUSIC, Carl E. Seashore. Classic work discusses music as a medium from psychological viewpoint. Clear treatment of physical acoustics, auditory apparatus, sound perception, development of musical skills, nature of musical feeling, host of other topics. 88 figures. 408pp. 5⅜ x 8½. 21851-1 Pa. $11.95

THE PHILOSOPHY OF HISTORY, Georg W. Hegel. Great classic of Western thought develops concept that history is not chance but rational process, the evolution of freedom. 457pp. 5⅜ x 8½. 20112-0 Pa. $9.95

THE BOOK OF TEA, Kakuzo Okakura. Minor classic of the Orient: entertaining, charming explanation, interpretation of traditional Japanese culture in terms of tea ceremony. 94pp. 5⅜ x 8½. 20070-1 Pa. $3.95

LIFE IN ANCIENT EGYPT, Adolf Erman. Fullest, most thorough, detailed older account with much not in more recent books, domestic life, religion, magic, medicine, commerce, much more. Many illustrations reproduce tomb paintings, carvings, hieroglyphs, etc. 597pp. 5⅜ x 8½. 22632-8 Pa. $12.95

SUNDIALS, Their Theory and Construction, Albert Waugh. Far and away the best, most thorough coverage of ideas, mathematics concerned, types, construction, adjusting anywhere. Simple, nontechnical treatment allows even children to build several of these dials. Over 100 illustrations. 230pp. 5⅜ x 8½. 22947-5 Pa. $8.95

THEORETICAL HYDRODYNAMICS, L. M. Milne-Thomson. Classic exposition of the mathematical theory of fluid motion, applicable to both hydrodynamics and aerodynamics. Over 600 exercises. 768pp. 6⅛ x 9¼. 68970-0 Pa. $20.95

SONGS OF EXPERIENCE: Facsimile Reproduction with 26 Plates in Full Color, William Blake. 26 full-color plates from a rare 1826 edition. Includes "TheTyger," "London," "Holy Thursday," and other poems. Printed text of poems. 48pp. 5¼ x 7. 24636-1 Pa. $4.95

OLD-TIME VIGNETTES IN FULL COLOR, Carol Belanger Grafton (ed.). Over 390 charming, often sentimental illustrations, selected from archives of Victorian graphics—pretty women posing, children playing, food, flowers, kittens and puppies, smiling cherubs, birds and butterflies, much more. All copyright-free. 48pp. 9¼ x 12¼. 27269-9 Pa. $9.95

PERSPECTIVE FOR ARTISTS, Rex Vicat Cole. Depth, perspective of sky and sea, shadows, much more, not usually covered. 391 diagrams, 81 reproductions of drawings and paintings. 279pp. 5⅜ x 8½. 22487-2 Pa. $9.95

DRAWING THE LIVING FIGURE, Joseph Sheppard. Innovative approach to artistic anatomy focuses on specifics of surface anatomy, rather than muscles and bones. Over 170 drawings of live models in front, back and side views, and in widely varying poses. Accompanying diagrams. 177 illustrations. Introduction. Index. 144pp. 8⅜ x11¼. 26723-7 Pa. $9.95

GOTHIC AND OLD ENGLISH ALPHABETS: 100 Complete Fonts, Dan X. Solo. Add power, elegance to posters, signs, other graphics with 100 stunning copyright-free alphabets: Blackstone, Dolbey, Germania, 97 more–including many lower-case, numerals, punctuation marks. 104pp. 8⅛ x 11. 24695-7 Pa. $9.95

HOW TO DO BEADWORK, Mary White. Fundamental book on craft from simple projects to five-bead chains and woven works. 106 illustrations. 142pp. 5⅜ x 8. 20697-1 Pa. $5.95

THE BOOK OF WOOD CARVING, Charles Marshall Sayers. Finest book for beginners discusses fundamentals and offers 34 designs. "Absolutely first rate . . . well thought out and well executed."–E. J. Tangerman. 118pp. 7¾ x 10⅝. 23654-4 Pa. $7.95

ILLUSTRATED CATALOG OF CIVIL WAR MILITARY GOODS: Union Army Weapons, Insignia, Uniform Accessories, and Other Equipment, Schuyler, Hartley, and Graham. Rare, profusely illustrated 1846 catalog includes Union Army uniform and dress regulations, arms and ammunition, coats, insignia, flags, swords, rifles, etc. 226 illustrations. 160pp. 9 x 12. 24939-5 Pa. $12.95

WOMEN'S FASHIONS OF THE EARLY 1900s: An Unabridged Republication of "New York Fashions, 1909," National Cloak & Suit Co. Rare catalog of mail-order fashions documents women's and children's clothing styles shortly after the turn of the century. Captions offer full descriptions, prices. Invaluable resource for fashion, costume historians. Approximately 725 illustrations. 128pp. 8⅜ x 11¼. 27276-1 Pa. $12.95

THE 1912 AND 1915 GUSTAV STICKLEY FURNITURE CATALOGS, Gustav Stickley. With over 200 detailed illustrations and descriptions, these two catalogs are essential reading and reference materials and identification guides for Stickley furniture. Captions cite materials, dimensions and prices. 112pp. 6½ x 9¼. 26676-1 Pa. $9.95

EARLY AMERICAN LOCOMOTIVES, John H. White, Jr. Finest locomotive engravings from early 19th century: historical (1804–74), main-line (after 1870), special, foreign, etc. 147 plates. 142pp. 11⅜ x 8¼. 22772-3 Pa. $12.95

THE TALL SHIPS OF TODAY IN PHOTOGRAPHS, Frank O. Braynard. Lavishly illustrated tribute to nearly 100 majestic contemporary sailing vessels: Amerigo Vespucci, Clearwater, Constitution, Eagle, Mayflower, Sea Cloud, Victory, many more. Authoritative captions provide statistics, background on each ship. 190 black-and-white photographs and illustrations. Introduction. 128pp. 8⅞ x 11¾. 27163-3 Pa. $14.95

LITTLE BOOK OF EARLY AMERICAN CRAFTS AND TRADES, Peter Stockham (ed.). 1807 children's book explains crafts and trades: baker, hatter, cooper, potter, and many others. 23 copperplate illustrations. 140pp. 4⅝ x 6.
23336-7 Pa. $4.95

VICTORIAN FASHIONS AND COSTUMES FROM HARPER'S BAZAR, 1867–1898, Stella Blum (ed.). Day costumes, evening wear, sports clothes, shoes, hats, other accessories in over 1,000 detailed engravings. 320pp. 9⅜ x 12¼.
22990-4 Pa. $16.95

GUSTAV STICKLEY, THE CRAFTSMAN, Mary Ann Smith. Superb study surveys broad scope of Stickley's achievement, especially in architecture. Design philosophy, rise and fall of the Craftsman empire, descriptions and floor plans for many Craftsman houses, more. 86 black-and-white halftones. 31 line illustrations. Introduction 208pp. 6½ x 9¼.
27210-9 Pa. $9.95

THE LONG ISLAND RAIL ROAD IN EARLY PHOTOGRAPHS, Ron Ziel. Over 220 rare photos, informative text document origin ( 1844) and development of rail service on Long Island. Vintage views of early trains, locomotives, stations, passengers, crews, much more. Captions. 8⅞ x 11¾.
26301-0 Pa. $14.95

VOYAGE OF THE LIBERDADE, Joshua Slocum. Great 19th-century mariner's thrilling, first-hand account of the wreck of his ship off South America, the 35-foot boat he built from the wreckage, and its remarkable voyage home. 128pp. 5⅜ x 8½.
40022-0 Pa. $5.95

TEN BOOKS ON ARCHITECTURE, Vitruvius. The most important book ever written on architecture. Early Roman aesthetics, technology, classical orders, site selection, all other aspects. Morgan translation. 331pp. 5⅜ x 8½. 20645-9 Pa. $9.95

THE HUMAN FIGURE IN MOTION, Eadweard Muybridge. More than 4,500 stopped-action photos, in action series, showing undraped men, women, children jumping, lying down, throwing, sitting, wrestling, carrying, etc. 390pp. 7⅞ x 10⅝.
20204-6 Clothbd. $29.95

TREES OF THE EASTERN AND CENTRAL UNITED STATES AND CANADA, William M. Harlow. Best one-volume guide to 140 trees. Full descriptions, woodlore, range, etc. Over 600 illustrations. Handy size. 288pp. 4½ x 6⅜.
20395-6 Pa. $6.95

SONGS OF WESTERN BIRDS, Dr. Donald J. Borror. Complete song and call repertoire of 60 western species, including flycatchers, juncoes, cactus wrens, many more–includes fully illustrated booklet. Cassette and manual 99913-0 $8.95

GROWING AND USING HERBS AND SPICES, Milo Miloradovich. Versatile handbook provides all the information needed for cultivation and use of all the herbs and spices available in North America. 4 illustrations. Index. Glossary. 236pp. 5⅜ x 8½.
25058-X Pa. $7.95

BIG BOOK OF MAZES AND LABYRINTHS, Walter Shepherd. 50 mazes and labyrinths in all–classical, solid, ripple, and more–in one great volume. Perfect inexpensive puzzler for clever youngsters. Full solutions. 112pp. 8⅛ x 11.
22951-3 Pa. $5.95

PIANO TUNING, J. Cree Fischer. Clearest, best book for beginner, amateur. Simple repairs, raising dropped notes, tuning by easy method of flattened fifths. No previous skills needed. 4 illustrations. 201pp. 5⅜ x 8½. 23267-0 Pa. $6.95

HINTS TO SINGERS, Lillian Nordica. Selecting the right teacher, developing confidence, overcoming stage fright, and many other important skills receive thoughtful discussion in this indispensible guide, written by a world-famous diva of four decades' experience. 96pp. 5³/₈ x 8¹/₂. 40094-8 Pa. $4.95

THE COMPLETE NONSENSE OF EDWARD LEAR, Edward Lear. All nonsense limericks, zany alphabets, Owl and Pussycat, songs, nonsense botany, etc., illustrated by Lear. Total of 320pp. 5⅜ x 8½. (Available in U.S. only.) 20167-8 Pa. $7.95

VICTORIAN PARLOUR POETRY: An Annotated Anthology, Michael R. Turner. 117 gems by Longfellow, Tennyson, Browning, many lesser-known poets. "The Village Blacksmith," "Curfew Must Not Ring Tonight," "Only a Baby Small," dozens more, often difficult to find elsewhere. Index of poets, titles, first lines. xxiii + 325pp. 5⅜ x 8¼. 27044-0 Pa. $12.95

DUBLINERS, James Joyce. Fifteen stories offer vivid, tightly focused observations of the lives of Dublin's poorer classes. At least one, "The Dead," is considered a masterpiece. Reprinted complete and unabridged from standard edition. 160pp. 5³/₁₆ x 8¼. 26870-5 Pa. $1.50

GREAT WEIRD TALES: 14 Stories by Lovecraft, Blackwood, Machen and Others, S. T. Joshi (ed.). 14 spellbinding tales, including "The Sin Eater," by Fiona McLeod, "The Eye Above the Mantel," by Frank Belknap Long, as well as renowned works by R. H. Barlow, Lord Dunsany, Arthur Machen, W. C. Morrow and eight other masters of the genre. 256pp. 5⅜ x 8½. (Available in U.S. only.) 40436-6 Pa. $8.95

THE BOOK OF THE SACRED MAGIC OF ABRAMELIN THE MAGE, translated by S. MacGregor Mathers. Medieval manuscript of ceremonial magic. Basic document in Aleister Crowley, Golden Dawn groups. 268pp. 5⅜ x 8½. 23211-5 Pa. $9.95

NEW RUSSIAN-ENGLISH AND ENGLISH-RUSSIAN DICTIONARY, M. A. O'Brien. This is a remarkably handy Russian dictionary, containing a surprising amount of information, including over 70,000 entries. 366pp. 4½ x 6¼. 20208-9 Pa. $10.95

HISTORIC HOMES OF THE AMERICAN PRESIDENTS, Second, Revised Edition, Irvin Haas. A traveler's guide to American Presidential homes, most open to the public, depicting and describing homes occupied by every American President from George Washington to George Bush. With visiting hours, admission charges, travel routes. 175 photographs. Index. 160pp. 8¼ x 11. 26751-2 Pa. $13.95

NEW YORK IN THE FORTIES, Andreas Feininger. 162 brilliant photographs by the well-known photographer, formerly with *Life* magazine. Commuters, shoppers, Times Square at night, much else from city at its peak. Captions by John von Hartz. 181pp. 9¼ x 10¾. 23585-8 Pa. $13.95

INDIAN SIGN LANGUAGE, William Tomkins. Over 525 signs developed by Sioux and other tribes. Written instructions and diagrams. Also 290 pictographs. 111pp. 6⅛ x 9¼. 22029-X Pa. $3.95

ANATOMY: A Complete Guide for Artists, Joseph Sheppard. A master of figure drawing shows artists how to render human anatomy convincingly. Over 460 illustrations. 224pp. 8⅜ x 11¼. 27279-6 Pa. $11.95

MEDIEVAL CALLIGRAPHY: Its History and Technique, Marc Drogin. Spirited history, comprehensive instruction manual covers 13 styles (ca. 4th century through 15th). Excellent photographs; directions for duplicating medieval techniques with modern tools. 224pp. 8⅜ x 11¼. 26142-5 Pa. $12.95

DRIED FLOWERS: How to Prepare Them, Sarah Whitlock and Martha Rankin. Complete instructions on how to use silica gel, meal and borax, perlite aggregate, sand and borax, glycerine and water to create attractive permanent flower arrangements. 12 illustrations. 32pp. 5⅜ x 8½. 21802-3 Pa. $1.00

EASY-TO-MAKE BIRD FEEDERS FOR WOODWORKERS, Scott D. Campbell. Detailed, simple-to-use guide for designing, constructing, caring for and using feeders. Text, illustrations for 12 classic and contemporary designs. 96pp. 5⅜ x 8½.
25847-5 Pa. $3.95

SCOTTISH WONDER TALES FROM MYTH AND LEGEND, Donald A. Mackenzie. 16 lively tales tell of giants rumbling down mountainsides, of a magic wand that turns stone pillars into warriors, of gods and goddesses, evil hags, powerful forces and more. 240pp. 5⅜ x 8½. 29677-6 Pa. $6.95

THE HISTORY OF UNDERCLOTHES, C. Willett Cunnington and Phyllis Cunnington. Fascinating, well-documented survey covering six centuries of English undergarments, enhanced with over 100 illustrations: 12th-century laced-up bodice, footed long drawers (1795), 19th-century bustles, 19th-century corsets for men, Victorian "bust improvers," much more. 272pp. 5⅜ x 8¼. 27124-2 Pa. $9.95

ARTS AND CRAFTS FURNITURE: The Complete Brooks Catalog of 1912, Brooks Manufacturing Co. Photos and detailed descriptions of more than 150 now very collectible furniture designs from the Arts and Crafts movement depict davenports, settees, buffets, desks, tables, chairs, bedsteads, dressers and more, all built of solid, quarter-sawed oak. Invaluable for students and enthusiasts of antiques, Americana and the decorative arts. 80pp. 6½ x 9¼. 27471-3 Pa. $8.95

WILBUR AND ORVILLE: A Biography of the Wright Brothers, Fred Howard. Definitive, crisply written study tells the full story of the brothers' lives and work. A vividly written biography, unparalleled in scope and color, that also captures the spirit of an extraordinary era. 560pp. 6⅛ x 9¼. 40297-5 Pa. $17.95

THE ARTS OF THE SAILOR: Knotting, Splicing and Ropework, Hervey Garrett Smith. Indispensable shipboard reference covers tools, basic knots and useful hitches; handsewing and canvas work, more. Over 100 illustrations. Delightful reading for sea lovers. 256pp. 5⅜ x 8½. 26440-8 Pa. $8.95

FRANK LLOYD WRIGHT'S FALLINGWATER: The House and Its History, Second, Revised Edition, Donald Hoffmann. A total revision–both in text and illustrations–of the standard document on Fallingwater, the boldest, most personal architectural statement of Wright's mature years, updated with valuable new material from the recently opened Frank Lloyd Wright Archives. "Fascinating"–*The New York Times*. 116 illustrations. 128pp. 9¼ x 10¾. 27430-6 Pa. $12.95

PHOTOGRAPHIC SKETCHBOOK OF THE CIVIL WAR, Alexander Gardner. 100 photos taken on field during the Civil War. Famous shots of Manassas Harper's Ferry, Lincoln, Richmond, slave pens, etc. 244pp. 10⅝ x 8¼. 22731-6 Pa. $10.95

FIVE ACRES AND INDEPENDENCE, Maurice G. Kains. Great back-to-the-land classic explains basics of self-sufficient farming. The one book to get. 95 illustrations. 397pp. 5⅜ x 8½. 20974-1 Pa. $7.95

SONGS OF EASTERN BIRDS, Dr. Donald J. Borror. Songs and calls of 60 species most common to eastern U.S.: warblers, woodpeckers, flycatchers, thrushes, larks, many more in high-quality recording. Cassette and manual 99912-2 $9.95

A MODERN HERBAL, Margaret Grieve. Much the fullest, most exact, most useful compilation of herbal material. Gigantic alphabetical encyclopedia, from aconite to zedoary, gives botanical information, medical properties, folklore, economic uses, much else. Indispensable to serious reader. 161 illustrations. 888pp. 6½ x 9¼. 2-vol. set. (Available in U.S. only.) Vol. I: 22798-7 Pa. $10.95
Vol. II: 22799-5 Pa. $10.95

HIDDEN TREASURE MAZE BOOK, Dave Phillips. Solve 34 challenging mazes accompanied by heroic tales of adventure. Evil dragons, people-eating plants, blood-thirsty giants, many more dangerous adversaries lurk at every twist and turn. 34 mazes, stories, solutions. 48pp. 8¼ x 11. 24566-7 Pa. $2.95

LETTERS OF W. A. MOZART, Wolfgang A. Mozart. Remarkable letters show bawdy wit, humor, imagination, musical insights, contemporary musical world; includes some letters from Leopold Mozart. 276pp. 5⅜ x 8½. 22859-2 Pa. $9.95

BASIC PRINCIPLES OF CLASSICAL BALLET, Agrippina Vaganova. Great Russian theoretician, teacher explains methods for teaching classical ballet. 118 illustrations. 175pp. 5⅜ x 8½. 22036-2 Pa. $6.95

THE JUMPING FROG, Mark Twain. Revenge edition. The original story of The Celebrated Jumping Frog of Calaveras County, a hapless French translation, and Twain's hilarious "retranslation" from the French. 12 illustrations. 66pp. 5⅜ x 8½. 22686-7 Pa. $4.95

BEST REMEMBERED POEMS, Martin Gardner (ed.). The 126 poems in this superb collection of 19th- and 20th-century British and American verse range from Shelley's "To a Skylark" to the impassioned "Renascence" of Edna St. Vincent Millay and to Edward Lear's whimsical "The Owl and the Pussycat." 224pp. 5⅜ x 8½. 27165-X Pa. $5.95

COMPLETE SONNETS, William Shakespeare. Over 150 exquisite poems deal with love, friendship, the tyranny of time, beauty's evanescence, death and other themes in language of remarkable power, precision and beauty. Glossary of archaic terms. 80pp. 5³⁄₁₆ x 8¼. 26686-9 Pa. $1.00

THE BATTLES THAT CHANGED HISTORY, Fletcher Pratt. Eminent historian profiles 16 crucial conflicts, ancient to modern, that changed the course of civilization. 352pp. 5⅜ x 8½. 41129-X Pa. $9.95

THE WIT AND HUMOR OF OSCAR WILDE, Alvin Redman (ed.). More than 1,000 ripostes, paradoxes, wisecracks: Work is the curse of the drinking classes; I can resist everything except temptation; etc. 258pp. 5⅜ x 8½.        20602-5 Pa. $6.95

SHAKESPEARE LEXICON AND QUOTATION DICTIONARY, Alexander Schmidt. Full definitions, locations, shades of meaning in every word in plays and poems. More than 50,000 exact quotations. 1,485pp. 6½ x 9¼. 2-vol. set.
Vol. 1: 22726-X Pa. $17.95
Vol. 2: 22727-8 Pa. $17.95

SELECTED POEMS, Emily Dickinson. Over 100 best-known, best-loved poems by one of America's foremost poets, reprinted from authoritative early editions. No comparable edition at this price. Index of first lines. 64pp. 5³⁄₁₆ x 8¼.
26466-1 Pa. $1.00

THE INSIDIOUS DR. FU-MANCHU, Sax Rohmer. The first of the popular mystery series introduces a pair of English detectives to their archnemesis, the diabolical Dr. Fu-Manchu. Flavorful atmosphere, fast-paced action, and colorful characters enliven this classic of the genre. 208pp. 5³⁄₁₆ x 8¼.        29898-1 Pa. $2.00

THE MALLEUS MALEFICARUM OF KRAMER AND SPRENGER, translated by Montague Summers. Full text of most important witchhunter's "bible," used by both Catholics and Protestants. 278pp. 6⅝ x 10.        22802-9 Pa. $12.95

SPANISH STORIES/CUENTOS ESPAÑOLES: A Dual-Language Book, Angel Flores (ed.). Unique format offers 13 great stories in Spanish by Cervantes, Borges, others. Faithful English translations on facing pages. 352pp. 5⅜ x 8½.
25399-6 Pa. $9.95

GARDEN CITY, LONG ISLAND, IN EARLY PHOTOGRAPHS, 1869–1919, Mildred H. Smith. Handsome treasury of 118 vintage pictures, accompanied by carefully researched captions, document the Garden City Hotel fire (1899), the Vanderbilt Cup Race (1908), the first airmail flight departing from the Nassau Boulevard Aerodrome (1911), and much more. 96pp. 8⅞ x 11¾.        40669-5 Pa. $12.95

OLD QUEENS, N.Y., IN EARLY PHOTOGRAPHS, Vincent F. Seyfried and William Asadorian. Over 160 rare photographs of Maspeth, Jamaica, Jackson Heights, and other areas. Vintage views of DeWitt Clinton mansion, 1939 World's Fair and more. Captions. 192pp. 8⅞ x 11.        26358-4 Pa. $14.95

CAPTURED BY THE INDIANS: 15 Firsthand Accounts, 1750-1870, Frederick Drimmer. Astounding true historical accounts of grisly torture, bloody conflicts, relentless pursuits, miraculous escapes and more, by people who lived to tell the tale. 384pp. 5⅜ x 8½.        24901-8 Pa. $9.95

THE WORLD'S GREAT SPEECHES (Fourth Enlarged Edition), Lewis Copeland, Lawrence W. Lamm, and Stephen J. McKenna. Nearly 300 speeches provide public speakers with a wealth of updated quotes and inspiration—from Pericles' funeral oration and William Jennings Bryan's "Cross of Gold Speech" to Malcolm X's powerful words on the Black Revolution and Earl of Spenser's tribute to his sister, Diana, Princess of Wales. 944pp. 5⅜ x 8⅜.        40903-1 Pa. $15.95

THE BOOK OF THE SWORD, Sir Richard F. Burton. Great Victorian scholar/adventurer's eloquent, erudite history of the "queen of weapons"—from prehistory to early Roman Empire. Evolution and development of early swords, variations (sabre, broadsword, cutlass, scimitar, etc.), much more. 336pp. 6⅛ x 9¼.
25434-8 Pa. $9.95

AUTOBIOGRAPHY: The Story of My Experiments with Truth, Mohandas K. Gandhi. Boyhood, legal studies, purification, the growth of the Satyagraha (nonviolent protest) movement. Critical, inspiring work of the man responsible for the freedom of India. 480pp. 5⅜ x 8½. (Available in U.S. only.) 24593-4 Pa. $9.95

CELTIC MYTHS AND LEGENDS, T. W. Rolleston. Masterful retelling of Irish and Welsh stories and tales. Cuchulain, King Arthur, Deirdre, the Grail, many more. First paperback edition. 58 full-page illustrations. 512pp. 5⅜ x 8½. 26507-2 Pa. $9.95

THE PRINCIPLES OF PSYCHOLOGY, William James. Famous long course complete, unabridged. Stream of thought, time perception, memory, experimental methods; great work decades ahead of its time. 94 figures. 1,391pp. 5⅜ x 8½. 2-vol. set.
Vol. I: 20381-6 Pa. $14.95
Vol. II: 20382-4 Pa. $16.95

THE WORLD AS WILL AND REPRESENTATION, Arthur Schopenhauer. Definitive English translation of Schopenhauer's life work, correcting more than 1,000 errors, omissions in earlier translations. Translated by E. F. J. Payne. Total of 1,269pp. 5⅜ x 8½. 2-vol. set. Vol. 1: 21761-2 Pa. $12.95
Vol. 2: 21762-0 Pa. $12.95

MAGIC AND MYSTERY IN TIBET, Madame Alexandra David-Neel. Experiences among lamas, magicians, sages, sorcerers, Bonpa wizards. A true psychic discovery. 32 illustrations. 321pp. 5⅜ x 8½. (Available in U.S. only.) 22682-4 Pa. $9.95

THE EGYPTIAN BOOK OF THE DEAD, E. A. Wallis Budge. Complete reproduction of Ani's papyrus, finest ever found. Full hieroglyphic text, interlinear transliteration, word-for-word translation, smooth translation. 533pp. 6½ x 9¼.
21866-X Pa. $12.95

MATHEMATICS FOR THE NONMATHEMATICIAN, Morris Kline. Detailed, college-level treatment of mathematics in cultural and historical context, with numerous exercises. Recommended Reading Lists. Tables. Numerous figures. 641pp. 5⅜ x 8½.
24823-2 Pa. $11.95

PROBABILISTIC METHODS IN THE THEORY OF STRUCTURES, Isaac Elishakoff. Well-written introduction covers the elements of the theory of probability from two or more random variables, the reliability of such multivariable structures, the theory of random function, Monte Carlo methods of treating problems incapable of exact solution, and more. Examples. 502pp. 5⅜ x 8½. 40691-1 Pa. $16.95

THE RIME OF THE ANCIENT MARINER, Gustave Doré, S. T. Coleridge. Doré's finest work; 34 plates capture moods, subtleties of poem. Flawless full-size reproductions printed on facing pages with authoritative text of poem. "Beautiful. Simply beautiful."–*Publisher's Weekly*. 77pp. 9¼ x 12. 22305-1 Pa. $7.95

NORTH AMERICAN INDIAN DESIGNS FOR ARTISTS AND CRAFTSPEOPLE, Eva Wilson. Over 360 authentic copyright-free designs adapted from Navajo blankets, Hopi pottery, Sioux buffalo hides, more. Geometrics, symbolic figures, plant and animal motifs, etc. 128pp. 8⅜ x 11. (Not for sale in the United Kingdom.) 25341-4 Pa. $9.95

SCULPTURE: Principles and Practice, Louis Slobodkin. Step-by-step approach to clay, plaster, metals, stone; classical and modern. 253 drawings, photos. 255pp. 8⅛ x 11.
22960-2 Pa. $11.95

THE INFLUENCE OF SEA POWER UPON HISTORY, 1660–1783, A. T. Mahan. Influential classic of naval history and tactics still used as text in war colleges. First paperback edition. 4 maps. 24 battle plans. 640pp. 5$\frac{3}{8}$ x 8$\frac{1}{2}$. 25509-3 Pa. $14.95

THE STORY OF THE TITANIC AS TOLD BY ITS SURVIVORS, Jack Winocour (ed.). What it was really like. Panic, despair, shocking inefficiency, and a little heroism. More thrilling than any fictional account. 26 illustrations. 320pp. 5$\frac{3}{8}$ x 8$\frac{1}{2}$. 20610-6 Pa. $8.95

FAIRY AND FOLK TALES OF THE IRISH PEASANTRY, William Butler Yeats (ed.). Treasury of 64 tales from the twilight world of Celtic myth and legend: "The Soul Cages," "The Kildare Pooka," "King O'Toole and his Goose," many more. Introduction and Notes by W. B. Yeats. 352pp. 5$\frac{3}{8}$ x 8$\frac{1}{2}$. 26941-8 Pa. $8.95

BUDDHIST MAHAYANA TEXTS, E. B. Cowell and others (eds.). Superb, accurate translations of basic documents in Mahayana Buddhism, highly important in history of religions. The Buddha-karita of Asvaghosha, Larger Sukhavativyuha, more. 448pp. 5$\frac{3}{8}$ x 8$\frac{1}{2}$. 25552-2 Pa. $12.95

ONE TWO THREE . . . INFINITY: Facts and Speculations of Science, George Gamow. Great physicist's fascinating, readable overview of contemporary science: number theory, relativity, fourth dimension, entropy, genes, atomic structure, much more. 128 illustrations. Index. 352pp. 5$\frac{3}{8}$ x 8$\frac{1}{2}$. 25664-2 Pa. $9.95

EXPERIMENTATION AND MEASUREMENT, W. J. Youden. Introductory manual explains laws of measurement in simple terms and offers tips for achieving accuracy and minimizing errors. Mathematics of measurement, use of instruments, experimenting with machines. 1994 edition. Foreword. Preface. Introduction. Epilogue. Selected Readings. Glossary. Index. Tables and figures. 128pp. 5$^3/_8$ x 8$^1/_2$. 40451-X Pa. $6.95

DALÍ ON MODERN ART: The Cuckolds of Antiquated Modern Art, Salvador Dalí. Influential painter skewers modern art and its practitioners. Outrageous evaluations of Picasso, Cézanne, Turner, more. 15 renderings of paintings discussed. 44 calligraphic decorations by Dalí. 96pp. 5$\frac{3}{8}$ x 8$\frac{1}{2}$. (Available in U.S. only.) 29220-7 Pa. $5.95

ANTIQUE PLAYING CARDS: A Pictorial History, Henry René D'Allemagne. Over 900 elaborate, decorative images from rare playing cards (14th–20th centuries): Bacchus, death, dancing dogs, hunting scenes, royal coats of arms, players cheating, much more. 96pp. 9$\frac{1}{4}$ x 12$\frac{1}{4}$. 29265-7 Pa. $12.95

MAKING FURNITURE MASTERPIECES: 30 Projects with Measured Drawings, Franklin H. Gottshall. Step-by-step instructions, illustrations for constructing handsome, useful pieces, among them a Sheraton desk, Chippendale chair, Spanish desk, Queen Anne table and a William and Mary dressing mirror. 224pp. 8$\frac{1}{8}$ x 11$\frac{1}{4}$. 29338-6 Pa. $16.95

THE FOSSIL BOOK: A Record of Prehistoric Life, Patricia V. Rich et al. Profusely illustrated definitive guide covers everything from single-celled organisms and dinosaurs to birds and mammals and the interplay between climate and man. Over 1,500 illustrations. 760pp. 7$\frac{1}{2}$ x 10$\frac{1}{8}$. 29371-8 Pa. $29.95

*Prices subject to change without notice.*

Available at your book dealer or write for free catalog to Dept. GI, Dover Publications, Inc., 31 East 2nd St., Mineola, N.Y. 11501. Dover publishes more than 500 books each year on science, elementary and advanced mathematics, biology, music, art, literary history, social sciences and other areas.